# Effective Small Business Management, 9/E

## Cases

**By Katherine Korman Frey**
*The George Washington University*

| Case | Entrepreneur & Company Name | Related Topics | Chapter Reference |
|------|------------------------------|----------------|-------------------|
| 1 | Ted Leonsis<br>Filmanthropy | *Industry: Film, social sector, technology*<br>• Entrepreneurship, "the big idea," life balance<br>• Strategic management<br>• Feasibility analysis<br>• Networking<br>• Large-scale growth | <br>1<br>2<br>6<br>11<br>2,19 |
| 2 | Brian Scudamore<br>1-800-Got-Junk | *Industry: Waste remediation*<br>• Business strategy and processes<br>• Franchising<br>• Growth strategy | <br>2<br>4<br>2,19 |
| 3 | Jason Beans<br>RISING Medical Solutions, Inc. | *Industry: Healthcare finance*<br>• Strategic management and accountability<br>• Human resource management, motivation<br>• Values and leadership | <br>2<br>19<br>21 |
| 4 | Josh Frey<br>On Sale Promos | *Industry: Promotional/marketing*<br>• Entrepreneurship, life balance<br>• Cash management<br>• Personal selling and sales strategies<br>• Pricing strategies | <br>1<br>9<br>10<br>11 |
| 5 | Kathryn From<br>Bravado! Designs | *Industry: Clothing, manufacturing*<br>• International business<br>• Sources of financing<br>• Manufacturing process/supply chain management | <br>12<br>14,15<br>17,18 |
| 6 | Kimberly Wilson<br>Tranquil Space | *Industry: Fitness/yoga*<br>• Management and leadership<br>• Forms of ownership<br>• Retail layout<br>• Staffing, human resources management | <br>2,19<br>3<br>16<br>19 |
| 7 | Laura Lee Williams-Murphy<br>Laura Lee Designs | *Industry: Fashion, retail, manufacturing*<br>• Entrepreneurship, starting a business<br>• Marketing strategies<br>• Pricing strategies<br>• Global marketing strategies | <br>1<br>9<br>11<br>12 |
| 8 | Susan Apgood<br>News Generation | *Industry: Public relations, radio*<br>• Entrepreneurship, life balance<br>• Financial planning, management, and analysis<br>• Outsourcing, staffing, and human resources management | <br>1<br>8<br>19 |
| 9 | Warren Myer<br>Myers Internet | *Industry: Technology, finance, and real estate*<br>• Entrepreneurship, life balance<br>• Competitive strategy<br>• Management and leadership<br>• Exit strategy<br>• E-commerce | <br>1<br>2<br>2,19<br>5<br>13 |
| 10 | Woodie Neiss<br>FLAVORx | *Industry: Pharmaceuticals*<br>• Selling a business, exit strategy<br>• Preparing for acquisition | <br>5<br>20 |

For printable cases, audio clips, and additional resources, go to www.VisionForward.com

# Effective Small Business Management

## An Entrepreneurial Approach

### Ninth Edition

---

**Norman M. Scarborough**
Presbyterian College

**Douglas L. Wilson**
University of Oregon

**Thomas W. Zimmerer**
Saint Leo University

PEARSON
Prentice Hall

Pearson Education International

**Acquisitions Editor:** Kim Norbuta
**Editorial Director:** Sally Yagan
**Editor in Chief:** David Parker
**Product Development Manager:** Ashley Santora
**Editorial Assistant:** Liz Davis
**Editorial Project Manager:** Claudia Fernandes
**Marketing Manager:** Nikki Jones
**Marketing Assistant:** Ian Gold
**Permissions Project Manager:** Charles Morris
**Senior Managing Editor:** Judy Leale
**Production Project Manager:** Kelly Warsak
**Senior Operations Specialist:** Arnold Vila
**Senior Art Director:** Janet Slowik
**Interior Design:** Karen Quigley
**Director, Image Resource Center:** Melinda Patelli
**Manager, Rights and Permissions:** Zina Arabia
**Manager, Visual Research:** Beth Brenzel
**Image Permission Coordinator:** Richard Rodrigues
**Photo Researcher:** Rachel Lucas
**Manager, Cover Visual Research & Permissions:** Karen Sanatar
**Composition:** S4Carlisle Publishing Services
**Full-Service Project Management:** Lynn Steines/S4Carlisle Publishing Services
**Printer/Binder:** Courier Kendallville, Inc.
**Cover Printer:** Lehigh Lithographers
**Typeface:** 10/12 Times

Credits and acknowledgments borrowed from other sources and reproduced, with permission, in this textbook appear on appropriate page within text.

If you purchased this book within the United States or Canada you should be aware that it has been wrongfully imported without the approval of the Publisher or the Author.

Pearson Education Ltd., London
Pearson Education Singapore, Pte. Ltd
Pearson Education, Canada, Inc.
Pearson Education—Japan
Pearson Education Australia PTY, Limited

Pearson Education North Asia Ltd., Hong Kong
Pearson Educación de Mexico, S.A. de C.V.
Pearson Education Malaysia, Pte. Ltd
Pearson Education Upper Saddle River, New Jersey

10 9 8 7 6 5 4 3 2 1
ISBN-13: 978-0-13-207951-8
ISBN-10: 0-13-207951-8

In memory of Lannie H. Thornley

To Louise T. Scarborough, Mildred Myers,
and John Scarborough. Your love, support,
and encouragement have made all the difference.

N.M.S.

To my wife and best friend, Judy,
whose love and support mean more
than words can ever express.

D.L.W.

# Brief Contents

# Contents

# Preface

The field of entrepreneurship is experiencing incredible rates of growth, not only in the United States but across the world as well. People of all ages, backgrounds, and nationalities are launching businesses of their own and, in the process, are reshaping the global economy. Entrepreneurs are discovering the natural advantages that result from their companies' small size—speed, agility, flexibility, sensitivity to customers' needs, creativity, a spirit of innovation, and many others—give them the ability to compete successfully with companies many times their size and that have budgets to match. As large companies struggle to survive wrenching changes in competitive forces by downsizing, merging, and restructuring, the unseen army of small businesses continues to flourish and to carry the nation's economy on its back. Entrepreneurs willing to assume the risks of the market to gain its rewards are at the heart of capitalism. These men and women, with their bold entrepreneurial spirits, have led our nation into prosperity throughout history. Entrepreneurship is a significant force throughout the world. We need to look no farther than those nations that are throwing off decades of control and central planning in favor of capitalism to see where the entrepreneurial process begins. In every case, it is the entrepreneurs who create small companies that lead those nations out of the jungles of economic oppression to higher standards of living and hope for the future.

In the United States, we can be thankful that the small business sector is strong and thriving. Small companies deliver the goods and services we use every day, provide jobs and training for millions of workers, and lead the way in creating the products and services that will make our lives easier and more enjoyable in the future. Small businesses were responsible for introducing to the world the elevator, the airplane, FM radio, the zipper, the personal computer, and a host of other marvelous inventions. The imaginations of the next generation of entrepreneurs of which you may be a part, will determine which other fantastic products and services may lie in our future! Whatever those ideas may be, we can be sure of one thing: entrepreneurs will be there to make them happen.

The purpose of this book is to open your mind to the possibilities, the challenges, and the rewards of owning your own business and to provide the tools you will need to be successful if you choose the path of the entrepreneur. It is not an easy road to follow, but the rewards—both tangible and intangible—are well worth the risks. Not only may you be rewarded financially for your business idea, but also like entrepreneurs the world over, you will be able to work at doing something you love!

*Effective Small Business Management: An Entrepreneurial Approach,* Ninth Edition, brings to you the material you will need to launch and manage a small business successfully in the hotly competitive environment of the twenty-first century. In writing this edition, we have worked hard to provide you with plenty of practical, "hands-on" tools and techniques to make your business venture a success. Many people launch businesses every year, but only some of them succeed. This book teaches you the *right* way to launch and manage a small business with the staying power to succeed and grow. Perhaps one day we'll be writing about *your* success story in future editions of this book!

## Text Features

*Effective Small Business Management,* Ninth Edition, contains many unique features that make it the ideal book for entrepreneurs who are serious about launching their businesses the right way. These features include the following:

- **Case studies.** This edition includes an exciting feature: 10 new cases, all of them featuring actual entrepreneurs and their business ventures, many of which you can research online. These cases are designed to give you the opportunity to apply the concepts that you have learned throughout the course. They challenge students on a variety of topics that are covered in the text, and they are ideal for either individual or group assignments. Case writer Kathy Korman Frey, whose cases have been published in a variety of venues, including the Harvard Business School Press, contributed the cases to this edition.

■ *Business Plan Pro.* Professors also can choose to bundle with this edition Business Plan Pro, the best-selling business planning software on the market. To many entrepreneurs, preparing a business plan seems at first to be an overwhelming task, but Business Plan Pro makes the job much easier by providing an easy-to-use guide that leads students through the process of building a solid business plan. At the end of every chapter, you will find exercises to help you integrate the topics that you have studied in the chapter with Business Plan Pro to create a powerful business plan. (Business Plan Pro – ISBN: 0-13-187484-5) Instructors also can choose to have Business Plan Pro bundled with the textbook at a special value price. Contact your local Prentice Hall sales representative for more information.

■ *A complete chapter on e-commerce and thorough coverage of the World Wide Web (WWW) as a business tool.* One of the most important business tools in existence today is the World Wide Web. Still in its infancy, it is already proving to be a powerful force in reshaping the face of business. *Effective Small Business Management,* Ninth Edition, offers the most comprehensive coverage of e-commerce of any book on the market. In these pages, you will find many references to the Web, ideas for using the Web as a business tool, and examples of entrepreneurs who are unleashing the power of the Web in creative ways.

■ *Text material that is relevant, practical, and key to entrepreneurial success.* Easy and interesting to read, this edition offers streamlined coverage of the topics you'll need to know about when you launch your own business without sacrificing the quality or the content of earlier editions.

■ *Lots of examples.* Because examples help people learn more effectively and efficiently, you will find plenty of examples that are new to this edition; they illustrate how entrepreneurs are using the concepts covered in the text to make their businesses more successful. These examples are also a great way to stimulate creativity.

■ *Emphasis on building and using a business plan.* Chapter 6, "Conducting a Feasibility Analysis and Crafting a Winning Business Plan," is devoted to building a business plan and features in many other chapters reinforce the business planning process.

■ *A sample business plan.* Many courses in entrepreneurship and small business management require students to write business plans. Students of entrepreneurship find it helpful to have a model to guide them as they build their own plans, and they can use the plan that appears in the Appendix as a resource. The plan is one written for My Friends Bookstore, a very successful business that was started and is operated by three college students. These young men used the previous edition of this book to help them launch their business.

■ *Features in every chapter that help students master the material more readily.* Learning objectives introduce each chapter, and they appear in the text margins at the appropriate places to keep students' attention focused on what they are learning. Chapter summaries are organized by learning objectives as well.

■ *Boxed features in every chapter that follow three important themes:*
  • "In the Entrepreneurial Spotlight"—cases that offer in-depth, interesting, and unique examples of entrepreneurs who are using the concepts covered in the text and reinforce the chapter learning objectives.
  • "Entrepreneurship in Action"—short cases that give students the opportunity to apply the concepts that they are learning in the course to an actual business.
  • "Gaining a Competitive Edge"—a "hands-on, how-to" feature designed to offer practical advice on a particular topic that students can use to develop a competitive edge for their businesses.
       Each feature presents thought-provoking issues that will produce lively class discussions and enhance students' learning experiences by asking them to (1) identify, (2) analyze, and (3) evaluate key issues related to entrepreneurship.

■ *Updated coverage of important topics such as:*
  • Conducting a feasibility analysis and building a business plan
  • E-commerce

- Strategic management
- Guerrilla marketing techniques
- Sources of financing, both equity and debt
- Business strategies for reaching global markets

In short, we have taken one of the most successful and time-tested books in the market and made it even better!

## Supplements

- **■ *Instructor's Resource Center.*** At www.prenhall.com/irc, instructors can access a variety of print, digital, and presentation resources available with this text in downloadable format. Registration is simple and gives you immediate access to new titles and new editions. As a registered faculty member, you can download resource files and receive immediate access and instructions for installing course management content on your campus server. If you ever need assistance, our dedicated technical support team is ready to help with the media supplements that accompany this text. Visit http://247.pearsoned.com/ for answers to frequently asked questions and toll-free user support phone numbers.

The following supplements are available to adopting instructors (for detailed descriptions, please visit www.prenhall.com/irc):

- Instructor's Manual with Test Item File—Also available in print (ISBN: 0-13-602834-91)
- TestGen test generating software—The TestGen allows instructors to easily create custom tests by choosing questions from the test bank. Files also available for course-management use. Available online at the IRC.
- PowerPoint Slides—Prepared by one of the authors and professionally designed for teaching, these presentations are available online at the IRC.

- **■ *Videos.*** A series of videos selected by one of the authors that is designed to illustrate the topics discussed in *Effective Small Business Management, 9/e.* These short videos are ideal for helping students master the concepts in the textbook and for launching meaningful class discussions. Available on DVD (ISBN: 0-13-602802-0)

- **■ *Companion Web site.*** An impressive Web site that both professors and students will find extremely useful. Locate the Web site for *Effective Small Business Management,* Ninth Edition, at www.prenhall.com/scarborough. Here, you'll find features for each chapter that are designed to get you onto the Web to research topics, solve problems, and engage in a variety of other activities that will make you a more "Web-savvy" entrepreneur. This companion site includes a multitude of useful features, including a Business Plan Evaluation Scale, a "Before You Start" checklist, and a list of hundreds of links to useful small business sites (organized by chapter). The World Wide Web Activities take students to the Web where they search for data, research relevant topics, and experience firsthand the power of the Web as a practical tool that will influence the way companies do business in the twenty-first century. The site also includes sample multiple-choice questions that help students determine how well they have mastered the subject matter and prepare for tests.

## Acknowledgments

Partnering with every author team is a staff of professionals who work extremely hard to bring a book to life. They handle the thousands of details involved in transforming a rough manuscript into the finished product you see before you. Their contributions are immeasurable, and we appreciate all they do to make this book successful. We have been blessed to work with the following outstanding publishing professionals:

David Parker, editor-in-chief, is one of the finest editors we have had the pleasure of working with over the course of more than 25 years. David's vision, dedication, and support made the process of creating this edition flow quite smoothly. He truly is an asset to the publishing industry.

Claudia Fernandes, project manager, who so capably handled a seemingly infinite number of details related to getting this edition ready for production and managed all of the components of the teaching package that plays a vital role in the success of this book. Claudia worked diligently to ensure that this edition is the best yet!

Kelly Warsak, production editor, who skillfully coordinated the production schedule for this edition of *Effective Small Business Management* and all of the ancillaries that accompany it. Kelly kept this project on schedule, which in publishing is never an easy task, and she always managed to do so in a friendly, caring manner. We have worked with Kelly on many editions in the past and look forward to working with her on future editions as well.

Rachel Lucas, photo researcher, whose dedication and persistence enabled her to track down the photos that appear in the chapters. Despite facing several challenges, Rachel was able to acquire the photos we needed.

Lynn Steines, project editor, S4Carlisle Publishing Services, who shepherded the manuscript through the copyediting process with aplomb. This is never a simple task, and we appreciate the outstanding job she did.

Janet Slowik, senior art director, who applied her ample creative talents to come up with an attractive, professional design for this edition. Janet understands that an appealing layout adds value to a quality product, and her design does just that.

Keri Jean Miksza, copy editor, who caught our mistakes and helped us polish the manuscript and transform it into the finished product you see before you.

Nikki Jones, marketing manager, who gave us many ideas based on her extensive contact with those who count most: our customers.

We also extend our appreciation to the army of Prentice Hall sales representatives, who work so hard to get our books into our customers' hands and who represent the front line in our effort to serve our customers' needs. They are the unsung heroes of the publishing industry.

Especially important in the development of the ninth edition of this book were the following professors, who reviewed the manuscript and provided valuable input that improved the final product. We incorporated many of their ideas and suggestions and value their insight.

Kimberly Brown-King, Southeast Arkansas College

Tony Bledsoe, Meredith College

Richard Judd, University of Illinois at Springfield

Jeff Hornsby, Ball State University

Howard Stroud, LeTourneau University

Bill Godair, Landmark College

Brian Dyk, Heritage College

Joyce Gallagher, Maysville Community and Technical College

Chris Howell, New Mexico Junior College

Herbert Sherman, Southampton College–LIU

Willie Williams, Tidewater Community College

Tanisha Washington, Wade College

Olene Fuller, San Jacinto College North

Randy Nichols, Sullivan University

Steve Varga-Sinka, Saint Leo University

Judy Beebe, Western Oregon University

Stephen Lovejoy, University of Maine at Augusta

Calvin Bacon,  University of South Alabama

Ronald Hagler, California Lutheran University

Lindsay Sholdar, Art Institute of California, San Diego

Corinne Asher, Henry Ford Community College

Mainuddin Afza, Bloomsburg University of Pennsylvania

Bill Wise, The Metropolitan State College of Denver

Joseph Adamo, Cazenovia College

Steven Bradley, Austin Community College

Eddie Hufft, Alcorn State University

We also are grateful to our colleagues who support us in the sometimes grueling process of writing a book: Foard Tarbert, Sam Howell, Jerry Slice, Meredith Holder, Suzanne Smith, Jody Lipford, Rickey Madden, and Kristy Hill of Presbyterian College. Finally, we thank Cindy Scarborough and Judy Wilson, for their love, support, and understanding while we worked many long hours to complete *Effective Small Business Management,* Ninth Edition. For them, this project represents a labor of love.

Norman M. Scarborough
William Henry Scott III Associate
Professor of Information Science
Presbyterian College
Clinton, South Carolina
e-mail: nmscarb@presby.edu

Douglas L. Wilson
Lundquist College of Business
University of Oregon
Eugene, Oregon
e-mail: douglw@lcbmail.uoregon.edu

> The greatest danger for most of us is not that our aim is too high and we miss it, but it is too low and we reach it.
> —Michelangelo

> There is nothing like a dream to create the future.
> —Victor Hugo

# Entrepreneurs: The Driving Force Behind Small Business

## Learning Objectives

**Upon completion of this chapter, you will be able to:**

1. Define the role of the entrepreneur in the economy.
2. Describe the entrepreneurial profile.
3. Explain how entrepreneurs spot business opportunities.
4. Describe the benefits of owning a small business.
5. Describe the potential drawbacks of owning a small business.
6. Explain the forces that are driving the growth in entrepreneurship.
7. Discuss the role of diversity in small business and entrepreneurship.
8. Describe the contributions small businesses make to the economy.
9. Put business failure into the proper perspective.
10. Explain how small business owners can avoid the major pitfalls of running a business.

**1.** Define the role of the entrepreneur in the U.S. economy.

elcome to the world of the entrepreneur! Every year, entrepreneurs around the world launch millions of businesses.[1] These people, who come from diverse backgrounds, are striving to realize the dream of owning and operating their own businesses. Some of them have chosen to leave the security of the corporate hierarchy in search of independence, others have been forced out of large corporations as a result of downsizing, and still others have from the start chosen the autonomy that owning a business offers. The impact of these entrepreneurs on the nation's economy goes far beyond their numbers, however. The resurgence of the entrepreneurial spirit they are spearheading is the most significant economic development in recent business history. These heroes of the new economy are introducing innovative products and services, pushing back technological frontiers, creating new jobs, opening foreign markets, and, in the process, sparking economies.

Scott Cook, cofounder of Intuit Inc., a highly successful publisher of personal financial software, explains the new attitude towards entrepreneurship and the vital role small businesses play:

> Small business is cool now, and I don't mean that lightly. . . . People are seeing that the stuff that makes our lives better comes from business more often than it comes from government. It used to be that there was an exciting part of big business that attracted people. But today it's the reverse; small companies are the heroes . . . and now the entrepreneurs get the attention.[2]

The last several decades have seen record numbers of entrepreneurs launching businesses. In 1969, U.S. entrepreneurs, for example, created 274,000 new corporations; today, the number of new U.S. incorporations exceeds 600,000 in a typical year![3] Another indicator of the popularity of entrepreneurship is the keen interest expressed by students in creating their own businesses. Increasing numbers of young people are choosing entrepreneurship as a career rather than joining the ranks of the pinstriped masses in major corporations. In short, the probability that you will become an entrepreneur at some point in your life has never been higher!

Research suggests that entrepreneurial activity remains vibrant not only in the United States but across the globe as well. According to the Global Entrepreneurship Monitor (GEM), a study of entrepreneurial activity across the globe, 10 percent of the U.S. population aged 18 to 64 is engaged in entrepreneurial activity. The study also found that 9.5 percent of people in the 42 GEM countries analyzed are involved in starting a new business (see Figure 1.1).[4]

Even countries that traditionally are not known as hotbeds of entrepreneurial activity are home to promising start-up companies:

**ENTREPRENEURIAL Profile**

*Chris Griffiths and Garrison Guitars*

St. John's, Newfoundland, is the home to Garrison Guitars, a start-up business that is credited with developing the first major technological advancement for the acoustic guitar, an instrument that has been around for hundreds of years. At age 19, company founder Chris Griffiths started Griffiths Guitar Works, a small maker of custom guitars, and a guitar retail store in St. John's. One day while on a commercial jetliner, Griffiths came up with the idea for the Active Brace System™, a revolutionary one-piece molded fiberglass unit encased in a traditional wood guitar body that allows all of the instrument's parts to vibrate in unison, producing a rich, full-bodied sound. He sketched his idea on a napkin and worked for the next six years to bring it to market. In 2000, with just five prototype models in hand, Griffiths rented a booth at the National Association of Music Merchants trade show and collected orders for more than 46,000 guitars! In less than one year, Griffiths raised $4 million to launch his company and build a factory. Garrison Guitars began shipping guitars with the Active Brace System in September 2001 and now employs 37 employees in its 20,000-square-foot factory. "I've transitioned from being a guitar builder to being a guitar CEO," says Griffiths.[5]

Productivity gains in recent years have made it possible for companies to accomplish more with fewer people, and America's largest companies have engaged in massive

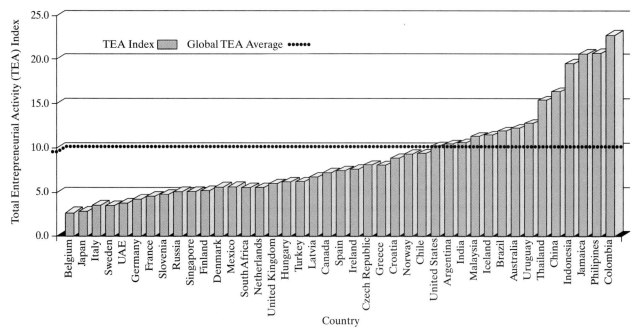

**FIGURE 1.1 Entrepreneurial Activity Across the Globe**
Persons per 100 Adults, 18–64 Years Old Engaged in Entrepreneurial Activity
*Source:* 2007 Global Entrepreneurship Monitor.

downsizing campaigns, dramatically cutting the number of managers and workers on their payrolls. This flurry of "pink slips" has spawned a new population of entrepreneurs—"castoffs" from large corporations (many of whom thought they would be lifetime ladder-climbers in their companies) with solid management experience and many productive years left before retirement.

One casualty of this downsizing has been the long-standing notion of job security in large corporations. As a result, members of Generation X (those born between 1965 and 1980) and Generation Y (those born between 1981 and 1995) in the United States no longer see launching a business as being a risky career path. Having witnessed large companies lay off their parents after many years of service, these young people see entrepreneurship as the ideal way to create their own job security and career success! They are eager to control their own destinies.

This downsizing trend among large companies also has created a more significant philosophical change. It has ushered in an age in which "small is beautiful." Twenty-five years ago, competitive conditions favored large companies with their hierarchies and layers of management; today, with the pace of change constantly accelerating, fleet-footed, agile, small companies have the competitive advantage. These nimble competitors can dart into and out of niche markets as they emerge and recede; they can move faster to exploit opportunities the market presents; and they can use modern technology to create within a matter of weeks or months products and services that once took years and all of the resources a giant corporation could muster. The balance has tipped in favor of small entrepreneurial companies.

Entrepreneurship also has become mainstream. Although launching a business is never easy, the resources available today make the job much simpler now than ever before. Thousands of colleges and universities offer courses in entrepreneurship, the Internet hosts a sea of information on launching a business, sources of capital that did not exist just a few years ago are now available, and business incubators hatch companies at impressive rates. Once looked down on as a choice for people unable to hold a job, entrepreneurship is now an accepted and respected part of our culture.

Another significant shift in the bedrock of the economic structures of many developed countries is influencing this swing in favor of small companies. These countries are rapidly moving away from industrial economies knowledge-based ones. What matters now is not so much the traditional factors of production but *knowledge* and *information*. A knowledge-based economy favors small businesses because the cost of managing and transmitting knowledge and information is very low, and computer and information technologies are driving these costs lower still.

No matter why they start their businesses, entrepreneurs continue to embark on one of the most exhilarating—and one of the most frightening—adventures ever known: launching a business. It's never easy, but it can be incredibly rewarding, both financially and emotionally. One successful business owner claims that an entrepreneur is "anyone who wants to experience the deep, dark canyons of uncertainty and ambiguity and wants to walk the breathtaking highlands of success. But I caution: Do not plan to walk the latter until you have experienced the former."[6] True entrepreneurs see owning a business as the real measure of success. Indeed, entrepreneurship often provides the only avenue for success to those who otherwise might have been denied the opportunity.

Who are these entrepreneurs, and what drives them to work so hard with no guarantee of success? What forces lead them to risk so much and to make so many sacrifices in an attempt to achieve an ideal? Why are they willing to give up the security of a steady paycheck working for someone else to become the last person to be paid in their own companies? This chapter will examine the entrepreneur, the driving force behind the American economy.

In the Entrepreneurial Spotlight

## ■ The Economics of Selling Garbage

The genesis of Tom Szaky's entrepreneurial idea was a high school project that involved growing plants and harvesting the buds. The project never succeeded, but Szaky and Jon Beyer, his partner on the project, kept working on it after they went off to college. Beyer finally achieved success by adding a home-grown fertilizer he made from vermicompost, a waste product generated when red worms eat garbage. Szaky, just a 19-year-old student at Princeton University in the United States, was looking for a business idea to enter a business plan competition when he realized the potential to sell the fertilizer made from red worm waste. The all-natural product would be the ideal alternative to harsh chemical fertilizers, and the market timing was right, with growing numbers of customers looking for organic, all-natural products. In addition, the worms worked for free, never took a day off, and produced an amount of compost that was equal to their body weight every day. Szaky and Beyer finagled $20,000 from friends and family and convinced a recycling expert to build a "worm gin," a device designed to deliver waste to an army of worms that would produce the organic fertilizer. The worm gin was a total failure, but their experiment allowed Szaky and Beyer to realize that their best business

opportunity was selling a liquid version of the fertilizer called vermicompost tea.

Szaky and Beyer entered Princeton's business plan competition but did not place or win any cash prize, which meant that their company, TerraCycle, was out of business before they really had a chance to start it. Fortunately, however, a local radio station interviewed Szaky and Beyer, and a local entrepreneur, Suman Sinha, contacted them about investing in the company. Sinha's $2,000 check, which bought him one percent of TerraCycle's stock, breathed life into the tiny company once again.

Szaky and Beyer kept the company afloat by entering—and winning—business plan competitions. Within a matter of just a few months, the entrepreneurs had won six competitions, netting them between $2,000 and $10,000 each. In April 2003, they achieved a major breakthrough when they won the intensely competitive Carrot Capital Business Plan Challenge in New York City, which carried with it a prize of $1 million! Szaky, however, was uncomfortable with the "strings" that the prize money carried with it (The deal would have required Szaky and Beyer to give up control of the company completely) and, making one of the toughest choices in his young entrepreneurial career, turned down the prize money.

With just $500 in the bank, TerraCycle again was on the verge of folding, but Szaky was more determined than ever to make the business a success. To keep costs low, Szaky hired a team of students to collect recycled soft drink bottles, and he discovered that there are only four bottle sizes made and that they all are of the same height and accept a universally-sized cap. "This was the big discovery," recalls Szaky. "It meant [that the bottles] could be run through a high-speed bottling machine. This was the moment when it all came together, when we crystallized what we could do in a powerful way. We realized we could make this product entirely from recycled waste. I thought, 'This is it. This is what we have to do.'" Within five months, Szaky had raised $1.2 million in capital from private investors.

Today, TerraCycle is growing fast. Its organic fertilizer, TerraCycle Plant Food, which still is packaged in reused soft drink bottles topped with sprayers that are rejects from other manufacturers, is sold in more than 7,000 locations, including both Home Depot and Wal-Mart. Even the boxes that TerraCycle uses to ship the product are recycled; they are the misprinted rejects from major companies. Not only does TerraCycle Plant Food provide environmental benefits to users, but it also works! An independent study by the Rutgers Eco-Complex concluded that TerraCycle Plant Food performs as well or better than the leading chemical fertilizer. Retailers find the product attractive as well because the company's low costs mean that it can offer its distributors higher profit margins than they can earn on chemical fertilizers.

TerraCycle's unique selling proposition is that its plant food is not only good for your plants, but it also is good for your planet. Szaky says that the all-natural fertilizer is goof-proof. Add too much chemical fertilizer to your plants, and the result is plant burn; add too much TerraCycle Plant Food, and your plants thrive. Since the company's inception, Szaky has raised a total of $4.3 million from private investors, and he expects sales to double to $5 million next year. Already he is making plans to take TerraCycle public or to sell it to a larger company in a few years. If that happens, Szaky, who still owns 11 percent of the company, could retire—before he turns 30.

1. Are TerraCycle's brushes with extinction typical of many business start-ups? What factors set apart those companies that survive these close calls and those that do not?
2. Visit the company's Web site (www.Terracycle.net) to learn more about TerraCycle. Work with a team of your classmates to develop an effective marketing pitch for TerraCycle and its plant food.

*Source:* Adapted from Bo Burlingham, "The Coolest Little Start-up in America," *Inc.*, July 2006, pp. 78–85; "Our Story," TerraCycle, www.TerraCycle.net/story.htm.

## What Is an Entrepreneur?

**2.** Describe the entrepreneurial profile.

At any given time, an estimated 10.1 million adults in the United States alone are engaged in launching a business, traveling down the path of entrepreneurship.[7] An **entrepreneur** is one who creates a new business in the face of risk and uncertainty for the purpose of achieving profit and growth by identifying opportunities and assembling the necessary resources to capitalize on those opportunities. Entrepreneurs usually start with nothing more than an idea—often a simple one—and then organize the resources necessary to transform that idea into a sustainable business. One business writer says that an entrepreneur is "someone who takes nothing for granted, assumes change is possible, and follows through; someone incapable of confronting reality without thinking about ways to improve it; and for whom action is a natural consequence of thought."[8]

**ENTREPRENEURIAL Profile**

*Hugh Brydges and StarChase Inc.*

Hugh Brydges struggled with the loss of his partner in a boating accessories start-up company who was an innocent victim of a crash in a high-speed police chase. Brydges began thinking about ways that police officers could apprehend offenders without risking their lives and the lives of others in high-speed chases. Borrowing an idea from paintball, he developed the StarChase, a sticky projectile that police can fire at a fleeing vehicle and that contains a GPS module equipped with its own power source. Once fired, the device immediately begins tracking the car's movement real-time, allowing police officers to track its exact location constantly and to move in for an arrest under safer, more controlled conditions.[9]

Because of Brydges' entrepreneurial spirit, officers are able to apprehend violators without the extreme risks associated with high-speed chases.

A recent study by Yahoo! and Harris Interactive reports that 72 percent of adults in the United States have considered starting their own businesses.[10] As this study suggests, many people not only in the United States but around the world dream of owning their own businesses, but most of them never actually launch a company. Those who do take the entrepreneurial plunge, however, will experience the thrill of creating something grand from nothing; they will also discover the challenges and the difficulties of building a business "from scratch." Whatever their reasons for choosing entrepreneurship, many recognize that true satisfaction comes only from running their own businesses the way they choose.

Researchers have invested a great deal of time and effort over the last decade studying these entrepreneurs and trying to paint a clear picture of the entrepreneurial personality. Although these studies have produced several characteristics entrepreneurs tend to exhibit, none of them has isolated a set of traits required for success. We now turn to a brief summary of the entrepreneurial profile.[11]

**1. *Desire and willingness to take initiative.*** Entrepreneurs feel a personal responsibility for the outcome of ventures they start. They prefer to be in control of their resources and to use those resources to achieve self-determined goals. They are willing to step forward and build businesses based on their creative ideas.

**2. *Preference for moderate risk.*** Entrepreneurs are not wild risk-takers, but are instead *calculating* risk-takers. Unlike "high rolling, riverboat gamblers," they rarely gamble. Entrepreneurs often have a different perception of the risk involved in a business situation. The goal may appear to be high—even impossible—from others' perspective, but entrepreneurs typically have thought through the situation and believe that their goals are reasonable and attainable. David Neeleman launched a low-cost airline, JetBlue, just when the industry was retrenching and suffering some of the greatest setbacks in its history. Many thought Neeleman was foolish to launch an airline in such a turbulent environment, but JetBlue is one of the few airlines that has been able to maintain its profitability.

This attitude explains why so many successful entrepreneurs failed many times before finally achieving their dreams. For instance, Milton Hershey, founder of one of the world's largest and most successful chocolate makers, started four candy businesses, all of which failed, before he launched the business that would make him famous. The director of an entrepreneurship center says that entrepreneurs "are not crazy, wild-eyed risk takers. Successful entrepreneurs understand the risks [of starting a business] and figure out how to manage them."[12] Good entrepreneurs become risk *reducers,* and one of the best ways to minimize the risk in any entrepreneurial venture is to create a sound business plan, which is the topic of Chapter 6.

**3. *Confidence in their ability to succeed.*** Entrepreneurs typically have an abundance of confidence in their ability to succeed, and they tend to be optimistic about their chances for business success. Entrepreneurs face many barriers when starting and running their companies, and a healthy dose of optimism can be an important component in their ultimate success.

**4. *Self-reliance.*** Entrepreneurs do not shy away from the responsibility for making their businesses succeed. Perhaps that is why many entrepreneurs persist in building businesses even when others advise them of the folly of their ideas. Their views reflect those of Ralph Waldo Emerson in his essay "Self Reliance:"[13]

> You will always find those who think they know what is your duty better than you know it. It is easy in the world to live after the world's opinion; it is easy in solitude to live after our own; but the great man is he who in the midst of the crowd keeps with perfect sweetness the independence of solitude.

**5. *Perseverance.*** Even when things don't work out as they planned, entrepreneurs don't give up. They simply keep trying. Real entrepreneurs follow the advice contained in the Japanese proverb, "Fall seven times; stand up eight."

*Gail Borden
and Borden Inc.*

Entrepreneur Gail Borden (1801–1874) was a prolific inventor, but most of his inventions, including the terraqueous wagon (a type of prairie schooner that could travel on land or water) and a meat biscuit (a mixture of dehydrated meat and flour that would last for months) never achieved commercial success. After witnessing a small child die from contaminated milk, Borden set out to devise a method for condensing milk to make it safer for human consumption in the days before refrigeration. For two years he tried a variety of methods, but every one of them failed. Finally, Borden developed a successful vacuum condensation process, won a patent for it, and built a company around the product. It failed, but Borden persevered. He launched another condensed milk business, this time with a stronger capital base, and it succeeded, eventually becoming Borden Inc., which in 1997 became part of Eagle Family Foods Inc., a company that still makes condensed milk using the process Borden developed 150 years ago. When he died, Borden was buried beneath a tombstone that reads, "I tried and failed. I tried again and succeeded."[14]

**6. *Desire for immediate feedback.*** Entrepreneurs like to know how they are doing and are constantly looking for reinforcement. Tricia Fox, founder of Fox Day Schools Inc., claims, "I like being independent and successful. Nothing gives you feedback like your own business."[15]

**7. *High level of energy.*** Entrepreneurs are more energetic than the average person. That energy may be a critical factor given the incredible effort required to launch a start-up company. Long hours—often 60 to 80 hours a week—and hard work are the rule rather than the exception. Building a successful business requires a great deal of stamina.

**8. *Competitiveness.*** Entrepreneurs tend to exhibit competitive behavior, often early in life. They enjoy competitive games and sports and always want to keep score!

**9. *Future orientation.*** Entrepreneurs tend to dream big and then formulate plans to transform those dreams into reality. They have a well-defined sense of searching for opportunities. They look ahead and are less concerned with what they accomplished yesterday than what they can do tomorrow. Ever vigilant for new business opportunities, entrepreneurs *observe* the same events other people do, but they *see* something different.

Taking this trait to the extreme are **serial entrepreneurs**, those who create multiple companies, often running more than one simultaneously. These entrepreneurs are masters at multi-tasking. Serial entrepreneurs get a charge from taking an idea, transforming it into a business, and repeating the process.

*Howard Yellen*

When asked how many businesses he has started, Howard Yellen says that he is not exactly sure. "It depends on how far back you want to go," he says, pointing out that he started several businesses as a kid. Yellen, now 43, has launched 6 companies in the past 15 years—many of them simultaneously, which also makes him a parallel entrepreneur—and has plans to launch several more in the future. Yellen keeps a list of business ideas and admits that his list currently includes 20 ideas for new businesses.[16]

**10. *Skill at organizing.*** Building a company "from scratch" is much like piecing together a giant jigsaw puzzle. Entrepreneurs know how to put the right people and resources together to accomplish a task. Effectively combining people and jobs enables entrepreneurs to bring their visions to reality.

**11. *Value of achievement over money.*** One of the most common misconceptions about entrepreneurs is that they are driven wholly by the desire to make money. To the contrary, *achievement* seems to be the primary motivating force behind entrepreneurs; money is simply a way of "keeping score" of accomplishments—a *symbol* of achievement. "Money is not the driving motive of most entrepreneurs," says Nick Grouf, the 28-year-old founder of a high-tech company. "It's just a very nice by-product of the process."[17]

Other characteristics entrepreneurs exhibit include:

■ *High degree of commitment.* Launching a company successfully requires total commitment from the entrepreneur. Business founders often immerse themselves completely in their businesses. "The commitment you have to make is tremendous; entrepreneurs usually put everything on the line," says one expert.[18] That commitment helps overcome business-threatening mistakes, obstacles, and pessimism from naysayers, however. Entrepreneurs' commitment to their ideas and to the businesses those ideas spawn determines how successful their companies ultimately become.

■ *Tolerance for ambiguity.* Entrepreneurs tend to have a high tolerance for ambiguous, ever-changing situations—the environment in which they most often operate. This ability to handle uncertainty is critical because these business builders constantly make decisions using new, sometimes conflicting information gleaned from a variety of unfamiliar sources.

■ *Flexibility.*    One hallmark of true entrepreneurs is their ability to adapt to the changing demands of their customers and their businesses. In this rapidly changing world economy, rigidity often leads to failure. As our society, its people, and their tastes change, entrepreneurs also must be willing to adapt their businesses to meet those changes. Successful entrepreneurs are willing to allow their business models to evolve as market conditions warrant.

**ENTREPRENEURIAL**
**Profile**

*Kevin Schaff and Thought Equity Management Inc.*

When Kevin Schaff launched Thought Equity Management Inc., his business plan said that the company would collect print ads from various advertising agencies and resell them online to newspapers, who could, in turn, offer creative print ads at affordable rates to small businesses. Although Schaff's company is in the advertising business, it focuses on a completely different service because Schaff spotted a different and better opportunity and was flexible enough to capitalize on it. Today, Thought Equity Management generates annual sales of more than $5 million by creating production-ready television commercials. The company also is a leading supplier of digitally mastered stock video footage and manages the video inventories for operations ranging from HBO, the cable television channel, to the U.S. National Collegiate Athletics Association.[19]

■ *Tenacity.* Obstacles, obstructions, and defeat typically do not dissuade entrepreneurs from doggedly pursuing their visions. Successful entrepreneurs have the willpower to conquer the barriers that stand in the way of their success.

What conclusion can we draw from the volumes of research conducted on the entrepreneurial personality? Entrepreneurs are not of one mold; no one set of characteristics can predict who will become entrepreneurs and whether or not they will succeed. Indeed, *diversity* seems to be a central characteristic of entrepreneurs. As you can see from the examples in this chapter, *anyone*—regardless of age, race, gender, color, national origin, or any other characteristic—can become an entrepreneur. There are no limitations on this form of economic expression, and Clyde Beasley is living proof.

**ENTREPRENEURIAL**
**Profile**

*Clyde Beasley and Beasley Creations*

While serving a sentence in Folsom State Prison for a drug-dealing conviction, Beasley was watching a golf tournament that was cancelled because of rain. He began wondering what golfers do when the weather prohibits them from playing outside and came up with the idea for a tabletop game that combines features of golf and billiards. The very day he was released from prison, Beasley began work on his idea. Armed only with rough blueprints, he purchased $200 worth of materials at a local building supply store and worked all night to build a prototype. Beasley borrowed $5,000 from a friend to lease a booth at the Billiards Congress of America trade show, where his game, which he calls the Original Tee and Cue, attracted attention from a manufacturer and a representative for the popular game show *The Price Is Right*. Today, Beasley sells his Original Tee and Cue through major retailers, and his company, Beasley Creations, generates annual sales of more than $5 million. "I want to let people know that anything is possible, regardless of your past and that it is never too late," says Beasley.[20]

Entrepreneurship is not a genetic trait; it is a skill that is learned. The editors of *Inc.* magazine claim, "Entrepreneurship is more mundane than it's sometimes portrayed. . . . You don't need to be a person of mythical proportions to be very, very successful in building a company."[21] As you read this book, we hope that you will pay attention to the numerous small business examples and will notice not only the creativity of the entrepreneurs behind them but also the diversity of those entrepreneurs.

## How to Spot Entrepreneurial Opportunities

**3.** Explain how entrepreneurs spot business opportunities.

One of the tenets of entrepreneurship is the ability to create new and useful ideas that solve the problems and challenges people face every day. Entrepreneurs achieve success by creating value in the marketplace when they combine resources in new and different ways to gain a competitive edge over rivals. Entrepreneurs can create value in a number of ways—inventing new products and services, developing new technology, discovering new knowledge, improving existing products or services, finding different ways of providing more goods and services with fewer resources, and many others. Indeed, finding new ways of satisfying customers' needs, inventing new products and services, putting together existing ideas in new and different ways, and creating new twists on existing products and services are hallmarks of the entrepreneur.

What is the entrepreneurial "secret" for creating value in the marketplace? In reality, the "secret" is no secret at all: it is applying creativity and innovation to solve problems and to exploit opportunities that people face every day. **Creativity** is the ability to develop new ideas and to discover new ways of looking at problems and opportunities. **Innovation** is the ability to *apply* creative solutions to those problems and opportunities to enhance or to enrich people's lives. Harvard's Ted Levitt says that creativity is *thinking* new things, and innovation is *doing* new things. In short, entrepreneurs succeed by *thinking and doing* new things or old things in new ways. Simply having a great new idea is not enough; turning the idea into a tangible product, service, or business venture is the essential next step.

Entrepreneurs' ability to build viable businesses around their ideas has transformed the world. From King Gillette's invention of the safety razor (Gillette) and Mary Kay Ash's use of a motivated team of consultants to sell her cosmetics (Mary Kay Cosmetics) to Steve Jobs and Steve Wozniak building the first personal computer in a California garage (Apple Inc.) and Fred Smith's concept for delivering packages overnight (FedEx), entrepreneurs have made the world a better place to live. How do entrepreneurs spot opportunities? Although there is no single process, the following techniques will help you learn to spot business opportunities in the same way these successful entrepreneurs did.

### Monitor Trends and Exploit Them Early On

Astute entrepreneurs watch both national and local trends that are emerging and then build businesses that align with those trends. Detecting a rising trend early on and launching a business to capitalize on it enables an entrepreneur to gain the advantage of being a "first mover."

*Michael Ryan and Spiro Baltas and Starwich*

Michael Ryan and Spiro Baltas observed how businesspeople stay connected with a multitude of electronic devices, ranging from cell phones and laptops to personal digital assistants and iPods. Targeting upscale businesspeople, the entrepreneurial duo launched Starwich, a chic sandwich lounge in New York City that offers a sophisticated menu in an equally sophisticated environment featuring overstuffed leather couches and international newspapers. Tapping into their target customers' needs, Starwich provides complimentary Wi-Fi connections and cell phone chargers at its tables and offers customers the use of fax machines and photocopiers.[22]

## Take a Different Approach to an Existing Market

Another way to spot opportunities is to ask if there is another way to reach an existing market with a unique product, service, or marketing strategy. Entrepreneurs are famous for finding new, creative approaches to existing markets and turning them into business opportunities.

*George Goodwin and
Goodwin Heart Pine*

George Goodwin, a master carpenter and homebuilder, spotted a business opportunity after he snagged and lost many fishing lures on underwater logs while fishing the shallow waters of several rivers. He learned that the logs had been harvested in the 1800s and had sunk to the river bottoms while loggers were floating them downstream to sawmills. Goodwin began researching the logs and discovered that they were perfectly preserved pieces of heart pine and heart cypress that were highly prized—and highly valued—by both the residential and commercial construction industries. Sensing a business opportunity, Goodwin and his wife invested their entire life savings to build a sawmill to clean, dry, and process these century-old logs and sell them to builders. Today, Goodwin Heart Pine supplies wood for flooring for houses, including celebrities such as musician Paul McCartney, actor Morgan Freeman, and the cable TV mogul Ted Turner. Their company now has 25 employees and annual sales that exceed $3 million.[23]

## Put a New Twist on an Old Idea

Sometimes entrepreneurs find opportunities by taking an old idea and giving it a unique twist. The result can lead to a profitable business venture.

*Peter Warhurst
and PODS*

Peter Warhurst owned a successful self-storage business in the United States and was looking for a second location, but finding land at a reasonable price proved to be a challenge. "Why not take the storage container to the customer?" he thought. He built a business plan based on his idea and in 1998 launched PODS, Portable On Demand Storage, a company that delivers storage containers to customers' homes for a monthly fee. The idea was a hit, and Warhurst's company now generates more than $200 million in annual sales and has franchisees in 45 states and Canada.[24]

## Look for Creative Ways to Use Existing Resources

Another way entrepreneurs uncover business opportunities is to find creative ways to use existing resources. This requires them to cast aside logic and traditional thinking.

*Lauren Padawer and
Alaska Glacial Mud
Company*

A resident of tiny Cordova, Alaska, Lauren Padawer often made float trips on the nearby Copper River. She always appreciated the river's beauty, but one day while on an excursion she was swimming in the river and noticed the rich mud swirling around her feet. The result of millions of years of glacial deposits, Padawer thought, "This is as luscious mud bath quality as you can find anywhere in the world." She began building a business plan and two years later launched the Alaska Glacial Mud Company, a business that sells the Glacial Facial Invigorating Mud Masque. "There is an enormous market for beauty products featuring natural and organic ingredients," says Padawer.[25]

## Realize That Others Have the Same Problem You Do

Another way to spot business opportunities is to recognize that other people face the same problems that you do. Providing a product or service that solves those problems offers the potential for a promising business.

*Lisa Druxman and
Stroller Strides*

After the birth of her son, Lisa Druxman decided not to return to her job as the manager of a health club. She wanted to spend time with her son but knew that she needed exercise to stay fit. Talking with friends and neighbors in the same situation, Druxman decided to start a small group exercise class that targeted mothers with infants. The class, which weaves together walking (with baby strollers) and exercises for the mothers with entertainment for the children, was a huge success. "That's when I knew I had touched on something big," says Druxman. Today, Druxman's company, Stroller Strides, has more than 300 franchised locations in the United States and Canada.[26]

## Notice What Is Missing

Sometimes entrepreneurs spot viable business opportunities by noticing what is *missing*. The first step is to determine whether a market for the missing product or service actually exists (perhaps the reason it does not exist is that there is not market potential), which is one of the objectives of building a business plan.

## Space: The Next Entrepreneurial Frontier?

In 1927, a $25,000 prize offered by New York business-man Raymond Orteig inspired a young airmail pilot named Charles Lindbergh to make the first non-stop transatlantic flight. "Lucky Lindy's" success launched the era of air travel, something that most people today take for granted.

On October 4, 2004, the $10 million X Prize, which was funded by the Ansari family and modeled after the Orteig Prize, motivated a team of explorers at Mojave Aerospace Adventures to build a spaceship capable of carrying three people at least 100 kilometers above the earth twice within two weeks. The craft, named SpaceShipOne, and the first private venture into space were the result of the joint efforts of famed pilot Burt Rutan, Microsoft cofounder Paul Allen, and British entrepreneur Sir Richard Branson, founder of Virgin Atlantic. Their historic flight has opened the doorway to the space tourism industry. In fact, Branson has launched his own company aimed at space travel, Virgin Galactic, and has signed a deal with Mojave Aerospace Adventures to purchase five spacecraft like SpaceShipOne with the goal of one day taking tourists on sub-orbital and orbital space flights. Branson's company is partnering with the U.S. state of New Mexico to build a spaceport that he says will operate as many as three Virgin Galactic flights a day. Rutan is currently testing SpaceShipTwo, a seven-passenger sub-orbital craft, and his company, Scaled Composites, plans to build a manufacturing facility in the Mojave desert to supply commercial spacecraft to his partner Branson and to any other pioneers willing to launch space tourism businesses.

Other entrepreneurs also have their sites set on space because they see it as a profitable business opportunity. Elon Musk, cofounder of PayPal, has started Space Exploration Technologies, a company that successfully launched a U.S. satellite into orbit at one-tenth the cost of a U.S. National Aeronautics and Space Administration launched rocket. Jeff Bezos, founder of Amazon.com, has created Blue Origin, a company that is building a spaceport in West Texas and operates a factory that is reported to be building a spacecraft designed specifically for space tourism. John Carmack, founder of Id Software, has invested millions of his own money to create Armadillo Aerospace, a company that aims to launch people more than 300,000 feet above the earth, where they can experience weightlessness. Jim Benson has launched Benson Space Company, a business that he says

will be able to take as many as six passengers on sub-orbital space flights using a spacecraft Benson designed called the Dream Chaser. "This is the most exciting thing I've ever done," says Benson of his space tourism work.

The entrepreneurial race into space promises to be an exciting one. Private-sector spending on space applications exceeded government spending on space for the first time in 1998, and the gap has been widening ever since. Although the price to play the space game can be significant, entrepreneurs see potential business opportunities in ideas that once seemed so far-fetched that they appeared only in science fiction novels, including space tourism, space hotels, solar satellites, and asteroid mining. Testifying before Congress recently on the future of private space ventures, Rutan estimated that as many as 100,000 people would be making sub-orbital space flights by 2020. Branson says that Virgin Galactic will sell its first tickets for sub-orbital flights for about $200,000. More than 100 people already have signed up and Benson predicts that tickets for similar flights with his company will cost between $100,000 and $300,000, including pre-flight training as well as the flight itself. As high as those prices seem to be, they are just a fraction of the $20 million that a handful of very wealthy space tourists have paid to travel to the International Space Station on a Russian Soyuz rocket. (Anousheh Ansari, whose family funded the X Prize, recently became the first female space tourist when she visited the International Space Station on a flight through another space pioneering company, Space Adventures Ltd.) Rutan says that competition will drive down costs to the point that large numbers of people can afford it, making space tourism a viable business. "Within 10 years," says Rutan, "the ticket price will be attractive enough that millions of people will want to leave the atmosphere."

Although many space ventures are financed by entrepreneurs who have built other successful companies, some space entrepreneurs are looking for private investors to provide capital to finance the cost of getting into space. Benson says he raised $1 million for his company "with less than a dozen phone calls" and that some investors said yes without even seeing his business plan. "If I had tried three or four years ago to solicit money for a private space flight, I wouldn't have had any luck," he says.

1. Use the resources of the Web to research space tourism. What do you predict for the future of this business?
2. What role did entrepreneurs play in industries such as air travel in the 1920s and what role do you foresee them playing in space travel in the twenty-first century? Based on your answer, what generalizations can you draw about entrepreneurs' role in society?

*Sources:* Chris Taylor, "The Entrepreneur's Guide to Outer Space," *Business 2.0,* March 2006, pp. 68–85; Kevin Maney, "Private Sector Enticing Public into Final Frontier," *USA Today,* June 17, 2005, pp. B1–B2; Andy Pasztor, "New Company Aims to Send Tourists to Space," *Wall Street Journal,* September 28, 2006, pp. B1, B5; Jeff Foust, "A New Chapter for a Space Entrepreneur," *The Space Review,* October 16, 2006, www.thespacerace.com/article/726/1; "Ansari X Prize," X Prize Foundation, www.xprize.org/xprizes/ansari_x_prize.html; Anousheh Ansari, Wikipedia, http://en.wikipedia.org/wiki/Anousheh_Ansari; "Charles Lindbergh: An American Aviator," www.charleslindbergh.com/plane/orteig.asp.

**Chris Vicino and Dogs on Wheels**

Chris Vicino, a native of New York City, grew tired of his career in finance and moved to Greenville, South Carolina, a small, fast-growing U.S. city of 60,000 people. While strolling the downtown district with his wife one day, Vicino noticed that there were no hot dog vendors like the ones he was so accustomed to seeing on most street corners in New York City. After purchasing all of the necessary licenses and a cart, Vicino opened Dogs on Wheels and began selling classic New York style hot dogs to hungry Southerners.[27]

No matter which methods they use to detect business opportunities, true entrepreneurs follow up their ideas with action, building companies to capitalize on their ideas.

## The Benefits of Owning a Small Business

**4.** Describe the benefits of owning a small business.

Surveys show that owners of small businesses believe they work harder, earn more money, and are happier than if they worked for a large company. Before launching any business venture, every potential entrepreneur should consider the benefits of owning a small business.

### Opportunity to Gain Control Over Your Own Destiny

Entrepreneurs cite controlling their own destinies as one of the benefits of owning their own businesses. Owning a business provides entrepreneurs the independence and the opportunity to achieve what is important to them. Entrepreneurs want to "call the shots" in their lives, and they use their businesses to bring this desire to life. A study by the Hartford Financial Services Group found that 53 percent of entrepreneurs cited "being my own boss" as the major incentive for starting their businesses (second only to "setting my own hours," which was cited by 62 percent of respondents).[28] Entrepreneurs reap the intrinsic rewards of knowing they are the driving forces behind their businesses.

### Opportunity to Make a Difference

Increasingly, entrepreneurs are starting businesses because they see an opportunity to make a difference in a cause that is important to them. Known as **social entrepreneurs**, these business builders seek to find innovative solutions to some of society's most pressing and most challenging problems. Whether it is providing low-cost, sturdy housing for families in developing countries, promoting the arts in small communities, or creating a company that educates young people about preserving the earth's limited resources, entrepreneurs are finding ways to combine their concerns for social issues and their desire to earn good livings. Although they see the importance of building viable, sustainable businesses, social entrepreneurs' primary goal is to use their companies to make a positive impact on the world.

*Earl Martin and
Building Educated
Leaders for Life (BELL)*

While attending Harvard Law School, Earl Martin Phalen volunteered as a mentor for kids from low-income families who were performing poorly in school. That experience led Phalen to launch a company, Building Educated Leaders for Life (BELL), whose purpose is to improve the academic performance, self-esteem, and career opportunities for children in kindergarten through grade six from low-income urban communities. Through his company, Phalen has built a network of teachers, mentors, parents, and community leaders to support the 7,000 children that BELL serves in four major U.S. cities. The program works; 82 percent of BELL scholars read at or above their grade level despite having started the program more than one year or more behind in their reading skills. "We have a program that has a demonstrable and positive impact on the lives of children," says Phalen, who won a President's Service Award for his work with BELL. "And we have a huge, huge waiting list of children who want to get into our program."[29]

## Opportunity to Reach Your Full Potential

Too many people find their work boring, unchallenging, and unexciting. But to most entrepreneurs, there is little difference between work and play; the two are synonymous. Roger Levin, founder of Levin Group, the largest dental practice management consulting firm in the world, says, "When I come to work every day, it's not a job for me. I'm having fun!"[30]

Entrepreneurs' businesses become the instrument for self-expression and self-actualization. Owning a business challenges all of an entrepreneur's skills, abilities, creativity, and determination. The only barriers to success are self-imposed. Entrepreneurs' creativity, determination, and enthusiasm—not limits artificially created by an organization (e.g., the "glass ceiling")—determine how high they can rise.

## Opportunity to Reap Impressive Profits

Although money is *not* the primary force driving most entrepreneurs, the profits their businesses can earn are an important motivating factor in their decisions to launch companies. If accumulating wealth is high on your list of priorities, owning a business is usually the best way to achieve it. When a survey asked the wealthiest one percent of Americans to identify the career path that offers young people the greatest potential for financial success, the number one response (46 percent) was starting a business.[31] Indeed, nearly 75 percent of those on the *Forbes* list of the 400 richest Americans are first-generation entrepreneurs![32] Self-employed people are four times more likely to become millionaires than those who work for someone else. According to researchers Thomas Stanley and William Danko, the typical American millionaire is first-generation wealthy, owns a small business in a less-than-glamorous industry such as welding, junk yards, or auctioneering, and works between 45 and 55 hours per week.[33]

*Mark Benioff and
Salesforce.com*

Marc Benioff has reaped the financial rewards from his entrepreneurial efforts. As a teenager, Benioff made enough money designing computer games to buy a car and to pay for his college education. After college, he went to work for software giant Oracle, where he became the youngest vice-president in the history of the company. Living up to his reputation as a "big-idea guy," Benioff left Oracle to launch Salesforce.com, a company that sells customer relationship management (CRM) software over the Web. Salesforce.com (where Benioff's golden retriever, Koa, is the CLO, "Chief Love Officer") has become the industry leader, with annual sales of more than $280 million and projections of $10 billion a year by 2012. Benioff, who owns 30 percent of the company's stock, has a net worth of hundreds of millions of dollars. Benioff also runs a global philanthropic organization based on the "one percent solution." Salesforce.com gives one percent of its profits, one percent of its net worth, and one percent of its employee hours back to the communities it serves.[34]

### Opportunity to Contribute to Society and Be Recognized for Your Efforts

Often, small business owners are among the most respected—and most trusted—members of their communities. Business deals based on trust and mutual respect are the hallmark of many established small companies. These owners enjoy the trust and the recognition they receive from the customers they have served faithfully over the years. Playing a vital role in their local business systems and knowing that the work they do has a significant impact on how smoothly our nation's economy functions is yet another reward for entrepreneurs.

### Opportunity to Do What You Enjoy Doing

A common sentiment among small business owners is that their work *really* isn't work. In fact, a survey conducted by the National Federation of Independent Businesses reports that 46 percent of business owners say they will never fully retire from their businesses![35] Most successful entrepreneurs choose to enter their particular business fields because they have an interest in them and enjoy those lines of work. They have made their avocations (hobbies) their vocations (work) and are glad they did! These entrepreneurs are living the advice Harvey McKay offers: "Find a job doing what you love, and you'll never have to work a day in your life."

**ENTREPRENEURIAL Profile**

*Blair Pethel and Earl Domaine Dublère*

Blair Pethel was raised in the United States, and although he was trained as a concert pianist, he landed a job in journalism in London, where he developed a passion for wine. Pethel's dream was to transform his passion for wine into a business, owning his own vineyard and producing wine under his own label. Eventually, he and his family moved to Beaune, France, the heart of the Burgundy wine country, where Pethel worked with other vintners to learn about the industry. In 2004, he purchased a small vineyard, from which he produced his first vintage, bottled under the name Earl Domaine Dublère ("du Blair"). Pethel, who already has invested $1.7 million in his venture, says that the work is extremely hard but is incredibly rewarding because he is living out his life's dream.[36]

## The Potential Drawbacks of Entrepreneurship

**5.** Describe the potential drawbacks of owning a small business.

Although owning a business has many benefits and provides many opportunities, anyone planning to enter the world of entrepreneurship should be aware of its potential drawbacks. "If you aren't 100 percent sure you want to own a business," says one business consultant, "there are plenty of demands and mishaps along the way to dissuade you."[37]

### Uncertainty of Income

Opening and running a business provides no guarantees that an entrepreneur will earn enough money to survive. Some small businesses barely earn enough to provide the owner-manager with an adequate income. In fact, the median income of small business owners is about the same ($30,000) as that of wage and salary workers. (However, business owners are more likely to earn high incomes than wage and salary workers.)[38] In the early days of a start-up, a business often cannot provide an attractive salary for its owner and meet all of its financial obligations, which means that the entrepreneur may have to live on savings for a time. The regularity of income that comes with working for someone else is absent because the owner is always the last one to be paid. The owner of a flavor and fragrances manufacturing operation recalls the

time his bank unexpectedly called the company's loans just before Thanksgiving, squeezing both the company's and the family's cash flow. "We had planned a huge Christmas party, but we canceled that," recalls his wife. "And Christmas. And our usual New Year's trip."[39]

### Risk of Losing Your Entire Invested Capital

The small business failure rate is relatively high. According to a study by the National Federation of Independent Businesses (NFIB), 35 percent of new businesses fail within two years, and 54 percent shut down within four years. Within six years, 64 percent of new businesses will have folded.[40]

A failed business can be financially and emotionally devastating. Before launching their businesses, entrepreneurs should ask themselves whether they can cope financially and psychologically with the consequences of failure. They should consider the risk/reward trade-off before putting their personal assets and their mental well-being at risk:

- What is the worst that could happen if I open my business and it fails?
- How likely is the worst to happen?
- What can I do to lower the risk of my business failing?
- If my business were to fail, what is my contingency plan for coping?

### Long Hours and Hard Work

The average U.S. small business owner, for example, works 52 hours per week, compared to the 34.2 hours per week the typical U.S. production employee works.[41] In many start-ups, 10- to 12-hour days and six- or seven-day workweeks with no paid vacations are the norm. For example, restaurateurs face not only traditionally high failure rates (one in two new restaurants fails within two years) but also long work hours; one in ten restaurant owners work more than 80 hours a week.[42]

Because they often must do everything themselves, owners experience intense, draining workdays. "I'm the owner, manager, secretary, and janitor," says Cynthia Malcolm, who owns a salon called the Hand Candy Mind and Body Escape.[43] Many business owners start down the path of entrepreneurship thinking that they will own a business only to discover later that the business owns them!

### Lower Quality of Life Until the Business Gets Established

The long hours and hard work needed to launch a company can take their toll on the remainder of an entrepreneur's life. Business owners often find their roles as husbands and wives or fathers and mothers take a back seat to their roles as company founders. Marriages and friendships are too often casualties of small business ownership. Part of the problem is that entrepreneurs are most likely to launch their businesses between the ages of 25 and 34, just when they start their families.

*Peyton Anderson
and Affinergy Inc.*

Peyton Anderson, owner of Affinergy Inc., a 12-person biotech firm, struggles to balance the demands of his young company and his family, which includes three children under the age of four. "I do a lot of work from 9 P.M. to midnight," says Anderson, "and I try to keep Saturday open to do things with the kids." He also uses flextime during the week to spend more time with his family, but maintaining balance is an ongoing battle, especially when managing a young company. "Even while I'm singing to them in the bathtub, in the back of my mind, I'm grinding on stuff at work," admits Anderson.[44]

Figure 1.2 provides a breakdown of the ages at which entrepreneurs start their businesses.

### High Levels of Stress

Launching and running a business can be an extremely rewarding experience, but it also can be a highly stressful one. Most entrepreneurs have made significant investments in their companies, have left behind the safety and security of a steady paycheck, and have mortgaged everything they own to get into business. Failure often means total financial ruin as well as a serious psychological blow, and that creates high levels of stress and anxiety. "Being an entrepreneur takes sheer guts and demands far more than an 'employee' mentality," says Jamie Kreitman, founder of Kreitman Knitworks Ltd., a company specializing in whimsical apparel and footwear.[45]

### Complete Responsibility

Owning a business is highly rewarding, but many entrepreneurs find that they must make decisions on issues about which they are not really knowledgeable. When there is no one to ask, pressure can build quickly. The realization that the decisions they make are the cause of success or failure of the business has a devastating effect on some people. Small business owners realize quickly that *they* are the business.

**FIGURE 1.2 Owner Age at Business Formation**

*Source:* National Federation of Independent Businesses and Wells Fargo Bank, 2002.

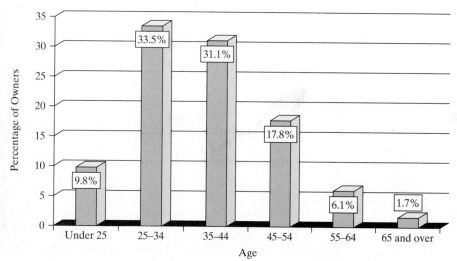

### Discouragement

Launching a business requires much dedication, discipline, and tenacity. Along the way to building a successful business, entrepreneurs will run headlong into many obstacles, some of which may appear to be insurmountable. Discouragement and disillusionment can set in, but successful entrepreneurs know that every business encounters rough spots and that perseverance is required to get through them.

## Why the Boom: The Fuel Feeding the Entrepreneurial Fire

**6.** Explain the forces that are driving the growth of entrepreneurship.

What forces are driving this entrepreneurial trend in our economy? Which factors have led to this age of entrepreneurship? Some of the most significant ones follow.

### Entrepreneurs as Heroes

An intangible but very important factor is the attitude that Americans have toward entrepreneurs. As a nation, we have raised them to hero status and have held out their accomplishments as models to follow. Business founders such as Niklas Zennström and Janus Friis (Skype), Michael Dell (Dell Inc.), Oprah Winfrey (Harpo Productions and Oxygen Media), Howard Schultz (Starbucks Corporation), Richard Branson (Virgin Group), and Phil Knight (Nike Inc.) are to entrepreneurship what David Beckham and Yao Ming are to sports.

### Entrepreneurial Education

People with more education are more likely to start businesses than those with less education, and entrepreneurship, in particular, is an extremely popular course of study among students at all levels. A rapidly growing number of college students see owning a business as an attractive career option, and in addition to signing up for entrepreneurship courses, many of them are launching companies while in school. Today, more than 2,100 colleges and universities offer at least one course in entrepreneurship or small business management, up from just 16 in 1970![46] More than 500 colleges and universities now offer entrepreneurship majors at both undergraduate and graduate levels, up from just 175 in 1990.[47] Many colleges and universities are having trouble meeting the demand for courses in entrepreneurship and small business management.

### Economic and Demographic Factors

As mentioned earlier, most entrepreneurs start their businesses between the ages of 25 and 44, and the number of U.S. citizens in that age range, for example, stands at more than 85 million! The economic growth that has occurred across the globe over the past 20 years has created many business opportunities and a significant pool of capital for launching companies.

### Shift to a Service Economy

In the United States, the service sector now accounts for about 80 percent of the jobs (up from 70 percent in the 1950s) and 64 percent of the gross domestic product (GDP).[48] Because of their relatively low start-up costs, service businesses have been very popular with entrepreneurs. The booming service sector has provided entrepreneurs with many business opportunities, from hotels and health care to computer maintenance and test preparation services.

**ENTREPRENEURIAL Profile**

*Joseph Jewell and PrepMe*

After making a perfect score on the Scholastic Aptitude Test (SAT), a college-entrance exam, and enrolling at the California Institute of Technology, Joseph Jewell, 24, launched an online SAT-preparation service called PrepMe using $20,000 he and his cofounders won in the University of Chicago's business plan competition. Despite intense competition from larger companies, PrepMe is growing fast because it offers students a customized approach to studying for this important college admissions test. PrepMe's system administers a diagnostic test to assess students' areas of weakness and then uses repetitive exercises to improve them and offers 20 to 60 more hours of instruction than its competition for the same price. PrepMe's courses also include live coaching via e-mail, instant messaging, and telephone on writing essays. "We're changing the way test preparation is taught," says Jewell.[49]

### Technology Advancements

With the help of modern business technology—personal and tablet computers, personal digital assistants, fax machines, copiers, color printers, instant messaging, and voicemail—even one person working at home can look like a big business. At one time, the high cost of such technological wizardry made it impossible for small businesses to compete with larger companies that could afford the hardware. Although entrepreneurs may not be able to manufacture heavy equipment in their spare bedrooms, they can run a service- or information-based company from their homes very effectively and look like any *Fortune* 500 company to customers and clients.

**ENTREPRENEURIAL Profile**

*Scott Adams and Dilbert*

Scott Adams, creator of the *Dilbert* cartoon strip that appears in more than 2,000 newspapers worldwide, operates his entire business from a home office near San Francisco that resembles nothing of the cubicles in which his cartoon characters exist. He runs the "Dilbert Empire," which includes the cartoon strip, books, and many Dilbert-related products, from his custom-made desk ("the world's coolest desk," says Adams), which is equipped with a host of high-tech gadgetry. Because he suffers from focal dystonia, a neurological movement disorder that affects his right (drawing) hand, Adams uses a high-tech interactive computer display to create his cartoon strips, making him one of the few cartoonists to use computer technology exclusively to produce his cartoons. Adams works 50 to 60 hours a week and when he gets tired, he often sleeps on the floor next to his desk. "I don't even bother walking to the couch," he says.[50]

### Independent Lifestyle

Entrepreneurship fits the way Americans want to live—independent and self-sustaining. Increasingly, entrepreneurs are starting businesses for lifestyle reasons. They want the freedom to choose where they live, the hours they work, and what they do. Although financial security remains an important goal for most entrepreneurs, lifestyle issues such as more time with family and friends, more leisure time, and more control over work-related stress also are important. To these "lifestyle entrepreneurs," launching businesses that give them the flexibility to work the hours they prefer and live where they want are far more important than money.

### E-Commerce and the World Wide Web

The proliferation of the **World Wide Web**, the vast network that links computers around the globe via the Internet and opens up endless oceans of information to its users, has spawned thousands of entrepreneurial ventures since its beginning in 1993. As online shopping becomes easier, more engaging, and more secure for shoppers, e-commerce will continue to grow rapidly.[51] Entrepreneurs see the power of the Web and are putting it to use. Interland, a Web hosting and Internet services provider, estimates that 72 percent of small businesses have established Web sites, approximately double the number of small businesses that had Web sites in 2002. Of those entrepreneurs who have Web sites, 78 percent say that their companies are healthier—having gained a competitive advantage or a stronger foothold in the marketplace—because they have Web sites.[52]

**ENTREPRENEURIAL Profile**

*Jacquelyn Tran and Perfume Bay*

As a young girl working in the cosmetics and perfume shop that her parents, both Vietnamese refugees, started in California, Jacquelyn Tran learned extensively about the industry, its suppliers, and customer preferences. In 1999, just as Tran was about to graduate from college, her father started a wholesale cosmetics and perfume division, which gave Tran the idea of launching a perfume store online. "I was interested in the Internet and thought it would be neat to have an online store," she recalls. After conducting extensive research and analyzing the competition, Tran, just 22 years old at the time, saw a market opportunity for an online store that offered a broad product line and a deep selection of products. She borrowed $50,000 from her parents to start Perfume Bay, an online store that sells more than 800 brands of perfume, cologne, and beauty products. With sales approaching $10 million, Perfume Bay has become so successful that Tran's parents have folded many of their businesses into her company.[53]

### International Opportunities

No longer are small businesses limited to pursuing customers within their own borders. The dramatic shift to a global economy has opened the door to tremendous business opportunities for those entrepreneurs willing to reach across the globe. Although the United States is an attractive market for entrepreneurs, approximately 95 percent of the world's population lives outside its borders. With so many opportunities in international markets, even the

## In the Entrepreneurial Spotlight

### ■ Collegiate Entrepreneurs

For growing numbers of students, college is not just a time of learning, partying, and growing into young adulthood; it is fast becoming a place for building a business. Today, more than 2,100 colleges and universities offer courses in entrepreneurship and small business management, and many of them have trouble meeting the demand for these classes. "Students used to come to college and assume that five to ten years down the road they'd start a business," says Gerry Hills, co-founder of the Collegiate Entrepreneurs Organization (CEO). "[Today], they come in preparing to get ideas and launch."

Many of these collegiate entrepreneurs' ideas come from their college experience. While attending the University of Iowa, Diana Reed became one of the top baton twirlers in the Big Ten (athletic) Conference, and, with the help of several entrepreneurship classes she took during her college career, Reed launched a for-profit baton-twirling school. Now a senior, Reed, with a double major in dance and business, says, "I learned to think about twirling as a market, not just a sport. My career as a competitive twirler may be coming to an end, but I can see there's almost unlimited potential in the twirling market."

Megan Wettach started a business while she was still in secondary school. Wettach opened a retail store to sell prom dresses in her hometown in the U.S. state of Iowa. After taking an entrepreneurship class in college, Wettach decided to launch another business, this time designing her own dresses. The 22-year-old negotiated a $150,000 line

of credit at a local bank, contracted with an apparel maker in China to produce her designs, and then convinced Nordstrom to sell her dresses. "My professors opened my eyes to the idea that I can be bigger than a little dress store in Iowa," says Wettach. "I can be a global force in fashion."

College was fertile ground for business ideas for entrepreneur Mark Cuban, who took his first class in entrepreneurship as a freshman. "It really motivated me," recalls Cuban, who apparently learned well. Cuban went on to launch Broadcast.com, a media company that he later sold to Yahoo! for $6 billion. Cuban is cofounder of HD-Net, a high definition television network, and is the animated owner of the Dallas Mavericks pro basketball team. "There is so much more to starting a business than just understanding finance, accounting, and marketing," he says. "Teaching kids what has worked with startup companies and learning about experiences that others have had could really make a difference. I know it did for me."

Budding entrepreneurs at a growing number of colleges can take advantage of special programs designed to create a culture for entrepreneurship. For instance, the University of Maryland's Hinman Campus Entrepreneurship Opportunities program provides space in a specially outfitted dormitory for 100 students who want to build their own companies. Students not only share living space with other like-minded entrepreneurial types, an ideal setting for encouraging start-ups, but they also have access to amenities such as professionally appointed conference rooms, wireless Internet access, SMART Boards, ample computer facilities, video-conferencing equipment, copiers, and a phone system that rings simultaneously home and cellular phones so that no one misses an important business call. Weekly presentations from entrepreneurs, venture capitalists, attorneys, and others help students define their business ideas and develop their business plans. Two hundred students recently applied for the 100 available spots in the dorm with its incubator-like business environment. The program, which won the Price Institute Innovative Entrepreneurship Educators Award, is working. Twenty of the students already have launched companies, including a medical software company and a textbook sales business. "It's often over those late-night pizzas where the best ideas are born," says one college administrator. One student entrepreneur in the program agrees, "A lot of it is the community. Being around people in the program inspires one to think about other opportunities out there. What I've learned here is how to plan, how to make a business actually work."

1. Some critics contend that entrepreneurship cannot be taught. What do you think?

2. In addition to the normal obstacles of starting a business, what other barriers do collegiate entrepreneurs face?
3. What advantages do collegiate entrepreneurs have when launching a business?
4. What advice would you offer a fellow college student about to start a business?
5. Work with a team of your classmates to develop ideas about what your college or university could do to create a culture that supports entrepreneurship on your campus or in your community.

*Sources:* Patricia B. Gray, Can Entrepreneurship Be Taught?" *FSB,* March 2006, pp. 34–51; Mark Henricks, "Honor Roll," *Entrepreneur,* April 2005, pp. 68–73; Nichole L. Torres, "Big Biz on Campus," *Entrepreneur B.Y.O.B.,* December 2004, p. 130; Nichole L. Torres, "Hit the Floor," *Entrepreneur,* May 2005, p. 122; Nichole L. Torres, "Inside Job," *Entrepreneur,* March 2005, p. 132; Michael Myser, "Giving College Kids a Smoother Move," *Business 2.0,* June 2004, p. 82; Ellen McCarthy, "A Dorm for Dreamers," *Washington Post,* October 30, 2002, p. E1; "Hinman CEOs Living-Learning Entrepreneurship Program," www.hinmanceos.umd.edu/.

smallest businesses can sell globally. Most small businesses do not take advantage of exporting opportunities, however. A study by the National Federation of Independent Businesses reports that just 13 percent of small businesses report making foreign sales within the previous three years. The most common barriers to international trade small business owners cited were difficulty locating potential customers and problems finding reliable foreign sales representatives to handle their products.[54] As business becomes increasingly global in nature, international opportunities for small businesses will continue to grow rapidly in the twenty-first century.

Although "going global" can be fraught with many dangers and problems, especially for small companies, many entrepreneurs are discovering that selling their products and services in foreign markets is not really as difficult as they originally thought. Patience, diligence, and a management commitment to exporting are essential elements.

**ENTREPRENEURIAL**
**Profile**

*Bob Piazza and Price Pump Manufacturing*

Bob Piazza, president of Price Pump Manufacturing, a small American maker of centrifugal pumps with 36 employees, says that until 1994, exporting accounted for just two percent of the company's sales. As a result of participating in a U.S. Department of Commerce trade show in Singapore that year, however, Piazza was able to find reliable trade intermediaries to handle the company's pumps in foreign markets. Today, Price Pump Manufacturing's markets span the globe, and exports now account for 25 percent of sales, which represents a significant change for a company that once was hesitant to look outside the borders of the United States for customers.[55]

## The Cultural Diversity of Entrepreneurship

**7.** Discuss the role of diversity in small business and entrepreneurship.

As we have seen, virtually anyone has the potential to become an entrepreneur. The entrepreneurial sector consists of a rich blend of people of all races, ages, backgrounds, and cultures. It is this cultural diversity that is one of entrepreneurship's greatest strengths. We turn our attention to those who make up this diverse fabric we call entrepreneurship.

### Young Entrepreneurs

Young people are setting the pace in entrepreneurship. Disenchanted with their prospects in corporate America and willing to take a chance to control their own destinies, scores of young people are choosing entrepreneurship as their primary career path. Generation X, made up of those people born between 1965 and 1980, is the most entrepreneurial generation in the history of the United States. Because members of this generation are responsible for 70 percent of all U.S. business start-ups, "Generation X" might be more appropriately called "Generation E."[56] There is no slowdown in sight as Generation Y (the Millenials), begins to flex its entrepreneurial muscles. The Global Entrepreneurship Monitor reports that globally entrepreneurial activity is highest among people between the ages of 25 and 34, but those in the 18-to-24 age group are a strong second.[57] In the United States, a recent survey by Junior Achievement reports that 69 percent of teenagers say they hope to launch their own businesses.[58]

*Mark Zuckerberg
and Facebook*

In his sophomore year at Harvard University, 19-year-old Mark Zuckerberg built a Web site that allowed Harvard students to post personal profiles, photographs, and share their hobbies and interests. Within two weeks, two-thirds of Harvard students had signed on, and Zuckerberg, who had never intended to build a business, realized that he had created a hit. Over the course of the next month, he opened the site to students at Columbia, Stanford, and Yale universities. The site, which Zuckerberg named Facebook, now has more than 7 million users, two-thirds of whom log on to the site daily, at more than 2,100 colleges and 22,000 high schools in the United States. Zuckerberg, who left college to run the company full-time, relied on private investors and venture capital companies to provide the funding to fuel his company's growth. Today, Facebook is valued at more than $2 billion![59]

### Women Entrepreneurs

Despite years of legislative effort, women still face discrimination in the workforce. However, small business has been a leader in offering women opportunities for economic expression through employment and entrepreneurship. Increasing numbers of women are discovering that the best way to break the "glass ceiling" that prevents them from rising to the top of many organizations is to start their own companies (see Figure 1.3). The freedom that owning their own companies gives them is one reason that women-owned businesses are growing at a rate that is nearly twice as fast as that of all private businesses.[60] Many of them are in fields that traditionally have been male dominated.[61]

**FIGURE 1.3 Women-Owned Businesses in the United States**
*Source:* National Federation of Women Business Owners, 2006.

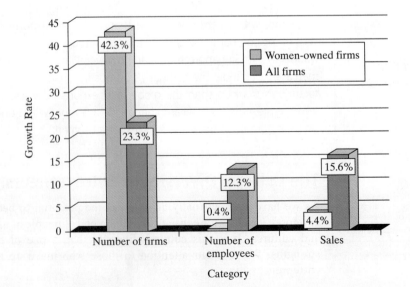

*Elizabeth Holmes and Theranos*

Elizabeth Holmes built her company, Theranos, around a device she designed that can prevent the 100,000 deaths that occur each year from adverse drug reactions. A patient places a small drop of blood into the Theranos 1.0, which analyzes the level of medicine in the person's system and sends it wirelessly to a secure database, which is available online to physicians. Just 19 when she designed the revolutionary apparatus, Holmes has raised $16 million in seed capital from venture capital firms and private equity firms to get Theranos up and running.[62]

Although the businesses women start tend to be smaller than those men start, their impact is anything but small. The 10.6 million women-owned companies across the United States employ 13 million workers and generate approximately $1.9 trillion in revenue.[63] Women entrepreneurs have even broken through the comic strip barrier. The comic-strip character Blondie Bumstead, long a typical suburban housewife married to Dagwood, now owns her own catering business with her best friend and neighbor, Tootsie Woodly!

*Beck Hickey and Beck(y)*

Beck Hickey saw a business opportunity in the old skateboards customers trade in when they purchase new ones. Hickey, herself an avid skateboarder, launched Beck(y), a company that takes the used boards off retailers' hands (paying only shipping charges) and then transforms the decks of the boards into one-of-a-kind Sk8bags, a line of handbags that ranges from evening bags and messenger totes to gym bags and iPod cases. Hickey sells her unique bags to boutiques and sport shops in Australia, Brazil, Europe, Canada, the United States, and Japan.[64]

### Minority Enterprises

Like women, U.S. minorities also are choosing entrepreneurship more often than ever before. Asians, African-Americans, and Hispanics, respectively, are most likely to become entrepreneurs. Like women, minorities cite discrimination as a principal reason for their limited access to the world of entrepreneurship. Minority-owned businesses have come a long way in the past decade, however. Increasingly, minorities are finding ways to overcome the barriers to business ownership. A recent study by the Ewing Marion Kaufman Foundation found that African-Americans are 50 percent more likely to start a business than whites, and Hispanic-Americans are 20 percent more likely.[65] Studies show that America's minority entrepreneurs own more than 4.1 million businesses that generate $668 billion in revenues and employ 4.7 million workers.[66] The future is promising for this new generation of minority entrepreneurs who are better educated, have more business experience, have more entrepreneurial role models, and are better prepared for business ownership than their predecessors.

*Shawn Prez and Power Moves Inc.*

When he worked for Bad Boy Entertainment, Shawn Prez handled promotions for rapper Sean "Diddy" Combs. Many clients were so impressed with Prez's work that they asked him to take on jobs after their contracts with Bad Boy Entertainment were finished. Prez knew it was time to start his own company and launched Power Moves Inc., a street promotion, marketing, and event-planning company. Prez's niche is helping companies find the best way to reach youth markets, who tend not to respond to traditional advertising technique. To stay on top of the ever-changing preferences of these customers, Prez employs "street teams," hip, trend-setting urbanites between the ages of 18 and 27, to cover 31 major cities in Europe, the United States, and Japan and report on the latest trends.[67]

### Immigrant Entrepreneurs

The United States has always been a "melting pot" of diverse cultures, and many immigrants have been lured to this nation by its economic freedom. Unlike the unskilled "huddled masses" of the past, today's immigrants arrive with more education and experience. Although many of them come to the United States with few assets, their dedication and desire to succeed enable them to achieve their entrepreneurial dreams.

*Chai Ling and Jenzabar*

Chai Ling's leadership role in the uprising against the Chinese government at Tiananmen Square in 1989 landed her on the government's most wanted list. Hidden inside a cargo crate, she escaped to the United States, where she earned degrees from Princeton and Harvard Universities and was nominated twice for the Nobel Peace Prize. When she graduated from Harvard in 1998, Ling launched Jenzabar (loosely translated from Mandarin as "best and brightest"), a company that provides Web-based software products and services for colleges. The company survived the dot-com implosion and other business obstacles, and its products are used in 20 percent of the universities across the United States, generating more than $50 million in annual sales.[68]

## Part-Time Entrepreneurs

Starting a part-time business is a popular gateway to entrepreneurship. Part-timers have the best of both worlds. They can ease into a business without sacrificing the security of a steady paycheck. Nearly 12 million entrepreneurs operate part-time businesses. A major advantage of going into business part-time is the lower risk in case the venture flops. Starting a part-time business and maintaining a "regular" job can challenge the endurance of the most determined entrepreneur, but it does provide a safety net in case the business venture fails. Many part-timers are "testing the entrepreneurial waters" to see whether their business ideas will work and whether they enjoy being self-employed. As they grow, many part-time enterprises absorb more of the entrepreneur's time until they become full-time businesses.

## Home-Based Business Owners

Home-based businesses are booming! Indeed, 49 percent of all businesses are home-based, but about 75 percent of them are very small companies with no employees.[69] However, when taken collectively, their impact is anything but small; these companies generate $102 billion in revenue per year.[70] The biggest advantage home-based businesses offer entrepreneurs is the cost savings of not having to lease or buy an external location. Home-based entrepreneurs also enjoy the benefits of flexible work and lifestyles. (One survey of home-based workers reports that 39 percent work in sweat pants and shirts, and 10 percent work naked!)[71]

In the past, home-based businesses tended to be rather unexciting cottage industries such as crafts or sewing. Today's home-based businesses are more diverse; modern home-based entrepreneurs are more likely to be running high-tech or service companies that can generate millions of dollars in sales. The typical home-based business generates average annual revenues of $62,500 and earns a net income of nearly $22,600.[72] Because of their low-cost locations, home-based businesses generate higher gross profit margins than companies that have locations outside the home. Less costly and more powerful technology, which is transforming many ordinary homes into "electronic cottages," will continue to drive the growth of home-based businesses.

*Jennifer Behar and Jennifer's Homemade*

The idea for Jennifer Behar's home-based business came to her one day while she was stuck in a traffic jam on the way home from her job as a marketing executive for a large company. "I saw the whole thing right in front of me," she recalls, "the packaging, the product, the business plan. I just ran with it." Behar's idea was to make gourmet biscotti and breadsticks and sell them on her company's Web site and through gourmet food shops. Behar, a single mother, launched Jennifer's Homemade from her home, where she baked all of the items she sold. Sales took off quickly, and Behar quit her corporate job to focus on her business. Within a year, she began leasing space in a commercial kitchen and hired nine employees to produce her company's products. Today, her customer base includes local gourmet shops as well as large chains such as Whole Foods and The Fresh Market. Behar also donates five percent of her company's sales to a local nonprofit food bank.[73]

## Family Business Owners

A **family-owned business** is one that includes two or more members of a family with financial control of the company. They are an integral part of the economy. For example, more than 90 percent of the 25.5 million businesses in the United States are family-owned and managed. These companies account for 60 percent of total employment in the United States, 78 percent of all new jobs, and generate more than 50 percent of the U.S. gross domestic product (GDP). Not all of them are small; 37 percent of the *Fortune* 500 companies are family businesses.[74]

"When it works right," says one writer, "nothing succeeds like a family firm. The roots run deep, embedded in family values. The flash of the fast buck is replaced with long-term plans. Tradition counts."[75]

**ENTREPRENEURIAL
Profile**

*Donna Grucci Butler
and Fireworks
by Grucci*

Fireworks by Grucci, a company now in its fifth generation of leadership, is one family business that has managed to beat the odds. Donna Grucci Butler, the great-great-great granddaughter of company founder Angelo Lanzetta, grew up working in the family business and is now its president. Fireworks by Grucci puts on more than 250 fireworks shows each year and generates more than $10 million in annual revenue. The company's list of credits includes six U.S. presidential inaugurations, three Olympics, and three World's Fairs.[76]

Despite their magnitude, family businesses face a major threat—a threat from within: management succession. Only 33 percent of family businesses survive to the second generation; just 12 percent make it to the third generation; and only 3 percent survive to the fourth generation and beyond.[77] Business periodicals are full of stories describing bitter disputes among family members that have crippled or destroyed once-thriving businesses, usually because the founder failed to create a succession plan. To avoid the senseless destruction of valuable assets, founders of family businesses should develop plans for management succession long before retirement looms before them. We will discuss family businesses and management succession in more detail in Chapter 20, "Management Succession and Risk Management."

## Copreneurs

"Copreneurs" are entrepreneurial couples who work together as co-owners of their businesses. Experts estimate that copreneurs operate approximately 30 percent of family businesses.[78] Unlike the traditional "mom and pop" (pop as "boss" and mom as "subordinate"), copreneurs divide their business responsibilities on the basis of their skills, experience, and abilities rather than on gender. Studies suggest that companies co-owned by spouses represent one of the fastest growing business sectors.

Managing a small business with a spouse may appear to be a recipe for divorce, but most copreneurs say not. "There are days when you want to kill each other," says Mary Duty, who has operated Poppa Rollo's Pizza with her husband for 20 years. "But there's nothing better than working side-by-side with the [person] you love."[79] Successful copreneurs learn to build the foundation for a successful working relationship *before* they ever launch their companies. Some of the characteristics they rely on include:

- An assessment of how well their personalities will mesh in a business setting.
- Mutual respect for each other and one another's talents.
- Compatible business and life goals—a common "vision."
- A view that they are full and equal partners, not a superior and a subordinate.
- Complementary business skills that each acknowledges in the other and that lead to a unique business identity for each spouse.
- A clear division of roles and authority—ideally based on each partner's skills and abilities—to minimize conflict and power struggles.
- The ability to keep lines of communication open, talking and listening to each other about personal as well as business issues.
- The ability to encourage each other and to lift up a disillusioned partner.
- Separate work spaces that allow them to escape when the need arises.
- Boundaries between their business life and their personal life so that one doesn't consume the other.

- A sense of humor.
- An understanding that not every couple can work together.

Although copreneuring isn't for everyone, it works extremely well for many couples and often leads to successful businesses.

*Barry John and Tara van der Maas and Luangwa River Lodge*

Former finance executive Barry John van der Maas and his wife, Tara, moved to the plains of Zambia and spent four years building and getting government approval to operate a guest lodge next to Zambia's second most popular tourist attraction, a national park in the Great Rift Valley. Barry John and Tara, who operate the business together, spent $850,000 to build the luxurious Luangwa River Lodge in the wilderness, where guests can gaze at leopards, lions, giraffes, monkeys, cape buffalo, and other animals, including more than 400 species of birds, while enjoying the comfort of a five-star hotel.[80]

## Corporate Castoffs

Concentrating on trying to operate more efficiently, corporations have been downsizing, shedding their excess bulk, and slashing employment at all levels in the organization. These downsizing victims or "corporate castoffs" have become an important source of entrepreneurial activity. Skittish about experiencing more downsizing at other large companies, many of these castoffs are choosing instead to create their own job security by launching their own businesses. They have decided that the best defense against future job insecurity is an entrepreneurial offense. Armed with years of experience, a tidy severance package, a working knowledge of their industries, and a network of connections, these former managers are setting out to start companies of their own. Some 20 percent of these discharged corporate managers become entrepreneurs, and many of those left behind in corporate America would like to join them.

## Corporate "Dropouts"

The dramatic downsizing in corporations has created another effect among the employees left after restructuring: a trust gap. The result of this trust gap is a growing number of "dropouts" from the corporate structure who then become entrepreneurs. Although their workdays may grow longer and their incomes may shrink, those who strike out on their own often find their work more rewarding and more satisfying because they are doing what they enjoy and they are in control. When one dropout left his corporate post, he invited his former coworkers to a bonfire in the parking lot—fueled by a pile of his expensive business suits! He happily passed out marshmallows to everyone who came. Today, he and his wife run an artists' gallery in California's wine country.[81]

Because they often have college degrees, a working knowledge of business, and years of management experience, both corporate castoffs and dropouts may ultimately increase the small business survival rate. Better-trained, more experienced entrepreneurs are less likely to fail in business. Many corporate castoffs and dropouts choose franchising as the vehicle to business ownership because it offers the structure and support with which these former corporate executives are most comfortable.

*Jim and Sally Hewell and AlphaGraphics*

Jim Hewell had spent 24 years at Texas Instruments (TI), working his way up to senior management, when he decided to leave the company to start his own business. After performing extensive research, Hewell and his wife, Sally, decided to open an AlphaGraphics franchise near their Dallas, Texas, home. Hewell says that opening the franchise, which has grown to include 27 employees, was the right decision. "My experience at Texas Instruments showed me the importance of discipline in budgeting and business, and I've been able to build that into my own organization," says Hewell. "The things I learned in those 24 years (at TI) have been a huge benefit to me."[82]

## Retired Baby Boomers

Members of the U.S. Baby Boom Generation (1946–1964) are retiring, but many of them are not idle; instead, they are launching businesses of their own (see Figure 1.4). A recent

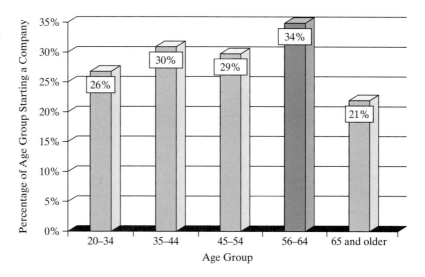

**FIGURE 1.4**
**Entrepreneurial Activity by Age Group**
*Source:* Kauffman Foundation, *Kauffman Index of Entrepreneurial Activity*, 2006, www.kauffman.org/pdf/KIEA_national_052206.pdf.

survey by the American Association of Retired Persons reports that 15 percent of baby boomers expect to own a business in retirement.[83] To finance their businesses, retirees often use some of their invested "nest eggs," or they can rely on the same sources of funds as younger entrepreneurs, such as banks, private investors, and others.

ENTREPRENEURIAL
Profile

*Franny Martin and Cookies on Call*

Franny Martin retired early from a 30-year career in marketing at several large companies, including McDonald's, and at age 56 launched Cookies on Call, a company that sells 47 types of all-natural, handmade chocolate chunk cookies online. Her company has grown rapidly, and with annual sales of more than $500,000, Martin is planning to hire more workers. Martin spent $3,000 to build the Cookies on Call Web site, which has expanded her market far beyond the local shops she would be limited to without the Web. She credits much of her company's success to the experience she gained throughout her career, although she outsources the activities she knows least about—accounting, legal, and Web site development. "I wouldn't want to be younger," she says as she picks up a tray laden with cookies. "I just wish my back was the back I had when I was 18."[84]

## The Contributions of Small Businesses

*8.* Describe the contributions small businesses make to the U.S. economy.

Of the 29.3 million businesses in the United States today, for example, approximately 29.2 million, or 99.7 percent, can be considered "small." Although there is no universal definition of a small business, a common delineation of a **small business** is one that employs fewer than 100 people. They thrive in virtually every industry, although the majority of small companies are concentrated in the service and retail industries (see Figure 1.5). Their contributions to the U.S. economy are as numerous as the businesses themselves. For example, small companies employ 52 percent of the nation's private sector workforce, even though they possess less than one-fourth of total business assets.[85] Small companies also pay 45 percent of the total private payroll in the United States. Because they are primarily labor intensive, small businesses actually create more jobs than do big businesses. The U.S. Small Business Administration estimates that from 1996 to 2006, small companies created between 60 percent and 80 percent of the net new jobs each year in the United States.[86] David Birch, president of the research firm Cognetics, says that the ability to create jobs is not distributed evenly across the small business sector, however. His research shows that just 6 percent of these small companies created 70 percent of the net new jobs, and they did so across all industry sectors—not just in "hot" industries. Birch calls these job-creating small companies "gazelles," those growing at 20 percent or more per year with at least $100,000 in annual sales. His research also identified "mice," small companies that never grow much and don't create many jobs. The majority of small companies are "mice."[87]

**FIGURE 1.5  Small
Businesses by Industry**
*Source:* U.S. Small Business
Administration, 2006.

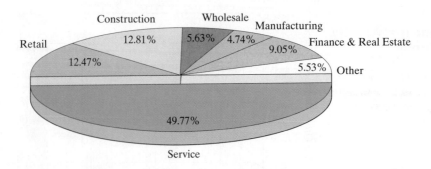

Construction   Wholesale   Manufacturing
Retail   12.81%   5.63%   4.74%   Finance & Real Estate
12.47%   9.05%
5.53%   Other
49.77%
Service

Not only do small companies lead the way in creating jobs, but they also bear the brunt of training workers for them. Small businesses provide 67 percent of workers with their first jobs and basic job training. Small companies offer more general skills instruction and training than large ones, and their employees receive more benefits from the training than do those in larger firms. Although their training programs tend to be informal, in-house, and on-the-job, small companies teach employees valuable skills—from written communication to computer literacy.[88]

## Gaining a Competitive Edge

### Bullet-Proofing Your Start-up

It happens thousands of times every day: Someone comes up with a great idea for a new business, certain that the idea is going to be "the next big thing." Technological advances, the Internet, increased global interconnectivity, and computer-aided-design tools that allow inventors to go from the idea stage to creating a prototype faster than ever have made transforming a great idea into reality much easier than at any point in the past. In addition, entrepreneurial training, improved access to information, and greater awareness of entrepreneurship as a career choice have made it easier than ever to launch a business. However, *succeeding* in business today is as challenging as it ever was.

What steps can a potential entrepreneur with a great idea take to build a "bullet-proof" start-up?

### Step 1. Test to see if your idea really is a good one

The reality is that transforming an idea into a successful business concept is much like trying to become a pop-music star. For every person who really is a great singer, there are 99 people who can't stay on key but who *think* they are great singers. This step involves getting a reality check from other people—and not just friends and relatives who may not tell you what they really think about your idea because they don't want to hurt your feelings. One key is to involve potential customers and people who are knowledgeable about the particular industry into which your idea fits in evaluating your idea.

This step requires potential entrepreneurs to maintain a delicate balance between getting valuable feedback on their idea and protecting it from those who might steal it. Before they reveal their ideas to other people, some would-be entrepreneurs rely on nondisclosure agreements, contracts in which the other party promises not to use the idea for their own gain or to reveal it to others. Typically, the feedback, input, and advice entrepreneurs get at this phase far outweigh the risks of disclosing their ideas to others. "If you are on a mission, your first concern shouldn't be what someone takes from you but to be aggressive in refining [your idea]," says Rich Sloan, co-host with his brother Jeff of Startup Nation.com and a nationally syndicated radio show designed to offer advice to entrepreneurs and inventors.

Sometimes entrepreneurs discover that Step 1 is as far as they should go; otherwise, they would be wasting time, talent, and resources. Other entrepreneurs receive confirmation that they really are on to something at this step. Ready to make a change from her career in a large marketing company, Wendy Almquist decided she wanted to be in business for herself. A fan of craft shows, she had noticed the popularity of soy candles, which burn more cleanly than petroleum-based wax candles, as home decorating accessories. She began researching the market while her husband, Brett, set up a shop in the family garage, where the Almquists experimented for months to perfect the proper formula and designs for their candles. Once they were satisfied that their formula was correct, Wendy created a company, BeansWax, and launched into a series of "informational interviews" with representatives from potential customers she had identified from her research. The Almquists incorporated the ideas and the feedback from these interviews into the product line. Encouraged by the responses from the interviews, Wendy then began making sales calls. The product testing paid off. From its start in the Almquist home, the company has grown to nearly $1 million in annual sales.

## Step 2. Start building your entrepreneurial team

Nearly half of all new business ventures are started by teams of people. As one business writer observes, "Launching a company isn't just a full-time job; in many cases, it's three full-time jobs." Indeed, launching a company is a demanding task that requires a diverse blend of skills, abilities, and experience that not every individual possesses. If that is the case, the best alternative is to launch your company with others whose skills, abilities, and experience *complement* rather than *mirror* yours. Picking the right entrepreneurial players is as essential to business success as picking the best kids to be on your kickball team was in grammar school! However many people it may require, ideally a start-up team includes a "big picture" strategic thinker, a top-notch networker with marketing and sales know-how, and a hands-on technical person who understands the business opportunity at the "nuts-and-bolts" level.

Although individually Jeff Bostic, Steve Bostic, nor Paul Noble possessed all of the skills and experience they needed to launch FirstArtWorks, a company that sponsors shows for art created by grade school children, they knew that together they had the right stuff for a successful start-up. Steve was an experienced entrepreneur who had built several companies, one of which made it to *Inc.* magazine's 500 list, and had the financial resources to contribute to the venture. Jeff had a background in the financial industry and the sales and marketing acumen the company needed.

Paul had spent more than a decade in the framing business and had the technical knowledge and the industry contacts to produce the quality of framing customers would expect while keeping costs down. The team launched FirstArtWorks ("We treat every student's art like a masterpiece"), and in its first year, the company generated $1 million in revenue. In just its third year of operation, the business is on track to generate $25 million in sales!

## Step 3. Do your research and create a business plan

After a dry cleaner ruined one of Robert Byerley's new $100 dress shirts without an apology or offering to replace it, Byerley decided to do something about it. Rather than complain, he chose to open a dry cleaning service that offered higher quality service in more convenient locations than existing dry cleaners were providing. An experienced businessperson, Byerley knew the importance of performing the necessary industry research and preparing a sound business plan. He even contacted the U.S. Better Business Bureau and learned that dry cleaners are near the top of the customer complaint list. The number one complaint? "Cleaners didn't stand behind what they did," he says. Byerley also learned about the environmental regulations that affected the way in which cleaners were required to handle their cleaning solutions. As he built his plan, Byerley hired a marketing company to conduct focus groups with customers concerning potential business names, locations, design, and services. Based on feedback from the focus groups, he chose the name Bibbentuckers. Byerley also made a list of 10 features that his business must have to be successful. First on the list: Standing behind everything the company did. Bibbentuckers also would offer drive-through service with curb-side delivery, a computerized tracking system to minimize the number of lost garments, and state-of-the-art, environmentally friendly cleaning compounds. Byerley's detailed business plan paid off. In its first year, his first location (the company has expanded to three units) was generating sales at a rate that was four times the industry average.

*Sources:* Adapted from Michael V. Copeland and Om Malik, "How to Build a Bulletproof Startup," *Business 2.0*, June 2006, pp. 76–92; Gwendolyn Bounds, "You Have a Great Idea. Now What?" *Wall Street Journal*, May 9, 2005, pp. R1, R3; Michael V. Copeland and Andrew Tilin, "The New Instant Companies," *Business 2.0*, June 2005, pp. 82–94; Daniel Roth, "The Amazing Rise of the Do-It-Yourself Economy," *Fortune*, May 30, 2005, pp. 45–46; "Panel Study on Entrepreneurial Dynamics," Kauffman Foundation Entrepreneurship Research Portal, http://research.kauffman.org/cwp/appmanager/research/researchDesktop?_nfpb=true&_pageLabel=research_dataDetail&awebcurl=Research/DataSet_01.htm.

Small businesses also produce 51 percent of the U.S.'s private sector Gross Domestic Product (GDP) and account for 47 percent of business sales.[89] In fact, the U.S small business sector is the world's third largest "economy," trailing only the economies of the United States and China. Small businesses also play an integral role in creating new products, services, and processes. Small companies produce 13 to 14 times more patents per employee than do large firms, and many of those patents are among the most significant inventions in their fields.[90] Many important inventions trace their roots to an entrepreneur; for example, the zipper, the personal computer, FM radio, air conditioning, the escalator, the light bulb, the helicopter, and the automatic transmission all originated in small businesses.

Entrepreneurs continue to create innovations designed to improve people's lives in areas ranging from energy and communications to clothing and toys. CuteCircuit, a small company that specializes in wearable technology, has developed the Hug Shirt, a shirt that allows someone using a Bluetooth-enabled cell phone to send a hug to the wearer. Responding to the wireless signal, sensors in the shirt simulate the warmth and pressure of an actual hug even though the sender and the Hug Shirt wearer may be thousands of miles apart![91] Drawing on their experience with technology and toy companies, Bob Christopher and Caleb Chung launched UGOBE, a small company that uses cutting edge robotic technology to create a groundbreaking line of animated toys called Life Forms. The company's first toy, Pleo, is a life-like dinosaur (a plant-eating Camarasaurus) that walks, blinks, yawns, sneezes, and exhibits various moods, depending on how his owner treats him. (Ignore Pleo and he sulks and sleeps all day; give him attention, and he wags his tail and purrs when you come home.)[92]

## Putting Failure into Perspective

**9.** Put business failure into proper perspective.

The median age of U.S. companies is 12 years, and nearly half of the companies in the United States have been in business for at least 15 years.[93] Many businesses don't last that long, however. Studies suggest that 54 percent of new businesses will have failed within four years. Because of their limited resources, inexperienced management, and lack of financial stability, small businesses suffer relatively high mortality rate (see Figure 1.6).

Because they are building businesses in an environment filled with uncertainty and shaped by rapid change, entrepreneurs recognize that failure is likely to be a part of their lives; yet, they are not paralyzed by that fear. "The excitement of building a new business from scratch is far greater than the fear of failure," says one entrepreneur who failed in business several times before finally succeeding.[94] Instead, they use their failures as a rallying point and as a means of defining their companies' reason for being more clearly. They see failure for what it really is: an opportunity to learn what doesn't work! Successful entrepreneurs

**FIGURE 1.6 Small Business Survival Rate**
*Source: NFIB Business Policy Guide* 2003, p. 16.

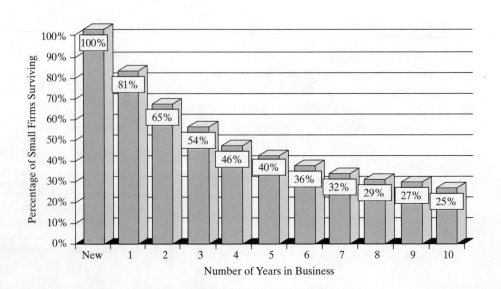

have the attitude that failures are simply stepping stones along the path to success. Walt Disney was fired from a newspaper job because, according to his boss, he "lacked ideas." Disney also went bankrupt several times before he created Disneyland.

Failure is a natural part of the creative process. The only people who never fail are those who never do anything or never attempt anything new. Baseball fans know that Babe Ruth held the record for career home runs (714) for many years, but how many know that he also held the record for strikeouts (1,330)? Successful entrepreneurs realize that hitting an entrepreneurial home run requires a few strikeouts along the way, and they are willing to accept that. Lillian Vernon, who started her mail-order company with $2,000 in wedding present money, says, "Everybody stumbles. . . . The true test is how well you pick yourself up and move on, and whether you're willing to learn from that."[95]

One hallmark of successful entrepreneurs is the ability to fail *intelligently,* learning why they failed so that they can avoid making the same mistake again. They know that business success does not depend on their ability to avoid making mistakes but to be open to the lessons each mistake brings. They learn from their failures and use them as fuel to push themselves closer to their ultimate target. Entrepreneurs are less worried about what they might lose if they try something and fail than about what they miss if they fail to try.

Entrepreneurial success requires both persistence and resilience, the ability to bounce back from failures. Thomas Edison discovered about 1,800 ways *not* to build a light bulb before hitting upon a design that worked—and would revolutionize the world. Entrepreneur Bryn Kaufman explains this "don't quit" attitude, "If you are truly an entrepreneur, giving up is not an option."[96]

## How to Avoid the Pitfalls

**10.** Explain how small business owners can avoid the pitfalls of running a business.

As valuable as failure can be to the entrepreneurial process, no one sets out to fail. We now examine the ways to avoid becoming another failure statistic and gain insight into what makes a start-up successful. Entrepreneurial success requires much more than just a good idea for a product or service. It also takes a solid plan of execution, adequate resources (including capital and people), the ability to assemble and manage those resources, and perseverance. The following suggestions for success follow naturally from the causes of business failures.

### Know Your Business in Depth

We have already emphasized the need for the right type of experience in the business. Get the best education in your business area you possibly can *before* you set out on your own. Read everything you can—trade journals, business periodicals, books, Web pages—relating to your industry. Personal contact with suppliers, customers, trade associations, and others in the same industry is another excellent way to get important knowledge.

*Stephanie Ann Kantis and Stephanie Ann Room to Grow*

Before she launched Stephanie Anne Room to Grow, a chain of stores selling upscale furniture for babies and children, Stephanie Anne Kantis had career stints at a major department store and a small interior design/furniture store. In both jobs, she picked up many valuable tips on everything from how to check in merchandise to establishing employee policy manuals and identified the key factors required for success in her industry.[97]

Like Stephanie Anne Kantis, successful entrepreneurs are like sponges, soaking up as much knowledge as they can from a variety of sources, and they continue to learn about their businesses, markets, and customers as long as they are in business.

### Prepare a Business Plan

To wise entrepreneurs, a well-written business plan is a crucial ingredient in business success. Without a sound business plan, a company merely drifts along without any real direction and often stalls out when it faces its first challenge. Yet, entrepreneurs, who tend to be people of action, too often jump right into a business venture without taking time to prepare a written plan outlining the essence of the business. "Most entrepreneurs don't have a solid business plan," says one business owner. "But a thorough business plan and timely financial information are critical. They help you make the important decisions about your business; you constantly have to monitor what you're doing against your plan."[98]

Although uncertainty is a part of any business start-up, preparing a business plan allows entrepreneurs to replace "I think" with "I know" in many important areas of a business. In many cases, entrepreneurs attempt to build businesses on faulty assumptions such as "I think there are enough customers in town to support an organic food store." Experienced entrepreneurs investigate these assumptions and replace them with facts before making the decision to go into business. We will discuss the process of developing a business plan in Chapter 6, "Crafting a Winning Business Plan."

### Manage Financial Resources

The best defense against financial problems is developing a practical financial information system and then using this information to make business decisions. No entrepreneur can maintain control over a business unless he is able to judge its financial health.

The first step in managing financial resources effectively is to have adequate start-up capital. Too many entrepreneurs begin their businesses with too little capital. One experienced business owner advises, "Estimate how much capital you need to get the business going and then double that figure." His point is well taken; it almost always costs more to launch a business than *any* entrepreneur expects. Establishing a relationship early on with at least one reliable lender who understands your business is a good way to gain access to financing when a company needs capital for growth or expansion.

The most valuable financial resource to any small business is *cash;* successful entrepreneurs learn early on to manage it carefully. Although earning a profit is essential to its long-term survival, a business must have an adequate supply of cash to pay its bills and obligations. Some entrepreneurs count on growing sales to supply their company's cash needs, but it almost never happens. Growing companies usually consume more cash than they generate; and the faster they grow, the more cash they gobble up! We will discuss cash management techniques in Chapter 9, "Managing Cash Flow."

### Understand Financial Statements

All business owners depend on records and financial statements to know the condition of their business. All too often, these records are used only for tax purposes and are not employed as vital control devices. To truly understand what is going on in the business, an owner must have at least a basic understanding of accounting and finance.

When analyzed and interpreted properly, these financial statements are reliable indicators of a small company's health. They can be quite helpful in signaling potential problems. For example, declining sales, slipping profits, rising debt, and deteriorating working capital are all symptoms of potentially lethal problems that require immediate attention. We will discuss financial statement analysis in Chapter 8, "Creating a Solid Financial Plan."

### Learn to Manage People Effectively

No matter what kind of business you launch, you must learn to manage people. Every business depends on a foundation of well-trained, motivated employees. No business owner can do everything alone. The people an entrepreneur hires ultimately determine the heights to which the company can climb—or the depths to which it can plunge. Attracting and retaining a corps of quality employees is no easy task, however; it remains a challenge for every small business owner. One entrepreneur alienated employees with a memo chastising them for skipping lines on interoffice envelopes (the cost of a skipped line was two-thirds of a penny) while he continued to use a chauffeur-driven luxury car and to stay at exclusive luxury hotels while traveling on business.[99] Entrepreneurs quickly learn that treating their employees with respect, dignity, and compassion usually translates into their employees treating customers in the same fashion. Successful entrepreneurs value their employees and constantly find ways to show it. We will discuss the techniques of managing and motivating people effectively in Chapter 19, "Staffing and Leading a Growing Company."

### Set Your Business Apart from the Competition

The formula for almost certain business failure involves becoming a "me-too business"—merely copying whatever the competition is doing. Most successful entrepreneurs find a way to convince their customers that their companies are superior to their competitors even if they sell similar products or services. It is especially important for small companies going up against larger, more powerful rivals with greater financial resources. Ideally, the basis for differentiating a company from its competitors is founded in what it does best. For small companies, that basis often is customer service, convenience, speed, quality, or whatever else is important to attracting and keeping happy customers. We will discuss the strategies for creating a unique footprint in the marketplace in Chapter 7, "Creating the Marketing Plan."

### Maintain a Positive Attitude

Achieving business success requires an entrepreneur to maintain a positive mental attitude toward business and the discipline to stick with it. Successful entrepreneurs recognize that their most valuable resource is their time, and they learn to manage it effectively to make themselves and their companies more productive. None of this, of course, is possible without passion—passion for their businesses, their products or services, their customers, their communities. Passion is what enables a failed business owner to get back up, try again, and make it to the top! One business writer says that growing a successful business requires entrepreneurs to have great faith in themselves and their ideas, great doubt concerning the challenges and inevitable obstacles they will face as they build their businesses, and great effort—lots of hard work—to make their dreams become reality.[100]

## Conclusion

As you can see, entrepreneurship lies at the heart of this nation's free enterprise system; small companies truly are the backbone of our economy. Their contributions are as many and as diverse as the businesses themselves. Indeed, diversity is one of the strengths of the U.S. small business sector. Although there are no secrets to becoming a successful entrepreneur, there are steps that entrepreneurs can take to enhance the probability of their success. The remainder of this book will explore those steps and how to apply them to the process of launching a successful business with an emphasis on building a sound business plan.

■ Section 2, "Building a Business Plan: Beginning Considerations" (Chapters 2–6), discusses the classic start-up questions every entrepreneur faces, particularly developing a strategy, choosing a form of ownership, alternative methods for becoming a business owner (franchising and buying an existing business), and building a business plan.

■ Section 3, "Building a Business Plan: Financial Issues" (Chapters 7 and 8), explains how to develop the financial component of a business plan, including creating projected financial statements and forecasting cash flow. These chapters also offer existing business owners practical financial management tools.

■ Section 4, "Building a Business Plan: Marketing Your Company" (Chapters 9–13), focuses on creating an effective marketing plan for a small company. These chapters address developing advertising and promotional campaigns, establishing pricing and credit strategies, penetrating global markets, and creating an effective e-commerce strategy.

■ Section 5, "Putting the Business Plan to Work: Finding Financing" (Chapters 14 and 15), explains how entrepreneurs can find the financing they need to launch their businesses. It covers sources of debt financing (borrowed capital) and equity financing (equity capital) and the implications of using them.

■ Section 6, "Location and Layout" (Chapter 16), describes how entrepreneurs should select a location for their businesses and how to create a layout that enhances sales and employee productivity.

■ Section 7, "Managing a Small Business: Techniques for Enhancing Profitability" (Chapters 17 and 18) explains the practical aspects of purchasing goods, materials and supplies and managing inventory.

■ Section 8, "Managing People: A Company's Most Valuable Resource" (Chapter 19), provides useful techniques for assembling a strong new venture team and leading its members to success.

■ Section 9, "Legal Aspects of Entrepreneurship" (Chapters 20–22), discusses the important topics of management succession and risk management, operating a business in an ethical, socially responsible manner, and avoiding legal and regulatory pitfalls.

As you can see, the journey down the road of entrepreneurship will be an interesting and exciting one. Let's get started!

## Chapter Review

1. Define the role of the entrepreneur in business.
   - Record numbers of people have launched companies over the past decade. The boom in entrepreneurship is worldwide; many nations across the globe are seeing similar growth in the small business sector. A variety of competitive, economic, and demographic shifts have created a world in which "small is beautiful."
   - Society depends on entrepreneurs to provide the drive and risk-taking necessary for the business system to supply people with the goods and services they need.

2. Describe the entrepreneurial profile.
   - Entrepreneurs have some common characteristics, including a desire for responsibility, a preference for moderate risk, confidence in their ability to succeed, desire for immediate feedback, a high energy level, a future orientation, skill at organizing, and a value of achievement over money. In a phrase, they are high achievers.

3. Describe the benefits of owning a small business.
   - Driven by these personal characteristics, entrepreneurs establish and manage small businesses to gain control over their lives, become self-fulfilled, reap unlimited profits, contribute to society, and do what they enjoy doing.

4. Describe the potential drawbacks of owning a small business.
   - Small business ownership has some potential drawbacks. There are no guarantees that the business will make a profit or even survive. The time and energy required to manage a new business may have dire effects on the owner and family members.

5. Explain the forces that are driving the growth in entrepreneurship.
   - Several factors are driving the boom in entrepreneurship, including entrepreneurs portrayed as heroes, better entrepreneurial education, economic and demographic factors, a shift to a service economy, technological advancements, more independent lifestyles, and increased international opportunities.

6. Discuss the role of diversity in small business and entrepreneurship.
   - Several groups are leading the drive toward entrepreneurship—women, minorities, immigrants, part-timers, home-based business owners, family business owners, copreneurs, corporate castoffs, corporate dropouts, and retired baby boomers.

7. Describe the contributions small businesses make to the economy.
   - The small business sector's contributions are many. They make up 99.7 percent of all businesses in the United States, for example, employ 52 percent of the private sector workforce, create between 60 percent and 80 percent of the new jobs in the economy, produce 51 percent of America's private gross domestic product (GDP), and account for 47 percent of business sales.

8. Explain the reasons small businesses fail.
   - The failure rate for small businesses is higher than for big businesses, and profits fluctuate with general economic conditions. Statistics show that 54 percent of new businesses will have failed within four years.

9. Put business failure into the proper perspective.
   - Because they are building businesses in an environment filled with uncertainty and shaped by rapid change, entrepreneurs recognize that failure is likely to be a part of their lives; yet, they are not paralyzed by that fear. Successful entrepreneurs have the attitude that failures are simply stepping stones along the path to success.

10. Explain how small business owners can avoid the major pitfalls of running a business.
    - There are several general tactics small business owners can employ to avoid failure. Entrepreneurs should know their business in depth, develop a solid business plan, manage financial resources effectively, understand financial statements, learn to manage people effectively, set the business apart from the competition, and keep in tune with themselves.

## Discussion Questions

1. What forces have led to the boom in entrepreneurship in the United States?
2. What is an entrepreneur? Give a brief description of the entrepreneurial profile.
3. *Inc.* magazine claims, "Entrepreneurship is more mundane than it's sometimes portrayed . . . you don't need to be a person of mythical proportions to be very, very successful in building a company." Do you agree? Explain.
4. What are the major benefits of business ownership?
5. Which of the potential drawbacks to business ownership are most critical?
6. Briefly describe the role of the following groups in entrepreneurship: women, minorities, immigrants, part-timers, home-based business owners, family business owners, copreneurs, corporate castoffs, and corporate dropouts.
7. What contributions do small businesses make to our economy?
8. Describe the small business failure rate.
9. Outline the causes of business failure. Which problems cause most business failures?

10. How can the small business owner avoid the common pitfalls that often lead to business failures?
11. Why is it important to study the small business failure rate?
12. Explain the typical entrepreneur's attitude toward failure.
13. One entrepreneur says that too many people "don't see that by spending their lives afraid of failure, they *become* failures. But when you go out there and risk as I have, you'll have failures along the way, but eventually the result is great success if you are willing to keep risking. . . . For every big 'yes' in life, there will be 199 'nos.'" Do you agree? Explain.
14. What advice would you offer an entrepreneurial friend who has just suffered a business failure?
15. Noting the growing trend among collegiate entrepreneurs launching businesses while still in school, one educator says, "A student whose main activity on campus is running a business is missing the basic reason for being here, which is to get an education." Do you agree? Explain.

## Business PlanPro

This book is accompanied by the best-selling business planning software, Business Plan Pro™ by Palo Alto Software, Inc. This end-of-chapter feature along with the software can assist you in four ways as you accomplish the goal of creating a business plan:

1. *Structure.* Business Plan Pro provides a structure to the process of creating a business plan. There are general business plan standards and expectations, and Business Plan Pro has a recognized and well-received format that lends credibility to your plan. A comprehensive plan that follows a generally recognized outline adds credibility and, if it is a part of the plan's purpose, increases its chances of being funded.

2. *Efficiency.* Business Plan Pro will save you time. Once you become familiar with the interface, Business Plan Pro creates all of the essential financial statements for you using the information the software prompts you to enter. The income statement, balance sheet, and profit and loss statement are formatted once the data is there.

3. *Examples.* Business Plan Pro includes dozens of example business plans. Seeing examples of other plans can be a helpful learning tool to create a plan that is unique to your product or service and your market.

4. *Appearance.* Business Plan Pro automatically incorporates relevant tables and graphs into the text. The result is a cohesive business plan that combines text, tables, and charts and enhances the impact of your document.

Writing a business plan is more than just creating a document. The process can be the most valuable benefit of all. A business plan "tells a story" about your business. It addresses why the business concept is viable, who your target market is, what you offer that market, why the business offers a unique value, how you are going to reach your market, how your business is going to be funded, and—based on your projections—how it will be financially successful.

Creating a business plan is a learning process. For a start-up business, completing a business plan allows you to better understand what to do before you start writing checks and seek funding. Owners of existing businesses can benefit from writing a business plan to better address the challenges they face and optimize the opportunities before them. Business Plan Pro is a tool to assist you with this process. The software guides you through the process by asking a series of questions with software "wizards" to help build your business plan as you put the vision of your business on paper.

At the end of each chapter, a Business Plan Pro activity applies the concepts discussed in that chapter. These activities will enable you to build your plan one step at a time in manageable components. You will be able to assemble your plan in a way that captures the information you know about your business and raise key questions that will push you to learn more in areas you may not have considered. Business Plan Pro will guide you through each step to complete your plan as you progress through this book. This combination of learning concepts and then applying them in your business plan can be powerful. It represents a critical step toward launching a business or establishing a better understanding of the business you now own.

The following exercises will lead you through the process of creating your own business plan. If you or your team does not have a business concept in mind, select a business idea and work through these steps. Future chapters will ask you to validate and change this concept as needed.

The EasyPlan Wizard™ within Business Plan Pro is another optional resource that will guide you through the process of creating your business plan and, just as you follow the guidance each chapter offers, this will not proceed chronologically through the business plan outline that appears in Business Plan Pro. Instead, it skips from section to section as you build concepts about your business, the products and services you offer, the markets you will serve, and your financial information. You can use the wizard or follow the sections of the business plan outline based on the guidance from each chapter. Both options will lead you through the entire process and help you create a comprehensive business plan.

## On the Web

First, visit the Companion Website designed for this book at www.prenhall.com/scarborough. Locate the "Business Plan Resource" tab at the top along with the chapters and review the information in that section. The information and links here will be a resource for you as you work through each chapter and develop your business plan.

## In the Software

Follow the instructions included on the CD to install Business Plan Pro. After you first open Business Plan Pro—preferably on a PC with an Internet connection—open the "Sample Plan Browser." The Sample Plan Browser allows you to preview a library of sample business plans. You will find numerous business plan examples ranging from restaurants to accounting firms to nonprofit organizations. A tool will help sort through these plans based on a specific industry or key words. Don't be concerned about finding a plan that is identical to your business concept. Instead, look for plans that contain parallel characteristics, such as a product or service plan, or one that is targeted to consumers rather than business customers. Review several of these plans to get a better idea of the outline and content. This may give you a clearer vision of what your business plan will look like.

Click on the "Sample Plan Browser" within the software and review these two plans: "The Daily Perc" and "Corporate Fitness."

1. Compare the table of contents of each plan. What differences do you notice?
2. Review the executive summary of each plan. What is the key difference in these two business concepts?
3. What similarities do the plans share regarding the reason the plans were written?
4. As you look through the plans, what are some common tables and charts you find embedded in the text? What value do these tables and charts offer the reader?

## Building Your Business Plan

Open Business Plan Pro and select the choice that allows you to start a new plan. You may want to view the movie that will give you an animated and audio overview of the software. Then allow the EasyPlan Wizard to "ask" you about your start date, the title of your plan, and other basic information including:

1. Do you sell products or services?
2. Is your business a profit of a nonprofit organization?
3. Is your business a start-up operation or an ongoing business?
4. What kind of business plan do you want to create? (Choose "complete business plan.")

5.  Do you want to include the SWOT analysis? (Check this box.)
6.  Will you have a Web site?
7.  A series of financial questions to structure the financial aspects of your plan with assistance throughout.
8.  Do you want to prepare a plan for three years (a standard plan) or a longer term plan of five years, both with a one-year monthly breakdown?

Save these decisions by using the drop-down menu under "File" and clicking on "Save" or by clicking on the "Save" icon at the top right of the menu bar. You can change your response to these decisions at any time as you build your plan.

Review the outline of your plan by clicking on the "Preview" icon on the top of your screen, or by clicking on "File," "Print," and then "Preview" within the Print window. Based on your responses to the wizard questions, you will now see the outline of your business plan. The software will enable you to change and modify the plan outline in any way you choose at any time. Business Plan Pro will help you build your plan one step at a time as you progress through each chapter.

A wise man will make more opportunities than he finds.

—Francis Bacon

The general who wins the battle makes many calculations in his temple before the battle is fought. The general who loses makes but few calculations beforehand.

—Sun Tzu

# Strategic Management and the Entrepreneur

## *Learning Objectives*

**Upon completion of this chapter, you will be able to:**

1 Understand the importance of strategic management to a small business.

2 Explain why and how a small business must create a competitive advantage in the market.

3 Develop a strategic plan for a business using the nine steps in the strategic planning process.

4 Discuss the characteristics of three basic strategies: low-cost, differentiation, and focus.

5 Understand the importance of controls such as the balanced scorecard in the planning process.

**1.** Understand the importance of strategic management to a small business.

ew activities in the life of a small business are as vital—or as overlooked—as that of developing a strategy for success. Too often, entrepreneurs brimming with optimism and enthusiasm launch businesses destined for failure because their founders never stop to define a workable strategy that sets them apart from their competition. Because they tend to be people of action, entrepreneurs often find the process of developing a strategy dull and unnecessary. Their tendency is to start a business, try several approaches, and see what works. Without a cohesive plan of action, however, these entrepreneurs have as much chance of building a successful business as a defense contractor attempting to build a jet fighter without blueprints. Companies lacking clear strategies may achieve success in the short-run, but as soon as competitive conditions stiffen or an unanticipated threat arises, they usually "hit the wall" and fold. Without a basis for differentiating itself from a pack of similar competitors, the best a company can hope for is mediocrity in the marketplace.

In today's global competitive environment, any business, large or small, that is not thinking and acting strategically is extremely vulnerable. Every business is exposed to the forces of a rapidly changing competitive environment, and in the future small business executives can expect even greater change and uncertainty. From sweeping political changes around the planet and rapid technological advances to more intense competition and newly-emerging global markets, the business environment has become more turbulent and challenging for entrepreneurs. Although this market turbulence creates many challenges for small businesses, it also creates opportunities for those companies that have in place strategies to capitalize on them. Small companies now have access to technology, tools, and techniques that once were available only to large companies, enabling them to achieve significant, sometimes momentous, results.

Historically important, entrepreneurs' willingness to create change, to experiment with new business models, and to break traditional rules have become more important than ever. Rather than merely respond to the chaos in the environment, small companies that are prepared actually can *create* the disruptions that revolutionize their industries and gain a competitive edge. Just as sales of music CDs were at their peak, Steve Jobs' Apple Inc. revolutionized the music industry with the introduction of the iPod. Apple now has a commanding 80 percent market share for MP3 players, and its iTunes Music Store accounts for 10 percent of all music sales in the United States. In addition, Apple does not wait on rivals to render its iPod products obsolete with better, more powerful versions. Instead, the company disrupts its own products! Apple introduced the iPod Nano just 18 months after it released the highly successful iPod Mini and continues that pattern today.[1]

Perhaps the biggest change entrepreneurs face is unfolding now: the shift in the world's economy from a base of *financial to intellectual* capital. Intellectual capital is the knowledge and information a company acquires and uses to create a competitive edge in its market segment. "Knowledge is no longer just a factor of production," says futurist Alvin Toffler. "It is the *critical* factor of production."[2] Most small companies have significant stockpiles of valuable knowledge that can help them gain an edge in the marketplace— from a key customer's purchasing criteria to how one department uses Excel to forecast product demand. The key is putting it to good use. Norm Brodsky, a serial entrepreneur who owns several successful businesses, discovered the importance of intellectual capital early on in his business career, and it is a competitive advantage that he continues to rely on today. "I found that I could close a significantly higher percentage of sales than my competitors simply by knowing more than they did about the customer, its representatives, and every other aspect of the deal," he says. "That's still true today." Brodsky explains what happens at his records storage business before a potential customer comes on site.

> We prepare thoroughly. Before the customer's people arrive, I go online and find out as much as I can about the organization's structure, mission, and history. My salespeople give me a full briefing on the visitors I'm about to meet—what they're like as individuals, whom else they're considering, how the decision will be made, and so on. I tailor my presentation accordingly.

The result of Brodsky's use of the knowledge in his company is a closing rate that exceeds 95 percent for all prospective customers who visit his company's facility.[3]

Unfortunately, much of the knowledge that resides in many small companies sits idle or is shared only by happenstance on an informal basis. This scenario is the equivalent of having a bank account without a checkbook or a debit card to access it! The key is learning how to manage and utilize the knowledge a company accumulates over time. **Knowledge management** is the practice of gathering, organizing, and disseminating the collective wisdom and experience of a company's employees for the purpose of strengthening its competitive position. "Organizations that harness knowledge and put it to good use are able to gain a clear competitive advantage," says Eric Lesser, a consultant at the Institute for Knowledge Management.[4] Knowledge management enables companies to get more innovative products to market faster, respond to customers' needs faster, and solve (or avoid altogether) problems more efficiently. Because of their size and simplicity, small businesses have an advantage over large companies when it comes to managing knowledge. Knowledge management requires a small company to identify what its workers know, incorporate that knowledge into the business, distribute it where it is needed, and leverage it into more useful knowledge.

Increasingly, a company's intellectual capital is likely to be the source of its competitive advantage in the marketplace. **Intellectual capital** is comprised of three components:[5]

1. *Human capital.* The talents, skills, and abilities of a company's workforce.
2. *Structural capital.* The accumulated knowledge and experience in its industry and in business in general that a company possesses. It can take many forms including processes, software, patents, copyrights, and, perhaps most importantly, the knowledge and experience of the people in a company.
3. *Customer capital.* The established customer base, positive reputation, ongoing relationships, and goodwill a company builds up over time with its customers.

Increasingly, entrepreneurs are recognizing that the capital stored in these three areas forms the foundation of their ability to compete effectively and that they must manage this intangible capital base carefully. Every business uses all three components in its strategy, but the emphasis they place on each component varies.

This knowledge shift will create as much change in the world's business systems as the Industrial Revolution did in the agricultural-based economies of the 1800s. The Knowledge Revolution will spell disaster for those companies that are not prepared for it, but it will spawn tremendous opportunities for those entrepreneurs who are equipped with the strategies to exploit these opportunities. Management legend Jack Welch, who masterfully guided General Electric for many years, says, "Intellectual capital is what it's all about. Releasing the ideas of people is what we've got to do if we are going to win."[6] However, in practice, releasing people's ideas is much more difficult than it appears. The key is to encourage employees to generate a large volume of ideas, recognizing that only a few (the best) will survive. According to Gary Hamel, author of *Inside the Revolution*, "If you want to find a few ideas with the power to enthrall customers, foil competitors, and thrill investors, you must first generate hundreds and potentially thousands of unconventional strategic ideas. Put simply, you have to crush a lot of rock to find a diamond."[7]

In short, the rules of the competitive game of business have changed dramatically. Entrepreneurs must recognize that the business forecast calls for continued chaos and disruption with the certainty of new opportunities and a slight chance of disaster. To be successful in this environment, entrepreneurs can no longer do things in the way they've always done them. They must learn to be initiators and agents of change. The late management guru Peter Drucker said that the key challenge for managers in the twenty-first century is leading change and that doing so successfully required leaders "to abandon yesterday," leaving behind the products, services, management styles, marketing techniques, and other ideas that no longer work.[8] Unfortunately, for most managers, abandoning yesterday is no easy task because it is what they know and are most comfortable with.

Fortunately, successful entrepreneurs have at their disposal a powerful weapon to cope with a chaotic environment filled with disarray and constant disruptions: the process of strategic management. **Strategic management** is a process that involves developing a game plan to guide the company as it strives to accomplish its vision, mission, goals, and objectives and to keep it from straying off its desired course. The idea is to give an entrepreneur a blueprint for matching the company's strengths and weaknesses to the opportunities and threats in the environment.

## Building a Competitive Advantage

*2.* Explain why and how a small business must create a competitive advantage in the market.

The goal of developing a strategic plan is to create for the small company a **competitive advantage**—the aggregation of factors that sets the small business apart from its competitors and gives it a unique and superior position in the market. From a strategic perspective, the key to business success is to develop a unique competitive advantage, one that creates value for customers, is sustainable, and is difficult for competitors to duplicate. No business can be everything to everyone. In fact, one of the biggest pitfalls many entrepreneurs stumble into is failing to differentiate their companies from the crowd of competitors. Entrepreneurs often face the challenge of setting their companies apart from their larger, more powerful competitors (who can easily outspend them) by using their creativity, speed, flexibility, and special abilities their businesses offer customers.

**ENTREPRENEURIAL Profile**

*Seth Goldman and Barry Nalebuff and Honest Tea*

Seth Goldman came up with the idea for his business after he and a friend had finished a run in New York City's Central Park. Thirsty, they stopped by a corner bodega to buy a drink but found only water and sugary sodas. Goldman contacted Barry Nalebuff, a former professor at Yale University, and suggested that they start a company that offered a healthier drink alternative. Nalebuff had been studying the tea industry and had come up with the ideal name for a company, Honest Tea, but he had no product. Goldman and Nalebuff raised $500,000 from family and friends and in 1998 launched Honest Tea in an industry dominated by giants such as Lipton and Nestea. Soon, Goldman saw a way to differentiate Honest Tea's products from those of its larger competitors and smaller firms, such as Arizona, Snapple, and SoBe, by making Honest Tea's product line with only organic ingredients. The decision was driven in part by research that showed that organic foods and beverages are the fastest-growing segment of food sales in the United States. About 30 percent of shoppers say that they regularly purchase organic foods. Creating a line of tea that is "certified organic" however was no easy task because the U.S. Department of

Agriculture uses a 500-plus–page manual that governs everything from the ingredients used and how organic companies must grow and process their products to how they clean their equipment and control pests. Honest Tea's strategy has paid off. Despite operating in a very competitive industry, Honest Tea's sales have climbed to more than $20 million, and the company continues to grow rapidly.[9]

Entrepreneurs must be certain that the competitive advantages on which they build their companies are the ones that matter most to their customers. Do customers want healthy products, fast delivery, superior quality, customized products, low prices, or something else? The best way to find out is to listen to customers and to observe their buying behavior. Once a company defines the source of its competitive advantage from its customers' perspective, everyone in the company must communicate the competitive advantage to customers at every opportunity. Doing so not only attracts new customers, but it also helps a small company retain the customers that it has.

As Honest Tea demonstrates, over the long run, a company gains a sustainable competitive advantage through its ability to develop a set of core competencies that enable it to serve its target customers better or to operate more efficiently than its rivals. **Core competencies** are a unique set of skills, knowledge, or abilities that a company develops in key areas, such as superior quality, customer service, innovation, engineering, team-building, flexibility, speed, responsiveness, and others that allow it to perform vital processes to world-class standards and to vault past competitors. They are the things that a company does best and does far better than its competitors. Palmetto Bank, a small community bank that has been in operation for more than 100 years, has built a core competency in credit-screening and lending skills and processes. Over time, the bank's top managers, almost all of whom made lending decisions as loan officers early in their careers, have developed unique expertise and have built screening systems that have resulted in an impressive loan-loss ratio of just 0.12 percent, which translates into an enviable profit margin for the company.

Typically, a company is likely to build core competencies in no more than five or six (sometimes fewer) areas. These core competencies become the nucleus of a company's competitive advantage and are usually quite enduring over time. Markets, customers, and competitors may change, but a company's core competencies are more durable, forming the building blocks for *everything* a company does. In fact, to be effective, these competencies must be sustainable over time. They also should be difficult for competitors to duplicate and must provide customers with a valuable perceived benefit. Small companies' core competencies often have to do with the advantages of their size—agility, speed, closeness to their customers, superior service, or ability to innovate. In short, they use their "smallness" to their advantage, doing things that their larger rivals cannot. A recent survey of small business owners conducted by Allbusiness.com confirms that entrepreneurs recognize the benefits of being small. Seventy-seven percent of business owners say that their companies have less bureaucracy than their larger competitors, which allows them to act more quickly and to operate with more flexibility than their larger rivals.[10] The key to success is to build core competencies (or to identify the ones a company already has) and then concentrate them on providing superior service and value for its target customers.

Developing core competencies does *not* necessarily require a company to spend a great deal of money. It does, however, require an entrepreneur to use creativity, imagination, and vision to identify those things that the business does best and that are most important to its target customers. Building a company's strategy around its core competencies allows a business to gain a sustainable competitive edge over its rivals and to ride its strategy to victory.

*Adam Blumenfeld and Collegiate Pacific*

Adam Blumenfeld has set his company, Collegiate Pacific, apart from competitors in the $5-billion-a-year sporting goods industry by focusing on the company's core competence: the ability to manufacture and ship products to fill customer orders rapidly. Collegiate Pacific's customers include both end users such as schools, municipal recreation departments, and country clubs and online retailers such as Wal-Mart and Amazon.com who do not want to stock an inventory of soccer nets, stadium bleachers, and batting cages. Blumenfeld learned early on that the company's primary target audience, coaches, are pressed for time and often wait until the last minute to order, which gives Collegiate Pacific an edge because of its rapid turnaround time on orders. Its online partners also value the company's short order cycle time when customers place orders through their Web sites. The results of building Collegiate Pacific's strategy on a core competence that is important to customers include annual revenues that exceed $106 million and an annual growth rate of 68 percent from the time the company was founded in 2001.[11]

When it comes to developing a strategy for establishing a competitive advantage, small companies have a variety of natural advantages over their larger competitors. The typical small business has fewer product lines, a more clearly-defined customer base, and a limited geographic market area. Entrepreneurs usually are in close contact with their markets, giving them valuable knowledge on how to best serve their customers' needs and wants. Because of the simplicity of their organization structures, small business owners are in touch with employees daily, often working side-by-side with them, allowing them to communicate strategic moves firsthand. Consequently, small businesses find that strategic management comes more naturally to them than to larger companies with their layers of bureaucracy and far-flung operations.

Strategic management can increase a small company's effectiveness, but entrepreneurs first must have a process designed to meet their needs and their business's special characteristics. It is a mistake to attempt to force a big company's strategic management process onto a small business because a small business is not merely a little big business. Because of their size and their particular characteristics—limited resources, a flexible managerial style, an informal organizational structure, and adaptability to change—small businesses need a different approach to the strategic management process. The strategic management procedure for a small business should include the following features:

- Use a relatively short planning horizon—two years or less for most small companies.
- Be informal and not overly structured; a shirt-sleeve approach is ideal.
- Encourage the participation of employees and outside parties to improve the reliability and creativity of the resulting plan.
- Not begin with setting objectives because extensive objective-setting early on may interfere with the creative process of strategic management.
- Maintain flexibility; competitive conditions change too rapidly for any plan to be considered permanent.
- Focus on strategic *thinking*, not just planning, by linking long-range goals to day-to-day operations.

## The Strategic Management Process

**3.** Develop a strategic plan for a business using the nine steps in the strategic planning process.

One of the most important tasks a business owner must perform is to look ahead—to peer into the future—and then devise a strategy for meeting the challenges and opportunities it presents. Strategic management, the best way to accomplish this vital task, is a continuous process that consists of nine steps:

**Step 1**    Develop a clear vision and translate it into a meaningful mission statement.

**Step 2**    Assess the company's strengths and weaknesses.

**Step 3**    Scan the environment for significant opportunities and threats facing the business.

**Step 4**    Identify the key factors for success in the business.

**Step 5**    Analyze the competition.

**Step 6**    Create company goals and objectives.

**Step 7**    Formulate strategic options and select the appropriate strategies.

**Step 8**    Translate strategic plans into action plans.

**Step 9**    Establish accurate controls.

### Step 1. Develop a Clear Vision and Translate It into a Meaningful Mission Statement

**VISION.** Throughout history, the greatest political and business leaders have been visionaries. Whether the vision is as grand as entrepreneur Richard Branson's endeavor to offer consumers trips into space or as simple as fast-food founder Ray Kroc's devotion to quality, service, cleanliness, and value at McDonald's, the purpose is the same: to focus everyone's attention and efforts on the same target. The vision touches everyone associated with the company—employees, investors, lenders, customers, and the community. It is an expression of what entrepreneurs believe in and the values on which they build their businesses. Highly successful entrepreneurs are able to communicate their vision and their enthusiasm about that vision to those around them.

A vision statement addresses the questions, "What do we stand for?" and "What kind of company do we want to become?" In his book, *Daring Visionaries: How Entrepreneurs Build Companies, Inspire Allegiance, and Create Wealth,* Ray Smilor describes the importance of vision:[12]

> Vision is the organizational sixth sense that tells us why we make a difference in the world. It is the real but unseen fabric of connections that nurture and sustain values. It is the pulse of the organizational body that reaffirms relationships and directs behavior.

A vision is the result of an entrepreneur's dream of something that does not exist yet and the ability to paint a compelling picture of that dream for everyone to see. A clearly defined vision helps a company in three ways:

1. *Vision provides direction.* Entrepreneurs who spell out the vision for their company focus everyone's attention on the future and determine the path the business will take to get there.
2. *Vision determines decisions.* The vision influences the decisions, no matter how big or how small, that owners, managers, and employees make every day in a business. This influence can be positive or negative, depending on how well defined the vision is. One writer explains, "Almost all workers are making decisions, not just filling out weekly sales reports or tightening screws. They will do what they think [is] best. If you want them to do as the company thinks best too, then you must [see to it that] they have an inner gyroscope aligned with the corporate compass."[13] That gyroscope's alignment depends on an entrepreneur's values and how well he or she transmits them throughout the company.
3. *Vision motivates people.* A clear vision excites and ignites people to action. People want to work for a company that sets its sights high and establishes targets that are worth pursuing.

Vision is based on an entrepreneur's values. Successful entrepreneurs build their businesses around a set of three to six core values, which might range from respect for the individual and encouraging innovation to creating satisfied customers and making the world a better place to live. These values become the foundation on which the entire company and its strategy are built. Indeed, truly visionary entrepreneurs see their companies' primary purpose as much more than just "making money." David Neeleman, founder of JetBlue Airways, built the company on five core values—safety, caring, integrity, fun, and passion—and empowers employees to make decisions based on these values.[14] Danny Meyer, an author and the owner of New York City's Union Square Café, compares a company's core values to the banks of a river. "[Core values] are the riverbanks that guide us as we refine and improve our performance. A lack of riverbanks creates estuaries and cloudy waters that are confusing to navigate. I want a crystal-clear, swiftly flowing stream."[15]

The best way to create that crystal clear, swiftly flowing stream of core values and to translate them into action is to create a written mission statement that communicates the company's values to everyone it touches.

**MISSION STATEMENT.** A mission statement addresses the first question of any business venture: "What business am I in?" Establishing the purpose of the business in writing must come first in order to give the company a sense of direction. The mission is the mechanism for making it clear to everyone the company touches "why we are here" and "where we are going." It helps create an emotional bond between a company and its stakeholders, especially its employees and its customers. Without a concise, meaningful mission statement, a small business risks wandering aimlessly in the marketplace, with no idea of where to go or how to get there.

*Bill Thomas and Bills Khakis*

While he was in college in 1984, Bill Thomas purchased a pair of World War II vintage khaki pants from an army surplus store. "It was the best pair of khakis I've ever had," says Thomas. When he discovered that the pants were no longer made, Thomas sensed a business opportunity, had 250 pairs of khakis made to the same specifications, and sold them out of his car while on business trips as an advertising executive. Eventually, Thomas returned to his hometown of Reading, Pennsylvania, and launched Bills Khakis as a full-time business. "It's a business that concentrates on a single, basic product, trying to make it better than other, bigger companies can," says Thomas. "We live or die on khakis." Although Thomas' company is recognized for designing, manufacturing, and marketing the best pair of khakis anywhere in the world, his business philosophy runs much deeper. "We don't consider ourselves as competition for the larger apparel manufacturers," Thomas says. "We are going about business in a very different way. . . . Bills Khakis is a basic product that is driven by ideals." The company's mission is based on several core values, including stellar quality that enables the company's pants to fetch retail prices nearing $100, superior customer service for both retailers who carry its products and the end customers who purchase them, and a company culture that is built on respect. "Our company culture is a source of pride as well as a competitive advantage," says Thomas. Thomas' strategy has proved to be quite successful; Bills Khakis employs 26 people and rings up annual sales of nearly $10 million by selling more than 200,000 pairs of khaki pants to more than 500 upscale retailers.[16]

A good mission statement essentially sets the tone for the entire company and guides the decisions its people make. Tom's of Maine, a successful small company that sells all natural consumer products such as toothpaste, deodorant, and soap, has relied heavily on its mission statement (which was written collaboratively by employees and owners in 1989) as a strategic and ethical compass. The statement expresses the importance of earning a profit while meeting the company's social responsibility. When Tom's of Maine, which founder Tom Chappell recently sold to Colgate-Palmolive, modified one of its deodorants, the company discovered that the new formula did not work. When deciding how to handle the problem, Chappell and his employees turned to the mission statement for guidance, paying close attention to its first

Tom Chappell, founder of Tom's of Maine.

phrase: "To serve our customers by providing safe, effective, innovative natural products of high quality." They decided to contact every customer who had purchased the deodorant and replace it with a newly formulated one. "We [made the decision] because our mission statement says that we will serve customers with safe, effective, and natural products," says Chappell.[17]

***Elements of a Mission Statement.*** A sound mission statement need not be lengthy to be effective. Three key issues entrepreneurs and their employees should address as they develop a mission statement for their businesses include:

- The *purpose* of the company: What are we in business to accomplish?
- The *business* we are in: How are we going to accomplish that purpose?
- The *values* of the company: What principles and beliefs form the foundation of the way we do business?

A firm's mission statement may be the most essential and basic communication that it puts forward. If the people on the plant, shop, retail, or warehouse floor don't know what a company's mission is, then, for all practical purposes, it does not have one! The mission statement expresses the company's character, identity, and scope of operations, but writing it is only half the battle, at best. The most difficult part is living that mission every day. *That's* how employees decide what really matters. To be effective, a mission statement must become a natural part of the organization, embodied in the minds, habits, attitudes, and decisions of everyone in the company every day. Consider the mission statement of Fetzer Vineyards, a vineyard whose acreage is 100 percent organic with no chemical pesticides, herbicides, fungicides, or fertilizers, and the message it sends to company stakeholders:

We are an environmentally and socially conscious grower, producer, and marketer of wines of the highest quality and value.

Working in harmony with respect for the human spirit, we are committed to sharing information about the enjoyment of food and wine in a lifestyle of moderation and responsibility.

We are dedicated to the continuous growth and development of our people and our business.[18]

© Mike Baldwin / Cornered

A company may have a powerful competitive advantage, but it is wasted unless (1) the owner has communicated that advantage to workers, who, in turn, are working hard to communicate it to customers and potential customers and (2) customers are recommending the company to their friends because they understand the benefits they are getting from it that they cannot get elsewhere. *That's* the real power of a mission statement.

### Step 2: Assess the Company's Strengths and Weaknesses

Having defined the vision and the mission of the business, entrepreneurs can turn their attention to assessing company strengths and weaknesses. Competing successfully demands that a business create a competitive strategy that is built on and exploits its strengths and overcomes or compensates for its weaknesses. **Strengths** are positive internal factors that contribute to the accomplishment of a company's mission, goals, and objectives. **Weaknesses** are negative internal factors that inhibit the accomplishment of its mission, goals, and objectives.

Identifying strengths and weaknesses helps entrepreneurs understand their businesses as they exist (or will exist). An organization's strengths should originate in its core competencies because they are essential to its ability to remain competitive in each of the market segments in which it competes. The key is to build a successful strategy by using the company's underlying strengths as its foundation and matching those strengths against competitors' weaknesses. Honest Tea, for instance, has built its strategy on its strengths—the quality, freshness, and health aspects of its all-natural, organic products and an understanding of its core customers' preferences—to compete successfully against much larger and more financially capable rivals in the intensely competitive beverage industry.

One effective technique for taking a strategic inventory is to prepare a balance sheet of the company's strengths and weaknesses (see Table 2.1). The positive side should reflect important skills, knowledge, or resources that contribute to the company's success. The negative side should record honestly any limitations that detract from the company's ability to compete. This balance sheet should analyze all key performance areas of the business—human resources, finance, production, marketing, product development, organization, and others. This analysis should give entrepreneurs a more realistic perspective of their businesses, pointing out foundations on which they can build future strategies and obstacles that they must remove for business progress. This exercise can help owners move from their current position to future actions.

### Step 3: Scan the Environment for Significant Opportunities and Threats Facing the Business

**OPPORTUNITIES.** Once entrepreneurs have taken an internal inventory of company strengths and weaknesses, they must turn to the external environment to identify any opportunities and threats that might have a significant impact on the business. **Opportunities** are positive external options that a company can exploit to accomplish its objectives. The number of potential opportunities is limitless, so managers need to analyze only factors significant to the business (probably two or three at most). Otherwise, they may jeopardize their core business by losing focus and trying to do too much at once.

### TABLE 2.1 Identifying Company Strengths and Weaknesses

| Strengths (Positive Internal Factors) | Weaknesses (Negative Internal Factors) |
| --- | --- |
| | |
| | |
| | |
| | |

When identifying opportunities, entrepreneurs must pay close attention to new potential markets. Are competitors overlooking a niche in the market? Is there a better way to reach customers? Are customers requesting new products or product variations? Are trends in the industry creating new opportunities to serve customers? Have environmental changes created new markets?

*John Beldock and Erico Motorsports*

As rising gasoline prices put pressure on families' budgets, entrepreneurs are discovering business opportunities by helping customers deal with the escalating cost of travel. John Beldock, founder of Erico Motorsports, a business that sells motor scooters and motorcycles, says that rising fuel prices are translating into record sales for his company. Beldock also saw an opportunity to launch a scooter rental program for customers who want to travel efficiently but do not want to purchase a scooter.[19]

**THREATS.**   Scientists say that sixty-five million years ago, a giant asteroid or comet smashed into the earth, causing catastrophic damage to the environment that lasted for years and wiped out the dinosaurs. Today, astronomers monitor the heavens with their telescopes, watching for "near earth objects" that pose the same threat to our planet today. In the same way, small businesses must be on the lookout for threats that could destroy their companies. **Threats** are negative external forces that hamper a company's ability to achieve its objectives. Threats to a business can take a variety of forms, such as new competitors entering the local market, a government mandate regulating a business activity, an economic recession, rising interest rates, technological advances making a company's product obsolete, and many others. Movie theater owners face serious threats to their business from a variety of sources, including increasingly sophisticated home-theater systems that contain DVD players and high-definition big-screen televisions, pay-per-view movies

What kind of threats do small businesses face?

**FIGURE 2.1**
**External Market Forces**

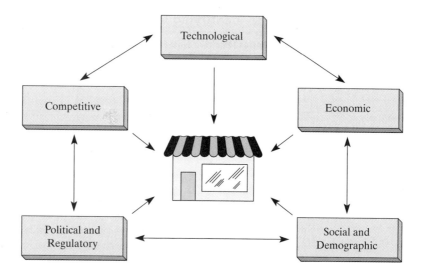

available on demand, criminals who distribute black-market copies of films (sometimes before the original is released), and other forms of entertainment, ranging from iPods and YouTube to sophisticated videogames and the Internet. The result has been an overall decline in movie ticket sales. In 1946, U.S. movie theaters, for example, sold 4 billion tickets (an average of 28 movies per year for each American); in a typical year, movie theaters sell about 1.4 billion tickets, which means that the average American goes to the movies less than five times per year.[20] Although theater owners cannot control the threats their businesses face, they must prepare a strategic plan that will shield their businesses from these threats.

Figure 2.1 illustrates that opportunities and threats are products of the interactions of forces, trends, and events outside the direct control of the business. These external forces will have direct impact on the behavior of the markets in which the business operates, the behavior of competitors, and the behavior of customers. By monitoring demographic trends as well as trends in their particular industries, entrepreneurs can sharpen their ability to spot most opportunities and threats well in advance, giving themselves time to prepare for them.

*Shari Redstone and Cinema De Lux*

To deal with the threats facing their businesses, theater owners are changing the way they do business in an effort to lure customers from their in-home theaters and back to the (really) big screen. "We are trying our hardest to get people out of the house to see a movie," says Shari Redstone, president of family-owned National Amusements, a chain of 1,000 movie theaters. "We simply must give people an experience they can't get elsewhere." To do that, Redstone has converted 11 theaters in the chain into Cinema De Lux (CDL) theaters that offer movie-goers amenities such as martini bars, upscale concessions (even a mini Ben & Jerry's ice cream outlet), a concierge desk to help patrons with tickets or cabs, "directors' halls" (reserved seating in premier locations with cushy leather rocking recliners), digital projection and high-tech sound systems, and a lobby that boasts a baby grand piano and a virtual football game for kids. Redstone's CDL theaters also include two private-function rooms that can be rented for birthday parties, social gatherings, or corporate events.[21]

Table 2.2 provides a form that allows entrepreneurs to take a strategic inventory of the opportunities and threats facing their companies.

Table 2.3 provides an analytical tool that is designed to help entrepreneurs to identify the threats that pose the greatest danger to their companies.

### Step 4: Identify the Key Factors for Success in the Business

**KEY SUCCESS FACTORS.** Every business is characterized by a set of controllable factors that determine the relative success of market participants. Identifying, understanding, and manipulating these factors allow a small business to gain a competitive advantage in its

**TABLE 2.2 Identifying Opportunities and Threats**

| Opportunities (Positive External Factors) | Threats (Negative External Factors) |
|---|---|
| | |
| | |
| | |
| | |

**TABLE 2.3 Identifying and Managing Major Threats**

Every business faces threats, but entrepreneurs cannot afford to be paranoid or paralyzed by fear when it comes to dealing with them. At the same time, they cannot afford to ignore threats that have the potential to destroy their businesses. The most productive approach to dealing with threats is to identify those that would have the most severe impact on a small company and those that have the highest probability of occurrence.

Research by Greg Hackett, president of management think tank MergerShop, has identified 12 major sources of risk that can wreak havoc on a company's future. The following table will help entrepreneurs determine the threats on which they should focus their attention.

| Source | Specific Threat | Severity (1 = Low, 10 = High) | Probability of Occurrence (0 to 1) | Threat Rating (Severity × Probability, Max = 10) |
|---|---|---|---|---|
| 1. Channels of distribution | | | | |
| 2. Competition | | | | |
| 3. Demographic changes | | | | |
| 4. Globalization | | | | |
| 5. Innovation | | | | |
| 6. Waning customer or supplier loyalty | | | | |
| 7. Offshoring or outsourcing | | | | |
| 8. Stage in product life cycle | | | | |
| 9. Government regulation | | | | |
| 10. Influence of special interest groups | | | | |
| 11. Influence of stake-holders | | | | |
| 12. Changes in technology | | | | |

Once entrepreneurs have identified specific threats facing their companies in the 12 areas (not necessarily all 12), they rate the severity of the impact of each one on their company on a 1 to 10 scale. Then, they assign probabilities (between 0 and 1) to each threat. To calculate the threat score, entrepreneurs simply multiply the severity of each threat by its probability. (Maximum threat score is 10.) The higher a threat's score is, the more attention it demands. Typically, one or two threats stand out above all of the others, and those are the ones on which entrepreneurs should focus.

*Source:* Adapted from Edward Teach, "Apocalypse Soon," *CFO*, September 2005, pp. 31–32.

## ■ What's Next for Netflix?

In 1999, entrepreneur Reed Hastings launched Netflix, an online video rental service that charges customers no shipping fees (either way), includes no late fees (customers can keep a DVD as long as they want), and offers an extensive library of 85,000 video titles (compared to just 2,000 titles at a typical neighborhood video rental store). In its first year of operation, Netflix signed up 239,000 movie lovers looking for the ultimate in convenience—getting the movies they wanted without having to visit a store. Today the company, which made an initial public offering in 2002, is the leader in the industry with nearly 9 million subscribers.

Even though it is still quite young, Netflix already is battle-tested, having fended off a competing service that retail giant Wal-Mart started in 2005 but soon folded. Netflix currently is locked in battle with Blockbuster, a company with more than 8,000 video rental outlets in 27 countries and an online rental service that is similar to the one Netflix offers. Netflix's impressive video library, which includes popular hit movies from major studios and lesser-known niche and foreign films from small studios, is larger than any of its competitors and is a major reason customers sign up for the company's service. With its 41 distribution centers, Netflix provides fast turnaround times for its subscribers; the company reaches nearly 95 percent of its customers with one-day delivery.

Another challenge faces Netflix, and this one is even more ominous than either Wal-Mart or Blockbuster: movie downloading from the Internet. Netflix's current strategy combines Internet technology with old-fashioned delivery methods—mailing DVDs to customers through the postal service. Although downloading movies via the Internet is in its infancy due to technology challenges, it is definitely the next big trend in the industry. Recognizing that Netflix must offer online video downloads or risk losing its competitive edge and face extinction, Hastings recently launched an online download service that offers more than 4,000 movie titles. Apple and online retail giant Amazon.com also offer movie downloads, but so far the service has attracted only a small number of early adopters with sufficient technology—and patience. At current download rates, a typical DVD with 7 gigabytes of digital information requires 10 hours to download; high-definition DVDs capable of broadcast on big-screen sets require 72 hours! "Movie downloading will evolve over the next decade, but it will do so slowly," says Hastings. "DVDs won't be dominant forever, but it will be dominant for a very long time. Movie downloading may be a miniscule market [at present], but Netflix intends to be the leader when it starts to grow."

Downloading movies over the Internet represents a major change in Netflix's business model. One positive aspect of the change is significantly lower distribution costs (shipping expenses) for Netflix. The move poses serious challenges for the company, however. Convincing movie studios that online distribution of their movies is secure, which protects their revenue stream, is paramount. Developing the technology that allows customers to download movies quickly, easily, and reliably is another key issue. Although company officials refuse to comment on the matter, industry experts say that Netflix is working on a set-top box that would allow subscribers to download movies with ease from the Internet.

Netflix has built its competitive advantage on two strengths: its expertise in technology and its ability for fast delivery from its 41 strategically located distribution centers. Netflix has built proprietary film suggestion software (29,000 lines of code) called CineMatch that uses customers' ratings from past films they have rented to suggest new ones. The CineMatch system works so well that its recommendations account for 70 percent of the movies Netflix customers rent. The company recently added a popular feature called Friends that allows movie buffs to share movie recommendations with one another.

Hastings has set a goal of 20 million subscribers by 2012, but he knows that Internet movie downloading represents the future for Netflix. "DVDs will continue to generate big profits in the near future," he says. "But movies over the Internet are coming, and at some point will be big business. We want to be ready when

(continued)

video-on-demand happens. That's why the company is called Netflix, not DVD-by-Mail."

1. What core competencies has Netflix developed? How has it used those core competencies to gain a competitive edge over its rivals?

2. Conduct a SWOT (Strengths, Weaknesses, Opportunities, and Threats) analysis for Netflix. (Refer to steps 2 and 3 of the strategic planning process.)

3. Work with a group of your classmates to brainstorm ideas for ways in which Netflix can capitalize on Internet movie downloading. What should the company's future strategy be?

*Sources:* Adapted from Larry Stevens, "Netflix IT Has to Deliver High Efficiency, Support Fast Growth," *CIO Insight,* October 15, 2005, pp. 11–13; "What's Next for Netflix?" *Knowledge@Wharton,* November 1, 2006, http://knowledge.wharton.upenn.edu/article.cfm?articleid=1593; "About Blockbuster," Blockerbuster.com, www.blockbuster.com.au/About_Blockbuster.htm; Reed Hastings, "How I Did It: The Envelope, Please," *Inc.,* December 2005, pp. 118–120; "Netflix Mulling Options for Downloading," *Reuters,* June 20, 2006, http://today.reuters.com/misc/type=technology; Andrew Simons, "Movie Downloads May Give Netflix New Competition," *Wall Street Journal,* October 18, 2006, p. B2C.

market segment. By focusing efforts to maximize their companies' performance on these key success factors, entrepreneurs can achieve dramatic strategic advantages over their competitors. Companies that understand these key success factors tend to be leaders of the pack, whereas those that fail to recognize them become also-rans.

**Key success factors** come in a variety of different patterns depending on the industry. Simply stated, they are the factors that determine a company's ability to compete successfully in an industry. Bruce Milletto, owner of Bellissimo Coffee Info-Group, a coffee business consulting firm, says that to be successful coffee shops must focus on three key success factors: high quality coffee products, stellar customer service, and a warm, inviting ambience that transforms a coffee house into a destination where people want to gather with their friends. Martin Mayorga started a coffee roasting business with his wife in 1998 and recently opened a retail coffee store that focuses on specialty imported coffee beans. With these key success factors in mind, Mayorga created a shop that looks more like a lounge than a retail store with its plush leather family-style seating. The Mayorgas also have added an entertainment factor by including musical entertainment and allowing customers to view the entire roasting process on its custom-made bean roaster, attractive extras for customers looking for a way to relax after a busy day at work.[22]

Simply stated, key success factors determine a company's ability to compete in the marketplace. Sometimes these sources of competitive advantages are cost factors such as manufacturing cost per unit, distribution cost per unit, or development cost per unit. More often these key success factors are less tangible but are just as important, such as level of product quality, customer services offered, convenient store locations, availability of customer credit, name recognition, and others. For example, one restaurant owner identified the following key success factors for his business:

- Tight cost control (labor, 15–18 percent of sales and food costs, 35–40 percent of sales)
- Trained, dependable, and honest in-store managers
- Close monitoring of waste
- Convenient location
- High food quality
- Consistent food
- Clean restaurants
- Friendly and attentive service from a well-trained waitstaff

These controllable variables determine the ability of any restaurant in his market segment to compete. Restaurants lacking these key success factors are not likely to survive, whereas those that build these factors into their strategies will prosper. However, before entrepreneurs can build a strategy on the foundation of the industry's key success factors, they must identify them. Table 2.4 presents a form to help entrepreneurs identify the most important success factors and their implications for the company.

**TABLE 2.4 Identifying Key Success Factors**

List the key success factors that your business must possess if it is to be successful in its market segment.

| Key Success Factor | How Your Company Rates |
|---|---|
| 1 | Low 1 2 3 4 5 6 7 8 9 10 High |
| 2 | Low 1 2 3 4 5 6 7 8 9 10 High |
| 3 | Low 1 2 3 4 5 6 7 8 9 10 High |
| 4 | Low 1 2 3 4 5 6 7 8 9 10 High |
| 5 | Low 1 2 3 4 5 6 7 8 9 10 High |
| Conclusions: | |

## Step 5: Analyze the Competition

Ask small business owners to identify the greatest challenge they face, and one of the most common responses is *competition*. A recent study of top executives by consulting firm McKinsey and Company reports that 85 percent say that their industries are becoming more competitive. What factors are driving the increased levels of competition? Smarter rivals, more companies competing on low price, and rising customer awareness top the list.[23] Small companies increasingly are under fire from larger, more powerful rivals, including general retailers such as Wal-Mart and specialty stores such as B&Q, PetSmart, and Electro World. Keeping tabs on rivals' strategic movements through competitive intelligence programs is a vital strategic activity. Indeed, in one study of fast-growing companies, 84 percent of entrepreneurs said that information about their competitors is an important factor in the growth of their companies' profits.[24] According to one small business consultant, "Business is like any battlefield. If you want to win the war, you have to know who you're up against."[25] The primary goals of a competitive intelligence program include the following:

- Avoiding surprises from existing competitors' new strategies and tactics
- Identifying potential new competitors
- Improving reaction time to competitors' actions
- Anticipating rivals' next strategic moves
- Improving your ability to differentiate your company's products and services from those of your competitors

Unfortunately, most small companies fail to gather competitive intelligence because their owners mistakenly assume that it is too costly or simply unnecessary. One study found that nearly 80 percent of business owners had no idea what their competitors were up to![26] In reality, the cost of collecting information about competitors typically is minimal, but it does require discipline.

**COMPETITOR ANALYSIS.** Sizing up the competition gives entrepreneurs a more realistic view of the market and their companies' position in it. Yet not every competitor warrants the same level of attention in a strategic plan. *Direct competitors* offer the same products and services, and customers often compare prices, features, and deals from these competitors as they shop. *Significant competitors* offer some of the same products and services. Although their product or service lines may be somewhat different, there is competition with them in several key areas. *Indirect competitors* offer the same or similar products or services only in a small number of areas, and their target customers seldom overlap yours. Entrepreneurs should monitor closely the actions of their direct competitors, maintain a solid grasp of where their significant competitors are heading, and spend only minimal resources tracking their indirect competitors. For instance, two of Philadelphia's landmark businesses, Pat's King of Steaks and Geno's Steaks, are direct competitors in the market for Philly cheesesteaks. Their locations—across the street from one another—make it easy for each to keep track of the other. Pat's and Geno's charge the same prices for their sandwiches, and both claim to be the home of the original Philly cheesesteak sandwich.[27]

A competitive intelligence exercise enables entrepreneurs to update their knowledge of competitors by answering the following questions:

- Who are your major competitors and where are they located? Bob Dickinson, president of Carnival Cruise Lines, considers his company's main competition to be land-based theme parks and casinos rather than other cruise lines. Why? Because 89 percent of American adults, for example, have never been on a cruise![28]
- What distinctive competencies have they developed?
- How do their cost structures compare to yours? Their financial resources?
- How do they market their products and services?
- What do customers say about them? How do customers describe their products or services; their way of doing business; the additional services they might supply?
- What are their key strategies?
- What are their strengths? How can your company surpass them?
- What are their primary weaknesses? How can your company capitalize on them?
- Are new competitors entering the market?

A small business owner can collect a great deal of information about competitors through low-cost competitive intelligence (CI) methods including the following:

- Read industry trade publications for announcements from competitors.
- Ask questions of customers and suppliers on what they hear competitors may be doing. In many cases, this information is easy to gather because some people love to gossip.
- Talk to employees, especially sales representatives and purchasing agents. Experts estimate that 70 to 90 percent of the competitive information a company needs already resides with employees who collect it in their routine dealings with suppliers, customers, and other industry contacts.[29]
- Attend trade shows and collect competitors' sales literature.
- Watch for employment ads from competitors; knowing what types of workers they are hiring can tell you a great deal about their future plans.
- Conduct patent searches for patents that competitors have filed. This gives important clues about new products they are developing.
- Review environmental reports. They can provide important information about the factories of manufacturing companies, including the amounts and the kinds of emissions released. A private group, Environmental Protection, also reports emissions for specific plants.[30]
- Learn about the kinds and amounts of equipment and raw materials competitors are importing by studying the *Journal of Commerce Port Import Export Reporting Service (PIERS)* database. These clues can alert an entrepreneur to new products a competitor is about to launch.
- If appropriate, buy competitors' products and assess their quality and features. Benchmark their products against yours. The owner of an online gift-basket company periodically places orders with his primary competitors and compares their packaging, pricing, service, and quality to his own.[31]
- Obtain credit reports on each of your major competitors to evaluate their financial condition. Dun & Bradstreet and other research firms also enable entrepreneurs to look up profiles of competitors that can be helpful in a strategic analysis.
- Visit the Web site of the agency that regulates the stock market in your country to view the perioidic financial reports that companies must file.
- Check out the resources of your local library, including articles and online databases. Press releases, which often announce important company news, can be an important source of competitive intelligence. Many companies supply press releases through the *PR Newswire*. For local competitors, review back issues of the area newspaper for articles on and advertisements by competitors.

- Use the vast resources of the World Wide Web to learn more about your competitors. The Web enables entrepreneurs to gather valuable competitive information at little or no cost. "Businesses need to make sure that they have the right people spending enough time looking for the right kind of information and that there is a mechanism for getting this intelligence into decision making loops," says one expert on business intelligence.[32] (Refer to our Web site at www.prenhall.com/scarborough for an extensive listing of more than 1,000 useful small business Web sites.)
- Visit competing businesses periodically to observe their operations. Sam Walton, founder of Wal-Mart, was famous for visiting competitors' operations to see what he could learn from them.

Using the information gathered, a business owner can set up teams of managers and employees to evaluate key competitors and make recommendations on strategic actions that will improve the company's competitive position against each one.

Entrepreneurs can use the results of the competitor intelligence analysis to construct a competitive profile matrix for each market segment in which the firm operates. A **competitive profile matrix** allows entrepreneurs to evaluate their firms against the major competitors on the key success factors for their market segments (refer to Table 2.4). The first step is to list the key success factors identified in Step 4 of the strategic planning process and to attach weights to them reflecting their relative importance. Table 2.5 shows a sample competitive profile matrix for a small company. (For simplicity, the weights in this matrix sum add up to 1.00.) In this example, notice that product quality is the most important key success factor, which is why its weight (.35) is the highest.

The next step is to identify the company's major competitors and to rate each one (and your company) on each of the key success factors:

| If factor is a: | Rating is: |
| --- | --- |
| Major weakness | 1 |
| Minor weakness | 2 |
| Minor strength | 3 |
| Major strength | 4 |

Once the rating is completed, the owner simply multiplies the weight by the rating for each factor to get a weighted score, and then adds up each competitor's weighted scores to get a total weighted score. The results will show which company is strongest, which is the weakest, and which of the key success factors each one is best and worst at meeting. The matrix shows entrepreneurs how their companies "measure up" against competitors on

**TABLE 2.5  Sample Competitive Profile Matrix**

**Key Success Factors**

| (from Step 5) | Weight | Your Business Rating | Weighted Score | Competitor 1 Rating | Weighted Score | Competitor 2 Rating | Weighted Score |
| --- | --- | --- | --- | --- | --- | --- | --- |
| Ability to Innovate | 0.25 | 4 | 1.00 | 2 | 0.50 | 1 | 0.25 |
| Customer Service | 0.10 | 3 | 0.30 | 3 | 0.30 | 4 | 0.40 |
| Convenience | 0.10 | 1 | 0.10 | 3 | 0.30 | 4 | 0.40 |
| Product Quality | 0.35 | 4 | 1.40 | 1 | 0.35 | 2 | 0.70 |
| Customer Loyalty | 0.20 | 2 | 0.40 | 3 | 0.60 | 2 | 0.40 |
| **Total** | 1.00 | | 3.20 | | 2.05 | | 2.15 |

the industry's key success factors and gives them an idea of which strategies they should employ to gain a competitive advantage over their rivals. For instance, the company in Table 2.5 should compete by emphasizing its product quality and its ability to innovate (both are major strengths for the company but are weaknesses for its rivals) and not its convenience (which is a major weakness for the company but is a strength for its rivals) or its customer loyalty (a minor weakness for the company).

### Step 6. Create Company Goals and Objectives

Before entrepreneurs can build a comprehensive set of strategies, they must first establish business goals and objectives, which give them targets to aim for and provide a basis for evaluating their companies' performance. Without them, entrepreneurs cannot know where their businesses are going or how well they are performing. Creating goals and objectives is an essential part of the strategic management process.

**GOALS.** **Goals** are the broad, long-range attributes that a business seeks to accomplish; they tend to be general and sometimes even abstract. Goals are not intended to be specific enough for a manager to act on but simply state the general level of accomplishment sought. What level of sales would you like for your company to achieve in five years? Do you want to boost your market share? Does your cash balance need strengthening? Would you like to enter a new market or increase sales in a current one? Do you want your company to be the leader in its market segment? Do you want to improve your company's customer retention level? Researchers Jim Collins and Jerry Porras studied a large group of businesses and determined that one of the factors that set apart successful companies from unsuccessful ones was the formulation of very ambitious, clear, and inspiring long-term goals. Collins and Porras called them BHAGs ("Big Hairy Audacious Goals," pronounced "bee-hags") and say that their main benefit is to inspire and focus a company on important actions that are consistent with its overall mission.[33] In their classic book, *Built to Last: Successful Habits of Visionary Companies,* Collins and Porras, explain the role of BHAGs to a company:

> A true BHAG is clear and compelling and serves as a unifying focal point of effort and acts as a catalyst for team spirit. It has a clear finish line, so the organization can know when it has achieved the goal; people like to shoot for finish lines. A BHAG engages people—it reaches out and grabs them in the gut. It is tangible, energizing, highly focused.[34]

Defining broad-based goals will help entrepreneurs to focus on the next phase—developing specific, realistic objectives.

**OBJECTIVES.** **Objectives** are more specific targets of performance. Common objectives address profitability, productivity, growth, efficiency, markets, financial resources, physical facilities, organizational structure, employee welfare, and social responsibility. Jim Collins suggests that the objectives a company sets determine the level of success it achieves. Establishing profitability targets is not enough. Instead, entrepreneurs must set objectives and measure performance in those critical areas that determine their companies' ability to be profitable—a concept he calls a company's true economic denominators. These economic denominators might be the cost of acquiring a customer, sales per labor hour, the customer retention rate, the rate of inventory turnover, or some other factor. Dell Inc., for instance, has left most of its competitors in the dust by focusing on one of its true economic denominators, achieving a phenomenal inventory turnover ratio of 90 times a year! As a result, Dell is able to keep inventory levels exceptionally low, just one-tenth that of some of its rivals, which is an essential component in its build-to-order strategy. "We typically run a factory with about five or six hours' worth of inventory on hand, including work in progress," says Dick Hunter, Dell's vice-president of supply chain management. "This has decreased the cycle time at our factories and reduced warehouse space—space that has been replaced by more manufacturing lines."[35] Unfortunately, Collins claims that, unlike Dell, fewer than 10 percent of all companies understand what their true economic denominators are. We will discuss the importance of identifying true economic denominators (also called critical numbers) in Chapter 7, "Creating a Solid Financial Plan."

Because objectives in one area of the company might conflict with one another, entrepreneurs must establish priorities. Which objectives are most important? Arranging objectives in a hierarchy according to their priority can help business owners resolve conflicts when they arise. Well-written objectives have the following characteristics:

***They are specific.*** Objectives should be quantifiable and precise. For example, "to achieve a healthy growth in sales" is not a meaningful objective; but "to increase retail sales by 12 percent and wholesale by 10 percent in the next fiscal year" is precise and spells out exactly what management wants to accomplish.

***They are measurable.*** Entrepreneurs should be able to plot their companies' progress toward its objectives; this requires a well-defined reference point from which to start and a scale for measuring progress.

***They are assignable.*** Unless an entrepreneur assigns responsibility for an objective to an individual, it is unlikely that the company will ever achieve it. Creating objectives without giving someone responsibility for accomplishing them is futile.

***They are realistic, yet challenging.*** Objectives must be within the reach of the organization or motivation will disappear. In any case, managerial expectations must remain high. In other words, the more challenging an objective is (within realistic limits), the higher the performance will be. Set objectives that will challenge yourself, your business, and your employees.

***They are timely.*** Objectives must specify not only what is to be accomplished but also when it is to be accomplished. A time frame for achievement is important.

***They are written down.*** This writing process does not have to be complex; in fact, the manager should make the number of objectives relatively small, from five to fifteen.

The strategic planning process works best when managers and employees are actively involved jointly in setting objectives. Developing a plan is top management's responsibility, but executing it falls to managers and employees; therefore, encouraging them to participate in the process broadens the plan's perspective and increases the motivation to make the plan work. Also, managers and employees know a great deal about the organization and usually are willing to share this knowledge.

## Step 7. Formulate Strategic Options and Select the Appropriate Strategies

**4.** Discuss the characteristics of three basic strategies: low-cost, differentiation, and focus.

By this point in the strategic management process, entrepreneurs should have a clear picture of what their businesses do best and what their competitive advantages are. Similarly, they should know their companies' weaknesses and limitations as well as those of their competitors. The next step is to evaluate strategic options and then prepare a game plan designed to achieve the company's mission, goals, and objectives.

**STRATEGY.** A **strategy** is a road map an entrepreneur draws up of the actions necessary to fulfill a company's mission, goals, and objectives. In other words, the mission, goals, and objectives spell out the *ends,* and the strategy defines the *means* for reaching them. A strategy is the master plan that covers all of the major parts of the organization and ties them together into a unified whole. The plan must be action-oriented—that is, it should breathe life into the entire planning process. Entrepreneurs must build a sound strategy based on the preceding steps that uses their company's core competencies as the springboard to success. Joseph Picken and Gregory Dess, authors of *Mission Critical: The 7 Strategic Traps That Derail Even the Smartest Companies,* write, "A flawed strategy—no matter how brilliant the leadership, no matter how effective the implementation—is doomed to fail. A sound strategy, implemented without error, wins every time."[36]

A successful strategy is comprehensive and well-integrated, focusing on establishing the key success factors that the entrepreneur identified in Step 4. For instance, if maximum

## How Blueprint Companies Break the $1 Billion Barrier

When entrepreneurs launch their businesses, they often dream that their companies will become industry leaders—the next Microsoft. One measure of that level of success is when a company crosses the $1 billion mark in annual sales. Only a handful of small companies grow to that size, and that fact intrigued researcher David Thomson, who set out to discover how the small companies that did achieve $1 billion in annual sales accomplished that feat. What Thomson discovered is that these (once) small companies, which he named blueprint companies, followed a similar path to reach this level of success. "My approach is to reverse-engineer success," says Thomson. The following seven "essentials" summarize the blueprint companies' pathway to success.

### Essential 1. Create and Sustain a Breakthrough Value Proposition

The entrepreneurs behind the blueprint companies are able to explain clearly and concisely why their companies have a competitive advantage over their rivals. Even more important, their customers recognize the blueprint companies' competitive advantages! Using his experience as a runner, Phil Knight worked with Bill Bowerman to create innovations in a product that had been long ignored: running shoes. Using lightweight nylon, cushioned midsoles, and waffle-bottom soles, Knight and Bowerman, co-founders of Nike, created a breakthrough value proposition that athletes recognized. The entrepreneurs also produced a major breakthrough in advertising when they signed a promising young professional basketball player named Michael Jordan to endorse and promote their athletic shoes. "Keeping an eye on your customer is the key to delivering a breakthrough value proposition," says Thomson.

### Essential 2. Exploit a High-Growth Market

Most blueprint companies operate in markets that are large enough to accommodate several billion-dollar companies. In the 1970s, Howard Lester spotted an opportunity in the kitchenware market as department stores expanded nationally and began selling standardized items. Lester launched Williams-Sonoma, a store that specializes in upscale kitchen gadgets and appliances, expanded quickly, and never looked back. Like Howard Lester, entrepreneurs must recognize that high-growth potential often exists in niches in mature markets and not just in new, emerging markets. Starbucks, Skype, and Office Depot also exploited high-growth markets to achieve their impressive records of success.

### Essential 3. Land Marquee Customers That Feed the Revenue Powerhouse

Blueprint companies achieve exponential growth early on in their lives and sustain their impressive growth rates by landing a limited number of highly valuable customers and taking good care of them. Sales to these marquee customers serve as a booster rocket for blueprint companies' sales. High customer retention rates also fuel their rapid growth. At the Cheesecake Factory, a restaurant with 111 locations in 30 states, founder David Overton says that 20 percent of the company's customers account for 80 percent of its sales.

### Essential 4. Leverage "Big Brother" Alliances to Break into New Markets

In the late 1970s, Bill Gates was a young entrepreneur who had developed an operating system for PCs, and IBM, a giant that was known for its mainframe computers, was getting into the PC business. When IBM shipped its first PC in the early 1980s, Microsoft's DOS was the operating system that ran on it, setting the stage for Microsoft's meteoric rise to the top of the software industry over the next three decades.

### Essential 5. Become the Master of Exponential Returns

Founders of blueprint companies recognize the importance of generating sales, but they also know that business success depends on earning a profit and achieving positive cash flow. These companies focus relentlessly on cash flow from day one in their operation, and they have been able to differentiate their products and services so that they create attractive profit margins. Howard Schultz, CEO of Starbucks, set out to create a business that not only sold a great cup of coffee but also a "third place" people go to hang out (in addition to home and work). Doing so enables Starbucks to charge prices for a "coffee experience" that are double (or more) those of other coffee sellers, which generates high rates of return and positive cash flow for the company.

### Essential 6. Manage by Inside-Outside Leadership

Creating a fast-growing business requires a diverse set of skills, and it is the rare individual who is blessed with the entire set. Founders of blueprint companies recognize this, and find someone whose leadership skills complement their own to help them manage their businesses. Their blend of skills makes them a dynamic duo—a "Mr./Ms. Inside" and a "Mr./Ms. Outside." At Cerner, a healthcare technology business, charismatic CEO Neil Patterson spends most of his time on the road, building client relationships and being the chief cheerleader for

the company. Vice-chairman Cliff Illig is Mr. Inside, focusing on internal operations and financial controls.

### Essential 7. Establish a Board of Essentials Experts

Founders of blueprint companies establish a board of directors for their companies, and they stack them with experts who can help them achieve the other six essentials. In his research of blueprint companies, Thomson says that he "found (marquee) customers, alliance partners, community members and CEOs (typically from other blueprint companies) who serve as battle-tested coaches guiding the team to exponential growth."

*Sources*: Adapted from Richard McGill Murphy, "Zero to $1 Billion," *FSB*, May 2006, pp. 34–45; David G. Thomson, "Blueprint to a Billion: 7 Essentials to Achieve Exponential Growth," *Kansas City Star*, September 26, 2006, www.kansascity.com/mld/kansascity/business/15611508.htm.

---

shelf space is a key success factor for a small manufacturer's product, the strategy must identify techniques for gaining more in-store shelf space (e.g., offering higher margins to distributors and brokers than competitors do, assisting retailers with in-store displays, or redesigning a wider, more attractive package).

**THREE STRATEGIC OPTIONS.** The number of strategies from which entrepreneurs can choose is infinite. When all the glitter is stripped away, however, three basic strategies remain. In his classic book, *Competitive Strategy*, Michael Porter defines these strategies: (1) cost leadership, (2) differentiation, and (3) focus.

*Cost Leadership.* A company pursuing a **cost leadership strategy** strives to be the lowest-cost producer relative to its competitors in the industry. Low-cost leaders have a competitive advantage in reaching buyers whose primary purchase criterion is price, and they have the power to set the industry's price floor. This strategy works well when buyers are sensitive to price changes, when competing firms sell the same commodity products, and when companies can benefit from economies of scale. Not only is a low-cost leader in the best position to defend itself in a price war, but it also can use its power to attack competitors with the lowest price in the industry. "You have to be the lowest-cost producer in your patch," says the president of a small company that sells the classic commodity product—cement.[37]

*Google*

Google, the well-known Web search engine, relies on a low-cost strategy to stay on top in a fiercely competitive industry. Google's Web site receives 7 billion page views a month and is the second most-visited Web site in the world. Yet the company's information technology budget is just 10 percent of the industry average. Google's secret: Its hardware system consists of several banks of more than 450,000 inexpensive servers linked together that, without monitors (no need!), run a bare-bones version of Linux. Google's real cost savings, however, lies in its IT maintenance; if a server breaks, Google simply throws it away and replaces it! The company has no need for costly service contracts or an extensive in-house IT department. As it has built new data centers across the United States, Google has incorporated technologies that are designed to reduce another major cost: electricity.[38]

There are many ways to build a low-cost strategy, but the most successful cost leaders know where they have cost advantages over their competitors, and they use these as the foundation for their strategies.

*JetBlue Airways*

Because its workforce currently is nonunion, JetBlue Airways has a significant advantage in labor costs, but not in fuel costs, over its larger, unionized competitors in the airline industry. The company's 1,100 call-center operators work from their homes, creating significant cost savings for themselves and for the company. Because the company offers stock options to its workers, employees often are willing to work for lower salaries. The result is that JetBlue's labor cost is just 25 percent of revenues compared to 33 to 44 percent of revenues for its competitors, and the company uses this to deploy its fleet of planes more efficiently and more profitably than its competition. JetBlue also gets more out of its employees' time than its competitors through cross-utilization, giving workers multiple assignments and job duties. JetBlue keeps its maintenance costs low by flying only two types of jets—Airbus A320s on long routes and Embraer 190s on short routes. Every JetBlue seat is upholstered in leather, a luxury that costs $15,000 more per plane but sends an important signal to passengers. In addition, the leather surfaces are easier to maintain and last much longer, lowering JetBlue's costs. The net effect of this cost leadership strategy is that JetBlue's operating cost is the lowest in the industry—just six cents per seat-mile compared with eight to twelve cents per seat-mile for older, "legacy" carriers. All of these factors mean that JetBlue jets are in the air (the only place they can make money!) longer than their competitors' planes are. The result is a successful low-cost strategy that has enabled JetBlue to remain profitable while many of its competitors have filed for bankruptcy.[39]

Of course, there are dangers in following a cost leadership strategy. Sometimes a company focuses exclusively on lower manufacturing costs, without considering the impact of purchasing, distribution, or overhead costs. Another danger is misunderstanding the company's true cost drivers. For instance, one furniture manufacturer drastically underestimated its overhead costs and, as a result, was selling its products at a loss. Finally, a company may pursue a low-cost leadership strategy so zealously that it essentially locks itself out of other strategic choices.

Under the right conditions, a cost leadership strategy executed properly can be an incredibly powerful strategic weapon. Small discount retailers that live in the shadows of Wal-Mart and thrive even when the economy slows succeed by relentlessly pursuing low-cost strategies. Small retail chains such as pound stores in Great Britain, for example, cater to low- and middle-income customers who live in inner cities or rural areas. They offer inexpensive products such as food, health and beauty products, cleaning supplies, clothing, and seasonal merchandise, and many of the items they stock are closeout buys (purchases made as low as 10 cents on the dollar) on brand name merchandise. They also are committed to squeezing unnecessary costs out of their operations. Every decision the founders of these companies make—from the low-cost locations of their headquarters with their spartan facilities to their efficient distribution centers—emphasizes cost containment and is designed to appeal to the bargain-hunting nature of their target audiences. For instance, 99 Cents Only, whose name describes its merchandising strategy, is housed in a no-frills warehouse in an older section of City of Commerce, California. Dollar General has reduced its cost with its EZStore system, a labor-saving strategy that streamlines inventory restocking by using pre-stocked carts that employees literally roll off of delivery trucks straight onto the retail floor.[40]

***Differentiation.*** A company following a **differentiation strategy** seeks to build customer loyalty by positioning its goods or services in a unique or different fashion. In other words, a company strives to be better than its competitors at something that its customers value. The primary benefit of successful differentiation is the ability to generate higher profit margins because of customers' heightened brand loyalty and reduced price sensitivity. There are many ways to create a differentiation strategy, but the key is to be special at something that is important to customers and offers them unique value such as quality, convenience, flexibility, performance, or style. "You'd better be on top of what it is your customers value and continually improve your offerings to better deliver that value," advises Jill Griffin, a strategic marketing consultant.[41] If a small company can offer products or services that larger competitors do not, improve a product's or service's performance, reduce the customer's risk of purchasing it, or both, it has the potential to differentiate. For instance, at PETCO, a chain of pet supply stores selling luxury pet products and services, only 40 of its more than 10,000 product offerings overlap the pet supply offerings of industry giant Wal-Mart.[42]

Even in industries in which giant companies dominate, small companies that differentiate themselves can thrive even when they cannot compete effectively on the basis of price.

*Pharmaca and Elephant Pharmacies*

Although the number of independent pharmacies has declined by 28 percent over the past decade (due primarily to intense competition from national chains), small drugstore chains such as Pharmaca and Elephant are growing fast by differentiating themselves from their larger rivals. In addition to traditional medicines that are available from any drugstore, both of these small drugstore chains sell natural remedies and services that are designed to heal their customers' bodies, minds, and spirits. At Pharmaca, for example, customers can consult with experts on naturopathy, homeopathy, acupuncture, and herbs, talk with registered nurses, take free classes on natural remedies, and use in-store kiosks to access a huge database of natural remedies, complete with information on potentially harmful interactions with prescription drugs. Pharmaca founder Barry Perzow knows that his target customers are well educated and have high incomes, and he selects the locations for the company's outlets with those characteristics in mind, looking for sites where median income levels are $85,000 or more. "I want to bring together the best of alternative and traditional medicines under one roof," says Perzow.[43]

Elephant, another drug chain that sells natural remedies in addition to regular prescription drugs, advertises itself as "the drugstore that prescribes yoga." Elephant stores have two separate pharmacies—one for prescription drugs and one for herbal remedies. Elephant pharmacies are large (about 11,000 square feet) and offer free health and wellness classes, yoga classes at in-store yoga studios, and wine and book sections. "Once people visit Elephant, they come back again and again due to our ability to help each customer individually and our unique and extraordinary product selection," says CEO Kathi Lentzsch. "We work hard to offer everything the community needs for health and wellness in a single location, while making the shopping experience educational and upbeat."[44]

Like Pharmaca and Elephant, small companies can use their size to their advantage and build their differentiation strategies on the principles that small businesses offer a more unique experience and are friendlier, more responsive to their customers, and more genuine than their larger rivals.

The key to a successful differentiation strategy is to build it on a *distinctive competence* (discussed earlier in this chapter)—something the small company is uniquely good at doing in comparison to its competitors. Common bases for differentiation include superior customer service, special product features, extensive product lines, a custom-tailored product or service, instantaneous parts availability, absolute product reliability, supreme product quality, in-depth product knowledge, and the ability to build long-term, mutually beneficial relationships with customers. To be successful, a differentiation strategy must create the perception of value to the customer. No customer will purchase a good or service that fails to produce a *perceived* value, no matter how *real* that value may be. One business consultant advises, "Make sure you tell your customers and prospects what it is about your business that makes you different. Make sure that difference is in the form of a true benefit to the customer."[45]

*Miguel Caballero Inc.*

Miguel Caballero, founder of the company that bears his name, sells a unique line of armored clothing that rivals any garment from an upscale designer but is designed to deflect point-blank gunfire. Caballero's business generates more than $7 million in annual sales by marketing bulletproof overcoats, business suits, suede jackets, and casual clothing to high-profile business executives, politicians, and undercover agents who don't want to look as if they are wearing bulletproof clothing. Rather than use traditional Kevlar (which can be quite heavy), Caballero has developed and patented a fabric made of woven polyester and nylon that can withstand gunfire without requiring the wearer to sacrifice style and comfort. (The first Kevlar suede jacket Caballero produced years ago weighed a hefty 11 pounds; that same garment made with his patented fabric weighs just 2.6 pounds.) "There are hundreds of companies that make bulletproof vests," says Caballero. "We make bulletproof fashion."[46]

Pursuing a differentiation strategy includes certain risks. One danger is trying to differentiate a product or service on the basis of something that does not boost its performance or lower its cost to the buyer. Another pitfall is trying to differentiate on the basis of something that customers do not perceive as important. Business owners also must consider how long they can sustain a product's or service's differentiation; changing customer tastes make the basis for differentiation temporary at best. Imitations and "knockoffs" from competitors also pose a threat to a successful differentiation strategy. For instance, designers of high-priced original clothing see much cheaper knock-off products on the market shortly after their designs hit the market. Another danger of this strategy is over-differentiating and charging so much that a company prices its products out of its target customers' reach. Another risk is focusing only on the physical characteristics of a product or service as a basis for differentiating it and ignoring important psychological factors—status, prestige, image, and style. For many successful companies, psychological factors are key elements in differentiating their products and services from those of competitors.

***Focus.*** A **focus strategy** recognizes that not all markets are homogeneous. In fact, in any given market, there are many different customer segments, each having different needs, wants, and characteristics. The principal idea of this strategy is to select one (or more) segment(s); identify customers' special needs, wants, and interests; and approach them with a good or service designed to excel in meeting these needs, wants, and interests. Focus strategies build on *differences* among market segments. Using a focus strategy, entrepreneurs concentrate on serving a niche in the market rather than trying to reach the entire market.

A successful focus strategy depends on a small company's ability to identify the changing needs of its targeted customer group and to develop the skills required to serve them. That means the owner and everyone in the organization must have a clear understanding of how to add value to the product or service for the customer. How does the product or service meet the customer's needs at each stage—from raw material to final sale?

Rather than attempting to serve the total market, a company pursuing a focus strategy specializes in serving a specific target segment or niche that larger companies are overlooking or underestimating. A focus strategy is ideally suited to many small businesses, which often lack the resources to reach a national market. Their goal is to serve their narrow target markets more effectively and efficiently than do competitors that pound away at the broad market. Common bases for building a focus strategy include zeroing in on a small geographic area, targeting a group of customers with similar needs or interests (e.g., left-handed people), or specializing in a specific product or service (e.g., petite clothing).

*Wayne and Marty Scott
and Clown Shoes & Props*

Wayne and Marty Scott, owners of Clown Shoes & Props, have captured about 20 percent of the U.S. market for clown shoes! The copreneurs learned their craft while working at the Ringling Brothers Circus in the 1960s and now fill orders from across the country for wingtips that are two feet long. The Scotts offer nine basic clown shoe styles, each a shoe within a shoe, and add accessories such as squirting flowers, trains, and mouths that open and close with each step. Making clown shoes is serious business for the Scotts, however—the average pair requires six hours to build and sells for $225. Before making a pair of shoes, the Scotts insist on a description of the clown's character and a picture of the clown in costume. "A clown isn't complete without the right shoes," says Peggy Williams, a former clown and now a manager at Ringling Brothers, "and you can't get these at the mall."[47]

Like the Scotts, the most successful focusers build a competitive edge by concentrating on specific market niches and serving them better than any other competitor can. Essentially, this strategy depends on creating value for the customer either by being the lowest-cost producer or by differentiating the product or service in a unique fashion, but doing so in a narrow target segment. Speedy service, a unique product or service, specialized knowledge, superior customer service, value pricing, and convenience are just some of the ways that companies using focus strategies meet their target customers' unique needs. To be worth targeting, a niche must be large enough to be profitable, reasonably reachable through marketing, and capable of sustaining a business over time (in other words, not a passing fad). Examples of small companies competing successfully in small, yet profitable, niches include the following:

- Copreneurs Jose and Karen Muñiz launched Amazing Butterflies, a distributor of live butterflies, in 1999 and now generate more than $1 million in annual revenues from their offices in Tamarac, Florida, San Jose, California, and Dallas, Texas. Amazing Butterflies charges customers as much as $95 for a dozen butterflies, which create a spectacular effect when released at weddings, funerals, charity or corporate events, and other special occasions. Muñiz, a former business consultant, says, "I could never go back to consulting. This is just too much fun."[48]
- Michael Quaranto and Andrew Brown, both airline pilots, operate 1570 Cinema Services on the 14 days off they have each month. Their company specializes in cleaning theater screens, which are eight stories tall, with customized equipment that the entrepreneurs built themselves, including a lamb's wool-covered cleaning head that is controlled by a winch and powered by an electric motor.[49]
- Citi Trends focuses on an often-overlooked niche in the clothing market: young hip-hop fans in low-income, urban areas. The company buys surplus merchandise from popular labels such as Phat Farm, Sean John, and Rocawear at huge discounts and sells them to cash-strapped inner-city teens at rock-bottom prices in its 250-plus retail stores. "Citi Trends has been able to drive growth not only by offering branded merchandise at a lower price point but [also] through a low-cost real estate strategy where the Big-Box chains can't compete," says one industry analyst.[50]
- Freed of London is a major player in a unique niche: pointe shoes, the slippers that ballet dancers wear that enable them to balance their weight on just two square inches of paper, fabric, and paste that make up a shoe's "box." At three factories in England, Freed employs 30 highly-skilled craftsmen, each of whom turn out 25 to 40 pairs of pointe shoes a day, which the company sells for $80 or more a pair. Large ballet companies such as the Moscow Ballet spend $500,000 or more a year on pointe shoes for their dancers, many of whom are fiercely loyal to the Freed brand and will perform in no other type of shoe.[51]

The rewards of dominating a niche can be huge, but pursuing a focus strategy does carry risks. Companies sometimes must struggle to capture a large enough share of a small market to be profitable. A niche must be big enough for a company to generate a profit. A successful focus strategy also brings with it a threat. If a small company is successful in its niche, there is the danger of larger competitors entering the market and eroding or controlling it. Sometimes a company with a successful niche strategy gets distracted by its success

## ■ Strategies for Success

Most entrepreneurs who launch businesses face established rivals with greater name recognition, more resources, bigger budgets, and existing customer bases. How can a small start-up company compete effectively against that? It all boils down to creating a winning strategy and then executing it. The entrepreneurs profiled here developed strategies for their companies that set them apart from their rivals and gave them a competitive edge in their respective markets.

### SavRow Bespoke Technology

The PC has long since become a commodity item, one for which customers' primary purchase criterion is low price. Yet 28-year-old Ali Raissi-Dehkordy, founder of SavRow Bespoke Technology, saw room in the market for a company offering customers top-of-the-line, custom-built, ultra-stylish PCs. Raissi-Dehkordy, a Londoner, quit his job as an investment banker with Goldman Sachs and launched SavRow by charging $150,000 in start-up costs on his credit cards. His company's name is derived from London's Savile Row, which is famous for its concentration of shops that produce custom-made clothing for wealthy customers, because it assembles by hand computers that are designed to match its clients' tastes, preferences, and technological requirements. In its most recent year of operation, the young company sold fewer than 400 computers but generated sales of more than $4 million! SavRow's mid-level computers sell for as much as $10,000, about 10 times the price of the average PC. The company's target customers are willing to pay premium prices for premium performance in a hand-made computer that they have a hand in designing. SavRow's Monza laptop more closely resembles a Grand Prix race car (including the flashy red, green, and white paint job) than a computer.

In addition to flashy, custom paint jobs (some of which costs $1,000), SavRow computers offer the latest technology inside. Rather than use traditional hard disk drives for storage, the company offers faster flash memory, which costs much more than traditional memory. For clients who want extra-quiet machines, SavRow adds a cooling paste made of diamonds to reduce the need for noisy fans. For a customer in London, SavRow built a custom desktop and then encased it in a hand-stitched leather case. A businessperson in Dubai ordered a special gold-plated PC from SavRow for his desk. Raissi-Dehkordy says that his company earns profit margins of 20 percent, a number that any company in the PC industry would envy. He expects sales at SavRow to triple in the near future now that it has opened a sales office in New York City. He also plans to open Gadget-Doc, a premium technical support service, for owners of "regular" PCs. "Your car and your suit are expressions of your personality," says Raissi-Dehkordy. "We see the computer the same way."

### Bacchus Caves

David Provost is in an unusual segment of the construction industry. As its name implies, his company, Bacchus Caves, builds caves—both underground and in hillsides. Provost initially built caverns for wineries that needed cool, stable climates to age their wines, but a new market segment emerged in 1999 when the company received a request from a customer who wanted to add a cave to his home. Although building a home cave costs from $150 to $375 per square foot, considerably more than the construction costs for a traditional home, home caves now comprise 65 percent of Bacchus Caves' sales. "People use them to store artwork or to have friends over," explains Provost. "One customer wants to put in a yoga studio; another wants to store his golf cart. One client said it really brings him back to his primal roots." Provost says that his Flintstones strategy produces an attractive profit on his company's annual sales of nearly $10 million.

1. Which of the three strategies described in this chapter are these companies using? Explain.
2. What advantages does successful execution of their strategies produce for SavRow Bespoke Technology and Bacchus Caves?
3. What are the risks associated with the strategies of these companies?

*Sources:* Adapted from Mark Halper, "Revving Up the PC," *Business 2.0,* November 2005, pp. 70–72; Geoff Williams, "The Good Old Days," *Entrepreneur,* November 2006, p. 28.

and tries to branch out into other areas. As it drifts farther away from its core strategy, it loses its competitive edge and runs the risk of confusing or alienating its customers. Muddying its image with customers puts a company in danger of losing its identity.

A successful strategic plan identifies a complete set of success factors—financial, operating, and marketing—that, taken together, produce a competitive advantage for the small business. The resulting action plan distinguishes the firm from its competitors by exploiting its competitive advantage. The focal point of this entire strategic plan is the customer. The customer is the nucleus of any business, and a competitive strategy will succeed only if it is aimed at serving customers better than the competitor does. An effective strategy draws out the competitive advantage in a small company by building on its strengths and by making the customer its focus. It also defines methods for overcoming a company's weaknesses, and it identifies opportunities and threats that demand action.

## Step 8. Translate Strategic Plans into Action Plans

When it comes to strategic planning, entrepreneurs typically do not lack vision. Success, however, requires matching vision with execution. No strategic plan is complete until it is put into action. Entrepreneurs must convert strategic plans into operating plans that guide their companies on a daily basis and become a visible, active part of their businesses. A small business cannot benefit from a strategic plan sitting on a shelf collecting dust.

**IMPLEMENT THE STRATEGY.**   To make the plan workable, business owners should divide the plan into projects, carefully defining each one by the following:

*Purpose.*  What is the project designed to accomplish?

*Scope.*  Which areas of the company will be involved in the project?

*Contribution.*  How does the project relate to other projects and to the overall strategic plan?

*Resource requirements.*  What human and financial resources are needed to complete the project successfully?

*Timing*.  Which schedules and deadlines will ensure project completion?

Once entrepreneurs assign priorities to these projects, they can begin to implement the strategic plan. Involving employees and delegating adequate authority to them is essential because these projects affect them most directly.

If an organization's people have been involved in the strategic management process to this point, they will have a better grasp of the steps they must take to achieve the organization's goals as well as their own professional goals. Early involvement of the workforce in the strategic management process is a luxury that larger businesses cannot achieve. Commitment to achieve the company's objectives is a powerful force for success, but involvement is a prerequisite for achieving total employee commitment. Without a committed, dedicated team of employees working together to implement it, a company's strategy, no matter how well planned, usually fails.

When putting their strategic plans into action, small companies must exploit all of the competitive advantages of their size by:

- Responding quickly to customers' needs.
- Remaining flexible and willing to change.
- Continually searching for new emerging market segments.
- Building and defending market niches.
- Erecting "switching costs" through personal service and special attention.
- Remaining entrepreneurial and willing to take risks.
- Acting with lightning speed to move into and out of markets as they ebb and flow.
- Constantly innovating.

Although it is possible for competitors to replicate a small company's strategy, it is much more difficult for them to mimic the way in which it implements and executes its strategy.

## Launching a New Airline:
## You Must Be Crazy!

The airline industry in the United States has been marked by chaos and cut-throat competition as companies struggle to survive. Many established, "legacy" carriers, including United Airlines, Delta Airlines, U.S. Airways, and Northwest Airlines, have declared bankruptcy and have formulated plans for restructuring their businesses. In fact, a passenger who buys an airline ticket has a 50 percent chance of flying on an airline that is operating under bankruptcy protection. Rising fuel prices, escalating labor costs, and rising customer complaints about lost luggage, food quality, and on-time performance only complicate struggling airlines' plans to return to profitability. American Airlines, the world's largest airline, recently posted its first annual profit in six years, a period in which it incurred losses totaling $8 billion!

Under these trying circumstances and industry conditions, surely no one would consider launching a new airline. Yet that's just what entrepreneurs David Spurlock and Gary Rogliano have done. Spurlock is the founder of EOS Airlines (named after the winged Greek goddess of the dawn), which offers premium business-class-only service between London's Stansted and New York's JFK airports. EOS's strategy is to attract business travelers with amenities such as seats that provide 21 square-feet of personal space and fold into six-foot six-inch flat beds along with compartments that have large credenza-style surfaces and "companion seats" for those travelers who want to work and conduct meetings in flight. Champagne flows freely, and passengers can order food whenever they are hungry. The company's Boeing 757s accommodate just 48 passengers, compared to a typical 757, which is configured for 180 passengers. Whereas a typical business-class ticket from the United States to Europe costs about $8,000, a ticket on EOS goes for $5,000 to $6,000.

MAXjet also flies the lucrative New York to London route because it is flush with price-insensitive business travelers and, like EOS, operates out of the same lower cost airports, JFK and Stansted. The carrier also has added flights from Washington's Dulles and Los Angeles airports to London. MAXjet uses only Boeing 767s but has configured them for just 102 passengers, less than half the 220 passengers a 767 carries on a typical airline. The carrier also targets business class fliers but aimsits flights at those business travelers who are more interested in value pricing and less interested in in-flight frills. Like EOS, MAXjet offers high-quality meals (although they are served according to the airline's schedule rather than on demand) and personal entertainment systems at every seat. MAXjet's seats are not as spacious as those on EOS, but MAXjet's prices are easier on travelers' budgets. MAXjet's fares start at $1,358, about 70 percent lower than a comparable business class fare on most legacy carriers. Legacy carriers are not sitting idly by, however. For them, business class travelers generate more revenue per seat-mile than any other category, which means they are likely to defend their markets with ferocity. In fact, many of the legacy carriers are in the process of renovating their business class cabins and services, primarily because of the competition from upstart carriers such as EOS and MAXjet.

Spurlock raised $87 million in venture capital, the second highest funding in the airline industry (behind David Neeleman, founder of JetBlue). To fund its launch, MAXjet raised $40 million from private investors. Despite an old saying that the fastest way to make a million dollars is to start with a billion dollars and launch an airline, many industry analysts think that both EOS and MAXjet have a good chance to succeed.

1. Use the resources of the Web to research EOS and MAXjet and their positions in the airline industry. Are their strategies proving to be successful? What threats do EOS and MAXjet face? What do you predict for the future of these two companies?
2. On a scale of 1 (high) to 10 (low), how would you rate the attractiveness of the airline industry to entrepreneurs who want to launch businesses? Explain.
3. Given the challenges the airline industry is facing, why would entrepreneurs such as David Spurlock and Gary Rogliano choose to launch start-up companies in such a challenging industry? What strategic recommendations would you make to these entrepreneurs?

*Sources:* Adapted from Susan Stellin, "A First-Class Production," *Fast Company,* September 2006, pp. 97–99; Sascha Segan, "Luxury Class Options Expand for Fliers and Prices Come Down a Notch," Frommers.com, December 20, 2005, www.frommers.com/articles/3314.html; Chris Isidore, "Northwest Files for Bankruptcy," CNNMoney.com, September 24, 2005, http://money.cnn.com/2005/09/14/news/fortune500/northwest/; Barney Gimbel, "New Kids in Class," *Fortune,* October 31, 2005, pp. 196–197.

## Step 9. Establish Accurate Controls

**5.** Understand the importance of controls such as the balanced scorecard in the planning process.

So far, the planning process has created company objectives and has developed a strategy for reaching them, but rarely, if ever, will a company's actual performance match its stated objectives. Entrepreneurs quickly realize the need to control actual results that deviate from its company's plans.

**CONTROLLING THE STRATEGY.**    Planning without control has little operational value, and a sound planning program requires a practical control process. The plans created in this process become the standards against which actual performance is measured. It is important for everyone in the organization to understand—and to be involved in—the planning and controlling process.

Controlling projects and keeping them on schedule means that the owner must identify and track key performance indicators. The source of these indicators is the operating data from the company's normal business activity; they are the guideposts for detecting deviations from established standards. Accounting, production, sales, inventory, and other operating records are primary sources of data an entrepreneur can use for controlling activities. For example, on a customer service project, performance indicators might include the number of customer complaints, orders returned, on-time shipments, and a measure of order accuracy.

To evaluate the effectiveness of their strategies and to link them to everyday performance, many companies are developing **balanced scorecards**, a set of measurements unique to a company that includes both financial and operational measures and gives managers a quick yet comprehensive picture of the company's total performance against its strategic plan. The key to linking strategy and day-to-day organizational performance is identifying the right factors and measurements to be included on the scorecard. (Recall the discussion of the true economic denominators or critical numbers in Step 6 of the strategic management process, creating goals and objectives.) One writer says that a balanced scorecard:

> . . . is a sophisticated business model that helps a company understand what's really driving its success. It acts a bit like the control panel on a spaceship—the business equivalent of a flight speedometer, odometer, and temperature gauge all rolled into one. It keeps track of many things, including financial progress and softer measurements—everything from customer satisfaction to return on investment—that need to be managed to reach the final destination: profitable growth.[52]

Rather than sticking solely to the traditional financial measures of a company's performance, the balanced scorecard gives managers a comprehensive view from *both a financial and an operational perspective*. The premise behind such a scorecard is that relying on any single measure of company performance is dangerous. Just as a pilot in command of a jet cannot fly safely by focusing on a single instrument, an entrepreneur cannot manage a company by concentrating on a single measurement. The complexity of managing a business demands that an entrepreneur be able to see performance measures in several areas simultaneously. Those measures might include traditional standards such as financial ratios or cash flow performance and gauges of product innovation, customer satisfaction, retention, and profitability as well as measures of vendor performance and inventory management.

When properly used, an entrepreneur can trace the elements on the company's balanced scorecard back to its overall strategy and its mission, goals, and objectives. The goal is to develop a reporting system that does not funnel meaningful information only to a few decision makers but to make it available in a timely manner throughout the entire company, enabling employees at *all* levels to make decisions based on strategic priorities. A balanced scorecard reporting system should collect, organize, and display meaningful information that managers and employees need to make daily decisions that are congruent with the company's overall strategy and it must do so in a concise, easy-to-read, timely manner. When creating a balanced scorecard for a company, the key is to establish goals for each critical indicator of company performance and then create meaningful measures for each one. Although some elements will apply to many businesses, a company's scorecard

**FIGURE 2.2**
**Balanced Scorecard**

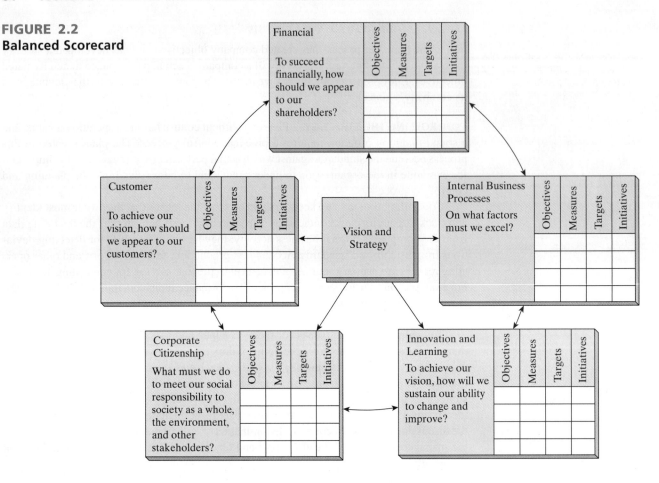

should be unique. The balanced scorecard looks at a business from five important perspectives (see Figure 2.2):[53]

**1.** *Customer perspective.* How do customers see us? Customers judge companies by at least four standards: time (how long it takes the company to deliver a good or service), quality (how well a company's product or service performs in terms of reliability, durability, and accuracy), performance (the extent to which a good or service performs as expected), and service (how well a company meets or exceeds customers' expectations of value). Because customer-related goals are external, managers must translate them into measures of what the company must do to meet customers' expectations.

**2.** *Internal business perspective.* On what factors must we excel? The internal factors that managers should focus on are those that have the greatest impact on customer satisfaction and retention and on company effectiveness and efficiency. Developing goals and measures for factors such as quality, cycle time, productivity, costs, and others that employees directly influence is essential.

**3.** *Innovation and learning perspective.* Can we continue to improve and create value? This view of a company recognizes that the targets required for success are never static; they are constantly changing. If a company wants to continue its pattern of success, it cannot stand still; it must continuously improve. A company's ability to innovate, learn, and improve determines its future. These goals and measures emphasize the importance of continuous improvement in customer satisfaction and internal business operations.

**4.** *Financial perspective.* How do we look to shareholders? The most traditional performance measures—financial standards—tell how much the company's overall strategy and its execution are contributing to its bottom line. These measures focus on factors such as profitability, growth, and shareholder value. On balanced scorecards, companies often break their financial goals into three categories: survival, success, and growth. Companies use these measures to make sure that their strategies drive their budgets rather than allowing their budgets to determine their strategies.

**5. *Corporate citizenship.*** How well are we meeting our social responsibility to society as a whole, the environment, the community, and other external stakeholders? Even the smallest companies must recognize that they have a responsibility to be good business citizens. This part of the scorecard focuses on measuring a small company's social and environmental performance.

Focusing on the factors that drive a company's overall performance on its critical numbers will improve its financial performance as well.

*John Garrett and Triad Distributing Northwest Inc.*

John Garrett, co-president of Triad Distributing Northwest Inc., a building supplies wholesaler, monitors hourly the balanced scorecard his company has developed. It incorporates an array of measures, including cash-on-hand, accounts payable and accounts receivable balances, inventory levels, new customer accounts, and several measures unique to both the industry and the company. As he sees key measures change, Garrett can act immediately by working with people throughout the company to address the changes. Recently when he opened the balanced scorecard, he noted a $9,000 sale to a new customer. Garrett called to congratulate the salesperson and then called the customer to introduce himself, starting off the new relationship on a positive note. "It's a great way to keep in touch with the pulse of the company," he says. "It gives you that quick overview of your business so, on the fly, you can see where your business is going."[54]

Although the balanced scorecard is a vital tool that helps managers keep their companies on track, it is also an important tool for changing behavior in an organization and for keeping everyone focused on what really matters. As conditions change, managers must make corrections in performances, policies, strategies, and objectives to get performance back on track. Increasingly, companies are linking performance on the metrics included in their balanced scorecards to employees' compensation. A practical control system is also economical to operate. Most small businesses have no need for a sophisticated, expensive control system. The system should be so practical that it becomes a natural part of the management process.

## Conclusion

The strategic planning process does *not* end with the nine steps outlined in this chapter; it is an on-going process that a small business owner must repeat. With each round, he or she gains experience, and the steps become much easier. The planning process outlined here is designed to be as simple as possible. No small business should be burdened with an elaborate, detailed formal planning process that it cannot easily use. Such programs require excessive amounts of time to operate, and they generate a sea of paperwork. The small business manager needs neither.

What does this strategic planning process lead to? It teaches entrepreneurs a degree of discipline that is important to their businesses' survival. It helps them learn about their businesses, their competitors, and, most important, their customers. It forces entrepreneurs to recognize and evaluate their companies' strengths and weaknesses as well as the opportunities and threats facing it. It also encourages entrepreneurs to define how they will set their businesses apart from the competition. Although strategic planning cannot guarantee success, it does dramatically increase the small firm's chances of survival in a hostile business environment.

## Chapter Review

1. Understand the importance of strategic management to a small business.
   - Strategic planning, often ignored by small companies, is a crucial ingredient in business success. The planning process forces potential entrepreneurs to subject their ideas to an objective evaluation in the competitive market.
2. Explain why and how a small business must create a competitive advantage in the market.
   - The goal of developing a strategic plan is to create for the small company a competitive advantage—the aggregation of factors that sets the small business apart from its competitors and gives it a unique position in the market. Every small firm must establish a plan for creating a unique image in the minds of its potential customers.
3. Develop a strategic plan for a business using the nine steps in the strategic planning process.
   - Small businesses need a strategic planning process designed to suit their particular needs. It should be relatively short, be informal and not structured, encourage the participation of employees, and not begin with extensive objective setting. Linking the purposeful action of strategic planning to an entrepreneur's ideas can produce results that shape the future.

     Step 1. *Develop a clear vision and translate it into a meaningful mission statement.* Highly successful entrepreneurs are able to communicate their vision to those around them. The firm's mission statement answers the first question of any venture: What business am I in? The mission statement sets the tone for the entire company.

     Step 2. *Assess the company's strengths and weaknesses.* Strengths are positive internal factors; weaknesses are negative internal factors.

     Step 3. *Scan the environment for significant opportunities and threats facing the business.* Opportunities are positive external options; threats are negative external forces.

     Step 4. *Identify the key factors for success in the business.* In every business, key factors determine the success of the firms in it, and so they must be an integral part of a company's strategy. Key success factors are relationships between a controllable variable (e.g., plant size, size of sales force, advertising expenditures, product packaging) and a critical factor influencing the firm's ability to compete in the market.

     Step 5. *Analyze the competition.* Business owners should know their competitors almost as well as they know their own company. A competitive profile matrix is a helpful tool for analyzing competitors' strengths and weaknesses.

     Step 6. *Create company goals and objectives.* Goals are the broad, long-range attributes that the firm seeks to accomplish. Objectives are quantifiable and more precise; they should be specific, measurable, assignable, realistic, timely, and written down. The process works best when subordinate managers and employees are actively involved.

     Step 7. *Formulate strategic options and select the appropriate strategies.* A strategy is the game plan the firm plans to use to achieve its objectives and mission. It must center on establishing for the firm the key success factors identified earlier.

     Step 8. *Translate strategic plans into action plans.* No strategic plan is complete until the owner puts it into action.

**Step 9.** *Establish accurate controls.* Actual performance rarely, if ever, matches plans exactly. Operating data from the business serve as guideposts for detecting deviations from plans. Such information is helpful when plotting future strategies.

The strategic planning process does not end with these nine steps; rather, it is an ongoing process that the owner will repeat.

4. Discuss the characteristics of three basic strategies: low-cost, differentiation, and focus.
   - A company pursuing a cost leadership strategy strives to be the lowest-cost producer relative to its competitors in the industry.
   - A company following a differentiation strategy seeks to build customer loyalty by positioning its goods or services in a unique or different fashion. In other words, the firm strives to be better than its competitors at something that its customers value.
   - A focus strategy recognizes that not all markets are homogeneous. The principal idea of this strategy is to select one (or more) segment(s); identify customers' special needs, wants, and interests; and approach them with a good or service designed to excel in meeting these needs, wants, and interests. Focus strategies build on differences among market segments.

5. Understand the importance of controls such as the balanced scorecard in the planning process.
   - Just as a pilot in command of a jet cannot fly safely by focusing on a single instrument, an entrepreneur cannot manage a company by concentrating on a single measurement. The balanced scorecard is a set of measurements unique to a company that includes both financial and operational measures and gives managers a quick yet comprehensive picture of the company's total performance.

## Discussion Questions

1. Why is strategic planning important to a small company?
2. What is a competitive advantage? Why is it important for a small business to establish one?
3. What are the steps in the strategic management process?
4. What are strengths, weaknesses, opportunities, and threats? Give an example of each.
5. What is knowledge management? What benefits does it offer a small company?
6. Explain the characteristics of effective objectives. Why is setting objectives important?
7. What are business strategies? Explain the three basic strategies from which entrepreneurs can choose. Give an example of each one.
8. Describe the three basic strategies available to small companies. Under what conditions is each most successful?
9. How is the controlling process related to the planning process?
10. What is a balanced scorecard? What value does it offer entrepreneurs who are evaluating the success of their current strategies?

# Business PlanPro

Chapter 2 is designed to help you think about your business from a strategic perspective. This involves describing your business objectives, drafting your mission statement, identifying "keys to success," conducting a SWOT analysis, and making initial comments about your strategy and your competitive advantage.

## On the Web

Visit the Companion Website at www.prenhall.com/scarborough and click on the "Business Plan Resources" tab. Scroll down and find the information with the heading "Standard Industry Classification Codes" (SIC codes). Step through the process to find the SIC code associated with your industry. Then, review the information associated with the "Competitor Analysis" section. This information may provide insight into learning more about your industry competitors on a global, national, or even on a local basis.

## In the Software

Open your plan in Business Plan Pro. Add text to the strategic areas mentioned in this chapter. Don't worry about perfecting this information. Instead, capture your main thoughts and ideas so you can revisit these topics, add detail, and make certain the sections are congruent with your entire plan. Reviewing some examples of each of these sections in one or more of the sample plans that you had selected earlier may be helpful.

Review the following sections, as they appear, in one or more of the sample plans that you identified earlier:

- Mission Statement
- Objectives
- SWOT Analysis
- Keys to Success
- Competition, Buying Patterns, and Main Competitors
- Value Proposition
- Competitive Edge
- Strategy & Implementation Summary

Note the information captured in these sections of the plans. The text in some areas may be quite elaborate while others might be brief and contain only bullet points. As you look at each plan, determine whether it provides the needed information under each topic and think about the type of information to include in your plan.

## Building Your Business Plan

Here are some tips you may want to consider as you tackle each of these sections:

*Mission Statement.* Use your mission statement to establish your fundamental goals for the quality of your business offering. The mission statement represents the opportunity to answer the questions: What business are you in and why does your business exist? This may include the value you offer and the role customers, employees, and owners play in providing and benefiting from that value. A good mission statement can be a critical element in defining your business and communicating this definition to key stakeholders including investors, partners, employees, and customers.

*Objectives.* Objectives should be specific goals that are quantifiable and measurable. Setting measurable objectives will enable you to track your progress and measure your results.

*SWOT Analysis.* What are the internal strengths and weaknesses of your business? As you look outside the organization, what are the external opportunities and threats? List the threats and opportunities and then assess what this tells you about your business. How can you leverage your strengths to take advantage of the opportunities ahead? How can you improve or minimize the areas of weaknesses?

*Keys to Success.* Virtually every business has critical aspects that make the difference between success and failure. These may be brief bullet point comments that capture key elements that will make a difference in accomplishing your stated objectives and realizing your mission.

*Competition, Buying Patterns, and Main Competitors.* Discuss your ideal position in the market. Think about specific kinds of features and benefits your business offers and how they are unique compared to what is available to your market today. Why do people buy your services instead of the services your competitors offer? Discuss your primary competitors' strengths and weaknesses. Consider their service offerings, pricing, reputation, management, financial position, brand awareness, business development, technology, and any other factors that may be important. What market segments do they occupy? What strategy do they appear to pursue? How much of a competitive threat do they present?

*Value Proposition.* A value proposition is a clear and concise statement that describes the tangible value-based result a customer receives from using your product or service. The more specific and meaningful this statement is from a customer's perspective, the better. Once you have your value proposition, look at your organization—and your business plan—in terms of how well you communicate it and fulfill your promise to your customers or clients.

***Your Competitive Edge.*** A competitive edge builds on your value proposition and seeks to capture the unique value—in whatever terms the customer defines that value—that your business offers. Your competitive edge may be through your product, customer service, method of distribution, pricing, or promotional methods. It describes how your business is uniquely different from all others in a way that is meaningful to customers and sustainable over time.

***Strategy & Implementation.*** This is a section that you will build upon and, for now, make comments that capture your plans for the business. This describes the game plan and provides focus to realize your venture's objectives and mission. Based on your initial strategic analysis, which of the three business strategies—low cost, differentiation, or focus—will you use to give your company a competitive advantage? How will this strategy capitalize on your company's strengths and appeal to your customer's need? Later you will build upon this information as you formulate action plans to bring this strategic plan to life.

Capture your ideas in each of these sections and continually ask yourself about the relevance of this information. If it does not add value to your business plan, there is no need to include this information.

# Choosing a Form of Ownership

> Whenever you see a
> successful business,
> someone once made a
> courageous decision.
> —Peter F. Drucker

> To survive, men and
> business and
> corporations must serve.
> —John H. Patterson

## Learning Objectives

**Upon completion of this chapter, you will be able to:**

1 Discuss the key issues to evaluate the different forms of ownership.

2 Describe the advantages and disadvantages of the sole proprietorship.

3 Describe the advantages and disadvantages of the partnership.

4 Describe the advantages and disadvantages of the corporation.

5 Describe the features of the alternative forms of ownership, such as the S corporation, the limited liability company, the joint venture, and the syndicate.

*1.* Discuss the key issues to evaluate the different forms of ownership.

S electing a form of business ownership is a landmark step in the creation of a venture. Most entrepreneurs, however, are not trained in the finer points of business law. Consequently, it is imperative that entrepreneurs carefully search the types of legal ownership and then consult an attorney, an accountant, or both to verify whether the choice addresses their specific needs. "One of the main reasons small businesses fail is they don't seek legal and accounting help at the beginning," says tax agent and eBay Silver PowerSeller Patrick Snetsinger. "How your company is structured will have long-term implications."[1] Although an entrepreneur may change the form of ownership later, this change can be expensive, time consuming, and complicated.

There is no single "best" form of business ownership. Each form has its own unique set of advantages and disadvantages. The key to choosing the optimal form of ownership is the ability to understand the characteristics of each business entity and how they affect an entrepreneur's business and personal circumstances.

The following are relevant issues the entrepreneur should consider in the evaluation process:

- **Tax considerations.** Graduated tax rates, the government's constant modification of the tax code, and the year-to-year fluctuations in a company's income require an entrepreneur to calculate the firm's tax liability under each ownership option every year. Changes in local or national tax codes may have a significant impact on a company's "bottom-line" and the entrepreneur's personal tax exposure.

- **Liability exposure.** Certain forms of ownership offer business owners greater protection from personal liability due to financial problems, faulty products, and a host of other difficulties. Entrepreneurs must evaluate the potential for legal and financial liabilities and decide the extent to which they are willing to assume personal responsibility for their companies' obligations. Individuals with significant personal wealth or a low tolerance for the risk of loss may benefit from forms of ownership that provide greater protection of their personal assets.

- **Start-up and future capital requirements.** The form of ownership can affect an entrepreneur's ability to raise start-up capital. Some forms of ownership are better when obtaining start-up capital, depending on how much capital is needed and the source from which it is obtained. As a business grows, capital requirements increase, and some forms of ownership make it easier to attract outside financing.

- **Control.** Certain forms of ownership require an entrepreneur to relinquish some control over the company. Before selecting a business entity, an entrepreneur must decide how much control he or she is willing to sacrifice in exchange for resources from other people or organizations.

- **Managerial ability.** Entrepreneurs must assess their own ability to successfully manage their companies. If they lack skill or experience in certain areas, they may need to select a form of ownership that allows them to involve people who possess those needed skills or experience in the company.

- **Business goals.** The projected size and profitability of a business influences the form of ownership chosen. Businesses often evolve into a different form of ownership as they grow, but moving from some formats can be complex and expensive. Legislation may change and make current ownership options less attractive.

- **Management succession plans.** When choosing a form of ownership, business owners must look ahead to the day when they will pass their companies on to the next generation or to a buyer. Some forms of ownership better facilitate this transition. In other cases, when the owner dies—so does the business.

- **Cost of formation.** The costs to create forms of ownership vary. Entrepreneurs must weigh the benefits and the costs of the form they choose.

Traditionally, in the United States, business owners have been able to choose from three major forms of ownership: the sole proprietorship, the partnership, and the corporation (see Figure 3.1). Entrepreneurs also can choose from other forms of ownership, including the S corporation, the limited liability company, the joint venture, and the syndicate.

**FIGURE 3.1**
**Forms of Business Ownership**

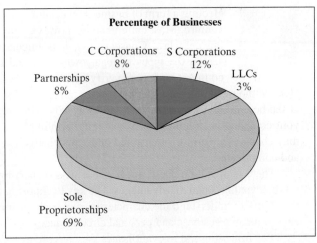

**Percentage of Businesses**

C Corporations 8%
S Corporations 12%
LLCs 3%
Partnerships 8%
Sole Proprietorships 69%

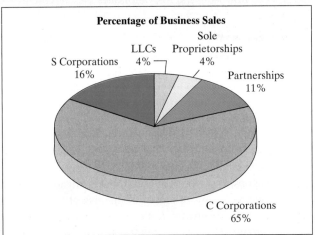

**Percentage of Business Sales**

S Corporations 16%
LLCs 4%
Sole Proprietorships 4%
Partnerships 11%
C Corporations 65%

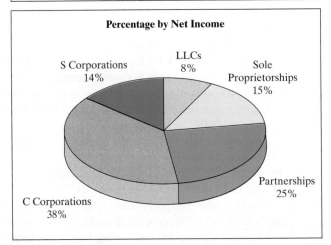

**Percentage by Net Income**

S Corporations 14%
LLCs 8%
Sole Proprietorships 15%
Partnerships 25%
C Corporations 38%

## The Sole Proprietorship

2. Describe the advantages and disadvantages of the sole proprietorship.

The sole proprietorship is the simplest and most popular form of ownership. This form of business ownership is designed for a business owned and managed by one individual. The sole proprietor is the only owner and ultimate decision maker for the business. The simplicity and ease of formation makes the sole proprietorship the most popular form of ownership, comprising nearly 70 percent of all businesses in the United States.[2]

One approach when naming a business is to visualize the company's target customers. What are they like? What are their ages, genders, lifestyles, and locations? What makes our company competitive or unique to those customers? Classic examples include

## What's in a Business Name?

Naming a business is like naming a child: You get only one shot, so you had better get it right the first time!

Choosing a memorable business name can be one of the most enjoyable—and most challenging—aspects of starting a business. Some entrepreneurs invest as much in creating their business names as they do their ideas, writing their business plans, and choosing a location. Ideally, a business name should convey the expertise, value, and uniqueness of the company's product or service.

There is controversy over what makes a good business name. Some experts believe that the best names are abstract, a blank slate upon which to create an image, but others think that names should be informative. In reality, almost any name can be effective if it is supported by a solid marketing and communication strategy.

Gerald Lewis' consulting firm CDI Designs specializes in helping retail food businesses. "In retailing," Lewis explains, "the market is so segmented that [a name must] convey very quickly what the customer is going after. For example, if it is a warehouse store, it has to convey that impression. If it's an upscale store selling high-quality food, it has to convey that impression. The name combined with the logo is very important in doing that."

Whatever image you want to communicate, the process of choosing a name that works involves a series of steps.

1. Decide the most appropriate single quality of the business that you want to convey to potential customers. Avoid sending a mixed or inappropriate message. Remember that a name is the most visible attribute of a company. The business name will be on all advertising and printed materials and if done effectively, will portray a personality, stand out in a crowd, and stick in the minds of customers.
2. Select a name that is short, attention getting, and memorable. Avoid names that are hard to spell, pronounce, or remember. This is especially true if the business is an Internet company with a Web site. Type "posiesbythedozenandthensomefromrosie. com" a few times before you decide this is *the* name for an online flower store! Rosiesposies.com may be a better choice.
3. Be creative. Entrepreneurs should devote as much creative effort to naming their businesses as they do to generating their product or service idea.

4. Make sure the name has longevity and will not become outdated. "Big Stiff Hair Salon" might have been a great name in the 1950s, but it would have died a horrible death in the 1960s, as long straight locks became the norm in many countries.
5. Select a name that creates a positive image. Is Rent-a-Wreck attractive because you think you will save money on a car rental, or does the name put you off because you question the reliability of their cars?
6. Practice using the name you are considering for a few days. Try it out on friends and family. See how the name sounds and "feels" to you.
7. Once you are comfortable with your choice, conduct a name search to make sure that no one else in your jurisdiction has already claimed the name. This is an especially tedious chore for a Web site. Registering a domain name can be daunting if a brilliant idea is already taken.

Creating a business name can prove beneficial to creating a brand image for your business. Choosing a name that is distinctive, memorable, and positive can go a long way toward helping you achieve success in your business venture. What's in a name? The future of your venture!

1. Consider the following business names and discuss the opportunities and challenges they presented in the marketplace to the entrepreneurs who created them.

   - Netflix
   - iPhone
   - O Magazine
   - 1-800-GOT-JUNK
   - YouTube
   - Starbucks

2. Kentucky Fried Chicken, also referred to as KFC, has tried to diversify its product line and is now attempting to transition to a healthier menu. Discuss the challenges the organization faces based on its name alone. What other business names have placed limitations on the future of the business?

*Sources:* Andrew Raskin, "The Name of the Game," *Inc.*, February 2000, pp. 31–32; Rhonda Adams, "Sometimes Business Success Is All in the Name," *Business*, July 23, 2000, p. 3; Thomas Edmark, "What's in a Name?" *Entrepreneur*, October 1999, pp. 163–165; "How to Name Your Business," *Entrepreneur*, April 23, 2005; Chris Penttila, "Small-Business Answer Book," *Entrepreneur*, December 2006, p. 66.

Service Master (home maintenance services), In-N-Out Burgers (fast food), and Bi-Lo (supermarkets). According to Dave Batt, president of marketing consulting firm Everest Communications Inc., "The more targeted your product or service is to a specific demographic, the more specific your name should be to appeal to that target." Batt provides perspective by stating, "In time, the name will be less important than what you make of it through hard work, dedication and customer satisfaction." It is at that point that you will know that you have selected the right name for your company and given birth to a brand.[3]

## Advantages of a Sole Proprietorship

**SIMPLE TO CREATE.** One attractive feature of the sole proprietorship is the ease and speed of its formation. For example, if an entrepreneur wants to form a business under his own name (Ron Johnston Mortgage), he must obtain the necessary business licenses from state, county, and/or local governments and may begin operation. In most cases, an entrepreneur can complete all of the necessary steps in a single day and, in many cases, do so online. Once all necessary licenses are in place, the entrepreneur can start conducting business immediately.

**LEAST COSTLY FORM OF OWNERSHIP TO ESTABLISH.** In addition to being easy to set up, the sole proprietorship is generally the least expensive form of ownership to establish. There is no need to create and file the legal documents, such as those recommended for partnerships and required for corporations. A U.S. entrepreneur, for example, may simply contact the secretary of state's office, select a business name, identify the location, describe the nature of the business, and pay the appropriate fees and license costs, which gives him or her the right to conduct business in that particular jurisdiction.

In many jurisdictions, entrepreneurs who plan to conduct business under a trade name are required to obtain a Certificate of Doing Business under an Assumed Name, or a "Doing Business As" (DBA) name from the secretary of state. This is also known as a fictitious business name. An entrepreneur functioning as a sole proprietor may want to use his or her own name for the company name, such as Bob Smith Towing Service. On the other hand, many entrepreneurs view their company names as a way of using creativity to distinguish themselves in the market.

The fee for the Certificate of Doing Business Under an Assumed Name is usually nominal. Acquiring this certificate involves conducting a search to determine that the name chosen for the business is not already registered as a trademark or service mark with the secretary of state. Filing this certificate also notifies the state of who owns the business. Additionally, most states now require notice of the trade name to be published in a newspaper serving the trading area of the business.

*David Polatseck and Business Licenses*

Download and store any of about 28,000 national, state, and local license and permit applications for sites around the United States—it is that easy for the users of Business Licenses at www.businesslicenses.com. By paying a series of fees, users can download business license applications, access the necessary surrounding documents, and file and archive the licenses online. According to co-owner David Polatseck, the 55-employee company has more than 10,000 small business clients and generates about $2 million in sales annually, a number he expects to increase as he works to sign up larger customers.[4]

**PROFIT INCENTIVE.** One major advantage of the proprietorship is that once the owner has paid all of the company's expenses, he or she can keep the remaining profits after taxes. The profit incentive is a powerful one, and among entrepreneurs, profits represent an excellent way of "keeping score" in the game of the business.

**TOTAL DECISION-MAKING AUTHORITY.** Because the sole proprietor is in total control of operations, he or she can respond quickly to changes. The ability to respond quickly is an asset in a rapidly shifting market, and the freedom to set the company's course of action is both a major motivational and strategic force. For people who thrive on seeking new opportunities, the freedom of fast, flexible decision making is vital. The entrepreneur solely directs the operations of the business.

**NO SPECIAL LEGAL RESTRICTIONS.**  The proprietorship is the least regulated form of business ownership. In a time when government requests for information seem never-ending, this feature has merit.

**EASY TO DISCONTINUE.**  If the entrepreneur decides to discontinue operations, he or she can terminate the business quickly, even though he or she will still be liable for all of the business's outstanding debts and obligations.

## Disadvantages of a Sole Proprietorship

Although the advantages of a proprietorship are extremely attractive to most individuals contemplating starting a new business, it is important to recognize that this form of ownership has some significant disadvantages.

**UNLIMITED PERSONAL LIABILITY.**  The greatest disadvantage of a sole proprietorship is the unlimited personal liability of the owner; the sole proprietor is *personally* liable for all business debts. In the eyes of the law and the public, the entrepreneur and the business are one in the same. The proprietor owns all of the business's assets, and if the business fails, creditors can force the sale of those assets to cover its debts. The *company's* debts are the *owner's* debts. If unpaid business debts remain, creditors can also force the sale of the proprietor's *personal* assets to cover repayment. U.S. state laws vary, but most states require creditors to leave the failed business owner a minimum amount of equity in a home, a car, and some personal property. The reality: *Failure of the business can ruin a sole proprietor financially.*

**LIMITED ACCESS TO CAPITAL.**  If a business is to grow and expand, a sole proprietor often needs additional financial resources. However, many proprietors already have invested their available resources into their businesses and may have used their personal assets as collateral on existing loans. Therefore, it can be difficult for sole proprietors to borrow additional funds. A sole proprietorship is limited to whatever capital the owner can contribute and whatever money the owner can borrow. Unless proprietors have substantial personal wealth, owners may find it difficult to raise additional money while maintaining sole ownership. Most banks and other lending institutions have well-defined formulas for determining a borrower's eligibility.

**LIMITED SKILLS AND ABILITIES.**  A sole proprietor may not possess the full range of skills running a successful business requires. An entrepreneur's education, training, and work experiences may have taught him or her a great deal, yet there are areas in which his or her decision-making ability will benefit from the insight of others. Many business failures occur because owners lack skill, knowledge, and experience in areas that are vital to business success. Owners tend to push aside problems they do not understand or do not feel comfortable with in favor of those they can solve more easily. Unfortunately, the problems they set aside seldom solve themselves. By the time an owner decides to ask for help in addressing these problems, it may be too late to take advantage of opportunities or, ultimately, save the company.

**FEELINGS OF ISOLATION.**  Running a business alone allows an entrepreneur maximum flexibility, but it also creates feelings of isolation; there is no one to turn to for help when solving problems or getting feedback on a new idea. Most entrepreneurs report that they sometimes feel alone and frightened when they must make decisions knowing that they have nowhere to turn for advice or guidance. The weight of each critical decision rests solely on the proprietor's shoulders.

**LACK OF CONTINUITY FOR THE BUSINESS.**   If the proprietor dies, retires, or becomes incapacitated, the business automatically terminates. Lack of continuity is inherent in a sole proprietorship. Unless a family member or employee can take over, the future of the business could be in jeopardy. Proprietorships often have trouble recruiting and retaining good employees because employees want secure employment with greater opportunities for advancement.

A sole proprietorship may be ideal for founders who do desire to keep their business relatively small and simple. Some entrepreneurs, however, find that forming partnerships is one way to overcome the disadvantages of the sole proprietorship. For instance, a person who lacks specific managerial skills or has insufficient access to needed capital can compensate for those weaknesses by forming a partnership with someone who has complementary management skills.

## The Partnership

*3.* Describe the advantages and disadvantages of the partnership.

A **partnership** is an association of two or more people who co-own a business for the purpose of making a profit. Partners legally share a business's assets, liabilities, and profits according to the terms of a partnership agreement.

U.S. law does not require a written partnership agreement, also known as the articles of partnership, but it is wise to work with an attorney to develop an agreement that documents the status, rights, and responsibilities of each partner. Partners may think they know what they are agreeing to, only to find that there was not a clear understanding about the role and obligations of each partner. The **partnership agreement** is a document that states all of the terms of operating the partnership for the protection of each partner involved. Every partnership should be based on a comprehensive written agreement. When problems arise between partners, the written document becomes an invaluable tool for resolving them.

When a partnership agreement does not exist, the U.S. Revised Uniform Partnership Act, which will be discussed later in this chapter, governs the partnership, but its provisions may not be as favorable as an agreement drafted by the partners. Creating a partnership agreement is not necessarily costly. In most cases, the partners can review example agreements and discuss each of the provisions in advance. Once they have reached an understanding, an attorney can draft the formal document.

Banks often want to review the partnership agreement before lending the business money. One important feature of the partnership agreement is that it addresses, in advance, sources of potential conflict that could result in partnership battles and the dissolution of a business that could have been successful. Documenting these details before they occur—especially for challenging issues such as profit splits, contributions, workloads, decision-making authority, dispute resolution, and others—will help avoid tension in a partnership that could lead to business failure or dissolution of the partnership. Over time, partners and partnerships experience change, and this foresight can save time and money, and minimize conflict.

A partnership agreement can include any legal terms the partners desire. The standard partnership agreement will likely include the following information:

1. *Name of the partnership.*
2. *Purpose of the business.* What is the reason the partners created the business?
3. *Location of the business.*
4. *Duration of the partnership.* How long will the partnership last?
5. *Names of the partners and their legal addresses.*
6. *Contributions of each partner to the business, at the creation of the partnership and later.* This would include each partner's investment in the business. In some situations, a partner may contribute assets that are not likely to appear on the balance sheet. Experience, sales contacts, or a good reputation in the community may be some reasons for asking a person to join a partnership.
7. *Agreement on how the profits or losses will be distributed.*
8. *Agreement on salaries or drawing rights against profits for each partner.*
9. *Procedure for expansion through the addition of new partners.*

10. *Distribution of the partnership's assets if the partners voluntarily dissolve the partnership.*

11. *Sale of the partnership interest.* How and to whom can partners sell their interests in the business?

12. *Absence or disability of one of the partners.* If a partner is absent or disabled for an extended period of time, should the partnership continue? Will the absent or disabled partner receive the same share of profits as he or she did before the absence or disability? Should the absent or disabled partner be held responsible for debts incurred while unable to participate?

13. *Voting rights.* In many partnerships, partners have unequal voting power. The partners may base their voting rights on their financial or managerial contributions to the business.

14. *Decision-making authority.* When can partners make decisions on their own, and when must other partners be involved?

15. *Financial authority.* Which partners are authorized to sign checks, and how many signatures are required to authorize bank transactions?

16. *Handling tax matters.* The U.S. Internal Revenue Service requires partnerships to designate one person to be responsible for handling the partnership's tax matters.

17. *Alterations or modifications of the partnership agreement.* No document is written to last forever. Partnership agreements should contain provisions for alterations or modifications. As a business grows and changes, partners often find it necessary to update their original agreement. Recall that when no written partnership agreement exists and a dispute arises, the courts will apply the Revised Uniform Partnership Act.

Some partners conduct regularly scheduled meetings to discuss the operation of the business and any issues that are producing conflict. These meetings encourage the partners to put the facts about the business on the table including current financial statements and any documented evaluations of the firm's operations. Sharing and discussing these facts provide a common focus for the owners so that they can deal openly with the issues that are causing conflict and can work together to find solutions. Thorough planning, honesty, openness, and a willingness to deal with issues causing conflict are critical elements in the long-term success of a partnership.

## The Revised Uniform Partnership Act

The **Revised Uniform Partnership Act (RUPA)** codifies the body of law dealing with partnerships in the United States. Under the RUPA, the three key elements of any partnership are common ownership interest in a business, sharing the business's profits and losses, and the right to participate in managing the operation of the partnership. Under the act, each partner has the right to:

1. Share in the management and operation of the business.
2. Share in any profits the business might earn from operations.
3. Receive interest on additional advances made to the business.
4. Be compensated for expenses incurred in the name of the partnership.
5. Have access to the business's books and records.
6. Receive a formal accounting of the partnership's business affairs.

The RUPA also describes the partners' general obligations. Each partner is obligated to:

1. Share in any losses sustained by the business.
2. Work for the partnership without salary.
3. Submit differences that may arise in the conduct of the business to majority vote or arbitration.
4. Give other partners complete information about all business affairs.
5. Give a formal accounting of the partnership's business affairs.
6. Live up to a fiduciary responsibility of the partnership and place the interest of the partnership above his or her personal interests.

7. Adhere to the provisions of the partnership agreement and the decisions made by the partnership.
8. Behave in ways that demonstrate the same level of care and skill that a reasonable co-owner in the same position would use under the same circumstances.

Beyond what the law prescribes, a partnership is based on mutual trust and respect. Any partnership missing those elements is destined to fail. Like sole proprietorships, partnerships also have advantages and disadvantages.

**ENTREPRENEURIAL Profile**

*Norm Brodsky and CitiStorage*

Norm Brodsky has often expressed the opinion that partnerships don't work, yet he took on Sam Kaplan as a partner in his records storage business. "I realized I needed the kind of help I couldn't get from an employee," says Brodsky. "Sam's arrival into the business had an immediate impact. Sam took over the management of our finances and introduced systems and practices that were rare in a company of our size. Beyond his contributions in finance, he serves as a reality check, a 'stabilizer' and a confidant," says Brodsky. "Although I still think it's a bad idea to start a business with one, I've come to realize that ending with a partner is another matter—especially if the other person is someone like Sam."[5]

## Advantages of the Partnership

**EASY TO ESTABLISH.** Like the proprietorship, the partnership is relatively easy and inexpensive to establish. Co-owners must obtain the necessary business license and submit a minimal number of forms. In most states, partners must file a Certificate for Conducting Business as Partners if the business operates under a trade name.

**ENTREPRENEURIAL Profile**

*Rick Bayless and Manny Valdes and Frontera Foods*

The partners at Frontera Foods, a company that operates restaurants and sells cookbooks and food products, are in a perpetual creative struggle—with each other. "We are very different," says Rick Bayless, host of the Public Broadcasting Service television show, *Mexico—One Plate at a Time*, as he describes the skills that he and his business partner, Manny Valdes, possess. Bayless' talents come out in the kitchen; Valdes has the business sense. The trio of successful companies they co-founded and run—Frontera Foods, Frontera Media Productions, and Frontera Fresco—now exceed $15 million in annual sales. Over the past decade, the partners have butted heads and the creative tug-of-wars continue. "I'm ready to kill an idea," says Valdes, "and he's ready to do it another way." Based on the performance of their businesses, they would not have it any other way.[6]

Chef Rick Bayless poses with Gorditas de Barbacoa, crispy masa pockets filled with red-chile goat barbacoa and avocado leaf scented black beans, avocado and queso anejo, top, and Trio Trio Trio, a sampling of Ceviche Pronterizo, Ceviche Yucateeo and Seaside Cocktail of shrimp and lime-marinated Hawaiian blue marlin, bottom, at his restaurant, Frontera Grill, in Chicago.

**COMPLEMENTARY SKILLS.** In successful partnerships, the parties' skills and abilities complement one another, strengthening the company's managerial foundation. The synergistic effect created when partners of equal skill and creativity collaborate effectively results in outcomes that reflect the contributions of all involved.

It is beneficial if at least one partner has intimate knowledge and experience at operating the business. Understanding the technological aspects of building a technology-based business, for example, must be equally supported by a sound understanding of the principles that govern marketing, finance, business management, human resources, supply chain management, and a myriad of other factors. Many technology-based firms fail because their founders lack basic business skills, even though they may otherwise have the technological expertise to succeed.

**DIVISION OF PROFITS.** There are no restrictions on how partners may distribute the company's profits as long as they are consistent with the partnership agreement and do not violate the rights of any partner. The partnership agreement should articulate the nature of each partner's contribution and proportional share of profits. If the partners fail to create an agreement, the RUPA states that the partners share equally in the partnership's profits, regardless of the proportional amount of their original capital contributions.

**LARGER POOL OF CAPITAL.** A partnership can significantly broaden the pool of capital available to a business. Each partner's asset base supports more borrowing capacity than any partner has alone. This may become a critical factor because undercapitalization is a common cause of business failure.

**ABILITY TO ATTRACT LIMITED PARTNERS.** Not every partner must take an active role in operating a business. Partners who take an active role in managing a company and who share in its rewards, liabilities, and responsibilities are **general partners**. Every partnership must have at least one general partner (although there is no limit on the number of general partners a business can have). General partners have unlimited personal liability for the company's debts and obligations and are expected to take an active role in managing the business.

**Limited partners** are financial investors who do not want to participate in the day-to-day affairs of the partnership and seek to limit their risk. Limited partners cannot take an active role in the operation of the company and have limited personal liability for the company's debts and obligations. If the business fails, limited partners lose only what they have invested in the partnership itself and no more. If limited partners are "materially and actively" involved in a business—defined as spending more than 500 hours a year in the company—in the United States, they will be treated as general partners and will lose their limited liability protection. Silent partners and dormant partners are special types of limited partners. **Silent partners** are not active in a business but generally are known to be members of the partnership. **Dormant partners** are neither active nor generally known to be associated with the business.

A limited partnership can attract many investors by offering them limited liability and the potential to realize a substantial return on their investments if the business is successful. Individuals may find it profitable to invest in high-potential small businesses, but *only* if they avoid the disadvantages of unlimited liability. Limited partnerships will be discussed in greater detail later in this chapter.

**MINIMAL GOVERNMENTAL REGULATION.** Like the proprietorship, the partnership form of ownership is not burdened with excessive reporting requirements.

**FLEXIBILITY.** Although not as flexible as sole proprietorships, partnerships can generally react quickly to changing market conditions. In large partnerships, however, getting all partners' approval on key decisions can slow down a company's ability to react.

**TAXATION.** The partnership itself is not subject to federal taxation. It serves as a conduit for the profit or losses it earns or incurs; its net income or losses are passed through the individual partners as personal income, and only the partners, not the business, pay income tax on their distributive shares. The partnership, like the proprietorship, avoids the "double taxation" disadvantage associated with the corporate form of ownership.

### Disadvantages of the Partnership

Business partnerships can be complicated, and the sins—and debts—of one partner can afflict the others. Entrepreneurs should double-check their decisions to take on a partner and make sure the prospective business partner is bringing real value to the business.[7] "I would never, ever, ever advise someone to go into a partnership," says Clay Nelson, a business and life coach who works with partners, "unless it's necessary. And sometimes it is."[8] Before entering into a business marriage, entrepreneurs must recognize the disadvantages of business partnerships.

**UNLIMITED LIABILITY OF AT LEAST ONE PARTNER.**  At least one member of every partnership must be a general partner. The general partner has unlimited personal liability, even though he or she is often the partner with the least personal resources. U.S. state laws commonly exempt certain personal property items from attachment by creditors. The most common is the homestead exemption, which allows the debtor's home to be sold to satisfy debt but stipulates that a certain dollar amount be reserved to allow the debtor to find other shelter. Household furniture (up to a specified amount), clothing and personal possessions, government or military pensions, and bonuses also are protected and cannot be taken to satisfy an outstanding business debt.

**CAPITAL ACCUMULATION.**  Although the partnership form of ownership is superior to the sole proprietorship when it comes to attracting capital, it also presents limitations. The partnership is not as effective at raising funds as the corporate form of ownership, which can acquire capital by selling shares of ownership to outside investors.

*Jason, Ken, and Katie Landau and Andrew Smas0h*

Partners Jason, Ken, and Katie Landau received a U.S. Small Business Administration (SBA) loan guarantee to finance their first restaurant—Andrew Smash. Their fresh-fruit smoothie concept was complemented by a vegetarian menu that appealed to health-oriented people seeking an attractive alternative to fast food. As their dream became a reality, they required additional capital to implement their growth strategy, but their bank informed them that they did not qualify for a loan. The bank perceived the owners as a risky investment because they did not have the necessary collateral to support additional debt, forcing the owners to turn to the SBA for the financing help they needed.[9]

**DIFFICULTY IN DISPOSING OF PARTNERSHIP INTEREST WITHOUT DISSOLVING THE PARTNERSHIP.**  Most partnership agreements restrict how partners can dispose of their shares of the business. Often, a partner is required to sell his or her interest to the remaining partners. Even if the original agreement contains such a requirement and clearly delineates how the value of each partner's ownership will be determined, there is no guarantee that other partners will have the financial resources to buy the seller's interest. When the money is not available to purchase a partner's interest, the other partners may be forced to either accept a new partner or to dissolve the partnership and distribute the remaining assets. When a partner withdraws from the partnership, the partnership will cease to exist unless there are specific provisions in the partnership agreement for a transition. If a general partner dies, becomes incompetent, or withdraws from the business, the partnership automatically dissolves, although it may not terminate. (This difference is discussed later in the chapter.) Even when there are numerous partners, if one wishes to disassociate his or her name from the business, the remaining partners will probably form a new partnership.

*Aaron Keller and Brian Aducci and Capsule*

Aaron Keller and his business partner Brian Aducci were working to establish their marketing and design firm, Capsule, with a third partner. However, when the partner left 18 months into the start-up, the pair had to scramble to keep the business intact. "It happened really quickly—basically over a weekend," remembers Keller. "And certain employees and clients were recruited away, so we went into high-action mode. We created a war room and got to work on saving every client and every employee we could." Today, their company is thriving.[10]

Capsule partners Brian Aducci (left) and Aaron Keller.

**LACK OF CONTINUITY.** If one partner dies, significant complications may arise. A partnership interest is often nontransferable through inheritance because remaining partners may not want to be in a partnership with the person who inherits the deceased partner's interest. Partners can make provisions in the partnership agreement to avoid dissolution due to death only if all parties agree to accept as partners those who inherit the deceased's interest.

**POTENTIAL FOR PERSONALITY AND AUTHORITY CONFLICTS.** A partnership is similar to a marriage. The compatibility of partners' work habits, goals, ethics, and general business philosophies are important to a healthy relationship. Friction among partners is inevitable and can be difficult to control. The key is to have a comprehensive partnership agreement and open lines of communication. The demise of many partnerships can be traced to interpersonal conflicts and the lack of a partnership agreement to resolve those conflicts. Knowing potential partners well and having a conflict resolution plan in place can result in better outcomes when dealing with the inevitable conflicts that eventually occur when there is a fundamental difference of opinion on one or more critical business decisions.

**PARTNERS ARE BOUND BY THE LAW OF AGENCY.** Each partner acts as an agent for the business and, in the United States, can legally bind the other partners to a business agreement. This agency power requires all partners to exercise good faith and reasonable care in performing their responsibilities. For example, if a partner signs a three-year lease for a business jet, dramatically increasing the operating costs of the business beyond what the company can afford, the partnership is legally bound to that agreement.

Some partnerships survive a lifetime, but others experience difficulties and ultimately are dissolved. In a general partnership, the continued exposure to personal liability for partners' actions may wear an entrepreneur down. Knowing that they could lose their personal assets because of a partner's bad business decision is a fact of life in partnerships. Conflicts between or among partners can force a business to close. Unfortunately, few partnerships have a mutually agreed upon means for conflict resolution. An arbitration of conflict mechanism is always valuable and may keep the business operating. Without such a mechanism, disagreements can escalate to the point where the partnership is dissolved and the business ceases to operate.

## ■ Until Death Do We Part?

Ariane Daguin was a college student when she met George Faison, a Texan with a temper and a taste for French food. She suggested that George, who had just completed his MBA, partner with her in a unique business venture. Foie gras—fattened goose or duck liver—had never been produced in or imported fresh to the United States due to restrictions on importing raw meat. Ariane had grown up on the delicacy in southwest France, and she and George believed Americans would want the luxury item as well. The two started their own foie gras distributorship out of the state of New Jersey and named it *D'Artagnan*, after Alexandre Dumas's musketeer—all for one and one for all.

On paper, their partnership looked strong. Ariane knew food and could talk in "chefspeak," and George ran the business side. Within two years, the company was profitable on sales of $2 million. Those were golden times with late nights of sharing the same office space, working hard, and driving a clanking delivery truck. They would uncork a bottle of Armagnac over despair or celebration. The partnership was going to last forever.

Then D'Artagnan began to take a toll on its owners. "There was not one day when one of us did not tell the other, 'I'm quitting,' and the other one would say, 'One more day, okay? Just show up tomorrow morning,'" says Ariane. Their relationship changed when Ariane had a baby, which marked the beginning of tumultuous times. Ariane, a single mother, brought her baby to work, but George thought that a baby in a business environment was inappropriate. Ultimately, Ariane agreed to let George take a larger salary for the next six months until she could hire a nanny.

Ariane and George continued to run the company as informally as they had at the outset. Unfortunately, they had not established clear roles, which led to them stepping on each other's toes. They took the advice of consultants and divided the business into two groups: Ariane handled sales and marketing, and George managed finance and operations.

D'Artagnan's attorney suggested the parties sign a buy-sell agreement. Ariane and George agreed that if one partner died, the survivor would purchase his or her shares at a determined price. "Initially," George says,

"the idea was to make sure that if one of us got hit by a truck, we wouldn't have any succession problems." As part of the buy-sell agreement, Ariane and George took out life insurance policies; if one partner died, the insurance payment would fund the survivor's share purchase. They also included a "shotgun clause" in their agreement. If the partnership failed, the shotgun clause provided a fair price for one partner to buy out the other as a way for the business to survive. Ariane and George may not have realized at the time how important this provision would be.

D'Artagnan was on track to produce $20 million in annual revenue and was still growing. Then at Christmas, the highest sales week of the year, some customers reported they had become ill from D'Artagnan products. An investigation by the Centers for Disease Control and Prevention found several D'Artagnan items from a single factory tested positive for Listeria, which causes Listeriosis— a serious infection caused by eating contaminated food. George and Ariane responded immediately. The impact of the contaminated products and the resulting investigation virtually shut down D'Artagnan for five months. For the first time in its history, the company lost money— a lot of money.

Hoping to rebuild the company's reputation, Ariane decided that opening a restaurant in New York City would help. George thought it was an excellent idea. Things did not go as planned, however, and eventually both had to invest more money than they had expected to keep the restaurant afloat. Once again, they began to argue about the venture. George complained that he was forced to make sales calls for D'Artagnan because Ariane was tied up at the restaurant all day.

As the dispute festered, a competitor offered to buy D'Artagnan. The partners asked an investment bank about the offer, and the bank confirmed that the price was too low. The partners rejected the offer, and Ariane assumed the talk of selling was over. "After that, he didn't talk about it anymore. I should have smelled something, but I didn't. I really didn't," she says.

In reality, George was warming to the notion of selling. He thought that D'Artagnan could be more profitable but did not believe that was going to happen with the two founders of the business at odds with each other.

Then, Ariane noticed that George had stopped arguing with her. She wrote it off to his focus on his approaching wedding. Once she dragged him to a long overdue lunch to try to learn what was wrong. "He was totally closed down," she says. It was not long before she found out why.

George walked into Ariane's office and handed her a certified letter. She read it and stared at him, flabbergasted. He was exercising the shotgun clause. By the provisions that they had agreed to, she had two choices: She had 30 days to sell her shares at the price he would offer or buy his shares at the price he offered, with another 30 days to raise the money. There could be no negotiating. "I never saw this coming," she says. "And then it was all kinds of feelings: How dare he? How could he do that?" But George believed Ariane had stopped listening to him and was trying to take D'Artagnan in the wrong direction. He believed that both he and the business had come to a dead end.

Ariane considered her options: buy or sell. She cold-called banks, which wanted a stake in the company, until a friend helped arrange a loan at a French bank. It required higher interest payments and a personal guarantee, but the bank did not want shares of stock in D'Artagnan. Adding her savings to the bank loan, Ariane met George's price. When she presented her counterproposal to the surprised George, she drew herself to her full six-foot height, and added, imperiously, "And by the way, thank you for your wedding invitation. I will come with pleasure."

The deal closed a month later. In a frosty finish to their relationship, George handed Ariane two letters. One said he accepted her purchase price, and the other asked that she not attend his wedding. The two have barely spoken since.

1. What steps might the two partners have taken initially when they established their partnership that could have helped them resolve their conflict?
2. What resources could they have used to assist them as they began experiencing conflict?
3. Could this partnership have been saved? Explain.

*Source:* Adapted from: Stephanie Clifford, "Until Death, or Some Other Sticky Problem, Do Us Part," *Inc. Magazine,* November 2006, www.inc.com/magazine/20061101/partnership.html.

## Dissolution and Termination of a Partnership

Partners expect their business relationships are going to last forever; however, most do not. Teaming up with others may be an easy solution for an entrepreneur who needs financial, operational, and moral support to get a business off the ground, but partnership problems may start when business problems arise. Problems may occur when the entrepreneur realizes he or she is not in charge of his or her own company. Even when partnerships work, there are always fears that the partners will develop different business goals.[11] As a result, partners may dissolve or terminate the partnership.

**Dissolution** occurs when a general partner ceases to be associated with the business. Dissolution of a partnership occurs as a result of one or more of the following events:

- Expiration of a time period or completion of the project undertaken as delineated in the partnership agreement.
- Expressed wish of any general partner to cease operation.
- Expulsion of a partner under the provisions of the agreement.
- Withdrawal, retirement, insanity, or death of a general partner (except when the partnership agreement provides a method of continuation).
- Bankruptcy of the partnership or of any general partner.
- Admission of a new partner resulting in the dissolution of the old partnership and establishment of a new partnership.
- A judicial decree that a general partner is insane or permanently incapacitated, making performance or responsibility under the partnership agreement impossible.
- Mounting losses that make it impractical for the business to continue.
- Impropriety or improper behavior of any general partner that reflects negatively on the business.

**Termination** is the final act of intentionally closing the partnership as a business. Termination occurs after the partners have agreed to cease operations and all affairs of the partnership have been concluded.

*John and Jim Martin
and Martin Bros.*

Brothers John and Jim Martin each own 50 percent of a partnership in a retail clothing shop that they began when they were young. The business proved successful and the brothers eventually opened two other shops. Five of the Martins' children are now involved in the business. Recently, Jim's family vetoed plans to open a fourth store, setting off a dispute that brought to the surface a range of underlying issues involving work practices and compensation, all of which had remained unresolved for years. The brothers attempted to resolve the dispute through direct negotiation over several months but were unsuccessful. Their accountant realized the impact the dispute was having on the business and suggested mediation. Both families agreed, and the mediator facilitated discussions regarding their concerns. For the first time in several years, the families began communicating. The mediation process led to the restoration of the relationship between the families, which had an immediate positive impact on the family business.

Like the Martins, partners must realize that unresolved issues or problems will surface at some stage and that it is better to address a problem when it occurs rather than ignore it. Unlike fine wines, most business problems do not get better with age.[12]

### Limited Partnerships

A **limited partnership** is a modification of a general partnership. Limited partnerships are composed of at least one general partner and at least one limited partner. The general partner is treated, under law, in the same manner as in a general partnership. Limited partners are treated as *investors* in the business venture with limited liability and, therefore, can lose only the amount they have invested in the business.

Most U.S. states recognize the ratified Revised Uniform Limited Partnership Act. To form a limited partnership, the partners must file a Certificate of Limited Partnership in the state in which the partnership plans to conduct business. The Certificate of Limited Partnership should include the following information.

- The name of the limited partnership.
- The general character of its business.
- The address of the office of the firm's agent authorized to receive summonses or other legal notices.
- The name and business address of each partner, specifying which ones are general partners and which are limited partners.
- The amount of cash contributions actually made, and agreed to be made in the future, by each partner.
- A description of the value of noncash contributions made or to be made by each partner.
- The times at which additional contributions are to be made by any of the partners.
- Whether and under what conditions a limited partner has the right to grant a limited partner status to an assignee of his or her interest in the partnership.
- If agreed upon, the time or the circumstances when a partner may withdraw from the firm (unlike the withdrawal of a general partner, the withdrawal of a limited partner does not automatically dissolve a limited partnership).
- If agreed upon, the amount of, or the method of determining, the funds to be received by a withdrawing partner.
- Any right of a partner to receive distributions of cash or other property from the firm, and the circumstances for such distributions.
- The time or circumstances when the limited partnership is to be dissolved.
- The rights of the remaining general partners to continue the business after the withdrawal of a general partner.
- Any other matters the partners want to include.

Although limited partners do not have the right to take an active role in managing the business, they can make management suggestions to general partners, inspect the business, and have access to and make copies of business records. A limited partner is, of course, entitled to a share of the business's profits as specified in the Certificate of Limited Partnership.

The primary disadvantage of limited partnerships is the complexity and cost of establishing this business entity.

### Master Limited Partnerships

A relatively new form of business structure is the **master limited partnership (MLP)**. MLPs are similar to regular limited partnerships except their shares are traded on stock exchanges like a corporation. Therefore, MLPs provide many of the advantages of a corporation, including limited liability. The United States originally allowed MLPs to be taxed as partnerships, but in 1987, ruled that MLPs would be taxed as corporations unless they were involved in natural resources or real estate, eliminating their ability to avoid the double taxation disadvantage. Master limited partnership profits are typically divided among the owners—potentially comprised of thousands of partners.

### Limited Liability Partnerships

Many states now recognize **limited liability partnerships (LLPs)**, in which all partners in the business are limited partners, having only limited liability for the debts and obligations of the partnership. Most states restrict LLPs to certain types of professionals such as attorneys, physicians, dentists, accountants, and others. Just as with any limited partnership, the partners must file a Certificate of Limited Partnership in the state in which the partnership plans to conduct business. Like every partnership, an LLP does not pay taxes; its income is passed through to the limited partners, who pay personal taxes on their shares of the company's net income.

## The Corporation

**4.** Describe the advantages and disadvantages of the corporation.

The **corporation** is the most complex of the three traditional forms of business ownership. Corporations make up only 8 percent of all businesses, but they account for 65 percent of all business sales (refer to Figure 3.1). A corporation is a legal entity that is separate from its owners. Operating as an "artificial being," a corporation can sue or be sued in its own name, enter into and enforce contracts, hold title to and transfer property, and be found civilly and criminally liable for violations of the law.[13] The life of the corporation is independent of its owners, a feature that allows shareholders to sell their interests in the business.

Corporations, also known as **C corporations**, are creations of the states, accepting the regulations and restrictions of the state in which they are incorporated and any other state in which they choose to conduct business. A corporation that conducts business in the state in which it is incorporated is a **domestic corporation**. When a corporation conducts business in another state, that state considers it to be a **foreign corporation**. Corporations that are formed in other countries and conduct business in the United States are referred to as **alien corporations**.

Corporations have the power to raise capital by selling shares of ownership to outside investors, but many corporations may have only a handful of shareholders. **Closely held corporations** have shares that are controlled by a relatively small number of people, often family members, relatives, or friends. Their stock is not traded on any stock exchange but instead, is passed from one generation to the next. Most small corporations are closely held. **Publicly held corporations** have a large number of shareholders, and their stock is usually traded on one of the large stock exchanges.

In general, a corporation must report annually its financial operations to its home state's secretary of state. These financial reports become public record. If a corporation's stock is sold in more than one state, the corporation must comply with federal regulations governing the sale of corporate securities. There are substantially more reporting requirements for a corporation than for the other forms of ownership.

### Requirements for Incorporation

Most U.S. states allow entrepreneurs to incorporate without the assistance of an attorney. Some states even provide incorporation kits to help in the incorporation process. Although it is less expensive for entrepreneurs to complete the process themselves, it may not be ideal as some provisions of incorporation may be overlooked. The application process in some states is complex, and the required forms are confusing. In these situations, entrepreneurs who choose this form of ownership usually benefit from hiring an attorney to guide them through the incorporation process.

Once the owners decide to form a corporation, they must choose the state in which to incorporate. If the business will operate in a single state, it usually makes sense to incorporate in that state. States differ—sometimes dramatically—in the requirements they place on the corporations they charter and in how they treat corporations chartered in other states. States also differ in the tax rate imposed on corporations, the restrictions placed on their activities, the capital required to incorporate, and the fees or organization tax charged to incorporate.

Every state requires a Certificate of Incorporation or charter to be filed with the secretary of state. The following information is generally required to be in the Certificate of Incorporation:

- *The corporation's name.* The corporation must choose a name that is not so similar to that of another firm in that state that it causes confusion or lends itself to deception. It must also include a term such as *corporation, incorporated, company,* or *limited* to notify the public that they are dealing with a corporation.
- *The corporation's statement of purpose.* The incorporators must state in general terms the intended nature of the business. The purpose must, of course, be lawful. For example, the owners of a retail furniture store may state the purpose of their corporation as follows: "to engage in the sale of office furniture and fixtures." The purpose should be broad enough to allow for some expansion in the activities of the business as it develops.
- *The company's time horizon.* Most corporations are formed with no specific termination date and continue "in perpetuity." However, it is possible to incorporate for a specific duration of time, for example, a period of 50 years.
- *Names and addresses of the incorporators.* The incorporators must be identified in the articles of incorporation and are liable under the law to attest that all information in the document is correct. In some states, one or more of the incorporators must reside in the state where the corporation is being created.
- *Place of business.* The post office address of the corporation's principal office must be listed.
- *Capital stock authorization.* The articles of incorporation must include the amount and class (or type) of capital stock the corporation wants to be authorized to issue. This is not the number of shares it *must* issue; a corporation can issue any number of shares up to the amount authorized. This section also must define the different classification of stock and any special rights, preferences, or limits each class has.
- *Capital required at the time of incorporation.* Some states require a newly formed corporation to deposit in a bank a specific percentage of the stock's par value before incorporating.
- *Provisions for preemptive rights, if any, that are granted to stockholders.* If arranged, **preemptive rights** state that stockholders have the right to purchase new shares of stock before they are offered to the public.
- *Restrictions on transferring shares.* Many closely held corporations—those owned by a few shareholders, often family members—require shareholders interested in selling their stocks to offer it first to the corporation. Shares the corporation itself owns are called **treasury stock**. To maintain control over their ownership, many closely held corporations exercise this right, known as **the right of first refusal**.
- *Names and addresses of the officers and directors of the corporation.*
- *Rules under which the corporation will operate.* **Bylaws** are the rules and regulations the officers and directors establish for the corporation's internal management and operation.

Once the secretary of state's office approves a request for incorporation and the corporation pays its fees, the articles of incorporation become its **corporate charter**. With the corporate charter as proof that the corporation legally exists, the next order of business is to hold an organizational meeting for the stockholders to formally elect directors, who, in turn, will appoint the corporate officers.

Corporations account for the majority of sales and profits among the various forms of ownership, but like the preceding forms of ownership, they have advantages and disadvantages.

## Advantages of the Corporation

**LIMITED LIABILITY OF STOCKHOLDERS.** The primary reason most entrepreneurs choose to incorporate is to gain the benefit of limited liability that allows investors to limit their liability to the total amount of their investment. This legal protection of personal assets beyond the business is of critical concern to many investors. The shield of limited liability may not be impenetrable, however. Because start-up companies generally present higher levels of risk, lenders and other creditors require the owners to *personally* guarantee loans made to the corporation. RMA, a national organization of bank loan officers, estimates that 95 percent of small business owners have to sign personal guarantees to get the financing they need. By making these guarantees, owners place their personal assets at risk (just as in a proprietorship) despite choosing the corporate form of ownership.

Court decisions have extended the personal liability of small corporation owners beyond the financial guarantees that banks and other lenders require, "piercing the corporate veil" more than ever before. Courts are increasingly holding corporate owners personally liable for environmental, pension, and legal claims against their corporations. Courts can hold owners liable for the company's debts and obligations if the owners deliberately commit criminal or negligent acts when handling corporate business. Corporate shareholders most commonly lose their liability protection, however, because owners and officers have commingled corporate funds with their own personal funds. Failing to keep corporate and personal funds separate is often a problem, particularly in closely held corporations.

Steps to avoid legal difficulties include the following:

- *File all of the reports and pay all of the necessary fees required by the state in a timely manner.* Most U.S. states require corporations to file reports with the secretary of state on an annual basis. Failing to do so jeopardizes the validity of a corporation and opens the door for personal liability problems for its shareholders.
- *Hold annual meetings to elect officers and directors.* In a closely held corporation, the officers elected may *be* the shareholders, but that does not matter. Corporations formed by an individual are not required to hold meetings, but the sole shareholder must file a written consent form.
- *Keep minutes of every meeting of the officers and directors, even if it takes place in the living room of the founders.* It is a good idea to elect a secretary who is responsible for recording the minutes.
- *Make sure that the corporation's board of directors makes all major decisions.* Problems arise in closely held corporations when one owner makes key decisions alone without consulting the elected board.
- *Make it clear that the business is a corporation by having all officers sign contracts, loan agreements, purchase orders, and other legal documents in the corporation's name rather than their own names.* Failing to designate their status as agents of the corporation can result in the officers being held personally liable for agreements they think they are signing on the corporation's behalf.
- *Keep corporate assets and the personal assets of the owners separate.* Few things make courts more willing to hold shareholders personally liable for a corporation's debts than commingling corporate and personal assets. In some closely held corporations, owners have been known to use corporate assets to pay their personal expenses (or vice versa) or to mix their personal funds with corporate funds in a single bank account. Protecting the corporation's identity by keeping it completely separate from the owners' personal identities is critical.

# ENTREPRENEURSHIP

## *In Action*

## Google: From Idea to Publicly Held Corporation

They named their new search engine Google after the biggest number they could imagine, but it may not have been big enough. Google is a library, an almanac, a settler of bets, a parlor game, a dating service, a shopping mall, and a Microsoft rival. It is also a verb. Google is a success story and has emerged as the leading Internet search engine—and a profitable stock investment.

As doctoral students at Stanford University, Google's founders Sergey Brin and Larry Page wrote a paper titled, "The Anatomy of a Large-Scale Hypertextual Web Search Engine." This document proved to be the foundation on which the Google search engine was constructed. In less than five years, Google evolved from a start-up corporation to the leading search engine in the market.

Google's search engine is attractive to those who admire the technology that drives it and to those who simply appreciate what it can do. "Google knows how to make geeks feel good about being geeks . . . but they didn't forget to make everyone else feel special too," says journalist Cory Doctorow. "They still do, by focusing relentlessly on the quality of the experience. Make it easy, make it fast. Make it work, and attack everything that gets in the way of perfection."

Growth in the quality of its product is linked to the people whom Google hires, a combination of PhDs with deep expertise in search-engine design and development and young, smart risk-takers who do not fear failure. Product performance is what counts. Google's founders understand that superior product performance attracts users, and users attract the money. Brin and Page are confident that their very unorthodox organization, which seems out of control to some observers, will continue to generate a significant revenue stream.

When Google went public in 2004, its executives were adamant about conducting an unusual initial public offering (IPO) auction that was intended to make the company's shares accessible to individual investors. In its IPO filing, Google said that it would sell 150 million shares of stock, a deal that would generate $2.7 billion in capital for the company and establish its market value in the $20 billion to $25 billion range. An unusual aspect of this offering was that there were two classes of stock, one with supervoting rights worth 10 times more than the voting rights of regular shareholders, a feature that was designed to keep power in the founders' hands. Brin and Page wanted as much control of their company as possible.

Google now boasts a market cap that exceeds $130 billion. Despite the company's success, some challenging questions remain. Is Google a company that can survive and remain focused and productive? Can Google make the transition from start-up to public company without losing its soul? Can the employees keep their perspective and still put the success of Google first until the next generation of employees arrives? Only time will tell. Just keep googling to find out.

1. What were some of the key characteristics that made Google an attractive business for an IPO?

2. Why do you think that Google's IPO was so successful? Could another company repeat the success of Google's IPO?

*Sources:* "How Google Grows . . . and Grows . . . and Grows," Keith H. Hammonds, *Fast Company,* April 2003, pp. 74–78; "Can Google Grow Up?" Fred Vogelstein, *Fortune,* December 8, 2003, pp. 102–112; "Surviving IPO Fever," Michael S. Malone, *Wired,* March 2004; "Google: Where's the Stock Split?" Elinor Mills, *CNET News,* January 5, 2006.

ENTREPRENEURIAL
**Profile**

*Dennis Kozlowski and
Tyco International Ltd.*

The former CEO of Tyco International Ltd., Dennis Kozlowski, and former Tyco finance chief Mark Swartz, were sentenced to 25 years in prison in a case that exposed the executives' extravagant personal lifestyles using company funds. For example, the corporation paid for a $2 million toga birthday party for Kozlowski's wife on a Mediterranean island and an $18 million Manhattan apartment with a $6,000 shower curtain. Kozlowski and Swartz were also accused of giving themselves more than $150 million in illegal bonuses, forgiving loans to themselves, and manipulating the company's stock price. After a four-month trial, the jury deliberated for 11 days before returning 22 guilty verdicts on counts of grand larceny, falsifying business records, securities fraud, and conspiracy.[14]

**ABILITY TO ATTRACT CAPITAL.** Corporations have proved to be the most effective form of ownership for accumulating large amounts of capital largely due to the protection of limited liability. Restricted only by the number of shares authorized in its charter (which can be amended), a corporation can raise money to begin business and expand as opportunity dictates by selling shares of its stock to investors. A corporation can sell its stock to a limited number of private investors, called a **private placement**, or to the public, referred to as a **public offering**.

**ABILITY TO CONTINUE INDEFINITELY.** As a separate legal entity, a corporation can continue indefinitely unless limited by its charter. Unlike a proprietorship or a partnership in which the death of a founder ends the business, the corporation lives beyond the lives of those who created it. This perpetual life gives rise to the next major advantage of the corporation, transferable ownership.

**TRANSFERABLE OWNERSHIP.** If stockholders in a corporation are displeased with the business's progress, they can sell their shares to someone else. Millions of shares of stock representing ownership in companies are traded daily on the world's stock exchanges. Shareholders can also transfer their stock through inheritance to a new generation of owners. Throughout these transfers of ownership, the corporation seamlessly continues to conduct business as usual. The resale of stock of closely held corporations—owned for example by company founders, family members, or employees—is limited and the transfer of ownership may be difficult.

## Disadvantages of the Corporation

**COST AND TIME INVOLVED IN THE INCORPORATION PROCESS.** Corporations can be costly and time-consuming to establish. As the owners "give birth" to this artificial legal entity, the gestation period can be prolonged. In most states, entrepreneurs can complete all of the required forms alone, but in others, an attorney must be involved in the incorporation process. Regardless, an owner must exercise great caution when incorporating without the help of an attorney. In addition to potential legal expenses, incorporating a business requires fees that are not applicable to proprietorships or partnerships. Creating a corporation can cost between $500 and $3,000, with an average cost of $1,500.

**"Thank you gentlemen for voting me as chairman."**

**DOUBLE TAXATION.** As a separate legal entity, a U.S. corporation must pay taxes on its net income to the federal, most state, and some local governments. Before stockholders receive any net income as dividends, a corporation must pay these taxes at the corporate tax rate. Then, stockholders must pay taxes on the dividends they receive from these same profits at the individual tax rate. Thus, a corporation's profits are taxed twice—once at the corporate level and again at the individual level. This **double taxation** is a distinct disadvantage of the corporate form of ownership.

**POTENTIAL FOR DIMINISHED MANAGERIAL INCENTIVES.** As a corporation grows, it may require additional managerial expertise beyond that which the founder can provide. The founding entrepreneur created the company and often has most of his or her personal wealth tied up in the business. These entrepreneurs have an intense interest in ensuring their success and are willing to make sacrifices for their businesses. They may bring in professional managers to help run the business as it grows, but those individuals do not always have the same degree of interest or loyalty to the company. As a result, the business may suffer without the founder's energy, care, and devotion. One way to minimize this potential problem is to link managers' and possibly employees' compensation to the company's financial performance through profit sharing or a bonus plan. Corporations can also stimulate managers' and employees' incentive on the job by creating an **employee stock ownership plan (ESOP)**, a plan in which managers and employees become owners in the company.

**LEGAL REQUIREMENTS AND REGULATORY RED TAPE.** Corporations are subject to more legal and financial requirements than other forms of ownership. Entrepreneurs must meet these stringent requirements to accurately record and report business transactions in a timely manner. They must hold annual meetings and consult the board of directors about major decisions that are beyond day-to-day operations. Managers may be required to submit some major decisions to the stockholders for approval. Corporations that are publicly held must also file quarterly and annual reports with the U.S. Securities and Exchange Commission (SEC), and these reports are available to the public, including a company's competitors.

**POTENTIAL LOSS OF CONTROL BY THE FOUNDERS.** When entrepreneurs sell shares of ownership in their companies, they relinquish some degree of control. This is magnified when they need large capital infusions for start-up or growth, when entrepreneurs may have to sell an amount of stock that causes them to become minority shareholders. Losing majority ownership—and therefore control—in their companies leaves founders in a precarious position. They no longer have the power to determine the company's direction; "outsiders" do. The founders' shares may become so diluted that a majority of shareholders can vote them out of their jobs.

**PIERCING THE CORPORATE VEIL.** If there is clear evidence that the corporation is merely set up as a mechanism to enable the owners to avoid paying debt, courts sometimes hold corporate owners personally liable for the debts of the business. This may occur when the owners have put very little money into the corporation or when they ignore the regulations and formalities of running a corporation.[15]

## The Professional Corporation

A **professional corporation** offers professionals—such as lawyers, doctors, dentists, accountants, and others—the advantage of the corporate form of ownership. Corporate ownership is ideally suited for licensed professionals, who must always be concerned about malpractice lawsuits, because it offers limited liability. For example, if three doctors form a professional corporation, although each would continue to be liable for his or her own actions, none of them would be liable for the malpractice of the other. Professional corporations are created in the same way as regular corporations. They often are identified by the abbreviations P.C. (professional corporation), P.A. (professional association), or S.C. (service corporation).

# Alternative Forms of Ownership

*5.* Describe the features of the alternative forms of ownership, such as the S corporation, the limited liability company, the joint venture, and the syndicate.

In addition to the sole proprietorship, the partnership, and the corporation, entrepreneurs can choose other forms of ownership, including the S corporation, the limited liability company, the joint venture, and the syndicate.

## The S Corporation

The U.S. Internal Revenue Service Code created the Subchapter S corporation in 1954. In recent years, the IRS has changed the title to S corporation and has made modifications in its qualifications. An **S corporation** is a distinction that is made only for federal income tax purposes and is, in terms of legal characteristics, no different from any other corporation. In 1996, the United States passed legislation to simplify or eliminate some of the restrictive rules and requirements for S corporations so that businesses seeking "S" status must meet the following criteria:

1. It must be a domestic (U.S.) corporation.
2. It cannot have a nonresident alien as a shareholder.
3. It can issue only one class of common stock, which means that all shares must carry the same rights (e.g., the right to dividends or liquidation rights). The exception is voting rights, which may differ. In other words, an S corporation can issue voting and nonvoting common stock.
4. It cannot have more than 100 shareholders (increased from 75).
5. No more than 20 percent of the corporation's income can be from passive investment income.
6. Corporations and partnerships cannot be shareholders.

Because the maximum number of shareholders allowed in S corporations is 100, succession planning is somewhat easier for business owners. Aging founders now can pass their stock on to their children and grandchildren without worrying about exceeding the maximum allowable number of owners. The larger number of shareholders also grants S corporations a greater ability to raise capital by attracting more investors. Updated laws allow S corporations to raise money more readily by permitting them to sell shares of their stock to certain tax-exempt organizations such as pension funds. (Previous rules limited ownership strictly to individuals, estates, and certain trusts.)

S corporations also can own subsidiary companies. Previously, the owners of S corporations had to establish separate businesses if they wanted to launch new ventures, even those closely related to the S corporation. This change is especially beneficial to entrepreneurs with several businesses in related fields. They can establish an S corporation as the "parent" company and then set up multiple subsidiaries as either C or S corporations as "offspring" under it. As separate corporations, the liabilities of one business cannot spill over and destroy the assets of another.

Violating any of the requirements for an S corporation automatically terminates a company's S status. If a corporation satisfies the definition for an S corporation, the owners must actually elect to be treated as one. The election is made by filing IRS Form 2553 (within the first 75 days of the tax year), and all shareholders must consent to have the corporation treated as an S corporation.

**ADVANTAGES OF AN S CORPORATION.**  S corporations retain all of the advantages of a regular corporation, including continuity of existence, transferability of ownership, and limited personal liability for its owners. The most notable provision of the S corporation is that it passes all of its profits or losses through to the *individual* shareholders and its income is taxed only *once* at the individual tax rate. Thus, electing S corporation status avoids the disadvantage of double taxation. In essence, the tax treatment of an S corporation is exactly like that of a partnership; its owners report their proportional shares of the company's profits on their individual income tax returns and pay taxes on those profits at the individual rate, even if they never take the money out of the business.

Another advantage of the S corporation is that it avoids the tax C corporations pay on the assets that have appreciated in value and are sold. Owners of S corporations also enjoy

**FIGURE 3.2 Tax Rate Comparison: C Corporation and S Corporation**

*Source:* Adapted from Jonathan Chapman, "Adopting the Business Structure—An Exercise with Care," *Construction Accounting & Taxation,* September/October 2003, p. 5.

---

### Tax Rate Comparison: C Corporation and S Corporation

S corporations do not pay taxes on income. Instead, the income, losses, deductions, and credits pass through to the owners. Therefore, the tax obligations for an owner of an S corporation may be considerably lower than that of a C corporation. Tax legislation has reduced the capital gains tax to 15 percent, reduced the top rate to 35 percent, and tax rates on dividends has been reduced to 15 percent—all lower than the corporate rate.

The following example illustrates the effect of these rate changes. This example assumes the S corporate shareholder is taxed at ordinary income rates and that the shareholder is married and filed jointly.

#### Capital Gains and Dividend Rates

|  | C Corp. | S Corp. |
|---|---|---|
| Corporate Income | $500,000 | $500,000 |
| Corporate Tax | 34% | 0% |
|  | (170,000) | - 0 - |
| After-tax Income | 330,000 | 500,000 |
| Shareholder Tax | 15.00% | 30.04% |
|  | (49,500) | (150,200) |
| **Net After-tax Income** | **$280,500** | **$349,800** |
| *S Corporate Savings* | | *$69,300* |

---

the ability to make year-end payouts to themselves if profits are high. In a C corporation, owners have no such luxury because the IRS watches for excessive compensation to owners and managers. The IRS, however, has concerns about the tax treatment of S corporations. Instead of classifying their income as salary, which is subject to Social Security and Medicare taxes, some S corporation owners distribute profits from their businesses as dividends. The IRS says that its most recent data indicate that this strategy by owners of S corporations costs the Treasury billions of dollars in lost revenue annually. As a result, the IRS randomly audits the returns of S corporations for this purpose.[16] Figure 3.2 shows the impact that the tax treatment of C corporations and S corporations has on a company's tax bill.

**DISADVANTAGES OF AN S CORPORATION.** Tax rates are established by laws passed by legislators and signed by the president or state governors. An S corporation would lose its attractiveness if either or both of the following occurred:

1. Personal income tax rates rose above those of C corporation rates, or
2. C corporation rates were lowered below personal income tax rates.

Currently neither of these conditions exists, but it is difficult to predict the future actions of the U.S. federal or state governments.

In addition to the tax implications of making the switch from an S corporation, owners should consider the following:

- The size of the company's net profits.
- The tax rates of its shareholders.
- Their strategic plans and their timing to sell the company or transition ownership.
- The impact of the C corporation's double taxation penalty on income distributed as dividends.

**WHEN IS AN S CORPORATION A WISE CHOICE?** Choosing S corporation status is usually beneficial to start-up companies anticipating net losses and highly profitable firms with substantial dividends to pay out to shareholders. In these cases, the owner can use the loss to offset other income or is in a lower tax bracket than the corporation, thus saving money in the long run. Companies that plan to reinvest most of their earnings to finance growth also find S corporation status favorable. Small business owners who intend to sell their companies in the near future will prefer S over C status because the taxable gains on the sale of an S corporation are generally lower than those on the sale of a C corporation.

Small companies with the following characteristics are *not* likely to benefit from S corporation status:

■ Highly profitable personal-service companies with large numbers of shareholders, in which most of the profits are passed on to shareholders as compensation or retirement benefits.

■ Fast-growing companies that must retain most of their earnings to finance growth and capital spending.

■ Corporations in which the loss of fringe benefits to shareholders exceeds tax savings.

■ Corporations in which the income before any compensation to shareholders is less than $100,000 a year.

■ Corporations with sizeable net operating losses that cannot be used against S corporation earnings.

## The Limited Liability Company

The **limited liability company (LLC)** possesses hybrid characteristics of a partnership and a corporation, similar to an S corporation, and is the fastest growing form of business ownership.[17] An LLC combines many of the benefits of the partnership and the corporate forms of ownership but is not subject to many of the restrictions imposed on an S corporation. For example, shareholder restrictions on S corporations do not apply to an LLC. Although an LLC can have one owner, most have multiple owners (called members). An LLC offers its owners limited liability without imposing any requirements on their characteristics or any ceiling on their numbers. An LLC does not restrict its members' ability to become involved in managing the company, unlike a limited partnership, which prohibits limited partners from participating in day-to-day management of the business.

An LLC offers it members the advantage of limited liability and avoids the double taxation imposed on a C corporation. Like an S corporation, an LLC does not pay income taxes; its income flows through to the members, who are responsible for paying income taxes on their shares of the LLC's net income. An LLC permits its members to divide income, and thus tax liability, as they see fit, just as in a partnership. An LLC is not subject to the many restrictions imposed on other forms of ownership and offers entrepreneurs another significant advantage: flexibility. This more flexible structure is not subject to the formalities of the S corporation. For these reasons, closely held companies are showing a preference for the LLC. According to the International Association of Commercial Administrators, LLC filings have increased in most states while corporate filings have declined.[18]

These advantages make the LLC an ideal form of ownership for companies in many diverse industries. Moviegoers might recognize the famous American production company, DreamWorks SKG. The SKG represents movie moguls Steven Spielberg, Jeffery Katzenberg, and David Geffen, who formed DreamWorks SKG as an LLC.

Creating an LLC is much like creating a corporation. Forming an LLC requires an entrepreneur to create two documents: the articles of organization and the operating agreement. The LLC's **articles of organization**, similar to the corporation's articles of incorporation, establish the company's name, its method of management (board-managed or member-managed), its duration, and the names and addresses of each organizer. In most states, the company's name must contain the words *limited liability company*, *limited company*, or the letters LLC or LC. An LLC can have a defined term of duration, or it can elect to be an "at-will" LLC that has no specific term of duration. However, the same factors that would cause a partnership to dissolve would also cause a term LLC to dissolve before its charter expired.

The LLC **operating agreement** is similar to a corporation's bylaws and outlines the provisions governing the way the LLC will conduct business. To ensure that an LLC is classified as a partnership for tax purposes, an entrepreneur must carefully draft the operating agreement. The operating agreement must create an LLC that has more characteristics of a partnership than of a corporation to maintain this favorable tax treatment. Specifically, an LLC cannot have any more than two of the following four corporate characteristics:

1. *Limited liability.* Limited liability exists if no member of the LLC is personally liable for the debts or claims against the company. Because entrepreneurs choosing this form of ownership usually get limited liability protection, the operating agreement almost always contains this characteristic.
2. *Continuity of life.* Continuity of life exists if the company continues to exist despite changes in stock ownership. To avoid continuity of life, any LLC member must have the power to dissolve the company. Most entrepreneurs choose to omit this characteristic from their LLC's operating agreements. Thus, if one member of an LLC resigns, dies, or declares bankruptcy, the LLC automatically dissolves and all remaining members must vote to keep the company going.
3. *Free transferability of interest.* Free transferability of interest exists if each LLC member has the power to transfer his or her ownership to another person without the consent from other members. To avoid this characteristic, the operating agreement must state the recipient of a member's LLC stock cannot become a substitute member without the consent of the remaining members.
4. *Centralized management.* Centralized management exists if a group that does not include all LLC members has the authority to make management decisions and to conduct company business. To avoid this characteristic, the operating agreement must state that the company elects to be "member-managed."

Despite their universal appeal to entrepreneurs, LLCs present some disadvantages. For example, they can be expensive to create. Although LLCs may be ideally suited for an entrepreneur launching a new company, it may pose problems for business owners who are considering converting an existing business to an LLC. Switching to an LLC from a general partnership, a limited partnership, or a sole proprietorship that is reorganizing to bring in new owners is usually not a problem. However, owners of corporations and S corporations would incur large tax obligations if they converted their companies to LLCs.

## Joint Ventures and Syndicates

The **joint venture** is very much like a partnership, except that it is formed for a specific, limited purpose. For instance, suppose that you have a 500-acre tract of land 60 miles from Chicago. This land has been cleared and is normally used for farming. One of your friends has solid contacts among major musical groups and would like to put on a concert. You expect prices for your agricultural products to be low this summer, so you and your friend form a joint venture for the specific purpose of staging a three-day concert. Your contribution will be the exclusive use of the land for one month, and your friend will provide all the performers, as well as the technicians, facilities, and equipment. All costs will be paid out of receipts, the net profits will be split, and you will receive 20 percent for the use of your land. When the concert is over, the facilities removed, and the accounting for all costs completed, you and your friend will split the profits 20–80, and the joint venture will terminate. The "partners" form a new joint venture for each new project they undertake. The income derived from a joint venture is taxed as if it had been generated from a partnership.

In any endeavor in which neither party can effectively achieve the purpose alone, a joint venture becomes the common form of ownership. That is why joint ventures have become increasingly popular in global business dealings. For instance, a small business in the United States may manufacture a product that is in demand in Brazil, but the U.S. firm has no knowledge of how to successfully conduct business in Brazil. Forming a joint venture with a Brazilian firm that knows the customs and laws of the country, has an established distribution network, and can promote the product effectively could result in a mutually beneficial joint venture.

## ■ The LLCs of the Travel Advantage Network Inc.

When Brad Callahan earned his undergraduate degree in psychology, he found himself in a similar situation to many graduating seniors: He was broke and working at a job that had little to do with his major. "I never planned on going into real estate," Callahan said. "Because of my degree, I thought I'd end up working with troubled kids." This newly minted graduate did not yet realize that the part-time college sales job—working for a vacation condominium-rental company—would dramatically alter his career plans.

Callahan quickly climbed the ranks at the real estate company and, within three years, was promoted to general manager. Soon, he came up with a business idea of his own, and the budding entrepreneur decided to set out on his own.

Callahan is now the sole owner of Travel Advantage Network Inc. (TAN), a business founded on a new approach to travel: a wholesale-priced condominium vacation program. The concept of prepaid vacation blocks has remained TAN's focus since its inception, but the company has evolved and now emphasizes providing quality accommodations at affordable rates. Today, the company provides prepaid, wholesale condominium vacations in Mexico, more than 20 U.S. states, and the Caribbean. TAN manages more than 500 properties and currently maintains a client base of nearly 50,000 families and individuals.

Due to his initial "shoe-string" budget, Callahan could not afford to purchase resort properties. He started by contacting owners and offering to manage their rental properties. This practice worked for a while, but Callahan quickly realized the path to larger profits lay with *owning* the rental properties. He began purchasing condominium units in prime vacation locations, primarily by using seller-based financing. In the beginning, all of the properties were in Callahan's name, but his accountant and attorney advised him to form LLCs to purchase each individual property. This would protect his personal assets and provide separate liability protection for each individual property.

TAN now not only creates an LLC for each property but also has an LLC to house its affiliated ventures. "By assigning separate LLCs, each business function can operate autonomously; managing taxes and filings, and assigning separate LLCs creates less of a burden to the overall finances of TAN," Callahan said.

1. Why did Callahan's accountant and attorney advise him not to hold the properties in his own name?
2. Discuss the advantages of multiple LLCs for Callahan, versus holding the business properties in his own name or under a single corporation.

*Source:* Adapted from Christine M. Matarese, "The Company Corporation," www.corporate.com/successStoryTravel.jsp.

A **syndicate**, much like a joint venture, is a private investment group that is formed for the purpose of financing a large commercial project whose scope is larger than the capacity of a single investor to finance alone. The members of the investment syndicate can come together quickly to seize an opportunity. One potential disadvantage is that if the project fails, the members of the syndicate may be held liable for a breach of agreement by a third party.

## Summary of Selecting the Form of Ownership

Selecting the optimal form of ownership involves these steps:

- Assess the nature, goals, and anticipated future of the business.
- Determine the resources, capabilities, and risk level of the owner.
- Review your current and expected tax situation.

- Understand the laws of your state and other jurisdictional regulations relating to forms of business ownership.
- Involve professional advisors, such as an attorney and accountant, to advise and assist with the decision process and take the appropriate action.

Table 3.1 summarizes the key features of the sole poprietorship, the partnership, the C corporation, the S corporation, and the limited liability company.

## TABLE 3.1 Characteristics of the Major Forms of Ownership

| Features | Sole Proprietorship | Partnership | C Corporation | S Corporation | Limited Liability Company |
|---|---|---|---|---|---|
| Owner's personal liability | Unlimited | Unlimited for general partners; limited for limited partners | Limited | Limited | Limited |
| Numbers of owners | 1 | 2 or more (at least 1 general partner required) | Any number | Maximum of 100 (with restrictions on who they are) | Any number (except in a few states which require 2 or more) |
| U.S. tax liability | Single tax: proprietor pays at individual rate | Single tax: partners pay on their proportional shares at individual rate | Double tax: corporation pays tax and shareholders pay tax on dividends distributed | Single tax: owners pay on their proportional shares at individual rate | Single tax: members pay on their pro-portional shares at individual rate |
| Maximum tax rate | 35% | 35% | 39% corporate plus 35% individual (on dividends) | 35% | 35% |
| Transferability of ownership | Fully transferable through sale or transfer of company assests | May require consent of all partners | Fully transferable | Transferable (but transfer may affect S status) | Usually requires consent of all members |
| Continuity of business | Ends on death or insanity of proprietor or upon termination by proprietor | Dissolves upon death, insanity, or retirement of a general partner (business may continue) | Perpetual life | Perpetual life | Perpetual life |
| Cost of formation | Low | Moderate | High | High | High |
| Liquidity of owner's investment in business | Poor to average | Poor to average | High | High | High |
| Complexity of formation | Extremely low | Moderate | High | High | High |
| Ability to raise capital | Low | Moderate | Very high | Moderate to high | High |
| Formation procedure | No special steps required other than buying necessary licenses | No written partnership agreements required (but highly advisable) | Must meet formal requirements specified by state law | Must follow same procedures as C corporation, then elect S status with IRS | Must meet formal requirements specified by state law |

# Chapter Review

**1.** Discuss the key issues to evaluate the different forms of ownership.
   - The key to choosing the "right" form of ownership is to understand the characteristics of each form and knowing how they affect an entrepreneur's personal and business circumstances.
   - Factors to consider include tax implications, liability expense, start-up and future capital requirements, control, managerial ability, business goals, management succession plans, and cost of formation.

**2.** Describe the advantages and disadvantages of the sole proprietorship.
   - A sole proprietorship is a business owned and managed by one individual and is the most popular form of ownership.
   - Sole proprietorships offer these advantages:
     - Simple to create
     - Least costly to begin
     - Owner has total decision-making authority
     - No special reporting requirement or legal restriction
     - Easy to discontinue
   - Sole proprietorships suffer from these disadvantages:
     - Unlimited personal liability of owner
     - Limited managerial skills and capabilities
     - Limited access to capital
     - Lack of continuity

**3.** Describe the advantages and disadvantages of the partnership.
   - A partnership is an association of two or more people who co-own a business for the purpose of making a profit.
   - Partnerships offer these advantages:
     - Easy to establish
     - Complementary skills of partners
     - Division of profits
     - Large pool of capital available
     - Ability to attract limited partners
     - Little government regulation
     - Flexibility
     - Tax advantages
   - Partnerships suffer from these disadvantages:
     - Unlimited liability of at least one partner
     - Difficulty in disposing of partnership interest
     - Lack of continuity
     - Potential for personal and authority conflicts
     - Partners are bound by the law of agency

**4.** Describe the advantages and disadvantages of the corporation.
   - A limited partnership operates like any other partnership except that it allows limited partners—primary investors who cannot take an active role in managing the business—to become owners without subjecting themselves to unlimited personal liability of the company's debts.
   - A corporation is a separate legal entity and the most complex of the three basic forms of ownership.
   - To form a corporation an entrepreneur must file the articles of incorporation with the state in which the company will incorporate.
   - Corporations offer these advantages:
     - Limited liability of stockholders
     - Ability to attract capital
     - Ability to continue indefinitely
     - Transferable ownership

- Corporations suffer from these disadvantages:
  - Cost and time of incorporating
  - Double taxation
  - Potential for diminished managerial incentives
  - Legal requirement and regulatory red tape
  - Potential loss of control by the founders
5. Describe the features of the alternative forms of ownership, such as the S corporation, the limited liability company, the joint venture, and the syndicate.
  - An S corporation offers its owners limited liability protection but avoids the double taxation of C corporations.
  - A limited liability company (LLC), like an S corporation, is a cross between a partnership and a corporation and offers many of the advantages of each. However, it operates without the restrictions imposed on an S corporation. To create an LLC, an entrepreneur must file the articles of organization and the operating agreement with the secretary of state.
  - A joint venture is like a partnership, except that it is formed for a specific purpose.
  - A syndicate, much like a joint venture, is a private investment group formed for the purpose of a large commercial project whose scope is larger than the capacity of a single investor to finance alone.

## Discussion Questions

1. What factors should an entrepreneur consider before choosing a form of ownership?
2. Why is the sole proprietorship the most popular form of ownership?
3. How does personal conflict affect partnerships? What steps might partners take to minimize personal conflict?
4. Why are the articles of partnership important to a successful partnership? What issues should the articles of partnership address?
5. Can one partner commit another to a business deal without the other's consent? Why, and what are the potential ramifications?
6. Explain the differences between a domestic corporation, a foreign corporation, and an alien corporation.
7. What issues should the Certificate of Incorporation cover?
8. How does an S corporation differ from a regular corporation?
9. What role do limited partners play in a partnership? What will happen if a limited partner takes an active role in managing the business?
10. What advantages does an LLC offer over an S corporation? Over a sole proprietorship?
11. How is an LLC created? How does this differ from creating an S corporation?
12. What criteria must an LLC meet to avoid double taxation?
13. How does a joint venture differ from a partnership?
14. In what circumstances might a joint venture or syndicate be applicable?

## Business PlanPro

Selecting the form of your business is an important decision. As the chapter describes, this decision will affect the number of business owners, tax obligations, the time and cost to form the entity, the ability to raise capital, and options to transfer ownership.

### On the Web

Review the business entity links associated with Chapter 3 at the Companion Website at www.prenhall.com/scarborough. This may provide additional information and resources to assist with your form of business. Enter the search term "business entity" in your favorite search engine and note the resources and information that this term generates.

Go to the Sample Plan Browser in Business Plan Pro and look at these three business plans: Calico Computer Consulting, a sole proprietorship; Lansing Aviation, a limited liability company; and Southeast Health Plans Inc., a corporation. After reviewing the executive summaries of each of these plans, why do you think the owners selected this form of ownership? Consider their respective industries: What are the advantages and disadvantages that each of these business entities offer the owners? Why are these choices a good match for the business entities relating to ease of starting, liability, control, ability to raise capital, and transfer of ownership?

## In the Software

Go to the section of Business Plan Pro called "Company Ownership." As you look at the comparison matrix of "Characteristics of the Major Forms of Ownership," Table 3.1 on page 116, consider the ramifications of your choice.

- If the business is a sole proprietorship or a partnership and the business is sued, you may be personally liable. Is the nature of your business one that may present this type of risk? Is this an appropriate business entity based on that potential outcome?
- Once your business becomes profitable, what are the potential tax ramifications compared to your current situation?
- If your goal is to retain control of the company over the long term, will the form of ownership you have chosen enable you to do so?

- How much should you budget for legal fees and other expenditures to form the business?
- How much time do you estimate you will need to invest to establish this business entity?
- Will you need to raise capital? How much capital will the venture require? Is this form of ownership optimal for accomplishing that objective?

As you review the instructions provided within Business Plan Pro, refer to the "Characteristics of the Major Forms of Ownership" in Table 3.1 to help you select the form of ownership that is best for you and your venture.

## Building Your Business Plan

Review the work that you have completed on your business plan to date. Does the form of ownership you have chosen "fit" your vision and the scope of the business? Will this choice of business entity offer the type of protection flexibility you desire for your business? You may also want to include comments in your plan regarding changing factors that may require you to reexamine your form of ownership in the future.

**4**

Experience is the name
every one gives to their
mistakes.
—Oscar Wilde

The big print giveth, the
fine print taketh away.
—Bishop Fulton J. Sheen

# Franchising and the Entrepreneur

*Learning Objectives*

**Upon completion of this chapter, you will be able to:**

1 Explain the importance of franchising in the U.S. and global economy.

2 Define the concept of franchising.

3 Describe the different types of franchises.

4 Describe the benefits and limitations of buying a franchise.

5 Describe the legal aspects of franchising, including the protection offered by the U.S. FTC's Trade Regulation Rule.

6 Explain the right way to buy a franchise.

7 Describe a typical franchise contract and its primary provisions.

8 Explain current trends shaping franchising.

9 Describe the potential of franchising a business as a growth strategy.

*1.* Explain the role of franchising in the U.S. and global economy.

ranchising is an important part of American business, and this powerful distribution and marketing system is also influencing the global economy. Franchises now dominate industries such as guest lodging, real estate brokerage, quick-serve restaurants, and convenience stores. The diversity of franchises allows consumers to purchase a wide range of goods and services, from waste-eating microbes and health care to hardware and supplemental education. Franchising accounts for more than $1 trillion in annual U.S. retail sales—an astonishing 50 percent of all retail sales nationwide.

The growth of franchising is also impacting the global economy. The International Franchise Association reports that over the past decade, almost half of all business units established by U.S. franchisors were outside the country.[1] The top 500 franchise companies alone have more than 358,000 business units that generate $400 billion in sales worldwide.[2] One study reports that 52 percent of U.S.-based franchise companies support international operations and that an average of 30 percent of their total franchise units are located in foreign countries. The hottest areas for international expansion among franchisors are Europe and the Pacific Rim countries, and many have high expectations for China in the future. Nearly 80 percent of franchisors plan to open new units outside the United States within the next three years.[3]

## What Is a Franchise?

*2.* Define the concept of franchising.

A **franchise** is a legal and business relationship between the owner of a trademark, service mark, trade name, or advertising symbol, and an entrepreneur who pays for the right to use that identification for his or her business. The franchise system provides business expertise and resources that otherwise would not be available to the entrepreneur. The franchise governs how the business operates and offers assistance to organize, train, merchandise, market, and manage in return for payment. The entrepreneur buying into the franchise system brings the investment, spirit, and drive necessary to make the franchise successful.[4]

Franchising involves a semi-independent business owner—the **franchisee**—who pays fees and royalties to a parent company—the **franchisor**—for the right to sell products or services under the franchisor's trade name. In most cases, the franchisee also uses the franchisor's business format and system. The franchisee buys a proven business model from the franchisor, which shows the franchisee how to use the model to provide a uniform level of quality and service. The franchise system provides a brand name, market research, location assistance, advertising support, training, group buying power, ongoing support, and other resources to increase the chances for success.

The word *franchise* is derived from a French word meaning "privilege" or "freedom." A franchise in the middle ages involved a local sovereign or lord granting the right for markets or fairs to take place. Later, kings would grant a franchise for commercial activity, such as building roads. Over time, the regulations governing franchises became a part of European Common Law. By the 1840s, major ale brewers in Germany were granting franchises to taverns, giving them exclusive rights to sell ale. This was the beginning of the franchising models we know today.

The first U.S. franchise began in 1851 when Isaac M. Singer devised a more efficient, less expensive way to sell his Singer sewing machines. Another successful example of franchising came in 1887 when Asa Candler, who purchased the rights to the soft drink that John S. Pemberton invented, began franchising the right to distribute Coca-Cola. Other examples of early American franchising include the telegraph system, which was operated by various railroad companies but controlled by Western Union, and the agreements between automobile manufacturers and operators of local dealerships that developed into successful franchises.

The 1950s and 1960s witnessed the appearance of many of the franchise giants of today, with the franchise expansion of Holiday Inn, Sheraton, Roto-Rooter, Dunkin Donuts, McDonald's, Burger King, Midas, 7-Eleven, Baskin-Robbins, Wendy's, and Kentucky Fried Chicken. During this period of growth, however, some franchisors began to abuse the system. In 1979, the U.S. Federal Trade Commission (FTC) required all franchisors to create a Uniform Franchise Offering Circular (UFOC), a document that provides valuable information to prospective franchisees so that they can make informed decisions before investing in a franchise. We will discuss this document, now called the Uniform Franchise Disclosure Document (UFDD), later in this chapter.

Today, retail outlets dominate franchising, accounting for about 85 percent of all franchise sales. The increasing demand for business and consumer services is producing a boom among service industries such as education, housecleaning, real estate, tax preparation, health care, and fitness, with both brick-and-mortar and online business models.

Buying a franchise is like going into business *for yourself* but *not by yourself*. Franchisees do not establish their own autonomous businesses. Instead, franchising requires franchisees to follow a defined system that imposes limitations on the operation of their businesses. For example, franchisees may not be able to independently shift advertising strategies, adjust product lines, or change suppliers. Successful franchisors claim that failing to follow the model is a common reason that franchisees fail. One writer explains:

> The science of franchising is an exacting one; products and services are delivered according to tightly-wrapped operating formulas. There is no variance. A product is developed and honed under the watchful eye of the franchisor, then offered by franchisees under strict quality standards. The result: a democratization of products and services. Hamburgers that taste as good in Boston as in Beijing. Quick lubes available to everyone, whether they drive a Toyota or a Treblinka.[5]

Nicholas A. Bibby, franchise consultant with The Bibby Group says, "First and foremost, franchising demands that you 'follow the system.' Whether the business is a major food brand or a home-based franchise, you must be a team player who is willing to follow the rules. If changing the order of things is among your favorite pastimes, think seriously about another form of self-employment. The best franchises simply have the best systems."[6]

Rich Premec invested $65,000 of his savings in a Sanford Rose executive recruiting franchise, recouped his investment, and was earning a six-figure income from his franchise within two years. The secret, according to Premec, is "following the recipe."[7] This standardized approach lies at the core of franchising success. It is one reason for the higher success rates of franchise businesses compared to independent ventures.[8]

## Types of Franchising

*3.* Describe the different types of franchises.

Franchising includes three basic types of systems: *trade name franchising*, *product distribution franchising*, and *pure franchising*. Each form of franchising allows franchisees to benefit from the parent company's identity.

**Trade name franchising** involves being associated with a brand name, such as True Value Hardware or Walking Culture footwear. Trade name franchising facilitates purchasing the right to become identified with the franchisor's trade name without distributing particular products exclusively under the manufacturer's name.

**Product distribution franchising** involves licensing the franchisee to sell specific products under the manufacturer's brand name and trademark through a selective, limited distribution network. This system is commonly used to market automobiles (General Motors and Toyota), gasoline products (BP and Chevron), soft drinks (Pepsi-Cola and Coca-Cola), bicycles, appliances, cosmetics, and other products.

**Pure franchising**, also referred to as **comprehensive** or **business format franchising**, involves providing the franchisee with a complete business format. This highly structured relationship includes a license for a trade name, the products or services to be sold, the physical plant, the methods of operation, a marketing plan, a quality control process, a two-way communications system, and the necessary business services. The franchisee purchases the right to use all the elements of a fully integrated business operation. Pure franchising, the most rapidly growing type of franchising, is common among fast-food restaurants, hotels, business service firms, car rental agencies, educational institutions, beauty aid retailers, and many others.

*Dresdene Flynn-White
and Action
International*

Dresdene Flynn-White's interest in an Action International franchise, a business coaching franchise that targets small and medium-size businesses, began with making calls to female Action International franchisees worldwide with some questions. "I wanted to know about the receptivity to diversity and to women, and I was thrilled with the response I got," says Flynn-White. Pursuing her goal allows her to serve minority business owners. "It's about relationships, and getting people to open up and say, 'I need help,'" says Flynn-White. Resources are available to help all minorities realize their dreams, including Count Me In, a New York City-based organization geared toward helping women establish their economic independence. Flynn-White says "If it's the franchise for you, if you've done the homework and you say, 'Yes, this is what I really want to do,' then dig in and find the resources to get what you need."[9]

## The Benefits of Buying a Franchise

**4-A.** Describe the benefits of buying a franchise.

Before entering into a franchise opportunity, an entrepreneur should ask, "What can a franchise do for me that I cannot do for myself?" One survey reports that the four most common categories of people who buy franchises are second-career executives, young entrepreneurs, women, and minorities.[10]

Some of the most important reasons franchising has been so successful are the benefits it offers both franchisors and franchisees. The ideal franchising relationship is a partnership between the franchisor and the franchisee that is based on trust and a willingness to work together for mutual success. In a franchising relationship, each party depends on the performance of the other. The most successful franchisors are those that consider their franchisees as partners—they know that their success depends on their franchisees' success. Noting the importance of maintaining a solid relationship with the company's franchisees, McDonald's founder Ray Kroc said, "None of us is as good as all of us."[11]

Franchisees benefit from the franchisor's business experience because the franchisee is essentially buying experience from the franchisor. The franchisor's industry knowledge and expertise offers a competitive advantage for franchisees. The franchisor already understands the most common problems, and franchisees benefit from that insight. Franchisors share their learning curve with franchisees, providing a proven successful business model. The ability to draw on the franchisor's experience acts as a safety net for entrepreneurs over which they can build their businesses. Therefore, franchisees with limited business experience have the opportunity to own a small business with a recognized brand name, participate in extensive training and support, and sell an established product. The value of these resources is one reason why many franchisees reach the breakeven point faster than an independent business.[12]

*Dennis Huff and Ed
Flanders and Aussie
Pet Mobile*

Dennis Huff, a sales and marketing executive, and Ed Flanders, an executive engineer, abandoned their corporate positions to become their own bosses. They took the plunge to open an Aussie Pet Mobile franchise. Within 18 months, they were among the top Aussie Pet Mobile franchisees—all without washing a single dog, but managing employees who do. They attribute their success to their ability to grasp the bigger franchise picture and enter with plans for aggressive growth. Their previous corporate experiences enabled them to embrace the importance of the business structure and prepare for the initial costs and time demands, factors Huff says many franchisees underestimate.[13]

The advantages of buying a franchise rely on the ability to replicate established, proven elements of a business model. Franchising offers a business system with management training and support of branded products and services with established promotional campaigns to help franchisees succeed.

## A Business System

One major benefit of joining a franchise is gaining access to a business system with a proven track record. In many instances, franchisors provide their franchisees with turnkey operations, allowing entrepreneurs to get their businesses up and running much faster, more efficiently, and more effectively than if they launched their own companies. With this business system as a guide, franchisees can succeed with limited business and industry experience. They have the advantage of relying on the franchisor's experience and the business system that results from that experience to build successful businesses.

*Fred DeLuca and
Peter Buck and Subway*

At the age of 17, Fred DeLuca and family friend Peter Buck opened Pete's Super Submarines in the northeastern United States. DeLuca's $1,000 loan from Buck came with the hope that the tiny sandwich shop would earn enough to put him through college. The struggling shop made a name change to Subway and within 9 years after its opening, DeLuca and Buck began franchising in 1974. Offering a fresh, healthy alternative to fast-food restaurants, Subway is now a leading U.S. franchise with nearly 29,000 locations in more than 85 countries.[14]

Subway founder Fred DeLuca
visits one of his franchise
restaurants.

## Management Training and Support

A leading cause of business failure is incompetent management, and franchisors are well aware of this challenge. They offer managerial training programs to franchisees prior to opening a new outlet to reduce the number of franchise casualties. Many franchisors also provide follow-up training and counseling services. These services are vital because most franchisors do not require a franchisee to have experience in the business. "Just putting a person in business, giving him a trademark, patting him on the [back], and saying, 'Good luck,' is not sufficient," says one franchise consultant.[15]

Training programs often involve both classroom and on-site instruction to teach franchisees the basic operations of the business—from producing and selling the goods or services to purchasing raw materials and completing paperwork. For example, Subway franchisees must complete a 55-hour course and spend an additional 34 hours in on-the-job training. As the training progresses, franchisees manage a store by themselves. Ultimately, they must pass a final exam before Subway gives them final approval to become franchisees.[16] Franchisees at the Golden Corral buffet chain learn how to manage a restaurant as well as how to perform every job in a typical 100-employee location. Dunkin' Donuts trains franchisees for as long as five weeks in everything from accounting to dough making. Franchisees at Plato's Closet, a chain of resale shops that focuses on clothing for teens and young adults, spend two weeks learning how to develop a business plan, secure financing, hire and manage employees, buy and sell inventory, and use the company's proprietary computer software system to manage their stores. The strength of that training program is one factor that gave Charlotte Knowles, a former schoolteacher with no experience in retail clothing, the confidence to open a Plato's Closet franchise.[17] Although these training programs are beneficial to running a successful franchise, franchisees should not expect to be "management experts" at the end of a two- to five-week program. The necessary management skills for any business are too complex to learn in any single course.

Many franchisors supplement their start-up training programs with ongoing instruction and support to ensure franchisees' continued success. Franchisors often provide field support to franchisees in customer service, quality control, inventory management, and general management. Franchisors may assign field consultants to guide new franchisees through the first week or two of operation after the grand opening. Franchisors offer this support because they realize the ultimate success of the system depends on the franchisee's success. Prospective franchisees should know exactly what the franchise contract says about the nature, extent, and frequency of field support the franchisor will provide.

Inherent dangers exist in the trainer/trainee relationship. A franchisee should be aware that, in some cases, "assistance" from the franchisor tends to drift into "control" over the franchisee's business. In addition, some franchisors charge fees for their training services; therefore, franchisees should clarify the cost of the specific training they will receive.

### Brand Name Appeal

Franchisees purchase the right to use a known and advertised brand name for a product or service, giving them the advantage of identifying their businesses with a widely recognized name. Customers recognize the identifying trademark, the standard symbols, the store design, and the products of an established franchise. A basic tenet of franchising is cloning the franchisor's success. Buying into this brand equity provides marketing power. A customer is confident that the quality and content of a meal at McDonald's in Dubai will be consistent with a meal at a Tokyo McDonald's. One franchising expert explains, "The day you open a McDonald's franchise, you have instant customers. If you choose to open [an independent] hamburger restaurant, . . . you'd have to spend a fortune on advertising and promotion before you'd attract customers."[18]

### Standardized Quality of Goods and Services

Because a franchisee purchases a license to sell the franchisor's product or service and the privilege of using the associated brand name, the quality of the goods or services sold determines the franchisor's reputation. Building a sound reputation in business takes time, but destroying a good reputation can happen quickly. Franchisors often demand strict compliance with uniform standards of quality and service to secure the image of the chain. Many franchisors conduct periodic inspections of local facilities to assist in maintaining acceptable levels of performance. Maintaining quality is so important that most franchisors retain the right to terminate the franchise contract and to repurchase the outlet if a franchisee fails to comply with established standards.

### National Advertising Programs

An effective advertising program is essential to the success of virtually all franchise operations. A regional or national advertising program benefits all franchisees. Most franchisors organize and control the advertising campaign. Advertising is financed by each franchisee's contribution of a percentage of monthly sales, usually 1 to 5 percent or a flat monthly fee. For example, Subway franchisees pay 3.5 percent of gross revenues to the Subway national advertising program. The franchisor uses this pool of funds to create a cooperative advertising program, which has a potentially greater impact than if the franchisees spent the same amount of money separately. The result is that franchisees of well-known franchises have greater recognition in the local marketplace than do independent owners.

Most franchisors also require franchisees to spend a minimum amount on local advertising. For example, to supplement their national advertising efforts, both Wendy's and Burger King require franchisees to spend at least 3 percent of gross sales on local advertising. Some franchisors assist franchisees in designing and producing local advertising. Many companies help franchisees create promotional plans and provide press releases, advertisements, and special materials such as signs and banners for grand openings and promotions.

### Financial Assistance

Franchisors vary considerably in the level of financial assistance they provide—from nothing to direct financing programs. Typically, franchisors are not interested in lending money to their franchisees. Rather, they rely on their franchisees' money to accelerate the growth of their own businesses. Fifty-two percent of franchisors offer financial guidance but only 20 percent of of them provide some form of *direct* financial assistance.[19] Few franchisors offer loans that enable franchisees to pay the initial franchise fee. However, once a franchisor locates a suitable franchisee, it may offer the qualified candidate direct financial assistance in specific areas, such as purchasing equipment and inventory, or even with the franchise fee. Because the total start-up costs of some franchises are already at breathtaking levels, some franchisors find that they *must* offer direct financial assistance if they are to continue to grow.

Many franchisors offer to help franchisees prepare a business plan or apply for a loan from a bank, the U.S. Small Business Administration, for example, or another lender. Franchisors usually are willing to assist qualified franchisees in establishing relationships with banks, private investors, and other sources of funds. In many instances, franchisors have established alliances with third-party lenders to make it easier for their franchisees to receive financing. For instance, the parent company of the ice cream franchise Baskin-Robbins, Dunkin' Donuts, and Togo's franchises has created an arrangement with three national small business lending programs in which its franchisees can qualify for up to 75 percent of the cost of a franchise. Franchisees can obtain loans to cover the initial franchise fee, fixtures, vehicles, working capital, and equipment purchases by completing a shorter, customized loan application designed just for them through this preferred lender relationship. Support from the franchisor enhances a franchisee's chances of getting the financing they seek because most lenders recognize the lower failure rate among reputable franchises.

The U.S. Small Business Administration (SBA) has simplified the loan application process for franchisees by working with FRANdata to create the **Franchise Registry** at *www.franchiseregistry.com*. The Franchise Registry is a central database of information about participating franchises that the SBA has certified and whose franchisees benefit from a streamlined loan review process. Likewise, the World Franchise Council (*www.worldfranchisecouncil.org*) serves as a gateway for information about the franchising industry and national franchise associations around the globe.[20]

**ENTREPRENEURIAL**
**Profile**

*Lei Kaniaupio and Dmitri Spadaccini and Robeks*

The husband-and-wife team of Lei Kaniaupio and Dmitri Spadaccini are franchisees and regional directors for Robeks in Hawaii, a franchise restaurant offering smoothies and a health-oriented menu. This dual involvement, which required the couple to take out two business loans, is a testimony to their belief in the Robeks concept. After exhausting their own funds and borrowing from family members and friends, the couple worked with Robeks to qualify for a loan from the Bank of Hawaii. Kaniaupio enjoys being part of a franchise that promotes healthy eating and living. "Hawaii's market is so perfect for this product," says Kaniaupio. "It's not just smoothies—it's sandwiches, soups, muffins, etc. Our whole concept is based on this healthy attitude."[21]

## Proven Products and Business Formats

A franchisee is purchasing the franchisor's experience, expertise, products, and support. A franchise owner does not have to build the business from scratch. Rather than relying solely on personal ability to establish a business and attract a clientele, the franchisee can depend on the methods and techniques of an established business. These standardized procedures and operations greatly enhance the franchisee's chances of success and avoid the most inefficient type of learning—trial and error. One Subway executive says, "When we say 'Do things our way,' it's not just an ego thing on the part of the franchiser. We've proven it works."[22]

Reputable franchisors also invest resources in researching and developing new products and services, improving existing ones, and tracking market trends that influence the success of its product line. Many franchisees cite this as another key benefit of the franchising arrangement.

## Centralized Buying Power

A franchisee may have a significant advantage over the independent business owner through the franchisor's centralized and large-volume buying power. Some franchisors sell goods and materials to franchisees, receive volume discounts, and pass on these cost savings to franchisees. For example, it is unlikely that a small, independent ice cream parlor could match the buying power of a franchise operation with thousands of ice cream stores. In many instances, economies of scale simply preclude independent owners from successfully competing head-to-head with franchise operations.

## Site Selection

A proper location is critical to the success of any business, and franchises are no exception. As is the case for retail stores, franchise experts also consider the three most important factors in franchising to be "location, location, location!" An affiliation with a franchisor may be the best way to get into prime locations. McDonald's, for example, is well known for its ability to obtain prime locations in high-traffic areas. Other fast-food competitors track new McDonald's locations, often attempting to acquire property as close as possible. Although choosing a location is the franchisee's responsibility, the franchisor usually reserves the right to approve the final site. Many franchisors will conduct an extensive location analysis for each new outlet (for a fee), including studies of traffic patterns, zoning ordinances, accessibility, and population density. Even if the franchisor does not conduct a site analysis, this is something that wise franchisees perform. A thorough demographic and statistical analysis of potential locations is essential to selecting the site that offers the greatest potential for success. We will discuss these topics in detail in Chapter 9, "Creating a Marketing Plan," and Chapter 16, "Location, Layout, and Physical Facilities."

## Territorial Protection

Franchisors may offer territorial protection, which gives the franchisee the right to exclusive distribution of brand name goods or services within a particular geographic area. Under such an agreement, a franchisor agrees not to sell another franchised outlet or to open a company-owned unit within the franchisee's defined territory. The size and description of a franchisee's territory varies from company to company. For example, a restaurant franchise may agree not to license another franchisee within a mile of existing locations. A dental franchise may define its franchisees' territories on the basis of postal code designations. BMW limits the number of dealerships that sell the MINI Cooper within geographic areas. The purpose of this protection is to prevent an invasion of existing franchisees' territories and the accompanying dilution of sales.

Unfortunately for franchisees, fewer franchisors now offer territorial protection, and franchise owners increasingly find themselves in close proximity to one other. As competition for top locations escalates, disputes over the placement of new franchise outlets have become a source of friction between franchisors and franchisees. Some franchisees charge that franchisors encroach on their territories by granting new franchises in such close proximity that it dilutes their sales. Franchise experts consistently cite territorial encroachment as a top concern for franchisees.[23] Although the new outlets franchisors grant lie outside the boundaries of

# ENTREPRENEURSHIP

## In Action

### Cold Stone Creamery: Scooping for Growth

One look and it's clear that Cold Stone Creamery is not your father's ice cream scoop shop. Customers choose from an assortment of ice cream "mix-ins" such as crumbled cookies, candies, fruits, and nuts, and watch crew members blend the ingredients into the ice cream on a cold granite slab before packing it into a cup or freshly baked waffle cone. When a happy customer places a tip in the tip jar, crew members break out into a Cold Stone song. "It's clear to see that Cold Stone is more than just ice cream," says industry analyst Donna Berry. "It's entertainment." Cold Stone Creamery's goal is to provide customers with similar service at every store by supplying instructional material and training videos to franchise owners.

Founded by Donald and Susan Sutherland, Cold Stone Creamery is for those who seek "smooth and creamy super-premium ice cream." The inspiration for Cold Stone's name comes from the frozen granite slab used to mix candy or other toppings into the ice cream. Cold Stone stores specialize in a customized ice cream "creation" tradition. Ice cream choices include basic flavors such as French Vanilla and Strawberry to more extravagant custom flavors such as Sweet Cream and Cake Batter.

Worldwide, people spend $51 billion a year on ice cream. "It's not a small category," said Harry Balzar, president of the NPD Group, a market research company. "These guys [at Stone Cold Creamery] are all hoping to be the next Starbucks," says Berry.

Former Procter & Gamble sales manager, Douglas A. Ducey, is Cold Stone's chief executive leading the expansion. "I saw an opportunity to reinvent a stagnant category like what happened with coffee," he says. Franchises such as Baskin-Robbins and Dairy Queen and the thousands of independent scoop shops have made certain there are plenty of places to satisfy a craving for ice cream. This new "ice cream slab" concept is scooping out a niche offering a high-priced, high-quality version of a relatively mundane product.

The Cold Stone Creamery franchise began as one store, which opened in 1988. The Sutherlands sold their first franchise in 1995, and today, Cold Stone includes more than 1,400 franchises across the United States, China, Japan, Korea, and Puerto Rico. Cold Stone plans to expand its market with a simple strategy: franchising more outlets and serving premium ice cream off of the cold granite slab, one scoop at a time.

1. What advantages does Cold Stone Creamery offer an entrepreneur compared to opening an independent store?
2. How might Cold Stone Creamery impose limitations on its franchisees?

*Source:* Kate Murphy, "Slabs Are Joining Scoops in Ice Cream Retailing," *New York Times,* October 26, 2006, p. C6.

existing franchisees' territories, their market coverage and reach may overlap those of existing territories, causing sales and profits to decline. When Naugles Inc., a Mexican restaurant chain, opened a company-owned outlet within 1.5 miles of an existing franchisee's location, the franchisee, Vylene Enterprises, charged that Naugles' opening of the new restaurant breached the franchise agreement and violated the implied requirement of fair dealing. Vylene testified that the new outlet caused a 35 percent sales decline at its store. Even though the franchise agreement did not grant Vylene an exclusive territory, the California Court of Appeals ruled in Vylene's favor, stating that "Naugles' construction of a competing restaurant within a mile and a half of Vylene's restaurant was a breach of the covenant of good faith and fair dealing."[24]

### Increased Chance for Success

Statistics suggest that franchising is less risky than building a business from the ground up. The U.S. Department of Commerce, for example, estimates that after five years, 90 percent of franchises are still in business, compared to just 40 percent of independent businesses

**FIGURE 4.1 Success Rate Comparison**

*Source:* Data compiled from the National Federation of Independent Businesses and the U.S. Department of Commerce.

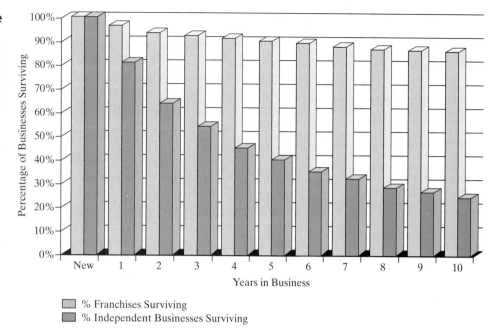

% Franchises Surviving
% Independent Businesses Surviving

(see Figure 4.1). The higher success rate for franchises is attributed to the broad range of services, assistance, guidance, and the business system franchisors provide. Many owners are convinced that franchising has been a crucial part of their success. Investing in a franchise is not risk-free, however. Between 200 and 300 new franchise companies enter the market each year, and many do not survive. One study found that one-fourth of new franchisors fail within ten years and that the franchisee failure rate is highest within the first four years.[25]

Franchising success statistics must be interpreted carefully. When a franchise outlet is in danger of failing, the franchisor may repurchase or relocate the outlet and does not have to report it as a failure. Franchisors may obscure the actual percentage rate of their failed franchised businesses through the reporting statistics in the Uniform Franchise Disclosure Document—describing these changes as "terminations," "sale-transfers," or "transfers"—but the reasons for this activity are not revealed. Terminations and sale-transfers may, in fact, be business failures.

Buying a franchise does not guarantee success. The franchisor provides franchisees with the business system and the tools to make it work, but the franchisees must use the system and the tools to their advantage. Table 4.1 describes the qualifications that franchisors look for in their franchisees.

**TABLE 4.1 What Franchisors Want in Their Franchisees**

A survey of franchisors reported the following qualities to be key to franchisees' success:

| | | |
|---|---|---|
| **1.** | People skills | 94% |
| **2.** | Ability to be coached | 87% |
| **3.** | General business skills | 86% |
| **4.** | Access to capital | 84% |
| **5.** | Entrepreneurial mind-set | 76% |
| **6.** | Specific industry skills | 29% |
| **7.** | Risk aversion | 29% |
| **8.** | Existing franchisee in system | 23% |
| **9.** | Ability to buy multiple units | 17% |

*Source:* Andrew A. Caffey, "Are You Franchisee Material?" *Entrepreneur, 2007 Franchise 500*, January 2007.

## Drawbacks of Buying a Franchise

**4-B.** Describe the limitations of buying a franchise.

The benefits of franchising can mean the difference between success and failure. However, franchisees must sacrifice some freedom to the franchisor. Prospective franchisees must explore the limitations of franchising before buying into this business system. Thoroughly researching potential franchise opportunities is the only way an entrepreneur can find a franchise that is a good match with his or her personality, likes, and dislikes.[26]

### Franchise Fees and Revenue Sharing

Virtually all franchisors impose some type of fees and demand a share of a franchisee's sales revenues in return for the use of the franchisor's name, products or services, and business system. Franchise fees and initial capital requirements vary among the different franchisors. The average total start-up cost for a franchise is approximately $200,000, and nearly 80 percent of franchise opportunities include initial investments of $250,000 or less (excluding real estate).[27] The U.S. Commerce Department reports that total investments for franchises range from $1,000 for business services up to $10 million for hotel and motel franchises. For instance, Jani-King, a home-based commercial cleaning service, sells franchises for $11,100 to $34,100, depending on the territory's size. A McDonald's franchise requires an investment that ranges from $506,000 to $1.6 million (but McDonald's owns the land and building).

Start-up costs for franchises often include additional fees. Most franchisors impose a franchise fee that ranges from $1,000 to $50,000 (sometimes more) up front for the right to use the company name. For instance, the franchise fee at Kumon Math and Reading Centers, an after-school educational service, is just $1,000. Culver's, a quick-service food franchise, charges a $55,000 franchise fee. Franchises may also charge fees for site purchase and preparation, construction, signs, fixtures, equipment, management assistance, and training. Some franchise fees include these costs whereas others do not. Before signing any contract, a prospective franchisee should determine the total cost of a franchise, something every franchisor is required to disclose in items 5, 6, and 7 of its UFDD.

Franchisors also receive income through ongoing royalty fees as revenue-sharing devices. The royalty fees usually involve a percentage of gross sales with a required minimum, or a flat fee levied on the franchise. Because the royalty percentage of *gross sales* determines the payment, franchisors receive payment even if the franchisee fails to earn a profit. Royalty fees typically range from 1 percent to 12 percent of sales, and most franchisors assess a rate between 3 percent and 7 percent. For example, Subway charges a franchise fee of $15,000 and a royalty fee of 8 percent of sales, payable weekly. Jiffy Lube's franchise fee is $35,000, and its royalty fee is 5 percent of each unit's sales. These fees can increase a franchisee's overhead expenses significantly. Sometimes unprepared franchisees discover—too late—that the franchisor's royalties and fees are about what the normal profit margin is for a franchise.

A prospective franchisee should find out which fees are required (some are merely recommended) and then determine the services and benefits the fees cover. One of the best ways to do this is to itemize what you are getting for your money and then determine whether the cost is reasonable. Getting details on all expenses—the amount, the time of payment, and the financing arrangements—is important. It is critical that entrepreneurs find out which items, if any, are included in the initial franchise fee and which ones require additional expenditures.[28]

### Strict Adherence to Standardized Operations

Although franchisees own their businesses, they do not have the autonomy of independent owners. The terms of the franchise agreement govern the franchisor-franchisee relationship. That agreement requires franchisees to operate their outlets according to the principles spelled out in the franchisor's operations manual. Typical topics covered in the manual include operating hours, dress codes, operating policies and procedures, product or service specifications, and confidentiality requirements.

To protect its public image, franchisors require their franchisees to maintain certain operating standards. Determining compliance with standards is usually accomplished by periodic inspections. If a franchise constantly fails to meet the minimum standards established for the business, the franchisor may terminate its license. Strict adherence to franchise standards may become a burden to the franchisee.

### Restrictions on Purchasing

Franchisors sometimes require franchisees to purchase products, supplies, or special equipment from the franchisor or from an approved supplier. The most common reason for this is to maintain quality standards. A poor image for the entire franchise could result from some franchisees using inferior products to cut costs. For example, KFC requires that franchisees use only seasonings blended by a particular company. The franchise contract spells out the penalty for using unapproved suppliers, which usually is termination of the franchise agreement.

Franchisees at some chains have filed antitrust suits alleging that franchisors overcharge their outlets for supplies and equipment and eliminate competition by failing to approve alternative suppliers. A franchisor can legally set the prices paid for the products it sells to franchisees but cannot establish the retail prices franchisees charge. Franchisors may suggest retail prices but cannot force the franchisee to abide by them.

*Chris Bray and Quiznos*

Chris Bray is a Quiznos franchise owner involved in a class-action lawsuit against the franchise, alleging that the company forces franchisees to buy Quiznos's food, supplies, and services at inflated prices while concurrently setting artificially low retail prices for its products, causing many stores to be unprofitable. "Quiznos has been taking advantage of its franchisees for years through practices that we contend are illegal and in violation of the franchise agreement," contends Bray, president of the Toasted Subs Franchisees Association, Inc. (TSFA). Bray, who owns two Quiznos, says the franchise "has slowly, methodically and deliberately modified the business model, year over year, to inflate corporate profits at the expense of franchisees system wide. This has led to a lack of franchisee profitability and excessive store closures." The lawsuit is the third class action by Quiznos franchisees in less than a year.[29]

### Limited Product Line

In most cases, the franchise agreement stipulates that franchisees can sell only those products approved by the franchisor. Franchisees must avoid selling unapproved products through their outlets unless they are willing to risk license cancellation. Franchisors strive for standardization in their product lines so that customers, wherever they may be, know what to expect. Some companies allow franchisees to modify their product or service offerings to suit regional or local tastes, but only with the franchisor's approval. When Heavenly Hams franchisee Felix Mirando spotted an opportunity to sell ready-made box lunches to employees at corporate offices near his franchise, he asked for and received approval from the franchisor to add the item to his menu.[30]

The franchise agreement may require franchisees to carry an unpopular product or prevent franchisees from introducing a desirable one. Although some franchises discourage franchisees from deviating from the standard "formula" in any way, including experimenting with new products and services, others encourage and solicit new ideas and innovations from their franchisees.

*Herb Peterson and McDonald's*

Herb Peterson, a McDonald's franchisee, created the highly successful Egg McMuffin while experimenting with a Teflon-coated egg ring that gave fried eggs rounded corners and a poached appearance. Peterson put his round eggs on English muffins, adorned them with Canadian bacon and melted cheese, and showed his creation to McDonald's chief, Ray Kroc. Kroc devoured two of them and was sold on the idea when Peterson's wife suggested the catchy name. In 1975, McDonald's became the first fast-food franchise to open its doors for breakfast, and the Egg McMuffin became a staple on the breakfast menu.[31] McDonald's franchisees are also responsible for the creation of the Big Mac and the Happy Meal.[32]

### Unsatisfactory Training Programs

Every would-be franchisee must be wary of unscrupulous franchisors who promise extensive services, advice, and assistance but deliver nothing. For instance, one owner pays a substantial technical assistance fee for what the franchisor describes as an "extensive, rigorous training program." The franchisee receives nothing but a set of pamphlets and do-it-yourself study guides. Common prey for dishonest franchisors are those impatient entrepreneurs who purchase franchises without investigating the business—and never hear from the franchisor again. Although disclosure rules have reduced the severity of the problem, dishonest franchisors still thrive on unprepared prospective franchisees.

### Market Saturation

Market saturation is a danger. Although some franchisors offer franchisees territorial protection, many do not. Territorial encroachment has become a hotly contested issue in franchising as growth-seeking franchisors have exhausted most of the prime locations and are now setting up new franchises in close proximity to existing ones. The biggest challenge to the growth potential of franchising is the lack of satisfactory locations.

Another challenge to territorial protection for franchisees is the Internet. Some franchisees complain that franchisors' Web sites are taking sales from their outlets and are in violation of their exclusive territory agreements. Franchisees of one drugstore chain recently filed arbitration claims to block the franchisor from competing with them by selling products over its Web site. The franchisor denied that its Web site was cannibalizing sales of its franchised outlets and claimed that the site would promote the entire company's brand.[33]

### Limited Freedom

When franchisees purchase their franchises and sign the contract, they agree to sell the franchisor's product or service by following its prescribed formula. When McDonald's rolls out a new national product, for instance, all franchisees add it to their menus. Franchisors want to ensure success, and most monitor their franchisees' performances closely. Strict uniformity is the rule rather than the exception. Highly independent entrepreneurs who want to be their own bosses and to avoid being subject to the control of others will most likely be frustrated as franchisees. Table 4.2 offers a Franchise Evaluation Quiz to help potential franchisees decide whether a franchise is right for them.

## Franchising and U.S. Laws

**5.** Describe the legal aspects of franchising, including the protection offered by the FTC's Trade Regulation Rule.

In 1971, the state of California was the first to respond to the potential for deception inherent in a franchise relationship by enacting the first Franchise Investment Law. This law, along with similar laws in 14 other states,* required franchisors to register a Uniform Franchise Offering Circular (UFOC), and deliver a copy to prospective franchisees before any offer or sale of a franchise. In 1979, the U.S. Federal Trade Commission (FTC) adopted similar legislation that established full disclosure guidelines for franchising companies and was designed to give potential franchisees the information they needed to protect themselves from unscrupulous franchisors.

In 2008, the FTC replaced the UFOC with a similar document, the **Uniform Franchise Disclosure Document (UFDD)** which requires all franchisors to disclose detailed information on their operations at least 14 days before a franchise contract is signed or any money is paid. The UFDD applies to all franchisors, even those in the 35 states lacking franchise disclosure laws. The purpose of the regulation is to assist the potential franchisee's investigation of the franchise deal and to introduce consistency into the franchisor's disclosure statements. The FTC also established a "plain English" requirement for the UFDD that prohibits legal and technical jargon and makes the document easy to read and understand. The FTC's philosophy is not to ferret out and prosecute abusers but to require

---

*The 15 U.S. states requiring franchise registration are: California, Hawaii, Illinois, Indiana, Maryland, Michigan, Minnesota, New York, North Dakota, Oregon, Rhode Island, South Dakota, Virginia, Washington, and Wisconsin.

**TABLE 4.2 A Franchise Evaluation Quiz**

Taking the emotion out of buying a franchise is the goal of this self-test developed by Franchise Solutions, Inc., a franchise consulting company. Circle the number that reflects your degree of certainty or positive feelings for each of the following 12 statements: 1 is low; 5 is high.

|  | Low    High |
|---|---|
| **1.** I would really enjoy being in this kind of business. | 1  2  3  4  5 |
| **2.** This franchise will meet or exceed my income goals. | 1  2  3  4  5 |
| **3.** My people-handling skills are sufficient for this franchise. | 1  2  3  4  5 |
| **4.** I understand fully my greatest challenge in this franchise, and I feel comfortable with my abilities. | 1  2  3  4  5 |
| **5.** I have met with the company management and feel compatible. | 1  2  3  4  5 |
| **6.** I understand the risks with this business and am prepared to accept them. | 1  2  3  4  5 |
| **7.** I have researched the competition in my area and feel comfortable with the potential market. | 1  2  3  4  5 |
| **8.** My family and friends think this is a great opportunity for me. | 1  2  3  4  5 |
| **9.** I have had an adviser review the disclosure documents and the franchise agreement. | 1  2  3  4  5 |
| **10.** I have contacted a representative number of the existing franchisees; they were overwhelmingly positive. | 1  2  3  4  5 |
| **11.** I have researched this industry and feel comfortable about the long-term growth potential. | 1  2  3  4  5 |
| **12.** My background and experience make this franchise an ideal choice. | 1  2  3  4  5 |

The maximum score on the quiz is 60. A score of 45 or below means that either the franchise opportunity is unsuitable or that you need to do more research on the franchise you are considering.

*Source:* Roberta Maynard, "Choosing a Franchise," *Nation's Business,* October 1996, p. 57.

franchisors to provide to prospective franchisees information to help them make intelligent decisions. Although the FTC requires every franchisor to provide a potential franchisee with a UFDD, it does not verify its accuracy. Even though the UFDD is an extremely important part of investigating any franchise, prospective franchisees should use this document only as a starting point for their investigations.

In addition to a cover page and a table of contents, the FTC requires a franchisor to include in the UFDD a sample franchise contract and statements on the following 23 major topics:

1. Information identifying the franchisor and its affiliates, and describing their business experience and the franchises being sold.
2. Information identifying and describing the business experience of each of the franchise's officers, directors, and management personnel responsible for the franchise program.
3. A description of the lawsuits in which the franchisor and its officers, directors, and managers have been involved in the last 10 years.
4. Information about any bankruptcies in which the franchisor and its officers, directors, and managers have been involved in the last 10 years.
5. Information about the initial franchise fee and other payments required to obtain the franchise, including the intended use of the fees and the franchisor's refund policy.
6. A table describing all other fees that franchisees are required to make after start-up, including royalties, service fees, training fees, lease payments, advertising charges, and others. The table also must include the due date for the fees.
7. A table showing the components of a franchisee's total initial investment. The categories covered are pre-opening expenses, initial franchise fee, training expenses, real property (purchased or leased), equipment, opening inventory, security deposits, business licenses, initial advertising fees, and other expenses such as working capital, legal, and accounting fees.
8. Information about quality restrictions on goods and services used in the franchise, where they may be purchased, and other details pertaining to purchasing agreements.

Franchisors often require franchisees to purchase goods, services, and supplies only from approved suppliers (including the franchisor).

9. A cross-reference table that shows the location of the description of the franchisee's obligations in the text of the UFDD and in the franchise contract.

10. A description of any financial assistance available from the franchisor in the purchase of the franchise, including the amount of financing offered and the interest rates on loans.

11. A description of all obligations the franchisor must fulfill in helping a franchisee prepare to open and operate a unit, with information covering site selection, advertising, computer systems, pricing, training (a table describing the length and type of training is required), and other forms of assistance provided to franchisees. This typically is the longest section of the UFDD.

12. A description of any territorial protection that will be granted to the franchise and a statement as to whether the franchisor may locate a company-owned store or other outlet in that territory. The franchisor must specify whether it offers exclusive or non-exclusive territories. Because market saturation and territorial encroachment have become such controversial issues in franchising, prospective franchisees should pay special attention to this section.

13. All relevant information about the franchisor's trademarks, service marks, trade names, logos, and commercial symbols, including where they are registered.

14. Similar information on any patents and copyrights the franchisor owns, and the rights to them that the franchisor transfers to franchisees.

15. A description of the extent to which franchisees must participate personally in the operation of the franchise. Some franchisors do not allow absentee owners.

16. A description of any restrictions on the goods or services franchisees are permitted to sell and with whom franchisees may deal. Many franchisors require franchisees to sell only those goods and services that the franchisor has approved.

17. A table that describes the conditions under which the franchise may be repurchased or refused renewal by the franchisor, transferred to a third party by the franchisee, and terminated or modified by either party. This section also spells out the process for resolving disputes between franchisees and the franchisor.

18. A description of the involvement of celebrities and public figures in the franchise.

19. A complete statement of the basis for any earnings claims made to the franchisee, including the percentage of existing franchises that have actually achieved the results that are claimed. Franchisors that make earnings claims must include them in the UFDD, and the claims must "have a reasonable basis" at the time they are made. However, franchisors are not required to make any earnings claims at all; in fact, 80 percent of franchisors do not make earnings claims in their disclosure documents, primarily because of liability concerns about committing such numbers to paper.[34]

20. A table that displays statistical information about the expansion or the contraction of the franchise over the past three years. This section also includes the current number of franchises, the number of franchises projected for the future and the states in which they are to be sold, the number of franchises terminated, the number of agreements the franchisor has not renewed, the number of franchises that have been sold to new owners, the number of outlets that the franchisor has repurchased, the number of franchises that have ceased operation, and a list of the names and addresses of other franchises. This section is particularly useful for the next phase of investigating a franchise: talking to existing franchisees about their experience with the franchisor.

21. The franchisor's audited financial statements.

22. A copy of all franchise and other contracts (leases, purchase agreements, and others) the franchisee will be required to sign.

23. A standardized, detachable "receipt" to prove that the prospective franchisee received a copy of the UFDD.

The typical UFDD is from 100 to 200 pages long, but every potential franchisee should read and understand it. Unfortunately, many do not, which results in unpleasant surprises for franchisees. The UFDD information neither fully protects potential franchises from deception, nor does it guarantee success. The UFDD does, however, provide a base of information to begin a thorough investigation of the franchisor and the franchise deal. Many experts recommend that potential franchisees have an experienced franchise attorney or consultant review a company's UFDD before they invest. The UFDD is a valuable tool for prospective franchisees, providing them the information they need to make informed decisions, saving them time and providing them with more complete information about a franchise.

## The Right Way to Buy a Franchise

*6.* Explain the right way to buy a franchise.

The UFDD can help potential franchisees identify and avoid dishonest franchisors. Preparation, common sense, and patience are the best defenses a prospective entrepreneur has against making a bad investment decision. A thorough investigation before investing in a franchise reduces the risk of deception. Asking the right questions and resisting the urge to rush into an investment decision helps a potential franchisee avoid unscrupulous franchisors.

Despite existing disclosure requirements, dishonest franchisors that take unsuspecting people's money and disappear may continue to operate, often moving from one state to another just ahead of authorities. Potential franchisees must beware. Franchise fraud can destroy the dreams of many hopeful franchisees and rob them of their life savings. Because dishonest franchisors tend to follow certain patterns, well-prepared franchisees can avoid this fate. The following clues should arouse the suspicion of an entrepreneur about to invest in a franchise:

- Claims that the franchise contract is "the standard one" and that "you don't need to read it." There is no standard franchise contract.
- A franchisor who fails to give you a copy of the required disclosure document, the UFDD, at your first face-to-face meeting.
- A marginally successful prototype store or no prototype at all.
- A poorly prepared operations manual outlining the franchise system or no manual (or system) at all.
- An unsolicited testimonial from "a highly successful franchisee." Scam artists will hire someone to pose as a successful franchisee, complete with a rented luxury car and expensive-looking jewelry and clothing, to "prove" how successful franchisees can be and to help close the sale. Use the list of franchisees in item 20 of the UFDD to find real franchisees and ask them plenty of questions.
- An unusual amount of litigation brought against the franchisor. In this litigious society, companies facing lawsuits is a common situation. However, too many lawsuits are a sign that something is amiss. This information is found in item 3 of the UFDD.
- Verbal promises of large future earnings without written documentation. Remember: If franchisors make earnings claims, they must document them in item 19 of the UFDD.
- A high franchisee turnover rate or a high termination rate. This information is described in item 20 of the UFDD.
- Attempts to discourage you from allowing an attorney to evaluate the franchise contract before you sign it.
- No written documentation to support claims and promises.
- A high pressure sale—sign the contract now or lose the opportunity. This tactic usually sounds like this: "Franchise territories are going fast. If you hesitate, you are likely to miss out on the prime locations."
- Claiming to be exempt from federal laws requiring complete disclosure of franchise details in a UFDD. If a franchisor has no UFDD, run—don't walk—away from the deal.
- "Get-rich-quick schemes"—promises of huge profits with only minimum effort.
- Reluctance to provide a list of present franchisees for you to interview.
- Evasive, vague answers to your questions about the franchise and its operation.

Not every franchise "horror story" is the result of dishonest franchisors. Most franchising problems are due to franchisees buying legitimate franchises without proper research and analysis. These entrepreneurs end up owning businesses they do not enjoy and that they are not well-suited to operate. The following steps will help any franchisee make the right franchise choice.

## Evaluate Yourself

Author and poet Henry David Thoreau's advice to "know thyself" is excellent advice for prospective franchisees. Before looking at any franchise, entrepreneurs should examine their own personalities, experiences, likes, dislikes, goals, and expectations. The following are valuable questions for the entrepreneur to ask:

- Will you be comfortable working in a structured environment?
- What kinds of franchises fit your desired lifestyle?
- Do you want to sell a product or a service?
- Do you want to work with the public?
- Do you enjoy selling?
- What hours do you expect to work?
- Do you want to work with people or do you prefer to work alone?
- Which franchise concepts mesh best with your past work experience?
- What activities and hobbies do you enjoy?
- What income do you expect a franchise to generate?
- How much can you afford to invest in a franchise?
- Will you be happy with the daily routine of operating the franchise?

A typical franchise contract runs for at least 10 years, making it imperative that prospective franchisees conduct a complete inventory of their interests, likes, dislikes, and abilities before buying a franchise.

## Research the Market

Entrepreneurs should research the market before shopping for a franchise and ask these questions:

- How fast is the surrounding area growing?
- In which areas is that growth occurring fastest?
- Is the market for the franchise's product or service growing or declining?
- Who are your potential customers?
- What are their characteristics?
- What are their income and education levels?
- What kinds of products and services do they buy?
- What gaps exist in the market?

These gaps may represent potential franchise opportunities. Without this market information, the potential franchisee is flying blind. Investing time in the library or on the Internet to develop a profile of the customers in the target area is essential.

Solid market research should tell a prospective franchisee whether a particular franchise is merely a passing fad. Steering clear of fads and into long-term trends is a key to sustained success in franchising. The secret to distinguishing between a fad that will soon fizzle and a meaningful trend that offers genuine opportunity is finding products or services that are consistent with fundamental demographic and lifestyle patterns of the population. That requires sound market research that focuses not only on local market opportunities but also on the "big picture." For instance, the prevalence of dual-career couples, available disposable income, and hectic schedules is creating a booming business for housecleaning, home improvement, and repair franchises.

**ENTREPRENEURIAL Profile**

*John McClurry and Fantastic Sam's*

With more than 20 years of work in the automotive sector, John McClurry knows a thing or two about the franchise game. "I was in the franchise automotive business with Midas," said McClurry, who now owns five Fantastic Sam's hair care franchises. "I wanted to get out of the automotive industry. I went with Fantastic Sam's because it does not rely on technology and is not subject to seasonal upturns and downturns." What advice would McClurry tell those considering a franchise? "My advice is to do your due diligence," he says. "Location is extremely important, as well as training your employees. . . . Staff for success. All of my employees were trained and were ready."[35]

## Consider Your Franchise Options

Tracking down information on prospective franchise systems is easier now than ever before. Franchisors publish information about their systems on the Internet, and these listings can help potential franchisees find a suitable franchise within their price ranges. Many cities host franchise trade shows throughout the year, where hundreds of franchisors gather to sell their franchises. Many business magazines such as *Entrepreneur, Inc., FSB,* and others devote at least one issue and a section of their Web sites to franchising, where they often list information on hundreds of franchises.

## Acquire a Copy of the UFDD and Study It

Once an entrepreneur identifies his or her top franchise choices, acquiring a copy of the franchise UFDD and reading it thoroughly is the next step. The UFDD is an important tool in searching for the right franchise. When evaluating a franchise opportunity, what should a potential franchisee look for? Although there's never a guarantee of success, the following characteristics make a franchise stand out:

- *A unique concept or marketing approach.* "Me-too" franchises are no more successful than "me-too" independent businesses. Pizza franchisor Papa John's has achieved an impressive growth rate by emphasizing the quality of its ingredients, whereas Domino's is known for its fast delivery.

- *Profitability.* A franchisor should have a track record of profitability and so should its franchisees. If a franchisor is not profitable, its franchisees are not likely to be either. Franchisees who follow the business format should expect to earn a reasonable rate of return.

- *A registered trademark.* Name recognition is difficult to achieve without a well-known and protected trademark.

- *A business system that works.* A franchisor should have in place a system that is efficient and is well documented in its manuals.

- *A solid training program.* One of the most valuable components of a franchise system is the training it offers franchisees. The system should be relatively easy to teach.

- *Affordability.* A franchisee should not have to take on an excessive amount of debt to purchase a franchise. Being forced to borrow too much money to open a franchise outlet can doom a business from the outset. Respectable franchisors verify prospective franchisees' financial qualifications as part of the screening process.

- *A positive relationship with franchisees.* The most successful franchises are those that see their franchisees as partners—and treat them accordingly.

The UFDD covers the 23 items discussed earlier and includes a copy of the company's franchise agreement and any contracts accompanying it. Although the law requires a UFDD to be written in plain English rather than "legalese," it is best to have an attorney with franchise experience review the UFDD. The franchise contract summarizes the details that will govern the franchisor-franchisee relationship over its life. The contract outlines exactly the rights and the obligations of each party and sets the guidelines that govern the franchise relationship. Franchise contracts typically are long term; 50 percent run for 15 years or more, which makes it extremely important for prospective franchisees to understand their terms before they sign them.

Entrepreneurs may benefit from focusing on particular items in the UFDD that describe the franchisor's experience (items 1 and 2), the current and past litigation against the franchisor (item 3), the fees and total investment (items 5, 6, and 7), and the franchisee turnover rate for the past three years (item 20). The **franchisee turnover rate**—the rate at which franchisees leave the system—is one of the most revealing items in the UFDD. A turnover rate of less than 5 percent is an indicator of a sound franchise. Higher rates raise questions, and a rate approaching 20 percent is a sign of serious underlying problems. Although virtually every franchisor has been involved in lawsuits, an excessive amount of litigation against a franchisor over a particular matter should also alert a prospective franchisee to potential problems. Determining the nature of the cases, their status, and whether this activity represents a trend is important.

## Talk to Existing Franchisees

Although the UFDD contains valuable information, it is only the starting point for researching a franchise opportunity thoroughly. Perhaps the best way to evaluate the reputation of a franchisor is to interview (in person) several franchise owners who have been in business at least one year. The entrepreneur should ask them about the positive and negative features of the agreement, and whether the franchisor delivered what it promised. Knowing what they know now, would they buy the franchise again? Item 20 of the UFDD lists all of a company's franchisees and their addresses by state, making it easy for potential franchisees to contact them.

It is also wise to interview former franchisees to get their perspectives on the franchisor-franchisee relationship. UFDD item 20 also lists those franchisees who have left the system within the past fiscal year. Understanding why they left may offer insight. Franchisees of some companies form associations, which may provide prospective franchisees with valuable information. Other sources of information include the American Association of Franchisees and Dealers (www.aafd.org), the American Franchise Association (www.franchisee.org), and the International Franchise Association (www.franchise.org).

## Ask the Franchisor Some Tough Questions

A potential franchisee should take time to visit the franchisor's headquarters and ask questions about the company and its relationship with its franchisees. Before entering a long-term relationship, the entrepreneur will benefit by knowing as much about it as possible. Questions that may offer valuable information include:

- What is the company philosophy concerning the franchisor-franchisee relationship?
- What is the company culture like?
- How much input do franchisees have into the system? Does the franchisor have a franchisee council, a group of franchisees who provide input and feedback to the franchisor?
- What are the franchisor's future expansion plans? How will they affect your franchise?
- What kind of profits can you expect? (If the franchisor made no earnings claims in item 19 of the UFDD, why not?)
- Does the franchisor have a well-formulated strategic plan?

## Make Your Choice

Prospective franchisees want to be sure that the franchise represents a solid business opportunity. The buyer should know that everything is in place to enhance their chances for a successful experience. The first lesson in getting involved in a franchise is "Do your homework before you get out your checkbook."[36]

Once a potential franchisee completes this level of due diligence, the next step is to develop a solid business plan to serve as a road map to success in the franchise he or she has selected. A business plan also is a valuable tool when searching for financing for a franchise, a topic we will discuss in Chapter 6, "Conducting a Feasibility Analysis and Crafting a Winning Business Plan."

**ENTREPRENEURIAL Profile**

*Rocco Valluzo and Microtel*

The leap from McDonald's to a Microtel Inns and Suites franchise may not seem intuitive, but it made perfect sense to Rocco Valluzo, a second generation McDonald's franchise operator. Valluzo did his homework before signing on with Microtel and US Franchise Systems, a lodging franchise that also operates Hawthorne Suites and Hyatt Hotels. "I toured properties and looked at the franchise cost and what the service fees would be," says Valluzo. The franchise was the first hotel company to receive the Fair Franchising Seal from the American Association of Franchisees & Dealers and achieved 88 percent conformance to AAFD's Fair Franchising Standards—the highest grade ever given.[37]

Table 4.3 on page 140 shows the most common mistakes that first-time franchisees make and how to avoid them.

## A Franchisee Checklist

When evaluating franchise options, the entrepreneur's goal is to know that the franchise offers high potential for success and has no major flaws. This checklist can help to determine whether a franchise represents a viable business opportunity:

1. *Responsiveness during the investigation process.* A professional and responsive reaction to your research into the franchise may be revealing. It is not a good sign if this initial phase includes frustration and delays in answering your requests for information.

2. *Direct operational training.* Make sure that the franchisor's training program addresses all of the operational areas that are essential to successfully delivering their product or service. Ask the existing franchisees about their ability to conduct business based on their training.

3. *Additional operations training.* Find out about the training the franchisor offers in other areas of running the business. Employee and payroll issues, cash management, and financial statement analysis are just a few examples of the topics that may be of value to franchisees.

4. *Marketing programs.* Review the marketing programs of the franchise system. Are they capable of attracting a sufficient base of customers? Have they been successful at creating name recognition in the marketplace for the franchise?

5. *Real estate and construction assistance.* Most franchisees have little experience in selecting a business location, yet for many franchises, this is a key to success. Determine the assistance that is available from the franchise company. Does the franchisor require the outlet to be built to certain specifications? Does the franchisor offer help with the construction process?

6. *Financing assistance.* Many franchisees must finance part of their investment in the franchise. A solid franchisor will have "paved the way" for the franchisees with standardized business plan templates or established relationships with prospective lenders.

7. *Litigation history.* Research the litigation history of the franchise. Carefully examine the franchisor's litigation history to determine clues about how the franchisor deals with conflict. A pattern of excessive litigation is a red flag for any franchise opportunity.

8. *Financial strength of the franchise company.* Examine the franchisor's financial statements, or have an accountant review them to make sure the company is financially sound and is able meet its commitments to franchisees.

9. *Financial strength of the unit operations.* Successful franchisors create the opportunity for their franchisees to generate a profit and to earn a reasonable return on their investments. Prospective franchisees should assess the average annual earnings of a typical franchisee in the first five years of operation.

10. *The attitude of existing franchisees.* Determine the attitudes of existing franchisees. Successful franchisees are satisfied with their businesses and with the franchising relationship. Find out how existing franchisees feel about their business, training and assistance programs, marketing efforts, financial results, and the relationship they have with the franchisor.

A franchise is worth consideration when it scores well on each of these indicators. When this research is complete, prospective franchisees can make an informed choice about the franchise that fits their goals and expectations. A franchise that successfully addresses these 10 indicators may in fact represent a solid franchise offering high potential.

*Source:* Adapted from Jeff Elgin, "Ten Signs of a Great Franchise," *Entrepreneur,* December 11, 2006, www.entrepreneur.com/article/printthis/171432.html.

**TABLE 4.3 Make Sure You Select the Right Franchise**

Finding the right franchise is no easy task, but the results are well worth the effort—*if* you make the right choice. First-time franchisees often make the following mistakes:

*Mistake 1.* Not knowing what they want in a franchise. Failing to define their goals increases the chance they will make the wrong choice.

*Mistake 2.* Buying a franchise they cannot afford. Franchises are expensive, and potential franchisees must know what they can afford before they begin reviewing franchises.

*Mistake 3.* Failing to ask existing and former franchisees about the franchise. This is one of the best ways to determine what the franchise experience will be.

*Mistake 4.* Failing to read the fine print. The UFDD is a valuable document for potential franchisees but only if they read it and use it to make the decision.

*Mistake 5.* Failing to get professional help. Inexperienced franchise shoppers believe that paying attorneys and accountants to help them understand the UFDD is a waste of money. Wrong!

*Mistake 6.* Buying in too early. Some new franchise operations simply have not worked the bugs out of their business systems or are not prepared to teach the system effectively.

*Mistake 7.* Falling for exaggerated earnings claims. Remember. Any earning claims franchisors make must be backed by facts.

*Mistake 8.* Neglecting to check the escape clause. Most franchise contracts include options for getting out of a franchise. Franchisees must know what they are.

Fanchisees who have made both wise and ill-advised franchise purchases offer the following advice to avoid making these common mistakes:

- Start by evaluating your own personal and business interest. What activities do you enjoy?
- Establish a budget. Know how much you can afford to spend before you ever go shopping for a franchise.
- Do your research. Study broad trends to determine which franchise concepts are likely to be most successful in the future.
- Identify potential franchise candidates. Create a profile of the most promising franchise that best fits both your interest and market trends.
- Review candidates' marketing literature and narrow your search to the top five or six.
- Get these companies' UFDDs and review them thoroughly. Get an experienced attorney to review the "fine print" in each UFDD.
- Visit existing franchisees and ask them lots of questions about the franchise system, the franchiser, and the franchisor-franchisee relationship.
- Study your local market. Use what you learned from existing franchises to determine whether the concept would be successful in the area you are considering. Don't forget to evaluate the level of competition present.
- Meet with company officials to discuss the details of buying a franchise. Look for depth and experience in the management team.
- Complete negotiations with the franchisor and close the deal.

*Source:* Adapted from Andrew A. Caffey, "Watch Your Step." *Entrepreneur B.Y.O.B.,* August 2002, p. 82; Todd D. Maddocks, "Write the Wrong," *Entrepreneur B.Y.O.B.,* January 2001, pp. 152–155; Kerry Pipes, "Franchise Lifestyles," Franchise UPDATE, www.franchise-update.com/fuadmin/article/rticleFranchiseeLifestyles5.htm.

## Franchise Contracts

7. Describe a typical franchise contract and some of its provisions.

Litigation between franchisors and franchisees is on the rise. A common source of this litigation is the interpretation of the franchise contract's terms. Most often, difficulties arise after the agreement is in operation. Because the franchisor's attorney prepares franchise contracts, the provisions favor the franchisor. Courts have relatively little statutory law and few precedents on which to base decisions in franchise disputes, resulting in minimal protection for franchisees. The problem is that the tremendous growth of franchising is faster than the growth of franchise law.

The franchise contract summarizes the details that will govern the franchisor-franchisee relationship over its life. It outlines exactly the rights and the obligations of each party and sets the guidelines that govern the franchise relationship. To protect potential franchisees from having to rush into a contract without clearly understanding it, the FTC requires that the franchisee receive the completed contract with all revisions at least five business days before it is signed. Despite such protection, one study by the FTC suggests that 40 percent of new franchisees sign contracts without reading them![38]

Every potential franchisee should have an attorney evaluate the franchise contract and review it with the investor before signing anything. Too many franchisees do not discover

**TABLE 4.4** **Advantages and Disadvantages of Buying a New versus an Established Franchise**

|  | Pros | Cons |
|---|---|---|
| New Franchise | ■ Can be new and exciting<br>■ Business concept can be fresh and different in the market<br>■ Possibility of getting lower fees as a "pioneer" of the concept<br>■ Potential for a high return on investment | ■ Business is not tested or established in the market<br>■ Unknown brand and trademark<br>■ Possibility that the concept is a fad with no staying power<br>■ Franchisor may lack the experience to deliver valuable services to franchisees |
| Established Franchise | ■ Business concept likely is well known to consumers and market for the products or services is already established.<br>■ Franchisor has experience in delivering services to franchisees<br>■ Franchisor has had time to work the "bugs" out of the business system | ■ High franchise fees and costs that often are non-negotiable<br>■ Concept may be on the wane in the market<br>■ Franchisor's brand and trademark may remind customers of an outdated concept<br>■ Franchisor's "trade dress" may be in need of updating and redesigning |

*Source:* Based on Andrew A. Caffey, "Age Issues," *Entrepreneur*, January 2002, p. 118.

unfavorable terms in their contracts until after investing in a franchise. By then, it is too late to negotiate changes. Although most large, established franchisors are not willing to negotiate the franchise contract's terms, many smaller franchises will, especially for highly qualified candidates.

Table 4.4 describes the advantages and the disadvantages of buying a new versus an established franchise.

Although franchise contracts cover everything from initial fees and continuing payments to training programs and territorial protection, three issues are responsible for most franchisor-franchisee disputes: termination of the contract, contract renewal, and transfer and buyback provisions.

### Termination

One of the most litigated subjects of a franchise agreement is the termination of the contract by either party. Most contracts prohibit termination "without just cause." However, prospective franchisees must be sure they know exactly when and under what conditions they—and the franchisor—can terminate the contract. Generally, the franchisor has the right to cancel a contract if a franchisee declares bankruptcy, fails to make required payments on time, or fails to maintain quality standards.

Terminations usually are costly to both parties. Most attorneys encourage franchisees to avoid conditions for termination or to use alternative routes to resolve disputes, such as formal complaints through franchise associations, arbitration, or ultimately selling the franchise.

### Renewal

Franchisors usually retain the right to renew or refuse to renew franchisees' contracts. If a franchisee fails to make payments on schedule or does not maintain quality standards, the franchisor has the right to refuse renewal. In some cases, the franchisor has no obligation to offer contract renewal to the franchisee when the contract expires.

When a franchisor grants renewal, the two parties must draw up a new contract. Frequently, the franchisee must pay a renewal fee and may be required to fix any deficiencies of the outlet or to modernize and upgrade it. The FTC's Trade Regulation Rule requires the franchisor to disclose these terms before any contracts are signed.

### Transfer and Buybacks

In any franchise system, franchisees will have outlets for sale. Franchisees typically are not free to sell their businesses to just anyone, however. Under most franchise contracts, franchisees cannot sell their franchises to a third party or transfer them to a relative without the franchisor's approval. In most instances, franchisors do approve a franchisee's request to sell an outlet to another person.

Most franchisors retain the right of first refusal in franchise transfers, which means the franchisee must offer to sell the franchise to the franchisor first. For example, McDonald's Corporation recently repurchased 13 restaurants under its first refusal clause from a franchisee who was ready to retire. If the franchisor refuses to buy the outlet, the franchisee may sell it to a third party who meets the franchisor's approval, applying the same standards that buyers of new franchises must meet.

## Trends in Franchising

8. Explain current trends shaping franchising.

Franchising has experienced four major growth waves since its beginning. The first wave occurred in the early 1970s when fast-food restaurants used the concept to grow rapidly. The fast-food industry was one of the first to discover the power of franchising, but other businesses soon took notice and adapted the franchising concept to their industries. The second wave took place in the United States in the mid-1980s as the U.S. economy shifted heavily toward the service sector. Franchises followed suit, springing up in every service business imaginable—from housecleaning services and copy centers to mailing services and real estate. The third wave began in the early 1990s. Characterized by new, low-cost franchises, this wave focused on specific market niches. In the wake of major corporate downsizing and the burgeoning costs of traditional franchises, these new franchises allowed would-be entrepreneurs to get into proven businesses faster and at lower costs. These companies featured start-up costs from $2,000 to $250,000 and span a variety of industries—from leak detection in homes and auto detailing to day care and tile glazing. The current wave that began in 2000 focuses on global franchising efforts. American franchise systems are expanding, and other countries are using this model for growth as well.[39]

### International Opportunities

The globalization of American franchise systems is a strong trend in franchising. Franchising is a major export industry for the United States. The globalization of American franchise networks is occurring because the markets outside the borders of the United States offer the greatest growth potential for these recognized and sought-after brands.[40] Highly competitive conditions in saturated domestic markets motivate franchisors to move into international markets to boost sales and profits. Others are taking their franchise systems abroad simply because of tremendous growth potential.

International expansion is a relatively new phenomenon in franchising, however; approximately 75 percent of franchisors established their first foreign outlet within the past

"I NO LONGER SELL LEMONADE. I'M A FRANCHISE OUTLET FOR A MULTI-NATIONAL."

10 years.[41] Canada is the primary market for U.S. franchisors, with Mexico, Japan, and Europe following. These markets are most attractive to franchisors because they are similar to the U.S. market with rising personal incomes, strong demand for consumer goods, growing service economies, and spreading urbanization. However, most franchisors recognize the difficulties of developing franchises in foreign markets and start slowly.

Franchising is in the early stages in many African countries, where more than 200 international franchises successfully operate in a market estimated at more than $300 million for food franchises alone. In Nigeria, for instance, food franchises are growing at an average annual rate of 40 percent. Franchisors entering the African market are learning to adapt their systems to reflect local culture and tastes by emulating the success of local franchises such as the Nigerian eatery, Mr. Biggs, and the Kenya-based bar and restaurant chain, Kengeles. One obstacle that international franchisors face in the African market is a lack of financing for prospective franchisees.[42]

As franchisors move into foreign markets, they learn that adaptation is one key to success. Although they keep their basic systems intact, franchises that are successful in foreign markets quickly learn how to change their concepts to adjust to local cultures and to appeal to local tastes. For instance, fast-food chains in other countries often must make adjustments to their menus to please locals' palates. Venezuelan diners prefer mayonnaise with their french fries, and in Chile, customers want avocado on their hamburgers. In Japan, McDonald's (known as "Makudonarudo") outlets sell teriyaki burgers, rice burgers, seaweed soup, vegetable croquette burgers, and katsu burgers (cheese wrapped in a roast pork cutlet topped with katsu sauce and shredded cabbage) in addition to their traditional American fare. In the Philippines, the McDonald's menu includes a spicy Filipino-style burger, spaghetti, and chicken with rice.

Other significant franchising trends include nontraditional locations, Internet franchises, conversion franchising, multiple-unit franchising, master franchising, piggybacking, and the opportunity to serve baby boomers (see Figure 4.2).

## Smaller, Nontraditional Locations

Franchisors are searching out nontraditional locations in which to build smaller, less expensive outlets as the costs of building full-scale locations escalates. Applying the principle of **intercept marketing**, franchisors position products or services directly in the path of potential customers. Franchises are placing scaled-down outlets on college campuses, in sports arenas, in hospitals, on airline flights, and in zoos. Customers are likely to find a mini-Wendy's inside a gas station, a Subway sandwich shop in a convenience store, a Dunkin' Donuts outlet in the airport, or a Maui Wowi kiosk at a sports stadium or arena. Auntie Anne's Pretzels has outlets inside some Wal-Mart stores, and the 7,000-member Brentwood Baptist Church in Houston, Texas, recently opened a McDonald's franchise in its lifelong learning center. The church co-owns the franchise with one of its members, who owns six McDonald's franchises.[43] Many franchisees have discovered that smaller outlets in these nontraditional locations generate nearly the same sales volume as full-sized outlets at just a fraction of the cost. Establishing outlets in innovative locations will be a key to continued franchise growth in the domestic market.

**FIGURE 4.2 Growing Franchise Categories**

*Source:* Sara Wilson, "In the Know," *Entrepreneur,* January 2006, pp. 88–93.

- Do-It-Yourself Meal Preparation—Converting cooking into a painless social activity.
- eBay Consignments Stores—Drop-off stores that help others sell merchandise on eBay.
- Kids' Specialty Services—Fitness, art classes, and science activities for kids.
- Fitness and Weight Loss—Resources for weight loss and fitness conscious people.
- Business Services—Ranging from tech consulting to advertising assistance for small business.
- Home Improvement—Home decorating services, furniture, and window treatment.
- Quick Service Restaurants—Continued interest in convenient access to meals on the go.

### Internet Franchises

The Internet presents an entirely new platform for franchises. Web-based franchises include a host of services such as online auction businesses, marketing consulting, child education, real estate, and technical resources. One attractive feature for tech-savvy entrepreneurs is that start-up investments for online franchises are typically more affordable than franchises requiring physical locations.

### Conversion Franchising

The trend toward **conversion franchising**, in which owners of independent businesses become franchisees to gain the advantage of name recognition, continues. One study found that 72 percent of North American franchise companies use conversion franchising in their domestic markets, and 26 percent use the strategy in foreign markets.[44] In a franchise conversion, the franchisor gets immediate entry into new markets and experienced operators; franchisees get increased visibility and often experience a significant sales boost.

### Multiple-Unit Franchising

Owning multiple franchise outlets, or **multiple-unit franchising (MUF)** became popular in the early 1990s, and this trend continues to accelerate. According to the International Franchise Association, 34 percent of franchisees own multiple outlets.[45] MUF occurs when a franchisee opens more than one unit in a territory within a specific time period. Franchising continues to attract more professional, experienced, and sophisticated entrepreneurs who have access to more capital—and who have their sights set on big goals that owning a single outlet cannot meet. Twenty-five years ago, a franchisee owning 10 or more outlets was rare; today, it is common for a single franchisee to own 50 or more outlets. The typical multiunit franchisee owns between three and six outlets, and some franchisees own many more.

**ENTREPRENEURIAL Profile**

*Shaquille O'Neal and 24 Hour Fitness and Auntie Ann's*

Professional basketball star Shaquille O'Neal is a multi-unit franchise owner. After delivering on his promise to bring the Miami Heat its first NBA championship, O'Neal opened a number of 24 Hour Fitness Shaq Sport gyms. Explaining how he became interested in the franchise, O'Neal explains, "I first fell in love with 24 Hour Fitness because, for one thing, it stays open 24 hours. I've got a lot of stuff to do during the day, so I like to go work out at night. O'Neal also recently purchased eight Auntie Ann's pretzel franchises.[46]

Multiple-unit franchising is an efficient way to expand quickly and is especially effective for franchisors targeting foreign markets, where having a local representative who knows the territory is essential. The time and cost to manage 10 franchisees each owning 12 outlets is much less than managing 120 franchisees each owning 1 outlet. MUF offers the opportunity for rapid growth without leaving the safety net of the franchise. In addition, franchisees may be able to get fast-growing companies for a bargain when franchisors offer discounts off their standard fees on multiple units.

### Master Franchising

A **master franchise** (or **subfranchise** or **area developer**) gives a franchisee the right to create a semi-independent organization in a particular territory to recruit, sell, and support other franchisees. A master franchisee buys the right to develop subfranchises within a broad geographic area or, sometimes, an entire country. Like MUF, subfranchising "turbocharges" a franchisor's growth.

Many franchisors use master franchising to open outlets in international markets because the master franchisees understand local laws and the nuances of selling in local markets. One master franchisee with TCBY International, a yogurt franchise, has 21 stores in China and Hong Kong. Based on his success in these markets, the company sold him the master franchise in India.

### Piggybacking or Combination Franchising

Some franchisors also are discovering new ways to reach customers by teaming up with other franchisors selling complementary products or services. A growing number of companies are **piggybacking** (or **co-branding**) **outlets**—combining two or more distinct franchises under one roof. This "buddy system" approach works best when the two franchise ideas are compatible and appeal to similar customers. This arrangement can lower fixed costs and increase customer traffic. At one location, a Texaco gasoline station, a Pizza Hut restaurant, and a Dunkin' Donuts—all owned by the same franchisee—work together in a piggyback arrangement to draw customers. Doughnut franchisor Dunkin' Donuts, ice cream franchisor Baskin-Robbins, and sandwich shop Togo's are working together to build hundreds of combination outlets, a concept that has proven highly successful.[47] Properly planned, piggybacked franchises can magnify many times over the sales and profits of individual, self-standing outlets.

### Serving Aging Baby Boomers

As dual-career couples have become the norm, the market for franchises offering convenience and time-saving services is booming. Customers are willing to pay for products and services that will save them time and offer convenience, and franchises are ready to provide them. Franchisees of Around Your Neck go into the homes and offices of busy male executives to sell men's apparel and accessories ranging from shirts and ties, to custom-made suits. Other franchising segments experiencing rapid growth include those targeting members of the aging U.S. baby boomer generation. An executive at a franchise consulting firm points out that "by 2010, 39 million Americans will be 65 or older; that's almost 20 percent of the population."[48] Franchises offering home delivery of meals, housecleaning and repair services, continuing education (especially computer and business training), leisure activities (crafts, hobbies, health spas, and travel-related activities), products and services aimed at home-based businesses, and health care (ranging from fitness and diet products and services to in-home elder care and medical services) will see sales grow rapidly.

## Franchising as a Growth Strategy

*9. Describe the potential of franchising a business as a growth strategy.*

Entrepreneurs with established business models can create a franchise as a growth strategy. The franchising advantage enables business owners to use other people's money to grow the venture. Franchising allows companies to grow with fewer resources and less risk. It enables expansion with minimal capital investment on the part of the franchisor. It is the franchisee, and not the franchisor, who signs the lease and commits to various service contracts. Franchisees put up the funds to start their businesses, infusing cash into the franchising organization, and generating continuous cash flow from royalty fees and other charges. Franchising can allow small companies to more effectively compete with much larger competitors. It also allows these companies to gain the advantages of highly motivated unit management while reducing overhead.[49]

**ENTREPRENEURIAL Profile**

*Mary Rogers and Computertots and Abrakadoodle*

More than 20 years ago, Mary Rogers launched Computertots, a small business that teaches young children to use computers. After expanding Computertots to 150 franchises in 11 countries, Rogers sold the company. Now Rogers is doing it again with Abrakadoodle, another business she started that offers art classes for children ages 2 to 12. Three years after selling the first franchise, Rogers and a partner now boast 70 Abrakadoodle locations around the United States—and the company continues to grow. Rogers believes that franchising is the best way for an entrepreneur with limited capital to expand beyond the start-up stage. "It's wonderful to have a business you can see replicated in multiple locations," she said. "You have people truly invested in building their own businesses."[50]

### Is the Business Model Replicable?

Entrepreneurs must first determine whether their business models can be replicated. Can potential franchisees do exactly what the original store does, regardless of location? In addition, is the owner willing to relinquish some control to these new owners? This

## Franchising the Taste of Yumm!

"Mary Anne has an amazing memory for taste," says Mark Beauchamp, her husband and business partner. "She can recall the moment when she experiences a new flavor—a particular tortellini soup in Italy or a rice treat in Japan." Mary Anne's culinary ability provided her with the momentum to open a restaurant, the Wild Rose Café & Deli. With continual culinary experimentation as a part of her existence, Mary Anne stumbled onto the creation of a type of "sauce," for lack of a better term. The sauce includes layers of ingredients from around the world—brown rice with red and black beans or jasmine rice with fresh soy beans, then topped with a variety of fresh and enticing combinations. It offers an inviting texture and an incredible flavor. Customers regularly exclaimed, "Yumm, what is this?"

Mary Anne first made the sauce for her own lunch at work, and word traveled. Employees began asking for the sauce, and then customers joined in with their requests. The word spread, and Yumm! Sauce changed the business in ways Mary Ann and Mark, then a commercial realtor, could not have imagined.

The opening of another restaurant, Café Yumm!, at a more central location was the next logical step. The entire menu featured versions of the Original Yumm! Sauce along with traditional soups and deli sandwiches. Variations on the theme include a beanless version with jasmine rice and fresh avocado; brown rice with chipotle chili; and zucchini-and-tomato stew with rice, beans, and sauce. Customers can top any of these off with cheese, tomato, avocado, sour cream, black olives, and cilantro for a satisfying, well-balanced meatless meal. Other menu options include chili or Chilean zucchini stew, flour tortilla wraps, and salads. Patrons can also purchase the Original Yumm! Sauce by the jar.

The new restaurant was immediately popular. The residents of Eugene, Oregon—a U.S. college town best known for its love for the sport of track and its organic culture—embraced the concept. Within two years, the exuberant reaction to a second restaurant validated the excitement for this newfound concept. The entrepreneurs realized they had a success story to tell about Café Yumm!

By this time, Mark had left his real estate career to join Mary Anne, who would much rather cook than manage a business. Their skills are complementary in every respect—Mary Anne is creative with an in-depth restaurant background, and Mark is a linear thinker with a business mind.

Growing pains and the logistics of making the sauce in large quantities presented problems for the couple. "With increases in demand and kitchens with only so much space, Mary Anne was just physically not able to make enough sauce to meet the needs of our customers," states Mark. He sought out a food manufacturer to produce the Original Yumm! Sauce in large volumes to meet the needs of the growing restaurants and enable them to sell Yumm! Sauce through specialty food stores, including Whole Foods. It was a natural fit.

The idea for franchising Café Yumm! was "organic" according to Mark. "We didn't intend to create a franchise; it just evolved with the business." Mark acknowledges that they were able to meet the basic needs of a franchise arrangement—to showcase profitable operations and to systematize, formulate, and transfer the philosophy and process to other people. Mark also realized that franchising Café Yumm! required them to create an entirely new kind of a business. Hiring a franchise consultant proved to be an essential resource for the Beauchamps to acquire financing and raise $1 million from investors to launch the franchise.

Today Mark is focusing on opening another restaurant that will serve as the state-of-the-art model for the franchise system. In addition, the Beauchamps have sold their first franchise, and several other prospective franchisees are interested in buying units. "We are just at the beginning stages of selling franchises and we are excited about what is ahead," says Mark. "As long as our customers continue to say 'yumm!,' we know we are on the right track."

1. How does the mind-set of the entrepreneurs change when they consider franchising their businesses?
2. What challenges will Café Yumm! face as an increasing number of franchisees join and expect to optimize the profitability of their restaurants?

*Source:* Personal contact with Mark Beauchamp, July 17, 2007.

means leaving the business's operation and reputation largely in the hands of others. "They have to be prepared to let a little bit go," said Matthew Shay, president of the International Franchise Association.[51]

### Have You Developed an Expansion Plan?

When a company makes a decision to franchise, it must develop a sound expansion plan. This plan must consider important issues confronting a new franchisor, such as the speed of growth, territorial development, support services, staffing, and fee structure. The entire plan requires rigorous financial analysis to fine-tune a solid strategy for growth.[52]

### Have You Performed the Necessary Due Diligence?

The next step involves an elaborate due diligence process—researching legal issues, trademarking their business names and symbols, creating a Web site, and writing training manuals for franchisees are just a few of the tasks that lie ahead. It requires time and attention to detail. There are numerous issues businesses must address to draft a good franchise agreement, and these decisions significantly influence the ultimate success of franchisees.

In the Entrepreneurial Spotlight

### ■ Franchising Trash

In the mind of Brian Scudamore, the recipe for success is straightforward. Take a fragmented business, add clean shiny trucks that act as mobile billboards, combine it with uniformed drivers, blend it with on-time service and up-front rates, and then mix in a culture of fun people focused on solid, healthy growth.

Brian Scudamore's story started with $700, a beat-up old pickup truck, a recent high school diploma, and a company name: 1-800-GOT-JUNK? "I wanted to build a company in which we were building something greater than any one of us could accomplish on our own. To this day, I continue to bring on the right employees to grow the company to maintain this vision of 'it's all about people,'" says Scudamore. Today, there are more than 300 franchise partners across North America as well as locations in the United Kingdom and Australia. System-wide franchise revenues exceed $106 million—not a bad return on his investment.

Scudamore is a risk-taker with focus. "The junk removal industry has traditionally been a fragmented industry full of 'man and truck operations.' I knew that by professionalizing the service, with a central call center, friendly uniformed drivers and reliable service I would be able to create a globally admired brand," says Scudamore.

The choice of franchising allows Scudamore to position the organization for rapid growth without having to turn to outside investors or other funding sources. "People pay you a fee up-front to help them grow. Rather than lose control of my vision by going public—I chose franchising. It's the ultimate growth model," states Scudamore.

Technology also plays a major role. A high-tech spin on a low-tech business allows the company to distinguish itself from its competition. Calls come into the 1-800-GOT-JUNK? call center where they do all the booking and dispatch for their franchise partners. Franchise partners then assess their real-time reports, schedules, customers, and other necessary information from JUNKNET, the corporate Intranet. This allows franchise partners to get into business quickly and focus on growth—working *on* the business versus working *in* the business.

Scudamore emphasizes environmental sustainability by recycling or reusing up to 60 percent of the junk the company collects. Thanks to Scudamore and his franchise, one man's trash can now become many people's treasures.

1. How does franchising complement Scudamore's goals?
2. What attributes add value to the success of Scudamore and his franchisees?

*Sources:* Personal contact with Lindsay Peroff, May 11, 2007; Scott Allen, "Your Guide to Entrepreneurs," About.com, http://entrepreneurs. about.com/od/casestudies/a/1800gotjunk.htm.

New franchisors must learn two new business roles: selling franchises and servicing franchisees.[53] "Franchising is like starting an entirely new business venture within the existing business structure," says Jim Thomas, former senior franchise vice president of Taco Time International. "The business now becomes a legally responsible support system with an entirely new set of responsibilities."[54]

### Do You Have Proper Legal Guidance?

Enlisting professional assistance from a franchise attorney is important. One role of the franchise attorney is to prepare the UFDD. This document is part disclosure and part franchise agreement. The UFDD helps the franchisor break down costs for equipment, marketing, and other fees. It also describes the franchisor's background and any litigation in which the company has been involved. Some 15 states require a franchisor to get state approval for the business. The initial cost for a franchisor to launch a franchise business ranges from $100,000 to $750,000.[55]

Once in motion, resources must be available to assist potential franchisees through the sales process, oversee the actual franchisee's purchase, train new owners, provide ongoing product support, conduct research and development, and meet the other ongoing needs franchisees present. Facilitating the role between the franchise and franchisees can be demanding, conflict-oriented, and unpredictable.[56] When all is in place, the franchise system has proved to be an effective, highly profitable growth model for both franchisors and franchisees.

## Conclusion

Franchising has proved its viability in the U.S. economy and has become a key part of the small business sector. It offers many would-be entrepreneurs the opportunity to own and operate a business with a greater chance for success. Despite its impressive growth rate to date, the franchising industry still has a great deal of room left to grow, especially globally. Current trends combined with international opportunities—China is one example—indicate that franchising will continue to play a vibrant role in the world business economy.

## Chapter Review

1. Explain the importance of franchising in the U.S. and global economy.
   - Through franchised businesses, consumers can buy nearly every good or service imaginable—from singing telegrams and computer training to tax services and waste-eating microbes.
   - Franchises account for more than 50 percent of all retail sales, totaling more than $1 trillion, and they employ more than 8 million people in more than 100 major industries.
2. Define the concept of franchising.
   - Franchising is a method of doing business involving a continuous relationship between a franchisor and a franchisee. The franchisor retains control of the distribution system, whereas the franchisee assumes all of the normal daily operating functions of the business.
3. Describe the different types of franchises.
   - There are three types of franchising: trade name franchising, where the franchisee purchases only the right to use a brand name; product distribution franchising, which involves a license to sell specific products under a brand name; and pure franchising, which provides a franchisee with a complete business system.
4. Describe the benefits and limitations of buying a franchise.
   - The franchisor has the benefits of expanding his or her business on limited capital and growing without developing key managers internally. The franchisee also receives many key benefits: management training and counseling;

customer appeal of a brand name; standardized quality of goods and services, national advertising programs, financial assistance, proven products and business formats, centralized buying power, territorial protection, and a greater chance for success.

- Potential franchisees should be aware of the disadvantages involved in buying a franchise: franchise fees and profit sharing, strict adherence to standardized operations, restrictions on purchasing, limited product lines, possible ineffective training programs, and less freedom.

5. Describe the legal aspects of franchising, including the protection offered by the FTC's Trade Regulation Rule.

- The FTC's Trade Regulation Rule is designed to help the franchisee evaluate a franchising package. It requires each franchisor to disclose information in a document covering 23 topics at least 10 days before accepting payment from a potential franchisee. This document, the Uniform Franchise Disclosure Document (UFDD), is a valuable source of information for anyone considering investing in a specific franchise.

6. Explain the right way to buy a franchise.

- To buy a franchise the right way requires that you evaluate yourself, research your market, consider your franchise options, get a copy of the franchisor's UFDD and study it, talk to existing franchisees, ask the franchisor some tough questions, and make your choice.

7. Describe a typical franchise contract and some of its provisions.

- The franchise contract summarizes the details that will govern the franchisor-franchisee relationship over its life. The contract outlines the rights and the obligations of each party and sets the guidelines that govern the franchise relationship. Although franchise contracts cover everything from initial fees and continuing payments to training programs and territorial protection, three issues are responsible for most franchisor-franchisee disputes: termination of the contract, contract renewal, and transfer and buyback provisions.

  *Termination.* Franchisees must know when and under what conditions they—and the franchisor—can terminate the contract. Generally, the franchisor has the right to cancel a contract if a franchisee declares bankruptcy, fails to make required payments on time, or fails to maintain quality standards.

  *Renewal.* Franchisors usually retain the right to renew or refuse to renew franchisees' contracts. If a franchisee fails to make payments on schedule or does not maintain quality standards, the franchisor has the right to refuse renewal. In some cases, the franchisor has no obligation to offer contract renewal to the franchisee when the contract expires.

  *Transfer and Buybacks.* Under most franchise contracts, franchisees cannot sell their franchises to a third party or will it to a relative without the franchisor's approval. In most instances, franchisors approve a franchisee's request to sell an outlet to another person. Most franchisors retain the right of first refusal in franchise transfers, which means the franchisee must offer to sell the franchise to the franchisor first.

8. Explain current trends shaping franchising.

- Trends influencing franchising include: international opportunities, the emergence of smaller, nontraditional locations, conversion franchising, multiple unit franchising (MUF), master franchising, piggyback franchising (or co-branding), and products and services targeting aging baby boomers.

9. Explain the advantages and challenges franchising offers a business as a growth strategy.

- Franchising a business can be an effective method to grow a business using the investments of the franchisees. It does involve a highly litigious and regulated process that demands specialized legal professionals and imposes an entirely new set of administrative demands on the business to establish and administer this complex system.

## Discussion Questions

1. What is franchising?
2. Describe the three types of franchising and provide an example of each.
3. How does franchising benefit the franchisor?
4. Discuss the advantages and the disadvantages of franchising for the franchisee.
5. How beneficial to franchisees is a quality training program? What types of entrepreneurs may benefit most from this training?
6. Compare the failure rates for franchises with those of independent businesses. What are some of the reasons for this difference?
7. Why might an independent entrepreneur be dissatisfied with a franchising arrangement?
8. What are the clues in detecting an unreliable franchisor?
9. Should a prospective franchisee investigate before investing in a franchise? If so, how and in what areas?
10. What is the function of the FTC's Trade Regulation Rule? What function does the UFDD perform?
11. Outline the rights the Trade Regulation Rule gives all prospective franchisees.
12. What is the source of most franchisor-franchisee litigation? Whom does the standard franchise contract favor?
13. Describe the current trends affecting franchising within the United States and internationally.
14. One franchisee says, "Franchising is helpful because it gives you somebody (the franchisor) to get you going, nurture you, and shove you along a little. However, the franchisor won't make you successful. That depends on what you bring to the business, how hard you are prepared to work, and how committed you are to finding the right franchise for you." Do you agree? Explain your response.
15. Why might an entrepreneur consider franchising as an attractive growth strategy?
16. How might an entrepreneur prepare when considering franchising as a viable alternative?

## Business Plan Pro

Most franchisors require a business plan as a part of the application process. In many cases, the franchisor will specify the elements that the business plan should include and may provide a business plan outline unique to the franchise. Determine the expectations regarding the content and structure of the business plan. Does the franchisor have a business plan outline or a sample plan available for review?

## On the Web

Go to the Companion Website www.prenhall.com/scarborough and click on the Chapter 4 tab. Review the online franchise resources that are available. One of those links is to "The World Franchise Directory." Click on that link and enter the first letter of a familiar franchise, the letter "S" for example. The number of franchise systems, many of them with an international presence, is staggering. Now, click on the sample plan tab and review the sample franchise plan in this section of Business Plan Pro. What unique characteristic do you notice about this business plan compared to others you have seen?

Select a franchise. Visit their corporate Web site and begin the process to request franchise information. Note specific questions regarding sources of capital. Access to capital will be a major qualification in determining whether an applicant is "franchise worthy."

## In the Software

To meet the needs of a specific franchise business plan, modify the outline in Business Plan Pro to match the franchisor's recommendation. First, view the outline in the left-hand navigation window and click on the "Plan Outline" icon, or go to the "View" menu and click on "Outline." Then, right-click on each of those topics that you need to change, move, or delete to meet the franchisors's requirements. Move topics up or down the outline with the corresponding arrows to place them in the correct sequence. To change topics from headings to subheadings, "Demote" the topic. Using the "Promote" option moves a subheading left to a more dominant position.

## Building Your Business Plan

Continue developing the franchise business plan based on that outline. Use the information and verbiage that is familiar to the franchise system whenever possible. This plan may be one of dozens received that week, and demonstrating knowledge, competence, and credibility is important. The franchise business plan can be a sales tool to position the applicant as an informed and attractive prospective franchise owner.

# Buying an Existing Business

Although our intellect always longs for clarity and certainty, our nature often finds uncertainty fascinating.

—Karl von Clausewitz

A pessimist sees the difficulty in every opportunity; an optimist sees the opportunity in every difficulty.

—Winston Churchill

## Learning Objectives

**Upon completion of this chapter, you will be able to:**

1 Understand the advantages and disadvantages of buying an existing business.

2 Define the steps involved in the *right* way to buy a business.

3 Describe the various methods used in the valuation of a business.

4 Discuss the process of negotiating the deal.

T he entrepreneurial experience involves risk. One way to minimize that risk is to purchase an existing business rather than create a new venture. Buying an existing business requires a great deal of analysis and evaluation to ensure that what the entrepreneur is purchasing meets his or her needs and expectations. It is important to exercise patience and invest time to conduct research before buying a business. Investing time in the evaluation process may help the entrepreneur avoid a business failure. Research shows that the average acquisition takes 19 months from the start of the search to the closing of the deal.[1] In too many cases, the excitement of making a "fast entry" into the market causes entrepreneurs to rush and make unnecessary mistakes in judgment.

Before signing a contract, it is critical that the entrepreneur learn everything that he or she can about the business and the market. According to Russell Brown, author of *Strategies for Successfully Buying or Selling a Business,* "You have access to the company's earnings history, which gives you a good idea of what the business will make, and an existing business has a proven track record; most established organizations tend to stay in business and keep making money."[2] If vital information, such as audited financial statements and legal clearances are not available, the entrepreneur must be especially diligent to acquire this background information.

The wise entrepreneur will conduct thorough research before negotiating a purchase price. As a starting point, the entrepreneur should consider the following questions:

- Is this type of business desirable?
- Will this business offer an attractive lifestyle?
- What are the critical factors that must exist for this business to be successful?
- Is this the best market and the best location for this business?
- What are negative aspects of this business?
- Are there any skeletons in the company closet?
- Do you have the experience required to operate this type of business? If not, will the current owner be willing to assist with the transition?
- Will the business or its operating procedures require changes to be successful, and, if so, at what expense?
- Does the present facility meet all state and federal accessibility guidelines, and if not, what will it take to bring the facility up to code?
- If the business is profitable, why does the current owner(s) want to sell? Does the reason given for selling the business make sense? If not, can you verify the reason given?
- If the business is currently in a decline, do you have a plan to return the business to a position of profitability?
- Are there other similar businesses currently for sale or that have sold recently to use as comparisons to determine what a "fair market price" should be?

These basic questions require the entrepreneur to examine whether the business will meet his or her expectations and whether he or she has the ability to operate the business successfully. It is one thing to watch others manage a business successfully and another to do it yourself.

## Buying an Existing Business

### Advantages of Buying an Existing Business

*1-A.* Understand the advantages of buying an existing business.

Buying an existing business may offer business "certainties" that do not exist when launching a new venture. The following are some of the most common advantages of purchasing an existing business.

**SUCCESSFUL BUSINESSES MAY CONTINUE TO BE SUCCESSFUL.** A business with a profitable history suggests the existence of a solid customer base and successful relationships with vendors and suppliers. A competent owner is a master of the day-to-day operations of the business and can help a buyer to make a smooth transition into business ownership. When things are going well, it is important to make changes slowly and retain the relationships with customers, suppliers, and staff that make the business a success. This attribute often accompanies the second advantage—using the experience of the previous owner.

**LEVERAGING THE EXPERIENCE OF THE PREVIOUS OWNER.** Most successful owners want the new owner to succeed. In cases in which a business has a history of success, the new owner may negotiate with the current owner to stay on in a consulting capacity for a period of time. During this transition, the current owner can introduce the new owner to customers or clients and vendors or suppliers. The owner also can train the incoming entrepreneur on the company's policies and procedures. The previous owner also can be helpful in unmasking the unwritten rules of business—whom to trust, expected business behavior, and other critical intangibles. Hiring the previous owner as a consultant for the first few months can be a valuable investment. If this option is not possible, the entrepreneur should at least review the key financial records with the owner to establish an understanding of the relationships between expenses and revenues. Learning from the previous owner's experience is extremely valuable.

**THE TURNKEY BUSINESS.** Buying an existing business can be one of the fastest pathways to entrepreneurship. When things go smoothly, purchasing an existing business saves time and energy. The buyer gets a business that is already generating cash, and sometimes profits. The day the entrepreneur takes over the business is the day revenues begin. Tom Gillis, an experienced business owner, entrepreneur, lawyer, accountant, and management consultant, says, "Acquisition of an established company becomes attractive in three situations: when you haven't found 'the idea' that really turns you on and you find it in an existing business; when you have more money than you have time to start a business from scratch; and when you want to grow but lack a compatible product, service, location or particular advantage that is available from an owner who wants out." According to Gillis, the critical question is: "What do I gain by acquiring this business that I would not be able to achieve on my own?"[3]

**SUPERIOR LOCATION.** When the location of the business is critical to its success, it may be wise to purchase a business that is already in the right location. In fact, the existing business's greatest asset may be its location. A location that provides a significant competitive advantage may cause an entrepreneur to decide to buy instead of build. Opening in a second-choice location and hoping to draw customers may prove fruitless. If purchasing the property is not a part of the transaction, entrepreneurs must investigate the terms of the lease or rental agreement and the relationship with the property owner.

**EMPLOYEES AND SUPPLIERS IN PLACE.** Experienced employees who choose to continue to work for the company can help the new owner learn the business. In addition, an existing business has relationships with suppliers and a history of business transactions. Vendors can continue to work with the business while the new owner assesses the products and services of other vendors. This allows the new owner to take time to evaluate alternative suppliers.

**INSTALLED EQUIPMENT WITH KNOWN PRODUCTION CAPACITY.** Acquiring and installing new equipment exerts a tremendous strain and uncertainty on a fledgling company's financial resources. A potential buyer of an existing business can determine the condition of the plant and equipment, its capacity, its remaining life, and its value before buying the business. The new owner has the option to use the existing production method or to improve it. In many cases, the entrepreneur can purchase the existing physical facilities and equipment at prices significantly below replacement costs. For some businesses, the purchase of these assets may be the best value of the entire arrangement.

**INVENTORY IN PLACE.** The proper mix and quantity of inventory is essential to cost control and sales volume. A business with too little inventory imposes limitations on its ability to satisfy customer demand. Too much inventory ties up excessive capital, increases costs, reduces profitability, and increases the danger of cash flow problems. Many successful business owners understand the balance between these two extremes. This may be highly valuable knowledge for buyers of businesses that experience seasonal fluctuations or that must meet the erratic needs of high-volume customers.

**ESTABLISHED TRADE CREDIT.** Previous owners also have trade credit relationships that may be advantageous to the new owner. The business's proven track record gives the new owner leverage when negotiating favorable trade credit terms. No supplier wants to lose a good customer.

**EASIER ACCESS TO FINANCING.** Investors and bankers often perceive the risk of buying an existing business with a solid history of performance to be lower than that of an unknown start-up. This may make it easier for the new owner to secure financing. A buyer can point to the existing company's track record and to the plans for improving the business to convince potential lenders to finance the purchase. Many lenders will fund 50 percent to 75 percent of the acquisition cost for businesses depending on a number of factors, including cash flow, assets, and available security.[4] In addition, in many buy-sell agreements, the buyer uses a "built-in" source of financing, the seller.

**HIGH VALUE.** Some existing businesses may be real bargains. If the current owners want to sell quickly, they may undervalue the business and sell for a price below its actual worth. Any special skills or training required to operate the business limit the number of potential buyers; therefore, the more specialized the business is, the greater is the likelihood that a buyer will find a bargain. If the owner wants a substantial down payment or the entire selling price in cash, there may be few qualified buyers. Those who do qualify may be able to negotiate a good deal.

Bill Broocke, founder of The Success Connection Inc. and an authority on buying and selling small businesses, says, "[Existing businesses] with a record of growth, trained employees, a good customer base, proper equipment, and an established inventory, are excellent business opportunities. In fact, the failure rates of businesses that have been around for at least five years are quite low."[5]

## Gaining a Competitive Edge

### Ten Tips for Buying a Business

An entrepreneur may find that buying an existing business is overwhelming. Following these 10 tips may make this transaction more manageable and, ultimately, more profitable for the new owner.

1. *Buy the assets, not the business.* If the acquisition target is a corporation or LLC, a buyer should not purchase the company's stock. Instead, he or she should offer to buy the assets of the business and form a separate company to act as the purchaser. There are two reasons this may be advantageous. First, the buyer will experience a better tax situation; the tax basis of the assets will be the amount the buyer actually paid for them rather than the amount the seller paid for them long ago. Second, if the seller owes money or is being sued, the buyer will not assume any of those liabilities.

2. *Ask about sales taxes and payroll taxes.* In many states, the tax authority may hold the buyer responsible if the seller owes sales taxes, use taxes, payroll taxes, and other business taxes. If the seller has employees, the buyer should make certain tax payments are current. The seller also should ask the state tax authority to issue a clearance letter that states that the seller is current in payment of the company's sales and use taxes on the closing date.

3. *Determine who will deal with accounts receivable.* Some customers may owe the seller

money on the closing date. Who will be responsible for collecting these debts? There are two ways to handle this: The buyer can purchase the accounts receivable at closing (for a discount, to reflect the fact that some of these may not be paid), or the seller can collect them.

4. *Explore assuming the seller's lease.* If the seller leases the business premises, the buyer needs to know the schedule of the lease term and whether the lease is assumable by the new owner. If the lease has less than two years remaining, for example, the buyer may want to negotiate a new lease with a 5- to 10-year term. In addition, the buyer should find out whether the landlord is holding a security deposit (usually two months' rent, but sometimes more). The seller will probably want the buyer to purchase the security deposit in addition to the agreed-on purchase price for the business assets. If the seller includes the security deposit in the purchase price, that should be in writing.

5. *Ask if there are any prepaid expenses.* The buyer should ask the seller for a list of "closing adjustments" that delineate the amounts the seller has prepaid so that they can be "pro rated." This will avoid nasty surprises at closing.

6. *Negotiate a "letter of intent."* Also called a "term sheet," a letter of intent (LOI) is an agreement between the buyer and the seller that spells out the important terms and conditions of the sale. For example, it may include the purchase price, how and when the purchase price will be paid, the assets that will be sold to the buyer (and those the seller will keep for his or her own use), and the terms of the seller's noncompete agreement. Although LOIs are not legally binding, it is worth the time and effort to address these issues in an LOI before the lawyers begin drafting the "definitive" legal contracts to document the sale. Without an LOI, the buyer may end up negotiating the business deal and the "legalese" of the definitive documents at the same time, requiring additional drafts of the sale documents and additional legal fees.

7. *Watch out for bulk sales laws.* Many states still require the buyer of a business to notify the seller's creditors that the transaction is taking place. Failure to get a list of the seller's creditors and to send "notices of sale" to them may give the seller's creditors a shot at undoing (or "rescinding") the transaction to prevent the seller's assets from being sold out from under them. Even if the seller has no creditors, the state tax authority may want a copy of the "bulk sales notice" to determine whether the seller owes any sales, use, or other business taxes. If the seller does owe taxes, he or she will have to pay them before closing.

8. *Get an indemnity from the seller.* The buyer should get an indemnity from the seller, promising to defend against any lawsuits and pay all judgments and fees from events that occurred *before* the sale. Likewise, the buyer should be prepared to give the seller an indemnity if sued because of something the buyer may do—or fail to do—*after* the closing takes place.

9. *Make sure the seller is available.* In many retail and service businesses, customers have a personal as well as business relationship with the owner. Be sure the seller is accessible after the closing to introduce customers, help figure out the books, and ensure a smooth and orderly transition of the business. The buyer may choose to compensate the seller for this time to create an incentive to assist.

10. *Get to know the employees.* Identify the key employees who are willing to stay. Take time to get to know them. These employees are often the ones who interact with customers, are most familiar with day-to-day operations, and know "where the bodies are buried."

*Source:* Cliffe Ennico, "10 Things to Look Out for When Buying a Business," Entrepreneur.com, November 23, 2005, www.entrepreneur.com/startingabusiness/selfassessment/whattypeof businessshouldyoustart/article81176.html.

## Disadvantages of Buying an Existing Business

Buying an existing business does have disadvantages that are important to consider.

*1-B.* Understand the disadvantages of buying an existing business.

**CASH REQUIREMENTS.** One of the most significant challenges to buying a business is acquiring the necessary funds for the initial purchase price. [Because] the business concept, customer base, brands, and other fundamental work have already been done, the financial costs of acquiring an existing business are usually greater then starting one.[6]

**THE BUSINESS IS LOSING MONEY.**    A business may be for sale because it is no longer—nor has it ever been—profitable. The seller of the business may not be honest about its lack of profitability. Owners can use various creative accounting techniques that make the company's financial picture appear much more positive than it actually is. The maxim "let the buyer beware" is sound advice in the purchase of a business. A buyer who fails to conduct a thorough analysis of the business may pay dearly for a foundering business.

Although buying a money-losing business is risky, it is not necessarily taboo. If the business analysis indicates that the company is struggling from poor management, suffering from neglect, or overlooking a prime opportunity, a new owner may be able to turn it around. However, buying a struggling business without a well-defined plan for solving the problems it faces is an invitation to disaster.

An evaluation of a business's profitability may include these potential problems:

- Excessive inventory levels
- Unnecessary personnel expenditures
- Overcompensation to the owners
- Inadequate collection efforts
- Recent rent or lease increases that are unaffordable
- Maintenance costs or service contracts that are too expensive
- Too many locations for the business to support
- Inefficient equipment
- New competitors that are reducing sales volumes
- New pricing structures that are reducing margins to unacceptable levels
- Low margins due to cost of goods increases or transportation
- Theft or other losses

If problems exist, the potential buyer can explore their source through an in-depth analysis of financial statements and additional research.[7] The primary objective is to determine whether the problems represent an opportunity or a warning to avoid buying a troubled business. Chapter 6, "Conducting a Feasibility Analysis and Crafting a Winning Business Plan," discusses the tasks of conducting a feasibility analysis and writing a business plan and addresses turnaround business opportunities.

# ENTREPRENEURSHIP
## In Action

### A Vintage Deal

Never underestimate the dreams of a couple of seven-year-olds. When they were elementary school classmates, Megan Knode and Shannon Ritchie wanted to own a restaurant. "We share the love of cooking," says Ritchie. "It was actually in second grade, and we said that when we grew up, we should start a restaurant." Knode and Ritchie are all grown up now.

Their dream started small. They reconnected shortly after Ritchie graduated from the Western Culinary Institute and Knode completed her bachelor's degree. They purchased a food trailer and named it "Pita Planet." Through this mobile venue, Knode and Ritchie offered a variety of pita sandwiches at fairs and other events. At the end of the festival season, the business partners sought a more permanent arrangement.

The entrepreneurs soon discovered a restaurant for sale in a vintage house from 1873. They quickly fell in love with the building, but not with the existing business. The restaurant had lost more than $50,000 in the previous year alone. The current owner wanted out—to literally walk away from the restaurant "as is." The two entrepreneurs took an objective look at the opportunity. The location and building were perfect, and everything for the restaurant was in place. Knode and Ritchie

Shannon Ritchie, left, and friend Megan Knode realized their childhood dream of opening a restaurant together when they opened Vintage Restaurant in 2006.

believed they could bring something more to the business. At the right selling price, the charming old house with the unsuccessful restaurant was ideal. Making an offer to purchase the building and the assets of the struggling restaurant made sense.

Knode and Ritchie did their homework. They researched the market value of the property, the building, and the assets and made an offer. With the advice of their accountant, they decided to make two separate purchases. They established a corporation to purchase the building and an LLC to purchase the assets of the restaurant. Knode and Ritchie also decided to own both entities equally.

The existing owner accepted Knode and Ritchie's offer, and they proceeded to raise the capital they needed to complete the deal. Knode and Ritchie met with a

bank loan officer who advised them to write a business plan. The next week, they returned with their plan and made a successful pitch to the bank. The sale of both the building and the restaurant's assets closed within the month, and Knode and Ritchie's dream of owning a restaurant became a reality.

Following the closing, the pair of entrepreneurs appropriately renamed the establishment "The Vintage" and began building the menu and remodeling the structure. "We've been collecting recipes for a long time, so we've brought them all together," Ritchie says. The Vintage's menu includes a variety of tapas and appetizer dishes along with dinner entrees, such as drunken clams and linguini and pizza pot pie. The house specialties are cheese and chocolate fondues and sweet and savory crepes. "We did a lot of crepe parties before opening to see which ones were popular," says Ritchie.

Knode and Ritchie anticipated that their restaurant would lose money for a period of time as they build their clientele. Fortunately, it didn't work out that way. The business was profitable in the first month, and they continue to operate in the black.

The dream of their restaurant was much like the vision of the two little girls. After a year in business, Knode and Ritchie look ahead and talk about what the next step is: keep the restaurant as is, expand, or sell. As they contemplate the future, neither has regrets about buying a failing business.

1. What questions should entrepreneurs ask before purchasing a building and a business?
2. What were the key advantages and risks of Knode and Ritchie's purchase?

*Sources:* Personal contact with Megan Knode and Shannon Ritchie, July 6, 2007; Joe Mosley, "Vintage Menu, Varied Menu," *Eugene Register Guard*, February 24, 2006, p. C-1.

**PAYING FOR ILL WILL.**    Just as proper business dealings can create goodwill, improper business behavior or unethical practices can create ill will. A business may look attractive on the surface, but customers, suppliers, creditors, or employees may have negative feelings about it. Too many business buyers discover—after the sale—that the purchase includes undisclosed credit problems, poor supplier relationships, soon-to-expire leases, pending lawsuits, building code violations, and other problems. Vital business relationships may have begun to deteriorate, but their long-term effects may not yet be reflected in the business's financial statements. Ill will can permeate a business for years. The only way to avoid these problems is to investigate a prospective purchase target thoroughly *before* moving forward in the negotiation process.

**CURRENT EMPLOYEES ARE UNSUITABLE.**    If the new owner plans to make changes in a business, the present employees may not suit future needs. Some workers may have a difficult time adapting to the new owner's management style and vision for the company. Marginal employees may be friends with the previous managers, or there may be other reasons they were not let go. The new owner, therefore, may have to make unpopular termination decisions. For this reason, employees may feel threatened by new ownership. In some cases, employees who want to buy the business themselves, but were unable to do so, may be resentful. They may see the new owner as the person who is "stealing" their opportunity. Bitter employees are not likely to be productive workers and may have difficulty fitting into the new management structure.

**LOCATION HAS BECOME UNSATISFACTORY.**   What was once an ideal location may have become obsolete as market and demographic trends change. The addition of large shopping malls, new competitors or traffic pattern changes can spell disaster, especially for a retail shop. Prospective buyers should always evaluate the current market in the area surrounding an existing business and its potential for future growth and expansion. Researching zoning, traffic, and land development plans with applicable jurisdictions such as the city, county, or state can avoid unpleasant surprises.

*Joe Rubinstein and Norwalk Furniture Store*

Joe Rubinstein knew that the ideal location for his Norwalk Furniture Store would offer high visibility and easy customer access. After researching the local real estate market, he selected the top location in a high-traffic commercial area serving an attractive demographic customer base. Rubinstein invested in a dramatic remodeling project, and sales were strong from the moment the store opened. After only a few years in operation, however, the government notified Rubinstein of a traffic change. Because of its proximity to a nearby freeway, the agency changed the classification of the street providing access to his parking lot to an "onramp." Rubinstein contested the decision, but the ruling stood. The government blocked the entrance with permanent curbing, forcing customers to access the store via an adjacent street through a maze of parking lots. The change severely reduced customer activity, sales, and profits, which forced Joe to close the once desirable location.[8]

**OBSOLETE OR INEFFICIENT EQUIPMENT AND FACILITIES.**   Potential buyers may neglect to have an expert evaluate a company's building and equipment before they purchase it. They may discover too late that the equipment is obsolete and inefficient, pushing operating expenses to excessively high levels. Modernizing equipment and facilities is often expensive. If the buyer is not trained and confident, employing experts to provide an objective assessment of the equipment and facilities is essential.

**CHANGE AND INNOVATION CHALLENGES.**   It is easier to plan for change than it is to implement it. The methods and procedures of the previous owner may have set precedents that can be difficult or awkward for a new owner to change. For example, if the previous owner grants volume-based discounts to customers, it may be difficult to eliminate that discount without losing some of those customers. The previous owner's policies—even those that are unwise—can influence the changes the new owner can make. Implementing changes to reverse a downward sales trend in a turnaround situation can be just as difficult as eliminating unprofitable procedures. Convincing alienated customers to return can be an expensive and laborious process that may take years.

**OBSOLETE INVENTORY.**   Inventory has value only when it is salable. Too many potential owners make the mistake of trusting a company's balance sheet to provide them with the value of its inventory. The inventory value reported on a company's balance sheet is seldom an accurate reflection of its real market value. A company's balance sheet may reflect the value of the inventory at the time of purchase, but the inventory probably has depreciated since that time. The value on the balance sheet reflects the original cost of the inventory, not its actual market value. In fact, inventory and other assets reported to have value may be absolutely worthless because they are outdated and obsolete. It is the

## TABLE 5.1 Valuing Accounts Receivable

A prospective buyer asked the current owner of a business about the value of her accounts receivable. The owner's business records showed $101,000 in receivables. However, when the prospective buyer aged them and then multiplied the resulting totals by his estimated probabilites of collection, he discovered their *real* value.

| Age of Accounts (days) | Amount | Probability of Collection | Value (Amount × Probability of Collection) |
|---|---|---|---|
| 0–30 | $40,000 | .95 | $38,000 |
| 31–60 | $25,000 | .88 | $22,000 |
| 61–90 | $14,000 | .70 | $ 9,800 |
| 91–120 | $10,000 | .40 | $ 4,000 |
| 121–150 | $ 7,000 | .25 | $ 1,750 |
| 151+ | $ 5,000 | .10 | $  500 |
| Total | $101,000 | | $76,050 |

Had he blindly accepted the "book value" of these accounts receivable, this prospective buyer would have overpaid by nearly $25,000 for them!

buyer's responsibility to assess the real value of the assets before negotiating a purchase price for the business.

**THE VALUE OF ACCOUNTS RECEIVABLE.**   Like inventory, accounts receivable are rarely worth their face value. The older the receivables are, the less likely they are to be collected and, consequently, the lower their actual value. Therefore, the prospective buyer should age the accounts receivable to determine the probability of collecting the outstanding receivables. Table 5.1 shows a simple but effective method of evaluating accounts receivable once the buyer ages them.

**THE BUSINESS MAY BE OVERPRICED.**   The purchase of most businesses is based on the purchase of the company's assets rather than the purchase of its stock. A buyer must be sure which assets are a part of the transaction and determine their real value. Many people purchase businesses at prices far in excess of their true value. A buyer who correctly values a business's accounts receivable, inventories, and other assets will be in a good position to negotiate a price that will allow the business to be profitable.

## The *Right* Way to Buy a Business

*2.* Define the steps involved in the *right* way to buy a busniess.

Purchasing an existing business can be a time-consuming process that requires a great deal of time and effort. Repeated studies report that more than half of all business acquisitions fail to meet the buyer's expectations. This statistic alone should provide a warning about the need to conduct a systematic and thorough analysis prior to negotiating any deal. The process for entrepreneurs who are considering buying a business includes the following seven steps:

1.   Conduct a self-inventory, objectively analyzing skills, abilities, and personal interests to determine the type(s) of business that offers the best fit.
2.   Develop a list of the criteria that define the "ideal business."
3.   Seek the help of others in developing a list of potential candidates for acquisitions that meet your criteria.
4.   Thoroughly investigate the potential acquisition targets that meet these criteria. This *due diligence process* involves practical steps, such as analyzing financial statements and making certain that the facilities are structurally sound. The goal is to minimize pitfalls and problems that may arise.
5.   After selecting the most acceptable candidate, begin the negotiation process with the existing owner.
6.   Explore various financing options that are beneficial to creating a profitable business.
7.   Once the deal is completed, be careful to ensure a smooth transition of ownership.

We will now address these important steps in detail.

### Self-Analysis of Skills, Abilities, and Interests

The first step in buying a business is conducting a "self-audit" to determine the ideal business. Consider, for example, how the following questions produce valuable insights into the best type of business for an entrepreneur. These answers will provide an important personal guide that might help avoid a costly mistake.

- What business activities do you enjoy most? What activities do you enjoy the least?
- Which industries interest you most? Which interest you the least?
- What kind of business do you want to buy?
- What kinds of businesses do you want to *avoid?*
- In what geographic area do you want to live and work?
- What do you expect to get out of the business?
- How much can you put into the business—in both time and money?
- What business skills and experience do you have? Which ones do you lack?
- How easily can you transfer your existing skills and experience to other types of businesses? In what kinds of businesses would that transfer be easiest?
- How much risk are you willing to take?
- What size company do you want to buy?

Answering these and other questions *beforehand* allows you to develop a list of criteria that a company must meet before it should be a purchase candidate.

### Develop a List of Criteria

Based on the answers to the self-inventory questions, the next step is to develop a list of criteria that a potential business acquisition must meet. The goal is to identify the characteristics of the "ideal business." Investigating every business for sale is a waste of time. Addressing these issues early in the search will save a great deal of time and trouble as the entrepreneur wades through a multitude of business opportunities. The evaluation process will apply the specific parameters of these criteria against potential acquisition candidates.

### Prepare a List of Potential Candidates

Once an entrepreneur knows the criteria and parameters for the ideal candidate, the search begins. One technique is to start at the macro level and work down. Draw on the resources from the Internet and the local library, such as government publications, industry trade associations, and reports, to discover which industries are growing fastest and offer the greatest potential in the future. For entrepreneurs without a clear idea of what they are looking for, another effective approach is to begin searching in an industry in which they have experience or knowledge.

Typical sources for identifying potential acquisition candidates include the following:

- The Internet, where several sites include listings of business brokers and companies for sale
- Business brokers
- Bankers
- Accountants
- Investment bankers
- Trade associations
- Industry contacts: suppliers, distributors, customers, and others
- Contact with the owners of desirable businesses (even if they're not advertised as being "for sale")
- Newspaper and trade journal listings of businesses for sale (e.g., the Business Opportunities section of the *Wall Street Journal*)
- "Networking" through social and business contact with friends and relatives

Buyers should consider all businesses that meet their criteria—even those that may not be for sale. For the right price, most businesses *are* for sale. In fact, the hidden market of unadvertised companies that might be for sale is one of the richest sources of top-quality businesses. Getting the word out that a buyer has interest in a specific type of business may lead to discovering opportunities that the entrepreneur must negotiate in complete confidence. The existing owners may not want anyone to know that they are considering selling the business.

*Randy Hoyle and Niche Equipment*

"For a long time I had thought about owning my own business, where I could make my own decisions," Randy Hoyle says. When Hoyle's employer notified him that he would be moving again, "I saw this as my chance." Rather than start a venture, "I wanted to have income faster than a startup would entail, so I focused on finding an ongoing business that also had a good upside." A key step in finding the right company is expanding the search beyond companies officially for sale. "None of the companies that we contacted was for sale," says Hoyle. "We got a listing of businesses for which my background could be a good fit, and we sent letters to those businesses to find out what interest they had in selling. We mailed 600 letters, narrowed it down to 20 to 25 that we actually visited, and then to three that were final candidates for which we did serious due diligence." The search, which took about nine months of full-time effort, ultimately led to Hoyle's purchase of Niche Equipment, a wholesale distributor of office equipment with six employees and more than $1 million in annual revenues.[9]

## The Due Diligence Process

Due diligence involves studying, reviewing, and verifying all of the relevant information concerning the top acquisition candidates. The due diligence process investigates the most attractive business candidates in greater detail. The goal of the due diligence process is to discover exactly what the buyer is purchasing and avoid any unpleasant surprises *after* the deal closes. Exploring a company's character and condition through the Better Business Bureau, credit-reporting agencies, the company's bank, its vendors and suppliers, accountants, attorneys, and other resources is a vital part of making certain the entrepreneur is going to get a good deal on a business with the capacity to succeed. It is important to invest in the due diligence process—the entrepreneur may choose to pay now or pay later.[10]

A thorough analysis of a potential acquisition candidate usually requires an entrepreneur to assemble a team of advisers. Finding a suitable business, structuring a deal, and negotiating the final bargain involves many complex legal, financial, tax, and business issues, and good advice is valuable. Many entrepreneurs enlist the professional assistance of an accountant, an attorney, an insurance agent, a banker, and a business broker to serve as consultants during the due diligence process.

The due diligence process involves investigating five critical areas of the business and the potential deal:

1. *Motivation.*   Why does the owner want to sell?
2. *Asset valuation.*   What is the true value of the company's assets?
3. *Market potential.*   What is the market potential for the company's products or services?
4. *Legal issues.*   What legal aspects of the business represent hidden risks?
5. *Financial state.*   Is the business financially sound?

**MOTIVATION.**   Every prospective business owner should investigate the *real* reason the business owner wants to sell. In addition to retirement, the most common reasons businesses are for sale usually fall into three categories:[11]

1. The seller is not making enough money.
2. The seller has a personal reason for selling—health, boredom, or burnout.
3. The seller is aware of pending changes in the business or the business environment that will alter the future of the business.

These changes may include a major competitor entering the market, a degraded location, lease problems, cash flow issues, supplier shifts, or a declining customer base. In other cases, owners decide to cash in their business investments and diversify into other types of assets. Every prospective buyer should *thoroughly* investigate any reason the seller gives for selling the business. Remember: Let the buyer beware!

Businesses do not last forever, and most owners know when the time has come to sell. Some owners may not disclose the entire story. In most business sales, the buyer bears the responsibility of determining whether the business is a good value. Visiting local business owners may reveal general patterns about the area and its overall vitality. The local Chamber of Commerce also may have useful information. Suppliers and competitors may be able to shed light on why the business is for sale. Combining this collection of information with an analysis of the company's financial records, a potential buyer should be able to develop a clear picture of the business and its real value.

**ASSET VALUATION.**   A prospective buyer should evaluate the business's assets to determine their value. Questions to ask about assets include:

- Are the assets reasonably priced?
- Are the assets obsolete?
- Will the assets have to be replaced soon?
- Do the assets operate efficiently?

The potential buyer should check the condition of all equipment and the building. It may be necessary to hire a professional to evaluate the major components of the building—its structure and the plumbing, electrical, and heating and cooling systems. Renovations are often expensive and time consuming.

Investigate the status of the company's existing inventory. Is it able to be sold at full price? How much of it would the buyer have to sell at a loss? Is it consistent with the image the new owner wants to project? A potential buyer may need to get an independent appraisal to determine the value of the company's inventory and other assets because the current owner may have priced them far above their actual value. Inventory typically constitutes the largest portion of a business's value, and a potential buyer should not accept the seller's asking price blindly. Remember: *Book value is not the same as market value.* Value is determined in the market, not on a balance sheet. It is common that a buyer can purchase equipment and fixtures at substantially lower prices than book value.

Other important factors that the potential buyer should investigate include the status of accounts receivable, the lease, business records, intangible assets, and the business location.

**1.** *Accounts receivable.* If the sale includes accounts receivable, the buyer should check their quality before purchasing them. How creditworthy are the accounts? What portion of them is past due? By aging the accounts receivable, the buyer can judge their quality and determine their value. (Refer to Table 5.1.)

**2.** *Lease arrangements.* If the business leases its space, determine whether the sale includes the lease. When does it expire? What restrictions does it have on renovation or expansion? What is the experience and status of the relationship with the property owner? The buyer should determine beforehand any restrictions the landlord has placed on the lease and the landlord's attitude regarding the transition of ownership. Even if the existing lease has a long time to run, the lease may not be assignable.[12] The buyer must check with the landlord to determine whether assignment is possible. Have the consent put in writing. All necessary changes should be negotiated prior to purchasing the business.

**3.** *Business records.* Accurate business records can be a valuable source of information and can tell the story of the company's pattern of success—or lack of it! Unfortunately, many business owners are poor record keepers, and the potential buyer and his or her team may have to reconstruct critical records. It is important to verify as much information about the business as possible. For instance, does the owner have current customer mailing lists? These can be valuable marketing tools for a new business owner.

**4.** *Intangible assets.* Determining the value of intangible assets is much more difficult than computing the value of the tangible assets; however, intangible assets can be one of the most valuable parts of a business acquisition. Does the sale include intangible assets such as trademarks, patents, copyrights, or goodwill? Edward Karstetter, director of valuation services at USBX says, "The value placed on intangible assets such as people, knowledge, relationships, and intellectual property is now a greater proportion of the total value of most businesses than is the value of tangible assets such as machinery and equipment."[13] Therefore, this is an important step in the valuation process.

**5.** *Location and appearance.* The location and appearance of the building are important to most businesses. It communicates a tremendous amount of information to customers and clients. What had been an outstanding location in the past may be unacceptable today. If the location of the business is in a declining area, it may not matter if the building and equipment are in good condition and are priced fairly. Every buyer should consider the location's suitability for today and for the future. The potential buyer should also check local zoning laws to ensure that any changes he or she wants to make are legal. In some areas, zoning laws are difficult to change and can restrict a business's growth.

**MARKET POTENTIAL.** No one wants to buy a business with a dying market. A thorough market analysis can lead to an accurate and realistic sales forecast. This research should tell the entrepreneur whether he or she should consider a particular business and help define the trend in the business's sales and customer base.

***Customer Characteristics and Composition.*** A business owner should analyze both the existing and potential customers before purchasing an existing business. Discovering why customers buy from the business and developing a profile of the customer base help a buyer identify a company's strengths and weaknesses. Prospective buyers should answer the following questions:

- Who are the company's customers in terms of race, age, gender, and income level?
- What do the customers want the business to do for them?
- What needs are they satisfying?
- How often do customers buy?
- Do they buy in seasonal patterns?
- How loyal are present customers?
- Why do some potential customers *not* buy from the business?
- Will it be practical to attract new customers? If so, will the new customers be significantly different from existing customers?

- Does the business have a well-defined customer base? Is it growing or shrinking?
- Does the customer base come from a large geographic area, or do they all live near the business?

Analyzing the answers to those questions can help the potential owner develop a marketing plan. Ideally, the entrepreneur will keep the business attractive to existing customers and change features of its marketing plan to attract new customers.

*Competitor Analysis.* A potential buyer must identify the company's direct competition, the businesses in the immediate area that sell the same or similar products or services. The potential profitability and survival of the business may depend on the behavior of these competitors.

In addition to analyzing direct competitors, a buyer should identify businesses that indirectly compete. For example, supermarkets and chain retail stores often carry a basic product line of automobile supplies (oil, spark plugs, and tune-up kits), competing with full-line auto parts stores. These chains often purchase bulk quantities at significant price reductions and do not incur the expense of carrying a full line of parts and supplies. As a result, they may be able to sell such basic products at lower prices. Even though these chains are not direct competitors, they may have an impact on local auto parts stores. Indirect competitors frequently limit their product lines to the most profitable segments of the market and, by concentrating on high-volume or high-profit items, they can pose a serious threat to other businesses.

A potential buyer should also evaluate the trends regarding competition and the market. The answers to the following questions provide insight:

- How many similar businesses have entered the market in the past five years?
- How many similar businesses have closed in the past five years?
- What caused these failures?
- Has the market already reached the saturation point?

Understanding these trends provides valuable insight regarding the future of the business. For example, being a late comer in a saturated market is plagued with challenges.

When evaluating the competitive environment, the prospective buyer should answer these questions:

- Which competitors are surviving and what characteristics make them successful?
- How do the competitors' sales volumes compare with those of the business the entrepreneur is considering?
- What unique services do the competitors offer?
- How effective are the marketing efforts of competitors?
- What are the competitors' reputations?
- What are the strengths and weaknesses of the competitors?
- How can a business gain market share in this competitive environment?

The intent of competitor analysis is to determine the company's current competitive situation, the competitive landscape that is evolving, and how the company may best compete.

**LEGAL ISSUES.** Business buyers face a myriad of legal pitfalls. The most significant legal issues involve liens, bulk transfers, contract assignments, covenants not to compete, and ongoing legal liabilities.

*Liens.* The key legal issue in the sale of any asset is typically the proper transfer of good title from seller to buyer. However, because most business sales involve a collection of assorted assets, the transfer of a good title is complex. Some business assets may have liens (creditors' claims) against them. Unless those liens are satisfied before the sale, the buyer must assume them and become financially responsible for those liens. One way to reduce

## Business Buying Tips

Picture this: The entrepreneur goes through the expense, sweat, and toil of starting a retail establishment. On opening day, he or she spends the day wondering if anyone will walk through the door. This image is quite different for an entrepreneur who buys an existing business. The following are six tips for buying an existing business:

■ *Buy a livelihood and a lifestyle.* Buyers of small businesses are not just buying assets, inventories, and leases; they are also choosing a lifestyle. "You have to look at the fact that you're buying a job and, hopefully, a decent return on investment," says Glen Cooper, a certified business appraiser. "Part of what you'll want to do is look at how much you can realistically expect the business to be able to pay you for your work and also how much of a return on your investment you can get in the form of additional profit beyond your own compensation." The business may be the single most significant determinant of a future lifestyle.

■ *Explore seller financing.* Banks may be hesitant to make loans for the purchase of a business. Business brokers say that down payments of 30 percent or more are not unusual. Cooper says it is usually a good sign when a seller is willing to finance the sale with a low down payment. A down payment of 20 percent or less, for example, indicates faith in their business and the buyer's potential success.

■ *Seek professional advice.* Look to other professionals for help—accountants, attorneys, and mentors can all provide valuable insight. "I strongly, strongly advise hiring professionals like attorneys and accountants to help you with the potential legal and financial issues or pitfalls of any purchase," says Nick Nicholson, business broker.

■ *Link the final price to customer retention.* A significant part of what the buyer is receiving is an existing client base. With some business sales, the price is based on retaining customers. A sales agreement could include a reduced price if the customer base declines after the buyer takes over.

■ *Get the seller to stick around.* The buyer may benefit from arranging to have the previous owner stay on during a transition period following any sale. The complexity of the business and the new owner's familiarity with the industry may determine if this is a few weeks or a few years. Basing part of the purchase price on retaining existing customers gives the seller incentive to assist the buyer through the initial stages of the purchase.

■ *Do your homework on the valuation of the business.* Educate yourself in advance about ways of valuing a prospective purchase. Two Internet sites that offer some rules of thumb are www.bizcomps.com and www.bvmarketdata.com.

*Source:* Adapted from Joseph Anthony, "Seven Tips for Buying a Business," Microsoft Small Business Center, www.microsoft.com/smallbusiness/resources/startups/business_opportunities/7_tips_for_buying_a_business.mspx#bio1.

this potential problem is to include a clause in the sales contract stating that any liability not shown on the balance sheet at the time of sale remains the responsibility of the seller. A prospective buyer should have an attorney thoroughly investigate all of the assets for sale and their lien status before buying any business.

***Bulk Transfers.*** A **bulk transfer** is a transaction in which a buyer purchases all or most of a business's inventory in a business sale. To protect against surprise claims from the seller's creditors after purchasing a business, the buyer should meet the requirements of a bulk transfer under Section 6 of the U.S. Uniform Commercial Code, for example. Suppose that an owner owing many creditors sells his business to a buyer. The seller, however, does not use the proceeds of the sale to pay his or her debts to business creditors. Instead, he "skips town," leaving his creditors unpaid. Without the protection of a bulk transfer, those creditors could make claim (within six months) to the assets that the buyer purchased to satisfy the previous owner's debts. To be effective, a bulk transfer must meet the following criteria:

- The seller must give the buyer a sworn list of existing creditors.
- The buyer and the seller must prepare a list of the property included in the sale.
- The buyer must keep the list of creditors and the list of property for six months.
- The buyer must give notice of the sale to each creditor at least 10 days before taking possession of the goods or paying for them (whichever is first).

By meeting these criteria, a buyer acquires a free and clear title to the assets, which are not subject to prior claims from the seller's creditors. Because Section 6 can create quite a burden on a business buyer, more than 30 U.S. states have repealed it, and more are likely to follow. Many states have revised Section 6 to make it easier for buyers to notify creditors. With this revision, if a business has more than 200 creditors, the buyer may notify them by public notice rather than by contacting them individually.

***Contract Assignments.*** A buyer must investigate the rights and the obligations that he or she would assume under existing contracts with suppliers, customers, employees, lessors and others. To continue the smooth operation of the business, the buyer must assume the rights of the seller under existing contracts. For example, if the current owner has 4 years left on a 10-year lease, he or she will need to assign this contract to the buyer. The seller can assign any contractual right unless the contract specifically prohibits the assignment or the contract is personal in nature. For instance, loan contracts sometimes prohibit assignments with **due-on-sale clauses**. These clauses require the buyer to pay the full amount of the remaining loan balance or to finance the balance at prevailing interest rates. Thus, the buyer cannot assume the seller's loan at a lower interest rate. In addition, a seller usually cannot assign his or her credit arrangements with suppliers to the buyer because they are based on the seller's business reputation and are personal in nature. If such contracts are crucial to the business operation and cannot be assigned, the buyer must negotiate new contracts.

The prospective buyer also should evaluate the terms of any other contracts the seller has, including the following:

- Patent, trademark, or copyright registrations
- Exclusive agent or distributor contracts
- Real estate leases
- Insurance contracts
- Financing and loan arrangements
- Union contracts

***Covenants Not to Compete.*** An important, and often overlooked, legal consideration for a prospective buyer is negotiating a covenant not to compete (or a restrictive covenant) with the seller. Under a restrictive covenant, the seller agrees not to open a new competing store within a specific time period and geographic area of the existing one. The buyer should negotiate the covenant directly with the owner, not the corporation; if the corporation signs the agreement, the owner may not be bound. However, the covenant must be part of a business sale and must be reasonable in scope to be enforceable. Without this protection, a buyer may find the new business eroding beneath his or her feet.

***Ongoing Legal Liabilities.*** Finally, a potential buyer must look for any potential legal liabilities the purchase might expose. These typically arise from three sources:

1. Physical premises
2. Product liability claims
3. Labor relations

*Physical Premises.* The buyer must first examine the physical premises for safety. Are the employees' health at risk because of asbestos or some other hazardous material? If a manufacturing environment is involved, does it meet government health and safety requirements and other regulatory agency requirements?

*Product Liability Claims.* The buyer must consider whether the product contains defects that could result in product liability lawsuits, which claim that a company is liable for damages and injuries caused by the products or services it sells. Existing lawsuits might be an omen of more to follow. In addition, the buyer must explore products that the company has discontinued because he or she might be liable for them if they prove to be defective. The final bargain between the parties should require the seller to guarantee that the company is not involved in any product liability lawsuits.

**LABOR RELATIONS.** The relationship between management and employees is key to a successful transition. Does a union represent employees in a collective bargaining agreement? The time to discover problematic management-labor relations is before the purchase, not after.

The existence of liabilities such as these does not necessarily eliminate the business from consideration. Insurance coverage can shift risks from the potential buyer, but the buyer should check to see whether the insurance covers lawsuits resulting from actions taken before the purchase. Despite conducting a thorough search, a buyer may purchase a business only to discover the presence of hidden liabilities—unpaid back taxes, delinquent bills, unpaid pension fund contributions, undisclosed lawsuits, or others. A clause in the purchase agreement assigning responsibility for such hidden liabilities to the seller protects a buyer from unpleasant surprises after the sale.

**FINANCIAL STATE.** A serious buyer must analyze the records of the business to determine its financial health. The buyer may benefit from enlisting the assistance of an accountant. Accounting systems and methods can vary tremendously and be confusing to a novice. Changes in a company's accounting procedure or in the method for recording sales can inflate its profits. For the buyer, the most dependable financial records are audited statements, statements prepared by a certified public accountant in accordance with International Accounting Standards Board requirements.

A buyer also must remember that he or she is purchasing the future profit potential of an existing business. To evaluate the company's profit potential, a buyer should review sales, operating expenses, profits, and the assets that generate those profits. The buyer must compare current balance sheets and income statements with previous ones and develop projected statements for the next two or three years. Sales tax records, income tax returns, and financial statements are valuable sources of information. Any investment in a company should produce a reasonable salary for the owner and a healthy return on the money invested. Otherwise, it makes no sense to purchase the business.

Profit trends are another area to analyze. Are profits consistent over the years or are they erratic? What has created these fluctuations? Is this pattern typical in the industry or is it a result of unique circumstances or poor management? Can the business survive with volatile changes in revenues, costs, and profits? If these fluctuations are caused by poor management, can a new manager make a difference? Some of the financial records that a potential buyer should examine include the income statement, balance sheet, tax returns, owner's compensation, and cash flow.

*Income Statements and Balance Sheets for at Least Three Years.* It is important to review data from several years prior; creative accounting techniques can distort financial data in any single year. Even though buyers are purchasing the future earnings of a business, they must remember that many business owners intentionally minimize profits to reduce their tax bills.

*Income Tax Returns for at Least Three Years.* Comparing basic financial statements with tax returns can reveal discrepancies of which the buyer should be aware. Some small business owners "skim" from their businesses; they take money from sales without reporting it as income. Owners who skim will claim their businesses are more profitable than their tax returns show. However, buyers should not pay for "phantom profits."

***Owner's and Family Compensation.*** Compensation to the owner is especially important in small companies; the smaller the company is, the more important the owner's compensation tends to be. Although many companies do not pay their owners what they are worth, others compensate their owners lavishly. Buyers must consider the impact of company benefits—company cars, insurance contracts, country club memberships, travel, and the like. It is important to adjust the company's income statements for the salary and benefits that the seller has paid himself or herself and others.

***Cash Flow.*** Most buyers understand the importance of evaluating a company's profit history, but few recognize the need to analyze its cash flow. They assume that if profits are adequate, there will be sufficient cash to pay all of the bills and to fund an adequate salary for them. *That is not necessarily the case.* Before closing any deal, a buyer should review the information with an accountant and convert the target company's financial statements into a cash flow forecast. This forecast must take into account not only existing debts and obligations but also any modifications or additional debts the buyer plans to make in the business. It should reflect the repayment of financing the buyer arranges to purchase the company. The critical question: Can the company generate sufficient cash to be self-supporting?

A potential buyer must look for suspicious deviations from the average (in either direction) for sales, expenses, profits, assets, and liabilities. Are sales increasing or decreasing? Does the equipment's value on the balance sheet reflect its real value? Are advertising expenses unusually high? How do the financial statements report depreciation?

This financial information offers the buyer the opportunity to verify the seller's claims about the business's performance. Prospective buyers must realize that some owners take short-term actions that produce healthy financial statements but that weaken their companies' long-term health and profit potential. For example, a seller might lower costs by gradually eliminating equipment maintenance or might boost sales by selling to marginal businesses that will never pay their bills. Techniques such as these artificially inflate assets and profits, but a well-prepared buyer should be able to see through them.

Finally, a potential buyer should always be wary of purchasing a business if the present owner refuses to disclose all financial records. Table 5.2 lists the records that a potential buyer should review before making a final decision about buying a business. Potential buyers may fail to review many of these important financial documents, records, and contracts. Such an oversight can result in unwelcome surprises after the deal is completed.

***Mark McDonnell and Superior X-Ray Tube Co.***

Former Motorola Inc. executive Mark McDonnell was ready to escape corporate life. However, he was not excited about launching a start-up from scratch or hanging out a shingle as a self-employed, one-person enterprise. McDonnell wound up pursuing a third, often-overlooked, option—becoming an entrepreneur via acquisition. McDonnell was seeking "an existing business where I could take advantage of skills that I had developed during my work in large organizations and that would allow me to go into that small company and take it to the next level." McDonnell notes that buying an existing business can be less risky than starting a business. "You have an existing customer base, you have a track record and you have employees in place. There are a whole lot of advantages to this. The trade-off is that you are going to have to pay for it."[14]

## Methods for Determining the Value of a Business

*3.* Describe the various methods used in the valuation of a business.

Business valuation is part art and part science. The number of variables that influence the value of a privately owned business makes establishing a reasonable price difficult. These factors include the nature of the business itself, its position in the market or industry, the outlook for the market or industry, the company's financial status and stability, its earning capacity, intangible assets (such as patents, trademarks, and copyrights), the value of similar companies, and many others.

**TABLE 5.2 Records a Business Buyer Should Review Before Committing to a Deal**

At a minimum, a business buyer should examine the following documents:

- *Organizational documents*—documents that show how the business is organized, such as partnership agreements, articles of incorporation, and business certificates, should be examined to determine how the business is structured and capitalized.
- *Contracts and leases*—documents such as property and machinery leases, sales contracts, and purchase contracts should be examined to determine the exact obligations the business is subject to.
- *Financial statements*—examine the financial statements for the past three years (and longer if available) to determine the financial condition of the business.
- *Tax returns*—examine the tax returns for the past three years (and longer if available) to determine the profitability of the business and whether any tax liability is outstanding.

However, a more complete investigation is recommended and should include the following:

- Asset list including real estate, equipment, and intangible assets such as patents, trademarks, and licenses
- Real and personal property documents (e.g., deeds, leases, appraisals, mortgages, loans, insurance policies)
- Bank account list
- Financial statements for the last three to five years
- Tax returns for as many years as possible
- Customer list
- Sales records
- Supplier/purchaser list
- Contracts that the business is a party to
- Advertisements, sales brochures, product packaging and enclosures, and any other marketing materials
- Inventory receipts (also take a look at the inventory itself to check the amount and condition)
- Organizational charts and résumés of key employees
- Payroll, benefits, and employee pension or profit-sharing plan information
- Certificates issued by federal, state, or local agencies (e.g., certificate of existence, certificate of authority to transact business, liquor license)
- Certificates, registration articles, and any amendments filed with any federal, state, or local agency (e.g., articles of incorporation for a corporation, articles of organization for a limited liability company)
- Organizational documents (e.g., corporate bylaws, partnership agreements, operating agreements for limited liability companies)
- List of owners, if more than one (e.g., all shareholders if a corporation, all partners if a partnership, all members if a limited liability company)

*Source:* Adapted from *Business Owner's Toolkit* at www.toolkit.cch.com/text/P01_0860.asp, 2004.

Assessing the value of the company's tangible assets is often straightforward. Assigning a price to the intangibles, such as goodwill, often creates controversy, however. The seller expects goodwill to reflect the hard work and long hours invested in building the business. The buyer, however, is willing to pay extra only for those intangible assets that produce exceptional income. How can the buyer and the seller arrive at a fair price? Each business sale is unique, and there is no single best method for determining a business's worth. There are few hard-and-fast rules in establishing the value of a business, but the following guidelines can help.

- Compute a company's value using several techniques, review those values, and then choose the one that makes the most sense.
- The deal must be financially feasible for both parties to be viable. The seller must consider the price acceptable, but the buyer cannot pay an excessively high price that would require heavy borrowing and strain cash flows from the outset.
- The buyer should have access to business records.

- Valuations should be based on facts, not feelings.
- The two parties should deal with one another openly, honestly, and in good faith.

The main reason that buyers purchase an existing business is to benefit from the company's future earnings potential. The second most common reason is to obtain an established asset base. It is often much easier to buy assets than to build them. Although evaluation methods should take these characteristics into consideration, too many business sellers and buyers depend on rules of thumb that ignore the unique features of many small companies. There is no "rule of thumb" or universal valuation method that fits every type of business.

This section describes three basic techniques—the balance sheet method, the earnings approach, and the market approach—and several variations on them for determining the value of a hypothetical business, Luxor Electronics.

## Balance Sheet Technique

The balance sheet method computes the book value of a company's net worth, or owner's equity (net worth = assets − liabilities) and uses this figure as the value. A criticism of this technique is that it oversimplifies the valuation process. The problem with this technique is that it fails to recognize reality: Most small businesses have market values that exceed their reported book values.

$$\text{Assets} - \text{Liabilities} = \text{Net Worth}$$

The first step is to determine which assets are included in the sale. In most cases, the owner has some personal assets that he or she does not want to sell. Professional business brokers can help the buyer and the seller arrive at a reasonable value for the collection of assets included in the deal. Remember that net worth on a financial statement will likely differ significantly from actual net worth in the market. Figure 5.1 shows the balance sheet for Luxor Electronics. This balance sheet shows that the company's net worth is:

$$\$278{,}990 - \$114{,}325 = \$164{,}665$$

**VARIATION: ADJUSTED BALANCE SHEET TECHNIQUE.**   A more realistic method for determining a company's value is to adjust the book value of net worth to reflect the actual market value. The values reported on a company's books may either overstate or understate the true value of assets and liabilities. Typical assets in a business sale include notes and accounts receivable, inventories, supplies, and fixtures. If a buyer purchases notes and accounts receivable, he or she should estimate the likelihood of their collection and adjust their value accordingly (refer to Table 5.1).

Inventory is usually the largest single asset in the sale in manufacturing, wholesale, and retail businesses. Taking a physical inventory count is the best way to determine accurately the condition and quantity of goods to be transferred. The sale may include three types of inventory, each having its own method of valuation: raw materials, work-in-process, and finished goods.

The buyer and the seller must arrive at a method for evaluating the inventory. First in, first out (FIFO), last in, first out (LIFO), and average costing are three frequently used techniques. The most common method uses the cost of last purchase and the replacement value of the inventory. Before accepting any inventory value, the buyer should evaluate the condition of the goods.

To avoid problems, some buyers insist on having a knowledgeable representative on an inventory team count the inventory and check its condition. Nearly every sale involves merchandise that cannot be sold, but by taking this precaution, a buyer minimizes the chance of buying worthless inventory.

Fixed assets transferred in a sale might include land, buildings, equipment, and fixtures. Business owners frequently carry real estate and buildings on their books at prices well below their actual market value. Equipment and fixtures, depending on their condition and usefulness, may increase or decrease the true value of the business. Appraisals of these assets on insurance policies are helpful guidelines for establishing market value. In addition, business brokers can be useful in determining the current value of fixed assets. Some

**FIGURE 5.1 Balance Sheet for Luxor Electronics, June 30, 20XX**

| ASSETS | | |
|---|---|---|
| **Current Assets** | | |
| Cash | $ 11,655 | |
| Accounts receivable | 15,876 | |
| Inventory | 56,523 | |
| Supplies | 8,574 | |
| Prepaid insurance | 5,587 | |
| Total current assets | | $ 98,215 |
| **Fixed Assets** | | |
| Land | | $ 36,900 |
| Buildings | $141,000 | |
| less accumulated depreciation | 51,500 | 89,500 |
| Office equipment | $ 12,760 | |
| less accumulated depreciation | 7,159 | 5,601 |
| Factory equipment | $ 59,085 | |
| less accumulated depreciation | 27,850 | 31,235 |
| Trucks and autos | $ 28,730 | |
| less accumulated depreciation | 11,190 | 17,540 |
| Total fixed assets | | $ 180,775 |
| **Total Assets** | | **$ 278,990** |
| | | |
| **LIABILITIES** | | |
| **Current Liabilities** | | |
| Accounts payable | $ 19,497 | |
| Mortgage payable | 5,215 | |
| Salaries payable | 3,671 | |
| Note payable | 10,000 | |
| Total current liabilities | | $ 38,383 |
| **Long-Term Liabilities** | | |
| Mortgage payable | $ 54,542 | |
| Note payable | 21,400 | |
| Total long-term liabilities | | $ 75,942 |
| **Total Liabilities** | | **$ 114,325** |
| | | |
| **OWNER'S EQUITY** | | |
| Owner's Equity [net worth] | | $ 164,665 |
| **Total Liabilities + Owner's Equity** | | **$ 278,990** |

brokers use an estimate of what it would cost to replace a company's physical assets (less a reasonable allowance for depreciation) to determine value. As indicated by the adjusted balance sheet in Figure 5.2, the adjusted net worth for Luxor Electronics is:

$$\$264,638 - \$114,325 = \$150,313$$

The difference of $114,325 compared to the initial balance sheet indicates that some of the entries on its books did not accurately reflect market value. In this case, the current assets are overstated on the balance sheet and, although the fixed asset value was actually higher on the adjusted balance sheet, the owner's equity was lower. The buyer will benefit from the adjusted balance sheet method.

**FIGURE 5.2 Adjusted Balance Sheet for Luxor Electronics to Reflect Market Value, June 30, 20XX**

| ASSETS | | |
|---|---:|---:|
| **Current Assets** | | |
| Cash | $ 11,655 | |
| Accounts receivable | 10,051 | |
| Inventory | 39,261 | |
| Supplies | 7,492 | |
| Prepaid insurance | 5,587 | |
| Total current assets | | $ 74,046 |
| **Fixed Assets** | | |
| Land | | $ 36,900 |
| Buildings | $177,000 | |
| less accumulated depreciation | 51,500 | 115,500 |
| Office equipment | $ 11,645 | |
| less accumulated depreciation | 7,159 | 4,486 |
| Factory equipment | $ 50,196 | |
| less accumulated depreciation | 27,850 | 22,346 |
| Trucks and autos | $ 22,550 | |
| less accumulated depreciation | 11,190 | 11,360 |
| Total fixed assets | | $ 190,592 |
| **Total Assets** | | **$ 264,638** |
| | | |
| **LIABILITIES** | | |
| **Current Liabilities** | | |
| Accounts payable | $ 19,497 | |
| Mortgage payable | 5,215 | |
| Salaries payable | 3,671 | |
| Note payable | 10,000 | |
| Total current liabilities | | $ 38,383 |
| **Long-Term Liabilities** | | |
| Mortgage payable | $ 54,542 | |
| Note payable | 21,400 | |
| Total long-term liabilities | | $ 75,942 |
| **Total Liabilities** | | **$ 114,325** |
| | | |
| **OWNER'S EQUITY** | | |
| Owner's Equity [net worth] | | $ 150,313 |
| **Total Liabilities + Owner's Equity** | | **$ 264,638** |

Business valuations based on any balance sheet method suffer one major drawback: They do not consider the future earnings potential of the business. These techniques value assets at current prices and do not consider them as tools for creating future profits. An additional omission is that balance sheet methods do not attach value to intangible assets of the business such as goodwill. The next method for computing the value of a business is based on its expected future earnings.

## Earnings Approach

The earnings approach is more refined than the balance sheet method because it considers the future income potential of the business. It considers this key element: The buyer of an existing business is purchasing its future income potential.

**VARIATION 1: EXCESS EARNINGS METHOD.**   This method combines both the value of the company's net worth and an estimate of its future earnings potential to determine the selling price for the business. One advantage of the excess earnings method is that it offers an estimate of goodwill. **Goodwill** is the difference between an established, successful business and one that has yet to prove itself. Goodwill is based on the company's reputation and its ability to attract customers. This intangible asset often creates problems in a business sale. The most common method of valuing a business is to compute its tangible net worth and then to add an often arbitrary adjustment for goodwill. A buyer should not blindly accept the seller's arbitrary adjustment for goodwill. It is likely to be inflated.

The excess earnings method provides a fairly consistent and realistic approach for determining the value of goodwill. It measures goodwill by the amount of profit the business earns above that of the average company in the same industry. It also assumes that the owner is entitled to a reasonable return on the company's adjusted tangible net worth.

**Step 1**    *Compute adjusted tangible net worth.*   Using the previous method of valuation, the buyer should compute the company's adjusted tangible net worth. Total tangible assets (adjusted for market value) minus total liabilities yields adjusted tangible net worth. In the Luxor Electronics example shown in Figure 5.2, the adjusted tangible net worth is:

$$\$264{,}638 - \$114{,}325 = \$150{,}313$$

**Step 2**    *Calculate the opportunity costs of investing in the business.*   **Opportunity costs** represent the cost of forgoing a choice; what revenues does the potential buyer give up by purchasing the business? If the buyer chooses to purchase the assets of a business, the buyer cannot invest his or her money elsewhere. Therefore, the opportunity cost of the purchase would be the amount that the buyer could have earned by investing the same amount *in a similar risk investment.*

There are three components in the rate of return used to value a business:

1. The basic, risk-free return
2. An inflation premium
3. The risk allowance for investing in the particular business.

The basic, risk-free return and the inflation premium are reflected in investments such as secure government bonds. To determine the appropriate rate of return for investing in a business, the buyer must add to this base rate a factor reflecting the risk of purchasing the company. The greater the risk is, the higher the rate of return. An average-risk business typically indicates a 20 to 25 percent rate of return. In the Luxor Electronics example, the opportunity cost of the investment is:

$$\$150{,}313 \times 25\% = \$37{,}578$$

The second part of the buyer's opportunity cost is the salary that he or she could have earned working for someone else. For the Luxor Electronics example, if the buyer purchases the business, the buyer must forgo a salary of, say, $25,000 that he or she could have earned working elsewhere. Adding these amounts yields a total opportunity cost of:

$$\$37{,}578 + \$25{,}000 = \$62{,}578$$

**Step 3**    *Project net earnings.*   The buyer must estimate the company's net earnings for the upcoming year before subtracting the owner's salary. Averages can be misleading, so the buyer must be sure to investigate the trend of net earnings. Have the earnings risen steadily over the past five years, dropped significantly, remained relatively constant, or fluctuated wildly? Past income statements provide useful guidelines for estimating earnings. In the Luxor Electronics example, the buyer and an accountant project net earnings to be $74,000.

**Step 4**    *Compute extra earning power.*    A company's extra earning power is the difference between forecasted earnings (Step 3) and total opportunity costs (Step 2). Many small businesses that are for sale do not have extra earning power (i.e., excess earnings) and they show marginal or no profits. The extra earning power of Luxor Electronics is:

$$\$74,000 - \$62,578 = \$11,422$$

**Step 5**    *Estimate the value of intangibles.*    The owner can use the business's extra earning power to estimate the value of its intangible assets: that is, its goodwill. Multiplying the extra earning power by a years-of-profit figure yields an estimate of the intangible assets' value. The years-of-profit figure for a normal-risk business ranges from three to four. A high-risk business may have a years-of-profit figure of one, whereas a well-established company might use a figure of seven. For Luxor Electronics, the value of intangibles (assuming normal risk) would be:

$$\$11,433 \times 3 = \$34,299$$

**Step 6**    *Determine the value of the business.*    To determine the value of the business, the buyer simply adds together the adjusted tangible net worth (Step 1) and the value of the intangibles (Step 5). Using this method, the value of Luxor Electronics is:

$$\$150,313 + \$34,299 = \$184,612$$

Both the buyer and seller should consider the tax implications of transferring goodwill. Because the buyer can amortize both the cost of goodwill and a covenant not to compete over 15 years, the tax treatment of either would be the same. However, the seller would prefer to have the amount of the purchase price in excess of the value of the assets allocated to goodwill, which is a capital asset. The gain on the capital asset would be taxed at lower capital gains rates. If that same amount were allocated to a covenant not to compete (which is negotiated with the seller personally, not the business), the seller must treat it as ordinary income, and regular tax rates apply that are higher than the capital gains rates.

**VARIATION 2: CAPITALIZED EARNINGS APPROACH.**    Another earnings approach capitalizes expected net income to determine the value of a business. The buyer should prepare his or her own projected income statement and should ask the seller to prepare one also. Many appraisers use a five-year weighted average of past sales (with the greatest weights assigned to the most recent years) to estimate sales for the upcoming year.

Once again, the buyer must evaluate the risk of purchasing the business to determine the appropriate rate of return on the investment. The greater the perceived risk, the higher the return the buyer will require. Risk determination is always somewhat subjective, but it is a necessary consideration for proper evaluation.

The capitalized earnings approach divides estimated net earnings (after subtracting the owner's reasonable salary) by the rate of return that reflects the risk level. For Luxor Electronics, the capitalized value (assuming a reasonable salary of $25,000) is:

$$\frac{\text{Net earnings (\textit{after deducting owner's salary})}}{\text{Rate of return}} = \frac{\$74,000 - \$25,000}{25\%} = \$196,000$$

Companies with lower risk factors offer greater certainty and, therefore, are more valuable. For example, a risk factor of 10 percent would yield a value of $490,000 for Luxor Electronics, and a risk factor of 50 percent would produce a value of $98,000. Most normal-risk businesses use a rate-of-return factor ranging from 20 percent to 25 percent. The lowest risk factor that most buyers would accept for a business is 15 percent.

**VARIATION 3: DISCOUNTED FUTURE EARNINGS APPROACH.** This variation of the earnings approach assumes that a dollar earned in the future will be worth less than that same dollar today. The discounted future earnings approach requires a buyer to estimate the company's net income for several years into the future and then discount these future earnings back to their present value. The resulting present value is an estimate of the company's worth. The present value represents the cost of the buyers' giving up the opportunity to earn a reasonable rate of return by receiving income in the future instead of today.

To visualize the importance of present value and the time value of money, consider two $1 million lottery winners. Rob wins $1 million in a lottery, and he receives it in $50,000 installments over 20 years. If Rob invests every installment at 15 percent interest, he will have accumulated $5,890,506 at the end of 20 years. Lisa wins $1 million in another lottery, but she collects her winnings in one lump sum. If Lisa invests her $1 million today at 15 percent, she will have accumulated $16,366,537 at the end of 20 years. The dramatic difference in their wealth—Lisa is now worth $10,476,031 more—is the result of the time value of money.

The discounted future earnings approach has five steps:

Step 1    *Project earnings for five years into the future.* One way is to assume that earnings will grow by a constant amount over the next five years. Perhaps a better method is to develop three forecasts—pessimistic, most likely, and optimistic—for each year and find a weighted average using the following formula:

$$\text{Forecasted earnings for year } i = \frac{\text{Pessimistic earnings for year } i + \text{Most Likely earnings for year } i \times 4 + \text{Optimistic earnings year } i}{6}$$

The Most Likely forecast is weighted four times greater than the pessimistic and optimistic forecast and, therefore, their sum is divided by 6 (based on the $1 + 4 + 1$ weighting). Using this weighting, the buyer's forecasts for Luxor Electronics are:

| Year | Pessimistic | Most Likely | Optimistic | Weighted Average |
|------|-------------|-------------|------------|------------------|
| XXX1 | $65,000 | $74,000 | $92,000 | **$75,500** |
| XXX2 | 74,000 | 90,000 | 101,000 | **89,167** |
| XXX3 | 82,000 | 100,000 | 112,000 | **99,000** |
| XXX4 | 88,000 | 109,000 | 120,000 | **107,333** |
| XXX5 | 88,000 | 115,000 | 122,000 | **111,667** |

The buyer must remember that the further into the future he or she forecasts, the less reliable the estimates will be.

Step 2    *Discount these future earnings using the appropriate present value factor.* The appropriate present value factor can be found by looking in published present value tables or by solving the equation:

$$1/(1 + k)^t$$

where        $k$ = rate of return

and          $t$ = time (year 1, 2, 3, ... $n$)

The rate that the buyer selects should reflect the rate he or she could earn on a similar risk investment. Because Luxor Electronics is a normal-risk business, the buyer chooses 25 percent.

| Year | Income Forecast Weighted Average | Present Value Factor at 25 Percent Value | Net Present Value |
|------|---------------------------------|------------------------------------------|-------------------|
| XXX1 | $75,500 | 0.8000 | $ 60,400 |
| XXX2 | 89,167 | 0.6400 | 57,067 |
| XXX3 | 99,000 | 0.5120 | 50,688 |
| XXX4 | 107,333 | 0.4096 | 43,964 |
| XXX5 | 111,667 | 0.3277 | 36,593 |
| **Total** | | | **$248,712** |

**Step 3**   *Estimate the income stream beyond five years.*   One technique suggests multiplying the fifth year income by 1 ÷ (rate of return). For Luxor Electronics, the estimate is:

Income beyond year 5: $111,667 × (1 ÷ 25%) = $446,668

**Step 4**   *Discount the income estimate beyond five years using the present value factor for the sixth year.*   For Luxor Electronics:

Present value of income beyond year 5: $446,668 × 0.2622 = $117,116

**Step 5**   *Compute the total value of the business.*

Total value: $248,712 + $117,116 = $365,828

The primary advantage of this technique is that it evaluates a business solely on the basis of its future earnings potential, but its reliability depends on making accurate forecasts of future earnings and on choosing a realistic present value factor. The discounted future earnings approach is especially well suited for valuing service businesses, whose asset bases are often small, and for companies experiencing high growth rates.

### Market Approach

The market approach (or Price/Earnings approach) uses the price/earnings ratios of similar businesses to establish the value of a company. The buyer must use businesses whose stocks are publicly traded to get a meaningful comparison. A company's **price/earnings ratio (P/E ratio)** is the price of one share of its common stock in the market divided by its earnings per share (after deducting preferred stock dividends). To get a representative P/E ratio, the buyer should average the P/Es of as many similar businesses as possible.

The buyer multiplies the average price/earnings ratio by the private company's estimated earnings to compute the company's value. For example, suppose that the buyer finds four companies comparable to Luxor Electronics whose stock is publicly traded. Their P/E ratios are:

| | |
|---|---|
| Company 1 | 3.300 |
| Company 2 | 3.800 |
| Company 3 | 4.700 |
| Company 4 | 4.100 |
| Average | 3.975 |

This average P/E ratio produces a value of $294,150:

Value average P/E ratio × Estimated net earnings

3.975 × $74,000 = $294,150

## In the Entrepreneurial Spotlight

### ■ Listen Up!

Kim and Chad's acoustics business, Sound Perspective, started out small and simple in a small and simple town. Kim designs sound isolation booths, and Chad constructs them in the back room of his auto body shop. Recording artists, voice-over talent, the government, and various manufacturers purchase an array of their sound-baffling products. The business is now for sale. The couple owns other businesses that they would prefer to concentrate on, and they are looking for a buyer who can take this company to the next level.

Sound Perspectives hit the million-dollar mark in its sixth year of operation, and the owners say the business is on pace to gross $1.5 million in year eight. They are in the early stages of building a new facility—adjacent to their present site—to double production capacity. Depending on the timing of a deal, they will build that facility to a buyer's specifications.

Currently Sound Perspective has seven employees. The sellers say they will help a new owner during a transition period. They have also prepared extensive manuals on how to operate the business and the manufacturing plant. The owners anticipate that most, if not all employees, will be interested in staying with the company.

Approximately 15 percent of their total revenues are government purchases, a figure that a new owner could increase, especially if the new owner has federal contracting knowledge. The company could also expand into the audiology market, representing another viable growth opportunity.

The asking price for the business is $2 million. The assets include plant and equipment, $70,000 in inventory, and three acres of land. The owners would consider financing up to $500,000 of the purchase. The business is well established but still relatively small. The plant and equipment are in good working order.

The company has no debt and for an owner seeking a small-town lifestyle, the location is also a plus. A state agency may help finance the deal, and a buyer who enjoys the outdoors will love the area. However, the region's labor pool is limited, constraining the owner's ability to recruit senior managers. "You don't find an M.B.A. anywhere in our town of 3,500 people," says Kim.

"This is a promising business if a buyer is patient," says Chad. To realize a reasonable rate of return, a new owner will have to focus on long-term growth. The following table shows some financial highlights for Sound Perspective for the last three years:

**Sound Perspective—Company Financials**

|  | Gross Revenue | EBITDA* | Owners' Compensation |
|---|---|---|---|
| **Year 5** | $928,986 | $153,605 | $55,278 |
| **Year 6** | $1,194,093 | $182,738 | $80,000 |
| **Year 7** | $1,087,715 | $92,216 | $80,000 |

*Earnings before interest, taxes, depreciation, and amortization.

1. What information should an entrepreneur know about the business and the current owners before purchasing the business?
2. Which valuation technique do you think can provide the most accurate assessment of the business? Use the technique to estimate the value of Sound Perspective.
3. Do you consider the asking price fair? If not, what price would you offer?

*Source:* Adapted from Elaine Appleton Grant, "Hush Money," *Inc.*, September 2006, www.inc.com/magazine/20060901/priority-biz4sale.html.

---

The most significant advantage of the market approach is its simplicity. However, the market approach method does have several disadvantages, including:

1. *Necessary comparisons between publicly traded and privately owned companies.* The stock of privately owned companies is illiquid, and therefore, the P/E ratio used is often subjective and lower than that of publicly held companies.

2. *Unrepresentative earnings estimates.*   A private company's net earnings may not realistically reflect its true earnings potential. To minimize taxes, owners usually attempt to keep profits low and rely on benefits to make up the difference.

3. *Finding similar companies for comparison.*   Often it is extremely difficult for a buyer to find comparable publicly held companies when estimating the appropriate P/E ratio.

4. *Applying the after-tax earnings of a private company to determine its value.*   If a prospective buyer is using an after-tax P/E ratio from a public company, he or she also must use the after-tax earnings from the private company.

Despite its drawbacks, the market approach is useful as a general guideline to establishing a company's value.

*Susan and James McIntyre and Cape Cod Marina*

Purchasing the Cape Cod Marina 10 years ago for $1.5 million was a risk for Susan and James McIntyre. It was no more than a "sleepy little boatyard" for commercial fishermen. Over the course of two years, the McIntyres changed their clientele demographic by catering to novice recreational boaters who "don't want to lift a finger" to maintain their high-end powerboats, which cost as much as $450,000. Today, the marina's 92 slips are booked solid with a three- to five-year waiting list. In addition to rental slips, the business also sells new and used boats and offers maintenance services. Selling ancillary items such as life jackets, fishing equipment, and charter services add to the bottom line with annual revenues of $2.7 million. The McIntyres have decided that it is time to move on, however, and the business is for sale at $9.15 million—not bad for a little fishing expedition.[15]

### The "Best" Method?

Which of these methods is best for determining the value of a small business? Simply stated, there is no single best method. These techniques will yield a range of values. Buyers should look for values that might cluster together and use their best judgment to determine their offering price. The final price will be based on both the valuation used and the negotiating skills of both parties. Like all assets, a business is ultimately worth what the highest bidder is willing to pay with terms and conditions that are most acceptable to the seller.

## Negotiating the Deal

*4.* Discuss the process of negotiating the deal.

Once an entrepreneur has a realistic value for the business, the next step in making a successful purchase is negotiating a suitable deal. Most buyers do not realize that the price they pay for a company is not as crucial to its continued success as the terms of the purchase. In other words, *the structure of the deal—the terms and conditions of payment—is more important than the actual price the seller agrees to pay.*

Wise business buyers will try to negotiate a reasonable price and focus on negotiating favorable terms. Examples of these terms include the answers to these questions:

- How much cash must the buyer pay and when must he or she pay it?
- How much of the price is the seller willing to finance and for how long?
- What is the interest rate for financing the deal?
- Which liabilities will the buyer assume?

The buyer's primary concern should be to make sure that the deal does not endanger the company's financial future (or their personal financial position) and that it preserves the company's cash flow.

Figure 5.3 sets forth the detailed sequence of events in a successful acquisition negotiation process.

On the surface, the negotiation process may appear to be strictly adversarial. Although each party may be trying to accomplish objectives that are at odds with those of the opposing party, the negotiation process does not have to be conflict-oriented. The negotiation process will go smoother and faster if the two parties work to establish a cooperative relationship based on honesty and trust from the outset. A successful deal requires both parties to examine and articulate their respective positions while trying to understand the other party's position. Recognizing that neither of them will benefit without a deal, both parties must work to achieve their objectives while making certain concessions to keep the negotiations alive.

To avoid a stalled deal, both buyer and seller should go into the negotiation with a list of objectives that is ranked in order of priority. Prioritizing increases the likelihood that both parties will get most of what they want from the bargain. Knowing which terms are most and least important enables the parties to make concessions without regret and avoid getting bogged down in unnecessary details. If, for example, the seller insists on a term that the buyer cannot agree to, the seller can explain why he cannot concede on that term and then offer to give up something in exchange. The following negotiating tips can help parties reach a mutually satisfying deal:

- ***Know what you want to have when you walk away from the table.*** What will it take to reach your business objectives? What would the perfect deal be? Although it may not be possible to achieve it, defining the perfect deal may help to identify which issues are most important.
- ***Develop a negotiation strategy.*** Once you know where you want to finish, decide where you will start and remember to leave some room to give. Avoid being the first to mention price. Let the other party do that; then negotiate from there.
- ***Recognize the other party's needs.*** For a bargain to occur, both parties must believe that they have met at least some of their goals. Asking open-ended questions can provide insight to the other's position.
- ***Be an empathetic listener.*** To truly understand what the other party's position is, you must listen attentively.
- ***Focus on the issue, not on the person.*** If the negotiation reaches an impasse, a natural tendency is to attack the other party. Instead, focus on developing a workable solution to accomplish your goals.
- ***Avoid seeing the other side as "the enemy."*** This type of an attitude reduces the negotiation to an "I win, you lose" mentality that only hinders the process.
- ***Educate; don't intimidate.*** Explain the reasoning and the logic behind your proposal, rather than trying to bully the other party into accepting your point of view.
- ***Be patient.*** Resist the tendency to become angry or insulted by the proposals the other party makes. Similarly, do not be in such a hurry to close the deal that you compromise on crucial points.
- ***Remember that "no deal" is an option.*** In most negotiations, walking away from the table is an option. What would happen if the negotiations failed to produce a deal? In some cases, it may be the best option. In all cases, this frame of mind is a powerful negotiation tool.
- ***Be flexible and creative.*** Always have a fallback position. This less-than-ideal alternative is still acceptable to both parties.

## FIGURE 5.3  Steps in the Acquisition Process

*Sources:* Adapted from *The Buying and Selling a Company Handbook* (New York: Price Waterhouse, 993), pp. 38–42; "Small Business Practices: How to . . . Buy a Business," Edgeonline, www.edgeonline.comlmalnlbizbuilders/BlZ/Sm_business/buybus.shtml; "Buying a Business;" www.ptbo.igs.net/~lbk/bab.htm; Ronaleen R. Roha, "Don't Start It, Buy It," *Kiplinger's Personal Finance Magazine,* July 1997, pp. 74–78; Robert F. Klueger, *Buying and Selling a Business: A Step by Step Guide* (Hoboken, NJ: John Wiley & Sons, Inc., 2004), pp. 179–188.

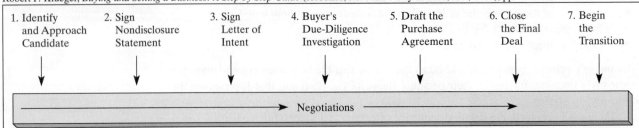

**Step 1: Approach the candidate company.** If a business is advertised for sale, the proper approach is through the channel defined in the ad. Sometimes buyers will contact business brokers to help them locate potential target companies. If you have targeted a company in the "hidden market," an introduction from a banker, accountant, or lawyer often is the best approach. During this phase, the seller checks out the buyer's qualifications, and the buyer begins to judge the quality of the company.

**Step 2: Sign a nondisclosure document.** If the buyer and the seller are satisfied with the results of their preliminary research, they are ready to begin serious negotiations. Throughout the negotiation process, the seller expects the buyer to maintain strict confidentiality of all of the records, documents, and information he or she receives during the investigation and negotiation process. The nondisclosure document is a legally binding contract that ensures the secrecy of the parties' negotiations.

**Step 3: Sign a letter of intent.** Before a buyer makes a legal offer to buy the company, the buyer typically will ask the seller to sign a letter of intent, or LOI. The letter of intent is a nonbinding document that says that the buyer and the seller have reached a sufficient "meeting of the minds" to justify the time and expense of negotiating a final agreement. The letter should state clearly that it is nonbinding, giving either party the right to walk away from the deal. It also should contain a clause calling for "good-faith negotiations" between the parties. A typical letter of intent addresses terms such as price, payment terms, categories of assets to be sold, and a deadline for closing the final deal. Typically, a letter of intent includes a "no-shop" clause. This clause states that the seller cannot use the deal that is being negotiated as leverage to raise an offer from other potential buyers for a given time frame, usually 90 days.

**Step 4: Conduct buyer's due diligence.** While negotiations are continuing, the buyer is busy studying the business and evaluating its strengths and weaknesses. In short, the buyer must do his or her homework to make sure that the business is a good value. The buyer should obtain an independent valuation of the business and conduct a detailed review of all company records, employment agreements, leases, and pending litigation.

**Step 5: Draft the purchase agreement.** The purchase agreement spells out the parties' final deal. It sets forth all of the details of the agreement and is the final product of the negotiation process. Typical purchase agreement provisions include:

- Definitions for terms in the agreement
- Description of assets (property) and timing of payment
- Purchase price
- Special conditions that the parties must satisfy to close the deal
- Allocation of purchase price to specific assets
- Whether the purchaser assumes any liabilities, and, if so which ones
- Lease transfers and their terms
- Warranties, representations, and agreements
- A clause addressing bulk transfer provisions, if appropriate
- Conduct of the business between the date of the purchase agreement and the closing date
- Conditions necessary to close the deal
- Provisions specifying procedures for resolving postclosing disputes and breaches of seller's warranties and representations
- Covenants restricting competition
- Miscellaneous matters regarding escrows, payment of broker commissions, and various legal and regulatory provisions
- Time and place of closing

**Step 6: Close the deal.** Once the parties have drafted the purchase agreement, all that remains to make the deal "official" is the closing. Both buyer and seller sign the necessary documents to make the sale final. The buyer delivers the required money, and the seller turns the company over to the buyer.

**Step 7: Begin the transition.** For the buyer, the real challenge now begins: Making the transition to a successful business owner!

Before beginning negotiations, a buyer should take stock of some basic issues.

- How strong is the seller's desire to sell?
- Is the seller willing to finance part of the purchase price?
- What terms does the seller suggest?
- Which terms are most important?
- Is it imperative that the seller closes the deal quickly?
- What deal structure best suits the buyer's needs?
- What are the tax consequences for both parties?
- Will the seller sign a restrictive covenant?
- Is the seller willing to stay on with the company for a time in a consulting role? What general economic conditions exist in the industry at the time of the sale? Sellers tend to have the upper hand in good economic times, and buyers will have an advantage during recessionary periods in an industry.

In general, the seller of the business is looking to accomplish these goals:

- Receiving the highest price possible for the company.
- Severing all responsibility for the company's liabilities.
- Avoiding unreasonable contract terms that might limit future opportunities.
- Maximizing the cash from the deal.
- Minimizing the tax burden from the sale.
- Making sure the buyer will make all future payments.

The buyer seeks to realize these goals:

- Buying the business at the lowest price possible.
- Negotiating favorable payment terms, preferably over time.
- Getting assurances that he or she is buying the business he or she thinks it is.
- Prohibiting the seller from opening a competing business.
- Minimizing the amount of cash paid up front.

Entrepreneurs who are most effective at acquiring a business know how important it is to understand the complex emotions that influence the seller's behavior and decisions. For the typical seller, the business often represents his or her life and defines his or her identity. He or she may be the original founder, having nurtured the business through its infancy to maturity to the point that it is time to "let go." The seller may ask; What will I do now? Where will I go each morning? Who will I be without "my business?" The negotiation process may raise these questions and require the seller to put a price tag on his or her life's work. For these reasons, a potential buyer must realize that the seller's emotions are entwined in the sale and negotiate with sensitivity and respect.

### The "Art of the Deal"

Both buyers and sellers must recognize that no one benefits without an agreement. Both parties must work to achieve their goals while making concessions to keep the negotiations alive.

Figure 5.4 is an illustration of two individuals preparing to negotiate for the purchase and sale of a business. The buyer and seller both have high and low bargaining points in this example.

- The buyer would like to purchase the business for $900,000 but would not pay more than $1,300,000.
- The seller would like to get $1,500,000 for the business but would not take less than $1,000,000.
- If the seller insists on getting $1,500,000, this buyer is not willing to make a deal.
- If the buyer offers only $900,000, there will be no deal.

The bargaining process may eventually lead both parties into the **bargaining zone**, the area in which the parties have the potential to reach an agreement. It extends from above the lowest price the seller is willing to take to below the maximum price the buyer is willing to pay. The dynamics of this negotiation process and the needs of each party ultimately determine whether the buyer and seller can reach an agreement and, if so, at what price.

**FIGURE 5.4 Identifying the Bargaining Zone**

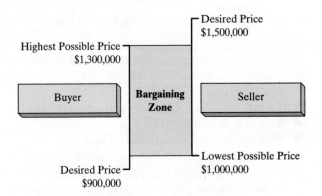

Learning to negotiate successfully means mastering "the art of the deal." The following guidelines will help both parties appreciate the negotiation as a conference, likely to produce positive results, rather than as a competition, likely to spiral downward into conflict.

*Establish the proper mind-set.* Trust is the foundation of successful negotiations. The first step in any negotiation should be to establish a climate of trust and communication. Too often, buyers and sellers rush into putting their chips on the bargaining table without establishing a rapport with one another.

*Understand the rules.* Recognize the "rules" of successful negotiations.

- Everything is negotiable.
- Take nothing for granted.
- Ask for as much as possible.
- Consider the other party's perspective.
- Explore a variety of options.
- Seek solutions that are mutually beneficial.

*Develop a negotiating strategy.* One of the biggest mistakes business buyers can make is entering negotiations with only a vague notion of the strategies they will employ. To be successful, it is necessary to know how to respond to a variety of situations that are likely to arise. Every strategy has an upside and a downside, and effective negotiators know what they are.

*Be creative.* When negotiations stall or come to an impasse, negotiators must seek creative alternatives that benefit both parties or, at a minimum, get the negotiations started again.

*Keep emotions in check.* A short temper and an important negotiation make ill-suited partners. The surest way to destroy trust and to sabotage a negotiation is to lose one's temper and lash out at the other party. Anger leads to poor decisions.

*Be patient.* Sound negotiations often take a great deal of time, especially when one is buying a business from the entrepreneur who founded it. The seller's ego is a part of the negotiation process, and wise negotiators recognize this. Persistence and patience are the keys to success in any negotiation involving the sale of the business.

*Don't become a victim.* Well-prepared negotiators are not afraid to walk away from deals that are not right for them.

### The Structure of the Deal

To make a negotiation work, the two sides must structure the deal in a way that is acceptable to both parties.

**STRAIGHT BUSINESS SALE.** A straight business sale may be best for a seller who wants to step down and turn over the reins of the company to someone else. A study of small business sales in 60 categories reported that 94 percent were asset sales and the remaining 6 percent involve the sale of stock. About 22 percent were for cash, and 75 percent included a down payment with a note carried by the seller. The remaining 3 percent relied on a note from the seller with no down payment. When the deal included a down payment, it averaged 33 percent of the purchase price. Only 40 percent of the business sales in the study included covenants not to compete.

Although selling a business outright is often the safest exit path for an entrepreneur, it includes several disadvantages. Sellers who want cash and take the money up front may face a significant tax burden. They must pay a capital gains tax on the sale price less their investments in the company. A straight sale is also not an attractive exit strategy for those who want to stay on with the company or for those who want to surrender control of the company gradually rather than all at once.

Ideally, a buyer has already begun to explore the options available for financing the purchase. Traditional lenders who are willing to finance business purchases normally lend only a portion of the value of the assets, and buyers often find themselves searching for alternative sources of funds. Fortunately, most business buyers discover an important source of financing built into the deal: the *seller*. Typically, a deal is structured so that the buyer makes a down payment to the seller, who then finances a note for the balance. The buyer makes regular principal and interest payments over time—perhaps with a larger balloon payment at the end—until the note is paid off. A common arrangement is when the seller is willing to finance 40 to 70 percent of the purchase price over time, usually 3 to 10 years. The terms and conditions of such a loan are vital to both buyer and seller. They cannot be so burdensome that they threaten the company's future; that is, the buyer must be able to make the payments to the seller out of the company's cash flow.

**SALE OF CONTROLLING INTEREST.**   Sometimes business owners sell the majority interest in their companies with an agreement that they will stay on after the sale. In this way a potential buyer might feel more confident about the acquisition if he or she knows that the owner will commit to a management contract for two to four years. Additionally, for the seller who does not want to retire or start a new business, a management contract can be an excellent source of income. This type of flexibility by the seller may result in negotiating a more lucrative final deal.

**RESTRUCTURE THE COMPANY.**   Another way for business owners to cash out gradually is to replace the existing corporation with a new one, formed with other investors. The owner is essentially performing a leveraged buyout of his or her own company. For example, suppose that you own a company worth $15 million. You form a new corporation with $12 million borrowed from a bank and $3 million in equity: $1.5 million of your own equity and $1.5 million in equity from an investor who wants you to stay on with the business. The new company buys your company for $15 million. You net $13.5 in cash ($15 million minus your $1.5 million equity investment) and still own 50 percent of the new leveraged business (see Figure 5.5). For a business whose financial statements can justify a significant bank loan, restructuring is an excellent alternative. This can be an option in cases where both parties agree that the seller should remain involved in the business.

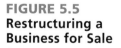
**FIGURE 5.5**
**Restructuring a Business for Sale**

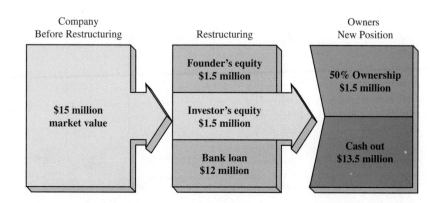

Company Before Restructuring

$15 million market value

Restructuring

Founder's equity $1.5 million

Investor's equity $1.5 million

Bank loan $12 million

Owners New Position

50% Ownership $1.5 million

Cash out $13.5 million

**USE A TWO-STEP SALE.**   For owners who want the security of a sales contract now but do not want to step down from the company's helm for several years, a two-step sale may be ideal. The buyer purchases the business in two phases, getting 20 percent to 70 percent today and agreeing to buy the remainder within a specific time period. Until the final transaction takes place, the entrepreneur retains at least partial control of the company.

### Other Alternatives

**FAMILY LIMITED PARTNERSHIP.**   Entrepreneurs who want to pass their businesses on to their children may benefit by forming a family limited partnership. Using this exit strategy, an entrepreneur can transfer the business to his or her children without sacrificing control. The owner takes the role of general partner while the children become limited partners. The general partner keeps just 1 percent of the company, but the partnership agreement gives him or her total control over the business. The children own 99 percent of the company, but have little or no say over how to run the business. Until the founder decides to step down and turn the reins of the company over to the next generation, the founder continues to run the business and sets up significant tax savings for the ultimate transfer of power.

**EMPLOYEE STOCK OWNERSHIP PLAN (ESOP).**   Some owners cash out by selling to their employees through an employee stock ownership plan (ESOP). An ESOP is a form of employee benefit plan that creates a trust for employees to purchase their employers' stock. Here's how an ESOP works: The company transfers shares of its stock to an ESOP trust, and the trust uses the stock as collateral to borrow enough money to purchase the shares from the company. The company guarantees payment of the loan principal and interest and makes tax-deductible contributions to the trust to repay the loan. The company then distributes the stock to employees' accounts on the basis of a predetermined formula (see Figure 5.6). In addition to the tax benefits an ESOP offers, the plan permits the owner to transfer all or part of the company to employees as gradually or as suddenly as preferred.

To use an ESOP successfully, a business should have pretax profits exceeding $100,000 and an annual payroll of at least $500,000. In general, companies with fewer than 15 to 20 employees do not find ESOPs beneficial. For companies that prepare properly, however, ESOPs offer significant financial and managerial benefits. Owners are able to sell their stock at whatever pace appeals to them. There is no cost to the employees, who eventually get to take over the company, and for the company the cost of the buyout is fully deductible. Setting up an ESOP can be expensive, however. Even a simple ESOP can cost $30,000 to establish.

**SELLING TO AN INTERNATIONAL BUYER.**   In an increasingly global marketplace, small domestic businesses have become attractive buyout targets for foreign companies. In many

**FIGURE 5.6  A Typical Employee Stock Ownership Plan (ESOP)**

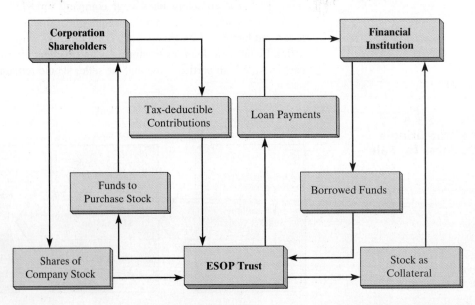

## Sprinkling Success

The chance to buy a business just fell into Ryan Berreth's lap. During summer breaks in high school, Berreth and a friend installed landscape sprinkler systems. Several years later, his father learned about a sprinkler installation company that was for sale, and Berreth thought it was a perfect fit. After studying the company, Berreth decided to leave his job as a sales representative and purchase Sprinkling Columbus Inc. from Donnie Coppedge, the company's founder, who was ready to retire.

Business broker Kevin Wilkerson facilitated the sale of Sprinkling Columbus, which Berreth renamed H2OME Irrigation Systems. Wilkerson believes the way potential buyers come across opportunities is not always through the most obvious pathways. "A lot of times there are businesses in the pipeline that aren't on the Internet," Wilkerson says. Simply talking to people—which is how things got started between Wilkerson and Berreth—can help prospective buyers find a business that fits.

When buying or selling a business, the buyer, the seller, and the broker must follow a process that includes collecting business information and screening potential buyers. Wilkerson believes that buyers should make sure they have a passion for the business. They should also examine the financials to make certain that the venture has the ability to generate enough cash to pay for debt service and a desired salary. It is also important that the prospective buyer find out why the business owner is selling the venture. Coppedge had operated Sprinkling Columbus for 22 years and wanted to find a buyer who would continue the company's tradition of success. When he met Berreth, he quickly gave the green light. The two agreed to have Coppedge stay on board for 40 working days so that Coppedge could help Berreth with the transition and introduce him to existing customers. "It was a smart part of the agreement because, hey, I'm the new guy," Berreth says. "There was a fear we'd lose half the clientele if they found out the company had been purchased by somebody else." Coppedge sent out a newsletter letting people know that he was retiring and that Berreth would be taking over the company.

Fortunately, most of Coppedge's customers remained. "It's a myth to think customers are tied to the owner," says Wilkerson. Customers are loyal to the quality the business offers, and if the new business owner continues to offer quality products or services, customers will most likely stay.

When it comes to buying a business versus starting one from scratch, Berreth and Wilkerson say there are both pros and cons for each. When buying a business, says Wilkerson, "The buyer has to be comfortable with the fact that because they're buying cash flow, they may have more debt initially." Berreth points out that legal and other fees add to the initial price.

Buying into a successful business with a proven model, immediate cash flow, an established customer list, and a marketable reputation offers significant benefits. "There's no way I would've picked up 300 clients on my own had I started it," Berreth stated.

Berreth has his own vision for H2OME Irrigation Systems. In the first three years, he wants to focus on the company as a service and repair business. Later, he will focus on sprinkler installation with plans to hire a crew to perform that work. In the meantime, Berreth says the business has been keeping him busy.

Some people might be afraid to take on the risks of buying an existing business like Berreth did, but sometimes success requires a leap of faith. "If you try to remove all the risk of starting or buying a business, you'll never buy a business," Wilkerson said. "At some point, you've got to jump."

Did Berreth think he made the right decision? "For someone who wants immediate business, immediate volume and immediate results, yes," Berreth said. "That's what I needed."

1. Make a list of the "pros and cons" of buying versus starting this type of a service business.
2. Discuss the potential risks that Berreth faces in the purchase of this business.

*Source:* Andrea Hernandez, "Buying an Existing Business Grows Confidence," Ledger-Inquirer.com, July 10, 2007, www.ledgerenquirer.com/102/story/80522.html.

instances, foreign companies buy domestic businesses to gain access to a lucrative, growing market. They look for a team of capable managers, whom they typically retain for a given time period. They also want companies that are profitable, stable, and growing. Selling to foreign buyers can have disadvantages, however. Foreign buyers typically purchase 100 percent of a company, allowing no ownership position for the previous owner. Relationships with foreign owners also can be more uncertain and difficult to manage.

### Ensure a Smooth Transition

Once the details of the negotiation are finalized, the challenge of facilitating a smooth transition is next. No matter how well planned the sale is, there are always surprises. For instance, the new owner may have ideas for changing the business—perhaps radically—that cause a great deal of stress and anxiety among employees and with the previous owner. Charged with emotion and uncertainty, the transition phase may be difficult, frustrating, and sometimes painful. To avoid a bumpy transition, a business buyer should do the following:

- *Communicate clearly.* Concentrate on communicating with employees. Business sales are fraught with uncertainty and anxiety, and employees need reassurance. Take the time to explain your plans for the company.
- *Be straightforward.* Be honest with employees. Avoid telling them only what they want to hear.
- *Listen carefully.* Listen to employees. They have intimate knowledge of the business and its strengths and weaknesses, and can usually offer valuable suggestions. Keep your door and your ears open and enter as somebody who is going to be good for the entire organization.
- *Sell the vision.* Devote time to selling the vision for the company to its key stakeholders, including major customers, suppliers, bankers, and others.
- *Seek advice.* Consider asking the seller to serve as a consultant until the transition is complete. The previous owner can be a valuable resource.

## Chapter Review

1. Understand the advantages and disadvantages of buying an existing business.
   - The *advantages* of buying an existing business include the following:
     - A successful business may continue to be successful.
     - The business may already have the best location.
     - Employees and suppliers are already established.
     - Equipment is installed and its productive capacity known.
     - Inventory is in place and trade credit established.
     - The owner hits the ground running.
     - The buyer can use the expertise of the previous owner.
     - The business may be a bargain.
   - The *disadvantages* of buying an existing business include the following:
     - An existing business may be for sale because it is deteriorating.
     - The previous owner may have created ill will.
     - Employees inherited with the business may not be suitable.
     - Its location may have become unsuitable.
     - Equipment and facilities may be obsolete.
     - Change and innovation are hard to implement.
     - Inventory may be outdated.
     - Accounts receivable may be worth less than face value.
     - The business may be overpriced.
2. Discuss the steps involved in the *right* way to buy a business.
   - Buying a business can be a treacherous experience unless the buyer is well prepared. The right way to buy a business includes the following actions:
     - Analyze your skills, abilities, and interests to determine the ideal business for you.

- Prepare a list of potential candidates, including those that might be in the "hidden market."
- Investigate and evaluate candidate businesses and evaluate the best one; explore financing options before you actually need the money.
- Ensure a smooth transition.
- Rushing into a deal can be the biggest mistake a business buyer can make. Before closing a deal, every business buyer should investigate five critical areas:
    1. Why does the owner wish to sell? Look for the real reason.
    2. Determine the physical condition of the business. Consider both the building and its location.
    3. Conduct a thorough analysis of the market for your products or services. Who are the present and potential customers? Conduct an equally thorough analysis of competitors, both direct and indirect. How do they operate and why do customers prefer them?
    4. Consider all of the legal aspects that might constrain the expansion and growth of the business. Did you comply with the provisions of a bulk transfer? Negotiate a restrictive covenant? Consider ongoing legal liabilities?
    5. Analyze the financial condition of the business, looking at financial statements, income tax returns, and especially cash flow.

**3.** Describe the various methods used in the valuation of a business.

- Placing a value on a business is partly an art and partly a science. There is no single best method for determining the value of a business. The following techniques (with several variations) are useful: the balance sheet technique (adjusted balance sheet technique), the earnings approach (excess earnings method, capitalized earnings approach, and discounted future earnings approach), and the market approach.

**4.** Discuss the process of negotiating the deal.

- Selling a business takes time, patience, and preparation to locate a suitable buyer, strike a deal, and make the transition. Sellers must always structure the deal with tax consequences in mind. Common exit strategies include a straight business sale, forming a family limited partnership, selling a controlling interest in the business, restructuring the company, selling to an international buyer, using a two-step sale, and establishing an employee stock ownership plan (ESOP). The first rule of negotiating is never confuse price with value. The party who is the better negotiator usually comes out on top. Before beginning negotiations, a buyer should identify the factors that are affecting the negotiations and then develop a negotiating strategy. The best deals are the result of a cooperative relationship based on trust.

## Discussion Questions

1. What advantages can an entrepreneur who buys a business gain over one who starts a business from scratch?
2. How would you go about determining the value of the assets of a business if you were unfamiliar with them?
3. Why do so many entrepreneurs run into trouble when they buy an existing business? Outline the steps involved in the *right* way to buy a business.
4. When evaluating an existing business that is for sale, what areas should an entrepreneur consider? Briefly summarize the key elements of each area.
5. How should a buyer evaluate a business's goodwill?

6. What is a restrictive covenant? Is it fair to ask the seller of a travel agency located in a small town to sign a restrictive covenant for one year covering a 20-square-mile area? Explain.
7. How much negative information can you expect the seller to give you about the business? How can a prospective buyer find out such information?
8. Why is it so difficult for buyers and sellers to agree on a price for a business?
9. Which method of valuing a business is best? Why?
10. Outline the different exit strategies available to a seller.

11. Explain the buyer's position in a typical negotiation for a business. Explain the seller's position. What tips would you offer a buyer about to begin negotiating the purchase of a business?

12. What benefits might an entrepreneur realize from using a business broker when purchasing a business? What are the potential disadvantages?

---

# Business PlanPro

This chapter addresses buying an existing business. If you are purchasing an existing business, determine whether the company has a business plan. If so, how recent is that plan? Is it representative of the current state of the organization? Is access available to other historical information including historical sales information and financial statements, such as the profit and loss, balance sheet, and cash flow statements? These documents are valuable resources to understand the business and develop a plan for its future.

## On the Web

If the business has a Web site, review that site to assess the "online personality" of the business. Gather as much information as possible about the business from the Web site. Does it match the information from the owner and other documents? Conduct an online search for the business name and the owners' names. Note what you find and, again, determine whether this information correlates with information from other sources.

Review the executive summaries of these ongoing business plans through the Sample Plan Browser in Business Plan Pro:

- Machine Tooling
- Salvador's Sauces
- Sample Software Company
- Take Five Sports Bar
- Web Solutions, Inc.

Scan the table of contents and find the section of the plan with information on the company's past performance. What might this historical information indicate about the future potential of the venture? Which of these businesses present the greatest profit potential based on their past performance? Which business represents the greatest risk based on these same criteria? How might this risk influence the purchase price?

## In the Software

If the company has sales, profits, and other information available, enter it into Business Plan Pro. First, select the "existing" business plan option in the opening window. If you have access to an electronic version of the company's plan you are considering purchasing, copy and paste text from a word processing document directly into Business Plan Pro by using the "Paste Special" option and then select the option "Without Formatting." This step will help to keep the formatting in order. Go to the "Company Summary" section and include the results of the due diligence process. The financial statements of the business, including the balance sheet, profit and loss, and cash flow statements from the past three years will be valuable. This will set a baseline for the future sales and expense scenarios. This process may help to better assess the business's future earning potential and its current value.

## Building Your Business Plan

One of the advantages of using Business Plan Pro is the ease of creating multiple financial scenarios. This can be an excellent way to explore multiple "what if" options. Once the business is up and running, updating the plan during the fiscal year and on an annual basis can be a quick and easy process. This will be an efficient way to keep the plan current and, by saving each of these files based on the date for the example, offer an excellent historical account of the business.

# 6

# Conducting a Feasibility Analysis and Crafting a Winning Business Plan

Planning is bringing the future into the present so that you can do something about it now.
—Alan Lakein

Good fortune is what happens when opportunity meets with planning.
—Thomas Alva Edison

## Learning Objectives

**Upon completion of this chapter, you will be able to:**

1 Describe the steps involved in conducting a feasibility analysis.

2 Explain the benefits of an effective business plan.

3 Describe the elements of a solid business plan.

4 Explain the three tests every business plan must pass.

5 Explain the "five Cs of credit" and why they are important to potential lenders and investors reviewing business plans.

6 Understand the keys to making an effective business plan presentation.

ne of the most important activities an entrepreneur should undertake before launching a company is to conduct a feasibility analysis, and based on a successful result, build a business plan. A **feasibility analysis** is the process of determining whether an idea is a viable foundation for creating a successful business. The business plan functions as a planning tool, taking a viable idea from the feasibility analysis and describing how to turn it into a successful business.

A feasibility analysis answers the question, "Should we proceed with this business idea?" It is primarily an investigative tool. The feasibility analysis gives an entrepreneur a picture of the market, sales, and profit potential of a particular business idea. Feasibility studies are particularly useful when an entrepreneur generates multiple ideas for business concepts and must make a "best choice." This analysis enables an entrepreneur to efficiently explore the viability of alternative business concepts and to assess the likelihood of transforming an idea into a successful business venture. The role of the feasibility analysis is to serve as a filter, screening out ideas that lack the potential for building a successful business, before an entrepreneur commits additional resources. When the result is the realization that an idea simply will not result in a viable business, the entrepreneur moves on to the next opportunity and avoids wasting valuable time, money, energy and other resources creating a full-blown business plan. More importantly, he or she avoids launching a business that is likely to fail because it is based on a flawed concept. In other cases, a feasibility study shows an entrepreneur that the business idea is sound, but it must be organized in a different fashion to be profitable.

If the idea proves feasible, the entrepreneur's next step is to leverage the findings of the feasibility analysis to build a business plan. The primary goal of the business plan is to guide the entrepreneur as he or she launches and operates a business venture. The business plan also helps the entrepreneur acquire the necessary financing to launch the venture. A well-constructed business plan may be the best possible insurance against failure. Research suggests that, whatever their size, companies that engage in business planning outperform those that do not. A business plan offers:

- A systematic, realistic evaluation of a venture's chances for success in the market.
- A way to determine the principal risks facing the venture.
- A "game plan" for managing the business successfully.
- A tool for comparing actual results against targeted performance.
- An important tool for attracting capital in the challenging hunt for money.

The feasibility study and the business plan play important, but separate, roles in the start-up process. This chapter describes how to build and use these vital business documents. It will help entrepreneurs create business plans that will guide them on their entrepreneurial journey and help them attract the capital they need to launch and grow their businesses.

## Conducting a Feasibility Analysis

*1.* Describe the steps involved in conducting a feasibility analysis.

A feasibility analysis consists of three interrelated components: an industry and market feasibility analysis, a product or service feasibility analysis, and a financial feasibility analysis as shown in Figure 6.1. "Making a critical evaluation of your business concept at an early stage will allow you to discover, address, and correct any fatal flaws before investing time in preparing your business plan," says Timothy Faley, managing director of the Samuel Zell & Robert H. Lurie Institute for Entrepreneurial Studies.[1]

### Industry and Market Feasibility Analysis

When evaluating the feasibility of a business idea, an entrepreneur finds a basic analysis of the industry and targeted market segments essential. The focus in this phase is twofold:

1. To determine how attractive an industry is overall as a "home" for a new business.
2. To identify possible niches a small business can occupy profitably.

**FIGURE 6.1 Elements
of a Feasibility Analysis**

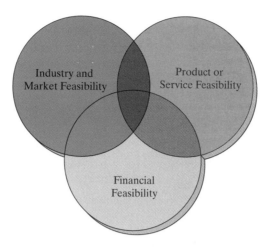

The first step in assessing industry attractiveness is to paint a picture of the industry with broad strokes, assessing it from a "macro" level. Answering the following questions will help establish this perspective:

- How large is the industry?
- How fast is it growing?
- Is the industry as a whole profitable?
- Is the industry characterized by high profit margins or razor-thin margins?
- How essential are its products or services to customers?
- What trends are shaping the industry's future?
- What threats does the industry face?
- What opportunities does the industry face?
- How crowded is the industry?
- How intense is the level of competition in the industry?
- Is the industry young, mature, or somewhere in between?

Addressing these questions helps entrepreneurs determine whether the potential for sufficient demand for their products and services exist.

A useful tool for analyzing an industry's attractiveness is the **five forces model** developed by Michael Porter of the Harvard Business School, shown in Figure 6.2. This model recognizes the influence of five industry forces:

1. Rivalry among the companies competing in the industry
2. Bargaining power of suppliers to the industry
3. Bargaining power of customers
4. Threat of new entrants to the industry
5. Threat of substitute products or services

These five forces interact with one another to determine the setting in which companies compete and the attractiveness of the industry.[2]

*Rivalry among companies competing in the industry.*   The strongest of the five forces in most industries is the rivalry that exists among the businesses competing in a particular market. Much like the horses running in a race, businesses in a market are jockeying for position in an attempt to gain a competitive advantage. When a company creates an innovation or develops a unique strategy that transforms the market, competing companies must adapt or run the risk of being forced out of business. This force makes markets a dynamic and highly competitive place. Generally, an industry is more attractive when:

- The number of competitors is large, or, at the other extreme, quite small (fewer than five).
- Competitors are not similar in size or capability.

**FIGURE 6.2 The Five Forces Model of Competition**

*Source:* Adapted from Michael E. Porter, "How Competitive Forces Shape Strategy," *Harvard Business Review,* March–April 1979, pp. 137–145.

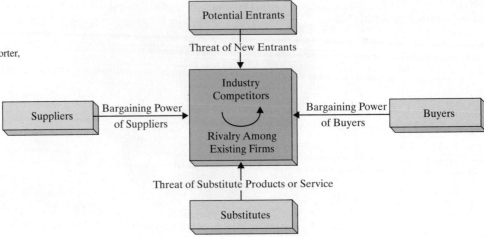

- The industry is growing at a fast pace.
- The opportunity to sell a differentiated product or service is present.

***Bargaining power of suppliers to the industry.*** The greater the leverage suppliers of key raw materials or components have, the less attractive is the industry. For instance, Intel and Advanced Micro Devices (AMD) exert a great deal of power over a number of computer manufacturers, which makes the industry less attractive for new entrants. These companies supply the chips that serve as the "brains" of PCs, and those chips make up a sizable portion of the cost of a computer. Generally, an industry is more attractive when:

- Many suppliers sell a commodity product to the companies in it.
- Substitute products are available for the items suppliers provide.
- Companies in the industry find it easy to switch from one supplier to another or to substitute products (i.e., "switching costs" are low).
- The items suppliers provide the industry account for a relatively small portion of the cost of the industry's finished products.

***Bargaining power of buyers.*** Just as suppliers to an industry can be a source of pressure, buyers also have the potential to exert significant power over a business, making it less attractive. When the number of customers is small and the cost of switching to competitors' products is low, buyers' influence on companies is high. Famous for offering its customers low prices, Wal-Mart, the largest company in the world, is also well known for applying relentless pressure to its 21,000 suppliers to offer price concessions.[3] Generally, an industry is more attractive when:

- Industry customers' "switching costs" to competitors' products or to substitute products are relatively high.
- The number of customers in the industry is large.
- Customers demand products that are differentiated rather than purchase commodity products that they can obtain from any supplier (and subsequently can pit one company against another to drive down price).
- Customers find it difficult to gather information on suppliers' costs, prices, and product features—something that is becoming much easier for customers in many industries to do by using the Internet.
- The items companies sell to the industry account for a relatively small portion of the cost of their customers' finished products.

***Threat of new entrants to the industry.*** The larger the pool of potential new entrants to an industry, the greater is the threat to existing companies in it. This is particularly true in industries in which the barriers to entry—such as capital requirements, specialized knowledge, access to distribution channels, and others—are low. Generally, an industry is more attractive to new entrants when:

- The advantages of economies of scale are absent. Economies of scale exist when companies in an industry achieve low average costs by producing huge volumes of items (e.g., computer chips).
- Capital requirements to enter the industry are low.
- Cost advantages are not related to company size.
- Customers are not extremely brand-loyal, making it easier for new entrants to the industry to draw them away from existing businesses.
- Governments, through their regulatory and international trade policies, do not restrict new companies from entering the industry.

***Threat of substitute products or services.***    Substitute products or services can turn an entire industry on its head. For instance, many makers of glass bottles have closed their doors in recent years as their customers—from soft drink bottlers to ketchup makers—have switched to plastic containers, which are lighter, less expensive to ship, and less subject to breakage. Printed newspapers have seen their readership rates decline as new generations of potential readers turn to online sources of news that are constantly updated. Generally, an industry is more attractive when:

- Quality substitute products are not readily available.
- The prices of substitute products are not significantly lower than those of the industry's products.
- Customers' cost of switching to substitute products is high.

After surveying the power these five forces exert on an industry, entrepreneurs can evaluate the potential for their companies to generate reasonable sales and profits in a particular industry. In other words, they can answer the question, "Is this industry a good home for my business?" Table 6.1 provides a sample matrix that allows entrepreneurs to assign quantitative scores to the five forces influencing industry attractiveness. Note that the lower the score for an industry, the more attractive it is.

### TABLE 6.1  Five Forces Matrix

Assign a value to rate the importance of each of the five forces to the industry on a 1 (not important) to 5 (very important) scale. Then assign a value to reflect the threat that each force poses to the industry. Multiply the importance rating in column 2 by the threat rating in column 3 to produce a weighted score. Add the weighted scores in column 3 to get a total weighted score. This score measures the industry's attractiveness. The matrix is a useful tool for comparing the attractiveness of different industries.

Minimum Score = 5 (Very attractive)
Maximum Score = 125 (Very unattractive)

| Force | Importance (1 to 5)* | Threat to Industry (1 to 5)** | Weighted Score Col 2 × Col 3 |
|---|---|---|---|
| Rivalry among companies competing in the industry | 5 | 5 | 25 |
| Bargaining power of suppliers in the industry | 2 | 2 | 4 |
| Bargaining power of buyers | 2 | 4 | 8 |
| Threat of new entrants to the industry | 3 | 4 | 12 |
| Threat of substitute products or services | 4 | 3 | 12 |
| | | Total | 61 |

*Scale of importance from 1 = not important to 5 = very important. **Scale of threat to the industry from 1 = low, 3 = medium, to 5 = high.

The next step in assessing an industry is to identify potentially attractive niches that exist in the industry. Many small businesses prosper by sticking to niches in a market that are too small to attract the attention of large competitors. Occupying an industry niche enables a business to shield itself, to some extent, from the power of the five forces. The key question for entrepreneurs is, "Can we identify a niche that is large enough to produce a profit, or can we position our company uniquely in the market to differentiate it from the competition in a meaningful way?" Entrepreneurs who have designed successful focus or differentiation strategies for their companies can exploit these niches to their advantage.

Questions entrepreneurs should address in this portion of the feasibility analysis include:

- Which niche in the market will we occupy?
- How large is this market segment, and how fast is it growing?
- What is the basis for differentiating our product or service from competitors?
- Do we have a superior business model that will be difficult for competitors to reproduce?

# ENTREPRENEURSHIP
# *In Action*

## Fighting for The End

Thanks to iTunes, YouTube, MySpace.com, satellite radio, Internet radio, and the vast underworld of illegal file sharing, never before has there been so much music floating around that is so accessible and in some cases, free. Music lovers, like Andreas Katsambas, appreciate that phenomena.

Katsambas remembers what a struggle it was to get his fill of his favorite rock artists when he was growing up on the Mediterranean island of Cyprus. Today as CEO of The End Records (www.theendrecords.com), a nine-year-old heavy-metal label, he holds a different view of the industry. Katsambas, now in his mid-thirties, fears for the life of his company.

Katsambas started this business within a business because he was unhappy with the mail-order distribution his label was getting from third parties. Today it is the biggest heavy-metal music mail-order site on the Web, handling dozens of labels that account for two-thirds of company sales and all its profits. "If it wasn't for mail order," Katsambas admits, "the label wouldn't work."

The story of The End began in Katsambas' bedroom in San Diego, California. The record label grew and three years later, he shifted operations to Salt Lake City, Utah. The next move came when Katsambas relocated to a new headquarters in Brooklyn, New York. Thirteen of The End's 14 loyal employees followed.

Annual sales were $3.5 million, up 25 percent over the year before, and the company was profitable. Katsambas signed a North America licensing agreement with celebrated Finnish monster-rocker group Lordi, whose members dress as mummies and vampires. Lordi's "Hard Rock Hallelujah" snatched first prize at the Eurovision Song Contest, an annual pan-European jamboree that launched the careers of the band ABBA and songstress Celine Dion. On the surface, you might think that The End was healthy, but a closer look at industry changes and corporate expenses paints a different picture.

When Tower Records folded, The End lost a major distributor that was friendlier to independent labels than the mainstream giants such as Best Buy and Wal-Mart. The fallout was immediate. "Suddenly all the big chains got very tight with their budgets," Katsambas says. Unfortunately, he cannot count on small record stores to pick up the slack. Hundreds of the neighborhood stores closed "and you don't see any new ones opening up," laments Katsambas.

Expenses are going through the roof in Brooklyn. The move from Salt Lake cost $30,000, and the $6,000 monthly office rent in New York is twice what he used to pay. Expenses for Internet access, taxes, and even trash pickup are significantly higher in Brooklyn as well. Katsambas says, "Every month I sit down with my accountant, and she says, 'Things are tight. How do we make it work?'"

However, Katsambas isn't panicking—yet. "In times of crisis, I make the best decisions," he says. But, he also realizes that he needs a road map. Katsambas is looking for answers to basic questions. "How do we maintain a steady cash flow?" Other questions center on the need for higher profit margins and allocating the available budget. If the traditional record-label business model of investing in studio sessions and concert tours and making the money back on CD and record sales is dead—and practically everyone agrees that it is—then what is next for The End?

Only 1 percent of the company's total sales are digital. In the digital, download environment, metal and hard-core fans still prefer to buy a full CD. They want to be able to read the lyrics and listen to the whole album. That is a mixed blessing. On the one hand, it means The End is less vulnerable to digital piracy than the major labels are. On the other, the company is losing out in profits that digital sales bring to major labels. For instance, digital sales account for 10 percent of total annual sales at a typical major label.

To give him insight, Katsambas brings in a consulting team. "I think you should continue to investigate digital sales," suggests one consultant. "The fact that digital hasn't taken off among this audience doesn't mean that it's not still going to be meaningful." They recommend that Katsambas experiment on The End's Web site, rather than waiting for iTunes to figure it out. Maybe the solution is digital content not available on CD, or digital prereleases available one month before a new CD hits the streets—but only to preferred customers. They all realize the best customer is somebody who already likes the band. They would rather market to somebody who already has records from The End and knows the label.

Another lesson from the majors is that the record label should think about forming a partnership with its artists, in which it can participate in touring income as well as merchandise such as hats, T-shirts, and collectibles. "That's something we want to establish," says Katsambas. He also realizes that licensing songs owned by the label for TV, film, and video games is a potential source of revenue.

The consultants agree that the Lordi signing is a key development, one that could make or break The End. The final conclusion is that The End is in a good position with its infrastructure and contacts—it has the ingredients to bring a large act into the company and amplify the base of success.

Following the session, Katsambas decides to implement a cash-generating idea of publishing a $40 limited-edition book/CD combo tied to the release of *The Novella Reservoir*, the latest album from the dark-metal band, Novembers Doom. Katsambas also plans to expand international distribution of the label's mail-order catalog. With the turbulence in the industry, the cash flow pressures of New York, and the need to identify new revenue streams, Katsambas also saw the need to update his business plan. He wants to be prepared for anything—except the end.

1. How are the dynamics of the industry affecting The End Records? What insights might Porter's five forces model offer Katsambas? Use the matrix in Table 6.1 to score and then comment on this industry's attractiveness.
2. What value might updating his business plan offer Katsambas?

*Source:* Adapted from David Whitford, "Heavy Metal Makeover," *FSB*, March 21, 2007, http://money.cnn.com/magazines/fsb/fsb_archive/2007/03/01/8402016/index.htm.

One technique for gauging the quality of a company's business model involves **business prototyping**, in which entrepreneurs test their business models on a small scale before committing serious resources to launch a business that might not work. Business prototyping recognizes that every business idea is a hypothesis that needs to be tested before an entrepreneur takes it to full scale. If the test supports the hypothesis and its accompanying assumptions, it is time to launch a company. If the prototype flops, the entrepreneur scraps the business idea with only minimal losses and turns to the next idea.

The Internet is a valuable prototyping resource. Entrepreneurs can test their ideas by selling their products on established sites, such as eBay or by setting up their own Web sites to gauge customers' response. Frank Ross, a home-based entrepreneur who dropped out of the corporate world, operates three successful online businesses. Before launching them, however, he tested his business concept on eBay. Ross explains:

If you're considering selling a product line online as your home-based business, there is really no better place to test a market than eBay. It's considerable trouble to set up a Web site, and it can be expensive if your product fails. (I've made that mistake.) If you want to be sure you have a viable, salable product line prior to going to the trouble and expense of setting up a Web site, try selling on eBay. For the price of a few listings, you will be able to tell very quickly what kind of market you have for your potential Web store, and it may also help you weed out any problems you had not thought of.[4]

## Product or Service Feasibility Analysis

Once entrepreneurs discover that sufficient market potential for their product or service idea actually exists, they sometimes rush in too quickly. With exuberant enthusiasm, they launch their businesses without actually considering whether they can actually produce the product or provide the service at a reasonable cost. A **product or service feasibility analysis** determines the degree to which a product or service idea appeals to potential customers. It also identifies the resources necessary to produce the product or provide the service. This portion of the feasibility analysis addresses two questions:

- ■ Are customers willing to purchase our goods and services?
- ■ Can we provide the product or service to customers at a profit?

Entrepreneurs need feedback from potential customers to successfully answer these questions. Acquiring that feedback might involve engaging in primary research such as customer surveys and focus groups, gathering secondary customer research, building prototypes, and conducting in-home trials.

**Primary research** involves collecting data firsthand and analyzing it; **secondary research** involves gathering data that has already been compiled and is available, often at a very reasonable cost or sometimes for free. Both types of research gather quantitative and qualitative information the entrepreneur can use to draw accurate conclusions about a product's or service's market potential. Primary research techniques include:

*Customer surveys and questionnaires.*   Keep surveys and questionnaires short. Word questions carefully to avoid biasing the results and use a simple ranking system. For example, a 1-to-5 scale, with 1 representing "definitely would not buy" and 5 representing "definitely would buy." Test the survey for problems on a small number of people before putting it to use. Many Web surveys are inexpensive, easy to conduct, and provide fast feedback from a large quantity of respondents. Monster.com, the online job search company, recently conducted an online survey of 30,000 customers and integrated the results from the survey into every aspect of the company's operation. "The survey results impact policy, process, product development and marketing efforts," says Chip Henry, Monster.com's vice president, voice of the customer. (Note the unique job title!) "There's nothing in the company that isn't touched as a result of the surveys."[5]

*Focus groups.*   A **focus group** involves enlisting a small number of potential customers (usually eight to twelve) to give you feedback on specific issues about your product or service (or the business idea itself). Listen carefully for what focus group members like and don't like about your product or service as they tell you what is on their minds. The founders of one small snack food company that produced apple chips conducted several focus groups to gauge customers' acceptance of the product and to guide many key business decisions, ranging from the product's name to its packaging.

The Web may also be a resource for focus groups by creating virtual focus groups on the Web. One small bicycle retailer conducts 10 online focus groups each year at virtually no cost, and gains valuable marketing information from them. Feedback from online customers is fast, convenient, and timely.

Secondary research, which usually is less expensive to conduct than primary research, includes the following sources:

*Trade associations and business directories.*   To locate a trade association, use *Business Information Sources* or the *Encyclopedia of Associations* (Thomson Gale). To find suppliers, use *The Thomas Register of American Manufacturers* (Thomas

Publishing Company) or *Standard & Poor's Register of Corporations, Executives, and Industries* (Standard & Poor Corporation).

*Direct mail lists.*    You can buy mailing lists for practically any type of business. *The Standard Rates and Data Service (SRDS) Directory of Mailing Lists* (Standard Rates and Data) is a good place to start looking.

*Demographic data.*    To learn more about the demographic characteristics of customers in general in the United States, use *The Statistical Abstract of the United States* (Government Printing Office and www.census.gov). Profiles of more specific regions are available in *The State and Metropolitan Data Book* (Government Printing Office). *The Sourcebook of Zip Code Demographics* (CACI Inc.) provides detailed breakdowns of the population in every zip code in the country. *Sales and Marketing Management's Survey of Buying Power* (Bill Communications) has statistics on consumer, retail, and industrial buying.

*Census data.*    The U.S. Bureau of the Census publishes a wide variety of reports that summarize the wealth of data found in its census database, which is available at most libraries and at the Census Bureau's Web site at www.census.gov.

*Forecasts.*    The *U.S. Global Outlook* traces the growth of 200 industries and gives a five-year forecast for each one. Many government agencies including the U.S. Department of Commerce offer forecasts on everything from interest rates to the number of housing starts. A government librarian can help you find what you need for your country.

*Market research.*    Someone may already have compiled the market research you need. *The FINDex Worldwide Directory of Market Research Reports, Studies, and Surveys* (Cambridge University Press) lists more than 10,600 studies available for purchase. Other directories of business research include *Simmons Study of Media and Markets* (Simmons Market Research Bureau Inc.) and the *ACNielsen Retail Index* (ACNielsen).

*Articles.*    Magazine and journal articles pertinent to your business are a great source of information. Use the *Reader's Guide to Periodical Literature*, the *Business Periodicals Index* (similar to the *Reader's Guide* but focuses on business periodicals), and *Ulrich's Guide to International Periodicals* to locate the ones you need.

*Local data.*    Your local Chamber of Commerce probably have useful data on the local market of interest to you. Call to find out what is available.

*The Internet.*    Entrepreneurs can benefit from the vast amount of marketing information available on the Web. This is an efficient resource with up-to-date information, and much of it is free.

**PRODUCT PROTOTYPES.**    An effective way to gauge the viability of a product is to build a prototype. A **prototype** is an original, functional model of a new product that entrepreneurs can put into the hands of potential customers so that they can see it, test it, use it, and provide feedback. Prototypes usually point out potential problems in a product's design, giving entrepreneurs the opportunity to address them in the product development process. The feedback customers give entrepreneurs based on prototypes often leads to design improvements and the identification of new features, some of which the entrepreneurs might never have discovered on their own. Makers of computer software frequently put prototypes of new products into customers' hands as they develop new products or improve existing ones. Known as *beta tests,* these trials result in an iterative design process in which software designers collect feedback from users and then incorporate their ideas into the product for the next round of tests. Existing companies can benefit from creating prototypes as well.

**IN-HOME TRIALS.**    One technique that reveals some of the most insightful information into how customers actually use a product or service is also the most challenging to coordinate: in-home trials. An **in-home trial** involves sending researchers into customers' homes to observe them as they use the company's product or service.

## ■ A Little Piece of the Planet

Ava DeMarco convinced her husband and business partner, Robert Brandegee, to give up his life as a ski instructor for a life in the city. After making the move, Brandegee decided to combine business with pleasure and enrolled in college to work toward a business degree. An assignment to write a business plan for one of Brandegee's entrepreneurship classes sparked the beginnings of their company, Little Earth. Brandegee and DeMarco put their heads together and came up with an idea for a company that they actually would want to start. DeMarco and Brandegee wanted to launch a creative business that is environmentally friendly—a business that could have a positive social impact. In fact, the idea of sustainability was the driving force behind the creation of Little Earth Productions Inc. (www.littlearth.com), a company that sells unique gifts and accessories including belts, bags, journals, and CD holders made from reused and recycled material.

"We had a gut feeling about recycled fashion accessories, and the research we did confirmed our instincts," says DeMarco. DeMarco and Brandegee used business prototyping to test their unique recycled retailing concept. "Before we invested a lot of time and money, we took a look at the market to make certain we were targeting the right buyers and offering products they wanted and could afford," says DeMarco. Their first move to explore the eco-friendly fashion concept was to set up booths displaying their unique products at various arts and crafts festivals in their local community. They were able to get face-to-face with buyers, learn what appeals to them, and find out what they are like—important steps to building a successful business.

They learned that their primary customers are people in their teens to mid-thirties who appreciate the recycling aspect of the company's products but are more interested in its distinctive fashion-forward accessories. "It was a good way to watch people use our products," says DeMarco. "We also got a lot of good feedback on price and comments on how our products worked or didn't work for them." Using the information from the festivals, they launched Little Earth Productions Inc., a company that makes distinctive fashion accessories such as belts, handbags, and wallets from recycled items such as bottle caps, license plates, tires, and hubcaps. DeMarco and Brandegee refined their business concept and rented a booth at a big industry trade show, where they came away with more than $24,000 worth of orders. They knew they had a market.

With a degree in design and 10 years experience in the graphic design field, DeMarco had seen too much waste. Her environmental sensibilities balked at the massive amount of waste produced from the beautiful paper brochures she created that were just thrown away. She decided that she wanted to make *things* instead of paper—things people would use, things that would make it easy for consumers to make the right environmental choices. DeMarco also understands the importance of flexibility and adaptability, especially in business. "I know this about business," DeMarco says, "it's always changing. What worked yesterday does not always work tomorrow."

Little Earth recycles more than 40 tons of rubber, 60,000 license plates, and over half a million bottle caps each year. The company has been featured on TV and in newspapers and magazines. Little Earth products have appeared in IKEA and American Eagle Outfitters catalogs; in magazines such as *Seventeen, Sassy,* and *Brides;* on television; and with celebrities such as Chelsea Clinton, Brooke Shields, Jay Leno, and the band members of Van Halen. They are also licensed to create designs for the U.S. national football and hockey leagues, and the Elvis Presley estate, with annual revenues in excess of $2 million.

Ava DeMarco and Rob Brandegee, founders of Little Earth.

Not only did the entrepreneurs' idea work, but their company introduced the world to a new term: eco-fashion. Little Earth is now a multi-building design and manufacturing complex in the SoHo district of Pittsburgh, Pennsylvania, with distributors in Australia, Germany, Japan, Mexico, New Zealand, and the United Kingdom. And it all started with an idea, a feasibility study, and a business plan.

1. What benefits did the feasibility analysis that DeMarco and Brandegee conducted give them?

2. What were the costs of the feasibility research and what might have the costs been without it?

*Sources:* Carla Goodman, "Can You Get There from Here?" *Entrepreneur*, December 1996, "Conveniently Green: Local Business Turns Trash to Cash," www.thepittsburghchannel.com/green-pages/13707818/detail.html; "About Little Earth," Little Earth Productions Inc., www.entrepreneur.com/article/0,4621,226677,00.html; "About Little Earth," Little Earth Productions Inc., www.littlearth.com/pages05/about.shtml; Jennifer McGuiggan, "When Duality Equals Balance," *Seaton Hall University, e-Magnify*, www.e-magnify.com/entrepreneurs_view.asp?ID=36.

## Financial Feasibility Analysis

The final component of a feasibility analysis involves assessing the financial feasibility of a proposed business venture. At this stage of the process, a broad financial analysis is sufficient. If the business concept passes the overall feasibility analysis, an entrepreneur should conduct a more thorough financial analysis when creating a full-blown business plan. The major elements in a financial feasibility analysis include the initial capital requirement, estimated earnings, and the resulting return on investment.

**CAPITAL REQUIREMENTS.** Just as a boy scout needs fuel to start a fire, an entrepreneur needs capital to start a business. Some businesses, such as manufacturing and retail businesses, require large amounts of capital. Other businesses, such as service businesses, require less capital to launch. Start-up companies often need capital to purchase equipment, buildings, technology, and other tangible assets as well as to hire and train employees, promote their products and services, and establish a presence in the market. A thorough feasibility analysis will provide an estimate of the amount of start-up capital an entrepreneur will need to get the business up and running.

**ENTREPRENEURIAL Profile**

*Shawn Donegan and Mike Puczkowski and Trac Tool Inc.*

For instance, Shawn Donegan and Mike Puczkowski needed $150,000 to launch Trac Tool Inc. and bring the Speed Rollers paint system to market. They spent most of that start-up capital to develop and test the prototype and to introduce the product at the Painting and Decorating Contractors of America trade show.[6]

You will learn more about finding sources of business funding, both debt and equity, in Chapters 14, "Sources of Equity Financing," and 15, "Sources of Debt Financing."

**ESTIMATED EARNINGS.** In addition to producing an estimate of the start-up company's capital requirements, an entrepreneur should forecast the earning potential of the proposed business. Industry trade associations and publications such as the *RMA Annual Statement Studies* offer guidelines on preparing sales and earnings estimates. From these, entrepreneurs can estimate the financial results they and their investors can expect to see from the business venture.

**RETURN ON INVESTMENT.** The final aspect of the financial feasibility analysis combines the estimated earnings and the capital requirements to determine the rate of return the venture is expected to produce. One simple measure is the rate of return on the capital invested, which is calculated by dividing the estimated earnings the business yields by the amount of capital invested in the business. Although financial estimates at the feasibility analysis stage typically are rough, they are an important part of the entrepreneur's ultimate "go" or "no go" decision about the business venture. A venture must produce an attractive rate of return relative to the level of risk it requires. This risk-return trade-off means that the higher the level of risk a prospective business involves, the higher the rate of return it must provide to the entrepreneur and investors. Why should an entrepreneur take on the risk of starting and running a business that produces a mere 3 percent or 4 percent rate of return when he or she could earn that much in a risk-free investment at a bank or other financial institution? You will learn more about developing detailed financial forecasts for a business start-up in Chapter 7, "Creating a Solid Financial Plan."

Wise entrepreneurs take the time to subject their ideas to a feasibility analysis lik : the one described here, whatever outcome it produces. If the analysis suggests that transforming the idea into a viable business is not feasible, the entrepreneur can move on to the next idea, confident that he or she has not wasted valuable resources launching a business destined to fail.

*Adaptive Hearing Solutions*

Will Anderson teamed up with Rory McDonald and Jared Archibald, two other Stanford business school students, and Stanford electrical engineering PhD candidate Paul Cuff to enter the Business Association of Stanford Engineering Students business plan contest. Their idea: to adapt a speech and noise separating filter technology being developed in Stanford's electrical engineering school to dramatically improve hearing aids. The team won the $25,000 grand prize and began to build a company around the idea. With $500,000 in venture capital, the Adaptive Hearing Solutions' team focused on its first task—to prove the quality of the new product to potential buyers. After a series of clinical trials, the new technology made only a small improvement in hearing aids, and the entrepreneurs decided to focus their energy on building other more viable businesses. "We were faced with whether we wanted a small business that might capture some value in the process, or whether we wanted to fold up while we were still ahead and move on to other pursuits. We chose the latter," says Anderson.[7]

If the analysis shows that the idea has potential as a profitable business, the entrepreneur can pursue it, using the information gathered during the feasibility analysis as the foundation for building a sound business plan. "As you work through this phase, you will identify factors that are essential to your venture's success while compiling the detailed, in-depth information you need to write your business plan, thereby immensely shortening the next phase in the process," says Timothy Faley, director of the first student-run venture capital fund in the United States.[8] We now turn our attention to the process of developing a business plan.

## The Benefits of a Business Plan

**2.** Explain the benefits of an effective business plan.

A business plan is a written summary of an entrepreneur's proposed business venture that describes its operational and financial details, its marketing opportunities and strategy, and its managers' skills and abilities. There is no substitute for a well-prepared business plan, and there are no shortcuts to creating one. The plan serves as an entrepreneur's road map on the journey toward building a successful business. One writer says "a business plan should be the place where the map is drawn, for, as every traveler knows, a journey is a lot less risky when you have directions."[9] In essence, a business plan describes the direction the company is taking, what its goals are, where it wants to be, and how it's going to get there. The plan documents the entrepreneur's thorough research of the business opportunity. A business plan is an entrepreneur's best insurance against launching a business destined to fail or mismanaging a potentially successful company. In the words of business plan consultant and author David H. Bangs, Jr., "Your business plan can help you avoid going into a business venture that is doomed to failure."[10]

The business plan serves two essential functions. First, it guides the company's operations by charting its future course and devising a strategy for direction. The plan provides a battery of tools—a mission statement, goals, objectives, budgets, financial forecasts, target markets, and strategies—to help managers successfully lead the company. In an ideal situation, the entrepreneur enlists the help of all involved in the venture to write and update the business plan, providing managers and employees a sense of direction. As more team members commit to making the plan work, it takes on special meaning. The business plan gives everyone targets to shoot for, and it provides metrics for measuring actual performance against those targets, especially in the crucial and chaotic start-up phase of the business. In addition, writing a business plan requires entrepreneurs to acquire an in-depth understanding of the industries in which they plan to compete and how their companies fit into them. The key to an effective business plan is to use it as a tool to guide everyone involved in the venture—making it a true planning document—as the business grows.[11]

The greatest waste of a business plan is to let it sit unused. When properly done, a plan becomes an integral and natural part of a company's planning process. In other words, successful entrepreneurs actually *use* their business plans to help them build strong companies.

*Craig Knouf and Associated Business Systems*

Every month, Craig Knouf, CEO of Associated Business Systems (ABS), an office-equipment supplier, distributes the company's business plan to his seven vice presidents. They compare their divisions' and the overall company's actual results to those established in the plan. When the plan and the actual results don't match, the managers try to determine why and then rewrite the business plan accordingly. Knouf and his top managers also devote two full days each year to a planning retreat where they discuss, evaluate, and revise ABS's mission and long-term goals. Knouf says this consistent approach to actually using the business plan plays a vital role to support more than $21.5 million in annual sales. With the help of the revised business plan, ABS scanning software sales doubled to $3.1 million in just one year.[12]

The second function of the business plan is to attract lenders and investors. Unfortunately, many small business owners approach potential lenders and investors without having prepared to sell themselves and their business concept. "Lenders [and investors] want to see solid, incisive business plans that clearly demonstrate an entrepreneur's creditworthiness and his ability to build and manage a profitable company," says a partner in a venture capital firm.[13] Scribbling some rough estimates on a note pad to support a loan application is not enough. Applying for loans or attempting to attract investors without a solid business plan rarely attracts needed capital. The best way to secure the necessary capital is to prepare a sound business plan. The quality of an entrepreneur's business plan weighs heavily in the final decision to lend or invest funds. It is also potential lenders' and investors' first impression of the company and its managers. Therefore, the finished product should be highly polished and professional in both form and content.

A business plan is a reflection of its creator or the team behind it. The plan should demonstrate that an entrepreneur has thought seriously about the venture and what will make it succeed. Preparing a solid plan demonstrates that an entrepreneur has taken the time to conduct the necessary research and to commit the idea to paper. Building a plan also forces an entrepreneur to consider both the positive and the negative aspects of the business. A detailed and thoughtfully developed business plan makes a positive first impression on those who read it. In most cases, potential lenders and investors read a business plan before they ever meet with the entrepreneur behind it. Sophisticated investors will not take the time to meet with an entrepreneur whose business plan fails to reflect a serious investment of time and energy in defining a promising business opportunity. They know that an entrepreneur who lacks the discipline to develop a good business plan likely lacks the discipline to run a business.

Although feedback from others may be valuable, entrepreneurs should not allow someone else to prepare their business plans. Outsiders cannot understand the business nor envision the proposed company as well. The entrepreneur is the driving force behind the business idea and is the one who can best convey the vision and the enthusiasm he or she has for transforming that idea into a successful business. Answering the often difficult questions potential lenders and investors ask requires entrepreneurs to understand all of the details of the business plan. Investors want to feel confident that an entrepreneur appreciates the risk of the new venture and has a strategy for addressing it. They also want to see proof that a business will become profitable and produce a reasonable return on their investment.

One way to understand the need for a business plan is to recognize the validity of the "two-thirds rule." This rule says that only two-thirds of the entrepreneurs with a sound and viable new business idea will find financial backing. Those who do find financial backing will only get two-thirds of what they initially requested, and it will take them two-thirds longer to get the financing than they anticipated.[14] An effective strategy for avoiding the two-thirds rule is to build a business plan!

Even after completing a feasibility analysis, sometimes it is the more detailed business plan that provides an entrepreneur with the realization that "it just won't work." The time to find out that a business idea will not succeed is in the planning stages *before* committing significant money, time, and effort. It is much less expensive to make mistakes on paper than in reality. In other cases, a business plan reveals important problems to overcome before launching a company. Exposing these flaws and then addressing them enhances the chances of a venture's success. Business plans can help nascent entrepreneurs nail down important aspects of their concept and sometimes prevent costly mistakes. Bill Evans, a counselor for SCORE, a group of retired business executives who counsel entrepreneurs, says one client wanted to start a business designing customer scrapbooks. It was not until she started formally planning that it became clear she would only average $3 an hour for her labor.[15]

The value in preparing a plan is not just in the document itself; it is in the *process* the entrepreneur goes through to create the plan. Although the final product is useful, the process of building the plan requires entrepreneurs to explore all areas of a business and subject their ideas to an objective, critical evaluation from many different angles. What entrepreneurs learn about their industries, target markets, financial requirements, competition, and other factors is essential to making their ventures successful. Building a business plan reduces the risk and uncertainty of launching a company by teaching an entrepreneur to do it the right way.

**ENTREPRENEURIAL Profile**

*Byron Myers, Ali Perry, and Brenton Taylor and Inogen*

Ali Perry's grandmother did not like to deal with her bulky, inconvenient oxygen tank. Working with friends Byron Myers and Brenton Taylor, Perry developed a solution—a portable oxygen concentrator that filters out nitrogen from room air to replace the oxygen tank. The team drew up a business plan, entered it in a business plan competition at the University of California at Santa Barbara—and they won! With this validation, the company Inogen was born. Inogen's machine plugs in anywhere and is portable, using a rechargeable lithium ion battery for power.[16]

## Gaining a Competitive Edge

### Using and Updating the Business Plan

A business plan can help spot future success or failure, attract suppliers and employees, and more. The process of writing a business plan forces you to take a thorough, careful, and comprehensive look at the most important facets of your business, including the contexts in which it operates. Merely raising questions can sometimes lead to a solution, or at least ensure that if conditions change, you will be better prepared to make an informed decision. The ongoing "what if this or that happens?" inherent in the planning process can be stimulating. In other words, the planning process itself can make the entrepreneur a more capable manager. Writing a business plan teaches you about aspects of the business that you may not learn through any other process—spotting future trouble areas, identifying opportunities, and recognizing organizational issues.

A business plan helps to:

- Evaluate a new venture—The plan can be used to develop strategy and create projections.
- Attract good people—Select portions of the plan can be a valuable communication tool for potential employees or potential business partners.
- Inform suppliers and customers—You can use your plan as a tool to develop deeper, stronger relationships with key suppliers and customers.
- Monitor your business's performance—Using a business plan to monitor your performance produces many benefits relating to cash flow, and

"plan-to-actual" analysis enables you to spot trouble early and develop action plans.
- Develop new strategies—The acts of reviewing and editing a plan can lead to strategic insights about the business and the changing environment in which it operates.

Therefore, updating a business plan can have numerous benefits. Here are eight reasons for updating your plan:

1. A new financial period is about to begin.
2. You need financing, or additional financing.
3. Significant market changes—shifting client tastes, consolidation trends among customers, and altered regulatory climates can trigger a need for plan updates.
4. New or stronger competitors are looking to take your customers for their growth.
5. The firm develops or is about to develop a new product, technology, service, or skill.
6. You have had a change in management, and new managers need fresh information.
7. Your company has crossed a threshold, such as moving out of your home office, reaching $1 million in sales, or employing 100 people.
8. Your old plan no longer reflects reality.

Using a business plan as an active, insightful tool can provide excellent returns for the entrepreneur and those involved in and around the business.

*Source:* David H. Bangs, "9 Ways to Use Your Business Plan," Entrepreneur.com, September 27, 2005, www.entrepreneur.com/startingabusiness/businessplans/article80098.html.

## The Elements of a Business Plan

*3.* Describe the elements of a solid business plan.

Wise entrepreneurs recognize that every business plan is unique and must be tailor-made. The elements of a business plan may be standard, but the way entrepreneurs tell their stories should be unique and reflect their enthusiasm for the new venture. For those making a first attempt at writing a business plan, it may be very helpful to seek the advice of individuals with experience in this process. Accountants, business professors, attorneys, and consultants U.S. small business development centers can be excellent sources of advice to create and refine a business plan. Remember, however, that the entrepreneur should be the one to author his or her business plan, not someone else.

Initially, the prospect of writing a business plan may appear to be overwhelming. Some entrepreneurs would rather launch their companies and "see what happens" than invest the necessary time and energy defining and researching their target markets, defining their strategies, and mapping out their finances. After all, building a plan is hard work—it requires time, effort, and thought. However, this investment pays dividends, and not all of them are immediately apparent. Entrepreneurs who invest their time and energy toward building a comprehensive business plan have an advantage when they compete in a hostile environment.

Entrepreneurs can benefit from business planning software available from several companies to create their plans. Some of the most popular programs include Business Plan Pro* (Palo Alto Software), PlanMaker (Power Solutions for Business), and Plan Write (Business Resources Software). Business Plan Pro, for example, covers every aspect of a business plan from the executive summary to the cash flow forecasts. The software helps entrepreneurs organize information, and provides helpful tips on plan writing with templates for creating financial statements. These planning packages can help to produce professional-looking business plans, but there is a potential drawback: The plans they produce may look as if they came from the same mold. That can be a turn-off for professional investors who review hundreds of business plans each year.

A business plan typically ranges from 25 to 50 pages in length. Shorter plans may be too brief to be of value, and longer plans run the risk of never getting used or read! This section explains the most common elements of a business plan. However, entrepreneurs must recognize that, like every business venture, every business plan is unique. An entrepreneur should view the following elements as a starting point for building a plan and modify the content to better tell the story of his or her new venture.

## Title Page and Table of Contents

A business plan should contain a title page with the company's name, logo, and address with the names and contact information of the company founders. Many entrepreneurs also include the copy number of the plan and the date on which it was issued on the title page. Business plan readers appreciate a table of contents that includes page numbers so that they can locate the sections of the plan in which they are most interested.

## The Executive Summary

An executive summary highlights the critical aspects of the plan. This section should be concise—a maximum of two pages—and should summarize all of the relevant points of the proposed deal. The executive summary is a synopsis of the entire plan, capturing its essence in a condensed form. It should explain the basic business model and the problem the business will solve for customers. It should briefly describe the owners and key employees, target market(s), and the company's competitive advantage. It should also include financial highlights including sales and earnings projections, the amount of funding needed, how the funds will be used, and how and when any loans will be repaid or investments cashed out. After reading the executive summary, the reader should be able to understand the entire business concept and what differentiates the company from the competition.

The executive summary is a written version of what is known as "the elevator pitch." Imagine an entrepreneur on an elevator with a potential lender or investor. The entrepreneur has that person's undivided attention for the duration of the ride, but the building is not very tall! To convince the investor that the business idea is a great investment, he or she must condense the message down to its essential elements: communicating key points in a matter of one or two minutes. The Babcock Elevator Competition at Wake Forest University has students actually ride an elevator with a venture capitalist with the opportunity to pitch their business ideas in just two minutes. "The competition was designed to simulate reality," says Stan Mandel, creator of the event and director of the Angell Center for Entrepreneurship. The object of the competition is to hone a two-minute "elevator pitch" and deliver it to a venture capitalist during the elevator ride. The winner receives the chance to

---

*Business Plan Pro is available at a nominal cost with this textbook

spend 30 minutes in face-to-face conversations with the venture capitalists who judge the competition.[17]

The executive summary is designed to capture the reader's attention. If it misses, the chances of the remainder of the plan being read are minimal. A coherent, well-developed summary introducing the rest of the plan establishes a favorable first impression of the business and the entrepreneur behind it, and can go a long way toward obtaining financing. A good executive summary should allow the reader to understand the business concept and how it will make money as well as answer the ultimate question from investors or lenders: "What's in it for me?" Although the executive summary is the first part of the business plan, it should be the last section written.

## Mission and Vision Statement

As discussed in Chapter 2, "Strategic Management: Gaining a Competitive Edge," a mission statement expresses in words an entrepreneur's purpose and direction for a company. The mission statement anchors a company in reality and serves as the thesis statement for the entire business plan. Every good plan captures an entrepreneur's passion and vision for the business, and the mission statement is the ideal place to express them. The mission statement answers the questions, "Why are we here?" and "Where are we going?" A vision statement complements this by addressing the questions, "What do we stand for?" and "What kind of company do we want to become?" A vision statement captures the entrepreneur's dream of something to come from the business

## Company History

The owner of an existing small business should prepare a brief history of the operation, highlighting the significant financial and operational events in the company's life. This section should describe when and why the company was formed, how it has evolved over time, and what the owner envisions for the future. It should highlight the successful accomplishment of past objectives and should convey the company's image in the marketplace.

## Business and Industry Profile

To acquaint lenders and investors with the industry in which a company competes, an entrepreneur should describe the industry in the business plan. This section should provide the reader with an overview of the industry or market segment in which the new venture will operate. Industry data such as market size, growth trends, and the relative economic and competitive strength of the major firms in the industry set the stage for understanding the viability of the new product or service. Strategic issues such as ease of market entry and exit, the ability to achieve economies of scale or scope, and the existence of cyclical or seasonal economic trends help readers further evaluate the new venture. This part of the plan also should describe significant industry trends and key success factors as well as an overall outlook for its future. Information about the evolution of the industry helps the reader comprehend its competitive dynamics.

The *U.S. Industrial Outlook Handbook* is an excellent reference that profiles a variety of industries and offers projections for future trends. Another useful resource of industry and economic information is the *Summary of Commentary on Current Economic Conditions,* more commonly known as *The Beige Book.* Published eight times a year, *The Beige Book* provides detailed statistics and trends in key business sectors and in the overall economy. It offers valuable information on topics ranging from tourism and housing starts to consumer spending and wage rates. Entrepreneurs can find this wealth of information at their fingertips on the Web at www.federalreserve.gov/FOMC/BeigeBook/2007.

This portion of the plan also should describe the existing and anticipated profitability of the industry. Any significant entry or exit of firms or consolidations and mergers should be discussed in terms of their impact on the competitive behavior of the market. In addition, the entrepreneur should mention any events that have significantly affected the industry in the past 10 years.

This section should contain a statement of the company's general business goals and then provide a narrower definition of its immediate objectives. Together, they should spell out what the business plans to accomplish, and how, when, and who will do it. **Goals** are broad, long-range statements of what a company plans to achieve in the future that guide its overall direction. In other words, they address the question, "What do I want my company to look like in three to five years?"

**Objectives** are short-term, specific performance targets that are attainable, measurable, and controllable. Every objective should reflect at least one business goal and include a technique for measuring progress toward its accomplishment. To be meaningful, an objective must have a time frame for achievement. Both goals and objectives should relate to the company's basic mission. In other words, accomplishing each objective should move a business closer to achieving its goals, which, in turn, should move it closer to its mission.

## Business Strategy

An even more important part of the business plan is the owner's view of the strategy needed to meet—and beat—the competition. The previous section discussed how entrepreneurs define where they want to take their businesses by establishing goals and objectives. This section addresses the question of how to get there—business strategy. Here, an entrepreneur must explain how he or she plans to gain a competitive edge in the market and what sets his or her business apart from the competition. Entrepreneurs should comment on how they plan to achieve business goals and objectives in the face of competition. A business strategy also addresses government regulation and identifies the image the business will project. An important theme in this section is what makes the company unique in the eyes of its customers. One of the quickest routes to business failure is trying to sell "me-too" products or services that offer customers nothing newer, better, bigger, faster, or different. The foundation for this part of the business plan comes from the material in Chapter 2.

This section of the business plan should outline the methods the company can use to meet the key success factors cited earlier. If, for example, making sales to repeat customers is critical to success, an entrepreneur must devise a plan of action for achieving a customer retention rate that exceeds that of existing companies in the market.

## Description of Firm's Product/Service

An entrepreneur should describe the company's overall product line, giving an overview of how customers use its goods or services. Drawings, diagrams, and illustrations may be valuable, particularly if the product is highly technical or original. It is best to write product and service descriptions so that laypeople can understand them. A statement of a product's position in the product life cycle might also be helpful. An entrepreneur should include a summary of any patents, trademarks, or copyrights protecting the product or service from infringement by competitors. Finally, the plan should include an honest comparison of the company's product or service with those of competitors. A plan should cite specific advantages or improvements that make the company's goods or services unique and describe plans for creating the next generation of goods and services that may evolve from the present product line. What competitive advantage does the venture's product or service offer? Ideally, a product or service offers high-value benefits to customers and is difficult for competitors to duplicate.

One danger entrepreneurs must avoid in this part of the plan is the tendency to dwell on the features of their products or services. This problem—the "fall-in-love-with-your-product" syndrome—often afflicts inventors. Customers, lenders, and investors do not care how much work, genius, and creativity went into a product or service; they care about what it will do for customers. This section should define the benefits customers receive by purchasing the company's products or services, rather than provide a "nuts and bolts" description of the features of those products or services. A **feature** is a descriptive fact about a product or service (e.g., "an ergonomically designed, more comfortable handle"). A **benefit** is what the customer gains from the product or service feature (e.g., "fewer problems with carpal tunnel syndrome and increased productivity"). Advertising legend Leo Burnett once

**TABLE 6.2 Transforming Features into Meaningful Benefits**

For many entrepreneurs, there's a big gap between what a business is selling and what its customers are buying. The following worksheet is designed to eliminate that gap.

First, develop a list of the features your company's product or service offers. List as many as you can think of, which may be 25 or more. Consider features that relate to price, performance, convenience, location, customer service, delivery, reputation, reliability, quality, features, and other aspects.

Next, group features with similar themes together by circling them with the same color ink. Then translate those groups of features into specific benefits to your customers by addressing the question "What's in it for me?" from the customer's perspective. (Note: It usually is a good idea to ask actual customers why they buy from you. They usually give reasons that you never thought of.) As many as six or eight product or service (or even company) features may translate into a single customer benefit, such as saving money or time or making life safer. Don't ignore intangible benefits such as increased status; they can be more important than tangible benefits.

Finally, combine all of the benefits you identify into a single sentence or paragraph. Use this statement as a key point in your business plan and to guide your company's marketing strategy.

| Features | Benefits |
|---|---|
|  |  |
|  |  |
| Benefit Statement: | |

*Source:* Adapted from Kim T. Gordon, "Position for Profits," *Business Start-Ups*, February 1998, pp. 18–20.

said, "Don't tell the people how good you make the goods; tell them how good your goods make them."[18] This part of the plan must describe how a business will transform tangible product or service features into important but often intangible customer benefits—for example, lower energy bills, faster access to the Internet, less time writing checks to pay monthly bills, greater flexibility in building floating structures, shorter time required to learn a foreign language, or others. Remember: *Customers buy benefits, not product or service features*. Table 6.2 offers an easy exercise designed to help entrepreneurs translate their products' or services' features into meaningful customer benefits.

Manufacturers should describe their production process, strategic raw materials required, sources of supply they will use, and their costs. They should also summarize the production method and illustrate the plant layout. If the product is based on a patented or proprietary process, a description (including diagrams, if necessary) of its unique market advantages is helpful. It is also helpful to explain the company's environmental impact and how the entrepreneur plans to mitigate any negative environmental consequences the process may produce.

*Håkan and Annika Olsson and First Penthouse*

While renovating their top-floor apartment in Stockholm, Sweden, civil engineers Håkan and Annika Olsson came up with a unique idea for creating high-quality modular penthouses that they could manufacture in factories and install on top of existing flat-roof buildings. When the couple moved to London, they purchased aerial photographs of the city and marked all of the flat-roof buildings in red ink. "We knew we had a good business idea when the whole picture was red," says Håkan. After conducting more research and building a business plan, the Olssons launched First Penthouse, a company specializing in rooftop development. Their business model adds value both for tenants, who get penthouse living quarters where none existed before, and for landlords, whose property values increase with the addition of the modular penthouses. First Penthouse offers the benefit of a convenient one-day installation and guarantees no disturbances to existing residents. To convince balking regulators, the Olssons use special "quiet" tools and place soundproof mats over the roofs as they work. As sales grow, the Olssons are planning to take their concept into other large urban markets around the world.[19]

## Marketing Strategy

One of the most important tasks a business plan must fulfill is proving that a viable market exists for a company's goods or services. A business plan must identify and describe a company's target customers and their characteristics and habits. Defining the target audience and its potential is one of the most important—and most challenging—parts of building a business plan. Narrowing its target market enables a small company to focus its limited resources on serving the needs of a specific group of customers rather than attempting to satisfy the desires of the mass market. Creating a successful business depends on an entrepreneur's ability to attract real customers who are willing and able to spend money to buy its products or services. Perhaps the worst marketing error an entrepreneur can commit is failing to define the target market and trying to make the business "everything to everybody." Companies are usually more successful when they focus on a specific market niche or niches where they can excel at meeting customers' special needs or wants.

Successful entrepreneurs know that a solid understanding of their target markets is the first step in building an effective marketing strategy. Indeed, every other aspect of marketing depends on their having a clear picture of their customers and their unique needs and wants. Defining a company's target market involves using the techniques described in more detail in Chapter 9, "Creating a Marketing Plan." Proving that a profitable market exists involves two steps: showing customer interest and documenting market claims.

**SHOWING CUSTOMER INTEREST.** An important element of any business plan is showing how a company's product or service provides a customer benefit or solves a customer problem. Entrepreneurs must be able to prove that their target customers actually need or want their goods or services and are willing to pay for them. After reviewing thousands of business plans, venture capitalist Kathryn Gould, says that she looks for plans that focus on "target customers with a compelling reason to buy. The product must be a 'must-have.'"[20]

Proving a viable market exists for a product or service is relatively straightforward for a company already in business, but can be quite difficult for an entrepreneur with only an idea or a prototype. In this case, an entrepreneur might offer the prototype to several potential customers in order to get written testimonials and evaluations to show to investors. Another option is to sell the product to several customers at a discount. This may prove that there are potential customers for the product and would allow demonstrations of the product in operation. Getting a product into customers' hands is also an excellent way to get valuable feedback that can lead to significant design improvements and increased sales down the road.

*Raymond Aranoff and Vektor*

Raymond Aranoff's work at the U.S. National Aeronautics and Space Administration's Johnson Space Center in Houston, Texas, used to include frustration due to the difficulties of integrating different types of engineering software and data management systems. "General Motors loses $1 billion [a year] because of the problem," says Aranoff. He noticed that software designers tended to ignore the poor integration in industries such as automotive, defense and contracting, and aerospace. To solve the problem, Aranoff created Vektor, a business that uses a Web-based software system that collects and interfaces data from multiple software platforms into one intuitive and customizable database. Aranoff was able to get Vektor into potential customers' hands and get feedback from them, which enabled him to prove that his business idea was valid.[21]

**DOCUMENTING MARKET CLAIMS.** Too many business plans rely on vague generalizations such as, "This market is so huge that if we get just 1 percent of it, we will break even in eight months." Statements such as these usually reflect nothing more than an entrepreneur's unbridled optimism, and in most cases, these statements are unrealistic. Entrepreneurs must support claims of market size and growth rates with *facts*. Gathering those facts requires market research. Results of market surveys, customer questionnaires, and demographic studies lend credibility to an entrepreneur's frequently optimistic sales projections. (Refer to the market research techniques and resources described earlier in this chapter.) Quantitative market data are important because they form the basis for all of the company's financial projections in the business plan. Recall from the section on feasibility analysis that one effective documentation technique involves business prototyping, in which entrepreneurs test their business models on a small scale before committing serious resources to a business that might not work.

One of the main purposes of the marketing section of the plan is to lay the foundation for the financial forecasts that follow. Sales, profit, and cash forecasts must come from more than wishful thinking. An effective market analysis should identify the following:

*Target market.*    Who are the company's target customers? How many of them are in the company's trading area? What are their characteristics (age, gender, educational level, income, and others)? What do they buy? Why do they buy? When do they buy? What expectations do they have about the product or service? How can the company set itself apart from the competition in its customers' minds?

*Advertising and promotion.*    Only after entrepreneurs understand their companies' target markets can they design a promotion and advertising campaign to reach those customers most effectively and efficiently. Which media are most effective in reaching the target market? How will they be used? How much will the promotional campaign cost? How will the promotional campaign position the company's products or services? How can the company benefit from publicity? How large is the company's promotional budget?

*Market size and trends.*    Assessing the size of the market is a critical step. How large is the potential market? Is it growing or shrinking? Why? Are customers' needs changing? Are sales seasonal? Is demand tied to another product or service?

*Neil Malhotra and NP Solutions*

One of the largest potential markets in the world of biotechnology is treating lower back pain. Many people begin to suffer some form of degenerative disc disease in their late twenties, but the majority of sufferers are not disabled severely enough for highly invasive and risky treatments such as spinal fusion. This led Neil Malhotra and the team at NP Solutions to see the market potential for a much less invasive form of treatment. The treatment they developed involves a tiny injection of a hydrogel treatment into the affected disc. "Lower back pain is responsible for 15 million physicians' visits a year," Malhotra says. The size of the potential market validates the business potential for the innovation.[22]

*Location.*    For many businesses, choosing the right location is a key success factor. For retailers, wholesalers, and service companies, the best location usually is one that is most convenient to their target customers. Using census data and other market research, entrepreneurs can determine the sites with the greatest concentrations of their target customers and locate there. Which sites put the company in the path of its target customers? Maps showing customer concentrations (available from census reports and other sources), traffic counts, or the number of customers using a particular train station may be available. This and other types of information help provide evidence that a solid and sizable customer base exists. Do zoning regulations restrict the use of a site? For manufacturers, the location issue often centers on finding a site near their key raw materials or near their primary customers. Using demographic reports and market research to screen potential sites takes the guesswork out of choosing the "right" location for a business. We will discuss the location decision in more detail in Chapter 16, "Location, Layout, and Physical Facilities."

*Pricing.* What does the product or service cost to produce or deliver? Before opening a restaurant, for example, an entrepreneur should know *exactly* what it will cost to produce each item on the menu. Failing to know the total cost (including the cost of the food as well as labor, rent, advertising, and other indirect costs) of putting a plate in front of a customer is a recipe for failure. As we will discover in Chapter 10, cost is just one part of the pricing equation. Another significant factor to consider is the image a company is trying to create in the market. "Price really is more of a marketing tool than it is a vehicle for cost recovery," says Peter Meyer, author of *Creating and Dominating New Markets.* "People will pay more for a high value product or solution, so be sure to research your [product's or service's] total value."[23]

*Ray Sidhom and Four Food Studio and Cocktail Salon*

Ray Sidhom, co-owner of Four Food Studio and Cocktail Salon, is one savvy owner who reviews his business plan frequently. "We have so many details to watch, from the food and liquor to staffing costs," says Sidhom. "If they're not where they should be, the business suffers. We look at the intricacies of the business plan often and use analysts who do projections and models."[24]

Other pricing issues include: What is the company's overall pricing strategy? Will the planned price support the company's strategy and desired image? (See Figure 6.3.) Given the company's cost structure, will the price produce a profit? How does the planned price compare to those of similar products or services? Are customers willing to pay it? What price tiers exist in the market? How sensitive are customers to price changes? Will the business sell to customers on credit? Will it accept credit cards? Will the company offer discounts? If so, what kinds and how much?

*Distribution.* The area of distribution addresses logistic questions. How will the company get the product or service to customers? Will distribution be extensive, selective, or exclusive? What is the average sale? How large will the sales staff be? How will the company compensate its sales force? What are the incentives for salespeople? How many sales calls does it take to close a sale? What can the company do to make it as easy as possible for customers to buy?

This portion of the plan also should describe the channels of distribution that the business will use (the Internet, direct mail, in-house sales force, sales agents, retailers, or others). An entrepreneur should summarize the company's overall pricing strategies and its warranties and guarantees for its products and services.

## Competitor Analysis

An entrepreneur should discuss the new venture's competition. Failing to assess competitors realistically makes entrepreneurs appear to be poorly prepared, naive, or dishonest, especially to potential lenders and investors. An analysis of each significant competitor should

**FIGURE 6.3 The Links Among Pricing, Perceived Quality, and Company Image**

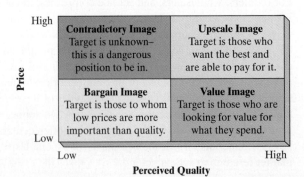

be presented. Entrepreneurs who believe they have no competitors are only fooling themselves and are raising a huge red flag to potential lenders and investors. Gathering information on competitors' market shares, products, and strategies is usually not difficult. Trade associations, customers, industry journals, marketing representatives, and sales literature are valuable sources of data. This section of the plan should focus on demonstrating that the entrepreneur's company has an advantage over its competitors and address these questions:

- Who are the company's key competitors?
- What are their strengths and weaknesses?
- What are their strategies?
- What images do they have in the marketplace?
- How successful are they?
- What distinguishes the entrepreneur's product or service from others already on the market, and how will these differences produce a competitive edge?

This section of the plan should demonstrate that the company's strategies are customer-focused. Firsthand competitor research is particularly valuable.

## Owners' and Managers' Résumés

The most important factor in the success of a business venture is its management, and financial officers and investors weigh heavily the ability and experience of a company's managers in financing decisions. A plan should include the résumés of business officers, key directors, and any person with at least 20 percent ownership in the company. This is the section of the plan in which entrepreneurs have the chance to sell the qualifications and the experience of their management team. Remember: *Lenders and investors prefer experienced managers.* Ideally, they look for managers with at least two years of operating experience in the industry they are targeting.

A résumé should summarize each individual's education, work history (emphasizing managerial responsibilities and duties), and relevant business experience. When compiling a personal profile, an entrepreneur should review the primary reasons for small business failure and show how the management team will use its skills and experience to avoid them. Lenders and investors look for the experience, talent, and integrity of the people who will breathe life into the plan. This portion of the plan should show that the company has the right people organized in the right fashion for success. One experienced private investor advises entrepreneurs to remember the following:

- Ideas and products don't succeed; people do. Show the strength of your management team. A top-notch management team with a variety of proven skills is crucial. Arthur Rock, a legend in the venture capital industry, says, "I invest in people, not ideas."[25]
- Show the strength of key employees and how you will retain them. Most small companies cannot pay salaries that match those at large businesses, but stock options and other incentives can improve employee retention.
- Enhance the strength of the management team with a capable, qualified board of advisers. A board of directors or advisers consisting of industry experts lends credibility and can complement the skills of the management team.

## Plan of Operation

To complete the description of the business, an entrepreneur should construct an organizational chart identifying the business's key positions and the people occupying them. Assembling a management team with the right stuff is difficult, but keeping it together until the company is established may be even harder. Thus, the entrepreneur should briefly describe the steps taken to encourage important officers to remain with the company. Employment contracts, shares of ownership, and perks are commonly used to keep and motivate key employees.

Finally, a description of the form of ownership—sole proprietorship, partnership, joint venture, C corporation, S corporation, or LLC, for example—and of any leases, contracts, and other relevant agreements pertaining to the operation is helpful.

## Pro Forma (Projected) Financial Statements

One of the most important sections of the business plan is an outline of the proposed company's financial statements. One survey found that 74 percent of bankers say that financial documentation is the most important aspect of a business plan for entrepreneurs seeking loans.[26] For an existing business, lenders and investors use past financial statements to judge the health of the company and its ability to repay loans or generate adequate returns; therefore, an owner should supply copies of the firm's financial statements from the past three years. Ideally, these statements should be audited by a certified public accountant because most financial institutions prefer that extra reliability. In some cases a financial review of the statements by an accountant may be acceptable.

Whether assembling a plan for an existing business or for a start-up, an entrepreneur should carefully prepare monthly projected (or pro forma) financial statements for the operation for the next year (and for two more years by quarter). An entrepreneur can use past operating data, published statistics, and research to derive three sets of forecasts of the income statement, balance sheet, cash forecast, and a schedule of planned capital expenditures. (You will learn more about creating projected financial statements in Chapter 7, "Creating a Financial Plan.") The forecasts should cover pessimistic, most likely, and optimistic conditions to reflect the uncertainty of the future. When in doubt, entrepreneurs should be up-front and include some contingencies for any costs that are in question.

It is essential that all three sets of forecasts be realistic. Entrepreneurs must avoid the tendency to inflate the numbers just to make their businesses look good. Lenders and investors compare these projections against published industry standards and can detect unrealistic forecasts. In fact, some venture capitalists automatically discount an entrepreneur's financial projections by as much as 50 percent. After completing these forecasts, an entrepreneur should perform a breakeven analysis and a ratio analysis on the projected figures.

It is also important to include a statement of the *assumptions* on which these financial projections are based. Potential lenders and investors want to know how an entrepreneur derives forecasts for sales, cost of goods sold, operating expenses, accounts receivable, collections, accounts payable, inventory, taxes, and other items. Spelling out realistic assumptions gives a plan more credibility and reduces the tendency to include overly optimistic estimates of sales growth and profit margins. Greg Martin, a partner in the venture capital company Redpoint Ventures, says, "I have problems with start-ups making unrealistic assumptions—how much money they need or how quickly they can ramp up revenue. Those can really kill a deal for me."[27]

In addition to providing valuable information to potential lenders and investors, projected financial statements help entrepreneurs run their businesses more effectively and more efficiently after the start-up. They establish important targets for financial performance and make it easier for an entrepreneur to maintain control over routine expenses and capital expenditures.

## The Loan or Investment Proposal

If an entrepreneur is seeking external financing, the loan or investment proposal section of the business plan should state the purpose of the financing, the amount requested, and the plans for repayment or, in the case of investors, an attractive exit strategy. When describing the purpose of the loan or investment, an entrepreneur must specify the planned use of the funds. General requests for funds using terms such as "for modernization," "working capital," or "expansion" are unlikely to win approval. Instead, entrepreneurs should use more detailed descriptions such as "to modernize production facilities by purchasing five new, more efficient looms that will boost productivity by 12 percent" or "to rebuild merchandise inventory for fall sales peak, beginning in early summer." Entrepreneurs should state the precise amount requested and include relevant backup data, such as vendor estimates of costs or past production levels. Entrepreneurs should not hesitate to request the amount of money they need but should not inflate the amount anticipating the financial officer to "talk them down." Remember: Lenders and investors are normally familiar with industry cost structures.

Another important element of the loan or investment proposal is the repayment schedule and exit strategy. A lender's main consideration in granting a loan is the reassurance that the applicant will repay, whereas an investor's major concern is earning a satisfactory rate of return. Financial projections must reflect a company's ability to repay loans and produce adequate returns for investors. Without this proof, a request for funding stands little chance of being approved. It is necessary for the entrepreneur to produce tangible evidence showing the ability to repay loans or to generate attractive returns. The plan should propose an exit strategy for investors—how they will get their money back plus an attractive return on their investments, such as the option to cash out through a public offering or acquistion by a larger company.

It is beneficial to include an evaluation of the risks of a new venture. Evaluating risk in a business plan requires an entrepreneur to walk a fine line, however. Dwelling on everything that can go wrong will discourage potential lenders and investors from financing the venture. Ignoring the project's risks makes those who evaluate the plan tend to believe an entrepreneur to be either naive, dishonest, or unprepared. The best strategy is to identify the most significant risks the venture faces and then to describe the plans the entrepreneur has developed to avoid them altogether or to overcome the negative outcome if the event does occur.

Finally, an entrepreneur should have a timetable for implementing the proposed plan. This should include a schedule showing the estimated start-up date for the project and noting any significant milestones along the way. Entrepreneurs tend to be optimistic; therefore, it is important to show why the timetable of events is realistic. The accompanying "Gaining the Competitive Edge" feature explains how two simple diagrams can communiate to investors both the risks and the rewards of a business venture.

There is a difference between a *working* business plan—the one the entrepreneur is using to guide the business—and the *presentation* business plan—the one he or she is using to attract capital. Although coffee rings and penciled-in changes in a working plan do not matter (in fact, they are a good sign that the entrepreneur is actually using the plan), they have no place on a plan going to someone outside the company. A plan is usually the tool that an entrepreneur uses to make a first impression on potential lenders and investors. To make sure that impression is a favorable one, an entrepreneur should follow these tips:

- Realize that first impressions are crucial. Make sure the plan has an attractive (not necessarily expensive) cover.
- Make sure the plan is free of spelling and grammatical errors and "typos." It is a professional document and should look like one.
- Make it visually appealing. Use color charts, figures, and diagrams to illustrate key points. Don't get carried away, however, and end up with a "comic book" plan.
- Leave ample "white space" in the margins.
- Include a table of contents with page numbers to allow readers to navigate the plan easily. Reviewers should be able to look through a plan and quickly locate the sections they want to review.
- Make it interesting. Boring plans seldom get read.
- Avoid overusing industry jargon and acronyms with which readers may not be familiar.
- A plan must prove that the business will make money. In one survey of lenders, investors, and financial advisors, 81 percent said that, first and foremost, a plan should prove that a venture will earn a profit.[28] Start-ups do not necessarily have to be profitable immediately, but sooner or later (preferably sooner), they must make money.
- Use computer spreadsheets to generate financial forecasts. They allow entrepreneurs to perform valuable "what if" (sensitivity) analysis in just seconds.
- *Always* include cash flow projections. Entrepreneurs sometimes focus excessively on their proposed venture's profit forecasts and ignore cash flow projections. Although profitability is important, lenders and investors are much more interested in cash flow because they know that's where the money to pay them back or to cash them out comes from.

## Gaining a Competitive Edge

### Visualizing a Venture's Risks and Rewards

When reviewing business plans, lenders and investors naturally focus on the risks and the rewards of a business venture. Rather than taking dozens of pages of text and charts to communicate these important concepts to investors, entrepreneurs can use the following simple graphs to accurately convey both the potential risk and the returns of their proposed businesses. The first diagram shows the amount of money an entrepreneur needs to launch the business, the time required to reach the point of positive cash flow, and the anticipated amount of the payoff.

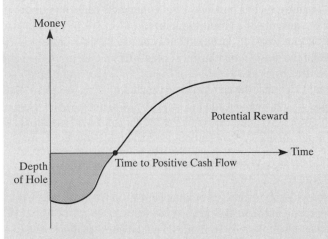

In this diagram, the "depth of hole" shows lenders and investors how much money it will take to start the business, and the length of the chasm shows how long it will take to reach positive cash flow. Experienced business owners know that cash flow is the lifeblood of any business. As we will learn in Chapter 8, "Managing Cash Flow," a company can operate (at least in the short run) without earning a profit, but it cannot survive without

cash flow. Shallow cash holes and short chasms to positive cash flow are ideal, but businesses can tolerate deeper holes and longer cash chasms *as long as their founders have a plan in place to carry the company through until cash flow does become positive*.

The second diagram that follows complements the first. It shows investors the range of possible returns and the probability of achieving them. In the following example, investors can see that there is a 15 percent chance that their investments will be complete losses. The flat section shows that there is a very small chance that investors will lose only a small amount of money. The hump in the middle says that investors have a significant chance of earning between 15 percent and 45 percent on their money. (Note the probability of these returns is about the same as that of a total loss.) Finally, there is a small chance that their initial investments will yield a 200 percent rate of return.

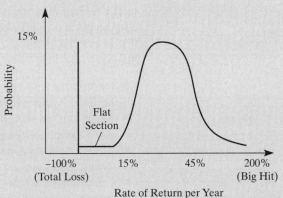

This diagram portrays what investors intuitively understand: Most companies either fail big or achieve solid success.

*Source:* Adapted from William A. Sahlman, "How to Write a Great Business Plan," *Harvard Business Review,* July/August 1997, pp. 98–108.

- The ideal plan is "crisp"—long enough to say what it should, but not so long that it is a chore to read.
- Tell the truth. Absolute honesty is always critical when preparing a business plan.

Business plans are forecasts about the future that an entrepreneur plans to create. One expert compares it to "taking a picture of the unknown," which is a challenging feat indeed! As uncertain and difficult to predict as the future may be, an entrepreneur who launches a business without a plan, arguing that "trying to forecast the future is pointless,"

## In the Entrepreneurial Spotlight

### ■ Muscling In

As a youngster in Mexico City, Rodrigo Alvarez enjoyed tinkering with the machines at his family's plastic bag plant and helping his father boost production. "That factory was my playground," Alvarez recalls. "That's where I learned to be inventive." Alvarez is hoping that his inventive talent will pay off.

While working on his master's degree in bioengineering, Alvarez created a new kind of flexible artificial muscle made of plastic. After joining up with two MBA students, Rahul Kothari and Howard Katzenberg, Alvarez launched MuscleMorph. The company's objective is to use an artificial muscle to transform the prosthetics industry by providing a new way to move artificial limbs.

Much like a human muscle, Alvarez's device uses thousands of strands of microfibers. These strands respond to electrical charges from a battery by contracting smoothly and silently. In the lab, the founders claim, MuscleMorph's prototype proves as strong and as responsive as human muscle. The company holds two provisional patents on the technology.

MuscleMorph's device comes at a critical time for the prosthetics industry. There are about 1.8 million amputees in the United States, and these numbers are increasing because of a rising incidence of heart disease and diabetes, in addition to returning veterans. Several motorized prosthetics already are on the market, but they are bulky, noisy, and power-hungry machines that cost between $50,000 and $100,000. Limbs using MuscleMorph's technology offer more lifelike motion, will cost signifi-

cantly less, and are completely silent, claims Kothari. "No one wants to sound like a cyborg," he says.

Alverez wrote a business plan and entered it in the *Fortune Small Business* business plan competition. He won first place and entered the plan in other business plan competitions. After accumulating $24,000 in start-up capital from contest prizes, Alverez knew he needed some serious funding. To speed its path to market, MuscleMorph is seeking $1.5 million from angel investors. The new venture is not the only company seeking to flex its muscle in the market. Artificial Muscle in Menlo Park, California, spun off from SRI International, is one of the world's largest contract research institutes, and has attracted about $10 million in venture capital. Artificial Muscle has a "muscle" product using technology similar to MuscleMorph's. Although Artificial Muscle says it does not intend to focus on the prosthetics market, but on the consumer electronics, automotive, and industrial markets, it is a force that MuscleMorph must recognize. As they work to implement their business plan, Alvarez and his cofounders believe that MuscleMorph has a good shot at putting millions of amputees back on their feet. Time will tell if MuscleMorph has the strength to accomplish its mission.

1. What benefits will a business plan offer MuscleMorph at this point of the venture's life?
2. What sections of the business plan would you consider the most critical for MuscleMorph and why?

*Source:* Patricia B. Gray, "Giving Amputees New Hope," *FSB*, November 2006, pp. 61–62, 64.

---

is misguided. In the *Harvard Business Review,* William Sahlman says that "the best business plans . . . are like movies of the future. They show the people, the opportunity, and the context from multiple angles. They offer a plausible, coherent story of what lies ahead. They unfold the possibilities of action and reaction."[29] That is the kind of "movie" an entrepreneur should strive to create in a plan.

## Can Your Plan Pass These Tests?

*4.* Explain the three tests every business plan must pass.

Preparing a sound business plan clearly requires time and effort, but the benefits greatly exceed the costs. Building the plan forces entrepreneurs to evaluate their business ideas in the harsh light of reality. It also requires entrepreneurs to assess their ventures' chances of success more objectively. A solid business plan helps prove to outsiders that a business idea can be successful. To get external financing, an entrepreneur's plan must pass three tests with potential lenders and investors: the reality test, the competitive test, and the value test.[30] The first two tests have both an external and an internal component:

1. *Reality test.* The external component of the reality test revolves around proving that a market for the product or service really does exist. It focuses on industry attractiveness, market niches, potential customers, market size, degree of competition, and similar factors. Entrepreneurs who pass this part of the reality test prove in the marketing portion of their business plans that there is strong demand for their business idea.

The internal component of the reality test focuses on the product or service itself. Can the company really build it for the cost estimates in the business plan? Is it truly different from what competitors are already selling? Does it offer customers something of value?

2. *Competitive test.* The external part of the competitive test evaluates the company's relative position to its key competitors. How do the company's strengths and weaknesses match up with those of the competition? How are existing competitors likely to react when the new business enters the market? Do these reactions threaten the new company's success and survival?

The internal competitive test focuses on the management team's ability to create a company that will gain an edge over existing rivals. To pass this part of the competitive test, a plan must prove the quality of the venture's management team. What other resources does the company have that give it a competitive edge in the market?

3. *Value test.* To convince lenders and investors to put their money into the venture, a business plan must prove to them that it offers a high probability of repayment or an attractive rate of return. Entrepreneurs usually see their businesses as good investments because they consider the intangibles of owning a business—gaining control over their own destinies, freedom to do what they enjoy, and others; lenders and investors, however, look at a venture in colder terms: dollar-for-dollar returns. A plan must convince lenders and investors that they will earn an attractive return on their money.

## What Lenders and Investors Look for in a Business Plan

*5.* Explain the "five Cs of credit" and why they are important to potential lenders and investors reviewing business plans.

To increase their chances of success when using their business plans to attract capital, entrepreneurs must be aware of the criteria lenders and investors use to evaluate the creditworthiness of entrepreneurs seeking financing. Lenders and investors refer to these criteria as the five Cs of credit: capital, capacity, collateral, character, and conditions.

*Capital.*   A small business must have a stable capital base before any lender will grant a loan. Otherwise the lender would be making, in effect, a capital investment in the business. Most lenders refuse to make loans that are capital investments because the potential for return on the investment is limited strictly to the interest on the loan, and the potential loss would probably exceed the reward. In fact, the most common reasons that banks give for rejecting small business loan applications are undercapitalization or too much debt. Investors also want to make sure that entrepreneurs have invested enough of their own money into the business to survive the tenuous start-up period.

*Capacity.*   A synonym for capacity is *cash flow*. The plan must convince lenders and investors of a company's ability to meet its regular financial obligations and to repay the bank loan—and that takes cash. In Chapter 8, you will see that more small businesses fail from lack of cash than from lack of profit. It is possible for a company to be earning a profit and run out of cash—to be technically bankrupt. Lenders expect a business to pass the test of liquidity, especially for short-term loans. Lenders closely study a small company's cash flow position to decide whether it has the capacity required to succeed.

*Collateral.*    Collateral includes any assets an entrepreneur pledges to a lender as security for repayment of the loan. If an entrepreneur defaults on the loan, the bank has the right to sell the collateral and use the proceeds to satisfy the loan. Typically, lenders make very few unsecured loans (those not backed by collateral) to business start-ups. Bankers view an entrepreneur's willingness to pledge collateral (personal or business assets) as an indication of dedication to making the venture a success.

*Character.*    Before putting money into a small business, lenders and investors must be satisfied with the owner's character. An evaluation of character is frequently based on intangible factors such as honesty, competence, polish, determination, knowledge, experience, and ability. Although the qualities judged are abstract, this evaluation plays a critical role in a lender's or investor's decision.

Lenders and investors know that most small businesses fail because of poor management; therefore they try to avoid extending loans to high-risk entrepreneurs. Preparing a solid business plan and a polished presentation can go far in convincing potential lenders and investors of an entrepreneur's ability to manage a company successfully.

*Conditions.*    The conditions surrounding a loan request also affect the owner's chance of receiving funds. Banks consider factors relating to the business operation such as potential growth in the market, competition, location, form of ownership, and loan purpose. Entrepreneurs should provide this information in an organized format in the business plan. Another important condition influencing the banker's decision is the shape of the overall economy, including interest rate levels, the inflation rate, and demand for money. Although these factors are beyond an entrepreneur's control, they still are an important component in a banker's decision.

The higher a small business scores on these five Cs, the greater is its chance of receiving a loan or an investment. Wise entrepreneurs keep this in mind when preparing their business plans and presentations.

## Making the Business Plan Presentation

*6. Understand the keys to making an effective business plan presentation.*

Lenders and investors are impressed by entrepreneurs who are informed and prepared when requesting a loan or investment. When entrepreneurs try to secure funding from lenders or investors, the written business plan almost always precedes the opportunity to meet face-to-face. The written plan must first pass muster before an entrepreneur gets the opportunity to present the plan in person. Usually, the time for presenting a business opportunity is short, often no more than just a few minutes. (When presenting a plan to a venture capital forum, the allotted time is usually less than 20 minutes and rarely more than 30.) When the opportunity arises, an entrepreneur must be well prepared. It is important to rehearse, rehearse, and then rehearse some more. It is a mistake to begin by leading the audience into a long-winded explanation about the technology on which the product or service is based. Within minutes most of the audience will be lost, along with the opportunity the entrepreneur has of obtaining the necessary financing for the new venture. A business plan presentation should cover five basic areas:

1. The company's background and its products or services.
2. A market analysis and a description of the opportunities it presents.
3. The company's competitive edge and the marketing strategies it will use to promote that edge.
4. The management team and its members' qualifications and experience.
5. A financial analysis that shows lenders and investors an attractive payback or payoff.

No matter how good a written business plan is, entrepreneurs who stumble through the presentation will lose the deal. Entrepreneurs who successfully raise the capital their

"This may help you understand my presentation."

companies need to grow have solid business plans and make convincing presentations of them. Some helpful tips for making a business plan presentation to potential lenders and investors include:

- Prepare in advance. Good presenters invest in preparing their presentations and knowing the points they want to get across to their audiences.
- Demonstrate enthusiasm about the business but don't be overemotional.
- Focus on communicating the dynamic opportunity your idea offers and how you plan to capitalize on it. Fight the temptation to launch immediately into a lengthy discourse about the details of your product or service or how much work it took to develop it. Otherwise, you'll never have the chance to describe the details to lenders and investors.
- Hook investors quickly with an up-front explanation of the new venture, its opportunities, and the anticipated benefits to them.
- Use visual aids. They make it easier for people to follow your presentation. Don't make the mistake of relying on visuals to communicate the entire message, however. Visual aids should punctuate your spoken message and focus the audience's attention on what you are saying.
- Hit the highlights; specific questions will bring out the details later. Don't get caught up in too much detail in early meetings with lenders and investors.
- Keep the presentation "crisp" just like your business plan. Otherwise, says one experienced investor, "Information that might have caused an investor to bite gets lost in the endless drone."[31]
- Avoid the use of technical terms that will likely be above most of the audience. Do at least one rehearsal before someone who has no special technical training. Tell that person to stop you anytime he or she does not understand what you are talking about. When this occurs (and it likely will), rewrite that portion of your presentation.
- Remember that every potential lender and investor you talk to is thinking "What's in it for me?" Be sure to answer that question in your presentation.
- Close by reinforcing the nature of the opportunity. Be sure you have sold the benefits the investors will realize when the business is a success.
- Be prepared for questions. In many cases, there is seldom time for a long "Q&A" session, but interested investors may want to get you aside to discuss the details of the plan.
- Anticipate the questions the audience is most likely to ask and prepare for them in advance.
- Be sensitive to the issues that are most important to lenders and investors by reading the pattern of their questions. Focus your answers accordingly. For instance, some

investors may be interested in the quality of the management team whereas others are more interested in marketing strategies. Be prepared to offer details on either.

■ Follow up with every investor to whom you make a presentation. Don't sit back and wait; be proactive. They have what you need—investment capital. Demonstrate that you have confidence in your plan and have the initiative necessary to run a business successfully.

## Conclusion

Although there is no guarantee of success when launching a business, the best way to insure against failure is to conduct a feasibility analysis and, if that analysis is positive, to create a business plan. A good plan serves as a strategic compass that keeps a business on course as it travels into an uncertain future. A solid business plan is essential to raising the capital needed to start a business; lenders and investors demand it. "There may be no easier way for an entrepreneur to sabotage his or her request for capital than by failing to produce a comprehensive, well-researched, and, above all, credible business plan," says one small business expert.[32] Of course, building a plan is just one step along the path to launching a business. Creating a successful business requires entrepreneurs to put the plan into action. The remaining chapters in this book focus on putting your business plan to work.

## Suggested Business Plan Format

Although every company's business plan will be unique, reflecting its individual circumstances, certain elements are universal. The following outline summarizes these components.

  **I.** Executive Summary (not to exceed two pages)
   A. Company name, address, and phone number
   B. Name(s), addresses, and phone number(s) of all key people
   C. Brief description of the business, its products and services, and the customer problems they solve
   D. Brief overview of the market for your products and services
   E. Brief overview of the strategies that will make your firm a success
   F. Brief description of the managerial and technical experience of key people
   G. Brief statement of the financial request and how the money will be used
   H. Charts or tables showing highlights of financial forecasts
  **II.** Vision and Mission Statement
   A. Entrepreneur's vision for the company
   B. "What business are we in?"
   C. Values and principles on which the business stands
   D. What makes the business unique? What is the source of its competitive advantage?
  **III.** Company History (for existing businesses only)
   A. Company founding
   B. Financial and operational highlights
   C. Significant achievements
  **IV.** Industry Profile and Overview
   A. Industry analysis
     1. Industry background and overview
     2. Major customer groups
     3. Regulatory restrictions, if any
     4. Significant trends
     5. Growth rate
     6. Barriers to entry and exit
     7. Key success factors in the industry
     8. Outlook for the future
   B. Stage of growth (start-up, growth, maturity)

   **V.** Business Strategy

      A. Desired image and position in market

      B. Company goals and objectives

         1. Operational

         2. Financial

         3. Other

      C. SWOT analysis

         1. Strengths

         2. Weaknesses

         3. Opportunities

         4. Threats

      D. Competitive strategy

         1. Cost leadership

         2. Differentiation

         3. Focus

  **VI.** Company Products and Services

      A. Description

         1. Product or service features

         2. Customer benefits

         3. Warranties and guarantees

         4. Uniqueness

      B. Patent or trademark protection

      C. Description of production process (if applicable)

         1. Raw materials

         2. Costs

         3. Key suppliers

         4. Lead times

      D. Future product or service offerings

 **VII.** Marketing Strategy

      A. Target market

         1. Problem to be solved or benefit to be offered

         2. Complete demographic profile

         3. Other significant customer characteristics

      B. Customers' motivation to buy

      C. Market size and trends

         1. How large is the market?

         2. Is it growing or shrinking? How fast?

      D. Personal selling efforts

         1. Sales force size, recruitment, and training

         2. Sales force compensation

         3. Number of calls per sale

         4. Amount of average sale

      E. Advertising and promotion

         1. Media used—reader, viewer, listener profiles

         2. Media costs

         3. Frequency of usage

         4. Plans for generating publicity

      F. Pricing

         1. Cost structure

            a. Fixed

            b. Variable

         2. Desired image in market

         3. Comparison against competitors' prices

         4. Discounts

         5. Gross profit margin

    G. Distribution strategy
       1. Channels of distribution used
       2. Sales techniques and incentives for intermediaries
    H. Test market results
       1. Surveys
       2. Customer feedback on prototypes
       3. Focus groups

**VIII.** Location and Layout
    A. Location
       1. Demographic analysis of location versus target customer profile
       2. Traffic count
       3. Lease/Rental rates
       4. Labor needs and supply
       5. Wage rates
    B. Layout
       1. Size requirements
       2. Legal compliance
       3. Ergonomic issues
       4. Layout plan (suitable for an appendix)

**IX.** Competitor Analysis
    A. Existing competitors
       1. Who are they? Create a competitive profile matrix
       2. Strengths
       3. Weaknesses
    B. Potential competitors: Companies that might enter the market
       1. Who are they?
       2. Impact on your business if they enter

**X.** Description of Management Team
    A. Key managers and employees
       1. Their backgrounds
       2. Experience, skills, and know-how they bring to the company
    B. Résumés of key managers and employees (suitable for an appendix)
    C. Future additions to management team
    D. Board of directors or advisers

**XI.** Plan of Operation
    A. Form of ownership chosen and reasoning
    B. Company structure (organization chart)
    C. Decision-making authority
    D. Compensation and benefits packages

**XII.** Financial Forecasts (suitable for an appendix)
    A. Key assumptions
    B. Financial statements (year 1 by month, years 2 and 3 by quarter)
       1. Income statement
       2. Balance sheet
       3. Cash flow statement
    C. Breakeven analysis
    D. Ratio analysis with comparison to industry standards (most applicable to existing businesses)

**XIII.** Loan or Investment Proposal
    A. Amount requested
    B. Purpose and uses of funds
    C. Repayment or "cash out" schedule (exit strategy)
    D. Timetable for implementing plan and launching the business

**XIV.** Appendices (Supporting documentation, including market research, financial statements, organization charts, résumés, and other items.)

# Chapter Review

1. Describe the steps in conducting a feasibility analysis.
   - A feasibility analysis consists of three interrelated components: (1) an industry and market feasibility analysis, (2) a product or service feasibility analysis, and (3) a financial feasibility analysis. The goal of the feasibility analysis is to determine whether or not an entrepreneur's idea is a viable foundation for creating a successful business.

2. Explain the benefits of an effective business plan.
   - A business plan serves two essential functions. First and most important, it guides the company's operations by charting its future course and devising a strategy for following it. The second function of the business plan is to attract lenders and investors. Applying for loans or attempting to attract investors without a solid business plan rarely attracts needed capital. Rather, the best way to secure the necessary capital is to prepare a sound business plan.

3. Describe the elements of a solid business plan.
   - Although a business plan should be unique and tailor-made to suit the particular needs of a small company, it should cover these basic elements: an executive summary, a mission statement, a company history, a business and industry profile, a description of the company's business strategy, a profile of its products or services, a statement explaining its marketing strategy, a competitor analysis, owners' and officers' résumés, a plan of operation, financial data, and the loan or investment proposal.

4. Explain the three tests every business plan should pass.
   - Reality test. The external component of the reality test revolves around proving that a market for the product or service really does exist. The internal component of the reality test focuses on the product or service itself.
   - Competitive test. The external part of the competitive test evaluates the company's relative position to its key competitors. The internal competitive test focuses on the management team's ability to create a company that will gain an edge over existing rivals.
   - Value test. To convince lenders and investors to put their money into the venture, a business plan must prove to them that it offers a high probability of repayment or an attractive rate of return.

5. Explain the "5 Cs of credit" and why they are important to potential lenders and investors reading business plans.
   - Small business owners need to be aware of the criteria bankers use in evaluating the creditworthiness of loan applicants—the five Cs of credit: capital, capacity, collateral, character, and conditions.
   - Capital—Lenders expect small businesses to have an equity base of investment by the owner(s) that will help support the venture during times of financial strain.
   - Capacity—A synonym for *capacity* is *cash flow*. The bank must be convinced of the firm's ability to meet its regular financial obligations and to repay the bank loan, and that takes cash.
   - Collateral—Collateral includes any assets the owner pledges to the bank as security for repayment of the loan.
   - Character—Before approving a loan to a small business, the banker must be satisfied with the owner's character.
   - Conditions—The conditions (interest rates, the health of the nation's economy, industry growth rates, etc.) surrounding a loan request also affect the owner's chance of receiving funds.

6. Understand the keys to making an effective business plan presentation.
   - Lenders and investors are favorably impressed by entrepreneurs who are informed and prepared when requesting a loan or investment.

- Tips include: Demonstrate enthusiasm about the venture, but don't be over-emotional; "hook" investors quickly with an up-front explanation of the new venture, its opportunities, and the anticipated benefits to them; use visual aids; hit the highlights of your venture; don't get caught up in too much detail in early meetings with lenders and investors; avoid the use of technological terms that will likely be above most of the audience; rehearse your presentation before giving it; close by reinforcing the nature of the opportunity; and be prepared for questions.

## Discussion Questions

1. What does a feasibility analysis encompass and what value might it provide?
2. Why should an entrepreneur develop a business plan?
3. Why do entrepreneurs who are not seeking external financing need to prepare business plans?
4. Describe the major components of a business plan.
5. How can an entrepreneur seeking funds to launch a business convince potential lenders and investors that a market for the product or service really does exist?
6. How would you prepare to make a formal presentation of your business plan to a venture capital forum?
7. What are the five C's of credit? How do lenders and investors use them when evaluating a request for financing?

# Business Plan Pro

This chapter begins with a discussion of the feasibility analysis to test the viability of your business concept. The following exercises will assist you in validating your business idea. You will also begin to work through the situation analysis part of the plan to enable you to better understand the market. Be as objective as possible as you work through these exercises. Rely on your ability to gather information and make realistic assessments and projections as the exercises require.

## On the Web

Go to the Companion Website at www.prenhall.com/scarborough and click on the "Business Plan Resource" tab. If you have not yet done so, find the Standard Industry Classification Code associated with your industry. You will find a link in the SIC Code information that will connect you to a resource to help you. Explore the information and links that are available on that site to learn more about the size of the industry, its growth, trends, and issues. Apply Porter's five forces model based on the the industry and its SIC code. Assess the power of the five forces—the bargaining power of buyers, the power of suppliers, threat of new entrants, the threat of substitute products, and the level of rivalry. Again, you will find additional information on Porter's five forces model in the "Strategy" section of this same site. Look for information on the Web that may assist you with this analysis. Based on this information, how attractive do you consider this industry? How would you assess the opportunity this industry presents? Does this information encourage you to become involved in this industry, or does it highlight significant challenges?

## In the Software

Your text may have come with "Business Feasibility Plan Pro." This software walks you through the essential steps of assessing the feasibility of your business concept. This software will address the overall feasibility of the product or service, help conduct an industry assessment, review management skills, and guide you through a preliminary financial analysis. The software provides "feedback-based" input in four components of the feasibility analysis with a numerical assessment. You can then export this information directly into Business Plan Pro.

Business Plan Pro is another resource to help you assess the feasibility of your business concept in the areas of product, service, market organization, and financial feasibility. For example, you can enter the initial capital requirements for the business in the start-up and expenses section. The sales forecast will help forecast revenues and help to determine the anticipated return on investment. If you have these estimates available, enter that information into your plan. Now look at the profit and loss statement. At what point, if any, does that statement indicate that your venture will begin generating a profit? In what year does that occur? Do you find that amount of time acceptable? If you are seeking investors, will they find that schedule attractive? Is the return on investment promising, and does this venture merit taking on the associated level of risk? We will talk more about these sections of the plan in the remaining chapters.

Review the start-up sample plans called "IntelliChild. com" and "Fantastic Florals."

1. What was the total amount of the start-up investment for each of these plans?
2. At what point, in months or years, did the plan indicate that it would begin making a profit?
3. What was the total profit projected in the following year after breakeven occurred?
4. Based on the breakeven point, which of these ventures is most attractive?
5. Based on the projections by year three, which plan appears to offer the greatest financial potential?
6. How does the scale and potential of these two opportunities compare to those in your plan?

## Building Your Business Plan

Review the information in the "Market Analysis" section. Continue to add information in this section based on the outline. Go to the "Sales Strategy" section and find information to help project expenses. You may enter the numbers in the table yourself or use the wizard that will pop up to assist you with this process. You may click and drag the visual graph to build that forecast base, or enter the actual data. If the business is a start-up venture, expenses will include those figures along with ongoing expense projections. At this point, do not worry about the accuracy of the projections. Enter the estimates you have even if they are just "rough" estimates; you can change them at any time. Look at the profit and loss statement. At what point in time will your business begin making a profit? Do you find this profit picture to be acceptable?

As you build your plan, check to see that the outline and structure of the plan tells your story. Although the outline in Business Plan Pro is not identical to the outline presented in the chapter, right clicking on the outline allows you to move, add, and delete any topic you choose to modify the plan outline.

# Creating a Solid Financial Plan

You can't tell who's swimming naked until after the tide goes out.

—David Darst

In the wake of numerous corporate financial scandals in which managers misrepresented their companies' financial positions, one pundit offers this definition of EBIT (in reality, earnings before interest and taxes): "earnings before irregularities and tampering."

—Mortimer B. Zuckerman

## *Learning Objectives*

**Upon completion of this chapter, you will be able to:**

1 Understand the importance of preparing a financial plan.
2 Describe how to prepare financial statements and use them to manage a small business.
3 Create projected financial statements.
4 Understand the basic financial statements through ratio analysis.
5 Explain how to interpret financial ratios.
6 Conduct a breakeven analysis for a small company.

*1.* Understand the importance of preparing a financial plan.

O
ne of the most important steps in launching a new business venture is fashioning a well-designed, practical, realistic financial plan. Potential lenders and investors expect to see a financial plan before putting their money into a start-up company. More important, however, a financial plan is a vital tool to help entrepreneurs manage their businesses more effectively, steering their way around the pitfalls that cause failure. Entrepreneurs who ignore the financial aspects of their businesses run the risk of watching their companies become another failure statistic. Many empirical studies have verified the positive correlation between the degree of planning (including financial planning) that entrepreneurs engage in and the success of their new ventures. These studies also show a significant positive relationship between formal planning by small companies and their financial performances.[1] One financial expert says of small companies, "Those that don't establish sound controls at the start are setting themselves up to fail."[2]

However, both research and anecdotal evidence suggest that a significant percentage of entrepreneurs run their companies without any kind of financial plan and never analyze their companies' financial statements as part of the decision making process. Why is the level of financial planning and analysis so low among entrepreneurs? The primary reason is the lack of financial know-how. One survey of small business owners by Greenfield Online found that accounting was the most intimidating part of managing their businesses and that more than half had no formal financial training at all.[3] To reach profit objectives, entrepreneurs cannot afford to be intimidated by financial management and must be aware of their companies' overall financial position and the changes in financial status that occur over time.

This chapter focuses on some very practical tools that will help entrepreneurs develop workable financial plans, keep them focused on their company's financial plan, and enable them to create a plan for earning a profit. They can use these tools to anticipate changes and plot an appropriate profit strategy to meet them head on. These profit planning techniques are not difficult to master, nor are they overly time consuming. We will discuss the techniques involved in preparing projected (pro forma) financial statements, conducting ratio analysis, and performing breakeven analysis.

## Basic Financial Reports

*2.* Describe how to prepare financial statements and use them to manage a small business.

Before we begin building projected financial statements, it would be helpful to review the basic financial reports that measure a company's overall financial position: the balance sheet, the income statement, and the statement of cash flows. Every business, no matter how small, will benefit from preparing these basic financial statements. Building them is the first step toward securing a small company's financial future. Most accounting experts advise entrepreneurs to use one of the popular computerized small business accounting programs such as Intuit's market-leading Quickbooks, Peachtree Accounting, or Microsoft's Small Business Accounting, and others to manage routine recordkeeping tasks that form the underlying framework of these financial statements. These programs make analyzing a company's financial statements, preparing reports, and summarizing data a snap. A survey by Microsoft, however, reports that less than half of small companies use dedicated accounting software; the balance use a combination of homemade spreadsheets and paper records to handle their accounting needs.[4] Working with an accountant to set up a smoothly functioning accounting system at the outset and then having an employee or a part-time bookkeeping service enter the transactions is most efficient for the businesses that use these packages.

### The Balance Sheet

Like a digital camera, the balance sheet takes a "snapshot" of a business, providing owners with an estimate of the company's worth on a given date. Its two major sections show the assets a business owns and the claims creditors and owners have against those assets. The balance sheet is usually prepared on the last day of the month. Figure 7.1 shows the balance sheet for a small business, Sam's Appliance Shop, for the year ended December 31, 20XX.

The balance sheet is built on the fundamental accounting equation: Assets = Liabilities + Owner's Equity. Any increase or decrease on one side of the equation must be offset

**FIGURE 7.1 Balance Sheet, Sam's Appliance Shop**

| Assets | | |
|---|---|---|
| **Current Assets** | | |
| Cash | | $ 49,855 |
| Accounts Receivable | $179,225 | |
| Less Allowance for Doubtful Accounts | $ 6,000 | $173,225 |
| Inventory | | $455,455 |
| Prepaid Expenses | | $ 8,450 |
| Total Current Assets | | $686,985 |
| **Fixed Assets** | | |
| Land | | $ 59,150 |
| Buildings | $ 74,650 | |
| Less Accumulated Depreciation | $ 7,050 | $ 67,600 |
| Equipment | $ 22,375 | |
| Less Accumulated Depreciation | $ 1,250 | $ 21,125 |
| Furniture and Fixtures | $ 10,295 | |
| Less Accumulated Depreciation | $ 1,000 | $ 9,295 |
| Total Fixed Assets | | $157,170 |
| Intangibles (Goodwill) | | $ 3,500 |
| Total Assets | | $847,655 |
| **Liabilities** | | |
| **Current Liabilities** | | |
| Accounts Payable | | $152,580 |
| Notes Payable | | $ 83,920 |
| Accrued Wages/Salaries Payable | | $ 38,150 |
| Accrued Interest Payable | | $ 42,380 |
| Accrued Taxes Payable | | $ 50,820 |
| Total Current Liabilities | | $367,850 |
| **Long-Term Liabilities** | | |
| Mortgage | | $127,150 |
| Note Payable | | $ 85,000 |
| Total Long-Term Liabilities | | $212,150 |
| **Owner's Equity** | | |
| Sam Lloyd, Capital | | $267,655 |
| Total Liabilities and Owner's Equity | | $847,655 |

by an equal increase or decrease on the other side, hence, the name *balance sheet*. It provides a baseline from which to measure future changes in assets, liabilities, and equity (or net worth). The first section of the balance sheet lists the company's **assets** (valued at cost, not actual market value) and shows the total value of everything the business owns. **Current assets** consist of cash and items to be converted into cash within one year or within the normal operating cycle of the company, whichever is longer, such as accounts receivable and inventory, and **fixed assets** are those acquired for long-term use in the business. **Intangible assets** include items that, although valuable, are not tangible, such as goodwill, copyrights, and patents.

The second section shows the business's **liabilities**—the creditors' claims against the company's assets. **Current liabilities** are those debts that must be paid within one year or within the normal operating cycle of the company, whichever is longer, and **long-term liabilities** are those that come due after one year. This section of the balance sheet also shows **owner's equity**, the value of the owner's investment in the business. It is the balancing factor on the balance sheet, representing all of the owner's capital contributions to the business plus all accumulated earnings not distributed to the owner(s).

## The Income Statement

The **income statement** (or profit and loss statement or "P&L") compares expenses against revenue over a certain period of time to show the company's net income or loss. Like a digital video recorder, the income statement provides a "moving picture" of a company's profitability over time. The annual P&L statement reports the bottom line of the business over the fiscal or calendar year. Figure 7.2 shows the income statement for Sam's Appliance Shop for the year ended December 31, 20XX.

To calculate net income or loss, owners record sales revenue for the year, which includes all income that flows into the business from the sale of goods and services. Income from other sources (rent, investments, interest) also must be included in the revenue section of the income statement. To determine net revenue, owners subtract the value of returned items and refunds from gross revenue. **Cost of goods sold** represents the total cost, including shipping, of the merchandise sold during the year. Wholesalers and retailers calculate cost of goods sold by adding purchases to beginning inventory and subtracting ending inventory. Service companies typically have no cost of goods sold.

Subtracting the cost of goods sold from net sales revenue results in a company's **gross profit**. Allowing the cost of goods sold to get out of control will whittle away its gross profit, virtually guaranteeing a net loss on the income statement. Dividing gross profit by net sales revenue produces the **gross profit margin**, a ratio that every business owner

**FIGURE 7.2 Income Statement, Sam's Appliance Shop**

| | | |
|---|---:|---:|
| Net Sales Revenue | | $1,870,841 |
| **Cost of Goods Sold** | | |
| Beginning Inventory, 1/1/XX | $   805,745 | |
| + Purchases | $   939,827 | |
| Goods Available for Sale | $1,745,572 | |
| − Ending Inventory, 12/31/XX | $   455,455 | |
| Cost of Goods Sold | | $1,290,117 |
| Gross Profit | | $   580,724 |
| **Operating Expenses** | | |
| Advertising | $   139,670 | |
| Insurance | $     46,125 | |
| Depreciation | | |
| Building | $     18,700 | |
| Equipment | $       9,000 | |
| Salaries | $   224,500 | |
| Travel | $       4,000 | |
| Entertainment | $       2,500 | |
| Total Operating Expenses | | $   444,495 |
| **General Expenses** | | |
| Utilities | $       5,300 | |
| Telephone | $       2,500 | |
| Postage | $       1,200 | |
| Payroll Taxes | $     25,000 | |
| Total General Expenses | | $     34,000 |
| **Other Expenses** | | |
| Interest Expense | $     39,850 | |
| Bad Check Expense | $       1,750 | |
| Total Other Expenses | | $     41,600 |
| Total Expenses | | $   520,095 |
| Net Income | | $     60,629 |

should watch closely. If a company's gross profit margin slips too low, it is likely that it will operate at a loss (negative net income). Many business owners whose companies are losing money mistakenly believe that the problem is inadequate sales volume; therefore, they focus on pumping up sales at any cost. In many cases, however, the losses are due to an inadequate gross profit margin, and pumping up sales only deepens their losses! Repairing a poor gross profit margin requires a company to raise prices, cut manufacturing or purchasing costs, refuse orders with low profit margins, or add new products with more attractive profit margins. *Increasing sales will not resolve the problem.* One business owner admits that he fell victim to this myth of profitability. His company was losing money, and in an attempt to correct the problem, he focused his efforts on boosting sales. His efforts were successful, but the results were not. The costs he incurred to add sales produced withering gross profit margins, and by the time he deducted operating costs, the business incurred an even greater net loss! Cash flow suffered, the business could not pay its bills on time, and the owner ended up filing for bankruptcy. Now a successful business owner, this entrepreneur says, "Ever since, I've tracked my gross [profit] margins like a hawk."[5] Monitoring the gross profit margin over time and comparing it to those of other companies in the same industry are important steps to maintaining a company's long-term profitability.

**Operating expenses** include those costs that contribute directly to the manufacture and distribution of goods. General expenses are indirect costs incurred in operating the business. "Other expenses" is a catch-all category covering all other expenses that don't fit into the other two categories. Total revenue minus total expenses gives the company's **net income (or loss)**. Reducing expenses increases a company's net income, and even small reductions in expenses can add up to big savings.

*Adobe Systems*

At the software company Adobe Systems, managers and employees have retrofitted their headquarters with so many energy-saving devices that the company recently became the first business to receive a platinum award from the U.S. Green Building Council. Automatic faucets equipped with sensors and waterless urinals in the restrooms, compact fluorescent bulbs replacing incandescent bulbs, motion detectors that switch on lights only when someone enters a room, and a weather-sensitive irrigation system are among the nearly 50 energy savings projects that the company has implemented. Taken together, Adobe has invested $1.1 million in these projects, which have produced an impressive annual savings in its energy bill of $1 million![6]

Adobe Systems' energy efficient headquarters saves the company $1 million annually.

Business owners must be careful when embarking on a cost-cutting mission, however. Cutting costs in areas that are vital to operating success—such as a retail jeweler cutting its advertising expenditures—can inhibit a company's ability to succeed and can lead to failure. In other cases, entrepreneurs on cost-cutting vendettas alienate employees and sap worker morale by eliminating nitpicking costs that affect employees but retaining expensive perks for themselves. One business owner enraged employees by cutting the budget for the company holiday party to $5 (for the whole event) and encouraging employees not to skip lines on interoffice envelopes (which, one worker calculated, cost the company $0.0064 per skipped line). Although his reasons for cutting costs were valid, this CEO lost all credibility because employees knew that when he traveled, he stayed only at upscale, butler-serviced hotels and had a chauffeur drive him to work every day![7]

### The Statement of Cash Flows

The **statement of cash flows** shows the changes in a company's working capital from the beginning of the accounting period by listing the sources of funds and the uses of these funds. Many small businesses never need such a statement; instead, they rely on a cash budget, a less formal managerial tool that tracks the flow of cash into and out of a company over time. (We will discuss cash budgets in Chapter 8.) Sometimes, however, creditors, lenders, investors, or business buyers may require this information.

To prepare the statement of cash flows, owners must assemble the balance sheets and the income statements summarizing the present year's operations. They begin with the company's net income for the accounting period (from the income statement). Then they add the sources of funds—borrowed funds, owner contributions, increases in accounts payable, decreases in inventory, depreciation, and any others. Depreciation is listed as a source of funds because it is a noncash expense that is deducted as a cost of doing business. Because the owners have already paid for the item being depreciated, its depreciation is a source of funds. Next the owners subtract the uses of these funds—plant and equipment purchases, dividends to owners, repayment of debt, increases in accounts receivable, decreases in accounts payable, increases in inventory, and so on. The difference between the total sources and the total uses of funds is the increase or decrease in working capital. By investigating the changes in their companies' working capital and the reasons for them, owners can create a more practical financial plan of action for the future.

These statements are more than just complex documents used only by accountants and financial officers. When used in conjunction with the analytical tools described in the following sections, they can help entrepreneurs map their companies' financial future and actively plan for profit. Merely preparing these statements is not enough, however; entrepreneurs and their employees must *understand and use* the information contained in them to make the business more effective and efficient.

## Creating Projected Financial Statements

**3.** Create projected financial statements.

Creating projected financial statements helps entrepreneurs transform their business goals into reality. These projected financial statements answer such questions as: What profit can the business expect to earn? If the founder's profit objective is $x$ dollars, what sales level must the business achieve? What fixed and variable expenses can the owner expect at that level of sales? The answers to these and other questions are critical in formulating a successful financial plan for the small business.

This section focuses on creating projected income statements and balance sheets for a small business. These projected (pro forma) statements estimate the profitability and the overall financial condition of a business for future months. They are an integral part of convincing potential lenders and investors to provide the financing needed to get the company off the ground. Also, because these statements forecast a company's financial position, they help entrepreneurs plan the route to improved financial strength and healthy business growth. In other words, they lay the foundation for a pathway to profitability.

Because an established business has a history of operating data from which to construct projected financial statements, the task is not nearly as difficult as it is for a start-up busi-

Entrepreneurs do not need a crystal ball to create projected financial statements.

ness. When creating projected financial statements for a business start-up, entrepreneurs typically rely on published statistics summarizing the operation of similar-size companies in the same industry. These statistics are available from a number of sources (described later), but this section draws on information found in *RMA Annual Statement Studies,* a compilation of financial data on thousands of companies across hundreds of industries (organized by North American Industry Classification [NAICS] and Standard Industrial Classification [SIC] Codes). Because conditions and markets change so rapidly, entrepreneurs developing financial forecasts for start-ups should focus on creating projections for two years into the future. Investors mainly want to see that entrepreneurs have realistic expectations about their companies' income and expenses and when they expect to start earning a profit.

## Projected Statements for the Small Business

One of the most important tasks confronting the entrepreneur launching a new enterprise is to determine the funds needed to begin operation as well as those required to keep going through the initial growth period. The amount of money needed to begin a business depends on the type of operation, its location, inventory requirements, sales volume, credit terms, and other factors. Every new firm must have enough capital to cover all start-up costs, including funds to rent or buy plant, equipment, and tools as well as to pay for advertising, licenses, utilities, travel, and other ongoing expenses until the company generates enough revenue to cover them. In addition, the owner must maintain a reserve of capital to carry the company until it begins to make a profit. Too often, entrepreneurs are overly optimistic in their financial plans and fail to recognize that expenses initially exceed income for most small firms. This period of net losses is normal and may last from just a few months to several years. During this time, entrepreneurs must be able to meet payrolls, maintain adequate inventory, take advantage of cash discounts, pay all other business expenses, grant customer credit, and meet personal obligations. Figure 7.3 provides a model that shows the

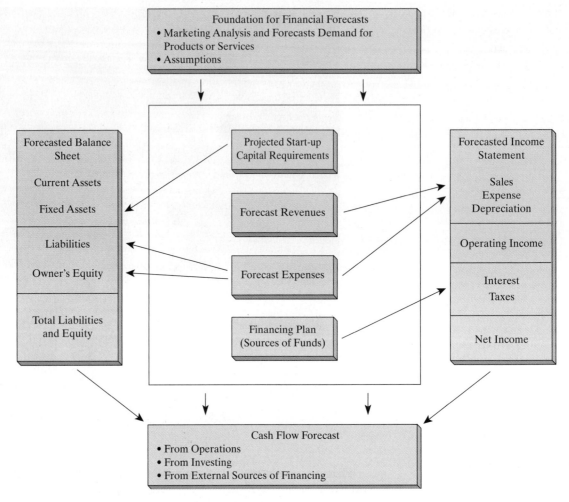

**FIGURE 7.3 Financial Forecasting Model**

*Source:* Adapted from Benjamin B. Gaunsel, "Toward a Framework of Financial Planning in New Venture Creation," presented at United States Association for Small Business and Entrepreneurship Annual Meeting, January 2005, Palm Springs, CA, www.sbaer. uca.edu/research/usasbe/2005/pdffiles/papers/25.pdf.

connections among the various financial forecasts entrepreneurs should include in their business plans.

**THE PROJECTED INCOME STATEMENT.**   When creating a projected income statement, an entrepreneur has two options: to develop a sales forecast and work down or set a profit target and work up. Many entrepreneurs prefer to use the latter method—targeting a profit figure and then determine the sales level they must achieve to reach it. Of course, it is important to compare this sales target against the results of the marketing plan to determine whether it is realistic. Although financial forecasts are projections, they must be based in reality; otherwise, they are nothing more than hopeless dreams. The next step is to estimate the expenses the business will incur to generate those sales. In any small business, the profit must be large enough to produce a return for the time the owners spend operating the business and a return on their investment in the business.

Entrepreneurs who earn less in their own business than they could earn working for someone else must weigh carefully the advantages and disadvantages of choosing the path of entrepreneurship. Why be exposed to all of the risks, sacrifices, and hard work of beginning and operating a small business if the rewards are less than those of remaining in the secure employment of someone else? Ideally, a small company's net income after taxes should be at least as much as the owner could earn by working for someone else.

An adequate profit must also include a reasonable return on the owner's total investment in the business. The owner's total investment is the amount contributed to the company at its inception plus any retained earnings (profits from previous years funneled back into the operation). If a would-be owner has $200,000 to invest and can invest it in securities and earn 10 percent, investing it in a small business that yields only 3 percent may not be the best course of action.

An entrepreneur's target income is the sum of a reasonable salary for the time spent running the business and a normal return on the amount invested in the firm. Determining how much this should be is the first step in creating the pro forma income statement.

The next step is to translate this target profit into a net sales figure for the forecasted period. To calculate net sales from a target profit, the owner needs published statistics for this type of business. Suppose an entrepreneur wants to launch a small retail bookstore and has determined that his target income is $30,000 for the upcoming year. Statistics gathered from *RMA Annual Statement Studies* show that the typical bookstore's net profit margin (net profit ÷ net sales) is 7.3 percent. Using this information, he can compute the sales level required to produce a net profit of $30,000:

$$\text{Net profit margin} = \frac{\text{Net profit}}{\text{Net sales (annual)}}$$

$$7.3\% = \frac{\$30,000}{\text{Net sales (annual)}}$$

$$\text{Net sales} = \frac{\$30,000}{0.073}$$

$$= \$410,959$$

Now the entrepreneur knows that to earn a net profit of $30,000 (before taxes), he must achieve annual sales of $410,959. To complete the projected income statement, he simply applies the appropriate statistics from *RMA Annual Statement Studies* to the annual sales figure. Because the statistics for each income statement item are expressed as percentages of net sales, he merely multiplies the proper statistic by the annual sales figure to obtain the desired value. For example, cost of goods sold usually comprises 61.4 percent of net sales for the typical small bookstore. So the owner of this new bookstore expects the cost of goods sold to be the following:

$$\text{Cost of goods sold} = \$311,828 \times 0.614 = \$252,329$$

The bookstore's complete projected income statement is shown as follows:

| | | |
|---|---|---|
| Net sales | (100%) | $410,959 |
| − Cost of goods sold | (61.4%) | 252,329 |
| Gross profit margin | (38.6%) | $158,630 |
| − Operating expenses | (31.3%) | 128,630 |
| Net income (before taxes) | (7.3%) | $ 30,000 |

At this point, the business appears to be a lucrative venture. But remember: This income statement represents a goal that the entrepreneur may not be able to attain. The next step is to determine whether this required sales volume is reasonable. One useful technique is to break down the required annual sales volume into daily sales figures. Assuming the store will be open six days per week for 52 weeks (312 days), the owner must average $1,317 per day in sales:

$$\text{Average daily sales} = \frac{\$410,959}{312 \text{ days}}$$

$$= \$1,317/\text{day}$$

This calculation gives the owner a better perspective of the sales required to yield an annual profit of $30,000.

To determine whether the profit expected from the business will meet or exceed the entrepreneur's target income, the prospective owner should create an income statement based on a realistic sales estimate. The previous analysis showed this entrepreneur what sales level is needed to reach the desired profit. But what happens if sales are lower or higher? To answer that question, he must develop a reliable sales forecast using the market research techniques described in Chapter 9, "Building a Guerilla Marketing Plan."

Suppose that after conducting a marketing survey of local customers and talking with nearby business owners, the prospective bookstore owner projects first year sales for the proposed business to be only $385,000. He must take this expected sales figure and develop a pro forma income statement.

| | | |
|---|---|---|
| Net Sales | (100%) | $385,000 |
| − Cost of Goods Sold | (61.4%) | 236,390 |
| Gross Profit Margin | (38.6%) | 148,610 |
| − Operating Expenses | (31.3%) | 120,505 |
| Net Income (before taxes) | (7.3%) | $ 28,105 |

Based on sales of $385,000, this entrepreneur should expect a net income (before taxes) of $28,105. If this amount is acceptable as a return on the investment of time and money in the business, he should proceed with his planning.

At this stage in developing the financial plan, the owner should create a more detailed picture of the company's expected operating expenses. One method is to use the statistics found in publications such as *Dun & Bradstreet's Cost of Doing Business* or reports from industry trade associations. These publications document selected operating expenses (expressed as a percentage of net sales) for different lines of businesses. Although publications such as these offer valuable guidelines for preparing estimates of expenses, the most reliable estimates of a start-up company's expenses are those that entrepreneurs develop for their particular situations and locations. Expenses such as rent, wages, salaries, benefits, utilities, and others vary dramatically from one part of the nation to another, and entrepreneurs must be sure that their forecasted expenses reflect the real cost of operating their particular businesses.

To ensure that they have overlooked no business expenses in preparing their business plans, entrepreneurs should list all of the initial expenses they will incur and have an accountant review the list. Figures 7.4 and 7.5 show two useful forms designed to help assign dollar values to anticipated expenses. Totals derived from this list of expenses should approximate the total expense figures calculated from published statistics. Naturally, an entrepreneur should be more confident of the total from his or her own list of expenses because this reflects his or her particular set of circumstances.

Entrepreneurs who follow the top-down approach to building an income statement—developing a sales forecast and working down to net income—must be careful to avoid falling into the trap of excessive optimism. Many entrepreneurs using this method overestimate their anticipated revenues and underestimate their actual expenses, and the results can be disastrous. To avoid this problem, some experts advise entrepreneurs to use the rule that many venture capitalists apply when they evaluate business start-ups: Divide revenues by two, multiply expenses by two, and if the business can still make it, it's a winner!

**THE PROJECTED BALANCE SHEET.**  In addition to projecting the small company's net profit or loss, the entrepreneur must develop a pro forma balance sheet outlining the fledgling company's assets and liabilities. Most entrepreneurs' primary focus is on the potential profitability of their businesses, but the assets their businesses use to generate profits are no less important. In many cases, small companies begin life on weak financial footing because their owners fail to determine their companies' total asset requirements. To prevent this major oversight, the owner should prepare a projected balance sheet listing every asset the business will need and all the claims against these assets.

**ASSETS.**  Cash is one of the most useful assets the business owns; it is highly liquid and can quickly be converted into other tangible assets. But how much cash should a small business have at its inception? Obviously, there is no single dollar figure that fits the needs of every small firm. One practical rule of thumb, however, suggests that the company's cash balance should cover its operating expenses (less depreciation, a noncash expense) for one

| Estimated Monthly Expenses | Your estimate of monthly expenses based on sales of $_____ per year. | Your estimate of how much cash you need to start your business. (See column 3.) | What to put in column 2. (These figures are typical for one kind of business. You will have to decide how many months to allow for in your business.) |
|---|---|---|---|
| **ITEM** | **COLUMN 1** | **COLUMN 2** | **COLUMN 3** |
| Salary of owner-manager | $ | $ | 2 times column 1 |
| All other salaries and wages | | | 3 times column 1 |
| Rent | | | 3 times column 1 |
| Advertising | | | 3 times column 1 |
| Delivery expense | | | 3 times column 1 |
| Supplies | | | 3 times column 1 |
| Telephone and telegraph | | | 3 times column 1 |
| Other utilities | | | 3 times column 1 |
| Insurance | | | Payment required by insurance company |
| Taxes, including Social Security | | | 4 times column 1 |
| Interest | | | 3 times column 1 |
| Maintenance | | | 3 times column 1 |
| Legal and other professional fees | | | 3 times column 1 |
| Miscellaneous | | | 3 times column 1 |
| Starting costs you have to pay only once | | | Leave column 2 blank |
| Fixtures and equipment | | | Fill in worksheet 3 and put the total here |
| Decorating and remodeling | | | Talk it over with a contractor |
| Installation of fixtures and equipment | | | Talk to suppliers from whom you buy these |
| Starting inventory | | | Suppliers will probably help you estimate this |
| Deposits with public utilities | | | Find out from utilities companies |
| Legal and professional fees | | | Lawyer, accountant, and so on |
| Licenses and permits | | | Find out from city offices what you have to have |
| Advertising and promotion for opening | | | Estimate what you'll use |
| Accounts receivable | | | What you need to buy more stock until credit customers pay |
| Cash | | | For unexpected expenses or losses, special purchases, etc. |
| Other | | | Make a separate list and enter total |
| Total Estimated Cash You Need to Start | | $ | Add up all the numbers in column 2 |

**FIGURE 7.4 Anticipated Expenses**

*Source:* U.S. Small Business Administration, *Checklist for Going into Business,* Small Marketers Aid No. 71 (Washington, DC: GPO, 1982), pp. 6–7.

**List of Furniture, Fixtures, and Equipment**

| Leave out or add items to suit your business. Use separate sheets to list exactly what you need for each of the items below. | If you plan to pay cash in full, enter the full amount below and in the last column. | If you are going to pay by installments, fill out the columns below. Enter in the last column your down payment plus at least one installment. | | | Estimate of the cash you need for furniture, fixtures, and equipment. |
|---|---|---|---|---|---|
| | | Price | Down payment | Amount of each installment | |
| Counters | $ | $ | $ | $ | $ |
| Storage shelves and cabinets | | | | | |
| Display stands, shelves, tables | | | | | |
| Cash register | | | | | |
| Safe | | | | | |
| Window display fixtures | | | | | |
| Special lighting | | | | | |
| Outside sign | | | | | |
| Delivery equipment if needed | | | | | |
| Total Furniture, Fixtures, and Equipment (enter this figure also in worksheet 2 under Starting Costs You Have to Pay Only Once) | | | | | $ |

**FIGURE 7.5 Anticipated Expenditures for Fixtures and Equipment**
*Source:* U.S. Small Business Administration, *Checklist for Going into Business,* Small Marketers Aid No. 71 (Washington, DC: GPO, 1982), pp. 6–7.

inventory turnover period. Using this rule, we can calculate the cash balance for the small bookstore as follows:

Operating expenses = $128,630 (from projected income statement)

Less depreciation (1.4% of annual sales) = $5,753 (a noncash expense)

Equals cash expenses (annual) = $122,877

$$\text{Cash requirement} = \frac{\text{Cash expenses}}{\text{Average inventory turnover ratio}}$$

$$= \frac{122,877}{3.6^*}$$

$$= \$34,132$$

*From *RMA Annual Statement Studies.*

Notice the inverse relationship between a small company's average inventory turnover ratio and its cash requirements. The faster a business turns its inventory, the shorter the time its cash is tied up in inventory, and the smaller is the amount of cash at start-up the company requires. For instance, if this bookstore could turn its inventory 5 times per year, its cash requirement would be $24,575 ($122,877 ÷ 5).

**INVENTORY.**    Another decision facing the entrepreneur is how much inventory the business should carry. An estimate of the inventory needed can be calculated from the information found on the projected income statement and from published statistics:

Cost of goods sold = $252,329 (from projected income statement)

$$\text{Average inventory turnover} = \frac{\text{Cost of goods sold}}{\text{Inventory level}}$$

$$= 3.6 \text{ times/year}$$

**FIGURE 7.6 Projected Balance Sheet for a Small Bookstore**

| Assets | | | Liabilities | |
|---|---|---|---|---|
| **Current Assets** | | | **Current Liabilities** | |
| Cash | $ 34,132 | | Accounts Payable | $ 48,796 |
| Inventory | 70,091 | | Note Payable | 3,750 |
| Miscellaneous | 1,800 | | | |
| Total Current Assets | $106,023 | | Total Current Liabilities | $52,546 |
| **Fixed Assets** | | | **Long-term Liabilities** | |
| Fixtures | $ 27,500 | | Note Payable | $ 40,000 |
| Office Equipment | 4,850 | | | |
| Computers/Cash Register | 3,125 | | Total Liabilities | $ 92,546 |
| Signs | 6,200 | | | |
| Miscellaneous | 1,500 | | | |
| Total Fixed Assets | $ 43,175 | | **Owner's Equity** | $ 56,653 |
| Total Assets | $149,198 | | **Total Liabilities and Owner's Equity** | $149,198 |

Substituting,

$$3.6 \text{ times/year} = \frac{\$252,329}{\text{Inventory level}}$$

Solving algebraically,

$$\text{Inventory level} = \$70,091$$

The entrepreneur also includes $1,800 in miscellaneous current assets. Suppose the estimate of fixed assets is as follows:

| | |
|---|---|
| Fixtures | $27,500 |
| Office Equipment | 4,850 |
| Computers/Cash Register | 3,125 |
| Signs | 6,200 |
| Miscellaneous | 1,500 |
| **Total** | **$43,175** |

**LIABILITIES.** To complete the projected balance sheet, the owner must record all of the small company's liabilities, the claims against the assets. The bookstore owner was able to finance 50 percent of inventory and fixtures ($48,796) through suppliers and has a short term note payable of $3,750. The only other major claim against the store's assets is a note payable to the entrepreneur's father-in-law for $40,000. The difference between the company's total assets ($149,198) and its total liabilities ($92,546) represents the owner's investment in the business (owner's equity) of $56,653.

The final step is to compile all of these items into a projected balance sheet, as shown in Figure 7.6.

## Ratio Analysis

*4.* Understand the basic financial statements through ratio analysis.

Would you be willing to drive a car on an extended trip without being able to see the dashboard displays showing fuel level, engine temperature, oil pressure, battery status, or the speed at which you were traveling? Not many people would! Yet, many small business owners run their companies exactly that way. They never take the time to check the vital signs of their businesses using their "financial dashboards." The result: Their companies develop engine trouble, fail, and leave them stranded along the road to successful entrepreneurship.

## Do You Know How Your Company Will Make Money?

When they launch their businesses, entrepreneurs instinctively know that their companies must make a profit to survive. However, many entrepreneurs never take the time to examine the factors in their business models that drive their companies' profitability. The following model is a useful tool for visualizing these factors, analyzing their impact on a company's profits, and identifying strategies for improving them so that a business can improve its profitability. Four factors determine a company's ability to produce an attractive profit: revenue drivers, margins, operating leverage, and volumes (see Figure 1).

**Revenue drivers** include all of the ways a company generates revenue. For instance, an automobile dealership's revenue drivers may be new cars sales, used cars sales, auto leases, service, parts, and short-term rentals. One small jewelry store identified its revenue generators as new jewelry, estate jewelry, watches, and gift items. Small companies with extensive inventories such as hardware stores can organize their revenue-generating product lines into a manageable number of major categories—for example, power tools, hand tools, lawn and garden, home repair, plumbing, electrical, and others. The next step is to assess the impact of each of the company's revenue drivers on total sales and their interaction with one another. For instance, an auto dealer may discover that the business generates more sales from used cars than from new cars.

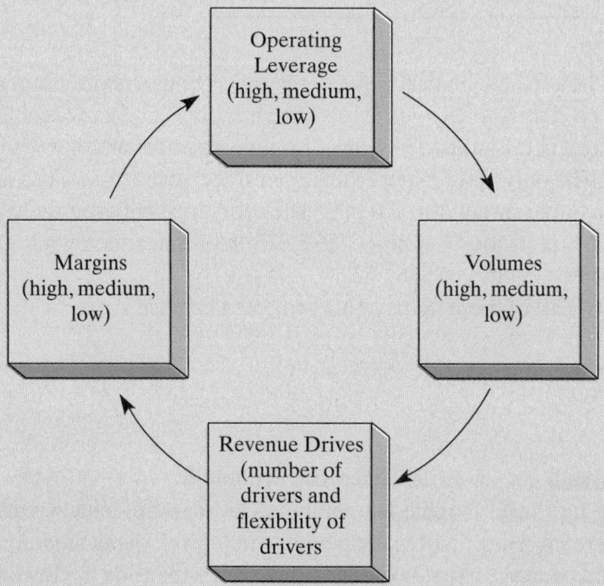

Entrepreneurs must then consider how much control they have over pricing their revenue drivers. Pricing may be either fixed or flexible. A company relies on fixed pricing if it sells goods or services at standard prices without negotiation or variation—for example, the items on the menu of a restaurant. Flexible pricing means that a company can offer different prices depending on when customers make a purchase, how many items they purchase, whether other items are bundled into the purchase, and other variables. Even though a restaurateur may be limited to fixed pricing on the menu, he or she would be able to use flexible pricing on catering jobs. Flexible pricing gives entrepreneurs greater ability to maximize total revenue (and profitability).

**Margins** reflect how much each revenue driver contributes to the profitability of a company. Margins are the price that a customer pays minus the cost to the company for providing that good or service. A small company can increase its margins either by raising its prices or by improving its efficiency and providing goods and services at lower costs. The goal is to determine which revenue drivers are capable of generating the greatest profit. For instance, an auto dealership may find that its profit margin on used cars is much higher than new cars and that the margin on auto repairs is higher still.

**Volumes** are another important determinant of a company's profitability. A small company's volume depends on the number of sales transactions it generates over a given time period and the value of each transaction. For instance, a fast-food restaurant counts on selling a large number of relatively low-priced meals, but an upscale restaurant generates revenue from a smaller number of meals at much higher average prices. At the fast-food restaurant, the average check may be $5.18, but at the upscale restaurant, the average check may be $45.80.

**Operating leverage** is the impact that a change in a company's sales volume has on its net income. If a

**FIGURE 1**

small company achieves positive operating leverage, its expenses as a percentage of sales revenues flatten or even decline as sales increase. As a result, the company's net profit margin will increase as it grows. Operating leverage is a function of a business's cost structure. Companies that have high levels of fixed costs have high operating leverage; conversely, companies that have high levels of variable costs have low operating leverage. Profits are more volatile when a company has high operating leverage because slight changes in revenue cause dramatic swings in profits as the company's sales fluctuate above and below its breakeven point.

Once entrepreneurs have analyzed the four components of a company's profitability, they can formulate strategies to enhance them (see Figure 2). For instance, if a company's current business model is characterized by a single revenue driver, low margins, low volumes, and high operating leverage, it is not likely to be a highly profitable venture. The entrepreneur in this situation, however, might change the business model to make it more profitable using the following questions:

- Can I add more revenue drivers to my business?
- How can I increase the number of transactions and/or the average transaction size that make up our volume?

- What can I do to reduce the level of fixed costs in my company?
- Can I change to a flexible pricing strategy and move away from a fixed pricing strategy?
- How can I improve the efficiency with which my company provides products and services to customers?
- In what other ways can I improve my company's profit margins?

Ron Towry, owner of Truck Gear SuperCenter, a small truck accessories business, was able to increase his company's sales by 25 percent and profits by 32 percent after making a strategic decision to begin selling his products at wholesale to truck and auto dealerships in addition to selling to his traditional retail customers. Although the company's wholesale prices and profit margins were lower, wholesale customers purchased in higher volumes, and Towry's company could sell to them at a lower cost per transaction, resulting in higher profits.

*Sources:* Adapted from April Murdoch and Michael Morris, "Is Your Economic Model Working?" *Orange Entrepreneur*, Fall 2006, pp. 16–19; Ron Stodghill, "Bolt Down Those Costs," *FSB*, May 2006, pp. 85–87.

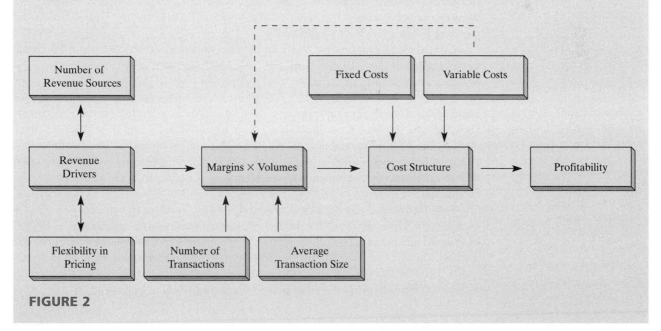

**FIGURE 2**

Smart entrepreneurs know that once they have their businesses up and running with the help of a solid financial plan, the next step is to keep the company moving in the right direction with the help of proper financial controls. Establishing these controls—and using them consistently—is one of the keys to keeping a business vibrant and healthy. Business owners who don't often are shocked to learn that their companies are in serious financial trouble *and they never knew it*.

A smoothly functioning system of financial controls is essential to achieving business success. These systems serve as an early warning device for underlying problems that could destroy a young business. They allow an entrepreneur to step back and see the big picture and to make adjustments in the company's strategic direction when necessary. According to one writer:

> A company's financial accounting and reporting system will provide signals, through comparative analysis, of impending trouble, such as:
>
> ■ Decreasing sales and falling profit margins.
> ■ Increasing corporate overhead.
> ■ Growing inventories and accounts receivable.
>
> These are all signals of declining cash flows from operations, the lifeblood of every business. As cash flows decrease, the squeeze begins:
>
> ■ Payments to vendors become slower.
> ■ Maintenance on production equipment lags.
> ■ Raw material shortages appear.
> ■ Equipment breakdowns occur.
>
> All of these begin to have a negative impact on productivity. Now the downward spiral has begun in earnest. The key is hearing and focusing on the signals.[8]

What are these signals, and how does an entrepreneur go about hearing and focusing on them? One extremely helpful tool is ratio analysis. **Ratio analysis**, a method of expressing the relationships between any two accounting elements, provides a convenient technique for performing financial analysis. When analyzed properly, ratios serve as barometers for a company's financial health. Using ratios as benchmarks allows entrepreneurs to determine, for example, whether their companies are carrying excessive inventory, experiencing heavy operating expenses, overextending credit, and managing to pay their debts on time. Ratio analysis also answers other questions relating to the efficient operation of their businesses. Unfortunately, few business owners actually use ratio analysis; one study discovered that only 27 percent of small business owners compute financial ratios and use them in managing their businesses![9]

Clever business owners use financial ratio analysis to identify problems in their businesses while they are still problems, not business-threatening crises. Tracking these ratios over time permits an owner to spot a variety of "red flags" that are indications of these problem areas. This is critical to business success because an entrepreneur cannot solve problems he or she does not know exist! Business owners also can use ratio analysis to increase the likelihood of obtaining bank loans. By analyzing their financial statements with ratios, entrepreneurs can anticipate potential problems and identify important strengths in advance. When evaluating a business plan or a loan request, lenders often rely on ratio analysis to determine how well managed a company is and how solid its financial footing is.

How many ratios should a small business manager monitor to maintain adequate financial control over the firm? The number of ratios an entrepreneur can calculate is limited only by the number of accounts recorded on the company's financial statements. However, tracking too many ratios only creates confusion and saps the meaning from an entrepreneur's financial analysis. The secret to successful ratio analysis is *simplicity*, focusing on just enough ratios to provide a clear picture of a company's financial standing.

## Twelve Key Ratios

In keeping with the idea of simplicity, we will describe twelve key ratios that will enable most business owners to monitor their companies' financial position without becoming bogged down in financial details. This chapter presents explanations of these ratios and examples based on the balance sheet and the income statement for Sam's Appliance Shop shown in Figures 7.1 and 7.2. We will group them into four categories: liquidity ratios, leverage ratios, operating ratios, and profitability ratios.

**LIQUIDITY RATIOS.**    **Liquidity ratios** tell whether a small business will be able to meet its maturing obligations as they come due. These ratios can forewarn entrepreneurs of impending cash flow problems. A small company with solid liquidity not only is able to pay its bills on time, but it also is in a position to take advantage of attractive business opportunities as they arise. The two most common measures of liquidity are the current ratio and the quick ratio.

**1. *Current ratio.*** The **current ratio** measures a small company's solvency by indicating its ability to pay current liabilities from current assets. It is calculated in the following manner:

$$\text{Current ratio} = \frac{\text{Current assets}}{\text{Current liabilities}}$$

$$= \frac{\$686,985}{\$367,850}$$

$$= 1.87:1$$

Sam's Appliance Shop has $1.87 in current assets for every $1 it has in current liabilities.

Current assets are assets that the entrepreneur expects to convert into cash in the ordinary business cycle, and normally include cash, notes/accounts receivable, inventory, and any other short-term marketable securities. Current liabilities are short-term obligations that come due within one year and include notes/accounts payable, taxes payable, and accruals.

The current ratio is sometimes called the working capital ratio and is the most commonly used measure of short-term solvency. Typically, financial analysts suggest that a small business maintain a current ratio of at least 2:1 (i.e., two dollars of current assets for every one dollar of current liabilities) to maintain a comfortable cushion of working capital. Generally, the higher a company's current ratio, the stronger its financial position, but a high current ratio does not guarantee that the company's assets are being used in the most profitable manner. For example, a business maintaining excessive balances of idle cash or overinvesting in inventory would likely have a high current ratio.

With its current ratio of 1.87:1, Sam's Appliance Shop could liquidate its current assets at 53.5% (1 ÷ 1.87 = 53.5%) of book value and still manage to pay its current creditors in full.

**2. *Quick ratio.*** The current ratio can sometimes be misleading because it does not show the quality of a company's current assets. For instance, a company with a large number of past-due receivables and stale inventory could boast an impressive current ratio and still be on the verge of financial collapse. The **quick ratio** (or the **acid test ratio**) is a more conservative measure of a firm's liquidity because it shows the extent to which its most liquid assets cover its current liabilities. It is calculated as follows:

$$\text{Quick ratio} = \frac{\text{Quick assets}}{\text{Current liabilities}} = \frac{\text{Current assets} - \text{Inventory}}{\text{Current liabilities}}$$

$$= \frac{\$686,985 - \$455,455}{\$367,850}$$

$$= 0.63:1$$

Sam's has 63 cents in quick assets for every $1 of current liabilities.

Quick assets include cash, readily marketable securities, and notes/accounts receivables—those assets that a company can convert into cash immediately, if needed. Most small firms determine quick assets by subtracting inventory from current assets because inventory cannot be converted into cash quickly. Also, inventory is the asset on which losses are most likely to occur in case of liquidation.

The quick ratio is a more specific measure of a company's ability to meet its short-term obligations and is a more rigorous test of its liquidity. It expresses capacity to repay current debts if all sales income ceased immediately. Generally, a quick ratio of 1:1 is considered satisfactory. A ratio of less than 1:1 indicates that the small company is overly dependent on inventory and on future sales to satisfy short-term debt. A quick ratio of more than 1:1 indicates a greater degree of financial security.

**LEVERAGE RATIOS.** **Leverage ratios** measure the financing supplied by a company's owners against that supplied by its creditors; they show the relationship between the contributions of investors and creditors to a company's capital base. Leverage ratios serve as gauges of the depth of a company's debt. These ratios show the extent to which an entrepreneur relies on debt capital (rather than equity capital) to finance operating expenses, capital expenditures, and expansion costs. Leverage ratios provide one measure of the degree of financial risk in a company. Generally, small businesses with low leverage ratios are less affected by economic downturns, but the returns for these firms are lower during economic booms. Conversely, small firms with high leverage ratios are more vulnerable to economic slides because their debt loads demolish cash flow; however, they have greater potential for large profits. "Leverage is a double-edged sword," says one financial expert. If it works for you, you can really build something. If you borrow too much, it can drag a business down faster than anything."[10] Companies that end up declaring bankruptcy most often take on more debt than the business can handle.

*Donald Trump and Trump Entertainment Resorts*

Real estate magnate and television celebrity Donald Trump historically has borrowed heavily to finance his company, Trump Entertainment Resorts, which operates hotels and casinos in various locations. Trump's business was forced to declare Chapter 11 bankruptcy for a second time to restructure a portion of the company's crushing $1.8 billion in debt. After negotiating a deal that gave creditors an equity stake in the company, Trump Entertainment Resorts emerged from bankruptcy with less debt, lower interest payments, and improved cash flow.[11]

The following ratios will help entrepreneurs keep their debt levels manageable.

**3.** *Debt ratio.* A small company's **debt ratio** measures the percentage of total assets financed by its creditors. The debt ratio is calculated as follows:

$$\text{Debt ratio} = \frac{\text{Total debt (or liabilities)}}{\text{Total assets}}$$
$$= \frac{\$367,850 + \$212,150}{847,655}$$
$$= 0.68:1$$

Creditors have claims of 68 cents against every $1 of assets that Sam's Appliance Shop owns.

Total debt includes all current liabilities and any outstanding long-term notes and bonds. Total assets represent the sum of the firm's current assets, fixed assets, and intangible assets. A high debt ratio means that creditors provide a large percentage of the firm's total financing. Owners generally prefer higher leverage ratios; otherwise, business funds must come either from the owners' personal assets or from taking on new owners, which means giving up more control over the business. Also, with a greater portion of the firm's assets financed by creditors, the owner is able to generate profits with a smaller personal investment. However, creditors typically prefer moderate debt ratios because a lower debt ratio indicates a smaller chance of creditor losses in case of liquidation. To lenders and creditors, high debt ratios mean a high risk of default.

**4.** *Debt to net worth ratio.* A small company's **debt to net worth ratio** also expresses the relationship between the capital contributions from creditors and those from owners. This ratio compares what the business "owes" to "what it is worth." It is a measure of a small company's ability to meet both its creditor and owner obligations in case of liquidation. The debt to net worth ratio is calculated as follows:

$$\text{Debt to net worth ratio} = \frac{\text{Total debt (or liabilities)}}{\text{Tangible net worth}}$$

$$= \frac{\$367,850 + \$212,150}{\$267,655 - \$3,500}$$

$$= 2.20:1$$

Sam's Appliance Shop owes creditors $2.20 for every $1 of equity that Sam owns.

Total debt is the sum of current liabilities and long-term liabilities, and tangible net worth represents the owners' investment in the business (capital + capital stock + earned surplus + retained earnings) less any intangible assets (e.g., goodwill) the company shows on its balance sheet.

The higher this ratio, the lower the degree of protection afforded creditors if the business should fail. Also, a higher debt to net worth ratio means that the firm has less capacity to borrow; lenders and creditors see the firm as being "borrowed up." In addition, carrying high levels of debt limits a company's options and restricts managers' flexibility. Quite simply, there isn't much "wiggle room" with a debt-laden balance sheet. Managers of a manufacturing company whose debt to equity ratio had climbed to 6:1 discovered just how crippling such a heavy debt load can be. The company was paying so much in interest on its debt that it lacked the cash to modernize its plant and equipment and to develop new products and product innovations, which made it difficult to keep up with its competitors. As sales slipped, earnings also fell, stretching the company's ability to make its interest payments, and its financial fortunes continued on a vicious downward spiral.[12]

A low debt to net worth ratio typically is associated with a higher level of financial security, giving the business greater borrowing potential. As a company's debt to net worth ratio approaches 1:1, its creditors' interest in the business approaches that of the owners'. If the ratio is greater than 1:1, the creditors' claims exceed those of the owners', and the business may be undercapitalized. In other words, the owners have not supplied an adequate amount of capital, forcing the business to take on too much debt.

**5. *Times interest earned ratio.*** The **times interest earned ratio** is a measure of a small company's ability to make the interest payments on its debt. It tells how many times the company's earnings cover the interest payments on the debt it is carrying. The times interest earned ratio is calculated as follows:

$$\text{Times interest earned ratio} = \frac{\text{Earnings before interest and taxes (or EBIT)}}{\text{Total interest expense}}$$

$$= \frac{\$60,629 + 39,850}{\$39,850}$$

$$= 2.52:1$$

Sam's Appliance Shop's earnings are 2.5 times greater than its interest expense.

EBIT is the company's net income (earnings) *before* deducting interest expense and taxes; the denominator measures the amount the business paid in interest over the accounting period.

A high times interest earned ratio suggests that the company would have little difficulty meeting the interest payments on its loans; creditors would see this as a sign of safety for future loans. Conversely, a low ratio is an indication that the company is overextended in its debts. A company's earnings are not able to cover its debt service if this ratio is less than one. "I look for a [times interest earned] ratio of higher than three-to-one," says one financial analyst, "which indicates that management has considerable breathing room to make its debt payments. When the ratio drops below one-to-one, it clearly indicates management is under tremendous pressure to raise cash. The risk of default or bankruptcy is very high."[13] Many creditors look for a times interest earned ratio of at least 4:1 to 6:1 before pronouncing a company a good credit risk.

Debt is a powerful financial tool, but companies must handle it carefully—just as a demolitionist handles dynamite. Denny's, the fast-food franchise, recently sold 60 of its

**FIGURE 7.7 The Right Amount of Debt Is a Balancing Act**

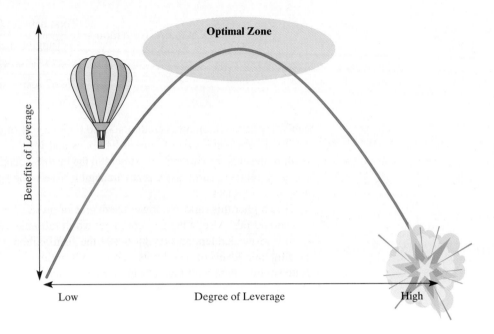

restaurants for $62 million, which the company used to reduce its "heavy debt burden." The move bolstered the company's performance and freed up cash for improving its operations, advertising, and enhancing customer service.[14] Like dynamite, too much debt can be dangerous. Trouble looms on the horizon for companies whose debt loads are so heavy that they must starve critical operations such as research and development, customer service, and others just to pay interest on the debt. Because their interest payments are so large, highly leveraged companies find that they are restricted when it comes to spending cash, whether on normal operations, acquisitions, or capital expenditures. Unfortunately, some companies go on borrowing binges, push their debt loads beyond the safety barrier (see Figure 7.7), and end up struggling for survival.

Some entrepreneurs are so averse to debt that they run their companies with a minimum amount of borrowing, relying instead on their businesses' cash flow to finance growth. Jerry Edwards, president of Chef's Expressions, a small catering company, manages to generate annual sales of $2 million with just a $20,000 line of credit. "We've always funded our growth out of cash flow," says Edwards. "I had a credit line that I didn't dip into for 10 years!"[15] Growth may be slower for these companies, but their owners do not have to contend with the dangers of debt. Managed carefully, however, debt can boost a company's performance and improve its productivity. Its treatment in the tax code also makes debt a much cheaper means of financial growth than equity. When companies with AA financial ratings borrow at 10 percent, the after-tax cost is just 7.2 percent (because interest payments to lenders are tax deductible); equity financing costs more than twice that.

**OPERATING RATIOS. Operating ratios** help entrepreneurs evaluate their companies' performances and indicate how effectively their businesses are using their resources. The more effectively its resources are used, the less capital a small business will require. These four operating ratios are designed to help entrepreneurs spot those areas they must improve if their businesses are to remain competitive.

**6.** *Average inventory turnover ratio.* A small company's **average inventory turnover ratio** measures the number of times its average inventory is sold out, or turned over, during the accounting period. This ratio tells owners how effectively and efficiently they are managing their companies' inventory. It tells them whether their inventory level is too low or too high and whether it is current or obsolete and priced correctly. The average inventory turnover ratio is calculated as follows:

$$\text{Average inventory turnover ratio} = \frac{\text{Cost of goods sold}}{\text{Average inventory}}$$

$$= \frac{\$1,290,117}{(\$805,745 + \$455,455) \div 2}$$

$$= 2.05 \text{ times/year}$$

Sam's Appliance Shop turns its inventory about two times a year, or once every 178 days.

Average inventory is found by adding a company's inventory at the beginning of the accounting period to the ending inventory and dividing the result by 2.

This ratio tells an entrepreneur how fast the merchandise is moving through the business and helps to balance the company on the fine line between oversupply and undersupply. To determine the average number of days units remain in inventory, the owner can divide the average inventory turnover ratio into the number of days in the accounting period (e.g., 365 ÷ average inventory turnover ratio, which for Sam's is 365 ÷ 2.05 times per year = 178 days). The result is called **days' inventory** (or **average age of inventory**). Auto dealerships often use days of inventory on hand as a measure of performance, but this is an important measure of performance for other companies as well.

*Michael's Inc.*

Michael's, a chain of arts and crafts stores, recently reported an inventory turnover ratio of 2.7 times per year, far below the industry average of 6.7 times per year. Industry analysts warned that the company could incur significant losses because of the price reductions that would be required to sell the obsolete and slow-moving inventory it held in stock.[16]

A below-average inventory turnover usually means an illiquid inventory characterized by obsolescence, overstocking, stale merchandise, or poor purchasing procedures. An above-average inventory turnover indicates that a small business has a healthy, salable, and liquid inventory and a balanced supply of merchandise supported by sound pricing policies.

**ENTREPRENEURIAL Profile**

*Dell Inc.*

Dell Inc., a computer maker that has used a build-to-order strategy to become a leader in the industry, turns its inventory an astonishing 76 times a year, or every five days. The company manages its inventory and its supplier relationships so closely that Dell has no more than two hours' worth of inventory at any particular moment. Because its inventory turnover rate is so high and because it collects payments from customers before it must pay suppliers, Dell's cash flow remains strong.[17]

Businesses that turn their inventories more rapidly than average require a smaller inventory investment to produce a particular sales volume. That means that these companies tie up less cash in inventory that sits idly on shelves. For instance, if Sam's could turn its inventory four times each year instead of just two, the company would require an average inventory of just $322,529 instead of the current level of $630,600 to generate sales of $1,870,841. Increasing the number of inventory turns would free up more than $308,000 currently tied up in excess inventory! Sam's would benefit from improved cash flow and higher profits.

The inventory turnover ratio can be misleading, however. For example, an excessively high ratio could mean the firm has a shortage of inventory and is experiencing stockouts. Similarly, a low ratio could be the result of planned inventory stockpiling to meet seasonal peak demand. Another problem is that the ratio is based on an inventory balance calculated from two days out of the entire accounting period. Thus, inventory fluctuations due to seasonal demand patterns are ignored, which may bias the resulting ratio. There is no universal, ideal inventory turnover ratio. Financial analysts suggest that a favorable turnover ratio depends on the type of business, its size, its profitability, its method of inventory valuation, and other relevant factors. The most meaningful basis for comparison is other companies of similar size in the same industry (more on this later in this chapter).

**7.** *Average collection period ratio.* A small company's **average collection period ratio** (or **days sales outstanding, DSO**) tells the average number of days it takes to collect accounts receivable. To compute the average collection period ratio, you must first calculate the firm's receivables turnover. If Sam's credit sales for the year were $1,309,589, then the receivables turnover ratio would be as follows:

$$\text{Receivables turnover ratio} = \frac{\text{Credit sales (or net sales)}}{\text{Accounts receivable}}$$

$$= \frac{\$1,309,589}{\$179,225}$$

$$= 7.31 \text{ times/year}$$

This ratio measures the number of times a company's accounts receivable turn over during the accounting period. Sam's Appliance Shop turns over its receivables 7.31 times per year. The higher a company's receivables turnover ratio, the shorter the time lag between making a sale and collecting the cash from it.

Use the following formula to calculate a company's average collection period ratio:

$$\text{Average collection period ratio} = \frac{\text{Days in accounting period}}{\text{Receivables turnover ratio}}$$

$$= \frac{365 \text{ days}}{7.31}$$

$$= 50.0 \text{ days}$$

Sam's Appliance Shop's accounts receivable are outstanding for an average of 50 days.

Typically, the higher a company's average collection period ratio, the greater is its chance of bad debt losses. Sales don't count unless a company collects the revenue from them!

*Lee Porter and Texas Auto Mart*

Lee Porter, owner of Texas Auto Mart, a small used car dealership that finances its customers' purchases, operates in an industry in which one-third of its customers typically default on their auto loans. With such a low collection rate, how does Porter stay in business? First, his gross profit margin is an impressive 60 percent; he buys cars for an average of $2,000 and then sells them for an average of $5,000. Also, most of his customers make a down payment and several monthly payments even if they do default on the loan (which gives Porter the right to repossess the car and sell it again). "It's not how much you sell," says Porter. "It's how much you collect."[18]

The most useful applications of the collection period ratio include comparing it to the industry average and to the firm's credit terms. This comparison will indicate the degree of the small company's control over its credit sales and collection techniques. One rule of thumb suggests that a company's collection period ratio should be no more than one-third greater than its credit terms. For example, if a small company's credit terms are "net 30," its average collection period ratio should be no more than 40 days. A ratio greater than 40 days would indicate poor collection procedures, such as sloppy record keeping or failure to send invoices promptly.

*Nick Ypsilantis and Accufile*

Nick Ypsilantis, CEO of AccuFile, a company that provides library staff and services to businesses, has learned the importance of sending invoices promptly. Before the company tightened its accounts receivable procedures, cash flow was a constant problem, forcing Ypsilantis to borrow money on a line of credit. By sending invoices sooner and following up promptly on past-due accounts, AccuFile has reduced its average collection period to 41 days and has not had to use its credit line at all.[19]

Just as Nick Ypsilantis has learned, slow payers represent great risk to small businesses. Many entrepreneurs proudly point to rapidly rising sales only to find that they must

Too often, entrepreneurs fail to recognize the importance of collecting their accounts receivable on time. After all, collecting accounts is not as glamorous or as much fun as generating sales. Lowering a company's average collection period ratio, however, can produce tangible—and often significant—savings. The following formula shows how to convert an improvement in a company's average collection period ratio into dollar savings:

$$\text{Annual savings} = \frac{(\text{Credit sales} \times \text{Annual interest rate} \times \text{Number of days average collection period is lowered})}{365}$$

where
  Credit sales = Company's annual credit sales in $.
  Annual interest rate = The interest rate at which the company borrows money.
  Number of days average collection period is lowered = The difference between the previous year's average collection period ratio and the current one.

**Example**

Sam's Appliance Shop's average collection period ratio is 50 days. Suppose that the previous year's average collection period ratio was 56 days, a six-day improvement. The company's credit sales for the most recent year were $1,309,589. If Sam borrows money at 10.25 percent, this six-day improvement has generated savings for Sam's Appliance Shop of:

$$\text{Savings} = \frac{\$1,309,589 \times 10.25\% \times 6 \text{ days}}{365} = \$2,207$$

By collecting his accounts receivable just six days faster on the average, Sam has saved his business more than $2,200! Of course, if a company's average collection period ratio rises, the same calculation will tell the owner how much that costs.

**FIGURE 7.8 How Lowering Your Average Collection Period Can Save You Money**
*Source:* "Days Saved. Thousands Earned," *Inc.,* November 1995, p. 98.

borrow money to keep their companies going because credit customers are paying their bills in 45, 60, or even 90 days instead of 30. Slow receivables often lead to a cash crisis that can cripple a business. Figure 7.8 shows how lowering its average collection period ratio can save a company money.

**8.** *Average payable period ratio.* The converse of the average collection period ratio, the **average payable period ratio**, tells the average number of days it takes a company to pay its accounts payable. Like the average collection period, it is measured in days. To compute this ratio, first calculate the payables turnover ratio. Sam's payables turnover ratio is as follows:

$$\text{Payables turnover ratio} = \frac{\text{Purchases}}{\text{Accounts payable}}$$
$$= \frac{\$939,827}{\$152,580}$$
$$= 6.16 \text{ times/year}$$

To find the average payable period, use the following computation:

$$\text{Average payable period ratio} = \frac{\text{Days in accounting period}}{\text{Payables turnover ratio}}$$
$$= \frac{365 \text{ days}}{6.16}$$
$$= 59.3 \text{ days}$$

Sam's Appliance Shop takes an average of 59 days to pay its accounts with vendors and suppliers.

An excessively high average payable period ratio may indicate that a company is enjoying extended credit terms from its suppliers or it may be a sign of a significant amount of past-due accounts payable. Although sound cash management calls for business owners to keep their cash as long as possible, slowing payables too drastically can severely damage a company's credit rating. Ideally, the average payable period would match (or exceed) the time it takes to convert inventory into sales and ultimately into cash. In this case, the company's vendors are financing its inventory and its credit sales. For example, Amazon.com reaps the benefits of this situation. On average, it does not pay its vendors until 31 days *after* it collects payment from its customers.[20]

One of the most meaningful comparisons for this ratio is against the credit terms offered by suppliers (or an average of the credit terms offered). If the average payable period ratio slips beyond vendors' credit terms, it is an indication that the company is suffering from cash shortages or a sloppy accounts payable procedure and its credit rating is in danger. If this ratio is significantly lower than vendors' credit terms, it may be a sign that a business is not using its cash most effectively.

**9.** *Net sales to total assets ratio.* A small company's **net sales to total assets ratio** (also called the **total assets turnover ratio**) is a general measure of its ability to generate sales in relation to its assets. It describes how productively the firm employs its assets to produce sales revenue. The total assets turnover ratio is calculated as follows:

$$\text{Total assets turnover ratio} = \frac{\text{Net sales}}{\text{Net total assets}}$$

$$= \frac{\$1,870,841}{\$847,655}$$

$$= 2.21:1$$

Sam's Appliance Shop generates $2.21 in sales for every dollar of assets.

The denominator of this ratio, net total assets, is the sum of all of the firm's assets (cash, inventory, land, buildings, equipment, tools, everything owned) less depreciation. This ratio is meaningful only when compared to that of similar firms in the same industry category. A total assets turnover ratio below the industry average suggests that a small company is not generating an adequate sales volume for its asset size.

**PROFITABILITY RATIOS. Profitability ratios** indicate how efficiently a small company is being managed. They provide the owner with information about a company's ability to generate a profit. They focus on a company's "bottom line"; in other words, they describe how successfully the firm is conducting business.

**10.** *Net profit on sales ratio.* The **net profit on sales ratio** (also called the **profit margin on sales**) measures a company's profit per dollar of sales. This ratio (which is expressed as a percentage) shows the number of cents of each sales dollar remaining after deducting all expenses and income taxes. The profit margin on sales is calculated as follows:

$$\text{Net profit on sales ratio} = \frac{\text{Net income}}{\text{Net sales}} \times 100\%$$

$$= \frac{\$60,629}{\$1,870,841} \times 100\%$$

$$= 3.24\%$$

For every dollar in sales that Sam's Appliance Shop generates, Sam keeps 3.24 cents in profit.

Many small business owners believe that a high profit margin on sales is necessary for a successful business operation, but this is a myth. To evaluate this ratio properly, entrepreneurs must consider their companies' asset base, their inventory and receivables turnover ratios, and their total capitalization. For example, the typical small supermarket earns an average net profit of only one or two cents on each dollar of sales, but its inventory may turn over as many as 30 times a year. If a company's profit margin on sales is below the industry average, it is a sign that its prices are relatively low or that its costs are excessively high, or both.

*Shelly Fireman and
Fireman Hospitality
Group*

Shelly Fireman, CEO of Fireman Hospitality Group, a company that owns several restaurants in New York City, including the Redeye Grill and Bond 45, says that rising costs are putting pressure on his restaurants' profit margins. "Sales are good," he says, "but the [profit] margin pressures are insane." Shelley points to rising costs for everything from food and rent to wages and insurance as the culprits that are draining his company's profit margins. Whatever industry they are in, businesses facing this dilemma can either pass along to their customers the increased costs of doing business in the form of higher prices or settle for lower profit margins. Fireman, like most of his competitors, has raised prices but is concerned about the dampening effect that might have on sales. He recently crossed an important psychological barrier when he reluctantly pushed the price of an entrée past the $40 mark. "I think the $40 entrée is here to stay," he says.[21]

If a company's net profit on sales ratio is excessively low, the owner should check the gross profit margin (net sales minus cost of goods sold expressed as a percentage of net sales). A reasonable gross profit margin varies from industry to industry, however. For instance, a service company may have a gross profit margin of 75 percent, whereas a manufacturer's may be 35 percent. If this margin slips too low, it puts the company's ability to generate a profit and stay in business in jeopardy.

**11.** *Net profit to assets ratio.* The **net profit to assets ratio** (also known as the **return on assets ratio**) tells how much profit a company generates for each dollar of assets that it owns. This ratio describes how efficiently a business is putting to work all of the assets it owns to generate a profit. It tells how much net income an entrepreneur is squeezing from each dollar's worth of the company's assets. It is calculated as follows:

$$\text{Net profit to assets ratio} = \frac{\text{Net income}}{\text{Total assets}} \times 100\%$$

$$= \frac{\$60,629}{\$847,655} \times 100\%$$

$$= 7.15\%$$

Sam's Appliance shop earns a return of 7.15 percent on its asset base. This ratio provides clues about the asset intensity of an industry. Return on assets ratios that are below 5 percent are indicative of asset-intense industries that require heavy investments in assets to stay in business (e.g., manufacturing and railroads). Return on assets ratios that exceed 20 percent tend to occur in asset-light industries such as business or personal services—for example, advertising agencies and computer services. A net profit to assets ratio that is below the industry average suggests that a company is not using its assets very efficiently to produce a profit. Another common application of this ratio is to compare it to the company's cost of borrowed capital. Ideally, a company's return on assets ratio (ROA) should exceed the cost of borrowing money to purchase those assets. Companies that experience significant swings in the value of their assets over the course of a year often use an average value of the asset base over the accounting period to get a more realistic estimate of this ratio.

**12.** *Net profit to equity ratio.* The **net profit to equity ratio** (or the **return on net worth ratio**) measures the owners' rate of return on investment. Because it reports the percentage of the owners' investment in the business that is being returned through profits annually, it is one of the most important indicators of a company's profitability or management's efficiency. The net profit to equity ratio is computed as follows:

$$\text{Net profit to equity ratio} = \frac{\text{Net income}}{\text{Owners' equity (or net worth)}} \times 100\%$$

$$= \frac{\$60,629}{\$267,655} \times 100\%$$

$$= 22.65\%$$

Sam is earning 22.65 percent on the money that he has invested in this business.

## Batting .1000 in the Auto Business

Dorian Boyland learned the value of hard work from his mother and role model, Alice. With his mother's help and encouragement, Boyland earned a degree in business administration and computer science while earning a name for himself as a college All-American baseball player. After graduation, Boyland played professional baseball, winning a World Series title with the Pittsburgh Pirates. When he retired from baseball after eight years, Boyland was set to begin work as a computer systems analyst at Intel when he received a call from Ron Tonkin, owner of one of the largest auto dealer groups in the United States. "He told me to come work for him for 60 days and if I liked it, I could stay," he recalls. "If I didn't, I still had my job at Intel."

Boyland was a natural. Within two months, he had been promoted to assistant manager and was making more money than he had made as a professional baseball player. "I loved the business from day one because it was like sports," he says. "It was competitive."

A few years later, when Tonkin approached Boyland with the idea of forming a partnership to buy an existing Dodge dealership, Boyland jumped at the chance. Two years later, Boyland sold his partnership interest and bought his own Dodge dealership. As a new owner, Boyland struggled at first, mainly because he lacked a plan and a disciplined approach for implementing it. "I had a lot of inventory, so manufacturers were happy," he says. "I spent a lot on advertising, so newspapers were happy. My commission structure was high, so my salespeople were happy. But I wasn't making any money, so I wasn't happy."

Boyland spent three days at home developing a business plan that established a bottom-up formula for earning a profit by controlling expenses and monitoring cash flow. He changed the way he handled inventory, advertising, and pricing—in short, the way he managed his entire business. Boyland's plan produced results: His Dodge dealership began earning a profit and has done so every year since, not an easy accomplishment in the retail auto industry. More importantly, Boyland, who now does business under the name Boyland Auto, has implemented that same plan at all seven of the dealerships he now owns.

Boyland is careful about how he spends his money so he can generate a profit. He keeps advertising expenditures to less than 10 percent of gross profit. His sales team receives no salaries; their compensation is commission-based. He allocates 35 percent of overhead expenses to new car sales, 30 percent to used car sales, 25 percent to service, and 10 percent to parts sales. His goal is to run his dealerships so that they produce a net profit margin of at least 3 percent of sales. "I never ask how many cars we sold," he quips. "I ask my sales managers how much profit we made." Although sales volume is important because automakers expect dealers to reach sales targets, Boyland focuses more on profitability. "You can be number one in terms of [sales] volume, but if you are constantly losing money, you'll be taken out of business."

Every month, Boyland sits down with the managers of all of his dealerships to review an extensive financial and operating report. The discussion is open and honest, but the real benefit comes from managers seeing the numbers their stores are generating and then exchanging ideas about how to improve them. Another important aspect of the meetings is the goal setting that takes place as managers set plans for the future.

Boyland learned early on a valuable lesson in maintaining the profitability of his auto dealerships, one that he continues to focus on every day. "You have to have a passion for this business," he says. "There's a lot of money to be made and a lot of money to be lost. Whether you are selling cars or shoes, you go into business to make money. That's the bottom line."

1. Why is monitoring a company's financial performance using the techniques described in this chapter important to operating a successful business?

2. Schedule a brief interview with a car dealer in your area. Describe the 12 ratios covered in this chapter. Which of these ratios are most important to running an auto dealership successfully?

3. What other "critical numbers" does the dealer monitor?

*Source:* Adapted from Carolyn M. Brown, "Maximum Overdrive," *Black Enterprise*, June 2003, pp. 156–162.

This ratio compares profits earned during the accounting period with the amount the owners have invested in the business during that time. If this interest rate on the owners' investment is excessively low, some of this capital might be better employed elsewhere. For instance, a business should produce a rate of return that exceeds its cost of capital. A company's cost of capital depends on the interest rates it must pay on debt capital and the return that shareholders expect on equity capital, both of which reflect the risk of providing that capital. For instance, if a small company's cost of capital is 13.5 percent, and its return on equity is just 6 percent, that business has not added any economic value to its owners.

A natural reaction to low profitability ratios is to embark on a cost-cutting effort. Although minimizing costs can improve profitability, entrepreneurs must be judicious in their cost-cutting, taking a strategic approach rather than imposing across-the-board cuts. Cutting costs in areas that are vital to operating success—such as a supermarket cutting its advertising expenditures—can inhibit a company's ability to succeed and can lead to failure. For instance, choosing to lay off workers, a common reaction for many companies facing financial challenges, often backfires. Not only does a company risk losing talented workers and the knowledge they have built up over time, but research also shows that repeated rounds of layoffs destroy the morale and the productivity of the remaining workers.[22] In other cases, entrepreneurs on cost-cutting vendettas alienate employees and sap worker morale by eliminating nitpicking costs that affect employees adversely and really don't save much money. Entrepreneurs also must consider the effect of their cost-cutting efforts on their customers, who often suffer when companies reduce staff or eliminate elements from the customer service equation. As airlines have abolished complementary in-flight meals, headsets, pillows, blankets, and other items (many now charge extra for these), customer complaints have climbed. "Five years ago, everyone was complaining about how lousy [airline] food was; now they're complaining that they're not getting their lousy food," says Debra Ward, an industry analyst.[23]

## Interpreting Business Ratios

*5.* Explain how to interpret financial ratios.

Ratios are useful yardsticks in measuring a small company's performance and can point out potential problems before they develop into serious crises. However, calculating these ratios is not enough to ensure proper financial control. In addition to knowing how to calculate these ratios, the owner must understand how to interpret them and apply them to managing the business more effectively and efficiently.

Not every business measures its success with the same ratios. In fact, key performance ratios vary dramatically across industries and even within different segments of the same industry. Entrepreneurs must know and understand which ratios are most crucial to their companies' success and focus on monitoring and controlling those. Many successful entrepreneurs identify or develop ratios that are unique to their own operations to help them achieve success. Known as **critical numbers**, these barometers of business success measure financial and operational aspects of a company's performance. When these critical numbers are headed in the right direction, a business is on track to achieve its objectives.

*Pat Croce and Sports Physical Therapists*

When Pat Croce founded Sports Physical Therapists, a business that grew into a chain of 40 sports medicine centers, he discovered that the number of new patient evaluations was the critical number he needed to track. This measure told Croce how much new business he could expect in the coming months. If the number climbed, he knew that he must begin adding staff immediately.[24]

Examples of critical numbers at other companies include:

- The load factor, the number of seats filled with passengers, on a luxury bus targeting business travelers with daily trips from Hong Kong Island to Shenzhen, China.[25]
- Sales per labor hour at a grocery store.
- Turnaround time on loan decisions at a community bank.
- Subscriber renewal rates at a magazine.
- The number of "full-season equivalent" ticket sales (or FSE, the equivalent of a season pass) for a Premier League.[26]
- Percentage of rework at a photo processor. Because the percentage of rework is an important determinant of profitability, this processor graphs this critical number and posts it weekly.

Critical numbers may be different for two companies in the same industry, depending on their strategies. The key is identifying *your* company's critical numbers, monitoring them, and then driving them in the right direction. That requires communicating the importance of critical numbers to employees and giving them feedback on how well the business is achieving them.

*Norm Brodsky and CitiStorage*

Over time, Norm Brodsky, owner of CitiStorage, a highly successful records-storage business that targets law firms, accounting firms, and hospitals, discovered that his company's critical number was the number of new boxes put into storage each week, so he began tracking it closely. "Tell me how many new boxes came in during [a month]," he says, "and I can tell you our overall sales figure for [that month] within one or two percent of the actual figure." That particular critical number surprised Brodsky because new boxes account for only a small percentage of total sales; yet new-box count was the key to allowing Brodsky to forecast his company's future. Once, during a period of rapid growth (about 55 percent a year), Brodsky saw on his Monday morning report that the new-box count had fallen by 70 percent in the previous week. Alarmed, Brodsky temporarily stopped expanding the company's workforce to see if the drop was an aberration or the beginning of a business slowdown. A few weeks later, he knew that the market had changed and that sales growth indeed had slowed to 15 percent. By using his company's critical number, Brodsky avoided excessive labor costs, a nasty cash crisis, and a morale-destroying layoff and was able to keep his company on track.[27]

One of the most valuable ways to utilize ratios is to compare them with those of similar businesses in the same industry. By comparing the company's financial statistics to industry averages, the owner is able to locate problem areas and maintain adequate financial controls. "By themselves, these numbers are not that meaningful," says one financial expert of ratios, "but when you compare them to [those of] other businesses in your industry, they suddenly come alive because they put your operation in perspective."[28]

The principle behind calculating these ratios and critical numbers and then comparing them to industry norms is the same as that of most medical tests in the health care profession. Just as a healthy person's blood pressure and cholesterol levels should fall within a range of normal values, so should a financially healthy company's ratios. A company cannot deviate too far from these normal values and remain successful for long. When deviations from "normal" do occur (and they will), a business owner should focus on determining the cause of the deviations. In some cases, deviations are the result of sound business decisions, such as taking on inventory in preparation for the busy season, investing heavily in new technology, and others. In other instances, however, ratios that are out of the normal range for a particular type of business are indicators of what could become serious problems for a company. When comparing a company's ratios to industry standards, entrepreneurs should ask the following questions:

- Is there a significant difference in my company's ratio and the industry average?
- If so, is this a *meaningful* difference?
- Is the difference good or bad?
- What are the possible causes of this difference? What is the most likely cause?
- Does this cause require that I take action?
- What action should I take to correct the problem?

Properly used, ratio analysis can help owners identify potential problem areas in their businesses early on—*before* they become crises that threaten their very survival. Several organizations regularly compile and publish operating statistics, including key ratios, summarizing the financial performance of many businesses across a wide range of industries. The local library should subscribe to most of these publications:

*RMA Annual Statement Studies.* The Risk Management Association publishes its *Annual Statement Studies,* showing ratios and other financial data for more than 740 different industrial, construction, wholesale, retail, and service categories.

*Dun & Bradstreet's Key Business Ratios.* Since 1932, Dun & Bradstreet has published *Key Business Ratios,* which covers more than 800 business categories.

*Almanac of Business and Industrial Financial Ratios.* Published by Prentice Hall, this almanac provides financial ratios and balance sheet and income statement data for 200 lines of business.

*Vest Pocket Guide to Business Ratios.* This handy guide, published by John Wiley & Sons, gives key ratios and financial data for a wide variety of industries.

*Industry Spotlight.* Published by Schonfeld & Associates, this publication, which can be customized for any one of more than 250 industries, contains financial

" THE GOOD NEWS IS, PROFITS ARE UP 74%, THE BAD NEWS IS, WE DON'T KNOW WHY. "

statement data and key ratios from more than 95,000 tax returns. *Industry Spotlight* also provides detailed financial information for both profitable companies and those with losses.

***Industry trade associations.*** Virtually every type of business is represented by a national trade association, which publishes detailed financial data compiled from its membership. For example, the owner of a small coffee shop could consult the National Coffee Association (and its newsletter, *The Coffee Reporter*), the International Coffee Organization, or a variety of regional coffee associations for financial statistics relevant to his operation.

***Government agencies.*** Government agencies offer a great deal of financial operating data on a variety of industries. For example, the U.S. Internal Revenue Service (IRS) annually publishes *Statistics of Income,* which includes income statement and balance sheet statistics compiled from income tax returns. The IRS also publishes the *Census of Business* that gives a limited amount of ratio information.

In the Entrepreneurial Spotlight

### ■ Critical Numbers

Critical numbers are key financial and operational indicators that determine a company's success. Although they vary from one industry to another and even from one company to another, when these critical numbers are moving in the right direction, a business is on track to achieve its objectives. Entrepreneurs must be sure to identify the right critical numbers and to track them *daily*. Ron Friedman, head of the accounting firm Stonefield Josephson, studies his company's critical numbers every day. "Every morning by 9:30, I receive a printed report that tracks certain key results from the day before," he says. "That's a tremendous management advantage. I can respond immediately to any problem signals."

A company's critical numbers depend on the business it is in. "Key numbers might be how much was sold each day, how much was shipped, how big your backlog is, and how much was collected," says Friedman. For instance, an airline's basic critical number might be its load factor, the percentage of seats it fills with passengers. A small manufacturer's basic critical number might be revenue per labor hour. Examples of critical numbers at other companies include:

- The call abandonment rate and the number of calls per paid hour at a toll-free caller service company.
- The gross profit margin at a manufacturer of pallets.
- Sales per labor hour at a supermarket.

How can entrepreneurs make critical numbers work for them? The first step is to conduct an analysis to determine the company's critical numbers. Asking managers and employees for input, studying industry standards, and using the management team's experience in the business are the most effective ways to determine the right critical numbers. Simplicity is the key. A company might have just one critical number, or several numbers may be important. Four critical numbers is probably the maximum.

Once managers determine their critical numbers, the next step is to set objectives for the numbers. Where should the numbers be at the end of the month, the quarter, the year?

Managers also must derive reliable and meaningful ways of measuring critical numbers. Whatever measure is appropriate, it must clearly link employees' actions to the critical numbers. For critical numbers to have an impact, everyone in the company must be able to see how their performance on the job affects the critical numbers. That means the method for measuring the critical numbers must be simple enough for everyone to understand. At one plant of printer R.R. Donnelley and Sons, press efficiency, a measure of output that also incorporates quality, is the critical number, and everyone understands how to measure it.

Finally, managers must give employees incentives to move critical numbers in the right direction. One retail chain established a daily customer count and average sale per customer as their critical numbers. The company organized a monthly contest with prizes and posted charts tracking each store's performance. Soon, employees were working hard to improve their stores' performances over the previous year and to outdo other stores in the chain. The healthy rivalry among stores boosted the company's performance significantly.

Focusing on critical numbers means keeping a company focused on what is essential for its success. Jack Clegg, CEO of Nobel Learning Communities, a for-profit company that operates 160 schools in 13 U.S. states, relies on three critical numbers to make sure his business achieves its goal of providing a quality education to children in kindergarten through secondary school. Nobel creates clusters of small, uniformly designed schools to maximize efficiency and emphasize small class sizes and teaching flexibility. At Nobel, maximum enrollment in a single school is 300, and class size is limited to 22 students. The three critical numbers Clegg uses to manage Nobel Learning Communities are general and administrative expenses (G&A) as a percentage of gross tuition, the school occupancy rate, and school personnel cost as a percentage of gross tuition. Maintaining control over these three numbers supports the company's overall strategy and, unlike many of its competitors, enables it to earn an attractive profit in a very challenging business. Every Friday morning,

Clegg convenes a meeting to review a "flash report" of these numbers for each school and to compare them against the objectives stated in Nobel's business plan. "That means that every single week I know how every single school is doing," says Clegg. "This allows us to make adjustments *within* the month, not after it."

1. What role do critical numbers play in running a business successfully?
2. How can business owners use critical numbers to make their businesses more successful?
3. Interview a local entrepreneur who has been in business for at least five years. Explain the concept of critical numbers and then ask him or her to identify the critical numbers in his or her business.

*Sources:* Adapted from Ilan Mochari, "When to Say When," *Inc.*, February 2001, p. 104; "A Daily Does of Numbers," *Inc.*, January 1, 1998, www2.inc.com/search/10147.html; John Case, "Swipe These Critical Numbers!" *Inc.*, December 11, 1999, www2.inc.com/search/15982.html; George Gendron, "FYI: Critical Numbers," *Inc.*, December 1, 2000, www2.inc.com/search/21103.html; John Case, "Figuring Out Your Critical Number," *Inc.*, July 24, 1996, www2.inc.com/search/13200.html; Edward O. Welles, "The ABCs of Profit," *Inc.*, December 1, 2000, www2.inc.com/search21116.html; John Case, "Critical Numbers in Action," *Inc.*, January 21, 2000, www2.inc.com/search/15981.html; John Case, "Boosting Performance with Critical Numbers," *Inc.*, December 11, 1999, www2.inc.com/search/15978-print.html; John Case, "Troubleshooting Your Critical Numbers," *Inc.*, December 13, 1999, www2.inc.com/search/15980.html.

## What Do All of These Numbers Mean?

Learning to interpret financial ratios just takes a little practice! This section will show you how it's done by comparing the ratios from the operating data already computed for Sam's Appliance Shop to those taken from the *RMA Annual Statement Studies*. (The industry median is the ratio falling exactly in the middle when sample elements are arranged in ascending or descending order.)

| **Sam's Appliance Shop** | **Industry Median** |
|---|---|

*Liquidity Ratios*—tell whether or not a small business will be able to meet its maturing obligations as they come due.

1. Current Ratio = 1.87:1                    1.50:1

Sam's Appliance Shop falls short of the rule of thumb of 2:1, but its current ratio is above the industry median by a significant amount. Sam's should have no problem meeting its short-term debts as they come due. By this measure, the company's liquidity is solid.

2. Quick Ratio = 0.63:1                    0.50:1

Again, Sam's is below the rule of thumb of 1:1, but the company passes this test of liquidity when measured against industry standards. Sam's relies on selling inventory to satisfy short-term debt (as do most appliance shops). If sales slump, the result could be liquidity problems for Sam's. Sam should consider building a cash reserve as a cautionary measure.

*Leverage Ratios*—measure the financing supplied by the company's owners against that supplied by its creditors and serve as a gauge of the depth of a company's debt.

3. Debt Ratio = 0.68:1                    0.64:1

Creditors provide 68 percent of Sam's total assets, very close to the industry median of 64 percent. Although Sam's does not appear to be overburdened with debt, the company might have difficulty borrowing additional money, especially from conservative lenders.

4. Debt to Net Worth Ratio = 2.20:1                                          1.90:1

Sam's Appliance Shop owes $2.20 to creditors for every $1.00 the owners have invested in the business (compared to $1.90 in debt to every $1.00 in equity for the typical business). Although this is not an exorbitant amount of debt, many lenders and creditors will see Sam's as "borrowed up." Borrowing capacity is somewhat limited because creditors' claims against the business are more than twice those of the owners. Sam should consider increasing his investment in the business through retained earnings or by paying down some of the company's debt.

5. Times Interest Earned = 2.52:1                                          2.0:1

Sam's earnings are high enough to cover the interest payments on its debt by a factor of 2.52, slightly better than the typical firm in the industry, whose earnings cover its interest payments just two times. Sam's Appliance Shop has a cushion (although a small one) in meeting its interest payments.

*Operating Ratios*—evaluate a company's overall performance and show how effectively it is putting its resources to work.

6. Average Inventory Turnover Ratio = 2.05 times/year                    4.0 times/year

Inventory is moving through Sam's at a very slow pace, *half* that of the industry median. The company has a problem with slow-moving items in its inventory and, perhaps, too much inventory. Which items are they, and why are they slow moving? Does Sam need to drop some product lines? Sam must analyze his company's inventory and inventory control procedures.

7. Average Collection Period Ratio = 50.0 days                          19.3 days

Sam's Appliance Shop collects the average accounts receivable after 50 days, compared with the industry median of 19 days, more than two-and-a-half times longer. A more meaningful comparison is against Sam's credit terms; if credit terms are net 30 (or anywhere close to that), Sam's has a dangerous collection problem, one that drains cash and profits and demands *immediate* attention! He must implement the cash management techniques that you will learn about in Chapter 8.

8. Average Payable Period Ratio = 59.3 days                             43 days

Sam's payables are nearly 40 percent slower than those of the typical firm in the industry. Stretching payables too far could seriously damage the company's credit rating, causing suppliers to cut off future trade credit. This could be a sign of cash flow problems or a sloppy accounts payable procedure. This problem also demands *immediate* attention. Using proper cash management techniques can help Sam to run his business more effectively.

9. Net Sales to Total Assets Ratio = 2.21:1                             2.7:1

Sam's Appliance Shop is not generating enough sales, given the size of its asset base. This could be the result of a number of factors—improper inventory, inappropriate pricing, poor location, poorly trained sales personnel, and many others. The key is to find the cause . . . *fast!*

*Profitability Ratios*—measure how efficiently a firm is operating and offer information about its bottom line.

10. Net Profit on Sales Ratio = 3.24%                                   7.6%

After deducting all expenses, 3.24 cents of each sales dollar remains as profit for Sam's—less than half the industry median. Sam should review his company's gross profit margin and investigate its operating expenses, checking them against industry standards and looking for those that are out of balance.

11. Net Profit to Assets Ratio = 7.15%                                  5.5%

Sam's generates just a return of 7.15% for every $1 in assets, which is 30 percent above the industry average. Given his asset base, Sam is squeezing an above-average return out of his company. This could be an indication that Sam's is highly profitable; however, given the previous ratio, this is unlikely. It is more likely that Sam's asset base is thinner than the industry average.

12. Net Profit to Equity Ratio = 22.65%                                 12.6%

Sam's Appliance Shop's owners are earning 22.65 percent on the money they have invested in the business. This yield is nearly twice that of the industry median, and, given the previous ratio, is more a result of the owner's relatively low investment in the business than an indication of its superior profitability. Sam is using O.P.M. (Other People's Money) to generate a profit.

When comparing ratios for their individual businesses to published statistics, entrepreneurs must remember that the comparison is made against averages. Owners should strive to achieve ratios that are at least as good as these average figures. The goal should be to manage the business so that its financial performance is better than the industry average. As owners compare financial performance to those covered in the published sta-

**FIGURE 7.9 Trend Analysis Ratios**

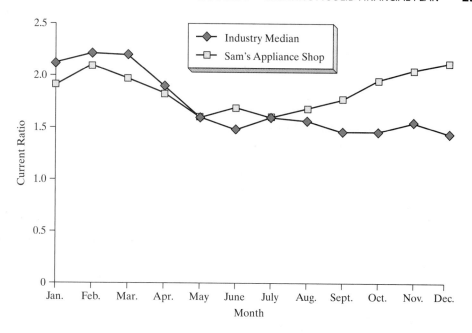

tistics, they inevitably will discern differences between them. They should note those items that are substantially out of line from the industry average. However, a ratio that varies from the average does not necessarily mean that a small business is in financial jeopardy. Instead of making drastic changes in financial policy, entrepreneurs must explore why the figures are out of line. Steve Cowan, co-owner of Professional Salon Concepts, a wholesale beauty products distributor, routinely performs such an analysis on his company's financial statements. "I need to know whether the variances for expenses and revenues for a certain period are similar," he says. "If they're not, are the differences explainable? Is an expense category up just because of a decision to spend more, or were we just sloppy?"[29]

In addition to comparing ratios to industry averages, owners should analyze their firms' financial ratios over time. By themselves, these ratios are "snapshots" of the firm's finances at a single instant; but by examining these trends over time, the owner can detect gradual shifts that otherwise might go unnoticed until a financial crisis is looming (see Figure 7.9).

## Breakeven Analysis

*6.* Conduct a breakeven analysis for a small company.

Another key component of every sound financial plan is a breakeven analysis (or cost-volume-profit analysis). A small company's **breakeven point** is the level of operation (sales dollars or production quantity) at which it neither earns a profit nor incurs a loss. At this level of activity, sales revenue equals expenses—that is, the company "breaks even." By analyzing costs and expenses, an entrepreneur can calculate the minimum level of activity required to keep a business in operation. These techniques can then be refined to project the sales needed to generate a desired level of profit. Most potential lenders and investors require entrepreneurs to prepare a breakeven analysis so that they can judge the earning potential of a new business and the likelihood that it will be successful. In addition to its being a simple, useful screening device for financial institutions, breakeven analysis also serves as a planning device for entrepreneurs. It can show an entrepreneur who might have unreasonable expectations about a business idea just how unprofitable a proposed business venture is likely to be.

### Calculating the Breakeven Point

A small business owner can calculate a firm's breakeven point by using a simple mathematical formula. To begin the analysis, the owner must determine fixed costs and variable costs. **Fixed expenses** are those that do not vary with changes in the volume of sales or production (e.g., rent, depreciation expense, insurance, salaries, lease or loan payments, and others). **Variable expenses**, on the other hand, vary directly with changes in the volume of sales or production (e.g., raw material costs, sales commissions, hourly wages, and others).

Some expenses cannot be neatly categorized as fixed or variable because they contain elements of both. These semivariable expenses change, although not proportionately, with changes in the level of sales or production (electricity would be one example). These costs remain constant up to a particular production or sales volume and then climb as that volume is exceeded. To calculate the breakeven point, an entrepreneur must separate these expenses into their fixed and variable components. A number of techniques can be used (which are beyond the scope of this text), but a good cost accounting system can provide the desired results.

Here are the steps an entrepreneur must take to compute the breakeven point using an example of a typical small business, the Magic Shop:

**Step 1**    *Determine the expenses the business can expect to incur.* With the help of a budget, an entrepreneur can develop estimates of sales revenue, cost of goods sold, and expenses for the upcoming accounting period. The Magic Shop expects net sales of $950,000 in the upcoming year, with a cost of goods sold of $646,000 and total expenses of $236,500.

**Step 2**    *Categorize the expenses estimated in Step 1 into fixed expenses and variable expenses and separate semivariable expenses into their component parts.* From the budget, the owner anticipates variable expenses (including the cost of goods sold) of $705,125 and fixed expenses of $177,375.

**Step 3**    *Calculate the ratio of variable expenses to net sales.* For the Magic Shop, this percentage is $705,125 ÷ $950,000 = 74 percent. The Magic Shop uses $0.74 out of every sales dollar to cover variable expenses, leaving $0.26 ($1.00 − 0.74) as a contribution margin to cover fixed costs and make a profit.

**Step 4**    *Compute the breakeven point by inserting this information into the following formula:*

$$\text{Breakeven sales (\$)} = \frac{\text{Total fixed cost}}{\text{Contribution margin expressed as a percentage of sales}}$$

For the Magic Shop,

$$\text{Breakeven sales} = \frac{\$177{,}375}{0.26}$$

$$= \$682{,}212$$

Thus, the Magic Shop will break even with sales of $682,212. At this point, sales revenue generated will just cover total fixed and variable expense. The Magic Shop will earn no profit and will incur no loss. To verify this, make the following calculations:

| | |
|---|---:|
| Sales at breakeven point | $682,212 |
| − Variable expenses (74% of sales) | −504,837 |
| Contribution margin | 177,375 |
| − Fixed expenses | −177,375 |
| Net income (or net loss) | $        0 |

Some entrepreneurs find it more meaningful to break down their companies' annual breakeven point into a daily sales figure. If the Magic Shop will be open 312 days per year, then the average daily sales it must generate just to break even is $682,212 ÷ 312 days = $2,187 per day.

## Adding in a Profit

What if the Magic Shop's owner wants to do *better* than just break even? The entrepreneur's analysis can be adjusted to consider such a possibility. Suppose the owner expects a reasonable profit (before taxes) of $80,000. What level of sales must the Magic Shop achieve to generate this? The owner can calculate this by treating the desired profit as if it were a fixed cost. In other words, the owner modifies the formula to include the desired net income:

$$\text{Sales (\$)} = \frac{\text{Total fixed expenses} + \text{Desired net income}}{\text{Contribution margin expressed as a percentage of sales}}$$

$$= \frac{\$177,375 + \$80\,000}{0.26}$$

$$= \$989,904$$

To achieve a net profit of $80,000 (before taxes), the Magic Shop must generate net sales of $989,904. Once again, if we transform this sales annual volume into a daily sales volume, we get: $989,904 ÷ 312 days = $3,173 per day.

## Breakeven Point in Units

Some small businesses may prefer to express the breakeven point in units produced or sold instead of in dollars. Manufacturers often find this approach particularly useful. The following formula computes the breakeven point in units:

$$\text{Breakeven volume} = \frac{\text{Total fixed costs}}{\text{Sales price per unit} - \text{Variable cost per unit}}$$

For example, suppose that Trilex Manufacturing Company estimates its fixed costs for producing its line of small appliances at $390 000. The variable costs (including materials, direct labor, and factory overhead) amount to $12.10 per unit, and the selling price per unit is $17.50. So, Trilex computes its contribution margin this way:

$$\text{Contribution margin} = \text{Price per unit} - \text{Variable cost per unit}$$

$$= \$17.50 \text{ per unit} - \$12.10 \text{ per unit}$$

$$= \$5.40 \text{ per unit}$$

Trilex's breakeven volume is as follows:

$$\text{Breakeven volume (units)} = \frac{\text{Total fixed costs}}{\text{Per unit contribution margin}}$$

$$= \frac{\$390,000}{\$5.40 \text{ per unit}}$$

$$= 72,222 \text{ units}$$

To convert this number of units to breakeven sales dollars, Trilex simply multiplies it by the selling price per unit:

$$\text{Breakeven sales} = 72,222 \text{ units} \times \$17.50 = \$1,263,889$$

Trilex could compute the sales required to produce a desired profit by treating the profit as if it were a fixed cost:

$$\text{Sales (units)} = \frac{\text{Total fixed costs} + \text{Desired net income}}{\text{Per unit contribution margin}}$$

For example, if Trilex wanted to earn a $60,000 profit, its required sales would be:

$$\text{Sales (units)} = \frac{\$390,000 + \$60,000}{5.40} = 83,333 \text{ units}$$

### Constructing a Breakeven Chart

The following outlines the procedure for constructing a graph that visually portrays the firm's breakeven point (that point where revenues equal expenses):

**Step 1**    *On the horizontal axis, mark a scale measuring sales volume in dollars (or in units sold or some other measure of volume).* The breakeven chart for the Magic Shop shown in Figure 7.10 uses sales volume in dollars because it applies to all types of businesses, products, and services.

**Step 2**    *On the vertical axis, mark a scale measuring income and expenses in dollars.*

**Step 3**    *Draw a fixed expense line intersecting the vertical axis at the proper dollar level parallel to the horizontal axis.* The area between this line and the horizontal axis represents the firm's fixed expenses. On the breakeven chart for the Magic Shop shown in Figure 7.10, the fixed expense line is drawn horizontally beginning at $177,375 (point A). Because this line is parallel to the horizontal axis, it indicates that fixed expenses remain constant at all levels of activity.

**Step 4**    *Draw a total expense line that slopes upward beginning at the point at which the fixed cost line intersects the vertical axis.* The precise location of the total expense line is determined by plotting the total cost incurred at a particular sales volume. The total cost for a given sales level is found by the following formula:

$$\text{Total expenses} = \text{Fixed expenses} + \text{Variable expenses}$$
$$\text{expressed as a percentage of sales} \times \text{Sales level}$$

Arbitrarily choosing a sales level of $950,000, the Magic Shop's total costs would be as follows:

$$\text{Total expenses} = \$177,375 + (0.74 \times \$950,000)$$
$$= \$880,375$$

Thus, the Magic Shop's total cost is $880,375 at a net sales level of $950,000 (point B). The variable cost line is drawn by connecting points A

**FIGURE 7.10 Break-Even Chart, the Magic Shop**

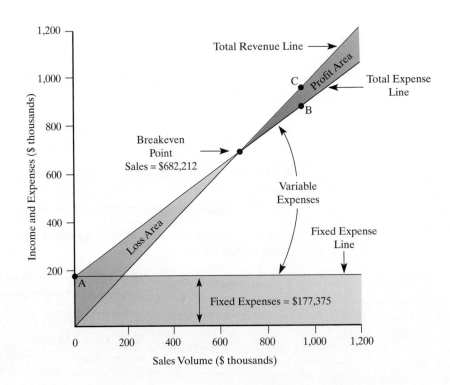

and B. The area between the total cost line and the horizontal axis measures the total costs the Magic Shop incurs at various levels of sales. For example, if the Magic Shop's sales are $850,000, its total costs will be $806,375.

**Step 5**  *Beginning at the graph's origin, draw a 45-degree revenue line showing where total sales volume equals total income.*

For the Magic Shop, point C shows that sales = income = $950,000.

**Step 6**  *Locate the breakeven point by finding the intersection of the total expense line and the revenue line.* If the Magic Shop operates at a sales volume to the left of the breakeven point, it will incur a loss because the expense line is higher than the revenue line over this range. This is shown by the triangular section labeled "Loss Area." On the other hand, if the firm operates at a sales volume to the right of the breakeven point, it will earn a profit because the revenue line lies above the expense line over this range. This is shown by the triangular section labeled "Profit Area."

### Using Breakeven Analysis

Breakeven analysis is a useful planning tool for the potential small business owner, especially when approaching potential lenders and investors for funds. It provides an opportunity for integrated analysis of sales volume, expenses, income, and other relevant factors. Breakeven analysis is a simple, preliminary screening device for the entrepreneur faced with the business start-up decision. It is easy to understand and use. With just a few calculations, an entrepreneur can determine the minimum level of sales needed to stay in business as well as the effects of various financial strategies on the business. It is a helpful tool for evaluating the impact of changes in investments and expenditures.

**ENTREPRENEURIAL**
**Profile**

*Fergus McCann*
*and LimoLiner*

Before launching LimoLiner, a company that provides luxury bus service aimed at business-people traveling between downtown Boston, Massachusetts, and New York City, entrepreneur Fergus McCann calculated his venture's breakeven point. Knowing that it would take a while to build a solid base of customers, McCann determined that to break even, his buses had to be only half-full on each one-way trip. McCann priced a LimoLiner trip at just $69, which is $30 less than the train, and $172.50 less than a full-fare airline ticket. Satisfied that he would be able to generate at least $483 per one-way trip within a short time of opening, McCann launched LimoLiner.[30]

Breakeven analysis does have certain limitations. It is too simple to use as a final screening device because it ignores the importance of cash flows. Also, the accuracy of the analysis depends on the accuracy of the revenue and expense estimates. Finally, the assumptions pertaining to breakeven analysis may not be realistic for some businesses. Breakeven calculations make the following assumptions: fixed expenses remain constant for all levels of sales volume; variable expenses change in direct proportion to changes in sales volume; and changes in sales volume have no effect on unit sales price. Relaxing these assumptions does not render this tool useless, however. For example, the owner could employ nonlinear breakeven analysis using a graphical approach.

## Chapter Review

1. Understand the importance of preparing a financial plan.
   - Launching a successful business requires an entrepreneur to create a solid financial plan. Not only is such a plan an important tool in raising the capital needed to get a company off the ground, but it also is an essential ingredient in managing a growing business.
   - Earning a profit does not occur by accident; it takes planning.

2. Describe how to prepare the basic financial statements and use them to manage the small business.
   - Entrepreneurs rely on three basic financial statements to understand the financial conditions of their companies:
     1. *The balance sheet.* Built on the accounting equation: Assets = Liabilities + Owner's equity (capital), it provides an estimate of the company's value on a particular date.
     2. *The income statement.* This statement compares the firm's revenues against its expenses to determine its net income (or loss). It provides information about the company's bottom line.
     3. *The statement of cash flows.* This statement shows the change in the company's working capital over the accounting period by listing the sources and the uses of funds.

3. Create projected financial statements.
   - Projected financial statements are a basic component of a sound financial plan. They help the manager plot the company's financial future by setting operating objectives and by analyzing the reasons for variations from targeted results. Also, the small business in search of start-up funds will need these pro forma statements to present to prospective lenders and investors. They also assist in determining the amount of cash, inventory, fixtures, and other assets the business will need to begin operation.

4. Understand the basic financial statements through ratio analysis.
   - The twelve key ratios described in this chapter are divided into four major categories: liquidity ratios, which show the small firm's ability to meet its current obligations; leverage ratios, which tell how much of the company's financing is provided by owners and how much by creditors; operating ratios, which show how effectively the firm uses its resources; and profitability ratios, which analyze the company's profitability.
   - Many agencies and organizations regularly publish these statistics. If there is a discrepancy between the small firm's ratios and those of the typical business, the owner should investigate the reason for the difference. A below average ratio does not necessarily mean that the business is in trouble.

5. Explain how to interpret financial ratios.
   - To benefit from ratio analysis, the small company should compare its ratios to those of other companies in the same line of business and look for trends over time.
   - When business owners detect deviations in their companies' ratios from industry standards, they should determine the cause of the deviations. In some cases, such deviations are the result of sound business decisions; in other instances, however, ratios that are out of the normal range for a particular type of business are indicators of what could become serious problems for a company.

6. Conduct a breakeven analysis for a small company.
   - Business owners should know their firm's breakeven point, the level of operations at which total revenues equal total costs; it is the point at which companies neither earn a profit nor incur a loss. Although just a simple screening device, breakeven analysis is a useful planning and decision making tool.

## Discussion Questions

1. Why is it important for entrepreneurs to develop financial plans for their companies?
2. How should a small business manager use the ratios discussed in this chapter?
3. Outline the key points of the 12 ratios discussed in this chapter. What signals does each give a business owner?
4. Describe the method for building a projected income statement and a projected balance sheet for a beginning business.

5. Why are pro forma financial statements important to the financial planning process?
6. How can breakeven analysis help an entrepreneur planning to launch a business? What information does it give an entrepreneur?

# Business PlanPro

One significant advantage Business Plan Pro offers is the efficient creation of pro forma (projected) financial statements, including the balance sheet, profit and loss statement, and cash flow statement. Once you enter the revenues, expenses, and other relevant figures in the step-by-step tables, your financial statements are done! This can save time, and the format is one that is commonly recognized and respected by bankers and investors. The simplicity of this process also enables you to create "what if" scenarios based on various levels of anticipated revenues and expenses simply by saving versions of your business plan under unique file names.

## On the Web

Go to www.bplans.com/bc/# or use the links called "Finance" and "Business Calculators" located on the Companion Website (www.prenhall.com/scarborough) under the "Business Plan Resource" tab. You will find a collection of online tools, including a breakeven calculator. Open this tool and enter the information it requests—the average per unit revenue, the average per unit cost, and the anticipated monthly fixed costs. This tool will calculate your breakeven point in units and revenue. Change the data and observe the difference the changes make in the breakeven point. What does this tell you about the level of risk that you may experience based on the most realistic financial projections you can make?

## In the Software

Select a sample plan that you found interesting. Go to the "Financial Plan" section and look at the financial statements that are contained in the business plan. Notice how the statements are organized. Month-to-month detail is provided for at least the first year, with annual totals for subsequent years. In addition, note the associated tables and graphics that appear within the financial plan. Graphics can be excellent tools for communicating information about financial trends and comparisons.

Click on the "Resources" icon at the top of your screen within Business Plan Pro. Then scroll down to "Research" and find the "Free Industry Profile" link. This information may help to compare your company's key ratios to industry averages. You can also get this information from *RMA Annual Statements Studies*, Dun & Bradstreet, trade associations, and other sources. This portion of your plan will help to prove the validity of your financial forecasts.

## Building Your Business Plan

Review the information in the "Financial Plan" section of the business plan. Add "Important Assumptions" to this section as you deem necessary. This is a good place to make notes and comments to test or further research any of these assumptions. If it is a start-up business, estimate the costs that you expect to incur to launch the business. The "Investment Offering" option may appear in the menu, based on your choice in the Plan Wizard, and you can complete that information. Review your information for your breakeven analysis and the financial statements including your profit and loss, cash flow, and balance sheet statements.

This chapter identifies 12 key business ratios. Based on your projections, calculate each of these ratios and compare them to industry standard ratios. Most, if not all, of these ratios are available through Business Plan Pro's "Ratio" section, the final topic in the "Financial Plan" section.

## RATIO ANALYSIS

| | Projected Ratio | Industry Ratio | Variance |
|---|---|---|---|
| 1. Current ratio | _____ | _____ | _____ |
| 2. Quick ratio | _____ | _____ | _____ |
| 3. Debt-ratio | _____ | _____ | _____ |
| 4. Debt to net worth ratio | _____ | _____ | _____ |
| 5. Times interest earned | _____ | _____ | _____ |
| 6. Average inventory turnover ratio | _____ | _____ | _____ |
| 7. Average collection period ratio | _____ | _____ | _____ |
| 8. Average payable period ratio | _____ | _____ | _____ |
| 9. Net sales to total assets ratio | _____ | _____ | _____ |
| 10. Net sales to working capital ratio | _____ | _____ | _____ |
| 11. Net profit on sales ratio | _____ | _____ | _____ |
| 12. Net profit to equity ratio | _____ | _____ | _____ |

If you notice significant differences in these comparisons, determine why those variances exist. Does this tell you something about the reality of your projections, or is this just due to the stage and differences of your business compared to the larger industry? These ratios can be excellent tools to help you question, test, and validate your assumptions and projections. Good business planning, solid projections, and a thorough analysis of these ratios can help launch a viable business with greater probability of success.

# Managing Cash Flow

Business isn't difficult—
be sure the incomings are
greater than the
outgoings.
—A wise Vermonter

No man's credit is as
good as his money.
—E. W. Howe

## Learning Objectives

**Upon completion of this chapter, you will be able to:**

1 Explain the importance of cash management to the success of a small business.

2 Differentiate between cash and profits.

3 Understand the five steps in creating a cash budget and use them to build a cash budget.

4 Describe the fundamental principles involved in managing the "Big Three" of cash management: accounts receivable, accounts payable, and inventory.

5 Explain the techniques for avoiding a cash crunch in a small company.

C ash—a four-letter word that has become a curse for many small businesses. Lack of this valuable asset has driven countless small companies into bankruptcy. Unfortunately, many more firms will become failure statistics because their owners have neglected the principles of cash management that can spell the difference between success and failure. One small business consultant says that "one of the most serious mistakes business owners make is trying to run their businesses without cash flow projections. This is like driving along on the freeway at 90 kilometers per hour with a blindfold on. It's not a question of whether you are headed for an accident. It's a question of how serious the accident will be and whether or not you will survive it."[1]

Developing cash forecasts is important for every small business but is essential for new businesses in particular because early sales levels usually do not generate sufficient cash to keep the company afloat. Too often, entrepreneurs launch their companies with insufficient cash to cover their start-up costs and the cash flow gap that results while expenses outstrip revenues. The result is business failure. Controlling the financial aspects of a business with the profit-planning techniques described in the previous chapter is immensely important; however, by themselves, these techniques are insufficient to achieve business success. Entrepreneurs are prone to focus on their companies' income statements—particularly sales and profits. The balance sheet and the income statement, of course, show an important part of a company's financial picture, but it is just that: only part of the total picture. It is entirely possible for a business to have a solid balance sheet and to make a profit and still go out of business by *running out of cash*. Even if a company's revenue exceeds its expenses for a given period, the cash flow from that revenue may not arrive in time to pay the company's cash expenses. Managing cash effectively requires an entrepreneur to look beyond the "bottom line" and focus on what keeps a company going—cash.

## Cash Management

*1.* Explain the importance of cash management to the success of a small business.

Managing cash flow is a struggle for many business owners (see Figure 8.1). In fact, research by the National Federation of Independent Businesses (NFIB) shows that managing cash flow consistently ranks among the top ten problems that small business owners face. **Cash management** involves forecasting, collecting, disbursing, investing, and planning for the cash a company needs to operate smoothly. Managing cash is a matter of timing—gaining control over when a company collects cash and when it pays it out. Managing cash

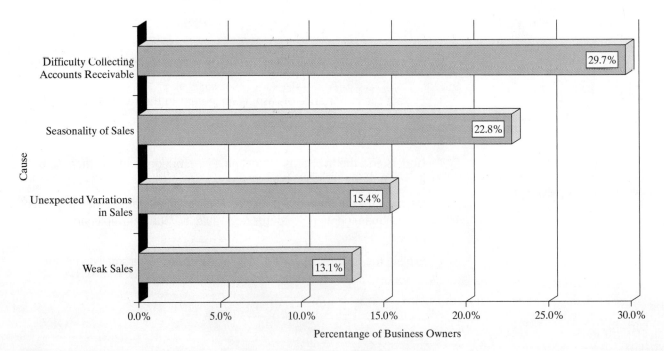

**FIGURE 8.1 Causes of Cash Flow Problems Among Small Businesses**

*Source: NFIB National Small Business Poll: The Cash Flow Problem* (National Federation of Independent Businesses: Washington, DC), 2003, p. 7.

is an important task because cash is the most important yet least productive asset that a small business owns. A business must have enough cash to meet its obligations as they come due or it will experience bankruptcy. Creditors, employees, and lenders expect to be paid on time, and cash is the required medium of exchange. Some firms retain an excessive amount of cash to meet any unexpected circumstances that might arise. This dormant cash has an income-earning potential that the owners are ignoring, and this restricts a company's growth and lowers its profitability. Proper cash management permits entrepreneurs to adequately meet the cash demands of their businesses, to avoid retaining unnecessarily large cash balances, and to stretch the profit-generating power of each unit of currency their companies own. Entrepreneurs must have the discipline to manage cash flow from their first day of operations.

*H. J. Heinz and the
H. J. Heinz Company*

Shortly after H. J. Heinz and two partners launched their first food business in 1875, their company's rapidly growing sales outstripped their start-up capital, and the company ran out of cash. A local newspaper called the entrepreneurs a "trio in a pickle." After the company failed, Heinz personally was liable for $20,000, a huge sum in that day. Undaunted, Heinz learned from his mistakes and launched a second food company the very next year. In this venture, he added the product that would eventually make him famous—ketchup—and with the help of careful cash management, the H. J. Heinz Company has become one of the largest food companies in the world.[2]

Although cash flow problems afflict companies of all sizes and ages, young businesses are prone to suffering cash shortages because they act like "cash sponges," soaking up all of the money and then some. The reason is that their cash-generating "engines" have not had the opportunity to "rev up" to full speed and cannot generate sufficient power to produce the cash necessary to cover rapidly climbing expenses.

Owners of fast growing businesses also must pay particular attention to cash management because the greatest potential threat to cash flow occurs when a company is experiencing rapid growth. If a company's sales are rising, the owner also must hire more employees, expand plant capacity, develop new products, increase the sales force and customer service staff, build inventory, and incur other drains on the firm's cash supply. However, collections from the increased sales often slip as a company grows, and the result is a cash crisis.

*Paul Moore and Cruise
Control Ltd.*

Paul Moore founded Cruise Control Ltd., a British company that sold travel cruises, in 1999 and took the business on a fast-growth path, reaching sales of £3.4 million in just seven months. Within five years, the company was generating £93 million in sales but was beginning to come apart at the seams under the strain of rapid growth. A year later Cruise Control Ltd. ran out of cash and folded.[3]

"Well you can't upset me.
Timpson - what's the bad news you've got?"

### TABLE 8.1 Five Cash Management Roles of the Entrepreneur

**Role 1. *Cash finder.*** This is the entrepreneur's first and foremost responsibility. You must make sure there is enough capital to pay all present (and future) bills. This is not a one-time task; it is an on-going job.

**Role 2. *Cash planner.*** As cash planner, an entrepreneur makes sure the company's cash is used properly and efficiently. You must keep track of its cash, make sure it is available to pay bills, and plan for its future use. Planning requires you to forecast the company's cash inflows and outflows for the months ahead with the help of a cash budget (discussed later in this chapter).

**Role 3. *Cash distributor.*** This role requires you to control the cash needed to pay the company's bills and the priority and the timing of those payments. Forecasting cash disbursements accurately and making sure the cash is available when payments come due is essential to keeping the business solvent.

**Role 4. *Cash collector.*** As cash collector, your job is to make sure your customers pay their bills on time. Too often, entrepreneurs focus on pumping up sales, while neglecting to collect the cash from those sales. Having someone in your company responsible for collecting accounts receivable is essential. Uncollected accounts drain a small company's pool of cash very quickly.

**Role 5. *Cash conserver.*** This role requires you to make sure your company gets maximum value for the money it spends. Whether you are buying inventory to resell or computers to keep track of what you sell, it is important to get the most for your money. Avoiding unnecessary expenditures is an important part of this task. The goal is to spend cash so it will produce a return for the company.

*Source:* Adapted from Bruce J. Blechman, "Quick Change Artist," *Entrepreneur*, January 1994, pp. 18–21.

Unfortunately, many small business owners do not engage in cash planning. One study of 2,200 small businesses found that 68 percent performed no cash flow analysis at all![4] The result is that many successful, growing, and profitable businesses fail because they become insolvent; they do not have adequate cash to meet the needs of a growing business with a booming sales volume. The head of the National Federation of Independent Businesses says that many small business owners "wake up one day to find that the price of success is no cash on hand. They don't understand that if they're successful, inventory and receivables will increase faster than profits can fund them."[5] The resulting cash crisis may force an entrepreneur to lose control of the business or, ultimately, declare bankruptcy and close. Table 8.1 describes the five key cash management roles every entrepreneur must fill.

The first step to managing cash more effectively is to understand the company's **cash flow cycle**—the time lag between paying suppliers for merchandise and receiving payment from customers (see Figure 8.2). The longer this cash flow cycle, the more likely the business owner is to encounter a cash crisis. Preparing a cash forecast that recognizes this cycle, however, will help avoid a crisis.

*John Fernsell and Ibex
Outdoor Clothing*

John Fernsell recognizes the importance of cash management because of the length of his company's cash flow cycle. Fernsell, a former stockbroker, is the founder of Ibex Outdoor Clothing, a company that makes outdoor clothing from high-quality European wool. Ibex's sales are growing rapidly, but cash is a constant problem because of its lengthy cash flow cycle. Fernsell orders wool from his European suppliers in February and pays for it in June. The wool then goes to garment makers in California, who ship finished clothing to Ibex in July and August, when Fernsell pays for the finished goods. Ibex ships the clothing to retailers in September and October but does not get paid until November, December, and sometimes January! Ibex's major cash outflows are from June to August, but its cash inflows during those months are virtually nil, making it essential for Fernsell to manage the company's cash balances carefully.[6]

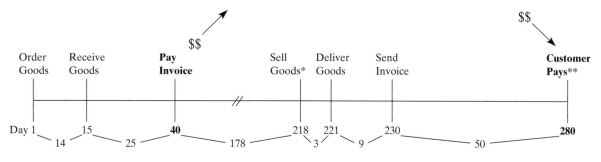

* Based on Average Inventory Turnover:

$$\frac{365 \text{ days}}{2.05 \text{ times/year}} = 178 \text{ days}$$

Cash Flow Cycle = **240 days**

** Based on Average Collection Period:

$$\frac{365 \text{ days}}{7.31 \text{ times/year}} = 50 \text{ days}$$

**FIGURE 8.2 The Cash Flow Cycle**

The next step in effective cash management is to begin cutting down the length of the cash flow cycle. In figure 8.2, reducing the cycle from 240 days to, say, 150 days would free up incredible amounts of cash that this company could use to finance growth and dramatically reduce its borrowing costs. What steps do you suggest the owner of the business whose cash flow cycle is illustrated in Figure 8.2 take to reduce the cycle's length?

## Cash and Profits Are Not the Same

*2.* Differentiate between cash and profits.

When analyzing cash flow, entrepreneurs must understand that cash and profits are not the same. Both are important financial concepts for entrepreneurs, but they measure very different aspects of a business. Profit (or net income) is the difference between a company's total revenue and its total expenses. It is an accounting concept designed to measure how efficiently a business is operating. On the other hand, cash is the money that is readily available to use in a business. **Cash flow** measures a company's liquidity and its ability to pay its bills and other financial obligations on time by tracking the flow of cash into and out of the business over a period of time. Many factors determine a company's cash flow, including its sales patterns, the timing of its accounts receivable and accounts payable, its inventory turnover rate, its debt repayment schedule, and its schedule of capital expenditures (e.g., fixtures, equipment, facilities expansion, and others).

Figure 8.3 shows the flow of cash through a typical small business. Decreases in cash occur when a business purchases, on credit or for cash, goods for inventory or materials for use in production. The resulting inventory is sold either for cash or on credit. When it takes in cash or collects accounts receivable, a company's cash balance increases. Notice that purchases for inventory and production *lead* sales; that is, these bills typically must be paid *before* sales are generated. However, collection of accounts receivable *lags* behind sales; that is, customers who purchase goods on credit may not pay until a month or more later.

As important as earning a profit is, no business owner can pay creditors, employees, and lenders in profits; that requires *cash*! "Cash flow is more important than earnings," says Evan Betzer, founder of a financial services firm.[7] A company can operate in the short run with a net loss showing on its income statement, but if its cash flow becomes negative, the business is in trouble. It can no longer pay suppliers, meet payroll, pay its taxes, or any other bills. In short, the business is out of business!

**FIGURE 8.3 Cash Flow**     Increase in Cash                              Decrease in Cash

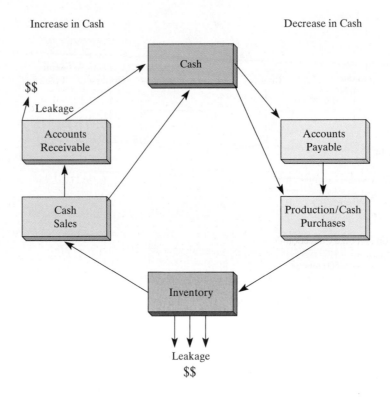

## Gaining a Competitive Edge

### Content to Be a Small Giant

It's a fact that sometimes growth gets the best of entrepreneurs: Fast-growing companies consume cash fast, which makes these fast-growing companies most vulnerable to cash crises. "If the money is coming in the front door at 100 kilometers per hour and going out the back door at 110 kilometers per hour, that's not a good thing," says entrepreneur Brian Hamilton, CEO of Sageworks, a financial research firm. Faced with the potential for fast growth in their companies, some entrepreneurs have decided to forego it, choosing instead to make their businesses "small giants," companies that grow at their own pace and place maximizing sales far below other, sometimes very different, goals.

Jay Goltz is one of those entrepreneurs. In 1997, Goltz, who founded Artists' Frame Service in 1978 at the age of 21, had become the most successful independent retailer of picture frames in the United States. He was a celebrity among those in the industry, had been featured in an article on "bizkids" in *Forbes* magazine, and had

been inducted into the Chicago Entrepreneurship Hall of Fame. Yet he was not content; he wanted his company to grow as big as possible as fast as possible.

Like many hard-driving entrepreneurs, Goltz was not satisfied with his accomplishments. He thought his company, which employed 75 people and generated sales of $7 million, was "dinky," especially when he compared it to really successful businesses like those founded by Michael Dell and Richard Branson. Because he was so focused on what he saw as his own inadequacies—and those of his company—Goltz could not see the contributions he had made to his industry, his local community, his customers, and his employees. Goltz's push for incessant growth led him into situations that were making his life miserable. Cash flow problems kept him awake at night and forced him to work long hours trying to fix things rather than spend time with his family. "I can't really describe it," he recalls. "It was circuit overload. I had so many things to worry about."

It was one of Goltz's employees, Lily Booker, who helped him see the light and put things in proper perspective. Lily was retiring after eight years with Artists' Frame Service, and she wanted to say a few words at her retirement party. She had come to work for Goltz after working for another custom frame company for 10 years and being laid off. "I was in my fifties," she told Goltz with tears in her eyes. "When you hired me, I never thought I'd get another job. I just want to thank you for giving me a chance."

Lily's heartfelt appreciation jolted Goltz into realizing that even though he and his company had experienced many setbacks, they also had achieved many successes, including providing good jobs for dozens of employees. "I'd always thought that for me to be happy, I had to have phenomenal growth [in my business] and turn this into a giant company," says Goltz. "It didn't occur to me that there are a lot of really happy people with very nice $10 million companies making good profits, and that those guys are way happier than guys with companies 10 times their size. That's what it comes down to. Happiness is not who's got the biggest company. Happiness is a whole lot of other things." It was a revelation for Goltz: He realized that he had a choice in how big and how fast his company grew and that growth for its own sake was not the ultimate achievement.

Many other entrepreneurs have come to the same realization that Goltz made. After Fritz Maytag bought Anchor Steam, a nearly bankrupt microbrewery in San Francisco, he worked hard to turn the company around. Within a few years, Anchor Steam's beers were recognized by San Franciscans as among the best anywhere, and demand for them grew so fast that Maytag ran out of production capacity and had to ration its supplies to distributors. Naturally, Maytag was busy making plans for his company to grow, including an initial public offering (IPO) of Anchor Steam stock. Just before the IPO was finalized, Maytag changed his mind and pulled out. "I realized we were doing the IPO out of desperation— because we thought we had to grow," he says. "It occurred to me that you could have a small, prestigious, profitable business, and it would be all right. We made the decision not to grow. This is not going to be a giant company—not on my watch."

Entrepreneurs who have made the decision to be "small giants" have five characteristics in common:

1. *They know themselves and what they want out of their businesses.* Rather than emphasize endless growth, the entrepreneurs behind these small giants focus more on providing excellent customer service,

creating workplaces that value employees and their contributions, being the best in their niches, and leading satisfying business and personal lives.

2. *They love their businesses.* The entrepreneurs behind these small giants have great passion for their companies and care deeply about making them the best businesses they can be.

3. *They are rooted in their communities.* Founders of small giants give back to their communities, but their connection to their communities runs much deeper than that. The companies and their communities have symbiotic relationships in which each benefits from the other.

4. *They cultivate and value relationships with their employees, customers, and suppliers.* These companies create a sense of unity and common purpose in their relationships with these key players and treat them with respect, dignity, and fairness.

5. *They stay private and closely held.* Founders of small giants know that if they sell stock to large numbers of outside investors, they will lose their independence and their ability to focus on the goals that matter most to them and their employees.

*Sources:* Adapted from Amy Feldman, "The Cash-Flow Crunch," *Inc.*, December 2005, pp. 51–52; Bo Burlingham, "There Is a Choice," *Inc.*, February 2006, pp. 80–89.

## The Cash Budget

The need for a reliable cash forecast arises because in every business the cash flowing in is rarely "in sync" with the cash flowing out. This uneven flow of cash creates periodic cash surpluses and deficits, making it necessary for entrepreneurs to track the flow of cash through their businesses so they can project realistically the pool of cash that is available throughout the year. Many owners operate their businesses without knowing the pattern of their cash flows, believing that the process is too complex or time consuming. In reality, entrepreneurs simply cannot afford to ignore cash management. They must ensure that an adequate, but not excessive, supply of cash is on hand to meet their companies' operating needs.

How much cash is enough? What is suitable for one business may be totally inadequate for another, depending on each company's size, sales, collections, expenses, and other factors. Entrepreneurs should prepare a **cash budget**, which is nothing more than a "cash map," showing the amount and the timing of the cash receipts and the cash disbursements week-by-week or month-by-month. It is used to predict the amount of cash a company will need to operate smoothly over a specific period of time, and it is a valuable tool in managing a company successfully.

## Preparing a Cash Budget

**3.** Understand the five steps in creating a cash budget and use them to build a cash budget.

Typically, a small business should prepare a projected monthly cash budget for at least one year and quarterly estimates one or two years beyond that. To be effective, a cash budget must cover all seasonal sales fluctuations. The more variable a company's sales pattern, the shorter its planning horizon should be. For example, a firm whose sales fluctuate widely over a relatively short time frame might require a weekly cash budget rather than a monthly one. The key to managing cash flow successfully is to monitor not only the *amount* of cash flowing into and out of a company but also the *timing* of those cash flows.

Regardless of the time frame selected, a cash budget must be in writing for an entrepreneur to visualize a company's cash position. Creating a written cash plan is not an excessively time-consuming task and can help the owner avoid unexpected cash shortages, a situation that can cause a business to fail. One financial consultant describes "a client who won't be able to make the payroll this month. His bank agreed to meet the payroll for him—but banks don't like to be surprised like that," he adds.[8] Preparing a cash budget will help business owners avoid unpleasant surprises such as that. It will also let owners know whether they are keeping excessive amounts of cash on hand. Computer spreadsheets such as Excel and Lotus 1-2-3 make the job fast and easy to complete and allow for instant updates and "what if" analysis.

A cash budget is based on the cash method of accounting, which means that cash receipts and cash disbursements are recorded in the forecast only when the cash transaction is expected to take place. For example, credit sales to customers are not reported until the company expects to collect the cash from them. Similarly, purchases made on credit are not recorded until the owner expects to pay them. Because depreciation, bad debt expense, and other noncash items involve no cash transfers, they are omitted entirely from the cash budget.

A cash budget is nothing more than a forecast of a company's cash inflows and outflows for a specific time period, and it will never be completely accurate. However, it does give a small business owner a clear picture of a company's estimated cash balance for the period, pointing out where external cash infusions may be required or where surplus cash balances may be available for investing. In addition, by comparing actual cash flows with projections, an entrepreneur can revise his forecast so that future cash budgets will be more accurate.

*Michael Koss and Koss Corporation*

Michael Koss, president and CEO of Koss Corporation, a manufacturer of stereo headphones, now emphasizes cash flow management after his company's brush with failure. In the 1980s, Koss Corporation expanded rapidly—so rapidly, in fact, that its cash flow couldn't keep pace. Debt climbed, and the company filed for reorganization under bankruptcy. Emergency actions saved the business, and today Koss manages with the determination never to repeat the same mistakes. "I look at cash every single day," he says. "That is absolutely critical."[9]

Formats for preparing a cash budget vary depending on the pattern of a company's cash flow. Table 8.2 shows a monthly cash budget for a small department store over a four-month period. Each monthly column should be divided into two sections—estimated and actual (not shown)—so that subsequent cash forecasts can be updated according to actual cash transactions. There are five steps to creating a cash budget:

1. Determining an adequate minimum cash balance.
2. Forecasting sales.
3. Forecasting cash receipts.
4. Forecasting cash disbursements.
5. Estimating the end-of-month cash balance.

## Step 1: Determining an Adequate Minimum Cash Balance

What is considered an excessive cash balance for one small business may be inadequate for another, even though the two firms are in the same industry. Some suggest that a company's cash balance should equal at least one-fourth of its current liabilities, but this simple guideline does not work for all small businesses. The most reliable method of deciding cash balance is based on past experience. Past operating records should indicate the proper cash cushion needed to cover any unexpected expenses after all normal cash outlays are deducted from the month's cash receipts. For example, past records may indicate that it is desirable to maintain a cash balance equal to five days' sales. Seasonal fluctuations may cause a company's minimum cash balance to change. For example, the desired cash balance for a retailer in December may be greater than in June.

## Step 2: Forecasting Sales

The heart of the cash budget is the sales forecast. It is the central factor in creating an accurate picture of a company's cash position because sales ultimately are transformed into cash receipts and cash disbursements. For most businesses, sales constitute the primary source of the cash flowing into the business. Similarly, sales of merchandise require entrepreneurs to use cash to replenish inventory. As a result, the cash budget is only as accurate as the sales forecast from which it is derived; an accurate sales forecast is essential to producing a reliable cash flow forecast.

*Dean Kamen and Segway LLC*

An overly optimistic sales forecast landed Segway LLC, the company that invented the futuristic upright motorized scooter, squarely in a cash flow bind. Known as the Segway Human Transporter, the scooter uses computer-driven gyroscopes and sensors that allow riders to stand upright and steer with simple body movements. Unveiled on live television to huge amounts of press fanfare, founder and inventor Dean Kamen projected that the company would be able to sell 50,000 to 100,000 Segways in its first year. The scooter's $4,000 price and lack of distribution outlets (People simply weren't willing to spend $4,000 on something they could not test-drive!) limited sales to just a total of 10,000 units two years after the Segway's introduction. The cash flow problems meant that Kamen had to raise $31 million to keep the company afloat in addition to the initial $100 million he raised to launch the company.[10]

For an established business, the sales forecast can be based on past sales, but entrepreneurs must be careful not to be excessively optimistic in their projections. Economic swings, increased competition, fluctuations in demand, and other factors can drastically alter sales patterns. A good cash budget must reflect the seasonality of a company's sales. Simply deriving a realistic annual sales forecast and then dividing it by 12 does not produce a reliable monthly sales forecast. Most businesses have sales patterns that are "lumpy" and not evenly distributed throughout the year. For instance, 40 percent of all toy sales take place during the last six weeks of the year, and companies that make fruitcakes typically generate 50 percent to 90 percent of their sales during the holiday season.[11] Super Bowl Sunday is the single largest revenue-generating day of the year for most U.S. pizzerias (and

## TABLE 8.2 Cash Budget for Small Department Store

*Assumptions:*

Cash balance on December 31 = $12,000

Minimum cash balance desired = $10,000

Sales are 75% credit and 25% cash.

Credit sales are collected in the following manner:

- 60% collected in the first month after the sale.
- 30% collected in the second month after the sale.
- 5% collected in the third month after the sale.
- 5% are never collected.

| Sales Forecasts Are as Follows: | Pessimistic | Most Likely | Optimistic |
|---|---|---|---|
| October (actual) | | $300,000 | |
| November (actual) | | 350,000 | |
| December (actual) | | 400,000 | |
| January | $120,000 | 150,000 | $175,000 |
| February | 160,000 | 200,000 | 250,000 |
| March | 160,000 | 200,000 | 250,000 |
| April | 250,000 | 300,000 | 340,000 |

The store pays 70% of sales price for merchandise purchased and pays for each month's anticipated sales in the preceding month.

Rent is $2,000 per month.

An interest payment of $7,500 is due in March.

A tax prepayment of $50,000 must be made in March.

A capital addition payment of $130,000 is due in February.

Utilities expenses amount to $850 per month.

Miscellaneous expenses are $70 per month.

Interest income of $200 will be received in February.

Wages and salaries are estimated to be

    January—$30,000

    February—$40,000

    March—$45,000

    April—$50,000

## Cash Budget—Pessimistic Sales Forecast

| | Oct. | Nov. | Dec. | Jan. | Feb. | Mar. | Apr. |
|---|---|---|---|---|---|---|---|
| *Cash Receipts:* | | | | | | | |
| Sales | $300,000 | $350,000 | $400,000 | $120,000 | $160,000 | $160,000 | $250,000 |
| Credit Sales | 225,000 | 262,500 | 300,000 | 90,000 | 120,000 | 120,000 | 187,500 |
| *Collections:* | | | | | | | |
| 60%—1st month after sale | | | | $180,000 | $ 54,000 | $ 72,000 | $ 72,000 |
| 30%—2nd month after sale | | | | 78,750 | 90,000 | 27,000 | 36,000 |
| 5%—3rd month after sale | | | | 11,250 | 13,125 | 15,000 | 4,500 |
| Cash Sales | | | | 30,000 | 40,000 | 40,000 | 62,500 |
| Interest | | | | 0 | 200 | 0 | 0 |
|   Total Cash Receipts | | | | $300,000 | $197,325 | $154,000 | $175,000 |
| *Cash Disbursements:* | | | | | | | |
| Purchases | | | | $112,000 | $112,000 | $175,000 | $133,000 |
| Rent | | | | 2,000 | 2,000 | 2,000 | 2,000 |
| Utilities | | | | 850 | 850 | 850 | 850 |
| Interest | | | | 0 | 0 | 7,500 | 0 |

**TABLE 8.2 Continued**

| | Oct. | Nov. | Dec. | Jan. | Feb. | Mar. | Apr. |
|---|---|---|---|---|---|---|---|
| Tax Prepayment | | | | 0 | 0 | 50,000 | 0 |
| Capital Addition | | | | 0 | 130,000 | 0 | 0 |
| Miscellaneous | | | | 70 | 70 | 70 | 70 |
| Wages/Salaries | | | | 30,000 | 40,000 | 45,000 | 50,000 |
| Total Cash Disbursements | | | | $144,920 | $284,920 | $280,420 | $185,920 |
| *End-of-Month Balance:* | | | | | | | |
| Cash (beginning of month) | | | | $ 12,000 | $167,080 | $ 79,485 | $ 10,000 |
| + Cash Receipts | | | | 300,000 | 197,325 | 154,000 | 175,000 |
| – Cash Disbursements | | | | 144,920 | 284,920 | 280,420 | 185,920 |
| Cash (end of month) | | | | 167,080 | 79,485 | (46,935) | (920) |
| Borrowing/Repayment | | | | 0 | 0 | 56,935 | 10,920 |
| Cash (end of month [after borrowing]) | | | | $167,080 | $ 79,485 | $ 10,000 | $ 10,000 |

## Cash Budget—Most Likely Sales Forecast

| | Oct. | Nov. | Dec. | Jan. | Feb. | Mar. | Apr. |
|---|---|---|---|---|---|---|---|
| *Cash Receipts:* | | | | | | | |
| Sales | $300,000 | $350,000 | $400,000 | $150,000 | $200,000 | $200,000 | $300,000 |
| Credit Sales | 225,000 | 262,500 | 300,000 | 112,000 | 150,000 | 150,000 | 225,000 |
| *Collections:* | | | | | | | |
| 60%—1st month after sale | | | | $180,000 | $ 67,500 | $ 90,000 | $ 90,000 |
| 30%—2nd month after sale | | | | 78,750 | 90,000 | 33,750 | 45,000 |
| 5%—3rd month after sale | | | | 11,250 | 13,125 | 15,000 | 5,625 |
| Cash Sales | | | | 37,500 | 50,000 | 50,000 | 75,000 |
| Interest | | | | 0 | 200 | 0 | 0 |
| Total Cash Receipts | | | | $307,500 | $220,825 | $188,750 | $215,625 |
| *Cash Disbursements:* | | | | | | | |
| Purchases | | | | $140,000 | $140,000 | $210,000 | $175,000 |
| Rent | | | | 2,000 | 2,000 | 2,000 | 2,000 |
| Utilities | | | | 850 | 850 | 850 | 850 |
| Interest | | | | 0 | 0 | 7,500 | 0 |
| Tax Prepayment | | | | 0 | 0 | 50,000 | 0 |
| Capital Addition | | | | 0 | 130,000 | 0 | 0 |
| Miscellaneous | | | | 70 | 70 | 70 | 70 |
| Wages/Salaries | | | | 30,000 | 40,000 | 45,000 | 50,000 |
| Total Cash Disbursements | | | | $172,920 | $312,920 | $315,420 | $227,920 |
| *End-of-Month Balance:* | | | | | | | |
| Cash [beginning of month] | | | | $ 12,000 | $146,580 | $ 54,485 | $ 10,000 |
| + Cash Receipts | | | | 307,500 | 220,825 | 188,750 | 215,625 |
| – Cash Disbursements | | | | 172,920 | 312,920 | 315,420 | 227,920 |
| Cash (end of month) | | | | 146,580 | 54,485 | (72,185) | (2,295) |
| Borrowing/Repayment | | | | 0 | 0 | 82,185 | 12,295 |
| Cash (end of month [after borrowing]) | | | | $146,580 | $ 54,485 | $ 10,000 | $ 10,000 |

## Cash Budget—Optimistic Sales Forecast

| | Oct. | Nov. | Dec. | Jan. | Feb. | Mar. | Apr. |
|---|---|---|---|---|---|---|---|
| *Cash Receipts:* | | | | | | | |
| Sales | $300,000 | $350,000 | $400,000 | $175,000 | $250,000 | $250,000 | $340,000 |
| Credit Sales | 225,000 | 262,500 | 300,000 | 131,250 | 187,500 | 187,500 | 255,000 |

*(continued)*

**TABLE 8.2 Continued**

|  | Oct. | Nov. | Dec. | Jan. | Feb. | Mar. | Apr. |
|---|---|---|---|---|---|---|---|
| *Collections:* | | | | | | | |
| 60%—1st month after sale | | | | $180,000 | $ 78,750 | $112,500 | $112,500 |
| 30%—2nd month after sale | | | | 78,750 | 90,000 | 39,375 | 56,250 |
| 5%—3rd month after sale | | | | 11,250 | 13,125 | 15,000 | 6,563 |
| Cash Sales | | | | 43,750 | 62,500 | 62,500 | 85,000 |
| Interest | | | | 0 | 200 | 0 | 0 |
|    Total Cash Receipts | | | | $313,750 | $244,575 | $229,375 | $260,313 |
| *Cash Disbursements:* | | | | | | | |
| Purchases | | | | $175,000 | $175,000 | $238,000 | $217,000 |
| Rent | | | | 2,000 | 2,000 | 2,000 | 2,000 |
| Utilities | | | | 850 | 850 | 850 | 850 |
| Interest | | | | 0 | 0 | 7,500 | 0 |
| Tax Prepayment | | | | 0 | 0 | 50,000 | 0 |
| Capital Addition | | | | 0 | 130,000 | 0 | 0 |
| Miscellaneous | | | | 70 | 70 | 70 | 70 |
| Wages/Salaries | | | | 30,000 | 40,000 | 45,000 | 50,000 |
|    Total Cash Disbursements | | | | $207,920 | $347,920 | $343,420 | $269,920 |
| *End-of-Month Balance:* | | | | | | | |
| Cash [beginning of month] | | | | $ 12,000 | $117,830 | $ 14,485 | $ 10,000 |
| + Cash Receipts | | | | 313,750 | 244,575 | 229,375 | 296,125 |
| − Cash Disbursements | | | | 207,920 | 317,920 | 343,120 | 269,920 |
| Cash (end of month) | | | | 117,830 | 14,485 | (99,560) | 36,205 |
| Borrowing/Repayment | | | | 0 | 0 | 109,560 | 0 |
| Cash (end of month [after borrowing]) | | | | $117,830 | $ 14,485 | $ 10,000 | $ 36,205 |

ranks second only to Thanksgiving as the largest food consumption day). In addition, as much as 25 percent of the sales at companies that supply exotic dancers for parties occur on Super Bowl Sunday.[12] Highly seasonal sales patterns such as these can make managing cash flow a challenge for entrepreneurs.

*Bob Groves and the Starlite Drive-In*

To combat a highly seasonal sales pattern and keep the Starlite Drive-In, one of only nine remaining drive-in theaters still in operation in the U.S. state of North Carolina, owner Bob Groves has added sideline businesses to generate cash flow during the slow winter months. The rather unusual combination of businesses includes a gun shop, a shooting range, a video rental store, and a flea-market-space rental business. Groves's unique approach to boosting cash flow during months with the slowest theater ticket sales works, and the 1930s-era theater has become a landmark in the area.[13]

Several quantitative techniques for forecasting sales, which are beyond the scope of this text (e.g., linear regression, multiple regression, time series analysis, and exponential smoothing), are available to owners of existing businesses with an established sales pattern. These methods allow business owners to extrapolate past and present sales trends to arrive at a fairly accurate sales forecast.

The task of forecasting sales for a new firm is difficult but not impossible. For example, an entrepreneur might conduct research on similar firms and their sales patterns in the first year of operation to come up with a forecast. The local chamber of commerce and trade associations in the various industries also collect such information. Market research is another source of information that may be used to estimate annual sales for the fledgling firm. Other potential sources that may help predict sales include: census reports; newspapers; radio and television customer profiles; polls and surveys; and local government statistics. Table 8.3 gives an example of how one entrepreneur used such marketing information to derive a sales forecast for his first year of operation in the automotive repair business.

No matter what techniques entrepreneurs use to forecast cash flow, they must recognize that even the best sales estimates will be wrong. Many financial analysts suggest that entrepreneurs create *three estimates*—an optimistic, a pessimistic, and a most likely sales estimate—and then make a separate cash budget for each forecast (a very simple task with a computer spreadsheet). This dynamic forecast enables entrepreneurs to determine the range within which their sales and cash flows will likely fall as the year progresses. By using the forecast that most closely reflects their sales patterns, entrepreneurs can project their companies' cash flow more accurately.

## Step 3: Forecasting Cash Receipts

As we mentioned earlier, sales constitute the major source of cash receipts. When a company sells goods and services on credit, a cash budget must count for the delay between the sale and the actual collection of the proceeds. Remember: You cannot spend cash you haven't collected yet! For instance, a company might not collect the cash from the sale of inventory made in February until March or April (or even later), and the cash budget must reflect this delay. To project accurately a firm's cash receipts, entrepreneurs must analyze their companies' accounts receivable to determine the collection pattern. For example, an entrepreneur may discover that 20 percent of sales are for cash, 50 percent are paid in the month following the sale, 20 percent are paid two months after the sale, 7 percent after three months, and 3 percent are never collected. In addition to cash and credit sales, a cash budget must include any other cash the company receives such as interest income, rental income, dividends, and others.

Some small business owners never discover the hidden danger in accounts receivable until it is too late for their companies. Receivables act as cash sponges, tying up valuable money until an entrepreneur collects them.

---

**TABLE 8.3  Forecasting Sales for a Business Start-up**

Robert Adler wants to open a repair shop for imported cars. The trade association for automotive garages estimates that the owner of an imported car spends an average of $485 per year on repairs and maintenance. The typical garage attracts its clientele from a trading zone (the area from which a business draws its customers) with a 20-kilometer radius. Census reports show that the families within a 20-kilometer radius of Robert's proposed location own 84,000 cars, of which 24 percent are imports. Based on a local market consultant's research, Robert believes he can capture 9.9 percent of the market this year. Robert's estimate of his company's first year's sales are as follows:

| | |
|---|---|
| Number of cars in trading zone | 84,000 |
| × Percent of imports | × 24% |
| = Number of imported cars in trading zone | 20,160 |
| Number of imports in trading zone | 20,160 |
| × Average expenditure on repairs and maintenance | × $485 |
| = Total import repair sales potential | $9,777,600 |
| Total import repair sales potential | $9,777,600 |
| × Estimated share of market | × 9.9% |
| = Sales estimate | $967,982 |

Now Robert Adler can convert this annual sales estimate of $967,982 into monthly sales estimates for use in his company's cash budget.

*Mary and Phil Baechler and Baby Jogger Company*

When Mary and Phil Baechler started Baby Jogger Company in 1983 to make strollers that would enable parents to take their babies along on their daily runs, Mary was in charge of the financial aspects of the business and watched its cash flow closely. As the company grew, the couple created an accounting department to handle its financial affairs. Unfortunately, the financial management system could not keep up with the company's rapid growth and failed to provide the necessary information to keep its finances under control. As inventory and accounts receivable ballooned, the company headed for a cash crisis. To ensure Baby Jogger's survival, the Baechlers were forced to reduce their workforce by half. Then they turned their attention to the accounts receivable and discovered that customers owed the business almost $700,000! In addition, most of the accounts were past due. Focusing on collecting the money owed to their company, the Baechlers were able to steer clear of a cash crisis and get Baby Jogger back on track.[14]

Figure 8.4 demonstrates how vital it is to act promptly once an account becomes past due. Notice how the probability of collecting an outstanding account diminishes the longer the account is delinquent. Table 8.4 illustrates the high cost of failing to collect accounts receivable on time.

### Step 4: Forecasting Cash Disbursements

Most owners of established businesses have a clear picture of a company's pattern of cash disbursements. In fact, many cash payments, such as rent, salaries, loan repayments, and insurance premiums, are fixed amounts due on specified dates. The key factor in forecasting disbursements for a cash budget is to *record them in the month in which they will be paid, not when the debt or obligation is incurred.* Of course, the number and type of cash disbursements varies with each particular business, but the following disbursement categories are standard: purchases of inventory or raw materials, wages and salaries, rent, taxes, loan repayments, interest, marketing and selling expenses, insurance, utility expenses, and miscellaneous expenses.

When preparing a cash budget, one of the worst mistakes entrepreneurs can make is to underestimate cash disbursements, which can result in a cash crisis. To prevent this, wise entrepreneurs cushion their cash disbursements, assuming they will be higher than expected. This is particularly important for entrepreneurs opening new businesses. In fact,

**FIGURE 8.4 Collecting Delinquent Accounts**

*Source:* Commercial Collection Agency Section of the Commercial Law League of America.

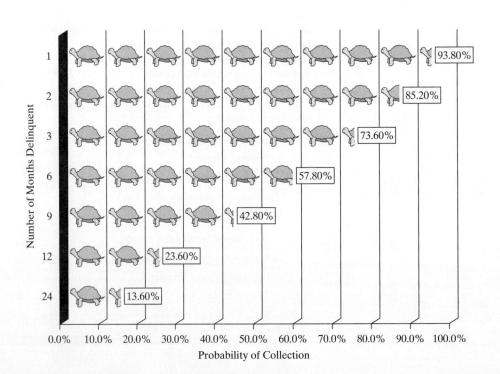

### TABLE 8.4 Managing Accounts Receivable

Are your customers who purchase on credit paying late? If so, these outstanding accounts receivable probably represent a significant leak in your company's profits. Regaining control of these late payers will likely improve your company's profits and cash flow.

Slow-paying customers, in effect, are borrowing money from your business interest free! They are using your money without penalty while you forgo opportunities to put it to productive use in your company or to place it in interest-bearing investments. Exactly how much are poor credit practices costing you? The answer may surprise you.

The first step is to compute the company's average collection period ratio (See the "Operating Ratios" section in Chapter 7), which tells the number of days required to collect the typical account receivable. Then you compare this number to your company's credit terms. The following example shows how to calculate the cost of past-due receivables for a company whose credit terms are "net 30":

| | |
|---|---:|
| Average collection period | 65 days |
| Less: credit terms | 30 days |
| Excess in accounts receivable | 35 days |
| Average daily sales of $21,500* × 35 days excess | $752,500 |
| Normal rate of return on investment | 10% |
| Annual cost of excess | $ 75,250 |

If your business is highly seasonal, quarterly or monthly figures may be more meaningful than annual ones.

$$*\text{Average daily sales} = \frac{\text{Annual sales}}{365} = \frac{\$7,487,500}{365} = \$21,500$$

some financial analysts recommend that people starting new businesses make the best estimates of their companies' cash disbursements and then add another 25 to 50 percent of that total as a contingency, recognizing that business expenses often run higher than expected. When setting up his company's cash budget, one entrepreneur included a line called "Murphy," an additional amount each month to account for Murphy's Law ("What can go wrong, will go wrong"). Whatever forecasting technique entrepreneurs use, the key is to avoid underestimating cash disbursements, which may lead to severe cash shortages and possibly bankruptcy.

Sometimes business owners have difficulty developing initial forecasts of cash receipts and cash disbursements. One of the most effective techniques for overcoming the "I don't know where to begin" hurdle is to make a *daily* list of the items that generated cash (receipts) and those that consumed it (disbursements).

*Susan Bowen and Champion Awards*

Susan Bowen, CEO of Champion Awards, a $9-million T-shirt screen printer, monitors cash flow by tracking the cash that flows into and out of her company every day. Focusing on keeping the process simple, Bowen sets aside a few minutes each morning to track updates from the previous day on four key numbers:

*Accounts receivable:* (1) What was billed yesterday? (2) How much was actually collected?

*Accounts payable:* (3) What invoices were received yesterday? (4) How much in total was paid out?

If Bowen observes the wrong trend—more new bills than new sales or more money going out than coming in—she makes immediate adjustments to protect her cash flow. The benefits produced (not the least of which is the peace of mind knowing no cash crisis is looming) more than outweigh the ten minutes she invests in the process every day. "I've tried to balance my books every single day since I started my company in 1970," says Bowen.[15]

## *In Action*

## Isis's Cash Budget

Isis Allam Rowdy had been in business for slightly more than two years, but she had never taken the time to develop a cash budget for her company. Based on a series of recent events, however, she knew the time had come to start paying more attention to her company's cash flow. The business was growing fast, with sales more than tripling from the previous year, and profits were rising. However, Isis often found it difficult to pay all of the company's bills on time. She didn't know why exactly, but she knew that the company's fast growth was requiring her to incur higher levels of expenses.

Last night, Isis attended a workshop on managing cash flow sponsored by the local chamber of commerce. Much of what the presenter said hit home with Isis. "This fellow must have taken a look at my company's financial records before he came here tonight," she said to a friend during a break in the presentation. On her way home from the workshop, Isis decided that she would take the presenter's advice and develop a cash budget for her business. After all, she was planning to approach her banker about a loan for her company, and she knew that creating a cash budget would be an essential part of her loan request. She started digging for the necessary information, and this is what she came up with:

| | |
|---|---|
| Current cash balance | $10,685 |
| Sales pattern | 63% on credit and 37% in cash |
| Collections of credit sales | 61% in 1 to 30 days |
| | 27% in 31 to 60 days |
| | 8% in 61 to 90 days |
| | 4% never collected (bad debts) |

**Sales Forecasts:**

| | Pessimistic | Most Likely | Optimistic |
|---|---|---|---|
| January (actual) | — | $24,780 | — |
| February (actual) | — | $20,900 | — |
| March (actual) | — | $21,630 | — |
| April | $19,100 | $23,550 | $25,750 |
| May | $21,300 | $24,900 | $27,300 |
| June | $23,300 | $29,870 | $30,000 |
| July | $23,900 | $27,500 | $29,100 |
| August | $20,500 | $25,800 | $28,800 |
| September | $18,500 | $21,500 | $23,900 |

| | |
|---|---|
| Utilities expenses | $950 per month. |
| Rent | $2,250 per month |
| Truck loan | $427 per month |

The company's wages and salaries (including payroll taxes) estimates are:

| | | | |
|---|---|---|---|
| April | $3,550 | July | $6,255 |
| May | $4,125 | August | $6,060 |
| June | $5,450 | September | $3,525 |

The company pays 66 percent of the sales price for the inventory it purchases, an amount that it actually pays in the following month. (Isis has negotiated "net 30" credit terms with her suppliers.)

Other expenses include:

| | |
|---|---|
| Insurance premiums | $1,200, payable in April and September. |
| Office supplies | $125 per month |
| Maintenance | $75 per month |
| Uniforms/cleaning | $80 per month |
| Office cleaning service | $85 per month |
| Internet and computer service | $225 per month |
| Computer supplies | $75 per month |
| Advertising | $450 per month |
| Legal and accounting fees | $250 per month |
| Miscellaneous expenses | $95 per month |

A tax payment of $3,140 is due in June. Isis has established a minimum cash balance of $1,500. If Isis must borrow money, she uses her line of credit at the bank which charges interest at an annual rate of 10.25 percent. Any money that Isis borrows must be repaid the next month.

1. Help Isis put together a cash budget for the six months beginning in April.

2. Does it appear that Isis's business will remain solvent, or could the company be heading for a cash crisis?
3. What suggestions can you make to help Isis improve her company's cash flow?

## Step 5: Estimating the End-of-Month Cash Balance

To estimate a company's final cash balance for each month, entrepreneurs first must determine the cash balance at the beginning of each month. The beginning cash balance includes cash on hand as well as cash in checking and savings accounts. The cash balance at the *end* of one month becomes the *beginning* balance for the following month. Next the owner simply adds to that balance the projected total cash receipts for the month and then subtracts projected total cash disbursements to obtain the end-of-month balance before any borrowing takes place. A positive balance indicates that the business has a cash surplus for the month, but a negative balance shows a cash shortage will occur unless the entrepreneur is able to collect, raise, or borrow additional cash.

Normally, a company's cash balance fluctuates from month to month, reflecting seasonal sales patterns. These fluctuations are normal, but entrepreneurs must watch closely any increases and decreases in the cash balance over time. A trend of increases indicates that the small firm has ample cash that could be placed in some income-earning investment. On the other hand, a pattern of cash decreases should alert the owner that the business is approaching a cash crisis.

Preparing a cash budget not only illustrates the flow of cash into and out of the small business, but it also allows a business owner to anticipate cash shortages and cash surpluses. By planning cash needs ahead of time, an entrepreneur is able to do the following:

- Increase the amount and the speed of cash flowing into the company.
- Reduce the amount and the speed of cash flowing out of the company.
- Develop a sound borrowing and repayment program.
- Impress lenders and investors with a plan for repaying loans or distributing dividends.
- Reduce borrowing costs by borrowing only when necessary.
- Take advantage of money-saving opportunities, such as economic order quantities and cash discounts.
- Make the most efficient use of the cash available.

- Finance seasonal business needs.
- Provide funds for expansion.
- Improve profitability by investing surplus cash.

The message is simple: Managing cash flow means survival for a business. Businesses tend to succeed when their owners manage cash effectively. Entrepreneurs who neglect cash flow management techniques are likely to see their companies fold; those who take the time to manage their cash flow free themselves of worrying about their companies' solvency to focus on what they do best: taking care of their customers and ensuring their companies' success.

## The "Big Three" of Cash Management

*4.* Describe the fundamental principles involved in managing the "big three" of cash management: accounts receivable, accounts payable, and inventory.

It is unrealistic for entrepreneurs to expect to trace the flow of every unit of currency through their businesses. However, by concentrating on the three primary causes of cash flow problems, they can dramatically lower the likelihood of experiencing a devastating cash crisis. The "big three" of cash management are accounts receivable, accounts payable, and inventory. When it comes to managing cash flow, entrepreneurs' goals should be to accelerate their companies' accounts receivable and to stretch out their accounts payable. As one company's chief financial officer states, the idea is to "get the cash in the door as fast as you can, cut costs, and pay people as late as possible."[16] Business owners also must monitor inventory carefully to avoid tying up valuable cash in an excess inventory. Figure 8.5 illustrates the interaction of the "big three" in a company's cash conversion cycle (inventory, accounts receivable, and accounts payable) and a measure for each one (days' inventory outstanding, days sales' outstanding, and days' payable outstanding).

### Accounts Receivable

Selling merchandise and services on credit is a necessary evil for most small businesses. Many customers expect to buy on credit, and entrepreneurs extend it to avoid losing customers to competitors. However, selling to customers on credit is expensive; it requires more paperwork, more staff, and *more cash* to service accounts receivable. Also, because extending credit is, in essence, lending money, the risk involved is higher. Every business owner who sells on credit will encounter customers who pay late or, worst of all, who never pay at all. This revenue leakage can be the source of severe cash flow problems for a small business. Much like a leak in a water pipe, revenue leakages from undisciplined collection procedures can become significant over time and cause serious damage. One expert estimates that revenue leakages rob companies of 2 percent of their sales. Health care and Web service providers, for instance, typically lose 5 to 10 percent of their revenues each year.[17]

Selling on credit is a common practice in business. Experts estimate that 90 percent of industrial and wholesale sales are on credit and that 40 percent of retail sales are on account. "Extending credit is a [double]-edged sword," says Robert Smith, president of his own public relations firm in Rockford, Illinois. "I give credit so more people can afford my publicity services. I also have people who still owe me money—and who will probably never pay."[18] Figure 8.6 shows that small business owners' greatest cash management challenge is collecting accounts receivable.

**FIGURE 8.5 The Cash Conversion Cycle**

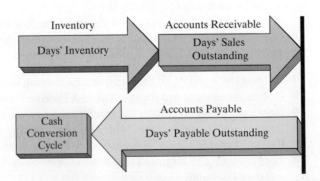

*Cash Conversion Cycle = Day's Inventory + Day's Sales Outstanding – Day's Payable Outstanding

**FIGURE 8.6 Which Cash Flow Process Is the Most Challenging to Manage?**

*Source: Visa Small Business Cash Management Survey, 2006.*

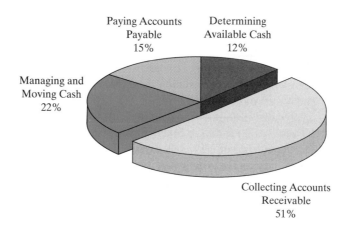

Paying Accounts Payable 15%

Determining Available Cash 12%

Managing and Moving Cash 22%

Collecting Accounts Receivable 51%

Because so many entrepreneurs sell on credit, an assertive collection program is essential to managing a company's cash flow. A credit policy that is too lenient can destroy a business's cash flow, attracting nothing but slow-paying and "deadbeat" customers. On the other hand, a carefully designed credit policy can be a powerful selling tool, attracting customers and boosting cash flow. "A sale is not a sale until you collect the money," warns the head of the National Association of Credit Management. "Receivables are the second most important item on the balance sheet. The first is cash. If you don't turn those receivables into cash, you're not going to be in business very long."[19]

**ENTREPRENEURIAL Profile**

*Bill Seidel and Seidel Flags and Flagpoles*

Bill Seidel, the second-generation owner of Seidel Flags and Flagpoles, won a contract for the installation of several flagpoles at a newly constructed downtown hotel and conference center. Three months after completing the work, Seidel, whose mother had started the company in 1971 in the family garage, was still waiting to be paid and was growing increasingly concerned after hearing rumors that the developer of the project was on the verge of bankruptcy. "I was really worried," says Seidel. "We're a small company, and that was a big project for us." To collect his cash, Seidel began calling the developer several times a day, asking for payment. His persistence finally paid off, and the developer paid most (but not all) of the project's cost. "If [the developer] had not paid me," says Seidel, "we would have been forced to file for bankruptcy." Seidel was fortunate because shortly after he received payment for the flagpoles, the developer declared bankruptcy, leaving creditors with more than $25 million in unpaid bills.[20]

**HOW TO ESTABLISH A CREDIT AND COLLECTION POLICY.** The first step to establishing a workable credit policy that preserves a company's cash flow is to screen customers carefully before granting credit. Unfortunately, few small businesses conduct any kind of credit investigation before selling to a new customer. According to one study, nearly 95 percent of small firms that sell on credit sell to anyone who wants to buy.[21] If a debt becomes past due and a business owner has gathered no information about the customer, the odds of collecting the account are virtually nil.

The first line of defense against bad debt losses is a detailed credit application. Before selling to any customer on credit, a business owner should have the customer fill out a customized application designed to provide the information needed to judge the potential customer's creditworthiness. At a minimum, this credit profile should include the following information about customers:

- Name, address, tax identification number, and telephone number.
- Form of ownership (proprietorship, S corporation, LLC, corporation, etc.) and number of years in business.
- Credit references (e.g., other suppliers), including contact names, addresses, and telephone numbers.
- Bank and credit card references.

After collecting this information, the business owner should use it by checking the potential customer's credit references! The savings from lower bad debt expenses can more than offset the cost of using a credit reporting service. Companies such as Dun & Bradstreet (D&B, www.dnb.com), Experian (www.experian.com), Equifax (www.equifax.com), TransUnion (www.transunion.com), Veritas Credit Corporation (www.veritas-usa.com), and TransUnion (www.transunion.com) enable entrepreneurs to gather credit information on potential customers. For entrepreneurs who sell to other business, D&B offers many useful services, including a Small Business Risk New Account Score, a tool for evaluating the credit risk of new businesses. The National Association of Credit Management (www.nacm.org) is another important source of credit information because it collects information on many small businesses that other reporting services ignore. The cost to check a potential customer's credit at reporting services such as these ranges from $15 to $85, a small price to pay when a small business is considering selling thousands of dollars worth of goods or services to a new customer.

The next step involves establishing a firm written credit policy and letting every customer know in advance the company's credit terms. The credit agreement must be in writing and should specify a customer's credit limit (which usually varies from one customer to another, depending on their credit ratings) and any deposits required (often stated as a percentage of the purchase price). It should state clearly all of the terms the business will enforce if the account goes bad, including interest, late charges, attorney's fees, and others. Failure to specify these terms in the contract means they *cannot* be added later after problems arise. When will you send invoices? How soon is payment due: immediately, 30 days, 60 days? Will you offer early-payment discounts? Will you add a late charge? If so, how much? The credit policies should be as tight as possible but remain within federal and state credit laws. According to some experts, if a business is writing off more than 5 percent of sales as bad debts, the owner should tighten its credit and collection policy.[22]

The third step in an effective credit policy is to send invoices promptly because customers rarely pay before they receive their bills. The sooner a company sends invoices, the sooner its customers will send payments. Manufacturers and wholesalers should make sure the invoice is en route to the customer as soon as the shipment goes out the door (if not before). Service companies should keep track of billable hours daily or weekly and bill as often as the contract or agreement with the client permits. Some businesses use **cycle billing**, in which a company bills a portion of its credit customers each day of the month to smooth out uneven cash receipts.

Small business owners can take several steps to encourage prompt payment of invoices:

- Ensure that all invoices are clear, accurate, and timely.
- State clearly a description of the goods or services purchased and an account number, if possible.
- Make sure that prices on invoices agree with the price quotations on purchase orders or contracts.
- Highlight the terms of sale (e.g., "net 30") on all invoices. One study by Xerox Corporation found that highlighting the "balance due" section of invoices increased the speed of collection by 30 percent.[23]
- Include a telephone number and a contact person in your organization in case the customer has a question or a dispute.
- Respond quickly and accurately to customers' questions about their bills.

Invoices that are well organized, easy to read, and allow customers to identify what is being billed are much more likely to get paid than those that are not. The key to creating "user-friendly" invoices is to design them from the customer's perspective.

Bob Dempster, cofounder of American Imaging Inc., a distributor of X-ray tubes, once handled receivables the same way most entrepreneurs do: When customers ignored the "net 30" terms on invoices, he would call them around the forty-fifth day to ask what the problem was. Payments usually would trickle in within the next two weeks, but by then 60 days had elapsed, and American Imaging's cash flow was always strained. Then Dempster decided to try a different approach. Now he makes a "customer relations call" on the twentieth day of the billing period to determine whether the customer is satisfied with the company's performance on the order. Before closing, he reminds the customer of the invoice due date and asks if there will be any problems meeting it. Dempster's proactive approach to collecting receivables has cut his company's average collection period by at least 15 days, improved cash flow, and increased customer satisfaction![24]

When an account becomes overdue, entrepreneurs must take immediate action. The longer an account is past due, the lower is the probability of collecting it. As soon as an account becomes overdue, many business owners send a "second notice" letter requesting immediate payment. If that fails to produce results, the next step is a telephone call. A better system is to call the customer the day after the payment is due to request payment. If the customer still refuses to pay the bill after 30 days, collection experts recommend the following:

- Send a letter from the company's attorney.
- Turn the account over to a collection agency.
- Hire a collection attorney.

Although collection agencies and attorneys will take a portion of any accounts they collect (typically around 30 percent), they are often worth the price. Collection agencies collect more than $39.3 billion annually for businesses.[25] According to the American Collector's Association, only 5 percent of accounts over 90 days delinquent will be paid voluntarily.[26]

Business owners must be sure to abide by the provisions of the federal Fair Debt Collection Practices Act, which prohibits any kind of harassment when collecting debts (e.g., telephoning repeatedly, issuing threats of violence, telling third parties about the debt, or using abusive language). When collecting past-due accounts, the primary rule in dealing with customers is, "Never lose your cool." Even if the debtor launches into an X-rated tirade when questioned about an overdue bill, the *worst* thing a collector can do is respond out of anger. Keep the call strictly business, and begin by identifying yourself, your company, and the amount of the debt. Ask the creditor what he or she intends to do about the past-due bill.

**TECHNIQUES FOR ACCELERATING ACCOUNTS RECEIVABLE.**  Small business owners can rely on a variety of techniques to speed cash inflow from accounts receivable:

- Speed up orders by having customers fax them to you.
- Subscribe to an electronic check conversion service that not only transfers purchase amounts immediately from customers' accounts to the company's account but also minimizes losses from check fraud.
- Send invoices when goods are shipped rather than a day or a week later; consider faxing or e-mailing invoices to reduce "in transit" time to a minimum.
- Indicate in conspicuous print or color the invoice due date and any late payment penalties imposed. (Check with an attorney to be sure all finance charges comply with state laws.)
- Restrict the customer's credit until past-due bills are paid. Salespeople should know which of their customers are behind in their payments. If not, they will continue to sell (most likely on credit) to those delinquent customers!
- Deposit customer checks and credit card receipts daily.
- Identify the top 20 percent of your customers (by sales volume), create a separate file system for them, and monitor them closely. Twenty percent of the typical company's customers generate 80 percent of all accounts receivable.
- Ask customers to pay a portion of the purchase price up front. Tired of chasing late payers after completing their public relations projects, Mike Clifford, founder of Clifford Public Relations, began checking potential clients' credit ratings and requiring an up-front payment of one-third of the cost of a job. Clifford also instituted a monthly billing system that tracks billable hours and related expenses. Since implementing the new system, Clifford has not experienced a single past-due account.[27]
- Watch for signs that a customer may be about to declare bankruptcy. Late payments from previously prompt payers and unreturned phone calls concerning late

payments usually are the first clues that a customer may be heading for bankruptcy. If that happens, creditors typically collect only a small fraction, on average just 10 percent, of the debt owed.[28] Cynthia McKay, owner of a Le Gourmet Gift Basket franchise lost thousands of dollars when five of her corporate clients filed for bankruptcy within a 10-month period. "That money is a weekly payroll for several employees," says McKay.[29]

■ If a customer does file for bankruptcy, the bankruptcy court notifies all creditors with a "Notice of Filing" document. If an entrepreneur receives one of these notices, he or she should create a file to track the events surrounding the bankruptcy and take action immediately. To have a valid claim against the debtor's assets in the United States, for example, a creditor must file a proof-of-claim form with the bankruptcy court within a specified time, often 90 days. (The actual time depends on which form of bankruptcy the debtor declares.) If, after paying the debtor's secured creditors, any assets remain, the court will distribute the proceeds to unsecured creditors who have legitimate proof-of-claim.

■ Consider using a bank's lockbox collection service (located near customers) to reduce mail time on collections. In a **lockbox** arrangement, customers send payments to a post office box the bank maintains. The bank collects the payments several times each day and deposits them immediately into the company account. The procedure sharply reduces processing and clearing times from the usual two to three days to just hours, especially if the lockboxes are located close to the company's biggest customers' business addresses. The system can be expensive to operate and is most economical for companies with a high volume of large checks (at least 200 checks each month).

■ Track the results of the company's collection efforts. Managers and key employees (including the sales force) should receive a weekly report on the status of the company's outstanding accounts receivable.

Another strategy that small companies, particularly those selling high-priced items, can use to protect the cash they have tied up in receivables is to couple a security agreement with a financing statement. A **security agreement** is a contract in which a business selling an asset on credit gets a security interest in that asset (the collateral), protecting the company's legal rights in case the buyer fails to pay. To get the protection it seeks in the security agreement in the United States, for example, the seller must file a financing statement called a UCC-1 form with the proper state or county office (a process the UCC calls "perfection"). The UCC-1 form gives notice to other creditors and to the general public that the seller holds a secured interest in the collateral named in the security agreement. The UCC-1 form must include the name, address, and signature of the buyer; a description of the collateral; and the name and address of the seller. If the buyer declares bankruptcy, the small business that sells the asset is not *guaranteed* payment, but the filing puts its claim to the asset ahead of those of unsecured creditors. A small company's degree of safety on a large credit sale is much higher with a security agreement and a properly-filed financing statement than if it does not file the security agreement.

### Accounts Payable

The second element of the "big three" of cash management is accounts payable. The timing of payables is just as crucial to proper cash management as the timing of receivables, but the objective is exactly the opposite. An entrepreneur should strive to stretch out payables as long as possible *without damaging the company's credit rating.* Paying late could cause suppliers to begin demanding prepayment or C.O.D. (cash on delivery) terms, which severely impair a company's cash flow. Small business owners should regulate their payments to vendors and suppliers to their companies' advantage. Ideally, a company will purchase an item on credit, sell it, and collect payment for it before the company must pay the supplier's invoice. In that case, the vendor's credit terms amount to an interest-free loan. That is exactly the situation that Dell Inc., the fast-growing computer maker, puts itself in. Its extremely high inventory turnover ratio of 76 times a year coupled with its abil-

**FIGURE 8.7 Dell Inc.'s Cash Conversion Cycle**

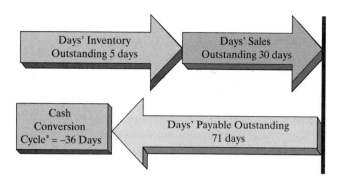

*Cash Conversion Cycle = Day's Inventory + Day's Sales Outstanding – Day's Payable Outstanding = 5 + 30 – 71 = –36

ity to negotiate favorable credit terms with its suppliers and to collect customers' payments quickly means that the company enjoys an industry-leading cash conversion cycle of *negative* 36 days. On average, Dell collects payments from its customers and gets to use that cash before having to pay its suppliers 36 days later (see Figure 8.7)![30]

Even when the cash flow timing isn't ideal, efficient cash managers benefit by setting up a payment calendar each month that allows them to pay their bills on time and to take advantage of cash discounts for early payment.

*Nancy Dunis and Dunis & Associates*

Nancy Dunis, CEO of Dunis & Associates, a marketing firm, recognizes the importance of controlling accounts payable. "Our payables must be functioning just right to keep our cash flow running smoothly," says Dunis. She has set up a simple five-point accounts payable system:

1. *Set scheduling goals.* Dunis strives to pay her company's bills 45 days after receiving them and to collect all her receivables within 30 days. Even though "it doesn't always work that way," her goal is to make the most of her cash flow.
2. *Keep paperwork organized.* Dunis dates every invoice she receives and carefully files it according to her payment plan. "This helps us remember when to cut the check," she says, and, "it helps us stagger our payments over days or weeks," significantly improving the company's cash flow.
3. *Prioritize.* Dunis cannot stretch out all of her company's creditors for 45 days; some demand payment sooner. Those suppliers are at the top of the accounts payable list.
4. *Be consistent.* "Companies want consistent customers," says Dunis. "With a few exceptions," she explains, "most businesses will be happy to accept 45-day payments, so long as they know you'll always pay your full obligation at that point."
5. *Look for warning signs.* Dunis sees her accounts payable as an early warning system for cash flow problems. "The first indication I get that cash flow is in trouble is when I see I'm getting low on cash and could have trouble paying my bills according to my staggered filing system," she says.[31]

Business owners should verify all invoices before paying them. Some unscrupulous vendors send out invoices for goods they never shipped, knowing that many business owners will simply pay the bill without checking its authenticity. Someone in the company—for instance, the accounts payable clerk—should have the responsibility of verifying every invoice received. In a common scam targeting small businesses, the accounts payable clerk at one company caught a bogus invoice for $322 worth of copier paper and toner it never ordered nor received.[32]

Generally, it is beneficial for owners to take advantage of cash discounts vendors offer. A cash discount (e.g., "2/10, net 30"—take a 2 percent discount if you pay the invoice within ten days; otherwise, total payment is due in 30 days) offers a price reduction if the owner pays an invoice early. The savings the discount provides usually exceed the cost of giving up the use of a company's cash by paying early.

*Jeff Schreiber and
Hansen Wholesale*

Jeff Schreiber, owner of Hansen Wholesale, a company that distributes home products, is in the habit of taking advantage of the cash discounts vendors offer his company. In one year alone, Schreiber, whose company generates $3.5 million in annual sales, saved $15,000 with cash discounts. "Your money works better if you take advantage of the discounts," says Schreiber.[33]

Clever cash managers also negotiate the best possible credit terms with their suppliers. Almost all vendors grant their customers trade credit, and entrepreneurs should take advantage of it. However, because trade credit is so easy to get, entrepreneurs must be careful not to abuse it, putting their businesses in a precarious financial position. Favorable credit terms can make a tremendous difference in a firm's cash flow. Table 8.5 shows the same most likely cash budget (from Table 8.2) with one exception: Instead of purchasing on C.O.D. terms (Table 8.2), the owner has negotiated "net 30" payment terms (Table 8.5). Notice the drastic improvement in this small company's cash flow that results from the improved credit terms.

If owners do find themselves financially strapped when payment to a vendor is due, they should avoid making empty promises that "the check is in the mail." Instead, they should discuss openly the situation with the vendor. Most suppliers are willing to work out payment terms for extended credit. One small business owner who was experiencing a cash crisis claims:

> One day things got so bad I just called up a supplier and said, 'I need your stuff, but I'm going through a tough period and simply can't pay you right now.' They said

### TABLE 8.5 Case Budget,[a] Most Likely Sales Forecast

|  | Jan. | Feb. | Mar. | Apr. |
|---|---|---|---|---|
| *Cash Receipts:* | | | | |
| Sales | $150,000 | $200,000 | $200,000 | $300,000 |
| Credit Sales | 112,500 | 150,000 | 150,000 | 225,000 |
| *Collections:* | | | | |
| 60%—1st month after sale | $180,000 | $ 67,500 | $ 90,000 | $ 90,000 |
| 30%—2nd month after sale | 78,750 | 90,000 | 33,750 | 45,000 |
| 5%—3rd month after sale | 11,250 | 13,125 | 15,000 | 5,625 |
| Cash Sales | 37,500 | 50,000 | 50,000 | 75,000 |
| Interest | 0 | 200 | 0 | 0 |
| Total Cash Receipts | $307,500 | $220,825 | $188,750 | $215,625 |
| *Cash Disbursements:* | | | | |
| Purchases[a] | $105,000 | $140,000 | $140,000 | $210,000 |
| Rent | 2,000 | 2,000 | 2,000 | 2,000 |
| Utilities | 850 | 850 | 850 | 850 |
| Interest | 0 | 0 | 7,500, | 0 |
| Tax Prepayment | 0 | 0 | 50,000 | 0 |
| Capital Addition | 0 | 130,000 | 3 | 0 |
| Miscellaneous | 70 | 70 | 70 | 70 |
| Wage/Salaries | 30,000 | 40,000 | 45,000 | 50,000 |
| Total Cash Disbursements[a] | $137,920 | $312,920 | $245,420 | $262,920 |
| *End-of-Month Balance:* | | | | |
| Cash (beginning of month)[a] | $ 12,000 | $181,580 | $ 89,485 | $ 32,815 |
| +Cash Receipts | 307,500 | 220,825 | 188,750 | 215,625 |
| −Cash Disbursements[a] | 137,920 | 312,920 | 245,420 | 262,920 |
| Cash (end of month)[a] | 181,580 | 89,485 | 32,815 | (14,480) |
| Borrowing | 0 | 0 | 0 | 24,480 |
| Cash (end of month [after borrowing])[a] | $181,580 | $ 89,485 | $ 32,815 | $ 10,000 |

[a]After negotiating "net 30" trade credit terms.

they wanted to keep me as a customer, and they asked if it was okay to bill me in three months. I was dumbfounded: They didn't even charge me interest.[34]

Entrepreneurs also can improve their firms' cash flow by scheduling controllable cash disbursements so that they do not come due at the same time. For example, paying employees every two weeks (or every month) rather than every week reduces administrative costs and gives the business more time to use its available cash. Owners of fledgling businesses may be able to conserve cash by hiring part-time employees or by using freelance workers rather than full-time, permanent workers. Scheduling insurance premiums monthly or quarterly rather than annually also improves cash flow.

### Inventory

Inventory is a significant investment for many small businesses and can create a severe strain on cash flow if not managed properly. Although inventory represents the largest capital investment for most businesses, many entrepreneurs do not use formal methods for managing it. As a result, the typical small business not only has too much inventory but also too much of the wrong kind of inventory! Because inventory is illiquid, it can quickly siphon off a company's pool of available cash. Small businesses need cash to grow and to survive, which is difficult to do if they have money tied up in excess inventory, which yields a zero rate of return. "The cost of carrying inventory is expensive," says one small business consultant. "A typical manufacturing company pays 25 percent to 30 percent of the value of the inventory for the cost of borrowed money, warehouse space, materials handling, staff, lift-truck expenses, and fixed costs. This shocks a lot of people. Once they realize it, they look at inventory differently."[35] Tracking inventory consistently enables a business owner to avoid purchasing or manufacturing goods unnecessarily. Experienced entrepreneurs often maintain different levels of inventory for different items depending on how critical they are to the company's operation and on how quickly they can be replenished. For instance, the owner of one small landscape company knew that hardwood mulch was one of his best-selling items in the spring, but he refused to purchase excessive amounts of it because his primary supplier was nearby and could deliver mulch within two hours of receiving an order.

Marking down items that don't sell will keep inventory lean and allow it to turn over frequently. Even though volume discounts lower inventory costs, large purchases may tie up the company's valuable cash. Wise business owners avoid overbuying inventory, recognizing that excess inventory ties up valuable cash unproductively. In fact, only 20 percent of a typical business's inventory turns over quickly, so owners must watch constantly for stale items.[36] Carrying unsold inventory costs businesses worldwide trillions a year.[37]

Carrying too much inventory increases the chances that a business will run out of cash.

*Dell Inc.*

When Tom Meredith joined Dell Inc. as its chief financial officer, he quickly discovered that excessive inventory was a major source of the cash flow problems the company was experiencing at the time. Because the company was focusing on growth, it held large inventories of costly computer components to make sure it could meet every sales opportunity. Meredith's top priority in his first few months at Dell was to cut inventory levels. "Low inventory equals high profit; high inventory equals low profit," he declares. Because the inventory that Dell carries becomes technologically obsolete so rapidly, losing 1 percent of its value each week, high inventory levels increase the likelihood of wasted cash.[38]

In addition to the cost of the inventory itself, the activities required to purchase, store, monitor, and control inventory are themselves costly. Efficient cash management calls for a business to commit just enough cash to inventory to meet demand. Paring down the number of suppliers enables a business to gain more bargaining power, minimize paperwork, and perhaps earn quantity discounts. Scheduling inventory deliveries at the latest possible date will prevent premature payment of invoices. Finally, given goods of comparable quality and price, entrepreneurs should purchase goods from those suppliers who are best at making fast, frequent deliveries to keep inventory levels low.

## ■ Watch Those Accounts Receivable!

When Randy Ringer developed the cash flow forecasts for the business plan he created for Verse Group, a New York City-based marketing and branding company, he assumed that the company's clients would pay their invoices in 30 days. As Ringer and his business partner learned more about the industry, however, they discovered that companies in their industry typically did not see any cash flow until 60 or more days after completing a job and billing the client. They quickly revised their business plan and increased the minimum cash balance they would keep on hand from three months' worth of expenses to six months' worth. They also established a policy that requires clients to prepay a portion of any projects that require Verse Group to pay substantial up-front costs. Their industry's collection patterns "have changed the way we do business," says Ringer.

Do you know the typical collection pattern for accounts receivable for the industry in which you are about to launch a business? Not knowing this important number could create significant cash flow problems for your company and even cost you your business. The following table shows the day's payable outstanding (DPO) ratio (which is calculated by dividing 365 days per year by the industry's average collection period ratio).

### Days' Payables Outstanding by Industry

| Industry | DPO | Industry | DPO |
|---|---|---|---|
| Aerospace and defense | 29.5 | Industrial technology | 26.5 |
| Airlines | 16.5 | Industrial diversified | 28.1 |
| Apparel retailers | 22.4 | Land transportation | 28.0 |
| Auto manufacturers | 49.9 | Machinery makers | 39.6 |
| Auto parts and suppliers | 38.3 | Medical devices | 17.5 |
| Biotechnology | 15.8 | Medical supplies | 20.2 |
| Building materials | 26.3 | Newspaper publishers | 14.0 |
| Chemicals, commodity | 29.6 | Oil drilling | 32.1 |
| Chemicals, specialty | 30.0 | Oil secondary | 37.9 |
| Clothing, fabrics | 27.6 | Other food | 19.5 |
| Communications technology | 30.0 | Other industrial and commercial services | 16.0 |
| Computer makers | 38.7 | Other oil equipment and services | 32.8 |
| Consumer and household services | 10.7 | Other recreational services | 16.8 |
| Containers and packaging | 33.3 | Other specialty retailers | 27.0 |
| Distributors | 39.4 | Paper and forest | 23.0 |
| Drug retailers | 27.3 | Pharmaceuticals | 18.0 |
| Electrical components | 33.1 | Pipelines | 41.2 |
| Food producers | 19.9 | Restaurants | 13.2 |
| Food retailers | 16.5 | Retailers, broadline | 27.5 |
| Footwear | 21.6 | Semiconductors | 22.8 |
| Healthcare providers | 12.2 | Soft drinks | 18.0 |
| Heavy construction | 28.4 | Software | 10.8 |
| Home construction | 19.3 | Steel | 26.6 |
| Home furniture | 18.1 | Telecom operators | 21.1 |
| Household products, nondurable | 25.5 | Trucking | 13.2 |

Note that a customer in the software industry with a DPO of 16 days would raise a red flag, but a customer in the pipeline business with a DPO of 36 days is paying its bills faster than the industry average.

What can entrepreneurs who operate businesses in industries characterized by longer payment periods do to protect their companies' cash flow? The following tips will help:

- *Increase your company's cash reserves.* Just as Randy Ringer did, entrepreneurs should plan to keep more cash on hand from the beginning to avoid being caught short. In addition, smart entrepreneurs establish a line of credit with a bank or other lending institution just in case they encounter a cash crisis. Note: The time to establish a line of credit is well before you need it!
- *Establish your company's credit and collection policy, tell your customers about it, and stick to it as closely as possible.* Doing so gives you more leverage when customers fall behind on their payments, as they inevitably will.
- *Monitor accounts receivable regularly—daily, if necessary.* Before Mike Edwards, founder of 5 Stones Group, a film production company, starts a project, he creates contracts that require clients to pay one-third of the price up front, one-third at mid-project, and one-third on completion. Still, to keep his company's cash flow positive, Edwards and his wife Tiffany, who manages 5 Stones Group's finances, have to monitor clients' accounts closely. "If the client says that [he] will make a payment next Friday, you have to call next Friday," he says. "You have to continually track payments."

- *Consider offering discounts for early payment.* These discounts, called cash discounts, will reduce a small company's total revenue, but that cost often is more than offset by the benefits of speeding up cash inflows.
- *If customers still won't comply with your terms, consider raising prices.* That's what Mitch Miller, president of Dynamic Computer Solutions of Topeka (DCST), a computer systems integrator that generates $3 million in annual sales, did when several of his long-time customers decided to pay their invoices in 45 days instead of the 20 days in DCST's selling terms. Although a few clients mentioned the price increase, none left. "You have to be bold," says Miller.

1. Why is it so important for small companies to monitor their accounts receivable? What are the implications for companies that fail to do so?
2. Contact a local entrepreneur whose company sells goods or services on credit. Ask him or her to explain the company's credit and collection policy. Are slow-paying customers a problem? How does the company deal with customers whose accounts are past due?
3. Why are some entrepreneurs hesitant to take bold actions to collect the money that customers owe them?

*Sources:* Adapted from "Managing Credit, Receivables, and Collections," *IOMA*, December 2006, p. 4; Amy Feldman, "The Cash-Flow Crunch," *Inc.*, December 2005, pp. 51–52.

---

Monitoring the big three of cash management can help every business owner avoid a cash crisis while making the best use of available cash. According to one expert, maximizing cash flow involves "getting money from customers sooner; paying bills at the last moment possible; consolidating money in a single bank account; managing accounts payable, accounts receivable, and inventory more effectively; and squeezing every penny out of your daily business."[39]

## Avoiding the Cash Crunch

**5.** Explain the techniques for avoiding a cash crunch in a small company.

Nearly every small business has the potential to improve its cash position with little or no investment. The key is to make an objective evaluation of a company's financial policies, searching for inefficiency in its cash flow and for ways to squeeze more cash out of their operations. Young firms cannot afford to waste resources, especially one as vital as cash. By utilizing these tools, an entrepreneur can get maximum benefit from the company's pool of cash.

### Barter

**Bartering**, the exchange of goods and services for other goods and services, is an effective way to conserve cash. An ancient concept, bartering began to regain popularity during recent recessions. Barter exchanges operate across the globe, catering primarily to small- and medium-sized businesses and many of them operating on the World Wide Web. Some 400,000 companies, most of them small, engage in bartering transactions worth more than $9 billion each year, trading everything from accounting services and computers to carpets and meals.[40] Every day, entrepreneurs use bartering to buy much needed materials, equipment, and supplies—*without using cash.* The president of one barter exchange estimates that business owners can save "between $5,000 and $150,000 in yearly business costs."[41] In addition to conserving cash, companies using bartering can transform slow-moving and excess inventory into much-needed goods and services. Often business owners who join barter exchanges find new customers for the products and services they sell.

Of course, there is a cost associated with bartering, but the real benefit is that entrepreneurs "pay" for products and services at their wholesale cost of doing business and get credit in the barter exchange for the retail price. In a typical arrangement, businesses accumulate trade credits when they offer goods or services through the exchange. Then they can use their trade credits to purchase other goods and services from other members of the exchange.

*Carlos Collins and CCI Industries*

Carlos Collins, president of CCI Industries, a Chicago-based wholesaler of sterling silver jewelry, says that bartering has saved his company thousands of dollars. "I use the barter dollars to purchase advertising for my business. Bartering allows CCI to "purchase much more advertising than I could afford to buy with cash. [Bartering is] one of the best things to happen to my business," says Carlos.[42]

The typical exchange charges a $500 membership fee and a 10 percent transaction fee (5 percent from the buyer and 5 percent from the seller) on every deal. The exchange tracks the balance in each member's account and typically sends a monthly statement summarizing account activity. Rather than join a barter exchange, many enterprising entrepreneurs choose to barter on an individual basis. The natural place to start is with the vendors, suppliers, and customers with whom a company normally does business.

### Trim Overhead Costs

High overhead expenses can strain a small company's cash supply to the breaking point. Frugal small business owners can trim their overhead in a number of ways:

**WHEN PRACTICAL, LEASE INSTEAD OF BUY.**   Of the $850 million that U.S. businesses spend annually on productive assets, for example, 27 percent is obtained through leases.[43] By leasing automobiles, computers, office equipment, machinery, and other assets rather than buying them, entrepreneurs can conserve valuable cash. The value of such assets is not in *owning* them but in *using* them. Leasing is popular among entrepreneurs because of its beneficial effects on a company's cash flow; a study by the Equipment Leasing Association found that 80 percent of U.S. businesses use leasing as a cash management strategy.[44] Leasing also gives business owners maximum flexibility when acquiring equipment and protection against the risk of purchasing assets that become obsolete quickly.

*Andy Fleischer and Alabanza Corporation*

Andy Fleischer, chief financial officer of the Web hosting business Alabanza Corporation, recently switched from purchasing the company's servers to leasing them. Not only does leasing conserve the fast-growing company's precious cash, but it also enables it to keep its technology up-to-date, a vital factor given the nature of Alabanza's business. "In the past, we bought large blocks of servers up front," explains Fleischer. Leasing, however, allows Alabanza to spread the payment terms over 36 months, freeing up sizable amounts of cash the company can use elsewhere.[45]

Although total lease payments often are greater than those for a conventional loan, most leases offer 100 percent financing, which means the owner avoids the large capital outlays required as down payments on most loans. Also, leasing is an "off-the-balance-sheet" method of financing; the lease is considered an operating expense on the income statement, not a liability on the balance sheet. Thus, leasing conserves not only a company's cash flow but also its borrowing capacity. Leasing companies typically allow businesses to stretch payments over a longer time period than those of a conventional loan. Lease agreements also are flexible; entrepreneurs can customize their lease payments to coincide with the seasonal fluctuations in their companies' cash balances.

Entrepreneurs can choose from two basic types of leases: operating leases and capital leases. At the end of an **operating lease**, a business turns the equipment back over to the leasing company with no further obligation. Businesses often lease computer and telecommunications equipment through operating leases because it becomes obsolete so quickly. At the end of a **capital lease**, a business may exercise an option to purchase the equipment, usually for a nominal sum. Table 8.6 compares the characteristics of leasing, borrowing, and paying cash for business assets.

**AVOID NONESSENTIAL OUTLAYS.**   Smart entrepreneurs spend cash only when it is necessary. By forgoing costly ego indulgences such as ostentatious office equipment, first-class travel, and flashy company cars, business owners can make efficient use of their companies' cash. Before putting scarce cash into an asset, every business owner should put the decision to the acid test by asking "What will this purchase add to the company's ability to compete and to become more successful?" Making across-the-board spending cuts to conserve cash is dangerous, however, because the owner runs the risk of cutting expenditures that literally drive the business. One common mistake during business slowdowns is cutting marketing and advertising expenditures. "As competitors pull back," says one adviser, "smart marketers will keep their ad budgets on an even keel, which is sufficient to bring increased attention to their products."[46] The secret to success is cutting nonessential

**TABLE 8.6  Lease, Borrow, or Pay Cash?**

When faced with the need to purchase equipment, many entrepreneurs wonder whether they should choose to lease the asset, borrow the money, or use the company's available cash to purchase it. The following table describes some of the characteristics of each option.

| Characteristic | Lease | Loan | Cash |
|---|---|---|---|
| **Capital Cost** | Net present value of lease payments typically is less than original equipment cost | Equipment cost plus interest expense | Equipment cost plus opportunity cost of tying up cash |
| **Initial Cash Outlay** | Small or no down payment | Significant down payment | 100% of equipment cost |
| **Payments** | Fixed monthly payments | Fixed monthly payments | None. Entire cost paid up front |
| **Impact on Borrowing Capacity** | None | Reduced borrowing capacity | None |
| **Risk of Obsolescence** | Low. Company returns equipment to lessor at end of lease | High. Company owns equipment after repaying loan | High. Company owns equipment up front |
| **Tax impact** | Lease expenses usually deductible as a business expense | Interest expenses deductible; equipment depreciated over time | Equipment depreciated over time |
| **Ownership** | Company does not own asset at end of lease | Company owns asset after paying off loan | Company owns asset immediately |

*Source:* Adapted from Hewlett-Packard, "Leasing Gives You More IT Bang for Your Buck," www3.hp.com/news_article.php?topiccode=20061212.

expenditures. "If the lifeblood of your company is marketing, cut it less," advises one advertising executive. "If it is customer service, that is the last thing you want to cut back on. Cut from areas that are not essential to business growth."[47]

**NEGOTIATE FIXED LOAN PAYMENTS TO COINCIDE WITH YOUR COMPANY'S CASH FLOW CYCLE.**   Many banks allow businesses to structure loans so that they can skip specific payments when their cash flow ebbs to its lowest point. Negotiating such terms gives businesses the opportunity to customize their loan repayments to their cash flow cycles. For example, Ted Zoli, president of Torrington Industries, a construction-materials supplier and contracting business, consistently uses "skipped payment loans" in his highly seasonal business. "Every time we buy a piece of construction machinery," he says, "we set it up so that we're making payments for eight or nine months, and then skipping three or four months during the winter."[48]

**BUY USED OR RECONDITIONED EQUIPMENT, ESPECIALLY IF IT IS "BEHIND-THE-SCENES" MACHINERY.**   Many shrewd entrepreneurs purchase their office furniture at flea markets and garage sales! One restaurateur saved significant amounts of cash in the start-up phase of his business by purchasing used equipment from a restaurant equipment broker.

*Mark Eshelman and
Smarte Solutions Inc.*

Mark Eshelman, cofounder of Smarte Solutions Inc., a company that markets anti-piracy software, purchases the diverse array of computers he needs to test the company's software from a used PC Web site. He was so impressed with the deal he got on those systems that he purchased another 30 used computers at drastically reduced prices for his programmers and office staff to use.[49]

**LOOK FOR SIMPLE WAYS TO CUT COSTS.**   Smart entrepreneurs are always on the lookout for ways to cut the cost of operating their businesses every day. One useful technique is to sit down with employees periodically with a list of company expenses and brainstorm ways the company could conserve cash without endangering product quality or customer service. Ideas might range from installing more energy-efficient equipment to adding more fuel-efficient cars to the company fleet.

**HIRE PART-TIME EMPLOYEES AND FREELANCE SPECIALISTS WHENEVER POSSIBLE.**
Hiring part-timers and freelancers rather than full-time workers saves on both the cost of salaries and employee benefits. Robert Ross, president of Xante Corporation, a maker of laser printer products, hires local college students for telemarketing and customer support positions, keeping his recruiting, benefits, and insurance costs down.

**OUTSOURCE.**   One way that many entrepreneurs conserve valuable cash is to outsource certain activities to businesses that specialize in performing them rather than hiring someone to do them in-house (or doing the activities themselves). In addition to saving cash, outsourcing enables entrepreneurs to focus on the most important aspects of running their businesses.

**CONTROL EMPLOYEE ADVANCES AND LOANS.**   A manager should grant only those advances and loans that are necessary and should keep accurate records on payments and balances.

**USE E-MAIL OR FAXES RATHER THAN MAIL.**   Whenever appropriate, entrepreneurs should use e-mails or faxes rather than mail to communicate with customers, suppliers, and others to reduce costs.

**USE CREDIT CARDS TO MAKE SMALL PURCHASES.**   Using a credit card to make small purchases from vendors who do not offer credit terms allows entrepreneurs to defer payment for up to 30 days. Entrepreneurs who use this strategy must be disciplined, however, and pay off the entire credit card balance each month. Carrying a credit card balance from month to month exposes an entrepreneur to annual interest rates of 15 percent to 30 percent—*not* a cash conserving technique!

**ESTABLISH AN INTERNAL SECURITY AND CONTROL SYSTEM.**   Too many owners encourage employee theft by failing to establish a system of controls. Reconciling the bank statement monthly and requiring special approval for checks over a specific amount, say $1,000, will help minimize losses. Separating record-keeping and check-writing responsibilities, rather than assigning them to a single employee, offers more protection.

**DEVELOP A SYSTEM TO BATTLE CHECK FRAUD.**   According to the American Collectors Association, Americans write about 1.7 million bad checks each day, totaling more than $50 million per day in bad check losses for U.S. businesses. About 70 percent of all "bounced" checks occur because nine out of ten customers fail to keep their checkbooks balanced; the remaining 30 percent of bad checks are the result of fraud. Companies lose more than $10 billion per year because of forged or fraudulent checks.[50] The most effective way to battle bad or fraudulent checks is to subscribe to an electronic check approval service. The service works at the cash register, and approval takes about a minute. The fee a small business pays to use the service depends on the volume of checks. For most small companies, charges range from a base of $25 to $100 per month plus a percentage of the cleared checks' value.

**CHANGE YOUR SHIPPING TERMS.**   Changing a company's shipping terms from "F.O.B. (free on board) buyer," in which the seller pays the cost of freight, to "F.O.B. seller," in which the buyer absorbs all shipping costs, will improve cash flow.

**SWITCH TO ZERO-BASED BUDGETING.**   **Zero-based budgeting (ZBB)** primarily is a shift in the philosophy of budgeting. Rather than build the current year budget on increases from the previous year's budget, ZBB starts from a budget of zero and evaluates the necessity of every item. The idea is to start the budget at zero and review all expenses, asking whether each one is necessary.

**START SELLING GIFT CARDS.**   Prepaid gift cards can be a real boost to a small company's cash flow. Customers pay for the cards up front, but the typical recipient does not redeem the gift card until later, sometimes much later, giving the company the use of the cash during that time. Gift cards are appropriate for many businesses, especially those in the retail or service sectors.

**INVEST SURPLUS CASH.**   Because of the uneven flow of receipts and disbursements, a company will often temporarily have more cash than it needs—for a week, month, quarter, or even longer. When this happens, most small business owners simply ignore the surplus because they are not sure how soon they will need it. They believe that relatively small amounts of cash sitting around for just a few days or weeks are not worth investing. However, this is not the case. Small business owners who put surplus cash to work *immediately* rather than allowing it to sit idle soon discover that the yield adds up to a significant amount over time. This money can help ease the daily cash crunch during business troughs. "Your goal . . . should be to identify every dollar you don't need to pay today's bills and to keep that money invested to improve your cash flow," explains a consultant.[51]

However, when investing surplus cash, an entrepreneur's primary objective should *not* be to earn the highest yield (which usually carries with it high levels of risk); instead, the focus should be on the safety and the liquidity of the investments. Making high-risk investments with a company's cash cushion makes no sense and could jeopardize its future. The need to minimize risk and to have ready access to the cash restricts an entrepreneur's investment options to just a few such as money market accounts, zero balance accounts, and sweep accounts. A **money market account** is an interest-bearing account offered by a variety of financial institutions ranging from banks to mutual funds. Money market accounts pay interest while allowing depositors to write checks (most have minimum check amounts) without tying their money up for a specific period of time. After surviving a cash crisis shortly after launching their branding and communications company,

Jaye Donaldson and her partner Chester Makoski now keep enough cash invested in a money market account to cover at least three to six months of expenses.[52]

A **zero balance account (ZBA)** is a checking account that technically never has any funds in it but is tied to a master account. The company keeps its money in the master account where it earns interest, but it writes checks on the ZBA. At the end of the day, the bank pays all of the checks drawn on the ZBA; then it withdraws enough money from the master account to cover them. ZBAs allow a company to keep more cash working during the float period, the time between a check being issued and its being cashed. A **sweep account** automatically "sweeps" all funds in a company's checking account above a predetermined minimum into an interest-bearing account, enabling it to keep otherwise idle cash invested until it is needed to cover checks.

**BE ON THE LOOKOUT FOR EMPLOYEE THEFT.**   Because small business owners often rely on informal procedures for managing cash (or no procedures at all) and often lack proper control procedures, they are most likely to become victims of employee theft, embezzlement, and fraud by their employees. Experts estimate that employee theft costs small businesses billions a year and that as much as 75 percent of all employee theft goes unnoticed![53] Although any business can be a victim of employee theft, retailers are particularly vulnerable. Retailers lose 1.5 percent of the value of their merchandise to employee theft and shoplifting each year.[54] One source of the problem is the entrepreneur's attitude that "we're all family here; no one would steal from family."

**KEEP YOUR BUSINESS PLAN CURRENT.**   Before approaching any potential lender or investor, a business owner must prepare a solid business plan. Smart owners keep their plans up-to-date in case an unexpected cash crisis forces them to seek emergency financing. Revising the plan annually also forces the owner to focus on managing the business more effectively.

## Conclusion

Successful owners run their businesses "lean and mean." Trimming wasteful expenditures, investing surplus funds, and carefully planning and managing the company's cash flow enable them to compete effectively in a hostile market. The simple but effective techniques covered in this chapter can improve every small company's cash position. One business writer says, "In the day-to-day course of running a company, other people's capital flows past an imaginative CEO as opportunity. By looking forward and keeping an analytical eye on your cash account as events unfold (remembering that if there's no real cash there when you need it, you're history), you can generate leverage as surely as if that capital were yours to keep."[55]

## Chapter Review

1. Explain the importance of cash management to the success of a small business.
   - Cash is the most important but least productive asset the small business has. Entrepreneurs must maintain enough cash to meet a company's normal operating requirements (plus a reserve for emergencies) without retaining excessively large, unproductive cash balances.
   - Without adequate cash, a small business will fail.
2. Differentiate between cash and profits.
   - Cash and profits are not the same. More businesses fail for lack of cash than for lack of profits.
   - Profit, the difference between total revenue and total expenses, is an accounting concept. Cash flow represents the flow of actual cash (the only thing businesses can use to pay bills) through a business in a continuous cycle. A business can be earning a profit and be forced out of business because it runs out of cash.

3. Understand the five steps in creating a cash budget and use them to build a cash budget.
   - The cash budgeting procedure outlined in this chapter tracks the flow of cash through the business and enables the owner to project cash surpluses and cash deficits at specific intervals.
   - The five steps in creating a cash budget are as follows: forecasting sales, forecasting cash receipts, forecasting cash disbursements, and determining the end-of-month cash balance.
4. Describe the fundamental principles involved in managing the "Big Three" of cash management: accounts receivable, accounts payable, and inventory.
   - Controlling accounts receivable requires business owners to establish clear, firm credit and collection policies and to screen customers before granting them credit. Sending invoices promptly and acting on past-due accounts quickly also improve cash flow. The goal is to collect cash from receivables as quickly as possible.
   - When managing accounts payable, an entrepreneur's goal is to stretch out payables as long as possible without damaging the company's credit rating. Other techniques include: verifying invoices before paying them, taking advantage of cash discounts, and negotiating the best possible credit terms.
   - Inventory frequently causes cash headaches for small business managers. Excess inventory earns a zero rate of return and ties up a company's cash unnecessarily. Owners must watch for stale merchandise.
5. Explain the techniques for avoiding a cash crunch in a small company.
   - Trimming overhead costs by bartering, leasing assets, avoiding nonessential outlays, using zero-based budgeting, and implementing an internal control system boost a firm's cash flow position.
   - In addition, investing surplus cash maximizes a company's earning power. The primary criteria for investing surplus cash are security and liquidity.

## Discussion Questions

1. Why must small business owners concentrate on effective cash flow management?
2. Explain the difference between cash and profit.
3. Outline the steps involved in developing a cash budget.
4. How can an entrepreneur launching a new business forecast sales?
5. Outline the basic principles of managing a small firm's receivables, payables, and inventory.
6. How can bartering improve a company's cash position?
7. One entrepreneur says, "We lease our equipment and technology because our core business is deploying it, not owning it." What does he mean? Is leasing a wise cash management strategy for small businesses? Explain.
8. What steps should business owners take to conserve cash in their companies?
9. What should be a small business owner's primary concern when investing surplus cash?
10. Fritz Maytag, owner of Anchor Steam, says, "Just because you are the best around doesn't mean that you have to franchise or even expand. You can stay as you are and have a business that's profitable and rewarding and a great source of pride." Do you agree? Do you think that most entrepreneurs would agree? Explain.

# BusinessPlanPro

Managing cash flow is a task that many entrepreneurs initially ignore—until they face a cash crisis. Cash is the resource that sustains a company, enabling it to grow and survive. Without cash, a business fails. Creating a cash flow forecast and using it to manage your company is critical. As this chapter points out, cash and profit are not the same, and there are aspects of understanding cash flow that are nonintuitive. In addition to being a valuable planning tool, your cash flow statement can help you assess the future health and potential of your venture. We will review the cash flow aspects of your plan and determine what you can learn from that cash flow statement. This is one step to assess how financially realistic your plan is based on the information that you have provided to date.

## On the Web

Go to the Companion Website at www.prenhall.com/ scarborough and review the links associated with Chapter 8. These online resources may offer additional information regarding the cash flow statement and the role it will play in your business plan.

## In the Software

Review the information that you have regarding your sales forecast and the expense information in your projected Profit and Loss statement. Change any numbers that you have determined to be unrealistic. Now go to the "Financial Statement" section of the plan and look at your "Projected Cash Flow Statement." Do any of these months show a negative cash flow? If this is the case, based on your projections, you do not have an adequate cash cushion. The lowest, most negative amount indicates the minimal amount of additional cash your business needs. Make sure your projections are realistic and that you have adequate cash to make it through this negative period. Advanced planning is your best opportunity to avoid bankruptcy. Conversely, are there months where your projections indicate an excess amount of cash? If so, have plans to use this cash to its best ability when that time comes.

Save any changes you have made in your plan. Assume that this version of your plan represents your "most likely" outcome based on realistic expense and revenue projections. Now create two additional "what if" scenarios—one using a pessimistic forecast and another using an optimistic forecast. Save this same file under a new name, for example, with the words "pessimistic" or "optimistic" after the file name. This will enable you to make changes in your plan and assess what that does to your cash flow. For example, lower your revenues by 25 percent. What does that do to your cash flow? Increase your expenses by 25 percent. What impact does that have regarding the amount of cash you will need to get through the most negative cash flow months? If you are extending credit to your customers, increase the accounts receivable lag time by 15 days, from 30 to 45 days, for example. What does your cash flow statement look like now? Make the changes that could paint a potentially negative picture for your venture and save the plan under the new "pessimistic" file name. Close that plan and open your original so we can start with your "most likely" scenario again.

Save your original under an "optimistic" file name. If you are planning to extend credit, decrease the number of collection days by seven. What does that change do to your cash flow? Increase your revenues by 15 percent. Decrease your projected expenses by 15 percent. Working through these scenarios can help test and validate your numbers and prepare you for contingencies as your plan becomes a reality. The goal is to create three scenarios that will provide a best, worst, and most likely view of your business.

## Building Your Business Plan

Review the data that affects your cash flow statement. Are there revisions you need to make based on your pro forma cash flow statement? What are some of the most significant cash demands of your business? Is it due to cash tied up in inventory? Is it your payroll? Are rent or lease expenditures disproportionately high based on your projected revenues? Can you take steps to reduce or better control these expenditures as you build your revenue stream? Once you have answered these questions, again determine whether you have adequate cash for your venture after allowing for potential cost overrun or revenues below your projections.

# Building a Guerrilla Marketing Plan

We see our customers as invited guests to a party, and we are the hosts. It's our job every day to make every important aspect of the customer experience a little bit better.
—Jeff Bezos, founder, Amazon.com

This may seem simple, but you need to give customers what they want, not what you think they want. If you do this, people will keep coming back.
—John Ilhan

## Learning Objectives

Upon completion of this chapter, you will be able to:

1 Describe the components of a guerrilla marketing plan and explain the benefits of preparing one.

2 Explain how small businesses can pinpoint their target markets.

3 Explain how to determine customer needs through market research and outline the steps in the market research process.

4 Describe the guerrilla marketing strategies on which a small business can build a competitive edge in the marketplace.

5 Discuss marketing opportunities the World Wide Web offers and how entrepreneurs can take advantage of them.

6 Discuss the "four Ps" of marketing—product, place, price, and promotion—and their role in building a successful marketing strategy.

T oo often, business plans describe in great detail what the entrepreneur intends to accomplish (e.g., "the financials") and pay little, if any, attention to the strategies to achieve those targets. Others entrepreneurs fail because they are not willing to invest the time and energy to identify and research their target markets and to assemble a business plan. These entrepreneurs squander enormous effort pulling together capital, staff, products, and services because they neglect to determine what it will take to attract and retain a profitable customer base. To be effective, a solid business plan must contain both a financial plan and a marketing plan. Like the financial plan, an effective marketing plan includes forecasts and analysis but from a different perspective. Rather than focus on cash flow, net income, and owner's equity, the marketing plan concentrates on a company's target customers, their buying power, and their buying behavior.

This chapter is devoted to creating an effective marketing plan, which is an integral part of a total business plan. Before producing reams of computer-generated spreadsheets of financial projections, entrepreneurs must determine what to sell, to whom and how often, on what terms and at what price, and how to get the product or service to the customer. In short, a marketing plan identifies a company's target customers and describes how it will attract and keep them. The process does not have to be complex. Figure 9.1 explains how to build a seven sentence marketing strategy.

## Creating a Guerrilla Marketing Plan

*1.* Describe the components of a guerrilla marketing plan and explain the benefits of preparing one.

**Marketing** is the process of creating and delivering desired goods and services to customers and involves all of the activities associated with winning and retaining loyal customers. The secret to successful marketing is to understand what the company's target customers' needs, demands, and wants are before competitors can; to offer them the products and services that will satisfy those needs, demands, and wants; and to provide those customers with quality, service, convenience, and value so that they will keep coming back. The marketing function cuts across the entire organization, affecting every aspect of its operation—from finance and production to hiring and purchasing.

Marketing strategies are not just for megacorporations competing in international markets; small companies need effective marketing strategies as much as their largest rivals do. Although they may be small in size and cannot match their larger competitors' marketing

**FIGURE 9.1 A Seven-Sentence Marketing Strategy**
*Source:* Adapted from Alan Lautenslager, "Write a Creative Marketing Plan in Seven Sentences," *Entrepreneur,* April 24, 2006, www.entrepreneur.com/marketing/marketingideas/guerrillamarketingcolumnistallautenslager/article159486.html.

Building a successful marketing plan does not have to be complex. One marketing expert says that entrepreneurs can create the foundation of a marketing plan with just seven sentences:

1. What is the purpose of your marketing?
2. Who is your target market?
3. What is your niche?
4. What are the benefits and competitive advantage?
5. What is your company's identity?
6. What tactics, strategies and weapons will you use to carry out your marketing?
7. How much money will you spend on your marketing; in other words, what is your marketing budget?

Answering these seven questions will give you an outline of your company's marketing plan. Implementing a successful marketing plan boils down to two essentials:

1. Having a thorough understanding of your target market, including what customers want and expect from your company and its products and services.
2. Identifying the obstacles that stand in your way of satisfying customers (competitors, barriers to entry, outside influences, budgets, knowledge, and others) and eliminating them.

budgets, entrepreneurial companies are not powerless when it comes to developing effective marketing strategies. By developing **guerrilla marketing** strategies that rely on unconventional, low-cost, creative techniques, small companies can wring as much or more "bang" from their marketing bucks.

**ENTREPRENEURIAL**
**Profile**

*Peter van Stolk*
*and Jones Soda*

Facing industry giants Coca-Cola and Pepsi Cola as well as a host of other competitors in the beverage industry, tiny Jones Soda has relied on a guerrilla marketing strategy since Peter van Stolk founded the company in 1996. When Jones Soda had trouble landing shelf space from traditional beverage outlets, Van Stolk turned to what he calls "an alternative distribution strategy" for his company's uniquely flavored drinks that carry names such as Blue Bubble Gum and Green Apple. The company lured customers by stocking its colorful drinks (neon-bright reds, yellows, blues, purples, and greens) with their retro long-necked bottles and unusual labels in nontraditional venues such as surf, skate, and snowboarding shops, music stores, tattoo parlors, and clothing stores—all places where Jones Soda's target customers were likely to be. Once customers started requesting the products, more traditional beverage outlets were willing to stock the company's drinks. To keep demand strong, the company has signed an array of extreme athletes, including BMX rider Matt Hoffman, surfer Benji Weatherley, and other rising stars, to promote its line of drinks. Employees also travel through cities in RVs handing out Jones Sodas and talking up the product line among customers. Van Stolk keeps customers interested in the brand with the help of a contest that encourages them to send in pictures of themselves for use on products labels! In another brilliant marketing move, van Stolk decided to introduce special Thanksgiving flavors (soft drink sales decline in winter months) as a gag that would get his company noticed. It worked! Several major network shows picked up the story, which featured the company's Brussels Sprout, Broccoli Casserole, and Turkey and Gravy flavors. (Jones Soda donates all of the profits from its holiday packs, which fly off of store shelves, to children's charities.) "I've been in the business 10 years and have launched 80 flavors, and none of the great-tasting ones ever got on Jay Leno's show," laughs van Stolk. The exposure translated directly into increased sales. With its innovative guerrilla strategy, Jones Soda has built a unique lifestyle brand with irreverent cult status among its customer base of young people in their teens and twenties.[1]

Developing a winning marketing strategy requires a business to master three vital resources: people, information, and technology. People are the most important ingredient in formulating a successful marketing strategy. Hiring and retaining creative, talented, well-trained people to develop and implement a marketing strategy is the first step. Just as in sports, implementing a successful marketing strategy relies on an entrepreneur's ability to recruit people with the talent to do the job and to teach them to work together as a team.

In today's more sophisticated and competitive markets, successful marketing relies on a company's ability to capture data and transform it into useful, meaningful information. Information is the fuel that feeds the marketing engine. Without it, a marketing strategy soon sputters and stops. Collecting more data than competitors, putting it into a meaningful form faster, and disseminating it to everyone in the business, especially those who deal with customers, can give a company a huge competitive edge. Unfortunately, too many small business owners fail to see the importance of capturing the information needed to drive a successful marketing strategy.

Technology has proved to be a powerful marketing weapon; yet, technology alone is not the key to marketing success. Competitors may duplicate or exceed the investment a small business makes in technology, but that may not guarantee their marketing success.

*NASCAR*

At all of its stock car races, NASCAR offers fans the ability to rent or to purchase the Nextel FanView, a hand-held electronic device that gives fans access to live video feeds from inside up to seven race cars, audio signals from the radio chatter between drivers and their pit crews, on-screen displays of drivers' real-time race statistics, and even personal profiles of drivers. Another technological innovation, TrackPass, enables fans who cannot attend a race to be there in a virtual sense. TrackPass is an online subscription service that combines a live race with a 3-D video game to give race fans real time race information (including the car's speedometer and tachometer readings) and allows them to watch a race from any of three virtual camera angles and to hear the live chatter between a driver and his crew. NASCAR's innovative use of technology has added "a new dimension of interactivity that brings fans closer to the race action on the track," says a NASCAR spokesperson.[2]

The way a company integrates the use of technology into its overall marketing strategy is what matters most. Smart entrepreneurs use technology to connect with their customers.

A marketing plan focuses the company's attention on the customer and recognizes that satisfying the customer is the foundation of every business. Indeed, the customer is the central player in the cast of every business venture. According to marketing expert Ted Levitt, the primary purpose of a business is not to earn a profit; instead, it is "to create and keep a customer. The rest, given reasonable good sense, will take care of itself."[3] Every area of the business must practice putting the customer first in planning and actions. A **guerrilla marketing plan** should accomplish four objectives:

1. It should pinpoint the target markets the small company will serve.
2. It should determine customer needs, wants, and characteristics through market research.
3. It should analyze a company's competitive advantages and build a marketing strategy around them.
4. It should help create a marketing mix that meets customer needs and wants.

This chapter focuses on building a customer orientation into these four objectives of the small company's marketing plan.

## Market Diversity: Pinpointing the Target Market

*2.* Explain how small businesses can pinpoint their target markets.

One of the first steps in building a marketing plan is identifying a small company's **target market**, the group of customers at whom the company aims its products and services. The more a business learns from market research about its local markets, its customers and their buying habits and preferences, the more precisely it can focus its marketing efforts on the group(s) of prospective and existing customers who are most likely to buy its products or services.

*Blane Nordahl*

Blane Nordahl, one of the most successful cat burglars ever (until he was caught), specialized in stealing only the finest sterling silver. What made Nordahl so difficult for police to catch was his meticulous market research that allowed him to target exactly the right homes to rob. Nordahl used local libraries and publications such as the duPont *Registry* and Sotheby's *Previews* to identify and learn about upscale neighborhoods. Then he would scout out the most likely "old money" homes in those neighborhoods, carefully selecting his targets to maximize his take and to minimize the likelihood of getting caught. Nordahl's systematic approach to selecting his target market worked for more than 15 years, netting him millions of dollars' worth of ill-gotten gain before a footprint left in a hasty exit allowed police to nab him. "Of all the burglars I've ever gone up against," says one police officer, "he is absolutely the best."[4]

Although Nordahl used a creative marketing approach to achieve illegal gain, small businesses can use a similar approach to make their marketing strategies more successful. Unfortunately, most marketing experts contend that the greatest marketing mistake that small businesses make is failing to define clearly the target market to be served. Failing to pinpoint their target markets is especially ironic because small firms are ideally suited to reaching market segments that their larger rivals overlook or consider too small to be profitable. Why, then, do so many small businesses fail to pinpoint their target markets? Because identifying, defining, and researching a target market requires market research and a marketing plan, both of which involve hard work! The result is that these companies follow a sales-driven rather than a customer-driven marketing strategy. To be customer driven, an effective marketing strategy must be based on a clear, well-defined understanding of a company's target customers.

### ENTREPRENEURIAL Profile

*Jeffrey Adler and Dlush*

After working as a retail consultant, Jeffrey Adler decided to launch a retail business of his own, one that bridged the gap between a coffee bar and a smoothie shop. Adler's idea was to reinvent the traditional beverage shop by creating a store that sold juice, smoothies, milkshakes, coffee, and tea that catered to the "iPod-listening, Nordstrom-wearing, MAC cosmetics kind of gal." He chose youthful San Diego, California, where the median age is just 33.5 (compared to a median age of 36.4 for the United States as a whole) and found a marquee location in Fashion Valley Mall, an area frequented by members of his target audience. (He knew that if he could attract young women to his stores the young men would follow.) Adler's business, Dlush, is housed in a 531-square-foot, circular building that pulsates with bright colors, bold graphics, thumping music, and intense energy—the perfect environment for his target customers—and generates an amazing $1 million in sales despite its size. Targeting 14- to 24-year-olds, Adler calls Dlush "MTV in a glass" and is planning to open locations in Las Vegas, Phoenix, Bangkok, and Dubai.[5]

A "one-size-fits-all" approach to marketing no longer works because the mass market is rapidly disappearing. The population of many countries, is becoming increasingly diverse. In the United States, for example, an increasingly fragmented market of multicultural customers including Hispanic Americans, African-Americans, Asian-Americans, Native Americans, and many other populations has replaced the mass market that dominated the business world 30 years ago. In fact, by 2010, Hispanics, African Americans, Asian Americans, and other minorities will account for one-third of the nation's population. To be successful, businesses must be in tune with the multicultural nature of the modern marketplace. Small businesses that take the time to recognize, understand, and cater to the unique needs, experiences, and preferences of these multicultural markets (and their submarkets) will reap immense rewards.

Increasingly diverse populations offer businesses of all sizes tremendous marketing opportunities if they target specific customers, learn how to reach them, and offer goods and services designed specifically for them. The key to success is learning about those target customers' unique, needs, wants, and preferences. The largest and fastest-growing minority sectors in the United States today, for example, are the Hispanic and Asian populations. The more than 41.3 million Hispanic Americans now comprise the nation's single largest minority group, edging out African Americans, and constitute one-seventh of the total population in the United States. As the number of minority Americans increases, so does their purchasing power (see Figure 9.2). "The fast-paced growth of minority buying power demonstrates the increasing economic clout of minority consumers," said Jeff Humphreys, Director of the Selig Center of Economic Growth and author of *The Multicultural Economy*.[6] With more than $1 trillion in purchasing power, the Hispanic American population is an extremely attractive target market for many entrepreneurs selling everything from groceries and perfumes to houses and entertainment.[7]

### ENTREPRENEURIAL Profile

*La Curacao*

La Curacao, Los Angeles-based department store that sells everything from furniture and household appliances to jewelry and toys, has achieved impressive levels of growth by targeting Hispanic customers. The stores, which feature Mayan and Aztec architecture, an inviting and colorful atmosphere, live entertainment (including mariachi bands playing Latino music), and fun-filled contests, are designed to make Hispanic shoppers feel at home. Because managers know that their Hispanic customers view shopping as an all-day,

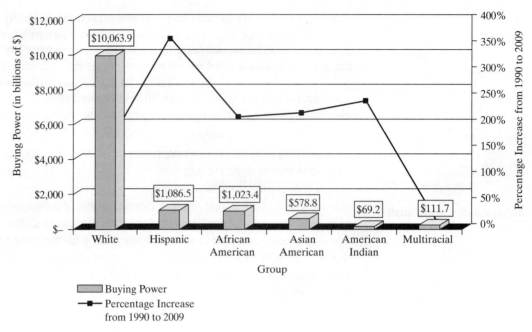

**FIGURE 9.2 U.S. Buying Power and Growth Rate**

*Source:* Jeffrey Humphrey, "The Multicultural Economy," Selig Center for Economic Growth, www.nmsdcus.org/infocenter/Multicult_Econ_2009.pdf.

family-oriented event, every store features a children's play area, where trained employees teach reading and computer skills. La Curacao stocks brands with which Hispanic shoppers are familiar, and every staff member speaks Spanish. The result is that many Hispanic customers drive past other department stores to shop at La Curacao, where they bring their families and spend the entire day.[8]

Like La Curacao, the most successful businesses have well-defined portraits of the customers they are seeking to attract. From market research, they know their customers' income levels, ages, lifestyles, buying patterns, education levels, likes and dislikes, and even their psychological profiles. At successful companies, the target customer permeates the entire business—from the merchandise it purchases and the ads it uses to the layout and décor of the store. These business owners have an advantage over their rivals because the images they have created for their companies appeal to their target customers, and that's why they prosper. Without a clear picture of its target market, a small company will try to reach almost everyone and usually will end up appealing to almost no one.

## Determining Customer Needs and Wants Through Market Research

*3-A.* Explain how to determine customer needs through market research.

The changing nature of the population is a potent force altering the landscape of business. Shifting patterns in age, income, education, race, and other population characteristics (which are the subject of demographics) have a major impact on companies, their customers, and the way they do business with those customers. Entrepreneurs who ignore demographic trends and fail to adjust their strategies accordingly run the risk of their companies' becoming competitively obsolete as their target customers pass them by.

A demographic trend is like a train; an entrepreneur must find out early on where it's going and decide whether to get on board. Waiting until the train is roaring down the tracks and gaining speed means it's too late to get on board. However, by checking the schedule early and planning ahead, an entrepreneur may wind up at the train's controls wearing the engineer's hat! Similarly, small companies that spot demographic trends early and act on them can gain a distinctive edge in the market. Entrepreneurs must align their businesses with as many demographic, social, and cultural trends as possible. Staying on trend means staying in synchronization with the market as it shifts and changes over time. The more

"Washrooms are down the hall."

trends a business converges with, the more likely it is to be successful. Conversely, a business moving away from significant trends in society is in danger of losing its customer base.

By performing some basic market research, entrepreneurs can detect key demographic, social, and cultural trends and zero in on the needs, wants, preferences, and desires of its target customers. Indeed, every business can benefit from a better understanding of its market, customers, and competitors. **Market research** is the vehicle for gathering the information that serves as the foundation for the marketing plan. It involves systematically collecting, analyzing, and interpreting data pertaining to the small company's market, customers, and competitors. Businesses face the challenge of reaching the highly fragmented markets that have emerged today, and market research can help them. Market research allows entrepreneurs to answer questions such as: Who are my customers and potential customers? What is their gender? To which age group(s) do they belong? What is their income level? What kind of people are they? Where do they live? Do they rent or own their own homes? What are they looking for in the products or services I sell? How often do they buy these products or services? What models, styles, colors, or flavors do they prefer? Why do or don't they buy from my store? How do the strengths of my product or service serve their needs and wants? What hours do they prefer to shop? How do they perceive my business? Which advertising media are most likely to reach them? How do customers perceive my business versus competitors? This information is an integral part of developing an effective marketing plan.

When marketing its goods and services, a small company must avoid mistakes because there is little margin for error when funds are scarce and budgets are tight. Small businesses simply cannot afford to miss their target markets, and market research can help them zero in on the bull's eye. That usually requires conducting market research up front, *before* launching a company. One of the worst—and most common—mistakes entrepreneurs make is *assuming* that a market exists for their products or services. The time to find out whether customers are likely to buy a product or a service is before investing thousands of dollars to launch it! Market research can tell entrepreneurs whether a sufficient customer base exists and how likely those customers are to buy their products and services. In addition to collecting and analyzing demographic data about their target customers, entrepreneurs can learn a great deal by actually observing, mingling with, and interviewing customers as they shop. One company videotapes customers while they are shopping to get a clear picture of their buying habits. This hands-on market research allows entrepreneurs to get past the barriers that customers often put up and to uncover their true preferences and hidden thoughts.

*Maker's Mark*

Researchers for Maker's Mark, a Kentucky bourbon distillery, have gathered some of their most meaningful data while talking to customers and potential customers in bars across the country. Their up-close-and-personal approach allows them to get a handle on customers' attitudes and behavior in a way that more traditional techniques cannot.[9]

Many entrepreneurs are discovering the speed, the convenience, and the low cost of conducting market research over the World Wide Web. Online surveys, customer opinion polls, and other research projects are easy to conduct, cost virtually nothing, produce quick responses, and help companies connect with their customers. Insight Express, an online market research firm, estimates that online surveys cost just 20 percent of what it costs to conduct a mail survey and only 10 percent of what it costs for a telephone survey.[10] With Web-based surveys, businesses can get real-time feedback from customers, often using surveys they have designed themselves. Web sites such as Survey Monkey and Zoomerang allow entrepreneurs to conduct low-cost (in some cases free) online surveys of existing or prospective customers. A recent comparison study of online and mail surveys found that response rates are higher for online surveys than for mail surveys.[11]

Market research does *not* have to be time consuming, complex, or expensive to be useful. Market research for a small business can be informal; it does not have to be highly sophisticated nor expensive to be valuable.

*Newbury Comics*

At Newbury Comics, a 21-year-old chain of music and novelty stores in the northeastern United States, managers see the necessity of keeping up with the rapidly changing tastes of their young target customers who are typically in their twenties. To stay plugged in, the company hosts small groups of customers at informal dinners of hamburgers and beers, where managers learn what their customers are thinking. Based on feedback from these meetings, Newbury Comics has shifted its advertising from newspapers and radio to transit ads and movie theater advertising.

## How to Conduct Market Research

**3-B.** Outline the steps in the market research process.

The goal of market research is to reduce the risks associated with making business decisions. It can replace misinformation and assumptions with facts. Opinion and hearsay are not viable foundations on which to build a solid marketing strategy. Successful market research consists of four steps:

### Step 1: Define the Objective

The first and most crucial step in market research is defining the research objective clearly and concisely. A common flaw at this stage is to confuse a symptom with the true problem. For example, dwindling sales is not a problem; it is a symptom. To get to the heart of the matter, an entrepreneur must consider all the possible factors that could have caused it. Is there new competition? Are the firm's sales representatives impolite or unknowledgeable? Have customer tastes changed? Is the product line too narrow? Do customers have trouble finding what they want? In other cases, an entrepreneur may be interested in researching a specific question. What are the characteristics of my customers? What are their income levels? What radio stations do they listen to? Why do they shop here? What factors are most important to their buying decisions? What impact do in-store displays have on their purchasing patterns? Do they enjoy their shopping experience? If so, why? If not, why not? What would they like to see my store do differently?

Business owners also can use market research to uncover new market opportunities as well. For example, when the owner of a fitness center surveyed his customers, he discovered that many had an interest in aerobic exercises. He added an aerobics program, and within a year his revenues had grown by 25 percent.

### Step 2: Collect the Data

The marketing approach that companies of all sizes strive to achieve is **individualized** (or **one-to-one**) **marketing**, a system of gathering data on individual customers and then developing a marketing plan designed specifically to appeal to their individual needs, tastes, and preferences. Its goal is not only to attract customers but also to keep them and to increase their purchases. In a society in which people feel so isolated and transactions are so impersonal, one-to-one marketing gives a business a competitive advantage. Companies following this approach know their customers, understand how to give them the value they want, and perhaps most important, know how to make them feel special and important. The goal is to treat each customer as an individual.

*The Ritz–Carlton*

The Ritz–Carlton hotel group uses a centralized computer network called Mystique that tracks its guests' preferences and spending habits with the company and provides information to all of the hotels in the chain so that they can offer guests individual attention. When a guest checks in, the desk clerk will know, for instance, that he or she prefers a queen-size bed with foam pillows, a stock of Le Bleu bottled water in the minibar, and a glass of orange juice and a copy of the *Wall Street Journal* with breakfast. Offering these "extras" without requiring the customer to ask for them makes hotel guests feel as though the hotel is catering specifically to their unique needs and preferences.[12]

Individualized marketing requires business owners to gather and assimilate detailed information about their customers. Fortunately, owners of even the smallest companies now have access to affordable technology that creates and manages computerized databases, allowing them to develop close, one-to-one relationships with their customers. Much like gold nuggets waiting to be discovered, significant amounts of valuable information about customers and their buying habits is hidden *inside* many small businesses, tucked away in computerized databases. For most business owners, collecting useful information about their customers and potential new products and markets is simply a matter of sorting and organizing data that are already floating around somewhere in their companies. "Most companies are data rich and information poor," claims one marketing expert.[13] The key is to mine these data and turn them into useful information that allows the company to "court" its customers with special products, services, ads, and offers that appeal most to them.

Thanks to advances in computer hardware and software, data mining, once available only to large companies with vast computer power, is now possible for even very small businesses. **Data mining** is a process that uses statistical analysis, database technology, and artificial intelligence to find hidden patterns, trends, and connections in data so that business owners can make better marketing decisions and predictions about their customers' behavior. Finding relationships among the many components of a data set, identifying clusters of customers with similar buying habits, and predicting customers' buying patterns, data mining gives entrepreneurs incredible marketing power. Popular data mining software packages include Clementine, DataScope Pro, GoldMine, MineSet, and many others.

For an effective individualized marketing campaign to be successful, business owners must collect and mine three types of information:

1. *Geographic.* Where are my customers located? Do they tend to be concentrated in one geographic region?
2. *Demographic.* What are the characteristics of my customers (age, education levels, income, sex, marital status, and many other features).
3. *Psychographic.* What drives my customers' buying behavior? Are they receptive to new products or are they among the last to accept them? What values are most important to them?

*Henry Singer Fashion Group*

The Henry Singer Fashion Group, a third generation, family-owned menswear retailer with two locations in Alberta, Canada, relies on its point of sale terminals, a well-trained, observant sales force, and data mining software to track the needs of its customers and to direct its marketing efforts with laser-like focus. Sifting through its database of 20,000 customers, Singer creates customized wardrobes for its best customers, using their lifestyles, careers, and hobbies as guides. The company also uses data mining to customize its direct mail campaigns. "We can [send] specific letters to our Canali, Brioni, or Giorgio [Armani] clients, on events such as a trunk show or a shoe clinic when a company's representative is coming in," says Elaine Saxer, Singer's information systems manager.[14]

Figure 9.3 explains how to become an effective individualized marketer.

### Step 3: Analyze and Interpret the Data

The results of market research alone do not provide a solution to the problem; the owner must attach some meaning to them. What do the facts mean? Is there a common thread running through the responses? Do the results suggest any changes needed in the way the business is run? Are there new opportunities the owner can take advantage of? There are no hard-and-fast rules for interpreting market research results; entrepreneurs must use judgment and common sense to determine what the numbers mean.

*William Pulte and Pulte Holmes*

William Pulte is owner of what has become the second largest home-building company in the United States by relying on market research to reveal where to locate housing developments and how to design the homes in them. Pulte's research has identified 11 distinct customer segments (ranging from "starters" to "retired/independents") and the features they most want in their homes. Market research also tells him in which markets these target segments are most underserved, allowing him to build homes there and sell them quickly, one of the keys to success in the industry. For instance, in San Francisco, Pulte recently identified an underserved market for "starters," first-time homeowners. Further research showed that these young professionals wanted stylish housing with a unique flair that was low-maintenance. Pulte purchased and renovated an old fruit-processing plant in a suburban area, transforming it into chic row houses and lofts. The night before the units went on sale, hopeful buyers camped out so they could be first in line to buy their dream homes.[15]

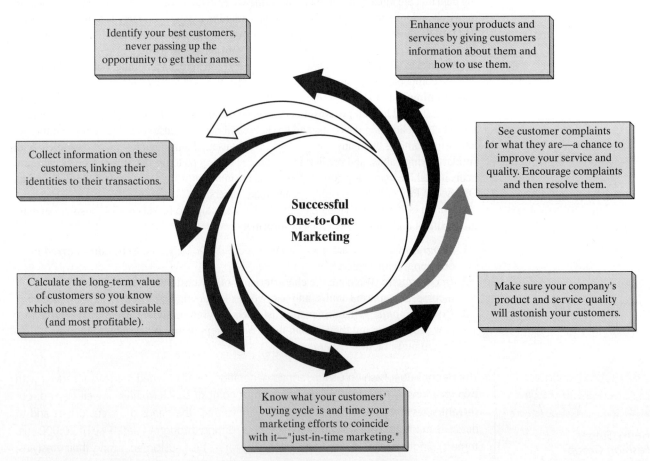

**FIGURE 9.3  How to Become an Effective One-to-One Marketer**

*Source:* Adapted from Susan Greco, "The Road to One-to-One Marketing," *Inc.*, October 1995, pp. 56–66.

### Step 4: Put the Information to Work

The market research process is not complete until business owners act on the information collected. Based on their understanding of what the facts really mean, owners must then decide how to use the information in their businesses. For example, the owner of a women's clothing shop discovered from a survey that her customers preferred evening shopping hours over early morning hours. She made the schedule adjustment, and sales began to climb.

## Plotting a Guerrilla Marketing Strategy: Building a Competitive Edge

*4.* Describe the guerrilla marketing strategies on which a small business can build a competitive edge in the marketplace.

A competitive edge is crucial for business success. A small business has a competitive edge when customers perceive that the company and its products or services are superior to those of its competitors. The right marketing strategy, not size or financial resources, is a key determinant of how successful a business is at achieving a competitive advantage. Although they may be smaller and lack the marketing budgets of their larger rivals, small companies can gain a competitive advantage using creative, low-cost guerrilla marketing strategies that hit home with their target customers. Independent bookstores have discovered that large chains use their buying power to get volume discounts and undercut the independents' prices. Individual shop owners are finding new ways, such as special ordering, adult reading groups, educational classes, children's story hours, newsletters, book-signing events, and targeting unique niches to differentiate themselves and to retain loyal customers. These entrepreneurs are finding that the best way to gain a competitive advantage is to create value by giving customers what they really want that they cannot get elsewhere.

Successful businesses often use the special advantages they have to build a competitive edge over their larger rivals. Their close contact with the customer, personal attention, focus on service, and organizational and managerial flexibility provide a solid foundation from which to build a towering competitive edge in the market. Small companies can exploit their size to become more effective than their larger rivals at **relationship marketing** or **customer relationship management (CRM)**—developing, maintaining, and managing long-term relationships with customers so that they will want to keep coming back to make repeat purchases. CRM puts the customer at the center of a company's thinking, planning, and action and shifts the focus from a product or service to customers and their needs and wants. CRM requires business owners to take the following steps:

- Collect meaningful information about existing customers and compile it in a database.
- Mine the database to identify the company's best and most profitable customers, their needs, and their buying habits. In most companies, a small percentage of customers account for the majority of sales and profits. These are the customers on whom a business should focus its attention and efforts.
- Focus on developing lasting relationships with these customers. This often requires entrepreneurs to "fire" some customers that require more attention, time, and expense than they generate in revenue for the business. Failing to do so reduces a company's return on its CRM effort.
- Attract more customers who fit the profile of the company's best customers.

Business owners are discovering that even though they may be providing their customers with satisfactory service and value, many of their customers do not remain loyal, choosing instead to buy from other companies. Businesses that provide poor customer service are in grave danger. Hepworth, a consulting firm that specializes in customer retention, measures its clients' **revenue at risk**, which calculates the sales revenue a company would lose by measuring the percentage of customers who would leave because of poor service. According to Hepworth's research, for companies that score in the top 25 percent on customer loyalty, revenue at risk averages just 3 percent. However, for companies that rate loyalty scores in the bottom 25 percent, poor customer service puts at risk an average of more than 12 percent of company revenue.[16] Today, earning customers' loyalty requires businesses

## FISHing for Success

If you ever find yourself in Pike Place in Seattle, Washington and you hear yelling, boisterous laughter, and thunderous applause, step closer, and you'll see an animated crowd of people from all walks of life at the Pike Place market having a blast! You'll see tourists who wandered by, amazed at the energy of the show they are enjoying, and the yogurt crowd, businesspeople from local offices who come by almost every day to eat their cups of yogurt (which they often hoist into the air as they cheer the fishmongers on). Most people's first reaction is "What is going on here? Is this place for real?" Indeed, it is for real, and the Pike Place Fish Market offers entrepreneurs a valuable lesson in employee relations and motivation and in creating a base of loyal customers.

Pike Place Fish is famous for its playful, bustling, and raucous atmosphere and for its success at creating an environment that has transformed its employees from bored fishmongers who took little pride in their smelly, monotonous work into fish-selling dynamos who derive a great deal of pleasure from their work in the joyful setting they have created for themselves. Pike Place Fish has become widely known as the subject of popular books, including *FISH!* and *FISH! TALES,* and of videos based on the best-selling books. Companies of all sizes and in a multitude of industries have become students of this humble fish market so they can learn the principles that have made it wildly successful. What are those principles?

*FISH! Principle 1. Choose your attitude.* There is always a choice about the way you do your work, even if there is not a choice about the work itself. The employees at the Pike Place Fish market discovered that even though they cannot change the nature of their work (i.e., selling fish is smelly, hard work with days that start very early and can stretch for long hours), they did have control about the attitudes they brought to work. "We can bring a grouchy attitude and irritate our coworkers and customers," says one employee, "or we can bring a sunny, playful, cheerful attitude and have a great day."

*FISH! Principle 2. Play.* At the Pike Place Fish Market, flying fish are a common occurrence! When a customer places an order, one of the employees yells out, "One salmon flying away to Minnesota!" All the other em-

ployees repeat in unison, "One salmon flying away to Minnesota!" The employee, decked out in his black rubber boots and white apron, grabs the salmon and then flings the fish through the air toward a coworker behind the counter, who makes an amazing one-handed catch before wrapping the fish for the customer. The crowd loves it, giving the cast of "fish performers" an enthusiastic round of applause. The scene is reminiscent of a playground—the only difference is that it's a group of adults at work who look like they're at recess. Still, the energy is electric.

*FISH Principle 3. Make their day.* The playful attitude of the employees at the Pike Place Fish Market allows them to connect with their customers. These workers don't stand back; they mingle with the crowd, making eye contact with potential customers and talking with them. They engage their customers! "We try not to stand apart from our customers," says one worker, "but to find ways to respectfully include them in our fun. When we are successful, it makes their day."

*FISH Principle 4. Be present.* The "fish guys" stay focused while working with customers. They are vigilant, focused on customers, looking for the next opportunity for action. *That's* what enables them to make a customer's day. They put their customers' needs before their own. Customers recognize that and respond.

Although most businesses can't throw fish around for fun, any business can use the FISH! Principles to become a better place. At a small hospital, nurses were having a difficult time with an elderly patient who was near death. He was incoherent, agitated, and trying to pull out his intravenous tubes. When nurse assistant Leo Carter found out that the man had been an orchestra conductor for many years, his FISH! training took over. He had an idea. "I have my clarinet in my car," he told a nurse, who offered to cover for him while he retrieved the instrument. Leo assembled the instrument, practiced for a few minutes, and then went into the elderly patient's room. He played a classical piece, "Peter and the Wolf," and then the theme from *The Muppet Show.* Almost immediately, the man stopped thrashing and began to settle down. He lay on his back, raised his hands, and began to move them as if conducting *his* orchestra as Leo played. After a few minutes, the man slowly moved his arms to his side, and he slept peacefully for the rest of the night. Leo had the next few days off, and when he returned to work, he learned that the man had died—peacefully, something for which his family credited Leo's kind gesture.

*Sources:* Adapted from Stephen C. Lundin, Harry Paul, and John Christensen, *FISH!* (New York: Hyperion Publishing Company, 2000); Stephen C. Lundin, Harry Paul, and John Christensen, *FISH!* (New York: ChartHouse Learning Publishers, 2002).

to take customer focus and service to unprecedented levels, and that requires building long-term relationships with customers.

### Guerrilla Marketing Principles

To be successful guerrilla marketers, entrepreneurs must be as innovative in creating their marketing strategies as they are in developing new product and service ideas. The following fourteen guerrilla marketing principles can help business owners develop a competitive edge: "niche-picking," "entertailing," building a consistent branding strategy, starting a blog, using online social networks, emphasizing their uniqueness, connecting with their customers, focusing on customers' needs, emphasizing quality, paying attention to convenience, concentrating on innovation, retaining existing customers, dedicating themselves to service, and emphasizing speed.

**FIND A NICHE AND FILL IT.**  As we saw in Chapter 2, "Strategic Management and the Entrepreneur," many successful small companies choose their niches carefully and defend them fiercely rather than compete head-to-head with larger rivals. A niche strategy allows a small company to maximize the advantages of its size and to compete effectively even in industries dominated by giants. Focusing on niches that are too small to be attractive to large companies or in which entrepreneurs have unique expertise are common recipes for success among thriving small companies.

**ENTREPRENEURIAL Profile**

*Jalem Getz and Buycostumes.com*

Jalem Getz launched Buycostumes.com, an online company that specializes in holiday costumes for both children and adults, in 1999 as a brick-and-mortar retail store. Earlier, Getz had operated a series of seasonal specialty stores in kiosks in shopping malls. "Our idea was that we would be the gypsies of retail," he says. "The whole model was seasonal." Getz saw the potential that the Web offered for his business and shifted his entire operation online, where he offers the most extensive selection of costumes anywhere—more than 10,000 costumes, 100 times the number that a typical retailer carries. By dominating a niche, Getz has guided Buycostumes.com from start-up to more than $30 million in annual sales.[17]

Jalem Getz, founder of Buycostumes.com

"Small business is uniquely positioned for niche marketing," says marketing expert Phil Kotler. "If a small business sits down and follows the principles of targeting, segmenting, and differentiating, it doesn't have to collapse to larger companies."[18]

**DON'T JUST SELL; ENTERTAIN.**   Numerous surveys have shown that consumers are bored with shopping and that they are less inclined to spend their scarce leisure time shopping than ever before. Winning customers today requires more than low prices and wide merchandise selection; increasingly, businesses are adopting strategies based on **"entertailing,"** the notion of drawing customers into a store by creating a kaleidoscope of sights, sounds, smells, and activities, all designed to entertain—and, of course, sell (think Disney). The primary goal of entertailing is to catch customers' attention and engage them in some kind of entertaining experience so that they shop longer and buy more goods or services. Entertailing involves "making [shopping] more fun, more educational, more interactive," says one retail consultant.[19] Research supports the benefits of entertailing's hands-on, interactive, educational, approach to selling; one study found that, when making a purchase, 34 percent of consumers are driven more by emotional factors such as fun and excitement than by logical factors such as price and convenience.[20]

*Maxine Clark and Build-A-Bear Workshop*

One small company that has successfully blended show business with the retail business is Build-A-Bear Workshop, a chain of retail stores where children of all ages can go to design and build their own teddy bears. As children enter a Build-A-Bear Workshop, they become Guest Bear Builders, and their first stop is the "Choose Me" station, where they select the unstuffed skin that will become their teddy bear (or monkey, frog, bunny, or other animal). The next stop is the "Hear Me" area, where children pick the sounds their animals will make. The message can be prerecorded, or the children can record the sounds themselves. Next, guests go to the "Stuff Me" station, where with the help of an employee (a Master Bear Builder), they fill their animals to just the right volume on a machine that resembles a large popcorn popper. Each child then picks a tiny pillowy heart to be inserted before the stuffed animal is stitched up. Kids groom their new creations into just the right shape at the "Fluff Me" station before moving on to a row of computers where they name their animals and complete a birth certificate for them. Customers can choose from an assortment of clothing options—from argyle sweaters to athletic shoes—and accessories such as toy cell phones for their stuffed animals. At the cash register, each guest receives a printed birth certificate signed by "Maxine Clark, C.E.B (Chief Executive Bear)." The customer's new friend is packed safely into a house-shaped box, ready for the journey to its new home. Clark's unique brand of entertailing has made Build-A-Bear Workshops highly successful. The chain averages sales of $600 per square foot of store space, twice that of the average mall store. "Retailing is entertainment, and the store is a stage," says Clark. "When customers have fun, they spend more money," says Clark.[21]

**CONNECT WITH CUSTOMERS ON AN EMOTIONAL LEVEL.**   Some of the most powerful marketers are those companies that have a clear sense of who they are, what they stand for, and why they exist. Defining their vision for their companies in a meaningful way is one of the most challenging tasks facing entrepreneurs. As we learned in Chapter 2, that vision stems from the beliefs and values of the entrepreneur and is reflected in a company's culture, ethics, and business strategy. Although it is intangible, this vision is a crucial ingredient in a successful guerrilla marketing campaign. Once this vision is firmly planted, guerrilla marketers can use it to connect with their customers. Harley-Davidson, the maker of classic motorcycles with that trademark throaty rumble, has established an emotional connection with its customers that many other businesses only dream of.

Companies that establish deeper relationships with their customers rather than one based merely on making a sale have the capacity to be exceptional guerrilla marketers. These businesses win because customers receive an emotional boost every time they buy the company's product or service. Companies connect with their customers emotionally by supporting causes that are important to their customer base, sponsoring events that are of interest to their customers, taking exceptional care of their customers, and making it fun and enjoyable to do business with them.

*Missy Park and
Title Nine*

When she was a collegiate athlete in the 1980s, Missy Park was disheartened by the absence of athletic gear made specifically for women. "We wore men's shorts," says the former Yale basketball player. "There was no women's basketball shoe. Jog bras didn't even exist." Spotting a business opportunity, Park launched a mail-order company that sold women's athletic apparel from the garage of her Emeryville, California, home in 1989. Today, Park's business, Title Nine, is a multi-million-dollar company with nine retail stores, a popular Web site, and thousands of loyal customers. Park finds many ways to connect with her company's customers. Title Nine's catalog and Web site feature "real women" as models (they include a full-time mom and a teacher), and the company organizes numerous athletic events, including hikes, bicycling tours, and a Mother's Day run, that are designed to transform regular customers into friends and ambassadors for the business. "As long as we are relevant [to our customers], they're going to choose to shop with us, spend Mother's Day with us, spend their evenings with us, and that, in the end, translates into a profitable, growing business," says Park.[22]

**BUILD A CONSISTENT BRANDING STRATEGY.**    Establishing an emotional bond with its customers is the first step to building a successful brand. Branding involves creating a distinct identity for a business and requires a well-coordinated effort at every touch point a company has with its customers. A brand represents a company's "personality," and entrepreneurs should spell out their companies' brand strategy in the business plan. In an age where companies find standing out from the crowd of competitors increasingly difficult, branding strategies have taken on much greater importance. The foundation of a successful brand is providing a quality product or superior customer service that meets or, preferably, exceeds customers' expectations. One way to do this is by defining exactly how your company's product or service solves a problem your customers face, preferably in a unique fashion. Although entrepreneurs don't have the resources to invest in building a brand as large as Coca-Cola and Nike (Coca-Cola's brand alone is estimated to be worth more than *$67 billion*), they can take steps to add value to their companies' images through branding. Another way is to develop consistent logos, letterheads, and graphics that serve as visual ambassadors for the company, communicating its desired image, values, and personality at a glance. Yet another aspect of creating a successful brand is to transform existing customers into evangelists for the company and its products by keeping them happy. Convincing celebrities to become customers also helps. Lisa Thurman and Sue Katz, founders of AmazingCosmetics, were able to convince a group of professional make-up artists to introduce their line of makeup to celebrities such as Demi Moore and Nicole Kidman, which provided a major sales boost to their young company. "Having celebrity clients is a great way to build a brand!" says Katz.[23]

**START A BLOG.**    A **Web log ("blog")** is a frequently updated online personal journal that contains a writer's ideas on a multitude of topics with links to related sites. The proliferation of blogs has been stupendous; everyone from teenagers to giant corporations has created blogs. Technorati, a company that tracks blogs, estimates that 60 million blogs exist online, with 100,000 more being added daily.[24] The most successful small business blogs

## ■ The Power of a Brand

Successful entrepreneurs understand the power of a brand. For companies that are able to build them, strong brands lead to higher sales levels, increased market share, and a significant competitive advantage. Coca-Cola's soft drinks, Apple's iPods, Subway's sandwiches, and Google's search engine have drawn on the power of their brands to become market leaders in their industries. Small companies don't have the marketing budgets that these companies have to build a recognizable brand, but the good news is that they don't have to! Small companies can build strong, effective brands without blistering their marketing budgets. The key is to understand the foundations on which a powerful brand is built. According to research by Landor Associates and BrandEconomics, both brand consulting firms, two components are significant to building a successful brand: strength and stature.

A brand's strength is a combination of two forces: differentiation and relevance. Differentiation is the degree to which a brand stands out from its competition. Relevance is the extent to which customers believe a brand meets their needs. Both factors are necessary to build a strong brand, but they do not always go together. For instance, Rolls Royce has excellent differentiation in the automotive market but has hardly any relevance because very few buyers are able to spend $300,000 on a car. Kleenex is a highly relevant brand but lacks differentiation because most customers see facial tissue as a commodity product. The best brands have both strength and relevance.

A brand's stature also is made up of two components: esteem and knowledge. Esteem is how highly customers regard a brand. Knowledge is the extent to which customers understand a brand. Once again, these two elements do not always go hand-in-hand. The packaged food Hamburger Helper is very easy for customers to understand, but it lacks esteem. Many high tech companies' products carry high esteem but are difficult for customers to understand. The strongest brands carry both high levels of knowledge and esteem.

The payoff for building a strong brand of high stature is huge. Research by BrandEconomics suggests that brands that score high on both strength and stature have an intangible value of 250 percent of a company's annual sales; the value of mediocre brands is just 70 percent of a company's annual sales. What steps can a small company with a modest marketing budget take to build a powerful brand?

### Define Your Company's Brand Message by Identifying Key Points of Differentiation for Your Company and Its Products and Services

One way to accomplish this is to study your key competitors' ads, press coverage, and Web sites. Then look at your own business and decide what sets it apart. These points of differentiation should become the foundation of your company's brand message. One caveat: Make sure that the points you identify are relevant to your customers' buying decisions.

When Stephanie Chandler decided to build a stronger brand for her business, Book Lovers Bookstore, she decided that the three factors that set her company apart were her shop's neatness, organization (which made it easy for customers to find the books they were looking for), and friendliness. Those three traits became the core of her company's brand message.

### Develop a Profile of Your Company's Target Customers

A company's products and services provide value for customers in many ways—from their performance (e.g., a glass cleaner that cleans glass really well) to their intangible characteristics (a clothing label that enhances a customer's self perception and status). Entrepreneurs must understand which factors drive their customers' buying behavior, and the best way to do that is to study them. Secondary research is helpful, but face-to-face contact with customers often is more revealing. The goal is to develop a clear portrait of your company's target customer.

At Book Lovers Bookstore, Stephanie Chandler already had many loyal customers who loved her bookstore; she just needed more of them. Once she understood the characteristics of her best (target) customers, she was able to focus her company's marketing efforts on attracting more customers who were like them.

## Deliver Value for Your Customers and Make Sure That They Know It

Few things destroy a business and its brand faster than making promises to customers in a marketing message and then failing to deliver on those promises. Your job is to ensure that your company lives up to the promises you make in your branding message. Do not assume that your customers understand the value that your company provides them; it's your job to show them! For Stephanie Chandler, that meant making sure that her bookstore was always neat and organized (including easy-to-understand signage) and that employees were friendly and well trained.

## Integrate Your Brand Messages into a Unified Whole

A company's brand message should project its desired image and tell customers what it stands for. Every interaction a customer has with a company should reinforce the brand message in a clear, consistent fashion—no matter what marketing channel or media it involves. Stephanie Chandler hired a team of marketing and design experts to create a new logo and brand image for Book Lovers Bookstore that reflected the unique elements of her shop: neatly stacked books, a friendly cat (to remind customers of the two "shop cats" that serve as the store's goodwill ambassadors), warm, inviting

colors, and a crisp, stylish font. Chandler now uses the design on everything associated with her company—letterhead, calendars, newsletters, the Web site, business sign, and the store interior. "[The new design] has captured the essence of my shop—whimsical and fun but professional," says a beaming Chandler.

1. Is it necessary for a company to spend large amounts of money to build a strong brand? Explain.
2. Select three brands that appeal to you and evaluate them on a scale of 1 (low) to 10 (high) on the following factors: differentiation, relevance, esteem, and knowledge. Which of the brands scored the highest? Ask a classmate to evaluate the same three brands. How does his or her score compare to yours? What are the implications of this?
3. Evaluate the impact of the following products on these brands: a Harley-Davidson cake decorating kit, an Everlast line of fragrances and grooming products, and Sylvester Stallone low-carb pudding. What predictions do you make about the success of these products? Explain.

*Sources:* Adapted from Kim T. Gordon, "Brand Slam," *Entrepreneur,* August 2006, pp. 81–82; Al Ehrbar, "Breakaway Brands," *Fortune,* October 31, 2005, pp. 153–170; Gwen Moran, "The Next Chapter," *Entrepreneur,* April 2006, pp. 35–38; Lucas Conley, "When Brand Extensions Go Bad," *Fast Company,* October 2006, p. 38.

are not just remakes of a company's Web site with thinly veiled marketing messages but instead are those that tell interesting stories from the perspective of an industry (and company) insider. The key to successful business blogging is to create a blog that provides useful industry information but that also is entertaining.

Business blogging can be an effective part of a guerrilla marketing strategy, enabling entrepreneurs to reach large numbers of potential customers very economically. Blogs can help establish a business owner as an expert in the field, attract the attention of potential customers, and boost a company's visibility and its sales. Companies post their blogs, promote them on their Web sites and on other blogs, and then watch as the viral nature of the Web takes over with visitors posting comments and e-mailing their friends about the blog. In fact many small companies allow customers to contribute to their blogs, offering the potential for one of the most valuable marketing tools: unsolicited endorsements from satisfied users. Blogging's informal dialogue is an ideal match for small companies, whose cultures and style tend to be informal.

Blogs can serve many business purposes, including keeping customers updated on new products, enhancing customer service, and promoting the company. Increasingly, they are becoming mainstream features on business Web sites. If monitored regularly, blogs also can give entrepreneurs keen insight into customers' viewpoints and preferences in ways that few other techniques can. One business writer says that blogs are "like never-ending focus groups."[25] Creating a blog is not risk-free, however. Companies must be prepared to deal with negative feedback from some visitors.

**USE SOCIAL NETWORKS.**   The immense popularity of social networking Web sites such as MySpace.com and Facebook provides a unique marketing opportunity for small businesses. These sites, which allow networks of friends to connect with one another, are the online version of word-of-mouth advertising: people who are passionate about a company and its products or services tell others about it. Social commerce recognizes a trend in online marketing: customers are becoming "friends" with the brands that are meaningful to them.

*Rob Washburn and Bones*

Rob Washburn, owner of Bones, a small skateboard shop, created a MySpace profile for his brand and maintains it daily, posting photos, stories, and links (including one to his company's Web site, of course). "I try not to make it obvious that I'm trying to push Bones," says Washburn. "I talk to kids about what's up and post bulletins to all of my 1,000-plus friends. It's great because it's all free." Washburn says that at least half of the hits that Bones' Web site receives originate on the link posted on his company's MySpace page.[26]

Companies that use social commerce as a marketing tool are taking an active approach to make sure that they become part of their customers' online networks. Business users of MySpace, for instance, often browse the site for "network neighbors," people who are connected to their existing customers or who have similar demographic characteristics as their existing customers. A study by the University of Pennsylvania's Wharton College found that existing customers' network neighbors were three to fives times more likely to purchase a new service than were potential customers who were contacted using traditional marketing techniques.[27]

**STRIVE TO BE UNIQUE.**   One of the most effective guerrilla marketing tactics is to create an image of uniqueness for your business. Entrepreneurs can achieve a unique place in the market in a variety of ways, including through the products and services they offer, the marketing and promotional campaigns they use, the store layouts they design, and the business strategies they employ. The goal is to stand out from the crowd; few things are as uninspiring to customers as a "me-too" business that offers nothing unique. At Buycostumes.com, the primary differentiating factor is the company's extensive product line. Costume selections range from Mickey Mouse and Santa Claus to sports team mascots and Barbie at prices that can accommodate any budget—from just a few dollars to more than $800. "Our selection sets us apart," says founder Jalem Getz.[28]

**FOCUS ON THE CUSTOMER.**   Too many companies have lost sight of the most important component of every business: the customer. Research shows that businesses often lose about half of their customer base every five years, and many of those defections are the result of companies failing to take care of their customers.[29] Businesses finally are waking up to the true costs of poor customer relations. For instance:

- Customers are five times more likely to leave because of poor service than they are for product quality or price.[30]
- Ninety-four percent of dissatisfied customers never complain to the business about rude or discourteous service, but . . .
  - Ninety-one percent will not buy from the business again.[31]
  - Thirty-one percent will tell others about their negative experience.
  - Forty-eight percent of customers say that they have avoided a store because of someone else's negative experience with it.

According to The Retail Customer Dissatisfaction Study, if 100 of a retailer's customers have a bad experience, the company stands to lose, on average, 34 current or potential customers.[32] Because most of a company's sales come from existing customers, no business can afford to alienate them.

The most successful small businesses have developed a customer orientation and have instilled an attitude of customer satisfaction throughout the company. Companies with world-class customer attitudes set themselves apart by paying attention to the little things. For example, at one dentist's office, staff members take photos on a patient's first visit. The photo, placed in the patient's file, allows everyone in the office to call him or her by name on subsequent visits. A small flower shop offers a special service for customers who forget that special event. The shop will insert a card reading, "Please forgive us! Being short-handed this week, we were unable to deliver this gift on time. We hope the sender's thoughtfulness will not be less appreciated because of our error. Again, we apologize."[33]

How do these companies focus so intently on their customers? They follow basic principles:

- When you create a dissatisfied customer, fix the problem fast. One study found that, given the chance to complain, 95 percent of customers will buy again if a business handles their complaints promptly and effectively.[34] The worst way to handle a complaint is to ignore it, to pass it off to a subordinate, or to let a lot of time slip by before dealing with it.
- *Encourage* customer complaints. You can't fix something if you don't know it's broken. Figure 9.4 describes nine ways to turn complaints into satisfied customers.
- Ask employees for feedback on improving customer service. A study by Technical Assistance Research Programs (TARP), a customer service research firm, found that frontline service workers can predict nearly 90 percent of the cases that produce customer complaints.[35] Put that expertise to work by involving frontline employees in process improvement efforts. Emphasize that *everyone* is part of the customer satisfaction team.
- Get total commitment to superior customer service from top managers and allocate resources appropriately.

**FIGURE 9.4 Ways to Turn Complainers into Satisfied Customers**

*Sources:* Adapted from Brian Caufield, "How to Win Customer Loyalty," *Business 2.0,* March 2004, pp. 77–78; Shirley Bednarz, "Fine Whine," *Entrepreneur,* February 1999, pp. 103–105; "Five Ways to Turn Complaints into Satisfied Customers," *Personal Selling Power,* April 1991, p. 53; "Handling Disgruntled Customers," *Your Company,* Spring 1993, p. 5.

When faced with a complaining customer, business owners naturally defend their companies. Don't do it! Here are nine ways to turn disgruntled buyers into loyal customers.

1. Let unhappy customers vent their feelings; don't interrupt; maintain eye contact and listen to them.
2. Remain objective; avoid labeling customers' emotions or passing judgment on them.
3. Promptly apologize and accept responsibility for the problem. Ask customers what they need to correct the error.
4. See the complaint for what it is. The customer is upset about something; zero in on what it is so you can fix it.
5. Wait until the customer finishes expressing a complaint and then respond with a solution.
6. Thank the customer; let him or her know you appreciate being told about the situation. Listen for suggestions the customer might have about resolving the complaint. Try to win a friend, not an argument.
7. Fix the problem quickly. The longer a business delays in resolving the problem, the less likely the customer is to be satisfied with the solution.
8. Follow up with the customer. Tell him or her what you're doing about the problem and make sure he or she is satisfied with the result. This shows that you really do care.
9. Ask yourself, "What changes do I need to make to our business system so this complaint does not occur again with this customer or other customers in similar situations?"

■ Allow managers to wait on customers occasionally. It's a great dose of reality. Dell CEO Michael Dell and his team of top managers meet periodically with the company's major customers to get a better understanding of how to serve their needs more effectively.[36]

■ Develop a service theme that communicates your attitude toward customers. Customers want to feel they are getting something special.

■ Reward employees "caught" providing exceptional service to customers. At ScriptSave, a company that manages prescription-drug benefit programs, managers hand out Bravo Bucks that are redeemable for gifts to employees who excel in providing superior customer service.[37]

■ Carefully select and train everyone who will deal with customers. View training for what it is: an investment rather than an expense. *Never* let rude employees work with customers. Charlie Horn, CEO of ScriptSave, requires all customer service representatives to go through three weeks of training before taking their first telephone call from a customer. Each representative also gets an additional 60 hours of classroom training in customer service techniques.[38]

**RETAIN EXISTING CUSTOMERS.** Loyal, long-term customers are the bedrock of every business. A study by the consulting firm Bain & Company shows that businesses that retain just 5 percent more customers experience profit increases of at least 25 percent, and in some cases, as much as 95 percent![39] Increasing a company's retention rate by just 2 percent has the same impact as cutting expenses by 10 percent![40] Studies by the Boston Consulting Group also show that companies with high customer retention rates produce above-average profits and superior growth in market share.[41]

Because about 20 to 30 percent of a typical companies' customers account for about 70 to 80 percent of its sales, it makes more sense to focus resources on keeping the best (and most profitable) customers than to chase "fair weather" customers who will defect to any better deal that comes along. Suppose that a company increases its customer base by 20 percent each year, but it retains only 85 percent of its existing customers. Its effective growth rate is just 5 percent per year [20% − (100% − 85%) = 5%]. If this same company can raise its customer retention rate to 95 percent, its net growth rate *triples* to 15 percent [20% − (100% − 95%) = 15%].[42] Shrewd entrepreneurs recognize that the greatest opportunity for new business often comes from existing customers.

Although winning new customers keeps a company growing, keeping existing ones is essential to success. Research shows that repeat customers spend 67 percent more than new customers. In addition, attracting a new customer actually costs the typical business *seven to nine times* as much as keeping an existing one.[43] Table 9.1 shows the high cost of lost customers.

Given these statistics, entrepreneurs are better off asking, "How can we improve customer value and service to encourage our existing customers to do more business with us?" rather than "How can we increase our market share by 10 percent?" One way that small companies can entice current customers to keep coming back is with a loyalty program

**TABLE 9.1 The High Cost of Lost Customers**

| If you lose . . . | Spending $5 weekly | Spending $10 weekly | Spending $50 weekly | Spending $100 weekly | Spending $200 weekly | Spending $300 weekly |
|---|---|---|---|---|---|---|
| 1 customer a day | $ 94,900 | $ 189,800 | $ 949,000 | $ 1,898,000 | $ 3,796,000 | $ 5,694,000 |
| 2 customers a day | 189,800 | 379,600 | 1,898,000 | 3,796,000 | 7,592,000 | 11,388,000 |
| 5 customers a day | 474,500 | 949,000 | 4,745,000 | 9,490,000 | 18,980,000 | 28,470,000 |
| 10 customers a day | 949,000 | 1,898,000 | 9,490,000 | 18,980,000 | 37,960,000 | 56,940,000 |
| 20 customers a day | 1,898,000 | 3,796,000 | 18,980,000 | 37,960,000 | 75,920,000 | 113,880,000 |
| 50 customers a day | 4,745,000 | 9,490,000 | 47,450,000 | 94,900,000 | 189,800,000 | 284,700,000 |
| 100 customers a day | 9,490,000 | 18,980,000 | 94,900,000 | 189,800,000 | 379,600,000 | 569,400,000 |

*Source:* Copyright 1989, Customer Service Institute, 1010 Wayne Avenue, Silver Spring, Maryland, 20910, (301)585-0730.

(e.g., a car wash offering a punch card that gives customers one free wash after they purchase nine washes). Perhaps the most effective way for a business to build customer loyalty is to sell quality products and to offer outstanding customer service. *That's* what keeps loyal customers returning to companies such as retail coffee icon Starbucks and Chick-fil-A, a company that has built a following of loyal customers by selling tasty chicken sandwiches in a fast-food market dominated by purveyors of hamburgers.

**DEVOTION TO QUALITY.** In this intensely competitive global business environment, quality goods and services are a prerequisite for success—and even survival. According to one marketing axiom, the worst of all marketing catastrophes is to have great advertising and a poor-quality product. Customers have come to expect and demand quality goods and services, and those businesses that provide them consistently have a distinct competitive advantage.

ENTREPRENEURIAL
Profile

*John Stollenwerk and Allen Edmonds Shoe Corporation*

Founded in 1922, shoe-maker Allen Edmonds has resisted the temptation to move its production to offshore locations, where costs are lower, choosing instead to focus on making quality men's footwear in the United States. In factories in the United States, highly skilled craftsman continue to build Allen Edmonds shoes, which sell for $200 to $400 a pair, by hand using a 212-step process. "It's all about the shoes," says CEO John Stollenwerk. "I believe that Allen Edmonds can make them better and serve customers faster in the United States."[44]

Today, quality is more than just a slogan posted on the company bulletin board; world-class companies treat quality as a strategic objective—an integral part of the company culture. This philosophy is called **total quality management (TQM)**—quality not just in the product or service itself but also in *every* aspect of the business and its relationship with the customer and in continuous improvement in the quality delivered to customers. Companies achieve continuous improvement by using statistical techniques to discover problems, determine their causes, and solve them; then they must incorporate what they have learned into improving the process. The ultimate goals of TQM are to *avoid* quality problems, reduce cycle time (the time between a customer's order and delivery of the finished product), reduce costs, and continuously improve the process. TQM's focus on continuous improvement is built on the "define, measure, analyze, improve, and control (DMAIC) process illustrated in Figure 9.5.

Companies on the cutting edge of the quality movement are developing new ways to measure quality. Manufacturers were the first to apply TQM techniques, but retail, wholesale, and service organizations have seen the benefits of becoming champions of quality.

**FIGURE 9.5 The Quality DMAIC Process**

*Source:* Adapted from Walter H. Ettinger, MD, "Six Sigma," *Trustee,* September 2001, p. 14.

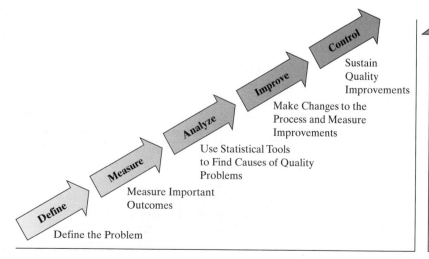

They are tracking customer complaints, contacting "lost" customers, and finding new ways to track the cost of quality and their return on quality (ROQ). ROQ recognizes that although any improvement in quality may improve a company's competitive ability, only those improvements that produce a reasonable rate of return are worthwhile. In essence, ROQ requires managers to ensure that the quality improvements they implement will more than pay for themselves. Using basic quality principles, Allen Edmonds recently revamped its entire production process, a move that not only improved quality but also increased worker productivity.[45]

The key to developing a successful TQM philosophy is seeing the world from the customer's point of view. In other words, quality must reflect the needs and wants of the customer. How do customers define quality? According to one survey, Americans rank quality components in this order: reliability (average time between failures), durability (how long it lasts), ease of use, a known or trusted brand name, and, last, a low price.[46] In services, customers are likely to look for similar characteristics: tangibles (equipment, facilities and people), reliability (doing what you say you will do), responsiveness (promptness in helping customers), and assurance and empathy (conveying a caring attitude). Companies successful in capturing a reputation for top-quality products and services follow certain guidelines to "get it right the first time":

- Build quality into the process; don't rely on inspection to obtain quality.
- Emphasize simplicity in the design of products and processes; it reduces the opportunity for errors to sneak in.
- Foster teamwork and dismantle the barriers that divide disparate departments.
- Establish long-term ties with select suppliers; don't award contracts on low price alone.
- Provide managers and employees the training needed to participate fully in the quality improvement program.
- Empower workers at all levels of the organization; give them authority and responsibility for making decisions that determine quality.
- Have managers commit to the quality philosophy. Otherwise, the program is doomed. Describing his role in his company's TQM philosophy, one CEO says, "People look to see if you just talk about it or actually do it."[47]
- Rethink the processes the company uses now to get its products or services to customers. Employees at Analog Devices redesigned its production process and significantly lowered the defect rate on its silicon chips, saving $1.2 million a year.[48]
- Reward employees for quality work. Ideally, employees' compensation is linked clearly and directly to key measures of quality and customer satisfaction.
- Develop a company-wide strategy for constant improvement of product and service quality.

**ATTENTION TO CONVENIENCE.** Ask customers what they want from the businesses they deal with and one of the most common responses is "convenience." In this busy, fast-paced world of dual-career couples and lengthy commutes to and from work (the average commute time is now 25.1 minutes), consumers have more disposable income but less time in which to enjoy it. A generation ago, married couples worked an average of 3,331 hours a year; today, the typical married couple works 3,719 hours a year, an average of 71.5 hours a week.[49] Anything a business can do to enhance convenience for its customers will give it an edge. Several studies have found that customers rank easy access to goods and services at the top of their purchase criteria. Unfortunately, many businesses fail to deliver adequate levels of convenience, and, as a result, they fail to attract and retain customers. One print and framing shop, for instance, alienated many potential customers with its abbreviated business hours—9 to 5 daily, except for Wednesday afternoons, Saturday, and Sunday when the shop was closed! Other companies make it a chore to do business with them, almost as if their owners have created an obstacle course for customers to negotiate. In an effort to defend themselves against a few unscrupulous customers, these businesses have created elaborate procedures for exchanges, refunds, writing checks, and other basic transactions that frustrate legitimate customers.

Successful companies go out of their way to make it easy for customers to do business with them.

*Dena Kaufel and Onsite Haircuts and Claudine and Brian Grumble and Caravan*

Dena Kaufel targets busy California technology workers and provides them with the ultimate convenience: onsite haircuts. Kaufel's aptly named business, Onsite Haircuts, operates three customized Winnebagos outfitted as traveling hair salons, complete with barber chairs, mirrors, and sinks, that make stops at some of Silicon Valley's top technology firms, including Yahoo!, Google, Genentech, and eBay. Customers schedule same-day haircuts at the company's Web site (of course!), www.onsitehaircuts.com. Since launching the convenient onsite service, Kaufel's sales have climbed 800 percent![50]

In New York City (and soon in Los Angeles and Miami, Florida), entrepreneurs Claudine and Brian Gumbel use the same business-on-wheels concept to take their boutique fashions directly to their customers. Their company, Caravan, takes trendy fashions straight to their customers' doorsteps (home or office) using specially outfitted trucks that, on the inside, look just like upscale boutiques, complete with wallpaper, dressing rooms, video screens playing runway fashion shows, and computers so that shoppers can check e-mail and download music. With its focus on convenience, Caravan became profitable within just eight months![51]

Dena Kaufel, owner of Onsite Haircuts, operates three mobile hair salons that make stops at some of Silicon Valley's top technology firms and offer customers the Ultimate in Convenience—on-site haircuts.

Many small companies have had success by finding simple ways to make it easier for customers to do business with them. How can entrepreneurs boost the convenience levels of their businesses? By conducting a "convenience audit" from the customer's point of view to get an idea of its ETDBW ("Easy To Do Business With") index:

- Is your business located near your customers? Does it provide easy access?
- Are your business hours suitable to your customers? Should you be open evenings and weekends to serve them better?
- Would customers appreciate pickup and delivery service? The owner of a restaurant located near a major office complex installed a Web site and a fax machine to receive orders from busy office workers; a crew of employees would deliver lunches to the workers at their desks!
- Does your business provide a sufficient number of checkout stations so that shoppers do not have to stand in long lines to make their purchases? Does your company make it easy for customers to make purchases on credit or with credit cards?
- Are you using technology to enhance customer convenience? At Stop & Shop, a grocery chain in New England, customers can save valuable time (and money) with

the Shopping Buddy, a shopping cart-mounted device that scans items as customers place them in their carts. The device makes grocery shopping more efficient by displaying each shopper's buying history by aisle. With the Shopping Buddy, customers also can send orders wirelessly to the deli or seafood departments, and the device will notify them when the order is ready to pick up.[52]

- Are your employees trained to handle business transactions quickly, efficiently, and politely? Waiting while rude, poorly trained employees fumble through routine transactions destroys customer goodwill.
- Do your employees use common courtesy when dealing with customers?
- Does your company offer "extras" that make customers' lives easier? With a phone call to one small gift store, customers in need of a special gift simply tell how much they wants to spend, and the owner takes care of the rest—selecting the gift, wrapping it, and shipping it. All customers have to do is pay the invoice when it arrives in the mail.
- Can you adapt existing products to make them more convenient for customers? When J. M. Smucker Company began test-marketing a pre-made, frozen peanut butter and jelly sandwich with no crust, CEO Tim Smucker was amazed at the results. The sandwiches, called Uncrustables, generated $20 million in sales, and Smucker now sells them as part of its regular product lineup.[53]
- Does your company handle telephone calls quickly and efficiently? Long waits "on hold," transfers from one office to another, and too many rings before answering signal customers that they are not important. Jerre Stead, CEO of Ingram Micro Inc., a distributor of computer products, expects every telephone call to the company to be answered within three seconds![54]

**CONCENTRATION ON INNOVATION.** Innovation is the key to future success. Markets change too quickly and competitors move too fast for small companies to stand still and remain competitive; they must constantly innovate. Because of their organizational and managerial flexibility, small businesses often can detect and act on new opportunities faster than large companies. Innovation is one of the greatest strengths of entrepreneurs, and it shows up in the new products, unique techniques, and unusual approaches they introduce. A recent study by the Product Development and Management Association of the top performing companies across more than 400 industries reveals that new products account for 49 percent of profits, more than twice as much as their less innovative competitors.[55] Innovation is an important source of competitive advantage for small companies in any industry, not just those in high-tech sectors.

*William and Pamela Rees and Harpsicle Harp Company*

William Rees had been building traditional harps since 1977 when he and his wife, Pamela, a physicist with a background in optical engineering, invented a small 26-string harp that was inexpensive to build yet was capable of producing tunes almost as true as large, professional harps. They playfully named their innovation the Harpsicle, which sells for less than $300 and comes in colors such as cherry, grape, lemon, and lime. Harpsicle sales have taken off, and the Rees say that their ability to blend traditional harp making and the principles of modern physics gives their company, the Harpsicle Harp Company, a distinct competitive edge. "Harps have been around for 4,000 years," says Pamela. "Who would have thought there would be an innovation in harps?"[56]

Small businesses have created a variety of world-changing innovations. For instance, small companies accounted for every significant breakthrough in the computer industry—including hand-held devices (Palm), microcomputers and MP3 players (Apple), and minicomputers (Digital). Small, innovative businesses also led the way in developing each generation of computer disk drives. In the hotly competitive pharmaceutical industry, the dominant drugs in many markets were discovered by small companies rather than by industry giants, such as Merck or GlaxoSmithKline, with their multi-million dollar R&D budgets. Recognizing that small businesses have the edge when it comes to innovation, large companies often purchase smaller ones that have developed new products, processes, and services. Cisco Systems, for instance, has purchased 75 small companies in recent years to help maintain a competitive edge in its high-tech sector.[57]

Although product and service innovation has never been more important to a small company's' success, it has never been more challenging. Companies of all sizes are feeling the pressure to develop new products and get them to market faster than ever before. More intense competition, often from across the globe, as well as rapid changes in technology and improvements in communication have made innovation more crucial to business success. "Today's innovation is tomorrow's imitation is next month's commodity," says one business writer.[58] Ely Callaway, founder of Callaway Golf, the company that makes the famous Big Bertha club, claimed that innovation was his "No. 1 priority and a core value outlined in the company's mission statement. That's because Callaway Golf's long-term success depends on satisfying our customers with a constant stream of innovative new products."[59]

There is more to innovation than spending megadollars on research and development. How do small businesses manage to maintain their leadership role in innovating new products and services? They use their size to their advantage, maintaining their speed and flexibility much like a martial arts expert does against a larger opponent. Their closeness to their customers enables them to read subtle shifts in the market and to anticipate trends as they unfold. Their ability to concentrate their efforts and attention in one area also gives small businesses an edge in innovation. "Small companies have an advantage: a dedicated management team focused solely on a new product or market," says one venture capitalist.[60]

*Woody Norris and American Technology Corporation*

Woody Norris, holder of 43 patents and founder of American Technology Corporation in San Diego, has developed a sound technology using sonic beams that enable sound to be shaped, directed, and focused, much like light beams. The innovative technology, called Hypersonic Sound, allows one person to hear sound beams aimed at him or her while another person standing nearby cannot. Norris sees a multitude of applications for his invention, some already in operation. The military currently is testing the technology, and Norris is working with automakers to develop speakers that allow passengers to listen to different music without disturbing fellow passengers. Some supermarkets currently use the technology to beam recorded messages to individual shoppers based on the products they select from the store's shelves![61]

To be an effective innovator, an entrepreneur should:

- Make innovation a strategic priority in the company by devoting management time and energy to it.
- Measure the company's innovative ability. Tracking the number of new products or services introduced and the proportion of sales products less than five years old generate can be useful measures of a company's ability to innovate.
- Set goals and objectives for innovation. Establishing targets and rewarding employees for achieving them can produce amazing results.
- Encourage new product and service ideas among employees. Workers have many incredible ideas, but they will lead to new products or services only if someone takes the time to listen to them.
- Listen to customers. A telephone call from the owner of a children's hair salon led Damon Carson, owner of Kiddie Rides, to a new market for the fiberglass figures his company makes for the children's rides that sit in shopping malls and centers: fun chairs for kids to sit in while they get their hair cut. Carson now actively seeks customer feedback as a source of new ideas for his company.[62]
- Always be on the lookout for new product and service ideas. They can come to you (or to anyone inside or outside the company) at any time. Victor and Janie Tsao, founders of Linksys Inc., a company that has become a leader in the market for affordable wireless routers and hubs study exactly what customers want networking technology to do and then roll out products rapidly to meet those needs. Linksys's size and flexibility are major competitive weapons. "We launch a new product a week," says one top manager. "By the time our competitors realize what's going on, we're already at work on the next one."[63]

■ Keep a steady stream of new products and services flowing. Even before sales of her safety-handle children's toothbrush took off, Millie Thomas, founder of RGT Enterprises, had developed other children's products using the same triangular-shaped handle, including a crayon holder, paintbrushes, and fingernail brushes.[64]

Table 9.2 describes a screening device for testing the viability of new product ideas.

**DEDICATION TO SERVICE AND CUSTOMER SATISFACTION.** Small companies have discovered that providing superior personalized customer service can be a powerful strategic weapon against their larger rivals in whose stores customers often are ignored and have to serve themselves. Small companies that lack the financial resources of their larger rivals have discovered that offering exceptional customer service is one of the most effective ways to differentiate themselves and to attract and maintain a growing customer base. "It doesn't take money to [provide] good customer service," says the head of one retail company. "It takes a commitment."[65] Unfortunately, the level of service in most companies is poor.[66]

*Mark Soderstrom and Southstream Seafoods*

Mark Soderstrom, founder of Southstream Seafoods, a small importer and wholesaler of frozen seafood, discovered early on that his business would have to set itself apart with superb customer service to thrive in an extremely competitive business. Rapid swings in fish prices can create both opportunities and problems for Southstream's customers, so Soderstrom began using a customer relationship management (CRM) software package to give customers updated information about changes in market prices so they could make good business decisions at purchase time. With the system, Southstream sends anywhere from 500 to 1,000 "customized" faxes a week with pricing information on products each customer is interested in. Customers find the information to be extremely valuable. "Knowledge is power," says Soderstrom, "and we're the people providing them with that power." Soderstrom credits his company's superior customer service as a major source of his company's success and growth, up from sales of $4 million to more than $60 million in just 10 years![67]

## TABLE 9.2 Testing the Viability of a New Product Idea

Testing the viability of new product ideas in their early stages of development can help entrepreneurs avoid expensive product failures later—after they have already invested significant amounts of cash in developing and launching them. The Chester Marketing Group Inc. of Washington Crossing, Pennsylvania, has developed the following test to determine the viability of a new product idea at each stage in the product development process. To calculate a new product idea's score, entrepreneurs simply multiply the score for each criterion by its weight and then add up the resulting weighted scores. For a product to advance to the next stage in the development process, its score should be at least 16.

| Criterion | Score | | | Weight | Weighted Score |
|---|---|---|---|---|---|
| Extent of Target Market Need | Below Average 1 | Average 2 | Above Average 3 | 2 | |
| Potential Profitability | Below Average 1 | Average 2 | Above Average 3 | 2 | |
| Likely Emergence of Competition | Below Average 1 | Average 2 | Above Average 3 | 1 | |
| Service Life Cycle | Below Average 1 | Average 2 | Above Average 3 | 1 | |
| Compatibility with Company Strengths | Below Average 1 | Average 2 | Above Average 3 | 2 | |
| | | | | Total Weighted Score | |

*Source:* Roberta Maynard, "Test Your Product Idea," *Nation's Business,* October 1997, p. 23.

Successful businesses recognize that superior customer service is only an intermediate step toward the goal of customer satisfaction. These companies seek to go beyond customer satisfaction, striving for *customer astonishment!* They concentrate on providing customers with quality, convenience, and service as their customers define those terms. Certainly, the least expensive—and the most effective—way to achieve customer satisfaction is through friendly, personal service. Numerous surveys of customers in a wide diversity of industries, from manufacturing and services to banking and high technology, conclude that the most important element of service is "the personal touch." Indeed, a study conducted by market research firm NFO WorldGroup found that friendly service, not the food, is the primary reason customers return to a restaurant![68] Whatever the nature of the business, calling customers by name, making attentive, friendly contact, and truly caring about customers' needs and wants are more essential than any other factor, even convenience, quality, and speed!

How can a company achieve stellar customer service and satisfaction?

***Listen to Customers.*** The best companies constantly listen to their customers and respond to what they hear! This allows them to keep up with customers' changing needs and expectations. The only way to find out what customers really want and value is to ask them. Businesses rely on a number of techniques including surveys, focus groups, telephone interviews, comment cards, suggestion boxes, toll-free hotlines, and regular one-on-one conversations with customers (perhaps the best technique). Starbucks founder Howard Schultz resisted using skim milk in the company's Italian lattes until he spent time working in a Starbucks outlet and listened to customers repeatedly ask for it.[69]

***Define Superior Service.*** Based on what customers say, managers and employees must decide exactly what "superior service" means in the company. Such a statement should (1) be a strong statement of intent, (2) differentiate the company from others, and (3) have value to customers. Deluxe Corporation, a printer of personal checks, defines superior service quite simply: "Forty-eight hour turnaround; zero defects."

***Set Standards and Measure Performance.*** To be able to deliver on its promise of superior service, a business must establish specific standards and measure overall performance against them. Satisfied customers should exhibit at least one of three behaviors: loyalty (increased customer retention rate), increased purchases (climbing sales and sales per customer), and resistance to rivals' attempts to lure them away with lower prices (market share and price tolerance).[70] Companies must track performance on these and other service standards and reward employees accordingly.

***Examine Your Company's Service Cycle.*** What steps must a customer go through to get your product or service? Business owners often are surprised at the complexity that has seeped into their customer service systems as they have evolved over time. One of the most effective techniques is to work with employees to flowchart each component in the company's service cycle, including everything a customer has to do to get your product or service. The goal is to look for steps and procedures that are unnecessary, redundant, or unreasonable and eliminate them.

***Hire the Right Employees.*** The key ingredient in the superior service equation is *people*. There is no substitute for friendly, courteous sales and service representatives. A customer service attitude requires hiring employees who believe in and embrace customer service. When it comes to the impact of customer retention on a company's profitability, a responsive, customer-oriented employee is worth many times the value of an employee who provides average (or, worse yet, below average) customer service. "You hire people for their inherent skill," says Gary Danko, owner of a restaurant that recently won a prestigious customer service award. "You can teach them the mechanics."

*T-Mobile*

When surveys showed a problem with its customer service, cell phone service provider T-Mobile instituted a set of hiring criteria aimed at recruiting employees with customer service attitudes. Managers also implemented a rewards program in which employees who exceed the company's stringent customer service standards earn treats ranging from free dinners to exotic trips. Since launching its customer service initiative, T-Mobile not only has seen employee absenteeism and attrition decline by 50 percent and productivity triple but also its customer service ranking now leads the industry.[71]

***Train Employees to Deliver Superior Service.*** Successful businesses train every employee who deals directly with customers; they don't leave the art of customer service to chance. Superior service companies devote 1 to 5 percent of their employees' work hours to training, concentrating on how to meet, greet, and serve customers. "Employees need to be trained to instinctively provide good service," says John Tschol, founder of the Service Quality Institute.[72]

***Empower Employees to Offer Superior Service.*** One of the biggest single variables determining whether employees deliver superior service is whether they perceive they have permission to do so. The goal is to push decision making down the organization to the employees who have contact with customers. This includes giving them the freedom to circumvent company policy if it means improving customer satisfaction. At Ritz-Carlton hotels, every employee is authorized to spend up to $2,000 to resolve a customer's complaint.[73] If frontline workers don't have the power to solve disgruntled customers' problems, they quickly become frustrated and the superior service cycle breaks down. To be empowered, employees need knowledge and information, adequate resources, and managerial support.

***Use Technology to Provide Improved Service.*** The role of technology is not to create a rigid bureaucracy but to free employees from routine clerical tasks, giving them more time and better tools to serve customers more effectively. Ideally, technology gives workers the timely information they need to help their customers and the freedom to serve them. To boost customer service, Best Buy's Geek Squad, a response team that provides 24-hour support for home and business computers and networks, issues Pocket PC phones to its agents. Agents use the phones to find directions to customers' homes and businesses, pull up technical information on the computers they are repairing, store handwritten notes on the work they have done, and connect wirelessly with the entire IT system at company headquarters. The high-tech phones allow service agents not only to offer better customer service faster but also to complete the entire transaction on the spot by submitting billing or credit card information.[74]

***Reward Superior Service.*** What gets rewarded gets done. Companies that want employees to provide stellar service must offer rewards for doing so.

***Get Top Managers' Support.*** The drive toward superior customer service will fall far short of its target unless top managers support it fully. Success requires more than just a verbal commitment; it calls for managers' involvement and dedication. Periodically, managers should spend time in customer service positions to maintain contact with customers, frontline employees, and the challenges of providing good service.

***Give Customers an Unexpected (and Pleasant) Surprise.*** Companies can make a lasting, favorable impression on their customers by providing them with an unexpected surprise periodically. The surprise does not have to be expensive to be effective. For instance, when customers of Tom Williams Lexus pick up their cars from the service department, they find bottled water and Hershey's kisses in the cupholders.[75] Cast members at one of Disney's theme parks are empowered to hand out "magic moments" to guests of their choice. The moment might be a ride on a float in a Disney parade, a special visit from a Disney princess, or a night's stay in a special suite in Cinderella's Castle.

## ■ The Ultimate Question

IPower, a Web hosting company founded by Thomas Gorny, had become a very successful business, hosting more than 400,000 Web sites and generating annual revenue of in excess of $25 million. As Gorny would soon learn, however, that success had come at a price. To achieve that level of success, IPower had grown too fast, and its level of customer service was slipping. Calls from disgruntled customers started trickling in, but soon the flow had turned into a raging torrent—some 15,000 unhappy customers a day! Gorny's initial reaction was to add features to the company's service and to offer discounts to unhappy customers, but things did not improve. That's when Gorny began to focus on improving IPower's customer service level using a simple measure called the Net Promoter Score (NPS). Developed by Fred Reichheld, a consultant for Bain and Company, the NPS asks customers no more than two questions:

1. How likely are you to recommend our company to friends and colleagues?
2. If you would not recommend us, why not?

On question 1, the NPS uses a 1 (not at all likely) to 10 (highly likely) scale. Customers who respond with nines and tens are considered "promoters"; those who score a company with sevens and eights are "passives." Any customer who rates a company below a seven is considered to be a "detractor." To calculate its NPS, a company subtracts the percentage of detractors from the percentage of promoters. Reichheld says that the NPS is a nearly ideal measure of a company's reputation in the marketplace and its ability to attract new customers and to retain existing ones. Most companies have NPS scores between 10 and 20; the best businesses score a commanding 80 to 90. "At small, fast-growing companies, more than half of new business comes from referrals, not advertising," explains Reichheld. "Our research reveals that in most industries, the firms with the highest NPS scores have the strongest profits and healthiest growth." According to Reichheld, on average, a 12-point increase in a company's NPS doubles its growth rate.

According to research by Bain, 80 percent of managers believe that their companies provide superior cus-

tomer service, but only 8 percent of their customers agree. "Most customers of the average firm—more than two-thirds—are either passive about the company or are downright detractors," Reichheld explains. "Once you find out who they are and why they're ticked off, you can take [corrective] action." NPS is an effective measure because it forces everyone in the company to focus on creating satisfied customers. "If customers are willing to promote you, that's the clearest indication of loyalty," says Reichheld. "If they're not going to promote you, follow up with more questions to determine why. Build a dialogue that turns them into promoters."

NPS surveys are ideal for small businesses. They are easy and inexpensive to administer by telephone, mail, e-mail, or in person. Response rates also tend to be high—20 to 30 percent compared to 10 percent or less for traditional surveys—because, unlike most customer satisfaction surveys, the NPS survey takes only moments to complete. The results are easy to tally, and entrepreneurs can communicate them to everyone in the company in an easy-to-understand way. When Gorny administered the NPS for the first time, he was shocked at the results; IPower's NPS was just 13. "It was eye-opening," he says. The number one customer complaint was the inability to talk about a problem with a live customer service representative. Gorny immediately began hiring and training 184 new customer service reps to handle customer calls and posting IPower's NPS for everyone to see. The changes are working. Within three months, IPower's NPS had climbed to 18 for existing customers and 24 for new ones. Gorny's goal is to push the company's NPS to at least 40 within one year. The benefits to the company have marched in step with the improvements in its NPS. Customer retention has improved by 33 percent, and sales have climbed to $40 million a year. "We finally have confidence that we can keep our customers for years," says Gorny.

1. Is the Net Promoter Score an effective way to measure customer satisfaction? What are the advantages and the disadvantages of using the NPS to measure customer satisfaction?
2. Select two companies in your area, one that you consider to offer superior customer service and one that does not. Select a (preferably random) sample of customers of each company and ask

*(continued)*

them to answer the NPS survey's questions. Tally the results. What conclusions can you draw from your analysis? What recommendations would you make to the business's owner?

*Sources:* Adapted from Darren Dahl, "Would You Recommend Us?" *Inc.,* September 2006, pp. 40–42; Russ Banham, "Angry and Bored? You Must Be a Customer," *CFO,* July 2006, pp. 62–67; Scott Thurm, "One Question, and Plenty of Debate," *Wall Street Journal,* December 4, 2006, p. B3.

**EMPHASIS ON SPEED.** We live in a world of instantaneous expectations. Technology that produces immediate results at the click of a mouse and allows for real-time communication has altered our sense of time and space. Speed reigns. Customers now expect companies to serve them at the speed of light! In such a world, speed has become a major competitive weapon. World-class companies recognize that reducing the time it takes to develop, design, manufacture, and distribute a product reduces costs, increases quality, and boosts market share. One study by McKinsey and Company found that high-tech products that come to market on budget but six months late will earn 33 percent less profit over five years. Bringing the product out on time but 50 percent over budget cuts profits just 4 percent ![76] Service companies also know that they must build speed into their business systems if they are to satisfy their impatient, time-sensitive customers.

This philosophy of speed is called **time compression management (TCM)**, and it involves three aspects: (1) speeding new products to market, (2) shortening customer response time in manufacturing and delivery, and (3) reducing the administrative time required to fill an order. Studies show plenty of room for improvement; most businesses waste 85 to 99 percent of the time it takes to produce products or services without ever realizing it![77] Although speeding up the manufacturing process is a common goal, companies using TCM have learned that manufacturing takes only 5 percent to 10 percent of the total time between taking an order and getting the product into the customer's hands. The rest is consumed by clerical and administrative tasks. The primary opportunity for TCM lies in its application to the administrative process.

Companies relying on TCM to help them turn speed into a competitive edge should:

- "Reengineer" the entire process rather than attempt to do the same things in the same way, only faster.
- Study every phase of the business process, whether it involves manufacturing, shipping, administration, or some other function, looking for small improvements that speed up the entire process.
- Create cross-functional teams of workers and give them the power to attack and solve problems. In world-class companies, product teams include engineers, manufacturers, salespeople, quality experts—even customers.
- Share information and ideas across the company. Easy access to meaningful information can speed a company's customer response time.
- Set aggressive goals for time reduction and stick to the schedule. Some companies using TCM have been able to reduce cycle time from several weeks to just a few hours!
- Instill speed in the culture. At Domino's Pizza, kitchen workers watch videos of the fastest pizza makers in the business.
- Use technology to find shortcuts wherever possible. Rather than build costly, time-consuming prototypes, many time-sensitive businesses use computer aided design and computer assisted manufacturing (CAD/CAM) to speed product design and testing.

*Apple Inc. and the iPod*

Speed can be a source of significant competitive advantage, something that Apple knows well. When it introduced the first iPod in 2002, it quickly dominated the market for MP3 players. Rather than wait for competitors to introduce new versions with improvements, Apple set out to make its own iPods obsolete by introducing new models to replace existing ones and doing it quickly. Recognizing that speed to market was a key to maintaining its market share, Apple has taken just eight months to introduce the last eight iPod models, compared to two years for the first six models.[78]

## Marketing on the World Wide Web

With its ability to display colorful graphics, sound, animation, and video as well as text, the World Wide Web is a powerful guerrilla marketing tool, allowing small companies to equal or even surpass their larger rivals' Web presence. Although small companies cannot match the marketing efforts of their larger competitors, a creative Web page can be the "great equalizer" in a small company's marketing program, giving it access to markets all across the globe. The Web gives small businesses the power to broaden their scope to unbelievable proportions. Web-based businesses are open around the clock, seven days a week and can reach customers anywhere in the world.

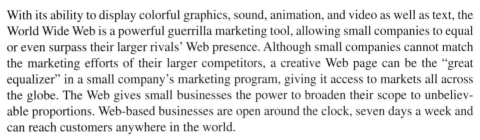

*Carlisle Wide Plank Floors*

Since its founding in 1966, Carlisle Wide Plank Floors had relied primarily on print advertising to drive customers to the company's toll-free telephone number. For the last several years, Carlisle had been steadily increasing its marketing budget, but sales were not growing. That's when managers decided to launch a carefully designed, interactive Web site that projected a "big company image" for the small, family-run business. The Web site began attracting an average of 17,000 unique visitors each month, causing sales leads to triple and company sales to increase by 40 percent. "The Web site hasn't changed the heart of our business," says Carlisle's marketing director, "but it has dramatically changed the way we do business."[79]

The Web has become a mainstream marketing medium, one that small business owners cannot afford to ignore, primarily because of its impressive power and reach.[80] As impressive as online business-to-consumer (B-to-C) sales are, sales in the business-to-business (B-to-B) sector exceed them! In fact, about two-thirds of all e-commerce activity is in the B-to-B sector. Whether they sell to other businesses or to consumers, small companies simply cannot ignore the potential of the online market.

Small companies that have had the greatest success selling on the Web have marketing strategies that emphasize their existing strengths and core competencies. Their Web marketing strategies reflect their "brick-and-mortar" marketing strategies, often focusing on building relationships with their customers rather than merely scouting for a sale. These companies understand their target customers and know how to reach them using the Web. They create Web sites that provide meaningful information to their customers, customize themselves based on each customer's interests, and make it easy for customers to find what they want. In short, their Web sites create the same sense of trust and personal attention customers get when dealing with a local brick-and-mortar small business. Poorly performing Web sites actually harm a company's marketing efforts. According to a study by Empirix, 20 percent of online shoppers say that a negative online experience had caused them to stop doing business—both online *and* offline—with a company.[81]

Using the Web as a marketing tool allows entrepreneurs to provide both existing and potential customers with meaningful information in an interactive rather than a passive setting. Well-designed Web sites include interactive features that allow customers to access information about a company, its products and services, its history, and other features such as question-and-answer sessions with experts or the ability to conduct e-mail or online conversations with company officials. To enhance their marketing reach, entrepreneurs can link their companies' home pages to other related Web sites, something advertisements in other media cannot offer. For instance, a company selling cookware might include links on its Web page to other pages containing recipes, cookbooks, foods, and other cooking resources. This allows small business owners to engage in cross-marketing with companies on the Web selling complementary products or services.

The Web also magnifies a company's ability to provide superior customer service at minimal cost. Innovative, customer-oriented Web sites allow customers to gather information about a product or service, have their questions answered, download diagrams and photographs, and track the progress of their orders. In fact, online companies are now shifting their online marketing strategies away from using the Web as a low-cost way to generate

## Can Two Bars Build a Brand?

After spending years designing golf clubs for large manufacturers, Guerin Rife left the corporate world to start a company to sell a unique putter that he claims contains enough physics-based innovations to shave a few strokes off of just about any golfer's score. The odd-looking club has two adjustable bars (hence its name, the Two Bar putter) that allow golfers to change the weight configuration of the putter to accommodate the speed of any green. Its weighting system provides more stability, even when a golfer's stroke is off-center, and its patented rollgroove technology reduced the ball's "skid," resulting in a straighter, more consistent roll.

Rife is president of Guerin Rife Putters, a company with sales of more than $3 million of its solo product, but Rife spends most of his time on the road, trailing the Professional Golf Association's (PGA) tour circuit, trying to convince professional golfers to use his Two Bar putter. Rife figures that convincing a few pro golfers to use his putter on the PGA circuit will translate into increased sales for the Two Bar. Experience proves that to be the case. When pro golfer Dana Quigley recently became the Champions Tour top money winner using the Two Bar, Rife's company saw sales increase. "Every time Dana wins with our putter," says Rife, "our sales spike, new retailers take notice, and it's just good for our business."

Convincing professional golfers, who not only are very particular about their equipment but also are quite superstitious about it, is no easy task. Large golf equipment companies also can afford to make endorsement deals with pro golfers to use their equipment, something that Rife struggles to do, given his company's size and limited marketing budget. Callaway Golf pays $1 million to LPGA champion Annika Sorenstam to use its Odyssey putter, and Aserta, a two-year-old company in San Jose, California, spends $1.5 million each year on "performance bonuses" (payments made to golfers who win using the company's clubs) and print ads. Rife's target is pro golfers who have not yet endorsed a particular putter or who have the flexibility to switch putters if their game is suffering. His success depends on his ability to find the right big name golfers, convince them that the Two Bar putter can improve their game, and offer to customize one to fit them.

Rife has managed to generate enough interest in his clubs to sell more than $3 million worth of them at $200 each. He took a gamble recently when he decided to spend $365,000 on an infomercial for the Two Bar putter starring pro golfer Dana Quigley. Shortly after Quigley played in the Kinko's classic using his Two Bar putter, the infomercial generated orders for 2,000 putters. Rife estimates that the infomercial has generated a return of 145 percent for his company, which Rife financed with his own money along with investments from private investors. "That's the kind of lightning we're looking for," says Jim Barfield, one of Rife's investors. Rife plans to continue using the infomercial, and this year, his company plans to spend $200,000 on a direct marketing campaign. Despite the company's inability to launch a major marketing campaign, the Two Bar putter has claimed the number-two spot in the putter market, behind giant Callaway but ahead of established companies such as Ping, Titleist, and TaylorMade. "It's the hottest new putter on the market right now," says Tony Duran, president of one of the industry's largest independent sales and marketing firms. "There's no other putter gaining distribution and market share like this one."

For now, Rife is dividing his focus between convincing golf pros to use his Two Bar putters and selling them to amateur golfers in an already-crowded marketplace. "We're just trying to get our putter into as many golfers' hands as we can," says Rife.

1. Is Guerin Rife's situation—a greater need for marketing than his budget allows—typical for small businesses? Explain.

2. What steps can entrepreneurs faced with the situation in the previous question take to market their companies' products and services?

3. Work with a small team of your classmates in a brainstorming session to devise a guerrilla marketing plan for Rife's Two Bar putter.

*Source:* Adapted from Ron Stodghill, "Roll Player," *FSB*, March 2006, pp. 90–93.

sales and towards enhancing customer service and retention. We will discuss using the Web as a business tool in Chapter 13, "E-Commerce and Entrepreneurship."

## The Marketing Mix

*6.* Discuss the "four Ps" of marketing—product, place, price, and promotion and their role in building a successful marketing strategy.

Implementing a marketing strategy requires entrepreneurs to determine how they will combine the "four Ps" of marketing—product, place, price, and promotion—into a successful **marketing mix**. The four elements of the marketing mix are self-reinforcing and, when coordinated, increase the sales appeal of a product or service. Entrepreneurs must integrate these elements into a coherent strategy to maximize the impact of their product or service on the consumer. All four Ps must reinforce the image of the product or service the company presents to the potential customer. One longtime retailer claims, "None of the modern marvels of computerized inventory control and point-of-sale telecommunications have replaced the need for the entrepreneur who understands the customer and can translate that into the appropriate merchandise mix."[82]

### Product

The **product** itself is an essential element in marketing. Products can have form and shape, or they can be services with no physical form. Products travel through various stages of development. The **product life cycle** (see Figure 9.6) measures these stages of growth, and these measurements enable the company's management to make decisions about whether to continue selling the product, when to introduce new follow-up products, and when to introduce changes to an existing product. For instance, clothing makers are adding hidden pockets and special holders to accommodate the growing numbers of electronic devices that people carry with them. Thomas Pink's commuter shirt features a hidden cuff pocket designed to hold a smart card, a concealed front pocket ideal for storing an iPod, cell phone, or PDA, and a special internal front placket that provides concealed routing for headphone cables.[83] Play Underwear makes iBoxers, men's and women's boxer shorts with a pocket designed to hold an iPod.[84]

In the *introductory stage,* marketers present their product to potential consumers. Initial high levels of acceptance are rare. Generally, new products must break into existing markets and compete with established products. Advertising and promotion help the new product gain recognition among potential customers, who must get information about the product and the needs it can satisfy. The cost of marketing a product at this level of the life cycle is usually high because small businesses must overcome customer resistance and inertia. Therefore, profits are generally low, or even negative, at the introductory stage.

After the introductory stage, the product enters the *growth and acceptance stage.* In this stage, customers begin to purchase the product in large numbers, allowing sales to rise and profits to increase. Products that reach this stage, however, do not necessarily become successful. If in the introductory or the growth stage the product fails to meet consumer needs, it does not generate adequate sales volume and eventually disappears from the marketplace. For a product to be successful, sales and profit margins must continue to rise through the growth stage.

In the *maturity and competition stage,* sales volume continues to rise, but profit margins peak and then begin to fall as competitors enter the market. Normally, this causes a reduction in the product's selling price to meet competitor's prices and to hold its share of the market.

Sales peak in the *market saturation stage* of the product life cycle and give the marketer fair warning that it soon will be time to introduce a new product innovation.

The final stage of the product life cycle is the *product decline stage* in which sales continue to drop, and profit margins fall drastically. However, when a product reaches this stage of the cycle, it does not mean that it is doomed to failure. Products that have remained popular are always being revised. No company can maintain its sales position without product innovation and change. Even the maker of Silly Putty, first introduced at the 1950 International Toy Fair (with lifetime sales of more than 300 million "eggs," a total of 4,500

**FIGURE 9.6 The Product Life Cycle**

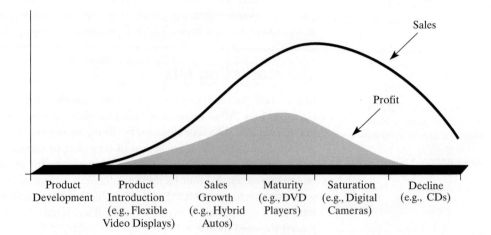

tons) has introduced new gold, Day-Glo, and glow-in-the-dark colors and a temperature-sensitive version that changes colors with the warmth of the hand. These innovations have attracted new generations of children to the classic toy.[85]

The time span of the stages in the product life cycle depends on the type of products involved. The life cycle for golf equipment has shrunk over the past decade from three or four years to less than one year today.[86] High-fashion and fad clothing has a short product life cycle, lasting for only four to six weeks. Products that are more stable such as appliances may take years to complete a life cycle. Research suggests that the typical product's life cycle lasts ten to fourteen years.

Understanding the product life cycle can help a business owner plan the introduction of new products to the company's product line. Too often, companies wait too late into the life cycle of one product to introduce another. The result is that they are totally unprepared when a competitor produces a "better mousetrap" and their sales decline. The ideal time to develop new products is early on in the life cycle of the current product (see Figure 9.7). Waiting until the current product is in the saturation or decline stages is like living on borrowed time.

### Place

**Place** (or method of distribution) has grown in importance as customers expect greater service and more convenience from businesses. Because of this trend, mail-order houses, home shopping channels, home shopping parties, and the Web which offer customers the ultimate convenience—shopping from home—have experienced booming sales in recent years. In addition, many traditionally stationary businesses have added wheels, becoming mobile animal clinics, computer repair shops, and dentist offices.

Any activity involving movement of goods to the point of consumer purchase provides place utility. Place utility is directly affected by the marketing channels of distribution, the path that goods or services take in moving from producer to consumer. Several companies,

**FIGURE 9.7 Time Between Introductions of Products**

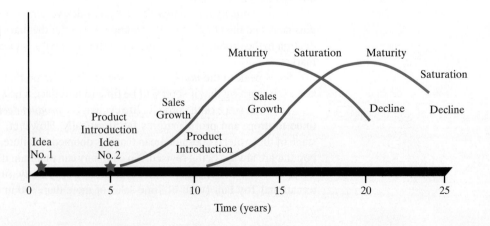

including the Pampered Chef, Tomboy Tools, and Bill Blass, are returning to the home shopping parties pioneered by Brownie Wise at Tupperware and Mary Kay Ash at Mary Kay Cosmetics in the 1940s and 1950s. Home parties, where an enterprising sales consultant invites her friends into her home for an evening of fun, fellowship, and shopping, account for nearly $8.3 billion in sales a year.[87] In 1980, Doris Christopher started The Pampered Chef, a company that sells kitchen tools through home parties, in her basement with a $3,000 loan from her husband's insurance policy. Today the company sells quality kitchen tools to more than 12 million customers worldwide through a network of more than 70,000 independent consultants who put on in-home cooking (and sales) demonstrations called Cooking Shows. Pampered Chef consultants sponsor more than one million cooking shows each year in the United States alone.[88]

Channels typically involve a number of intermediaries who perform specialized functions that add valuable utility to the goods or service. Specifically, these intermediaries provide time utility (making the product available when customers want to buy it) and place utility (making the product available where customers want to buy it).

For consumer goods, there are four common channels of distribution (see Figure 9.8).

1. ***Manufacturer to consumer.*** In some markets, producers sell their goods or services directly to consumers. Services, by nature, follow this channel of distribution. Dental care and haircuts, for example, go directly from provider to consumer.
2. ***Manufacturer to retailer to consumer.*** Another common channel involves a retailer as an intermediary. Many clothing items, books, shoes, and other consumer products are distributed in this manner.

*Howard Kruse and Blue Bell Creameries*

Blue Bell Creameries ("We eat all we can and we sell the rest"), the third largest ice cream retailer in the United States, currently sells its luscious line of ice cream in just 14 southern states, where second-generation owner Howard Kruse maintains tight control over distribution. The company buys its own refrigerated trucks, and only Blue Bell drivers can stock freezers in the grocery and convenience stores that account for most of the company's sales. Many customers in states outside the company's territory order online and pay $89 to have four half-gallons of their favorite flavors packed in dry ice and shipped to them via overnight delivery.[89]

3. ***Manufacturer to wholesaler to retailer to consumer.*** This is the most common channel of distribution for consumer goods. Prepackaged food products, hardware, toys, and other items are commonly distributed through this channel.
4. ***Manufacturer to wholesaler to wholesaler to retailer to consumer.*** A few consumer goods (e.g., agricultural goods and electrical components) follow this pattern of distribution.

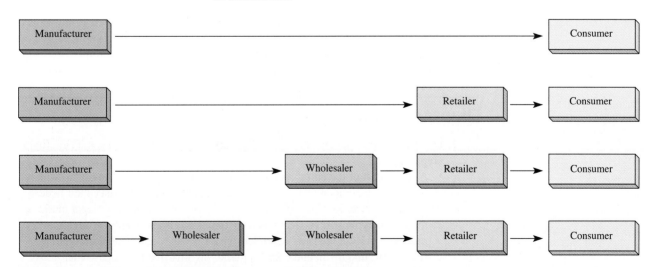

**FIGURE 9.8 Channels of Distribution: Consumer Goods**

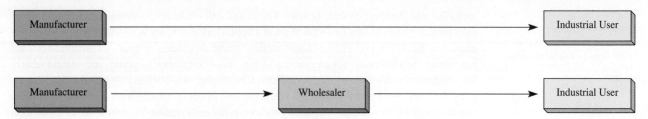

**FIGURE 9.9 Channels of Distribution: Industrial Goods**

Two channels of distribution are common for industrial goods (see Figure 9.9).

1. *Manufacturer to industrial user.* The majority of industrial goods are distributed directly from manufacturers to users. In some cases, the goods or services are designed to meet the user's specifications.
2. *Manufacturer to wholesaler to industrial user.* Most expense items (paper clips, paper, rubber bands, cleaning supplies) that firms commonly use are distributed through wholesalers. For most small manufacturers, distributing goods through established wholesalers and agents is often the most effective route. With their limited resources, entrepreneurs sometimes have to rely on nontraditional distribution channels and use their creativity to get their products into customers' hands.

### Price

Almost everyone agrees that the price of the product or service is a key factor in the decision to buy. **Price** affects both sales volume and profits, and without the right price, both sales and profits will suffer. As we will see in Chapter 11, "Pricing and Credit Strategies," the right price for a product or service depends on three factors: (1) a small company's cost structure, (2) an assessment of what the market will bear, and (3) the desired image the company wants to create in its customers' minds.

For many small businesses, non-price competition, focusing on factors other than price, is a more effective strategy than trying to beat larger competitors in a price war. Non-price competition, such as free trial offers, free delivery, lengthy warranties, and money-back guarantees, intends to play down the product's price and stress its durability, quality, reputation, or special features.

### Promotion

**Promotion** involves both advertising and personal selling. Advertising communicates to potential customers through some mass medium the benefits of a good or service. Personal selling involves the art of persuasive sales on a one-to-one basis.

The goals of a small company's promotional efforts are to create a brand image, to persuade customers to buy, and to develop brand loyalty. Promotion can take many forms and is put before the public through a variety of media. Entrepreneurs often must find ways to use low-cost guerrilla tactics to create promotions that get their companies noticed by both local and national media. Chapter 10, "Creative Use of Advertising and Promotion," is devoted to creating an effective advertising and promotion campaign for a small company.

---

## Chapter Review

1. Describe the components of a guerrilla marketing plan and explain the benefits of preparing one.
   - A major part of the entrepreneur's business plan is the marketing plan, which focuses on a company's target customers and how best to satisfy their needs and wants. A solid marketing plan should pinpoint the specific target markets the company will serve, determine customer needs and wants through market research, analyze the firm's competitive advantages and build a marketing strategy around them, and create a marketing mix that meets customer needs and wants.

2. Explain how small businesses can pinpoint their target markets.
   - Sound market research helps the owner pinpoint his target market. The most successful businesses have well-defined portraits of the customers they are seeking to attract.

3. Explain how to determine customer needs through market research and the steps in the market research process.
   - Market research is the vehicle for gathering the information that serves as the foundation of the marketing plan. Good research does not have to be complex and expensive to be useful. The steps in conducting market research include:

     **Step 1.** Defining the problem: "What do you want to know?"

     **Step 2.** Collecting the data from either primary or secondary sources.

     **Step 3.** Analyzing and interpreting the data.

     **Step 4.** Drawing conclusions and acting on them.

4. Describe the guerrilla marketing strategies on which a small business can build competitive edge in the marketplace.
   - When plotting a marketing strategy, owners must strive to achieve a competitive advantage, some way to make their companies different from and better than the competition. Successful small businesses rely on ten guerrilla marketing strategies to develop a competitive edge: "niche-picking," "entertailing," building a consistent branding strategy, starting a blog, using online social networks, emphasizing their uniqueness, connecting with their customers, focusing on customers' needs, retaining existing customers, emphasizing quality; paying attention to convenience, concentrating on innovation; dedicating themselves to service; and emphasizing speed.

5. Discuss the marketing opportunities the World Wide Web offers and how entrepreneurs can best take advantage of them.
   - The Web offers small business owners tremendous marketing potential on par with their larger rivals. Entrepreneurs are just beginning to uncover the Web's profit potential, which is growing rapidly. Successful Web sites are attractive, inviting, easy to navigate, interactive, and offers users something of value.

6. Discuss the "four Ps" of marketing—product, place, price, and promotion—and their role in building a successful marketing strategy.
   - The marketing mix consists of the "4 Ps":
     *Product.* Entrepreneurs should understand where in the product life cycle their products are.
     *Place.* The focus here is on choosing the appropriate channel of distribution and using it most efficiently.
     *Price.* Price is an important factor in customers' purchase decisions, but many small businesses find that non-price competition can be profitable.
     *Promotion.* Promotion involves both advertising and personal selling.

## Discussion Questions

1. What is a marketing plan. What lies at its center?
2. What objectives should a marketing plan accomplish?
3. How can market research benefit a small business owner? List some possible sources of market information.
4. Does market research have to be expensive and sophisticated to be valuable? Explain.
5. Why is it important for small business owners to define their target markets as part of their marketing strategies?
6. What is a competitive edge? How might a small company gain a competitive edge?
7. Describe how a small business owner could use the following sources of a competitive advantage: "niche-picking," "entertailing," building a consistent branding strategy, emphasizing their uniqueness, connecting with their customers, focusing on customers' needs, emphasizing quality; paying attention to convenience, concentrating on innovation; dedicating themselves to service; and emphasizing on speed.
8. Describe the marketing potential of the World Wide Web for small businesses.
9. Explain the concept of the marketing mix. What are the four Ps?

10. List and explain the stages in the product life cycle. How can a small firm extend its product's life?

11. With a 70 percent customer retention rate (average for most U.S. firms according to the American Management Association), every $1 million of business in 2005 will grow to more than $4 million by the year 2015. If you retain 80 percent of your customers, the $1 million will grow to a little over $6 million. If you can keep 90 percent of your customers, that $1 million will grow to more than $9.5 million. What can the typical small business do to increase its customer retention rate?

---

# Business PlanPro

Incorporate the marketing concepts from the chapter along with those from previous chapters as you continue to build your business plan. The marketing section of your plan will add greater depth to your situation analysis and offer additional insight into your business strategy. For most business plans, 25 to 35 percent of the plan is devoted to the marketing plan, emphasizing the importance of this information. Your business plan should describe how you determined that a market exists for the products or services of your business, identify the market segments you are targeting, establish the unique selling proposition to differentiate your products and services, and describe how you will reach the market and motivate customers to purchase.

## On the Web

The Internet is a great place to begin conducting market research. In addition to the resources it offers, the Web can also help determine which form of market research is most suitable for your plan. Your market research should provide specific information about your target market and the key factors that influence customers' buying decisions. Your business plan will benefit from even the most elementary market research and, if it does not provide new information, that research may validate what you already know.

The Internet can also help you identify your industry's trade associations. Assess the information that is available on their Web sites. Does the industry association have publications available? Does it sponsor seminars and workshops? What benefits does it provide to its members? What does it cost to join the association? Industry associations can be a valuable source of market research.

As this chapter mentions, excellent data that can assist with your plan is available through U.S. government Web sites, including the following:

- Small Business Administration (SBA)
  www.sba.gov
- Small Business Development Center (SBDC)
  www.sba.gov/sbdc
- U.S. Census Bureau
  www.census.gov
- U.S. Department of Commerce
  www.trade.gov
- U.S. Chamber of Commerce
  www.uschamber.com

For example, the U.S. Census Bureau's Web site at www.census.gov provides a menu of available demographic reports that includes detailed information on various cities, towns, industries, county-specific economic surveys, business patterns for specific zip codes, and others.

Private market research sources are plentiful on the Web as well. Although most provide this information for a fee, many sites offer preliminary information at no cost. One example is geocluster data called PRIZM, an acronym for Potential Rating Index by Zip Markets. This market data, available from Claritas Inc., offers descriptions of consumers by zip code beyond that of traditional demographic data. PRIZM data classifies U.S. neighborhoods into 62 distinct lifestyle groups based on education, affluence, family life cycle, urbanization, mobility, race, and ethnicity. You can look up PRIZM information by going to www.claritas.com/MyBestSegments and clicking on the "Zip Code Look-Up" tab at the top. Enter your zip code into the search window for your results and you may be impressed by what you find—all at no cost. Other market research information is available through sites such as Zap Data at www.zapdata.com. Here you will find industry data reports with preliminary information, also available at no charge. This information, sorted by Standard Industry Classification (SIC) code, tracks how many companies are in the industry, their average sales, the number of employees, the company size, and their locations.

Online magazines, newspapers, and other publications offer an efficient way to search for articles and other information related to your business and the industry in which it operates. Many industry-specific magazines publish statistical editions and market reviews at regular intervals. Search the indexes to identify published information that might help the marketing section of your business plan. You may find an index listing for an article that includes forecasts your industry or addresses industry economics or trends. You can also contact magazine editorial departments for additional information using the information on their Web sites.

## In the Software

Review some of the sample business plans that have been the most helpful to date. Review the marketing section of these plans and note the type and depth of market information they include. This information is essential to establish a solid understanding of the market your business will serve and to use as the basis for developing and validating your strategy. Now go to each of the following sections in your business plan:

*Your Company.* Review the work that you began in the "Your Company" section of your business plan. As you review that information, does it capture a marketing focus? Does this section place the necessary emphasis on building lasting customer relationships? Add to and edit your work to reflect this critical perspective.

*What You Are Selling?* Make certain this section presents the goods and services you are selling to your customer. It must concisely communicate the value that your customers will realize by doing business with your company and the benefits they receive from your company's products and services.

*Service Summary.* Think about the unique nature of the services your business provides. How will your services offer more customer benefits than those of your competitors? How will your services be superior and provide meaningful value to your customers that will enhance their loyalty? Address these questions in this section of your plan.

*Your Market.* Add information that you have gleaned from your marketing research to describe your market in as much detail as possible.

*Target Market Segment.* Review the chapter concepts regarding target marketing. Use those concepts to help you develop a clear picture of your target customers. You should incorporate these profiles into this section to describe your target market segment.

*Competition.* A detailed and thorough discussion and analysis of each of your company's current and potential competitors is critical. The business plan must demonstrate that you have evaluated this critical factor and can identify, in realistic and practical terms, how your business will compete successfully. Demonstrate your knowledge of how customers make purchasing decisions and how your proposed venture can gain their business. Be honest and objective as you describe your competitors' strengths and weaknesses. Discuss the customer appeal, pricing strategies, advertising campaigns, and the products and services your competitors offer.

*Competitive Edge.* Based on that information, review the "Competitive Edge" section of your plan. What unique attributes does your business offer that will provide real or perceived benefits for your customers? Make sure you capture those thoughts in this section. Be as detailed as possible and explain your strategies to create this advantage. Incorporate material from your marketing and sales plan that will show how these strategic advantages support your sales forecast.

*The Sales Forecast.* Review the sales forecast that you entered in the previous chapters. Is that forecast realistic? Is your company's cost of goods accurate? Go to the narrative section of the sales forecast and explain the numbers in the sales forecast. Include any assumptions on which you have developed your sales forecast. Explain why your sales are projected to change over time. Include any key events that may affect your sales and how and why they will influence the sales forecast. Finally, as you evaluate your numbers and the assumptions that support them, ask yourself if they are realistic. Developing financial forecasts using published statistics from sources such as RMA Annual Statement Studies (www.rmahq.org), market research, industry studies, and other sources lends credibility to your plan. Once again, you will find links at the Companion Website (www.prenhall/scarborough.com) to information that may be helpful.

*Marketing Plan Summary.* A marketing strategy should present a clear link to forecasts of sales revenue. Use a detailed analysis and explanation of all assumptions on which the analysis rests. Your company's product, pricing, distribution, and promotion plans combined should produce a unified marketing strategy.

## Building Your Business Plan

Continue to build your business plan with the new information you have acquired. Step back to assess whether you have a solid understanding of your market and whether your business plan effectively communicates that understanding.

# Creative Use of Advertising and Promotion

Advertising is salesmanship mass produced. No one would bother to use advertising if he could talk to all of his prospects face-to-face. But he can't.
—Morris Hite

The man who stops advertising to save money is like the man who stops the clock to save time.
—Anonymous

*Learning Objectives*

Upon completion of this chapter, you will be able to:

1   Define your company's unique selling proposition (USP).
2   Explain the differences among promotion, publicity, personal selling, and advertising.
3   Describe the advantages and disadvantages of the various advertising media.
4   Identify four basic methods for preparing an advertising budget.
5   Explain practical methods for stretching an entrepreneur's advertising budget.

dvertising is not just a business expense; it is an investment in a company's future. Without a steady advertising and promotional campaign, a small business's customer base will soon dry up. Advertising can be an effective means of increasing sales by telling customers about a business and its goods or services, by improving the image of the firm and its products, and by persuading customers to purchase its goods or services. A mega-budget is not a prerequisite for building an effective advertising campaign. With a dose of creativity and ingenuity, a small company can make its voice be heard above the clamor of its larger competitors—and stay within a limited budget! A company's promotional strategy, which is comprised of advertising, publicity, and personal selling, must deliver the same clear, consistent, and compelling message about the business and its products or services. Customers respond best to a positive message that is delivered consistently by each component of the strategy. One goal of a company's promotional strategy is to create brand equity, which is measured by customer loyalty and its customers' willingness to pay a premium for its products and services.

Developing an effective advertising program has become more of a challenge for business owners recently. Because of media overflow, overwhelming ad clutter, increasingly fragmented audiences, more advertising options, and more skeptical consumers, companies have had to become more innovative and creative in their advertising campaigns. Rather than merely turning up the volume on their advertising campaigns, companies are learning to change their frequencies and try out new approaches in different advertising media.

A company's promotional efforts must differentiate its products and services from those of competitors. Some of the most effective advertisers have enhanced their brand loyalty by emphasizing in their promotional strategies the unique customer benefits that their products or services provide. For example, Nordstrom department stores are defined by friendly customer service, Volvo is known for automotive safety, and FedEx is recognized for guaranteed overnight delivery. One of the first steps in creating a promotional strategy is for a company to carefully and thoughtfully define its *unique selling proposition*.

## Define Your Company's Unique Selling Proposition

*1.* Define your company's unique selling proposition (USP).

Entrepreneurs should build their advertising messages on a **unique selling proposition (USP)**, a key customer benefit or a product or service that sets it apart from its competition. To be effective, a USP must actually *be* unique—something the competition does not (or cannot) provide—and compelling enough to encourage customers to buy. One technique is to replace your company's name and logo with those of your top competitor. Does the ad still make sense? If so, the ad is not based on your company's unique selling proposition! Unfortunately, many business owners never define their companies' USP, and the result is an uninspiring "me-too" message that cries out "buy from us" without offering customers any compelling reasons to do so.

A successful USP answers the critical question every customer asks: "What's in it for me?" A USP should express in no more than 10 words what a business can do for its customers. Can your product or service save your customers time or money, make their lives easier or more convenient, improve their self-esteem, or make them feel better? If so, you have the foundation for building a USP. The most effective ads are *not* just about a company's products and services; instead, they focus on the company's customers and how its products and services can improve their lives.

The USP becomes the heart of a company's advertising message. For instance, the owner of a quaint New England bed and breakfast came up with a four-word USP that captures the essence of the escape her business offers guests from their busy lives: "Delicious beds, delicious breakfasts." Sheila Paterson, co-founder of Marco International, a marketing consulting firm, says her company's USP is "Creative solutions for impossible marketing problems."[1] At Enterprise Rent-a-Car, founded in 1957 by Jack Taylor and now one of the largest privately held companies in the United States with sales of more than $9 billion, the USP reflects the company's emphasis on customer service and convenience: "We'll

© Mike Baldwin / Cornered

Winner of the Worst Slogan Contest.

pick you up." The most effective USPs are simple, concrete, believable, emotional, and easy to communicate to prospective customers.

The best way to identify a meaningful USP is to describe the primary benefit a product or service offers customers and then to list other secondary benefits it provides. Most businesses will have no more than three primary benefits. Smart entrepreneurs look beyond the physical characteristics of their products or services. Sometimes the most powerful USP is the *intangible or psychological* benefit a product or service offers customers—for example, safety, security, acceptance, status, and others. Entrepreneurs must be careful, however, to avoid stressing minuscule differences that are irrelevant to customers. Before creating a promotional campaign, entrepreneurs should develop a brief list of the facts that support the company's USP—for example, 24-hour service, a fully trained, experienced staff, industry awards won, and others. By focusing the message on

### TABLE 10.1  A Six-Sentence Advertising and Promotion Strategy

Do your advertising and promotion deliver the message you want to the audience you are targeting? If not, try stating your strategy in six sentences:

*Primary purpose.* What is the primary purpose of your ad? "The purpose of Rainbow Tours' ads is to get people to call or write for a free video brochure."

*Primary benefit.* What USP can you offer customers? "We will stress the unique and exciting places our customers can visit."

*Secondary benefits.* What other key benefits support your USP? "We will also stress the convenience and value of our tours and the skill and experience of our tour guides."

*Target audience.* At whom are we aiming the ad? "We will aim our ads at adventurous male and female singles and couples, 21 to 34, who can afford our tours."

*Audience reaction.* What response do you want from your target audience? "We expect our audience to call or write to request our video brochure."

*Company personality.* What image do you want to convey in your ads? "Our ads will reflect our innovation, excitement, conscientiousness, and our warm, caring attitude toward our customers."

*Source:* Adapted from Jay Conrad Levinson, "The Six Sentence Strategy," *Communication Briefings,* December 1994, p. 4.

these top benefits and the facts that support them, entrepreneurs can communicate their USPs to their target audiences in meaningful, attention-getting ways. Building a firm's marketing message around a USP spells out for customers the benefits they can expect if they buy the company's product or service and why they should do business with a company rather than with its competition.

Table 10.1 describes a six-sentence advertising and promotion strategy designed to create powerful ads that focus on a USP.

## Creating a Promotional Strategy

**2.** Explain the differences among promotion, publicity, personal selling, and advertising.

The terms *advertising* and *promotion* are often confused. **Promotion** is any form of persuasive communication designed to inform consumers about a product or service and to influence them to purchase these goods or services. It includes publicity, personal selling, and advertising.

### Publicity

**Publicity** is any commercial news covered by the media that boosts sales but for which the small business does not pay. "[Publicity] is telling your story to the people you want to reach—namely the news media, potential customers, and community leaders," says the head of a public relations firm. "It is not haphazard . . . It requires regular and steady attention."[2] Publicity has power because it is from an unbiased source. For example, a news feature about a company or a product appearing in a newspaper or magazine has more impact on people's buying decisions than an advertisement does. Exposure in any medium raises a company's visibility and boosts sales, and, best of all, publicity is free! It does require some creativity and effort, however.

*Jody Hall and Vérité Coffee*

After working at Starbucks for 12 years, Jody Hall saw first-hand the value of publicity and decided to emphasize it when she launched her own Seattle-based coffee shop, Vérité Coffee. In addition to selling coffee, Hall included a unique gourmet cupcake bakery in her store, which has generated articles in both the *Los Angeles Times* and *Food & Wine* magazine. During elections, Hall hands out free cupcakes to voters, advertising the offer in local papers with catchy slogans such as "Legalize Frostitution." Hall also generated publicity for her Vérité Coffee by donating 1,000 cupcakes to the local zoo for an elephant's birthday party and to auctions at local schools. Her efforts have paid off; Vérité Coffee generates sales of more than $1 million, and several local supermarkets have approached her about carrying her company's products.[3]

The following tactics can help entrepreneurs stimulate publicity for their companies.

- *Write an article that will interest your customers or potential customers.* One investment advisor writes a monthly column for the local newspaper on timely topics such as "Retirement Planning," "Minimizing Your Tax Bill," and "How to Pay for College." Not only do the articles help build her credibility as an expert, but they also have attracted new customers to her business.
- *Sponsor an event designed to attract attention.* In 1982, Bob Bisbee, owner of a small fuel dock and fishing store in Newport Beach, California, created a fishing tournament, Bisbee's Black and Blue Tournament (the focus was on black marlin and blue marlin), in an attempt to boost sales for his business. Before long, the event was picked up by major media outlets. The public relations strategy was so successful that the fishing tournament, now one of the world's richest and best-known fishing events, has replaced Bisbee's original business![4]
- *Involve celebrities "on the cheap."* Few small businesses can afford to hire celebrities as spokespersons for their companies. Some companies have discovered other ways to get celebrities to promote their products, however. For instance, when Karen Neuburger, owner of Karen Neuburger's Sleepwear, learned that U.S. talk show host

Oprah Winfrey is a "pajama connoisseur," she sent the talk show host a pair of her pajamas. The move paid off; Neuburger has appeared on Oprah's popular television show on three separate occasions, generating hundreds of thousands of dollars' worth of publicity for her company.[5]

- **Contact local TV and radio stations and offer to be interviewed.** Many local news or talk shows are looking for guests to talk about topics of interest to their audiences (especially in January and February). Even local shows can reach new customers.

- **Publish a newsletter.** With a personal computer and desktop publishing software, any entrepreneur can publish a professional-looking newsletter. Freelancers can offer design and editing advice. Use the newsletter to reach present and potential customers.

- **Contact local business and civic organizations and offer to speak to them.** A powerful, informative presentation can win new business. (Be sure your public speaking skills are up to par first! If not, consider joining Toastmasters International, www. toastmasters.org)

- **Offer or sponsor a seminar.** Teaching people about a subject you know a great deal about builds confidence and goodwill among potential customers. The owner of a landscaping service and nursery offers a short course in landscape architecture and always sees sales climb afterwards!

- **Write news releases and fax or e-mail them to the media.** The key to having a news release picked up and printed is finding a unique angle on your business or industry that would interest an editor. Keep it short, simple, and interesting. E-mail press releases should be shorter than printed ones—typically four or five paragraphs rather than one or two pages—and they should include a link to the company's Web site.

*Richard Mori and Mori Books*

When New Hampshire switched to a new toll road system, the U.S. state declared all outstanding highway toll tokens worthless. Sensing a public relations opportunity, Richard Mori, owner of a bookstore, offered to redeem the outdated tokens at double their face value for up to half the price of any book in his store and sent out press releases announcing the deal. Within days, newspapers and television and radio stations across New Hampshire were featuring Mori's business. The exposure led to a 25 percent increase in sales.[6]

- **Volunteer to serve on community and industry boards and committees.** You can make your town a better place to live and work and raise your company's visibility at the same time.

- **Sponsor a community project or support a nonprofit organization or charity.** Not only will you be giving something back to the community, but you will also gain recognition, goodwill, and, perhaps, customers for your business. Appearance Plus, a dry cleaning business in Cincinnati, Ohio, received the equivalent of thousands of dollars' worth of advertising from the publicity generated by its Coats for Kids campaign. Customers donated winter coats and blankets, which the company cleaned for free and then distributed to the needy.[7]

- **Promote a cause.** By engaging in cause marketing, entrepreneurs can support a cause that is important to them and generate publicity for their companies at the same time. The key is choosing a cause that is important to your customers. One marketing expert offers the following formula for selecting the right cause: Mission statement + personal passion + customer demographics = ideal cause.[8] REI, a retailer of outdoor gear, generates goodwill among its customers and publicity for its business by donating both money and employees' time to worthy outdoor nonprofit programs such as Big City Mountaineers, which leads wilderness adventures for urban teens, and conservation causes such as the Continental Divide Trail Alliance and the Leave No Trace Center for Outdoor Ethics.[9]

## Personal Selling

Advertising often marks the beginning of a sale, but personal selling usually is required to close the sale. **Personal selling** is the personal contact between salespeople and potential customers that comes from sales efforts. Effective personal selling can give a small company a definite advantage over its larger competitors by creating a feeling of personal attention. Personal selling deals with the salesperson's ability to match customer needs to the company's goods and services. Top salespeople have the following characteristics:

- *They are enthusiastic and alert to opportunities.* Star sales representatives demonstrate deep concentration, high energy, and drive.
- *They are experts in the products or services they sell.* They understand how their product lines or services can help their customers.
- *They concentrate on their best accounts.* Top salespeople focus on customers with the greatest sales potential first. They understand the importance of the 80/20 rule: Approximately 80 percent of their sales comes from about 20 percent of their customers.
- *They plan thoroughly.* On every sales call, the best representatives act with a purpose to close the sale.
- *They use a direct approach.* They get right to the point with customers.
- *They approach the sales call from their customers' perspectives.* They have empathy for their customers and know their customers' businesses and their needs. Rather than sell the features of a product or service, they emphasize the benefits those features offer their customers.
- *They offer proof of the benefits their product or service provides.* The best salespeople provide tangible evidence such as statistics, facts, and testimonies from other customers about how their product or service will benefit the customer.
- *They are good listeners.* Great salespeople ask questions and listen. By listening, sales representatives are able to identify customers' "hot buttons," key issues that drive their purchase decisions. "Questions are the key to selling," says one experienced salesperson. "Nobody ever listened themselves out of a sale!"[10]
- *They use past success stories.* Top salespeople encourage customers to express their problems and then present solutions using examples of past successes.
- *They leave sales material with clients.* The material gives the customer the opportunity to study company and product literature in more detail.
- *They see themselves as problem solvers, not just vendors.* Their perspective is "How can I be a valuable resource for my customers?" In fact, smart salespeople take the time to ask their existing customers, "Is there anything I am not doing that I could be doing to serve you better?" A study by Cahners Research found that sales representatives who understand the business needs and pressures that their customers face are 69 percent more likely to close a sale.[11]
- *They measure their success not just by sales volume but by customer satisfaction.*

One extensive study of salespeople found that just 20 percent of all salespeople have the ability to sell and are selling the "right" product or service. That 20 percent of sales reps makes 80 percent of all sales. The study also concluded that 55 percent of sales representatives have "absolutely no ability to sell"; the remaining 25 percent have sales ability but are selling the wrong product or service.[12]

A study by Cahners Research found that it takes an average of 5.12 sales calls to close a deal.[13] Common causes of sales rejections include the representative's failure to determine customers' needs, talking too much, and neglecting to ask for the order. Given the high cost of making a sales call (an average of nearly $400), those missed opportunities are quite costly. Figure 10.1 shows how sales representatives spend their time. (Note that they spend only 10 percent of their time engaged in active selling!)

**FIGURE 10.1 How Sales Representatives Spend Their Time**

*Source:* Proudfoot Consulting, 2006.

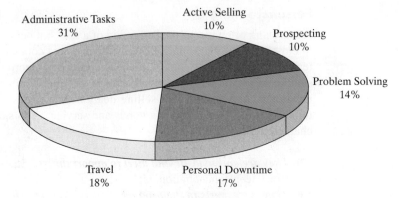

Administrative Tasks 31%

Active Selling 10%

Prospecting 10%

Problem Solving 14%

Travel 18%

Personal Downtime 17%

Entrepreneurs can improve their sales representatives' "closing averages" by following some basic guidelines:

- *Hire the right people.* A successful sales effort starts well before a sales representative calls on a potential customer. The first step is hiring capable salespeople who demonstrate empathy for customers, are motivated, persistent, and focused.

- *Train sales representatives.* Too often, business owners send sales representatives out into the field with little or no training and then wonder why they cannot produce. Training starts with teaching salespeople every aspect of the products or services they will be selling before moving on to teach them how to build relationships with customers. Training also must include the two most important selling skills of all: listening to the customer and closing the sale. Many business owners find that role playing exercises are an effective sales training technique.

- *Develop a selling system.* To be successful, sales representatives must develop an effective selling system. To build a winning selling system, entrepreneurs can take the following steps:

  1. *Prepare.* The best sales representatives know that what they do *before* they make a sales call can significantly influence their success. In fact, the top complaint about sales representatives among buyers is a salesperson who is unprepared. Unfortunately, according to a study by Knowledge Anywhere, nearly 63 percent of sales representatives spend less than 20 minutes preparing for a sales call.[14] Smart salespeople take the time to research their customers (most often using the Internet) and to learn about the companies where their customers work.

  2. *Approach.* Establish rapport with the prospect. Customers seldom buy from salespeople they dislike or distrust.

  3. *Interview.* Get the prospect to do most of the talking; the goal is to identify his or her needs, preferences, and problems. The key is to *listen* and then to ask follow-up questions that help determine exactly what the customer wants. Norm Brodsky, founder of six companies, including a highly successful records storage business, says, "When I call on a prospect for the first time, I don't even talk about our company. I spend the whole visit just trying to learn all I can about the people I'm dealing with. I look to build rapport and understand how the customer likes to do business."[15]

  4. *Demonstrate, explain, and show.* Make clear the features and benefits of your product or service and point out how they meet the prospect's needs or solve his problems.

  5. *Validate.* Prove the claims about your product or service. If possible, offer the prospect names and numbers of other satisfied customers (with their permission, of course). Testimonials really work.

  6. *Negotiate.* Listen for objections from the prospect. Objections can be the salesperson's best friend; they tell him or her what must be "fixed" before the

prospect will commit to an order. The key is to determine the *real* objection and confront it.

   7. *Close.* Ask for a decision. Good sales representatives know when the prospect flashes the green light on a sale. They stop talking and ask for the order.

■ *Be empathetic.* The best salespeople look at the sale from the customer's viewpoint, not their own! Doing so encourages the sales representative to stress *value* to the customer.

■ *Set multiple objectives.* Before making a sales call, salespeople should set three objectives:

   1. *The primary objective* is the most reasonable outcome expected from the meeting. It may be to get an order or to learn more about a prospect's needs.

   2. *The minimum objective* is the very least the salesperson will leave with. It may be to set another meeting or to identify the prospect's primary objections.

   3. *The visionary objective* is the most optimistic outcome of the meeting. This objective forces the salesperson to be open-minded and to shoot for the top.

■ *Monitor sales efforts and results.* Selling is just like any other business activity and must be controlled. At a minimum, entrepreneurs should know the following numbers for their companies:

   1. Actual sales versus projected sales
   2. Sales generated per call made
   3. Average cost of a sales call
   4. Total sales costs
   5. Sales by product, salesperson, territory, customer, and so on
   6. Profit contribution by product, salesperson, territory, customer, and so on

## Advertising

**Advertising** is any sales presentation that is non-personal in nature and is paid for by an identified sponsor. A company's target audience and the nature of its message determine the advertising media it will use. However, the process does not end with creating and broadcasting an ad. Entrepreneurs also must evaluate an ad campaign's effectiveness. Did it accomplish the objectives it was designed to accomplish? Immediate-response ads can be evaluated in a number of ways. For instance, a business owner can include coupons that customers redeem to get price reductions on products and services. Dated coupons identify customer responses over certain time periods. Some firms use "hidden offers," statements hidden somewhere in an ad that offer customers special deals if they mention an ad or bring in a coupon from an ad. For example, Scott Fiore, owner of the Herbal Remedy, an all-natural pharmacy uses a "bring this ad in for 10 percent off" message in his print ads so he can track each ad's success rate and adjust his advertising expenditures accordingly.

Business owners can also gauge an ad's effectiveness by measuring the volume of store traffic generated. Effective advertising should increase store traffic, which boosts sales of advertised and non-advertised items. Of course, if an advertisement promotes a particular bargain item, the owner can judge its effectiveness by comparing sales of the items to preadvertising sales levels. Remember: The ultimate test of an ad is whether or not it increases sales!

Ad tests allow entrepreneurs to determine the most effective methods of reaching their target customers. An owner can design two different ads (or use two different media or broadcast times) that are coded for identification and see which one produces more responses. For example, a business owner can use a split run of two different ads in a local newspaper. That is, he can place one ad in part of the paper's press run and another ad in the remainder of the run. Then he can measure the response level to each ad to compare its effectiveness. Table 10.2 offers 12 tips for creating an effective advertising campaign.

The remainder of this chapter will focus on selecting advertising media, developing an advertising plan, and creating an advertising budget. Figure 10.2 illustrates the characteristics of a successful ad.

## TABLE 10.2 Twelve Tips for Effective Advertising

1. *Plan more than one advertisement at a time.* An advertising campaign is likely to be more effective if it is developed from a comprehensive plan for a specific time period. A piecemeal approach produces ads that lack continuity and a unified theme.

2. *Set long-run advertising objectives.* One cause of inadequate planning is the failure to establish specific objectives for the advertising program. If an entrepreneur never defines what is expected from advertising, the program is likely to lack a sense of direction.

3. *Use advertisements, themes, and vehicles that appeal to diverse groups of people.* Although personal judgment influences every business decision, business owners cannot afford to let bias interfere with advertising decisions. For example, you should not use a particular radio station simply because you like it. What matters is whether the company's target customers listen to the station.

4. *View advertising expenditures as investments not as expenses.* In an accounting sense, advertising is a business expense, but money spent on ads tends to produce sales and profits over time that might not be possible without advertising. An effective advertising program generates more sales than it costs to create and implement. You must ask, "Can I afford *not* to advertise?"

5. *Use advertising that is different from your competitors' advertising.* Some managers tend to "follow the advertising crowd" because they fear being different from their competitors. "Me-too" advertising frequently is ineffective because it fails to create a unique image for the firm. Don't be afraid to be different!

6. *Choose the media vehicle that is best for your business even if it's not number one.* It is not uncommon for several media within the same geographic region to claim to be "number one." Different media offer certain advantages and disadvantages. Entrepreneurs should evaluate each according to its ability to reach their target audiences most effectively.

7. *Consider using someone else as the spokesperson in your TV and radio commercials.* Although being your own spokesperson may lend a personal touch to your ads, the commercial may be seen as nonprofessional or "homemade." The ad may detract from the company's image rather than improve it.

8. *Limit the content of each ad.* Some entrepreneurs think that to get the most for their advertising money, they must pack their ads full of facts and illustrations. But overcrowded ads confuse customers and are often ignored. Simple, well-designed ads that focus on your USP are much more effective.

9. *Devise ways of measuring your ads' effectiveness that don't depend on just two or three customers' responses.* Measuring the effectiveness of advertising is an elusive art at best. But the opinions of a small unrepresentative sample of customers, whose opinions may be biased, is not a reliable gauge of an ad's effectiveness. The techniques described earlier offer a more objective measurement of an ad's ability to produce results.

10. *Don't stop the ad if something does not happen immediately.* Some ads are designed to produce immediate results, but many ads require more time because of the lag effect they experience. One rule of advertising is: It's not the size; it's the frequency. The head of one advertising agency claims, "The biggest waste of money is stop-and-start advertising." With advertising, patience is essential, and entrepreneurs must give an advertising campaign a reasonable time to produce results. One recent study concluded that sales increases are most noticeable four to six months after an advertising campaign begins. One advertising expert claims that successful advertisers "are not capricious ad-by-ad makers; they're consistent ad campaigners."

11. *Emphasize the benefits that the product or service provides to the customer.* Too often, ads emphasize only the features of the products or services a company offers without mentioning the benefits they provide customers. Customers really don't care about a product's or service's "bells and whistles"; they are much more interested in the *benefits* those features can give them! Their primary concern is "What's in it for me?"

12. *Evaluate the cost of different advertising medium.* Entrepreneurs must understand the difference between the absolute and relative cost of an ad. The medium that has a low absolute cost may actually offer a high relative cost if it does not reach your intended target audience. Evaluate the cost of different media by looking at the cost per thousand customers reached. Remember: No medium is a bargain if it fails to connect you with your intended customers.

*Sources:* Adapted from Sue Clayton, "Advertising," *Business Start-Ups*, December 1995, pp. 6–7; *Marketing for Small Business*, The University of Georgia Small Business Development Center: Athens, Georgia, 1992, p. 69; "Advertising Leads to Sales," *Small Business Reports*, April 1988, p 14; Shelly Meinhardt, "Put It in Print," *Entrepreneur*, January 1989, p.54; Danny R. Arnold and Robert H. Solomon, "Ten 'Don'ts' in Bank Advertising"; *Burroughs Clearing House*, September 1980, pp. 20–24, 43–43; Howard Dana Shaw, "Success with Ads," *In Business*, November/December 1991, pp. 48–49; Jan Alexander and Aimee L. Stern, "Avoid the Deadly Sins in Advertising"; *Your Company*, August/September 1997, p. 22.

## Selecting Advertising Media

*3. Describe the advantages and disadvantages of the various advertising media.*

Entrepreneurs quickly discover a wide array of advertising media options, including newspapers, magazines, radio, television, direct mail, the Web, as well as many specialty media. One of the most important decisions an entrepreneur must make is which media to use to disseminate the company's message. The medium used to transmit the message influences the customer's perception—and reception—of it. The right message broadcast in the wrong

**FIGURE 10.2**
**Fundamentals of a**
**Successful Advertisement**

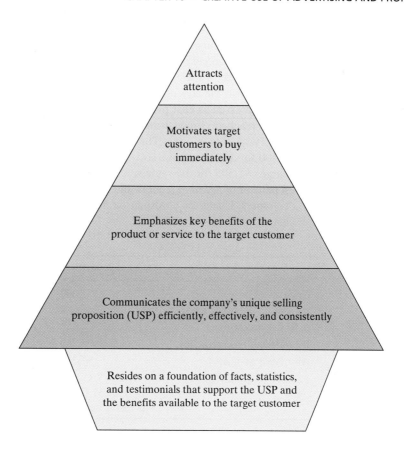

medium is ineffective. Before selecting the vehicle for the message, entrepreneurs should consider several important questions:

- *How large is my company's trading area?*  How big is the geographical region from which the firm will draw its customers? The size of this area influences the choice of media.

- *Who are my target customers and what are their characteristics?*  Determining a customer profile often points to the appropriate medium to use to get the message across most effectively.

- *With which media will my target customers most likely interact?*  Until they know who their target audience is, business owners cannot select the proper advertising media to reach it.

- *What budget limitations do I face?*  Entrepreneurs must direct their advertising programs within the restrictions of their operating budgets. Certain advertising media cost more than others.

- *Which media do my competitors use?*  Is it helpful for small business owners to know the media their competitors use, although they should *not* automatically assume that those media are the best choices. An approach that differs from the traditional one may produce better results.

- *How important is repetition and continuity of my advertising message?*  Generally, an ad becomes effective only after it is repeated several times, and many ads must be continued for some time before they produce results. Some experts suggest that an ad must be run at least six times in most mass media before it becomes effective.

- *How does each medium compare with others in its audience, its reach, and its frequency?*  **Audience** measures the number of paid subscribers a particular medium attracts and is called *circulation* in most print media such as newspapers and magazines. **Reach** is the total number of people exposed to an ad at least once in a period of time, usually four weeks. **Frequency** is the average number of times a person is exposed to an ad in that same time period.

■ *What does the advertising medium cost?* There are two types of advertising costs entrepreneurs must consider: the absolute cost and the relative cost. **Absolute cost** is the actual money outlay a business owner must make to place an ad in a particular medium for a specific time period. An even more important measure is an ad's **relative cost**, the ad's cost per potential customer reached. Relative cost is most often expressed as **cost per thousand (CPM)**, the cost of the ad per 1,000 customers reached. Suppose an entrepreneur decides to advertise his product in one of two newspapers in town. The *Sentinel* has a circulation of 21,000 and charges $1,200 for a quarter-page ad. The *Independent* has a circulation of 18,000 and charges $1,300 for the same space. Reader profiles of the two papers suggest that 25 percent of *Sentinel* readers and 37 percent of *Independent* readers are potential customers. Using this information, the manager computes the following relative costs:

|  | Sentinel | Independent |
|---|---|---|
| Circulation | 21,000 | 18,000 |
| Percentage of readers who are potential customers | $\times$ 25% | $\times$ .37% |
| Potential customers reached | 5,250 | 6,660 |
| Absolute cost of ad | $1,200 | $1,300 |
| Relative cost of ad (CPM) | $1,200/5,250 = .22857 or $228.57 per thousand potential customers reached | $1,300/6,660 = .19520 or $195.20 per thousand potential customers reached |

Although the *Sentinel* has a larger circulation and a lower absolute cost for running the ad, the *Independent* offers this entrepreneur a better advertising deal because of its lower cost per thousand potential customers (CPM) reached. It is important to note that this technique does not give a reliable comparison across media; it is a meaningful comparison only *within* a single medium. Differences among the format, presentation, and coverage of ads in different media are so vast that cross-comparisons are not meaningful.

## Media Options

The world of advertising is changing; traditional methods of advertising are not as effective as they once were because of increased advertising clutter, skepticism among customers, and competition for buyers' attention. Business owners are looking to supplement or even replace traditional methods of advertising with innovative, sometimes offbeat, techniques that capture buyers' attention. Choosing advertising media is no easy task because each has distinctive advantages, disadvantages, and costs. The "right" message in the "wrong" medium will miss its mark. Figure 10.3 gives a breakdown of U.S. business advertising expenditures by medium.

**WORD-OF-MOUTH ADVERTISING.** Perhaps the most effective and certainly the least expensive form of advertising is **word-of-mouth advertising** in which satisfied customers recommend a business to friends, family members, and acquaintances. Unsolicited testimonials are powerful because they are impartial and score high on importance and credibility among potential customers. The best way for a company to generate positive word-of-mouth advertising is to provide superior quality and service, giving customers a reason to talk about the company in a positive way. Providing high levels of service and quality leads to loyal customers who become walking advertisements for the companies they believe in. Word-of-mouth advertising can make or break a business because *dissatisfied* customers also speak out against businesses that treat them poorly. To ensure

**FIGURE 10.3 Advertising Expenditures by Medium**
*Source:* McCann-Erickson Inc., *Statistical Abstract of the United States,* 2003, www.census.gov.

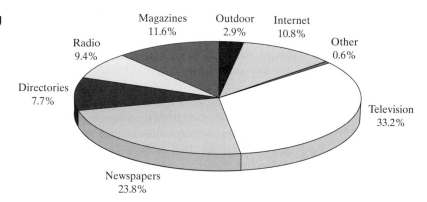

- Magazines 11.6%
- Outdoor 2.9%
- Internet 10.8%
- Other 0.6%
- Radio 9.4%
- Television 33.2%
- Directories 7.7%
- Newspapers 23.8%

that the word-of-mouth advertising a company generates is positive, business owners must actually do what they want their customers to say they do.

### ENTREPRENEURIAL Profile

*Shelly Hwang and Young Lee and Pinkberry*

When Shelly Hwang and Young Lee opened Pinkberry, a shop that sells all-natural, non-fat yogurt in West Hollywood, California, in a location that was less than ideal, they knew that they would have to rely on word-of-mouth advertising to build a customer base. Their yogurt, which comes in plain and green tea flavors with 18 toppings, ranging from kiwi and mango to fruity pebbles and carob chips, is served in a modern environment with upscale Italian furniture, Scandinavian light fixtures, and hip European music. Everything about Pinkberry resonates with the entrepreneurs' target customers, and the result was rampant word-of-mouth advertising. "When residents tasted the yogurt, their mouths were like machine guns," says Lee. "They talked about it; they brought their friends. Business has been just phenomenal from the first month." Word-of-mouth advertising has been so effective for Pinkberry that Hwang and Lee are busy planning to open other locations in the U.S. states of California, Arizona, New York, and Texas.[16]

A customer endorsement is an effective way of converting the power of word-of-mouth to an advertising message. The more recognized the person making the endorsement is, the more potential customers will be influenced to buy. Of course, unpaid and unsolicited endorsements are the most valuable. In a cynical world, many potential customers are turned off by what they believe is simply a paid statement from a person who may or may not have used the product.

The Holy Grail of word-of-mouth advertising is "buzz." Buzz occurs when a product is hot and everyone is talking about it. From the mood rings of the 1970s to the redesigned Volkswagon beetle of the 1990s, buzz drives the sales of many products. The Internet has only magnified the power of buzz to influence a product's sales. Buzz on the Web has become a powerful force in influencing the popularity of a firm's products or services. What can business owners do to start a buzz about their companies or their products or services? Sometimes buzz starts on its own, leaving a business owner struggling to keep up with the fury it creates. More often than not, however, business owners can give it a nudge by creating interest, mystique, and curiosity in a product or service by employing the following tips:

- **Make your business buzz-worthy.** If your company has nothing to set it apart, customers have no incentive to create buzz about it. Does your company sell a novel product, have a unique marketing approach, offer stellar customer service, use a wacky logo, or anything else that can set it apart? If so, that can be the basis for buzz.

- *Promote your company to "Influencers" in your market.* Influencers are high-profile customers that are on the front edge of every trend. They are the first to wear the hottest athletic shoe, master the coolest video game, or make the hippest restaurant their new hangout. They also are willing to tell their friends. Promoting your company's products and services to Influencers increases the likelihood that your company will be the subject of buzz.

- *Make it easy for satisfied customers to spread the word about your company.* Ask customers periodically to tell a friend about your business and their positive experience with it. Put a "Tell-a-friend" link on every page of your company's Web site. Reward customers who do refer customers to your business by offering them something special in return.

- *Use the Web to encourage viral marketing and amplify your company's word-of-mouth advertising.* One of the easiest ways to accomplish this is through e-mail because it is so easy for people to pass along to their friends. Another technique is to publicize news about your company on a blog and to include links to your company's Web site. Entrepreneurs also can use company sponsored message boards and instant messaging to engage customers and encourage word-of-mouth advertising.

- *Tap into the power of YouTube.* Video-oriented Web sites such as YouTube, which draws 8 million page views per day, can be a powerful tool for creating buzz for a company's products and services, particularly if its target customers are young people. Videos on YouTube often become the subject of e-mail, blogs, and instant messaging and are an important source of buzz for small companies.

**ENTREPRENEURIAL Profile**

*Kevork Kouyoumjian and WorldTrading23.com*

After a remote-controlled toy helicopter, the Picco Z, manufactured by Silverlit Toys, appeared with a cat in a YouTube video, bloggers began writing about it, and the video became the subject of millions of e-mails. Even though Silverlit Toys had not used "traditional" advertising techniques, the buzz generated from the amateur video created so much demand for the product that Silverlit had difficulty meeting it! WorldTrading23.com, a toy retailer, posted its own video on YouTube and sold 18,000 Picco Z helicopters in just two weeks! "It's the hottest item we've ever sold," says owner Kevork Kouyoumjian.[17]

**SPONSORSHIPS, SPECIAL EVENTS, AND PRODUCT PLACEMENT.** Although sponsorships and special events are a relatively new promotional medium for small companies, a growing number of small businesses are finding that sponsoring special events attracts a great deal of interest and provides a lasting impression of the company in customers' minds. In fact, sponsorship is the fastest growing form of advertising in the United States. As customers become increasingly harder to reach through any single advertising medium, companies of all sizes are finding that sponsoring special events—from wine tastings and beach volleyball tournaments to fitness walks and car races—is an excellent way to reach their target audiences.

There is a wide range in the cost of sponsorships. Sponsoring a hole at a charitable golf outing may cost as little as $100, but landing the name of your business or product on the hood of a car driven by a National Association for Stock Car Auto Racing (NASCAR) legend may cost as much as $7 million. (Flash memory makers SanDisk and Imation recently signed on as sponsors for teams competing in the NASCAR Sprint Cup Series.[18]) Sponsorships and participation in special events can be very cost effective if the entrepreneur supports events where attendees are potential customers. Local festivals and events gain the sponsor a great deal of positive public relations. Support for charity functions enhance the sponsor's community image, boost sales, and often attracts new customers.

**ENTREPRENEURIAL Profile**

*Gathering Tribes*

In Berkeley, California, small businesses can become sponsors in the community's popular Chocolate and Chalk Art Festival, which includes music, entertainment, food (including chocolate, of course), and sidewalk art. Sponsorships range from just $25 to $1,500, and the show brings in thousands of potential customers. The owner of Gathering Tribes, a retail store that sells Native American art, jewelry, and pottery, says that her company's sales increase 30 percent on the day of the festival, making the event worthwhile for Gathering Tribes.[19]

## ■ YouTube and the Power of Viral Video

MerlynDHZ (actually David Chau), an employee of Heeling Sports, the company that makes Heelys, the athletic shoes with retractable heels hidden in their soles, recently recorded a video of himself and his buddies performing a variety of acrobatic stunts in their Heelys. He uploaded the video onto YouTube.com, the popular video sharing Web site. What happened next was every advertiser's dream. Within a month, more than 2,000 people had watched the 90-second video clip. Some loyal fans linked to the video from their personal MySpace.com pages, and the exposure cost Heeling Sports nothing!

Every small business counts on positive word-of-mouth advertising from satisfied customers to bring in new business. The Internet, with its extensive social networking ability, gives entrepreneurs the ability to amplify the power of word-of-mouth advertising. One of the most effective ways to tap into Internet-powered word-of-mouth advertising is using video posting sites such as YouTube and MySpace. Video viral marketing is becoming a part of many small companies' advertising strategies because the homemade style of the videos appeals to customers who have been so inundated with traditional ads that they have begun to ignore many of them.

A study by the Online Publishers Association reports that 67 percent of Internet users have watched an online video (see Figure 10.4) and that 30 percent of those people have shared a video with friends. The study also shows that 66 percent of people who have watched an online video have seen an ad clip. Of those people, one-third have visited the advertiser's Web site, and 8 percent of them have actually made a purchase. Because of the impressive results they are getting from online video ads, some companies are shifting their advertising budgets away from traditional media to offbeat techniques such as viral video.

On YouTube alone, users upload 65,000 new video clips each day. What steps can a small company take to increase the odds that its video ad clips get noticed?

- *Keep your video short.* Visitors to the site are more likely to spend 55 seconds watching a video than they are to spend 8 minutes and 55 seconds to watch one.
- *Be creative.* Videos that are innovative and funny tend to be the most popular and the most viral among YouTube and Google Video users. One of the most popular ad videos online was a spot called "Tea Partay," a spoof that featured a "gang" of upscale preppies in their tennis togs rapping about finger sandwiches, Ivy League educations, multiple course meals, croquet, and, of course, the sponsor's product.

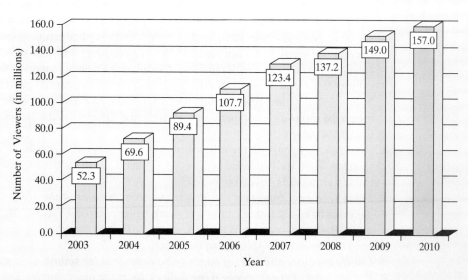

FIGURE 10.4 **Number of Viewers of Online Video**

*(continued)*

■ *Use key words and your company or product name in the tags and titles of your video.* When members of Team Heelys, the skate team that performs stunts in the company's shoes, post their videos to YouTube, they always include the word "Heelys" in the title to make it easy for fans to find their videos among the millions that are already posted at the site.

■ *Display your company's URL at the beginning and at the end of your video.* The goal is to drive customer traffic to your Web site; make it easy for customers to find it!

■ *Post notices of your newly posted video on your company's Web site.* Shoppers may decide to share the video with their friends, which may generate more customers for your company.

■ *Mention the video (and include a link to it) in your company blog or MySpace page.* (MySpace has more than 100 million accounts and adds another 250,000 users per day!) Don't make the mistake of posing as a customer who is offering an unsolicited endorsement of your company's product or service, however. Web users are far too smart for that, and the backlash can be brutal.

The video advertising strategy has proved to be quite successful for Heeling Sports; the company receives maximum exposure at a minimum cost, and sales have climbed rapidly. "It's helping us build brand recognition," says Brooks Radighieri, the company's marketing manager.

1. What advantages do video Web sites offer small companies as an advertising medium? Disadvantages?

2. What other tips would you offer entrepreneurs who are considering using video Web sites such as YouTube and Google Video?

*Sources:* Adapted from Jennifer Gill, "Contagious Commercials: How to Get in on the YouTube Craze," *Inc.*, November 2006, pp. 31–32; Jennifer Alsever, "Flying Off the Shelves," *Business 2.0*, December 2006, pp. 47–49; Nicholas Hoover and Larry Greenemeir, "YouTooCan Tube," *Information Week*, October 2, 2006, pp. 25–27.

Small companies do not have to rely on other organizations' events to generate advertising opportunities; they can create their own special events. The owner of Quadrille Quilting partnered with the owners of two other quilting shops to create Shop Hops, an event in which customers buy "passports" to all three stores that entitle them to refreshments and special prizes. The first Shop Hop, which took place on a Super Bowl weekend, generated an entire month's sales in just one day for Quadrille Quilting.[20]

Creativity and uniqueness are essential ingredients in any special event promotion, and entrepreneurs excel at those. The following tips will help entrepreneurs get the greatest promotional impact from event sponsorships:

■ *Do not count on sponsorships for your entire advertising campaign.* Sponsorships are most effective when they are part of a coordinated advertising effort. Most sponsors spend no more than 10 percent of their advertising budgets on sponsorships.

■ *Look for an event that is appropriate for your company and its products and services.* The owner of a small music store in an upscale mountain resort sponsors a local jazz festival every summer during the busy tourist season and generates lots of business among both residents and tourists. Ideally, an event's audience should match the sponsoring company's target audience. Otherwise, the sponsorship will be a waste of money.

■ *Research the event and the organization hosting it before agreeing to become a sponsor.* How well attended is the event? What is the demographic profile of the event's visitors? Is it well organized?

■ *Try to become a dominant (or, ideally, the only) sponsor of the event.* A small company can be easily lost in a crowd of much larger companies sponsoring the same event. If sole sponsorship is too expensive, make sure that your company is the only one from its industry sponsoring the event.

■ *Clarify the costs and level of participation required for sponsorship up front.*

■ *Get involved.* Do not simply write a check for the sponsorship fee and then walk away. Find an event that is meaningful to you, your company, and its employees and take an active role in it. Your sponsorship money will produce a higher return if you do.

In recent years, entrepreneurs have begun to explore new methods of getting their products or services in front of their target customers in a more subtle fashion. Many companies are engaged in product placement strategies in which their products or services appear in television shows, movies, video games, and other media that their target customers are likely to see. For example, Apple's laptop computers and iPods have received valuable exposure on popular U.S. TV shows such as *24, Heroes,* and *The Office.*[21] Product placement is effective because it relies on highly sophisticated yet subtle brand exposure. One of the earliest and most successful cases of product placement occurred in the 1982 movie, *E.T.—The Extra-Terrestrial,* in which the main character (E.T., the alien) discovers an affinity for Reese's Pieces candy. After the movie's premiere, sales of Reese's Pieces increased 65 percent![22]

Apple has benefited from a product placement strategy in which its laptop computers have appeared in popular television shows such as *24*.

**NEWSPAPERS.** Traditionally, the local newspaper has been the medium that most small companies rely on to get their messages across to customers. Although the number of newspapers sold in some countries has declined in recent years, the medium provides several *advantages* to small business advertisers:

*Selected geographical coverage.* Newspapers are geared to a specific geographic region, and they reach potential customers across all demographic classes. In general, they provide extensive coverage of a company's immediate trading area.

*Flexibility.* Newspaper advertisements can be changed readily on very short notice. Entrepreneurs can select the size of the ad, its location in the paper, and the days on which it runs. For instance, auto repair shops often advertise their tune-up specials in the sports section on weekends, and party shops display their ads in the entertainment section.

*Timeliness.* Papers almost always have very short closing times, the publication deadline prior to which the advertising copy must be submitted. Many newspapers allow advertisers to submit their copy as late as 24 hours before the ad runs.

*Communication potential.* Newspaper ads can convey a great deal of information by employing attractive graphics and copy. Properly designed, they can be very effective in attracting attention and persuading readers to buy.

*Low costs.* Newspapers normally offer advertising space at low absolute cost and, because of their blanket coverage of a geographic area, at low relative cost as well.

*Prompt responses.* Newspaper ads typically produce relatively quick customer response. A newspaper ad is likely to generate sales the very next day, and advertisers who use coupons can track the response to an ad. This advantage makes newspapers an ideal medium for promoting special events such as sales, grand openings, or the arrival of a new product.

*Growing popularity of free newspapers.* Most communities have at least one free (to readers) newspaper, and their reach can be significant, an important consideration for advertisers. Studies show that 60 percent of consumers say that they read a free paper at least once a week.[23]

Newspaper advertisements also have *disadvantages:*

*Wasted readership.* Because newspapers reach a wide variety of people, at least a portion of an ad's coverage will be wasted on readers who are not potential customers. This nonselective coverage makes it more difficult for newspapers to reach specific target markets than ads in other media.

*Reproduction limitations.* The quality of reproduction in newspapers is limited, especially when it is compared with that of magazines and direct mail. Recent technological advances, however, are improving the quality of reproduction in newspaper ads.

*Lack of prominence.* One frequently cited drawback of newspapers is that they carry so many ads that a small company's message might be lost in the crowd. The typical newspaper is 62 percent advertising. This disadvantage can be overcome by increasing the size of the ad or by adding color to it. Color can increase the reading of ads by as much as 80 percent over black-and-white ads. Studies show that two-color ads do "pull" better than black-and-white ones but only by a small margin. The *real* increase in ad recall and response comes from using full four-color ads. Bold headlines, illustrations, and photographs also increase an ad's prominence. Proper placement in the newspaper can also increase an ad's effectiveness. The best locations are on a right-hand page, near the right margin, above the half-page mark, or next to editorial articles. The most-read sections in the typical newspaper are the front page and the comics.

*Declining readership.* U.S. newspaper circulation, for example, has dropped from 98 percent in 1970 to less than 50 percent today. Newspaper ads are more effective with older adults and those with higher education and income. They are less effective with younger adults; studies show that just 35 percent of 18- to 34-year-old adults read a daily newspaper.[24]

*Short ad life.* The typical newspaper is soon discarded and, as a result, an ad's life is extremely short. Business owners can increase the effectiveness of their ads by giving them greater continuity. Spot ads can produce results, but maintaining a steady flow of business requires some degree of continuity in advertising.

**Buying Newspaper Ad Space.** Newspapers typically sell ad space by lines and columns or inches and columns. For instance, a 4-column by 100-line ad occupies four columns and 100 lines of space (14 lines are equal to 1 column inch). For this ad, a small business owner would pay the rate for 400 lines. If the newspaper's line rate is $3.50, this ad would cost $1,400 (400 lines × $3.50 per line). Most papers offer discounts for bulk, long-term and frequency contracts, and full-page ads. Advertising rates vary from one paper to another, depending on factors such as circulation and focus. Entrepreneurs should investigate the circulation statements, advertising rates, and reader profiles of a newspaper to see how well it matches the company's target audience before selecting one as an advertising medium.

**RADIO.** Newspapers offer blanket advertising coverage of a region, but radio permits advertisers to reach specific audiences over large geographic areas. By choosing the appropriate station, program, and time for an ad, a small company can reach virtually any target market.
Radio advertising offers several *advantages:*

*Universal infiltration.* The radio's nearly universal presence gives advertisements in this medium a major advantage. Nearly every home and car in the United States is equipped with a radio, which means that radio ads receive a tremendous amount of exposure in the target market. The average adult spends 20 hours each week listening to the radio. According to the Radio Advertising Bureau, radio reaches 74.2 percent of adults each day and 94 percent of customers each week![25]

*Market segmentation.* Radio advertising is flexible and efficient because advertisers can choose stations directed toward a specific market within a broad geographic region. Radio stations design their formats to appeal to specific types of audiences. (Ever notice how the stations you listen to are not the same ones your parents listen to?) AM stations, which once ruled the airways, now specialize mainly in "talk formats" such as call-in, news, religion, sports, and automotive shows. On the FM dial, country, top 40, rap, easy listening, modern rock, rhythm and blues, Spanish, and "golden oldies" stations have listener profiles that give entrepreneurs the ability to pinpoint practically any advertising target.

*Flexibility and timeliness.* Radio commercials have short closing times and can be changed quickly. Small firms dealing in seasonal merchandise or advertising special sales or events can change their ads on short notice to match changing market conditions.

*Friendliness.* Radio ads are more "active" than ads in printed media because they use the spoken word to influence customers. Vocal subtleties used in radio ads are impossible to convey through printed media. Spoken ads can suggest emotions and urgency, and they lend a personalized tone to the message.

Radio advertisements also have some *disadvantages:*

*Poor listening.* Radio's intrusiveness into the public life almost guarantees that customers will hear ads, but they may not listen to them. Listeners are often engaged in other activities while the radio is on and may ignore the message.

*Need for repetition.* Listeners usually do not respond to radio ads after a single exposure to them. Radio ads must be broadcast repeatedly to be effective. Consistency in radio ads is the key to success.

*Limited message.* Radio ads are limited to one minute or less, which means that entrepreneurs must keep their messages simple, covering only one or two points. Also, radio spots do not allow advertisers to demonstrate their products or services. Although listeners can hear the engine purr, they can't see the car; spoken messages can only describe the product or service.

*Buying Radio Time.* Entrepreneurs can zero in on a specific advertising target audience by using the appropriate radio station. Stations follow various formats—from rap to rhapsodies—and appeal to specific audiences. Radio advertising time usually sells in 15-second, 30-second, and 60-second increments. Many radio stations now offer five-second spots called "adlets" and even super-short one- or two-second "blinks" that are designed to increase the awareness of a brand among listeners. Fixed spots are guaranteed to be broadcast at the times specified in the owner's contract with the station. Preemptible spots are cheaper than fixed spots, but the advertiser risks being preempted by an advertiser willing to pay the fixed rate for a time slot. Floating spots are the least expensive, but the advertiser has no control over broadcast times. Many stations offer package plans, using flexible combinations of fixed, preemptible, and floating spots. Table 10.3 offers a guide to producing effective radio copy.

Radio rates vary depending on the time of day they are broadcast and, like television, there are prime-time slots known as drive-time spots. Although exact hours may differ from station to station, the following classifications are common (listed in descending order of cost):

Class AA: Morning drive time—6 A.M. to 10 A.M.

Class A: Evening drive time—4 P.M. to 7 P.M.

Class B: Home worker time—10 A.M. to 4 P.M.

Class C: Evening time —7 P.M. to Midnight

Class D: Nighttime—Midnight to 6 A.M.

**TABLE 10.3 Guidelines for Effective Radio Copy**

- *Mention the business often.* This is the single most important and inflexible rule in radio advertising. Also make sure listeners know how to find your business. If the address is complicated, use landmarks.
- *Stress the benefit to the listener.* Don't say "Dixon's has new fall fashions." Say "Dixon's fall fashions make you look fabulous."
- *Use attention-getters.* One key to a successful radio ad is grabbing listeners' attention from the start and holding it. Radio gives the options of music, sound effects, and unusual voices. Crack the barrier with sound.
- *Zero in on your audience.* Know to whom you're selling. Radio's selectivity attracts the right audience. It's up to you to communicate in the right language.
- *Keep the copy simple and to the point.* Don't try to impress listeners with vocabulary. "To be or not to be" may be the best-known phrase in the language . . . and the longest word has just three letters.
- *Sell early and often.* Don't back into the selling message. At most, you've got 60 seconds. Make the most of them. Don't be subtle.
- *Write for the ear.* Forget the rules of grammar; write conversationally.
- *Prepare your copy.* Underline words you want to emphasize so that the announcer knows how the ad should read.
- *Triple space.* Type clean, legible copy. Make sure the announcer rehearses the ad.
- *Use positive action words.* Use words such as *now* and *today,* particularly when you're writing copy for a sale. Radio has qualities of urgency and immediacy. Take advantage of them by including a time limit or the date the sale ends.
- *Put the listener in the picture.* Radio's theater of the mind means you don't have to talk about a new car. With sounds and music, you can put the listener behind the wheel.
- *Focus the spot on getting a response.* Make it clear what you want the listener to do. Don't try to get a mail response. Use phone numbers or Web site addresses only, and repeat them at least three times. End the spot with the phone number or the Web address.
- *Don't stay with a loser.* Direct-response ads produce results right way—or not at all. Don't stick with a radio spot that is not generating sales. Change it.

*Sources:* Kim T. Gordon, "Turn It Up," *Entrepreneur*, January 2004, pp. 80–81; *Radio Basics*, Radio Advertising Bureau.

Some stations may also have different rates for weekend time slots.

**TELEVISION.** In advertising money spent, television ranks first in popularity of all media. Although the cost of national TV ads precludes their use by most small businesses, local spots can be an extremely effective means of broadcasting a small company's message. A 30-second commercial on network television may cost more than $500,000 (a 30-second spot during the Super Bowl sells for $2.6 million, up from $600,000 in 1987), but a 30-second spot on local cable television, which now is in 59 percent of U.S. homes, may go for as little as $10 in small markets.[26]

*Terri and Al Merrick and Channel Island Surfboards*

Terri and Al Merrick, owners of Channel Island Surfboards in Santa Barbara, California, recently ran a television commercial that helped them nearly double sales in the last three months of the year. They purchased the ad from Spot Runner, a company that makes a variety of pre-made, customizable, 30-second television spots available to small companies for as little as $499. In three months, Channel Island's ad ran 432 times in the greater Santa Barbara area on national cable channels such as ESPN and MTV. Total cost of the entire advertising campaign, including the television time: just $3,000. Total time from start to airtime: just five days. "I still laugh when I think about how easy and affordable it was," says Terri. The television ad was so successful that the Merricks are planning an even bigger television ad campaign for the summer, their prime sales season, that will include family channels as well as sports and youth-oriented channels. "I never knew advertising could be so painless," says Terri.[27]

Television advertising offers a number of distinct *advantages:*

**Broad coverage.** Television ads provide extensive coverage of a sizeable region, and they reach a significant portion of the population. Television reaches 89.9 percent of adults every day, exceeding the reach of all other major advertising media.[28] In fact, the average household spends 8 hours and 11 minutes each day tuned to television.[29]

**Ability to focus on a target audience.** Because many cable channels focus their broadcasting in topical areas—from home and garden or food to science or cartoons—cable television offers advertisers the ability to reach specific target markets much as radio ads do. Because an inverse relationship exists between time spent in television viewing and education level, television ads overall are more likely to reach people with lower educational levels.

**Visual advantage.** The primary benefit of television is its capacity to present the advertiser's product or service visually. With TV ads, entrepreneurs are not limited to mere descriptions of a product or service; instead, they can demonstrate their uses and show firsthand their advantages. For instance, a small retail store selling a hydraulic log splitter can design a television commercial to show how easily the machine works. The ability to use sight, sound, and motion makes TV ads a powerful selling tool.

**Flexibility.** Television ads can be modified quickly to meet the rapidly changing conditions in the marketplace. Advertising on TV is a close substitute for personal selling. Like a sales representative's call, television commercials can use "hard sell" techniques, attempt to convince through logic, appeal to viewers' emotions, persuade through subtle influence, or use any number of other strategies. In addition, advertisers can choose the length of the spot (30-second ads are most common), its time slot, and even the program during which to broadcast the ad.

**Design assistance.** Few entrepreneurs have the skills to prepare an effective television commercial. Although professional production firms might easily charge $50,000 to produce a commercial, the television station from which an entrepreneur purchases air time often is willing to help design and produce an ad very inexpensively.

Television advertising also has several *disadvantages:*

**Brief exposure.** Most television ads are on the screen for only a short time and require substantial repetition to achieve the desired effect. One of the realities is that television viewers often avoid or ignore the commercial messages. The commercial is the time to get up and do whatever needs to be done before the program returns.

**"Clutter."** By the age of 65, the average person has seen more than 2 million television commercials, and more ads are on the way![30] With so many television ads beaming across the airwaves, a small company's advertising message easily could become lost in the shuffle.

**"Zapping." "Zappers,"** television viewers who flash from one channel to another, especially during commercials, or those who use digital video recording devices such as TiVo to bypass commercials, pose a real threat to TV advertisers. Zapping can cut deeply into an ad's reach. A study by Yankelovich and Forrester of people who own television recording devices such as Tivo reports that 92 percent fast-forward through commercials.[31] Zapping prevents TV advertisers from reaching the audiences they hope to reach.

**Fragmented audience.** As the number of channels available proliferates, the question of where to advertise becomes more difficult to answer. The average household in the U.S. alone now receives 104 television channels, up from just 33 in 1990![32] This dramatic increase in the number of channels available has fragmented the audience that an ad run on a single channel will reach.

**Costs.** TV commercials can be expensive to create. A professionally done 30-second ad can cost several thousand dollars to develop, even before an entrepreneur purchases airtime. Advertising agencies and professional design firms offer design assistance—sometimes at hefty prices—leading many small business owners to hire less expensive

**TABLE 10.4 Guidelines for Creative TV Ads**

- *Keep it simple.* Avoid confusing the viewer by sticking to a simple concept.
- *Have one basic idea.* The message should focus on a single, important benefit to the customer. Why should people buy from your business?
- *Make your point clear.* The customer benefit should be obvious and easy to understand.
- *Make it unique.* To be effective, a television ad must reach out and grab the viewer's attention. Take advantage of television's visual experience.
- *Get viewers' attention.* Unless viewers watch the ad, its effect is lost.
- *Involve the viewer.* To be most effective, an ad should portray a situation to which the viewer can relate. Common, everyday experiences are easiest for people to identify with.
- *Use emotion.* The most effective ads evoke an emotion from the viewer—a laugh, a tear, or a pleasant memory.
- *Consider production values.* Television offers vivid sights, colors, motions, and sounds. Use them to your advantage!
- *Prove the benefit.* Television allows an advertiser to prove a product's or service's customer benefit by actually demonstrating it.
- *Identify your company well and often.* Make sure your store's name, location, and product line stand out. The ad should portray your company's image.

*Source:* Adapted from *How to Make a Creative Television Commercial,* Television Bureau of Advertising.

freelance ad designers or turn to the stations on which they buy air time for help with their ads. Table 10.4 offers some suggestions for developing creative television commercials.

***Using Television Creatively.*** Although television ads are not affordable for every small business, many entrepreneurs have found creative ways to use the power of television advertising without spending a fortune. Two popular methods include creating infomercials and using home shopping networks. **Infomercials** (also called direct-response television) are full-length (nearly 30 minutes) television commercials packed with information, testimonials, and a sales pitch asking for an immediate response. They are popular tools for selling everything from mops to computers. The length of these ads allows entrepreneurs to demonstrate and explain their products in detail and to show customers the benefits of using them, a particularly important consideration for a new or complex product. Producing and airing a half-hour infomercial can be expensive, often costing $40,000 to $600,000, depending on the length, format, content, and celebrity involvement. Because most infomercials ask for an immediate response from viewers, entrepreneurs can gauge their success at landing customers right away. Research suggests that viewers' perceptions of infomercials is becoming more positive. A recent study by market research company The Leading Edge reports that 73 percent of viewers say that infomercials are a good way to get information about a product and that 74 percent liked infomercials "when the product is relevant."[33]

*Kate Adams and Snap-Saver LLC*

After Kate Adams invented the Snap-Saver, a food-storage container that makes it easier to keep kitchen cupboards organized because its lid snaps to the bottom of the container and the containers snap to each other, she knew that landing orders required her to let customers see firsthand the benefits of the product. Adams, a homemaker, knew that an infomercial was the ideal way to promote her clever new product, dubbed "the no-brainer container." The success of the infomercial led to coverage in newspapers such as the *Wall Street Journal* and the *Toronto Star* and to interest from major retailers such as Sears and home shopping channel QVC. Today Snap-Saver LLC generates annual sales of more than $6 million from a variety of distribution channels, including retail stores, the company's Web site, and home shopping channels.[34]

To become an infomercial star, a product should meet the following criteria:

- Be unique and of good quality.
- Solve a common problem.

■ Be easy to use and easy to demonstrate.
■ Appeal to a mass audience.
■ Have an "aha! factor" that makes customers think "What a great idea!"

Shopping cable TV networks such as QVC and Shop TV offer entrepreneurs another route to television. Time on these networks is free, but getting a product accepted is tough. Only a small percentage of the products reviewed by QVC or Shop TV are featured on the show. Shopping networks look for products that offer quality, have "demonstration appeal," and are typically priced between $15 and $50 (although there are exceptions). Landing a product on one of these networks may be a challenge, but entrepreneurs who do often sell thousands of units in a matter of minutes.

**John Abdo and AB-Doer**

John Abdo, inventor of the AB-Doer, an aerobic machine that exercises users' mid-sections without putting undue strain on their backs, landed a spot on the home shopping channel HSN. Acting as the spokesman for the product, Abdo sold 21,500 units in his first day on the network, generating $2.5 million in sales for his small company! Repeat performances on HSN also were successful, and Abdo has sold more than $320 million worth of AB-Doers on HSN.[35]

**MAGAZINES.** Another advertising medium available to the small business owner is magazines. Today, customers have more than 18,300 magazine titles from which to choose. Magazines have a wide reach, and their readers tend to be more educated and have higher incomes than consumers of other advertising media such as television.[36]

Magazines offer several *advantages* for advertisers:

*Long life spans.* Magazines have a long reading life because readers tend to keep them longer than other printed media. Few people read an entire magazine at one sitting. Instead, most pick it up, read it at intervals, and come back to it later. The result is that each magazine ad has a good chance of being seen several times.

*Multiple readership.* The average magazine has a readership of 3.9 adults, and each reader spends about one hour and 33 minutes with each copy. Many magazines have a high "pass-along" rate; they are handed down from reader to reader. For instance, the in-flight magazines on jets reach many readers in their lifetimes.

*Target marketing.* Within the past 20 years, magazines have become increasingly focused. Advertisers can select magazines aimed at customers with specific interests—from wooden boats and black-and-white photography to container gardening and body-building. By selecting the appropriate special-interest periodical, small business owners can reach those customers with a high degree of interest in their goods or service. Once business owners define their target markets, they can select magazines whose readers most closely match their customer profiles. For instance, *Home Magazine* reaches a very different audience than *PC Gamer*.

*Ad quality.* Magazine ads usually are of high quality. Photographs and drawings can be reproduced very effectively, and high-quality color ads are readily available. Advertisers can also choose the location of their ads in a magazine and can design creative ads that capture readers' attention. The most effective locations for magazine ads are the back cover, the inside front cover, and the inside back cover. Multiple page spreads also increase ad recall among readers.[37]

Magazines also have several *disadvantages:*

*Costs.* Magazine advertising rates vary according to their circulation rates; the higher the circulation, the higher the rate. Thus, local magazines, whose rates are often comparable to newspaper rates, may be the best bargain for small businesses.

*Long closing times.* Another disadvantage of magazines is the relatively long closing times they require. For a weekly periodical, the closing date for an ad may be several weeks before the actual publication date, making it difficult for advertisers to respond quickly to changing market conditions.

## How Should We Advertise?

With its unique blend of limited-edition graphic T-shirts and casual clothing aimed at young urban men and women, Brooklyn Industries (BKI), a Brooklyn, New York, apparel design and retail company, has achieved sales of $10.1 million. In their mission statement, cofounders Lexy Funk and Vahap Avsar, who now have eight stores in Manhattan and Brooklyn, say that one of their company's guiding principles is to create the most innovative and artistic designs for everyday living. They expect sales to grow to $15 million within the next year but are concerned about the effectiveness of their advertising strategy. Funk and Avsar spend about 2 percent of their annual sales each year on advertising, but recently they decided to shift the focus of their ad spending (see accompanying table).

| | This Year | Last Year |
| --- | --- | --- |
| Marketing budget | $301,000 | $201,000 |
| Marketing budget as a percentage of revenue | 2% | 2% |
| Catalogs | $100,000 | $57,000 |
| Store window displays | $60,000 | $12,000 |
| Installing window displays | $38,000 | $30,000 |
| Magazine ads | $40,000 | $80,000 |
| Direct mail | $26,000 | $6,000 |
| Photography | $21,000 | $12,000 |
| Product placement | $16,000 | $16,000 |
| Major change from last year | Reducing magazine advertising by one-half | |
| New this year | Hiring a window stylist to create window displays | |

Last year, BKI relied heavily on advertising in alternative New York magazines such as *BPM*, *Vice*, and *L* to reach their target customers, but after conducting online surveys and focus group sessions with customers, Funk and Avsar realized that very few of their customers read those magazines. Instead, they read *The New York Times* and *Esquire*, but the cost of placing ads in those magazines was more than BKI's budget could handle. Their research also revealed that customers were drawn to BKI because they noticed one of the company's eight stores and were intrigued by its interesting window displays that have an artistic flair. (Both Funk and Avsar are professional artists.)

Drawing on the customer feedback, Funk and Avsar decided to stop advertising in magazines, except for one, *Nylon*. "We were shocked to see how little impact our [magazine] ads had," says Avsar. "It was a painful decision, but we cut them off." Listening to what their customers told them, Funk and Avsar increased spending on window displays for their eight stores from $12,000 to $60,000, an amount that includes a salary for a display designer. Last year, BKI changed its window displays 10 times per year. This year, the couple plans to change them every month, giving their stores a fresh look that they hope will entice customers to visit more frequently.

Funk and Avsar also have increased their spending on catalogs, which will incorporate many of the same visual effects as their store windows, and BKI will publish them more frequently. Last year, BKI published four catalogs that averaged 48 pages each and distributed 22,000 copies of each one. This year, Funk and Avsar plan to print five 64-page catalogs and to mail 30,000 copies of each one. They are considering printing the catalogs in a larger trim size and on high quality, glossy paper, which will cost more. Even then, they do not expect the catalogs to generate a large percentage of their company's sales. Instead, Funk and Avsar hope that the catalogs will occupy a prominent spot on their customers' coffee tables and serve as a reminder of their stores. "When you advertise through store windows and a catalog, you can speak directly to the customer," says Funk.

1. Visit Brooklyn Industry's Web site at www.brooklynindustries.com. How would you describe the company's target customer?
2. Evaluate the advertising plan that Funk and Avsar have developed for Brooklyn Industries. Would you recommend any changes to the plan? Explain.
3. Are there other advertising media and techniques that you would suggest Funk and Avsar consider using to boost Brooklyn Industry's sales and profits? Explain your reasoning.

*Source:* Adapted from Beth Kwon, "Sales More Than Doubled Last Year. So Why Are They Changing Tactics?" *Inc.,* January 2007, pp. 54–55.

*Lack of prominence.* Another disadvantage of magazine ads arises from their popularity as an advertising vehicle. The effectiveness of a single ad may be reduced because of a lack of prominence; 47.2 percent of the typical magazine content is devoted to advertising.[38] Proper ad positioning, therefore, is critical to an ad's success. Research shows that readers "tune out" right-hand pages and look mainly at left-hand pages.

**SPECIALTY ADVERTISING.** As advertisers have shifted their focus to "narrowcasting" their messages to target audiences and away from "broadcasting," specialty advertising has grown in popularity. This category includes all customer gift items imprinted with the company's name, address, telephone number, and slogan. Specialty items are best used as reminder ads to supplement other forms of advertising and help to create goodwill among existing and potential customers.

Specialty advertising offers several *advantages:*

*Reaching select audiences.* Advertisers have the ability to reach specific audiences with well-planned specialty items.

*Personalized nature.* By carefully choosing a specialty item, business owners can "personalize" their advertisements. When choosing advertising specialties, an entrepreneur should use items that are unusual, related to the nature of the business, and meaningful to customers. For instance, a small software company generated a great deal of recognition by giving existing and potential customers flash memory sticks imprinted with its company logo and Web site address.

*Versatility.* The rich versatility of specialty advertising is limited only by the business owner's imagination. Advertisers print their logos on everything from pens and scarves to wallets and caps.

There also are *disadvantages* to specialty advertising:

*Potential for waste.* Unless business owners choose the appropriate specialty item, they will be wasting time and money. The options are virtually unlimited.

*Cost.* Some specialty items can be quite expensive. In addition, some owners have a tendency to give advertising materials to anyone—even to those people who are not potential customers. Proper distribution of give-away items is an important aspect of enhancing the effectiveness of and controlling the cost of specialty advertising.

**POINT-OF-PURCHASE ADS.** In-store advertising has become popular as a way of reaching the customer at a crucial moment—the point of purchase. Research suggests that consumers make 74 percent of all buying decisions at the point of sale.[39] Self-service stores are especially well suited for in-store ads because they remind people of the products as they walk the aisles. These in-store ads are not just simple signs or glossy photographs of the product in use. Some businesses use in-store music interspersed with household hints and, of course, ads. Another technique involves shelves that contain tiny devices that sense when a customer passes by and triggers a prerecorded sales message. Some self-service stores are experimenting with floor graphics, point-of-purchase ads that transform their floors into advertising space.

**OUT-OF-HOME ADVERTISING.** Out-of-home or outdoor advertising is one of the oldest forms of advertising in existence. Archeological evidence shows that merchants in ancient Egypt chiseled advertising messages on stone tablets and placed them along major thoroughfares. Out-of-home advertising remains popular today; advertisers spend more than $7.5 billion on this medium annually.[40] The United States is one of a number of countries that is a highly mobile society, and out-of-home advertising takes advantage of this mobility. Out-of-home advertising is popular among small companies, especially retailers, because well-placed ads serve as reminders to shoppers that the small business is nearby and ready to serve their needs. Very few small businesses rely solely on out-of-home advertising; instead, they supplement other advertising media with out-of-home ads such as

Wilkins' Oklahoma Truck Supply's unusual out-of-home ad attracts lots of attention—and potential customers.

billboards and transit ads. With a creative out-of-home ad campaign, a small company can make a big impact with only a small budget.

*Rob Bennett and
Bennett Infiniti Inc.*

Rob Bennett, owner of Bennett Infiniti in Lehigh Valley, Pennsylvania, saw his inventory of luxury cars building up and knew that he had to do something to attract customers and boost sales. Although Bennett never had used out-of-home advertising, he realized that the medium was ideal for reaching his target audience: upscale, well-educated professionals who enjoy driving. Research showed that although these buyers are affluent, they are value conscious in their purchases. Bennett launched an outdoor ad campaign that emphasized the low monthly lease payments that were available on the most popular luxury models, concentrating the ads in upscale areas near his dealership. Sales climbed almost immediately. In the first four weeks, Bennett Infiniti's sales jumped from an average of just two cars per week to seven cars per week! The initial campaign was such a hit that Bennett conducted a follow-up ad campaign that proved to be even more successful.[41]

Outdoor advertising offers certain *advantages* to a small business:

*High exposure.* Outdoor advertising offers a high-frequency exposure, especially among people who commute to work. The average one-way commute to work in the United States is just over 25 minutes.[42] Most people tend to follow the same routes in their daily traveling, and billboards are there waiting for them when they pass by.

*Broad reach.* The typical billboard reaches an adult 29 to 31 times each month. The nature of outdoor ads makes them effective devices for reaching a large number of potential customers within a specific area. Not only has the number of cars on the road increased, but the number of daily vehicle trips people take has also climbed. In addition, the people outdoor ads reach tend to be younger, wealthier, and better educated than the average person.

*Attention-getting.* The introduction of new technology such as 3-D, fiber optics, and other creative special effects to outdoor advertising has transformed billboards from flat, passive signs to innovative, attention-grabbing promotions that passers-by cannot help but notice.

*Flexibility.* Advertisers can buy outdoor advertising units separately or in a number of packages. Through its variety of graphics, design, and unique features, outdoor advertising enables the small advertiser to match his message to the particular audience.

*Cost efficiency.* Outdoor advertising offers one of the lowest costs per thousand customers reached of all advertising media. Experts estimate the cost per thousand viewers (CPM) for outdoor ads is about $4, compared to $5 for drive-time radio spots, $8 for magazine ads, and $10 to $20 for newspaper ads and prime-time television spots.[43]

Outdoor ads also have several *disadvantages:*

*Brief exposure.* Because billboards are immobile, the reader is exposed to the advertiser's message for only a short time—typically only one or two seconds. As a result, the message must be short and to the point.

*Limited ad recall.* Because customers often are zooming past outdoor ads at high speed, they are exposed to an advertising message very briefly, which limits their ability to retain the message.

*Legal restrictions.* Outdoor billboards are subject to strict regulations and to a high degree of standardization. Many cities place limitations on the number and type of signs and billboards allowed along the roadside.

*Lack of prominence.* A clutter of billboards and signs along a heavily traveled route tends to reduce the effectiveness of a single ad that loses its prominence among the crowd of billboards.

***Using Out-of-Home Advertising.*** Technology has changed the face of outdoor advertising dramatically in recent years. Computerized painting techniques render truer, crisper, and brighter colors and have improved the quality of outdoor ads significantly. Vinyl surfaces accept print-quality images and are extremely durable. Digital technology, three-dimensional effects, computerized lighting, and other advances allow companies to create animated, continuous motion ads that really capture viewers' attention at reasonable cost. Because the outdoor ad is stationary and the viewer is in motion, a small business owner must pay special attention to its design. An outdoor ad should:

- Identify the product and the company clearly and quickly.
- Use a simple background. The background should not compete with the message.
- Rely on large illustrations that jump out at the viewer.
- Include clear, legible type. All lowercase or a combination of uppercase and lowercase letters works best. Very bold or very thin typefaces become illegible at a distance.
- Use black-and-white designs. Research shows that black-and-white outdoor ads are more effective than color ads. If color is important to the message, pick color combinations that contrast both hue and brightness—for example, black on yellow.
- Emphasize simplicity; short copy and short words are best. Don't try to cram too much onto a billboard. Because of their brief window of exposure, ads with just three to five words are most effective, and ads containing more than 10 words are ineffective.
- Use illumination so that passers-by can read them at night. By using illuminated billboards, advertisers can increase the reach of outdoor ads by 16 percent.[44]
- Be located on the right-hand side of the highway.

Two of the latest trends in outdoor advertising are Internet-connected digital boards and billboards that send messages to customers' cell phones via Bluetooth. Less than 1 percent of the 450,000 billboards in the United States are digital, but their numbers are expected to grow rapidly in the next several years. With digital billboards, ad content is virtually unlimited; advertisers can include eye-catching graphics and streaming media in their ads. (Digital billboards are common in Shanghai, for example, where much of the traffic includes pedestrians, whose travel speeds are slower than cars.) Digital billboards offer advertisers great flexibility. For instance, a restaurant could change the messages it displays to advertise its breakfast offerings in the morning, lunch specials at mid-day, and dinner menu in the evening.

The latest outdoor ads include a computer chip that interacts with a Web browser that is common to many cell phones, which enables advertisers to send messages to passersby's cell phones. For instance, a movie theater's smart billboard could send messages to customers' cell phones with show times for the feature films it is running.

**TRANSIT ADVERTISING.** A variation of out-of-home advertising is transit advertising, which includes advertising signs on the inside and outside of the public transportation vehicles such as trains, buses, and subways throughout the country's urban areas. The medium is likely to grow as more cities look to public transit systems to relieve traffic congestion.

Transit ads offer a number of *advantages:*

*Wide coverage.* Transit advertising offers advertisers mass exposure to a variety of customers. The message literally goes to where the people are.

*Repeat exposure.* Transit ads provide lengthy and repeated exposure to a message, particularly for inside cards, the ads that appear inside the vehicle.

*Low cost.* Even small business owners with limited budgets can afford transit advertising.

*Flexibility.* Transit ads come in a wide range of sizes, numbers, and duration. With transit ads, an owner can select an individual market or any combination of markets across the country.

Transit ads also have several *disadvantages:*

*Generality.* Although entrepreneurs can choose the specific transit routes on which to advertise, they cannot target a particular segment of the market through transit advertising as effectively as they can with other media. The effectiveness of transit ads depends on the routes that public vehicles travel and on the people they reach, which, unfortunately, the advertiser cannot control. Overall, transit riders tend to be young, affluent, and culturally diverse.

*Limited appeal.*  Unlike many media, transit ads are not beamed into the potential customer's residence or business. The result is that customers cannot keep them for future reference.

*Brief message.*  Transit ads do not permit advertisers to present a detailed description or a demonstration of the product or service for sale. Although inside ads have a relatively long exposure (the average ride lasts 22.5 minutes), outside ads must be brief and to the point.

**DIRECT MAIL.**  Direct mail has long been a popular method of direct marketing and includes tools such as letters, postcards, catalogues, discount coupons, brochures, and CDs that are mailed to homes or businesses. The earliest known catalogs were printed by fifteenth-century printers. Although Internet sales have surpassed direct-mail catalog sales, direct mail remains strong. Companies sell virtually every kind of product imaginable through direct mail, from trees and lobsters to furniture and clothing (the most popular mail-order purchase). Responding to the convenience of "shopping at home," 167 million stay-at-home shoppers purchase more than $150 billion worth of goods and services through direct-mail catalogs each year.[45]

Direct mail offers some distinct *advantages* to entrepreneurs:

*Flexibility.*  An advantage of direct mail is its capacity to tailor the message to the target. The advertiser's presentation to the customer can be as simple or as elaborate as necessary. One custom tailor shop achieved a great deal of success with fliers it mailed to customers on its mailing list when it included a swatch of material from the fabric for the upcoming season's suits. With direct mail, the tone of the message can be personal, creating a positive psychological effect. In addition, the advertiser controls the timing of the campaign; the company can send the ad when it is most appropriate.

*Reader attention.*  With direct mail, an advertiser's message does not have to compete with other ads for the reader's attention. People enjoy getting mail, and a majority of households open and read some or all of the direct mail that they receive.[46] For at least a moment, direct mail gets a recipient's undivided attention. If the message is on the mark and sent to the right audience, direct-mail ads can be a powerful advertising tool.

*Rapid feedback.*  Direct-mail advertisements produce quick results. In most cases, the ad will generate sales within three or four days after customers receive it. Business owners should know whether a mailing has produced results within a relatively short time period.

*Measurable results and testable strategies.*  Because they control their mailing lists, direct marketers can readily measure the results their ads produce. Also, direct mail allows business owners to test different ad layouts, designs, and strategies (often within the same "run") to see which one "pulls" the greatest response. The best direct marketers are always fine-tuning their ads to make them more effective. Table 10.5 offers guidelines for creating direct-mail ads that really work.

*Effectiveness.*  The right message targeted at the right mailing list can make direct mail one of the most efficient forms of advertising. Direct mail sent to the right people produces results.

Direct-mail ads also suffer from several *disadvantages:*

*Inaccurate mailing lists.*  The key to the success of the entire mailing is the accuracy of the customer list. Using direct-mail ads with a poor mailing list is a guaranteed waste of money. Experienced direct-mail marketers cite the 60–30–10 rule, which says that 60 percent of a campaign's success depends on the quality of the list, 30 percent on the offer, and 10 percent on the creativity of the ad.[47] Make sure the mailing list you use is accurate and up-to-date.

**TABLE 10.5 Guidelines for Creating Direct-Mail Ads That Really Work**

In many industries, a successful direct-mail campaign is one that produces a response rate of at least 2.5 percent, which means that 97.5 percent of the customers who received the ad do *not* respond to it! What steps can entrepreneurs take to improve the results of their direct-mail campaigns?

*Realize that repetition is one key to success.* Experts estimate that customers must receive at least three direct mail pieces per month from a business before they really notice the ad.

*Provide meaningful incentives.* Direct mail succeeds by getting prospects to respond to a written offer. To do that, a direct-mail ad must offer potential customers something of value—a free sample, a special price, a bonus gift, or anything that a company's target customers value. Twenty percent of prospects who do not open the direct-mail ads they receive say that they have no reason to open them. Make sure your offer gives them a reason!

*Write copy that will get results.* Try the following proven techniques:

- Promise readers your most important benefit in the headline or first paragraph.
- Use short "action" words and paragraphs and get to the point quickly.
- Make the copy look easy to read with lots of "white space."
- Use eye-catching words such as *free, you, save, guarantee, new, profit, benefit, improve,* and others.
- Consider using computerized "handwriting" somewhere on the page or envelope; it attracts attention.
- Forget grammatical rules; write as if you were speaking to the reader.
- Repeat the offer three or more times in various ways.
- Back up claims and statements with proof and endorsements whenever possible.
- Ask for the order or a response.
- Ask attention-getting questions such as "Would you like to lower your home's energy costs?" in the copy.
- Use high-quality copy paper and envelopes (those with windows are best) because they stand a better chance of being opened and read. Brown envelopes that resemble government correspondence work well, too.
- Envelopes that resemble bills almost always get opened.
- Address the envelope to an individual, not "Occupant."
- Avoid mailing labels, which shout "direct-mail ad piece." The best campaigns print addresses directly on the envelopes.
- Use stamps if possible. They get more letters opened than metered postage.
- Use a postscript (P.S.)—always. They are the most often read part of a printed page. Make sure the P.S. contains a "hook" that will encourage the recipient to read on. This is the perfect place to restate a unique selling proposition.
- Include a separate order form that passes the following "easy" test:

  *Easy to find.* Consider using brightly colored paper or a unique shape.

  *Easy to understand.* Make sure the offer is easy for readers to understand. Marketing expert Paul Goldberg says, "Confuse 'em and you lose 'em."

  *Easy to complete.* Keep the order form simple and unconfusing.

  *Easy to pay.* Direct-mail ads should give customers the option to pay by whatever means is most convenient.

  *Easy to return.* Including a postage-paid return envelope (or at a minimum a return envelope) will increase the response rate.

*Build and maintain a quality mailing list over time.* The right mailing list is the key to a successful direct-mail campaign. You may have to rent lists to get started, but once you are in business, use every opportunity to capture information about your customers. Constantly focus on improving the quality of your mailing list.

*Test your campaigns and track their results.* "Testing is everything," says the founder of a company that used direct-mail ads as part of a marketing strategy that led to $10 million in annual sales. Monitoring the response rate from each mailing is essential for knowing which ads and which lists actually produce results.

*Sources:* Adapted from *What's in the Mailbox? The Impact of One-to-One Marketing on Consumer Response*, Winterberry Group, January 2007, p. 7; "Direct Mail Tips for Manufacturers' Letters," Koch Group, www.kochgroup.com/directmail.html; Kim T. Gordon, "Copy Right," *Business Start-Ups*, June 1998, pp. 18–19; Paul Hughes, "Profits Due," *Entrepreneur*, February 1994, pp. 74–78; "Why They Open Direct Mail," *Communications Briefings*, December 1993, p. 5; Ted Lammers, "The Elements of Perfect Pitch," *Inc.*, March 1992, pp. 53–55: "Special Delivery," *Small Business Reports*, February 1993, p. 6; Gloria Green and James W. Peltier, "How to Develop a Direct Mail Program, "*Small Business Forum*, Winter 1993/1994, pp. 30–45; Susan Headden, "The Junk Mail Deluge," *U.S. News & World Report*, December 8, 1997, pp. 40–48; Joanna L. Krotz, "Direct-Mail Tips for Sophisticated Marketers," Microsoft Small Business Center, www.microsoft.com/smallbusiness/resources/marketing/customer_service_acquisition/direct_mail_tips_for_sophisticated_marketers.mspx.

*Clutter.* The average household in the United States alone receives more than 960 pieces of direct mail each year.[48] With that volume of direct mail, it can be difficult for an advertisement to get customers' attention.

*High relative costs.* Relative to the size of the audience reached, the cost of designing, producing, and mailing an advertisement via direct mail is high. But if the mailing is well planned and properly executed, it can produce a high percentage of returns, making direct mail one of the least expensive advertising methods in terms of results.

*High throwaway rate.* Often called junk mail, direct-mail ads become "junk" when an advertiser selects the wrong audience or broadcasts the wrong message. According to the Direct Mail Association, the average response rate for a direct-mail campaign is 2.5 percent.[49] By supplementing traditional direct-mail pieces with toll-free numbers and carefully timed follow-up phone calls, companies have been able to increase their response rates.

***How to Use Direct Mail.*** The key to a direct mailing's success is the right mailing list. Even the best direct-mail ad will fail if sent to the "wrong" customers. Owners can develop lists themselves, using customer accounts, telephone books, city and trade directories, and other sources, including companies selling complementary but not competing products, professional organizations' membership lists, business or professional magazines' subscription lists, and mailing list brokers who sell lists for practically any need. Advertisers can locate list brokers through *The Direct Marketing List Source* from the Standard Rate and Data Service found in most public libraries. In a world in which the average adult receives literally kilograms of direct mail each year, the key to success with a direct-mail campaign is to get your ad noticed, and the right mailing list is the ideal starting point.

*Michael Greco and Dartmouth Pharmaceuticals*

Dartmouth Pharmaceuticals, launched in 1991 as a maker of cold and allergy medications, developed a line of all-natural skin and nail care products called Elon Essentials, but annual sales were a measly $5,000. To pump up sales, CEO Michael Greco decided to use direct-mail ads sent to dermatologists. To increase the probability that the busy doctors would look at the ads, Greco sent them by priority mail. The direct-mail campaign helped Dartmouth increase sales of its Elon Essentials line to more than $1.5 million in just a few years, and the company is now gearing up to add a national sales force to sell its products.[50]

**THE WORLD WIDE WEB.** Just as the Web has become a common tool for conducting business, it also has become a popular medium for advertisers. Internet advertising is growing rapidly because advertisers are recognizing that their target customers are spending more and more of their time and because advertisers can easily track the effectiveness of online advertising campaigns (see Figure 10.5).

*Tina and George Showalter and the Blonde Bear Bed & Breakfast*

Tina and George Showalter, owners of the Blonde Bear Bed & Breakfast in Kenai, Alaska (population 7,000), relied on a word-of-mouth advertising strategy when they launched their business, but their remote location limited its success. In their second year of operation, the Showalters, along with 50 other Kenai small businesses, joined MerchantCircle, a convergence Web site that includes local business listings, directories, and links to members' Web sites. "When we got involved in Internet advertising, our sales exploded," says Tina. "Now MerchantCircle is a huge part of our advertising plan."[51]

The Web's multimedia capabilities make it an ideal medium for companies to demonstrate their products and services with full motion, color, and sound and to get customers involved in the demonstration. Businesses that normally use direct mail can bring the two-dimensional photos and product descriptions in their print catalogues to life, avoid the expense of mailing them, and attract new customers that traditional mailings might miss.

Advertisements on the Web take five basic forms: banner ads, display ads, contextual ads, pay-per-click ads, and e-mail ads. **Banner ads** are small rectangular ads that reside

**FIGURE 10.5 Online Advertising Expenditures**

*Source:* "Online Ad Spending to Total $19.5 Billion in 2007," *eMarketer,* February 28, 2007, www.emarketer.com/Article.aspx? 1004635.

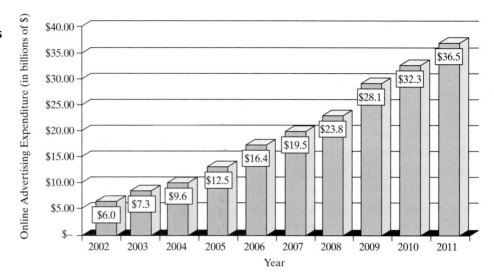

on Web sites, much like roadside billboards, touting a company's product or service. When visitors to a site click on the banner ad, they go straight to the advertiser's home page. One measure of a banner ad's effectiveness is the number of impressions it produces. An **impression** occurs every time an ad appears on a Web page, whether or not the user clicks on the ad to explore it. Another common way of judging the effectiveness of banner ads is the **click-through rate**, which is calculated by dividing the number of times customers actually click on the banner ad by the number of impressions for that ad. For instance, if an ad is displayed 1,000 times, and 20 customers actually click on the ad to go to the advertiser's Web site, the ad's click-through rate is 2 percent (20 ÷ 1,000). The cost of a banner ad to an advertiser depends on the number of prospects who actually click on it.

Banner ads do not have to be expensive to be effective. Many small business owners increase the exposure their banner ads receive by joining a banner exchange program that is similar to an advertising cooperative. In a banner exchange program, member companies can post their banners on each other's sites. These programs work best for companies selling complementary products or services. For instance, a small company that sells gourmet food products over the Web could exchange banner ads with a company using the Web to sell fine wines or one that sells upscale kitchen tools and appliances.

The primary disadvantage of banner ads is that Web users can easily ignore them. These ads have become such a part of the landscape of the Web that users tend to ignore them. Web designers search for the best page placement for banner ads and the "bells and whistles" that will attract browsers and encourage them to click through. Another form of Web advertising that is more difficult to ignore are **display ads**, which include both pop-up, interstitial ads, and contextual ads. A **pop-up ad** appears on a separate window that pops up spontaneously, blocking the site behind it. It is designed to grab consumers' attention for the few nanoseconds it takes them to close the window. One danger is that the attention the pop-up ad gets is not necessarily positive. Most Internet users perceive these ads as an annoying intrusion. A slight variation on this ad is the "pop-under" ad that immediately goes behind the active screen but stays open until the browser window is closed. An **interstitial ad** is an ad page that appears for a short time before a user-requested page appears. These ads are also called transition ads, splash pages, and flash pages.

**Contextual ads** appear on users' screens when they download information such as news, sports, or entertainment from another site, and the ad is correlated to the user's interest or online behavior. For instance, a Web user downloading sports information might receive an ad for athletic shoes or T-shirts with the information, and one conducting a search for vitamins might receive an ad for green tea or herbal remedies. To catch the attention of Web users, many advertisers, particularly those companies that aim their products at young customers, are using video ads rather than traditional display ads.

**Pay-per-click ads** require companies to bid on top search engine listings using key words that they expect Internet users to type into a search engine when they are interested in purchasing a particular product or service. The higher a company's bid is for a key word, the more prominent is the location of its ad on the results that the search engine returns. Companies pay for an ad only when a prospect actually clicks on it. Entrepreneurs who advertise on the Internet should consider making pay-per-click ads a part of their advertising strategies. Studies by Jupiter Media Metrix show that 77 percent of Internet shoppers go straight to a search engine to find the products and services they want. Unfortunately, business owners invest less than 1 percent of their marketing budget in landing highly placed spots on popular search engines.[52] Google, MSN, and Yahoo! are the three leading search engines, and advertisers who want to increase the odds of reaching their target audiences should advertise on all three. The minimum bid is one cent per click on Google's AdWords, five cents per click on MSN Keywords, and 10 cents per click on Yahoo! Sponsored Search.

Used properly, pay-per-click ads can drive customers to a company's Web site even before the search engines discover it and include it in their natural or organic listings. Pay-per-click ads also allow advertisers to test the effectiveness of different ads by running several variations at once (for instance, one version might include a discounted price and another might include a free accessory). These ads are efficient because advertisers pay for an ad only when a customer actually clicks on it.

One threat to the effectiveness of pay-per-click ads is **click fraud**, which occurs when a person or a computer program generates ad clicks even though they have no interest in the advertiser's product or service. Experts estimate that the click fraud rate on search engines is between 15 percent and 20 percent.[53] Click fraud artificially inflates an advertiser's cost but produces no benefits.

E-mail is the most common application on the Internet, and e-mail advertising capitalizes on that popularity. The Radicati Group estimates that Internet users send more than 171 billion e-mails per day![54] **E-mail advertising**, in which companies broadcast their advertising messages by e-mail, is growing rapidly because it is so effective and so inexpensive. E-mail advertising takes two forms: permission e-mail and spam. As its name suggests, **permission e-mail** involves sending e-mail ads to customers with their permission; **spam** is unsolicited commercial e-mail. The Radicati Group also estimates that 71 percent of all e-mail messages are spam.[55] Because most e-mail users see spam as a nuisance, they often view companies that use it in a negative fashion. Smart entrepreneurs do not rely on spam in their marketing strategies. Permission e-mail, however, can be an effective and money-saving advertising tool. Permission e-mail messages often produce very high response rates.

Building an e-mail list simply requires attention to the basics of marketing. The goal is to encourage potential buyers to share their e-mail addresses. The reward may be a one-time discount, special offer, special report, entry in a sweepstakes, or drawing for a prize. Once a small company obtains potential customers' e-mail addresses, the next step is to send messages that are useful and interesting to them. The message must be geared to their interests and should highlight the product's unique selling proposition.

Many companies have success with e-mail ad campaigns that produce immediate results but are very inexpensive to conduct.

*Nan Vardaro and Balance Spa*

Nan Vardaro, owner of Balance Spa, a spa retreat aimed at both women and men, is unwavering in her effort to collect customers' e-mail addresses both on her company's Web site and in the spa. As a result, she has built an e-mail list of nearly 3,000 people, to whom she sends notices of daily specials and upcoming events. "Clients love our daily specials in which we offer a discount of up to 25 percent on treatments for certain time slots that very day. Because e-mail is so immediate, I can look at my schedule for the day, determine what last-minute openings we have, and offer services to my valued clients at a great discount." Vardaro's e-mail ad campaign has been so successful at increasing Balance Spa's sales volume that she now devotes 100 percent of her advertising budget to this medium.[56]

**DIRECTORIES.** Directories may seem old-fashioned compared to newer high-tech tools, but both are valuable ways for businesses to reach commercial or industrial customers. Directories are an important medium for reaching those customers who have already made purchase

## E-Mail Ads That Produce Results

While Josh Molinari and Anthony Green were students in college, they began making plans to open a restaurant that served fresh food fast. After graduating, the young entrepreneurs launched Fajita Grill, a restaurant that prepares high-quality, fresh southwestern food "assembly-line" style in Syracuse, New York. A few months later, they opened a second location in nearby Oswego, New York. Looking for an inexpensive yet effective way to advertise their new restaurants, Molinari and Green decided to try e-mail advertising.

With a concerted effort by all employees and the help of e-mail marketing firm Constant Contact, Fajita Grill increased the size of its e-mail list from 480 names to 950 names. "I doubled my subscriber list by sending out interesting e-mails that people would want to forward to friends, having a sign-up form on our Web site, and putting information about the e-mails on the restaurants' signs," says Abby Weaver, Fajita Grill's marketing manager. Even the employees are excited about it. They're telling customers and are helping to grow the list too."

Fajita Grill's e-mail ads not only include daily specials but also discount coupons. "Before I tried e-mail, I put a coupon in the local newspaper and had fewer than 10 people redeem it. I put the same coupon in an e-mail, sent it to 400 people, and saw 100 of the e-mail coupons redeemed that month!" In addition to the high (and measurable) response rate, Weaver enjoys the flexibility and speed of e-mail ad campaigns. "I don't need a designer," she says. "I don't have to wait for a printer or the Postal Service to get it delivered. I can hit 'send' at 10 A.M. and watch how many people open the e-mail and where they click on the Fajita Grill Web site."

Entrepreneurs who want to reproduce the success that Fajita Grill has created using an e-mail advertising campaign should consider the following tips:

***Make a concerted effort to collect customers' (and potential customers') e-mail addresses.*** Every contact that anyone in your company has with a customer presents an opportunity to collect another e-mail address. Seize them! Ensure that everyone in the company understands the importance of building an accurate and reliable e-mail list.

***Make sure the e-mail's subject line is short, meaningful, and to-the-point.*** Without the right subject line, e-mail recipients may never open the e-mail. One rule of thumb suggests that the subject line should not exceed 40 characters, including spaces. The best subject lines suggest the product's or service's unique selling proposition. For example, "Fresh lunch FAST—just $5.99!" in the subject line of an e-mail expresses several product features to potential customers.

***Make sure your e-mail's look and feel are consistent with your company's overall image.*** Every component of a company's advertising campaign should have a consistent look and feel, even though the ads may appear in many diverse media. The design of a company's ads should rely on similar colors, themes, slogans, and appearances.

***Send e-mails when customers are most likely to make their purchases.*** Proper timing of e-mail ads can improve customer response rates dramatically. Friday is the day of the week on which recipients are most likely to read e-mails. January, July, August, and December are the months in which customers are least likely to pay attention to e-mail ads (although there are exceptions). Marketing research firm Atlas reports in a study that lunch time and the late evening were the times of day that resulted in the highest response rates to e-mail ads in general. Companies must time their e-mail ads to correspond to their customers' demand for their products and services. One company saw sales climb when it began sending e-mail messages advertising beer on Friday afternoons, and a fast-food company realized success by promoting its breakfast products in early morning e-mails.

***Write copy that produces the results you seek.*** Start by concentrating on one idea. Before writing any copy, develop a mental picture of your target customer. Give him or her a name and try to envision how your company's product or service can benefit him or her. This will help you keep your ad copy focused on the USP you put in the subject line of the e-mail. When appropriate, consider including an endorsement from an existing customer (perhaps with a photo) to add credibility to your claims. Be

*(continued)*

sure to provide clearly visible links to your company's Web site at several places in the e-mail ad, including at the top and the bottom of the page.

***Use value-added items to increase your campaign's response rate.*** In the typical inbox, there are dozens of messages (if not more) competing for a person's attention. One way to boost your campaign's response rate is to offer recipients something of value—for example, a coupon, a newsletter, or a white paper. Betsy Harper, CEO of Sales and Marketing Search, an executive search firm that specializes in sales and marketing positions, says that publishing a monthly e-mail newsletter that includes hiring trends and tips has improved her company's visibility, reputation, and sales. Recently, says Harper, "within two minutes (literally!) of sending our email newsletter, I got an email from a fellow in New York. He asked me to call him right away about

filling a senior sales position. We talked, signed an agreement to work together the very next day, and started the search. We finished the search in record time and received a $22,000 fee."

Properly executed, e-mail advertising campaigns can be highly effective and very cost efficient.

*Sources:* Adapted from Michelle Keegan, " Real Life Small Business Newsletter Tips," *Constant Contact,* www.constantcontact.com/learning-center/hints-tips/volume10-issue2.jsp; Gail Goodman, "Writing Compelling Promotional Copy," *Constant Contact,* www.constantcontact.com/learning-center/hints-tips/ht-2006-07.jsp; "Success Stories: Fajita Grill," *Constant Contact,* www.constant contact.com/email-marketing-success/case-studies/fajita-grill.jsp; David Kesmodel, "More Marketers Place Web Ads by Time of Day," *Wall Street Journal,* June 23, 2006, pp. B1, B3; Ivan Levison, "Five Common E-mail Mistakes and How to Avoid Them," *Levison Letter,* April 2002, www.levison.com/email-advertising.htm; Ben Fesxbe, "Small Business E-mail Advertising—3 Keys to Success," *Ezine@Articles,* http://ezinearticles.com/?Small-Business-Email-Advertising—3-Keys-To-Success&id=519407.

decisions. The directory simply helps these customers locate the specific product or service they have decided to buy. Directories include telephone books, industrial guides, buyer guides, annuals, catalogue files, and yearbooks that list various businesses and the products they sell.

Directories offer several *advantages* to advertisers:

***Prime prospects.*** Directory listings reach customers who are prime prospects, because they have already decided to purchase an item. The directory just helps them find what they are looking for.

***Long life.*** Directory listings usually have long lives. A typical directory may be published annually.

However, there are certain *disadvantages* to using directories:

***Lack of flexibility.*** Listings and ads in many directories offer only a limited variety of design features. Business owners may not be as free to create unique ads as in other printed media.

***Ad clutter.*** In many directories, ads from many companies are clustered together so closely that no single ad stands out from the rest.

***Obsolescence.*** Because directories commonly are updated only annually, some of their listings become obsolete. This is a problem for a small firm that changes its name, location, or phone number.

When choosing a directory, the small business owner should evaluate several criteria:

- ***Completeness.*** Does the directory include enough listings that customers will use it?
- ***Convenience.*** Are the listings well organized and convenient? Are they cross-referenced?
- ***Evidence of use.*** To what extent do customers actually use the directory? What evidence of use does the publisher offer?
- ***Age.*** Is the directory well established and does it have a good reputation?
- ***Circulation.*** Do users pay for the directory or do they receive complimentary copies? Is there an audited circulation statement?

**TRADE SHOWS.** Trade shows provide manufacturers and distributors with a unique opportunity to advertise to a pre-selected audience of potential customers who are inclined to buy.

Thousands of trade shows take place each year, and carefully evaluating and selecting the right shows can produce profitable results for a business owner. Trade show success does *not* depend on how much an exhibitor spends; instead, success is a function of planning, preparation, and follow-up.

Trade shows offer the following *advantages:*

*A natural market.* Trade shows bring together buyers and sellers in a setting in which exhibitors can explain and demonstrate their products. Comparative shopping is easy, and the buying process is efficient for customers.

*Pre-selected audience.* Trade exhibits attract potential customers with a genuine interest in the goods or services on display. There is a high probability that trade show attendees will make a purchase. A study by Exhibit Surveys reports that 53 percent of trade show attendees plan to purchase at least one of the products on display within one year.[57]

*New customer market.* Trade shows offer exhibitors a prime opportunity to reach new customers and to contact people who are not accessible to sales representatives.

*Cost advantage.* As the cost of making a field sales call continues to escalate, companies are realizing that trade shows are an economical method of generating leads and making sales presentations.

There are, however, certain *disadvantages* associated with trade shows:

*Increasing costs.* The cost of exhibiting at trade shows is rising. Registration fees, travel and setup costs, sales salaries, and other expenditures may be a barrier to some small firms.

*Wasted effort.* A poorly planned exhibit ultimately costs the small business more than its benefits are worth. Too many firms enter exhibits in trade shows without proper preparation, and they end up wasting their time, energy, and money on unproductive activities.

To avoid these disadvantages, entrepreneurs should:

- Research trade shows to find the ones that will put you in front of the best prospects for your product or service.
- Establish objectives for every trade show. Do you want to generate 100 new sales leads, make new product presentations to 500 potential customers, or make $5,000 in sales?
- Communicate with key potential customers *before* the show; send them invitations or invite them to stop by your booth for a special gift.
- Plan your display with your target audience in mind and make it memorable. Be sure your exhibit shows your company and its products or services in the best light. Do everything to maximize the visibility of your exhibit and keep the display neat.
- Staff your booth with knowledgeable salespeople. Attendees appreciate meeting face-to-face with knowledgeable and friendly staff.
- Do something to attract a crowd to your booth. Demonstrate your product or service so that customers can see it in action, sponsor a drawing for a prize, or set up an interactive display. Drawing a crowd creates "buzz" for your company among attendees.
- Learn to distinguish between serious customers and "tire-kickers."
- Make it easy for potential customers to get information about your company and its products and services. Distribute literature that clearly communicates the benefits of your products or services.
- Project a professional image at all times. Salespeople who man the booth should engage prospects in conversation and ask qualifying questions.
- Follow up promptly on sales leads. The most common mistake trade-show participants make is failing to follow up on the sales leads the show generated. If you are not going to follow up leads, why bother to attend the show in the first place?

## ■ Bob-Bob-Bobble(head) Along

Founded in 1982, Richardson, a company that provides sales training and consulting, grew rapidly during the 1990s. However, by the time Jim Brodo took over as the company's marketing manager, its minimal marketing and advertising efforts over the years had left Richardson moribund. Brodo's first task was to plan the company's display at the major industry trade show. He had to do something to generate traffic and quality sales leads at the display booth and to promote the company's new Quickskills sales training program—and he had to do it with a budget of just $7,500!

Pulling together several staff members at the small company, Brodo and CEO David DiStefano led a brainstorming session. As they looked around the office, members of the group noticed the extensive collection of bobblehead toys that the two executives had on display. "Perhaps we could build our promotion around bobbleheads," they reasoned. "We could imprint them with our company name, logo, and a catchy slogan and give them to potential customers at our trade show booth." The team came up with a figure of a businessman named "The Trusted Advisor" because he personified the characteristics that Richardson's products and services offered its customers. They set objectives for the trade show, ordered 500 bobbleheads, and hoped for the best. Two weeks before the show, Brodo and his team sent a direct mail ad to the show's attendees that explained Richardson's products and services, where its booth would be located, and how potential customers could win a promotional bobblehead.

When the show opened, Brodo and his team realized that they had a promotional hit on their hands. The buzz at the show was all about Richardson's bobbleheads, and attendees were lining up to get a free bobblehead. Much to his amazement, says Brodo, "as I walked around the show, people would call out to me, 'Hey, you're the bobblehead guys, right? Love those bobbles! What a great idea!'" Well before the show was over, booth workers had distributed all 500 bobbleheads and collected more than 200 sales leads, double the goal they had set.

Every year since then, Richardson has introduced a new bobblehead figure to distribute at the trade show. (Brodo also has increased the number of bobbleheads he orders for the show to 2,000.) Recent figurines have included The Win-Win Negotiator, The Call Center Agent, The Prospector, and The Sales Coach. Each new bobblehead figure has generated the same level of enthusiasm and interest at the show. Since the company began using the bobblehead campaign at the trade show, Richardson has gone from being a name in the sales training industry that almost no one recognized to the third most recognized name in the business. It may be hard to believe, but much of the credit for that tremendous accomplishment goes to a group of 7-inch tall figurines and the creativity of the people who dreamed them up.

Since Richardson's initial appearance with the bobbleheads at the trade show, its brand recognition has increased significantly. In addition, the promotion increased sales leads by an impressive 1,367 percent and helped land two major clients that have generated sales of more than $35 million for the company. "Not many people believed that promoting a service by giving away something like bobbleheads would generate interest and excitement while maintaining credibility and the brand message," says Brodo. "This promotion has allowed us to become more creative and to start to think outside the box."

1. Learn more about Richardson by visiting the company's Web site at www.richardson.com. How would you define the company's unique selling proposition?

2. What role did creativity play in the success of the trade show advertising campaign that Richardson ran? What lessons can other entrepreneurs learn from Richardson's experience?

3. Work with a team of your classmates to generate ideas for Richardson that would generate publicity for the company.

*Source:* Adapted from Travis Stanton and T. Wayne Waters, "What About Bobbleheads?" *Exhibitor*, March 2007, www.exhibitoronline.com/exhibitormagazine/print.asp?ID=1187.

## How to Prepare an Advertising Budget

**4.** Identify four basic methods for preparing an advertising budget.

One of the most challenging decisions confronting a small business owner is how much to spend on advertising. The amount entrepreneurs want to spend and the amount they can afford to spend usually differ significantly. There are four methods of creating an advertising budget: *what-is-affordable, matching competitors, percentage of sales,* and *objective and task.*

Under the **what-is-affordable method**, business owners see advertising as a luxury. They view it completely as an expense rather than as an investment that generates sales and profits in the future. As the name implies, entrepreneurs who use this method spend on advertising whatever their companies can afford. Too often, business owners determine their advertising budgets after they have funded all of the other budget items. The result is an advertising budget that is inadequate for getting the job done. This method also fails to relate the advertising budget to the company's advertising objectives.

Another approach is to match the advertising budget of the company's competitors, either in a flat amount or as a percentage of sales. This method assumes that a company's advertising needs and strategies are the same as those of its competitors, which is rarely the case. Although competitors' actions can be helpful in establishing a floor for advertising expenditures, relying on this technique can lead to blind imitation instead of a budget suited to a small company's circumstances.

The most commonly used method of establishing an advertising budget is the simple **percentage-of-sales approach**. This method relates advertising expenditures to actual sales results. Tying advertising expenditure to sales rather than to profits creates greater consistency in advertising because most companies' sales tend to fluctuate less than profits. One

| | | | October | | | |
|---|---|---|---|---|---|---|
| Sun | Mon | Tue | Wed | Thu | Fri | Sat |
| Advertising Budget for October:<br>9% of Sales = $2,275<br>Co-op Ads = $ 550<br>Total = $2,825 | | October Advertising<br>Expenditures: $2,845<br>Under/(Over) Budget: $20<br>Remaining Balance: $6,400 | | **1**<br>WPCC Radio<br>5 Spots, $125<br>Billboard, $350 | **2**<br>*The Chronicle*<br>140 Lines, $100 | **3** |
| **4** | **5** | **6** | **7** | **8** | **9**<br>*The Chronicle*<br>140 Lines, $100 | **10** |
| **11** | **12** | **13**<br>Meet w/ Leslie<br>re: November<br>Ad Campaigns,<br>2 P.M. | **14** | **15**<br>Envelope<br>"Stuffer" in<br>Invoices:<br>Halloween Sale,<br>$175 | **16**<br>*The Chronicle*<br>140 Lines, $100 | **17**<br>WPCC Radio,<br>5 Spots, $100 |
| **18** | **19** | **20**<br>WPCC Radio,<br>5 Spots, $125 | **21** | **22**<br>Direct Mail,<br>Halloween Sale<br>Promo "Preferred<br>Customers," $120 | **23**<br>*The Chronicle*<br>140 Lines, $100 | **24**<br>WPCC Radio,<br>5 Spots, $100 |
| **25** | **26**<br>WPCC Radio,<br>5 Spots, $125 | **27**<br>WPCC Radio,<br>5 Spots, $125 | **28**<br>WPCC Radio,<br>5 Spots, $125 | **29**<br>WPCC Radio,<br>5 Spots, $125 | **30**<br>*The Chronicle*<br>Half-page<br>Spread, Sale,<br>$300 | Halloween<br>Sale **31**<br>WPCC Radio,<br>Live Remote<br>Broadcast, $425 |

**FIGURE 10.6** **A Sample Advertising Calendar**

rule of thumb for establishing an advertising budget is spending 10 percent of projected sales the first year of business, seven percent the second year and at least five percent in each successive year. Relying totally on broad rules like these can be dangerous, however. They may not be representative of a small company's advertising needs.

The **objective-and-task method** is the most difficult and least used technique for establishing an advertising budget. It also is the method most often recommended by advertising experts. With this method, an entrepreneur links advertising expenditures to specific business objectives. The objective-and-task method builds up an advertising budget from the bottom up by analyzing what it will cost to accomplish an entrepreneur's business objectives. For example, suppose that an entrepreneur wants to boost sales of a particular product 10 percent by attracting local college students. He may determine that a nearby rock radio station would be the best advertising medium to use. Then he must decide on the number and frequency of the ads and estimate their costs.

Entrepreneurs follow this process for each advertising objective. A common problem with the method is the tendency for entrepreneurs to be overly ambitious in setting advertising objectives, which leads to unrealistically high advertising expenditures. Entrepreneurs may be forced to alter objectives or the plans to reach them to bring their advertising budgets back to a reasonable level.

Once they establish their advertising objectives and budget, many entrepreneurs find it useful to plan in advance their advertising expenditures week by week for an entire year. This comprehensive plan ensures a consistent advertising effort throughout the year. A calendar such as the one illustrated in Figure 10.6 on page 373 is one of the most valuable tools for planning a small company's advertising campaign. The calendar enables the owner to prepare for holidays and special events, to monitor actual and budgeted expenditures, and to ensure that ads are scheduled in the appropriate media at the proper times.

## How to Advertise Big on a Small Budget

*5.* Explain practical methods for stretching a small business owner's advertising budget.

The typical small business does not have the luxury of an unlimited advertising budget. Most cannot afford to hire a professional ad agency. This does not mean, however, that a small company should assume a second-class advertising posture. Most advertising experts say that, unless a small company spends more than $10,000 to $15,000 a year on advertising, it probably doesn't need an ad agency. For most, hiring freelance copywriters and artists on a per-project basis is a much better bargain. With a little creativity and a dose of ingenuity, small business owners can stretch their advertising money and make the most of what they spend. Four useful techniques are cooperative advertising, shared advertising, stealth advertising, and publicity.

### Cooperative Advertising

In **cooperative advertising**, a manufacturing company shares the cost of advertising with a retailer if the retailer features its products in those ads. Both the manufacturer and the retailer get more advertising for the money by sharing expenses. Cooperative advertising not only helps small businesses stretch their advertising budgets, but it also offers another source of savings: the free advertising packages that many manufacturers supply to retailers. These packages usually include photographs and illustrations of the product as well as professionally prepared ads to use in different media.

### Shared Advertising

In **shared advertising**, a group of similar businesses forms a syndicate to produce generic ads that allow the individual businesses to dub in local information. The technique is especially useful for small businesses that sell relatively standardized products or services such as legal assistance, autos, and furniture. Because the small firms in the syndicate pool their funds, the result usually is higher-quality ads and significantly lower production costs.

### Stealth Advertising

In Chapter 9, you learned about guerrilla marketing principles, offbeat, low-cost techniques for marketing a small company's goods and services. In advertising, these techniques are called **stealth advertising**, which includes innovative ads that do not necessarily look like traditional ads and often are located in unexpected places. Ads now appear on electrical outlets in airport terminals, on eggs (gently printed directly onto the shells with lasers), clothes hangars from laundries, in urinals in public restrooms (using a device called Wizmark that plays sounds and pictures when a guest arrives), and other unusual places.[58] "People are getting hit with so many messages," says one advertising executive. "They are zapping commercials and [are] not looking at print ads. Marketers want what is going to make customers stop and look."[59] One consumer products company achieved success with a campaign that involved painting manhole covers in New York City to look like steaming hot cups of coffee. Bamboo Lingerie attracted a great deal of attention for its brand by stenciling on New York City sidewalks the message "From here it looks like you could use some new underwear" and its name and logo.[60]

### Publicity

The press can be either a valuable friend or a fearsome foe to small businesses, depending on how well owners handle their companies' publicity. Too often, entrepreneurs take the attitude, "My business is too small to be concerned about public relations." However, wise entrepreneurs recognize that investing time and money in public relations (publicity) benefits both the community and the company. The community gains the support of a good business citizen, and the company earns a positive image in the marketplace.

Many small businesses rely on media attention to get noticed, and getting that attention takes a coordinated effort. Publicity doesn't just happen; business owners must work at getting their companies noticed by the media. Although such publicity may not be free, it can lower the company's advertising expenditures and still keep its name before the public. Because small companies' advertising budgets are limited, publicity takes on significant importance.

**OTHER WAYS TO SAVE.** Other cost-saving suggestions for advertising expenditures include the following:

- *Repeat ads that have been successful.* In addition to reducing the cost of ad preparation, repetition may create a consistent image in a small firm's advertising program.
- *Use identical ads in different media.* If a billboard has been an effective advertising tool, an owner should consider converting it to a newspaper or magazine ad or a direct-mail flier.
- *Hire independent copywriters, graphic designers, photographers, and other media specialists.* Many small businesses that cannot afford a full-time advertising staff buy their advertising services a la carte. They work directly with independent specialists and usually receive high-quality work that compares favorably with that of advertising agencies without paying a fee for overhead.
- *Concentrate advertising during times when customers are most likely to buy.* Some small business owners make the mistake of spreading an already small advertising budget evenly—and thinly—over a 12-month period. A better strategy is to match advertising expenditures to customers' buying habits.

---

## Chapter Review

**1.** Define your company's unique selling proposition (USP)
- Branding a company's products or services depends on communicating the correct *unique selling proposition* (USP).
- Answers the customer's ultimate question: What's in it for me?

2. Explain the differences among promotion, publicity, personal selling, and advertising.
   - Promotion is any form of persuasive communication designed to inform consumers about a product or service and to influence them to purchase these goods or services. It includes publicity, personal selling, and advertising.
   - Publicity is any commercial news covered by the media that boosts sales but for which the small business does not pay.
   - Personal selling is the personal contact between salespeople and potential customers that comes from sales efforts.
   - Advertising is any sales presentation that is non-personal in nature and is paid for by an identified sponsor. A company's target audience and the nature of its message determine the advertising media it will use.

3. Describe the advantages and disadvantages of various advertising media.
   - The medium used to transmit an advertising message influences customers' perception—and reception—of it.
   - Media options include word of mouth, sponsorships and special events, newspapers, radio, television, magazines, specialty advertising, point-of-purchase ads, out-of-home advertising, transit advertising, direct mail, the World Wide Web, directories, and trade shows.

4. Discuss the four basic methods for preparing an advertising budget.
   - Establishing an advertising budget presents a real challenge to the small business owner.
   - There are four basic methods: what is affordable, matching competitors, percentage of sales, and objective and task.

5. Explain practical methods for stretching a business owner's advertising budget.
   - Despite their limited advertising budgets, small businesses do not have to take a second-class approach to advertising. Three techniques that can stretch a small company's advertising money are cooperative advertising, shared advertising, and publicity.

## Discussion Questions

1. What are the three elements of promotion? How do they support one another?
2. What factors should a small business manager consider when selecting advertising media?
3. What is a unique selling proposition? What role should it play in a company's advertising strategy?
4. Review the advantages and disadvantages of the following advertising media:
   - Newspapers
   - Radio
   - Television
   - Magazines
   - Specialty advertising
   - Direct mail
   - Out-of-home advertising
   - Transit advertising
   - Directories
   - Trade shows

   Assume you are a small business owner who has an advertising budget of $1,500 to invest in a campaign promoting a big July 4th "Blowout" sale. Where would you be most likely to invest your advertising budget if you were trying to reach customers in the 25-to-45 age range with higher than average disposable income who are likely to be involved in boating activities in a local resort town? Explain. How would you generate free publicity to extend your advertising budget?

5. What are fixed spots, preemptible spots, and floating spots in radio advertising?
6. Describe the characteristics of an effective out-of-home advertisement.
7. Briefly outline the steps in creating an advertising plan. What principles should the small business owner follow when creating an effective advertisement?
8. Describe the common methods of establishing an advertising budget. Which method is most often used? Which technique is most often recommended? Why?
9. What techniques can small business owners use to stretch their advertising budgets?

# Business PlanPro

A coordinated and consistent advertising and promotion effort is essential to an entrepreneur's success. Companies that fail to maintain a high profile among their target customers are soon forgotten. As an entrepreneur, your job is to leverage the advertising and promotion ideas from the chapter. Review the concepts and company examples in the chapter to determine whether they provide insight and ideas that may work to promote your business. How do you anticipate promoting your business? Which advertising media do you plan to use? Why?

## On the Web

If you anticipate using the Web to promote your business, you will want to invest time to determine how best to do that. Search for similar businesses on the Internet. Identify three favorite sites. Note the appearance, layout, and navigation tools on these sites. What do you find attractive? What do you find distracting? Use this to develop ideas about how your site should look and what it should accomplish for your business. Chapter 13 will discuss developing an online presence, which you can build based on your research.

## In the Software

Determine how much you plan to invest in your advertising and promotional activities. Will you use newspapers, radio, television, sponsorships, or other media? What role will publicity play in promoting your business? Include estimates of the cost of your advertising and promotional activities in your business plan. Once again, reviewing sample plans may help to get ideas of where you want to invest your advertising budget. You also will need to do some additional research to help determine how much your advertising and promotional efforts are going to cost. Once you have come up with some preliminary figures, go to the marketing section and develop your unique selling proposition. Review other information to test for consistency throughout the plan.

## Building Your Business Plan

Continue to build your business plan with the new information you have acquired. Step back to assess whether you have a solid understanding of your market and whether your business plan effectively communicates that understanding.

# Pricing and Credit Strategies

Cheap is the last refuge
of a product developer or
marketer who is out of
great ideas.

—Seth Godin

There is hardly anything
in the world that
someone cannot make a
little worse and sell a
little cheaper, and the
people who consider
price alone are this
man's prey.

—John Ruskin

## Learning Objectives

**Upon completion of this chapter, you will be able to:**

1 Explain why pricing is both an art and a science.

2 Discuss the relationships among pricing, image, competition, and value.

3 Discuss various pricing strategies for both new and existing products and services.

4 Explain the pricing techniques used by retailers.

5 Explain the pricing techniques used by manufacturers.

6 Explain the pricing techniques used by service firms.

7 Describe the impact of credit on pricing.

# Pricing: A Creative Blend of Art and Science

*1.* Explain why pricing is both an art and a science.

One of the most challenging yet most important decisions entrepreneurs must make involves pricing their products and services. Studies by consulting firm Accenture show that increasing prices by just 1 percent can produce an 11 percent increase in a company's profit, a result that is much greater than that produced by a comparable 1 percent decrease in costs.[1] Pricing mistakes can destroy an otherwise promising business. Prices that are too high can drive customers away and hurt a small company's sales. Pricing products and services too low, a common tendency among start-up companies, robs a business's ability to earn a profit, leaves customers with the impression that its goods and services are of inferior quality, and threatens its long-term success. Customers' demand for value-priced goods and services, their ability to make easy price comparisons using the Internet, and constantly rising costs of raw materials only complicate an entrepreneur's pricing decisions.

Determining the most appropriate price for a product or service requires entrepreneurs to consider how the following factors interact to provide clues about the proper price to charge:

- The total cost associated with providing the product or service.
- Target customers' characteristics, including their buying power and their perceptions of the product or service.
- The current and anticipated market forces that determine both supply and demand.
- The pricing strategies of competitors and their competitive behavior.
- The company's anticipated sales volume and the impact of that production volume on unit cost.
- The entrepreneur's desired image for the company and customers' expectations regarding product or service quality and price.
- Normal cycles or seasonality in the market.
- Customers' sensitivity to price changes.
- Psychological factors that influence customers' perceptions of price and quality.
- Substitute products or services that are available to customers.
- Traditional and expected credit terms and discount policy.

Notice that some of the factors such as costs and competitors' prices are relatively easy to quantify, but others, such as customers' sensitivity to price changes and desired image are much less tangible. This is where the creative blending of art and science comes into play and leads to a final pricing decision. In pure economic terms, **price** is the monetary value

A Bugatti Veryon. Top speed: 253 mph. Price: $1.4 million.

of a good or service; it is a measure of what a customer must give up to obtain a good or service. For an individual, price is a reflection of value. Customers will pay no more for a product or service than what they perceive it to be worth. Value, like beauty, is in the eye of the beholder. The process of setting the price for any good or service must involve an analysis of how customers view its value. For instance, a select few people (135 worldwide, to be exact) are willing to pay $1.4 million for a Bugatti Veryon, a 1001-horsepower sports car made by the VW Group that is capable of going from zero to 60 miles per hour in just 2.5 seconds, faster than many current Formula One cars. The car's top speed is 253 miles per hour. For these ultra-luxury car buyers, the Veryon offers value, even at a price of $1.4 million. When asked why he purchased a Veryon, one customer says, "This car is about dedication to perfection."[2]

Entrepreneurs must develop a keen sensitivity to both the psychological and economic characteristics of their customers. Without being in tune with customers' psychological and economic motivators, they cannot price their goods and services correctly. This customer orientation is an important factor in a successful pricing process. What the process produces is seldom *the* ideal price, but an ideal price *range*. This **price range** is the area between the **price floor** that is established by a company's total cost to produce the product or provide the service and the **price ceiling**, which is the most the target customers are willing to pay (see Figure 11.1).

The price floor depends on a company's cost structure, which can vary considerably from one business to another, even though they may be in the same industry. Although their cost structures may be different from their competitors', many entrepreneurs play follow-the-leader with their prices, simply charging what their competitors do on similar or identical products or services. Although this strategy simplifies the pricing decision, it can be very dangerous. Determining the price floor for a product or service requires entrepreneurs to have access to timely, accurate information about the cost of producing or selling a product or providing a service.

The price ceiling depends on entrepreneurs' ability to understand their customers' characteristics and buying behavior, the benefits that the product or service offers customers, and the prices of competing products. The best way to learn about customers' buying behavior is to conduct ongoing market research and to spend time with customers, listening to the feedback they offer. Small companies with effective pricing strategies tend to have a clear picture of their target customers and how their companies' products and services fit into their customers' perception of value. A company that begins losing valued customers who complain that its prices are too high has bumped into the price ceiling, and the owner should consider cutting prices.

An entrepreneur's goal is to position the company's prices within this acceptable price range that falls between the price floor and the price ceiling. The final price that entrepreneurs set depends on the desired image they want to create for their products or services: discount (bargain), middle-of-the-road (value), or prestige (luxury). A prestige pricing strategy is not

**FIGURE 11.1 What Determines Price?**

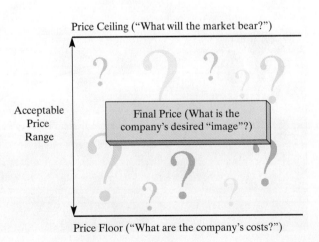

Price Ceiling ("What will the market bear?")

Acceptable Price Range

Final Price (What is the company's desired "image"?)

Price Floor ("What are the company's costs?")

necessarily better or more effective than a no-frills, value pricing strategy. What matters most is that the company's pricing strategy matches the image the owner wants to create for it.

Some entrepreneurs compete in markets in which the cost of raw material and supplies can fluctuate wildly due to forces beyond their control. That's the situation Danny O'Neill, owner of The Roasterie, a wholesale coffee business that sells to upscale restaurants, coffee houses, and supermarkets, found his company in when coffee prices nearly doubled in just three months.[3] Businesses faced with rapidly rising raw materials costs should consider the following strategies:

- ■ *Communicate with customers.* Let your customers know what's happening. The Roasterie's O'Neill was able to pass along the rising costs of his company's raw material to customers without losing a single one. He sent his customers a six-page letter and copies of newspaper articles about the increases in coffee prices. The approach gave The Roasterie credibility and helped show customers that the necessary price increases were beyond his control.

- ■ *Rather than raise the price of the good or service, include a surcharge.* Price increases tend to be permanent, but if higher costs are the result of a particular event (e.g., a hurricane that disrupted the nation's ability to process oil and resulted in rapidly rising fuel costs), a company can include a temporary surcharge. If the pressure on its costs subsides, the company can eliminate the surcharge. When fuel prices began climbing rapidly, John Bunch, owner of a fishing guide service, added a $50 fuel surcharge to his charter boat fishing rates, which start at $375 for four hours.[4]

- ■ *Rather than raise prices, consider eliminating customer discounts, coupons, and "freebies."* Eliminating discounts, coupons, and other freebies is an invisible way of raising prices, which can add significantly to a small company's profit margin. Borders Books recently restructured its generous discount program because it had begun to cut too deeply into the company's profitability. Loyal customers still earn discounts (as do loyal customers at Borders' competitors), but the discounts are smaller and expire faster.[5]

- ■ *Focus on improving efficiency everywhere in the company.* Although raw materials costs may be beyond a business owner's control, other costs within the company are not. One way to cope with the effects of a rapid increase in costs is to find ways to cut costs and to improve efficiency in other areas. These improvements may not totally offset higher raw materials costs, but they can dampen their impact. Rather than raise prices, the owners of Jen-Mor Florists, a family-run flower shop, decided to cut the number of deliveries to the edge of their territory to just one per day to reduce the company's delivery expenses.[6]

- ■ *Consider absorbing raw material cost increases to keep valuable customer accounts.* Saving a large account might be more important than keeping pace with rising costs. Companies that absorb the rising cost of raw materials often find ways to cut costs in other areas and to operate more efficiently.

- ■ *Emphasize the value your company provides to customers.* Unless a company reminds them, customers can forget the benefits and value its products offer.

*Russell Pike and Advanced Cart Technology*

When some casinos balked at paying premium prices ($2,000 to $2,600) for his company's portable carts that dispense change to slot machine players, Russell Pike, owner of Advanced Cart Technology, emphasized to casino managers the value his carts offer. He showed them how the convenient carts would pay for themselves in a single weekend by letting casinos use them for two weeks free of charge. He then showed them how his prices compared with their increased profits. "Even though our prices are high," says Pike, "they are not high for what we are doing for them."[7]

- ■ *Anticipate rising materials costs and try to lock in prices early.* It pays to keep tabs on raw materials prices and be able to predict cycles of inflation. Entrepreneurs who can anticipate rising prices may be able to make purchases early or lock in long-term contracts before prices take off. After Hurricane Katrina devastated the U.S. Gulf

Coast and disrupted the production of gasoline, fuel prices skyrocketed both for motorists and for airlines. Because Southwest Airlines had locked in contracts for fuel at pre-Katrina prices, the low-cost carrier was able to post impressive profits even though the rest of the industry's fuel cost had climbed 57 percent.[8]

## Three Powerful Pricing Forces: Image, Competition, and Value

### Price Conveys Image

**2.** Discuss the relationships among pricing, image, competition, and value.

A company's pricing policy can be a powerful tool for establishing a brand and for creating a desired image among its target customers. Whether they are seeking an image of exclusivity or one that reflects bargain basement deals, companies can use price to enhance their brands. Some companies emphasize low prices, but others establish high prices to convey an image of quality, exclusivity, and prestige, all of which appeal to a particular market segment. For example, price reflects the notion of perceived value nowhere better than in the Swiss watch industry. Companies such as Bulgari, Rolex, Cartier, Patek Philippe, Blanepain, and Corum are legendary brands of ultrapremium, handmade watches that sell from $5,000 to $375,000. Bulgari created a limited edition of just 24 ASIOMA Multi-Complications Tourbillon watches and priced them at $134,000. The IWC II Destriero Scafusia is one of the most complicated watches in the world with 750 moving parts and is priced between $350,000 and $375,000. Although these watches are not as accurate at keeping time as a $10 quartz-driven Timex, their owners don't seem to mind.[9] Owning one of these watches is a mark of financial success. Value for these buyers is not found in superior technical performance of the product but in their scarcity, uniqueness, and "Wow" factor. Although the scope of the market for these ultraluxury items is extremely limited, the ego-satisfying ownership of limited edition watches, pens, cars, jewelry, and other items is the psychological force driving these customers' buying behavior.

Too often, small companies underprice their products and services, believing that low prices is the only way they can gain an advantage in the marketplace. According to management consulting firm McKinsey and Company, 80 to 90 percent of the pricing mistakes that companies make involve setting prices that are too low.[10] Companies that fall into this trap fail to recognize the extra value, convenience, service, and attention that they give their customers—things that many customers are willing to pay extra for. Many of these businesses attempt to compete solely on price when they lack the volume that results in lower cost per unit. It is a recipe for failure. Shoppers usually equate low prices with low quality.

**Rene Lacoste and Lacaoste Inc.**

Discounting prices on its once popular Izod polo shirts nearly cost Lacoste its entire business. Demand for the shirts, which sported a unique crocodile logo, slumped as prices fell; discounting had eroded the company's distinctive and once upscale image. Company founder Rene Lacoste bought back the company and began rebuilding its upscale image and the cachet of its shirts by charging premium prices. Under the new pricing strategy, sales are climbing.[11]

The secret to setting prices properly is based on understanding the company's target market, the customer groups at which the small company is aiming its goods or services. Target market, business image, and price are closely related.

**ENTREPRENEURIAL Profile**

**Max Barenbrug and Eduard Zanen and Bugaboo**

When Amsterdam-based Bugaboo, a company co-founded by brothers-in-law Max Barenbrug and Eduard Zanen, introduced its $795 Cameleon baby stroller, some experts wondered whether parents would pay a premium for it. After all, the price was nearly double that of other "premium" strollers. Prices quickly top $1,500 after adding on accessories such as custom fabric, cupholders, a parasol, and a fleece-lined foot muff. Although privately-owned Bugaboo won't reveal sales of the Cameleon, the company says that U.S. revenues have doubled every year since it launched the upscale stroller. "The Bugaboo carries not only a child, but, thanks to a range of hooks and attachments, all of the accompanying stuff parents need," says one satisfied customer. "It's solid and sturdy, and its sleek, minimalist design and all-terrain wheels appeal to both women and men." One father says, "It's a stroller I'm not ashamed to push." The key to Bugaboo's success lies in its ability to differentiate its strollers from other similar products and to market those differences to well-to-do parents who have children later in life and want only the best for them.[12]

## Competition and Prices

An important part of setting appropriate prices is tracking competitors' prices regularly; however, the prices that competitors are charging is just *one* variable in the pricing mix (and often not the most important one at that). When setting prices, entrepreneurs should take into account their competitors' prices, but they should *not* automatically match or beat them. Businesses that offer customers extra quality, value, service, or convenience can charge higher prices as long as customers recognize the "extras" they are getting. In other words, companies that can implement successfully a differentiation strategy (refer to Chapter 2) can charge higher prices for their products and services.

*Damon Risucci and Synergy Fitness Clubs*

When Damon Risucci opened his first health club, he was 24 years old. Despite tough competition from chains such as New York Sports Clubs and Equinox Fitness, he built Synergy Fitness Clubs into a successful business, with three stylish New York City locations, $7 million in revenue, and 9,500 members. But when it came to raising prices, Risucci was positively a wimp. Obsessed with being a value leader, he was determined to provide customers with a comparable experience to the chain fitness centers while charging rock-bottom prices. For almost a decade, membership fees remained at $49.99 a month—nearly half those of his rivals—despite an upscale Midtown Manhattan flagship location and ever-rising rent and utility bills. "We thought our prices had to be low," Risucci says. "It was almost a core belief." Finally, after poring over his financials and holding extensive interviews with customers and staffers, Risucci built up his courage and took action. Prompted by withering margins and a hunch that his customers were willing to pay more, he raised monthly fees 16 percent for new members and the cost of personal training sessions 20 percent. The result: No one complained and not a single one of his members threatened to jump ship.[13]

Two factors are vital to studying the effects of competition on a small firm's pricing policies: the location of the competitors and the nature of the competing goods. In most cases, unless a company can differentiate the quality and the quantity of the extras it provides, it must match the prices charged by nearby competitors for identical items. For example, if a self-service station charges a nickel more for a gallon of gasoline than the self-service station across the street charges, customers will simply go across the street to buy. Without the advantage of a unique business image—quality of goods sold, value of service provided, convenient location, favorable credit terms—a small company must match local competitors' prices or lose sales. Although the prices that distant competitors charge are not nearly as critical to the small business as are those of local competitors, it can be helpful to know them and to use them as reference points. Before matching any competitor's price change, however, entrepreneurs should consider the rivals' strategies. The competition may be establishing its prices on the basis of a unique set of criteria and a totally different strategy.

The nature of competitors' goods also influences a small company's pricing policies. Entrepreneurs must recognize those products that are substitutes for those they sell and strive to keep prices in line with them. For example, the local sandwich shop should consider the hamburger restaurant, the taco shop, and the roast beef shop as competitors because they all serve fast foods. Although none of them offer the identical menu of the sandwich shop, they're all competing for the same quick-meal dollar.

Whenever possible, entrepreneurs should avoid head-to-head price competition with other firms that can more easily offer lower prices because of their lower cost structures.

Most locally owned drugstores cannot compete with the prices of large national drug chains. However, many local drugstores operate successfully by using non-price competition such as personal service, free delivery, credit sales, and other extras that the chains have eliminated. Non-price competition can be an effective strategy for a small business in the face of larger, more powerful enterprises because there are many dangers in experimenting with prices. For instance, price shifts cause fluctuations in sales volume that the small firm may not be able to tolerate. Also, frequent price changes may damage the company's image and its customer relations.

One of the deadliest games a small business can get into with competitors is a price war. Price wars can eradicate companies' profit margins and scar an entire industry for years. The global microchip industry, which supplies the chips that power computers, cell phones, and many other electronic devices, has been marred by price wars. In an attempt to hold onto market share, two of the industry's most fierce competitors, Intel and AMD, often battle one another with price cuts that affect the entire industry rather than by emphasizing product features and performance. Recently, as AMD began to cut into Intel's market share, Intel cut prices on its chips, AMD followed suit, and both companies' profit margins declined significantly.[14]

Price wars usually begin when one competitor believes that it can achieve a higher volume through lower price, or it believes it can exert enough pressure on its competitors' profits to drive them out of business. In most cases, entrepreneurs overestimate the power of price cuts to increase sales sufficiently to improve net profitability.

### ENTREPRENEURIAL Profile

*McDonald's*

McDonald's infamous "Campaign 55," in which it planned to lower to 55 cents the price of a different sandwich each month, launched another volley in an ongoing fast food price war that no company seemed to be winning. The 55-cent price was a throwback to the prices in 1955, the year McDonald's was founded. The company kicked off the campaign by selling Big Macs (which cost around 40 cents to make) for 55 cents and hoped to increase store traffic and boost sales on other menu items enough to offset the lower margin on the sandwich. Unfortunately, the increased traffic never materialized and same-store sales fell 6 percent from the year before. In less than two months amid the complaints of its franchisees, McDonald's abandoned the promotion.[15]

In a price war, a company may cut its prices so severely that it is impossible to achieve the volume necessary to offset the lower profit margins. If a company that has a 25 percent gross (profit) margin cuts prices by 10 percent, it would have to *triple* its sales volume just to break even. Even when price cuts work, their effects are often temporary. Customers lured by the lowest price usually have almost no loyalty to a business. The lesson: The best way to survive a price war is to stay out of it by emphasizing the unique features, benefits, and value your company offers its customers!

### Focus on Value

Ultimately, the "right" price for a product or service depends on one factor: the value that it provides for a customer. There are two aspects of value, however. Entrepreneurs may recognize the *objective* value of their products and services, which is the price customers would be willing to pay if they understood perfectly the benefits that a product or service delivers for them. Unfortunately, few, if any, customers can see a product's or a service's true objective value; instead, they see only its *perceived* value, which determines the price they are willing to pay for it. Research into purchasing decisions has revealed a fundamental problem that adds to the complexity of a business owner's pricing decision: People faced with pricing decisions often act irrationally. In one classic study, researchers asked shoppers if they would travel an additional 20 minutes to save $5 on a calculator that costs $15; most said they would. When asked the same question about a $125 jacket, most of the shoppers said no, even though they would be saving the exact same amount of money! "People make [purchasing] decisions piecemeal, influenced by the context of the choice," says Richard Thaler, who won a Nobel Prize for his work in behavioral economics.[16]

## Should We Engage in a Price War?

In India, as much as 90 percent of the annual rainfall occurs during the three or four months of the monsoon season. For instance, in Mumbai (formerly Bombay), rainfall averages between 20 and 30 inches per month during the summer monsoon season. With rainfall totals that high, it pays to have a well-made umbrella. Ebrahim Currim & Sons, a company still managed by descendants of founder Ebrahim Currim himself, has provided Mumbaikars with quality umbrellas since 1860. Currim's original business model resembled that of Henry Ford in the early days of the automobile industry: Customers could buy the sturdy, affordable Stag umbrella in any color they wanted as long as it was black.

By the end of the twentieth century, however, Currim found itself facing a very different competitive situation. The company's Stag umbrella confronted intense competition from cheaper products imported from China that were made with less sturdy frames and with less durable and less water-resistant polyester fabric than the water-shedding but more expensive nylon that Currim used. Soon, the average price of an umbrella in Mumbai fell from about 100 rupees ($2.27) to just 70 rupees ($1.59). Customers began snapping up the cheaper Chinese imported umbrellas, causing Currim's market share to slide, and the company began losing money for the first time since the 1940s.

To compete with the import onslaught, Aziz Currim and his brother Abbas decided to cut the price of its Stag umbrella, which meant that the company also had to scrimp on quality, something that the Currims were loathe to do, but they believed that they had little choice with the cheap imports eating into their sales and market share. Customers began to notice the changes immediately. "Quality had been our mainstay all along, and customer satisfaction [with poor quality] pained us," says Aziz. Before they knew it, the Currims were in a price war with their Chinese competitors, who often engage in price wars (even with companies within the borders of China). "Chinese customers are very price sensitive," says John Zhang, a professor at Wharton and an expert on marketing in China. "When you lower a price, you generate more sales, a lot more sales. In China, anytime you lower the price a little, you draw a larger buying audience." Shoppers in other countries such as the United States, where markets are more mature, tend not to be as price sensitive. "When you lower the price there, you gain some sales but not on the scale triggered by price-sensitive Chinese consumers," says Zhang.

Before long, the Currims began to reconsider their business and pricing strategies. Given their company's reputation for quality, does it make sense for them to compete with cheaper imports by engaging in a price war? Who ultimately wins a price war, if anybody?

As they talked about their strategic options, the Currims considered ditching the mentality that they had to match the low prices of their Chinese competitors and emphasizing quality and innovative designs. There were risks associated with that strategy as well. A generation earlier, the company had attempted to launch a line of "designer" umbrellas, but they never caught on with customers. Perhaps, the Currim brothers reasoned, we could identify different customer segments, target them with high-quality, specialized products, and forget about competing on price with foreign companies whose competitive advantage is low cost. Working with their staff, the Currims began to identify potential markets, ranging from umbrellas that play music and come in brightly colored, funky patterns for teens to security umbrellas that are equipped with glare lights, emergency blinkers, and an alarm for women. Pursuing this strategy would necessitate an increase in prices to compensate for the increased cost of producing innovative, high-quality umbrellas.

1. What course of action do you recommend the Currims take? Explain your reasoning.

2. Use the Web to research price wars. What conditions usually prompt price wars? What impact do price wars have on an industry and the companies in it? What outcomes are typical in a price war?

*(continued)*

**385**

3. Many companies compete successfully without focusing on providing the lowest prices, even in industries in which customers view product or service prices as important purchasing criteria. What tactics do these companies use to compete successfully without relying on the lowest prices?

*Source:* Adapted from Anupam Mukerji, "Monsoon Marketing," *Fast Company,* April 2007, p. 22; "Preparing for the Pitter Patter," *Cybernoon,* June 1, 2007, www.cybernoon.com/DisplayArticle. asp?section=fromthepress&subsection=inbombay&xfile=June2007_ inbombay_standard13110; "How and Why Chinese Firms Excel in 'The Art of the Price War,'" *Knowledge@Wharton,* December 13, 2006, http://knowledge.wharton.upenn.edu/article.cfm?articleid=1625.

Note that value does not necessarily correspond to low price, however. Businesses that underprice their products and services or run special discount price promotions may be short circuiting the value proposition they are trying to communicate to their customers. Customers may respond to price cuts, but companies that rely on them to boost sales risk undermining the perceived value of their products and services. In addition, once customers grow accustomed to buying products and services during special promotions, the habit can be difficult to break. They simply wait for the next sale. Some companies in the auto industry have faced this problem as customers became accustomed to buying autos with large rebates and postponed buying new cars until automakers offered them special incentives. The result has been fluctuating sales and a diminished value of those automotive brands.

One of the most important determinants of customers' response to a price is whether they perceive the price to be a fair exchange for the value they receive from the product or service. Customers are willing to pay more for goods they perceive as more valuable.

*Peter Cucchiara and Uncle Pete's Hickory Ribs*

Peter Cucchiara, owner of Uncle Pete's Hickory Ribs in Revere, Massachusetts, was surprised when customers kept asking why baby back ribs were missing from his restaurant's menu. "It's the same meat as the other ribs, but you cannot convince people of that," he says. Cucchiara finally succumbed to customers' requests and soon discovered that he could charge more for baby back ribs, which are priced at $26.95 per rack compared with $21.95 for a rack of regular ribs. The menu addition has increased sales; baby back ribs now account for 20 percent of the restaurant's rib sales.[17]

The good news is that companies can influence through marketing and other efforts customers' perception of value. "The price you get for a product is a function of what it's truly worth—and how good a job you do communicating that value to the end user," says one entrepreneur.[18] Indeed, setting a product's or a service's price is another way a company can communicate value to its customers. For most shoppers, three reference points define a fair price: the price they have paid for the product or service in the past, the prices competitors charge for the same or similar product or service, and the costs a company incurs to provide the product or service. The price that customers have paid in the past for an item serves as a baseline reference point, but people often forget that inflation causes a company's costs to rise from year to year. Therefore, it is important for business owners to remind customers periodically that they must raise prices to offset the increased cost of doing business. "Over time, costs always go up," says Norm Brodsky, owner of a successful document storage company. "I'd rather raise prices a little every year or with every new contract than be forced to demand a big increase down the road."[19]

As we have seen already, companies often find it necessary to match competitors' prices on the same or similar items unless they can establish a distinctive image in customers' minds. One of the most successful strategies for companies facing direct competition is to differentiate their products or services by adding value for customers and then charging for it. For instance, a company might offer faster delivery, a longer product warranty, extra service, or something else that adds value to an item for its customers and allows the business to charge a higher price.

Perhaps the least understood of the three reference points is a company's cost structure. Customers often underestimate the costs businesses incur to provide products and services, whether it is a simple cotton T-shirt on a shelf in a beachfront shop or a life-saving drug that may have cost hundreds of millions of dollars and many years to develop. They forget that business owners must make or buy the products they sell, market them, pay their employees, and cover a host of other operating expenses, ranging from health care to legal fees.

## Pricing Strategies and Tactics

*3.* Discuss various pricing strategies for both new and existing products and services.

There is no limit to the number of variations in pricing strategies and tactics. The wide variety of options is exactly what allows entrepreneurs to be so creative with their pricing. This section will examine some of the more commonly used tactics under a variety of conditions. Pricing always plays a critical role in a firm's overall strategy; pricing policies must be compatible with a company's total marketing plan.

### New Product Pricing: Penetration, Skimming, or Life-Cycle Pricing

Most entrepreneurs approach setting the price of a new product with a great deal of apprehension because they have no precedent on which to base their decisions. If a new product's price is too high, it is in danger of failing because of low sales volume. However, if its price is too low, the product's sales revenue might not cover costs. Establishing a price that is too low is far more dangerous. Not only does the company forego revenues and profits, but it also limits the product's value in the eyes of its target customers.

The price a company can charge depends, in part, on the type of product it introduces:

- *Revolutionary products* are so new that they transform an industry. Companies that introduce these innovative products usually have the ability to charge prices that are close to the price ceiling although they may have to educate customers about the product's benefits.
- *Evolutionary products* involve making enhancements and improvements to products that are already on the market. Companies that introduce these products do not have the ability to charge premium prices unless they can use the enhancements they have made to differentiate their products from their competitors'. Establishing a price for an evolutionary product that is too low can lead to a price war.
- *Me-too products* are products that companies introduce just to keep up with competitors. Because they offer customers nothing new or unique, me-too products offer companies the least amount of pricing flexibility. Achieving success with these products means focusing on cost control and targeting the right market segments.

When pricing any new product, an entrepreneur must satisfy three objectives:

1. *Get the product accepted.* No matter how unique a product is, its price must be acceptable to the company's potential customers.
2. *Maintain market share as competition grows.* If a new product is successful, competitors will enter the market, and a small company must work to expand or at least maintain its market share. Continuously reappraising a product's price in conjunction with special advertising and promotion techniques helps the company maintain market share.
3. *Earn a profit.* A small company must establish a price for the new product that is higher than its cost. Entrepreneurs should not introduce a new product at a price below cost because it is much easier to lower the price than to increase it once the product is on the market. Pricing their products too low is a common and often fatal mistake for new businesses; entrepreneurs are tempted to underprice their products and services when they enter a new market to ensure its acceptance.

*Linda Calder and Calder
& Calder Promotions*

Linda Calder, owner of Calder & Calder Promotions, a company that produces trade shows, knows how difficult it can be to raise prices. When she launched her company, Calder decided to set her price below the average price of competing trade show production companies because she thought that would give her a competitive edge. "My fee was so low . . . I sold out but did not make a profit," she says. Realizing her mistake, Calder raised prices in her second year, but her customers balked. Her sales fell by 50 percent.[20]

Entrepreneurs have three basic strategies to choose from in establishing a new product's price: penetration, skimming, and life-cycle pricing.

**PENETRATION.** When a company introduces a new product in which customers are price sensitive, a **penetration pricing strategy** enables the business to build market share quickly and establish itself as the market leader. In other words, it sets the price just above total unit cost to develop a wedge in the market and quickly achieve a high volume of sales. The resulting low profit margins may discourage other competitors from entering the market with similar products.

In most cases, a penetration pricing strategy is used to introduce relatively low-priced goods into a market in which no elite segment and little opportunity for differentiation exist. Penetration pricing also works when a company's competitors are locked into high cost structures that result from the channels of distribution they use, labor agreements, or other factors. For instance, since its inception, Southwest Airlines has relied on its lower cost structure to compete with older, "legacy" carriers by emphasizing low prices. When it entered the market as a build-to-order computer company that took orders over the phone and online rather than incurring the cost of establishing retail outlets, Dell was able to beat competitors' prices and still earn higher profit margins.

Entrepreneurs must recognize that penetration pricing is a long-range strategy; until a company achieves customer acceptance for the product, profits are likely to be small. When a young college student launched a carpet cleaning business to help pay for his education, he decided to be the low-cost provider in his area. Although he landed plenty of work for his part-time business, he found that his company generated very little profit after deducting the expenses of doing business. Realizing that his customers would be willing to pay more for quality work, he raised his prices and began earning a reasonable profit.[21]

A danger of a penetration pricing strategy is that it attracts customers who know no brand loyalty. Companies that garner customers by offering low introductory prices must wonder what will become of their customer bases if they increase their prices or if a competitor undercuts their prices. If a penetration pricing strategy succeeds and the product achieves mass-market penetration, sales volume increases, economies of scale result in lower unit cost, and the company earns attractive profits. The objective of the penetration strategy is to achieve quick access to the market to generate high sales volume as soon as possible.

**SKIMMING.** A **skimming pricing strategy** often is used when a company introduces a unique product into a market with little or no competition. Sometimes a company uses this tactic when introducing a product into a competitive market that contains an elite group that is willing and able to pay a premium price. A company sets a higher-than-normal price in an effort to quickly recover the initial developmental and promotional costs of the product. The idea is to set a price well above the product's total unit cost and to promote the product heavily to appeal to the segment of the market that is not sensitive to price. This pricing tactic often reinforces the unique, prestigious image of a store and projects a quality picture of the product.

*Sylvie Chantecaille
and Chantecaille*

When Sylvie Chantecaille, owner of a cosmetic company that bears her name, launched a new biodynamic lifting cream aimed at female baby boomers who are fighting the aging process, she decided to price the product at $295 for 1.7 ounces. "Can we really sell it for that much?" Chantecaille recalls thinking as she pondered her pricing decision. Her concern was unfounded; her company sells more than 20,000 units of the special cream each year through Neiman Marcus, Barneys New York, and small, upscale cosmetic shops and is preparing to introduce another product at a significantly higher price![22]

In cases in which product development costs are extremely high, such as for new drugs and high-tech products, a skimming strategy helps a company recoup its research and development costs in a shorter time span. As sales volume increases with the broad acceptance of the new products, the firm can lower its price.

**LIFE-CYCLE PRICING.** One variation of the skimming pricing strategy is called **life-cycle pricing**. Using this technique, a company introduces a product at a high price. Then as the product moves through its life cycle, the company relies on technological advances, the learning curve effect, and economies of scale to lower its cost and to reduce the product's price faster than its competitors can. By beating other businesses in a price decline, the company discourages competitors and, over time, becomes a high-volume producer. Computers, DVD players, and other electronic components are prime examples of products introduced at a high price that quickly cascaded downward as companies forged important technological advances.

Life-cycle pricing assumes that competition will emerge over time. Even if no competition arises, companies almost always lower the product's price to attract a larger segment of the market. For instance, when the DVD collection of the hit television comedy *Seinfeld* was released in November, it was priced at $49.99. As the Christmas holidays drew closer, retailers cut the price of the collection to $44.99; after the holidays, the price fell to $39.99. By early spring, customers could purchase the DVD set for just $29.99.[23] In a sliding strategy, the initial high price contributes to the rapid return of start-up or development costs and generates a pool of funds to finance expansion and technological advances.

## Pricing Techniques for Established Products and Services

Entrepreneurs have a variety of pricing techniques or tactics available to them to apply to established products and services.

**ODD PRICING.** Although studies of consumer reactions to prices are mixed, many entrepreneurs use the technique known as **odd pricing**. They set prices that end in odd numbers (frequently 5, 7, or 9) because they believe that an item selling for $12.69 appears to be much cheaper than an item selling for $13.00. Some studies show no benefits from using odd pricing, but others have concluded that the technique can produce significant increases in sales.

**PRICE LINING.** **Price lining** is a technique that greatly simplifies pricing decisions. Under this system, the manager stocks merchandise in several different price ranges or price lines. Each category of merchandise contains items that are similar in appearance, quality, cost, performance, or other features. For example, many electronics stores use price lines for their DVDs to make it easier for customers to select items and to simplify stock planning. Many lined products appear in sets of three—good, better, and best—at prices designed to satisfy different market segments' needs and incomes. Price lining can boost a store's sales because it makes goods available to a wide range of shoppers, simplifies the purchase decision for customers, and allows them to keep their purchases within their budgets.

**DYNAMIC PRICING.** For many businesses, the pricing decision has become more challenging because the World Wide Web gives customers access to incredible amounts of information about the prices of items ranging from cars to computers. Increasingly, customers are using the Web to find the lowest prices available. To maintain their profitability, companies have responded with **dynamic (or customized) pricing**, in which they set different prices on the same products and services for different customers using the information they have collected about their customers. Rather than sell their products at fixed prices, companies using dynamic pricing rely on fluid prices that may change based on supply and demand and on which customer is buying or when a customer makes a purchase. For instance, a first-time customer making a purchase at an online store may pay a higher price for an item than a regular customer who shops there frequently.

Dynamic pricing is not a new concept. The standard practice in ancient bazaars involved merchants and customers haggling until they came to a mutually agreeable price,

©Mike Baldwin/Cornered

which meant that different customers paid different prices for the same goods. Although the modern version of dynamic pricing often involves sophisticated market research or the Internet, the goal is the same: to charge the right customer the right price at the right time. For example, travelers can use Priceline and similar Web sites to purchase last minute airline tickets at significant discounts—e.g., a round trip ticket from Paris to Tokyo for just $500 rather than for the full-fare price of $1,000. Travelers benefit from lower prices, and the airlines are able to generate revenue from seats that otherwise would have gone unsold.

**LEADER PRICING. Leader pricing** is a technique in which the small retailer marks down the customary price (i.e., the price consumers are accustomed to paying) of a popular item in an attempt to attract more customers. The company earns a much smaller profit on each unit because the markup is lower, but purchases of other merchandise by customers seeking the leader item often boost sales and profits. In other words, the incidental purchases that consumers make when shopping for the leader item boosts sales revenue enough to offset a lower profit margin on the leader. Grocery stores often use leader pricing, particularly around holidays.

**GEOGRAPHIC PRICING.** Small businesses whose pricing decisions are greatly affected by the costs of shipping merchandise to customers across a wide range of geographic regions frequently employ one of the **geographic pricing** techniques. For these companies, freight expenses constitute a substantial portion of the cost of doing business and often cut deeply into already narrow profit margins. One type of geographic pricing is **zone pricing**, in which a company sells its merchandise at different prices to customers located in different territories. For example, a manufacturer might sell at one price to customers in the eastern part of the country and at another to those in the western part of the country. The parcel post charges are a good example of zone pricing. The small business must be able to show a legitimate basis (e.g., difference in selling or transportation costs) for the price discrimination or risk violating the law in some countries.

Another variation of geographic pricing is the **uniform delivered pricing**, a technique in which a company charges all customers the same price regardless of their location, even though the cost of selling or transporting merchandise varies. The company calculates freight charges for each region in which it sells and combines them into a uniform fee. The result is that local customers subsidize shipping costs to distant customers.

A final variation of geographic pricing is **F.O.B. factory**, in which the small company sells its merchandise to customers on the condition that they pay all shipping costs. Using this technique, a company can set a uniform price for its products and let each customer cover the freight cost.

**OPPORTUNISTIC PRICING.** When products or services are in short supply, customers are willing to pay more for products they need. Some businesses use such circumstances to maximize short-term profits by engaging in price gouging. Many customers have little choice but to pay the higher prices. **Opportunistic pricing** may backfire, however, because customers know that a company that charges unreasonably high prices is exploiting them. For instance, after a major hurricane, a convenience store owner jacked up prices on virtually every item, selling packs of batteries for $10 each. Neighborhood residents had little choice but to pay the higher prices. After the incident, customers remembered the store's price gouging and began to shop elsewhere. The convenience store's sales never recovered, and the store eventually went out of business.

**DISCOUNTS.** Many small businesses use **discounts (or markdowns)**, reductions from normal list prices, to sell stale, outdated, damaged, or slow-moving merchandise. A seasonal discount is a price reduction designed to encourage shoppers to purchase merchandise before an upcoming season. For instance, many retail clothiers offer special sales on winter coats in late summer. Some firms grant purchase discounts to special groups of customers, such as senior citizens or students, to establish a faithful clientele and to generate repeat business. Merchants in many college towns offer special discounts to students, and the discounts help these businesses generate a large volume of student business. Large retailers commonly offer discounts to senior citizens or they set aside a particular day of the month for special discounts for senior shoppers.

**MULTIPLE UNIT PRICING.** **Multiple unit pricing** is a promotional technique that offers customers discounts if they purchase in quantity. Many products, especially those with a relatively low unit value, are sold using multiple unit pricing. For example, instead of selling an item for 50 cents, a small company might offer five for $2.

**BUNDLING.** Many small businesses have discovered the marketing benefits of **bundling**, grouping together several products or services, or both, into a package that offers customers extra value at a special price. For instance, many software manufacturers bundle several computer programs (such as a word processor, spreadsheet, database, presentation graphics, and Web browser) into "suites" that offer customers a discount over purchasing the same programs separately. The tourism industry has discovered a large market for travelers who want their entire vacation bundled into a one-price experience. One company, Funjet Vacations, includes airfare, ground transportation, hotel accommodations, and discounts on local attractions in one reasonably priced travel package.

*First Steps*

To compete with industry leader Baby Einstein, several entrepreneurs who have created educational DVDs aimed at babies and young children have banded together to bundle their products under the brand name First Steps. Single titles from First Steps sell for $9.99 each, but customers can purchase a box set that includes a bundle of three DVDs for just $19.99. All of the members of First Steps say that both their sales and their profits have increased since they began bundling their titles into box sets.[24]

**Optional-product pricing** involves selling the base product for one price but selling the options or accessories at a much higher percentage markup. Automobiles are often sold at a base price with each option priced separately. In many cases, the car is sold with some of the options bundled together.

*Don and Joseph Saladino
and Drive 495*

Drive 495, an upscale fitness and golf center in New York City started by brothers Don and Joseph Saladino, offers three simulation bays where urban golfers can practice their swings on 31 famous courses from around the world, including Pebble Beach and St. Andrews. Drive 495 uses optional-product pricing; standard one-year memberships start at $5,000, an annual membership with unlimited golf and fitness lessons costs $25,000, and a lifetime membership with unlimited lessons for one year is $100,000.[25]

**Captive-product pricing** is the granddaddy of all pricing tactics in which the basic product is useless without the appropriate accessories. King Gillette, the founder of the company that manufactures Gillette razors, taught the business world that the *real* money is not in the razor (the product) itself but in the blades (the accessory). Today we see the same pricing strategy used by Nintendo and other electronic game manufacturers that have a very small profit margin on the game system but substantially higher margins on the game cartridges. When Nintendo launched its popular Wii game station, the company's strategy was to sell a simpler game station with games that players could enjoy without having to invest dozens of hours to learn them. This strategy enabled Nintendo to introduce its game station at a price of just $249, well below the $500 price tag on Sony's PlayStation 3 and Microsoft's $400 Xbox 360. Nintendo's real money-maker, however, is the games that it sells to Wii owners that are priced at $50 each (still below the $60 price tag on most PlayStation games). Nintendo's pricing strategy worked, and sales of Wii stations and games outstripped those of Sony's and Microsoft's products.[26]

**By-product pricing** is a technique in which the revenues from the sale of by-products allow a firm to be more competitive in its pricing of the main product. For years, owners of sawmills considered bark chips to be a nuisance. Today they package them and sell them as ground cover to homeowners, gardeners, and landscapers. Zoos across the globe offer one of the most creative examples of by-product pricing, packaging once-worthless exotic animal droppings and marketing it as fertilizer under the clever name "Zoo Doo."

**SUGGESTED RETAIL PRICES.** Many manufacturers print suggested retail prices on their products or include them on invoices or in wholesale catalogs. Small business owners frequently follow these suggested retail prices because doing so eliminates the need to make a pricing decision. Nonetheless, following prices established by a distant manufacturer may create problems for the small firm. For example, a haberdasher may try to create a high-quality, exclusive image through a prestige pricing policy, but manufacturers may suggest discount outlet prices that are incompatible with the small firm's image. Another danger of accepting the manufacturer's suggested price is that it does not take into consideration a small company's cost structure or competitive situation. In the United States, for example, a manufacturer cannot force a business to accept a suggested retail price or require a business to agree not to resell merchandise below a stated price because such practices violate the Sherman Antitrust Act and other laws.

**FOLLOW-THE-LEADER PRICING.** Some businesses make no effort to be price leaders in their immediate geographic areas and simply follow the prices that their competitors establish. Entrepreneurs wisely monitor their competitors' pricing policies and individual prices by reviewing their advertisements or by hiring part-time or full-time comparison shoppers. However, these entrepreneurs use this information only to establish a "me too" pricing policy, which eradicates any opportunity to create a special price image for their businesses. Maintaining a follow-the-leader pricing policy may not be healthy for a small business because it robs the company of the opportunity to create a distinctive image in its customers' eyes.

A small company's pricing strategy must be compatible with its marketing objectives, its marketing mix, and its cost structure. Also, the pricing strategy must be consistent with

## ■ Whoa! Did I Read That Price Tag Correctly?

Looking for the ideal gift for that hard-to-buy-for person on your list? How about a trip into space for him or her and 11 friends on Virgin Galactic's SpaceShip Two? In addition to having breathtaking views of the earth from 63 miles high and experiencing weightlessness, after landing the group will enjoy four nights of luxurious accommodations on Necker Island, Sir Richard Branson's (founder of Virgin Atlantic) private paradise in the British Virgin Islands. Branson himself will present the members of the group with a set of pilot's wings. Price: a mere $1,764,000 and available through Neiman Marcus.

Upscale retailer Neiman Marcus is famous for its annual fantasy gift list that the company publishes in time for the Christmas season. Some of the items for sale have ranged from the exotic such as his and hers submarines, hot-air balloons, Chinese junks (ships) to more "practical" purchases such as a limited edition 500-horsepower BMW convertible priced at $139,000 (All 50 sold out in a record 92 seconds!) and a Monopoly game made from chocolate (Christy Hefner purchased one for her father, Hugh, founder of *Playboy* magazine).

Company co-founder Stanley Marcus came up with the idea of extravagant "fantasy" gifts in the late 1950s as a way to generate publicity for his upscale retail stores. The idea was that even if customers could not afford to purchase any of the fantasy gifts, they would want to purchase more affordable items from a company whose name was synonymous with luxury. Marcus's strategy worked, and today, many retailers, ranging from toy store FAO Schwarz and lingerie company Victoria's Secret to handbag maker Coach and entrepreneur Taysha Smith Valez's small cosmetic company, H. Couture Beauty, are using similar strategies to court customers at the extreme upper end of the market. Companies of all sizes are adapting their pricing strategies to the "barbell market," the migration of large numbers of customers from the "middle market" to both extremes—the discount and luxury ends of the market. Currently, the fastest growth is occurring at the extremes of the market: discount outlets at one end and luxury retailers at the other.

FAO Schwarz offers custom-made Lionel model train sets that start at $10,000, and Victoria's Secret made the headlines when it offered a diamond-studded bra for $6.5 million. (Actually, Victoria's Secret has sold only one super-bra, a $3 million jewel-encrusted model that included a 42-carat Harry Winston pear-shaped diamond, but the publicity the company gets from the press is worth many times that.)

After market research revealed that truly upscale customers considered Coach bags to be too "pedestrian" for their chic tastes (After all, their bags typically sold for a mere $350), managers decided to introduce the Legacy line of products aimed at the top of the market. Legacy customers can purchase limited edition bags, accessories, and clothing made from exotic materials or sporting unique designs. For instance, a Legacy satchel made from python skin sells for $2,500 and one made from ostrich skin sells for $4,500. The bags look great with a pair of $800 Legacy jeans and a $1,300 sweater coat.

A wealthy socialite herself, entrepreneur Taysha Smith Valez, 25, understands what the customers who make up the ultraluxury market want. Having made her first million by age 21, Smith Valez launched the Socialite Collection, a line of luxury cosmetics with cases that are adorned with hand-placed Swarovski crystals, and one year of concierge service is included with every purchase. A tube of Socialite lipstick sells for $300, mascara goes for $1,589, and bronzer sells for $1,440. Too pricey? Not for Smith Valez's upscale target market. Within four months of launching the Socialite Collection, sales had reached $15 million.

1. What forces are driving the barbell market effect—customers migrating to the extremes of the market, discount outlets and the luxury shops?
2. Use the Web to research some of the products described in this feature. Are the costs of producing and marketing these items that much more than producing and marketing items for the mainstream market?
3. What benefits do companies that pursue ultraluxury pricing strategies realize in other segments of the market, even among customers who cannot afford their ultraluxury items?

*Sources:* Adapted from Vanessa O'Connell, "It's the Publicity That Counts," *Wall Street Journal*, November 17, 2006, pp. B1, B4; Rachel Dodes and Cherly Lu-Lien Tan, "What Price Beauty? Costly Face Creams Lift Prices, Spirits," *Wall Street Journal*, December 19, 2006, pp. A1, A12; Allison Fass, "Trading Up," *Forbes*, January 29, 2007, pp. 48–49; "Sometimes a Fantasy: Behind the Neiman Marcus Christmas Book," *MultiChannel Merchant*, December 1, 2006, http://multichannelmerchant.com/holiday_resource_2006/sometimes_fantasy_122006/; Sara Wilson, "The Finer Things," *Entrepreneur*, May 2007, www.entrepreneur.com/magazine/entrepreneur/2007/may/177126.html.

the competitive realities of the marketplace and the shifting forces of supply and demand. The forces that shape the pricing decision can change rapidly and, therefore, a company's pricing strategy is never completely fixed.

The underlying forces that dictate how a business prices its goods or services vary greatly among industries. The next three sections will investigate pricing techniques used in retailing, manufacturing, and service firms.

## Pricing Techniques for Retailers

*4.* Explain the pricing techniques used by retailers.

Because retail customers have become more price conscious and the Internet has made prices more transparent, retailers have changed their pricing strategies to emphasize value. This value-price relationship allows for a wide variety of highly creative pricing and marketing practices. Delivering high levels of recognized value in products and services is one key to retail customer loyalty. To justify paying a higher price than those charged by competitors, customers must perceive a company's products or services as giving them greater value.

### Markup

The basic premise of a successful business operation is selling a good or service for more than it costs to produce it. The difference between the cost of a product or service and its selling price is called **markup** (or **markon**). Markup can be expressed in dollars or as a percentage of either cost or selling price:

$$\text{Dollar markup} = \text{Retail price} - \text{Cost of the merchandise}$$

$$\text{Percentage (of retail price) markup} = \frac{\text{Dollar markup}}{\text{Retail price}}$$

$$\text{Percentage (of cost) markup} = \frac{\text{Dollar markup}}{\text{Cost of unit}}$$

For example, if a man's shirt costs $15, and the manager plans to sell it for $25, markup would be as follows:

$$\text{Dollar markup} = \$25 - \$15 = \$10$$

$$\text{Percentage (of retail price) markup} = \frac{\$10}{\$25}$$

$$= 40\%$$

$$\text{Percentage (of cost) markup} = \frac{\$10}{\$15}$$

$$= 66.67\%$$

The cost of merchandise used in computing markup includes not only the wholesale price of the merchandise but also any incidental costs (e.g., selling or transportation charges) that the retailer incurs and a profit minus any discounts (quantity, cash) that the wholesaler offers.

Once entrepreneurs have a financial plan in place, including sales estimates and anticipated expenses, they can compute their companies' initial markup. The **initial markup** is the *average* markup required on all merchandise to cover the cost of the items, all incidental expenses, and a reasonable profit.

$$\text{Initial dollar markup} = \frac{\text{Operating expenses} + \text{Reductions} + \text{Profits}}{\text{Net sales} + \text{Reductions}}$$

Operating expenses are the cost of doing business, such as rent, utilities, and depreciation; reductions include employee and customer discounts, markdowns, special sales, and the cost of stockouts. For example, if a small retailer forecasts sales of $980,000, expenses of $140,000, and $24,000 in reductions, and he or she expects a profit of $58,000, the initial markup percentage will be:

$$\text{Initial markup percentage} = \frac{\$540,000 + \$24,000 + \$58,000}{\$980,000 + \$24,000}$$

$$= 62\%$$

Thus, this retailer knows that an average markup of 62 percent is necessary to cover costs and generate an adequate profit.

Some businesses use a standard markup on all of their merchandise. This technique, which is usually used in retail stores carrying related products, applies a standard percentage markup to all merchandise. Most stores find it much more practical to use a flexible markup, which assigns different markup percentages to different types of products. Because of the wide range of prices and types of merchandise they sell, department stores frequently rely on a flexible markup. It would be impractical for them to use a standard markup on all items because they have such a diverse cost and volume range. For instance, the markup percentage for socks is not likely to be suitable as a markup for washing machines.

Once owners determine the desired markup percentage, they can compute the appropriate retail price. Knowing that the markup of a particular item represents 60 percent of the retail price:

$$\text{Cost} = \text{Retail price} - \text{Markup}$$
$$= 100\% - 60\%$$
$$= 40\% \text{ of retail price}$$

Assuming that the cost of the item is $18.00, the retailer can rearrange the percentage (of retail price) markup formula:

$$\text{Retail price} = \frac{\text{Dollar cost}}{\text{Percentage cost}}$$

Solving for retail price, the retailer computes the following price:

$$\text{Retail price} = \frac{\$18.00}{40\%} = \$45.00$$

Thus, the owner establishes a retail price of $45.00 for the item using a 60 percent markup.

Finally, retailers must verify that the computed retail price is consistent with their planned initial markup percentage. Will it cover costs and generate the desired profit? Is it congruent with the firm's overall price image? Is the final price in line with the company's strategy? Is it within an acceptable price range? How does it compare with the prices charged by competitors? Perhaps most important, are the customers willing and able to pay this price?

## Pricing Techniques for Manufacturers

*5.* Explain the pricing techniques used by manufacturers.

For manufacturers, the pricing decision requires the support of accurate, timely accounting records. The most commonly used pricing technique for manufacturers is **cost-plus pricing**. Using this method, manufacturers establish a price composed of direct materials, direct labor, factory overhead, selling and administrative costs, plus a desired profit margin. Figure 11.2 illustrates the components of cost-plus pricing.

The primary advantage of the cost-plus pricing method is its simplicity. Given the proper cost accounting data, computing a product's final selling price is relatively easy. Also, because it adds a profit onto the top of the firm's costs, a manufacturer is guaranteed

**FIGURE 11.2**
**Components of Cost-Plus Pricing**

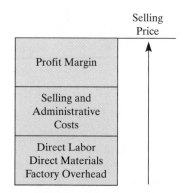

to achieve the desired profit margin. This process, however, does not encourage the manufacturer to use its resources efficiently. Even if the company fails to use its resources in the most effective manner, it will still earn a reasonable profit, and thus, there is no motivation to conserve resources in the manufacturing process. Finally, because manufacturers' cost structures vary so greatly, cost-plus pricing fails to consider the competition sufficiently. Despite its drawbacks, however, the cost-plus method of establishing prices remains prominent in many industries such as construction and printing.

### Direct Costing and Pricing

One requisite for a successful pricing policy in manufacturing is a reliable cost accounting system that can generate timely reports to determine the costs of processing raw materials into finished goods. The traditional method of product costing is called **absorption costing** because all manufacturing and overhead costs are absorbed into the finished product's total cost. Absorption costing includes direct materials and direct labor, plus a portion of fixed and variable factory overhead costs, in each unit manufactured. Full-absorption financial statements, used in published annual reports and tax reports, are very useful in performing financial analysis. However, full-absorption statements are of little help to a manufacturer when determining prices or the impact of price changes.

A more useful technique for managerial decision making is **variable (or direct) costing**, in which the cost of the products manufactured includes only those costs that vary directly with the quantity produced. In other words, variable costing encompasses direct materials, direct labor, and factory overhead costs that vary with the level of the company's output of finished goods. Factory overhead costs that are fixed (for instance rent, depreciation, and insurance) are *not* included in the costs of finished items. Instead, they are considered to be expenses of the period.

A manufacturer's goal when establishing prices is to discover the cost combination of selling price and sales volume that exceeds the variable costs of producing a product and contributes enough to cover fixed costs and earn a profit. Using full-absorption costing clouds the true relationships among price, volume, and costs by including fixed expenses when calculating unit cost. Using direct-costing yields a constant unit cost of the product no matter what the volume of production is. The result is a clearer picture of the price-volume-costs relationship.

The starting point for establishing product prices is the direct-cost income statement. As Table 11.1 indicates, the direct-cost statement yields the same net income as does the full-absorption income statement. The only difference between the two statements is the format. The full-absorption statement allocates costs such as advertising, rent, and utilities according to the activity that caused them, but the direct-cost income statement separates expenses into fixed and variable costs. Fixed expenses remain constant regardless of the production level, but variable expenses fluctuate according to production volume.

When variable costs are subtracted from total revenues, the result is the manufacturer's **contribution margin**, the amount remaining that contributes to covering fixed expenses and earning a profit. Expressing this contribution margin as a percentage of total revenue yields the company's contribution percentage. Computing the contribution percentage is a critical step when establishing prices through the direct-costing method. This manufacturer's contribution percentage is 36.5 percent, which is calculated as follows:

$$\text{Contribution percentage} = 1 - \frac{\text{Variable expenses}}{\text{Revenues}}$$

$$= 1 - \frac{\$502,000}{\$790,000} = 36.5\%$$

### Computing a Breakeven Selling Price

A manufacturer's contribution percentage tells what portion of total revenue remains after covering variable costs to contribute toward meeting fixed expenses and earning a profit. This manufacturer's contribution percentage is 36.5 percent, which means that variable costs absorb 63.5 percent of total revenues. In other words, variable costs represent

## TABLE 11.1  Full-Absorption versus Direct-Cost Income Statement

### Full-Absorption Income Statement

| | | |
|---|---:|---:|
| Sales Revenue | | $790,000 |
| Cost of Goods Sold | | |
|    Materials | $250,500 | |
|    Direct Labor | 190,200 | |
|    Factory Overhead | 120,200 | 560,900 |
| Gross Profit | | $229,100 |
| Operating Expenses | | |
|    General and Administrative | $ 66,100 | |
|    Selling | 112,000 | |
|    Other | 11,000 | |
| Total Operating Expenses | | 189,100 |
| Net Income (before taxes) | | $ 40,000 |

### Direct-Cost Income Statement

| | | |
|---|---:|---:|
| Sales Revenue (100%) | | $790,000 |
| Variable Costs | | |
|    Materials | $250,500 | |
|    Direct Labor | 190,200 | |
|    Variable Factory Overhead | 13,200 | |
|    Variable Selling Expenses | 48,100 | |
| Total Variable Costs (63.5%) | | 502,000 |
| Contribution Margin (36.5%) | | 288,000 |
| Fixed Costs | | |
|    Fixed Factory Overhead | $107,000 | |
|    Fixed Selling Expenses | 63,900 | |
|    General and Administrative | 66,100 | |
|    Other Fixed Expenses | 11,000 | |
| Total Fixed Expenses (31.4%) | | 248,000 |
| Net Income (before taxes) (5.1%) | | $ 40,000 |

63.5 percent $(1.00 - 0.365 = 0.635)$ of the product's selling price. Suppose that this manufacturer's variable costs include the following:

| | |
|---|---|
| Material | $2.08/unit |
| Direct labor | $4.12/unit |
| Variable factory overhead | $0.78/unit |
| Total variable cost | $6.98/unit |

The minimum price at which the manufacturer would sell the item is $6.98. Any price below that would not cover variable costs. To compute the breakeven selling price for his product, find the selling price using the following equation:

$$\text{Breakeven selling price} = \frac{\text{Profit} + \left( \begin{array}{c} \text{Variable cost} \\ \text{per unit} \end{array} \times \begin{array}{c} \text{Quantity} \\ \text{produced} \end{array} \right) + \begin{array}{c} \text{Total} \\ \text{fixed cost} \end{array}}{\text{Quantity produced}}$$

To break even, the manufacturer assumes $0 profit. Suppose that its plans are to produce 50,000 units of the product and that fixed costs will be $248,000. The breakeven selling price is as follows:

$$\text{Breakeven selling price} = \frac{\$0 + (\$6.98/\text{unit} \times 50,000 \text{ units}) + \$248,000}{50,000 \text{ units}}$$

$$= \frac{\$597,000}{50,000 \text{ units}}$$

$$= \$11.94 \text{ per unit}$$

Thus, $4.96 ($11.94/unit – $6.98/unit) of the $11.94 breakeven price goes toward meeting fixed production costs. Suppose the manufacturer wants to earn a $50,000 profit. Then the required selling price is:

$$\text{Selling price} = \frac{\$50,000 + (6.98/\text{unit} \times 50,000 \text{ units}) + \$248,000}{50,000 \text{ units}}$$

$$= \frac{\$647,000}{50,000 \text{ units}}$$

$$= \$12.94/\text{unit}$$

Now the manufacturer must decide whether customers will purchase 50,000 units at $12.94. If the manufacturer thinks they won't, managers must decide either to produce a different, more profitable product or lower the selling price by lowering either its cost or its profit target. Any price above $11.94 will generate some profit although less than that desired. In the short run, the manufacturer could sell the product for less than $11.94 if competitive factors dictate, but *not* below $6.98 because a price below $6.98 would not cover the variable costs of production.

Because the manufacturer's capacity in the short run is fixed, pricing decisions should be aimed at using resources most efficiently. The company cannot avoid the fixed cost of operating the plant, and the variable costs can be eliminated only if the firm ceases to offer the product. Therefore, the selling price must be at least equal to the variable costs (per unit) of making the product. Any price above that amount contributes to covering fixed costs and providing a reasonable profit.

Of course, over the long run, the manufacturer cannot sell below total costs and continue to survive. A product's selling price must cover total product costs—both fixed and variable—and generate a reasonable profit.

## Pricing Techniques for Service Businesses

**6.** Explain the pricing techniques used by service firms.

Service businesses must establish their prices on the basis of the materials used to provide the service, the labor employed, an allowance for overhead, and a profit. As in a manufacturing operation, a service firm must have a reliable and accurate accounting system to keep a tally of the total costs of providing the service. Most service firms base their prices on an hourly rate, usually the actual number of hours required to perform the service. For most firms, labor and materials constitute the largest portion of the cost of the service. To establish a reasonable and profitable price for service, the small business owner must know the cost of materials, direct labor, and overhead for each unit of service. Using these basic cost data and a desired profit margin, the owner of the small service firm can determine the appropriate price for the service.

Consider a simple example for pricing a common service—television repair. Ned's TV Repair Shop uses the direct-costing method to prepare an income statement for exercising managerial control (see Table 11.2). Notice that Ned's total expenses are $172,000 ($104,000 in variable expenses and $68,000 in fixed expenses). Ned estimates that he and his employees spend about 9,250 hours in the actual production of television repair service. The total cost per productive hour for Ned's TV Repair Shop is as follows:

$$\text{Total cost per hour} = \frac{\$172,000}{9,250 \text{ hours}} = \$18.59/\text{hour}$$

## TABLE 11.2  Direct-Cost Income Statement, Ned's TV Repair Shop

| | | |
|---|---:|---:|
| Sales Revenue | | $199,000 |
| Variable Expenses | | |
| Labor | $52,000 | |
| Materials | 40,500 | |
| Variable Factory Overhead | 11,500 | |
| Total Variable Expenses | | $104,000 |
| Fixed Expenses | | |
| Rent | $ 2,500 | |
| Salaries | 38,500 | |
| Fixed Overhead | 27,000 | |
| Total Fixed Expenses | | 68,000 |
| Net Income | | $ 27,000 |

Now Ned must add in an amount for his desired profit. He expects a net operating profit margin of 18 percent on sales. To compute the final price, he uses the following equation:

$$\text{Price per hour} = \text{Total cost per productive hour} \times \frac{1.00}{(1 - \text{net profit target as \% of sale})}$$

$$= \text{Total cost per productive hour} \times \frac{1.00}{(1 - .18)}$$

$$= \$18.59 \times 1.219$$

$$= \$22.68/\text{hour}$$

A price of $22.68 per hour will cover Ned's costs and generate the desired profit. Smart service shop owners compute the cost per production hour at regular intervals throughout the year because they know that rising costs can eat into their profit margins very quickly. Rapidly rising labor costs and materials prices dictate that the service firm's price per hour be computed even more frequently. As in the case of the retailer and the manufacturer, Ned must evaluate the pricing policies of competitors and decide whether his price is consistent with the firm's image.

Of course, the price of $22.68 per hour assumes that all jobs require the same amount of materials. If this is not a valid assumption (and it probably is not), Ned must recalculate the price per hour without including the cost of materials.

$$\text{Cost per productive hour} = \frac{\$172,000 - \$40,500}{9,250 \text{ hours}}$$

$$= \$14.22/\text{hour}$$

Adding in the desired 18 percent net operating profit on sales yields:

$$\text{Price per hour} = \$14.22/\text{hour} \times \frac{1.00}{(1 - 0.18)}$$

$$= \$14.22/\text{hour} \times 1.219$$

$$= \$17.34/\text{hour}$$

Under these conditions Ned would charge $17.34 per hour plus the actual cost of materials used and a markup on the cost of materials. For instance, a repair job that takes four hours to complete would have the following price:

| | |
|---|---:|
| Cost of service (4 hours × $17.34/hour) | $ 50.08 |
| Cost of materials | $ 41.00 |
| Markup on materials (60%) | $ 24.60 |
| Total price | $115.68 |

Because services are intangible, their pricing offers more flexibility than do tangible products. One danger that entrepreneurs face is pricing their services too low because prospective customers' perceptions of a service are influenced heavily by its price. In other words, establishing a low price for a service actually may harm a service company's sales!

To avoid this problem, Reid Carr, founder of Red Door Interactive, a company that specializes in Web services, prices each project that his company takes on by estimating the number of hours it will take to complete and multiplying that number by an hourly rate and then including some "wiggle room" for unforeseen cost overruns. If the flow of work slows, Carr allows his employees to work on pro bono projects to raise the visibility of his company and to show the quality of work his employees create. "Pro bono work is free advertising," explains Carr.[27]

## The Impact of Credit on Pricing

**7.** Describe the impact of credit on pricing.

In today's business environment, linking a company's pricing strategy with its credit strategy has become essential because many customers expect to "pay with plastic" rather than with cash. Consumers crave convenience when they shop, and one of the most common conveniences they demand is the ability to purchase goods and services on credit. Small businesses have three options for selling to customers on credit: credit cards, installment credit, and trade credit.

### Credit Cards

The average number of credit cards per person in the U.K. is 2.4. By contrast, nearly 144 million Americans have credit cards, and the average person has four credit cards carrying an average interest rate of more than 19 percent per year.[28] Approximately 14 percent of Americans carry more than 10 credit cards! Three out of four U.S. households have at least one credit card, and customers use them to purchase $1.8 trillion worth of goods and services annually.[29] The message is clear: Customers expect to make purchases with credit cards, and small companies that fail to accept credit cards run the risk of losing sales to competitors who do. Research shows that customers who use credit cards make purchases that are 112 percent higher than if they had used cash.[30]

Companies that accept credit cards incur additional expenses for offering this convenience, however. Businesses must pay to use the system—typically 1 to 6 percent of the total credit card charges, which they in turn must factor into the prices of their products or services. They also pay a transaction fee of 5 to 50 cents per charge and must purchase or lease equipment to process transactions. Given customer expectations, small businesses find it difficult to refuse major cards, even when the big card companies raise the fees that merchants must pay to process them. Fees operate on a multi-step process. On a $100 Visa or MasterCard purchase at a typical business, a processing bank buys the credit card slip from the retailer for $97.44. Then that bank sells the slip to the bank that issued the card for about $98.80. The remaining $1.20 discount is called the interchange fee, which is what the processing bank passes along to the issuing bank. The prices entrepreneurs charge must reflect the higher costs associated with credit card transactions.

Before it can accept credit cards, a business must obtain merchant status from either a bank or an **independent sales organization (ISO)**. The accompanying "Gaining a Competitive Edge" feature describes how a small company can obtain merchant status.

As customers' use of debit cards grows, small businesses also are equipping their stores to handle debit card transactions, which act as electronic checks, automatically deducting the purchase amount from a customer's checking account. The equipment is easy to install and to set up, and the cost to the company is negligible. The payoff can be big, however, in the form of increased sales.

**E-COMMERCE AND CREDIT CARDS.** When it comes to online business transactions, the most common method of payment is the credit card. Internet vendors are constantly challenged by the need to provide secure methods of transacting business in a safe environment. As you will learn in Chapter 13, "E-Commerce and Entrepreneurship," many shoppers are

## How to Obtain Merchant Status

Whether they sell online or offline, entrepreneurs must acquire merchant status to accept credit card payments for goods and services. Offering customers the convenience of paying with credit cards enhances a company's reputation and translates directly into higher sales, especially for online sellers. Qualifying for a merchant account is not easy for many small companies, however, because merchant service providers (MSPs) such as banks view it in the same manner as making a loan to a business. "When we give you the ability to accept credit cards," explains one banker, "we are giving you the use of funds before we get them." Although small storefront businesses with operating histories of less than two years may have difficulty establishing merchant accounts, home-based businesses and mail-order companies or entrepreneurs doing business over the World Wide Web typically have the greatest difficulty convincing banks to set them up with credit card accounts.

For instance, when Steve and Shelly Bloom, owners of Crystal Collection, a small glass art importer, applied for merchant status, their bank denied their request because their company is home-based. The Blooms then turned to an independent sales organization (ISO) the bank recommended, and the ISO helped them get merchant status through another bank. Because their business represents a higher-than-normal risk to credit card-issuing banks, the Blooms pay higher fees than small storefront companies. Their fees include either 2.5 percent of their monthly credit card transactions or $25 (whichever is higher), a 20 cent per transaction handling fee, a $15 monthly fee, and $32 per month to rent the point-of-sale terminal to process credit card transactions.

What can business owners do to increase their chances of gaining merchant status so that they can accept customers without driving their costs sky-high? Try these tips:

■ *Recognize that business start-ups and companies that have been in business less than three years face the greatest obstacles in gaining merchant status.* Entrepreneurs just starting out in business should consider applying for merchant status when they approach a bank for start-up capital. Existing companies can boost their chances of success by preparing a package to present to the bank—credit references, financial statements, business description, and an overview of the company's marketing plan, including a detailed customer profile.

■ *Apply with your own bank first.* The best place to begin the application process is with your own bank; ISOs typically charge higher fees than banks. "When we look at an application," says one banker, "we consider three critical things: the principal, the product, and the process. In other words, we need to know about you, what you are selling, and how you are selling it." If your banker cannot set up a credit card account for your business, ask for a referral to an ISO that might be interested.

■ *Know what information the MSP is looking for and be prepared to provide it.* Before granting merchant status, banks and ISOs want to make sure that a business is a good credit risk. Treat the application process in the same way you would an application for a loan—because, in essence, it is. In addition to the package mentioned above, business owners should be able to estimate their companies' credit card volume and their average transaction size.

■ *Make sure you understand the costs involved.* When merchants accept credit cards, they do not receive the total amount of the sale; they must pay a transaction charge to the bank. Costs typically include start-up fees ranging from $50 to $200; interchange fees of 25 cents to 70 cents per credit purchase; the discount rate, which is a percentage of the actual sales amount and usually ranges from 1 to 6 percent; monthly statement fees of $4 to $20; equipment rental or purchase costs, which can range from $250 to $1,500 or more; and miscellaneous fees.

Some MSPs also hold back a percentage of a merchant's transactions to cover chargebacks, contested fees that are settled in favor of the credit card holder. Many chargebacks are the result of credit card fraud. Because the cost of accepting credit cards can be substantial, business owners must be sure that accepting them will produce valuable benefits.

*(continued)*

■ *Evaluate the MSP's online security system.* Online merchants are more vulnerable to credit card fraud than merchants who operate brick-and-mortar stores; therefore, it is important to investigate MSPs' online security procedures and policies on payments and transfers.

■ *Shop around.* Too often, business owners take the first deal offered to them, only to regret it later. "One of the problems is that merchants are forced by society to give people credit, and they get panicky if they can't take credit cards," says one expert. "So they make a pact with the devil and don't do their due diligence before signing [the merchant status agreement]." If a company fails to respond to your inquiry within 24 hours, drop it from consideration. The inattention to your request is indicative of the company's approach to serving its customers. Look for a company that *wants* your business!

■ *Have a knowledgeable attorney look over your contract before you sign it.* Otherwise, you may not discover clauses that work a hardship on your business until it's too late.

Accepting credit cards may not be important for every business, but for those whose customers expect that convenience, acquiring merchant status can spell the difference between making a sale and losing it.

*Sources:* Adapted from Olga Karpman, "Things Good to Know When Setting Up a Merchant Account," *Shop-Script Blog,* May 22, 2007, http://blog.shop-script.com/things-good-to-know-when-setting-up-a-merchant-account/; "Merchant Accounts 101," *Small Business Computing,* July 17, 2003; Charles Gajeway, "Finished Business," *Small Business Computing,* January 2001, pp. 58–59; Johana S. Billings, "Taking Charge," *Business Start-Ups,* November 1997, pp. 16–18; Lin Gresing-Pophal, "Let Them Use Plastic," *Business Start-Ups,* May 1996, pp. 16–18; Cynthia E. Griffin, "Charging Ahead," *Entrepreneur,* April 1997, pp. 54–57; Frances Cerra Whittelsey, "The Minefield of Merchant Status," *Nation's Business,* January 1997, pp. 38–40; Charles Gajeway, "Finished Business," *Small Business Computing,* January 2001, pp. 58–59; Michael Bloch, "Payment Gateways, Internet Merchant Accounts, and Third-Party Credit Card Processors," *Taming the Beast,* www.tamingthebeast.net/articles2/back-end-ecommerce.htm.

suspicious of online transactions for reasons of security and privacy. Therefore, online merchants must ensure their customers' privacy and the security of their credit card transactions by using computer encryption software.

Online merchants also face another obstacle: credit card fraud. Because they lack the face-to-face contact with their customers, online merchants face special challenges to avoid credit card fraud. According to consulting firm Celent Communications, about 2 percent of online credit card transactions are fraudulent and online credit card fraud cost merchants more than $3.2 billion a year![31] The following steps can help online merchants reduce the probability that they will become victims of credit card fraud:

■ Use an address verification system (AVS) to compare every customer's billing information on the order form with the billing information in the bank or credit card company's records.

■ Require customers to provide the CVV2 number from the back of the credit card. Although crooks can get access to this number, it can help screen out some fraudulent orders.

■ Check customers' Internet protocol (IP) addresses. If an order contains a billing address in Rome, but the IP address from which the order is placed is in China, chances are that the order is fraudulent.

■ Monitor activity on the Web site with the help of a Web analytics software package. There are many packages available, and analyzing log files can help online entrepreneurs to pinpoint the sources of fraud.

■ Verify large orders. Large orders are a cause for celebration but only if they are legitimate. Check the authenticity of large orders, especially if the order is from a first-time customer.

■ Post notices on the Web site that your company uses anti-fraud technology to screen orders. These notices make legitimate customers feel more confident about placing their orders and crooks trying to commit fraud tentative about running their scams.

■ Contact the credit card company or the bank that issued the card. If you suspect that an order may be fraudulent, contact the company *before* processing it. Taking this step could save a company thousands of dollars in losses.[32]

### Installment Credit

Small companies that sell big-ticket consumer durables—major appliances, cars, and boats—frequently rely on installment credit. Because very few customers can purchase these items in a single lump-sum payment, small businesses finance them over time. The time horizon may range from just a few months up to 25 or more years. Most companies require the customer to make an initial down payment for the merchandise and then finance the balance for the life of the loan. The customer repays the loan principal plus interest on the loan. One advantage of installment loans for a small business is that the owner retains a security interest as collateral on the loan. If the customer defaults on the loan, the owner still holds the title to the merchandise. Because installment credit absorbs a small company's cash, many entrepreneurs rely on financial institutions such as banks and credit unions to provide the installment credit. When a business has the financial strength to "carry its own paper," the interest income from the installment loan contract often yields more than the initial profit on the sale of the product. For some businesses, such as auto dealerships and furniture stores, financing is an important source of revenue.

### Trade Credit

Companies that sell small-ticket items frequently offer their customers trade credit; that is, they create customer charge accounts. The typical small business invoices its credit customers monthly. To speed collections, some offer cash discounts if customers pay their balances early; others impose penalties on late payers. Before deciding to use credit as a competitive weapon, the small business owner must make sure that the firm's cash position is strong enough to support that additional pressure.

For manufacturers and wholesalers, trade credit is traditional. Chapter 7, "Creating a Solid Financial Plan," showed how the potential problems of being unable to control the amount of accounts payable outstanding is a major cause of lost profitability and even total failure. In reality, trade credit is a double-edged sword. Small businesses must be willing to grant credit to purchasers to get and keep their business, but they must manage carefully credit accounts to make sure that their customers pay as they promised.

---

## Chapter Review

1. Explain why pricing is both an art and a science.
   - Pricing requires a knowledge of accounting to determine the firm's cost, strategy to understand the behavior of competitors, and psychology to understand the behaviors of customers
2. Discuss the relationships among pricing, image, and competition.
   - Company pricing policies offer potential customers important information about the firm's overall image. Accordingly, when developing a marketing approach to pricing, business owners must establish prices that are compatible with what their customers expect and are willing to pay. Too often, small business owners *underprice* their goods and services, believing that low prices are the only way they can achieve a competitive advantage. They fail to identify the extra value, convenience, service, and quality they give their customers— all things many customers are willing to pay for.
   - An important part of setting appropriate prices is tracking competitors' prices regularly; however, what the competition is charging is just one variable in the pricing mix. When setting prices, business owners should take into account their competitors' prices, but they should not automatically match or beat them. Businesses that offer customers extra quality, value, service, or convenience can charge higher prices as long as customers recognize the "extras" they are getting. Two factors are vital to studying the effects of competition on the small firm's pricing policies: the location of the competitors and the nature of the competing goods.

3. Discuss effective pricing strategies for both new and existing products and services.
   - Pricing a new product is often difficult for the small business manager, but it should accomplish three objectives: getting the product accepted, maintaining market share as the competition grows, and earning a profit.
   - There are three major pricing strategies generally used to introduce new products into the market: penetration, skimming, and life-cycle pricing.
   - Pricing techniques for existing products and services include odd pricing, price lining, leader pricing, geographic pricing, opportunistic pricing, discounts, multiple pricing, bundling, and suggested retail pricing.

4. Explain the pricing techniques used by retailers.
   - Pricing for the retailer means pricing to move merchandise. Markup is the difference between the cost of a product or service and its selling price.
   - Some retailers use retail price, but others put a standard markup on all their merchandise; more frequently, they use a flexible markup.

5. Explain the pricing techniques used by manufacturers.
   - A manufacturer's pricing decision depends on the support of accurate cost accounting records. The most common technique is cost-plus pricing, in which the manufacturer charges a price that covers the cost of producing a product plus a reasonable profit. Every manufacturer should calculate a product's breakeven price, the price that produces neither a profit nor a loss.

6. Explain the pricing techniques used by service firms.
   - Service firms often suffer from the effects of vague, unfounded pricing procedures and frequently charge the going rate without any idea of their costs. A service firm must set a price based on the cost of materials used, labor involved, overhead, and a profit. The proper price reflects the total cost of providing a unit of service.

7. Describe the impact of credit on pricing.
   - Offering customer credit enhances a small company's reputation and increases the probability, speed, and magnitude of customers' purchases. Small firms offer three types of customer credit: credit cards, installment credit, and trade credit (charge accounts).

## Discussion Questions

1. What does the price of a good or service represent to the customer? Why is a customer orientation to pricing important?
2. How does pricing affect a small firm's image?
3. What competitive factors must the small firm consider when establishing prices?
4. Describe the strategies a small business could use in setting the price of a new product. What objectives should the strategy seek to achieve?
5. Define the following pricing techniques: odd pricing, price lining, leader pricing, geographic pricing, and discounts.
6. Why do many small businesses use the manufacturer's suggested retail price? What are the disadvantages of this technique?
7. What is markup? How is it used to determine prices?
8. What is a standard markup? A flexible markup?
9. What is follow-the-leader pricing? Why is it risky?
10. What is cost-plus pricing? Why do so many manufacturers use it? What are the disadvantages of using it?

11. Explain the difference between full-absorption costing and direct costing. How does absorption costing help a manufacturer determine a reasonable price?
12. Explain the techniques for a small service firm setting an hourly price.
13. What is the relevant price range for a product or service?
14. What advantages and disadvantages does offering trade credit provide to a small business?
15. What are the most commonly used methods to purchase online using credit? What reasons can you give for consumer uncertainty when giving credit card information online as opposed to via the telephone?
16. What advantages does accepting credit cards provide a small business. What costs are involved?
17. What steps should a small business owner take to earn merchant status?

# Business PlanPro

Determining an "ideal" price for a product or service is challenging. Setting a price that is too low can generate high sales volume but also can reduce profit margins and may impede the company's ability to generate a positive cash flow. Setting a price that is too high may send potential customers to competitors, and sales may never materialize. Pricing is both an art and a science. The first step is to determine what it costs to provide your product or service to customers, and the second step is to establish a price that covers total costs, generates a profit, and creates the desired image for your business. Setting the price of your products and services and knowing your company's breakeven point is a fundamental element of your business plan. Resources and information are available within Business Plan Pro that may help you better understand the impact that pricing will have on your business.

## On the Web

Do some competitive pricing research on the Web. Search for products and services that are similar to those that you are offering and list their price points. Check to see that you are making parallel comparisons of these products. For example, are you considering the entire price that may include shipping, handling, complementary products, and other attributes that will influence the final price to the customer? Do you consider these businesses to be direct competitors? If not, why? What does this information tell you about your price point? Is your price strategy consistent with your business strategy?

## In the Software

Open your business plan and locate the "Break-Even" section under "Financial Plan." Follow the instructions and enter the information that will enable you to determine your breakeven point. This will require you to have estimated figures for your fixed costs, variable costs, and prices. Once you have entered that information, look at the breakeven point shown in units and revenue. Is this breakeven point realistic? How long would you expect it would take to reach your breakeven point? Is this timeframe acceptable? Now increase your price by 10 percent. How does this change your breakeven point? The software is an excellent tool to experiment with your breakeven by entering different price points and costs to see the impact price will have on the breakeven point when you will begin making a profit.

## Building Your Business Plan

Go to the "Sales Forecast" table under the "Sales Strategy" section. An optional wizard will appear that you may select to help you through the process, or you can enter your information directly on the worksheet. If you have not done so yet, enter your price information in that section. Work through the rest of the table as you estimate your direct unit costs. The instructions and examples will assist you through that process.

# 12

# Global Marketing Strategies

The world is getting smaller and smaller, and the competition is getting tougher every day.

—Martha Layne Collins

It is easier to go to the moon than it is to enter the world of another civilization. Culture—not space—is the greatest distance between two people.

—Jamake Highwater

## Learning Objectives

**Upon completion of this chapter, you will be able to:**

1 Explain why "going global" has become an integral part of many small companies' strategies.

2 Describe the nine principal strategies small businesses can use to go global.

3 Explain how to build a successful export program.

4 Discuss the major barriers to international trade and their impact on the global economy.

5 Describe the trade agreements that have the greatest influence on foreign trade.

ntil recently, the world of international business was much like the world of astronomy before Copernicus, who revolutionized the study of the planets and the stars with his theory of planetary motion. In the sixteenth century, his Copernican system replaced the Ptolemaic system, which held that the earth was the center of the universe with the sun and all the other planets revolving around it. The Copernican system, however, placed the sun at the center of the solar system with all of the planets, including the earth, revolving around it. Astronomy would never be the same.

In the same sense, business owners across the globe were guilty of having Ptolemaic tunnel vision when it came to viewing international business opportunities. Like their pre-Copernican counterparts, owners saw an economy that revolved around the nations that served as their home bases. Market opportunities stopped at their homeland's borders. Global trade was only for giant corporations that had the money and the management talent to tap foreign markets and enough resources to survive if the venture flopped. That scenario no longer holds true in the twenty-first century. Indeed, a recent survey by consulting firm Grant Thornton of medium-size businesses reports that 56 percent of CEOs view globalization as an opportunity for their companies; just 19 percent of CEOs see it as a threat.[1]

Fifteen years ago, if a company was considered to be multinational, everyone knew that it was a giant corporation; today, that is no longer the case. In 1990, approximately 30,000 companies operated as multinational businesses; today, that number has grown to more than 60,000, but perhaps more important is the fact that the average size of multinational companies is shrinking.[2] In other words, the global marketplace is as much the territory of small, upstart companies as it is that of giant multinational corporations. Powerful, affordable technology, the Internet, increased access to information on conducting global business, and the growing interdependence of the world's economies have made it easier for companies of all sizes, many of which had never before considered going global, to engage in international trade.

*Philip Clemmons and Elk River Inc.*

In 1988, Elk River Safety Belt Company was a start-up company with a handful of employees producing safety belts for use in the construction industry. Today, the U.S.–based company continues to manufacture products that prevent falls and accidents in the construction industry, but its product line has grown extensively, and the company now employs more than 100 people. Elk River, as the company is now known, recently began exploring the possibility of exporting its products to foreign markets. CEO Philip Clemmons started Elk River's global expansion by targeting Europe but soon recognized the tremendous potential for the company's products in Asia, where construction is booming but safety standards are nowhere near what they are in the United States and Europe. "We plan to get in on the ground floor with our products and help protect local workers and save lives," says Clemmons. With help from the U.S. Small Business Administration and the Alabama International Trade Center, Clemmons attended an international trade show in Malaysia, where he opened a world of opportunities for his small company. Although Elk River faces trade barriers such as high tariffs in some countries, international sales are climbing and are becoming a significant part of the company's total sales.[3]

Just a few years ago, military might governed world relationships; today, commercial trade and economic benefit have become the forces that drive global interaction. Since 1948, the value of world merchandise exports has risen from $58.0 billion to $10.2 *trillion*.[4] Countries at every stage of development are reaping the benefits of increased global trade. In China, where economic growth has been among the fastest in the world, per-capita income has grown from just $16 per year in 1978 to more than $2,000 per year today thanks to global trade.[5] The future of international business appears to be bright. According to management consulting firm McKinsey and Company, global markets produced and consumed 20 percent of the world's $28 trillion gross domestic product in 2000; by 2027, gross domestic product will be $73 trillion, and global markets will account for 80 percent of total world output.[6]

Political, social, cultural, technological, and economic changes continue to sweep the world, creating a new world order—and a legion of both threats and opportunities for businesses of all sizes. Market economies are replacing centralized economies in countries where only decades ago private ownership of productive assets was unthinkable. Technological advances have cut the cost of long-distance communications and transactions so low that conducting business globally often costs no more than doing business locally. Companies are buying raw materials and services from all over the globe, wherever the deals are best. Jack Stack, CEO of Springfield Remanufacturing Corporation, a Springfield, Missouri-based company that refurbishes automotive engines and parts, was surprised when he learned that the company was purchasing parts from suppliers in 56 different countries! "Here we were, minding our business in Springfield, Missouri," says Stack, "and suddenly we discover that we've gone global."[7] Entrepreneurs are seeing new markets emerge around the world as the ranks of their middle class surge. These business owners realize that the size of these fast-growing markets is small today compared to their potential in the near future. Changes such as these are creating instability for businesses of *any* size going global, but they also are creating tremendous opportunities for those small companies ready to capitalize on them. One writer explains why entrepreneurs, with their unique perspective on risk taking, stand ready to embrace going global:

> Globalizing is risky. The risks include potential spoilers such as an unfamiliar language, an alien business landscape, untested partners, and political volatility. Still, the chance to try new things in new places is like a jumper cable to the entrepreneurial engine. Like the Internet companies of a decade ago, company owners [who go global] are working out the rules as they go, drawing lessons from the failures and the successes alike. They see the scale of battle growing, and they are girding for it.[8]

Expanding a business beyond its domestic borders actually enhances a small company's overall performance. Several studies have concluded that small companies that export earn more money, grow faster, create higher paying jobs, and are more likely to survive than their purely domestic counterparts.

## Why Go Global?

**1.** Explain why "going global" has become an integral part of many small companies' strategies.

Small companies can no longer consider themselves to be strictly domestic businesses in this hotly competitive global environment. "In the global economy, the competitor six time zones away is potentially as serious a threat as the competitor six blocks away," says one expert.[9] For companies across the world, going global is a matter of survival, not preference. No matter where a company's home base is, competitors are forcing it to think globally. "There are an awful lot of people in the rest of the world who think they are pretty good at doing your business," warns Lester Thurow.[10] Companies that fail to see the world as a global marketplace risk being blindsided in their markets both at home and abroad.

Failure to cultivate global markets can be a lethal mistake for modern businesses—whatever their size. In short, to thrive in the twenty-first century, small businesses must take their place in the world market. To be successful, companies must consider themselves to be businesses without borders.

*Brad Oberwager and Sundia Inc.*

Brad Oberwager, CEO of Sundia, a company that sells cut fruit and fruit juices to upscale grocery stores around the world, operates the business from an office in the basement of his home in San Francisco, California, but employs workers across the United States, India, and the Philippines. From the outset, Oberwager set up Sundia to be a micro-multinational business, and he relies on Web-based business systems to coordinate the company's far-flung activities. For instance, suppose that a customer in Europe orders several cases of watermelon-pomegranate juice (which is processed in the U.S. state of Washington from fruit grown in Mexico and California) by calling Sundia's San Francisco telephone number. The call is forwarded to a customer service center in the Philippines, where a representative takes the order and submits it to a warehouse that is closest to the customer, in this case, London. The warehouse ships the order to the customer and notifies the accounting department, which is housed in India. The accounting department generates a customer invoice, sends it to company headquarters in San Francisco, which forwards the invoice to the customer in Europe. In less than two years, Oberwager's global strategy has made Sundia the largest watermelon brand in the world and the fastest growing produce brand in the United States.[11]

Going global can put a tremendous strain on a small company, but entrepreneurs who take the plunge into global business can reap the following benefits:

- *Offset sales declines in the domestic market.* Markets in foreign countries may be booming when those in the United States are sagging, becoming a counter-cyclical balance for small companies.
- *Increase sales and profits.* Two forces are working in tandem to make global business increasingly attractive for small companies: rising income levels in many nations that are creating large middle classes that are hungry for products and services and the realization that 95 percent of the world's population lies outside of the United States.
- *Extend products' life cycles.* Many consumers across the world have an affinity for anything American, which has allowed some companies to take products that have reached the maturity stage of the product life cycle in the United States and sell them successfully in foreign markets.
- *Lower manufacturing costs.* In industries characterized by high levels of fixed costs, businesses that expand into global markets can lower their manufacturing costs by spreading these fixed costs over a larger number of units.
- *Lower the cost of their products.* Many companies find that purchasing goods or raw materials at the lowest cost requires them to shop the global marketplace for the best deals.

**ENTREPRENEURIAL Profile**

*Sonia Seye and Art of Braiding & Extensions LLC*

Sonia Seye, owner of Los Angeles-based Art of Braiding & Extensions LLC, recently began buying the hair that goes into her company's human-hair extensions from suppliers in India, which use Hindu temples as a primary source of women's hair. (Many women in India go to Hindu temples to make offerings of their hair as a symbol of surrendering their egos.) Seye says that going directly to suppliers in India has allowed her to cut in half the cost of the extensions that she was purchasing from her domestic suppliers, which allows her to sell her company's stylish extensions at $28 per ounce rather than the $40 per ounce her competitors charge. "You don't have to be big to be global," says Seye. Since making the switch to global suppliers, Art of Braiding and Extension's sales have grown by 60 percent and profits have doubled.[12]

- *Improve their competitive position and enhance their reputation.* Going up against some of the toughest competition in the world forces a company to hone its competitive skills.
- *Raise quality levels.* Customers in many global markets are much tougher to satisfy than those in the United States. One reason Japanese products have done so well worldwide is that Japanese companies must build products to satisfy their customers at home, who demand extremely high quality and are sticklers for detail. Businesses that compete in global markets learn very quickly how to boost their quality levels to world-class standards. "Japan is the most demanding market in the world," says one global manager doing business there. "Japanese consumers look for quality in the tiniest details. Products that survive there have a better chance of succeeding in other markets."[13]

"MAKING A PROFIT WAS A LOT EASIER BEFORE SO MANY COUNTRIES ABANDONED SOCIALISM AND STARTED COMPETING!"

- ■ *Become more customer oriented.* Delving into global markets teaches business owners about the unique tastes, customs, preferences, and habits of customers in many different cultures. Responding to these differences imbues these businesses with a degree of sensitivity toward their customers, both domestic and foreign.
- ■ *Increase their chances of success.* Companies that are engaged in international trade experience faster growth and higher survival rates than those companies whose business focus remains solely domestic.[14] Going global helps small companies become stronger competitors.

Unfortunately, many entrepreneurs have not learned to view their companies from a global perspective. Indeed, learning to *think globally* may be the first—and most challenging—obstacle an entrepreneur must overcome on the way to creating a truly global business. One British manager explains:

> If you are operating in South America, you'd better know how to operate in conditions of hyperinflation. If you're operating in Africa, you'd better know a lot about government relations and the use of local partners. If you're operating in Germany, you'd better understand the mechanics of codetermination and some of the special tax systems that one finds in that country. If you're operating in China, it's quite useful in trademark matters to know how the People's Court of Shanghai works. . . . If you're operating in Japan, you'd better understand the different trade structure.[15]

Gaining a foothold in newly opened foreign markets or maintaining a position in an existing one is no easy task, however. Until an entrepreneur develops the attitude of operating a truly global company rather than a domestic company that happens to be doing business abroad, achieving success in international business is difficult. That attitude starts at the top in the chief executive's office. Success in the global economy also requires constant innovation; staying nimble enough to use speed as a competitive weapon; maintaining a high level of quality and constantly improving it; being sensitive to foreign customers' unique requirements; adopting a more respectful attitude toward foreign habits and customs; hiring motivated, multilingual employees; and retaining a desire to learn constantly about global markets. In short, the path to success requires businesses to become "insiders" rather than just "exporters."

Before venturing into the global marketplace, an entrepreneur should consider six questions:

1. Is there a profitable market in which our company has the potential to be successful over the long run? Table 12.1 shows a country screening matrix designed to help entrepreneurs decide which countries offer the best opportunities for their products.

## TABLE 12.1  A Country Screening Matrix

For an entrepreneur considering launching a global business venture, getting started often is the hardest step. "The world is such a big place! Where do I start?" is a typical comment from entrepreneurs considering global business. The following matrix will help you narrow down your options. Based on preliminary research, select three to five countries that you believe have the greatest market potential for your products. Then, use the following factors to guide you as you conduct more detailed research into these countries and their markets. Rate each factor on a scale of 1 (lowest) to 5 (highest). Based on your ratings, which country has the highest score?

| Market Factor | Country 1 Rating | Country 2 Rating | Country 3 Rating |
|---|---|---|---|
| **Demographic/Physical Environment** | | | |
| ■ Population size, growth, density | | | |
| ■ Urban and rural distribution | | | |
| ■ Climate and weather variations | | | |
| ■ Shipping distance | | | |
| ■ Product-significant demographics | | | |
| ■ Physical distribution and communication network | | | |
| ■ Natural resources | | | |
| **Political Environment** | | | |
| ■ System of government | | | |
| ■ Political stability and continuity | | | |
| ■ Ideological orientation | | | |
| ■ Government involvement in business | | | |
| ■ Attitudes toward foreign business (trade restrictions, tariffs, non-tariff barriers, bilateral trade agreements) | | | |
| ■ National economic and developmental priorities | | | |
| **Economic Environment** | | | |
| ■ Overall level of development | | | |
| ■ Economic growth: GNP, industrial sector | | | |
| ■ Role of foreign trade in the economy | | | |
| ■ Currency: inflation rate, availability, controls, stability of exchange rate | | | |
| ■ Balance of payments | | | |
| ■ Per capita income and distribution | | | |
| ■ Disposable income and expenditure patterns | | | |
| **Social/Cultural Environment** | | | |
| ■ Literacy rate, educational level | | | |
| ■ Existence of middle class | | | |
| ■ Similarities and differences in relation to home market | | | |
| ■ Language and other cultural considerations | | | |
| **Market Access** | | | |
| ■ Limitations on trade: high tariff levels, quotas | | | |
| ■ Documentation and import regulations | | | |
| ■ Local standards, practices, and other non-tariff barriers | | | |
| ■ Patents and trademark protection | | | |
| ■ Preferential treaties | | | |
| ■ Legal considerations for investment, taxation, repatriation, employment, code of laws | | | |

2. Do we have and are we willing to commit adequate resources of time, people, and capital to a global campaign?

3. Are we considering going global for the right reasons? Are domestic pressures forcing our company to consider global opportunities?

4. Do we understand the cultural differences, history, economics, values, opportunities, and risks of conducting business in the country(s) we are considering?

5. Do we have a viable exit strategy for our company if conditions change or the new venture does not succeed?

6. Can we afford *not* to go global?

## Going Global: Strategies for Small Businesses

*2.* Describe the nine principal strategies small businesses can use to go global.

The globalization of business actually *favors* small businesses because it creates an abundance of niche markets that are ideal for small companies to serve. "In this global economy, the competitive edge is swiftness to market and innovation," says John Naisbitt, trend-spotting author of *The Global Paradox*, and those are characteristics that are hallmarks of entrepreneurs. "Small [companies] are much better at speed to market and innovation. As a result, they can innovate faster, not just in products but in internal operations, to take advantage of the new technologies."[16] Their agility and adaptability gives small firms the edge in today's highly interactive, fast-paced global economy. "The bigger the world economy, the more powerful its smallest players," concludes Naisbitt.[17]

Becoming a global business depends on instilling a global culture throughout the organization that permeates *everything* the company does. Entrepreneurs who conduct international business successfully have developed a global mind-set for themselves and their companies. As one business writer explains:

> The global [business] looks at the whole world as *one market*. It manufactures, conducts research, raises capital, and buys supplies wherever it can do the job best. It keeps in touch with technology and market trends around the world. National boundaries and regulations tend to be irrelevant, or a mere hindrance. [Company] headquarters might be anywhere.[18]

As cultures across the globe become increasingly interwoven, companies' ability to go global will determine their degree of success. Small companies pursuing a global presence have nine principal strategies available: creating a presence on the Web, relying on trade intermediaries, establishing joint ventures, engaging in foreign licensing arrangements, franchising, using counter trading and bartering, exporting products or services, establishing international locations, and importing and outsourcing (see Figure 12.1).

**FIGURE 12.1 Nine Strategies for Going Global**

Creating a Web Site

Importing and Outsourcing

Relying on Trade Intermediaries

Establishing International Locations

Creating Joint Ventures

Exporting

Foreign Licensing

Countertrading and Bartering

International Franchising

### Creating a Presence on the Web

The simplest and least expensive way for a small business to begin conducting business globally is to create a Web site. The Web gives small businesses tremendous marketing potential all across the globe without having to incur the expense of opening international locations. With a well-designed Web site, a small company can extend its reach to customers anywhere in the world—without breaking the budget! A Web site is available to anyone,

## In the Entrepreneurial Spotlight

### ■ A Global Focus

After being laid off by giant drug company Pfizer, Robert Gadwood and David Zimmermann launched Kalexsym, a company that specializes in providing focused chemical research for large drug companies. Shortly after they started their company, recalls Gadwood, "all of our customers disappeared." To reduce costs, large drug companies were outsourcing much of their early-stage medicinal chemistry research to low-cost labs in India and China. As they called on potential clients in the United States, the entrepreneurs heard repeatedly, "If you can match the cost of an Indian chemical lab, we'll talk to you."

Gadwood and Zimmermann needed a new strategy fast, and they decided that taking their small company global was the key. The entrepreneurs discovered that European drug companies were spending billions of dollars a year outsourcing their own chemical research to companies in the United States. Although price is an important factor for companies deciding where to send their chemical research, it is not the only consideration; quality counts even more. Gadwood and Zimmermann knew that they had to find chemical companies in the United States and in Europe for whom quality of research was more important than low price. Relying on the contacts of a French economic development director whom he had met at a scientific meeting in Paris, Zimmermann began making sales calls on French companies. They were interested in Kalexsym's high-quality services, and the favorable exchange rate (a weak dollar compared to the euro) made Kalexsym's prices even more attractive.

While Gadwood focused on operations in the United States, Zimmermann spent time marketing the company's services in France. Success required much patience. Scheduling meetings with decision makers was difficult because Zimmermann and his company were unknown and were . . . American. "Opening the first door was the

hardest," says Zimmermann. "European companies tend to rely on the references of people they know and trust." Zimmermann's perseverance and his contacts in the economic development office began to open more doors, however, and he was constantly learning the keys to conducting business successfully in France. One mistake he made was discussing pricing in initial meetings with potential clients, something that he was accustomed to doing in meetings with U.S. clients. French executives, Zimmermann learned, prefer to spend early meetings getting to know the executives of the companies with which they may be doing business. The company finally landed a contract with Cytomics Systems, a French biotech company that had become frustrated with the European labs that had been performing its chemical research. To overcome the biotech company's hesitance to do business with a small company based in Kalamazoo, Michigan, Zimmermann offered to allow Cytomics to make a small up-front payment with the balance due on delivery. If Kalexsym failed to deliver, Zimmermann and Gadwood would bear the expense. Kalexsym delivered. Within two weeks, Kalexsym delivered 15 times more chemical compounds than Cytomics had requested.

Zimmermann used the success of the relationship with Cytomics to land deals with other biotech companies in France and Austria. His next target: Japan. "We're in a global market," says Zimmermann. "We need to continue to devise our business strategies and our goals with that as our focus."

1. What steps should Zimmerman and Gadwood take to market their company's services in Japan?
2. Use the resources described in the chapter to research the culture and customs of doing business in Japan. Use what you learned to prepare a "tip sheet" to help Zimmermann and Gadwood as they prepare to conduct business there.

*Source:* Adapted from Alison Stein Wellner, "Turning the Tables," *Inc.,* May 2006, pp. 55–57.

**FIGURE 12.2A World Internet Users by Region**

*Source:* "Internet Usage Statistics: The Big Picture," Internet World Stats 2007, www.internetworldstats. com,stats.htm.

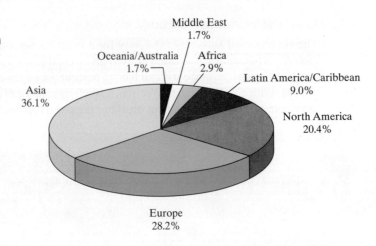

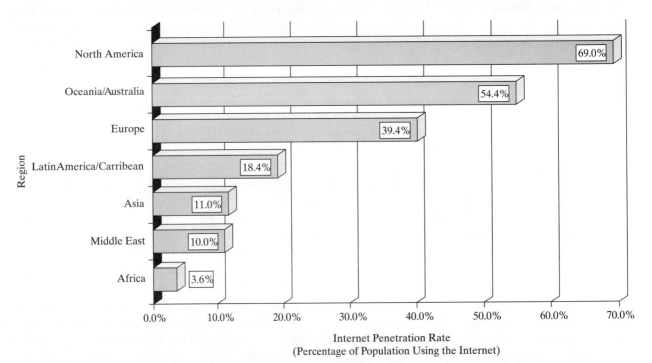

**FIGURE 12.2B  Internet Penetration Rate Percentage of Population Using the Internet**

*Source:* "Internet Usage Statistics: The Big Picture," Internet World Stats, 2007, www.internetworldstats.com/stats.htm.

anywhere in the world and provides 24-hour-a-day exposure to a company's products or services, making global time differences meaningless.

Establishing a presence on the Web is an essential ingredient in the strategies of small companies trying to reach customers outside their borders. Although Internet usage varies greatly by region of the world (see Figure 12.2), the number of Internet users (and potential online customers) is growing extremely fast—nearly 31 percent a year worldwide. Another important factor for North American entrepreneurs to note is that 80 percent of the estimated 1.13 billion Internet users worldwide live *outside* of North America.

Before the advent of the Internet, small businesses usually took incremental steps toward becoming global businesses. They began selling locally, and, then, after establishing a reputation, expanded regionally and perhaps nationally. Only after establishing themselves domestically did small businesses begin to think about selling their products or services internationally. The Web makes that business model obsolete because it provides small companies with a low-cost global distribution channel that they can utilize from the day they are launched. Designed properly, a Web site can be an engaging marketing tool.

*Greg Jackson and Carolina Classic Boats*

Shortly after starting his company, Greg Jackson created a Web site (www.carolina-classic-boats.com) for his boat brokering business, Carolina Classic Boats, that specializes in buying, selling, and trading antique wooden boats made from the 1920s to the 1950s by manufacturers such as Chris Craft, Gar Wood, Hacker Craft, and Riva. Although Jackson operates from a small southern town of just 10,000 residents, his company operates globally with the help of the Web site, where customers can see photographs and read detailed descriptions of the boats they are considering. Jackson has bought, sold, and shipped classic boats all over the world, from Europe to Australia.

Entrepreneurs who do not want to take the time to set up their own Web sites can still sell to international customers through the Internet giant eBay, which has a wide global reach. Even though eBay is a U.S.-headquartered company, half of all eBay buyers live outside the United States, and eBay's international sales are growing twice as fast as its domestic sales.

Birgit Conlen is an eBay PowerSeller who operates Afternoon Daydreams, a business that sells body and health products, food, toys, and collectibles to shoppers around the world from her home. "eBay enables buyers to go on a shopping spree around the globe and allows sellers to advertise their products to a worldwide audience," says Conlen.[19]

*Birgit Conlen and Afternoon Daydreams*

### Relying on Trade Intermediaries

Another alternative for low cost and low risk entry into international markets is to use a trade intermediary. Trade intermediaries serve as distributors in foreign countries for domestic companies of all sizes. They rely on their networks of contacts, their extensive knowledge of local customs and markets, and their experience in international trade to market products effectively and efficiently all across the globe. Although a broad array of trade intermediaries is available, the following are ideally suited for small businesses:

**EXPORT MANAGEMENT COMPANIES (EMCs).** **Export management companies (EMCs)** are an important channel of foreign distribution for small companies just getting started in international trade or for those lacking the resources to assign their own people to foreign markets. Most EMCs are merchant intermediaries, working on a buy-and-sell arrangement with domestic small companies. They provide small businesses with a low-cost, efficient, independent international marketing department, offering services ranging from market research on foreign countries and advice on patent protection to arranging financing and handling shipping. Many of them specialize in particular products or product lines. The chief advantage of using an export management company is that a small business's products get international exposure without having to tie up its own resources excessively.

*Neil Archer and Arch Environmental Equipment*

In 1975, Neil Archer founded Arch Environmental Equipment (AEE), a manufacturer of conveyor-belt systems and components that are used in mining, cement manufacturing, food processing, and other industries. Recognizing the opportunity to sell its products in foreign markets but lacking the experience to go global alone, the Paducah, Kentucky-based company recently hired IMPEX, an export management company started by Richard Grana, to act as its international sales department. Grana sells to 35 companies in Chile and is developing relationships with potential customers in Argentina and Brazil. Both AEE's and IMPEX's foreign sales are climbing rapidly.[20]

The greatest benefits that EMCs offer small companies are ready access to global markets and an extensive knowledge base on foreign trade, both of which are vital for entrepreneurs who are inexperienced in conducting global business. In return for their services, EMCs usually earn an extra discount on the goods they buy from their clients or, if they operate on a commission rate, a higher commission than domestic distributors earn on what they sell. EMCs charge commission rates of about 10 percent on consumer goods and 15 percent on industrial products. Although EMCs rarely advertise their services, finding one is not difficult. The Federation of International Trade Associations (FITA) provides useful information for small companies about global business and trade intermediaries on its Web site (http://fita. org/emc.html), including a *Directory of Export Management Companies*. Industry trade associations and publications and the Export Assistance Centers* also can help entrepreneurs to locate EMCs and other trade intermediaries.

**EXPORT TRADING COMPANIES (ETCs).** Another tactic for getting into international markets with a minimum of cost and effort is through an export trading company (ETC). ETCs have been an important vehicle in international trade throughout history. The Hudson's Bay Company and the East India Company, both export trade companies, were dominant powers in world trade in the sixteenth, seventeenth, and eighteenth centuries.

**Export trading companies** are businesses that buy and sell products in a number of countries, and they typically offer a wide range of services such as exporting, importing, shipping, storing, distributing, and others to their clients. Unlike EMCs, which tend to focus on exporting, ETCs usually perform both import and export trades across many countries' borders. However, like EMCs, ETCs lower the risk of exporting for small businesses. Some of the largest trading companies in the world are based in the United States and Japan. In fact, many businesses that have navigated successfully Japan's complex system of distribution have done so with the help of ETCs.

In 1982, the U.S. passed the Export Trading Company Act to allow producers of similar products to form ETC cooperatives without the fear of violating antitrust laws. The goal was to encourage U.S. companies to export more goods by allowing businesses in the same industry to band together to form export trading companies.

**MANUFACTURER'S EXPORT AGENTS (MEAs).** **Manufacturer's export agents (MEAs)** act as international sales representatives in a limited number of markets for various noncompeting domestic companies. Unlike the close, partnering relationship formed with most EMCs, the relationship between an MEA and a small company is a short-term one, in which the MEA typically operates on a commission basis.

**EXPORT MERCHANTS.** **Export merchants** are domestic wholesalers who do business in foreign markets. They buy goods from many domestic manufacturers and then market them in foreign markets. Unlike MEAs, export merchants often carry competing lines, which means they have little loyalty to suppliers. Most export merchants specialize in particular industries—office equipment, computers, industrial supplies, and others.

**RESIDENT BUYING OFFICES.** Another approach to exporting is to sell to a **resident buying office**, a government- or privately owned operation established in a country for the purpose of buying goods made there. Many foreign governments and businesses have set up buying offices in the United States. Selling to them is just like selling to domestic customers because the buying office handles all of the details of exporting.

**FOREIGN DISTRIBUTORS.** Some small businesses work through foreign distributors to reach international markets. Domestic small companies export their products to these distributors who handle all of the marketing, distribution, and service functions in the foreign country.

*Mark Chaplin and Disc-Go-Tech*

When Mark Chaplin, founder of Disc-Go-Tech, a company that sells machines that repair damaged CDs, DVDs, and game disks, began expanding into global markets, he decided to use foreign distributors who could help his company penetrate the European market efficiently and effectively. Today, Chaplin continues to rely on foreign distributors, and his company now does business in more than 50 countries, including Australia, Egypt, Japan, and South Africa from its Canadian headquarters. Disc-Go-Tech's sales now exceed $5.3 million. "The biggest challenge working with distributors is [navigating] different languages and time zones," says Chaplin.[21]

---

*A searchable list of the Export Assistance Centers is available at the Export.gov Web site www.export.gov/comm_svc/eac.html.

**THE VALUE OF USING TRADE INTERMEDIARIES.** Trade intermediaries such as these are becoming increasingly popular among businesses attempting to branch out into world markets because they make that transition much faster and easier. Most small business owners simply do not have the knowledge, resources, or confidence to go global alone. Intermediaries' global networks of buyers and sellers allow their small business customers to build their international sales much faster and with fewer hassles and mistakes. Entrepreneurs who are inexperienced in global sales and attempt to crack certain foreign markets quickly discover just how difficult the challenge can be. However, with their know-how, experience, and contacts, trade intermediaries can get small companies' products into foreign markets quickly and efficiently. The primary disadvantage of using trade intermediaries is that doing so requires entrepreneurs to surrender control over their foreign sales. Maintaining close contact with intermediaries and evaluating their performance regularly help to avoid major problems, however.

The key to establishing a successful relationship with a trade intermediary is conducting a thorough screening to determine what type of intermediary—and which one in particular—will serve a small company's needs best. A company looking for an intermediary should compile a list of potential candidates using some of the sources listed in Table 12.2. The 50 World Trade Centers and the Export Assistance Centers located in more than 100 cities across the United States and in 80 countries around the world offer valuable advice and assistance to small businesses wanting to get started in conducting global business. In addition, entrepreneurs can

## TABLE 12.2  Resources for Locating a Trade Intermediary

Trade intermediaries make doing business around the world much easier for small companies, but finding the right one can be a challenge. Fortunately, several government agencies offer a wealth of information to businesses interested in reaching into global markets with the help of trade intermediaries. Entrepreneurs looking for help in breaking into global markets should contact the International Trade Administration (www.ita.gov), the U.S. Commercial Service (www.buyusa.gov), the Export Trade Portal (www.export.gov), and the U.S. Small Business Administration (www.sba.gov) to take advantage of the following services:

- *U.S. Commercial Service.* The trade promotion unit of the International Trade Administration, the U.S. Commercial Service (http://trade.gov/cs/) provides trade specialists in 107 cities in the United States and in more than 80 countries worldwide who work with small companies that want to start exporting or to increase their sales to new global markets.
- *Export.gov.* The U.S. government's export portal provides a vast amount of useful information for both novice and experienced exporters. Topics range from the basics of exporting and market research to international finance and tariffs.
- *Commercial Service International Contacts (CSIC) List.* Provides contact and product information for more than 82,000 foreign agents, distributors, and importers interested in doing business with U.S. companies.
- *Country Directories of International Contacts (CDIC) List.* Provides the same kind of information as the CSIC List but is organized by country.
- *Global Diversity Initiative (GDI).* Offered by the U.S. Commercial Service, the Global Diversity Initiative is aimed at helping minority-owned companies become exporters. Contact your local Export Assistance Center or visit www.buyusa.gov/globaldiversity/.
- *Industry Sector Analyses (ISAs) and International Market Insights (IMIs).* ISAs are free reports from the BuyUSA.gov Web site, which is sponsored by the U.S. Commercial Service, that offer in-depth information on industries in foreign countries, including information on distribution practices, end-users, and top sales prospects. IMIs include information on foreign market conditions, upcoming opportunities for companies, trade contacts, trade show schedules, and other information. Visit www.buyusa.gov for access to information on particular countries.
- *Trade Opportunity Program (TOP).* Provides up-to-the-minute, prescreened sales leads around the world for businesses, including joint venture and licensing partners, direct sales leads, and representation offers. To find leads for a particular country, entrepreneurs can visit the U.S. Commercial Service Web site, select a country and/or an industry and click the "view leads" button.
- *International Company Profiles (ICPs).* Commercial specialists will investigate potential partners, agents, distributors, or customers for companies and will issue profiles on them.

*(continued)*

**TABLE 12.2 Continued**

- **Commercial News USA.** A government-published magazine that promotes U.S. companies' products and services to 400,000 business readers in 176 countries at a fraction of the cost of commercial advertising. Small companies can use *Commercial News USA* to reach new customers around the world for as little as $495.
- **Gold Key Service.** For a small fee, business owners wanting to target a specific country can use the U.S. Commercial Service's Gold Key Service, in which experienced trade professionals arrange meetings for U.S. business owners with prescreened contacts whose interests match their own.
- **Platinum Key Service.** The U.S. Commercial Service's Platinum Key Service is more comprehensive than its Gold Key Service, offering business owners long-term consulting services on topics such as building a global marketing strategy, deciding which countries to target, and how to reach customers in foreign markets.
- **Matchmaker Trade Delegations Program.** This program helps small companies establish business relationships in major markets abroad by introducing them to the right contacts. Destinations on past trips have included Spain, Italy, India, China, and many others.
- **Multi-State/Catalog Exhibition Program.** Working with state economic development offices, the U.S. Commercial Service presents companies' product catalogs and sales literature to hundreds of interested business prospects in foreign countries for as little as $450.
- **International Trade Fair Certification Program.** This U.S. Commercial Service program promotes companies' participation in a "U.S. Pavilion" at foreign trade shows that represent the best marketing opportunities for them.
- **Globus and National Trade Data Bank (NTDB).** Globus and the NTDB, services of the U.S. Department of Commerce, include the U.S. government's most comprehensive database of world trade data. Through Globus and the NTDB, small companies have access to information that only *Fortune* 500 companies once could afford. At this Web site (www.stat-usa.gov/tradtest.nsf), subscribers can access the International Trade Library, where they can learn about currency exchange rates, find business leads for particular industries, country and market research, read Country Commercial Guides, and access a treasure trove of information on doing business globally.
- **U.S Export Assistance Centers.** The Department of Commerce has established 104 export centers (USEACs) around the country to serve as one-stop shops for entrepreneurs needing export help. To find the Export Assistance Center nearest you, visit www.export.gov/eac/index.asp.
- **Office of International Trade.** At the Web site for the Office of International Trade (www.sba.gov/aboutsba/sbaprograms/internationaltrade/index.html), the Small Business Administration provides a variety of export assistance, including information on foreign markets and export financing.
- **Export Hotline.** Provided by a private company called International Strategies, the Export Hotline (www.exporthotline.com/) is a comprehensive library of global trade content that provides trade data on 140 countries and hundreds of industry sectors on topics ranging from market entry strategies, import and export regulations, culture and business protocol, country risk, and many others.
- **American Chambers of Commerce Abroad.** The goal of the American Chambers of Commerce Abroad is to promote U.S. businesses in foreign markets. More than 100 American chambers of commerce operate in 91 countries, and they are an excellent point of contact for entrepreneurs who want to learn more about a particular country, its culture, its business system, and opportunities for exporting.

find reliable intermediaries by using their network of contacts in foreign countries and by attending international trade shows while keeping an eye out for potential candidates.

### Joint Ventures

Joint ventures, both domestic and foreign, lower the risk of entering global markets for small businesses. They also give small companies more clout in foreign lands. In a **domestic joint venture**, two or more domestic small businesses form an alliance for the purpose of exporting their goods and services abroad. For export ventures, participating companies get antitrust immunity, allowing them to cooperate freely. The businesses share the responsibility and the costs of getting export licenses and permits, and they split the venture's profits. Establishing a joint venture with the right partner has become an essential part of maintaining a competitive position in global markets for a growing number of industries.

In a **foreign joint venture**, a domestic small business forms an alliance with a company in the target nation. The host partner brings to the joint venture valuable knowledge of the local market and the customs and the tastes of local customers, making it much easier to conduct business in the foreign country. Forming a joint venture with a local company often is the best way for a business to negotiate the maze of government regulations in some countries. Some foreign countries place limitations on how joint ventures operate. Some nations, for example, require domestic (host) companies to own at least 51 percent of the venture. Sometimes, says one international manager, "the only way to be German in Germany, Canadian in Canada, and Japanese in Japan is through alliances."[22] When Subway, one of the leading franchises in the world, enters foreign markets with one of its sandwich shops, it often looks for a local company with which to form a joint venture. "Nobody knows an area like a local partner," says Don Fertman, a director of international development at Subway.[23]

The most important ingredient in the recipe for a successful joint venture is choosing the right partner(s). A productive joint venture is much like a marriage, requiring commitment, trust, and understanding. In addition to picking the right partner(s), a second key to creating a successful alliance is to establish common objectives. Defining *exactly* what each party in the joint venture hopes to accomplish at the outset will minimize the opportunity for misunderstandings and disagreements later on. One important objective should always be to use the joint venture as a learning experience, which requires a long-term view of the business relationship. Issues to address *before* entering into a joint venture include:

■ What contributions will each party make?
■ Who will be responsible for making which decisions?
■ How much control will each party have over the joint venture's direction?
■ How will the earnings from the joint venture be allocated?
■ How long will the joint venture last? Under what circumstances can the parties terminate the relationship?

*Impart Media Group and China Media Ltd.*

Impart Media Group, a Seattle, Washington-based company that provides out-of-home (outdoor) and other advertising solutions for businesses, recently entered into a joint venture with China Media Ltd., a company that sells digital advertising media in China. Under the agreement, Impart Media will contribute business and technology management, intellectual property such as its trademark, software, and training. China Media's contribution to the joint venture will be seed capital, facilities in Shanghai, and manufacturing, sales, and administrative staff. Laird Laabs, Impart's president of the Asia-Pacific division, says that China's unparalleled growth rate and the careful choice of China Media as a partner make the joint venture the ideal way to enter this foreign market. "The upside is huge," says China Media's Goodwin Wang, who will manage the venture's daily operations. "The revenue potential is staggering."[24]

Unfortunately, most joint ventures fail. That makes it essential for the companies in an alliance to establish a contingency plan for getting out in case the joint venture doesn't work. Common problems leading to failure include improper selection of partners, incompatible management styles, failure to establish common goals, inability to be flexible, and failure to trust one another. What can entrepreneurs do to avoid these pitfalls in joint ventures?

■ Understand their partner's reasons and objectives for joining the venture.
■ Select a partner that shares their company's values and standards of conduct.
■ Spell out in writing exactly how the venture will work, what each partner's responsibilities are, and where decision-making authority lies.
■ Select a partner whose skills are different from but compatible with those of their own companies.
■ Prepare a "prenuptial agreement" that spells out what happens in case of a "business divorce."

## Foreign Licensing

Rather than sell their products or services directly to customers overseas, some small companies enter foreign markets by licensing businesses in other nations to use their patents, trademarks, copyrights, technology, processes, or products. In return for licensing its assets, a small company collects royalties from the sales of its foreign licenses. Licensing is a relatively simple way for even the most inexperienced business owners to extend their reach into global markets. Licensing is ideal for companies whose value lies in its intellectual property, unique products or services, recognized name, or proprietary technology. Although many businesses consider licensing only their products to foreign companies, the licensing potential for intangibles such as processes, technology, copyrights, and trademarks often is greater. Some entrepreneurs earn more money from licensing their know-how for product design, manufacturing, or quality control than they do from actually selling their finished goods in a highly competitive foreign market with which they are not familiar. Foreign licensing enables a small business to enter foreign markets quickly, easily, and with virtually no capital investment. Risks to the company include the potential loss of control over its manufacturing and marketing processes and creating a competitor if the licensee gains too much knowledge and control. Securing proper patent, trademark, and copyright protection beforehand can minimize those risks, however.

*George Duke and Zippo Manufacturing*

Faced with stagnant sales, George Duke, chairman of the board of Zippo Manufacturing and grandson of the cigarette lighter company's founder, began extending the company's product line to include products such as flashlights, watches, sunglasses, stoves, and clothing. Zippo has licensed the well-known Zippo name to foreign companies who will manufacture and sell the products in China, Japan, and Italy. Since forging the licensing agreement, Zippo's sales in China have doubled to $10 million.[25]

## International Franchising

Franchising has become a major export industry for the United States. Over the past decade, a growing number of franchises have been attracted to international markets to boost sales and profits as the domestic market has become increasingly saturated with outlets and much tougher to wring growth from. International franchisors sell virtually every kind of product or service imaginable—from fast food to child day care—in global markets. In some cases, the products and services sold in international markets are identical to those sold in the United States. However, most franchisors have learned that they must adapt their products and services to suit local tastes and customs. Fast-food chains operating in other countries often must make adjustments to their menus to please locals' palates.

*McDonald's and Domino's Pizza*

In Japan, McDonald's (known as "Makudonarudo") outlets sell teriyaki burgers, rice burgers, and katsu burgers (cheese wrapped in a roast pork cutlet topped with katsu sauce and shredded cabbage) in addition to their traditional American fare. In the Philippines, the McDonald's menu includes a spicy Filipino-style burger, spaghetti, and chicken with rice. In Switzerland, McDonald's reaches hungry commuters in transit. The company has commissioned two railroad dining cars, each seating about 40 people, that run on two routes—from Geneva to Basel and Geneva to Brig. In addition to Big Macs, diners have a choice of red or white wine and beer. Because Egg McMuffins don't appeal to Swiss palates, the rolling restaurants offer the more traditional Swiss breakfast of croissant, marmalade, butter, and hard cheese. In Germany, McDonald's restaurants sell beer, and in Great Britain they offer British Cadbury chocolate sticks. Domino's Pizza operates more than 3,200 restaurants in 55 countries, where local managers have developed new pizza flavors such as mayonnaise and potato (Japan), lamb and pickled ginger (India), tuna and sweet corn (England), and reindeer sausage (Iceland) to cater to customers' preferences.

McDonald's, which opened its first international location in Canada in 1967, now has nearly 12,000 locations in foreign countries, such as this one in China.

Although franchise outlets span the globe, Canada is the primary market for U.S. franchisors, with Japan and Europe following. These markets are most attractive to franchisors because they are similar to the U.S. market—a large middle-class population, rising personal incomes, strong demand for consumer goods, growing service economies, and spreading urbanization. Europe also holds special interest for many U.S. franchises as trade barriers there continue to topple, opening up the largest—and one of the most affluent—markets in the world. Although large franchisors are already well established in many European nations, a new wave of smaller franchisors is seeking to establish a foothold there. Growth potential is the primary attraction. Franchisors that decide to expand internationally should take these steps:

1. *Identify the country or countries that are best suited to the franchisor's business concept.* Factors to consider include a country's business climate, demographic profile, level of economic development, rate of economic growth, degree of legal protection, language and cultural barriers, and market potential. Franchisors making their first forays into global markets should consider focusing on a single nation or a small group of similar nations.
2. *Generate leads for potential franchisees.* Franchisors looking for prospective franchisees in foreign markets have many tools available to them, including international franchise trade shows, their own Web sites, trade missions, and brokers. Many franchisors have had success with trade missions such as those sponsored by trade groups such as the International Franchise Association, the U.S. Department of Commerce's Gold Key Program, or various state programs. These trade missions are designed to introduce franchisors to qualified franchise candidates in target countries. Other franchisors rely on brokers who have extensive business contacts in specific countries.
3. *Select quality candidates.* Just as in any franchise relationship, the real key to success is choosing the right franchisee. Because of the complexity and cost of international franchising, selecting quality franchisees is essential to success.
4. *Structure the franchise deal.* Franchisors can structure international franchise arrangements in a variety of ways, but three techniques are most popular: direct franchising, area development, and master franchising.

- **Direct franchising**, so common in domestic franchise deals, involves selling single-unit franchises to individual operators in foreign countries. Although dealing with individual franchisees makes it easier for the franchisor to maintain control, it also requires more of the franchisor's time and resources.
- **Area development** is similar to direct franchising except that the franchisor allows the franchisee to develop multiple units in a particular territory, perhaps a province, a county, or even an entire nation. A successful area development strategy depends on a franchisor selecting and then supporting quality franchisees.
- **Master franchising** is the most popular strategy for companies entering international markets. In a master franchising deal, a franchisor sells to a franchisee the right to develop sub-franchises within a broad geographic area or, sometimes, an entire foreign country. In short, master franchising turbocharges a franchisor's growth. Many franchisors use this method to open outlets in international markets more quickly and efficiently because their master franchisees understand local laws and the nuances of selling in local markets.

*California Pizza Kitchen and Grupo Calpik S.A. de C.V.*

The California Pizza Kitchen (CPK), founded by former attorneys Rick Rosenfeld and Larry Flax in 1985, recently signed agreements with master franchisees who will develop CPK restaurants in Mexico and Korea over the next decade. CPK selected Grupo Calpik S.A. de C.V., a company that operates 17 casual dining restaurants in Mexico, to develop at least 15 CPK franchises throughout Mexico. California Pizza Kitchen currently operates more than 200 restaurants in 29 states and six countries, and the new agreements will expand the franchise's global reach while minimizing the company's risk exposure.[26]

Although master franchising simplifies a franchisor's expansion into global markets, it gives franchisors the least amount of control over their international franchisees.

## Countertrading and Bartering

As business becomes increasingly global, companies are discovering that attracting customers is just one part of the battle. Another problem global businesses face when selling to some countries is that their currencies are virtually worthless outside their borders, so getting paid in a valuable currency is a real challenge! Companies that want to reach these markets must countertrade or barter. A **countertrade** is a transaction in which a company selling goods and services in a foreign country agrees to help promote investment and trade in that country. The goal of the transaction is to help offset the capital drain from the foreign country's purchases. As entrepreneurs enter more developing nations, they will discover the need to develop skill at implementing this global trading strategy.

Countertrading does suffer from numerous drawbacks. Countertrade transactions can be complicated, cumbersome, and time consuming. They also increase the chances that a company will get stuck with useless merchandise that it cannot move. They can lead to unpleasant surprises concerning the quantity and quality of products required in the countertrade. Still, countertrading offers one major advantage: Sometimes it's the only way to make a sale!

Entrepreneurs must weigh the advantages against the disadvantages for their companies before committing to a countertrade deal. Because of its complexity and the risks involved, countertrading is not the best choice for a novice entrepreneur looking to break into the global marketplace.

**Bartering**, the exchange of goods and services for other goods and services, is another way of trading with countries lacking convertible currency. In a barter exchange, a company that manufactures electronics components might trade its products for the coffee that a business in a foreign country processes, which it then sells to a third company for cash. Barter transactions require finding a business with complementary needs, but they are much simpler than countertrade transactions.

*Howard Dahl and
Amity Technology*

Howard Dahl, owner of Amity Technology, a U.S.-based manufacturer of farm equipment, was part of the first wave of entrepreneurs to enter Russia after the communist regime in the former Soviet Union collapsed. Conducting business in those early years was challenging, and Dahl's company often relied on bartering. "[The Russians] would trade rapeseed, which you could use to make vegetable oil, for our machinery," he says. "We would then sell the seeds to a German agribusiness in a back-to-back transaction." Dahl is glad that he didn't give up the Russian export market. Today, exports to Russia account for 40 percent of Amity Technology's total sales.[27]

## Exporting

*3.* Explain how to build a successful export program.

For years, small businesses in the United States could afford the luxury of conducting business at home in the world's largest market, never having to venture outside its borders. However, a growing number of small companies, realizing the incredible profit potential that exporting offers, are making globalization an ever-expanding part of their marketing plans. The number of small companies that export is growing twice as fast as the number of large businesses that export, but large companies still dominate exporting.[28] For example, although small companies account for 97 percent of all U.S. businesses that export goods and services, they generate only 29 of the nation's export sales.[29]

Similarly, more than 250,000 U.S. companies currently export; however, experts estimate that at least twice as many are capable of exporting but are not doing so.[30] The biggest barrier facing companies that have never exported is not knowing where or how to start. Paul Hsu, whose company sells ginseng across the globe, explains, "Exporting starts with a global mind-set, which unfortunately, is not all that common among owners of small- and medium-sized businesses in the United States. Most entrepreneurs in the United States envision markets only within domestic and sometimes even state borders, while foreign entrepreneurs look at export markets first."[31]

Breaking the psychological barrier to exporting is the first—and most difficult—step in setting up a successful program. The U.S. Chamber of Commerce's Trade Roots initiative, an international trade leadership program that networks more than 3,000 local U.S. chambers of commerce, is a useful resource for entrepreneurs looking to launch into global business. The program provides information on the benefits and methods for its members who want to engage in international trade but aren't sure where to start. The U.S. Commercial Service's *Export Programs Guide* provides entrepreneurs with a comprehensive list of federal programs designed to help U.S. exporters. Another valuable source of information are the U.S. Export Assistance Centers (www.sba.gov/oit/export/useac.html) that serve as single contact points for information on the multitude of federal export programs that are designed to help entrepreneurs who want to start exporting. Entrepreneurs who want to learn more about exporting should investigate *A Basic Guide to Exporting* (www.unzco.com/basicguide/), which is published by the Department of Commerce and Unz and Company. The U.S. government export portal (www.export.gov) gives entrepreneurs access to valuable information about exporting in general (finance, shipping, documentation, and others) as well as details on individual nations (market research, trade agreements, statistics, and more). Learning more about exporting and realizing that it is within the realm of possibility for small companies—even *very* small companies—is the first, and often most difficult, step in breaking the psychological barrier to exporting.

The next challenge is to create a sound export strategy. In fact, a recent study of 346 small exporting companies by Pierre-André Julien and Charles Ramangahahy found that small companies with well-defined export strategies outperformed those that merely dabbled in exporting.[32] What steps must entrepreneurs take to build a successful export strategy?

**1.** *Recognize that even the tiniest companies and least experienced entrepreneurs have the potential to export; help is available.* Size and experience are not prerequisites for a successful export program.

*John and Nancy Kleppe
and J&N Enterprises*

In 1985, when John and Nancy Kleppe launched J&N Enterprises, a company that sells the Gas Trac, a portable combustible gas detector, in the spare bedroom of their home in the U.S. state of Indiana, they had no intention of operating their tiny business on a global scale. J&N Enterprises grew over time, and in 2003, the company moved into a new high-tech 14,000-square-foot building in a nearby town. With the help of state agencies, president Scott Kleppe, the couple's son, attended a trade show in China, which led to orders that increased the company's sales by 22 percent. Today, J&N Industries exports its expanded product line to 16 countries, including Australia, Korea, Mexico, and Turkey and recently was named the Indiana Exporter of the Year by the U.S. Small Business Administration.[33]

2. *Analyze your product or service.* Is it special? New? Unique? High quality? Priced favorably due to lower costs or exchange rates? Does it appeal to a particular niche? In which countries would there be sufficient demand for it? In many foreign countries, products from the United States are in demand because they have an air of mystery about them! Exporters quickly learn the value foreign customers place on quality. Ron Schutte, president of Creative Bakers of Brooklyn, New York, a company that makes pre-sliced cheesecakes for restaurants, saw an opportunity to sell in Japan. The only modification Schutte made to his high-quality cheesecakes was reducing the portion size from 4.5 ounces to 2.25 ounces to accommodate Japanese diners' smaller appetites.[34]

3. *Analyze your commitment.* Are you willing to devote the time and the energy to develop export markets? Does your company have the necessary resources to capitalize on market opportunities? In any international venture, patience is essential. One expert estimates that penetrating a foreign market requires at least three years.[35] Laying the groundwork for an export operation can take from six to eight months (or longer), but entering foreign markets isn't as tough as most entrepreneurs think. "One of the biggest misconceptions people have is that they can't market overseas unless they have a big team of lawyers and specialists," says one export specialist. "That just isn't true."[36] Table 12.3 summarizes key issues managers must address in the export decision.

4. *Research markets and pick your target.* Nearly two-thirds of small- and medium-sized companies export to just one foreign market (see Figure 12.3). Before investing in a costly sales trip abroad, entrepreneurs should make a trip to the local library or the nearest branch of their department of commerce and the International Trade Administration. Exporters can choose from a multitude of guides, manuals, books, statistical reports, newsletters, videos, and other resources to help them research potential markets. Armed with research, small business owners can avoid wasting time and money on markets with limited potential for their products and can concentrate on those with the greatest promise. According to the Economist Intelligence Unit, the fastest growing economies in the world between 2006 and 2020 will be China, the United States, India, Brazil, and Russia. Asian economies in particular will be attractive markets for small exporters, increasing their share of global GDP from 35 percent today to 43 percent in 2020.[37]

Research shows export entrepreneurs whether they need to modify their existing products and services to suit the tastes and preferences of their foreign target customers. Sometimes foreign customers' lifestyles, housing needs, body sizes, and cultures require exporters to make alterations in their product lines. For instance, when Rodney Robbins, CEO of Robbins Industries, a maker of measuring cups and spoons, was negotiating with a distributor prior to entering the Swedish and British markets, he learned that he would have to modify his products slightly. The British use measuring utensils labeled in milliliters while the Swedes prefer deciliters.[38] Making modifications such as these often spells the difference between success and failure in the global market. In other cases, products destined for export need little or no modification. Experts estimate that one-half of exported products require little modification; one-third require moderate modification; only

### TABLE 12.3 Management Issues in the Export Decision

**I. Experience**
  1. With what countries has your company already conducted business (or from what countries have you received inquiries about your product or service)?
  2. What product lines do foreign customers ask about most often?
  3. Prepare a list of sale inquiries for each buyer by product and by country.
  4. Is the trend of inquiries or sales increasing or decreasing?
  5. Who are your primary domestic and foreign competitors?
  6. What lessons has your company learned from past export experience?

**II. Management and Personnel**
  1. Who will be responsible for the export entity's organization and staff? (Do you have an export "champion"?)
  2. How much top management time
      a. should you allocate to exporting?
      b. can you afford to allocate to exporting?
  3. What does management expect from its exporting efforts? What are your company's export goals and objectives?
  4. What organizational structure will your company require to ensure that it can service export sales properly? (Note the political implications, if any.)
  5. Who will implement the plan?

**III. Production Capacity**
  1. To what extent is your company using its existing production capacity? Is there any excess? If so, how much?
  2. Will filling export orders hurt your company's ability to make and service domestic sales?
  3. What will additional production for export markets cost your company?
  4. Are there seasonal or cyclical fluctuations in your company's workload? When? Why?
  5. Is there a minimum quantity foreign customers must order for a sale to be profitable?
  6. To what extent would your company need to modify its products, packaging, and design specifically for its export targets? Is your product quality adequate for foreign customers?
  7. What pricing structure will your company use? Will prices be competitive given currency exchange rates?
  8. How will your company collect payment on its export sales?

**IV. Financial Capacity**
  1. How much capital will your company need to begin exporting? Where will it come from?
  2. How will you allocate the initial costs of your company's export effort?
  3. Does your company have other expansion plans that would compete with an exporting effort?
  4. By what date do you expect your company's export program to pay for itself?

*Source:* Adapted from *A Basic Guide to Exporting* (Washington, DC: U.S. Department of Commerce, 1986), p. 3.

**FIGURE 12.3 Number of Countries to Which Small and Medium Businesses Export**

*Source:* Elizabeth Clark, *Small and Medium-Sized Exporting Companies: A Statistical Handbook*, International Trade Administration, Office of Trade and Industry Information (Washington, DC: U.S. Government Printing Office, 2005), p. 19.

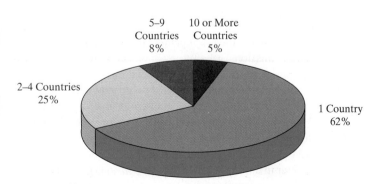

5–9 Countries 8%
10 or More Countries 5%
2–4 Countries 25%
1 Country 62%

**TABLE 12.4  Questions to Guide International Market Research**

- Is there an overseas market for your company's products or services?
- Are there specific target markets that look most promising?
- Which new markets abroad are most likely to open up or expand?
- How big is the market your company is targeting, and how fast is it growing?
- What are the major economic, political, legal, social, technological, and other environmental factors affecting this market?
- What are the demographic and cultural factors affecting this market: e.g., disposable income, occupation, age, gender, opinions, activities, interests, tastes, and values?
- Who are your company's present and potential customers abroad?
- What are their needs and desires? What factors influence their buying decisions: price, credit terms, delivery terms, quality, brand name, etc.?
- How would they use your company's product or service? What modifications, if any, would be necessary to sell to your target customers?
- Who are your primary competitors in the foreign market?
- How do competitors distribute, sell, and promote their products? What are their prices?
- What are the best channels of distribution for your product?
- What is the best way for your company to gain exposure in this market?
- Are there any barriers such as tariffs, quotas, duties, or regulations to selling your product in this market? Are there any incentives?
- Are there any potential licensing or joint venture partners already in this market?

*Source:* Adapted from *A Basic Guide to Exporting* (Washington, DC: Department of Commerce, 1986), p.11.

a few require major changes. Table 12.4 offers questions to guide entrepreneurs as they conduct export research.

**5. *Develop a distribution strategy.***  Should you use an export intermediary or sell directly to foreign customers? As you learned earlier in this chapter, many small companies just entering international markets prefer to rely on trade intermediaries or a joint venture partner to break new ground. Using intermediaries or joint ventures often makes sense until an entrepreneur has the chance to gain experience in exporting and to learn the ground rules of selling in foreign lands.

**6. *Find your customer.***  Small businesses can rely on a host of export specialists to help them track down foreign customers. (Refer to Table 12.1 for a list of some of the resources available from the government.) The U.S. Department of Commerce and the International Trade Administration should be the first stops on an entrepreneur's agenda for going global. These agencies have market research available through the U.S. Commercial Service Web site (www.buyusa.gov) that can help entrepreneurs locate the best target markets for its products or services and specific customers within those markets. Industry Sector Analysis (ISAs), International Market Insights (IMIs), and Customized Market Analysis (CMAs) are just some of the reports and services that global entrepreneurs find most useful. These agencies also have knowledgeable staff specialists experienced in the details of global trade and in the intricacies of foreign cultures. Through the Platinum Key Service, Commercial Service agents consult with companies as they build their global strategies, evaluate markets, and decide how to reach foreign markets.

One of the most efficient and least expensive ways for entrepreneurs to locate potential customers for their companies' products and services is to participate in a trade mission. These missions usually are sponsored by either a government economic development agency or an industry trade association for the purpose of cultivating international trade by connecting domestic companies with potential trading partners overseas. A trade mission may focus on a particular industry or may cover several industries but target a particular country. "We set up meetings for them with distributors, suppliers, manufacturers, customers, accountants, law firms, the whole gamut, to be able to provide them with the necessary resources to get into that market," says Christian Bartley, president of the World Trade Center in the U.S. state of Wisconsin, an organization that regularly sponsors trade missions to foreign countries for Wisconsin entrepreneurs who are interested in exploring export markets.[39] Fourteen small companies participated in a recent trade mission to China sponsored by Automation Alley, an organization that specializes in trade missions for high-tech companies. The trip resulted in 15 sales contracts from Chinese companies and added nearly $18.5 million in export sales to the participating companies' revenue streams. "As a direct result of the China Trade Mission, we signed up four highly qualified distributors," says Lee King, a top manager at Numatics Inc., one of the trade mission participants." "We have generated $500,000 in sales and, as a result of exporting, we have hired 15 more employees."[40]

**7. Find financing.** One of the biggest barriers to small business exports is lack of financing. Access to adequate financing is a crucial ingredient in a successful export program because the cost of generating foreign sales often is higher and collection cycles are longer. The trouble is that bankers and other sources of capital don't always understand the intricacies of international sales and view financing them as highly risky ventures. In addition, among major industrialized nations, the U.S. government spends the least per capita to promote exports.

Several federal, state, and private programs are operating to fill this export financing void, however. Loan programs from the U.S. Small Business Administration include its Export Working Capital program (90 percent loan guarantees up to $1,500,000) and International Trade Loan program (75 percent loan guarantees up to $1,500,000). In addition, the Export-Import Bank (www.exim.gov), the Overseas Private Investment Corporation, and a variety of state-sponsored programs offer export-minded entrepreneurs both direct loans and loan guarantees. (Recall that the *Export Programs Guide* provides a list of the 20 government agencies that help companies to develop their export potential.) The Export-Import Bank, which has been financing the sale of exports for more than 70 years, provides small exporters with export credit insurance and loans through its working capital line of credit and a variety of pre-export loan programs. The Bankers Association for Foreign Trade (www.baft.org/jsps/) is an association of 150 banks around the world that matches exporters needing foreign trade financing with interested banks.

**ENTREPRENEURIAL Profile**

*Teri Gautier (standing) founder of Pharmaceutical Trade Services Inc.*

In 1998, just three months after launching Pharmaceutical Trade Services Inc. (PTSI), a small company that sells specialized prescription drugs and supplements, president Teri Gautier was using export credit insurance from the Export-Import bank to sell to European customers. In 2005, after Hurricane Katrina devastated the U.S. community where the company is headquartered, Gautier needed a boost to rebuild her business. Using financing and insurance from the Export-Import Bank, PTSI was able to increase its export sales from $713,000 a year to nearly $6 million a year over the next eight years. Today, Gautier's company exports its products to customers in Europe, the Middle East, Southeast Asia, Africa, and Latin America.[41]

**8. Ship your goods.** Export novices usually rely on international freight forwarders and custom-house agents—experienced specialists in overseas shipping—for help in navigating the bureaucratic morass of packaging requirements and paperwork demanded by customs. These specialists, also known as **transport architects**, are to exporters what travel agents are to passengers and normally charge relatively small fees for a valuable service. They move shipments of all sizes to destinations all over the world efficiently, saving entrepreneurs many headaches. Good freight forwarders understand export regulations, foreign import requirements, shipping procedures (such as packing, labeling, documenting, and insuring goods), customs processes, and maintaining proper records for paying tariffs. In addition, because they work for several companies, freight forwarders can aggregate payloads to negotiate favorable rates with shippers. "[A freight forwarder] is going to be sure that his client conforms with all of the government regulations that apply to export cargo," explains the owner of an international freight forwarding business. "He acts as an agent of the exporter, and, in most circumstances, is like an extension of that exporter's traffic department." The Johnston Sweeper Company, a manufacturer of street sweepers, ships its 20,000-pound pieces of equipment worldwide with the help of an international freight forwarder.[42]

Table 12.5 features common international shipping terms and their meaning.

**9. *Collect your money.*** Collecting foreign accounts can be more complex than collecting domestic ones; however, by picking their customers carefully and checking their credit references closely, entrepreneurs can minimize bad-debt losses. Businesses engaging in international sales can use four primary payment methods (ranked from least risky to most risky): cash in advance, a letter of credit, a bank (or documentary) draft, and an open account. The safest method of selling to foreign customers is to collect cash in advance of the sale. This is the safest option for the seller because it eliminates the risk of collection

**TABLE 12.5  Common International Shipping Terms and Their Meaning**

| Shipping Term | Seller's Responsibility | Buyer's Responsibility | Shipping Method(s) Used |
|---|---|---|---|
| FOB ("Free on Board") Seller | Deliver goods to carrier and provide export license and clean on-board receipt. Bear risk of loss until goods are delivered to carrier. | Pay shipping, freight, and insurance charges. Bear risk of loss while goods are in transit. | All |
| FOB ("Free on Board") Buyer | Deliver goods to the buyer's place of business and provide export license and clean on-board receipt. Pay shipping, freight, and insurance charges. | Accept delivery of goods after documents are tendered. | All |
| FAS ("Free Along Side"), Vessel | Deliver goods alongside ship. Provides an "alongside" receipt. | Provide export license and proof of delivery of the goods to the carrier. Bear risk of loss once goods are delivered to the carrier. | Ship |
| CFR ("Cost and Freight") | Deliver goods to carrier, obtain export licenses, and pay export taxes. Provide buyer with clean bill of lading. Pay freight and shipping charges. Bear risk of loss until goods are delivered to buyer. | Pay insurance charges. Accept delivery of goods after documents are tendered. | Ship |
| CIF ("Cost, Insurance, and Freight") | Same as CFR plus pay insurance charges and provide buyer with insurance policy. | Accept delivery of goods after documents are tendered. | Ship |
| CPT ("Carriage Paid to . . . ") | Deliver goods to carrier, obtain export licenses, and pay export taxes. Provide buyer with clean transportation documents. Pay shipping and freight charges. | Pay insurance charges. Accept delivery of goods after documents are tendered. | All |
| CIP ("Carriage and Insurance Paid to . . .") | Same as CPT plus pay insurance charges and provide buyer with insurance policy. | Accept delivery of goods after documents are tendered. | All |
| DDU ("Delivered Duty Unpaid") | Obtain export license, pay insurance charges, and provide buyer documents for taking delivery. | Take delivery of goods and pay import duties. | All |
| DDP ("Delivered Duty Paid") | Obtain export license and pay import duty, pay insurance charges, and provide buyer documents for taking delivery. | Take delivery of goods. | All |

*Source:* Adapted from *Guide to the Finance of International Trade*, edited by Gordon Platt (HBSC Trade Services, Marine Midland Bank, and the Journal of Commerce), http://infoserv2.ita.doc.gov/efm/efm.nsf/503d177e3c63f0b48525675900112e24/6218a8703573b32985256759004c41f3/$FILE/Finance_.pdf, pp. 6–10.

**FIGURE 12.4 How a
Letter of Credit Works**

Seller          Buyer

Foreign buyer agrees to buy
products; seller agrees to ship
goods if buyer arranges a letter
of credit.

Seller ships goods to buyer
according to letter of credit's
terms and submits shipping
documents to bank issuing letter
of credit.

Seller's bank          Buyer's bank

Letter of credit

Buyer requests that his bank grant a letter of
credit, which assures exporter payment if she
presents documents proving goods were
actually shipped. Bank makes out letter of
credit to seller and sends it to seller's bank
(called the confirming bank).

Buyer's bank makes payment
to seller's (confirming) bank.
Confirming bank then pays
seller amount specified in
letter of credit.

problems and provides immediate cash flow. However, requiring cash payments up front
may limit severely a small company's base of foreign customers.

Financing foreign sales often involves special credit arrangements such as letters of
credit and bank (or documentary) drafts. A **letter of credit** is an agreement between an exporter's bank and the foreign buyer's bank that guarantees payment to the exporter for a
specific shipment of goods. In essence, a letter of credit reduces the financial risk for the
exporter by substituting a bank's creditworthiness for that of the purchaser (see Figure 12.4).
A **bank draft** is a document the seller draws on the buyer, requiring the buyer to pay the
face amount (the purchase price of the goods) either on sight (a sight draft) or on a specified date (a time draft) once the goods are shipped. Rather than use letters of credit or
drafts, some exporters simply sell to foreign customers on open account. In other words,
they ship the goods to a foreign customer without any guarantee of payment. This method
is riskiest because collecting a delinquent account from a foreign customer is even more
difficult than collecting past-due payments from a domestic customer. The parties to an international deal should always come to an agreement in advance on an acceptable method
of payment.

### Establishing International Locations

Once established in international markets, some small businesses set up permanent locations there. Establishing an office or a factory in a foreign land can require a substantial investment reaching beyond the budgets of many small companies. In addition, setting up an
international office can be an incredibly frustrating experience in some countries. Business
infrastructures are in disrepair or are nonexistent. Getting a telephone line installed can take
months in some places, and finding reliable equipment to move goods to customers is
nearly impossible. Securing necessary licenses and permits from bureaucrats often takes
more than filing the necessary paperwork; in some nations, bureaucrats expect payments to
"grease the wheels of justice." One study by the World Bank of "grease payments" for the

purpose of minimizing the red tape imposed by foreign regulations concludes that the payments do not work; in fact, companies that actually used them experienced greater government scrutiny and red tape in their international transactions.[43] In another study, risk management company Simmons & Simmons reports that 35.4 percent of companies said that they had refused to make investments in certain country's because of the nation's reputation for corruption.[44] Finally, finding the right person to manage an international office is crucial to success; it also is a major challenge, especially for small businesses. Small companies usually have lean management staffs and cannot afford to send key people abroad without running the risk of losing their focus.

*Paul Hoffman and
the Hoffman Agency*

The Hoffman Agency, a small public relations firm founded by Paul Hoffman, works primarily with high tech companies based in California. As he watched many of his company's clients go global, Hoffman saw opportunities for his business in international markets. Market research pointed him to Asia, and Hoffman selected China as an early international expansion target. Hoffman conducted several exploratory trips to China, but found the business climate and culture baffling. "After three days, I came back dazed," he recalls. "The divide between East and West was too dramatic. I thought, 'There's no way in a million years we're going to figure this out.'" Hoffman persisted, however, and decided to find someone who could open an office in China. He hired Zhong Li, a Chinese national who had worked at a large Chinese petroleum company, and put her to work in the company's California office for more than a year, where she learned about the company, its mission, and its culture and conducted seminars for Hoffman's clients on doing business in China. Li then returned to Beijing, where she established the company's first Chinese office. Today the Hoffman Agency has 10 international locations (seven of them in Asia and three of those in China), and nearly half of the company's revenues come from international sales. "Every country has it own vignette," says Hoffman. "I'm always learning. If it weren't for the global expansion, I would have sold the business by now."[45]

Small companies that establish international locations can reap significant benefits. Start-up costs are lower in some foreign countries (but not all!), and lower labor costs can produce significant savings as well. In addition, by locating in a country, a business learns firsthand how its culture influences business and how it can satisfy customers' demands most effectively. In essence, the business becomes a local corporate citizen.

Going global by employing one or more of these nine strategies can put tremendous strain on a small company, but the benefits of cracking international markets can be significant. Not only does going global offer attractive sales and profit possibilities, but it also strengthens the company's competitive skills and enhances its overall reputation. Pleasing tough foreign customers also keeps companies on their competitive toes.

### Importing and Outsourcing

In addition to selling their goods in foreign markets, small companies also buy goods from distributors and manufacturers in foreign markets. In fact, the intensity of price competition in many industries—from textiles and handbags to industrial machinery and computers—means that more companies now shop the world market, looking for the lowest prices they can find. Because labor costs in countries such as China and India are far below those in other nations, businesses there offer goods and services at very low prices. Increasingly, these nations are home to well-educated, skilled workers that are paid far less than comparable workers in the more developed countries. For instance, a computer programmer in a developed country might earn $100,000 a year, but in India, a computer programmer doing the same work earns $20,000 a year or less. As a result, many companies either import goods or outsource work directly to manufacturers in countries where costs are far lower than they would be domestically. According to market research company Gartner, global outsourcing is a $429.2 billion per year industry.[46]

## ■ Things Are a Bit Different Here

Although the closest he had ever lived to China was in Taipei, Taiwan, Harry Tsao, whose parents had once lived in Shanghai, thought he understood Chinese culture. After all, he was fluent in Mandarin and in Shanghaiese (the local dialect spoken in Shangai) and he understood the basics of Chinese business etiquette. While interviewing potential employees for software engineering jobs with his comparison pricing Web site, however, the reality and the complications of doing business globally came into focus. Tsao was shocked when several candidates brought their mothers with them to the interviews. None of them seemed to understand the entrepreneurial spirit, and most candidates' résumés included four to six jobs in just two years, exhibiting the "*Qi lu zhao ma*" mentality— "Ride a mule as you seek a horse."

Tsao came to China because he and his business partner, Talmadge O'Neill, knew that for their start-up Web site, Smarter.com, to be competitive, they had to hire software engineers and editors at bargain prices, and China was the ideal place for that. After wading through scores of résumés and interviews, Tsao was able to hire Chinese software engineers for an average of $750 to $1,000 a month—about 75 percent less than the start-up company would have to pay for the same skill level in the United States. As employees' résumés had hinted, Smarter.com experienced high turnover as employees left for jobs at larger companies, and Tsao was constantly training new workers.

Tsao realized that the traditional Western style of managing employees in China was not working, and he decided to change his approach. He gave employees a meal subsidy of $26 per month, which in China was enough for them to purchase lavish lunches every day. He hired a full-time trainer to teach workers a multitude of business skills, from making presentations and handling e-mail to working in teams and keeping projects on schedule. He awarded every department a "fun budget," money that managers can spend on staff outings such as skiing trips and karaoke nights. Tsao and O'Neill offer none of these perks to their U.S. employees, but they find that Chinese workers respond to them.

Tsao also discovered that although Chinese employees were quick to identify problems and potential solutions to them, they were hesitant to take action on their own to solve problems. Chinese workers are not comfortable questioning authority. Naturally, he tried a Western solution to encourage employees to take initiative to assume more responsibility and to take the initiative in solving problems: financial rewards. Employees' response to the bonus incentives was lukewarm; instead, Tsao discovered that his Chinese employees respond much better to praise. Managers began recognizing employees who did solve problems in group e-mails and in front of managers. He also realized that inviting employees to offer ideas and suggestions was fruitless. Now in meetings, he asks each person for specific feedback. "Then you get a lot of opinions," says Tsao, "although you really have to pull it out of them."

The management techniques that Tsao has developed over time for managing in China have begun to bear fruit. Smarter.com's employee turnover rate is down to just 20 percent per year, and Tsao has hired two Chinese managers, both with experience in the West, to oversee the Shanghai office. The company now has 125 employees in China, 25 in the United States, and 5 in Japan, and its annual revenue exceeds $40 million. Smarter.com is profitable, says Tsao, thanks, in large part, to the cost savings of operating in China. With the knowledge it has gained by operating in the Asian market, the company also has been able to launch Chinese, Korean, and Japanese versions of the Smarter.com Web site.

1. What steps could Tsao and O'Neill have taken to avoid some of the problems they encountered in China?
2. Use the resources described in the chapter to research the culture and customs of doing business in a country that interests you. Prepare a one-page summary of recommendations for entrepreneurs who might be interested in doing business there.

*Source:* Adapted from Michelle Tsai, "Shanghai Surprises: The Perils of Opening an Office in China," *Inc.*, March 2007, pp. 47–49.

A recent study by the newspaper *USA Today* reports that nearly 40 percent of technology start-ups employ skilled workers in a foreign country, where labor costs are low.[47] Fieldglass, a software development business founded by Jai Shekhawat in 2000, included plans for outsourcing some of the company's software development to India from the outset. Shekhawat, says that, without the ability to outsource certain jobs to foreign countries, he would never have launched Fieldglass, which employs more than 60 employees in its Chicago headquarters.[48]

Entrepreneurs who are considering importing goods and service or outsourcing their service or manufacturing jobs to foreign countries should follow these steps:

- ■ *Make sure that importing or outsourcing is right for your business.* Even though foreign manufacturers often can provide items at significant cost savings, using them may not always be the best business decision. Entrepreneurs sometimes discover that achieving the lowest price may require a tradeoff of other important factors such as quality and speed of delivery. When Patrick Kruse, owner of Ruff Wear, a business that sells dog booties, began outsourcing many of his company's products to Chinese factories, he discovered that the quality of the goods was poor. "We actually had to refuse some shipments, which really hurt our business," he says.[49] In addition, some foreign manufacturers require sizeable minimum orders, perhaps $200,000 or more, before they will produce a product.

- ■ *Establish a target cost for your product.* Before setting off on a global shopping spree, entrepreneurs first should determine exactly what they can afford to spend on manufacturing a product and make a profit on it. Given the low labor costs of many foreign manufacturers, products that are the most labor intensive make good candidates for outsourcing.

- ■ *Do your research before you leave home.* Investing time in basic research about the industry and potential suppliers in foreign lands is essential before setting foot on foreign soil. Useful resources are plentiful, and entrepreneurs should use them. Refer to Table 12.2 for a list of some of the most popular sources of information on foreign countries and the companies that are based there.

- ■ *Be sensitive to cultural differences.* When making contacts, setting up business appointments, or calling on prospective manufacturers in foreign lands, make sure you understand what is accepted business behavior and what is not. Once again, this is where your research pays off; be sure to study the cultural nuances of doing business in the countries you will visit.

- ■ *Do your groundwork.* Once you locate potential manufacturers, contact them to set up appointments, and go visit them. Preliminary research is essential to finding reliable sources of supply, but "face time" with representatives from various companies allows entrepreneurs to judge the intangible factors that can make or break a relationship.

- ■ *Protect your company's intellectual property.* A common problem that many entrepreneurs have encountered with outsourcing is "knockoffs." Some foreign manufacturers see nothing wrong with agreeing to manufacture a product for a company and then selling their own "knockoff" version of it. Securing a nondisclosure agreement and a contract that prohibits such behavior helps, but experts say that securing a patent for the item in the source country itself (not just the United States) is a good idea.

- ■ *Select a manufacturer.* Using quality, speed of delivery, level of trust, degree of legal protection, costs, and other factors, select the manufacturer that can do the best job for your company. Be aware that delivery times may be longer—sometimes much longer—for outsourced goods. Items that domestic suppliers can supply within a week or two may take months to arrive from some foreign countries.

- ■ *Provide an exact model of the product you want manufactured.* Providing a manufacturer with an actual model of the item to be manufactured will save lots of time, mistakes, and problems. One entrepreneur learned this lesson the hard way when he submitted a rough prototype of a product to a Chinese factory with which he had contracted for production. When the first shipment of the products arrived, he was shocked to see that they were exact duplicates—including imperfections and flaws—of the prototype that he had submitted!

# ENTREPRENEURSHIP

# *In Action*

## Where Do We Start?

Specialty Building Supplies is a small company with $6.4 million in annual sales that manufactures and sells a line of building supply products such as foundation vents, innovative insulation materials, and fireplace blowers to building supply stores in the northeastern United States. The eight-year-old company, founded by Tad Meyers, has won several awards for its unique and innovative products and has earned a solid reputation among its supply store customers and the builders and homeowners who ultimately buy its products.

Before launching the company, Meyers had been a home builder. As he watched the price of home heating fuels climb dramatically over time, Meyers began to incorporate into the houses he built simple, inexpensive ways to help homeowners save energy. He began tinkering with existing products, looking for ways to improve them. The first product he designed (and the product that ultimately led him to launch Specialty Building Supplies) was an automatic foundation vent that was thermostatically controlled (no electricity needed). The vent would automatically open and close based on the outside temperature, keeping cold drafts from blowing under a house. Simple and inexpensive in its design, the Autovent was a big hit in newly constructed homes in the Northeast because it not only saved energy but it also avoided a major headache for homeowners in cold climates: water pipes that would freeze and burst. Before long, Meyers stopped building houses and focused on selling the Autovent. Its success prompted him to add other products to the company's line.

Specialty's sales have been lackluster for more than a year now, primarily due to a slump in new home construction in its primary market. Tad Meyers recently met the company's top marketing managers and salespeople to talk about their options for getting Specialty's sales

and profit growth back on track. "What about selling our products in international markets?" asked Dee Rada, the company's marketing manager. "I read an article just last week about small companies doing good business in other countries, and many of them were smaller than we are."

"Interesting idea," Meyers said, pondering the concept. "I've never really thought about selling anything overseas. In fact, other than my years in the military, I've never traveled overseas and don't know anything about doing business there."

"It's a big world out there. Where should we sell our products?" said Hal Milam, Specialty's sales manager. "How do we find out what the building codes are in foreign countries? Would we have to modify our designs to meet foreign standards?"

"I don't know," shrugged Meyers. "Those are some good questions."

"How would we distribute our products?" asked Rada. "We have an established network of distributors here in the United States, but how do we find foreign distributors?"

"I wonder if exporting is our only option," Meyers said. "There must be other ways to get into the global market besides exporting. What do you think? Where do we start?"

1. What advice would you offer Meyers and the other managers at Specialty Building Supplies about their prospects of going global?

2. How would you suggest these managers go about finding the answers to the questions they have posed? What other questions would you advise them to answer?

3. Outline the steps these managers should take to assemble an international marketing plan.

■ ***Stay in constant contact with the manufacturer and try to build a long-term relationship.*** Communication is a key to building and maintaining a successful relationship with a foreign manufacturer. Weekly teleconferences, e-mails, and periodic visits are essential to making sure that your company gets the performance you expect from a foreign manufacturer.

## Barriers to International Trade

**4.** Discuss the major barriers to international trade and their impact on the global economy.

Governments have always used a variety of barriers to block free trade among nations in an attempt to protect businesses within their own borders. The benefit of protecting their own companies, however, comes at the expense of foreign businesses, which face limited access to global markets. Ultimately, customers in nations that restrict free trade pay the price in the form of higher prices and smaller supplies of goods available. Numerous trade barriers—both domestic and international—restrict the freedom of businesses in global trading. Despite these barriers, international trade has grown to nearly $15 trillion per year.[50]

### Domestic Barriers

Sometimes the biggest barriers potential exporters face are right here at home. Three major domestic roadblocks are common: attitude, information, and financing. Perhaps the biggest barrier to small businesses exporting is the attitude: "I'm too small to export. That's just for big corporations." The first lesson of exporting is "Take nothing for granted about who can export and what you can and cannot export." The first step to building an export program is recognizing that the opportunity to export exists.

Another reason entrepreneurs neglect international markets is a lack of information about how to get started. The key to success in international markets is choosing the correct target market and designing the appropriate strategy to reach it. That requires access to information and research. Although a variety of government and private organizations make volumes of exporting and international marketing information available, many small business owners never use it. A successful global marketing strategy also recognizes that not all international markets are the same. Companies must be flexible and willing to make adjustments to their products and services, promotional campaigns, packaging, and sales techniques.

Another significant obstacle is the lack of export financing available. A common complaint among small exporters is that they lose export business simply because they cannot get the financing to support it. Financial institutions that serve small companies often do not have experience in conducting international business and simply deny loans for international transactions as being too risky.

### International Barriers

Domestic barriers are not the only ones export-minded entrepreneurs must overcome. Trading nations also erect obstacles to free trade. Two types of international barriers are common: tariff and nontariff.

**TARIFF BARRIERS.** A **tariff** is a tax, or duty, that a government imposes on goods and services imported into that country. Imposing tariffs raises the price of the imported goods—making them less attractive to consumers—and protects the makers of comparable domestic products and services. The United States imposes tariffs on thousands of items ranging from brooms and fish fillets to costume jewelry and fence posts. The average tariff on goods imported into the United States is just 1.4 percent, but the U.S. International Trade Commission estimates that eliminating tariffs would expand U.S. exports by $13.5 billion and increase imports by $19.6 billion. It's not just the U.S. that imposes tariffs, however. Higher tariffs on agricultural products, for example, are most prevalent in East Asian countries.[51]

Nations across the globe rely on tariffs to protect local manufacturers of certain products. If a small company's products are subject to those tariffs, exporting to that nation becomes much more difficult because remaining price competitive with products made by local manufacturers is virtually impossible.

**NONTARIFF BARRIERS.** Many nations have lowered the tariffs they impose on products and services brought into their borders, but they rely on other nontariff structures as protectionist trade barriers.

***Quotas.*** Rather than impose a direct tariff on certain imported products, nations often use quotas to protect their industries. A **quota** is a limit on the amount of a product imported into a country. After lifting the quotas on clothing and textile products from China on January 1, 2005, the European Union and United States saw textile imports soar by 40 percent within one year. Concerned about the impact on their own textile industries, both the EU and U.S. quickly reinstituted quotas (the agreements called them "safeguards") on half of the textile products China exported to these nations, including bras, bath towels, socks, wool suits, and many other items.[52] China also relies on quotas. For instance, China allows only 20 foreign films to be released each year. In addition, foreigners can invest in Chinese cinemas, but they can own no more than 49 percent of the joint venture.[53]

***Embargoes.*** An **embargo** is a total ban on imports of certain products or all products from a particular nation. The motivation for embargoes is not always economic but it also can involve political differences, environmental disputes, terrorism, and other issues. For instance, the United States imposes embargoes on products from nations it considers to be adversarial, including Cuba, Iran, Iraq, and North Korea, among others. An embargo on trade with Cuba that began in 1962 still exists today. In other cases, embargoes originate from cultural differences or health reasons. Many countries imposed embargoes on live birds from nations where avian influenza outbreaks have occurred.

***Dumping.*** In an effort to grab market share quickly, some companies have been guilty of **dumping** products, including steel, televisions, shoes, and computer chips—that is, selling large quantities of them in foreign countries below cost. More than 60 nations now have antidumping laws. Under the U.S. Antidumping Act, a company must prove that the foreign company's prices are lower here than in the home country and that U.S. companies are directly harmed. In response to a complaint from U.S.-based companies, the U.S. International Trade Commission ruled that Chinese manufacturers were dumping color televisions in the United States at unfairly low prices, and, as a result, were damaging the ability of U.S. producers to compete. In just two years, the companies claimed, sales fell 81 percent, and they were forced to lay off more than 7,000 workers. The ITC imposed tariffs ranging from 5 percent to 78 percent on color televisions imported from China.[54]

## Political Barriers

Entrepreneurs who go global quickly discover a labyrinth of political tangles. Although many American business owners complain of excessive government regulation in the United States, they are often astounded by the complex web of governmental and legal regulations and barriers they encounter in foreign countries.

Companies doing business in politically risky lands face the very real dangers of government takeovers of private property; attempts at coups to overthrow ruling parties; kidnappings, bombings, and other violent acts against businesses and their employees; and other threatening events. Employees of several companies working to rebuild Iraq after the war there were killed in uprisings by militants loyal to the former regime. Companies' investments of millions of dollars may evaporate overnight in the wake of a government coup or the passage of a law nationalizing an industry (giving control of an entire industry to the government).

## Business Barriers

Companies doing business internationally quickly learn that business practices and regulations in foreign lands can be quite different. Simply duplicating the practices they have adopted (and have used successfully) in the domestic market and using them in foreign markets is not always a good idea. Perhaps the biggest shock comes in the area of human resources management, where international managers discover that practices common in many countries such as overtime, women workers, and employee benefits are restricted, disfavored, or forbidden in other cultures. Business owners new to international business sometimes are shocked at the wide range of labor costs they encounter and the accompanying wide range of skilled labor available. In some countries, what appear to be "bargain" labor rates turn out to be excessively high after accounting for the quality of the labor force and the mandated benefits their governments impose—from company-sponsored housing, meals, and clothing to required profit sharing and extended vacations. For instance, in most European nations, workers are accustomed to four to six weeks of vacation compared to two weeks in the United States.

*Harry Tsao and Talmadge O'Neill and Smarter.com*

In 2003, Harry Tsao and Talmadge O'Neill launched Smarter.com, a comparison-shopping Web site, in the United States. The entrepreneurs thought that by hiring software engineers in China, they could keep their operating costs low. They opened a branch in Shanghai to handle the back office of their e-commerce operation and hired 10 engineers at bargain salaries. Then Tsao and O'Neill discovered that companies operating in China must pay exorbitant payroll taxes, an unforeseen technicality that cost their fledgling company an unexpected $26,000. "I had no choice," recalls Tsao. "I had to take on those costs."[55]

In many nations, labor unions represent workers in almost every company, yet they play a very different role from the unions in other countries. In other countries, including the United Arab Emirates and Saudi Arabia, unions are banned. Although management-union relations need not be hostile, unions can greatly complicate a company's ability to compete effectively.

### Cultural Barriers

The **culture** of a nation includes the beliefs, values, views, and mores that its inhabitants share. Differences in cultures among nations create another barrier to international trade. The diversity of languages, business philosophies, practices, and traditions make international trade more complex than selling to the business down the street. Entrepreneurs wanting to do business in international markets must have a clear understanding and appreciation of the cultures in which they plan to do business. Consider the following examples:

- A South American entrepreneur, eager to expand into the European Union, arrives at his company's potential business partner's headquarters in France. Confidently, he strides into the meeting room, enthusiastically pumps his host's hand, slaps him on the back, and says "Tony, I've heard a great deal about you; please, call me Fabrizio." Eager to explain the benefits of his product, he opens his briefcase and gets right down to business. The French executive politely excuses himself and leaves the room before negotiations ever begin, shocked by the American's rudeness and ill manners. Rudeness and ill manners? Yes—from the French executive's perspective.
- A European business owner flies to Tokyo to close a deal with a Japanese executive. He is pleased when his host invites him to play a round of golf shortly after he arrives. He plays well and manages to win by a few strokes. The Japanese executive invites him to play again the next day, and again he wins by a few strokes. Invited to play another round the following day, the European asks, "But when are we going to start doing business?" His host, surprised by the question, says, "But we *have* been doing business."
- The CEO of a successful small U.S. company is in China negotiating with several customers on deals, any of which would be significant to the company. On the verge of closing one deal, the CEO sends in his place to the negotiation a young sales representative, thinking that the only thing that remained is to sign the contract. At the meeting, the manager of the Chinese company remarks, "Ah, you are about the same age as my son." Much to the U.S. entrepreneur's surprise, the deal falls through.[56]

When businesspeople enter international markets for the first time, they often are amazed at the differences in foreign cultures' habits and customs. In the first scenario described, for instance, had the entrepreneur done his homework, he would have known that the French are very formal (back slapping is *definitely* taboo!) and do not typically use first names in business relationships (even among long-time colleagues). In the second scenario, a global manager would have known that the Japanese place a tremendous importance on developing personal relationships before committing to any business deals. Thus, he would have seen the golf games for what they really were: an integral part of building a business relationship. In the final scenario, the U.S. entrepreneur did not understand that status (*shehui dengji*) is extremely important to the Chinese. The Chinese executive would consider negotiating a deal with an executive whose rank in the organization did not at least equal his to be a great insult. That particular deal was doomed the minute the lower-level salesperson walked into the room.

Understanding and heeding these often subtle cultural differences is one of the most important keys to international business success. "There's more to business than just business," says one writer, "particularly when confronting the subtleties of deeply ingrained cultural customs, conventions, and protocols that abound in today's global marketplace."[57] Conducting a business meeting with a foreign executive in the same manner as one with an American businessperson could doom the deal from the outset. Business customs and behaviors that are acceptable—even expected—in this country may be taboo in others.

Entrepreneurs who fail to learn the differences in the habits and customs of the cultures in which they hope to do business are at a distinct disadvantage. When it comes to conducting international business, a lack of understanding of cultures and business practices can be as great a barrier to structuring and implementing a business transaction as an error in the basic assumptions of the deal. Consider, for instance, the American who was in the final stages of contract negotiations with an Indonesian company. Given the size of the contract and his distance from home, the American business executive was nervous. Sitting across from his Indonesian counterpart, the American propped his feet up. Obviously angered, the Indonesian business owner stormed out of the room, refusing to sign the contract and leaving the American executive totally bewildered. Only later did he discover that exposing the soles of one's shoes to an Indonesian is an insult. Profuse apologies and some delicate negotiations salvaged the deal.[58] In another incident, an American went to Malaysia to close a sizable contract. In an elaborate ceremony, he was introduced to a man he thought was named "Roger." Throughout the negotiations, he called the man "Rog," not realizing that his potential client was a "rajah," a title of nobility, not a name.[59]

An American businesswoman in London was invited to a party hosted by an advertising agency. Unsure of her ability to navigate the streets and subways of London alone, she approached a British colleague who was driving to the party and asked him, "Could I get a ride with you?" After he turned bright red from embarrassment, he regained his composure and politely said, "Lucky for you I know what you meant." Unknowingly, the young woman had requested a sexual encounter with her colleague, not a lift to the party![60]

Inaccurate translations of documents into other languages often pose embarrassing problems for companies conducting international business.

Interactive Magic, an American software company, had introduced several computer games in Germany that had been quite successful. Executives at the small company expected that their newest release, "Capitalism," would be the best-selling game yet. After the game hit store shelves in Germany, however, managers discovered that the instructions told customers to use a nail file to get the game running on their computers. In the translation from English to German, the word "file" somehow lost its electronic meaning and became a beauty accessory![61]

In other cases, mistranslated ads have left foreign locals scratching their heads, wondering why a company's advertising message would say *that!* For example, when an ad for Kentucky Fried Chicken that was supposed to say "Finger lickin' good" was translated into Chinese, it came out as "Eat your fingers off." An ad for the Parker Pen Company that was supposed to say "Avoid embarrassment" in Spanish actually said "Avoid pregnancy," leaving Parker Pen executives quite embarrassed themselves.[62]

The accompanying "Gaining a Competitive Edge" feature shows the importance of learning about a nation's culture before conducting business there.

## The Secret Language of International Business

When businesspeople enter international markets for the first time, they often are amazed at the differences in foreign cultures' habits and customs. Understanding and heeding these often subtle cultural differences is one of the most important keys to international business success. The maze of cultural variables from one country to another can be confusing, but with proper preparation and a little common sense, any manager can handle international transactions successfully. In short, before you pack your bags, do your homework. In most cases, conducting international business successfully requires managers to have unlimited patience, a long-term commitment, and a thorough knowledge of the local market, business practices, and culture. The key for entrepreneurs is learning to be sensitive to the business cultures in which they operate. Consider these pointers.

- Patience is a must for doing business in Spain. Like the French, Spaniards want to get to know business associates before working with them. In the United States, business comes before pleasure, but in Spain business is conducted after dinner, when the drinks and cigars are served. "I've known American businessmen who have shocked their Spanish host by pulling out their portfolios and charts before dinner is even served," says one expert. In Spain, women should avoid crossing their legs; it is considered unladylike. Men usually cross their legs at the knees.

- Appearance and style are important to Italian businesspeople; they judge the polish and the expertise of the company's executives as well as the quality of its products and services. Italians expect presentations to be organized, clear, and exact. A stylish business wardrobe also is an asset in Italy. Physical contact is an accepted part of Italian society. Don't be surprised if an Italian businessperson uses a lingering handshake or touches you occasionally when doing business.

- In Great Britain, businesspeople consider it extremely important to conduct business "properly" with formality and reserve. Boisterous behavior such as backslapping or overindulging in alcohol and ostentatious displays of wealth are considered ill-mannered. The British do not respond to hard-sell tactics but do appreciate well-mannered executives. Politeness and impeccable manners are useful tools for conducting business successfully in Great Britain.

- In Mexico, making business appointments through a well-connected Mexican national will go a long way to assuring successful business deals. "People in Mexico do business with somebody they know, they like, or they're related to," says one expert. Because family and tradition are top priorities for Mexicans, entrepreneurs who discuss their family heritages and can talk knowledgeably about Mexican history are a step ahead. In business meetings, making extended eye contact is considered impolite.

- In China, entrepreneurs will need an ample dose of the "three Ps": patience, patience, patience. Nothing in China—especially business—happens fast! In conversations and negotiations, periods of silence are common; they are a sign of politeness and contemplation. The Chinese view personal space much differently than Americans; in normal conversation, they will stand much closer to their partners. Before doing business with someone, especially foreigners, Chinese business people look to build a personal relationship (*renji hexie*) that demonstrates trust and harmony. Doing so often involves invitations to sporting events, sightseeing, long dinners that involve talking about everything but business, and home visits, all of which may take months. A traditional part of Chinese culture involves haggling over the terms of a deal, and Chinese negotiators are very good at it!

- Entrepreneurs doing business in the Pacific Rim should avoid hard-sell techniques, which are an immediate turnoff to Asian businesspeople. Harmony, patience, and consensus make good business companions in this region. It is also a good idea to minimize the importance of legal documents in negotiations. Although getting deals and trade agreements down in writing always is advisable, attempting to negotiate detailed contracts would insult most Asians, who base their deals on mutual trust and benefits.

■ Japanese executives conduct business much like the British: with an emphasis on formality, thoughtfulness, and respect. Don't expect to hear Japanese executives say "no," even during a negotiation; they don't want to offend or to appear confrontational. Instead of saying "no," a Japanese negotiator will say, "It is very difficult," "Let us think about that," or "Let us get back to you on that." Similarly, a "yes" from a Japanese executive doesn't necessarily mean that. It could mean, "I understand," "I hear you," or "I don't understand what you mean, but I don't want to embarrass you."

■ In Japan and South Korea, exchanging business cards, known in Japan as *meishi*, is an important business function (unlike Great Britain, where exchanging business cards is less popular). A Western executive who accepts a Japanese companion's card and then slips it into his pocket or scribbles notes on it has committed a major blunder. Tradition there says a business card must be treated just as its owner would be—with respect. Travelers should present their own cards using both hands with the card positioned so the recipient can read it. (The flip side should be printed in Japanese, an expected courtesy.)

■ Greeting a Japanese executive properly includes a bow and a handshake—showing respect for both cultures. In many traditional Japanese businesses, exchanging gifts at the first meeting is appropriate. Also, a love of golf (the Japanese are crazy about the game) and a willingness to participate in karaoke are a real plus for winning business in Japan.

*Source:* Adapted from John L. Graham and N. Mark Lam, "The Chinese Negotiation," *Harvard Business Review*, October 2003, pp. 82–91; Laura Fortunato, "Japan: Making It in the USA, " *Region Focus*, Fall 1997, p. 15; David Stamps, "Welcome to America," *Training*, November 1996, p. 30; Barbara Pachter, "When in Japan, Don't Cross Your Legs," *Business Ethics*, March/April 1996, p. 50; Tom Dunkel, "A New Breed of People Gazers," *Insight*, January 13, 1992, pp. 10–14; M. Katherine Glover, "Do's and Taboos," *Business America*, August 13, 1990, pp. 2–6; Deidre Sullivan, "An American Businesswoman's Guide to Japan," *Overseas Business*, Winter 1990, pp. 50–55; Stephanie Barlow, "Let's Make a Deal," *Entrepreneur*, May 1991, p. 40; "Worldy Wise," *Entrepreneur*, March 1991, p. 40; David Altany, "Culture Clash," *Industry Week*, October 2, 1998, pp. 13–20; Edward T. Hall, "The Silent Language of Overseas Business," *Harvard Business Review*, May–June 1960 pp. 5–14; John S. McClenahen, Andrew Rosenbaum, and Michael Williams, "As Others See U.S.," *Industry Week*, January 8, 1990, pp. 80-82; James Bredin, "Japan Needs to be Understood," *Industry Week*, April 20, 1992, pp. 24–26; David L. James, "Don't Think about Winning" *Across the Board*, April 1992, pp. 49–51; "When in Japan, " *Small Business Reports*, January 1992, p. 8; Bernie Ward, "Other Climates, Other Cultures," *Sky*, March 1992, pp. 72–86; Roger E. Axtell, *Gestures: The Do's and Taboos of Body Language around the World* (Hoboken, NJ: John Wiley and Sons, 1991); Suzanne Kreiter, "Customs Differ Widely from Those in the U.S., " *Greenville News*, September 26, 1993, p. 15D; Bradford W. Ketchum, "Going Global: East Asia-Pacific Rim," *Inc.* (Special Advertising Section), May 20, 1997; Valerie Frazee, "Getting Started in Mexico," *Global Workforce*, January 1997, pp. 16–17.

## International Trade Agreements

**5.** Describe the trade agreements that have the greatest influence on foreign trade.

In an attempt to boost world trade, nations have created a variety of trade agreements over the years. Although hundreds of agreements are paving the way for free trade across the world, the following stand out with particular significance: the World Trade Organization (WTO), the North American Free Trade Agreement (NAFTA), and the Central American Free Trade Agreement (CAFTA).

### World Trade Organization

The World Trade Organization (WTO) was established in January 1995 and replaced the General Agreement of Tariffs and Trade (GATT), the first global tariff agreement, which was created in 1947 and designed to reduce tariffs among member nations. The WTO, currently with 151 member countries, is the only international organization that establishes rules for trade among nations. Its member countries represent more than 97 percent of all world trade. The rules and agreements of the WTO, called the **multilateral trading system**, are the result of negotiations among its members. The WTO actively implements the rules established by the Uruguay Round negotiations of General Agreement on Tariffs and Trade from 1986 to 1994 and continues to negotiate additional trade agreements.

Through the agreements of the WTO, members commit themselves to nondiscriminatory trade practices. These agreements spell out the rights and obligations of each member country. Each member country receives guarantees that its exports will be treated fairly and consistently in other member countries' markets. The WTO's General Agreement on Trade in Services (GATS) addresses specific industries, including banking, insurance, telecommunications, and tourism. In addition, the WTO's intellectual property agreement, which covers patents, copyrights, and trademarks, defines rules for protecting ideas and creativity across borders. The WTO also includes an Antidumping Agreement that allows governments to take action against companies that dump their products into foreign markets at prices that are much lower than in their home markets.

In addition to the development of agreements among members, the WTO is involved in the resolution of trade disputes among members. The WTO system is designed to encourage dispute resolutions through consultation. If this approach fails, the WTO has a stage-by-stage procedure that can culminate in a ruling by a panel of experts.

## NAFTA

The North American Free Trade Agreement (NAFTA) created the world's largest free trade zone among Canada, Mexico, and the United States. A **free trade zone** is an association of countries that have agreed to eliminate trade barriers—both tariff and nontariff—among partner nations. Under the provisions of NAFTA, these barriers were eliminated for trade among the three countries, but each remained free to set its own tariffs on imports from nonmember nations.

NAFTA forged a unified U.S.-Canada-Mexico market of 406 million people with a total annual output of more than $11 trillion of goods and services. This important trade agreement binds together the three nations on the North American continent into a single trading unit stretching from the Yukon to the Yucatan. Today, Canada and Mexico are the largest trading partners for companies in the United States.

NAFTA's provisions include:

- *Tariff reductions.* Immediate reduction and then a gradual phasing out of most tariffs on goods traded among the three countries.
- *Nontariff barriers eliminated.* Elimination of most nontariff barriers to free trade by 2008.
- *Simplified border processing.* Mexico, in particular, opens its border and interior to U.S. truckers and simplifies border processing.
- *Tougher health and safety standard.* Industrial standards involving worker health and safety become more stringent and more uniform.

## The Central America Free Trade Agreement

The Central America Free Trade Agreement (CAFTA) is to Central America what NAFTA is to North America. The agreement, which took effect on August 2, 2005, is designed to promote free trade among the United States and seven Central American countries: Costa Rica, El Salvador, Guatemala, Honduras, Dominican Republic, Panama, and Nicaragua.[63] In addition to reducing tariffs among these nations, CAFTA protects companies' investments and intellectual property in the region, simplifies the export process for companies, and provides easier access to Central American markets.

*Big Ass Fan Company*

Working with the U.S. Department of Commerce to cultivate international contacts, the Big Ass Fan Company (BAFC), a Lexington, Kentucky-based maker of oversized fans (8- to 24-feet) that are used in large industrial and commercial buildings, has increased its export sales to 10 percent of the company's total sales. The company recently landed its first sale in Honduras as a result of CAFTA, and Bill Buell, the "international guy" for BAFC expects sales to Central America to grow.[64]

## Conclusion

For a rapidly growing number of small businesses, conducting business on a global basis will be the key to future success. A small company going global exposes itself to certain risks, but, if planned and executed properly, a global strategy can produce huge rewards. To remain competitive, businesses of all sizes must assume a global posture. Global effectiveness requires managers to be able to leverage workers' skills, company resources, and customer know-how across borders and throughout cultures across the world. Managers also must concentrate on maintaining competitive cost structures and a focus on the core of every business—the *customer*! Robert G. Shaw, CEO of International Jensen Inc., a global maker of home and automobile stereo speakers, explains the importance of retaining that customer focus as his company pursues its global strategy: "We want [our customers] to have the attitude of [our] being across the street. If we're going to have a global company, we have to behave in that mode—whether [the customer is] across the street—or seven miles, seven minutes, or 7,000 miles away."[65]

Few businesses can afford the luxury of basing the definition of their target market on the boundaries of their home organization's borders. The manager of one global business, who discourages the use of the word *domestic* among his employees, says, "Where's 'domestic' when the world is your market?"[66] Although there are no sure-fire rules for going global, small businesses wanting to become successful international competitors should observe these guidelines:

- Make yourself at home in all three of the world's key markets—Asia, North America, and Europe. This triad of regions is forging a new world order in trade that will dominate global markets for years to come. Small companies that focus on business opportunities in the fast-growing economies of Brazil, Russia, India, and China are likely to benefit most because forecasts call for these four nations to account for 44 percent of global GDP by 2050.[67]
- Appeal to the similarities within the various regions in which you operate but recognize the differences in their specific cultures. Although the European Union is a single trading bloc comprised of 27 countries with a combined population of 490 million people, smart entrepreneurs know that each country has its own cultural uniqueness and do not treat them as a unified market.
- Be willing to commit the necessary resources to make your global efforts successful. Going global requires an investment of time, talent, money, and patience.
- Develop new products for the world market. Make sure your products and services measure up to world-class quality standards.
- Use the many resources available such as the International Trade Administration to research potential markets and to determine the ideal target market for your products.
- Familiarize yourself with foreign customs and languages; constantly scan, clip, and build a file on the cultures of countries where you are likely to do business—their lifestyles, values, customs, and business practices.
- Learn to understand your customers from the perspective of *their* culture, not your own. Bridge cultural gaps by being willing to adapt your business practices to suit their preferences and customs.
- "Glocalize." Make global decisions about products, markets, and management, but allow local employees to make tactical decisions about packaging, advertising, and service. Building relationships with local companies that have solid reputations in a region or a country can help overcome resistance, lower risks, and encourage residents to think of them as local companies.
- Make positive and preferably visible contributions to the local community. A company's social responsibility does not stop at the borders of its home country. Seattle-based Starbucks enhances its reputation in the Chinese communities in which it does business by donating coffee and snacks for local celebrations such as the Autumn Moon Festival. Once, when a group of protesters approached the U.S. Embassy in

Beijing, they stopped at a nearby Starbucks café to buy coffee. Rather than being the object of a protest, the branch actually saw sales climb![68]

■ Train employees to think globally, send them on international trips, and equip them with state-of-the-art communications technology.

■ Hire local managers to staff foreign offices and branches.

■ Do whatever seems best wherever it seems best, even if people at home lose jobs or responsibilities.

■ Consider using partners and joint ventures to break into foreign markets you cannot penetrate on your own.

By its very nature, going global can be a frightening experience for an entrepreneur considering the jump into international markets. Most of those who have already made the jump, however, have found that the benefits outweigh the risks and that their companies are much stronger because of it.

## Chapter Review

1. Explain why "going global" has become an integral part of many entrepreneurs' marketing strategies.
   - Companies that move into international business can reap many benefits, including offsetting sales declines in the domestic market by increasing sales and profits; extending their products' life cycles; lowering manufacturing costs; improving competitive position; raising quality levels; and becoming more customer oriented.

2. Describe the nine principal strategies for going global.
   - Perhaps the simplest and least expensive way for a small business to begin conducting business globally is to establish a site on the World Wide Web. Companies wanting to sell goods on the Web should establish a secure ordering and payment system for online customers.
   - Trade intermediaries such as export management companies, export trading companies, manufacturer's export agents, export merchants, resident buying offices, and foreign distributors can serve as a small company's "export department."
   - In a domestic joint venture, two or more domestic small companies form an alliance for the purpose of exporting their goods and services abroad. In a foreign joint venture, a domestic small business forms an alliance with a company in the target area.
   - Some small businesses enter foreign markets by licensing businesses in other nations to use their patents, trademarks, copyrights, technology, processes, or products.
   - Over the past decade, a growing number of franchises have been attracted to international markets to boost sales and profits as the domestic market has become increasingly saturated with outlets and much tougher to wring growth from. International franchisers sell virtually every kind of product or service imaginable in global markets. Most franchisers have learned that they must modify their products and services to suit local tastes and customs.
   - Some countries lack a hard currency that is convertible into other currencies, so companies doing business there must rely on countertrading or bartering. A countertrade is a transaction in which a business selling goods in a foreign country agrees to promote investment and trade in that country. Bartering involves trading goods and services for other goods and services.
   - Although small companies account for 97 percent of the companies involved in exporting, they generate only 29 percent of the nation's export sales. However, small companies, realizing the incredible profit potential it offers, are making exporting an ever-expanding part of their marketing plans.

- Once established in international markets, some small businesses set up permanent locations there. Although they can be very expensive to establish and maintain, international locations give businesses the opportunity to stay in close contact with their international customers.
- In addition to selling their goods in foreign markets, small companies also buy goods from distributors and manufacturers in foreign markets. Many companies either import goods or outsource work directly to manufacturers in countries where costs are far lower than they would be domestically.

**3.** Explain how to build a thriving export program.
- Building a successful export program takes patience and research. Steps include: realize that even the tiniest firms have the potential to export; analyze your product or service; analyze your commitment to exporting; research markets and pick your target; develop a distribution strategy; find your customer; find financing; ship your goods; and collect your money.

**4.** Discuss the major barriers to international trade and their impact on the global economy.
- Three domestic barriers to international trade are common: the attitude that "we're too small to export," lack of information on how to get started in global trade, and a lack of available financing.
- International barriers include tariffs, quotas, embargoes, and dumping.
- Other barriers to international trade include political, business, and cultural barriers.

**5.** Describe the trade agreements that will have the greatest influence on foreign trade into the twenty-first century.
- Created in 1947, the General Agreement on Tariffs and Trade (GATT), the first global tariff agreement, was designed to reduce tariffs among member nations and to facilitate trade across the globe. The World Trade Organization (WTO) was established in 1995 and replaced GATT. The WTO has 151 member nations and represents over 97 percent of all global trade. The WTO is the governing body that resolves trade disputes among members.
- The North American Free Trade Agreement (NAFTA) created a free trade area among Canada, Mexico, and the United States. The agreement created an association that knocked down trade barriers, both tariff and nontariff, among these partner nations.
- The Central America Free Trade Agreement (CAFTA) is to Central America what NAFTA is to North America. The agreement, which took effect on August 2, 2005, is designed to promote free trade among the United States and seven Central American countries: Costa Rica, El Salvador, Guatemala, Honduras, Dominican Republic, Panama, and Nicaragua.

## Discussion Questions

1. Why must entrepreneurs learn to think globally?
2. What forces are driving small businesses into international markets?
3. What advantages and risks does going global offer a small business owner?
4. Outline the nine strategies that small businesses can use to go global.
5. Describe the various types of trade intermediaries small business owners can use. Explain the functions they perform.
6. What is a domestic joint venture? A foreign joint venture? What advantages does taking on an international partner through a joint venture offer? Disadvantages?
7. What mistakes are first-time exporters most likely to make? Outline the steps a small company should take to establish a successful export program.
8. What are the benefits of establishing international locations? Disadvantages?
9. Describe the barriers businesses face when trying to conduct business internationally. How can a small business owner overcome these obstacles?
10. What is a tariff? A quota? What impact do they have on international trade?

11. Thirty furniture makers in the United States recently asked the U.S. International Trade Commission to impose high tariffs on Chinese makers of wooden bedroom furniture for dumping their products in the U.S. market at extremely low prices. The U.S. manufacturers claimed that the Chinese imports single-handedly sent their industry into a deep tailspin. The Chinese factory owners contend that their low-cost furniture is the result of taking a labor-intensive product and building it with low-priced workers in high-tech modern factories. Identify the stakeholders in this trade dispute. What are the consequences for each stakeholder likely to be if the ITC were to impose tariffs on Chinese furniture? What impact do tariffs have on international trade? If you served on the International Trade Commission, what factors would you consider in making your decision? How would you vote in this case? Explain.

12. What impact have the WTO and NAFTA had on small companies wanting to go global? What provisions are included in these trade agreements?

13. What advice would you offer an entrepreneur interested in launching a global business effort?

---

# Business PlanPro

Are there global opportunities for your business? If so, include them as an "opportunity" in your SWOT analysis. Review the other sections that will benefit from incorporating these global plans into your business plan strategy. For example, you may need to address your global strategy in the marketing strategy and the Web site sections of your business plan. You may need to include additional expenses in the financial section of your business plan relating to your global strategy.

## On the Web

There are a number of Web resources that may assist with developing global strategies. You will find several of those links at the Companion Website www.prenhall.com/scarborough. One specific site that may be helpful is a management portal for global strategy at www.themanager.org/Knowledgebase/Strategy/Global.

## In the Software

If you plan to employ a global strategy, make certain that you have addressed that intent in your business plan. International activity of any kind will have implications to several sections of your business plan, including your products and services, market analysis, strategy, implementation, Web plans, management, and financial sections.

This is also an excellent time to review your entire plan, paying specific attention to the summary sections at the beginning of each major section. You may have used these areas for notes and now is a good time to review what you have written in each of these sections. Make certain the summaries provide a brief overview of what each section contains. Those sections include:

- Company
- Product and Services
- Market Analysis
- Strategy and Implementation
- Web Plan
- Management Plan
- Financial Plan

These initial introductory statements will add flow to your plan. You may also want to review each section to avoid redundancy and optimize the efficiency of your overall plan.

## Building Your Business Plan

As you near the final stages of creating your business plan, have others review your plan. Do they understand the "story" your business plan is telling? Do they follow your rationale? Do they have questions that the plan should address? Based on their comments, assess whether the plan is successful at communicating your message. If there are deficiencies, make the necessary changes to improve your plan.

# E-Commerce and Entrepreneurship

Almost overnight, the Internet's gone from a technical wonder to a business must.

—Bill Schrader

In the mental geography of e-commerce, distance has been eliminated. There is only one economy and one market.

—Peter Drucker

## *Learning Objectives*

**Upon completion of this chapter, you will be able to:**

1 Describe the benefits of selling on the World Wide Web.

2 Understand the factors an entrepreneur should consider before launching into e-commerce.

3 Explain the 12 myths of e-commerce and how to avoid falling victim to them.

4 Explain the basic strategies entrepreneurs should follow to achieve success in their e-commerce efforts.

5 Learn the techniques of designing a killer Web site.

6 Explain how companies track the results from their Web sites.

7 Describe how e-businesses ensure the privacy and security of the information they collect and store from the Web.

-commerce is creating a new economy, one that is connecting producers, sellers, and customers via technology in ways that have never been possible before. The result is a new method of doing business that is turning traditional methods of commerce and industry on their heads. Companies that ignore the impact of the Internet on their markets run the risk of becoming as relevant to customers as rotary-dial telephones. The most successful small companies are embracing the Internet, not as merely another advertising medium or marketing tool but as a mechanism for transforming their companies and changing *everything* about the way they do business. As these companies discover new, innovative ways to use the Internet, computers, and communications technology to connect with their suppliers and to serve their customers better, they are creating a new industrial order. In short, e-commerce has launched a revolution. Just as in previous revolutions in the business world, some old players are being ousted, and new leaders are emerging. The winners are discovering new business opportunities, new ways of designing work, and new ways of organizing and operating their businesses.

Perhaps the most visible changes are occurring in the world of retailing. Although e-commerce will not replace traditional retailing, no retailer, from the smallest corner store to industry giant Wal-Mart, can afford to ignore the impact of the Web on its business. Companies can take orders at the speed of light from anywhere in the world and at any time of day. The Internet enables companies to collect more information on customers' shopping and buying habits than any other medium in history. This ability means that companies can focus their marketing efforts like never before—for instance, selling garden supplies to customers who are most likely to buy them and not wasting resources trying to sell to those who have no interest in gardening. The capacity to track customers' Web-based shopping habits allows companies to personalize their approaches to marketing and to realize the benefits of individualized (or one-to-one) marketing (refer to Chapter 9, "Building a Guerrilla Marketing Plan"). Ironically, the same Web-based marketing approach that allows companies to get so personal with their customers also can make shopping extremely impersonal. Entrepreneurs who set up shop on the Web will likely never meet their customers face-to-face or even talk to them. Yet those customers, who can live anywhere in the world, will visit the online store at all hours of the day or night and expect to receive individual attention. Making a Web-based marketing approach succeed requires a business to strike a balance, creating an e-commerce strategy that capitalizes on the strengths of the Web while meeting customers' expectations of convenience and service.

In this fast-paced world of e-commerce, size no longer matters as much as speed and flexibility do. One of the Web's greatest strengths is its interactive nature, the ability to provide companies with instantaneous customer feedback, giving them the opportunity to learn and to make necessary adjustments. Businesses, whatever their size, that are willing to experiment with different approaches to reaching customers and are quick to learn and adapt will grow and prosper; those that cannot will fall by the wayside. The Internet is creating a new industrial order, and companies that fail to adapt to it will soon become extinct.

E-commerce is redefining even the most traditional industries such as the retail grocery business. Despite the legacy of Webvan, an Internet grocer that proved to be one of the greatest failures of the dot-bomb era (burning through nearly $1 billion in venture capital before flaming out), several grocers are challenging the traditional industry model with Web-based ventures.

*FreshDirect Inc.*

FreshDirect Inc. in New York City has 100,000 customers in Manhattan for its Web grocery service, which offers more than 8,000 types of fresh meats, vegetables, and other grocery items delivered directly to shoppers' homes for a flat $3.95 fee. Using the business model perfected by computer maker Dell Inc., FreshDirect fills online orders as customers place them and then delivers them using its fleet of trucks. Business is going so well that the company plans to begin selling gourmet foods such as caviar, fancy meats, and cheeses to customers across the country from its Web site. "We're about food," says cofounder and CEO Joe Fedele. "The Internet is just a tool. The only reason we chose the Internet was that it helped us reach people at a lower transaction cost."[1]

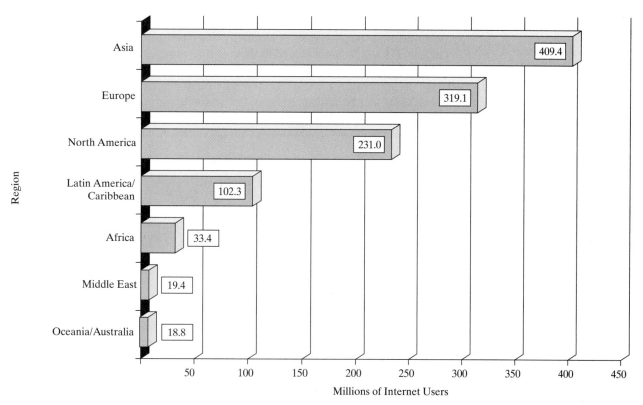

**FIGURE 13.1  Number of Internet Users (in Millions)**

*Source:* Data from Internet Usage Statistics: The Big Picture, Internet World Stats, 2007, www.internetworldstats.com/stats.htm.

High-volume, low-margin commodity products tend to be best suited for selling on the Web. Although the most popular items purchased online vary from one country to another, the items that customers purchase most often online include books, music, travel services, clothing, computer hardware and software, consumer electronics, cosmetics, and jewelry. However, companies can—and do—sell practically anything over the Web, from antiques and pharmaceuticals to popcorn and drug-free urine.

Companies of all sizes are establishing a presence on the Web because that's where their customers are. The number of Internet users worldwide now stands at more than 1.1 billion (see Figure 13.1), up from 147 million at the end of 1998.[2] Forrester Research reports that consumers in North America spend more time online than they do watching television, reading magazines, and listening to the radio combined.[3] Consumers have adopted the Internet much more quickly than any other major innovation in the past. It

**"First of all—you need a Web site."**

reached 50 percent penetration in the United States in just seven years, compared to 30 years for the computer, 40 years for electricity, and more than 100 years for steam power.[4] In the United States, e-commerce sales, both business-to-business (B2B) and business-to-consumer (B2C), will reach $144 billion in 2010, which amounts to a 12 percent annual growth rate. In addition, a survey by JupiterResearch reports that by 2010, 49 percent of total purchases will be influenced by online research, up from 27 percent in 2005.[5] Although the torrid growth rates of online sales will not last indefinitely, the Web represents a tremendous opportunity that businesses simply cannot afford to ignore.

## Benefits of Selling on the Web

*1.* Describe the benefits of selling on the World Wide Web.

According to a study by Interland, a company that provides online services for small businesses, 78 percent of small business owners whose firms have Web sites report that their businesses benefit by having a site. The major benefits they cite include enhanced credibility, improved marketing efforts, higher sales, and lower costs.[6] Although a Web-based sales strategy does not guarantee success, small companies that have established Web sites realize many benefits, including the following:

■ *The opportunity to increase revenues.*  For many small businesses, launching a Web site is the equivalent of opening a new sales channel. Companies that launch e-commerce efforts soon discover that their sites are generating additional sales from new customers.

**ENTREPRENEURIAL**
**Profile**

*The Cheesecake Factory*

The Cheesecake Factory, a California company that operates a chain of restaurants, had been selling its specialty desserts through traditional mail-order channels when managers decided in 2002 to begin offering them on the company's Web site. The boost from the Web enabled the Cheesecake Factory to double its catalog sales in less than one year, and Web-based orders now account for more than 70 percent of all catalog orders. Because the cost of placing online orders is minimal, the Cheesecake Factory earns a higher profit margin on Web orders than on traditional telephone or mail orders.[7]

■ *The chance to attract new customers.*  In its *State of Retailing Online* study, Forrester Research reports that 38 percent of the customers that the typical online company attracts to its Web site are new customers for that business.[8]

■ *The ability of brick-and-mortar retailers to drive online customers into their stores and increase sales there.*  Owners of retail stores have discovered that setting up a Web site leads not only to increased online sales but also to higher in-store sales. Some retailers offer customers the convenience of ordering products online and then picking them up in the store. According to Forrester Research, customers pick up in person 31 percent of the orders they place online, and 27 percent of those customers make additional purchases in the store.[9]

■ *The ability to expand their reach into global markets.*  The Web is the most efficient way for small businesses to sell their products to the millions of potential customers who live outside the borders of their countries. Tapping into these global markets through more traditional methods would be too complex and too costly for the typical small business. Yet on the Web, a small company can sell its products efficiently to customers anywhere in the world at any time of day.

■ *The ability to remain open 24 hours a day, seven days a week.*  More than half of all retail sales occur after 6 P.M., when many traditional stores close. Extending the hours a brick-and-mortar store remains open can increase sales, but it also takes a toll on the business owner and the employees. With a Web site up and running, however, a small company can sell around the clock without having to incur additional staffing expenses. Customers never have to worry about whether or not an online store is "open."

■ *The capacity to use the Web's interactive nature to enhance customer service.*  Although selling on the Web can be highly impersonal because of the lack of human interaction, companies that design their sites properly can create an exciting, interactive experience for their online visitors. Customers can contact a company at any time of the day, can control the flow of information they get, and in some cases can interact with company representatives in real time. In addition, technology now allows companies to "personalize" their sites to suit the tastes and preferences of individual customers. Drawing on a database containing information customers have provided in the past, modern Web sites can customize themselves, displaying content that appeals to an individual visitor. For instance, a site selling clothing can greet a returning customer by name and ask if she is shopping for herself or for someone on her personal shopping list. Based on her response, the site can recall appropriate sizes and favorite styles and colors and can even make product recommendations.

■ ***The power to educate and to inform.*** Far more than most marketing media, the Web gives entrepreneurs the power to educate and to inform customers. Women and members of Generation Y, especially, crave product information before they make purchases. The Web allows business owners to provide more detailed information to visitors than practically any other medium. For instance, a travel company advertising an Alaskan tour in a newspaper or magazine might include a brief description of the tour, a list of the destinations, a telephone number, the price, and perhaps a photo or two. A Web-based promotion for the same tour could include all of the information just mentioned as well as a detailed itinerary with dozens of breathtaking photographs; descriptions and photographs of all accommodations; advice on what to pack; airline schedules, seating configurations, and availability; information on optional side trips; comments from customers who have taken this tour before; and links to other Web sites about Alaska, the weather, and fun things to do in the region.[10] Companies that provide shoppers with useful information have an edge when it comes to attracting and retaining customers.

■ ***The ability to lower the cost of doing business.*** The Web is one of the most efficient ways of reaching both new and existing customers. Properly promoted, a Web site can reduce a company's cost of generating sales leads, providing customer support, and distributing marketing materials. For instance, sending customers an e-mail newsletter is much less expensive than paying the printing and postage costs of sending the same newsletter by "snail mail."

■ ***The capacity to improve the efficiency of purchasing and inventory control processes.*** The Internet also has the potential to improve the efficiency of small companies' purchasing and inventory control processes. In a study by BuyerZone, an online marketplace for business purchasing, more than 75 percent of small business owners say that using the Internet in their purchasing decisions allows them to save both money and time making buying decisions.[11] By integrating its Web site and its inventory control system, a company also can shorten its sales cycle and reduce its inventory costs. Linking its Web orders directly to suppliers enables a business to cut purchasing costs even more.

---

**ENTREPRENEURIAL**
**Profile**

*FreshDirect Inc.*

FreshDirect Inc., the online grocer, uses the Internet to shorten its supply chain for seafood, resulting in higher-quality products for its customers and a smaller investment inventory for the company. As boats arrive at the docks in New York City in the early evening, FreshDirect representatives place initial orders. At midnight, FreshDirect stops taking customer orders for the next day and provides exact orders and quantities to its seafood buyers. The shipments arrive around 3 A.M. at the company's 300,000-square-foot processing center, where employees cut and package them into customers' desired orders, a process that is completed by mid-morning. Customer deliveries begin at 4 P.M. that same day, often resulting in a "dock-to-door" time of less than 24 hours! FreshDirect typically has just one day's worth of seafood inventory in stock, compared to seven to nine days' worth at a traditional grocery store.[12]

■ *The ability to spot new business opportunities and to capitalize on them.* E-commerce companies are poised to give customers just what they want when they want it. As the number of dual-career couples rises and the amount of available leisure time shrinks, consumers are looking for ways to increase the convenience of shopping, and the Web is fast becoming the solution they seek. Increasingly, customers view shopping as an unpleasant chore that cuts into already scarce leisure time, and they are embracing anything that reduces the amount of time they must spend shopping. (One study of New York shoppers by Visa reports that 42 percent of people prefer to clean their bathrooms and 18 percent would rather visit the dentist than stand in a checkout line![13]) Entrepreneurs who tap into customers' need to buy goods more conveniently and with less hassle are winning the battle for market share. New opportunities to serve customers' changing needs and wants are arising constantly, and the Web is the birthplace of many of them.

■ *The power to track sales results.* The Web gives businesses the power to track virtually any kind of activity on their Web sites, from the number of visitors to the click-through rates on their banner ads. With modern Web analytics tools, entrepreneurs can track not only the number of visitors to their sites but also how they got there, how they maneuver around the site, and what they buy. Web entrepreneurs can experiment with different designs and layouts for their sites to determine their impact on the site's **conversion rate**, the percentage of visitors to a Web site who actually make a purchase. This timely information allows entrepreneurs to judge the value their sites are producing for their companies and to improve the effectiveness of their sites.

■ *The opportunity to build credibility and a brand identity among customers.* Many entrepreneurs who operate off-line businesses have discovered that launching a Web site enhances their company's reputation among existing and potential customers. A well-designed Web site can help a small company differentiate itself from its competitors, especially those that lack Web sites, whether or not the company does business online. One business writer says, "A company that neglects its Web site may be committing commercial suicide. A Web site is increasingly becoming the gateway to a company's brand, products, and services—even if the firm does not sell online." [14]

*Charlie and Eddie Bakhash and American Pearl*

In 1950, Charlie Bakhash started American Pearl, a wholesale business that imported high-quality pearls from Japan, setting up shop in a tiny storefront in the diamond district in the heart of Manhattan. Charlie moved to Japan in 1952 so that he could expand his network of suppliers and maintain a steady supply of the best pearls available. Over the course of the next 50 years, Charlie became one of the most respected dealers in the global pearl business, and during that time, his company handled more than one million pearl strands. In 1990, Charlie's son, Eddie, took over the family business, opened a retail operation, and in a radical move for 1997—the very early days of the Internet—went online. (Charlie still goes on buying trips to the Far East.) Eddie knew that in a "hands-on" business such as jewelry, creating a Web site (www.americanpearl.com) that built customer confidence in the company was essential. To establish that level of confidence, Eddie devoted much of the site's content to educating visitors about pearls, buying them, and caring for them. American Pearl's e-commerce strategy worked and has been the driving force behind the company's impressive 10-year annual growth rate of 20 percent. Sales now exceed $20 million a year, with 20 percent originating in the retail store and 80 percent from online sales.[15]

## Factors to Consider Before Launching into E-Commerce

*2. Understand the factors an entrepreneur should consider before launching into e-commerce.*

Despite the many benefits the Web offers, not every small business owner has embraced e-commerce. According to a study by the National Small Business Association, 40 percent of small companies do not have Web sites, and only 36 percent of small businesses actually engage in e-commerce.[16] Why are so many small companies hesitant to use the Web as a business tool? For many entrepreneurs, the key barrier is not knowing where or how to start an e-commerce effort, whereas for others cost concerns are a major issue. Other roadblocks include the fear that customers will not use the Web site and the problems associated with ensuring online security.

Whatever the size of their companies, entrepreneurs are realizing that establishing a presence on the Web is no longer a luxury. "A Web site is your ticket to get into the game," says the CEO of one high-tech company. "If you don't have one, you might as well not even name your business."[17] Indeed, business owners who are not at least considering creating a Web presence or integrating the Web creatively into their operations are putting their companies at risk. However, before launching an e-commerce effort, business owners should consider the following important issues:

- How a company exploits the Web's interconnectivity and the opportunities it creates to transform relationships with its suppliers and vendors, its customers, and other external stakeholders is crucial to its success.
- Web success requires a company to develop a plan for integrating the Web into its overall strategy. The plan should address issues such as site design and maintenance, creating and managing a brand name, marketing and promotional strategies, sales, and customer service.
- Developing deep, lasting relationships with customers takes on even greater importance on the Web. Attracting customers on the Web costs money, and companies must be able to retain their online customers to make their Web sites profitable.
- Creating a meaningful presence on the Web requires an ongoing investment of resources—time, money, energy, and talent. Establishing an attractive Web site brimming with catchy photographs of products is only the beginning.
- Measuring the success of its Web-based sales effort is essential to remaining relevant to customers whose tastes, needs, and preferences are always changing.

Doing business on the Web takes more time and energy than many entrepreneurs think. Answering the following questions will help entrepreneurs make sure they are ready to do business on the Web and avoid unpleasant surprises in their e-commerce efforts:

- What exactly do you expect a Web site to do for your company? Will it provide information only, reach new customers, increase sales to existing customers, improve communication with customers, enhance customer service, or reduce your company's cost of operation? Will customers be able to place orders from the site, or must they call your company to buy?
- How much can you afford to invest in an e-commerce effort?
- What rate of return do you expect to earn on that investment?
- How long can you afford to wait for that return?
- How well suited are your products and services to sell on the Web?
- How will the "back office" of your Web site work? Will your site be tied into your company's inventory control system?
- How will you handle order fulfillment? Can your fulfillment system handle the increase in volume you are expecting?
- What impact, if any, will your Web site have on your company's traditional channels of distribution?
- What mechanism will your site use to ensure secure customer transactions?
- How will your company handle customer service for the site? What provisions will you make for returned items?
- How do you plan to promote the site to draw traffic to it?
- What information will you collect from the visitors to your site? How will you use it? Will you tell visitors how you intend to use this information?
- Have you developed a privacy policy? Have you posted that policy on your company's Web site for customers?
- Have you tested your site with real, live customers to make sure that it is easy to navigate and easy to order from?
- How will you measure the success of your company's Web site? What objectives have you set for the site?

# Twelve Myths of E-Commerce

*3.* Explain the 12 myths of e-commerce and how to avoid falling victim to them.

Although many entrepreneurs have boosted their businesses with e-commerce, setting up shop on the Web is no guarantee of success. Scores of entrepreneurs have plunged unprepared into the world of e-commerce only to discover that there is more to it than merely setting up a Web site and waiting for the orders to start pouring in. Make sure that you do not fall victim to one of the following e-commerce myths.

## Myth 1. Setting Up a Business on the Web Is Easy and Inexpensive

Using one of the many do-it-yourself Web services, entrepreneurs can design their own bare-bones sites and find a Web host for less than $10 per month. Although practically anyone using these services can post a Web site in just a few minutes, creating an effective, professional, and polished Web site designed for e-commerce can be a more expensive, time-consuming project. Designing, maintaining, advertising, and promoting a Web site that can handle a company's e-commerce transactions ranges from just a few hundred dollars to many thousands of dollars.

*Lois Riske and General Cleaning Inc.*

Lois Riske, president of General Cleaning Inc., a 75-year-old commercial contract cleaning business in Homestead, Pennsylvania, considered building a Web site for her company and asked several Web designers for proposals. The designs did not impress her, and the estimated cost of operating the site—about $1,000 per month—convinced Riske to remain a conventional brick-and-mortar business. Because her business counts on a sales team and word-of-mouth advertising from satisfied customers, Riske did not believe that a Web site would pay for itself. "It's hard to justify that expense," she says.[18]

Hiring a Web designer to build an e-commerce site from scratch can cost more than $5,000. However, unless they need a site to handle large numbers of products or one that projects a sophisticated or unique image, many entrepreneurs use do-it-yourself design services that rely on pre-designed templates. Many companies provide templates that are aimed at small companies. Yahoo! Merchant Solutions, for example, allows entrepreneurs to select a domain name, create a Web site using one of 12 templates, establish a payment processor or a merchant account, and select a shipping company. eBay's ProStores gives Internet entrepreneurs 180 design templates from which to choose, their own Web address, a secure checkout process, and the option to adopt more sophisticated e-commerce tools at prices that range from $7 per month to $250 per month.

*Marc Derosiers and Racewax.com*

After repeatedly spending $50 for bars of wax for his son's snow ski competitions, chemist Marc Derosiers began studying the labels of the bars and realized that he could formulate his own ski wax. He whipped up several batches and began supplying them to his son and to the members of his son's ski team. "They said, 'You should sell this stuff,'" recalls Derosiers. In 1999, Derosiers built a simple Web site, racewax.com, that offered free samples and included an order form for his company, Racewax, which specializes in affordable ski and snowboard wax products. Recently, Derosiers recognized that his Web site was in need of a makeover and turned to Web hosting company ProStores to help him. ProStores helped Derosiers develop a comprehensive Web strategy that included a catchy new logo and a newly designed, more functional site that allows customers to compute shipping costs from many countries. Another bonus is that the site allows Derosiers to capture better information about his customers and their buying habits.[19]

Designing a Web site and taking it live are just the initial costs of an entrepreneur's e-commerce efforts. Companies often spend more advertising and promoting their Web sites than they spend on their initial setup. Because most Web users rely on search engines to find the products or services they are looking for online, businesses must invest in a viable search engine optimization (SEO) strategy to make their Web sites pay off. Bidding on key words so that your company's Web site pops up at the top of a user's search listing can be a significant cost of doing business online (More on this later in this chapter). Advertising and promoting the site ads to the cost of maintaining an effective Web site, but both are essential activities. Building a Web site and then failing to invest money in promoting it is pointless; online shoppers cannot buy from small companies if they do not know that they exist!

Companies that decide to operate their own e-commerce businesses quickly learn that setting up a site is only the first investment required. Sooner or later, most companies encounter follow-up investments, including updating and revising the Web site, buying more hardware to support the Web site, automating or expanding their warehouses to meet customer demand, integrating their inventory control system into the Web site, and increasing customer call-center capacity. When it comes to e-commerce, the lesson for entrepreneurs is this: Focus your efforts on the core competencies that your company has developed, whether they reside in "traditional" business practices or online, and outsource all of the other aspects of doing business online to companies that have the expertise to make your e-commerce business successful.

### Myth 2. If I Launch a Site, Customers Will Flock to It

Some entrepreneurs think that once they set up their Web sites, their expenses end there. Not true! Without promotional support, no Web site will draw enough traffic to support a business. With an estimated 600 billion Web pages already in existence and the number of new Web documents growing by 6 million per day, getting a site noticed has become increasingly difficult. Experts estimate that only about half of the Web's content is indexed and therefore retrievable by search engines.[20] Merely listing a site with popular Web search engines cannot guarantee that Web users will find a small company's site. Just like traditional retail stores seeking to attract customers, virtual companies have discovered that drawing sufficient traffic to a Web site requires promotion—and lots of it! "No one will know you're on the Web unless you tell them and motivate them to visit," explains Mark Layton, owner of a Web-based distributor of computer supplies and author of a book on e-commerce.[21]

Entrepreneurs with both physical and virtual stores must promote their Web sites at every opportunity by printing their URLs on everything related to their physical stores—on signs, in print and broadcast ads, in store windows, on shopping bags, on merchandise labels, and anywhere else their customers will see. Virtual shop owners should consider buying ads in traditional advertising media as well as using banner ads, banner exchange programs, and cross-marketing arrangements with companies selling complementary products on their own Web sites. Other techniques include creating some type of interactivity with customers such as a Web-based newsletter, posting a video about your company's products on YouTube, writing articles that link to the company's site, hosting a chat room that allows customers to interact with one another and with company personnel, incorporating a bulletin board or customer-generated reviews, establishing a Web log (or "blog," a regularly updated online journal), or sponsoring a contest. For instance, one small pet store has had success promoting both its Web site and its retail store with Howl-O-Ween, an online photo contest featuring people's dogs dressed in Halloween costumes.

Blogs are easy to create, but they require regular updating to attract visitors. Technorati, a company that tracks blogs, estimates that the Web hosts more than 75 million blogs and that bloggers are adding 175,000 new blogs per day![22] Blogs with fresh, entertaining content and a soft-sell approach can be an effective way to draw potential customers to a company's Web site. Video blogs or "vlogs," video versions of blogs, are another attention-getting tool for a small company's Web site.

*Southwest Airlines*

Low-cost airline Southwest Airlines launched a company blog called "Nuts About Southwest" to connect with its employees and customers, to promote its business, and to encourage people to visit its official Web site. Because the blog developed a loyal readership very quickly, about 30 employees, ranging from president Colleen Barrett and mechanics to pilots and flight attendants, now update it daily. Nearly two-thirds of the posts on the blog are from customers and others outside of the company. Southwest managers have discovered another benefit of the blog; it serves as a very inexpensive virtual focus group, giving them valuable feedback from customers on a variety of issues.[23]

The key to promoting a Web site successfully is networking, building relationships with customers, other companies, trade associations, online directories, and other Web sites the company's customers visit. "You need to create relationships with the businesses and people with whom you share common customers," says Barbara Ling, author of a book on e-commerce. "Then you need to create links between sites to help customers find what they are looking for."[24]

### Myth 3. Making Money on the Web Is Easy

Promoters who hawk "get-rich-quick" schemes on the Web lure many entrepreneurs with the promise that making money on the Web is easy. It isn't. Doing business online can be quite lucrative, but it takes time and requires an up-front investment. As hundreds of new Web sites spring up every day, getting a company's site noticed requires more effort and marketing muscle than ever before.

Entrepreneurs engaging in e-commerce recognize the power that the Internet gives customers. Pricing, for example, is no longer as simple as it once was for companies. Auction sites such as eBay and Priceline.com mean that entrepreneurs can no longer be content to take into account only local competitors when setting their own prices. With the Web, price transparency is now the rule of the day. With a few mouse clicks, customers can compare the prices of the same or similar products and services from companies across the globe. In this wired and connected economy, the balance of power has shifted to customers, and new business models recognize this fact.

### Myth 4. Privacy Is Not an Important Issue on the Web

The Web allows companies to gain access to almost unbelievable amounts of information about their customers. Many sites offer visitors "freebies" in exchange for information about themselves. Companies then use this information to learn more about their target customers and how to market to them most effectively. Concerns over the privacy and the use of this information have become the topic of debate by many interested parties, including government agencies, consumer watchdog groups, customers, and industry trade associations.

Companies that collect information from their online customers have a responsibility to safeguard their customers' privacy, to protect that information from unauthorized use, and to use it responsibly. That means that businesses should post a privacy statement on their Web sites, explaining to customers how they intend to use the information they collect. One of the surest ways to alienate online customers is to experience a security breach that allows their personal information to be stolen, to abuse the information collected from them by selling it to third parties, or to spam customers with unwanted solicitations. A recent survey by Internet research firm Gartner Inc. reports that 46 percent of online adults in the United States say that concerns about information theft, data breaches, and Internet-based attacks have affected their Internet purchasing behavior. The result is that online companies in the United States lose nearly $2 billion in potential sales each year because of customers' concerns about security.[25] BBBOnLine offers a useful resource center that is designed to help small business owners who want to establish or upgrade their Web site's privacy policies (www.bbbonline.org/UnderstandingPrivacy/PMRC/).

Businesses that publish privacy policies and then adhere to them build trust among their customers, an important facet of doing business on the Web. According to John Briggs, director of e-commerce for the Yahoo! Network, customers "need to trust the brand they are buying and believe that their online purchases will be safe transactions. They need to feel comfortable that [their] personal data will not be sold and that they won't get spammed by giving their e-mail address. They need to know about shipping costs, product availability, and return policies up front."[26] Privacy *does* matter on the Web, and businesses that respect their customers' privacy will win their customers' trust. Trust is the foundation on which companies build the long-term customer relationships that are so crucial to Web success.

### Myth 5. The Most Important Part of Any E-Commerce Effort Is Technology

Although understanding the technology of e-commerce is an important part of the formula for success, it is *not* the most crucial ingredient. What matters most is the ability to understand the underlying business and to develop a workable business model that offers customers something of value at a reasonable price while producing a reasonable return for the company. The entrepreneurs who are proving to be most successful in e-commerce are those who know how their industries work inside and out and then build an e-business around that knowledge. They know that they can hire Webmasters, database experts, and fulfillment companies to design the technical aspects of their online businesses, but that nothing can substitute for a solid understanding of their industry, their target market, and the strategy needed to pull the various parts together. The key is seeing the Web for what it really is: another way to reach and serve customers with an effective business model and to minimize the cost of doing business.

**ENTREPRENEURIAL**
**Profile**

*Dell Inc.*

Dell Inc., the pioneer of the online build-to-order model, has integrated the Web into its business strategy very effectively. Dell allows shoppers to customize their PCs at Dell.com, get a delivery date, and track the status of their orders at any time. Dell also uses the Web to control one of the most challenging aspects of its business: managing inventory. Dell's component suppliers log onto a special Web site to get instructions about which parts to deliver, how many to ship, and where and when to deliver them. Using the Web to tie together its supply chain, Dell keeps its inventory levels so low that it turns its inventory an amazing 60 times a year![27]

The key to Dell's success on the Web is the company's knowledge of the computer industry to which it then applies the technology of the Web. Unfortunately, many entrepreneurs tackle e-commerce by focusing on technology first and then determine how that technology fits their business idea. "If you start with technology, you're likely going to buy a solution in search of a problem," says Kip Martin, program director of META Group's Electronic Business Strategies. Instead, he suggests, "Start with the business and ask yourself what you want to happen and how you'll measure it. *Then* ask how the technology will help you achieve your goals. Remember: Business first, technology second."[28]

### Myth 6. "Strategy? I Don't Need a Strategy to Sell on the Web! Just Give Me a Web Site, and the Rest Will Take Care of Itself."

Building a successful e-business is no different than building a successful brick-and-mortar business, and that requires a well-thought-out strategy. Building a strategy means that an entrepreneur must first develop a clear definition of the company's target audience and a thorough understanding of customers' needs, wants, likes, and dislikes. To be successful, a Web site must be appealing to the customers it seeks to attract just as a traditional store's design and décor must draw foot traffic. Before your Web site can become the foundation for a successful e-business, you must create it with your target audience in mind.

Recall from Chapter 2, "Strategic Management and the Entrepreneur," that one goal of developing a strategy is to set a business apart from its competitors. The same is true for creating a strategy for conducting business online. It is just as important, if not more important, for an online business to differentiate itself from the competition if it is to be successful. Unlike customers in a retail store, who must exert the effort to go to a competitor's store if they cannot find what they want, online customers only have to make a mouse click or two to go to a rival Web site. Therefore, competition online is fierce, and to succeed, a company must have a sound strategy.

**ENTREPRENEURIAL**
**Profile**

*Nick Swinmurn and Zappos*

Zappos bills itself as the Web's most popular shoe store. The company, founded in 1999 by Nick Swinmurn after a frustrating and fruitless trip to a local mall in search of shoes, offers online customers a huge selection of shoes, including dress and athletic shoes for men and women, extra-wide shoes for hard-to-fit feet, and even "vegetarian" shoes made from materials other than leather. Swinmurn's strategy for Zappos is simple: offer customers the greatest variety and selection of shoes possible to gain an edge over brick-and-mortar stores that are limited in the stock that they can carry. Zappos stocks more than 90,000 styles in a wide array of sizes of more than 500 brands for a total inventory of nearly 2 million pairs of shoes. As part of Zappos' commitment to customer service, the company offers free expedited shipping (even on shoes that customers return) and a so-phisticated warehouse system that provides shoppers real-time information on the availability of any particular shoe. CEO Tony Hsieh says that Zappos' focus on its customers (evidenced by its free shipping policy, which costs more than $100 million annually) is the reason that 65 percent of Zappos shoppers are repeat customers. Its strategy is working. The company now has 4 million customers and commands 20 percent of the $3 billion online footwear market.[29]

Zappos CEO Tony Hsieh.

### Myth 7. On the Web, Customer Service Is Not as Important as It Is in a Traditional Retail Store

The Web offers shoppers the ultimate in convenience. With just a few mouse clicks, people can shop for practically anything anywhere in the world and have it delivered to their doorsteps within days. In fact, more than 70 percent of online shoppers say that they do so because it is easier and more convenient than other shopping methods.[30] As convenient as online shopping is, customers still expect high levels of customer service. Unfortunately, many e-commerce companies treat customer service as an afterthought, an attitude that costs businesses in many ways, including lost customers and a diminished public image. In one recent study, 82 percent of shoppers who had experienced a frustrating online shopping experience reported that they were not likely to return to the online store. The study also revealed 28 percent of shoppers said that they were less likely to shop at the retailer's physical store, and 55 percent said that their negative online experience had a negative impact on their perception of the company.[31]

The average conversion rate for e-commerce sites is just 2.4 percent, down from 3.1 percent in 2001.[32] In other words, out of 1,000 visitors to the typical company's Web site, just 24 of them actually make a purchase! Sites that are difficult to navigate, slow to load, offer complex checkout systems, or confuse shoppers will turn customers away quickly, never to return. Online merchants must recognize that customer service is just as important (if not more so) on the Web as it is in traditional brick-and-mortar stores.

There is plenty of room for improvement in customer service on the Web. Research shows that 48 percent of Web shoppers who fill their online shopping carts become frustrated and abandon them without checking out.[33] The most common reasons for leaving a site without purchasing include the following: (1) the customer was simply comparison shopping, (2) shipping and handling charges were too high, (3) the checkout process required too much time and too much information to make a purchase, (4) the product was out of stock, and (5) the customer was uncomfortable with the sites' buying process. Even more alarming is the fact that 47 percent of the owners of e-businesses do not know their sites' shopping cart abandonment rate.[34]

E-commerce entrepreneurs can reduce the likelihood that customers will leave their companies' Web sites frustrated and unlikely to return by taking the following steps: [35]

- Consider providing free shipping if a customer's order exceeds some minimum purchase. Research by Wharton professor David Bell shows that companies that want to fill relatively few orders should establish higher free shipping thresholds; firms that want customers to visit regularly—perhaps so that they can sell ads on their site—should use lower shipping thresholds. Approximately 60 percent of online retailers say that providing free shipping (with conditions) is their most successful marketing tool.[36]
- If you do not offer free shipping, provide multiple shipping methods and be sure to include a table that shows shoppers the cost of each shipping option—and do it early in the checkout process.
- Reduce the number of steps required to complete the checkout process. Just as in regular retail stores, online customers appreciate a quick, efficient checkout process that is as simple as possible. A convoluted checkout process is an invitation to customers to abandon their shopping carts.
- Include a progress indicator on each checkout page. Clearly numbering the steps in the process and letting customers know where they are in that process will improve customer retention rates during checkout.
- Provide a link back to the items in the customers' shopping cart. This allows customers to return to the product page to make sure they selected the correct item without losing their place in the checkout process.
- Allow customers to see whether an item is in stock on the product page. Customers become frustrated when they learn that an item is out of stock *after* having clicked through most or all of the checkout process.
- Include product photos in the shopping cart. Research shows that simply including product photos increases a company's conversion rate by as much as 10 percent.
- Make it easy for customers to change the contents of their shopping carts. The cart page should allow customers to change quantities, colors, sizes, and other options or to delete an item from the cart (believe it or not!) with just one mouse click.
- Give customers the option of calling to resolve problems they encounter during checkout. A toll-free line enables a company to track the number of problem-solving calls, which can point out flaws in the design of the Web site or the checkout process.
- Make it easy for customers to pay for their online purchases. Credit cards are a popular online payment method, but many small online merchants do not generate enough revenue to justify the costs of gaining credit card merchant status. If a small company's credit card sales are no more than $250 per month, a credit card company charges about 35 percent of each transaction, compared to just 3 to 5 percent of monthly credit card sales of at least $7,500 per month. Electronic payment services such as Google's Checkout or PayPal, which is owned by eBay, allow customers to send payments to anyone with an e-mail address through their checking accounts or their credit cards. Customers who sign up for the free service can use their PayPal accounts to buy products online conveniently, and PayPal charges the company

making the sale a fee that ranges from 1.9 percent to 2.9 percent of the transaction, depending on its monthly transaction volume. When a merchant signs on with PayPal, it simply adds PayPal's "Buy Now" button to its site, which customers click on to pay with their PayPal accounts.

*Kurt Denke and Pam Moore and Blue Jeans Cable*

Kurt Denke and Pam Moore launched Blue Jeans Cable, a company that sells high-quality video and audio cable and connectors as a part-time, home-based, e-Bay business. Sales grew quickly, and in 2002, the copreneurs decided to launch their own Web site, but they needed a low-cost, convenient, and secure payment processing system. "We looked at all kinds of payment processing solutions," recalls Denke. "The initial fees to set up a merchant [account] and payment processing gateway were just too much." Denke and Moore settled on PayPal, which charges no up-front or monthly fees, offers very competitive processing rates, and provides a free shopping cart feature. The couple frequently downloads their merchant sales report and analyzes it to understand better their customers' buying habits. Denke and Moore's home-based business has "exceeded our wildest expectations," says Denke. Sales are rising fast, and 95 percent of Blue Jeans Cable's sales are processed through PayPal.[37]

■ Incorporate a short survey of randomly chosen customers who abandon their shopping carts. The results can help companies to improve their online shopping experience and to lower their cart abandonment rates.

In an attempt to improve the level of service they offer, many sites provide e-mail links to encourage customer interaction. Unfortunately, e-mail takes a very low priority at many e-businesses. One study by JupiterResearch found that 42 percent of business Web sites took longer than five days to respond to e-mail inquiries, never replied at all, or simply were not accessible by e-mail![38] The lesson for e-commerce entrepreneurs is simple: Devote time, energy, and money to developing a functional mechanism for providing superior customer service. Those who do will build a sizable base of loyal customers who will keep coming back. Perhaps the most significant actions online companies can take to bolster their customer service efforts are providing a quick online checkout process, creating a well-staffed and well-trained customer response team, offering a simple return process, and providing an easy order-tracking process so customers can check the status of their orders at any time.

### Myth 8. Flash Makes a Web Site Better

Businesses that fall into this trap pour most of their e-commerce budgets into designing flashy Web sites with all of the "bells and whistles." The logic is that to stand out on the Web, a site really has to sparkle. That logic leads to a "more is better" mentality when designing a site. On the Web, however, "more" does *not* necessarily equate to "better." Although fancy graphics, bright colors, playful music, and spinning icons can attract attention, they also can be quite distracting and very slow to download. Sites that download slowly may never have the chance to sell because customers will click to another site. Research by JupiterResearch shows that 33 percent of dissatisfied Web shoppers' major complaints concerned Web sites that are too slow to load. The lesson: Keep the design of your site simple so that pages download in no more than four seconds.[39]

*Travelocity*

Travelocity, once the largest online travel agency, recently revamped its Web site after studies showed that it lacked distinction and overloaded customers with information that was poorly organized. "Consumers said, 'You're all cluttered, almost like a Turkish bazaar,'" says Jeff Glueck, the company's chief marketing officer. The redesigned site cuts the information on the Travelocity home page by half, organizes that information in a more intuitive manner, and uses more subdued colors. Rather than being overwhelmed with information when they arrive at the site, customers now use drop-down menus to access the travel and booking information they need.[40]

### Myth 9. It's What's Up Front That Counts

Designing an attractive Web site is important to building a successful e-business. However, designing the back office, the systems that take over once a customer places an order on a Web site, is just as important as designing the site itself. If the behind-the-scenes support is not in place or cannot handle the traffic from the Web site, a company's entire e-commerce effort will come crashing down. Although e-commerce can lower many costs of doing business, it still requires a basic infrastructure somewhere in the channel of distribution to process orders, maintain inventory, fill orders, and handle customer service. Many entrepreneurs hoping to launch virtual businesses are discovering the need for a "clicks-and-mortar" approach to provide the necessary infrastructure to serve their customers. "The companies with warehouses, supply-chain management, and solid customer service are going to be the ones that survive," says Daryl Plummer, head of the Gartner Group's Internet and new media division.[41]

To customers, a business is only as good as its last order, and many e-companies are not measuring up. Many small e-tailers' Web sites do not offer real-time inventory look-up, which gives online shoppers the ability to see whether an item they want to purchase is actually in stock. In addition, many have not yet linked their Web sites to an automated back office, which means that processing orders takes longer and that errors are more likely. As software to integrate Web sites with the back office becomes easier to use and more affordable, more businesses will offer these features, but in the meantime some customers will have to endure late shipments, incorrect orders, and poor service.

Web-based entrepreneurs often discover that the greatest challenge their businesses face is not necessarily attracting customers on the Web but creating a workable order fulfillment strategy. Order fulfillment involves everything required to get goods from a warehouse into a customer's hands and includes order processing, warehousing, picking and packing, shipping, and billing. Some entrepreneurs choose to handle order fulfillment in-house with their own employees, whereas others find it more economical to hire specialized fulfillment houses to handle these functions. **Virtual order fulfillment** (or dropshipping) suits many e-tailers perfectly. When a customer orders a product from its Web site, the company forwards the order to its wholesaler or distributor, which then ships the product to the customer with the online merchant's label on it.

*Michael Baum and The Guild*

For Michael Baum, president of The Guild, a U.S.-based e-tailer of original artwork, a virtual order fulfillment strategy is central to his company's success. From The Guild's Web site, customers can browse through more than 12,000 unique handmade works of art created by some 1,200 artists across the United States. The artists, whose work ranges from jewelry and paintings to furniture and lighting, are connected to The Guild by an extranet that operates with special proprietary software. When a customer makes a purchase, The Guild notifies the artist, who ships the item directly to the customer. "We couldn't run a business like ours any other way," notes Baum.[42]

Although e-tailers such as The Guild avoid the risks and problems associated with managing inventory, they lose control over delivery times and service quality. In addition, for some small businesses, finding a fulfillment house willing to handle a relatively small volume of orders at a reasonable price can be difficult. Major fulfillment providers include FedEx, UPS, NewRoads, and NFI Interactive.

### Myth 10. E-Commerce Will Cause Brick-and-Mortar Retail Stores to Disappear

The rapid growth of e-commerce does pose a serious threat to some traditional retailers, especially those that fail to find ways to capitalize on the opportunities the Web offers them. However, it is unlikely that Web-based shopping will replace completely customers' need and desire to visit real stores selling real merchandise that they can see, touch, and try on. That's why e-commerce research firm JupiterResearch estimates that online sales will never exceed 15 percent of total retail sales.[43] Currently, online retail sales in the United States, for example, account for less than 7 percent of total retail sales, an amount that is less than the annual revenues of Wal-Mart.[44]

Some products simply lend themselves to selling in real stores more naturally than in online shops, but with the right strategies, entrepreneurs are finding success selling online almost every product imaginable. Virtual stores have, and will, continue to drive out of existence some traditional companies that resist creating new business models or are too slow to change. To remain competitive, traditional bricks-and-mortar stores must find ways to blend their operations with an online presence to become clicks-and-mortar businesses that can make the convenience, the reach, and the low transaction costs of the Web work for them.

**ENTREPRENEURIAL Profile**

*REI Inc.*

REI Inc., a retailer of outdoor gear and apparel with nearly 100 stores, was one of the first companies to integrate its Web presence into its retail outlets using in-store kiosks that give customers access to more than 178,000 items on its Web site. Both online and in-store customers can access hundreds of "how-to" articles and clinics to help them evaluate and select the right products for their needs. The "Expert Advice" feature of REI's Web site provides valuable advice on a variety of topics ranging from rock climbing to fly fishing. Customers' response to in-store Web access has been phenomenal. REI, which consistently ranks consistently in the "Internet Retailer Top 500" list, reports that the revenue generated by its in-store kiosks is equivalent to that generated by a 25,000-square-foot retail store! "We've combined years of retail experience and years on the Web to create a successful multi-channel approach to serving our customers," says former CEO Dennis Madsen. REI's latest goal is increasing online sales by adding videocasts that show shoppers products' special features and allow them to see the products in action.[45]

### Myth 11. The Greatest Opportunities for E-Commerce Lie in the Retail Sector

As impressive as the growth rate and total volume for online retail sales are, they are dwarfed by those in the online business-to-business (B2B) sector, where businesses sell to one another rather than to retail customers. In fact, B2B sales account for more than 90 percent of all e-commerce transactions.[46] Entrepreneurs who are looking to sell goods to other businesses on the Web will find plenty of opportunities available in a multitude of industries.

B2B e-commerce is growing so rapidly because of its potential to boost productivity, slash costs, and increase profits. This brand of e-commerce is transforming the way companies design and purchase parts, supplies, and materials as well as the way they manage inventory and process transactions. The Web's power to increase the speed and the efficiency of the purchasing function represents a fundamental departure from the past. Experts estimate that transferring purchasing to the Web can cut total procurement costs by 10 percent and transaction costs by as much as 90 percent.[47] For instance, Chris Cogan, CEO of GoCo-op, an Internet purchasing site for hotels, restaurants, and health care companies, explains, "We estimate [that] the average cost of executing a paper purchase order is $115." Businesses using his company's Web-based purchasing system "get that cost down to $10," he says.[48]

B2B e-commerce is growing because of the natural link that exists with business-to-consumer (B2C) e-commerce. As we have seen, one of the greatest challenges Web-based retailers face is obtaining and delivering the goods their customers order fast enough to satisfy customers' expectations. Increasingly, Web-based retailers are connecting their front office sales systems and their back office purchasing and order fulfillment systems with those of their suppliers. The result is a faster, more efficient method of filling customer orders. So far the most successful online B2B companies are those that have discovered ways of tying their front offices, their back offices, their suppliers, and their customers together into a single, smoothly functioning, Web-based network.

### Myth 12. It's Too Late to Get on the Web

A common myth, especially among small business owners, is that those companies that have not yet moved onto the Web have missed a golden opportunity. One Internet entrepreneur who has launched two multi-million-dollar companies, compares e-commerce to

# Don't Make These Common E-Commerce Mistakes

Online shoppers are more savvy today than in the early days of the Internet, and the entrepreneurs who are trying to sell to them also must be smarter in their approaches to attracting, serving, and retaining those customers. Following are some of the most common traps e-commerce entrepreneurs fall into; make sure you don't commit these mistakes.

## Selling the Wrong Product Online

Although businesses are selling almost every product and service online, some items are much better suited to the Internet than others. Low-cost items that people purchase locally and with high levels of frequency or products that have to be specially fitted or custom-made may be too difficult to sell online. The most successful online products are those that offer high value to purchasers and are difficult to obtain locally. Before launching an online company around a particular product or product line, conduct some marketing tests to see whether customers are willing to make those purchases online.

## Lack of Marketing

Some entrepreneurs believe that merely posting a really cool Web site will draw thousands of customers and millions of dollars. With more than 6 billion Web pages online, getting your site noticed takes hard work and marketing know-how. Although some companies do quite well using organic listings from popular search engines, to truly succeed in an online business requires a concerted marketing effort to generate traffic. The key to success is building on your company's competitive advantage and telling customers how that advantage benefits them.

## Poorly Designed Web Site

Some companies work hard to attract customers to their Web sites only to aggravate them with a poorly designed site that causes customers so much frustration that they leave and never return. The best Web sites are "works in progress." Their owners are constantly revising, improving,

and upgrading them. Sites that are simple, clean, professional looking, load fast, and make it easy for customers to find the items they are looking for keep online customers happy. Doing business online boils down to building trust and confidence among customers, and a professional site goes a long way towards accomplishing that goal.

## Failing to Stay Current

Getting a Web site up and running is only the beginning of an e-commerce effort. Keeping it current requires dedication, time, and energy. Sites that regularly post new items and update their content give customers a reason to return—and often. A successful e-commerce site is one that is always changing, vibrant, and up-to-date.

## Clumsy Checkout Procedure

Online shoppers have dozens, sometimes thousands, of places they can shop, all of them just a mouse click away. Companies that establish convoluted, confusing checkout procedures are inviting customers to abandon their shopping carts. Don't present customers with obstacles to making a purchase. Make your checkout process as simple as possible, preferably accomplished in no more than five clicks.

## No Privacy Policy

As you have seen in this chapter, privacy *does* matter on the Web. Companies that fail to post—and then follow—a privacy policy run the risk of turning away customers. Make sure that your company's privacy policy is available from every page on the Web site, and make sure that you abide by it to protect your customers' information.

## Poorly Planned Order Fulfillment

Some entrepreneurs launch their Web sites without having thought through exactly how they plan to fill the orders that customers place. Before launching a site, make sure that you have the "back office" in order to minimize errors and delays in filling customer orders. Remember: online customer service counts! Customers who experience it are unlikely to return.

*(continued)*

### Lack of Focus

Becoming the next Amazon.com of the Internet is not a practical goal for most e-commerce entrepreneurs. The most successful small companies doing business on the Internet are those that focus on a niche and serve the customers in it well. Doing business on the Web is like being located next to Wal-Mart. A small company that sells the same items as Wal-Mart doesn't stand a chance; however, one that specializes in a profitable niche such as wildflower seeds, antique boats, and others can prosper even in the backyard of a giant competitor.

### Failure to Recognize the Importance of Security

Security concerns cost online businesses billions of dollars in sales each year. The most successful online companies are those that treat security as a top priority. They are willing to make investments in technology and solutions to keep their customers' transactions and personal information safe. Security must be a top priority for every company's Web site, no matter how small its operation.

*Sources:* Adapted from "Top 10 E-Commerce Mistakes," *AllBusiness,* www.allbusiness.com/sales/internet-e-commerce/3972-1.html; Paul Graham, "Ten E-Commerce Mistakes," www.paulgraham.com/mistakes.html; Nach M. Maravilla, "Top 10 E-Commerce Mistakes," *PowerHomeBiz.com,* www.powerhomebiz.com/vol87/ecommerce.htm.

the California gold rush in the mid-nineteenth century, "The [e-commerce] landscape looks like California must have looked in 1850. The gold rush is over, and the easy money is gone. However, much more gold was mined in California after 1850 than before; so it is with e-commerce. Enormous opportunities are still available online to those smart enough to take advantage of them."[49] The reality is that e-commerce is still very young, and companies are still figuring out how to succeed on the Web. For every e-commerce site that exists, many others have failed. An abundance of online business opportunities exists for those entrepreneurs insightful enough to spot them and clever enough to capitalize on them.

One fact of e-commerce that has emerged is the importance of speed. Companies doing business on the Web have discovered that those who reach customers first often have a significant advantage over their slower rivals. "The lesson of the Web is not how the big eat the small, but how the fast eat the slow," says a manager at a venture capital firm specializing in Web-based companies.[50]

Succumbing to this myth often leads entrepreneurs to make a fundamental mistake once they finally decide to go online: They believe they have to have a "perfect" site before they can launch it. Few businesses get their sites "right" the first time. In fact, the most successful e-commerce sites are constantly changing, removing what does not work and adding new features to see what does. Successful Web sites are much like a well-designed flower garden, constantly growing and improving, yet changing to reflect the climate of each season. Their creators worry less about creating the perfect site at the outset than about getting a site online and then fixing it, tweaking it, and updating it to meet changing customer demands.

## Strategies for E-Success

*4.* Explain the basic strategies entrepreneurs should follow to achieve success in their e-commerce efforts.

The typical Internet user spends an average of 14 hours a week online, and people between the ages of 18 and 24 spend twice as much time online as they do watching television.[51] By comparison, the typical person spends an average of two hours per week reading newspapers, one hour per week reading magazines, and five hours per week listening to radio.[52] In other words, people now spend more time online than ever before. However, converting these Web surfers into online customers requires a business to do more than merely set up a Web site and wait for the hits to start rolling up. Doing business from a Web site is like setting up shop on a dead-end street or a back alley. You may be ready to sell, but no one knows you are there! Building sufficient volume for a site takes energy, time, money, creativity, and, perhaps most importantly, a well-defined strategy. Many entrepreneurs choose to start their e-commerce efforts small and simple and then expand them as sales grow and their needs become more sophisticated. Others make major investments in creating full-blown, interconnected sites at the outset. The cost of setting up a Web site varies significantly, depending on which options an entrepreneur chooses.

Although the Web is a unique medium for creating a company, launching an e-business is not much different from launching a traditional off-line company. The basic drivers of a successful business are the same on the Web as they are on Main Street. To be successful, both off-line and online companies require solid planning and a well-formulated strategy that emphasizes customer service. The goals of e-commerce are no different from traditional off-line businesses—to increase sales, improve efficiency, and boost profits. Yet the Web has the power to transform businesses, industries, and commerce itself. How a company integrates the Web into its overall business strategy determines how successful it ultimately will become. Following are some guidelines for building a successful Web strategy for a small e-company.

### Focus on a Niche in the Market

Many small businesses are finding success on the Web by focusing on one thing. Rather than try to compete head-to-head with the dominant players on the Web who have the resources and the recognition to squash smaller competitors, smart entrepreneurs focus on serving market niches. Small companies' limited resources usually are better spent serving niche markets than trying to be everything to everyone (recall the discussion of the focus strategy in Chapter 2). The idea is to concentrate on serving a small corner of the market the giants have overlooked. Niches exist in every industry and can be highly profitable, given the right strategy for serving them. A niche can be defined in many ways, including by geography, by customer profile, by product, by product usage, and many others.

The Web allows small businesses to attract niche customers that would have been impossible to reach in sufficient volume without it.

**The Garlic Store**

As its name implies, the Garlic Store, located in Fort Collins, Colorado, sells everything garlic to customers across the globe. The company's inventory includes everything from fresh garlic (of course!) and garlic sauces to garlic jams and books on garlic. The site even boasts a "garlic cam" so visitors can "watch" a crop of garlic grow!

Recall from Chapter 2 that one disadvantage of a focus strategy is being so narrowly focused that attracting a large enough customer base can be a challenge. Without the power of the Web, it is unlikely that the Garlic Store would be able to survive from its single location on Weld County Road 13 in Fort Collins![53] Because of its broad reach, the Web is the ideal mechanism for implementing a focus strategy because small companies can reach large numbers of customers with a common interest.

### Develop a Community

On the Web, competitors are just a mouse click away. To attract customers and keep them coming back, e-companies have discovered the need to offer more than just quality products and excellent customer service. Many seek to develop a community of customers with similar interests, the nucleus of which is their Web site. The idea is to increase customer loyalty by giving customers the chance to interact with other like-minded visitors or with experts to discuss and learn more about topics they are passionate about. E-mail lists, chat rooms, customer polls ("What is your favorite sports drink?"), Web logs, guest books, and message boards are powerful tools for building a community of visitors at a site because they give visitors the opportunity to have conversations about products, services, and topics that interest them.

Small businesses that are most successful at building a community enlist their most passionate customers as company evangelists.

*Alan and Hanz Scholz and Bike Friday*

Brothers Alan and Hanz Scholz, co-founders of Green Gear Cycling (more commonly known by its product name, Bike Friday), a small maker of folding travel bicycles, have created a cadre of customers who are evangelical about using Bike Friday products on adventure treks around the world and then telling others about their journeys. The Scholzes encourage this community of company zealots by giving them a forum through which they spread praise for the small company and its bicycles: the Bike Friday Web site. The main page poses the question "What do you do on a Friday?" and satisfied customers submit blogs, stories, and photos of their adventures. The site, which focuses as much on Bike Friday's community of loyal customers as it does on selling bicycles and accessories, includes an e-mail list (Yak!), a forum where users post comments and tips, a community news page, and an events calendar that features upcoming company-sponsored outings. The site also allows customers to locate the Bike Friday Club of America (and Beyond) nearest them.[54]

Like Bike Friday, companies that successfully create a community around their Web sites turn their customers into loyal fans who keep coming back and, better yet, invite others to join them.

## Attract Visitors by Giving Away "Freebies"

One of the most important words on the Internet is "free." Many successful e-merchants have discovered the ability to attract visitors to their site by giving away something free and then selling them something else. One e-commerce consultant calls this cycle of giving something away and then selling something "the rhythm of the Web."[55] The "freebie" must be something that customers value, but it does *not* have to be expensive nor does it have to be a product. In fact, one of the most common giveaways on the Web is *information*. (After all, that's what most people on the Web are after!) Creating a free online or e-mail newsletter with links to your company's site, of course, and to others of interest is one of the most effective ways of drawing potential customers to a site. Meaningful content presented in a clear, professional fashion is a must. Experts advise keeping online newsletters short—no more than about 600 words. *Poor Richard's E-Mail Publishing*, by Chris Pirillo (Top Floor Publishing) offers much useful advice on creating online newsletters.

*Jennifer Gehrt and Communiqué Public Relations*

When Jennifer Gehrt was revamping the Web site for her company, Communiqué Public Relations, she and her staff decided to launch an e-newsletter aimed at keeping her company's name in the minds of the owners of small businesses whom she targets. Gehrt and her staff of six contribute articles to the newsletter, which they send out every six weeks. Within eight months of launching the newsletter, Communiqué's subscriber list grew from 150 to 450, and the newsletter's open rate, the percentage of e-mails opened in an e-mail marketing campaign, is an above average 47 percent. The newsletter is paying off in increased sales. "We are working on a project now [for which we] would never have been considered if it had not been for our newsletter," says Gehrt. "Every time we send a newsletter, we get responses from people who are interested in learning more about our business. Our e-mail newsletter has played a critical role in our growth."[56]

### Make Creative Use of E-Mail, but Avoid Becoming a "Spammer"

Used properly and creatively, e-mail can be an effective, low-cost way to build traffic on a Web site. Spending on e-mail campaigns ranks second only to search engine optimization in online companies' marketing budgets, yet e-mail **click-through rates**, the percentage of recipients who open an e-mail and click on the link to the company's Web site, average only 6.5 percent. (E-mails sent on Fridays have the highest combination of open and click-through rates.)[57] Just as with newsletters, an e-mail's content should offer something of value to recipients. Supported by online newsletters or chat rooms, customers welcome well-constructed permission e-mail that directs them to a company's site for information or special deals, unlike unsolicited and universally despised e-mails known as spam. Unfortunately, getting legitimate e-mails noticed has become more challenging for business owners because spam is on the rise. The Threat Research and Content Engineering (TRACE) team, an Australian-based Internet security company, estimates that 85 percent of all e-mails sent are spam.[58]

Companies often collect visitors' e-mail addresses when they register to receive a "freebie." To be successful at collecting a sufficient number of e-mail addresses, a company must make clear to customers that they will receive messages that are meaningful to them and that the company will not sell e-mail addresses to others (which should be part of its posted privacy policy). Once a company has a customer's permission to send information in additional e-mail messages, it has a meaningful marketing opportunity to create a long-term customer relationship. Table 13.1 includes a spam test to which every company should submit its e-mail campaigns.

### Make Sure Your Web Site Says "Credibility"

Many studies have concluded that trust and security issues are the leading inhibitors of online shopping. Unless a company can build among customers *trust* in its Web site, selling is virtually impossible. Visitors begin to evaluate the credibility of a site as soon as they arrive. Does the site look professional? Are there misspelled words and typographical errors? If the site provides information, does it note the sources of that information? If so, are those sources legitimate? Are they trustworthy? Is the presentation of the information fair and objective, or is it biased? Has the site been updated recently? Does the company include a privacy policy posted in an obvious place?

One of the simplest ways to establish credibility with customers is to use brand names they know and trust. Whether a company sells nationally recognized brands or its own well-known private brand, using those names on its site creates a sense of legitimacy. People buy brand names they trust, and online companies can use that to their advantage. Another effective way to build customer confidence is by joining an online seal program such as TRUSTe or BBBOnLine (Better Business Bureau Online). The seals mean that a company meets certain standards concerning the privacy of customers' information and the resolution of customer complaints. Finally, providing a street address, an e-mail address, and a toll-free telephone number sends a subtle message to shoppers that a legitimate business is behind a Web site. Many small companies include photographs of their brick-and-mortar stores and of their employees to combat the Web's anonymity and to give shoppers the feeling that they are supporting a friendly small business.

**TABLE 13.1 Does Your E-Mail Measure Up to the Anti-Spam Test?**

1. Is the content of your e-mail appropriate for your audience? Are recipients likely to be interested in the offers or articles you are sending? The biggest problem with sales-oriented e-mails and the primary cause of low open and click-through rates is irrelevant content.

2. Does the e-mail offer something of value to recipients—an invitation to a special sale, a free newsletter filled with useful information, or something similar? Sending frivolous e-mails that pack little or no value to customers is one sure-fire way to send your company's click-through rate plummeting.

3. Has your e-mail provider been black-listed by spam screening tools?

4. Have the recipients on your e-mail list opted into your e-mail list? Trolling Internet user lists for e-mail addresses is *not* an acceptable way to build a recipient list.

5. Does the subject line include your company's name? Is the subject line accurate and not misleading? Do *not* include "$$$" in the subject line as so many spam messages do.

6. Is the e-mail readable? Some e-mails sent in HTML format can appear garbled and unreadable on some computers.

7. Is the frequency of the e-mail appropriate? Customers do not appreciate being hammered by 20 e-mails from a company in one week.

8. Is the timing of your e-mail appropriate? Monday mornings, when people are returning to work from the weekend and their inboxes are full of messages, is *not* the best time to send an e-mail.

9. Can recipients opt out of your e-mail list if they choose to?

10. Does the e-mail contain your company's valid mailing address? In 2003, the U.S. passed the CAN-SPAM Act, which did not ban spam but put limitations on how marketers can use e-mail as part of their marketing tools. This is one of the act's requirements.

## Consider Forming Strategic Alliances

Most small companies seeking e-commerce success lack the brand and name recognition that larger, more established companies have. Creating that sort of recognition on the Web requires a significant investment of both time and money, two things that most small companies find scarce. If building name recognition is one of the keys to success on the Web, how can small companies with their limited resources hope to compete? One option is to form strategic alliances with bigger companies that can help a small business achieve what it could not accomplish alone. One expert says, "The question is no longer, 'Should I consider an alliance?' Now the questions are 'What form should the alliance take?' and 'How do I find the right partner?' "[59]

One of the easiest ways to begin forging alliances online is through an **affiliate marketing program**. Also known as referral or associate marketing, this technique involves an online merchant paying a commission to another online business (the affiliate) for directing customers to the merchant's Web site. A study by Forrester Research found that more than half of all online retailers used an affiliate program and 99 percent of them reported that it was an effective method of driving sales. When coordinated properly with the right affiliates, a referral marketing program can generate 10 percent to 40 percent of a company's online sales.[60]

*Dan "The Lobster Man" Zawacki and Lobster Gram*

Dan "The Lobster Man" Zawacki, founder of Lobster Gram, a Chicago-based retailer of lobsters, has seen his company's sales grow by more than 30 percent annually for the last several years to more than $8 million because of the company's affiliate marketing program. After years of counting on radio and print ads to attract customers, Zawacki believes that traditional advertising media are no longer sufficient. Zawacki pays an affiliate management company to place links to his company's Web site on more than 2,000 affiliate sites. Affiliates collect a 10 percent commission on any sales to customers who are directed to Lobster Gram from their sites. Thanks to the affiliate marketing program, Lobster Gram is the most-visited lobster site on the Web. Recently, Zawacki paid affiliates $50,700 but their leads generated $390,000 in sales. He estimates that the company's annual return on investment on its affiliate marketing program is an impressive 112 percent![61]

## Make the Most of the Web's Global Reach

The Internet has reduced dramatically the cost of launching a global business initiative; even the tiniest of businesses can engage in international business with a well-designed Web site. Still, despite the Web's reputation as an international marketplace, many Web entrepreneurs fail to utilize fully its global reach. For example, nearly 90 percent of the 1.13 billion people around the world who use the Internet live outside the United States. Only 31.7 percent of Web users speak English.[62] It does not make sense for entrepreneurs to limit their Web sites to just a small percentage of the world because of a language barrier. A top manager at Travelocity, a travel planning Web site, says that whenever his company adds country-specific features to its site, sales in that country typically double![63]

*Peter Justen and
MyBizHomePage.com*

When Peter Justen launched MyBizHomePage.com, a company that offers a Web-based financial dashboard reporting system for small business owners, he focused solely on the U.S. market. Before long, Justen began to see business owners around the world logging in to use his company's financial dashboard measures, particularly after *Forbes* and the *Wall Street Journal* ran favorable reviews of the site. Justen was surprised by his small company's global reach. "The big 'duh' moment for me was the international side," he admits. "I didn't see any of that coming." Today, small business owners in 23 countries account for 35 percent of MyBizHomePage.com's subscribers, and Justen is busy launching international language editions of the site to accommodate the needs of his growing list of international customers.[64]

E-companies wanting to draw significant sales from foreign markets must design their sites with customers from other lands and cultures in mind. A common mechanism is to include several "language buttons" on the opening page of a site that take customers to pages in the language of their choice. Virtual companies trying to establish a foothold in foreign markets by setting up Web sites dedicated to them run the same risk that actual companies do: offending international visitors by using the business conventions and standards they are accustomed to. Business practices, even those used on the Web that are acceptable, even expected, in some countries, may be taboo in other countries. Color schemes can be important, too. Selecting the "wrong" colors and symbols on a site targeting people in a particular country can hurt sales and offend visitors. A little research into the subtleties of a target country's culture and business practices can save a great deal of embarrassment and money! Creating secure, simple, and reliable payment methods for foreign customers also will increase sales.

When translating the content of their Web pages into other languages, entrepreneurs must use extreme caution. This is *not* the time to pull out their notes from an introductory Spanish course and begin their own translations. Hiring professional translation and localization services to convert a company's Web content into other languages minimizes the likelihood of a company unintentionally offending foreign customers.

## Promote Your Web Site Online and Off-line

E-commerce entrepreneurs have to use every means available—both online and off-line—to promote their Web sites and to drive traffic to it. In addition to using traditional online techniques such as registering with search engines, creating banner ads, and joining banner exchange programs, Web entrepreneurs must promote their sites off-line as well. Ads in other media such as direct mail or newspapers that mention a site's URL will bring customers to it. It is also a good idea to put the company's Web address on *everything* a company publishes, from its advertisements and letterhead to shopping bags and business cards. A passive approach to generating Web site traffic is a recipe for failure. On the other hand, entrepreneurs who are as innovative at promoting their e-businesses as they are at creating them can attract impressive numbers of visitors to their sites.

Cross promotions in which a physical store promotes the Web site and the Web site promotes the physical store can boost sales in both venues.

*Jenny Craig*

Weight-loss company Jenny Craig recently added to its Web site a "Click to Call" button that takes customers to a contact form where they can request a telephone contact from the company. The company distributes the contact information from customers who complete the form to the nearest franchisee, who contacts the customer by telephone. Since launching the tie-in between its physical stores and its Web site, Jenny Craig has seen in-store sales and its online conversion rate increase.[65]

### Develop an Effective Search Engine Optimization (SEO) Strategy

Because of the growing popularity of search engines among Internet shoppers, Web search strategies have become an essential part of online companies' promotion strategies. Because the sheer number of Web pages is overwhelming, it is no surprise that Internet shoppers use search engines extensively. Studies by Forrester Research show that 67 percent of Internet shoppers go straight to a search engine to find the products and services they want.[66] As a result, companies are devoting more of their marketing budgets to search engine listings that are focused on landing their Web sites at or near the top of the most popular search engines. Search engine marketing is the fastest growing sector of advertising spending among businesses.[67] For a company engaged in e-commerce, a well-defined search marketing strategy is an essential part of its overall marketing strategy. Figure 13.2 shows that search engines are the leading source of new online customers.

One of the biggest challenges facing e-commerce entrepreneurs is maintaining the effectiveness of their search engine marketing strategies. Because the most popular search engines are constantly updating and refining their algorithms, the secretive formulas and

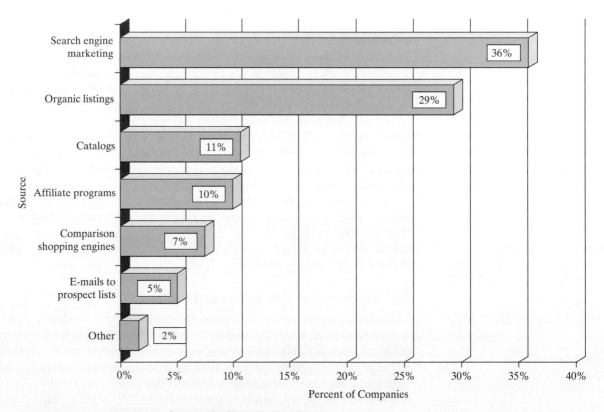

**FIGURE 13.2  Sources of New Online Customers**
*Source: State of Retailing Online 2006,* Forrester Research and shop.org, 2007.

methodology search engines use to find and rank the results of Web searches, Web entrepreneurs also must evaluate and refine constantly their search strategies. Allan Keiter, owner of MyRatePlan.com, a company that helps customers compare cellular phone plans, traditionally had relied on natural listings on the search engine giant Google to direct customers to his company's Web site. His company almost always appeared in the top ten results list for customers looking for information on calling plans. Then Google engineers changed the algorithm used to produce search results, and MyRatePlan.com virtually disappeared from its search results. Keiter watched helplessly as his company's revenues plunged by 20 percent. "There was nothing I could do," he says.[68]

A company's Web search strategy must recognize the three basic types of search engine results: natural or organic listings, paid or sponsored listings, and paid inclusion. **Natural (or organic)** listings often arise as a result of "spiders," powerful programs search engines use to crawl around the Web, analyzing sites for key words, links, and other data. Based on what they find, spiders index Web sites so that a search engine can display a listing of relevant Web sites when a person enters a key word in the engine to start a search. Some search engines use people-powered searches rather than spider-powered ones to assemble their indexes. With natural listings, an entrepreneur's goal is to get his or her Web site displayed at or near the top of the list of search results, a technique known as search engine optimization (SEO). The reason: JupiterResearch reports that 62 percent of search engine users click on a link to a site that appears on the first page of the search results.[69] About 500,000 small online companies rely on natural listings for the majority of their sales revenue.[70]

Companies can use the following tips to improve their search placement results:

- Conduct brainstorming sessions to develop a list of key words and phrases that searchers are likely to use when using a search engine to locate a company's products and services and then use those words and phrases on your Web pages. Usually, simple terms are better than industry jargon.
- Visit competitors' sites for key word ideas, but avoid using the exact phrases. Simply right-clicking on a competitor's Web page and choosing "View Source" will display the key words used in the meta tags on the site.
- Consider using less obvious key words and brand names. For instance, rather than use just "bicycles," a small bicycle retailer should consider key words such as "racing bikes" or "LeMond."
- Ask customers which words and phrases they use when searching for the products and services the company sells.
- Use data analysis tools to review Web logs to find the words and phrases (and the search engines) that brought visitors to the company's Web site.
- Check blogs and bulletin boards related to the company's products and services for key terms.
- Don't forget about misspellings; people often misspell the words they type into search engines. Include them in your list.
- Hire services such as Wordtracker that monitor and analyze Web users' search engine tendencies.

Paid or sponsored listings are short text advertisements with links to the sponsoring company's Web site that appear on the results pages of a search engine when a user types in a key word or phrase. Entrepreneurs should use paid search listings to accomplish what natural listings cannot. As we have explained, the top three search engines in the world are Google, Yahoo!, and MSN.[71] Google, the most popular search engine, displays paid listings as "sponsored links" at the top and down the side of each results page, and Yahoo! shows "sponsored results" at the top and the bottom of its results pages. Some 350,000 small companies participate in Google's paid search program. Advertisers bid on key words to determine their placement on a search engine's results page. The highest bidder for a key word gets the most prominent placement (at the top) on the search engine's results page when a user types in that key word on the search engine. An advertiser pays only when a shopper clicks through to its Web site from the search engine. For this reason, paid listings also are called pay for placement, pay per click, and pay for performance ads. At one popular search engine, the average bid for key words in its paid listings is 40 cents, but some words can bring as much as $100!* The average cost for a pay-per-click key word has risen from 39 cents in 2004 to 58 cents today.[72] Although they can be expensive, one advantage of paid listings is their ability to allow advertisers to evaluate the effectiveness of the listings.

*Ray Allen and American Meadows*

Ray Allen, who left the world of corporate advertising to start American Meadows, a wildflower-seed company, has changed the way he promotes his business. Ten years ago, Allen spent $300,000 annually on magazine ads and printed catalogs to generate $1 million in sales. Today, he spends just $120,000 per year on pay-per-click ads with major search engines Google and Yahoo! to direct customers to the company Web site, and American Meadows' sales have increased to $2 million annually. "It's a total revolution," says Allen.[73]

One problem facing companies that rely on paid listings to generate Web traffic is **click fraud**, which occurs when a company pays for clicks that are generated by someone with no interest in or intent to purchase a product or service. "Clickbots," programs that can generate thousands of phony clicks on a Web site are a common source of click fraud. Experts estimate that the pay-per-click fraud rate is between 14 percent and, for more expensive key search terms (those priced at more than $2), 20 percent.[74] Web analytics software can help online merchants detect click fraud, which can be quite costly. Large numbers of visitors who leave within seconds of arriving at a site, computer IP addresses that appear from all over the world, and pay-per-click costs that rise without any corresponding increase in sales are clues that a company is a victim of click fraud.

Another alternative for increasing a Web site's visibility is paid inclusion. In **paid inclusion**, a company pays a search engine for the right to submit either selected pages or the content of its entire Web site. To keep their natural listings current, search engines regularly crawl through the Internet in the hunt for new and updated Web sites and material to include in their databases, but searching through the huge volume of pages on the Web means that it may take weeks or even months to locate a company's Web site. Because a company pays to submit its Web content into the search engine's database, a paid inclusion eliminates the necessity of waiting for a search engine to find its site. Not every search engine (including Google) accepts paid inclusions, however.

*Heather Walls and Lippincott Williams & Wilkins*

Lippincott Williams & Wilkins, a publisher of medical information, offered such a wide variety of products that describing them with a reasonable number of key words was impractical. Heather Walls, the company's Internet content specialist, decided to try paid inclusions instead, which allowed search engines to draw on the entire content of the company's site. Since Walls began using paid inclusions, traffic to the publisher's Web site has risen 15 percent. In addition, she discovered that visitors who come to the site by way of the search engines are twice as likely to make a purchase as those the company reaches through other media.[75]

## Designing a Killer Web Site

**5.** Learn the techniques of designing a killer Web site.

World Wide Web users are not a patient lot. They sit before their computers, surfing the Internet, their fingers poised on their mouse buttons, daring any Web site to delay them with files that take a long time to load (anything more than four to eight seconds). Slow-loading sites or sites that fail to deliver on their promises will cause a Web user to move on faster than a bolt of lightning can strike. With more than 600 billion Web sites online and more

---

*An online merchant's cost per sale = cost per click ÷ merchant's conversion rate. For example, a merchant with a 1 percent conversion rate who submits a key word bid of 10 cents per click is paying $10 per sale ($0.10 ÷ 0.01 = $10).

## ■ A Web Site with Personality: More Than a Bare Necessity

In 2001, Noah Wrubel took over the family business, Bare Necessities, a retail lingerie shop with four stores located in the northeast and a Web site, www.barenecessities.com. Bare Necessities generates $15 million in annual sales, about one-tenth of the sales of market leader Victoria's Secret. The retail outlets—and the entire company—are profitable, but 80 percent of Bare Necessities' sales are online. However, Wrubel, who sees the Web as the future of his company, is dissatisfied with his company's online presence. "It lacks personality," he explains. "It has no voice."

Fortunately, online shoppers who type in key words such as "women's underwear" will see Bare Necessities' site near the top of the results page. Those who click on the link see a very functional site that includes a large stock of bras, panties, nightgowns, bustiers, and other lingerie items—all displayed in a very antiseptic way. The site could just as easily sell office furniture or industrial supplies. "When the transaction is over, I think the customer barely remembers our name," laments marketing director Dan Sakrowitz. Wrubel has tried to revamp the site numerous times in an attempt to give it more personality and to make it more memorable. "Nothing really worked," he admits.

Enter a group of consultants to work with Bare Necessities' staff. Consultant Luke Williams splits the employees and managers into two groups and, presenting them with a collection of images clipped from magazines, asks them to build two collages: one that shows shoppers' actual online experience and another that demonstrates the ideal online shopping experience. The collage showing the actual shopping experience includes a photo of a woman wearing a helmet, suggesting the combative, challenging experience purchasing underwear on the company Web site is. Another photo of lampshades represents the fact that women of all shapes and sizes, not just glamorous supermodels, purchase underwear—and for many different purposes. As the groups compare the actual buying experience to the ideal one, they realize that, for most women, buying underwear is a highly frustrating—and often boring—experience. It also becomes clear that the Bare Necessities Web site does not do enough to make buying underwear easier or more fun for its customers.

"Why don't we include an instant messaging link on the site so that customers can ask questions or get more information about an item they are considering buying?" asks one employee. Another asks, "What kind of image are we trying to project with our site?" Wrubel admits that so far Bare Necessities has avoided projecting any image at all with its site. "It's a functional site by design," he says, "but we don't impact the mood."

Next Williams asks the groups to list Bare Necessities' three major competitors and to list brief descriptions of those sites. The list includes terms such as "sexy," "low quality," "generic," "cheesy," "too many markdowns," "messy," and others. To help the group develop a unique selling proposition for its Web site, Stuart Hogue, another consultant, asks the groups to list antonyms for the words and phrases they used to describe the competition. The energy level in the room increases as employees set about their task. If a competitor's products are of inferior quality, Bare Necessities' site should emphasize its high-end brands such as Versace and La Perla. One rival uses only gorgeous supermodels in its photos, and the team counters with the idea of showing that Bare Necessities caters to women of all body shapes and sizes. The employees note that one competitor sells generic products, and they suggest that Bare Necessities emphasize its trendy niche products such as its Scanty line of sleepwear or upscale lingerie from British manufacturer Spoylt.

Hogue asks the employees if they spot any recurring themes. Almost in unison, they point out that Bare Necessities' site should provide more guidance and information to shoppers. The idea is to position the company as an expert on women's underwear: "If you've had problems buying the right underwear in the past, relax; you are in the right place." One employee suggests creating a wise fictional character to guide customers through the process of selecting the right products for their needs. Wrubel elaborates on the idea, suggesting that the site include several characters, each one representing a shopper with a different need or in a different mood. As the session begins to wind down, the team draws a diagram with the word "sage" (suggesting wisdom and expertise) at the center and, around it, the words "intimate," which suggests that Bare Necessities

*(continued)*

serves women of all sizes and body shapes, and "sensual," which suggests that the company can help women be more attractive. Wrubel is ready to redesign the Bare Necessities' Web site. "Instead of just 'free slippers' [with an order]," says Wrubel, "it's 'the ten best bras to go with T-shirts' or 'eight solutions for your prom dress.'"

1. Work with a group of your classmates to brainstorm ideas for redesigning Bare Necessities'

Web site. Use the concepts covered in this chapter to help you generate ideas.

2. How should Bare Necessities link its online marketing strategy to the marketing strategy for its retail outlets?

*Source:* Adapted from Brian O'Reilly, "Taking on Victoria's Secret," *FSB*, June 2006, pp. 56–64.

added every day, how can an entrepreneur design a Web site that will capture and hold potential customers' attention long enough to make a sale? What can they do to keep customers coming back on a regular basis? There is no surefire formula for stopping Web surfers in their tracks, but the following suggestions will help.

### Start with Your Target Customer

Before launching into the design of their Web sites, entrepreneurs must paint a clear picture of their target customers. Only then are they ready to design a site that will appeal to their customers. The goal is create a design in which customers see themselves when they visit. Creating a site in which customers find a comfortable fit requires a careful blend of market research, sales know-how, and aesthetics. The challenge for a business on the Web is to create the same image, style, and ambiance in its online presence as in its offline stores.

### Give Customers What They Want

Although Web shoppers are price conscious, they rank fast, reliable delivery high on their list of criteria in their purchase decisions. Studies also show that surfers look for a large selection of merchandise available to them immediately. Remember that the essence of selling on the Web is providing *convenience* to customers. Sites that allow them to shop whenever they want, to find what they are looking for easily, and to pay for it conveniently and securely will keep customers coming back. Furniture maker Herman Miller's Web site not only makes it easy for shoppers to browse and to buy its products, but the site also offers research on the benefits of ergonomic designs and allows visitors to try various furniture layouts in rooms created with a special 3-D design tool.[76] One of the reasons Amazon.com has become the largest online retailer is that its five-point strategy is designed to give online shoppers exactly what they want: low prices, wide selection, product availability, shopping convenience, and extensive information about the products it sells.[77]

Figure 13.3 shows the features that make shoppers in the United States most likely to buy from a Web site.

### Select the Right Domain Name

Choose a domain name that is consistent with the image you want to create for your company and register it. Entrepreneurs should never underestimate the power of the right domain name or universal resource locator (URL), which is a company's address on the Internet. It not only tells Web surfers where to find a company, but it also should suggest something about the company and what it does. Even the casual Web surfer could guess that the "toys.com" name belongs to a company selling children's toys. (It does; it belongs to eToys Inc., which also owns "etoys.com," "e-toys.com," and several other variations of its name.) The ideal domain name should be:

- **Short.** Short names are easy for people to remember, so the shorter a company's URL is, the more likely potential customers are to recall it.
- **Memorable.** Not every short domain name is necessarily memorable. Some business owners use their companies' initials as their domain name (for example, www.sbfo.

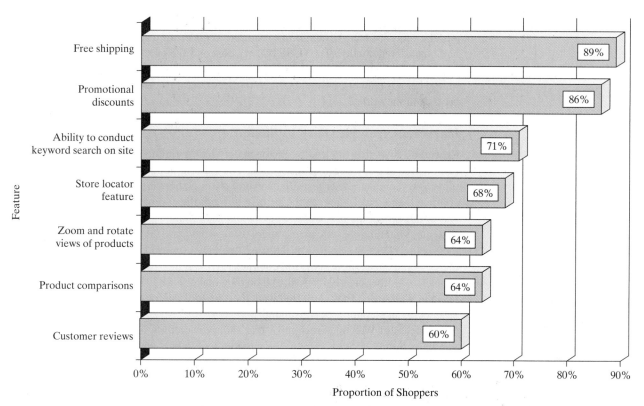

**FIGURE 13.3 Features That Make U.S. Shoppers More Likely to Buy from a Web Site**
*Source: Multi-Channel Shopping Transformation Study,* The e-tailing Group/J. C. Williams Group/Start Sampling, 2006.

com for Stanley Brothers Furniture Outlet). The problem with using initials for a domain name is that customers rarely associate the two, which makes a company virtually invisible on the Web.

- ■ *Indicative of a company's business or business name.* Perhaps the best domain name for a company is one that customers can guess easily if they know the company's name. For instance, mail order catalogue company L.L.Bean's URL is www. llbean.com, and New Pig, a maker of absorbent materials for a variety of industrial applications, uses www.newpig.com as its domain name. (The company carries this concept over to its toll-free number, which is 1-800-HOT-HOGS.)
- ■ *Easy to spell.* Even though a company's domain name may be easy to spell, it is usually wise to buy several variations of the correct spelling simply because some customers are not likely to be good spellers!

Just because entrepreneurs come up with the perfect URL for their companies' Web sites does not necessarily mean that they can use it. Domain names are given on a first-come, first-served basis. Before business owners can use a domain name, they must ensure that someone else has not already taken it. The simplest way to do that is to go to a domain name registration service such as Network Solutions at www.networksolutions.com, NetNames at www.netnames.com, or Go Daddy (www.godaddy.com) to conduct a name search. Entrepreneurs who find the domain name they have selected already registered to someone else have two choices: They can select another name, or they can try to buy the name from the original registrant.

Finding unregistered domain names can be a challenge, but several new top-level domain names recently became available: .aero (airlines), .biz (any business site), .coop (business cooperatives), .info (any site), .museum (museums), .name (individuals' sites), and .pro (professionals' sites). Once an entrepreneur finds an unused name that is suitable, she must register it (plus any variations of it)—and the sooner, the better! Finding unregistered domain names is becoming more difficult; 98 percent of the words in *Webster's English Dictionary* have been registered as Internet domain names![78] Registering is quite easy: Simply use one of the registration services listed previously to fill out a form and pay the required fee. Although not required, registering the domain name with the U.S. Patent and Trademark Office (USPTO) at a cost of $275 provides maximum protection for a company's domain name. The USPTO's Web site (www.uspto.gov) not only allows users to register a trademark online, but it also offers useful information on trademarks and the protection they offer.

### Make Your Web Site Easy to Navigate

Research shows that the leading factor in convincing online shoppers to make a purchase from a Web site is its ease of navigation. The starting point for evaluating a site's navigability is to conduct a user test. Find several willing shoppers, sit them down in front of a computer, and watch them as they cruise through the company's Web site to make a purchase. It is one of the best ways to get meaningful, immediate feedback on the navigability of a site. Watching these test customers as they navigate the site also is useful. Where do they pause? Do they get lost in the site? Are they confused by the choices the site gives them? Is the checkout process too complex? Are the navigation buttons from one page of the site to another clearly marked, and do they make sense? "Eighty percent of visitors will leave [a Web site] if they can't find what they are looking for after three pages," says Bryan Eisenberg, an e-commerce consultant.[79]

Successful Web sites recognize that shoppers employ different strategies to make a purchase. Some shoppers want to use a search tool, others want to browse through product categories, and still others prefer a company to make product recommendations. Effective sites accommodate all three strategies in their design.

### Create a Gift Idea Center

Online retailers have discovered that one of the most successful tools for improving their conversion rates is to offer a gift idea center. A gift idea center is a section of a Web site that includes a variety of gift ideas where shoppers can browse for ideas based on price, gender, or category. Gift centers can provide a huge boost for e-tailers, particularly around holidays, because they offer creative suggestions for shoppers looking for the perfect gift. Other variations of this approach that have proved to be successful for e-commerce entrepreneurs include suggested items pages, bargain basement sale pages, and featured sale pages.

### Build Loyalty by Giving Online Customers a Reason to Return to Your Web Site

The typical e-commerce site experiences a 60 percent turnover rate among its customers every six weeks![80] Just as with brick-and-mortar retailers, e-tailers that constantly have to incur the expense of attracting new customers find it difficult to remain profitable because of the extra cost required to acquire customers. One of the most effective ways to encourage customers to return to a site is to establish an incentive program that rewards them for repeat purchases. "Frequent-buyer" programs that offer discounts or points toward future purchases, giveaways such as T-shirts emblazoned with a company's logo, or special services are common components of incentive programs. Incentive programs that are properly designed with a company's target customer in mind really work. A study by market research firm NFO Interactive found that 53 percent of online customers say they would return to a particular site to shop if it offered an incentive program.[81]

### Establish Hyperlinks with Other Businesses, Preferably Those Selling Products or Services That Complement Yours

Establish hyperlinks with other businesses, preferably those selling products or services that complement yours. Listing the Web addresses of complementary businesses on a company's site and having them list its address on their sites offers customers more value and can bring traffic to your site that you otherwise would have missed. For instance, the owner of a site selling upscale kitchen gadgets should consider a cross-listing arrangement with sites that feature gourmet recipes, wines, and kitchen appliances.

### Include an E-Mail Option and a Telephone Number on Your Site

Include an e-mail option, an address, and a telephone number in your site. Customers appreciate the opportunity to communicate with your company. If you include e-mail access on your site, however, be sure to respond to it promptly. Nothing alienates cyber-customers faster than a company that is slow to respond or fails to respond to their e-mail messages. Also be sure to include an address and a toll-free telephone number for customers who prefer to write or call with their questions. Unfortunately, many companies either fail to include their telephone numbers on their sites or bury them so deeply within the sites' pages that customers never find them.

### Offer Shoppers Online Order Tracking

Give shoppers the ability to track their orders online. Many customers who order items online want to track the progress of their orders. One of the most effective ways to keep a customer happy is to send an e-mail confirmation that your company received the order and another e-mail notification when you ship the order. The shipment notice should include the shipper's tracking number and instructions on how to track the order from the shipper's site. Order and shipping confirmations instill confidence in even the most Web-wary shoppers.

### Offer Web Specials

Give Web customers a special deal that you don't offer in any other advertising piece. Change your specials often (weekly, if possible) and use clever "teasers" to draw attention to the offer. Regular special offers available only on the Web give customers an incentive to keep visiting a company's site. Also provide product prices and shipping charges early in the transaction. Customers do not like to be surprised by high charges at checkout.

### Look for Opportunities to Cross-Sell

Sales clerks in brick-and-mortar retail stores quickly learn the art of cross-selling, offering, for example, a customer who purchases a shirt the opportunity to purchase a matching tie as well. Online merchants can use the same tactic. Amazon.com employs this sales strategy extremely well with its display that reads "Others who purchased this book also bought the following books . . ." making it appear as more of a service to shoppers than a clever selling tactic.

### Use Customer Testimonials

Customer testimonials about a company and its products and services lend credibility to a site, but the testimonials must be genuine and believable.

### Follow a Simple Design

Catchy graphics and photographs are important to snaring customers, but designers must choose them carefully. Designs that are overly complex take a long time to download, and customers are likely to move on before they appear. Web Site Garage (http://websitegarage. netscape.com), a Web site maintenance company, offers companies a free evaluation of how their sites measure up in terms of speed.

Specific design tips include:

- Avoid clutter. The best designs are simple and elegant with a balance of both text and graphics. "The minimalist approach makes a site appear more professional," says one design expert.[82]
- Avoid huge graphic headers that must download first, prohibiting customers from seeing anything else on your site as they wait (or, more likely, *don't* wait). Use graphics judiciously so that the site loads quickly; otherwise, impatient customers will abandon the site.
- Include a menu bar at the top of the page that makes it easy for customers to find their way around your site.

■ Make the site easy to navigate by including easy-to-follow navigation buttons at the bottom of pages that enable customers to return to the top of the page or to the menu bar. This avoids "the pogo effect," where visitors bounce from page to page in a Web site looking for what they need. Without navigation buttons or a site map page, a company runs the risk of customers getting lost in its site and leaving. Organizing a Web site into logical categories also helps.

■ Minimize the number of clicks required for a customer to get to any particular page in the site. Long paths increase the likelihood of customers bailing out before they reach their intended destination.

■ Incorporate meaningful content in the site that is useful to visitors, well organized, easy to read, and current. The content should be consistent with the message a company sends in the other advertising media it uses. Although a Web site should be designed to sell, providing useful, current information attracts visitors, keeps them coming back, and establishes a company's reputation as an expert in the field.

■ Include a "frequently asked questions (FAQ)" section. Adding this section to a page can reduce dramatically the number of telephone calls and e-mails customer service representatives must handle. FAQ sections typically span a wide range of issues— from how to place an order to how to return merchandise—and cover whatever topics customers most often want to know about.

■ Be sure to include privacy and return policies as well as product guarantees the company offers.

■ Avoid fancy typefaces and small fonts because they are too hard to read.

■ Be vigilant for misspelled words, typographical errors, and formatting mistakes; they destroy a site's credibility in no time and send customers fleeing to competitors' sites.

■ Don't put small fonts on "busy" backgrounds; no one will read them!

■ Use contrasting colors of text and graphics. For instance, blue text on a green background is nearly impossible to read.

■ Be careful with frames. Using frames that are so thick that they crowd out text makes for a poor design.

■ Test the site on different Web browsers and on different size monitors. A Web site may look exactly the way it was designed to look on one Web browser and be a garbled mess on another. Sites designed to display correctly on large monitors may not view well on small ones.

■ Use your Web site to collect information from visitors, but don't tie up customers with a tedious registration process. Most will simply leave the site never to return. Offers for a free e-mail newsletter or a contest giveaway can give visitors enough incentive to register with a site.

■ Incorporate a search function that allows shoppers to type in the items they want to purchase. Unlike in-store shoppers, who might browse until they find the item, online shoppers usually want to go straight to the products they seek. Ideally, the search function acknowledges common misspellings of key terms, avoiding the dreaded "No Results Found" message.

■ Include company contact information and an easy-to-find customer service telephone number.

■ Avoid automated music that plays continuously and cannot be cut off.

■ Make sure the overall look of the site is consistent and appealing. "When a site is poorly designed, lacks information, or cannot support customer needs, that [company's] reputation is seriously jeopardized," says one expert.[83]

■ Remember: Simpler usually is better.

### Assure Customers That Online Transactions Are Secure

If you are serious about doing business on the Web, make sure that your site includes the proper security software and encryption devices. Computer-savvy customers are not willing to divulge their credit card numbers on sites that are not secure. E-commerce companies should avoid storing their customers' credit card information. With attacks from hackers increasingly prevalent, the risk is just too high.

# ENTREPRENEURSHIP

## *In Action*

## Web Site Makeovers

### Spirit Work Knitting

Pam Huber-Hauck is an entrepreneurial corporate dropout, having left a secure position in top management at a telecommunications company to pursue her passion, owning a knitting and yarn shop. Huber-Hauck's management experience served her well as she built a business plan for her retail shop, Spirit Work Knitting and Designs, located in Rochester, New York. In 2003, she opened a small 400-square-foot retail store but quickly outgrew the space. Within a year, she relocated to a 2,400-square-foot building that now houses one of the largest retail yarn shops in New York state. "Our whole strategy around the brick-and-mortar store was finding what we could do that's different and innovative," says Huber-Hauck. "We brought in couches and seating and coffee and spa music."

Faced with a sales decline in the retail store, Huber-Hauck knew that one key to the company's growth was its Web site (www.spiritworkknit.com). Because she initially had focused on her retail store, Spirit Work's Web site was very simple, geared primarily toward local shoppers. The challenge she faces now is transforming the company's Web site into a genuine e-commerce initiative with broad appeal. Rather than offer postings of upcoming in-store events, Huber-Hauck wants the site to become a full-service online retail space for yarn and knitting accessories. After evaluating the site, a business advisor says, "It is hard to tell if you could actually purchase products [online]. We have to find a way to take the warm, fuzzy feeling of the retail store and put it in the online setting."

### Busted Knuckle Garage

In 1996, when Warren Tracy stumbled out of bed and wrote down on a piece of paper the idea that had come to him during the night, he did not realize that he had just begun a journey to start a business. At the time,

Tracy, an avid auto and motorcycle enthusiast, was the manager of the Phantom Ranch, the lodge located at the bottom of the Grand Canyon. Within a year of his midnight revelation, Tracy launched the Busted Knuckle Garage, a gift company that sells more than 150 distinctive items aimed at car and motorcycle enthusiasts. Tracy's initial product line was built on hand- and skin-care products that he sold to local river guides when he worked at the Phantom Ranch; he thought that mechanics (professional and "shadetree") would enjoy them as well. His company started very small, placing ads in automotive magazines, but sales grew. Once the business reached a tipping point, Tracy quit his job at the Phantom Ranch and sold his collection of cars and motorcycles to expand the Busted Knuckle Garage into a full-time enterprise. The company's product line now includes items ranging from garage signs with a vintage look and mechanic's work shirts to car polishes and cookie jars that look like gas pumps.

The company's revenue has been growing, but Tracy knows that sales through the company's Web site (www. bustedknucklegarage.com) could be better. "We didn't really customize the Web site but watched it grow every year," says Tracy. "We need someone to come in and bring it up a level."

1. How can a small business transfer the personality and ambience of its retail location to its Web site? What are the challenges to accomplishing this?
2. What steps can Spirit Work Knitting and the Busted Knuckle Garage take to promote their Web sites to attract new customers and generate more business?
3. Visit the Web sites for these two companies. Work with a small team of your classmates to develop a list of ideas for improving the sites.

*Source:* Adapted from Gwen Moran, "Time for a Change," *Entrepreneur*, November 2006, pp. 67–71.

### Post Shipping and Handling Charges Up Front

A common gripe among online shoppers is that some e-tailers fail to reveal their shipping and handling charges early in the checkout process. Responsible online merchants keep shipping and handling charges reasonable and display them early on in the buying process.

### Create a Fast, Simple Checkout Process

One sure-fire way to destroy an online company's conversion rate is to impose a lengthy, convoluted checkout process that requires customers to wade through pages of forms to fill out just to complete a purchase. When faced with a lengthy checkout process, customers simply abandon their shopping carts and make their purchases elsewhere. E-commerce experts suggest that the top performing sites require a maximum of five clicks to check out, but the fewer the steps required for customers to check out, the more successful will be the site at generating sales.[84]

### Confirm Transactions

Order-confirmation e-mails, which a company can generate automatically, let a customer know that the company received the online order and can be an important first line of defense against online fraud. If the customer claims not to have placed the order, the company can cancel it and report the credit card information as suspicious.

### Keep Your Site Updated

Customers want to see something new when they visit stores, and they expect the same when they visit virtual stores as well. Delete any hyperlinks that have disappeared and keep the information on your Web site current. One sure way to run off customers on the Web is to continue to advertise your company's "New Year's Special" in August! On the other hand, fresh information and new specials keep customers coming back.

### Test Your Site Often

Smart e-commerce entrepreneurs check their sites frequently to make sure they are running smoothly and are not causing customers unexpected problems. A good rule of thumb is to check your site at least monthly—or weekly if its content changes frequently.

### Consider Hiring a Professional Designer

Pros can do it a lot faster and better than you can. However, don't give designers free rein to do whatever they want to with your site. Make sure it meets your criteria for an effective site that can sell.

Entrepreneurs must remember that on the World Wide Web every company, no matter how big or small it is, has the exact same screen size for its site. What matters most is not the size of your company but how you put that screen size to use.

## Tracking Web Results

### Software Solutions

6. Explain how companies track the results from their Web sites.

Web sites offer entrepreneurs a treasure trove of valuable information about how well their sites are performing—if they take the time to analyze it. **Web analytics**, tools that measure a Web site's ability to attract customers, generate sales, and keep customers coming back, help entrepreneurs to know what works—and what doesn't—on their sites. Online companies that use Web analytics have an advantage over those that do not. Their owners can review the data collected from their customers' Web site activity, analyze them, make adjustments to the Web site, and then start the monitoring process over again to see whether the changes improve the site's performance. In other words, Web analytics give entrepreneurs the ability to apply the principles of continuous improvement to their sites. In addition, the changes these e-business owners make are based on facts (the data from the Web analytics) rather than on mere guesses about how customers interact with a site. There are many Web analytics software packages, but effective ones offer the following types of information:

- *Commerce metrics.* These are basic analytics such as sales revenue generated, number of items sold, which products are selling best (and which are not), and others.
- *Visitor segmentation measurements.* These measurements provide entrepreneurs valuable information about online shoppers and customers, including whether they

are return customers or new customers, how they arrived at the site (for example, via a search engine or a pay-per-click ad), which search terms they used (if they used a search engine), and others.

■ *Content reports.* This information tells entrepreneurs which products customers are looking for and which pages they view most often (and least often), how they navigate through the site, how long they stay, which pages they are on when they exit, and more. Using this information, an entrepreneur can get an idea of how effective the site's design is.

■ *Process measurements.* These metrics help entrepreneurs to understand how their Web sites attract visitors and convert them into customers. Does the checkout process work smoothly? How often do shoppers abandon their carts? At what point in the process do they abandon them? These measures can lead to higher conversion rates for an online business.

In the early days of e-commerce, entrepreneurs tried to create sites that were both "sticky" and "viral." A **sticky site** is one that acts like electronic flypaper, capturing visitors' attention and offering them useful, interesting information that makes them stay at the site. The premise of stickiness is that the longer customers stay in a site, the more likely they are to actually purchase something and to come back to it. A **viral site** is one that visitors are willing to share with their friends. This "word-of-mouse" advertising is one of the most effective ways of generating traffic to a company's site. As the Web has matured as a marketing channel, however, the shortcomings of these simple measures have become apparent, and other e-metrics continue to emerge. E-businesses now focus on **recency**, the length of time between a customer's visits to a Web site. The more frequently customers visit a site, the more likely they are to become loyal customers. Other common measures of Web site performance include the following:

■ The **click-through rate (CTR)** is the proportion of people who see a company's online ad and actually click on it to reach the company's Web site. Each time an ad is displayed is called an impression; therefore:

$$CTR = \text{Number of clicks} \div \text{Number of impressions}$$

For instance, if a company's ad was displayed 500 times in one day and 12 people clicked on it, the CTR is $12 \div 500 = .024 = 2.4\%$

■ The **cost per acquistion (CPA)** is the cost a company incurs to generate each purchase (or customer registration):

$$CPA = \text{Total cost of acquiring a new customer} \div \text{Number of new customers}$$

For example, if a company purchases an advertisement in an e-magazine for $200, and it yields 15 new customers, then the cost of acquistion is $200 \div 15 = \$13.33$.

■ The **conversion** (or **browse-to-buy**) **rate** is the proportion of visitors to a site who actually make a purchase. It is one of the most important measures of Web success and is calculated as follows:

Conversion rate $=$ Number of customers who make a purchase $\div$ Number of visitors to the site

Although conversion rates vary dramatically across industries, the average conversion rate is 2.4 percent. In other words, out of every 1,000 people who visit a Web site, 24 of them actually make a purchase.

## Collecting Performance Indicators

How do online entrepreneurs know if their Web sites are successful? Answering that question means that entrepreneurs must track the visitors to their sites, their paths within the site, and the activity they generate while there. A variety of methods for tracking Web results are available, but the most commonly used ones include counters and log-analysis software. The simplest technique is a **counter**, which records the number of "hits" a Web site receives. Although counters measure activity on a site, they do so only at the broadest level.

If a counter records 10 hits, for instance, there is no way to know if those hits came as a result of 10 different visitors or as a result of just one person making 10 visits.

A more meaningful way to track activity on a Web site is through **log-analysis software**, which has the goal of helping entrepreneurs understand visitors' online behavior. Server logs record every page, graphic, audio clip, or photograph that visitors to a site access, and log-analysis software analyzes these logs and generates reports describing how visitors behave when they get to a site. With this software, entrepreneurs can determine how many unique visitors come to their site and how often repeat visitors return. Owners of e-stores can discover which FAQ customers click on most often, which part of a site they stayed in the longest, which site they came from, and how the volume of traffic at the site affected the server's speed of operation. The result is the ability to infer what visitors think about a Web site, its products, its content, its design, and other features. Feedback from log-analysis software helps entrepreneurs redesign their sites to eliminate confusing navigation, unnecessary graphics, meaningless content, incomplete information, and other problems that can cause visitors to leave.

Other tracking methods available to owners of e-businesses include:

- *Clustering.* This software observes visitors to a Web site, analyzes their behavior, and then groups them into narrow categories. Companies then target each category of shoppers with products, specials, and offers designed to appeal to them.
- *Collaborative filtering.* This software uses sophisticated algorithms to determine visitors' interests by comparing them to other shoppers with similar tastes. Companies then use this information to suggest products an individual customer would most likely be interested in, given his or her profile.
- *Profiling systems.* These programs tag individual customers on a site and note their responses to the various pages in the site. Based on the areas a customer visits most, the software develops a psychographic profile of the shopper. For instance, a visitor who reads an article on massage techniques might receive an offer for a book on alternative medicine or a magazine focusing on environmental issues.
- *Artificial intelligence (AI).* This software, sometimes called neural networking, is the most sophisticated of the group because it actually learns from users' behavior. The more these programs interact with customers, the "smarter" they become. Over time, they can help online marketers know which special offers work best with which customers, when customers are most likely to respond, and how to present the offer.

## Ensuring Web Privacy and Security

### Privacy

7. Describe how e-businesses ensure the privacy and security of the information they collect and store from the Web.

The Web's ability to track customers' every move naturally raises concerns over the privacy of the information companies collect. E-commerce gives businesses access to tremendous volumes of information about their customers, creating a responsibility to protect that information and to use it wisely. The potential for breaching customers' privacy is present in any e-business. To make sure they are using the information they collect from visitors to their Web sites legally and ethically and are safeguarding it adequately, companies should take the following steps:

**TAKE AN INVENTORY OF THE CUSTOMER DATA COLLECTED.** The first step to ensuring proper data handling is to assess exactly the type of data the company is collecting and storing. How are you collecting the information? Why are you collecting it? How are you using it? Do visitors know how you are using the data? Do you need to get their permission to use the data in this way? Do you use all of the data you are collecting?

**DEVELOP A COMPANY PRIVACY POLICY FOR THE INFORMATION YOU COLLECT.** A **privacy policy** is a statement explaining the type of information a company collects online, what it does with that information, and the recourse customers have if they believe the company is misusing the information. *Every* online company should have a privacy policy, but many do not. Several online privacy firms such as TRUSTe (www.truste.org) and BetterWeb (www.betterweb.com), offer Web "seal programs," or a Good House-keeping seal of privacy approval. To earn a privacy seal of approval, a company must adopt a privacy policy, implement it, and monitor its effectiveness. Many of these privacy sites also provide online policy wizards, automated questionnaires that help e-business owners create comprehensive privacy statements.

**POST YOUR COMPANY'S PRIVACY POLICY PROMINENTLY ON YOUR WEB SITE AND FOLLOW IT.** Creating a privacy policy is not sufficient; posting it in a prominent place on the Web site (accessible from every page on the site) and then abiding by it make a policy meaningful. Whether a company has a privacy policy posted prominently often determines whether customers will do online business with it. One study reports that shoppers are more likely to purchase from online merchants who have sound privacy policies and post them.[85] One of the worst mistakes a company can make is to publish its privacy policy online and then fail to follow it. Not only is this unethical, but it also can lead to serious damage awards if customers take legal action against the company.

### Security

Concerns about security and fraud present the greatest obstacles to the growth of e-commerce. Determining the extent of online security breaches is difficult because only 20 percent of companies report breaches of computer security to authorities, according to the Computer Security Institute.[86] Every company with a Web site—no matter how small—is a potential target for hackers and others seeking to cause harm. A test of randomly, chosen Web sites by Acunetix, a Web site security company, shows that 70 percent of Web sites have vulnerabilities rated from medium-risk to high-risk and that the probability of hackers being able to use these weak points to steal information is "extremely high."[87] A company doing business on the Web faces two conflicting goals: (1) to establish a presence on the Web so that customers from across the globe can have access to its site and the information maintained there and (2) to preserve a high level of security so that the business, its site, and the information it collects from customers are safe from hackers and intruders intent on doing harm. Companies have a number of safeguards available to them, but hackers with enough time, talent, and determination usually can beat even the most sophisticated safety measures. If hackers manage to break into a system, they can do irreparable damage, stealing programs and sensitive customer data, modifying or deleting valuable information, changing the look and content of sites, or crashing sites altogether. In the largest data breach to date, hackers broke into the database at one retail company and stole information that included more than 45 million debit and credit card numbers.[88] Hackers also flooded Amazon.com's Web site with so many hits that legitimate users were locked out (a denial of service attack), costing the company an estimated $244,000 in lost sales every hour it was out of service.[89] In addition to the actual losses these scams cause, another real danger is that scams such as these erode customers' confidence in e-commerce, posing real threats to online entrepreneurs.

Security threats are real for companies of every size, and entrepreneurs must contend with that reality. To minimize the likelihood of invasion by hackers and viruses, e-companies rely on several tools, including virus detection software, intrusion detection software, and firewalls. At the most basic level of protection is **virus detection software**, which scans computer drives for viruses, nasty programs written by devious hackers and designed to harm computers and the information they contain. The severity of viruses ranges widely, from relatively harmless programs that put humorous messages on a user's screen to those that erase a computer's hard drive or cause the entire system to crash. Because hackers are *always* writing new viruses to attack computer systems, entrepreneurs must keep their virus detection software up-to-date and must run it often. An attack by one virus can bring a company's entire e-commerce platform to a screeching halt in no time! One virus which was sent by e-mail with the subject line "I love you" infected computer systems across the globe, leaving companies with an estimated $15 billion in damages and downtime.

**Intrusion detection software** is essential for any company doing business on the Web. These packages constantly monitor the activity on a company's network server and sound an alert if they detect someone breaking into the company's computer system or if they detect unusual network activity. Intrusion detection software not only can detect attempts by unauthorized users to break into a computer system while they are happening, but it also can trace the hacker's location. Most packages also have the ability to preserve a record of the attempted break-in that will stand up in court so that companies can take legal action against cyber-intruders. Web security companies such as ScanAlert provide software that scans a small business's Web site daily to certify that it is "Hacker Safe." Online companies using the software are able to post a certification mark signifying that their sites are protected from unauthorized access.

A **firewall** is a combination of hardware and software operating between the Internet and a company's computer network that allows authorized employees to have access to the Internet but keeps unauthorized users from entering a company's network and the programs and data it contains. Establishing a firewall is essential for any company operating on the Web, but entrepreneurs must make sure that their firewalls are set up properly. Otherwise, they are useless! Even with all of these security measures in place, it is best for a company to run its Web page on a separate server from the network that runs the business. If hackers break into the Web site, they still do not have access to the company's sensitive data and programs.

The Computer Security Institute (www.gocsi.com) offers articles, information, and seminars to help business owners maintain computer security. The *Business Security e-Journal* (www.lubrinco.com) is a free monthly newsletter on computer security, and *Information Security Magazine* (www.infosecuritymag.com), published by the International Computer Security Association (www.icsa.net), also offers helpful advice on maintaining computer security. For entrepreneurs who want to test their sites' security, the ICSA offers its Security Snapshot system (free of charge) that runs various security tests on a site and then e-mails a "Risk Index" score in six different categories, including the site's risk of hacker intrusion.

In e-commerce just as in traditional retailing, sales do not matter unless a company gets paid! On the Web customers demand transactions they can complete with ease and convenience, and the simplest way to allow customers to pay for e-commerce transactions is with credit cards. From a Web customer's perspective, however, one of the most important security issues is the security of his or her credit card information. To ensure the security of their customers' credit card information, online retailers typically use **secure sockets layer (SSL) technology** to encrypt customers' transaction information as it travels across the Internet. By using secure shopping cart features from storefront-building services or Internet service providers, even the smallest e-commerce stores can offer their customers secure online transactions.

Processing credit card transactions requires a company to obtain an Internet merchant account from a bank or financial intermediary. Setup fees for an Internet merchant account typically range from $500 to $1,000, but companies also pay monthly access and statement fees of between $40 and $80 plus a transaction fee of 10 to 60 cents per transaction. Once an online company has a merchant account, it can accept credit cards from online customers.

Online credit card transactions also pose a risk for merchants; online companies lose an estimated $2.8 billion a year to online payment fraud each year, most of it from **charge-backs**, online credit card transactions that customers dispute.[90] Illegitimate chargebacks usually are the result of thieves stealing credit card numbers and then using them to make online purchases. Unlike credit card transactions in a retail store, those made online involve no signatures, and Internet merchants incur the loss when a customer disputes the transaction. For example, Raymond Attipa, founder of topautoparts.com, a Web-based seller of aftermarket automotive parts, closed his online business after incurring $35,000—one-fourth of the company's annual sales—in fraudulent credit card charges in a single year.[91]

One way to prevent fraud is to ask customers for their card verification value (CVV, CID, or CVV2), the three-digit number above the signature panel on the back of the credit card, as well as their card number and expiration date. Online merchants also can subscribe to a real-time credit card processing service that authorizes credit card transactions, but the fees can be high. In addition, using a shipper that provides the ability to track shipments so online merchants can prove that the customer actually received the merchandise can help minimize the threat of payment fraud.

# Chapter Review

E-commerce is creating a new economy, one that is connecting producers, sellers, and customers via technology in ways that have never been possible before. In this fast-paced world of e-commerce, size no longer matters as much as speed and flexibility do. The Internet is creating a new industrial order, and companies that fail to adapt to it will fall by the wayside.

1. **Describe the benefits of selling on the World Wide Web.** Although a Web-based sales strategy does not guarantee success, the companies that have pioneered Web-based selling have realized many benefits, including the following:
   - The opportunity to increase revenues.
   - The ability to expand their reach into global markets.
   - The ability to remain open 24 hours a day, seven days a week
   - The capacity to use the Web's interactive nature to enhance customer service.
   - The power to educate and to inform.
   - The ability to lower the cost of doing business.
   - The ability to spot new business opportunities and to capitalize on them.
   - The power to track sales results.

2. **Understand the factors an entrepreneur should consider before launching into e-commerce.** Before launching an e-commerce effort, business owners should consider the following important issues:
   - How a company exploits the Web's interconnectivity and the opportunities it creates to transform relationships with its suppliers and vendors, its customers, and other external stakeholders is crucial to its success.
   - Web success requires a company to develop a plan for integrating the Web into its overall strategy. The plan should address issues such as site design and maintenance, creating and managing a brand name, marketing and promotional strategies, sales, and customer service.
   - Developing deep, lasting relationships with customers takes on even greater importance on the Web. Attracting customers on the Web costs money, and companies must be able to retain their online customers to make their Web sites profitable.
   - Creating a meaningful presence on the Web requires an ongoing investment of resources—time, money, energy, and talent. Establishing an attractive Web site brimming with catchy photographs of products is only the beginning.
   - Measuring the success of Web-based sales efforts is essential to remaining relevant to customers whose tastes, needs, and preferences are always changing.

3. **Explain the 12 myths of e-commerce and how to avoid falling victim to them.**
   The 12 myths of e-commerce are:
   Myth 1. Setting up a business on the Web is easy and inexpensive.
   Myth 2. If I launch a site, customers will flock to it.
   Myth 3. Making money on the Web is easy.
   Myth 4. Privacy is not an important issue on the Web.
   Myth 5. The most important part of any e-commerce effort is technology.
   Myth 6. "Strategy? I don't need a strategy to sell on the Web! Just give me a Web site, and the rest will take care of itself."
   Myth 7. On the Web, customer service is not as important as it is in a traditional retail store.
   Myth 8. Flash makes a Web site better.
   Myth 9. It's what's up front that counts.
   Myth 10. E-commerce will cause brick-and-mortar retail stores to disappear.
   Myth 11. The greatest opportunities for e-commerce lie in the retail sector.
   Myth 12. It's too late to get on the Web.

4. **Explain the basic strategies entrepreneurs should follow to achieve success in their e-commerce efforts.** Following are some guidelines for building a successful Web strategy for a small e-company:
   - Focus on a niche in the market.

- Develop a community of online customers.
- Attract visitors by giving away "freebies."
- Make creative use of e-mail, but avoid becoming a "spammer."
- Make sure your Web site says "credibility."
- Consider forming strategic alliances with larger, more established companies.
- Make the most of the Web's global reach.
- Promote your Web site online and off-line.
- Develop an effective search engine optimization (SEO) strategy.

5. **Learn the techniques of designing a killer Web site.** There is no surefire formula for stopping surfers in their tracks, but the following suggestions will help:
   - Start with your target customer.
   - Give customers what they want.
   - Select a domain name that is consistent with the image you want to create for your company and register it.
   - Make your Web site easy to navigate.
   - Create a gift idea center.
   - Build loyalty by giving online customers a reason to return to your Web site.
   - Establish hyperlinks with other businesses, preferably those selling products or services that complement yours.
   - Include an e-mail option and a telephone number in your site.
   - Give shoppers the ability to track their orders online.
   - Offer Web specials.
   - Look for opportunities to cross-sell.
   - Use customer testimonials.
   - Follow a simple design for your Web page.
   - Assure customers that their online transactions are secure.
   - Post shipping and handling charges up front.
   - Create a fast, simple checkout process.
   - Confirm transactions.
   - Keep your site updated.
   - Consider hiring a professional to design your site.

6. **Explain how companies track the results from their Web sites.** The simplest technique for tracking the results of a Web site is a counter, which records the number of "hits" a Web site receives. Another option for tracking Web activity is through log-analysis software. Server logs record every page, graphic, audio clip, or photograph that visitors to a site access, and log-analysis software analyzes these logs and generates reports describing how visitors behave when they get to a site.

7. **Describe how e-businesses ensure the privacy and security of the information they collect and store from the Web.** To make sure they are using the information they collect from visitors to their Web sites legally and ethically, companies should take the following steps:
   - Take an inventory of the customer data collected.
   - Develop a company privacy policy for the information you collect.
   - Post your company's privacy policy prominently on your Web site and follow it.
     To ensure the security of the information they collect and store from Web transactions, companies should rely on virus and intrusion detection software and firewalls to ward off attacks from hackers.

## Discussion Questions

1. How has the Internet and e-commerce changed the ways companies do business?
2. Explain the benefits a company earns by selling on the Web.
3. Discuss the factors entrepreneurs should consider before launching an e-commerce site.
4. What are the 12 myths of e-commerce? What can an entrepreneur do to avoid them?
5. Explain the five basic approaches available to entrepreneurs for launching an e-commerce effort. What are the advantages, the disadvantages, and the costs associated with each one?

6. What strategic advice would you offer an entrepreneur about to start an e-company?
7. What design characteristics make for a successful Web site?
8. Explain the characteristics of an ideal domain name.
9. Describe the techniques that are available to e-companies for tracking results from their Web sites. What advantages does each offer?

10. What steps should e-businesses take to ensure the privacy of the information they collect and store from the Web?
11. What techniques can e-companies use to protect their banks of information and their customers' transaction data from hackers?
12. Why does evaluating the effectiveness of a Web site pose a problem for online entrepreneurs?

---

# Business PlanPro

The Internet has transformed the way entrepreneurs operate, giving them the ability to sell their goods and services 24/7 and to reach customers around the world. Web-based businesses can connect with suppliers, provide higher levels of customer service, understand and respond to customer's preferences, and gain insight into their customers' online buying behavior to improve the experience. One of the initial questions asked in the initial Business Plan Pro wizard relates to your business Web site. What was your response to that question—yes or no? Use the contents of this chapter to review your decision. Think about the online presence that you would like your business to have. Is your Web site going to be an information only site, or do you plan to have a robust online store that is capable of conducting e-commerce? As you look through the list of the 12 myths mentioned in this chapter, ask yourself if you have fallen prey to any of these myths. What benefits do you expect to realize from your online presence?

## On the Web

If you are planning to create a Web site that is for information only purposes, go to sites that accomplish that goal. For example, you may want to visit www.epinions.com. Note the layout and navigation of the site and how it presents this information. If you plan to have a dynamic online store, Amazon.com's site was a pioneer in the evolution of online shopping. Go to www.amazon.com and take a fresh look at the attributes of the site. What attributes on the site make it simple, efficient, and "safe" for new and returning buyers? Think back to the three Web sites that you found in the Chapter 10 exercise. Again, identify those qualities and explore how your site might also benefit from those attributes.

## In the Software

Open your plan in Business Plan Pro and go to the "Web Summary" section. If you will create a Web site, click on "View" and "Wizard" and change that decision. Business Plan Pro will update the outline of your business plan by adding a "Web Summary" section. Read the instructions within the software and click on the sample plan link in the upper right-hand section of the instructions. Add content to this section. The following questions may help you as you build your e-commerce strategy:

- Do you have a URL registered for your business? If not, how will you begin the process to secure and register a Web address?
- How would you assess the general level of comfort that your target market has with the Web? For example, are they a technologically savvy group that uses the Web as a part of their daily life, or is this group an older audience that is just learning how to leverage the power of the Web?
- List the objectives you hope to realize through your Web site.
- Is your site going to have an online store? If so, explore how to implement credit card or other online payment options. What are the costs associated with the method of accepting payments online that you have chosen?
- Who will design and update the site? Will you or someone in your organization, or will you outsource that work?
- How will you measure, track, and assess the performance of your site and how often that will occur?
- Are you going to incorporate Web analytics tools and resources that may help you to measure your Web site's performance?
- Does your business plan demonstrate that you have planned and budgeted for your Web site based on the required resources to design, launch, and maintain your site?

## Building Your Business Plan

The additions you have made regarding your Web site may be significant or minimal. Step back and review the information that you have captured in your plan to date. With these additions, does your plan continue to tell a consistent and coherent story about your business? Review and edit other sections that may be affected by your additions to the Web section. Some of those sections may include areas that relate to marketing promotions, communications, expenses, and revenues.

14

# Sources of Equity Financing

Rule # 1: You can never have too much equity.

Rule # 2: You can never have too much capital.

Rule # 3: When Rules 1 and 2 conflict, choose Rule # 2.

—Peg Wyant, venture capitalist

If you don't know who the fool is in a deal, it's you.

—Michael Wolff

## *Learning Objectives*

**Upon completion of this chapter, you will be able to:**

1 Explain the differences in the three types of capital small businesses require: fixed, working, and growth.

2 Describe the various sources of equity capital available to entrepreneurs, including personal savings, friends and relatives, angels, partners, corporations, venture capital, and public stock offerings.

3 Describe the process of "going public," as well as its advantages and disadvantages.

4 Explain the various simplified registrations, exemptions from registration, and other alternatives available to entrepreneurs wanting to sell shares of equity to investors.

aising the money to launch a new business venture has always been a challenge for entrepreneurs. Capital markets rise and fall with the stock market, overall economic conditions, and investors' fortunes. These swells and troughs in the availability of capital make the search for financing look like a wild roller-coaster ride. Entrepreneurs, especially those in less glamorous industries or those just starting out, soon discover the difficulty of finding outside sources of financing. Many banks shy away from making loans to start-ups, venture capitalists are looking for ever-larger deals, private investors have grown cautious, and making a public stock offering remains a viable option for only a handful of promising companies with good track records and fast-growth futures. The result has been a credit crunch for entrepreneurs looking for small to moderate amounts of start-up capital. Entrepreneurs and business owners needing between $100,000 and $3 million are especially hard hit because of the vacuum that exists at that level of financing.

In the face of this capital crunch, business's need for capital has never been greater. Experts estimate the small business financing market to be $170 billion a year; yet, that still is not enough to satisfy the capital appetites of entrepreneurs and their cash-hungry businesses.[1] When searching for the capital to launch their companies, entrepreneurs must remember the following "secrets" to successful financing:

- *Choosing the right sources of capital for a business can be just as important as choosing the right form of ownership or the right location.* It is a decision that will influence a company for a lifetime, and entrepreneurs must weigh their options carefully and understand the consequences of the deal before committing to a particular funding source.

When he launched his technology company, one entrepreneur convinced 10 of his former college buddies to make an equity investment of $150,000 in the business. Unfortunately, the entrepreneur failed to realize that he had given up control over any future financing arrangements that would affect the original investors' shares. Later, when a venture capital firm wanted to invest $5 million in the fast-growing business, the 10 investors vetoed the deal. "They thought that VCs (venture capitalists) were vampires, trying to steal their money," says the entrepreneur. Ultimately, the entrepreneur and the 10 investors agreed to restructure the company's financing. The business survived, but their friendships did not.[2]

- *The money is out there; the key is knowing where to look.* Entrepreneurs must do their homework *before* they set out to raise money for their ventures. Understanding which sources of funding are best suited for the various stages of a company's growth and then taking the time to learn how those sources work are essential to success.
- *Creativity counts.* To find the financing their businesses demand, entrepreneurs must use as much creativity in attracting financing as they did in generating the ideas for their products and services.
- *The World Wide Web puts at entrepreneurs' fingertips vast resources of information that can lead to financing.* The Web offers entrepreneurs, especially those looking for relatively small amounts of money, the opportunity to discover sources of funds that they otherwise might miss. The Web site created for this book (www.prenhall.com/scarborough) provides links to many useful sites related to raising both start-up and growth capital. The Web also provides a low-cost, convenient way for entrepreneurs to get their business plans into potential investors' hands anywhere in the world. When searching for sources of capital, entrepreneurs must not overlook this valuable tool!
- *Be thoroughly prepared before approaching potential lenders and investors.* In the hunt for capital, tracking down leads is tough enough; don't blow a potential deal by failing to be ready to present your business idea to potential lenders and investors in a clear, concise, convincing way. That, of course, requires a solid business plan.
- *Looking for "smart" money is more important than looking for "easy" money.* Some entrepreneurs have little difficulty attracting investors' money. However, easy money is not always smart money. Even though it may be easy to acquire, money from the wrong

investor can spell disaster for a small company. Entrepreneurs cannot overestimate the importance of making sure that the "chemistry" among themselves, their companies, and their funding sources is a good one. Too many entrepreneurs get into financial deals because they needed the money to keep their businesses growing only to discover that their plans do not match those of their financial partners.

ENTREPRENEURIAL Profile

*Brian Carlton and New Breed Wireless*

When Brian Carlton launched CEIG, a company that sells content and applications for mobile phones under the brand name New Breed Wireless, he accepted an offer from a private investor who put up $400,000, payable in two installments, in exchange for 25 percent of the company. The relationship was rocky from the beginning, and the investor made clear his expectations of the company's performance. When CEIG missed one benchmark one year into the deal, the investor refused to invest the second installment, and Carlton was forced to scramble for money to keep the company afloat. "That investor didn't understand how technology businesses grow," says Carlton, whose company ultimately received the remaining $200,000 from the investor. Wiser for the experience, Carlton has revised his capital searching strategy, relying on smaller amounts of money and screening carefully every potential investor. With his new approach, Carlton has raised $1.1 million from 25 investors and has retained 75 percent of the equity in his business.[3]

Rather than rely primarily on a single source of funds as they have in the past, entrepreneurs must piece together capital from multiple sources, a method known as **layered financing**. They have discovered that raising capital successfully requires them to cast a wide net to capture the financing they need to launch their businesses. Much like assembling a patchwork quilt using fabric from many different sources, financing a small business often requires entrepreneurs to find capital from many different sources.

ENTREPRENEURIAL Profile

*Bige Doruk and Gaia Power Technologies*

Bige Doruk discovered that investors had a high level of interest in her company, Gaia Power Technologies, a company that manufactures devices that help companies reduce energy costs and acquire reliable backup power. Demand for the company's products was rising in step with energy prices. To launch her company, Doruk invested her own money and obtained a $1.5 million development grant from the New York State Energy Research and Development Authority. Within a year, she received a $250,000 loan from a consortium of New York banks to complete Gaia's product development effort. As the company grew, Doruk began talking with private investors and venture capital firms (VCs), which led to a group of both investing $2.25 million in Gaia to expand both manufacturing and marketing. In just four years, Doruk has raised more than $4 million for her company from multiple sources.[4]

For most entrepreneurs, raising the money to start or expand their businesses is a challenge that demands time, energy, creativity, and a measure of luck. "Raising money is a marathon, not a sprint," says one entrepreneur who has raised $4 million for her four-year-old company.[5] This chapter and the next one will guide you through the myriad of financing options available to entrepreneurs, focusing on both sources of equity (ownership) and debt (borrowed) financing.

## Planning for Capital Needs

*1.* Explain the differences in the three types of capital small businesses require: fixed, working, and growth.

Becoming a successful entrepreneur requires one to become a skilled fund-raiser, a job that usually requires more time and energy than most business founders anticipate. In start-up companies, raising capital can easily consume as much as one-half of the entrepreneur's time and can take many months to complete. Most entrepreneurs are seeking less than $1 million (indeed, most need less than $100,000), which may be the toughest money to secure. Where to find this seed money depends, in part, on the nature of the proposed business and on the amount of money required. For example, the creator of a computer software firm would have different capital requirements than the founder of a coal mining operation. Although both entrepreneurs might approach some of the same types of lenders or investors, each would be more successful targeting specific sources of funds best suited to their particular financial needs.

**Capital** is any form of wealth employed to produce more wealth. It exists in many forms in a typical business, including cash, inventory, plant, and equipment. Entrepreneurs need three different types of capital:

### Fixed Capital

**Fixed capital** is needed to purchase a business's permanent or fixed assets such as buildings, land, computers, and equipment. Money invested in these fixed assets tends to be frozen because it cannot be used for any other purpose. Typically, large sums of money are involved in purchasing fixed assets, and credit terms usually are lengthy. Lenders of fixed capital expect the assets purchased to improve the efficiency and, thus, the profitability of the business, and to create improved cash flows that ensure repayment.

### Working Capital

**Working capital** represents a business's temporary funds; it is the capital used to support a company's normal short-term operations. Accountants define working capital as current assets minus current liabilities. The need for working capital arises because of the uneven flow of cash into and out of the business due to normal seasonal fluctuations. Credit sales, seasonal sales swings, or unforeseeable changes in demand will create fluctuations in *any* small company's cash flow. Working capital normally is used to buy inventory, pay bills, finance credit sales, pay wages and salaries, and take care of any unexpected emergencies. Lenders of working capital expect it to produce higher cash flows to ensure repayment at the end of the production/sales cycle.

### Growth Capital

**Growth capital**, unlike working capital, is not related to the seasonal fluctuations of a small business. Instead, growth capital requirements surface when an existing business is expanding or changing its primary direction. For example, a small manufacturer of silicon microchips for computers saw his business skyrocket in a short time period. With orders for chips rushing in, the growing business needed a sizable cash infusion to increase plant size, expand its sales and production workforce, and buy more equipment. During times of such rapid expansion, a growing company's capital requirements are similar to those of a business start-up. Like lenders of fixed capital, growth capital lenders expect the funds to improve a company's profitability and cash flow, thus ensuring repayment.

Although these three types of capital are interdependent, each has certain sources, characteristics, and effects on the business and its long-term growth that entrepreneurs must

**TABLE 14.1 Equity Capital Sources at Various Stages of Company Growth**

|  | Start-Up | Early | Expansion | Profitability |
|---|---|---|---|---|
| Characteristics | Business is in conceptual phase and exists only on paper. | Business is developing one or more products or services but is not yet generating sales. | Business is selling products or services and is generating revenue and is beginning to establish a customer base. | Company has established a customer base and is profitable. |
| **Possible Sources of Funding** | Likelihood of using each source: H = Highly likely; P = Possible; U = Unlikely | | | |
| Personal savings | H | H | H | H |
| Retained earnings | U | U | U | H |
| Friends and relatives | H | H | P | P |
| Angel investors | H | H | P | U |
| Partners | H | H | P | U |
| Corporate venture capital | P | H | H | H |
| Venture capital | U | P | H | H |
| Initial public offering (IPO) | U | U | P | H |
| Regulation S-B offering | U | U | P | H |
| Small Company Offering Registration (SCOR) | U | P | P | H |
| Private placements | U | P | P | H |
| Intrastate offerings (Rule 147) | U | P | P | H |
| Regulation A | U | P | P | H |

recognize. Table 14.1 shows the various stages of a company's growth and the sources of capital most suitable in each stage.

## Sources of Equity Financing

**2.** Describe the various sources of equity financing available to entrepreneurs.

**Equity capital** represents the personal investment of the owner (or owners) in a business and is sometimes called *risk* capital because these investors assume the primary risk of losing their funds if the business fails. For instance, private investor Victor Lombardi lost the $3.5 million he invested in a start-up called NetFax, a company that was developing the technology to send faxes over the Internet. However, when NetFax's patent application stalled, the company foundered. Just three years after its launch, NetFax ceased operations, leaving Lombardi's investment worthless.[6]

If a venture succeeds, however, founders and investors share in the benefits, which can be quite substantial. The founders of and early investors in Yahoo!, FedEx, and Microsoft became multi-millionaires when the companies went public and their equity investments finally paid off. To entrepreneurs, the primary advantage of equity capital is that it does not have to be repaid like a loan does. Equity investors are entitled to share in the company's earnings (if there are any) and usually to have a voice in the company's future direction.

The primary disadvantage of equity capital is that the entrepreneur must give up some—perhaps *most*—of the ownership in the business to outsiders. Although 50 percent of something is better than 100 percent of nothing, giving up control of your company can be disconcerting and dangerous. Many entrepreneurs who give up majority ownership in their companies in exchange for equity capital find themselves forced out of the businesses they started! Entrepreneurs are most likely to give up equity in their businesses in the start-up phase than in any other.

We now turn our attention to nine common sources of equity capital.

### Personal Savings

The *first* place entrepreneurs should look for start-up money is in their own pockets. It's the least expensive source of funds available! Entrepreneurs apparently see the benefits of self-sufficiency; the most common source of equity funds used to start a small business is the entrepreneur's pool of personal savings. The Global Entrepreneurship Monitor (GEM) study reports that in the United States, for example, the average cost to start a business is $70,200 and that the typical entrepreneur provides 67.9 percent of the initial capital requirement.[7]

Lenders and investors *expect* entrepreneurs to put their own money into a business start-up. If an entrepreneur is not willing to risk his own money, potential investors are not likely to risk their money in the business either. Furthermore, failing to put up sufficient capital of their own means that entrepreneurs must either borrow excessive amounts of capital or give up significant shares of ownership to outsiders to fund their businesses properly. Excessive borrowing in the early days of a business puts intense pressure on its cash flow, and becoming a minority shareholder may dampen a founder's enthusiasm for making a business successful. Neither outcome presents a bright future for the company involved. Using their own money at start-up allows entrepreneurs to minimize the debt their companies take on and to retain control of their companies' future.

Because they are not able to attract capital from outside sources, entrepreneurs often must "bootstrap" their companies, launching them with little or no money. It takes creativity, boldness, and a certain degree of brashness and moxie, but it works.

*Mark D'Amelio
and Madsoul*

Mark D'Amelio launched his urban streetwear company, Madsoul, from his New York City apartment in 2000 with just $1,000, all of it his own money. D'Amelio opened an account with UPS and received an unlimited supply of blank UPS labels. He purchased a Tektronix printer and received a free supply of black ink. Then he began printing thousands of stickers with his company name and logo, distributing them at rap concerts and art festivals around New York City. D'Amelio approached hip-hop record labels and found that he could get the rights to use unreleased songs for free if he agreed to include both well-known stars and new artists on the album. D'Amelio had the rappers include briefs plugs for Madsoul between tracks and began handing out free CDs to prospective customers. D'Amelio even hired graffiti artists to create graphics for his clothing, offering them a 10 percent royalty or a flat fee not to exceed $500. When he struck a deal with the New York Knicks to sell Madsoul T-shirts at home games, he convinced a screen printer to print the T-shirts without any deposits and to accept payment after the Knicks paid Madsoul. D'Amelio's bootstrapping strategy worked; Madsoul clothing is distributed through more than 400 retail outlets worldwide.[8]

### Friends and Family Members

Although most entrepreneurs look to their own bank accounts first to finance a business, few have sufficient resources to launch their businesses alone. After emptying their own pockets, entrepreneurs should look to friends and family members who might be willing to invest in a business venture. Because of their relationships with the founder, these people are most likely to invest.

*Dave and Catherine
Cook and
MyYearbook.com*

While flipping through their high school yearbooks, 17-year-old Dave Cook and his 15-year-old sister, Catherine, envisioned a social networking Web site where young people could post photos, stories, and other memorabilia. Over dinner one evening, the budding entrepreneurs described their idea to their older brother Geoff, who had started his own Internet company while in college in 1997 and sold it in 2002. "As soon as I heard the idea, I thought it was very cool and put in $250,000," says Geoff, 28. "We got another

$250,000 from an angel investor whom I had worked with on my previous company." The Cooks used the money to launch MyYearbook, hire staff (including programmers in India), set up headquarters in quaint New Hope, Pennsylvania, and market the company's Web site (www.myyearbook.com). Within months of the site's launch, thousands of teenagers had signed up for the site. MyYearbook now has 1.7 million members, generates annual sales of more than $1 million, and recently landed $4.1 million in venture capital from U.S. Venture Partners and First Round Capital to finance its rapid growth.[9]

The Global Entrepreneurship Monitor, a study of entrepreneurial trends across the globe, reports that family members and friends are the biggest source of external capital used to launch new businesses. Investments from family and friends are an important source of capital for entrepreneurs, but the amounts invested typically are small, often no more than just a few thousand dollars. Across the globe, the average amount that family members and friends invest in start-up businesses averages just $3,000.[10] In the United States alone, family members and friends invest an average of $27,715 in a typical small business start-up for an astonishing total of $100 billion per year![11]

Family members and friends are more patient than other outside investors and are less meddlesome in a business's affairs than many other types of investors. Investments from family and friends are an excellent source of seed capital and bridge financing, the money that gets a young business far enough along to attract money from private investors or venture capital companies. Inherent dangers lurk in friend and family business investments, however. Unrealistic expectations or misunderstood risks have destroyed many friendships and have ruined many family reunions. To avoid this problem, an entrepreneur must honestly present the investment opportunity and the nature of the risks involved to avoid alienating friends and family members if the business fails. On the other hand, some investments return more than friends and family members ever could have imagined. In 1995, Mike and Jackie Bezos invested $300,000 into their son Jeff's start-up business, Amazon.com. Today, Mike and Jackie own 6 percent of Amazon.com's stock, and their shares are worth billions of dollars![12]

Table 14.2 offers suggestions for structuring family and friendship financing deals.

### Angels

After dipping into their own pockets and convincing friends and relatives to invest in their business ventures, many entrepreneurs still find themselves short of the seed capital they need. Frequently, the next stop on the road to business financing is private investors. These **private investors** (or **angels**) are wealthy individuals, often entrepreneurs themselves, who invest in business start-ups in exchange for equity stakes in the companies. Alexander Graham Bell, inventor of the telephone, used angel capital to start Bell Telephone in 1877. More recently, companies such as Google, Apple, Starbucks, FedEx Kinko's, and the Body Shop relied on angel financing in their early years to finance growth. Today, angel capital is the largest source of external financing for companies in the seed and start-up phases.

In many cases, angels invest in businesses for more than purely economic reasons (often because they have experience and a personal interest in the industry), and they are willing to put money into companies in the earliest stages, long before venture capital firms and institutional investors jump in. Angel financing, the fastest-growing segment of the small business capital market, is ideal for companies that have outgrown the capacity of investments from friends and family but are still too small to attract the interest of venture capital companies. For instance, after raising the money to launch Amazon.com from family and friends, Jeff Bezos turned to angels because venture capital firms were not interested in a business start-up. Bezos attracted $1.2 million from a dozen angels before landing $8 million from venture capital firms a year later.[13]

Angels are a primary source of capital for companies in the start-up stage through the growth stage, and their role in financing small businesses is significant. The Center for Venture Research estimates that 234,000 angels invest $25.6 billion a year in 51,000 small companies, most of them in the start-up phase (see Figure 14.1).[14] Angels invest more

### TABLE 14.2 Suggestions for Structuring Family and Friendship Financing Deals

Tapping family members and friends for start-up capital, whether in the form of equity or debt financing, is a popular method of financing business ideas. In a typical year, some 6 million individuals in the United States invest about $100 billion in entrepreneurial ventures. Unfortunately, these deals don't always work to the satisfaction of both parties. For instance, when actor Don Johnson needed seed capital to launch DJ Racing, a company that designs and races speedboats, he approached a wealthy friend who made a $300,000 interest-free loan on nothing but a handshake. Within a year, a dispute arose over when Johnson was to pay back the loan. A lawsuit followed, which the two now former friends settled out of court. The following suggestions can help entrepreneurs avoid needlessly destroying family relationships and friendships:

- *Consider the impact of the investment on everyone involved.* Will it work a hardship on anyone? Is the investor putting up the money because he wants to or because he feels obligated to? Can all parties afford the loan if the business folds? Convincing your aunt to invest her retirement nest egg in a high risk start-up is not the best financing strategy. Lynn McPhee used $250,000 from family members to launch Xuny, a Web-based clothing store. "Our basic rule of thumb was, if [the investment is] going to strap someone, we won't take it," she says.
- *Keep the arrangement strictly business.* The parties should treat all loans and investments in a business-like manner, no matter how close the friendship or family relationship, to avoid problems down the line. If the transaction is a loan exceeding $10,000, it must carry a rate of interest at least as high as the market rate; otherwise the IRS may consider the loan a gift and penalize the lender.
- *Educate "naïve" investors.* Family members and friends usually invest in a business because of their relationships with the founder not because they understand the business itself. Take the time to explain to potential investors the basics of the business idea, how it will make money, and the risks associated with investing in it.
- *Settle the details up front.* Before any money changes hands, both parties must agree on the details of the deal. How much money is involved? Is it a loan or an investment? How will the investor cash out? How will the business pay off the loan? What happens if the business fails?
- *Never accept more than investors can afford to lose.* No matter how much capital you may need, accepting more than family members or friends can afford to lose is a recipe for disaster—and perhaps financial hardship or even bankruptcy for the investors.
- *Create a written contract.* Don't make the mistake of closing a financial deal with just a handshake. The probability of misunderstandings skyrockets! Putting an agreement in writing demonstrates the parties' commitment to the deal and minimizes the chances of disputes from faulty memories and misunderstandings.
- *Treat the money as "bridge financing."* Although family and friends can help you launch your business, it is unlikely that they can provide enough capital to sustain it over the long term. Sooner or later, you will need to establish a relationship with other sources of credit if your company is to survive and thrive. Consider money from family and friends as a bridge to take your company to the next level of financing.
- *Develop a payment schedule that suits both the entrepreneur and the lender or investor.* Although lenders and investors may want to get their money back as quickly as possible, a rapid repayment or cash-out schedule can jeopardize a fledgling company's survival. Establish a realistic repayment plan that works for the parties without putting excessive strain on the young company's cash flow.
- *Have an exit plan.* Every deal should define exactly how investors will "cash out" their investments.
- *Keep everyone informed.* Entrepreneurs should keep investors informed about the company's progress, its successes and failures, and the challenges it faces. Investors will want to know both good news and bad news.

*Source:* Adapted from Jenny McCune, "Tips for Feud-Free Financing from Friends and Family," *Bankrate,* July 24, 2000, www.bankrate.com/brm/news/biz/Capital_borrowing/20000724.asp; Andrea Coombes, "Retirees as Venture Capitalists," CBS.MarketWatch.com, November 2, 2003, http://netscape. marketwatch.com/news/story.asp?dist=feed&siteid=netscape&guid={1E1267CD-32A4-4558-9F7E-40E4B7892D01}; Paul Kvinta, "Frogskins, Shekels, Bucks, Moolah, Cash, Simoleans, Dough, Dinero: Everybody Wants It. Your Business Needs It. Here's How to Get It," *Smart Business,* August 2000, pp. 74–89. Alex Markels, "A Little Help from Their Friends," *Wall Street Journal,* May 22, 1995, p. R10; Heather Chaplin, "Friends and Family," *Your Company,* September 1999, p. 26.

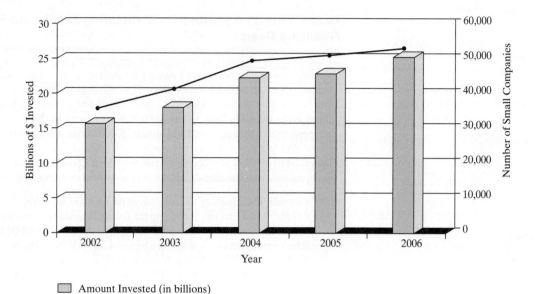

**FIGURE 14.1 Angel Financing**

*Source:* Center for Venture Financing, Whittemore School of Business, University of New Hampshire, www.unh.edu/cvr.

money in small companies than do venture capital firms, and they put it into 15 times as many companies as venture capital firms. Former Beatle Paul McCartney has joined the ranks of angel investors, putting an undisclosed amount of money into Magex, a company that encrypts digital material on the World Wide Web.[15] Because the angel market is so fragmented and, in many cases, built on anonymity, we may never get a completely accurate estimate of its investment in business start-ups. However, experts concur on one fact: Angels are a vital source of equity capital for small businesses.

Angels fill a significant gap in the seed capital market. They are most likely to finance start-ups with capital requirements in the $10,000 to $2 million range, well below the $3 million to $10 million minimum investments most professional venture capitalists prefer. Because a $500,000 deal requires about as much of a venture capitalist's time to research and evaluate as a $5 million deal does, venture capitalists tend to focus on big deals, where their returns are bigger. Angels also tolerate risk levels that would make venture capitalists shudder; as many as 90 percent of angel-backed companies fail.[16] One angel investor, a retired entrepreneur, says that of the 31 companies he has invested in, "more than half have gone under, but four were home runs, returning 25 times my investment. The others gave me a small return or at least some of my money back."[17] That's why angel financing is so important: Angels often finance deals that no venture capitalist will consider. Because of the inherent risks in start-up companies, many venture capitalists have shifted their investment portfolios away from start-ups toward more established firms.

While working as a server in a restaurant, Stacey Belkin met Scott Adams, creator of the Dilbert cartoon, who was a regular customer at the California eatery. Belkin casually mentioned that one day she wanted to start her own restaurant, and Adams said that if she put together a business plan, he would consider making an investment in her business. "She followed up the next day," recalls Adams. Before long, Belkin was launching Stacey's Café in Pleasanton, California, with financing provided by angel investor Scott Adams. The restaurant was so successful that, with Adams's support, Belkin has opened a second location in Dublin, California. One benefit of having a famous cartoonist as an investor is that both restaurants sell personalized Dilbert products signed by the author![18]

Because angels prefer to maintain a low profile, the real challenge lies in *finding* them. Most angels have substantial business and financial experience, and many of them are entrepreneurs or former entrepreneurs. The typical angel invests in companies at the seed or start-up growth stages and accepts 12 percent of the investment opportunities presented, makes an average of two investments every three years, and has invested an average of $80,000 of equity in 3.5 firms. Ninety percent say they are satisfied with their investment decisions.[19] When evaluating a proposal, angels look for a qualified management team ("We invest in people," says one angel), a business with a clearly defined niche, the potential to dominate the market, and a competitive advantage. They also want to see market research that proves the existence of a sizable and profitable customer base.

Potential angels are everywhere, including in a small company's customer base.

*Andrew Zenoff and DayOne*

Andrew Zenoff turned to his customers for capital when he wanted to expand DayOne, a retail store that caters to expectant and new parents with a mix of education, community, and selling. Even though his flagship store was profitable, venture capital companies saw the expansion as too risky. "The outside investor community wanted more proof," says Zenoff, "so who better to go to [for capital] than people who have the proof: my customers?" He contacted 60 customers, and within 30 days, 28 of them agreed to invest in DayOne, which now generates annual sales of $10 million and continues to add new locations.[20]

Because angels frown on "cold calls" from entrepreneurs they don't know, locating them boils down to making the right contacts. Asking friends, attorneys, bankers, stockbrokers, accountants, other business owners, and consultants for suggestions and introductions is a good way to start. "Angels are more likely to invest in a company that was referred to them by someone they know and trust," says Marianne Hudson, director of the angel initiative at the Kauffman Foundation.[21] Networking is the key. One entrepreneur who has successfully raised an average of $120,000 a month for his growing business has developed a list of more than 100 potential angels through an extensive network of contacts in the industry.[22] Angels almost always invest their money locally, so entrepreneurs should look close to home for them—typically within a 50- to 100-mile radius. Angels also look for businesses they know something about, and most expect to invest their knowledge, experience, and energy as well as their money in a company. In fact, the advice and the network of contacts that angels bring to a deal can sometimes be as valuable as their money!

*Sharelle Klaus and Dry Soda*

When Sharelle Klaus launched Dry Soda, a company that produces and distributes non-alcoholic beverages to upscale restaurants and retailers, she used her network of contacts to arrange meetings with potential angel investors. She raised $1.5 million in angel financing, but Klaus says that the advice and professional contacts that her company's investors brought to the table have proved to be as valuable as their money. Klaus' investors helped her find key employees and locate distributors for her line of nonalcoholic beverages.[23]

Angel investing has become more sophisticated, with investors pooling their resources to form angel networks and operating in some ways like very small venture capital firms. Today, nearly 300 angel capital networks operate in cities of all sizes across the United States (up from just 10 in 1996) with as many operating in other countries.[24] Entrepreneurs can find angel networks in their areas with the help of the Angel Capital Association's directory (www.angelcapitalassociation.org). With the right approach, an entrepreneur can attract more money and a larger network of advisors from an angel capital group than from individual investors.

*Hans Severiens and the Band of Angels*

In 1995, Hans Severiens, a professional investor, created the Band of Angels, a group of about 150 angels who meet monthly in Portola Valley, California, to listen to entrepreneurs pitch their business plans. The Band of Angels reviews about 30 proposals each month before inviting a handful of entrepreneurs to make brief presentations at its monthly meeting. Interested members often team up with one another to invest in the businesses they consider most promising. The Band of Angels' average investment is $604,000, which usually nets the investors between 15 percent and 20 percent of a company's stock. Since its inception, the Band of Angels has invested more than $117 million in promising young companies, most of them in the high-tech sector.[25]

The Internet has expanded greatly the ability of entrepreneurs in search of capital and angels in search of businesses to find one another. Dozens of angel networks have opened on the World Wide Web, including AngelMoney.com, Business Angels International, Garage Technology Ventures, CommonAngels.com, The Capital Network, Women Angels.net, and many others. The Small Business Administration's Active Capital Network (www.activecapital.org) is a Web-based listing service that provides a marketplace for entrepreneurs seeking between $250,000 and $5 million in capital and angels looking to invest in promising businesses. Entrepreneurs pay $450 a year to list information about their companies on the site, which potential angels can access at any time.

Angels are an excellent source of "patient money," often willing to wait five to seven years or longer to cash out their investments. They earn their returns through the increased value of the business, not through dividends and interest. For example, more than 1,000 early investors in Microsoft Inc. are now millionaires, and the original investors in Genentech Inc. (a genetic engineering company) have seen their investments increase more than 500 times.[26] Angels' return-on-investment targets tend to be lower than those of professional venture capitalists. Although venture capitalists shoot for 60 percent to 75 percent returns annually, private investors usually settle for 20 percent to 50 percent (depending on the level of risk involved in the venture). The average rate of return for angels is 30 percent a year.[27] Private investors typically take less than 50 percent ownership, leaving the majority ownership to the company founder(s). The lesson: If an entrepreneur needs relatively small amounts of money to launch a company, angels are an excellent source to consider.

Table 14.3 offers useful tips for attracting angel capital.

### Partners

As we saw in Chapter 3, "Choosing a Form of Ownership," entrepreneurs can take on partners to expand the capital base of a business.

*Lan Tran Cao and Viet Café*

After spending nearly 30 years in various IT jobs for major corporations, Lan Tran Cao decided to return to her first love—cooking. Raised in Saigon, Cao started cooking for the 13 members of her family when she was just 12 and then went on to study the art of cooking in France. Cao used her experience starting restaurants (She launched two of them while in college in Sydney, Australia) to open Viet Café in New York City. She used money from her savings to finance most of the start-up costs of the restaurant, which serves traditional Vietnamese dishes such as lemongrass chicken rolls and roast lacquered duck. Starting a restaurant in New York City is extremely expensive, however, and Cao needed more capital. She decided to bring in a partner, who owns 30 percent of Viet Café, but Cao is both the chef and the CEO of the company.[28]

Before entering into any partnership arrangement, however, entrepreneurs must consider the impact of giving up some personal control over operations and of sharing profits with others. Whenever entrepreneurs give up equity in their businesses (through whatever mechanism), they run the risk of losing control over it. As the founder's ownership in a company becomes increasingly diluted, the probability of losing control of its future direction and the entire decision-making process increases.

### TABLE 14.3  Tips for Attracting Angel Financing

Although they are an important source of small business financing, angels can be extremely difficult to locate. You won't find them listed under "Angels" in the telephone directory. Patience and persistence—and connections—pay off in the search for angel financing, however. How does an entrepreneur who needs financing find an angel to help launch or expand a company and make the deal work?

- *Start looking for potential investors early—before you need the money.* Finding private investors takes a lot longer than most entrepreneurs think. Starting early is one key to success.
- *Have a business plan ready.* Once you find potential private investors, don't risk them losing interest while you put together a business plan. Have the plan ready to go *before* you begin your search.
- *Look close to home.* Most angels prefer to invest their money locally, so conduct a thorough search for potential angels within a 50-to-100-kilometer radius of your business.
- *Canvass your industry.* Angels tend to specialize in particular industries, usually ones they know a lot about.
- *Recognize that, in addition to the money they invest, angels also want to provide their knowledge and expertise.* Indeed, angels' experience and knowledge can be just as valuable as their money *if* entrepreneurs are willing to accept it.
- *Remember that angels invest for more than just financial reasons.* Angels want to earn a good return on the money they invest in businesses, but there's usually more to it than that. Angels often invest in companies for personal reasons.
- *Join local philanthropic organizations, chambers of commerce, nonprofit organizations, and advisory boards.* Potential investors often are involved in such organizations.
- *Ask business professionals such as bankers, lawyers, stockbrokers, accountants, and others for names of potential angels.* They know people who have the money and the desire to invest in business ventures.
- *Network, network, network.* Finding angel financing initially is a game of contacts—getting an introduction to the right person from the right person.
- *Investigate the investors and their past deals.* Never get involved in a deal with an angel you don't know or trust. Be sure you and your investors have a common vision of the business and the deal.
- *Summarize the details of the deal in a letter of intent.* Although a letter of intent is not legally binding, it outlines the basic structure of the deal and exposes the most sensitive areas being negotiated so that there are no surprises. What role, if any, will the angel play in running the business? Angels can be a source of valuable help, but some entrepreneurs complain of angels' meddling.
- *Talk about the risks up front.* Some entrepreneurs do everything they can to disguise the risks associated with their businesses from potential investors. Smart entrepreneurs disclose the risks early on. Don't dwell on the downside, but be honest about the risk of the investment.
- *Keep the deal simple.* The simpler the deal is, the easier it will be to sell to potential investors. Probably the simplest way to involve angels is to sell them common stock.
- *Nail down the angels' exit path.* Angels make their money when they sell their ownership interests. Ideally, the exit path should be part of structuring the deal. Will the company buy back the angels' shares? Will the company go public so the angels can sell their shares on the market? Will the owners sell out to a larger company? What is the time frame for doing so?
- *Avoid intimidating potential investors.* Most angels are turned off by entrepreneurs with an attitude of "I have someone else who will do the deal if you don't." In the face of such coercion, many private investors simply walk away from the deal.
- *Always be truthful.* Overpromising and underdelivering will kill a deal and spoil future financing opportunities.
- *Develop alternative financing arrangements.* Never back an angel into a corner with "take this deal or leave it." Have alternative plans prepared in case the investor balks at the outset.
- *Don't take the money and run.* Investors appreciate entrepreneurs who keep them informed—about how their money is being spent and the results it shows. Prepare periodic reports for them.
- *Stick to the deal.* It's tempting to spend the money where it's most needed once it is in hand. Resist! If you promised to use the funds for specific purposes, do it. Nothing undermines an angel's trust as quickly as violating the original plan.

## ■ Running in Circles in Search of Capital

Janet Kraus and Kathy Sherbrooke met as graduate students at Stanford Business School before classes began and quickly struck up a friendship. The two discovered that they had much in common, including an admiration of Anita Roddick, founder of The Body Shop. Sherbrooke had written her admissions essay on Roddick's ability to balance business success with both social and environmental responsibility. Kraus admired Roddick's approach to business and aspired to work for her one day, which she ultimately did.

While at Stanford, the pair of entrepreneurs-to-be were influenced by the school's emphasis on entrepreneurship. They took a class on financing start-ups that was taught by Irv Grousbeck, founder of Continental Cablevision. They also took a class by Jim Collins, who was compiling what would become his best-selling book, *Built to Last*, and learned how to build a company that not only would be successful but also would make a difference.

When Kraus and Sherbrooke graduated in the spring of 1994, they did what many college students dream about: they took a cross-country road trip. They loaded up Kraus' Honda Accord and headed east, but it was not a typical college road trip. Kraus and Sherbrooke were *working*. They were on a journey of discovery; rather than be consumed with reading a roadmap for their trip, the two were creating a map for their future as entrepreneurs. A business partnership, says Kraus, "is like a marriage. You want to make sure you're doing it with someone you trust through and through." While one drove, the other took notes on their intense discussions.

They talked about business philosophies, launch strategies, financing options, and exit strategies. What they did not talk about, however, was perhaps the most obvious question: What kind of business will we start together? They didn't really know, nor did they think that was essential at that point to answer that question. From their 3,000-mile journey, Kraus and Sherbrooke realized that they wanted to start a company that would have a positive impact on its customers, its employees, its community, and even the world.

Before launching a company, however, their plan called for both of them to get business experience. They established a three-year timetable. Sherbrooke returned to California to work as a product manager for a software company, and Kraus landed her dream job as Director of Values and Vision for The Body Shop. By the summer of 1996, the two were meeting every morning planning to launch their business. At that point, the question, "What business do we launch?" became essential. They considered many options and settled on the booming concierge industry, but they envisioned something much grander than a local personal shopping and dog-walking service. Instead, they decided that their company, Circles, would target credit card and financial services companies, offering to provide top-notch concierge services for their clients' best customers. Need a table at one of New York's hottest restaurants on a moment's notice? Circles can get it. Have to have a vintage gown for the ball tonight delivered to your hotel room? Circles can handle it. Want tickets to a sold-out concert or musical? Circles can deliver. Need a magician for your kid's birthday party? Circles can do it.

Following their plan, Kraus and Sherbrooke began using their network of contacts to set up meetings with venture capital firms to discuss financing for their company. They knew that women-owned businesses received only 5 percent of private equity investments, but they were undeterred. In meetings with venture capitalists (VCs), they told their story and pitched their business plan.

They were successful. Boston-based Circles now has more than 500 employees. The company usually connects with its 2.5 million customers by phone and then turns its staff loose to meet customers' needs. Their competitive advantage is their willingness to go to almost any extreme for their customers. They once coordinated a helicopter rescue for a climber in distress on a Himalayan mountain. Kraus and Sherbrooke launched Circles in 1997 with their own money and nearly $500,000 from friends and family members. In their first round of formal financing, they raised $15 million from two venture capital firms and have since landed $11 million more in VC financing. Their business began earning a profit in 2001 and has remained profitable ever since.

1. Like many entrepreneurs, Kraus and Sherbrooke used money from family members and friends to launch Circles. Professor David Deeds says of

investments in business start-ups from family members and friends, "It's the highest-risk money you'll ever get. The venture may succeed or fail, but either way, you still have to go to Thanksgiving dinner." What does he mean?

2. What advice would you offer to an entrepreneur seeking capital from family members and friends to launch a business?

3. Suppose that early in their business, Kraus and Sherbrooke came to you for advice on where to find, say $5 million, for their business. What would you tell them?

*Source:* Adapted from David Whitford, "We Can Fix Anything," *FSB*, April 2006, pp. 30–33.

## Corporate Venture Capital

Large corporations are in the business of financing small companies. Today about 19 percent of all venture capital deals involve corporate venture capital. The average investment that large corporations make in small companies is $2.97 million, an amount that represents 7.7 percent of total venture capital investments.[29] Approximately 300 large corporations across the globe, including Intel, Motorola, Cisco Systems, Siemens, Dow Chemical, Nokia, UPS, and General Electric, have venture capital divisions that invest nearly $2 billion a year in young companies, most often those in the product development and growth stages. The large companies are looking not only for financial returns from the small companies in which they invest but also innovative products that can benefit them. Young companies get a boost from the capital injections large companies give them, but they also stand to gain many other benefits from the relationship. The right corporate partner may share technical expertise, distribution channels, marketing know-how, and provide introductions to important customers and suppliers. Another intangible yet highly important advantage that an investment from a large corporate partner gives a start-up is credibility, often referred to as "market validation." Doors that otherwise would be closed to a small company magically open when the right corporation becomes a strategic partner.

Foreign corporations also are interested in investing in small businesses abroad. Often these corporations are seeking strategic partnerships to gain access to new technology, new products, or access to lucrative markets. In return, the small companies they invest in benefit from the capital infusion as well as from their partners' international experience and connections. Some small companies are turning to their customers for the resources they need to fuel their rapid growth. Recognizing how interwoven their success is with that of their suppliers, corporate giants such as AT&T, JCPenney, and Ford now offer financial support to many of the small businesses from which they buy. Figure 14.2 shows recent trends in corporate venture capital.

*Virtual Iron and Intel*

Virtual Iron, a small company that makes virtual storage software, recently landed $3 million in funding from the venture capital division of giant computer chipmaker Intel that it is using to develop new products and to expand its marketing efforts. Because Virtual Iron's technology is "strategic to Intel," the investment led to a collaboration agreement between the two companies. Since 1991, Intel has invested more than $4 billion in nearly 1,000 promising young companies whose products or services align with its strategy.[30]

## Venture Capital Companies

**Venture capital companies (VCs)** are private, for-profit organizations that purchase equity positions in young businesses they believe have high-growth and high-profit potential, producing annual returns of 300 to 500 percent over five to seven years. More than 1,300 venture capital firms operate across the United States today, investing in promising small companies in a variety of industries (see Figure 14.3). Forty-two states also operate venture capital funds. New Mexico's venture capital fund recently invested $10 million in Eclipse

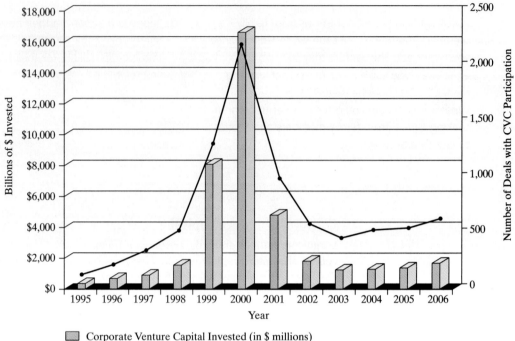

**FIGURE 14.2  Corporate Venture Capital**

*Source:* PricewaterhouseCoopers, *MoneyTree Report,* 2007, www.pwcmoneytree.com.

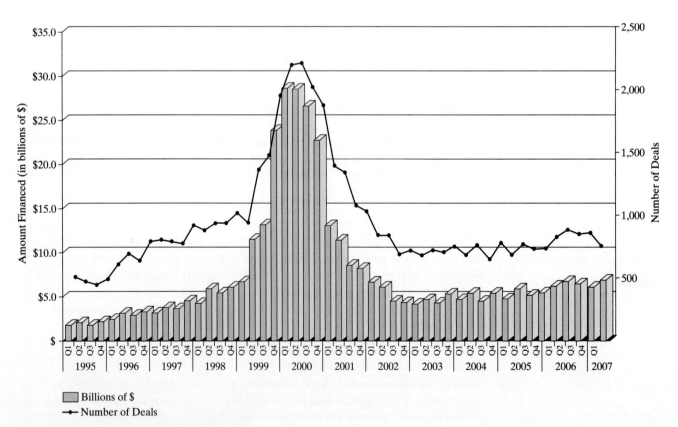

**FIGURE 14.3  Venture Capital Financing**

*Source:* PricewaterhouseCoopers, *MoneyTree Report*, 2007, www.pwcmoneytree.com.

Aviation, a company based in Albuquerque that makes small, low-cost, fuel-efficient jets and counts billionaire Bill Gates among its investors.[31] Many colleges and universities across the nation have created venture funds designated to invest in promising businesses started by their students, alumni, faculty, and others. A number of business schools operate venture capital funds that are co-managed by students, faculty, and professional venture capitalists. "We don't mandate that capital go to alumni," says the manager of one such fund, "but we certainly give preferential treatment to people associated with the universities."[32]

Even government entities such as the U.S. Central Intelligence Agency (CIA), the U.S. Army, the Defense Advanced Research Project Agency (DARPA), and the National Security Agency (NSA) have launched venture capital firms to invest in promising small businesses that are creating technologies to fight the war on terrorism. For instance, DARPA has invested in a company that has developed strength-enhancing body armor, a mechanically powered exoskeleton (remember RoboCop?) that allows people to carry heavy objects and travel great distances with ease.[33]

*Sourcefire Network Security*

Since its founding in 1999, the CIA's venture fund, In-Q-Tel, has invested in several small companies including Sourcefire Network Security, a computer network security firm that has developed products designed to protect computer networks from attacks by cyber-terrorists. The boost from In-Q-Tel's investments has enabled Sourcefire to raise $18 million from other venture capital firms.[34]

Venture capital firms, which provide about 7 percent of all funding for private companies, have invested billions in high-potential small companies over the years, including notable businesses such as Apple, Microsoft, Intel, and Outback Steakhouse. Although companies in high-tech industries such as the Internet, communications, computer hardware and software, medical care, and biotechnology are the most popular targets of venture capital, a company with extraordinary growth prospects has the potential to attract venture capital, whatever its industry. Table 14.4 offers a humorous look at how venture capitalists decipher the language of sometimes overly optimistic entrepreneurs.

**POLICIES AND INVESTMENT STRATEGIES.** VCs usually establish stringent policies to govern their overall investment strategies.

*Investment Size and Screening.* The average venture capital firm's investment in a small company is $7.4 million. Depending on the size of the venture capital company and its cost structure, minimum investments range from $50,000 to $5 million. Investment ceilings, in effect, do not exist. Most firms seek investments in the $3 million to $10 million range to justify the cost of screening the large number of proposals they receive.

In a normal year, VCs invest in only 3,500 of the 25.5 million small businesses in the United States! The venture capital screening process is *extremely* rigorous. The typical venture capital company invests in less than 1 percent of the applications it receives. For example, the average venture capital firm screens about 1,200 proposals a year, but more than 90 percent are rejected immediately because they do not match the firm's investment criteria. The remaining 10 percent are investigated more thoroughly at a cost ranging from $2,000 to $3,000 per proposal. At this time, approximately 10 to 15 proposals will have passed the screening process, and these are subjected to comprehensive review. The venture capital firm will invest in three to six of these remaining proposals.

*Ownership.* Most venture capitalists prefer to purchase ownership in a small business through common stock or convertible preferred stock. Typically, a venture capital company seeks to purchase 15 percent to 40 percent of a business, but in some cases, VCs may buy 70 percent or more of a company's stock, leaving its founders with a minority share

**TABLE 14.4  Deciphering the Language of the Venture Capital Industry**

By nature, entrepreneurs tend to be optimistic. When screening business plans, venture capitalists must make an allowance for entrepreneurial enthusiasm. Here's a dictionary of phrases commonly found in business plans and their accompanying venture capital translations.

*Exploring an acquisition strategy*—Our current products have no market.

*We're on a clear P2P (pathway to profitability)*—We're still years away from earning a profit.

*Basically on plan*—We're expecting a revenue shortfall of 25 percent.

*Internet business model*—Potentially bigger fools have been identified.

*A challenging year*—Competitors are eating our lunch.

*Considerably ahead of plan*—Hit our plan in one of the last three months.

*Company's underlying strength and resilience*—We still lost money, but look how we cut our losses.

*Core business*—Our product line is obsolete.

*Currently revising budget*—The financial plan is in total chaos.

*Cyclical industry*—We posted a huge loss last year.

*Entrepreneurial CEO*—He is totally uncontrollable, bordering on maniacal.

*Facing challenges*—Our sales continue to slide, and we have no idea why.

*Facing unprecedented economic, political, and structural shifts*—It's a tough world out there, but we're coping the best we can.

*Highly leverageable network*—No longer works but has friends who do.

*Ingredients are there*—Given two years, we might find a workable strategy.

*Investing heavily in R&D*—We're trying desperately to catch the competition.

*Limited downside*—Things can't get much worse.

*Long sales cycle*—Yet to find a customer who likes the product enough to buy it.

*Major opportunity*—It's our last chance.

*Niche strategy*—A small-time player.

*On a manufacturing learning curve*—We can't make the product with positive margins.

*Passive investor*—Someone who phones once a year to see if we're still in business.

*Positive results*—Our losses were less than last year.

*Refocus our efforts*—We've blown our chance, and now we have to fire most of our employees.

*Repositioning the business*—We've recently written off a multi-million-dollar investment.

*Selective investment strategy*—The board is spending more time on yachts than on planes.

*Solid operating performance in a difficult year*—Yes, we lost money and market share, but look how hard we tried.

*Somewhat below plan*—We expect a revenue shortfall of 75 percent.

*Expenses were unexpectedly high*—We grossly overestimated our profit margins.

*Strategic investor*—One who will pay a preposterous price for an equity share in the business.

*Strongest fourth quarter ever*—Don't quibble over the losses in the first three quarters.

*Sufficient opportunity to market this product no longer exists*—Nobody will buy the thing.

*Too early to tell*—Results to date have been grim.

*A team of skilled, motivated, and dedicated people*—We've laid off most of our staff, and those who are left should be glad they still have jobs.

*Turnaround opportunity*—It's a lost cause.

*Unique*—We have no more than six strong competitors.

*Volume-sensitive*—Our company has massive fixed costs.

*Window of opportunity*—Without more money fast, this company is dead.

*Work closely with the management*—We talk to them on the phone once a month.

*A year in which we confronted challenges*—At least we know the questions even if we haven't got the answers.

*Sources:* Adapted from Scott Herhold, "When CEOs Blow Smoke," *e-company*, May 2001, pp. 125–127; Suzanne McGee, "A Devil's Dictionary of Financing," *Wall Street Journal*, June 12, 2000, p. C13; John F. Budd Jr., "Cracking the CEO's Code," *Wall Street Journal*, March 27, 1995, p. A20; "Venture-Speak Defined," *Teleconnect*, October 1990, p. 42; Cynthia E. Griffin, "Figuratively Speaking," *Entrepreneur*, August 1999, p. 26.

of ownership. Entrepreneurs must weigh the positive aspects of receiving needed financing against the disadvantages of owning a smaller share of the business.

When Form + Function, an information technology firm, was looking to expand, founder Bob Bernard and his management team convinced a venture capital firm, Wheatley Partners, to invest $8.5 million in the company in exchange for 27 percent of its stock. Two years later, the company acquired another consulting firm for $6 million using a second round of venture capital and changed its name to Whittman-Hart Inc.[35]

***Stage of Investment.*** Most venture capital firms invest in companies that are either in the early stages of development (called early stage investing) or in the rapid-growth phase (called expansion stage investing); few invest in businesses that are only in the start-up phase (see Figure 14.4). According to the Global Entrepreneurship Monitor, only one in 10,000 entrepreneurs worldwide receives venture capital funding at start-up.[36] Some venture capital firms specialize in acquisitions, providing the financing for managers and employees of a business to buy it out. About 98 percent of all venture capital goes to businesses in the early, expansion, and later stages, although some venture capital firms are showing more interest in companies in the start-up phase because of the tremendous returns that are possible by investing then.[37] Most venture capital firms do not make just a single investment in a company. Instead, they invest in a company over time across several stages, where their investments often total $10 to $15 million or more.

***Advice and Contacts.*** In addition to the money they invest, venture capital companies provide the small companies in their portfolios with management advice and access to valuable networks of contacts of suppliers, employees, customers, and other sources of capital. One of their goals in doing so is to strengthen the companies in which they have invested, thereby increasing their value.

**FIGURE 14.4 Venture Capital Funding by Stage**

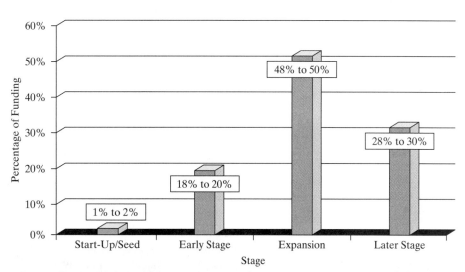

**Start-Up/Seed**—This is the initial stage in which companies are just beginning to develop their ideas into products or services. Typically, these businesses have been in existence less than 18 months and are not yet fully operational.

**Early Stage**—These companies are refining their initial products or services in pilot tests or in the market. Even though the product or service is available commercially, it typically generates little or no revenue. These companies have been in business less than three years.

**Expansion Stage**—These companies' products or services are commercially available and are producing strong revenue growth. Businesses at this stage may not be generating a profit yet, however.

**Later Stage**—These companies' products or services are widely available and are producing ongoing revenue and, in most cases, positive cash flow. Businesses at this stage are more likely to be generating a profit. Sometimes these businesses are spin-offs of already established successful private companies.

*Yuchun Lee, Unica Corporation, and Summit Partners*

When Summit Partners, a U.S.-based venture capital firm, invested $6.5 million in Unica Corporation, a small company that created direct marketing software, it helped Unica's management team build a strong board of directors and recruited a respected software industry veteran to serve as chairman of the board. For the next five years, Summit Partners coached Unica's managers in the nuances of financial management and shepherded the company's growth, making it possible for Unica to make an initial public offering (IPO). "Summit helped us run like a public company from the start, which helped build investor confidence as we prepared for an IPO," says Unica cofounder and CEO Yuchun Lee.[38]

*Control.* In exchange for the financing they receive from venture capitalists, entrepreneurs must give up a portion of their businesses, sometimes surrendering a majority interest and control of its operations. Most venture capitalists prefer to let the founding team of managers employ its skills to operate a business *if* they are capable of managing its growth. However, it is quite common for venture capitalists to join the boards of directors of the companies they invest in or to send in new managers or a new management team to protect their investments. In other words, venture capitalists are *not* passive investors! Some serve only as financial and managerial advisers, whereas others take an active role managing the company—recruiting employees, providing sales leads, choosing attorneys and advertising agencies, and making daily decisions—which can cause friction with the founding entrepreneur(s). The majority of these active venture capitalists say they are forced to step in because the existing management team lacked the talent and experience to achieve growth targets.

**ENTREPRENEURIAL Profile**

*Joan Lyman and SecureWorks Inc.*

Joan Lyman, cofounder of SecureWorks Inc., was CEO of the Internet security company when she decided to relinquish control of the business in exchange for a $30 million capital infusion from venture capital firms. Two years later, she came to regret her decision when the investors replaced her as CEO. Having learned a valuable lesson, Lyman has since launched another technology company with her own money, and this time, she says she will not give up a majority interest in her company.[39]

*Investment Preferences.* The venture capital industry has undergone important changes over the past two decades. Venture capital funds are larger, more numerous, more professional, and more specialized. As the industry grows, more venture capital funds are focusing their investments in niches—everything from low-calorie custards to the Internet. Some will invest in almost any industry but prefer companies in particular stages, including the start-up phase. Traditionally, however, only about 2 percent of the companies receiving venture capital financing are in the start-up (seed) stage when entrepreneurs are forming a company or developing a product or service. Most of the start-up businesses that attract venture capital today are technology companies and life science companies (e.g., biotechnology firms and medical device makers).

**WHAT VENTURE CAPITALISTS LOOK FOR.** Entrepreneurs must realize that it is very difficult for any small business, especially start-ups, to pass the intense screening process of a venture capital company and qualify for an investment. Two factors make a deal attractive to venture capitalists: high returns and a convenient (and profitable) exit strategy. When evaluating potential investments, venture capitalists look for the following features:

*Competent Management.* Attracting venture capital takes more than just a good idea; it requires a management team that can transform an idea into a viable business. Venture capitalists believe in the adage "Money follows management." To them, the most important ingredient in the success of any business is the ability of the management team. "Our business is about investing in people who can get it done," explains Steve Domenik of venture capital fund Sevin Rosen. "The [business] idea is almost secondary."[40] From a venture capitalist's perspective, the ideal management team has experience, managerial skills, commitment, and the ability to build effective teams. When the managers at the venture capital firm Wheatley Partners decided to invest in Form + Function, they cited the quality of the management team as a major factor in their decision.[41]

***Competitive Edge.*** Investors are searching for some factor that will enable a small business to set itself apart from its competitors. This distinctive competence may range from an innovative product or service that satisfies unmet customer needs to a unique marketing or R&D approach. It must be something with the potential to make the business a leader in its field. A study by Global Insight shows how dominant venture-funded businesses are in their industries. Companies that received venture funding between 1980 and 2000 generated 11 percent of the entire U.S. gross domestic product in 2000! The report cited the importance of these companies in terms of their total sales, exports, investments in R&D, and contributions to the tax base.[42]

***Growth Industry.*** Hot industries attract profits—and venture capital. Most venture capital funds focus their searches for prospects in rapidly expanding fields because they believe the profit potential is greater in these areas. Venture capital firms are most interested in young companies that have enough growth potential to become at least $100 million businesses within three to five years. Venture capitalists know that most of the businesses they invest in will flop, so their winners have to be *big* winners.

***Viable Exit Strategy.*** Venture capitalists not only look for promising companies with the ability to dominate a market, but they also want to see a plan for a feasible exit strategy, ideally to be executed within three to five years. Venture capital firms realize the return on their investments when the companies they invest in either make an initial public offering or sell out to a larger business. For instance, Cisco Inc. recently purchased Ironport, a company that makes Internet spam filters, for $830 million, creating a handsome payout for Ironport's founders and the venture capital companies that had invested in it.[43] "If your vision is to run a company and hand it over to your kids, VC funding is out of the question," says Mike Simon, CEO of LogMeIn Inc., a remote software company that has raised $20 million in capital, half of it from venture capital firms.[44] The exit strategy that Wheatley Partners defined for its investment in Form + Function was for the company to make an initial public offering of its stock within five years.[45]

***Intangible Factors.*** Some other important factors considered in the screening process are not easily measured; they are the intuitive, intangible factors the venture capitalist detects by gut feeling. This feeling might be the result of the small company's solid sense of direction, its strategic planning process, the chemistry of its management team, or a number of other factors.

**ENTREPRENEURIAL Profile**

*Rick Holt and David Grano and APTUS Financial LLC*

Rick Holt and David Grano, cofounders of APTUS Financial LLC, a company on the cutting edge of technology designed for wireless banking transactions, parlayed their experience in both the banking and high-tech industries into venture capital to fuel the growth of their business. The pair had launched APTUS Financial with their own money and had developed a leading position with their unique products, but they needed growth capital to retain that edge. With sales of $4.2 million, the company had a successful track record, and both entrepreneurs had relevant management experience. Holt says that the credibility that their experience and the investment of their own capital provided was key to their ability to raise $1.5 million in venture capital.[46]

Despite its many benefits, venture capital is not suitable for every entrepreneur. "VC money comes at a price," warns one entrepreneur. "Before boarding a one-way money train, ask yourself if this is the best route for your business and personal desires, because investors are like department stores the day after Christmas—they expect a lot of returns in a short period of time."[47]

In the Entrepreneurial Spotlight

## ■ Private Equity to the Rescue

Kurt Koloseike and James Samter were at a crossroads. The two had founded FlagZone, a maker of flags and banners, in Pottstown, Pennsylvania, in 1999, and with annual sales of $14.5 million, the company was successful and growing. Samter, now 60, owned 55 percent of the company and was ready to retire, but Koloseike, just 37, did not have the money to purchase Samter's majority share of FlagZone. Koloseike had visions of building FlagZone into the largest maker of flags in the United States but was wondering whether he would be able to achieve that vision.

The cofounders evaluated their options for several months and were considering selling their company outright. Then their financial advisor suggested that they recapitalize FlagZone with the help of private equity investors, enabling Samter to retire and Koloseike to retain control of the business. Recapitalizing, he explained, involves reorganizing a company's capital structure. Deals usually take from 3 to 12 months to close, and legal and accounting fees typically are 1 percent of the deal amount but can be higher depending on the complexity of the deal.

Koloseike spent three months putting together a 20-page proposal that amounted to a mini-business plan, describing FlagZone's strategy, manufacturing process, profiles of its major customers, historical financial statements, and financial forecasts. He sent the proposal to five private equity firms, companies that include both institutional and accredited individual investors and are willing to purchase shares of ownership in promising small companies. Most private equity firms expect to earn 20 percent to 35 percent on their investments and look to sell their equity shares in three to seven years as an exit strategy. "It's not just a funding source," says Koloseike. "You're looking for a financial partner who understands your business."

Koloseike's proposal resulted in two bids from private equity firms, and after careful evaluation, he went with an offer that involved $8 million in both equity and debt financing. He used most of the money to buy out Samter's share of the business and to take some money out of the company for himself to put into a college fund for his three daughters—"sleep well money," he calls it.

After the restructuring, Koloseike owns 55 percent of FlagZone, and his private equity partners own the remaining 45 percent, which allows him to retain control of the business. The cost of completing the recapitalization was $550,000, money that Koloseike considers well spent. Already he has plowed $2 million into expanding the company's staff and purchasing new equipment and is planning to enter the specialty advertising market. Although the process took time, money, and effort, Koloseike is pleased with the outcome. "Now I can focus on running the company," he says.

1. What other financing options could Koloseike have used to buy out Samter? What are the advantages and disadvantages of each option?

*Source:* Adapted from Dalia Fahmy, "Want Money and Power?" *Inc.,* April 2006, pp. 44–46.

## Public Stock Sale ("Going Public")

*3.* Describe the process of "going public" as well as its advantages and disadvantages.

In some cases, small companies can "go public" by selling shares of stock to outside investors. In an **initial public offering (IPO)**, a company raises capital by selling shares of its stock to the general public for the first time. A public offering is an effective method of raising large amounts of capital, but it can be an expensive and time-consuming process filled with regulatory nightmares. "An IPO can be a wonderful thing," says one investment banker, "but it's not all sweetness and light."[48] Once a company makes an initial public offering, *nothing* will ever be the same again. Managers must consider the impact of their decisions not only on the company and its employees but also on shareholders and the value of their stock.

Going public isn't for every business. In fact, most small companies do not meet the criteria for making a successful public stock offering. Since 2000, the average number of companies that make initial public offerings each year is 211, and only about 20,000 companies in the United States—less than 1 percent of the total—are publicly held. Few companies with less than $25 million in annual sales manage to go public successfully. It is extremely difficult for a start-up company with no track record of success to raise money in a public offering. Instead, investment bankers who underwrite public stock offerings typically look for established companies with the following characteristics:

- Consistently high growth rates.
- High profit potential. Strangely enough, profitability at the time of the IPO is not essential; from 2002 to 2006, 45 percent of companies making IPOs had negative earnings.[49]
- Audited financial statements that meet or exceed a nation's standards. After the Enron and WorldCom scandals, investors are demanding impeccable financial statements.
- A solid position in a rapidly-growing industry. In 1999, the median age of companies making IPOs was 4 years; today, it is 13 years.[50]
- A sound management team with experience and a strong board of directors.

Figure 14.5 shows the trend in the number of IPOs and the amount of capital raised. Entrepreneurs who are considering taking their companies public should first consider carefully the advantages and the disadvantages of an IPO. The *advantages* include the following:

***Ability to Raise Large Amounts of Capital.*** The biggest benefit of a public offering is the capital infusion the company receives. After going public, the corporation has the cash to fund R&D projects, expand plant and facilities, repay debt, or boost working capital balances without incurring the interest expense and the obligation to repay associated with debt financing. For instance, when Heely's, the maker of wheeled footwear, went public, the sale of 6.4 million shares at $21 per share generated more than $134 million for the company (before subtracting the expenses of making the offering).[51]

***Improved Corporate Image.*** All of the media attention a company receives during the registration process makes it more visible. In addition, becoming a public company in some industries improves its prestige and enhances its competitive position, one of the most widely recognized, intangible benefits of going public.

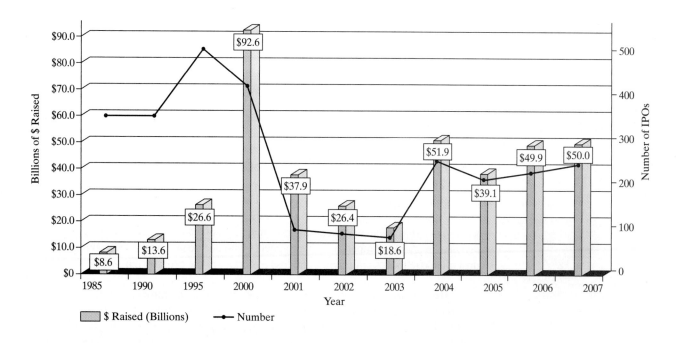

**FIGURE 14.5  Initial Public Offerings**
*Source:* PricewaterhouseCoopers, *US IPO Watch 2006: Analysis and Trends*, p. 2.

***Improved Access to Future Financing.*** Going public boosts a company's net worth and broadens its equity base. Its improved stature and financial strength make it easier for the firm to attract more capital—both debt and equity—and to grow.

***Attracting and Retaining Key Employees.*** Public companies often use stock-based compensation plans to attract and retain quality employees. Stock options and bonuses are excellent methods for winning employees' loyalty and for instilling a healthy ownership attitude among them. Employee stock ownership plans (ESOPs) and stock purchase plans are popular recruiting and motivational tools in many small corporations, enabling them to hire top-flight talent they otherwise would not be able to afford.

***Using Stock for Acquisitions.*** A company whose stock is publicly traded can acquire other businesses by offering its own shares rather than cash. Acquiring other companies with shares of stock eliminates the need to incur additional debt. When search engine giant Google purchased YouTube, the small company that popularized online video, for $1.65 billion (Google's largest acquisition to date), it used Google stock rather than cash to complete the transaction. YouTube founders Chad Hurly, Steve Chen, and Jawed Karim had been considering an IPO for YouTube, but Google's offer was attractive enough to change their minds.[52]

***Listing on a Stock Exchange.*** Being listed on an organized stock exchange, even a small regional one, improves the marketability of a company's shares and enhances its image. World Wrestling Entertainment's stock trades on the New York Stock Exchange, giving it more clout in its market. Most small companies' stocks, however, do not qualify for listing on their nation's largest exchanges. However, some countries have smaller exchanges. In the United States, for example, the American Stock Exchange (the AMEX) offers a market for small-company stocks, The Emerging Company Marketplace. Most small companies' stocks are traded on either the National Association of Securities Dealers Automated Quotation (NASDAQ) system's National Market System (NMS) and its emerging small-capitalization exchange or one of the nation's regional stock exchanges.

The *disadvantages* of going public include the following:

***Dilution of Founder's Ownership.*** Whenever entrepreneurs sell stock to the public, they automatically dilute their ownership in their businesses. Most owners retain a majority interest in the business, but they may still run the risk of unfriendly takeovers years later after selling more stock.

An initial public offering by Heeley's, a maker of wheeled footwear, generated $134 million in capital for the company.

***Loss of Control.*** If enough shares are sold in a public offering, the company founder risks losing control of the company. If a large block of shares falls into the hands of dissident stockholders, they could vote the existing management team (including the founder) out. The board of directors at JetBlue, the discount air carrier, recently voted to relieve company founder David Neeleman, who owned 6 percent of the company's stock, of his duties as CEO and give him the title of chairman of the board, citing the need for "new processes."[53]

***Loss of Privacy.*** Taking their companies public can be a big ego boost for owners, but they must realize that their companies are no longer solely theirs. Information that was once private must be available for public scrutiny. The initial prospectus and the continuous reports filed with the government agencies disclose a variety of information about the company and its operations—from financial data and raw material sources to legal matters and patents to *anyone*—including competitors. Entrepreneurs who decide not to take their companies public most often cite the loss of privacy and loss of control as the primary reasons.

***Regulatory Requirements and Reporting to the SEC.*** Operating as a publicly held company is expensive, especially in the United States since the Sarbanes-Oxley Act was passed in 2002. The U.S. traditionally has required publicly held companies to file periodic reports with it, which often requires a more powerful accounting system, a larger accounting staff, and greater use of attorneys and other professionals. Created in response to ethical fiascoes such as Enron and WorldCom, Sarbanes-Oxley was designed to improve the degree of internal control and the level of financial reporting by publicly held companies. Although many executives agree with the intent of the law, they contend that the cost of complying with it is overbearing. A study by Financial Executives International reports that the cost of complying with the most significant section of Sarbanes-Oxley to public companies with $25 million to $99 million in annual revenues averages $740,000 per year.[54]

**ENTREPRENEURIAL**
**Profile**

*Paymaxx and CompuPay*

The high cost of regulatory compliance dissuades many potential companies from going public. Paymaxx, founded in 1991, became one of the largest payroll provider companies in the United States, and the fast-growing company was considering an IPO to acquire the capital necessary to fuel its growth. Its founders made an abrupt U-turn in their plans when they discovered the cost of complying with Sarbanes-Oxley, choosing instead to sell the company to a larger payroll processing company, CompuPay.[55]

Publicly held companies incur additional costs because they must file periodic reports with their governments, which often requires a more powerful accounting system, a larger accounting staff, and greater use of attorneys, auditors, and other professionals. Complying with the accounting and filing requirements alone can cost $150,000 or more a year.

***Filing Expenses.*** A public stock offering usually is an expensive way to generate funds to finance a company's growth. For the typical small company, the cost of a public offering is about 15 percent of the capital raised. On small offerings, costs can eat up as much as 40 percent of the capital raised, whereas on larger offerings, those above $25 million, only 10 to 12 percent will go to cover expenses. Once an offering exceeds $15 million, its relative issuing costs drop. The largest cost is the underwriter's commission, which is typically 6.5 to 7 percent of the proceeds on offerings less than $10 million and 13 percent on those over that amount. Critics claim that the underwriting fees that U.S. investment banks charge are the highest in the world, which when combined with the reporting requirements of the Sarbanes-Oxley Act, dissuade companies, particularly small ones, from making IPOs in the United States. A study on Small Business and Entrepreneurship shows a decline in the proportion of small company IPOs in recent years. In 1999, companies with revenues of less than $25 million accounted for 70 percent of all IPOs; within five years, that percentage had dropped to just 46 percent.[56]

***Accountability to Shareholders.*** The capital that entrepreneurs manage and risk is no longer just their own. The managers of a publicly held firm are accountable to the company's shareholders. Indeed, the law requires that managers recognize and abide by a relationship built on trust. Profit and return on investment become the primary concerns for investors. If the stock price of a newly public company falls, shareholder lawsuits are inevitable. Investors whose shares decline in value often sue the company's managers for fraud and the failure to disclose in the IPO prospectus the potential risks of their investments.

**ENTREPRENEURIAL**
**Profile**

*Vonage*

When VoIP provider Vonage went public, the offering price of its shares was $17, and the company set aside 13.5 percent of the 31.25 million shares it was offering for its customers. However, when Vonage shares fell to $14.85 on its first day of trading and then plummeted in the months that followed, more than 10,000 customers filed a lawsuit against Vonage, claiming that the company made false and misleading statements about its financial condition during the IPO. As part of its agreement with the issue's underwriters, Vonage also had to pay $11.7 million to cover the cost of the shares for which disgruntled customers refused to pay when the stock price fell.[57]

***Pressure for Short-Term Performance.*** In privately held companies, entrepreneurs are free to follow their strategies for success, even if those strategies take years to produce results. When a company goes public, however, entrepreneurs quickly learn that shareholders are often impatient and expect results immediately. In publicly held companies, quarterly results matter. Founders are under constant pressure to produce short-term results, which can have a negative impact on a company's long-term strategy. The United States Chamber of

Commerce recently called the emphasis on the short term "one of the biggest threats to America's competitiveness."[58] David Klock, who took his once publicly held company Comp Benefits private, says, "I am glad we're private because [it gives us] the ability to make investments that may take two or three quarters to give a good return. That's difficult to do as a public company."[59]

*Loss of Focus.* As impatient as they can be, entrepreneurs often find the time demands of an initial public offering frustrating and distracting. Managing the IPO takes time away from managing the company. Working on an IPO can consume as much as 75 percent of top managers' time, robbing them of their ability to manage the business effectively. "The most common mistake [in an IPO] is the failure to understand the amount of time and effort that is required and the amount of distraction from the primary business," says one IPO expert.[60]

*Timing.* The median time required between a small company receiving its first round of financing and an IPO is now 6.2 years, twice the 3.0 years it took in 2000.[61] During that time, many things that are beyond the company's control, such as declines in the stock market and potential investors' jitters, can quickly slam shut a company's "window of opportunity" for an IPO even after top managers have spent months and many thousands of dollars working on the offering.

*Neatgear Inc.*

Netgear Inc., a manufacturer of networking hardware, filed for an IPO just before the market for high-tech stocks soured. Three years later, after the stock market and the economy recovered, Netgear managed to complete its IPO, selling 7 million shares of stock at $7 per share and raising $98 million. Netgear was fortunate in some respects; many companies planning IPOs were forced to withdraw their proposed stock offerings altogether.[62]

**THE REGISTRATION PROCESS.** Taking a company public is a complicated, bureaucratic process that usually takes several months to complete. Many experts compare the IPO process to running a corporate marathon, and both the company and its management team must be in shape and up to the grueling task. The typical entrepreneur *cannot* take his company public alone. It requires a coordinated effort from a team of professionals, including company executives, an accountant, a securities attorney, a financial printer, and at least one underwriter. Following are key steps in taking a company public.

*Choose the Underwriter.* The single most important ingredient in making a successful IPO is selecting a capable **underwriter** (or **investment banker**). The underwriter serves two primary roles: helping to prepare the registration statement for the issue and promoting the company's stock to potential investors. The underwriter works with the company managers as an adviser in preparing the registration statement that must be filed with the SEC, promoting the issue in a road show, pricing the stock, and providing after-market support. Once the registration statement is finished, the underwriter's primary job is selling the company's stock through an underwriting syndicate of other investment bankers it develops.

*Leslie Blodgett and Bare Escentuals*

Bare Escentuals, a company established in 1976 as a retail storefront and now under the leadership of Leslie Blodgett, CEO, sells premium mineral-based, all-natural makeup and recently made an initial public offering. The company, whose shares trade on the NASDAQ under the symbol "BARE," selected Goldman Sachs and CIBC World Market as its lead underwriters to manage the offering of $16 million shares that generated $352 million to fuel the company's rapid growth.[63]

***Negotiate a Letter of Intent.*** To begin an offering, the entrepreneur and the underwriter must negotiate a **letter of intent**, which outlines the details of the deal. The letter of intent covers a variety of important issues, including the type of underwriting, its size and price range, the underwriter's commission, and any warrants and options included. It almost always states that the underwriter is not bound to the offering until it is executed—usually the day before or the day of the offering. However, the letter usually creates a binding obligation for the company to pay any direct expenses the underwriter incurs relating to the offer.

There are two types of underwriting agreements: firm commitment and best effort. In a **firm commitment agreement**, the underwriter agrees to purchase all of the shares in the offering and then resells them to investors. This agreement *guarantees* that the company will receive the required funds, and most large underwriters use it. In a **best efforts agreement**, the underwriter merely agrees to use its best efforts to sell the company's shares and does not guarantee the company will receive the needed financing. The managing underwriter acts as an agent, selling as many shares as possible through the syndicate. Some best effort contracts are all or nothing—if the underwriter cannot sell all of the shares, the offering is withdrawn. Another version of the best efforts agreement is to set a minimum number of shares that must be sold for the issue to be completed. These methods are riskier because the company has no guarantee of raising the required capital.

The company and the underwriter must decide on the size of the offering and the price of the shares. To keep the stock active in the aftermarket, most underwriters prefer to offer a *minimum* of 400,000 to 500,000 shares. A smaller number of shares inhibits sufficiently broad distribution. Most underwriters recommend selling 25 percent to 40 percent of the company in the IPO. They also strive to price the issue so that the total value of the offering is at least $8 to $15 million. (Although there are exceptions, some underwriters, especially regional ones, are interested in doing IPOs in the $2 to $5 million range.) To meet these criteria and to keep interest in the issue high, the underwriter usually recommends an initial price between $10 and $20 per share. The underwriter establishes an estimated price range for the company's IPO in the underwriting agreement, but it does not establish the final price until the day before the offering takes place. Depending on anticipated demand for the company's shares, the condition of the market, and other factors, the actual price may be outside the estimated range. For instance, in Heely's IPO, lead underwriter Bear Stearns estimated the stock price to be $16 to $18 per share, but because of strong demand for the issue, the final offering price was $21 per share.[64]

Most letters of intent include a **lock-up agreement** that prevents the sale of insider shares, those owned by directors, managers, founders, employees, and other insiders, for 12 to 36 months. The sale of these shares early in a company's public life could send negative signals to investors, eroding their confidence in the stock and pushing its price downward.

***Prepare the Registration Statement.*** After a company signs the letter of intent, the next task is to prepare the **registration statement** to be filed with the government and the prospectus to be distributed to potential investors. These documents describe both the company and the stock offering and disclose information about the risks of investing. It includes information on the use of the proceeds, the company's history, its financial position, its capital structure, the risks it faces, its managers, and many other details. The statements are extremely comprehensive and may take months to develop. To prepare them, entrepreneurs must rely on their team of IPO professionals.

***File with the SEC.*** When the statement is finished (with the exception of pricing the shares, proceeds, and commissions, which cannot be determined until just before the issue goes to market), the company officially files the statement with the SEC and awaits the review of the Division of Corporate Finance. The division sends notice of any deficiencies in the registration statement to the company's attorney in a comment letter. The company and its team of professionals must address all of the deficiencies noted in the comment letter and prepare an amended registration statement. Finally, the company files the revised registration statement, along with a pricing amendment (giving the price of the shares, the proceeds, and the underwriter's commission).

*Wait to Go Effective.* While waiting for the SEC's approval, the managers and the underwriters are busy. The underwriters are building a syndicate of other underwriters who will market the company's stock. (No sales can be made prior to the effective date of the offering, however.) The SEC also limits the publicity and information a company may release during this **quiet period** (which officially starts when the company reaches a preliminary agreement with the managing underwriter and ends 90 days after the effective date).

Securities laws do permit a **road show**, a gathering of potential syndicate members sponsored by the managing underwriter. Its purpose is to promote interest among potential underwriters in the IPO by featuring the company, its management, and the proposed deal. The managing underwriter and key company officials barnstorm major cities, and sometimes foreign cities at a grueling pace.

*Unica Corporation*

During the road show for Unica Corporation, a company that sells enterprise marketing management software, top managers courted potential investors in 12 cities in just 14 days! Their efforts were exhausting but productive: Unica sold 4.8 million shares of its stock and raised $48 million.[65]

On the last day before the registration statement becomes effective, the company signs the formal underwriting agreement. The final settlement, or closing, takes place a few days after the effective date for the issue. At this meeting the underwriters receive their shares to sell and the company receives the proceeds of the offering.

Typically, the entire process of going public takes from 60 to 180 days, but it can take much longer if the issuing company is not properly prepared for the process.

*Meet State Requirements.* In addition to satisfying the SEC's requirements, a company also must meet the securities laws in all states in which the issue is sold. These state laws (or "blue sky" laws) vary drastically from one state to another, and the company must comply with them.

## Gaining a Competitive Edge

### Eight Rules for Financing a Business

Raising the money to launch or expand a business is a challenge. The following "rules" will help you avoid many pitfalls along the way.

*Be sure that you raise enough capital to sustain your business.* One of the most basic mistakes that entrepreneurs make is failing to raise enough capital to keep their businesses going until they begin to generate positive cash flow. In a recent survey by Wells Fargo and Gallup Small Business Index, 53 percent of business owners said that they would have had an easier time in their businesses if they had had access to more capital at the outset. A solid business plan with realistic financial forecasts is the key to knowing how much money your venture will need. When preparing financial forecasts, remember that it is better to stay on the pessimistic side of "realistic."

*Start looking for money before you need it.* Entrepreneurs put themselves in a bind when they wait until the last minute to look for financing. When you are desperate for financing, *any* deal that brings in capital looks like a good one, even if it is not. When Robert Kiyosaki was seeking capital for a gold mining operation in China, he and his partner started explaining the venture to potential investors months before they would need the money. "We let

[them] know how much we required," he says. "Then about a month before we needed the money, we made personal phone calls to see if the prospects were still interested."

*Realize that raising money will take longer than you think.* This is the reason behind the previous rule. Potential investors usually are not in a huge hurry to invest in the small companies that they are considering. They need time to investigate, evaluate, and study the company, its business plan, and the market. The process is called "due diligence," and it takes time to complete. Entrepreneurs who push investors to make quick decisions will get a quick answer, and it's almost always "no."

*Be cautious about giving up too much equity too soon.* Some entrepreneurs are so eager to land financing for their businesses that they hand over a majority interest in their companies to investors at the outset. "Once you sell a percentage of your company, recovering it is very, very difficult and very, very expensive," says one financing expert. In some cases, recovering equity from investors is impossible. An entrepreneur who hands over the majority of the ownership in his or her company also is handing over *control* of the companies to outsiders whose vision for the company may be quite different from the entrepreneur's.

*Don't take money from the wrong investors.* Entrepreneurs can turn to many sources for funding their businesses, but not all of them are a good fit. What constitutes a good fit between a business and its investors often depends on how much money the entrepreneur is seeking, what stage the company is in (seed vs. expansion), and what the investors expect in return. Before signing a deal, make sure that your investors' expectations are a solid match with your company's needs and goals. In addition, accept capital only from those people whom you trust and respect. Entrepreneurs and their investors often have to go through the desert of uncertainty together before they reach the oasis of business success. The journey is much easier if you are traveling with someone you trust and respect.

*Be willing to compromise, but don't give up the farm.* The final deal between entrepreneurs and their investors is the result of a process of negotiation. You must be willing to compromise, but you should not blindly accept every proposal that investors want to include in the deal.

*Keep good records and use them to keep your investors informed.* Be sure that your company prepares accurate, timely financial statements and that you report the results of the company's performance to investors. Naturally, entrepreneurs are hesitant to bring bad news back to their investors. That's a mistake! The right investors can help entrepreneurs find ways to deal with the inevitable setbacks that occur in business.

*Look for investors who can bring something of value to your business—something other than just money.* Clever entrepreneurs see potential investors as potential advisors, consultants, mentors, and ambassadors for their companies.

*Sources:* Adapted from Susan Schreter, "Biggest Financing Mistakes by First-Time Entrepreneurs," Microsoft Office Live, July 2007, http://office.microsoft.com/en-us/officelive/FX102282321033.aspx; Robert Kiyosaki, "Reel 'Em In," *Entrepreneur,* June 2007, p. 152; "How Much It Takes to Start a Business," CNNMoney, August 17, 2006, http://money.cnn.com/2006/08/17/smbusiness/wells_fargo_study/index.htm; Perri Capell, "Typical Funding Mistakes That You Should Avoid," *Startup Journal,* November 9, 2004, http://startup.wsj.com/financing/trends/20041109-capell.html; Christine Comaford-Lynch, "Rules for Raising Capital," *Business Week,* January 22, 2007, www.businessweek.com/smallbiz/content/jan2007/sb20070122_060956_page_2.htm.

## Simplified Registrations and Exemptions

*4.* Explain the various simplified registrations, exemptions from registration, and other alternatives available to entrepreneurs wanting to sell shares of equity to investors.

The IPO process described previously (called an S-1 filing in the United States) requires maximum disclosure in the initial filing and costly compliance with federal regulations, discouraging most small businesses from using it. Fortunately, in the United States, at least, the SEC allows several exemptions from this full-disclosure process for small businesses. Many small businesses that go public choose one of these simplified options the SEC has designed for small companies. The SEC has established the following simplified registration statements and exemptions from the registration process:

**REGULATION S-B.** Regulation S-B is a simplified registration process for small companies seeking to make initial or subsequent public offerings in the U.S. Not only does this regulation simplify the initial filing requirements with the SEC, but it also reduces the ongoing disclosure and filings required of companies. Its primary goals are to open the doors to capital markets to smaller companies by cutting the paperwork and the costs of raising capital. Companies using the simplified registration process have two options: Form SB-1, a "transitional" registration statement for companies issuing less than $10 million worth of securities over a 12-month period, and Form SB-2, reserved for small companies seeking more than $10 million in a 12-month period.

To be eligible for the simplified registration process under Regulation S-B, a company must:

- Be based in the United States or Canada.
- Have revenues of less than $25 million.
- Have outstanding publicly held stock worth no more than $25 million.
- Not be an investment company.
- Provide audited financial statements for two fiscal years.

The goal of Regulation S-B's simplified registration requirements is to enable smaller companies to go public without incurring the expense of a full-blown registration. Total costs for a Regulation S-B offering are approximately $35,000.

**REGULATION D (RULE 504): SMALL COMPANY OFFERING REGISTRATION (SCOR).** Created in the late 1980s, the U.S. Small Company Offering Registration (also known as the Uniform Limited Offering Registration, ULOR) now is available in all 50 states and the District of Columbia. A little known tool, SCOR is designed to make it easier and less expensive for small companies to sell their stock to the public by eliminating the requirement for registering the offering with the SEC. The whole process typically costs less than half of what a traditional public offering costs. Entrepreneurs using SCOR will need an attorney and an accountant to help them with the issue, but many can get by without a securities lawyer, which can save tens of thousands of dollars. Some entrepreneurs even choose to market their companies' securities themselves (for example, to customers), saving the expense of hiring a broker. However, selling an issue is both time- and energy-consuming, and most SCOR experts recommend hiring a professional securities or brokerage firm to sell the company's shares. The SEC's objective in creating SCOR was to give small companies the same access to equity financing that large companies have via the stock market while bypassing many of the same costs and filing requirements.

The capital ceiling on a SCOR issue is $1 million (except in Texas, where there is no limit), and the price of each share must be at least $5. That means that a company can sell no more than 200,000 shares (making the stock less attractive to stock manipulators). A SCOR offering requires only minimal notification to the SEC. The company must file a standardized disclosure statement, the U-7, which consists of 50 fill-in-the-blank questions. The form, which asks for information such as how much money the company needs, what the money will be used for, what investors receive, how investors can sell their investments, and other pertinent questions, closely resembles a business plan but also serves as a state securities offering registration, a disclosure document, and a prospectus. Entrepreneurs using SCOR may advertise their companies' offerings and can sell them directly to any investor with no restrictions and no minimums. An entrepreneur can sell practically any kind of security through a SCOR, including common stock, preferred stock, convertible preferred stock, stock options, stock warrants, and others.

*Dwayne Fosseen and Mirenco*

Dwayne Fosseen, founder of Mirenco, Inc., a company that has developed patented technology to improve the fuel economy, reduce the emissions, and lower the maintenance costs associated with cars and trucks, relied on a SCOR offering to secure an early round of outside capital for his business. After launching Mirenco with his own funds, Fosseen obtained patents for his technology and then landed a grant from the Department of Energy. Needing more capital for expansion, Mirenco raised money through both SB-2 and SCOR offerings. Based in tiny Radcliffe, Iowa, Mirenco, whose shares trade on the OTC Bulletin Board, used the proceeds of its offerings to build a new headquarters, to fund more research and development, and to expand the market for its innovative products.[66]

A SCOR offering offers entrepreneurs needing equity financing several *advantages:*

■ Access to a sizable pool of equity funds (up to $1 million in a year) without the expense of full registration with the SEC. Companies often can complete a SCOR offering for less than $25,000.
■ Few restrictions on the securities to be sold and on the investors to whom they can be sold.
■ The ability to market the offering through advertisements to the public.
■ Young or start-up companies can qualify.
■ No requirement of audited financial statements for offerings less than $500,000.
■ Faster approval of the issue from regulatory agencies.
■ The ability to make the offering in several states at once.

There are, of course, some *disadvantages* to using SCOR to raise needed funds:

■ Partnerships cannot make SCOR offerings.
■ A company can raise no more than $1 million in a 12-month period.
■ An entrepreneur must register the offering in every state in which shares of stock will be sold to comply with their blue sky laws, although current regulations allow simultaneous registration in multiple states.
■ The process can be time-consuming, distracting an entrepreneur from the daily routine of running the company. A limited secondary market for the securities may limit investors' interest. Currently, SCOR shares must be traded through brokerage firms that make small markets in specific stocks. However, the NASDAQ's electronic bulletin board now list SCOR stocks, and the secondary market for them has broadened.

**REGULATION D (RULES 505 AND 506): PRIVATE PLACEMENTS.** Rules 505 and 506 of Regulation D, also known as the Private Placement Memorandum, are exemptions from U.S. registration requirements that give emerging companies the opportunity to sell stock through private placements without actually going public. In a private placement, a company sells its shares directly to accredited private investors without having to register them with the SEC or incur the expenses of an IPO. Instead, an attorney simply draws up an investment agreement that meets state and federal requirements between the company and its private investors. Most companies offer private investors "book deals," proposals with terms that are made on a take-it-or-leave-it basis.

A *Rule 505* offering has a higher capital ceiling than a SCOR offering ($5 million) in a 12-month period but imposes more restrictions (no more than 35 non-accredited investors, no advertising of the offer, and more stringent disclosure requirements).

*Rule 506* imposes no ceiling on the amount that can be raised, but, like a Rule 505 offering, limits the issue to 35 non-accredited investors and prohibits advertising the offer to the public. There is no limit on the number of accredited investors, however. Rule 506 also requires detailed disclosure of relevant information, but the extent depends on the size of the offering.

*Gordon McGilton and
Force Protection Inc.*

Force Protection Inc. (FPI) that makes armored vehicles for military applications, was growing so fast that cash flow was a constant problem. The company needed a capital infusion to sustain its growth. Rather than make an IPO, company managers sold 13 million shares of FPI stock to a group of institutional investors in a private placement that raised more than $152 million. CEO Gordon McGilton says that FPI will use the money to expand the production capacity of its existing life-saving armored vehicles, the Buffalo and the Cougar, and to develop a new vehicle line, the Cheetah. The investment banking firm C.E. Unterberg Towbin handled the details of the private placement for FPI.[67]

Regulation D rules minimize the expense and the time required to raise equity capital for small businesses. Fees for private placements typically range from 1 to 5 percent rather than the 7 to 13 percent underwriters normally charge for managing a public offering. Offerings made under Regulation D do impose limitations and demand certain disclosures, but they only require a company to file a simple form (Form D) with the SEC within 15 days of the first sale of stock.

**SECTION 4(6).** Section 4(6) covers private placements and is similar to Regulation D, Rules 505 and 506. It does not require registration on offers up to $5 million if they are made only to accredited investors.

**INTRASTATE OFFERINGS (RULE 147).** Rule 147 governs intrastate offerings, those sold only to investors in a single state by a company doing business in that state. To qualify, a company must be incorporated in the state, maintain its executive offices there, have 50 percent of its assets there, derive 50 percent of its revenues from the state, and use 50 percent of the offering proceeds for business in the state. There is no ceiling on the amount of the offering, but only residents of the state in which the issuing company operates can invest. The maximum number of shareholders is 500, and a company's asset base cannot exceed $10 million.

*Martin Lightsey and Specialty Blades Inc.*

Specialty Blades, a closely held company that Martin Lightsey had founded in 1985 had increased in value so much that several shareholders, including his daughters, wanted to cash out some of their stock. Lightsey, however, did not have the cash available to buy back their shares. Lightsey considered an IPO for Specialty Blades until he learned that the regulatory and reporting costs for the company if it were publicly held would be $500,000 a year. Instead, Lightsey decided to use an intrastate offering to sell stock to residents of Virginia, where the company is based. Specialty Blades' existing shareholders could cash out their investments, and Lightsey could diversify the company's pool of investors beyond its existing family members and friends. To make the intrastate offering, Lightsey had to switch from an S corporation to a C corporation; then, he hired a Richmond, Virginia, brokerage firm to value Specialty Blades. A few months later, Lightsey invited 40 potential investors, most of whom he knew from church and community events, to a presentation about the company's strategy and growth potential. Within a few weeks, investors purchased 6 percent of Specialty Blades stock, generating $600,000 in growth capital, and the entire process cost Lightsey just $15,000, a fraction of the cost of an IPO. In the years since, Specialty Blades has made two more intrastate offerings under Rule 147, and the company now has more than 200 shareholders and a market capitalization of $33.9 million. Lightsey, who owns 5.6 percent of Specialty Blades' stock is considering acquiring another company. If he does, he plans to make another intrastate offering of up to $10 million to finance it.[68]

**REGULATION A.** Regulation A, although currently not used often, allows an exemption for offerings up to $5 million over a 12-month period. Regulation A imposes few restrictions, but it is more costly than the other types of exempted offerings, usually running between $80,000 and $120,000. The primary difference between a SCOR offering and a Regulation A offering is that a company must register its SCOR offering only in the states where it will sell its stock; in a Regulation A offering, the company also must file an offering statement with the SEC. Like a SCOR offering, a Regulation A offering allows a company to sell its shares directly to investors.

**DIRECT STOCK OFFERINGS.** Many of the simplified registrations and exemptions discussed previously give entrepreneurs the power to sidestep investment bankers and sell their companies' stock offerings directly to investors and, in the process, save themselves thousands of dollars in underwriting fees. By going straight to investors rather than through underwriters, entrepreneurs cut out the underwriter's commission, many legal expenses, and most registration fees. Entrepreneurs willing to handle the paperwork requirements and to market their own shares can make direct public offerings (DPOs) for about 6 percent of the total amount of the issue, compared with 15 percent for a traditional stock offering, and raise as much or more money as a private placement generates.

*Ann Ruethling and
Chinaberry Inc.*

Chinaberry Inc., founded in 1982 by Ann Ruethling, a former airline executive turned stay-at-home mom, at her kitchen table, markets children's books with positive, wholesome messages through its Web site, book fairs, and catalogs that are mailed to 3.6 million customers three times a year. With sales growing fast (they more than doubled between 1998 and 2005), Chinaberry needed capital to support its online marketing efforts, reduce its debt, and expand call center and warehouse and shipping facilities. Ruethling turned to Drew Fields Direct Public Offerings for help and sent an e-mail prospectus, a frequently asked questions document, and an order form to prospective investors (including customers). Chinaberry also marketed the DPO in its print catalogs. Loyal customers responded, and Chinaberry raised $284,200 through its DPO.[69]

The World Wide Web (WWW) has opened a new avenue for direct public offerings and is one of the fastest-growing sources of capital for small businesses. Much of the Web's appeal as a fund-raising tool stems from its ability to reach large numbers of prospective investors very quickly and at a low cost. The Web enables a small company to make its investment prospectus available to the world at a minimal cost. Companies making direct stock offerings on the Web most often make them under either Regulation A or Regulation D and usually generate between $300,000 and $4 million for the company.

# ENTREPRENEURSHIP
# In Action

## Would You Invest?

Daniel Carroll, 25, and Christopher Carlevato, 24, are the cofounders of HedgeStop, a start-up that combines the social networking appeal of Facebook and MySpace.com with the opportunity to learn about the financial world of investing and managing portfolios. Members, who can sign up for free, have access to the first social networking stock market game on the Web, in which they can manage their own imaginary hedge fund and interact with other members as they manage their funds. "We at HedgeStop are about one thing: making investing fun, and heck, if you can learn how to trade, meet some friends, and have a good time in the process, we are all for it," says Carroll. "Investing will never be boring again."

Members can send e-mails to one another through the site, track friends' investing patterns, read business and financial news, blogs, and profiles on recording artists. "We're trying to sex up business news by creating an online community for young people [who are] interested in finance, from casual investors to business professionals," says Carroll. HedgeStop has 2,200 members and adds an average of 400 new users each week. Revenue in its first full year of operation was just $48,000, almost all

of it from advertisements placed on its site by other companies. "Five years down the line, we'd like to be the destination for 3 million young people with $5 million in sponsorships and advertising revenue each year," says Carlevato. Carroll and Carlevato are seeking $2.5 to $3 million to hire a marketing staff, a public relations firm, and software engineers to enhance their company's Web site with features such as streaming video.

1. Visit the HedgeStop Web site (www.hedgestop.com) to learn more about the company. On a scale of 1 (low) to 10 (high), how would you rate HedgeStop's chances of attracting the capital it needs? Explain your reasoning.

2. Would you consider investing in HedgeStop? Why or why not?

3. What questions would you want answered before considering an investment in HedgeStop?

4. What sources of financing do you recommend that Carroll and Carlevato consider to raise the money they are seeking for HedgeStop?

*Source:* Adapted from Ryan McCarthy, "Elevator Pitch," *Inc.*, February 2007, pp. 32–33.

**TABLE 14.5 Is a Direct Public Offering for You?**

Drew Field, an expert in direct public offerings, has developed the following 10-question quiz to help entrepreneurs decide whether or not their companies are good candidates for a DPO.

1. Does your company have a history of consistently profitable operations under the present management?
2. Is your company's present management team honest, socially responsible, and competent?
3. In 10 words or fewer, can you explain the nature of your business to laypeople new to investing?
4. Would your company excite prospective investors, making them want to share in its future?
5. Does your company have natural affinity groups, such as customers with strong emotional loyalty?
6. Do members of your natural affinity groups have discretionary cash to risk for long-term gains?
7. Would your company's natural affinity groups recognize your company's name and consider your offering materials?
8. Can you get the names, addresses, and telephone numbers of affinity group members, as well as some demographic information about them?
9. Can a high-level company employee spend half-time for six months as a DPO project manager?
10. Does your company have—or can you obtain—audited financial statements for at least the last two fiscal years?

The more questions you can answer with "yes," the more likely it is that a direct public offering could work for your company.

*Sources:* Drew Field Direct Public Offers, Screen Test for a Direct Public Offering, www.dfdpo.com/screen.htm; Stephanie Gruner, "Could You Do a DPO?" *Inc.*, December 1996, p. 70.

Direct public offerings work best for companies that have a single product or related product lines, a base of customers who are loyal to the company, good name recognition, and annual sales between $3 million and $25 million. The first company to make a successful DPO over the Internet was Spring Street Brewing, a microbrewery founded by Andy Klein. Klein raised $1.6 million in a Regulation A offering in 1996. Companies that make successful direct public offerings of their stock over the Web must meet the same standards as companies making stock offerings using more traditional methods. Experts caution Web-based fund seekers to make sure that their electronic prospectuses meet government requirements. Table 14.5 provides a brief quiz to help entrepreneurs determine whether their companies would be good candidates for a DPO.

### Foreign Stock Markets

Some foreign stock markets offer entrepreneurs access to equity funds more readily than exchanges in their domestic markets. The London Stock Exchange's AIM (Alternative Investment Market) is geared to small companies with its lower costs and less extensive reporting and regulatory requirements. "Smaller deals can get done on the AIM," says one U.S.-based securities attorney. "They're cheaper, and there are fewer requirements. The deals I've seen there could not have been done here." Similarly, stock exchanges in Canada (Toronto and Vancouver), Germany, Korea, and Singapore are attracting small companies that are hungry for capital. These foreign exchanges encourage equity listings of small companies because the cost of offerings is about half that in the United States.

**ENTREPRENEURIAL Profile**

*Bruce Khouri and Solar Integrated Systems*

Bruce Khouri, founder of Solar Integrated Technologies, a company that makes unique solar-electric roofing systems, was struggling to fund his company's rapid growth from retained earnings and his own pocket. He needed a significant amount of capital to finance the assembly and installation of solar systems for several large corporate clients and to develop markets in foreign countries. An IPO in the United States was not practical. With annual sales of just $8 million, "we were a guppy in a large ocean," says Khouri. He began exploring London's AIM and making contacts in Britain's financial markets. Within five months, Solar Integrated Technologies completed an initial public offering on the AIM that generated $22 million at a total cost of $2.9 million.[70]

Securing capital to launch or to expand a small business is no easy task. However, entrepreneurs who understand the equity funding options that are available and are prepared to go after them stand a much better chance of getting the financing they seek than those who don't.

---

## Chapter Review

1. Explain the differences in the three types of capital small businesses require: fixed, working, and growth.
   - Capital is any form of wealth employed to produce more wealth. Three forms of capital are commonly identified: fixed capital, working capital, and growth capital.
   - Fixed capital is used to purchase a company's permanent or fixed assets; working capital represents the business's temporary funds and is used to support the business's normal short-term operations; growth capital requirements surface when an existing business is expanding or changing its primary direction.

2. Describe the various sources of equity capital available to entrepreneurs, including personal savings, friends and relatives, angels, partners, corporations, venture capital, and public stock offerings.
   - The most common source of financing a business is the owner's personal savings. After emptying their own pockets, the next place entrepreneurs turn for capital is family members and friends. Angels are private investors who not only invest their money in small companies, but they also offer valuable advice and counsel to them. Some business owners have success financing their companies by taking on limited partners as investors or by forming an alliance with a corporation, often a customer or a supplier. Venture capital companies are for-profit, professional investors looking for fast-growing companies in "hot" industries. When screening prospects, venture capital firms look for competent management, a competitive edge, a growth industry, and important intangibles that will make a business successful. Some owners choose to attract capital by taking their companies public, which requires registering the public offering.

3. Describe the process of "going public," as well as its advantages and disadvantages
   - Going public involves: (1) choosing the underwriter, (2) negotiating a letter of intent, (3) preparing the registration statement, (4) filing with the national government, and (5) meeting local government requirements.
   - Going public offers the advantages of raising large amounts of capital, improved access to future financing, improved corporate image, and gaining listing on a stock exchange. The disadvantages include dilution of the founder's ownership, loss of privacy, reporting and filing expenses, and accountability to shareholders.

4. Explain the various simplified registrations and exemptions from registration available to small businesses wanting to sell securities to investors.
   - Rather than go through the complete registration process, some companies use one of the simplified registration options and exemptions available to small companies: U.S. Regulation S-B, Regulation D (Rule 504) Small Company Offering Registration (SCOR), Regulation D (Rule 505 and Rule 506) Private Placements, Section 4(6), Rule 147, Regulation A, direct stock offerings, and stock markets in other countries.

## Discussion Questions

1. Why is it so difficult for most small business owners to raise the capital needed to start, operate, or expand their ventures?
2. What is capital? List and describe the three types of capital a small business needs for its operations.
3. Define equity financing. What advantage does it offer over debt financing?
4. What is the most common source of equity funds in a typical small business? If an owner lacks sufficient equity capital to invest in the firm, what options are available for raising it?
5. What guidelines should entrepreneurs follow if friends and relatives choose to invest in their businesses?
6. What is an angel investor? Assemble a brief profile of the typical private investor. How can entrepreneurs locate potential angels to invest in their businesses?
7. What advice would you offer an entrepreneur on how to strike a deal with a private investor and avoid problems?
8. What types of businesses are most likely to attract venture capital? What investment criteria do venture capitalists use when screening potential businesses? How do these compare to the typical angel's criteria?
9. How do venture capital firms operate? Describe their procedure for screening investment proposals.
10. Summarize the major exemptions and simplified registrations available to small companies wanting to make public offerings of their stock.

# Business PlanPro

A business plan is an important instrument in the search for capital; therefore, one of the most common motivations for creating a business plan is to secure equity financing. The business plan can be an excellent communication tool to convince investors of a business's stability and convey its potential earning power. A business plan adds credibility to your vision and the investments that others may make in it. Think about the financial needs of your company. Do you need start-up funding beyond the amount that you can provide? Is your business going to need working capital? Does your business need additional financing for growth? If you have the need to raise capital for any purpose, your business plan can help you clarify those needs and formulate a strategy for raising capital.

## On the Web

If you need start-up or growth capital for your venture, visit the Companion Website at www.prenhall.com/scarborough for Chapter 14 and review these equity financing options. Determine whether these sources may be useful to you as you explore financing opportunities. You will also find additional information regarding bootstrap and non-traditional funding.

Review some sample plans in Business Plan Pro and note the financial sections in them. If you are creating a start-up plan, you may want to review these sample plans: Elsewares Promotional, Westbury Storage, Inc., and Southeast Health Plans. If you are going to be searching for financing for an ongoing business, these plans may be of interest: Coach House Bed & Breakfast, The Daily Perc, and Bioring SA. These diverse plans present financial information in ways that may give you ideas how to best communicate your company's financial needs and potential. Use approaches that fit your plan as you consider the elements that potential investors will find enticing so that they will want to learn more about the growth and earning potential of your business. Leverage each aspect of the financial section—the breakeven analysis, projected profit and loss, projected cash flow, projected balance sheet, and business rations—to prove your company's attractiveness as an investment opportunity.

## In the Software

Open your plan in Business Plan Pro and go to the "Financial Plan" section. You may want to begin this section by providing an overview of your financial situation and needs. State your assumptions about the existing financial environment. Your assumptions will help to identify general facts upon which you are basing your plan, such as anticipated economic conditions, current short interest term, long term interest rates, expected tax rates, personnel expenses, cash expenses, sales on credit, and others. Let the software lead you through this section.

Next consider which of the following sources you plan to use as a source of equity capital:

- Friends and family member
- Private investors or "angels"
- Partners
- Corporate venture capitalist

- Venture capital companies
- Public stock sale
- Simplified registrations and exemptions

## Building Your Business Plan

One of the most valuable aspects of developing the financial section of your business plan is to determine the amount of capital your business will need and to describe the use of that capital in the business. In addition, you must consider the implications of accepting capital from outside investors. There always are costs associated with using other people's money; make sure that you know what they are in your situation. Keep in mind that potential investors will also be assessing the qualifications of your management team, the industry's growth potential, the proposed exit strategy, and other factors as they assess the financial stability and potential of your business venture. A business plan is an effective way to expand your equity financing options and to help you strike a deal with the options that are best for your situation.

# Sources of Debt Financing

Always borrow from pessimists. They never expect to get it back.
—Anonymous

Don't ever borrow a little bit of money because when you borrow a little bit of money, you have a serious creditor if you run short. And, if you borrow a lot of money, you have a partner when you get into trouble.
—Fred Smith, founder, FedEx

## Learning Objectives

**Upon completion of this chapter, you will be able to:**

1 Describe the various sources of debt capital and the advantages and disadvantages of each.

2 Explain the types of financing available from nonbank sources of credit.

3 Identify the sources of government financial assistance and the loan programs these agencies offer.

4 Describe the various loan programs available from the Small Business Administration.

5 Discuss state and local economic development programs.

6 Discuss valuable methods of financing growth and expansion internally with bootstrap financing.

7 Explain how to avoid becoming a victim of a loan scam.

**ebt financing** involves the funds that the small business owner borrows and must repay with interest. Small companies in the United States, for example, rely heavily on debt capital to start and feed their growing businesses. The U.S. Small Business Administration estimates that lenders make $600 billion worth of loans of less than $1 million to small companies each year. Add to that amount loans from family members and friends and credit card borrowing, and total small business borrowing approaches $1 trillion a year.[1] Lenders of capital are more numerous than investors, but small business loans can be just as difficult (if not more difficult) to obtain. Although borrowed capital allows entrepreneurs to maintain complete ownership of their businesses, it must be carried as a liability on the balance sheet as well as be repaid with interest at some point in the future. In addition, because small businesses are considered to be greater risks than bigger corporate customers, they must pay higher interest rates because of the risk-return tradeoff—the higher the risk, the greater the return demanded. Most small firms pay the **prime rate**, the interest rate banks charge their most creditworthy customers, *plus* two or more percentage points. Still, the cost of debt financing often is lower than that of equity financing. Because of the higher risks associated with providing equity capital to small companies, investors demand greater returns than lenders. In addition, unlike equity financing, debt financing does not require entrepreneurs to dilute their ownership interest in the company.

The need for debt capital can arise from a number of sources, but financial experts identify the following reasons business owners should consider borrowing money:[2]

- *Increasing the company's workforce and/or inventory to boost sales.* Sufficient working capital is the fuel that feeds a company's growth.
- *Gaining market share.* Businesses often need extra capital as their customer bases expand and they incur the added expense of extending credit to customers.
- *Purchasing new equipment.* Financing new equipment that can improve productivity, increase quality, and lower operating expenses often takes more capital than a growing company can generate internally.
- *Refinancing existing debt.* As companies become more established, they can negotiate more favorable borrowing terms compared to their start-up days, when entrepreneurs take whatever money they can get at whatever rate they can get. Replacing high-interest loans with loans carrying lower interest rates can improve cash flow significantly.
- *Taking advantage of cash discounts.* Suppliers sometimes offer discounts to customers who pay their invoices early. As you will learn in Chapter 17, "Purchasing, Quality Management, and Vendor Analysis," business owners should take advantage of cash discounts in most cases.
- *Buying the building in which the business is located.* Many entrepreneurs start out renting the buildings that house their businesses; however, if location is crucial to their success, it may be wise to purchase the location.
- *Establishing a relationship with a lender.* If a business has never borrowed money, taking out a loan and developing a good repayment and credit history can pave the way for future financing. Smart business owners know that bankers who understand their businesses play an integral role in their companies' ultimate success.
- *Retiring debt held by a "non-relationship" creditor.* Entrepreneurs find that lenders who have no real interest in their companies' long-term success or do not understand their businesses can be extremely difficult to work with. They prefer to borrow money from lenders who are willing to help them achieve their business mission and goals.
- *Foreseeing a downturn in business.* Establishing access to financing before a business slowdown hits insulates a company from a serious cash crisis and protects it from failure.

Entrepreneurs seeking debt capital are quickly confronted with an astounding range of credit options varying greatly in complexity, availability, and flexibility. Not all of these sources of debt capital are equally favorable, however. By understanding the various sources of capital—both commercial and government lenders—and their characteristics, entrepreneurs can greatly increase the chances of obtaining a loan.

We now turn to the various sources of debt capital.

## Peer-to-Peer Lending

Chris Larsen, cofounder of mortgage and auto loan Web site E-Loan, had the vision to combine the global trend in microlending, the process of lending entrepreneurs small amounts of money to start businesses, with the popularity of auction site eBay and launched Prosper.com, a Web site that brings together groups of people who lend money to those who need it. Larsen calls Prosper "America's first people-to-people lending marketplace."

Although borrowers on Prosper make loan requests for cars, home improvements, debt consolidation, and many other purposes, one of the most active sections of the site is the small business loan section. When borrowers sign up for a free membership at Prosper, the company performs a credit check and assigns each member a credit rating that ranges from AA (highest) to HR ("high risk," lowest). Borrowers then are free to post their loan requests, which include the loan amount, maximum interest rate they are willing to pay, and the use of the loan proceeds. Prosper provides potential lenders with borrowers' credit scores and their income-to-debt ratios. All loans carry three-year terms with fixed monthly payments, and the maximum loan amount is $25,000.

Prospective lenders bid on specific amounts of money they are willing to lend and the interest rate they are willing to accept. (As more lenders bid, the interest rate on the loan is driven down.) Auctions usually run from three to seven days. If a loan is fully funded, the winning bidders' (lenders') money, which usually is in small increments of $100 or less, is packaged into a single loan that is granted to the borrower. The interest rates that most borrowers end up paying is three to five percentage points lower than the rates they could get using credit cards. Prosper receives an up-front fee of 1 to 2 percent from borrowers and an annual fee of 0.50 to 1.0 percent of the annual loan balance from lenders. Prosper deposits loans into successful borrowers' accounts within a few days of an auction's close and handles all of the loan's payment collections as well.

Even though most of its members are at the "iffier" end of the loan qualification spectrum, Prosper boasts more than 480,000 members and has facilitated more than $100 million in loans. One expert predicts that person-to-person lending sites such as Prosper and British-owned Zopa will assist in more than 124,000 loans totaling $978 million in 2010, many of them to entrepreneurs who want to launch or to expand businesses.

Charles and Laura Staley of Modesto, California, turned to Prosper to find lenders for the $25,000 they needed to start a wine shop. Because the Staleys had filed bankruptcy in the past, banks "looked at us like black sheep," says Charles. Staley originally listed his $25,000 loan request on Prosper at 12.99 percent interest, but his listing received so many bids (544) that the final interest rate fell to 11.45 percent. In the end, 241 bidders extended the $25,000 loan to the Staleys, who feel a personal connection to each one. "They're like co-owners in the store," says Charles. Explaining why he was willing to lend money to the Staleys, one successful bidder says, "A lot of people have stories about how their credit scores don't capture their true worth. The detail that Staley went into describing his and his wife's plans [for the wine shop] and experience solidified my involvement." The appeal to another lender was the Staleys entrepreneurial ambitions. "As an entrepreneur, it's exciting to see other people start their own businesses," he says.

1. Would you consider bidding on a loan for the Staleys' wine shop? Why or why not?

2. How important is it for entrepreneurs looking for loans on Prosper.com to post an executive summary of their business plans? Explain.

3. Visit Prosper's Web site at www.prosper.com. Search for several loan requests from entrepreneurs who want to launch or to expand a business. Find one in which you would participate in the pool of bidders and another in which you would not participate. Write a one-page report explaining the loan requests and why you would or would not invest in each one.

*Sources:* Adapted from Carol Tice, "Peer Power," *Entrepreneur,* July 2007, p. 25; Christopher Steiner, "The eBay of Loans," *Forbes,* March 12, 2007, pp. 68–70; Alex Salkever, "Brother, Can You Spare a Dime?" *Inc.,* August 2006, pp. 33–35; Thomas Claburn, "Lending Peer to Peer," *Information Week,* May 22, 2006, p. 18; Michael A. Prospero, "A Borrower or Lender Be," *Fast Company,* April 2007, p. 24.

# Sources of Debt Capital

## Commercial Banks

Commercial banks are the very heart of the financial market, providing the greatest number and variety of loans to small businesses. One study found that commercial banks provide 64.7 percent of all traditional debt to small businesses, compared to 12.3 percent supplied by commercial finance companies, the next most prominent source of small business lending.[3] For small business owners, banks are lenders of *first* resort, especially as their companies grow. Most small business bank loans are for less than $100,000 (see Figure 15.1).

Banks tend to be conservative in their lending practices and prefer to make loans to established small businesses rather than to high-risk start-ups. A study by Wells Fargo/Gallup Small Business Index reports that 12 percent of entrepreneurs received bank loans to start their businesses.[4] Because start-ups are so risky, bankers prefer to make loans to companies that have successful track records. They are concerned with a small company's operating past and will scrutinize its records to project its position in the immediate future. They also want proof of a company's stability and its ability to generate adequate cash flows that ensure repayment of the loan. If they do make loans to a start-up venture, banks like to see significant investment from the owner, sufficient cash flows to repay the loan, ample collateral to secure it, or a guarantee from an organization such as the U.S. Small Business Administration (SBA) to insure it. Studies suggest that small banks (those with less than $500 million in assets) are most likely to lend money to small businesses.[5]

ENTREPRENEURIAL
Profile

*Benjamin Richter and Bradford Airport Logistics Ltd.*

Benjamin Richter, CEO of Bradford Airport Logistics Ltd. (BAL) applied for a $250,000 loan at a major bank with which he had been dealing for some time to purchase equipment for an installation for an important client. The bank approved the loan, but the day before the deal was to close, the bank postponed the loan. "The bank said it was working on $100 million deals and took ours off of the table because we weren't big enough," says Richter. Richter quickly contacted a small community bank, the Bank of Houston, which provided the $250,000 Richter needed in just three days, keeping his project on track and his customer happy.[6]

**FIGURE 15.1 Commercial Bank Loans to Small Business by Loan Size**

*Source: Banking and SME Financing in the United States*, SBA Office of Advocacy, June 2006, www.sba.gov/advo/research/rs277tot.pdf.

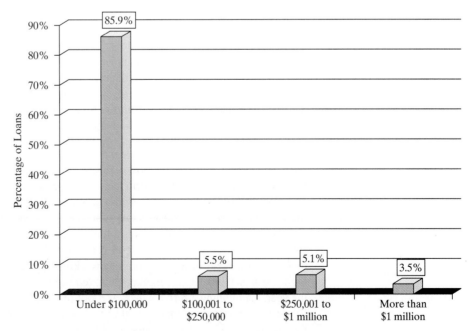

When evaluating a loan application, banks focus on a company's capacity to create positive cash flow because they know that's where the money to repay their loans will come from. The first question in most bankers' minds when reviewing an entrepreneur's business plan is "Can this business generate sufficient cash to repay the loan?" Even though they rely on collateral to secure their loans, the last thing banks want is for a borrower to default, forcing them to sell the collateral (often at "fire sale" prices) and use the proceeds to pay off the loan. *That's why bankers stress cash flow when analyzing a loan request, especially for a business start-up.* "Cash is more important than your mother," jokes one experienced borrower.[7]

Banks, as well as many other lenders, also require that entrepreneurs sign a personal guarantee for any loan they make to small businesses. By making a personal loan guarantee, an entrepreneur is pledging that he or she will be personally liable for repaying the loan in the event that the business itself cannot repay the loan. Recall from Chapter 3, "Choosing a Form of Ownership," that in the eyes of the law a sole proprietor or a general partner and the business are one and the same; therefore, for them, personal loan guarantees are redundant. However, because the owners of S corporations, C corporations, and LLCs, for example, are separate from their businesses, they are not automatically responsible for the company's debts. Once the owners of these businesses sign a personal loan guarantee, however, they become liable for their companies' loans. (It is as if these individuals have "cosigned" the loan with the business.)

**Rosalind Resnick and NetCreations**

Working with a partner, Rosalind Resnick launched NetCreations, an Internet marketing company, using money from various sources, including bank loans. The bank "required us to provide personal guarantees for [NetCreations'] credit line and equipment lease—loans that totaled $2 million," says Resnick. "It wasn't until our company went public that the bank let us off the hook for those loans."[8]

### Short-Term Loans

Short-term loans, extended for less than one year, are the most common type of loans banks make to small companies. These funds typically are used to replenish the working capital account to finance the purchase of inventory, boost output, finance credit sales to customers, or take advantage of cash discounts. As a result, an owner repays the loan after converting inventory and receivables into cash. There are several types of short-term loans.

**COMMERCIAL LOANS (OR TRADITIONAL BANK LOANS).** The basic short-term loan is the commercial bank's specialty. It is usually repaid as a lump sum within three to six months and is unsecured because secured loans are much more expensive to administer and maintain. In other words, the bank grants a loan to the small business owner without requiring him or her to pledge any specific collateral to support the loan in case of default. The owner is expected to repay the total amount of the loan at maturity. Sometimes the interest due on the loan is prepaid—deducted from the total amount borrowed. Until a small business is able to prove its financial strength and liquidity (cash flow) to the bank's satisfaction, it will probably not qualify for this kind of commercial loan.

**LINES OF CREDIT.** One of the most common requests entrepreneurs make of banks is to establish a **line of credit**, a short-term loan with a preset limit that provides much needed cash flow for day-to-day operations. With a commercial (or revolving) line of credit, business owners can borrow up to the predetermined ceiling at any time during the year quickly and conveniently by writing themselves a loan. Banks set up lines of credit that are renewable for anywhere from 90 days to several years, and they usually limit the open line of credit to 40 to 50 percent of a firm's present working capital although they will lend more for highly seasonal businesses. Bankers may require a company to rest its line of credit during the year, maintaining a zero balance, as proof that the line of credit is not a perpetual crutch. Like commercial loans, lines of credit can be secured or unsecured. Small lines of credit often are unsecured, and large ones usually are secured by accounts receivable, inventory, equipment, or other business assets. A business typically pays a small handling fee (1 to

2 percent of the maximum amount of credit) plus interest on the amount borrowed—usually prime-plus-three points or more. One study by the National Federation of Independent Businesses reports that when small business owners borrow money because of cash flow problems, 70 percent of them rely on their lines of credit.[9]

Tara Olson and Sherrie Aycock, co-owners of AllPoints Research, a marketing research firm, rely on a line of credit to keep their company's cash flowing smoothly. Many of their clients are *Fortune* 500 companies with stellar credit ratings, but most of AllPoints' projects take months to complete, stretching its cash flow thin. "We'll be working on a project that is worth a couple of hundred thousand dollars, but, because of their payment policy, that client is going to pay in 60 days," explains Olson. "During that time, we're spending money. We need a line of credit to help us cover those expenses while we're waiting for the collections to come in."[10]

Table 15.1 shows one method for determining how large a line of credit a small company should seek.

## TABLE 15.1 How Large Should Your Line of Credit Be?

Determining how large a small company's line of credit should be is an important step for a growing business. As a company's sales grow, so will its inventory and accounts receivable balances, both of which tie up valuable cash. To avoid experiencing a cash crisis, many growing companies rely on a line of credit. How large should that line of credit be? The following formula will help you answer that question:

Average collection period ratio + Average inventory turnover ratio
− Average payable period ratio = Cash flow cycle

Cash flow cycle × Average daily sales − Forecasted annual profit = Line of credit requirement

Example:

Suppose that Laramie Corporation has an average collection period ratio of 49 days and an average inventory turnover ratio of 53 days. The company's average payable period is 39 days, its annual sales are $5,800,000, and its net profit margin is 6.5 percent. What size line of credit should Laramie seek?

| | |
|---|---|
| Average collection period ratio | 49 days |
| Plus average inventory turnover ratio | 53 days |
| Total | 102 days |
| Minus average payable period ratio | 39 days |
| Cash flow cycle | 63 days |
| Annual sales | $5,800,000 |
| Average daily sales (annual sales ÷ 365 days) | $ 15,890 |
| Cash flow cycle | 63 days |
| Times average daily sales | $ 15,890 |
| Equals | $1,001,096 |
| Minus forecasted profit (annual sales × net profit margin) | 377,000 |
| Equals line of credit requirement | $ 624,096 |

Laramie Corporation should seek a line of credit of $624,000.

*Source:* Adapted from George M. Dawson, "It Figures," *Entrepreneur Start-Ups*, December 2000, p. 27.

"Never mind how much we have - how much do you want to borrow?"

**FLOOR PLANNING.** Floor planning is a form of financing frequently employed by retailers of "big ticket items" that are easily distinguishable from one another (usually by serial number), such as automobiles, recreational vehicles, boats, and major appliances. For example, Thrifty Car Sales makes a floor plan financing program available to the network of franchised dealers who sell the used cars that are taken out of service from its Thrifty Car Rental system. Bombadier Capital, the provider of the floor plan, finances Thrifty Car Sales dealers' purchases of automobiles from Thrifty Car Rental and maintains a security interest in each car by holding its title as collateral.[11] Dealers pay interest on the loan monthly and repay the principal as the cars are sold. The longer a floor-planned item sits in inventory, the more it costs a business owner in interest expense. Banks and other floor planners often discourage retailers from using their money without authorization by performing spot checks to verify prompt repayment of the principal as items are sold.

### Intermediate and Long-Term Loans

Banks primarily are lenders of short-term capital to small businesses, although they will make certain intermediate and long-term loans. Intermediate and long-term loans are extended for one year or longer and are normally used to increase fixed- and growth-capital balances. Commercial banks grant these loans for starting a business, constructing a plant, purchasing real estate and equipment, and other long-term investments. Loan repayments are normally made monthly or quarterly.

**TERM LOANS.** Another common type of loan banks make to small businesses is a **term loan**. Typically unsecured, banks grant these loans to businesses whose past operating history suggests a high probability of repayment. Some banks make only secured term loans, however. Term loans impose restrictions (called **covenants**) on the business decisions an entrepreneur makes concerning the company's operations. For instance, a term loan may set limits on owners' salaries, prohibit further borrowing without the bank's approval, or require the company to maintain certain financial ratios. An entrepreneur must understand all of the terms attached to a loan before accepting it.

**INSTALLMENT LOANS.** These loans are made to small firms for purchasing equipment, facilities, real estate, and other fixed assets. In financing equipment, a bank usually lends the small business from 60 to 80 percent of the equipment's value in return for a security interest in the equipment. The loan's amortization schedule typically coincides with the length of the equipment's usable life. When financing real estate (commercial mortgages), banks typically will lend up to 75 to 80 percent of the property's value and will allow a longer repayment schedule of 10 to 30 years.

**DISCOUNTED INSTALLMENT CONTRACTS.** Banks also extend loans to small businesses when the owner pledges installment contracts as collateral. The process operates in the same manner as discounting accounts receivable (discussed later). For example, Acme Equipment Company sells several pieces of heavy equipment to General Contractors Inc. on an installment basis. To obtain a loan, Acme pledges the installment contract as collateral and receives a percentage of the contract's value from the bank. As Acme receives installment payments from General Contractors, it transfers the proceeds to the bank to satisfy the loan. If the installment contract is with an established, reliable business, the bank may lend the small company 100 percent of the contract's value.

**CHARACTER LOANS.** Banking regulatory changes intended to create jobs by increasing the credit available to small- and medium-sized companies now allow banks to make **character loans**. Rather than requiring entrepreneurs to prove their creditworthiness with financial statements, evaluations, appraisals, and tax returns, banks making character loans base their lending decisions on the borrower's reputation and reliability (i.e., "character"). Two entrepreneurs who cofounded a river touring business received a character loan from a small local bank. Because of their solid reputations in the community and their overall business experience, they were able to borrow $20,000 to purchase canoes, supplies, and safety equipment and to hire guides without even pledging any collateral. "We simply signed our names on the loan agreement and got the money to launch the company," says one of the partners.

The accompanying "Gaining a Competitive Edge" feature describes how small business owners can maintain positive relationships with their bankers.

## Gaining a Competitive Edge

### Maintaining a Positive Relationship with Your Banker

Too often, entrepreneurs communicate with their bankers only when they find themselves in a tight spot and need money. Unfortunately, that's not the best way to manage a working relationship with a bank. "Businesspeople have a responsibility to train their bankers in their businesses," says one lending adviser. "A good banker will stay close to the business, and a good business will stay close to the banker." A good banking relationship has the power to influence in a significant way the success of a small business.

How can business owners develop and maintain a positive relationship with their bankers? The first step is picking the right bank and the right banker. Some banks are not terribly enthusiastic about making small business loans, and others target small businesses as their primary customers. It's a good idea to visit several banks—both small community banks and large national banks—and talk with a commercial loan officer about your banking needs and the bank's products and services. After finding the right banker, an entrepreneur must focus on maintaining effective *communication*. The best strategy is to keep bankers informed—*of both good news and bad*.

Tim Chen, owner of Keys Fitness Products, knows that's the secret to keeping bankers in his company's corner. He is always finding ways to show his bank that his company has proper financial controls in place. The former financial analyst makes it a point to send his bankers regular financial reports. He calls them twice each month to discuss "our supply sources, our pricing strategy, our marketing channels. We want them to be confident about our long-term growth prospects as well as our short-term results," says

*(continued)*

Chen. That means he also lets them know when problems arise in his wholesale exercise equipment business.

Chen's approach has impressed his bankers so much that they have raised his firm's line of credit from $50,000 to $4 million! What else can entrepreneurs do to manage their banking relationships?

*Understand the factors that influence a banker's decision to lend money.* Bankers *want* to lend money to businesses; that's how they generate a profit. However, they want to lend money to businesses they believe offer a very high probability of repaying their loans on time. Bankers look for companies that are good credit risks and have clear plans for success.

*Invite the banker to visit your company.* An on-site visit gives the banker the chance to see exactly what a company does and how it does it. It's also a great opportunity to show the bank where and how its money is put to use.

*Make a good impression.* A company's physical appearance can go a long way toward making either a positive (or a negative) impression on a banker. Lenders appreciate clean, safe, orderly work environments and view sloppily maintained facilities (such as spills, leaks, and unnecessary clutter) as negatives.

*Send customer mailings to the banker as well.* "Besides the numbers, we try to give our bankers a sense of our vision for the business," says Mitchell Goldstone, president of Thirty-Minute Photos Etc. Goldstone sends customer mailings to his bankers "so they know we're thinking about opportunities to generate money."

*Send the banker samples of new products.* "I try to make my banker feel as if he's a partner," says Drew Santin, president of a product-development company. "Whenever we get a new machine, I go out of my way to show the banker what it does."

*Show off your employees.* Bankers know that one of the most important components of building a successful company is a dedicated team of capable employees. Giving bankers the opportunity to visit with employees and ask them questions while touring a company can help alleviate fears that they are pumping their money into a high-risk "one-person show."

*Know your company's assets.* Almost always interested in collateral, bankers judge the quality of your company's assets—property, equipment, inventory, accounts receivable, and others. Be sure to point them out. "As you walk the lender through your business," says one experienced banker, "it's always a good idea to identify assets the banker might not think of."

*Be prepared to personally guarantee any loans the bank makes to your business.* Even though many business owners choose the corporate form of ownership for its limited liability benefits, some are surprised when a banker asks them to make personal guarantees on business loans. It's a common practice, especially on small business loans.

*Keep your business plan up-to-date and make sure your banker gets a copy of it.* Bankers lend money to companies that can demonstrate that they will use the money wisely and productively. They also want to make sure that the company offers a high probability of repayment. The best way to provide bankers with that assurance is with a solid business plan.

*Know how much money you need and how you will repay it.* When a banker asks "How much money do you need?" the correct answer is not "How much can I get?"

*Sources:* Adapted from Keith Lowe, "Keep Your Banker Informed," *Entrepreneur*, April 1, 2002, www.entrepreneur.com/article/0,4621,298380,00.html; David Worrell, "Attacking a Loan," *Entrepreneur*, July 2002, www.entrepreneur.com/article/0,4621,300734, 00.html; Maggie Overfelt, "How to Raise Cash During Crunch Time," *FSB*, March 2001, pp. 35–36; Jenny McCune, "Getting Banks to Say 'Yes.'" Bankrate.com, March 19, 2001, www.bankrate.com/ brm/news/biz/Capital_borrowing/200010319a.asp; Joan Pryde, "Lending a Hand with Financing," *Nation's Business*, January 1998, pp. 53–59; Joseph W. May, "Be Frank with Your Bank," *Profit*, November/December 1996, pp. 54–55; "They'll Up Your Credit If ..." *Inc.*, April 1994, p. 99; Jane Easter Bahls, "Borrower Beware," *Entrepreneur*, April 1994, p. 97; Jacquelyn Lynn, "You Can Bank on It," *Business Start-Ups*, August 1996, pp. 56–61; Stephanie Barlow, "Buddy System," *Entrepreneur*, March 1997, pp. 121–125; Carlye Adler, "Secrets from the Vault," *FSB*, June 2001, p. 33.

## Nonbank Sources of Debt Capital

**2.** Explain the types of financing available from nonbank sources of credit.

Although they are usually the first stop for entrepreneurs in search of debt capital, banks are not the only lending game in town. We now turn our attention to other sources of debt capital that entrepreneurs can tap to feed their cash-hungry companies.

## Asset-Based Lenders

**Asset-based lenders**, which are usually smaller commercial banks, commercial finance companies, or specialty lenders, allow small businesses to borrow money by pledging otherwise idle assets such as accounts receivable, inventory, or purchase orders as collateral. This form of financing works especially well for manufacturers, wholesalers, distributors, and other companies with significant stocks of inventory, accounts receivable, equipment, real estate, or other assets. Even unprofitable companies whose income statements could not convince loan officers to make traditional loans can get asset-based loans. These cash-poor but asset-rich companies can use normally unproductive assets—accounts receivable, inventory, equipment, and purchase orders—to finance rapid growth and the cash crises that often accompany it. Even large companies such as Levi Strauss, Michelin, and Tesco rely on asset-based loans.[12]

Like banks, asset-based lenders consider a company's cash flow, but they are much more interested in the quality of the assets pledged as collateral. The amount a small business can borrow through asset-based lending depends on the **advance rate**, the percentage of an asset's value that a lender will lend. For example, a company pledging $100,000 of accounts receivable might negotiate a 70 percent advance rate and qualify for a $70,000 asset-based loan. Advance rates can vary dramatically depending on the quality of the assets pledged and the lender. Because inventory is an illiquid asset (i.e., hard to sell), the advance rate on inventory-based loans is quite low, usually 10 percent to 50 percent. Steven Melick, CEO of the Sycamore Group, an e-business software developer, gets an 85 percent advance rate on his company's loans from GE Capital by pledging high-quality accounts receivable as collateral.[13] The most common types of asset-based financing are discounting accounts receivable and inventory financing.

**DISCOUNTING ACCOUNTS RECEIVABLE.** The most common form of secured credit is accounts receivable financing. Under this arrangement, a small business pledges its accounts receivable as collateral; in return, the lender advances a loan against the value of approved accounts receivable. The amount of the loan tendered is not equal to the face value of the accounts receivable, however. Even though the lender screens the firm's accounts and accepts only qualified receivables, it makes an allowance for the risk involved because some will be written off as uncollectible. A small business usually can borrow an amount equal to 55 to 80 percent of its receivables, depending on their quality. Generally, lenders will not accept receivables that are past due.

**INVENTORY FINANCING.** Here, a small business loan is secured by its inventory of raw materials, work in process, and finished goods. If an owner defaults on the loan, the lender can claim the firm's inventory, sell it, and use the proceeds to satisfy the loan (assuming the bank's claim is superior to the claims of other creditors). Because inventory usually is not a highly liquid asset and its value can be difficult to determine, lenders are willing to lend only a portion of its worth, usually no more than 50 percent of the inventory's value. Most asset-based lenders avoid inventory-only deals; they prefer to make loans backed by inventory *and* more secure accounts receivable.

*John Calicchio and Argo International*

Argo International, a distributor of electrical and mechanical equipment and components, has counted on asset-based financing to help finance its growth. "[Asset-based financing] has been an essential element in our company's expansion," says chairman John Calicchio. "We've borrowed against accounts receivable, inventory, and fixed assets, and the strategy has allowed us to expand our business worldwide by taking advantage of the value of our assets."[14]

Asset-based financing is a powerful tool. A small business that could obtain a $1 million line of credit with a bank would be able to borrow as much as $3 million by using accounts receivable as collateral. It is also an efficient method of borrowing because entrepreneurs borrow only the money they need when they need it. Asset-based borrowing is an excellent just-in-time method of borrowing, one that often is available within just hours.

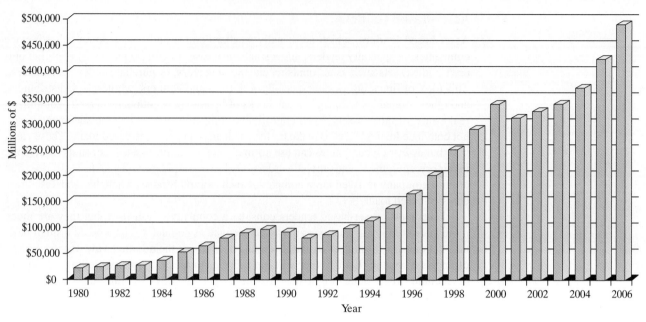

**FIGURE 15.2 Asset-Based Loans**
*Source:* Commercial Finance Association.

However, asset-based loans are more expensive than traditional bank loans because of the cost of originating and maintaining them and the higher risk involved. To ensure the quality of the assets supporting the loans they make, lenders must monitor borrowers' assets, perhaps as often as weekly, making paperwork requirements on these loans intimidating, especially to first-time borrowers. Rates usually run from two to eight percentage points (or more) above the prime rate. Because of this rate differential, small business owners should not use asset-based loans over the long term; their goal should be to establish their credit through asset-based financing and then to move up to a line of credit. Figure 15.2 shows the trend in asset-based borrowing since 1980.

### Trade Credit

Because of its ready availability, trade credit is an extremely important source of financing to most entrepreneurs. Trade credit involves convincing vendors and suppliers to sell goods and services without requiring payment upfront. When banks refuse to lend money to a small business because they see it as a bad credit risk, an entrepreneur may be able to turn to trade credit for capital. Getting vendors to extend credit in the form of delayed payments (for example, "net 30" credit terms) usually is much easier for small businesses than obtaining bank financing. Essentially, a company receiving trade credit from a supplier is getting a short-term, interest-free loan for the amount of the goods purchased.

It is no surprise that businesses receive three dollars of credit from suppliers for every two dollars they receive from banks as loans.[15] Vendors and suppliers usually are willing to finance a small business owner's purchase of goods from 30 to 90 days, interest free. The key to maintaining trade credit as a source of funds is establishing a consistent and reliable payment history with every vendor.

ENTREPRENEURIAL
Profile

*Vikas Goel and eSys Technologies*

Vikas Goel launched Singapore-based eSys Technologies, a global distributor of computer and electronic components, with virtually no capital, and vendor financing was the key. Goel realized that vendor financing is the cheapest financing available (at zero percent interest, it is far cheaper than bank loans)—if an entrepreneur can get it. Goel approached the suppliers of the electronic components his company would sell and explained his business plan, showed them how eSys Technologies would become a loyal—and eventually large—customer, and asked them to extend trade credit to his start-up company. To lower their level of risk, Goel offered to purchase insurance to cover the amount that eSys Technologies owed each vendor. It worked, and five years later, eSys Technologies' capital structure was made up of $350 million in vendor financing and $150 million in bank lines of credit. Goel's company had no long-term debt, and Goel had retained 100 percent of the equity in the business, which now generates sales of $2 billion annually.[16]

## Equipment Suppliers

Most equipment suppliers encourage business owners to purchase their equipment by offering to finance the purchase over time. This method of financing is similar to trade credit but with slightly different terms. Usually, equipment vendors offer reasonable credit terms with only a modest down payment and the balance financed over the life of the equipment (often several years). In some cases, the vendor will repurchase equipment for salvage value at the end of its useful life and offer the business owner another credit agreement on new equipment. Start-up companies often use trade credit from equipment suppliers to purchase equipment and fixtures such as counters, display cases, refrigeration units, machinery, and the like. It pays to scrutinize vendors' credit terms, however; they may be less attractive than those of other lenders.

## Commercial Finance Companies

When denied bank loans, small business owners often look to commercial finance companies for the same type of loan. Commercial finance companies are second only to banks in making loans to small businesses and, unlike their conservative counterparts, are willing to tolerate more risk in their loan portfolios.[17] For instance, Chris Lehnes, a top manager at CIT Small Business Lending, says that his company regularly makes loans to small businesses with debt to equity ratios of 10:1 (10 times as much debt as equity), a situation that would send most bankers scurrying back to their vaults.[18] Of course, like banks, finance companies' primary consideration is collecting their loans, but finance companies tend to rely more on obtaining a security interest in some type of collateral, given the higher risk loans that make up their portfolios. Because commercial finance companies depend on collateral to recover most of their losses, they do not always require a complete set of financial projections of future operations as most banks do. However, this does *not* mean that they neglect to evaluate carefully a company's financial position, especially its cash balance, before making a loan. "We're looking at the projected cash flow—the ability of the business to repay us," says CIT's Lehnes. "We put a lot of weight on what the business has done in the past couple of years."[19]

Approximately 150 large commercial finance companies such as AT&T Small Business Lending, UPS Capital, GE Capital Solutions, CIT Small Business Lending, and others make a variety of loans to small companies, ranging from asset-based loans and business leases to construction and Small Business Administration loans. Dubbed "the Wal-Marts of finance," commercial finance companies usually offer many of the same credit options as commercial banks do, including intermediate and long-term loans for real estate and fixed assets as well as short-term loans and lines of credit. Biscuits and Burgers LLC, a company formed by long-time franchisees Steve Rosenfield and Buddy Brown, recently obtained a long-term $6.5 million loan from GE Capital Solutions to purchase 18 Hardee's fast-food franchises in the U.S. state of Georgia, and a $2 million line of credit for working capital.[20]

Finance companies offer small business borrowers faster turnaround times, longer repayment schedules, and more flexible payment plans than traditional lenders, all valuable benefits to cash-hungry small companies. However, because their loans are subject to more risks, finance companies charge higher interest rates than commercial banks. Rates on loans from commercial finance companies can run as high as 15 to 30 percent (including fees), depending on the risk a particular business presents and the quality of the assets involved. Their most common methods of providing credit to small businesses are asset-based—accounts receivable financing and inventory loans. Because many of the loans they make are secured by collateral, finance companies often impose more onerous reporting requirements, sometimes requiring weekly (or even daily) information on a small company's inventory levels or accounts receivable balances. However, entrepreneurs who cannot secure financing from traditional lenders because of their short track records, less than perfect credit ratings, or fluctuating earnings often find the loans they need at commercial finance companies.

*Ian Johnson and
MedHelp Inc.*

MedHelp Inc., a $1.8 million medical billing service, turned to Butler Capital, a finance company, for a $50,000 loan to purchase high-end computer servers that were part of a special limited-time sale. "We saved $10,000 on the purchase of those servers because [Butler Capital] was able to get the funding in place within 24 hours," says Ian Johnson, the company's vice-president of operations. MedHelp has used loans from Butler Capital on many other occasions as well and plans to continue to do so.[21]

### Savings and Loan Associations

Savings and loan associations (S&Ls) specialize in loans for real property. In addition to their traditional role of providing mortgages for personal residences, savings and loan associations offer financing on commercial and industrial property. In the typical commercial or industrial loan, the S&L will lend up to 80 percent of the property's value with a repayment schedule of up to 30 years. Minimum loan amounts are typically $50,000, but most S&Ls hesitate to lend money for buildings specially designed for a particular customer's needs. S&Ls expect the mortgage to be repaid from the firm's future profits.

### Stock Brokerage Houses

Stockbrokers also make loans, and many of them offer loans to their customers at lower interest rates than banks. These **margin loans** carry lower rates because the collateral supporting them—the stocks and bonds in the customer's portfolio—is of high quality and is highly liquid. Moreover, brokerage firms make it easy to borrow. Usually, brokers set up a line of credit for their customers when they open a brokerage account. To tap that line of credit, a customer simply writes a check or uses a debit card. Typically, there is no fixed repayment schedule for a margin loan; the debt can remain outstanding indefinitely, as long as the market value of the borrower's portfolio of collateral meets minimum requirements. Aspiring entrepreneurs can borrow up to 50 percent of the value of their stock portfolios, up to 70 percent of their bond portfolios, and up to 90 percent of the value of their government securities. For example, one woman borrowed $60,000 to buy equipment for her New York health club, and a St. Louis doctor borrowed $1 million against his brokerage account to help finance a medical clinic.[22]

There is risk involved in using stocks and bonds as collateral on a loan. Brokers typically require a 30 percent cushion on margin loans. If the value of the borrower's portfolio drops, the broker can make a **margin call**—that is, the broker can call the loan in and require the borrower to provide more cash and securities as collateral. Recent swings in the stock market have translated into margin calls for many entrepreneurs, requiring them to repay a significant portion of their loan balances within a matter of days—or hours. If an account lacks adequate collateral, the broker can sell off the customer's portfolio to pay off the loan.

### Insurance Companies

For many small businesses, life insurance companies can be an important source of business capital. Insurance companies offer two basic types of loans: policy loans and mortgage loans. **Policy loans** are extended on the basis of the amount of money paid through premiums into the insurance policy; with a policy loan, a business owner serves as his or her own bank, borrowing against the money accumulated in the investment portion of an insurance policy. It usually takes about two years for an insurance policy to accumulate enough cash surrender value to justify a loan against it. Once he or she accumulates cash value in a policy, an entrepreneur may borrow up to 95 percent of that value for any length of time. Interest is levied annually, but the entrepreneur determines the repayment rate, or repayment may be deferred indefinitely. However, the amount of insurance coverage is reduced by the amount of the loan. Policy loans typically offer very favorable interest rates, sometimes below the prime rate. Only insurance policies that build cash value—that is, combine a savings plan with insurance coverage—offer the option of borrowing. These include whole life (permanent insurance), variable life, universal life, and many corporate-owned life insurance policies. Term life insurance, which offers only pure insurance coverage, has no borrowing capacity.

Insurance companies make **mortgage loans** on a long-term basis on real property worth a minimum of $500,000. They are based primarily on the value of the real property being purchased. The insurance company will extend a loan of up to 75 or 80 percent of the real estate's value and will allow a lengthy repayment schedule over 25 or 30 years so that payments do not strain the firm's cash flows excessively. Many large real estate developments such as shopping malls, office buildings, and theme parks rely on mortgage loans from insurance companies.

### Credit Unions

**Credit unions**, nonprofit financial cooperatives that promote saving and provide loans to their members, are best known for making consumer and car loans. However, many are also willing to lend money to their members to launch businesses, especially since many banks have restricted loans to higher-risk start-ups.[23] Today, in the United States, 8,500 federally and state-chartered credit unions operate in the United States, and nearly 2,000 of them make business loans, many of them in amounts smaller than commercial banks typically make. In fact, the average credit union business loan is $175,000, but some credit unions have made business loans in the millions of dollars.[24] Because credit unions are exempt from federal income tax, they often charge lower interest rates than banks.

Credit unions have more than $25.3 billion in small business loans outstanding, but they don't make loans to just anyone; in most cases, to qualify for a loan, an entrepreneur must be a member.[25] Lending practices at credit unions are very much like those at banks, but they are subject to restraints that banks are not. For instance, credit unions are prohibited from making business loans that total more than 12.25 percent of their assets. Recent changes in U.S. legislation, however, exempt certain business loans from that limitation. In another move favoring entrepreneurs, the U.S. Small Business Administration recently opened its 7(a) loan programs to credit unions, providing even more avenues for entrepreneurs seeking financing. Because of this change, credit unions now make more than $120 million in SBA-guaranteed loans each year.[26] The Export-Import Bank is exploring ways to work with credit unions that want to provide export financing to small businesses.

Increasingly, entrepreneurs are turning to credit unions to finance their businesses' capital needs.

**ENTREPRENEURIAL**
**Profile**

*Ross Johnson and Mobilight Inc.*

Ross Johnson, inventor of a portable light tower used for nighttime events (including the Winter Olympic Games), has used loans from credit unions for a variety of business purposes—from purchasing commercial property to securing short-term working capital for his company, Mobilight Inc. When Johnson needed $1.8 million to expand Mobilight's manufacturing plant and warehouse space, he turned to Mountain America Credit Union, which also had financed a company vehicle and a real estate purchase for Mobilight in the past. The loan, which is backed by an SBA guarantee, is financing the construction of the company's new 24,000-square-foot facility.[27]

Entrepreneurs searching for a credit union near them can use the online database at the Credit Union National Association's Web site, www.cuna.org.

## Bonds

Bonds, which are corporate IOUs, have always been a popular source of debt financing for large companies, but few small business owners realize that they can also tap this valuable source of capital. Although the smallest businesses are not viable candidates for issuing bonds, a growing number of small companies are finding the funding they need through bonds when banks and other lenders say no. Because of the costs involved, issuing bonds usually is best suited for companies generating annual sales between $5 million and $30 million and have capital requirements between $1.5 million and $10 million. Although they can help small companies raise much needed capital, bonds have certain disadvantages. The issuing company must follow the same regulations that govern businesses selling stock to public investors. Even if the bond issue is private, the company must register the offering and file periodic reports with the SEC.

**Convertible bonds**, bonds that give the buyer the option of converting the debt to equity by purchasing the company's stock at a fixed price in the future, have become more popular for small companies. In exchange for offering the option to convert the bond into stock, the small company issuing the convertible bonds gets the benefit of paying a lower interest rate on the bond than on a traditional bond.

Small manufacturers needing money for fixed assets with long repayment schedules have access to an attractive, relatively inexpensive source of funds in **industrial development revenue bonds (IDRBs)**. A company wanting to issue IDRBs must work with a government agency, which issues the bonds on the company's behalf. The company is responsible for repaying both the principal and the interest on the bond issue. Typically, the amount of money companies that issue IDRBs seek to raise is at least $1 million, but some small manufacturers have raised as little as $500,000 using a mini-bond program that offers a simple application process and short closing times. Each government entity has its own criteria, such as job creation, expansion of the tax base, and others that companies must meet to be eligible to issue mini-bonds.

*Ned Golterman*

Ned Golterman used mini-bonds to finance the expansion of his building materials company in St. Louis, Missouri. Working with the St. Louis County Economic Authority, Golterman was able to close the deal in about the same time it would have taken to close a bank loan, and he was able to borrow money at 2 percent below the bank's best interest rate! "My mini-bond [issue] gave me the money I needed for expansion, [and] it allowed me to pay over a much longer period than any commercial bank would allow," says Golterman.[28]

To open IDRBs up to even smaller companies, some states pool the industrial bonds of several small companies too small to make an issue alone. By joining together to issue composite industrial bonds, companies can reduce their issuing fees and attract a greater number of investors. The issuing companies typically pay lower interest rates than they would on conventional bank loans, often below the prime interest rate.

## Private Placements

In the previous chapter, we saw how companies can raise capital by making private placements of their stock (equity). Private placements are also available for debt instruments. A private placement involves selling debt to one or a small number of investors, usually insurance companies or pension funds. Private placement debt is a hybrid between a conventional loan and a bond. At its heart, it is a bond, but its terms are tailored to the borrower's individual needs, as a loan would be.

Privately placed securities offer several advantages over standard bank loans. First, they usually carry fixed interest rates rather than the variable rates banks often charge. Second, the maturity of private placements is longer than most bank loans: 15 years rather than 5. Private placements do not require hiring expensive investment bankers. Finally, because private investors can afford to take greater risks than banks, they are willing to finance deals for fledgling small companies.

*Sweet Success
Enterprises*

Sweet Success Enterprises, a small company that sells all-natural health drinks, recently completed a $3.3 million private placement of debt at 8 percent annual interest with a group of accredited investors with the help of Econor Investments Ltd, a Swiss private placement company. The debt is convertible into shares of company stock, and the company is using the money to develop and market its line of drinks and to expand the number of retail distributors that handle its products.[29]

### Small Business Investment Companies (SBICs)

The U.S. Small Business Investment Company program was started after Russia's successful launch of the first space satellite, Sputnik, in 1958. Its goal was to accelerate the United States' position in the space race by funding high technology start-ups. Created by the 1958 Small Business Investment Act, **small business investment companies (SBICs)** are privately owned financial institutions that are licensed and regulated by the SBA. The 396 SBICs operating across the United States use a combination of private capital and federally guaranteed debt to provide long-term venture capital to small businesses. In other words, SBICs operate like any other venture capital firm, but, unlike traditional venture capital firms, they use private capital and borrowed government funds to provide both debt and equity financing to small businesses. There are two types of SBICs: regular SBICs and Specialized SBICs (SSBICs). More than 100 SSBICs provide credit and capital to small businesses that are at least 51 percent owned by minorities and socially or economically disadvantaged people. Since their inception in 1969, SSBICs have helped finance more than 25,000 minority-owned companies with investments totaling $2.34 billion.

Since 1958, SBICs have provided $48 billion in long-term debt and equity financing to more than 100,000 small businesses, adding many thousands of jobs to the U.S. economy.[30] Most SBICs prefer later-round financing and leveraged buyouts (LBOs) over funding raw start-ups. Because of changes in their financial structure made a few years ago, however, SBICs now are better equipped to invest in start-up companies. In fact, 33 percent of SBIC investments go to companies that are less than two years old.[31] Funding from SBICs helped launch companies such as Apple, FedEx, Whole Foods Market, Sun Microsystems, Outback Steakhouse, and Build-A-Bear Workshop.

Both SBICs and SSBICs must be capitalized privately with a minimum of $5 million to $10 million, at which point they qualify for up to four dollars in long-term SBA loans for every dollar of private capital invested in small businesses. As a general rule, both SBICs and SSBICs may provide financial assistance only to small businesses with a net worth of less than $18 million and average after-tax earnings of $6 million during their past two years. However, employment and total annual sales standards vary from industry to industry. SBICs are limited to a maximum investment or loan amount of 20 percent of their private capital to a single client, but SSBICs may lend or invest up to 30 percent of their private capital in a single small business.

Operating as government-backed venture capitalists, SBICs provide both debt and equity financing to small businesses. Currently, the average amount of SBIC financing in a company is $768,800.[32] Because of SBA regulations affecting the financing arrangements an SBIC can offer, many SBICs extend their investments as loans with an option to convert the debt instrument into an equity interest later. Most SBIC loans are between $100,000 and $5 million, and the loan term is longer than most banks allow. When they make equity investments, SBICs are prohibited from obtaining a controlling interest in the companies in which they invest (no more than 49 percent ownership). The most common forms of SBIC financing (in order of their frequency) are equity only investments (51.0%), debt instruments combined with equity investments (28.5%), and straight debt instruments (20.5%).[33]

*Roy and Bertrand Sosa
and NetSpend*

Brothers Roy and Bertrand Sosa moved with their mother from Mexico to Austin, Texas, in 1986 and, after earning degrees, launched NetSpend in 1998 from their apartment with just $750. Today, their company is the fastest growing provider of prepaid debit cards in the United States, ringing up sales of more than $50 million per year. The brothers originally targeted teenagers who wanted to make purchases on the Internet but soon discovered a much larger target market—adults who had no banking relationships but needed access to a credit card. As it has grown, NetSpend has relied on alliances with strategic partners such as MasterCard and has engaged in three separate rounds of financing, including funding from several SBICs. NetSpend was honored with the "Portfolio Company of the Year" award by the National Association of Small Business Investment Companies.[34]

### Small Business Lending Companies (SBLCs)

Small Business Lending Companies (SBLCs) make only intermediate and long-term SBA-guaranteed loans. They specialize in loans that many banks would not consider and operate on a nationwide basis. For instance, most SBLC loans have terms extending for at least 10 years. The maximum interest rate for loans of seven years or longer is 2.75 percent above the prime rate; for shorter-term loans, the ceiling is 2.25 percent above prime. Another feature of SBLC loans is the management expertise that SBLCs offer the companies to which they make loans. Corporations own most of the nation's SBLCs, which gives them a solid capital base.

## Federally Sponsored Programs

**3.** Identify the sources of government financial assistance and the loan programs these agencies offer.

Federally sponsored lending programs have suffered from budget reductions in the past several years. Current trends suggest that the federal government is reducing its involvement in the lending business, but many programs are still quite active and some are actually growing.

### Economic Development Administration (EDA)

The Economic Development Administration, a branch of the U.S. Commerce Department, offers loan guarantees to create new business and to expand existing businesses in areas with below average income and high unemployment. Focusing on economically distressed communities, the EDA finances long-term investment projects needed to stimulate economic growth and to create jobs by making loan guarantees. The EDA guarantees up to 80 percent of business loans between $750,000 and $10 million. Entrepreneurs apply for loans through private lenders, for whom an EDA loan guarantee significantly reduces the risk of lending. Small companies must supply at least 15 percent of the guaranteed amount in the form of equity. Small businesses can use the loan proceeds in a variety of ways, including supplementing working capital and purchasing equipment to buying land and renovating buildings.

EDA business loans are designed to help replenish economically distressed areas by creating or expanding small businesses that provide employment opportunities in local communities. To qualify for a loan, a business must be located in a disadvantaged area and its presence must directly benefit local residents. Some communities experiencing high unemployment or suffering from the effects of devastating natural disasters have received EDA Revolving Loan Fund (RLF) Grants to create loan pools for local small businesses. Lending policies vary depending on community lending agency; some loans can be as small as just a few thousand dollars, and others can be several hundreds of thousands of dollars. Most loans are for business expansion.

### U.S. Department of Housing and Urban Development (HUD)

HUD sponsors several loan programs to assist qualified entrepreneurs in raising needed capital. Community Development Block Grants (CDBGs) are extended to cities and towns that, in turn, lend or grant money to entrepreneurs to start small businesses that will strengthen the local economy. Grants are aimed at cities and towns in need of revitalization and economic stimulation. Some grants are used to construct buildings and plants to be leased to entrepreneurs, sometimes with an option to buy. Others are earmarked for revitalizing a crime-ridden area or making start-up loans to entrepreneurs or expansion loans to existing business owners. No ceilings or geographic limitations are placed on CDBG loans and grants, but projects must benefit low- and moderate-income families.

HUD also makes loan guarantees through its Section 108 provision of the Community Block Development Grant program. The agency has funded more than 1,200 projects since its inception in 1978. These loan guarantees allow a community to transform a portion of

CDBG funds into federally guaranteed loans large enough to pursue economic revitalization projects that can lead to the renewal of an entire town. For instance, one southeastern U.S. city used government funds to renovate a public market designed to serve as an anchor in its West End section that was targeted for revitalization. Since its construction, 16 small businesses have located in the market, creating new jobs and stimulating economic growth in the area.[35]

### U.S. Department of Agriculture's Rural Business-Cooperative Service

The U.S. Department of Agriculture provides financial assistance to certain small businesses through the Rural Business-Cooperative Service (RBS). The RBS program is open to all types of businesses (not just farms) and is designed to create nonfarm employment opportunities in rural areas—those with populations below 50,000 and not adjacent to a city where densities exceed 100 people per square mile. Entrepreneurs in many small towns, especially those with populations below 25,000, are eligible to apply for loans through the RBS program, which makes $900 million in loan guarantees each year.

**ENTREPRENEURIAL**
**Profile**

*Frederick James and Sanco Rembert and Church Manufacturing Corporation*

Frederick James and Sanco Rembert received financing from the RBS to expand and improve their church furnishings business, Church Manufacturing Corporation. The company, which builds and installs pews, pulpits, and other furnishings in churches across the country, used the funding to earn ISO 9000 certification and to upgrade its equipment and facilities.[36]

The RBS does make a limited number of direct loans to small businesses, but the majority of its activity is in loan guarantees. Through its Business and Industry Guaranteed Loan Program, the RBS will guarantee as much as 80 percent loans up to $25 million (although actual guarantee amounts are almost always far less) for qualified applicants. Entrepreneurs apply for loans through private lenders, who view applicants with loan guarantees much more favorably than those without such guarantees. The RBS guarantee reduces the lender's risk dramatically because the guarantee means that the government agency would pay off the loan balance (up to the ceiling) if the entrepreneur defaults on the loan.

To make a loan guarantee, the RBS requires much of the same documentation as most banks and most other loan guarantee programs. Because of its emphasis on developing employment in rural areas, the RBS requires an environmental-impact statement describing the jobs created and the effect the business has on the area. The Rural Business-Cooperative Service also makes grants available through several other programs to businesses and communities for the purpose of encouraging small business development and growth.

### Small Business Innovation Research (SBIR) Program

Started as a pilot program by the National Science Foundation in the 1970s, the U.S. Small Business Innovation Research (SBIR) program has expanded to 11 government agencies. The total SBIR budget across all 11 agencies is more than $2 billion annually. These agencies award cash grants or long-term contracts to small companies wanting to initiate or to expand their research and development (R&D) efforts. SBIR grants give innovative small companies the opportunity to attract early-stage capital investments *without* having to give up significant equity stakes or taking on burdensome levels of debt.

The SBIR process includes three phases. Phase I (project feasibility) grants, which determine the feasibility and commercial potential of a technology or product (called "proof of concept"), last for up to six months and have a ceiling of $100,000. Phase II (prototype development) grants, designed to develop the concept into a specific technology or product, run for up to 24 months with a ceiling of $750,000. Approximately 40 percent of all Phase II applicants receive funding. Phase III is the commercialization phase, in which the company pursues commercial applications of the research and development conducted in phases I and II and must use private or non-SBIR federal funding to bring a product to market.

Competition for SBIR funding is intense; only 12 percent of the small companies that apply for Phase I financing receive funding. So far, more than 36,000 SBIR awards totaling in excess of $10 billion have gone to small companies that traditionally have had difficulty competing with big corporations for federal R&D dollars. The government's dollars have been well invested. About one in four small businesses receiving SBIR awards have achieved commercial success for their products.[37]

**Dick Albert and Digiray Corporation**

Dick Albert was fascinated by X-ray technology and actually built his own X-ray machine, which he tested on a chicken bone. With the help of two SBIR grants from the U.S. National Aeronautics and Space Administration (NASA) Langley Research Center, Albert started Digiray, a Danville, California-based small company that developed a reverse geometry digital X-ray system that allows engineers to detect hidden stress cracks and weak spots in aging aircraft components. Building on its success in the aircraft market, Digiray is exploring applications for its newest X-ray systems for Homeland Security in airports around the world. Compared to the X-ray systems currently in place in airports, Digiray's screening and detection systems are smaller, faster, and are able to produce higher levels of detail and even 3-D images of the items it scans. Digiray also is looking at ways of putting its digital X-ray technology to work in medical imaging.[38]

## In the Entrepreneurial Spotlight

### ■ "Hey Buddy, Wanna Buy a Jet?"

After watching the number of disgruntled commercial airline passengers increase over the years, in 2004 recreational pilot William Herp launched Linear Air, an airplane chartering service in the U.S. state of Massachusetts. Linear has a fleet of six Cessna Caravan airplanes, three that are leased and the other three that the company owns. Herp wants to expand Linear, bringing the company into the world of "air taxis," providing clients with customized air travel in fast, low-cost "light" jets manufactured by Eclipse Aviation in the U.S. state of New Mexico. The jets, which carry as many passengers as the planes in Linear's current fleet but can fly twice as fast, cost about the same as the Cessna Caravans: $1.7 million each. In addition, Eclipse Aviation, like most jet makers, requires that customers pay 60 percent of the price of a jet six months before the scheduled delivery date.

For Herp, the key question is: Where can he get the capital to purchase a fleet of light jets? "Banks would never touch it," he says. Herp, whose business generates $2.3 million in annual revenue, approached several finance companies about a loan, but the amount they were willing to lend was not enough to cover the cost of the jets. Even with the loans, "we'd still have to go out and raise cash by selling part of the business," he says.

Then Herp came up with an idea for financing the acquisition of the jets his company needs. The technique is a twist on the buy-and-lease-back strategy that some companies use to acquire fixed assets. Linear Air would enter into leasing arrangements with wealthy individuals who would be likely to use the company's air taxi service. The individuals purchase the jets from Eclipse Aviation and lease them to Linear Air. During the lease, the individuals get discounts on using the jet and beneficial tax treatment because of the jet's depreciation expense. Linear Air, in turn, gets to use the jets that it needs without incurring the interest expense on a loan or giving up valuable equity in the business.

Murray Low, an entrepreneurship professor at Columbia Business School, says that leasing is relatively low cost and, because it is considered "off-balance-sheet financing," it does not tie up the rest of a company's balance sheet. So far, two customers have signed up for Linear Air's leasing agreement. Several others have expressed interest in the deal, but Eclipse Aviation is running behind schedule on delivery of the jets, causing them to delay their investment.

1. Discuss the advantages and the disadvantages for both the company and the individuals of the leasing arrangement that Linear Aviation is offering.
2. What other financing strategies do you recommend that Herp consider to acquire the jets that Linear Air needs?

*Source:* Adapted from Simona Covel, "Lease Deal Helps Plane Expansion Take Off," *Wall Street Journal*, July 30, 2007, p. B4.

### The Small Business Technology Transfer Program

The U.S. Small Business Technology Transfer (STTR) program complements the Small Business Innovation Research program. Whereas the SBIR focuses on commercially promising ideas that originate in small businesses, the STTR allows small companies to exploit the vast reservoir of commercially promising ideas that originate in universities, government funded R&D centers, and nonprofit research institutions. Researchers at these institutions can join forces with small businesses and can spin off commercially promising ideas while remaining employed at their research institutions. Six federal agencies award grants in two phases (up to $100,000 in phase I and up to $500,000 in phase II) to these research partnerships. The STTR's annual budget is approximately $1.5 billion.

## Small Business Administration (SBA)

*4.* Describe the various loan programs available from the Small Business Administration.

The U.S. Small Business Administration (SBA) has several programs designed to help finance both start-up and existing small companies that cannot qualify for traditional loans because of their thin asset base and their high risk of failure. In its 50-plus years of operation, the SBA has helped 20 million companies through a multitude of programs get the financing they need for start-up or for growth.

Daniel Lieberman started Dynamic Student Services, a college textbook business, in his dormitory room. Sales grew, and Lieberman formed a partnership with his parents to open the company's first official retail store. Dynamic Student Services received a $562,500 loan with the help of the SBA's popular 7(a) loan guarantee program, and the company has since expanded to three locations.[39]

The SBA's $45 billion loan portfolio makes it the largest single financial backer of small businesses in the nation.[40] To be eligible for SBA funds, a business must be within the SBA's criteria for defining a small business. In addition, some types of businesses, such as those engaged in gambling, pyramid sales schemes, or real estate investment, among others, are ineligible for SBA loans. The loan application process can take from between three days to many months, depending on how well prepared the entrepreneur is and which bank is involved. To speed up processing times, the SBA has established a Certified Lender Program (CLP) and a Preferred Lender Program (PLP). About 850 lenders across the United States are certified lenders, and another 500 qualify as preferred lenders.[41] Both are designed to encourage banks and other lenders to become frequent SBA lenders. When a lender makes enough good loans to qualify as a **certified lender**, the SBA promises a fast turnaround time for the loan decision—typically three to ten business days. When a lender becomes a **preferred lender**, it makes the final lending decision itself, subject to SBA review. In essence, the SBA delegates the application process, the lending decision, and other details to the preferred lender. The SBA guarantees up to 75 percent of PLP loans in case the borrower fails and defaults on the loan. The minimum PLP loan guarantee is $100,000, and the maximum is $500,000. Using certified or preferred lenders can reduce the processing time for an SBA loan considerably.

The **SBA*Express* Program**, in which participating lenders use their own loan procedures and applications to make loans of up to $350,000 to small businesses, also helps streamline the application process for SBA loan guarantees. Because the SBA guarantees up to 50 percent of the loan, banks are often more willing to make smaller loans to entrepreneurs who might otherwise have difficulty meeting lenders' standards. Lenders can charge up to 6.5 percent above the prime interest rate on SBA*Express* loans below $50,000 and up to 4.5 percent above prime on loans above $50,000. Maturities on these loans typically are seven years. Mike Robillard, president of the San Antonio Clippers in San Antonio, Texas, used an SBA*Express* loan to add two locations to his Sports Clips hair salon franchise operation. Robillard needed growth capital quickly to secure the best locations, a key to success in his industry. "We had to start laying out money quickly to lock down those locations," he says.[42]

**PATRIOT EXPRESS PROGRAM.** The SBA recently launched as a pilot program the Patriot Express loan program, which is designed to assist some of the nation's 25 million veterans who want to become entrepreneurs. The loan ceiling is $500,000, and the SBA guarantees up to 85 percent of the loan amount in case the borrower defaults. Like SBA*Express* loans, the turnaround time on loan applications is just 36 hours. Patriot Express loans carry interest rates that range from 2.25 percent to 4.75 percent above the prime interest rate.

### SBA Loan Programs

**7(A) LOAN GUARANTY PROGRAM.** The SBA works with local lenders (both bank and nonbank) to offer a variety of loan programs all designed to help entrepreneurs who cannot get capital from traditional sources to gain access to the financing they need to launch and grow their businesses. By far, the most popular SBA loan program is the **7(A) loan guaranty program** (see Figure 15.3), which makes partial guarantees on loans up to $2 million to small businesses. Private lenders actually extend these loans to companies, but the SBA guarantees them (85 percent of loans up to $150,000; 75 percent of loans above $150,000 up to the loan guarantee ceiling of $1,500,000). In other words, the SBA does not actually lend any money; it merely acts as an insurer, guaranteeing the lender a certain level of repayment in case the borrower defaults on the loan. Because the SBA assumes most of the credit risk, lenders are more willing to consider riskier deals that they normally would refuse. In a typical year, the SBA guarantees loans to about 43,000 small businesses that would have difficulty getting loans without the help of the SBA guarantee.

*Eugene Kane and Kane Is Able*

Edward Kane started Kane Is Able, a small trucking company in 1930 at the peak of the Great Depression. In 1955, Kane's son, Eugene, took over the family business and, with the help of a loan from the SBA, began offering customers warehousing services. Over the next several decades, Kane received three loans from the 7(a) program to fuel the company's fast growth. In addition to its traditional trucking and warehousing services, this successful family-run business has diversified into packaging, serves thousands of customers across the northeast, employs more than 600 people, and has $70 million in annual sales.[43]

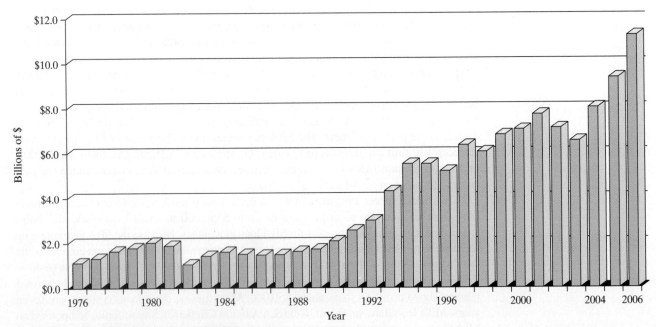

**FIGURE 15.3  SBA 7(a) Guaranteed Loans**
*Source:* U.S. Small Business Administration.

Qualifying for an SBA loan guarantee requires cooperation among the entrepreneur, the participating bank, and the SBA. The participating bank determines the loan's terms and sets the interest rate within SBA limits. Contrary to popular belief, SBA guaranteed loans do *not* carry special deals on interest rates. Typically, rates are negotiated with the participating bank, with a ceiling of prime-plus-2.25 percent on loans of less than 7 years and prime-plus-2.75 percent on loans of 7 to 25 years. Interest rates on loans of less than $25,000 can go up to prime-plus-4.75 percent. The average interest rate on SBA-guaranteed loans is prime-plus-2 percent (compared to prime-plus-1 percent on conventional bank loans). The SBA also assesses a one-time guaranty fee of between 2.5 percent and 3.5 percent for all loan guarantees, depending on the loan amount.

The size of an average loan through the 7(A) guaranty program has dropped from $232,500 in 2002 to $157,500, and the average duration of an SBA loan is 12 years—longer than the average commercial small business loan. In fact, longer loan terms are a distinct advantage of SBA loans. At least half of all bank business loans are for less than one year. By contrast, SBA real estate loans can extend for up to 25 years (compared to just 10 to 15 years for a conventional loan), and working capital loans have maturities of seven years (compared with 2 to 5 years at most banks). These longer terms translate into lower payments, which are better suited for young, fast-growing, cash-strapped companies.

**ENTREPRENEURIAL Profile**

*Ted Clarke and Pat Easter and Jet Stream Car Wash*

Ted Clarke and Pat Easter, former fighter pilots and squadron mates in the military, became commercial airline pilots after their military careers, but both men wanted to own their own business. With the help of a 25-year SBA-guaranteed 7(a) loan from Business Loan Express, Clarke and Easter constructed a Jet Stream touchless car wash that operates 24 hours a day.[44]

**THE CAPLINE PROGRAM.** In addition to its basic 7(a) loan guarantee program (through which the SBA makes about 80 percent of its loans), the SBA provides guarantees on small business loans for start-up, real estate, machinery and equipment, fixtures, working capital, exporting, and restructuring debt through several other methods. About two-thirds of all SBA's loan guarantees are for machinery and equipment or working capital. The **CAPLine Program** offers short-term capital to growing companies that need to finance seasonal buildups in inventory or accounts receivable under five separate programs, each with maturities of up to five years: seasonal line of credit (provides advances against inventory and accounts receivable to help businesses weather seasonal sales fluctuations), contract line of credit (finances the cost of direct labor and materials costs associated with performing contracts), builder's line of credit (helps small contractors and builders finance labor and materials costs), standard asset-based line of credit (an asset-based revolving line of credit for financing short-term needs), and small asset-based line of credit (an asset-based revolving line of credit up to $200,000). CAPLine is aimed at helping cash-hungry small businesses by giving them a credit line to draw on when they need it. Loans built around lines of credit are what small companies need most because they are so flexible, efficient, and, unfortunately, so hard for small businesses to get from traditional lenders.

**LOANS INVOLVING INTERNATIONAL TRADE.** For small businesses going global, the SBA has the **Export Working Capital (EWC) Program**, which is designed to provide working capital to small exporters by providing loan guarantees of 90 percent of the loan amount up to $1.5 million. The SBA works in conjunction with the Export-Import Bank to administer this loan guarantee program. Applicants file a one-page loan application, and the response time normally is 10 days or less. Loan proceeds must be used to finance small business exports.

*Venkee Sharma and Aquatech International Corporation*

Aquatech International Corporation, a small company that makes cutting-edge water purification systems, used a $25 million export working capital loan to land millions of dollars in export contracts, including a $75 million deal with Italian utility company ENEL. PNC Financial Group, the Ex-Im Bank, and the SBA partnered to complete the financing for Aquatech in less than 90 days. "Without this prompt support, Aquatech would not have been able to secure the $75 million contract for environmental exports to ENEL," says CEO Venkee Sharma.[45]

The **International Trade Program** is for small businesses that are engaging in international trade or are adversely affected by competition from imports. The SBA allows global entrepreneurs to combine loans from the Export Working Capital Program with those from the International Trade Program for a maximum guarantee of $1,750,000. The loan ceiling is $2 million, and maturities run up to 25 years.

**SECTION 504 CERTIFIED DEVELOPMENT COMPANY PROGRAM.** Established in 1980, the SBA's Section 504 program is designed to encourage small businesses to expand their facilities and to create jobs. Section 504 loans provide long-term financing at fixed rates to small companies to purchase land, buildings, or equipment. Because they are designated for fixed asset purchases that provide basic business infrastructure to small companies that otherwise might not qualify, 504 loans are intended to serve as a catalyst for economic development. Three lenders play a role in every 504 loan: a bank, the SBA, and a **certified development company (CDC)**. A CDC is a nonprofit organization licensed by the SBA and designed to promote economic growth in local communities. Some 270 CDCs now operate across the United States. An entrepreneur generally is required to make a down payment of just 10 percent of the total project cost. The CDC puts up 40 percent at a low, long-term, fixed rate, supported by an SBA loan guarantee in case the entrepreneur defaults. The bank provides at market rates long-term financing for the remaining 50 percent, which also is supported by an SBA guarantee. The major advantages of Section 504 loans are their fixed rates and terms, their 10 to 20 year maturities, and the low down payment required.

*Tom and Ellen Haglan and Lindar Corporation*

In 1979, Tom and Ellen Haglan started Lindar Corporation, a small manufacturer of plastic trays and liners used in the food and paint industries. Today the company's customer list includes many notable businesses, including Pillsbury, Target, Wal-Mart, and Sherwin-Williams. Lindar was growing so fast that it had run out of room in its small factory, and the Haglans began working with the Minnesota Business Finance Corporation, a certified development company in Baxter, Minnesota, to put together a loan package to finance the construction of a new $2.9 million, 54,000-square-foot factory, more than twice the size of the old one. The Haglans put up just $30,000, the CDC contributed $1.2 million, Wells Fargo Bank added $1.4 million, and a local economic development agency supplied the balance. Sales continue to climb, and the Haglans are adding a third shift and plan to hire 65 more employees. "Because we could use SBA 504 financing as part of our funding package, we got favorable, long term interest rates that contributed to our financial stability," says Tom.[46]

As attractive as they are, 504 loans are not for every business owner. The SBA imposes several restrictions on 504 loans:

- For every $50,000 ($100,000 for small manufacturers) the CDC loans, the project must create at least one new job or achieve a public policy goal such as rural development, expansion of exports, minority business development, and others.
- Machinery and equipment financed must have a useful life of at least 10 years.
- The borrower must occupy at least two-thirds of a building constructed with the loan, or the borrower must occupy at least half of a building purchased or remodeled with the loan.

■ The borrower must qualify as a small business under the SBA's definition and must not have a tangible net worth in excess of $7 million and does not have an average net income in excess of $2.5 million after taxes for the preceding two years.

Because of strict equity requirements, existing small businesses usually find it easier to qualify for 504 loans than do start-ups.

**MICROLOAN PROGRAM.** Recall from the previous chapter that the majority of entrepreneurs need less than $100,000 to launch their businesses. Indeed, research suggests that most entrepreneurs require less than $50,000 to start their companies. Unfortunately, loans of that amount can be the most difficult to get. Lending these relatively small amounts to entrepreneurs starting businesses is the purpose of the SBA's microloan program. Called **microloans** because they range from just a hundred dollars to as much as $35,000, these loans have helped thousands of people take their first steps toward entrepreneurship. Banks typically have shunned loans in such small amounts because they considered them to be unprofitable. In 1992, the SBA began funding microloan programs at 96 private nonprofit lenders in 44 states in an attempt to "fill the void" in small loans to start-up companies, and the program has expanded from there. Since its inception, the microloan program has made loans totaling more than $286 million!

Today, more than 150 authorized lenders make SBA-backed microloans. The average size of a microloan is $13,000, with a maturity of three years (the maximum term is six years), and lenders' standards are less demanding than those on conventional loans. About 37 percent of all microloans go to business start-ups.[47] All microloans are made through nonprofit intermediaries approved by the SBA such as Trickle Up and ACCION International. The typical microloan recipient is a small company with five or fewer employees and collateral that bankers shun for traditional loans: for example, earthworms from a fish bait farmer or a grocery store's frozen fish inventory.[48] Although microloans are available to anyone, the SBA hopes to target those entrepreneurs who have the greatest difficulty getting start-up and expansion capital: women, minorities, and people with low incomes.

*Richard Shell and Budget Blinds*

After being laid off by a large company after 20 years, Richard Shell decided that owning a franchise would be the best way to realize his entrepreneurial dream. After months of intense searching and evaluation, Shell decided that a Budget Blinds franchise best fit his experience in making home improvements and his desire to help people. Coming up with the money to pay the initial franchise fees and to get the business up and running was a challenge for Shell, however. After taking a class on business planning, Shell worked with a Small Business Development Center to apply for an SBA microloan. His application was approved, and Shell received the maximum $35,000 microloan. Sales at his Budget Blinds franchise are growing, and Shell is planning to increase the size of his franchise area.[49]

**PREQUALIFICATION LOAN PROGRAM.** The **Prequalification Loan Program** is designed to help disadvantaged entrepreneurs, such as those in rural areas, minorities, women, the disabled, those with low incomes, veterans, and others, prepare loan applications and "prequalify" for SBA loan guarantees before approaching banks and lending institutions for business loans. Because lenders are much more likely to approve loans that the SBA has prequalified, these entrepreneurs have greater access to the capital they need. The maximum loan under this program is $250,000, and loan maturities range from 7 to 25 years. A local Small Business Development Center usually helps entrepreneurs prepare their loan applications at no charge.

**DISASTER LOANS.** As their name implies, **disaster loans** are made to small businesses devastated by financial or physical losses from hurricanes, floods, tornados, and other disasters. Business physical disaster loans are designed to help companies repair or replace damage to physical property (buildings, equipment, inventory, etc.) caused by the disaster, and economic injury loans provide working capital for businesses throughout the disaster period. For businesses, the maximum disaster loan usually is $1.5 million, but the U.S. government, for example, often raises that ceiling when circumstances warrant. Disaster loans carry below-market interest rates and long payback periods. Loans for physical damage above $10,000 and financial damage of more than $5,000 require the entrepreneur to pledge some kind of collateral, usually a lien on the business property. In the aftermath of the hurricanes that destroyed, damaged, or disrupted an estimated 16,100 businesses along the U.S. Gulf Coast, the SBA approved a record $1.4 billion in disaster loans.[50]

**SBA'S 8(A) PROGRAM.** The SBA's 8(a) business development program is designed to help minority-owned businesses become more competitive and get a fair share of government contracts. Through this program, the SBA directs about $4.5 million each year to small businesses with "socially and economically disadvantaged" owners. Once a small business convinces the SBA that it meets the program's criteria, it finds a government agency needing work done. The SBA then approaches the federal agency that needs the work done and arranges for a contract to go to the SBA. The agency then subcontracts the work to the small business. Government agencies cooperate with the SBA in its 8(a) program because the law requires them to set aside a portion of their work for minority-owned firms.

## U.S. State and Local Loan Development Programs

**5.** Discuss state and local economic development programs.

Just when many federally funded programs are facing cutbacks, state-sponsored loan and development programs are becoming more active in providing funds for business start-ups and expansions. Many U.S. states have decided that their funds are better spent encouraging small business growth rather than "chasing smokestacks"—trying to entice large businesses to locate in their boundaries. These programs come in many forms, but they all tend to focus on developing small businesses that create the greatest number of jobs and economic benefits.

*Sandy and Tom Hood and HoodCo*

When Sandy and Tom Hood were looking for a bigger and better location for their commercial door and hardware distribution business, they were surprised to learn that their state offered commercial loans for established small companies that were expanding and creating jobs. After the Hoods found the ideal location for their $4-million-a-year business in an industrial park, they applied for a loan from the state of Pennsylvania's Small Business First Fund. The state fund approved a loan for $200,000, half of the cost of the new location, which enabled the entrepreneurial couple to convince a private lender to provide the balance. The only requirement for the loan from the Small Business First Fund was that HC HoodCo create one new job for every $25,000 it received.[51]

Like the Hoods, entrepreneurs who apply for state and local funding must have patience and must be willing to slog through some paperwork. The Hoods began their application process in March and received their loan in August. One advantage, however, was the lower down payment required. Any bank would require a 20 to 25 percent down payment on a project like one the Hoods had in mind, but the state required only a 10 percent down payment.

Although each state's approach to economic development and job growth is unique, one common element is some kind of small business financing program: loans, loan guarantees, development grants, venture capital pools, and others. One approach many states have had success with is **Capital Access Programs (CAPs)**. First introduced in 1986 in Michigan, 22 states now offer CAPs that are designed to encourage lending institutions to make loans to businesses that do not qualify for traditional financing. Under a CAP, a bank and a borrower each pay an up-front fee (a portion of the loan amount) into a loan-loss reserve fund at the participating bank, and the state matches this amount. The reserve fund, which normally ranges from 6 to 14 percent of the loan amount, acts as an insurance policy against the potential loss a bank might experience on a loan and frees the bank to make loans that it otherwise might refuse. One study of CAPs found that 55 percent of the entrepreneurs who received loans under a CAP would not have been granted loans without the backing of the program.[52]

## ■ A Community Loan Fund to the Rescue

Leo White had been an executive in the manufacturing industry for many years, and when he had the chance to purchase Bortech, a small company based in the U.S. state of New Hampshire, that had been making industrial welders since 1989, he was ready to take advantage of the opportunity. Bortech's annual sales had never broken $5 million, but White saw the small company's potential and believed that under his leadership, it could grow significantly. He took his business plan to his local bank, which, with the backing of a Small Business Administration guarantee, agreed to a $500,000 loan to help with the purchase of the company. At the last minute, however, the bank withdrew its loan, and the deal was in danger of collapsing.

Then one of White's friends introduced him to John Hamilton, director of the New Hampshire Community Loan Fund (NHCLF), a non-profit community development financial institution (CDFI) based in Concord, New Hampshire, that finances businesses that cannot attract capital from banks and other sources. CDFIs across the United States hold more than $739 million in loans and investments to small companies. Some CDFIs specialize in loans to particular industries, and others focus on making loans to companies in specific geographic areas. Because they are not subject to banking regulations, CDFIs typically make riskier loans than banks can. As a result, the interest rates they charge usually are higher. Many entrepreneurs, however, are willing to pay the higher interest rates because they know that, for one reason or another, their businesses are considered to be "unbankable." Bortech, for example, had very few assets that were of any value to a bank, and, even though it had been profitable for nine out of ten years, the one "off" year became the focus of most bankers. "Banks look mainly at the past," says NHCLF's Hamilton. "They want to know 'What kind of collateral do you have? What's the secondary way [that] I'm going to be repaid if the business doesn't go forward as expected?'"

Unlike the banks in Keene, Hamilton's NHCLF was willing to take a chance on White and Bortech. "We're more like venture capitalists," he explains. "The key question is 'Do I believe in your growth proposition?'" Hamilton did believe in Bortech's growth potential and offered White a 10-year loan at 9 percent interest with royalty payments based on sales. If Bortech met its growth goals, both the company and NHCLF would benefit. Even though the deal was not exactly "cheap" money, White readily accepted Hamilton's offer. "I knew I could afford the higher payment," says White. "Since I knew there was no other way of doing the deal, it became that much more attractive."

In addition to the loans that they provide, most CDFIs also make available to the entrepreneurs they deal with valuable management training and advice—"insurance" on the loans they make. "We are here to grow companies not to sell loans," says Barbara Nagy, director of Enterprise Finance Funds, a CDFI that makes loans to small companies in economically distressed parts of Cuyahoga County, Ohio. "We know that without sound management training, companies won't be able to grow." Hamilton began consulting with White regularly and offered him a spot in the CEO discussion group that NHCLF held each month.

NHCLF's investment in Bortech paid off. In White's first three years of operating Bortech, the company experienced an unprecedented growth rate of 40 percent per year. Since White took over at Bortech, sales have tripled, and the company has expanded its workforce to 15 employees. At the end of the third year, White repaid the entire loan to NHCLF and qualified for an SBA-guaranteed bank loan. Sales are growing at 20 percent a year now, and White is able to finance that growth from the company's internal operations. He still attends the monthly CEO discussion group at NHCLF, however. "The advice and guidance I'm getting from that group is just amazing," he says.

NHCLF's Hamilton is satisfied with the loan he made to Bortech, which allowed the company to grow and to create jobs in the community. He also realizes that if it were not for CDFIs such as his, many entrepreneurs would never have the chance to realize their dreams. "Good growth plans don't always fit with bankable debt or equity," he explains. "We're keeping good growth plans from being shelved."

1. Why do small companies such as Bortech have difficulty qualifying for loans from banks and other traditional lenders?
2. What advantages and disadvantages did Leo White encounter by relying on a loan from a non-profit community development financial institution? What other sources of funding should an entrepreneur in White's position consider?

*Source:* Adapted from Elaine Appleton Grant, "High Risk Loans from Nonprofit Community Fund Are Filling a Gap," *Inc.*, June 2007, pp. 42–44.

Even cities and small towns have joined in the effort to develop small businesses and help them grow. More than 7,500 communities across the United States, for example, operate **revolving loan funds (RLFs)** that combine private and public funds to make loans to small businesses, often at below-market interest rates. As money is repaid into the funds, it is loaned back out to other entrepreneurs. The city of Columbia, South Carolina, has made loans totaling $2 million in an effort to revitalize its downtown business district. Tom Prioreschi received $1.2 million from the city's commercial revolving loan fund to transform vacant commercial buildings into apartments. Entrepreneurs Barry and Susan Walker tapped the revolving loan pool to purchase and renovate an old building, transforming it into upscale offices, meeting rooms, and a jazz and blues restaurant called Mac's on Main.[53]

In addition to RLFs, nearly 1,000 communities across the United States have created **community development financial institutions (CDFIs)** that designate at least some of their loan portfolios for entrepreneurs and small businesses. CDFIs provide loans to people who do not meet traditional lenders' criteria; 68 percent of CDFI borrowers are from low income backgrounds.[54] Because the loans that they make are higher risk, the interest rates that CDFIs charge are higher than those charged by traditional lenders.

## Internal Methods of Financing

*6.* Discuss valuable methods of financing growth and expansion internally with bootstrap financing.

Small business owners do not have to rely solely on financial institutions and government agencies for capital. Instead, the business itself has the capacity to generate capital. This type of financing, called **bootstrap financing**, is available to virtually every small business and encompasses factoring, leasing rather than purchasing equipment, using credit cards, and managing the business frugally.

### Factoring Accounts Receivable

Rather than carry credit sales on its own books (some of which may never be collected), a small business can sell outright its accounts receivable to a factor. A **factor** buys a company's accounts receivable and pays for them in two parts. The first payment, which the factor makes immediately, is for 50 to 80 percent of the accounts' agreed-upon value, which is typically discounted at a rate of 3 to 5 percent of the value of the invoice. The factor makes the second payment of 15 to 18 percent, which makes up the balance less the factor's service fees, when the original customer pays the invoice. Because factoring is a more expensive type of financing than loans from either banks or commercial finance companies, many entrepreneurs view factors as lenders of last resort. However, for businesses that cannot qualify for those loans, factoring may be the only choice!

Factoring has become an important source of capital for many small businesses that depend on fast billing turnaround across a multitude of industries ranging from hardware stores and pharmacies to pest control firms and employment agencies (see Figure 15.4). Factoring deals are either with recourse or without recourse. Under deals arranged with recourse, a small business owner retains the responsibility for customers who fail to pay their accounts. The business owner must take back these uncollectible invoices. Under deals arranged without recourse, however, the owner is relieved of the responsibility of collecting them. If customers fail to pay their accounts, the factor bears the loss. Because the factoring company assumes the risk of collecting the accounts, it normally screens the firm's credit customers, accepts those judged to be creditworthy, and advances the small business owner a portion of the value of the accounts receivable. Factors will discount anywhere from 2 to 40 percent of the face value of a company's accounts receivable, depending on a small company's:

- Customers' financial strength, credit ratings, and their ability to pay their invoices on time.
- Industry and its customers' industries because some industries have a reputation for slow payments.
- History and financial strength, especially in deals arranged with recourse.
- Credit policies.

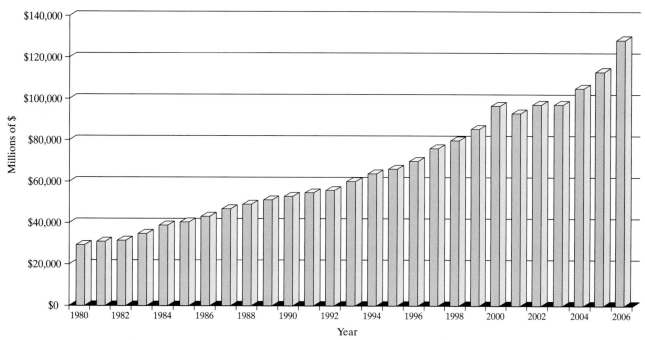

**FIGURE 15.4 Factoring Volume**

Source: *Annual Asset-Based Lending and Factoring Surveys 2006,* Commercial Finance Association, July 2, 2007, p. 15.

The discount rate on deals without recourse usually is higher than on those with recourse because of the higher level of risk they carry for the factor.

Although factoring is more expensive than traditional bank loans (a 2 percent discount from the face value of an invoice due in 30 days amounts to an annual interest rate of 24.5 percent), it is a source of quick cash and is ideally suited for fast-growing companies, especially start-ups that cannot qualify for bank loans. "Factoring provides a business with immediate cash for accounts receivable because a business can sell receivables as soon as they are generated," explains the head of one factoring operation.[55] Small companies that sell to government agencies and large corporations, both famous for stretching out their payments for 60 to 90 days or more, also find factoring attractive because they collect the money from the sale (less the factor's discount) much faster.

*Dennis Hauser, Jr. and DCH Roofing*

Dennis Hauser, Jr., owner of DCH Roofing, has 70 employees, and short-term cash flow, particularly for meeting payroll, was a constant concern in the early days of his business. "Banks didn't want to talk to us," he says. That's when Hauser turned to a factor to speed up his company's cash flow. Hauser sold DCH Roofing's accounts receivable to Hennessey Capital Southeast and received the cash in a matter of hours. Within just three years, Hauser has seen sales at his small company nearly double to $6 million. More important, DCH Roofing's cash flow now is more stable. "I don't have the stress of making sure that I have money in the bank every week to make payroll," he says.[56]

## Leasing

Leasing is another common bootstrap financing technique. Today, small businesses can lease virtually any kind of asset—from office space and telephones to computers and heavy equipment. By leasing expensive assets, a small business owner is able to use them without tying up valuable capital for an extended period of time. In other words, entrepreneurs can reduce the long-term capital requirements of their businesses by leasing equipment and facilities, and they are not investing their capital in depreciating assets. Also, because no down payment is required and because the cost of the asset is spread over a longer time (lowering monthly payments), the company's cash flow improves.

### Credit Cards

Unable to find financing elsewhere, some entrepreneurs have launched their companies using the fastest and most convenient source of debt capital available: credit cards! A survey by payroll service SurePayroll reports that 90 percent of small business owners use credit cards to cover business expenses.[57] Because they cannot get financing anywhere else, many entrepreneurs launch their companies by charging their start-up expenses to credit cards. Putting business start-up costs on credit cards charging 21 percent or more in annual interest is expensive, risky, and can lead to severe financial woes, but some determined entrepreneurs have no other choice. Credit cards are a ready source of temporary financing that can carry a company through the start-up phase until it begins generating positive cash flow. Entrepreneurs who do finance their companies with credit cards should use different cards for business and personal expenses.

*Nathan Newman (left) and Michael Epstein, cofounders of eDimensional*

Like most college students, Michael Epstein and Nathan Newman did not have the capital to launch a business. However, the two computer gamers were persistent in making their dream of making video games as realistic as possible using 3-D technology. Using credit cards, they began purchasing 3-D medical imaging glasses at wholesale and worked with a software developer to make them compatible with computer video games. They convinced a friend to design a Web site for their company, eDimensional, for free and began selling the 3-D glasses online. The product received rave reviews from key gaming Web sites, and sales took off, now surpassing $5 million a year.[58]

## Where *Not* to Seek Funds

**7.** Explain how to avoid becoming a victim of a loan scam.

Entrepreneurs searching for capital must be wary of con artists whose targets frequently include financially strapped small businesses. The swindle usually begins when the con artist scours an area for "DEs"—Desperate Entrepreneurs—in search of quick cash injections to keep their businesses going. Usually, the small business scheme follows one of two patterns (although a number of variations exist). Under one scheme, the small business owner is guaranteed a loan for whatever amount he needs from a nonexistent bank with false credentials. The con artist tells the owner that loan processing will take time, and that in the meantime he must pay a percentage of the loan amount as an advance fee. Of course, the loan never materializes, and the small business owner loses his deposit, sometimes several hundred thousand dollars.

Richard Gould, owner of a small chain of drive-through restaurants, believed that his business was an ideal candidate for franchising, but he needed the money to finance the expansion. He answered an ad in an industry trade journal from a company claiming to have capital to invest in growing businesses. When the company officials told Gould that he would have to pay a $60,000 fee up front, he refused. Ultimately, however, he paid the company $18,000 for the promise of attracting as much as $3 million from investors it supposedly represented. Gould never received a dime in investments from the company.[59]

Another common scam begins with a con artist who claims to be a representative of the Small Business Administration and promises the cash-hungry small business owner an SBA loan if the owner pays a small processing fee. Again, the loan never appears, and the small business owner loses his deposit.

Unfortunately, scams by con artists preying on unsuspecting business owners in need of capital are more common than ever. The World Wide Web has made crooks' jobs easier. On the Web, they can establish a legitimate-looking presence, approach their targets anonymously, and vanish instantly—all while avoiding mail fraud charges if they happen to get caught. These con artists move fast, cover their trails well, and are extremely smooth. The best protection against such scams is common sense and remembering "If it sounds too good to be true, it probably is." Experts offer the following advice to business owners:

■ Be suspicious of anyone who approaches you—unsolicited—with an offer for "guaranteed financing."

■ Watch out for red flags that indicate a scam: "guaranteed" loans, credit, or investments; up-front fees; pitches over the World Wide Web; Nigerian-letter scams (promises to cut you in for a share if you help transfer large amounts of money from distant locations, such as Nigeria. Of course, the con artists will need the numbers for your account, which they promptly clean out.)

■ Conduct a thorough background check on any lenders, brokers, or financiers you intend to do business with. Does the company have a listing in the telephone book? Does the Better Business Bureau have a record of complaints against the company? Does the company have a physical location? If so, visit it.

■ Ask the lender or broker about specific sources of financing. Then call to verify the information.

■ Make sure you have an attorney review all loan agreements before you sign them.

■ *Never* pay advance fees for financing, especially on the Web unless you have verified the lender's credibility.

## Chapter Review

1. Describe the various sources of debt capital and the advantages and disadvantages of each.
   - Commercial banks offer the greatest variety of loans, although they are conservative lenders. Typical short-term bank loans include commercial loans, lines of credit, discounting accounts receivable, inventory financing, floor planning, and character loans.
2. Explain the types of financing available from nonbank sources of credit.
   - Asset-based lenders allow small businesses to borrow money by pledging otherwise idle assets such as accounts receivable, inventory, or purchase orders as collateral.
   - Trade credit is used extensively by small businesses as a source of financing. Vendors and suppliers commonly finance sales to businesses for 30, 60, or even 90 days.

- Equipment suppliers offer small businesses financing similar to trade credit, but with slightly different terms.
- Commercial finance companies offer many of the same types of loans that banks do, but they are more risk oriented in their lending practices. They emphasize accounts receivable financing and inventory loans.
- Savings and loan associations specialize in loans to purchase real property—commercial and industrial mortgages—for up to 30 years.
- Stock-brokerage houses offer loans to prospective entrepreneurs at lower interest rates than banks because they have high-quality, liquid collateral—stocks and bonds in the borrower's portfolio.
- Insurance companies provide financing through policy loans and mortgage loans. Policy loans are extended to the owner against the cash surrender value of insurance policies. Mortgage loans are made for large amounts and are based on the value of the land being purchased.
- Small Business Investment Companies are privately owned companies licensed and regulated by the SBA that qualify for SBA loans to be invested in or loaned to small businesses.
- Small Business Lending Companies make only intermediate and long-term loans that are guaranteed by the SBA.

3. Identify the various federal loan programs aimed at small businesses.
- The Economic Development Administration, a branch of the Commerce Department, makes loan guarantees to create and expand small businesses in economically depressed areas.
- The Department of Housing and Urban Development extends grants (such as Community Development Block Grants) to cities that, in turn, lend and grant money to small businesses in an attempt to strengthen the local economy.
- The Department of Agriculture's Rural Business-Cooperative Service loan program is designed to create nonfarm employment opportunities in rural areas through loans and loan guarantees.
- The Small Business Innovation Research Program involves 10 federal agencies that award cash grants or long-term contracts to small companies wanting to initiate or to expand their research and development (R&D) efforts.
- The Small Business Technology Transfer Program allows researchers at universities, federally funded R&D centers, and non-profit research institutions to join forces with small businesses and develop commercially promising ideas.

4. Describe the various loan programs available from the U.S. Small Business Administration.
- Almost all SBA loan activity is in the form of loan guarantees rather than direct loans. Popular SBA programs include: the SBA*Express* program, the Patriot Express program, the 7(A) loan guaranty program, the CAPLine Program, the Export Working Capital program, the International Trade program, the Section 504 Certified Development Company program, the Microloan program, the Prequalification Loan Program, the disaster loan program, and the 8(a) program.

5. Discuss U.S. state and local economic development programs.
- In an attempt to develop businesses that create jobs and economic growth, most states offer small business financing programs, usually in the form of loans, loan guarantees, and venture capital pools.

6. Discuss valuable methods of financing growth and expansion internally with bootstrap financing.
- Small business owners may also look inside their firms for capital. By factoring accounts receivable, leasing equipment instead of buying it, and by minimizing costs, owners can stretch their supplies of capital.

7. Explain how to avoid becoming a victim of a loan scam.
- Entrepreneurs hungry for capital for their growing businesses can be easy targets for con artists running loan scams. Entrepreneurs should watch out for promises of "guaranteed" loans, up-front fees, pitches over the World Wide Web, and Nigerian letter scams.

## Discussion Questions

1. What role do commercial banks play in providing debt financing to small businesses? Outline and briefly describe the major types of short-term, intermediate, and long-term loans commercial banks offer.
2. What is trade credit? How important is it as a source of debt financing to small firms?
3. Explain how asset-based financing works. What is the most common method of asset-based financing? What are the advantages and disadvantages of using this method of financing?
4. What function do SBICs serve? How does an SBIC operate? What methods of financing do SBICs rely on most heavily?
5. Briefly describe the loan programs offered by the following:
   a. Economic Development Administration
   b. Department of Housing and Urban Development
   c. Department of Agriculture
   d. Local development companies
6. Explain the purpose and the methods of operation of the Small Business Innovation Research Program and the Small Business Technology Transfer Program.
7. Which of the Small Business Administration's loan programs accounts for the majority of its loan activity? How does the program work?
8. Explain the purpose and the operation of the SBA's microloan program.
9. How can a firm employ bootstrap financing to stretch its current capital supply?
10. What is a factor? How does the typical factor operate? Explain the advantages and the disadvantages of factoring. What kinds of businesses typically use factors?

# Business PlanPro

Many entrepreneurs are reluctant to give up a percentage of ownership in their companies that equity capital requires and turn instead to debt capital as a source of funds. Almost every lending institution expects to see a quality business plan. A business plan adds credibility and is testimony that you have invested thought and time in your business idea. If you need debt capital for your venture, a business plan can help you clarify how much money you will need, formulate a financing strategy for acquiring the funds, and communicate to potential lenders why you are worth the risk.

## On the Web

If you need start-up or growth capital for your venture, visit the Companion Website at www.prenhall.com/scarborough for Chapter 15 and review some equity financing options. Determine whether these sources may be useful as you explore financing opportunities. You will also find additional information regarding bootstrap and non-traditional funding.

## Sample Plans

As in the previous chapter, you should review sample plans in Business Plan Pro for companies that are seeking debt financing. Lenders will want to confirm that you have a sound business or business idea, that you are motivated enough to make the business successful, and that you will be able to make your payments on time! They also will want to know about any collateral that you have to bring to the table. Use each aspect of the financial section—the breakeven analysis, projected profit and loss, projected cash flow, projected balance sheet, and business ratios—to tell your company's financial story to your lending audience.

## In the Software

Open your plan in Business Plan Pro and go to the "Financial Plan" section. Review the assumptions you made in the previous chapter. Once again, these assumptions will state anticipated economic conditions, current short interest term, long-term interest rates, expected tax rates, personnel expenses, cash expenses, sales on credit, or any areas that you hope to develop and confirm through further research. You will then assess the type and amount of debt financing that you will need. Will this be short- or long-term financing? Work through the finance section and review the numbers in your breakeven point calculation, balance sheet, projected profit and loss statement, and cash flow forecast. This section also will enable you to review industry ratios and to compare them to your company's anticipated performance. These ratio comparisons may be helpful for lenders. Make certain this section clearly tells your financial story. Providing relevant information that will be meaningful to the potential lenders who will review your plan is critical.

## Building Your Business Plan

The business plan will help to assess the amount of debt financing needed, describe the use of these funds, and make certain that you can live with the financial consequences of these decisions. This "financial road map" helps you to analyze your funding options. Expect potential lenders to review your pro forma statements and, like investors, to assess the qualifications of your management team, the industry's growth potential, your proposed exit strategy, and other factors as they assess the financial stability of your venture.

# 16

# Location, Layout, and Physical Facilities

I believe life is a series of near misses. A lot of what we ascribe to luck is not luck at all. It's seizing the day and accepting responsibility for your future. It's seeing what other people don't see and pursuing that vision.

— Howard Schultz

Don't open a shop unless you like to smile.

—Chinese Proverb

*Learning Objectives*

**Upon completion of this chapter, you will be able to:**

1  Explain the stages in the location decision.

2  Describe the location criteria for retail and service businesses.

3  Outline the basic location options for retail and service businesses.

4  Explain the site selection process for manufacturers.

5  Discuss the benefits of locating a start-up company in a business incubator.

6  Describe the criteria used to analyze the layout and design considerations of a building, including legal requirements such as the Americans with Disabilities Act.

7  Explain the principles of effective layouts for retailers, service businesses, and manufacturers.

here are few decisions that entrepreneurs make that have as lasting and as dramatic an impact on their businesses as the choice of a location. Selecting the right location increases the chances that a company will succeed, but choosing the wrong location may place a business at a distinct disadvantage from the start. A company's location influences a number of critical variables. The quality of the labor pool, customer exposure, logistic issues, and tax rates are just a few of the considerations in the location selection process. The location decision is an important one that can influence the growth rate and the ultimate success of a company. Retailers, service-based companies, and manufacturers must invest time and resources to ensure the location they select meets their needs.

The characteristics that make for an ideal location vary from one company to another. A recent study concluded that the factors that make an area most suitable for starting and growing small companies include access to dynamic universities, an ample supply of skilled workers, a nearby airport, a temperate climate, and a high quality of life.[1] The key to finding a suitable location is identifying the characteristics that can give a company a competitive edge and then locating potential sites that meet those criteria. Data is available from a variety of sources—much of it at no cost—to help make this critical decision. The key is to use relevant information to make an informed location choice.

For example, businesses that depend on face-to-face contact with customers must identify locations that attract high volumes of well-qualified walk-in customers. Although online shopping continues to increase, brick-and-mortar businesses with physical stores continue to dominate consumer sales, accounting for 93 percent of all retail sales.[2] One reason for the staying power of physical locations is their real-world presence. An inviting physical location enables people to drive by, walk through, touch, feel, and experience the products and services the business offers. Potential buyers can feel and smell the merchandise, try it on, and compare it side-by-side with other items. An optimal location provides a destination point and a gathering place. People value these shared experiences and one-on-one exchanges. The ability to look someone in the eye and ask questions or watch a demonstration appeals to human nature and provides a powerful sales tool for the business. A purchase results in instant gratification because buyers can carry their goods home—without shipping charges. A well-chosen physical location provides credibility as a solid and reliable business that can complement an online presence.[3] Investing time collecting and analyzing the data relevant to choosing a location will pay off in customer traffic, higher sales, and greater efficiencies.

The first step is to list the information needed to conduct a comparison of locations. What data provide real insight into the buying behaviors of your potential target audience? Which information will be useful in determining the basic demographic, competitive, and regulatory environment of potential locations? When searching for demographic and market information, entrepreneurs must act much like prospectors panning for gold, searching for the nuggets of information among the piles of rubble.

*Jeremy Wunsch and LuciData*

Jeremy Wunsch never planned to expand his business beyond the U.S. city of Minneapolis. "I started in my basement and thought that was where the company would stay," says the founder and CEO of LuciData, which sells data products and services to aid forensic investigations and protect intellectual property. However, when Wunsch received an inquiry from a prospective customer in the state of Colorado, he changed his mind and opened an office there. "I was losing business because I did not have a local presence," says Wunsch. He opened an office in Colorado, which now has $1.8 million in sales, and is considering expansion to the U.S. East Coast and California markets.[4]

This chapter serves as a guide to help an entrepreneur identify the ideal location for his or her business.

# The Logic of Location: From Region to State to City to Site

*1.* Explain the stages in the location decision.

An entrepreneur's ultimate goal is to locate the company at a site that will maximize the likelihood of success. The more that entrepreneurs invest in researching potential locations, the higher is the probability that they will find the location that is best suited for their businesses. The challenge is to keep an open mind about where the best location might be. As with most decisions affecting a business, the needs of customers drive the choice of the "best" location for a business. Choosing an appropriate location is essentially a matter of selecting a site that best serves the needs of the business's target customers. Is there a location where the new business will have the greatest number of customers who need, want, and can afford the products or services the business provides? Entrepreneurs who know and understand their target customers' characteristics, demographic profiles, and buying behavior have a greater chance to identify the right location from which to serve them.

The search for the ideal location involves research that entrepreneurs can conduct on the Internet, in libraries, by telephone, and in person. Some entrepreneurs may limit the locations they consider to those where they currently live or consider to be attractive areas. However, the ideal way to choose a location is to begin with a broad regional search and then systematically narrow the decision to a specific site (see Figure 16.1).

**FIGURE 16.1 The Location Decision**
*Source:* From Dale M. Lewison and M. Wayne DeLozier, *Retailing* (Columbus, OH: Merrill/Macmillan Publishing, 1984), p. 341.

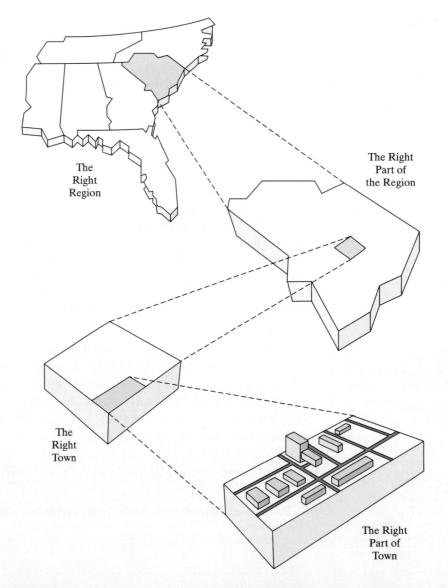

The Right Region

The Right Part of the Region

The Right Town

The Right Part of Town

## Selecting the Region

The first step in selecting the best location is to focus at the regional level. Which region of the country has the characteristics necessary for your business to succeed? Common requirements include rapid growth in the population of a certain age group, rising disposable incomes, the existence of specific infrastructure, a pool of skilled workers, and low operating costs. Each of these factors impacts revenues and cost.

At the broadest level of the location decision, entrepreneurs usually identify regions of the country that are experiencing substantial population growth. Business publications and census data offer useful reports about the regions of the nation that are growing, stagnant, and declining. Studying shifts in population and industrial growth will give an entrepreneur an idea of where the greatest opportunities lie. Some of the questions that may help in the analysis are:

- What is the total population of the region?
- How fast is it growing?
- What is the demographic makeup of the overall population?
- Which segments are growing fastest?
- Which are growing the slowest?
- What is the population's average income?
- Are the income levels increasing or decreasing?
- Are other businesses moving into the region? If so, what kinds of businesses are they?

In general, owners want to avoid regions that are struggling; these regions may not be able to provide a broad base of potential customers. A company's customer base is comprised of people, businesses, and government. If it is to be successful, the business must locate in a place that is convenient to them.

One of the most useful resources for conducting a regional evaluation is the census bureau information and Web site. Many of these Web sites offer a wealth of important demographic and economic information—and it is *free*. Entrepreneurs can view summary tables and handy maps for practically any of the bureau's available data at many levels of detail, ranging from the nation as a whole to individual provinces, parishes, census tracts, and even city blocks. The U.S. Census Bureau conducts the Decennial census for every household in the United States in years that end in "0." Reports based on the Decennial census are some of the most useful tools for selecting a location. This database contains both demographic and economic information about the residents of a particular area, including age, gender, ancestry, marital status, language spoken, education level, occupation, travel time to work, income level, and many other population characteristics. This census also includes a housing report that contains household information including the number of rooms, the number of bedrooms, the age of the home, the utility costs, the home's value, the number of cars owned, and other characteristics.

In addition to the Decennial census, the bureau takes nearly 100 other surveys and censuses that entrepreneurs can use to find the ideal location for their businesses. For instance, in an effort to provide reliable annual updates to the Decennial census, the Census Bureau conducts the American Community Survey (ACS), which includes about three million households. Using the ACS, entrepreneurs can judge how rapidly an area is growing and how quickly its population makeup is changing.

The Census Bureau also conducts the Economic Census every five years in years that end in 2 and 7. This information provides a portrait of businesses in local communities across the nation. The Economic Census is helpful to entrepreneurs developing business plans for start-up ventures, existing business owners who want to learn about their competitors and their potential business customers, or those in search of a location near potential customers or away from competitors. The information is organized using the popular North American Industry Classification System (NAICS) and includes such data as the number of establishments in an industry, their sales, shipments, number of employees, and annual payroll. The Annual Survey of Manufacturers (ASM) provides similar information for makers of more than 1,800 classes of products.

These Web resources give entrepreneurs instant access to important site location information. *American Demographics* magazine (www.demographics.com) is another exceptional source of information on current demographic trends that impact U.S. society.

This publication provides in-depth articles that allow the entrepreneur to gain valuable insights into the changes in our society that produce valuable business opportunities. Access to most of the articles requires a subscription to *American Demographics*.

Ameristat (www.ameristat.org) provides a detailed breakdown of the most relevant data collected from the most recent census. The site also includes helpful articles that discuss the implications of the changing demographic and economic profile of the nation's population, such as the impact of aging baby boomers on business and the changing composition of the U.S. workforce. STAT-USA (www.stat-usa.gov) is a service of the United States Department of Commerce that offers both financial and economic data about the United States as well as trade data for the nation and for Europe. Here entrepreneurs can locate everything from the latest consumer price index and the number of housing starts to leads for global trading partners and tips on conducting business in practically any country in the world.

Other helpful resources are also available. *Demographics USA* is a three-edition series covering the United States, its counties, and postal code areas. This useful publication provides market surveys on various segments of U.S. demographics, including purchasing power, retail sales by type of merchandise, employment and payroll data, and forecasts of economic conditions down to the county level. Entrepreneurs can use *Demographics USA* to analyze the level of competition in a particular area, assess the sales potential of a particular location, compare consumers' buying power across a dozen categories, and more. *Lifestyle Market Analyst,* an annual publication, matches population demographics with lifestyle interests. Section 1 gives demographics and lifestyle information by "Areas of Dominant Influence," Section 2 gives demographic and geographic information according to 57 lifestyle interests, and Section 3 lists areas of dominant influence and lifestyles according to 42 demographic segments. It is wise to consult the introductory material on how to use this source. Entrepreneurs can use *Lifestyle Market Analyst* to determine, for example, how likely members of a particular market segment are to own a dog, collect antiques, play golf, own a vacation home, fly frequently, invest in stocks or bonds, or participate in a host of other activities.

*Rand McNally Commercial Atlas & Marketing Guide* is an annual publication that features maps, transportation, communication, and population data as well as a variety of economic data. Rand McNally also offers this guide in an online, interactive version on its Web site. The *Commercial Atlas & Marketing Guide* includes population, income, buying power, and sales data by store type for most areas in the United States, including small towns not covered in detail by the U.S. Census data. It also lists the largest U.S. companies in a variety of industries. Each state map includes an analysis of business and manufacturers by county and a list of banks. The *Community Sourcebook of County Demographics* is another annual publication that provides up-to-date estimates for more than 80 economic and demographic characteristics such as age distribution, population, education, employment, housing, income distribution, race, household income, and others as well as consumer spending indexes for 20 product and service categories for every U.S. Postal code or county. This publication also breaks down the population into 65 distinct segments and provides lifestyle and life stage descriptions of consumers living in each zip code area.

Sales and Marketing Management's *Survey of Buying Power,* published annually, provides statistics, rankings, and projections for every county and media market in the United States with demographics segmented by age, race, city, county, and state. This publication also includes current information on retail spending and forecasts for each category. The data are divided into 323 metropolitan markets as defined by the Census Bureau and 210 media markets, which are television or broadcast markets defined by Nielsen Media Research. The *Survey* also includes several unique statistics. Effective buying income (EBI) is a measure of disposable income, and the buying power index (BPI), for which the *Survey* is best known, is a unique measure of spending power that takes population, EBI, and retail sales into account to determine a market's ability to buy goods and services. The *Editor and Publisher Market Guide* is similar to the *Survey of Buying Power,* but provides additional information on markets. This guide includes detailed information on key cities.

The U.S. Small Business Administration's Small Business Development Center (SBDC) program also offers location analysis assistance to entrepreneurs. More than 1,100 SBDC offices throughout the nation provide training, counseling, research, and other specialized assistance to entrepreneurs and existing business owners on a wide variety of subjects—all at no charge. To locate the nearest SBDC, contact the SBA office in your state or go to the SBA's Small Business Development Center home page at www.sba.gov/sbdc.

A growing number of entrepreneurs are relying on geographic information systems (GISs), powerful software programs that combine map drawing with database management capability, to pinpoint the ideal location for their businesses. GIS programs enable entrepreneurs to plot an existing customer base on a map with various colors representing the different population densities. Then they can zoom in on the areas with the greatest concentration of customers, mapping a detailed view of postal code borders or even city streets. Geographic information system street files originate in the U.S. Census Bureau's TIGER (Topological Integrated Geographic Encoding Referencing) file, which contains map information for every street in the country and detailed block statistics for the 345 largest urban areas. In essence, TIGER is a computerized map of the entire United States and, when linked with a database, gives small business owners incredible power to pinpoint existing and potential customers as well as competitors. With either mapping or GIS software to access and use the TIGER files, this digital map can be downloaded at no cost and be tailored to reflect census tracts, railroads, highways, waterways, and other physical attributes of any area in the United States. Many private vendors offer GIS software packages with additional enhancements that are based on TIGER files.

*World Savings Bank*

World Savings Bank, California-based bank with branches in 38 states, uses a product called iSite to examine potential locations for new branches. iSite allows managers to evaluate business opportunities in a trade area, understand the demographic profile of customers in that area, determine how many branches it can sustain, decide where to locate them, and estimate the performance of a branch in any given location. According to Jim Stone, CEO of geoVue, the company that developed iSite, "We deliver a software solution that integrates maps and market data to support decisions involving location." The iSite program contains locations throughout the United States as well as some international locations. Enter an address, and the software automatically finds that location on a map along with information about the vicinity, such as the location of nearby shopping centers, retail businesses, and other employers.[5]

## Selecting the State

Every state has a business development office to recruit new businesses. Even though the publications produced by these offices will be biased in favor of locating in that state, they still are an excellent source of facts and can help entrepreneurs assess the business climate in each state. Some of the key issues to explore include the laws, regulations, and taxes that govern businesses and any incentives or investment credits the state may offer to businesses locating there. In some cases, government incentives are dependant upon using "clawback" provisions that let the government recover their money if companies fail to create jobs they promised.[6]

*Instinet Group*

Instinet Group, a stock brokerage firm, decided to move some of its operations from New York City to the U.S. state of New Jersey, when the state offered incentives based on the company's investment in facilities and the number of jobs created. Within two years, Instinet Group had created 233 jobs and had leased 144,000 square feet of office space. In return, the state of New Jersey and the city in which the company relocated gave the company $542,856 in cash grants. Two years later, however, the NASDAQ Stock Market acquired part of the firm, and the jobs left New Jersey. New Jersey's clawback provisions required NASDAQ to repay the state 100 percent of the incentives that Instinet had received.[7]

Other factors to consider when selecting a state in which to locate include proximity to markets, proximity to raw materials, wage rates, quantity and quality of the labor supply, general business climate, and tax rates.

**PROXIMITY TO MARKETS.** Locating close to the markets they plan to serve is critical to manufacturers, especially when the cost of transporting finished goods is high relative to their value. Locations near customers offer a competitive advantage. Service firms often find that proximity to their clients is essential. If a business is involved in repairing equipment used in a specific industry, it should be located where that industry is concentrated. The more specialized a business, or the greater the relative cost of transporting the product to the customer, the more likely it is that proximity to the market will be of importance in the location decision.

**PROXIMITY TO NEEDED RAW MATERIALS.** A business that requires raw materials that are difficult or expensive to transport may need a location near the source of those materials. Some companies locate close to the source of raw materials because of the cost of transporting heavy low-value materials over long distances. For instance, a company that produces kitty litter selected a location near a large vein of kaolin, the highly absorbent clay and the principal raw material used to make the finished product. In situations in which bulk or weight is not a factor, locating close to suppliers can facilitate quick deliveries and reduce inventory holding costs. The value of products and materials, their cost of transportation, and their unique functions interact to determine how close a business must be to its sources of supply.

**LABOR SUPPLY.** Two factors are important for entrepreneurs analyzing the labor supply in a potential location: the number of workers available in the area and their level of education, training, and experience. Business owners should know how many qualified people are available in the area to do the work required in the business. The size of the local labor pool determines a company's ability to fill jobs at reasonable wages. Companies that require workers with special skills, education, or knowledge often find it beneficial to locate in clusters. "Companies that operate in clusters have greater access to talent," explains Jeffrey Grogan, partner at the Monitor Group, a Boston strategy consulting firm.[8] That's why Bangalore, India is home to so many high-tech companies; the area offers companies one of the largest pools of highly educated, experienced workers in the nation and ready access to some of the leading research universities in the world.

Knowing the exact nature of the labor needed and preparing job descriptions and job specifications in advance will help business owners to determine whether there is a good match between their companies' needs and the available labor pool. Checking educational statistics in the state to determine the number of graduates in relevant fields of study will provide an idea of the local supply of qualified workers.

**WAGE RATES.** Wage rates provide another measure for comparison among states. Entrepreneurs should determine the wage rates for jobs that are related to their particular industry or company. In addition to published government surveys, the help wanted ads in local newspapers can give entrepreneurs an idea of the wages local companies must pay to attract workers. What trends have emerged in wage rates over time? How does the rate of increase in wage rates compare among states? Another factor influencing wage rates is the level of union activity in a state. How much union organizing activity has the state seen within the past two years? Is it increasing or decreasing? Which industries have unions targeted in the recent past? Entrepreneurs must determine whether the depth of the workforce is sufficient to supply the growth needs of their businesses without resulting in an exorbitant increase in wages.

**BUSINESS CLIMATE.** Assessing the business climate provides important information about the environment. What is the province's overall attitude toward this type of business? Has it passed laws that impose restrictions on the way a company can operate? Does the state impose a corporate income tax? Is there an inventory tax? Does the province or state offer small business support programs or financial assistance to entrepreneurs? Some states have created environments that are much more "entrepreneur friendly" than others.

For example, several business publications have named Austin, Texas, as one of the best areas for small businesses, citing its positive attitude toward growing and developing

## ■ The Place for Replacements

Bangalore, India has computers, China has TVs, and the undisputed world capital of orthopedic devices is Warsaw, in the U.S. state of Indiana. This city of 12,500 people is home to three of the world's five largest makers of artificial joints. Related surgical tool manufacturers also have their headquarters here amid the lakes and fields of northeastern Indiana. The local industry has grown so much that it is now a regional force, with orthopedics companies locating in nearby farm towns and the suburbs of Fort Wayne, about 50 miles away. An estimated 60 percent of the workers who live within seven miles of Warsaw are in some way engaged in orthopedics manufacturing, says Joy McCarthy-Sessing, president of the local chamber of commerce.

A Canadian pharmacist, Revra DePuy, planted the orthopedic seed more than a century ago. He had the idea of making flexible splints to replace the wooden barrel staves then used to set broken bones. The company he created still exists today as DePuy Inc., a unit of Johnson & Johnson. It even spawned other companies, as people left to start competing operations. For instance, a DePuy salesman left DePuy in the 1920s to launch Zimmer Holdings Inc., which is now Warsaw's largest employer. Orthopedics makers opening up shop in Warsaw found a ready supply of skilled workers, particularly in recent years as the more-traditional industrial sectors have slumped.

Memphis, Tennessee, and northern New Jersey are other hotspots for orthopedics products, but none rivals Warsaw for sheer concentration. Alhough major orthopedics companies are looking overseas for cheaper places to produce items such as basic bone screws and metal plates, the United States retains a firm grip on the industry. A major reason for this continued concentration is that the United States, with its population of fast-aging baby boomers, injury-prone weekend athletes, and overweight people is the world's biggest market for artificial hips and knees, accounting for more than 60 percent of the world market. The United States also effectively protects manufacturers in the sector with strict regulations for devices that go inside the human body. Rather than risk problems—and crippling lawsuits—U.S. health care providers buy their artificial joints from companies they know, which generally means buying American.

A concentration of one industry in such a small town is unusual, but the larger phenomenon is common. Many of the strongest U.S. manufacturers set up production far away from urban centers, with their high taxes, labor, and utility costs, and instead look for locations in small towns that are close to major highways and railways. Proximity to transportation hubs allows for smooth logistics in an age of just-in-time deliveries.

Profits are strong in the orthopedics industry because there is little pressure on suppliers to shave costs by setting up operations abroad. "The reason this business is in Warsaw and not Mexico is because margins are 70 percent or better," says Ron Clark, an orthopedic surgeon who founded his own company in Fort Wayne so he could be closer to Warsaw. Dr. Clark says savings from going abroad simply are not worth the logistical and quality problems those locations create.

However, the industry's dynamics may be changing as health care providers start to push back against the industry's steady price increases, raising concerns among investors about whether profits for Warsaw companies and others can keep up the brisk growth. But for now, Warsaw's orthopedics businesses continue to move and bend right along.

1. Use the Web to research Warsaw, Indiana. List the advantages that the community offers this collection of orthopedic manufacturers.
2. What are some of the potential challenges orthopedic manufacturers face with the shared location of Warsaw, Indiana?

Zimmer Holdings, the largest orthopedics employer in the industry capital, Warsaw, Indiana.

*Source:* Adapted from Timothy Aeppel, "Sticks and Stones May Break Bones, But Warsaw, Ind., Makes Replacements," *Wall Street Journal,* October 26, 2006, pp. B1, B4.

**561**

small companies as major assets. Many factors make Austin a desirable location for start-up companies, including its diversified economic base, a strong core of *Fortune 500* companies, including Dell, Motorola, and IBM, a significant population of private investors ready to invest in promising small companies, and several state and local government support systems offering entrepreneurial assistance and advice. The University of Texas system supplies companies with a steady crop of highly creative college graduates. Business incubators and a large pool of retired executives ready to offer business advice also provide important pieces of business infrastructure. "Austin has a strong venture capital community, the legal and accounting systems to support start-ups, a good university with technologies coming out of it, and a nice quality of life," says Carolyn Stark, head of the Austin Technology Council. It is no surprise that Austin is home to more than 1,800 technology companies, 1,100 of which are small businesses.[9]

Table 16.1 provides an abbreviated example of an evaluation matrix that entrepreneurs can use to evaluate various states as potential locations. Because of the unique nature of each business venture, an entrepreneur should modify the table to include location criteria that are relevant to his or her business and then attach weights to each criterion in the appropriate manner. This simple evaluation tool allows entrepreneurs to transform a location decision based solely on subjective feelings into one based on objective criteria.

**TAX RATES.** Another important factor entrepreneurs must consider is the tax burden that states impose on businesses and individuals. Income taxes may be the most obvious tax states impose on both business and individual residents, but entrepreneurs also must evaluate the impact of payroll taxes, sales taxes, property taxes, and specialized taxes on the cost of their operations.[10] In some cases, provinces and states offer special tax rates or are willing to negotiate fees in lieu of taxes for companies that will create jobs and stimulate the local economy.

**INTERNET ACCESS.** Fast and reliable Internet access is another important factor in the location decision. Internet access through high-speed cable or DSL lines is essential for high-tech companies and those engaging in e-commerce. Even those companies that may not do business over the Web use the Internet as a daily business tool for e-mail and information access. Companies that fall behind in high-tech communications will find themselves at a severe competitive disadvantage.

Most entrepreneurs are amazed at the amount of helpful information that exists about each state if they search the right places and ask the right questions. Obtaining and analyzing

## TABLE 16.1 State Evaluation Matrix

| Location Criterion | Weight 10 = High 1 = Low | Score 5 = High 1 = Low | State Weighted Score (Weight × Score) | | |
|---|---|---|---|---|---|
| | | | Florida | Georgia | South Carolina |
| Quality of labor force | | 1  2  3  4  5 | | | |
| Wage rates | | 1  2  3  4  5 | | | |
| Union activity | | 1  2  3  4  5 | | | |
| Energy costs | | 1  2  3  4  5 | | | |
| Tax burden | | 1  2  3  4  5 | | | |
| Educational/training assistance | | 1  2  3  4  5 | | | |
| Start-up incentives | | 1  2  3  4  5 | | | |
| Quality of life | | 1  2  3  4  5 | | | |
| Availability of raw materials | | 1  2  3  4  5 | | | |
| Other | | 1  2  3  4  5 | | | |
| Other | | 1  2  3  4  5 | | | |
| **Total score** | | | | | |

Assign to each location criterion a weight that reflects its relative importance (10 high to 1 low). Then score each state on a scale of 1 (low) to 5 (high). Calculate the weighted score (weight × score) for each state. Finally, add up the total weighted score for each state. The state with the highest total weighted score is the best location for your business.

regional and state information—and screening that information for bias—will provide entrepreneurs with a clear picture of the most favorable locations for their companies.

### Selecting the City

The next stage in the location process involves selecting the right city within the right region. This process involves a more personal, hands-on aspect of the research. Data will provide the entrepreneur with leads for potential locations, but entrepreneurs must visit them so that they can see first hand what a location has to offer. Who are your potential neighbors? Is the area safe? Is it bustling and energetic or lethargic and dying? What is the traffic flow like at various times of day? What is the parking situation like? Conducting this research before signing a lease is critical. In addition, entrepreneurs must factor into their decisions the population density and growth trends, the nature of competition, the location's potential to attract customers, the cost of the location, and other factors.

**POPULATION TRENDS.** An entrepreneur should know more about a city and its neighborhoods than do the people who live there. By analyzing population and demographic data, an entrepreneur can develop a revealing profile of a city, and the location decision becomes more than just "a shot in the dark." Studying the characteristics of a city's residents, including population sizes and density, growth trends, family size, age breakdowns, education, income levels, job categories, gender, religion, race, and nationality gives entrepreneurs the facts they need to make an informed location decision. A company's location should match the market for its products or services, and assembling a demographic profile will tell an entrepreneur how well a particular site measures up to his or her target market's profile. For example, with basic census data, entrepreneurs can determine the value of the homes in an area, how many rooms they contain, how many bedrooms they contain, what percentage of the population own their homes, and the amount residents' monthly rental or mortgage payments are. Imagine how useful such information would be to someone about to launch a home accessories store!

**ENTREPRENEURIAL**
**Profile**

*Dept. of the Interior Decorator Fabric LLC*

Dept. of the Interior Decorator Fabric LLC (DIDF) decided to make a move after 10 years in its initial location. The Oregon retail store offers decorator fabric, home accessories, and furniture, and the existing location was providing the level of customer exposure needed for growth. However, research indicated that Oakway Center, a newly remodeled lifestyle center, presented a better location. Although the move would reduce the space available from 5,600 to 4,300 square feet and cost more than three times the monthly lease, the busy center had become a local retail attraction and was well positioned to serve the growing number of affluent residential areas with attractive demographic profiles. The research and the move paid off for the small company. In the first six months at the new location, DIDF experienced a 38 percent increase in revenue and a substantial increase in profitability.[11]

Trends or shifts in population components may have more meaning than total population trends. A city may be experiencing rapid growth in the population of high-income, professional young people. This is the case in Atlanta, Georgia, where the median age of residents is 35, which is below the median age of the United States as a whole. The city has seen an explosion of businesses aimed at young people with rising incomes and hearty appetites for consumption. Beihai, China, and Ghaziabad, India, are the two fastest-growing cities in the world, with annual growth rates of 10 and 5 percent, respectively.[12]

**ENTREPRENEURIAL**
**Profile**

*The World Jewelry Center*

The World Jewelry Center selected Las Vegas, Nevada, for its new location. This 50-plus story jewelry marketplace in downtown Las Vegas is located across the street from the World Market Center, a furniture convention showplace, to attract corporate jewelry and gem companies from around the world. "The philosophy is pretty simple: build an enormous trade tower in Las Vegas offering security and one-stop shopping for the jewelry industry," says project manager Bill Boyajian, former president of the Gemological Institute of America. The jewelry mart also includes a separate three-story retail center offering jewelry for public sale and a jewelry and gem museum.[13]

**POPULATION DENSITY.** The number of people per square kilometer can be another important factor that determines the optimal business location. In many older cities, people live or work in very high-density areas. Businesses that need high traffic volume benefit by locating in these high-density areas. Knowing the population density within a few kilometers of a potential location can give entrepreneurs a clear picture of whether the city can support their businesses. It can also help them develop the appropriate marketing strategies to attract customers. For instance, fitness club owners have discovered that population density is one of the most important factors in selecting a suitable location. Experience has taught them that customers are willing to drive or walk only so far to visit a fitness club.

*Rita Hunter and Pulze
Fitness Center*

Rita Hunter recently opened Pulze Fitness Center in the heart of Greenville, South Carolina's downtown business district. She wanted her fitness center to be in a location that was convenient for her customers, but finding the right location proved to be a challenge. Space requirements and parking needs for these facilities are demanding. "I knew the space was available, and after some research, I realized there was a void in the full-service fitness center department for the area," says Hunter. Other factors Hunter considered when choosing the location for her center included the number of new houses, a growing population in the city's central business district, rising interest in corporate-sponsored physical training programs, and the number of businesses in the surrounding area.[14]

**COMPETITION.** Locations near competitors may offer labor pool advantages for manufacturers and service-based businesses. Retailers may find that having similar businesses located near one another increases traffic flow. This location strategy, known as **clustering**, works well for products for which customers are most likely to comparison shop. In many towns, auto dealers locate next to one another in an effort to create a shopping magnet for customers. The convenience of being able to shop for dozens of brands of cars, all within a few hundred yards of one another, draws customers from a sizable trading area.

Of course, this strategy has limits. An area that is saturated with businesses of the same type can limit the profitability of all competing firms. Entrepreneurs must weigh these criteria and may prefer to locate where little or no competition exists.

Studying the size of the market for a product or service and the number of existing competitors helps entrepreneurs determine whether they can capture a sufficiently large market share. Again in the United States, U.S. Census Bureau reports can be valuable. The bureau's *County Business Patterns Economic Profile* shows the breakdown of businesses in manufacturing, wholesale, retail, and service categories and estimates companies' annual payrolls and number of employees. The *Economic Census,* which covers 15 million businesses, gives an overview of the businesses in an area, including their sales or other measure of output, employment, payroll, and form of organization. It covers eight industry categories including retail, wholesale, service, manufacturing, and construction and gives statistics at not only the national level but also by state, metropolitan markets, county, places with 2,500 or more inhabitants, and postal code. The *Economic Census* is a useful tool for helping entrepreneurs determine whether the areas they are considering as a location are already saturated with competitors. One chain of food stores uses data from the Economic Census to estimate its market share in the trading area for each of its existing stores and to forecast sales in potential locations before opening new ones.[15]

The amount of available data on the population of any city or town is staggering. These statistics allow a potential business owner to compare a wide variety of cities or towns and to narrow the choices to those few that warrant further investigation. The mass of data may make it possible to screen out undesirable locations, but it does not make a decision for an entrepreneur. Entrepreneurs must see potential locations firsthand. Only by personal investigation can an entrepreneur add the intangible factor of intuition to the decision-making process.

**COSTS.** For many businesses, the cost of locating and operating is always critical to success. Some entrepreneurs search for locations that are in the process of revitalization and locate there while the entry cost is very low. Entrepreneurs who are able to find opportunities to locate their businesses at the "right place at the right time" can lower their cost dramatically.

Trina Sheridan cried when her husband-to-be, Sean, bought a building in the decayed Andersonville neighborhood north of downtown Chicago with plans to open a business. "I was very depressed," says Trina, recalling the gangs, graffiti, and crumbling storefronts around the two-story retail and living space. The Sheridans opened their cookware store, The Wooden Spoon, and now preside over a healthy business with four employees and six-figure sales that are growing 10 percent annually. More new businesses are moving into the reviving neighborhood. "There used to be a lot of vacant stores and businesses that people didn't take care of," Trina says. "And they're all gone." Although gentrification can benefit entrepreneurs, some business owners—like the Sheridans—are essential to the process, notes Ellen Shepard, executive director of the Andersonville Chamber of Commerce. "They took a risk in opening stores in a neighborhood that some people thought was weak."[16]

**LOCAL LAWS AND REGULATIONS.** Before selecting a particular site within a city, small business owners must explore local zoning laws to determine whether there are any ordinances that would place restrictions on business activity or that would prohibit establishing a business altogether. **Zoning** is a system that divides a city or county into small cells or districts to control the use of land, buildings, and sites. Its purpose is to contain similar activities in suitable locations. For instance, one section of a city may be zoned industrial to house manufacturing operations, whereas another section may be zoned commercial for retail businesses. In addition to limiting the activities that can take place at a site, zoning also may control the hours of operation, parking requirements, noise limitations, and size of the businesses located there. In some cases, an entrepreneur may appeal to the local zoning commission to rezone a site or to grant a **variance**, a special exception to a zoning ordinance. This tactic is risky, potentially time consuming, and could be devastating if the commission disallows the variance.

**COMPATIBILITY WITH THE COMMUNITY.** One of the intangibles that an entrepreneur can determine only by visiting a particular city is the degree of compatibility that a business has with the surrounding community. It is best if a company's image fits the character of the town and the needs and wants of its residents. Consider the costs associated with opening a retail business in an upscale, high-income community. To succeed, the business would have to match the flavor of the surrounding businesses and create an image that would appeal to upscale customers. Rents, along with fixtures and other decor items, would likely be expensive. The entrepreneur must determine whether there will be an adequate markup on the merchandise to justify these additional costs.

**QUALITY OF LIFE.** One of the most important, yet most difficult to measure, criteria for a city is the quality of life it offers. Entrepreneurs have the freedom and the flexibility to locate their companies in cities that suit not only their business needs but also their personal preferences. When choosing locations for their companies, entrepreneurs often consider factors such as cultural events, outdoor activities, entertainment opportunities, safety, and the city's "personality." A city that offers a high quality of life away from the workplace allows businesses to attract and retain a quality workforce. For instance, San Diego, California, has become a hub for the biotech industry as companies of all sizes have clustered there. Capitalizing on the proximity of several key biotech research institutes such as Salk Institute and the Scripps Research Institute, and the pool of talent at the University of California, these businesses also cite San Diego's quality of life as a key reason for their location choice. The nearby ocean, mild temperatures, and diverse opportunities for entertainment make San Diego an easy place for recruiting top-notch talent. "We have almost as many bookstores as surf shops," quips one business owner.[17]

**TRANSPORTATION NETWORKS.** Manufacturers and wholesalers in particular must investigate the quality of local transportation systems. If a company receives raw materials or ships finished goods by rail, is a location with rail access available in the city under consideration? What kind of highway access is available, and are there any plans in the future for major construction that might impact the desired location? Will transportation costs be reasonable and does the transportation infrastructure allow for efficient distribution? The availability of loading zones may be an important feature for a product-based business location.

**POLICE AND FIRE PROTECTION.** Does the community in which you plan to locate offer adequate police and fire protection? An absence of adequate police and fire protection will reflect in higher insurance costs and increased risks for the owner.

**PUBLIC SERVICES.** Some entity that provides water and sewer services, trash collection, and other utilities should serve the location. Streets should be in good repair with adequate drainage. Not having these services in place translates into higher costs for a business over time.

**THE LOCATION'S REPUTATION.** Like people, a city or parts of a city can have a bad reputation. In some cases, the reputation of the previous business will lower the value of the location. Sites where businesses have failed repeatedly create negative impressions in customers' minds. These negative impressions are hard to overcome and may prevent customers from giving the new business a try.

### The Final Site Selection

Successful entrepreneurs develop a site evaluation system that is both detailed and methodical. Each type of business has different evaluation criteria, and experience has taught successful entrepreneurs to analyze the facts about each potential location in search of the best possible site. A manufacturer may consider access to customers, raw material, suppliers, labor, and suitable transportation. Service firms need access to customers but can generally survive in lower-rent areas, whereas a retailer's prime consideration is customer traffic. The one element common to all three is the need to locate where customers want to do business.

## Location Criteria for Retail and Service Businesses

**2.** Describe the location criteria for retail and service businesses.

Few decisions are as important for retailers and service firms as the choice of a location. Because their success depends on a steady flow of customers, retail and service businesses must locate with their target customers' convenience and preferences in mind. It is important to realize that unless the company is a destination retailer, a business must locate where its customers are. Questions to address include:

- Where is the strongest concentration of potential customers who fit the profile of the target market?
- Among these various potential locations, where are competitors weakest?
- What, if any, are the physical or psychological barriers to operating in these potential locations?
- What are the comparative costs of the location options?
- What are the long-term prospects for the site?

The answers to these questions come only from research.

The choice of a location can influence what products to carry, what segments to target, how to position brands in the marketplace, how to compete against rivals, and which areas to target with advertising and promotional efforts. For a retail business, location actually can be a competitive advantage if an entrepreneur takes the time to conduct the necessary research. Trade area size, volume of customer traffic, parking, expansion potential, and visibility are important considerations when determining the ideal business location.

## Trade Area Size

Every retail business should determine the extent of its **trading area**, the region from which a business can expect to draw customers over a reasonable time span. The primary variables that influence the scope of a trading area are the type and size of the operation. If a retailer offers a broad range of products, he or she may draw customers from a great distance. In contrast, a convenience store with a general line of merchandise may have a small trading area because it is unlikely that customers would drive across town to purchase what is available within blocks of their homes or businesses. Generally speaking, the larger the store and the greater its selection of merchandise, the broader is its trading area.

The *Survey of Buying Power* published annually by *Sales and Marketing Management* provides a structure to conduct a side-by-side evaluation of the retail trading areas under consideration. Two key statistics that are traditionally used are **effective buying power**, which is equivalent to disposable personal income, and the buying power index. The **buying power index** is a weighted measure that combines effective buying income, retail sales, and population size into a single economic indicator of an area's sales potential as compared with total U.S. sales. The higher an areas's buying power index, the greater is its residents' purchasing potential. The following environmental factors influence the retail trading area size.

*Retail compatibility.* Shoppers tend to be drawn to clusters of related businesses. That is one reason shopping malls, lifestyle centers, and outlet shopping centers are popular destinations for shoppers and are attractive locations for retailers. The concentration of businesses pulls customers from a larger trading area than a single free-standing business does. Retail compatibility describes the benefits a company receives by locating near other businesses selling complementary products and services. Clever retailers choose their locations with an eye on the surrounding mix of businesses.

*Degree of competition.* The size, location, and activity of competing businesses also influence the size of the trading area. If a business is the first of its kind in a location, its trading area might be extensive. However, if the area already has multiple stores nearby that directly compete with a business, its trading area might be very small. How does the size of your planned operation compare with those that presently exist? Your business may be significantly larger and have more drawing power, giving it a competitive advantage.

*Transportation network.* The transportation networks are the highways, roads, and public service routes that presently exist or are planned. An inconvenient location reduces the business's trading area. Entrepreneurs should check to see whether the transportation system works smoothly and is free of barriers that might prevent customers from reaching their store. Is it easy for customers traveling in the opposite direction to cross traffic? Do signs and lights allow traffic to flow smoothly?

*Physical, cultural, or emotional barrier.* Physical barriers may be parks, rivers, lakes, or any other obstruction that hinders customers' access to the area. Locating on one side of a large park may reduce the number of customers who will drive around it to get to the store. In urban areas, new immigrants tend to cluster together, sharing a common culture and language. These trading areas are defined by cultural barriers, where inhabitants patronize only the businesses in their neighborhoods. The Little Havana section of Miami or the Chinatown sections of Paris, San Francisco, New York, and London are examples. Another powerful emotional barrier is fear. If high-crime areas exist around a location, most of a company's potential customers will not travel through those neighborhoods to reach the business. The mayors of many large cities have recognized that economic viability depends on the attitudes of both entrepreneurs and customers. The leaders of these cities are focusing their efforts on reducing crime and eliminating barriers to potential shoppers.

*Political barriers.* Local, regional, and national boundaries—and the laws within those boundaries—can influence the size of a company's trading area. Different laws across borders also created conditions where customers cross over from one to the next to save money. For instance, some U.S. states impose a very low cigarette tax, and shops located on their borders do a brisk business in the product.

**TABLE 16.2 Retail Trading Area Analysis**

| Characteristics | Relative Importance 1 = Low, 10 = High | Trading Area Score 1 = Negative, 5 = Positive | Area A | Area B |
|---|---|---|---|---|
| Population size and density | | | | |
| Per capita disposable income | | | | |
| Total disposable income | | | | |
| Educational levels of the population | | | | |
| Age distribution | | | | |
| Number and size of existing competitors | | | | |
| Evaluation of existing competitors' strength | | | | |
| Level of market saturation | | | | |
| Population growth projections | | | | |
| Ease of access | | | | |
| Other: | | | | |
| **Total score** | | | | |

Table 16.2 is a helpful tool for conducting a location analysis. Once entrepreneurs rank each factor in relative importance and assign a score on the 1 to 5 scale, they simply multiply the two values to get a score for each characteristic. Adding up the scores produces a total score. (Higher is better.)

**THE INDEX OF RETAIL SATURATION.** The **index of retail saturation (IRS)** is a measure of the potential sales per square foot of store space for a given product within a specific trading area. This measure combines the number of customers in a trading area, their purchasing power, and the level of competition. The index is the ratio of a trading area's sales potential for a particular product or service to its sales capacity:

$$IRS = \frac{C \times RE}{RF}$$

where:

C = Number of customers in the trading area

RE = Retail expenditures (the average expenditure per person [$] for the product in the trading area)

RF = Retail facilities (the total square meters of selling space allocated to the product in the trading area)

This computation is an important one for any retailer to make. Locating in an area already saturated with competitors results in dismal sales volume and often leads to failure.

To illustrate the IRS, suppose that an entrepreneur looking at two sites for a sports store finds that he needs sales of $175 per square meter to be profitable. Site 1 has a trading area with 25,875 potential customers, each of whom spends an average of $42 on sports annually; the only competitor in the trading area has 6,000 square meters of selling space. Site 2 has 27,750 potential customers spending an average of $43.50 on sports annually; two competitors occupy 8,400 square meters of space. The IRS of site 1 is:

$$IRS = \frac{25,875 \times 42}{6,000}$$

= $182.12 sales potential per square meter

The IRS of site 2 is:

$$IRS = \frac{27,750 \times 43.50}{8,400}$$

= $143.71 sales potential per square meter

Although site 2 appears to be more favorable on the surface, site 1 is supported by the index; site 2 fails to meet the minimum standard of $175 per square meter.

**REILLY'S LAW OF RETAIL GRAVITATION. Reilly's Law of Retail Gravitation**, a classic work in market analysis published in 1931 by William J. Reilly, uses the analogy of gravity to estimate the attractiveness of a particular business to potential customers. The ability to draw customers is directly related to the extent to which customers see it as a "destination" and is inversely related to the distance customers must travel to reach the business. Reilly's model also provides a way to estimate the trade boundary between two market areas by calculating the "break point" between them. The break point between two primary market areas is the boundary between the two where customers become indifferent about shopping at one or the other. The key factor in determining this point of indifference is the size of the communities. If two nearby cities have the same population sizes, then the break point lies halfway between them. The following is the equation for Reilly's Law:[18]

$$BP = \frac{d}{1 + \sqrt{\frac{P_b}{P_a}}}$$

where:

  BP = Distance from location A to the break point

  d = Distance between locations A and B

  $P_a$ = Population surrounding location A

  $P_b$ = Population surrounding location B

For example, if city A and city B are 22 kilometers apart, and city A has a population of 22,500 and city B has a population of 42,900, the break point according to Reilly's law is:

$$BP = \frac{22}{1 + \sqrt{\frac{42,900}{22,500}}} = 9.2 \text{ kilometers}$$

The outer edge of city A's trading area lies about 9 kilometers between city A and city B. Although only a rough estimate, this simple calculation using readily available data can be useful for screening potential locations.

## Customer Traffic

Perhaps the most important screening criterion for a potential retail or service location is the number of potential customers passing by the site during business hours. To be successful, a business must be able to generate sufficient sales to surpass its breakeven point, and doing that requires an ample volume of traffic. One of the key success factors for a convenience store, for instance, is a high-traffic location with easy accessibility. Entrepreneurs should know the traffic counts (pedestrian and auto) at the sites they are considering. Shoeshine stands and kiosks in airports are examples of service businesses in which the customer comes directly to the entrepreneur. The high volume of people passing by creates a prime customer base for these businesses.

## Adequate Parking

If customers cannot find convenient and safe parking, they are not likely to stop in the area. Many downtown areas have lost customers because of inadequate parking. Although a U.S. shopping mall might average five parking spaces per 1,000 square feet of shopping space, many U.S. central business districts get by with 3.5 spaces per 1,000 square feet. Customers generally will not pay to park if parking is free at shopping centers or in front of competing stores. Even when a business provides free parking, some potential customers may not feel safe on the streets, especially after dark. Many large city business districts become virtual ghost towns at the end of the business day. A location where traffic vanishes after 6 P.M. may not be as valuable as mall and shopping center locations that mark the beginning of the prime sales at 6 P.M.

### Expansion Potential

A location should be flexible enough to provide for expansion. Failure to consider this factor can force a successful business to open a second store when it would have been advantageous to expand its original location.

### Visibility

No matter what a retailer sells or how well it serves customers' needs, it cannot survive without visibility. Highly visible locations simply make it easy for customers to find a business. A site lacking visibility puts a company at a major disadvantage before it even opens its doors. In a competitive marketplace, customers seldom are willing to search for a business when equally attractive alternatives are easier to locate.

# ENTREPRENEURSHIP

# *In Action*

## Growing with Chocolates

Whoever would have thought to put dragon fruit into a chocolate bar? Oakland, California, chocolatier Michael Mischer has. His line of 20 oversized Criollo chocolate bars are studded with traditional and exotic delights such as caramelized nibs, Montmorency cherries, roasted nuts, and spicy mango. Mischer also fashions rich Belgian-style shell-molded truffles, all of which he sells at his stylish Grand Avenue store in downtown Oakland.

Born and raised in Northern Germany, Michael Mischer entered the pastry and confection business as an apprentice to Swiss Master Pastry Chef Andreas Haertle at Konditorei in Braunschweig, Germany. "When I first started, I did not know anything about confections, except really enjoying freshly made chocolates and pastries from local shops," says Michael. After moving to California and working in small pastry shops as well as his own pastry shop, Michael decided that it was time for a challenge. With a love for the craft of producing fresh products, the idea for a small chocolate shop was born.

Mischer had to contend with high fixed costs from the very beginning. He opened Michael Mischer Chocolates in a space that offered long-term growth potential—all 1,700 square feet of it. It was then he realized that facility came with an unavoidable rental price tag of $2,800 a month. That gave him 2,800 reasons to keep the rest of his expenses as low as possible. "I was very confident I could get this going with what I had," he says.

Mischer spent $75,000 to renovate the former office space. About half of his budget went into electrical and plumbing systems, both of which had to be installed by professionals to meet local codes. Mischer did as much of the work as he could, saving $2,000, for instance, by yanking out old carpeting. Fortunately for his budget, Mischer prefers "the lean look" in store design. Rather than shelling out for fancy glass cases, he displays his sweets on white plates. The one exception: He spent $12,000 on a showcase for gelato.

Mischer stayed stingy with his operating budget. He has yet to hire a full-time employee but instead has three part-timers to tend the counter. He prefers to be in the back, where he makes the chocolates using machinery that is mostly left over from an earlier bakery venture. In his third year of operation, the space continues to meet the needs of the business, and Mischer does not expect that to change any time soon. Mischer has received rave reviews for his chocolate throughout the San Francisco Bay Area, and with annual revenues of about $250,000, the business is already profitable.

1. What was Mischer's total investment in the space for the first year, including the remodel, fixtures, and rent?

2. Mischer chose to invest in space that would meet his long-term needs. Discuss the trade-offs of that decision.

*Sources:* Personal contact, Michael Mischer, September 6, 2007; Joshua Hyatt, "How to Get Rich in America–Lean Cuisine," *Money,* June 6, 2007, http://money.cnn.com/galleries/2007/moneymag/0706/gallery.success_stories.moneymag/5.html.

Some service businesses, however, can select sites with less visibility if the majority of their customer contacts are by telephone, fax, or the Internet. For example, customers usually contact plumbers by telephone; rather than locating close to their customer bases, plumbers have flexibility in choosing their locations. Similarly, businesses that work at their customers' homes, such as swimming pool services, can operate from their homes and service vans.

## Location Options for Retail and Service Businesses

*3.* Outline the basic location options for retail and service businesses.

There are six basic areas where retail and service business owners can locate: the central business district, neighborhoods, shopping centers and malls, near competitors, outlying areas, and at home.

### Central Business District

The **central business district (CBD)** is the traditional center of town—the downtown concentration of businesses established early in the development of most towns and cities. Entrepreneurs derive several advantages from a downtown location. Because businesses are centrally located, they attract customers from the entire trading area of the city. In addition, small businesses benefit from the traffic generated by other stores clustered in the downtown district. However, locating in a CBD does have certain disadvantages. Intense competition, high rental rates, traffic congestion, and inadequate parking facilities characterize some CBDs. In addition, many cities have experienced difficulty in preventing the decay of their older downtown business districts. Downtown districts withered as residents moved to the suburbs and began shopping at newer, more convenient shopping centers and malls.

Today, many cities are working to restore the unique atmosphere of their traditional downtown shopping districts. Many customers find the charming atmosphere that central business districts offer irresistible with their rich mix of shops, their unique architecture and streetscapes, and their historic charm. Cities across the United States, for example, have begun to reverse the urban decay of their downtown business districts through proactive revitalization programs designed to attract visitor and residents alike to cultural events by locating major theaters and museums in the downtown area. In addition, many cities are providing economic incentives to real estate developers to build apartment and condominium complexes in the heart of the downtown area. Vitality is returning as residents live and shop in the once nearly abandoned downtown areas. The "ghost-town" image is being replaced by residents who love the convenience and excitement of life at the center of the city. As residents have become more interested in preserving their downtown districts, retailers have returned to cities in the United States and elsewhere.

*Borders Group*

Borders Group has opened a Borders Bookstore in downtown Detroit on the ground floor of Compuware Corporation's world headquarters building. Although shuttered storefronts and empty buildings are scattered throughout the area, the bookstore draws many of its customers from the more than 4,000 employees who work at Compuware and from other downtown workers. In other cities, large retailers such as Talbots, Gap, J. Crew, Williams-Sonoma, Eddie Bauer, Starbucks, and others are opening stores in traditional CBDs, locations they typically have shunned in the past.[19]

### Neighborhood Locations

Small businesses that locate near residential areas rely heavily on the local trading areas for business. For example, many grocers and convenience stores located just outside residential subdivisions count on local clients for successful operation. One study of food stores found that the majority of the typical grocers' customers live within a five-mile radius. The primary advantages of a neighborhood location include relatively low operating costs and rents and close contact with customers.

## Shopping Centers and Malls

A shopping center is a group of retail and other commercial establishments that is planned, developed, owned, and managed as a single property with on-site parking. The center's size and orientation are determined by the market characteristics of the trade area served by the center. A mall is typically enclosed, climate-controlled and lighted, flanked on one or both sides by storefronts, and gives meaning to the term "one-stop shopping." Onsite parking is usually provided around the perimeter. Shopping centers and malls have become part of the fabric of retail life in the United States, for example, and more than 48,000 of them occupy 6.06 billion square feet of retail space. According to the International Council of Shopping Centers, more than 2.28 billion adults visit shopping centers and malls each year.[20] The world's two largest malls are Chinese. They are the South China Mall in Dongguan and Golden Resources Mall in Beijing. Both include features like windmills and kids' theme parks.[21]

Although malls are booming in Asia and still account for the majority of retail sales in the United States, their popularity has declined in the United States in recent years. A mall location is no longer a guarantee of success. Enclosed malls have been under pressure lately, and many weaker ones have closed. Part of the problem is the bland feel that malls exhibit in their designs and the sameness of the stores they offer. In addition, the demographic makeup of malls' shoppers has changed over time, and many traditional mall shoppers are unhappy with the traffic congestion and sprawling parking lots that characterize many mall shopping experiences. Other malls have undergone extensive renovations, adding entertainment features to their existing retail space in an attempt to generate more traffic.

There are eight types of shopping centers (see Table 16.3).[22]

***Neighborhood Center.*** This center is designed to provide convenience shopping for the day-to-day needs of consumers in the immediate neighborhood. Typically containing 3 to 12 stores, they often are anchored by a supermarket, and about a third have a drugstore anchor. A neighborhood center is usually configured as a straight-line strip

© Mike Baldwin / Cornered

**TABLE 16.3 Shopping Center Descriptions**

| Type of Shopping Center | Concept | Square Feet (Including Anchors) | Acreage | Primary Trade Area |
|---|---|---|---|---|
| OPEN-AIR CENTERS | | | | |
| Neighborhood Center | Convenience | 30,000–150,000 | 3–15 acres | 3 miles |
| Community Center | General merchandise; convenience | 100,000–350,000 | 10–40 acres | 3–6 miles |
| Power Center | Category-dominant anchors: few small tenants | 250,000–600,000 | 25–80 acres | 5–10 miles |
| Theme/Festival Center | Leisure; tourist-oriented; retail and service | 80,000–250,000 | 5–20 acres | N/A |
| Outlet Center | Manufacturers' outlet stores | 50,000–40,000 | 10–50 acres | 25–75 miles |
| Lifestyle Center | Upscale national chains specialty store; dining and entertainment in outdoor setting | 150,000–500,000 and can vary | 10–40 acres | 8–12 miles |
| MALLS | | | | |
| Regional Center | General merchandise; fashion | 480,000–800,000 | 40–100 acres | 5–15 miles |
| Superregional Center | Similar to regional center with more variety and assortment | 800,0000+ | 60–120 acres | 5–25 miles |

*Source:* "ISCS Shopping Center Definitions—U.S.," International Council of Shopping Centers, http://icsc.org/srch/about/impactofshoppingcenters/03_Definitions.pdf#xml=http://icscsearch.icsc.org/texis/search/pdfhi.txt?query=ICSC+Shopping+Center+Definitions&pr=IcscLiveNew&prox=page&rorder=500&rprox=500&rdfreq=500&rwfreq=500&rlead=500&sufs=0&order=r&cq=&id=46ddeab6a9.

with no enclosed walkway or mall area and parking in the front. Centers may have a canopy or other façade treatment to provide shade and protection from inclement weather or to tie the center together.

***Community Center.*** A community center contains from 12 to 50 stores and offers a wider range of apparel and other soft goods than the neighborhood center. Common anchors are supermarkets, super drugstores, and discount department stores. Community center tenants sometimes contain value-oriented, big-box, category-dominant retailers selling such items as apparel, home improvement/furnishings, toys, electronics, or sporting goods. The center is usually configured in a straight line as a strip or may be laid out in an L- or U-shape, depending on the site. Of the eight types of shopping centers, community centers encompass the widest range of formats.

***Power Center.*** A power center is dominated by several large anchors, including discount department stores, off-price stores, warehouse clubs, or "category killers"—stores that offer a vast selection in related merchandise categories at very competitive retail prices. Power centers typically consist of several anchors, some of which may be freestanding (unconnected), and only a small number of small specialty tenants. Anchor stores usually account for 80 percent of a power center space, compared with 50 percent in the typical strip shopping center.

***Theme/Festival Center.*** These centers typically employ a unifying theme that is carried out by the individual shops in their architectural design and, to an extent, in their merchandise. Entertainment is often a common element of such centers, although it may come in the shopping experience as much as in the tenants themselves. Theme/festival centers are often targeted toward tourists, but may also attract local customers who might be drawn by the center's unique nature. They may be anchored by restaurants and entertainment facilities and are generally located in urban areas where they adapt older, sometimes historic, buildings, to be part of mixed-use projects.

*Outlet Center.* This center type consists of manufacturers' and retailers' outlet stores selling brand-name goods at a discount. Outlet centers typically have no anchor stores although certain brand-name stores may serve as "magnet" tenants. The majority of outlet centers are open-air, configured either in a strip or as a village cluster, although some are enclosed.

*Lifestyle Center.* Most often located near affluent residential neighborhoods, the lifestyle center caters to the retail needs and "lifestyle" pursuits of consumers in its trading area. It has an open-air configuration and typically includes at least 50,000 square feet of retail space occupied by upscale national chain specialty stores. Other elements differentiate the lifestyle center in its role as a multi-purpose leisure-time destination, including restaurants, entertainment, and design ambience and amenities such as fountains and street furniture that are conducive to casual browsing. These centers may be anchored by one or more conventional or fashion specialty department stores.

Open canopies may connect the storefronts, but an open-air center does not have enclosed walkways linking the stores. The most common variations of this configuration are linear, L-shaped, U-shaped, Z-shaped, or cluster.[23] The cluster form and its variations have led to the emergence of new classes of centers in which the physical layout and open design are differentiating features, emulating a "village main street" feel. The typical lifestyle center generates between $400 and $500 in sales per square foot compared with $330 in sales per square foot in traditional malls.

*Regional shopping malls.* A regional center serves a large trading area, usually from 5 to 15 miles in all directions. These enclosed malls contain from 50 to 100 stores and serve a population of 150,000 or more that lives within a 20- to 40-minute drive. Its main attraction is the combination of anchors, which may be traditional, mass merchant, discount, or fashion department stores, with numerous fashion-oriented specialty stores.

*Superregional shopping malls.* A superregional mall is similar to a regional mall but is bigger, containing more anchor stores and a greater variety of shops selling deeper lines of merchandise. Its trade area stretches up to 25 miles out.[24] The South China Mall in Dongguan, China, for example, has 7.1 million square feet of floor space and more than 1,000 stores.[25]

**HYBRID CENTERS.** Hybrid centers combine elements from two or more of the main shopping center types. Common hybrids include value-oriented mega-malls (combining mall, power center, and outlet elements), power-lifestyle centers (combining power center and lifestyle center elements), and entertainment-retail centers (combining retail uses with megaplex movie theaters, theme restaurants, and other entertainment uses).[26]

Because the cost of locating in any of these areas can be high, it is important for an entrepreneur to consider the following questions:

- Is there a good fit with other products and brands sold in the mall or center?
- Who are the other tenants? Which stores are the anchors that will bring people into the mall or center?
- What are its customer demographics?
- Do these demographics match the company's target market?
- How much foot traffic does the mall or center generate?
- How much traffic passes the specific site being considered?
- How much vehicle traffic does the mall or center generate?
- Check its proximity to major population centers, the volume of tourists it draws, and the volume of drive-by freeway traffic.
- What is the vacancy rate?
- What is the turnover rate, and is there a consistent reason for these departures?
- Is the mall or center considered to be successful overall?
- How much money in sales does it generate per square meter? Compare its performance against the industry average.

### Near Competitors

One of the most important factors when choosing a retail or service location is the compatibility of nearby stores with the retail or service customer. For example, stores selling high-priced goods such as cars or merchandise that requires comparisons, such as antiques, find it advantageous to locate near competitors to facilitate comparison shopping. Locating near competitors might be a key factor for success in businesses that sell goods that customers compare on the basis of price, quality, color, and other factors.

Although some small business owners seek to avoid locations near direct competitors, others prefer to locate near rivals. For instance, restaurateurs know that restaurants attract other restaurants, which, in turn, attract more customers. In many cities, at least one "restaurant row" develops as each restaurant feeds off of the customers that the cluster of restaurants draw.

There are limits to locating near competitors, however. Clustering too many businesses of a single type into a small area ultimately will erode their sales once the market reaches the saturation point. As the number of gourmet coffee shops has exploded in recent years, many have struggled to remain profitable, often competing with three or four similar shops, all within easy walking distance of one another. When an area becomes saturated with competitors, the stores cannibalize sales from one another, making it difficult for them to survive.

### Outlying Areas

In general, small businesses should not locate in remote, hard-to-find areas. Accessibility and traffic flow are vital to retail and service success, but there are exceptions. Some businesses, however, have turned their remote locations into trademarks. Cabela's, a successful chain of sporting goods stores, has used some of its remote locations to become local attractions in small outlying towns or areas.

Outlying locations become a distinct disadvantage if potential customers cannot find your location, if they believe that there is no overriding reason to travel to your location, or if they fear for their safety either at your location or on the way to and from your location.

### Home-Based Businesses

According to some sources, every 11 seconds someone starts a home-based business.[27] Locating a service business at home can offer several benefits. Perhaps the biggest benefit is the low cost of setting up the business. Most often, home-based entrepreneurs set up shop in a spare bedroom or basement, avoiding the cost of renting, leasing, or buying a building. With a phone, a computer and a printer, a lone entrepreneur can be open for business. Many service companies do not have customers come to their places of business, making an expensive office location unnecessary. For instance, customers typically contact plumbers or exterminators by telephone, and the work is performed in customers' homes.

Choosing a home location has disadvantages, however. It may affect family life, interruptions are more frequent, the refrigerator is all too handy, work is always just a few steps away, and isolation can be a problem. Another difficulty some home-based entrepreneurs may face involves zoning laws. As their businesses grow and become more successful, entrepreneurs' neighbors often complain about the increased traffic, noise and disruptions from deliveries, employees, and customers who drive through their residential neighborhoods to conduct business. Many communities now face the challenge of passing updated zoning laws that reflect the reality of today's home-based businesses while protecting the interests of residential homeowners.

*4.* Explain the site selection process for manufacturers.

## The Location Decision for Manufacturers

The criteria for the location decision for manufacturers are very different from those of retailers and service businesses; however, the decision can have just as much impact on the company's success. Many manufacturers have special needs that influence their choice of location. In other cases, the decision is influenced by municipal regulations.

Labor productivity is a critical factor for manufacturers when labor cost is a significant component of a product's total cost. Labor productivity in cost per unit of production is a simple calculation:

$$\text{Cost per unit} = \frac{\text{Labor cost per day}}{\text{Productivity (in units/day)}}$$

Areas with lower labor costs may seem at first glance to be a good choice, but the lower levels of productivity associated with less trained or poorly motivated workers may result in higher cost per unit of production.

*Hutchinson Technology*

Hutchinson Technology, a company that makes the tiny suspension systems that are used in computer disk drives, maintains all four of its manufacturing plants within a 200-mile radius of tiny Hutchinson in the U.S. state of Minnesota, despite the fact that all of its competitors manufacture their products in Asia to take advantage of lower labor costs. Hutchinson's highly automated manufacturing process relies on high-quality, skilled workers to produce the tiny stainless steel strips that hold the head of computer disk drives just 8 nanometers above the surface of the spinning disk. In the face of intense competition, Hutchinson maintains 55 percent market share and ships 98 percent of its output to computer makers that are located in the Far East. The company's aggressive investment in automation enables it to keep labor costs at less than 15 percent of its cost of goods sold, even though wage rates for its workers in the United States are far greater than those of workers in East Asia. In addition, because the finished product is so small, shipping costs are minimal. "Our location is one of our competitive advantages," says CEO Wayne Fortun.[28]

Local zoning ordinances limit a manufacturer's choice of location. If the manufacturing process creates offensive odors or noise, a business may be even further restricted in its choices. City and area planners can show potential manufacturers the areas of the city or county set aside for industrial development. Some cities have developed industrial parks in cooperation with private industry. These industrial parks typically are equipped with sewage and electrical power sufficient for manufacturing. Many locations are not so equipped, and it can be extremely expensive for a small manufacturer to have such utilities brought to an existing site.

The type of transportation network that a company requires sometimes dictates the location of a manufacturing operation. Some manufacturers must locate along a railroad siding; others may only need reliable trucking service. Bulk materials are sometimes shipped by barge and, consequently, require a facility convenient to a navigable river or lake. The added cost of using multiple shipping options, such as rail-to-truck or barge-to-truck, can significantly increase shipping costs and make a location unfeasible for a manufacturer.

### Foreign Trade Zones

Foreign trade zones can be an attractive location for many small manufacturers that are engaged in global trade and are looking to lower the tariffs they pay on the materials and parts they import and on the goods they export. A **foreign trade zone** is a specially designated area that allows resident companies to import materials and components from foreign countries; assemble, process, package, or manufacture them; and then ship finished products out while incurring low tariffs and duties or, in some cases, paying no tariffs or duties at all. For instance, a bicycle maker might import parts and components from around the world and assemble them onto frames made in the United Kingdom. If located in a foreign trade zone, the manufacturer pays no duties on the parts it imports or on the finished bicycles it exports.

# In Action

## Does the Buck Stop Here?

Basalt columns flank the drive to the lobby with the spectacular chandelier built of antlers. The building looks like it belongs here, in the rugged U.S. state of Idaho. The Buck Knives factory in the Idaho panhandle looks like a native company of the U.S. northwest, but, in fact, is a well-orchestrated California transplant. The story of how CJ Buck moved the family knife-making business from California to this rugged patch of Idaho is a case study in business relocation.

For generations, Buck Knives enjoyed loyal customers, great name recognition, and a tradition of quality forged by CJ Buck's great-grandfather, a blacksmith apprentice named Hoyt Buck who grew tired of sharpening grub hoes and in 1902 decided to grind his own blades instead. After years of experimentation, Hoyt Buck came up with a secret tempering technique that produced knives that were so sharp and so hard that they could whack a steel bolt in two. He co-founded the company with his son, Al Buck, in 1947. From its origin in a wooden lean-to, the business had grown into a California institution with $33 million in annual sales and 260 employees cranking out more than a million knives a year.

A few months before his 39th birthday, CJ Buck took over the family business. For someone who had spent his entire professional life working for the company, it should have been a magical moment. It was not. CJ inherited as many headaches as he did traditions. Low-cost foreign competitors were putting pressure on the company's profit margins, and cash flow was a constant problem. Energy costs, a key factor in tempering blades, were creeping up. The company's workforce was experienced, but it also was expensive. "We were losing money," CJ says. "And it looked like there was no end in sight."

Working closely with his father, Chuck, Buck's chairman of the board, CJ streamlined the manufacturing process at Buck's sprawling plant in California and began to make some low-end knives in Taiwan. In fact, Buck's new manufacturing process proved to be a real asset. It organized workers into small groups rather than a single assembly line using space more efficiently and freeing up 40,000 square feet of the company's 170,000-square-foot factory. That meant Buck could save money by moving

into a smaller facility. As members of the executive team pondered new locations, they were struck by a more radical notion—getting out of California altogether.

At first, a move seemed inconceivable. Buck Knives had deep roots in California. However, deep roots do not mean much if a company cannot stay in business. Electricity bills, workers' compensation, labor costs, and taxes were high everywhere in California, and the board of directors told CJ to discreetly explore the idea of moving out of the state.

CJ received a call from Bob Potter, who ran economic development for Kootenai County in the Idaho panhandle. Potter had heard that Buck was scouting locations around the Northwest and called to see if Buck might consider moving to Idaho. He offered to perform a cost analysis and a few weeks later, flew to California to present his report.

The numbers made CJ take notice. Electricity rates were about half, workers' compensation was a third, and wages for manufacturing jobs were 20 percent less than what Buck was paying in California. According to Potter's figures, Buck could shave at least $600,000 off its manufacturing costs every year by moving to Idaho. "It's a tough decision—especially for family-owned companies," Potter told CJ. "Uprooting a company is a tough thing to go through. You're uprooting families."

One day as he drove to work, CJ surveyed the California plant that his father had built, and a terrible thought entered his mind: "This place is sinking." CJ knew that he had to move the factory out of the state—soon. "It's like having an operation that can save your life," he says. "We had to do the move before it was too late."

The hunt for a new location took on a sense of urgency. Buck's executives drew up a wish list for the ideal location: Cheap electricity, a good climate for business, low taxes, a plentiful supply of labor, good highway and rail connections, proximity to a major airport, and access to a major port through which to import cheaper knives from Taiwan. In addition, it had to offer a good quality of life. Post Falls, Idaho, a growing suburb of Coeur d'Alene, Idaho, was one of the top three considerations. Positioned on Interstate 90 just west of Coeur

*(continued)*

d'Alene, Post Falls is a small but fast-growing town that measured up well against the board's wish list. After some discussion, the board and top management decided to move the Buck knife factory to Post Falls, Idaho.

Buck estimated that building a factory in Idaho would cost about $8.5 million with another $4 million to relocate key employees and equipment. Offsetting that was the capital Buck could realize from selling the factory in California, which CJ hoped to sell to another manufacturer for $11 million. If that happened, the move would pay for itself in three years. After more than a year Buck found a buyer, but the offer was only $7.5 million. CJ bit his lip and made the deal.

Meanwhile, the company had to confront the painful process of deciding who would move to Idaho— and who would be left behind. Moving everyone would simply be too expensive. Eventually, 200 workers would lose their jobs, but Buck tried to ease the pain by giving workers a year's notice, providing severance packages, and working with the California Department of Industrial Relations to provide retraining. At the same time, the company had to woo the workers it needed to move north. In the end, 58 workers and their families decided to make the move to Idaho.

Buck broke ground on its new factory more than a year later than CJ originally wanted, but the new,

128,000-square-foot building is impressive. Located in an industrial park along the I-90 corridor, it was designed from the ground up to implement lean manufacturing in which workers operate in "cells," with emphasis on quality and flexibility. Employees soon settled into their jobs, and within a year, efficiency figures in the new factory passed the mark set in California. Electric bills are roughly 30 percent what they would have been if Buck had stayed there; workers' compensation is 10 percent less; and labor costs 75 percent of what it cost in California. The move reduced overhead and freed up capital for investment and product development. "It has reinvigorated this company, from the engineers to the factory floor," CJ says. We're excited. We're kicking butt. [The move has] reanimated a sense of pride in the company."

1. What were the greatest risks that Buck faced in making the decision to relocate?

2. Why was it important for the company to define the ideal location and what it would offer? How did this criteria influence Buck's location selection?

3. Do you agree with CJ's decision to move the factory to Idaho? Explain.

*Source:* Adapted from Chris Lydgate, "The Buck Stopped Here," *Inc.*, May 2006, pp. 86–95.

The only duty the manufacturer would pay is on the bicycles it sells in the United Kingdom (see Figure 16.2).

### Enterprise and Empowerment Zones

Originally created to encourage companies to locate in economically blighted areas, **enterprise zones and empowerment zones** offer entrepreneurs tax breaks on investments they make within geographic zone boundaries. Companies can have access to tax credits for hiring workers living in empowerment zones and for investments they make in plant and equipment in the zones. Free zones are located in many countries around the world. Often, the goal of these programs is to halt the blight that has resulted in the exodus of many residents by encouraging businesses to locate in these economically challenged areas and revitalize them.[29]

**FIGURE 16.2 How a Foreign Trade Zone Works**

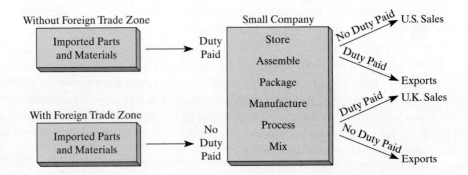

*Kevin Forrester and
Forestone Inc.*

Kevin Forrester says that California's Enterprise Zone program allowed him to open Forestone Inc., a stone veneer manufacturing company, in the small town of Brawley, California. To keep manufacturing costs low, Forrester originally had planned to open his factory just across the border in Mexico, but Brawley's enterprise zone gave him incentives and allowed him to take advantage of tax credits by locating there. Less than two years after start-up, Forestone already is shipping its stone veneer products to distributors in Mexico from its factory in California rather than the other way around.[30]

## Business Incubators

**5.** Discuss the benefits of locating a start-up company in a business incubator.

A **business incubator** is an organization that combines low-cost, flexible rental space with a multitude of support services for its small business residents. For some start-up companies, an incubator may make the ideal initial location. Business incubators house several businesses under one roof or in a campus setting. They commonly offer resident companies reduced rents, shared services and, in many instances, formal or informal access to financing. The shared resources incubators typically provide their tenants include secretarial services, a telephone system, a computer and software, fax machines, meeting facilities, and, sometimes, management consulting services. Some incubators also provide assistance to resident businesses interested in exporting.

Approximately 1,400 incubators in North America cater to high- and low-tech businesses. Of these, about 80 percent report that they provide formal or informal access to capital. Therefore, business incubators may be ideal for pre-revenue-stage companies to early-stage companies that are selling products or services.[31] Most receive some type of financial assistance from their sponsors to continue operations. The investment that supports the incubator is generally a wise one because firms that graduate from incubators have only a 13 percent failure rate.

*Martek Biosciences*

Martek Biosciences develops and sells products derived from microalgae, including nutritional oils contained in infant formula that aid in the development of newborns' eyes and central nervous systems. Martek was a part of the Technology Advancement Program at a U.S. University. The program enabled Martek to access specialized facilities and equipment that served as a pilot development lab for its early products. What was the key to Martek's successful incubator experience? Former incubator director Ed Sybert believes it was the company's willingness to seek help from the incubator and the university. "This company has always been desirous of the university's help," Sybert says. "They were always pulling toward us—asking for help."[32]

The primary reason that government and other entities establish incubators is to enhance economic development in an area and to diversify the local economy. Common sponsors of incubators include government agencies, colleges or universities, partnerships among government agencies, nonprofit agencies, private developers, and private investment groups. Business and technical incubators vary to some degree as to the types of clients they attempt to attract, but most incubator residents are engaged in light manufacturing, service businesses, and technology or research-related fields (see Figure 16.3).[33] The ease of becoming an incubator tenant varies. The typical incubator has entry requirements that are tied to its purpose and that detail the nature and scope of permissible business activities. Incubators also have criteria that establish the conditions a business must meet to remain in the facility as well as the expectations for graduation as the business leaves the incubator site.

Business incubators facilitate entrepreneurs' search for capital from angel investors, state and government agencies, economic-development coalitions, and other lenders and investors. In addition to reduced rents and support services, incubators also offer their fledgling tenants another valuable resource: access to the early-stage capital that young

**FIGURE 16.3 Business Incubators by Industry**
*Source:* National Business Incubation Association, 2007.

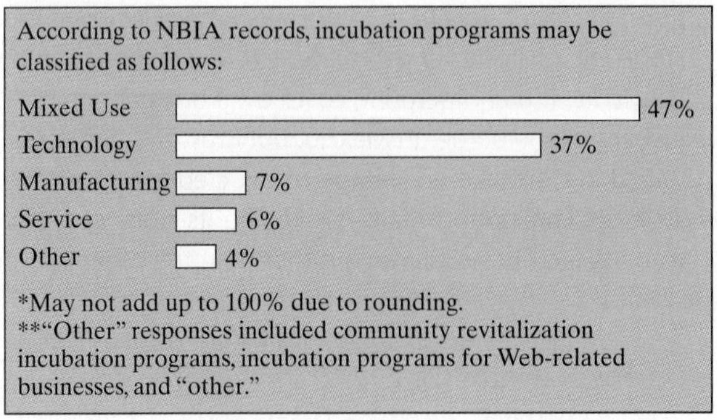

According to NBIA records, incubation programs may be classified as follows:

| | |
|---|---|
| Mixed Use | 47% |
| Technology | 37% |
| Manufacturing | 7% |
| Service | 6% |
| Other | 4% |

*May not add up to 100% due to rounding.
**"Other" responses included community revitalization incubation programs, incubation programs for Web-related businesses, and "other."

companies need to grow. A recent survey by the National Business Incubation Association found that 83 percent of incubators provide some kind of access to seed capital, ranging from help with obtaining federal grants to making connections with angel investors.[34]

## Layout and Design Considerations

*6.* Describe the criteria used to analyze the layout and design considerations of a building, including the Americans with Disabilities Act.

Once an entrepreneur chooses the best location for the business, the next question deals with designing the proper layout to maximize sales (retail) or productivity (manufacturing or service). **Layout** is the logical arrangement of the physical facilities in a business that contributes to efficient operations, increased productivity, lower energy usage, and higher sales. Planning for the most effective and efficient layout in a business environment can produce dramatic improvements in a company's operating effectiveness and efficiency.

One study conducted by the American Association of Interior Designers found that employees rated the look and feel of their workspaces as the third most important consideration—after salary and benefits—when deciding whether or not to accept or to quit a job.[35] Another survey of more than 2,000 office workers commissioned by Gensler, a leading design firm, illustrates both the problems and the promise of workplace design. More than 90 percent reported that their office space affected their attitudes about work and that a different setup could make their companies more competitive. Nearly half of the respondents said they would work an extra hour a day if they had a better workplace environment. Only 38 percent of workers said they would be proud to show important customers their workspace. Approximately one-third of the employees complained that the environment did not promote health and well-being, and almost half concluded that creating a productive workplace was not a company priority.[36]

When customers have access to the workplace, the impact on their attitudes and behaviors are just as dramatic. Building size, adaptability, appearance, entrances, accessibility, signage, lighting, and even the scent and sound of the environment are important layout and design considerations.

### Size and Adaptability

A building must offer adequate space and be adaptable to accommodate a business's daily operations. If the space is too small at the outset of operations, efficiency will suffer. There must be room enough for customers' movement, inventory, displays, storage, work areas, offices, and restrooms. Inefficient layouts undermine employee productivity and can create organizational chaos.

As a business expands, a lack of adequate room or an inefficient configuration may limit future growth. Some businesses wait too long before moving into larger quarters, and they fail to plan their new space arrangements properly. To avoid this problem, experts recommend that new business owners plan their space requirements one to two years ahead and update the estimates every six months. When preparing the plan, entrepreneurs should include the expected growth in the number of employees, manufacturing, selling, or storage space requirements, and the number and location of branches to be opened.

*Gravity Tank*

When Gravity Tank, a Chicago design strategy firm, needed a flexible layout for project teams that work together for months at a time, owners created an innovative office design. Groups of four or five employees cluster in semi-enclosed "bays" constructed of thick cardboard. The bays are easily reconfigured to suit the needs of each team. Each bay houses two small desks and a conference table with power outlets, Ethernet cables, and trays for office supplies for optimal access. The cardboard dividing panels also provide bulletin board surfaces to display drawings, project timetables, and works in progress. This design is considered ideal for start-ups or small professional services with a need for flexibility and collaboration on a budget. Gravity Tank built the entire workspace on a $20,000 budget.[37]

## External Appearance

The physical appearance of a building provides customers with their first impression of a business and contributes significantly to establishing its identity in the customer's mind. The building's appearance should be consistent with the entrepreneur's desired image for the business. This is especially true for retail businesses. Retailers must recognize the importance of creating the proper image for their stores and how their shop's layout and physical facility influence this image. In many ways, the building's appearance sets the tone for the customer's quality and service expectations. The appearance should reflect the "personality" of the business. Should the building project an exclusive image or an economical one? Is the atmosphere informal and relaxed, or is it formal and businesslike? Externally, the storefront's architectural style and color, signs, entrances, and general appearance give important clues to customers about a business's image. For example, a glass front enables a retail business to display merchandise easily and to attract potential customers' attention. Passersby can look in and see attractive merchandise displays or, in some cases, dedicated employees working.

Communicating the right signals through layout and physical facilities is an important step in attracting a steady stream of customers. Retail consultant Paco Underhill advises merchants to "seduce" passersby with their storefronts. "The seduction process should start a minimum of 10 paces away," he says. "A store's interior architecture is fundamental to the customer's experience—the stage upon which a retail company functions."[38]

Williams-Sonoma, an upscale retailer of kitchenware, seduces passersby with window displays that look more like someone's kitchen than a retail shop. Stores in the chain change their eye-catching displays frequently to reflect the foods of the season. The goal is not only to sell but also to make customers feel welcome and to put them in a positive frame of mind. "If you have a positive feeling," says Julie Irwin, a marketing professor, you're going to associate it with everything you see." Once inside a Williams-Sonoma store, an array of aromas rising from freshly-baked foods or hot beverages also lure customers and encourage them to stay, which increases the probability that they will make a purchase.[39]

The following tips help entrepreneurs create displays that will sell:

- *Keep displays simple.* Simple, uncluttered arrangements of merchandise will draw the most attention and will have the greatest impact on potential customers.
- *Keep displays clean and up to date.* Dusty, dingy displays or designs that are outdated send the wrong message to customers.
- *Promote local events.* Small companies can show their support of the community by devoting part of the display window to promoting local events.
- *Change displays frequently.* Customers don't want to see the same merchandise every time they visit a store. Experts recommend changing window displays at least

quarterly. Businesses that sell fashionable items, however, should change their displays at least twice a month, if not weekly.

■ *Get expert help, if necessary.* Some business owners have no aptitude for design! In that case, their best bet is to hire a professional to design window and in-store displays. If a company cannot afford a professional designer's fees, the entrepreneur should check with the design departments at local colleges and universities. There might be a faculty member or a talented student willing to work on a freelance basis.

■ *Appeal to all of a customer's senses.* Effective displays engage more than one of a customer's senses. Who can pass up a bakery case of freshly baked, gooey cinnamon buns with their mouth-watering aroma wafting up to greet passersby?

■ *Contact the companies whose products you sell to see if they offer design props and assistance.* These vendors may offer additional insight and are aware of industry trends and competitor tactics.

### Entrances

All entrances to a business should invite customers in. Wide entryways and attractive merchandise displays that are set back from the doorway can draw customers into a business. A store's entrance should catch passing customers' attention and draw them inside. "That's where you want somebody to slam on the brakes and realize they're going someplace new," says retail consultant Paco Underhill.[40] Retailers with heavy traffic flows, such as supermarkets or drugstores, often install automatic doors to ensure a smooth traffic flow into and out of their stores. Retailers should remove any barriers that interfere with customers' easy access to the storefront. Broken sidewalks, sagging steps, mud puddles, and sticking or heavy doors not only create obstacles that might discourage potential customers but they also create legal hazards for a business if they cause customers to be injured.

### Government Regulations and the U.S. Americans with Disabilities Act

The **Americans with Disabilities Act (ADA)**, for example, passed in 1990 by the United States, requires most businesses to make their facilities available to physically challenged customers and employees. In addition, the law requires businesses with 15 or more employees to accommodate physically challenged candidates in their hiring practices. Most states have similar laws, many of them more stringent than the ADA, that apply to smaller companies as well. The rules of these state laws and the ADA's Title III are designed to ensure that mentally and physically challenged customers have equal access to a firm's goods or services. For instance, the act requires business owners to remove architectural and communication barriers when "readily achievable." The ADA allows flexibility in how a business achieves this equal access, however. For example, a restaurant either could provide menus in Braille or could offer to have a staff member read the menu to blind customers. A small dry cleaner might not be able to add a wheel-chair ramp to its storefront without incurring significant expense, but the owner could comply with the ADA by offering curbside pickup and delivery services for disabled customers at no extra charge.

Although the law allows a good deal of flexibility in retrofitting existing structures, buildings that were occupied after January 25, 1993, must be designed to comply with all aspects of the law. For example, buildings with three stories or more must have elevators; anywhere the floor level changes by more than one-half inch, an access ramp must be in place. In retail stores, checkout aisles must be wide enough—at least 36 inches—to accommodate wheelchairs. Restaurants must have 5 percent of their tables accessible to wheelchair-bound patrons.

Complying with the ADA does not necessarily require businesses to spend large amounts of money. The Justice Department estimates that more than 20 percent of the cases customers have filed under Title III involved changes the business owners could have made at no cost, and another 60 percent would have cost less than $1,000![41] In addition, companies with $1 million or less in annual sales or with 30 or fewer full-time employees that invest in making their locations more accessible to all qualify for a tax credit. The credit is 50 percent of their expenses between $250 and $10,500. Businesses that remove physical, structural, and transportation barriers for disabled employees and customers also qualify for a tax deduction of up to $15,000.

The Americans with Disabilities Act also prohibits any kind of employment discrimination against anyone with a physical or mental disability. A physically challenged person is considered to be "qualified" if he can perform the essential functions of the job. The employer must make "reasonable accommodation" for a physically challenged candidate or employee without causing "undue hardship" to the business. Following are some of the specific provisions of Title III of the act.

- Restaurants, hotels, theaters, shopping centers and malls, retail stores, museums, libraries, parks, private schools, daycare centers, and other similar places of public accommodation may not discriminate on the basis of disability.
- Physical barriers in existing places of public accommodation must be removed if readily achievable (i.e., easily accomplished and able to be carried out without much difficulty or expense). If not, alternative methods of providing services must be offered, if those methods are readily achievable.
- New construction of places of public accommodation and commercial facilities (nonresidential facilities affecting commerce) must be accessible.
- Alterations to existing places of public accommodation and commercial facilities must be done in an accessible manner. When alterations affect the utility of or access to a "primary function" area of a facility, an accessible path of travel must be provided to the altered areas. The restrooms, telephones, and drinking fountains serving the altered areas must also be accessible, to the extent that the cost of making these features accessible does not exceed 20 percent of the cost of the planned alterations. The additional accessibility requirements for alterations to primary function areas do not apply to measures taken solely to comply with readily achievable barrier removal.
- Elevators are not required in newly constructed or altered buildings under three stories or with less than 3,000 square feet per floor, unless the building is a shopping center; shopping mall; professional office of a health care provider; terminal; depot, or station used for public transportation; or an airport passenger terminal.

Most businesses have found that making these reasonable accommodations for customers and employees creates a more pleasant environment and offers additional conveniences for all.

The Americans with Disabilities Act has positively affected how businesses deal with this segment of its customers and employees. The U.S. Department of Justice offers a technical assistance program that provides business owners with free information and technical assistance concerning the ADA. The Department of Justice also has an ADA Information Line that owners can call for information and publications on the ADA (800-514-0301).

### Signage

One of the lowest-cost and most effective methods of communicating with customers is a business sign. Signs communicate what a business does, where it is, and what it is selling. America is a very mobile society, and a well-designed, well-placed sign can be a powerful vehicle for reaching potential customers.

A sign should be large enough for passersby to read from a distance, taking into consideration the location and speed of surrounding traffic arteries. To be most effective, the message should be short, simple, and clear. A sign should be legible in both daylight and at night; proper illumination is a must. Contrasting colors and simple typefaces are best. The most common problems with business signs are that they are illegible, poorly designed, improperly located, poorly maintained, and have color schemes that are unattractive or are hard to read.

Before investing in a sign, an entrepreneur should investigate the local community's sign ordinances. In some cities and towns, local regulations impose restrictions on the size, location, height, and construction materials used in business signs.

### Interiors

The functional aspects of building interiors are very important and require careful attention to detail. Designing a functional, efficient interior is not as easy as it seems. Technology has changed the way employees, customers, and the environment interact with one another, and smart entrepreneurs realize that they can influence the effectiveness of those interactions with well-designed layouts. The result can be a boost to a company's sales and profits. For instance, as their customers have changed, department stores and clothing retailers have modified the layouts of their stores. Because shoppers are busier than ever and want an efficient shopping experience, stores have moved away from the traditional departments and are organizing their merchandise by "lifestyle categories" such as sports, women's contemporary, and men's business casual. These displays expose customers to additional merchandise and make it easier for them to make complementary purchases. Studies have shown that men and women tend to shop differently and redesigned stores feature separate entrances for each. Women's sections are organized into lifestyle sections, and accessories are scattered throughout the store to encourage browsing. The men's side features signage showing how to build the outfits on display, and individual items are neatly displayed and organized by size for efficiency.[42]

Although designing an effective layout is a combination of art and a science, it is not a haphazard process. **Ergonomics**, the science of adapting work and the work environment to complement employees' strengths and to suit customers' needs, is an integral part of a successful design for office environments. For example, chairs, desks, and table heights that allow people to work comfortably help employees perform their jobs faster and more easily. Design experts claim that improved lighting, better acoustics, and proper climate control benefit the company as well as employees. An ergonomically designed workplace can improve workers' productivity significantly and lower days lost due to injuries and accidents. Unfortunately, many businesses fail to incorporate ergonomic design principles into their layouts, and the result is costly. Every year, 1.8 million workers experience injuries related to repetitive motion or overexertion. The most frequent and most expensive workplace injuries are musculoskeletal disorders (MSDs).[43] Workers who spend their days staring at computer monitors (a significant and growing proportion of the workforce) often are victims of MSDs.

When planning store, office, or plant layouts, business owners usually focus on minimizing costs. Although staying within a budget is important, minimizing injuries and enhancing employees' productivity with an effective layout should be the overriding issues. Many exhaustive studies have concluded that changes in office design have a direct impact on workers' performance, job satisfaction, and ease of communication. In a reversal of the trend toward open offices separated by nothing more than cubicles, businesses are once again creating private offices in their workspaces. Many businesses embraced open designs, hoping that they would lead to greater interaction among workers. Many companies, however, have discovered that most office workers need privacy and quiet surroundings to be productive. Michael Brill, an office space consultant, studied 11,000 workers to determine the factors that most affect their productivity and found that the ability to do distraction-free work topped the list.[44] Rather than encourage teamwork, open offices leave workers distracted, frustrated, and less productive—just like the characters in the Dilbert cartoon strip. "Open offices do lead to more unstructured communication, but those same offices can lead to problems of [employee] concentration," says Babson College's Tom Davenport, whose research shows that workplace design has a direct impact on white-collar workers' performances and productivity.[45]

When evaluating an existing building's interior, an entrepreneur must be sure to determine the integrity of its structural components. Are the building's floors sufficiently strong to hold the business's equipment, inventories, and personnel? Strength is an especially critical factor for manufacturing firms that use heavy equipment. When multiple floors exist, are the upper floors anchored as solidly as the primary floor? Can inventory be moved safely and easily from one area of the plant to another? Is the floor space adequate for safe and efficient movement of goods and people? Consider the cost of maintaining the floors. Hardwood floors may be extremely attractive but require expensive and time-consuming maintenance. Carpeted floors may be extremely attractive in a retail business but may be impractical for a manufacturing firm. Entrepreneurs must consider utility, durability, maintenance requirements, attractiveness, and, if important, effectiveness in reducing noise.

Like floors, walls and ceilings must be both functional and attractive. On the functional side, walls and ceilings should be fireproof and soundproof. Are the colors of walls and ceilings compatible, and do they create an attractive atmosphere here for customers and employees? For instance, many high-tech companies use bright, bold colors in their designs because they appeal to their young employees. On the other hand, more conservative companies such as accounting firms and law offices decorate with more subtle, subdued tones because they convey an image of trustworthiness and honesty. Upscale restaurants that want their patrons to linger over dinner use deep, luxurious tones and soft lighting to create the proper ambiance. Fast-food restaurants, on the other hand, use strong, vibrant colors and bright lighting to encourage customers to get in and out quickly, ensuring the fast table turnover they require to be successful. In most cases, ceilings should be done in light colors to reflect the store's lighting.

For many businesses, a drive-through window adds another dimension to the concept of customer convenience and is a relatively inexpensive way to increase sales. Although drive-through windows are staples at fast-food restaurants and banks, they can add value for customers in a surprising number of businesses. Owners of building supply stores and wedding chapels have experienced sales increases from the addition of drive-through windows.

### Lighting

Good lighting allows employees to work at maximum efficiency and comfort. Proper lighting is measured by what is ideal for the job being done. Proper lighting in a factory may be quite different from that required in an office or retail shop. Retailers often use creative lighting to attract customers to a specific display. Jewelry stores provide excellent examples of how lighting can be used to display merchandise effectively. Lighting provides a good return on investment when considering its overall impact on a business. Few people seek out businesses that are dimly lit because they convey an image of untrustworthiness. The use of natural light gives a business an open and cheerful look and actually can boost sales. A series of studies by energy research firm Heschong Mahone Group found that stores using natural light experience sales that are 40 percent higher than those of similar stores using fluorescent lighting.[46] In a retail environment, proper lighting can draw attention to featured products.

### Scent

Research shows that scents can have a powerful effect in retail stores. The Sense of Smell Institute reports that the average human being can recognize 10,000 different odors and can recall scents with 65 percent accuracy after one year, a much higher recall rate than visual stimuli produce. In one experiment, a researcher diffused a subtle scent of vanilla into the women's department of a store and rose maroc into the men's department and discovered that sales nearly doubled. He also discovered that if he switched the scents, sales in both departments fell well below their normal average.[47] Many companies—from casinos to retail stores—are beginning to understand the power of using scent as a marketing tool. Almost every bakery uses a fan to push the smell of fresh-baked breads and sweets into pedestrian traffic lanes, tempting them to sample some of their delectable goodies. "Smell has a greater impact on purchasing than everything else combined," Says Alan Hirsch, neurological director of the Smell & Taste Treatment & Research Foundation in Chicago. "If something smells good, the product is perceived as good."[48] "Scent marketing gives companies a competitive advantage over ads on the Internet," says Arthur Sherwood, managing partner at sensory marketing consultancy Scent ID.[49]

*Hard Rock Hotel*

Orlando's Hard Rock Hotel was having difficulty getting people to visit an out-of-the-way ice cream shop. It turned to ScentAir Technologies, a company specializing in offering 1,480 different fragrances to enhance business environments for customers. The shop installed a device from ScentAir that released waffle-cone and sugar-cookie aromas in hopes of luring visitors to the shop. It worked; sales jumped 45 percent in the first six months.[50]

### Sound

In addition to focusing on influencing shoppers with alluring displays and smells, more businesses are paying attention to the smart use of sound. Background music can be a merchandising tool if the type of music playing in a store matches the demographics of its target customers. Research shows that music is a stimulant to sales because it reduces resistance, warps the sense of time allowing shoppers to stay longer in the store, and helps to produce a positive mental association between the music and the intended image of the store.[51] One rule is clear for retail soundscapes: slow is good. As people's biorhythms often mirror the sounds around them, a gently meandering mix of classical music or soothing ambient noise encourages shoppers to slow down and relax. Classical music, in particular, makes shoppers feel affluent and boosts sales more than other types of music.[52] Shopping psychologists say that unhurried customers are exactly what retailers want because they are more likely to make purchases. The growing competition for the attention of time-pressed consumers is forcing businesses to focus more on the total sensory experience they provide: "Retailers will have to make their stores more stimulating," says retail consultant Tim Dennison.[53]

*Bob Finigan and Muzak*

Muzak used to be the butt of jokes for its bland elevator music, but the company now supplies some 400,000 shops, restaurants and hotels around the world—including Gap, McDonald's, and Burger King—with songs tailored to reflect their identity. "What we're trying to capture is a brand's essence," says Bob Finigan, Muzak's vice president of product and marketing. "We express the intangibles of a brand's identity—their company values, their position in the market—through the emotional power of music." Two years ago, Muzak formed a partnership with ScentAir, a firm that specializes in installing inviting aromas in hotels, restaurants, and stores. "Instead of asking a customer, 'How does it sound?' when they walk into a business, we're now saying, 'How do you feel?'" says Muzak's Finigan.[54]

## Layout: Maximizing Revenues, Increasing Efficiency, and Reducing Costs

**7.** Explain the principles of effective layouts for retailers, service businesses, and manufacturers.

The ideal layout depends on the type of business and on the entrepreneur's strategy for gaining a competitive edge. Retailers design their layouts with the goal of maximizing sales revenue; manufacturers design theirs to increase efficiency and productivity and to lower costs.

### Layout for Retailers

Retail layout is the arrangement of merchandise in a store. A retailer's success depends, in part, on well-designed floor displays. The displays should pull customers into the store and make it easy for them to locate merchandise; compare price, quality, and features; and ultimately to make a purchase. Paco Underhill, retail consultant and author of *Why We Buy: The Science of Shopping,* calls a store's interior design "the stage on which a retail company functions."[55] Unfortunately, according to Underhill, most retailers set that stage with a greater focus on their own needs for convenience than on creating an engaging, satisfying shopping experience for their customers.[56] A retail layout should pull customers into the store and make it easy for them to locate merchandise, compare price, quality, and features, and ultimately make a purchase. In addition, a floor plan should take customers past displays of other items that they may buy on impulse. Between 65 and 70 percent of all buying decisions are made once a customer enters a store, which means that the right layout can boost sales significantly. One study found that 68 percent of the items bought on major shopping trips (and 54 percent on smaller trips) were impulse purchases. Shoppers in this study were heavily influenced by in-store displays, especially those at the ends of aisles, called end-cap displays.[57]

Smart retailers recognize that some locations within a store are superior to others. Customer traffic patterns give the owner a clue to the best location for the highest gross margin

## Retail Espionage

Paco Underhill is something of a retail spy. He surreptitiously trolls stores, supermarkets, banks, hotels, stadiums, and malls to observe the behavior of consumers in physical spaces. Underhill, founder, CEO, and president of Envirosell, a behavioral market research firm, has been conducting research on consumer shopping behavior for more than 25 years. "Merchants and marketers like to measure the efficacy of their efforts through advertising research, such as stopping people while leaving the store, calling them on the phone, or sending them e-mails," he says. However, there is a problem with that approach: What consumers think they did and what they actually did are often quite different.

Underhill's research focuses on the space and human factors that govern how consumers move in a store, how visual acuity and perception of time impact the way they shop, what makes a female-friendly environment, shoppers' unspoken inclinations, and the retail differences between different parts of the world. Using a combination of in-store video recording and observation, each year Underhill and his colleagues observe 50,000 people and record more than 70,000 hours of some of the most boring, yet revealing, videotape.

Envirosell's vast collection of research provides this advice for retailers:

*Design matters.* A good example of knowing what to design is knowing what *not* to design. "Where is the *real* mall entrance?" asks Underhill. "It's not the magnificent doorway, but it's the dark, dismal parking lot." Overdesign is problematic. "If I look at the architecture of the [retail] complex and the design of the store, including fixtures, the point of sales, store windows, packaging, signage, flat-screen televisions—it adds up to a visual cacophony that is not commercially or aesthetically satisfying," says Underhill. Too many signs take the discovery out of shopping. He recommends clear and crisp signage, particularly at the cash registers where people are "held captive," but not at the entrance, where they are not inclined to take in much information. Window signs, displays, and mannequins, he said, best communicate when angled 10 to 15 degrees to face the direction in which people are moving.

*The human factor.* In the United States, for example, shoppers tend to turn to the right as they enter a store. "If you want to get my attention, it better be to my right," says Underhill. In addition, there should be more open spaces for places to sit and eat, especially at malls, where, says Underhill, 40 percent of food is taken to a quiet spot and consumed in a space that was never intended to serve as a dining area.

*Traffic patterns.* Underhill also challenges mall traffic patterns. "There is a prescribed walking pattern of up the right and down the left, yet we design our malls as if we walk sideways." Underhill also suggests that malls and department stores group similar products and services, a concept known as retail gravity. Furthermore, Underhill predicts that developers will soon emulate European-style malls, which he refers to as "alls" because they incorporate businesses that serve a wide variety of shoppers' needs conveniently in one location. "People are more time-pressed than money-pressed, so the idea of crossing a Jiffy Lube with a nail salon is not out of the question," says Underhill.

*Gender appreciation.* "We live in a world that is designed by men, yet we expect women to participate," says Underhill. The majority of shoppers are women, not men. "Whether I am looking at a hotel, airport, Exxon station, or Victoria's Secret, the question should be: What will make it female-friendly? You may be designing a hardware store, but you better ask yourself: 'How do I sell to the wife?'" For example, stores can provide more chairs in convenient locations, especially for husbands and boyfriends who are uninterested in their female partner's shopping. If a woman knows the man is comfortable somewhere, then she is more comfortable continuing to shop. Additional chairs also give a woman "a place to put her bags down," which in turns also motivates her to keep shopping.

*(continued)*

Studies indicate that space is also an important factor for women. "Women want more space and privacy," Underhill says. "They don't want to be bumped from behind (the "butt-brush factor") or crowded. The bigger the physical shopping space, the better." Underhill also recognizes a difference between male and female in terms of sensitivity. "A woman comes equipped with radar—if a woman stands to look at a display or signage, how long she stands there is defined by how close the traffic pattern moves behind her. Underhill suggests avoiding designing narrow aisles and tight display areas because women, in particular, prefer to shop where they have space to roam.

*Kids count.* "Kids can be your allies or your enemies," Underhill says. "If a child feels welcome, the parent will come in." Underhill recalls having a Disney executive crawl on the floor to get a three-year-old's perspective. "Many stores from a three-year-old's perspective are just not that fabulous. So make sure there's something for them to see at their eye level." Projecting a virtual hopscotch pattern or dinosaur on the floor is all it takes to turn a boring shopping trip for a child into a friendly experience.

*Source:* Russell Boniface, "I Spy a Shopper," *AIArchitect,* June 23, 2006, www.aia.org/aiarchitect/thisweek06/0623/0623paco.cfm.

items. Merchandise purchased on impulse and convenience goods should be located near the front of the store. Items people shop around for before buying and specialty goods will attract their own customers and should not be placed in prime space. Prime selling space should be restricted to products that carry the highest markups.

**ENTREPRENEURIAL Profile**

*Target*

Research revealing that customers purchase 40 percent of all the wine sold in the United States in discount retail stores and supermarkets caught the attention of managers at Target. They decided to devote part of their SuperTarget stores' retail space to attractive wine displays. Aimed at the company's core customers, women of the baby boom generation, the large display cases are well organized and hold more than 100 different types of wine. The centerpiece of the displays is a series of giant posters that take those who may not be familiar with the nuances of purchasing wine through a four-step process for selecting just the right wine. The displays include easy-to-understand text with graphics that explain the terms commonly used to describe wines' tastes. A "wine wheel" helps shoppers match a wine with everyday meals such as canned soup or macaroni and cheese. Because of the effective design of the displays, wine sales have exceeded Target's expectations.[58]

Retail store layout evolves from a clear understanding of customers' buying habits. If customers come into the store for specific products and have a tendency to walk directly to those items, placing complementary products in their path will boost sales. Observing customer behavior can help the owner identify the "hot spots" where merchandise sells briskly and "cold spots" where it may sit indefinitely. By experimenting with factors such as traffic flow, lighting, aisle size, music type and audio levels, signs, and colors, an owner can discover the most productive store layout.

**ENTREPRENEURIAL Profile**

*Ray Davis and Umpqua Bank*

Umpqua Bank considers itself a retailer. As competition for deposits intensifies, Umpqua is capturing customers' attention by revamping its buildings to look more like coffeehouses and retail boutiques and less like the stodgy fortresses of banks in the past. The new designs offer more open spaces and softer lines to create a less formal environment with common areas and activities to encourage people to linger. Customers at Umpqua Bank's stores—versus branches—in the U.S. states of Oregon and California discover couches, coffee service, and Wi-Fi. Some even have a movie screen for community "movie nights."[59] CEO Ray Davis says, "The neighborhood bank store concept represents a dramatic shift away from the traditional approach of building bank locations." Not only is the new store design more welcoming to customers, but it also is more convenient for them. The bank stores also fit into existing neighborhoods more easily, the way a coffee shop or cafe would.[60]

With their inviting interiors and open layouts, Umpqua Bank stores are quite different from traditional bank branches.

Retailers have three basic layout patterns to choose from: the grid, the free-form layout, and the boutique.

**GRID LAYOUT.** The **grid layout** arranges displays in rectangular fashion so that aisles are parallel. It is a formal layout that controls the traffic flow through the store. Most supermarkets and many discount stores use the grid layout because it is well suited to self-service stores. This layout uses the available selling space efficiently, creates a neat and organized environment, and facilitates shopping by standardizing the location of items. Figure 16.4 shows a typical grid layout.

**FREE-FORM LAYOUT.** Unlike the grid layout, the **free-form layout** is informal, using displays of various shapes and sizes. As illustrated in Figure 16.5, the free-form layout's primary advantage is the relaxed, friendly shopping atmosphere it creates, which encourages

**FIGURE 16.4 The Grid Layout**

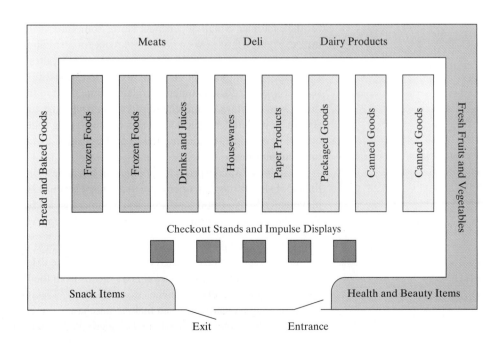

**FIGURE 16.5 The Free-Form Layout**

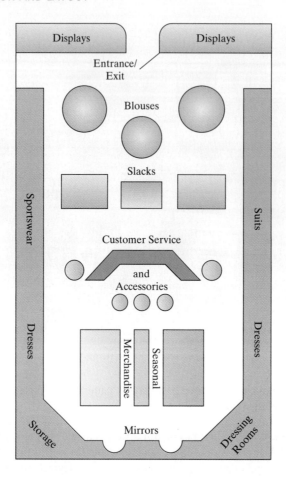

customers to shop longer and increases the number of impulse purchases they make. Still, the free-form layout is not as efficient as the grid layout in using selling space, and it can create security problems if not properly planned.

**BOUTIQUE LAYOUT.** The **boutique layout** divides the store into a series of individual shopping areas, each with its own theme. It is like building a series of specialty shops into a single store. The boutique layout is informal and can create a unique shopping environment for the customer. Small department stores sometimes use this layout to create a distinctive image. Figure 16.6 shows a boutique layout for a small department store.

Business owners should display merchandise as attractively as their budgets will allow. Customers' eyes focus on displays, which tell them the type of merchandise the business sells. It is easier for customers to relate to one display than to a rack or shelf of merchandise. Open displays of merchandise can surround the focal display, creating an attractive selling area. Retailers can boost sales by displaying together items that complement each other. For example, displaying ties near dress shirts or handbags next to shoes often leads to multiple sales.

Spacious displays provide shoppers an open view of merchandise and reduce the likelihood of shoplifting. An open, spacious image is preferable to a cluttered appearance. Display height is also important because customers won't buy what they cannot see or reach. When planning in-store displays, retailers should remember the following:

■ The average man is 68.8 inches tall, and the average woman is 63.6 inches tall. The average person's normal reach is 16 inches, and the extended reach is 24 inches. The average man's standing eye level is 62 inches from the floor, and the average woman's standing eye level is 57 inches from the floor.[61] Placing merchandise on high shelves discourages customers from making purchases. For example, putting hearing aid batteries on bottom shelves where the elderly have trouble getting to them or placing

**FIGURE 16.6 The Boutique Layout**

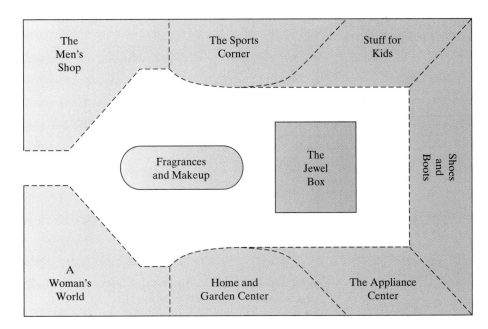

popular children's toys on top shelves where little ones cannot reach them hurts sales. Smart retailers keep items within easy reach of shoppers.

- One study found that shoppers, especially women, are reluctant to enter narrow aisles in a store. Narrow aisles force customers to jostle past one another (experts call this the "butt-brush factor"), which creates anxiety, especially among women shoppers.
- Placing shopping baskets in several areas around a store can increase sales. Seventy-five percent of shoppers who pick up a basket buy something, compared to just 34 percent of customers who do not pick up a basket.[62] Smart retailers make shopping baskets available to customers throughout the store, not just at the entrance.
- Making shoppers hunt for the items they want to buy lowers the probability that they will purchase an item and that they will return to a particular store. Easy-to-read signs, clearly marked aisles, and displays of popular items located near the entrance make it easy for shoppers to find their way around a store.
- Whenever possible, allow customers to touch the merchandise; they are much more likely to buy items if they can pick them up. The probability that customers shopping for clothing will make a purchase increases if they try on the garments. It pays to have friendly clerks who offer to "start a dressing room" for customers who pick up an article of clothing.[63]

Retailers must remember to separate the selling and non-selling areas of a store. They should never waste prime selling space with non-selling functions such as storage, office, and fitting areas. Although non-selling activities are necessary for a successful retail operation, they should not take precedence and occupy valuable selling space. Many retailers place their non-selling departments in the rear of the building or in the center of the floor, recognizing the value of each foot of space in a retail store and locating their most profitable items in the best-selling areas.

The various areas within a small store's interior space are not equal in generating sales revenue. Certain areas contribute more to revenue than others. The value of store space depends on floor location in a multistory building, location with respect to aisles and walkways, and proximity to entrances. Space values decrease as distance from the main entry-level floor increases. Selling areas on the main level contribute a greater portion to sales than do those on other floors because they offer greater exposure to customers than either basement or higher-level locations. Therefore, main-level locations carry a greater share of rent than other levels.

The layout of aisles in the store has a major impact on the customer exposure that merchandise receives. Items located on primary walkways should be assigned a higher share of rental costs and should contribute a greater portion to sales revenue than those displayed

**FIGURE 16.7 The Space Value for a Small Store**

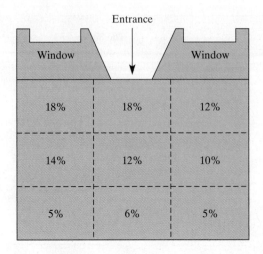

along secondary aisles. Space value also depends on the space's relative position to the store entrance, which serves as the "landing strip" for shoppers. A critical moment occurs when shoppers walk into a store as they slow down, try to orient themselves, and expand their peripheral vision to get a panoramic view of the retail spaces. An effective layout allows them to familiarize themselves with the retail landscape as quickly as possible.

Many shoppers turn to the right when entering a store and move around it counter-clockwise.[64] That makes the front right-hand section of a retail store the "retail sweet spot." Retailers should put their best selling and highest profit margin items in this prime area. Only about one-fourth of a store's customers will go more than halfway into the store. Therefore, the farther away an area is from the entrance, the lower its value. Using these characteristics, Figure 16.7 illustrates space values for a typical small-store layout.

Understanding the value of store space ensures proper placement of merchandise. The items placed in the high-rent areas of the store should generate adequate sales and contribute enough profit to justify their high-value locations. The decline in value of store space from front to back of the shop is expressed in the 40–30–20–10 rule. This rule assigns 40 percent of a store's rental cost to the front quarter of the shop, 30 percent to the second quarter, 20 percent to the third quarter, and 10 percent to the final quarter. Similarly, each quarter of the store should contribute the same percentages of sales revenue.

For example, suppose that the owner of a small department store anticipates $920,000 in sales this year. Each quarter of the store should generate the following sales volume:

| | |
|---|---|
| Front quarter | $920,000 × 0.40 = $368,000 |
| Second quarter | $920,000 × 0.30 = $276,000 |
| Third quarter | $920,000 × 0.20 = $184,000 |
| Fourth quarter | $920,000 × 0.10 = $ 92,000 |
| **Total** | **$920,000** |

### Layout for Manufacturers

Manufacturing layout decisions take into consideration the arrangement of departments, workstations, machines, and stock-holding points within a production facility. The general objective is to arrange these elements to ensure a smooth workflow (in a production area) or a particular traffic pattern (in a service area).

Manufacturing facilities have come under increased scrutiny as companies attempt to improve quality, decrease inventories, and increase productivity through facilities that are integrated, flexible, and controlled. Facility layout has a dramatic effect on product mix, product processing, materials handling, storage, control, and production volume and quality. Some manufacturers use 3-D simulation software (based on the same technology as the 3-D video games people play) to test the layout of their factories and its impact on employees and their productivity *before* they ever build them. These highly realistic simulations tell designers how well a particular combination of people, machinery, and environment interacts with one another. The software can identify potential problem areas, such as layouts that force workers into awkward positions that would cause injuries, equipment designs that cause workers to reach too far for materials, and layouts that unnecessarily add extra time to the manufacturing process by requiring extra materials handling or unneeded steps.[65]

**FACTORS IN MANUFACTURING LAYOUT.** The ideal layout for a manufacturing operation depends on several factors, including the following:

- *Type of product.* Product design and quality standards; whether the product is produced for inventory or for order; and physical properties such as the size of materials and products special handling requirements, susceptibility to damage, and perishability
- *Type of production process.* Technology used; types of materials handled; means of providing a service; and processing requirements in terms of number of operations involved and amount of interaction between departments and work centers
- *Ergonomic considerations.* To ensure worker safety; to avoid unnecessary injuries and accidents; and to increase productivity
- *Economic considerations.* Volume of production; costs of materials, machines, workstations, and labor; pattern and variability of demand; and length of permissible delays
- *Space availability within facility itself.* Ensure the space will adequately meet current and future manufacturing needs.

**TYPES OF MANUFACTURING LAYOUTS.** Manufacturing layouts are categorized either by the work flow in a plant or by the production system's function. There are three basic types of layouts that manufacturers can use separately or in combination—product, process, and fixed position—and they differ in their applicability of different levels of manufacturing volume.

- *Product Layouts.* In a **product (or line) layout**, a manufacturer arranges workers and equipment according to the sequence of operations performed on the product. Conceptually, the flow is an unbroken line from raw materials input to finished goods. This type of layout is applicable to rigid-flow, high-volume, continuous, or mass-production operations or when the product is highly standardized. Automobile assembly plants, paper mills, and oil refineries are examples of product layouts. Product layouts offer the advantages of lower materials handling costs; simplified tasks that can be done with low-cost, lower-skilled labor; reduced amounts of work-in process inventory; and relatively simplified production control activities. All units are routed along the same fixed path, and scheduling consists primarily of setting a production rate.

  Disadvantages of product layouts include their inflexibility, monotony of job tasks, high fixed investment in specialized equipment, and heavy interdependence of all operations. A breakdown in one machine or at one workstation can idle the entire line. Such a layout also requires the owner to duplicate many pieces of equipment in the manufacturing facility; duplication can be cost prohibitive for a small firm.

- *Process Layouts.* In a **process layout**, a manufacturer groups workers and equipment according to the general function they perform, without regard to any particular product. Process layouts are appropriate when production runs are short, when demand shows considerable variation and the costs of holding finished goods inventory are high, or when the product is customized. Process layouts have the advantages of being flexible for doing customized work and promoting job satisfaction by offering employees diverse and challenging tasks. Its disadvantages are the higher costs of materials handling, lower productivity, and more complex production control. Because the workflow is intermittent, each job must be individually routed through the system and scheduled at the various work centers, and its status must be monitored individually.

■ *Fixed-position layouts.* The bulk or weight of the final product is assembled in one spot in a **fixed position layout**; materials do not move down a line as in a product layout. Workers and equipment go to the materials rather than having the materials flow down a line to them. Aircraft assembly shops and shipyards typify this kind of layout.

**DESIGNING LAYOUTS.** The starting point in layout design is determining how and in what sequence product parts or service tasks flow together. One of the most effective techniques is to create an overall picture of the manufacturing process using process flowcharts. Given the tasks and their sequence, plus knowledge of the volume or products that can be produced, an entrepreneur can analyze space and equipment needs to get an idea of the facility's demand. When a product layout is being used, these demands take precedence, and manufacturers must arrange equipment and workstations to fit the production tasks and their sequence. If a process layout is used, different products place different demands on the facility. Rather than having a single best flow, there may be one flow for each product, and compromises will be necessary. As a result, any one product may not get the ideal layout.

**ANALYZING PRODUCTION LAYOUTS.** Although there is no general procedure for analyzing the numerous interdependent factors that enter into layout design, specific layout problems lend themselves to detailed analysis. Two important criteria for selecting and designing a layout are worker effectiveness and materials handling costs.

Designing layouts ergonomically so that they maximize workers' strengths is especially important for manufacturers. Creating an environment that is comfortable and pleasant for workers will pay big benefits over time in the form of higher productivity, lower absenteeism and tardiness, and fewer injuries. Designers must be sure that they match the environment they create to workers' needs rather than trying to force workers to adapt to the environment.

Manufacturers can lower materials handling costs by using layouts designed to automate product flow whenever possible and to minimize flow distances and times. The extent of automation depends on the level of technology and amount of capital available, as well as behavioral considerations of employees. Flow distances and times are usually minimized by locating sequential processing activities or interrelated departments in adjacent areas. The following features are important to a good manufacturing layout:

1. Planned materials flow pattern
2. Straight-line layout where possible
3. Straight, clearly marked aisles
4. Backtracking kept to a minimum
5. Related operations close together
6. Minimal in-process inventory
7. Easy adjustment to changing conditions
8. Minimal materials handling distances
9. Minimal manual handling
10. No unnecessary rehandling of material
11. Minimal handling between operations
12. Materials delivered to production employees quickly
13. Use of gravity to move materials whenever possible
14. Materials efficiently removed from the work area
15. Materials handling done by indirect labor
16. Orderly materials handling and storage
17. Good housekeeping

## Chapter Review

1. Explain the stages in the location decision.
   • The location decision is one of the most important decisions an entrepreneur will make, given its long-term effects on the company. An entrepreneur should

look at the choice as a series of increasingly narrow decisions: Which region of the country? Which state? Which city? Which site?

- Demographic statistics are available from a wide variety of sources, but government agencies such as census bureaus have a wealth of detailed data that can guide an entrepreneur in his or her location decision.

2. Describe the location criteria for retail and service businesses.

- For retailers and many service businesses, the location decision is especially crucial. They must consider the size of the trade area, the volume of customer traffic, number of parking spots, availability of room for expansion, and the visibility of a site.

3. Outline the basic location options for retail and service businesses.

- Retail and service businesses have six basic location options: central business districts (CBDs), neighborhoods, shopping centers and malls, near competitors, outlying areas, and at home.

4. Explain the site selection process for manufacturers.

- A manufacturer's location decision is strongly influenced by local zoning ordinances. Some areas offer industrial parks designed specifically to attract manufacturers. Two crucial factors for most manufacturers are the accessibility to (and the cost of transporting) raw materials and the quality and quantity of available labor.

5. Discuss the benefits of locating a start-up company in a business incubator.

- Business incubators are locations that offer flexible, low-cost rental space to their tenants as well as business and consulting services. Their goal is to nurture small companies until they are ready to "graduate" into the larger business community. Many government entities and universities offer incubator locations.

6. Describe the criteria used to analyze the layout and design considerations of a building, including legal requirements, such as the Americans with Disabilities Act.

- When evaluating the suitability of a particular building, an entrepreneur should consider several factors:
  - Size: Is the structure large enough to accommodate the business with some room for growth
  - Construction and external appearance: Is the building structurally sound, and does it create the right impression for the business
  - Entrances: Are they inviting
  - Legal issues: Does the building comply with the Americans with Disabilities Act, for example, and, if not, how much will it cost to bring it up to standard
  - Signage: Are they legible, well located, and easy to see
  - Interior: Does the interior design contribute to your ability to make sales and is it ergonomically designed
  - Lights and fixtures: Is the lighting adequate to the tasks workers will be performing, and what is the estimated cost of lighting

7. Explain the principles of effective layout for retailers, service businesses, and manufacturers.

- Layout for retail stores and service businesses depends on the owner's understanding of customers' buying habits. Retailers have three basic layout options from which to choose: grid, free-form, and boutique layouts. Some areas of a retail store generate more sales per square foot and are, therefore, more valuable than others.
- The goal of a manufacturer's layout is to create a smooth, efficient workflow. Three basic options exist: product layout, process layout, and fixed position layout. Two key considerations are worker productivity and materials handling costs.

## Discussion Questions

1. How do most small business owners choose a location? Is this wise?
2. What factors should a manager consider when evaluating a region in which to locate a business? Where are such data available?
3. Outline the factors entrepreneurs should consider when selecting a state in which to locate a business.
4. What factors should a seafood-processing plant, a beauty shop, and an exclusive jewelry store consider in choosing a location? List factors for each type of business.
5. What intangible factors might enter into the entrepreneur's location decision?
6. What are zoning laws? How do they affect the location decision?

7. What is the trade area? What determines a small retailer's trade area?
8. Why is it important to discover more than just the number of passersby in a traffic count?
9. What types of information can an entrepreneur collect from census data?
10. Why may a cheap location not be the best location?
11. What function does a small firm's sign serve? What are the characteristics of an effective business sign?
12. Explain the statement: "The portions of a small store's interior space are not of equal value in generating sales revenue." What areas are most valuable?
13. What are some of the major features that are important to a good manufacturing layout?

## Business PlanPro

For many businesses, analyzing the value of a potential business site is critical. Owners of retail- or service-based companies usually want high traffic locations for optimal exposure. Owners of manufacturing, repair, or storage businesses must address issues regarding the location's suitability for their specific needs. Selecting the wrong location places a company at a disadvantage before it ever opens for business. This chapter emphasizes that selecting the right location is crucial to any business venture.

## On the Web

The Web offers valuable information regarding location information. One resource mentioned earlier in Chapter 9, "Building a Guerrilla Marketing Plan" was the PRIZM information from Claritas, Inc. (www.claritas.com/MyBest Segments). This information identifies the most common market segments in your postal code and may be a way to validate whether your location is in proximity to your target customers. PRIZM has categorized American consumer markets based on demographic and customer segmentation profiling research data by zip code. A restaurant or a retail business, for example, will find that locating close to their target customers is a key success factor. Additional infor-

mation, such as traffic counts and other location attributes, are important factors to include in your business plan.

## In the Software

Open your business plan and go to the "Your Company" section. Here is where you will describe your ideal, potential, or existing location. If the location you have chosen possesses many of the positive attributes mentioned in the chapter, identify your location as a strength. If your location has negative characteristics, recognize it as a weakness and develop a plan to address how you will overcome the challenges your location presents. If you determine that your location is a critical component for the success of the business, you should assess your location under the "Keys to Success" section. Remember to include the expense for your location—rent, lease, or mortgage payments—into the financial section of your plan.

## Building Your Business Plan

Selecting your location is an important strategic business decision for most business ventures. Your business plan will help you profile, describe, and ultimately decide on the most attractive business location available. Once you have secured a location, your plan can leverage that location's strongest attributes to optimize customer exposure, sales, and profits.

The buyer needs a hundred eyes; the seller but one.
—Italian proverb

Quality is the result of a carefully constructed cultural environment. It has to be the fabric of the organization, not part of the fabric.
—Philip Crosby

# Supply Chain Management

## Learning Objectives

1 Understand the components of a purchasing plan.

2 Explain the principles of total quality management (TQM) and Six Sigma and their impact on quality.

3 Conduct economic order quantity (EOQ) analysis to determine the proper level of inventory.

4 Differentiate among the three types of purchase discounts that vendors offer.

5 Calculate a company's reorder point.

6 Develop a vendor rating scale.

7 Describe the legal implications of the purchasing function.

T his chapter discusses the activities involved in managing a small company's supply chain—purchasing, quality management, and vendor analysis. Although none of these is the most glamorous or exciting job an entrepreneur undertakes, they form an important part of the foundation that supports every small business. When entrepreneurs begin producing products or providing services, they quickly learn how much their products or services depend on the quality of the components and services they purchase from their suppliers. Success today depends on higher levels of collaboration among the businesses that make up a company's supply chain. Few successful companies are freestanding entities; instead, thriving companies operate as part of seamless networks of alliances and partnerships with customers, suppliers, and distributors. For many businesses, the quality of the supply chain determines their ability to satisfy their customers and to compete effectively. "Competition is not really company vs. company," says one expert, "but supply chain vs. supply chain."[1] In other words, supply chain management has become an important strategic issue rather than merely a tactical matter for companies.

Companies spend nearly trillions on goods and services each year. Selecting the right vendors and designing a fast and efficient supply chain influences a small company's ability to produce and sell quality products and services at competitive prices. These decisions have far-reaching effects for a business as well as a significant impact on its bottom line. Depending on the type of business involved, the purchasing function can consume anywhere from 25 percent to 85 percent of total sales. By shaving just 2 percent off of its cost of goods sold, a typical small company can increase its net income by more than 25 percent! To realize these savings, entrepreneurs must create a purchasing plan, establish well-defined measures of product or service quality, and select vendors and suppliers based on objectively determined criteria.

When a company's supply chain breaks down, the result can be devastating in both immediate and future costs such as recalling dangerous or defective products and lost sales from customers who turn to substitute products. Some of those lost customers never return, and worse yet, the company's name and reputation are tarnished forever. For instance, Menu Foods Corporation, a Canada-based producer of pet foods for other companies, recently was forced to recall more than 100 brands of pet food after they were found to be contaminated with melamine, an industrial chemical that caused kidney and liver damage to pets. Officials traced the contaminant to wheat gluten that Menu Foods had purchased from a domestic supplier, which, in turn, had outsourced to factories in China. Surveys taken in the weeks following the recall showed that millions of pet owners had changed the way they feed their pets, often shifting to organic pet food or homemade pet food.[2]

Both man-made and natural disasters pose a threat to companies' supply chains. In a study of companies across a variety of industries conducted by the Aberdeen Group, 82 percent of managers say that their companies had experienced a supply disruption or outage within the previous two years.[3] Companies located along the Gulf Coast of the United States that were in the paths of hurricanes Rita and Katrina, for example, were devastated

Selecting the right vendors and designing a fast and efficient supply chain influences a company's ability to produce and sell quality products and services at competitive prices.

by the floods and high winds of the storms, but thousands of other businesses located far away from the strike zone also were affected when their sources of raw materials and supplies were cut off. Before the storms struck, factories near New Orleans supplied 12 percent of the nation's cement supply.[4] After the storms, construction firms across the nation engaged in building projects faced lengthy delays. Before the hurricanes, Louisiana provided 85 percent of the world's supply of alligator skins. After the storm surge damaged alligator nesting grounds, companies such as Ralph Lauren, Louis Vuitton, Hermes, Gucci, and others that use the hides to make bags, belts, luggage, and other items faced shortages and rapidly rising prices. Many businesses were forced to turn to substitute products such as crocodile, ostrich, and even eel and fish skins.[5] Minimizing problems from disruptions in a company's supply chains as a result of disasters and unexpected events requires a sound purchasing plan.

## Creating a Purchasing Plan

*1.* Understand the components of a purchasing plan.

**Purchasing** involves the acquisition of needed materials, supplies, services, and equipment of the right quality, in the proper quantities, for reasonable prices, at the appropriate time, and from the right vendor. A major objective of purchasing is to acquire enough (but not too much) stock to ensure smooth, uninterrupted production or sales and to see that the merchandise is delivered on time. Companies large and small are purchasing goods and supplies from all across the globe, making their supply chains longer and more challenging to manage. Coordinating the pieces of the global puzzle requires a comprehensive purchasing plan. The plan must identify a company's quality requirements, its cost targets, and the criteria for determining the best supplier, considering such factors as reliability, service, delivery, and cooperation.

ENTREPRENEURIAL
Profile

*McCormick & Company*

McCormick & Company, a business that sells spices ranging from allspice to turmeric, literally spans the globe to purchase from hundreds of suppliers the raw materials it requires for its product line. For more than 100 years, company buyers have traveled to Uganda and Madagascar for vanilla, to China and Nigeria for ginger, to Yugoslavia and Albania for sage, and to India, Turkey, Pakistan, and Syria for cumin seed. McCormick makes significant investments to find suppliers that can deliver quality materials in a timely manner and engages in extensive testing and security practices to ensure the quality and the safety of the raw materials it purchases.[6]

A purchasing plan is closely linked to the other functional areas of managing a small business: production, marketing, sales, engineering, accounting, finance, and others. A purchasing plan should recognize this interaction and help integrate the purchasing function into the total organization. A small company's purchasing plan should focus on the five key elements of purchasing: quality, quantity, price, timing, and vendor selection (see Figure 17.1).

**FIGURE 17.1**
**Components of a Purchasing Plan**

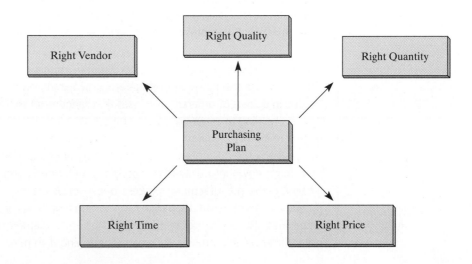

## Quality

**2.** Explain the principles of total quality management (TQM) and Six Sigma and their impact on quality.

Not long ago businesses saw quality products and services as luxuries for customers who could afford them. Many companies mistakenly believed that producing or purchasing high-quality products and services was too costly. The last few decades have taught businesspeople that quality goods and services are absolutely *essential* to remaining competitive. The benefits that companies earn by creating quality products, services, and processes come not only in the form of fewer defects but also in lower costs, higher productivity, and higher customer retention rates. W. Edwards Deming, one of the founding fathers of the modern quality movement, always claimed that higher quality resulted in lower costs. Internally, companies with a focus on quality report significant improvements in work-related factors such as increased employee morale, lower employee turnover, and enhanced quality of work life. Benefits such as these can result in earning a significant competitive advantage over rivals of *any* size.

Total quality companies believe in and manage with the attitude of continuous improvement, a concept the Japanese call *kaizen*. The *kaizen* philosophy holds that small improvements made continuously over time accumulate into a radically reshaped and improved process. When defective items do occur, managers and employees who are engaged in continuous improvement do not simply rework or repair them. Instead, they see defectives as an opportunity to improve the entire process. Their goal is to identify the root cause of the defect and to change the process so that the same problem does not occur again. According to the *Industry Week*/Manufacturing Performance Institute's Census of Manufacturers, continuous improvement programs are the most commonly used (72.9 percent of companies) quality improvement strategies among manufacturers.[7]

Scotsman Ice Systems is a small company that manufactures both high-end residential and commercial ice machines and refrigerators. Scotsman produces more than 300 different models in dozens of different processes that range from sheet metal fabrication and plastic roto-molding to assembly and shipping. In the late 1980s, the company began using a system of continuous improvement to maintain a competitive edge in its market. As part of its *kaizen* efforts, employees from the factory floor analyzed the manufacturing process, breaking it down into distinct components, and redesigning it into more logical "cells." Analyzing the manufacturing process one step at a time and implementing small improvements throughout resulted in faster production times, less waste, and higher quality. Employees also undertook a "poka yoke" effort, a method of identifying the sources of potential errors in a process and then redesigning it to minimize the probability of those errors. Scotsman relies on employee teams, invests heavily in employee training, and encourages employee involvement in improving every process in the plant. Managers expect hourly employees to implement at least 36 improvement suggestions each year. Scotsman's continuous improvement efforts have paid off. Since 2000, employees have reduced scrap by 46 percent and have improved productivity by 41 percent and quality measures by 53 percent.[8]

As Scotsman Ice System's experience shows, quality has an impact on both costs and revenues. Improved quality leads to less scrap and rework time, lower warranty cost, and increased worker productivity. On the revenue side of the equation, quality improves a company's reputation, attracts customers, and often affords it the opportunity to charge higher prices. The bottom-line impact of quality is increased profitability.

### Tools for Ensuring Quality: Total Quality Management and Six Sigma

**TOTAL QUALITY MANAGEMENT.** Under the total quality management (TQM) philosophy, companies define a quality product as one that conforms to predetermined standards that satisfy customers' demands. That means getting *everything* from delivery and invoicing to installation and follow-up right the first time. Although these companies know that they may never reach their targets of perfect quality, they never stop striving for perfection, recognizing that even a 99.9 percent level of quality is not good enough (see Table 17.1). The businesses that have effectively implemented these programs understand that the process involves a total commitment from the top of the organization to the bottom.

Rather than trying to inspect quality into products and services after they are completed, TQM instills the philosophy of doing the job right the first time. Although the concept is simple, implementing such a process is a challenge that requires a very different kind of thinking and a very different culture than most organizations are comfortable with. Because the changes TQM requires are so significant, patience is a must for companies adopting the philosophy. Consistent quality improvements rarely occur over night. Yet too many small business managers think, "We'll implement TQM today and tomorrow our quality will soar." TQM is *not* a "quick-fix," short-term program that can magically push a company to world-class-quality status overnight. Because it requires fundamental, often drastic, changes in the way a company does business, TQM takes time both to implement and to produce results. Although some small businesses that use TQM begin to see some improvements within just a matter of weeks, the *real* benefits take longer to realize. It takes

### TABLE 17.1 Why 99.9 Percent Quality Isn't Good Enough

Many businesses strive for zero defects in their manufacturing and service processes even though they know that they are not likely to achieve perfection. Most companies would settle for 99.9 percent quality, but is that good enough? What would be the result if some things were done right "only" 99.9 percent of the time? Consider the implications:

- Two unsafe landings at Heathrow Airport per day.
- 16,000 lost pieces of mail per hour.
- 200,000 incorrectly filled drug prescriptions per year.
- 5,000 incorrect surgical procedures performed each week.
- 22,000 checks deducted from the wrong accounts every hour.
- 1,314 telephone calls misdirected every minute.
- 14 babies delivered to the wrong parents each day.
- 2,488,200 magazines published with the wrong covers every year.

If you are the customer who falls into the unlucky one-tenth of one percent, the error affects you 100 percent. In addition, unless a company strives for 100 percent product or service quality, there is little chance that it will ever achieve 99.9 percent quality.

*Sources*: Adapted from Lieca Brown, "Sigma Management," *Point of Beginning*, August 2001, p. 6; *On the Job Performance* (Chicago: Dartnell Corporation, 1997), p. 3; San Marino, "Is 'Good Enough' Good Enough?" *Industry Week*, February 3, 1997, p. 22.

at least three or four years before TQM principles gain acceptance among employees, and as much as eight years are necessary to fully implement TQM in a company.

To implement TQM successfully, a small business owner must rely on these fundamental principles:

■ *Employ benchmarking to achieve quality outcomes.* **Benchmarking** is the process of identifying world-class processes or procedures other companies (often in other industries) currently are using and building higher-quality standards around these for your business. This search for best practices is ongoing. As part of their quality initiative, employees at Scotsman Ice Systems benchmark other manufacturing operations. To make sure that they do not miss anything, they have developed a benchmarking booklet that contains a list of key questions to take with them on benchmarking trips.[9]

■ *Shift from a management-driven culture to a participative, team-based one.* Two basic tenets of TQM are employee involvement and teamwork. Business owners must be willing to push decision-making authority down the organization to where the real experts are. Teams of employees working together to identify and solve problems can be a powerful force in an organization of any size. Experience with TQM has taught entrepreneurs that the combined knowledge and experience of workers is much greater than that of only one person. Tapping into the problem-solving capabilities of the team produces profitable results.

■ *Modify the reward system to encourage teamwork and innovation.* Because the team, not the individual, is the building block of TQM, companies often have to modify their compensation systems to reflect team performance. Traditional compensation methods pit one employee against another, undermining any sense of cooperation. Often they are based on seniority rather than on how much an employee contributes to the company. Compensation systems under TQM usually rely on incentives, linking pay to performance. However, rather than tying pay to individual performance, these systems focus on team-based incentives. Each person's pay depends on whether the entire team (or, sometimes, the entire company) meets a clearly defined, measurable set of performance objectives.

■ *Train workers constantly to give them the tools they need to produce quality and to upgrade the company's knowledge base.* One of the most important factors in making long-term, constant improvements in a company's processes is teaching workers the philosophy and the tools of TQM. Admonishing employees to "produce quality" or offering them rewards for high quality is futile unless a company gives them the tools and know-how to achieve that end. Managers must be dedicated to making their companies "learning organizations" that encourage people to upgrade their skills and give them the opportunities and incentives to do so. The most successful companies spend anywhere from 1 to 5 percent of their employees' time on training, most of it invested in workers, not managers. To give employees a sense of how the quality of their job fits into the big picture, many TQM companies engage in **cross-training**, teaching workers to do other jobs in the company.

■ *Train employees to measure quality with the tools of statistical process control (SPC).* The only way to ensure gains in quality is to measure results objectively and to trace the company's progress toward its quality objectives. That requires teaching employees how to use statistical process control techniques such as fishbone charts, Pareto charts, control charts, and measures of process capability.* (Without knowledgeable workers using these quantitative tools, TQM cannot produce the intended results.)

■ *Use Pareto's Law to focus TQM efforts.* One of the toughest questions managers face in companies embarking on TQM for the first time is "Where do we start?" The best way to answer that fundamental question is to use Pareto's Law (also called the 80/20 Rule), which states that 80 percent of a company's quality problems arise from just 20 percent of all causes. By identifying this small percentage of

---

*To learn more about total quality management and the tools of statistical quality control, look in modern statistics or operations management textbooks or visit the following Web sites: http://deming.eng.clemson.edu/pub/den/deming_map.htm and www.isixsigma.com/me/tqm/.

causes and focusing quality improvement efforts on them, a company gets maximum return for minimum effort. This simple yet powerful rule forces workers to concentrate resources on the most significant problems first, where payoffs are likely to be biggest, and helps build momentum for a successful TQM effort.

■ *Share information with everyone in the organization.* Asking employees to make decisions and to assume responsibility for creating quality necessitates that the owner share information with them. Employees cannot make sound decisions consistent with the company's quality initiative if managers are unwilling to give them the information they need to make those decisions.

■ *Focus quality improvements on astonishing the customer.* The heart of TQM is customer satisfaction—better yet, customer astonishment. Unfortunately, some companies focus their quality improvement efforts on areas that never benefit the customer. Quality improvements with no customer focus (either internal or external customers) are wasted.

■ *Don't rely on inspection to produce quality products and services.* The traditional approach to achieving quality was to create a product or service and then to rely on an army of inspectors to "weed out" all of the defects. Not only is such a system a terrible waste of resources (consider the cost of scrap, rework, and no-value-added inspections), but it gives managers no opportunity for continuous improvement. The only way to improve a process is to discover the cause of poor quality, fix it (the sooner, the better), and learn from it so that workers can *avoid* the problem in the future. Using the statistical tools of the TQM approach allows a company to learn from its mistakes with a consistent approach to constantly improving quality.

■ *Avoid using TQM to place blame on those who make mistakes.* In many firms, the only reason managers seek out mistakes is to find someone to blame for them. The result is a culture based on fear and the unwillingness of workers to take chances to innovate. The goal of TQM is to improve the processes in which people work, *not* to lay blame on workers. Searching out "the guilty party" doesn't solve the problem. The TQM philosophy sees each problem that arises as an opportunity for improving the company's system.

■ *Strive for continuous improvement in processes as well as in products and services.* There is no finish line in the race for quality. A company's goal must be to improve the quality of its processes, products, and services constantly, no matter how high it currently stands!

Many of these principles are evident in quality guru W. Edwards Deming's 14 points, a capsulized version of how to build a successful TQM approach (see Table 17.2).

Implementing a TQM program successfully begins at the top. If the owner or chief executive of a company doesn't actively and visibly support the initiative, the employees who must make it happen will never accept it. TQM requires change: change in the way a company defines quality, in the way it sees its customers, in the way it treats employees, and in the way it sees itself. Successful implementation involves modifying an organization's culture as much as in the work processes.

**SIX SIGMA.** Like TQM, Six Sigma uses data-driven statistical techniques to improve the quality and the efficiency of any process and to increase customer satisfaction. The quality threshold that Six Sigma programs set is high: just an average of 3.4 defects per one million opportunities! Although initially used by large corporations, Six Sigma can be adapted to work in small businesses as well. The four key tenets of Six Sigma are:

1. *Delight customers with quality and speed.* Six Sigma recognizes that the customer's needs come first. The goal is to produce products that are of the highest quality in a process that is efficient and fast.
2. *Constantly improve the process.* Six Sigma builds on the concept of continuous improvement. According to W. Edwards Deming, most quality problems are the result of the *process* (which management creates) rather than the *employees* (who work within the process that management builds). The goal is to reduce the variation of the

**TABLE 17.2 Deming's 14 Points**

Total quality management cannot succeed as a piecemeal program or without true commitment to its philosophy. W. Edwards Deming, the man most visibly connected to TQM, drove home these concepts with his 14 points, the essential elements for integrating TQM successfully into a company. Deming's message was straightforward: Companies must transform themselves into customer-oriented, quality-focused organizations in which teams of employees have the training, the resources, and the freedom to pursue quality on a daily basis. The goal is to track the performance of a process, whether manufacturing a clock or serving a bank customer, and to develop ways to minimize variation in the system, eliminate defects, and spur innovation. The 14 points are:

1. *Constantly strive to improve products and services.* This requires total dedication to improving quality, productivity, and service—*continuously.*
2. *Adopt a total quality philosophy.* There are no shortcuts to quality improvement; it requires a completely new way of thinking and managing.
3. *Correct defects as they happen,* rather than relying on mass inspection of end products. Real quality comes from improving the process, not from inspecting finished products and services. At that point, it's too late. Statistical process control charts can help workers detect when a process is producing poor-quality goods or services. Then they can stop it, make corrections, and get the process back on target.
4. *Don't award business on price alone.* Rather than choosing the lowest-cost vendor, businesses should work toward establishing close relationships with the vendors who offer the highest quality.
5. *Constantly improve the system of production and service.* Managers must focus the entire company on customer satisfaction, measure results, and make adjustments as necessary.
6. *Institute training.* Workers cannot improve quality and lower costs without proper training to erase old ways of doing things.
7. *Institute leadership.* The supervisor's job is not to boss workers around; it is to lead. The nature of the work is more like coaching than controlling.
8. *Drive out fear.* People often are afraid to point out problems because they fear the repercussions. Managers must encourage and reward employee suggestions.
9. *Break down barriers among staff areas.* Departments within organizations often erect needless barriers to protect their own turf. Total quality requires a spirit of teamwork and cooperation across the entire organization.
10. *Eliminate superficial slogans and goals.* These only offend employees because they imply that workers could do a better job if only they would try.
11. *Eliminate standard quotas.* They emphasize quantity over quality. Not everyone can move at the same rate and still produce quality.
12. *Remove barriers to pride of workmanship.* Most workers want to do quality work. Eliminating "de-motivators" frees them to achieve quality results.
13. *Institute vigorous education and retraining.* Managers must teach employees the new methods of continuous improvement, including statistical process control techniques.
14. *Take demonstrated management action to achieve the transformation.* Although success requires involvement of all levels of the organization, the impetus for change must come from the top.

These 14 interrelated elements contribute to a chain reaction effect. As a company improves its quality, costs decline, productivity increases, the company gains additional market share due to its ability to provide high-quality products at competitive prices, and the company and its employees prosper.

*Source:* Deming, W. Edwards, *Out of the Crisis*, pp. 23–24: "The 14 Points," © 2000 W. Edwards Deming Institute, by permission of the MIT Press.

process, which is measured by the standard deviation (denoted by the Greek letter sigma, $\sigma$).

3. *Use teamwork to improve the process.* Like TQM, Six Sigma counts on teams of employees working together to improve a process. People working together to share their knowledge can generate better solutions to quality problems than individuals can.
4. *Make changes to the process based on facts, not guesses.* To improve a process, employees must have quantifiable measures of results (e.g., quality of output) and of the process itself (e.g., how the process operated to produce those results).[10]

In the Entrepreneurial Spotlight

## ■ Entrepreneurship: The Grape Escape

Chuck McMinn has made the jump from the world of high tech to the world of wine. When McMinn worked at computer chip maker Intel, he often heard one of then-CEO Andy Grove's favorite sayings: "If you can't measure it, you can't improve it." His new career has taken him far away from the world of computer chips, but he still puts into practice Grove's wisdom even though he operates a business in an industry that for centuries has relied on old-world techniques: winemaking.

McMinn owns a small California winery, Vineyard 29, that produces about 3,000 cases of fine wine annually and is one of the region's most technologically advanced vineyards. Every piece of equipment at Vineyard 29 is designed to help McMinn treat his vines, the harvested grapes, and eventually the wine itself with supreme care, a practice that old world vintners called "elevage," raising each vintage as one would raise a child.

"The ultimate goal in the use of technology," says McMinn, "is to augment and precisely control the techniques and ideals used in old-world winemaking to produce wines of the highest quality." Vineyard 29 has moisture probes that monitor water use and weather stations that send statistics to a Web site that employees can check. The company's consulting winemaker, Phillipe Melka, has enlisted a French Ph.D. student to install sap-flow sensors on some of the vines to track how much water they consume. McMinn uses a system called Tanknet that links thermostats on the fermenting tanks to Web-based software to monitor the aging process. During the grape harvest, when temperatures in the tanks are crucial, winemakers can monitor them constantly from any computer, wherever they may be. The Vineyard 29 lab even has a $15,000 titrator, which tracks key characteristics of the wines, including its pH and its sulfur content. "What we're doing is making wine the old-fashioned way," explains McMinn. "We just use technology to do it."

Roger Boulton, a professor of enology (the science of winemaking) at the University of California at Davis calls

McMinn's approach to making wine "quantitative, data-driven, hypothesis thinking." Many old world vintners look with disdain on the technology that companies such as Vineyard 29 use to make wine, but that does not discourage winemakers such as McMinn and Bill Murphy, who also relies on technology to produce wine for his California vineyard, Clos LaChance. "The French learned [to make wine] empirically over hundreds of years," says Murphy. "I don't have hundreds of years. Technology means that we can learn so much faster."

1. Discuss the advantages and the disadvantages of using high-tech solutions to make wine.
2. Vineyard 29 and Clos LaChance are using technology in creative ways to produce wine. Write a one-page report explaining how these vintners can use the techniques discussed in this chapter to improve their business models.

Adapted from Kate Bonamici, "The Grapes of Math," *Fortune*, August 21, 2006, pp. 131–134.

Table 17.3 explains the DMAIC (define, measure, analyze, improve, and control) process (refer to Figure 9.5, "The Quality DMAIC Process," on page 319) on which the Six Sigma approach is built. For small companies, the goal of this process is to understand their core business processes better so that managers and employees can work together to make significant improvements to them over time.

**TABLE 17.3 The Six Sigma DMAIC Approach**

| Principle | Process Improvement Technique |
| --- | --- |
| **Define** | Identify the problem<br>Define the requirements<br>Set the goal for improvement |
| **Measure** | Validate the process problem by mapping the process and gathering data about it<br>Refine the problem statement and the goal<br>Measure current performance by examining the relevant process inputs, steps, and output to establish a baseline |
| **Analyze** | Develop a list of potential root causes<br>Identify the vital few<br>Use data analysis tools to validate the cause and effect connections between root causes and the quality problem |
| **Improve** | Develop potential solutions to remove root causes by making changes to the process<br>Test potential solutions and develop a plan for implementing those that are successful<br>Measure the results of the improved process |
| **Control** | Establish standard measures for the new process<br>Establish standard procedures for the new process<br>Review performance periodically and make adjustments as needed. |

*Source:* Adapted from Andrew Spanyi and Marvin Wurtzel, "Six Sigma for the Rest of Us," *Quality Digest*, July 2003, www.qualitydigest.com/july03/articles/01_article.shtml.

The last few decades have been trying times for manufacturers as outsourcing to lower cost foreign manufacturers has accelerated. Nevertheless, many domestic manufacturers that are using quality improvement processes have not only been able to survive but to thrive. From 1996 to 2006, U.S. manufacturers, for example, increased their productivity by at least 4 percent a year.[11] Data from the Census of Manufacturers show widespread progress, including higher quality, faster cycle times, and lower manufacturing costs, when companies use improvement strategies such as continuous improvement, TQM, and Six Sigma.

World-class organizations in the twenty-first century have made continuous improvement a fundamental element of their competitive strategies. International standards for quality have emerged in the form of ISO 9001 standards that establish quality management procedures, detailed documentation, work instruction, and record keeping. The International Organization for Standardization also has created ISO 14001 standards as environmental management principles that are becoming accepted worldwide.

### Quantity: The Economic Order Quantity (EOQ)

*3.* Conduct economic order quantity (EOQ) analysis to determine the proper level of inventory.

The typical small business has its largest investment in inventory. But an investment in inventory is not profitable because money spent returns nothing until the inventory is sold. In a sense, a small company's inventory is its largest non-interest-bearing investment. Entrepreneurs must focus on controlling this investment and on maintaining proper inventory levels.

*Peter Nygard and Nygard International*

A few years ago, Peter Nygard, founder of Nygard International, a women's clothing manufacturer in Toronto, Canada, was concerned about the high and increasing level of inventory in his warehouse. The company's inventory had ballooned to its highest level ever, and what concerned Nygard even more than the amount of stock was the imbalance of the inventory. Nygard was overstocked with out-of-style fashions but was running short of items that were popular. To solve the inventory problem, Nygard developed a purchasing plan designed to create a more efficient flow of goods from "the sheep and the silkworms to the consumer," he says. Nygard invested in software that tracked both actual and forecasted sales of specific products, and he shifted the company's ordering, manufacturing, shipping, and selling operations online. The company cut its manufacturing costs by one-third and reduced the time required to fill a customer's order from three weeks to just one day! Nygard estimates that making these changes in the company's supply chain has added about $10 million a year to his company's bottom line. In addition, he says, "We can gather information and make decisions based on what is actually selling with the snap of a finger as opposed to philosophizing or assuming."[12]

A primary objective of this portion of the purchasing plan is to generate an adequate turnover of merchandise by purchasing proper quantities. Tying up capital in extra inventory limits a company's working capital and exerts pressure on its cash flows. In addition, a business risks being stuck with spoiled or obsolete merchandise, an extremely serious problem for many small businesses. Excess inventory also takes up valuable storage or selling space that could be used for items with higher turnover rates and more profit potential. On the other hand, maintaining too little inventory can be extremely costly. An entrepreneur may be forced to reorder merchandise too frequently, which escalates total inventory costs. In addition, inventory stockouts will occur when customer demand exceeds a company's supply of merchandise, causing customer ill will. Persistent stockouts are inconvenient for customers, and many of them eventually choose to shop elsewhere. Manufacturers that run out of inventory must shut down temporarily and incur huge costs. For instance, Toyota, which operates an extremely lean production process, was forced to shut down production when the factory that supplies all of its brake shoes was damaged by an earthquake. The supply shortage cost Toyota an estimated $200 million in revenue.[13] Carrying either too much or too little inventory both are expensive mistakes that lead to serious problems in other areas of the business.

The goal is to maintain enough inventory to meet customer demand and to satisfy production needs but not so much that storage costs and inventory investments are excessive. The analytical techniques used to determine **economic order quantities (EOQs)** help entrepreneurs to compute the amount of stock to purchase with an order or to produce with each production run to minimize total inventory costs. To compute the proper amount of stock to order or to produce, an entrepreneur must first determine the three principal elements of total inventory costs: the cost of the units, the holding (or carrying) cost, and the setup (or ordering) cost.

### Cost of Units

The cost of the units is simply the number of units demanded for a particular time period multiplied by the cost per unit. Suppose that a small manufacturer of lawnmowers forecasts demand for the upcoming year to be 100,000 mowers. He needs to order enough wheels at $4.15 each to supply the production department. He computes:

$$\text{Total annual cost of units} = D \times C$$

where:

$$D = \text{Annual demand (in units)}$$
$$C = \text{Cost of a single unit (\$)}$$

In this example,

$$D = 100{,}000 \text{ mowers} \times 4 \text{ wheels per mower} = 400{,}000 \text{ wheels}$$
$$C = \$4.15/\text{wheel}$$

Total annual cost of units $= D \times C$
$$= 400{,}000 \text{ wheels} \times \$4.15$$
$$= \$1{,}660{,}000$$

### Holding (Carrying) Costs

The typical costs of holding inventory include the costs of storage, insurance, taxes, interest, depreciation, damage or spoilage, obsolescence, and pilferage. The expense involved in physically storing the items in inventory is usually substantial, especially if the inventories are large. An entrepreneur may have to rent or build additional warehousing facilities, pushing the cost of storing the inventory even higher. The company also may incur expenses in transferring items into and out of inventory. The cost of storage also includes the expense of operating the facility (e.g., heating, lighting, refrigeration), as well as the depreciation, taxes, and interest on the building. Most small business owners purchase insurance on their inventories to shift the risk of fire, theft, flood, and other disasters to an insurer. The premiums paid for this coverage also are included in the cost of holding inventory. In general, the larger a company's average inventory, the greater is its storage cost. For most companies, holding costs for an item range from 15 percent to 35 percent of its actual cost.

Many small business owners fail to recognize the interest expense associated with carrying large inventories. In many cases the interest expense is evident when a company borrows money to purchase inventory. However, a less obvious interest expense is the opportunity cost associated with investing in inventory. In other words, the entrepreneur could have used the money invested in inventory (a non-interest-bearing investment) for some other purpose, such as plant expansion, research and development, or reducing debt. Thus, the cost of buying and holding inventory is the cost of forgoing the opportunity to use those funds elsewhere. A substantial inventory investment ties up a large amount of cash unproductively.

Depreciation costs represent the reduced value of inventory over time. Some businesses are strongly influenced by the depreciation of inventory. For example, a small auto dealer's inventory is subject to depreciation because he must sell models left over from one year at reduced prices.

Holding inventory is costly. Retailers, especially those that sell trendy merchandise, run the risk of being stuck with obsolete merchandise unless they manage their inventories carefully.

Spoilage, obsolescence, and pilferage also add to the costs of holding inventory. Some small firms, especially those that deal in trendy merchandise, assume an extremely high risk of obsolescence. For example, a fashion merchandiser with a large inventory of the latest styles may be left with worthless merchandise if styles suddenly change. In addition, unless the entrepreneur establishes sound inventory control procedures, the business will suffer losses from employee theft and shoplifting.

Small companies selling perishables must always be aware of the danger of spoilage. For example, the owner of a small fish market must plan purchases carefully to ensure a fresh inventory and avoid being stuck with a costly (and smelly) problem.

Let us return to the lawnmower manufacturer example to illustrate the cost of holding inventory:

$$\text{Total annual holding (carrying) costs} = \frac{Q}{2} \times H$$

where:

$$Q = \text{Quantity of inventory ordered}$$
$$H = \text{Holding cost per unit per year}$$

The greater the quantity ordered, the greater is the inventory carrying costs. This relationship is shown in Table 17.4, assuming that the cost of carrying a single unit of inventory for one year is $1.25.

**TABLE 17.4 Holding (Carrying) Costs**

| If $Q$ Is . . . | $Q/2$, Average Inventory, Is . . . | $Q/2 \times H$, Holding Cost, Is . . . |
|---|---|---|
| 500 | 250 | $312.50 |
| 1,000 | 500 | 625.00 |
| 2,000 | 1,000 | 1,250.00 |
| 3,000 | 1,500 | 1,875.00 |
| 4,000 | 2,000 | 2,500.00 |
| 5,000 | 2,500 | 3,125.00 |
| 6,000 | 3,000 | 3,750.00 |
| 7,000 | 3,500 | 4,375.00 |
| 8,000 | 4,000 | 5,000.00 |
| 9,000 | 4,500 | 5,625.00 |
| 10,000 | 5,000 | 6,250.00 |

## Setup (Ordering) Costs

The various expenses incurred in actually ordering materials and inventory or in setting up the production line to manufacture them determine the level of setup or ordering costs of a product. The costs of obtaining materials and inventory typically include preparing purchase orders; analyzing and choosing vendors; processing, handling, and expediting orders; receiving and inspecting items; and performing all the necessary accounting and clerical functions. Even if the small company produces its own supply of goods, it encounters most of these same expenses. Ordering costs are usually relatively fixed, regardless of the quantity ordered.

Setup or ordering costs are found by multiplying the number of orders made in a year (or the number of production runs in a year) by the cost of placing a single order (or the cost of setting up a single production run). In the lawnmower manufacturing example, the annual requirement is 400,000 wheels per year, the cost to place an order is $9.00, and the ordering costs are as follows:

$$\text{Total annual setup (ordering) costs} = \frac{D}{Q} \times S$$

where:

$$D = \text{Annual demand}$$
$$Q = \text{Quantity of inventory ordered}$$
$$S = \text{Setup (ordering) costs for a single run (or order)}$$

The greater the quantity ordered, the smaller the number of orders placed. This relationship is shown in Table 17.5, assuming an ordering cost of $9.00 per order.

## Solving for EOQ

If carrying costs were the only expense involved in obtaining inventory, the entrepreneur would purchase the smallest number of units possible in each order to minimize the cost of holding the inventory. For example, if the lawnmower manufacturer purchased just four wheels per order, carrying cost would be minimized:

$$\text{Carrying cost} = \frac{Q}{2} \times H$$

$$= \frac{4}{2} \times \$1.25$$

$$= \$2.50$$

**TABLE 17.5 Holding (Carrying) Costs**

| If $Q$ Is ... | $D/Q$, Number of Orders per Year, Is ... | $D/Q \times S$, Setup (Ordering) Cost, Is ... |
|---|---|---|
| 500 | 800 | $7,200.00 |
| 1,000 | 400 | 3,600.00 |
| 5,000 | 80 | 720.00 |
| 10,000 | 40 | 360.00 |

but ordering cost would be outrageous:

$$\text{Ordering cost} = \frac{D}{Q} \times S$$

$$= \frac{400{,}000}{4} \times \$9$$

$$= 900{,}000$$

Obviously this is not the small manufacturer's ideal inventory solution.

Similarly, if ordering costs were the only expense involved in procuring inventory, the entrepreneur would purchase the largest number of units possible to minimize the ordering cost. In our example, if the lawnmower manufacturer purchased 400,000 wheels per order, ordering cost would be minimized:

$$\text{Ordering cost} = \frac{D}{Q} \times S$$

$$= \frac{400{,}000}{400{,}000} \times \$9$$

$$= \$9$$

but his carrying cost would be tremendously high:

$$\text{Carrying cost} = Q \times H$$

$$= \frac{400{,}000}{2} \times \$1.25$$

$$= \$250{,}000$$

A quick inspection shows that neither of those solutions minimizes the total cost of the manufacturer's inventory. Total cost is composed of the cost of the unit, carrying cost, and ordering costs:

$$\text{Total cost} = (D \times C) + \left( \frac{Q}{2} \times H \right) + \left( \frac{D}{Q} \times S \right)$$

These costs are graphed in Figure 17.2. Notice that as the quantity ordered increases, the ordering costs decrease and the carrying costs increase.

The EOQ formula simply balances the ordering cost and the carrying cost of the small business owner's inventory so that total costs are minimized. Table 17.6 summarizes the total costs for various values of $Q$ for our lawnmower manufacturer.

As Table 17.6 and Figure 17.2 illustrate, the EOQ formula locates the minimum point on the total cost curve, which occurs where the cost of carrying inventory ($Q/2 \times H$) equals the cost of ordering inventory ($D/Q \times S$). If the small business places the smallest number of orders possible each year, its ordering cost is minimized but its carrying cost is maximized. Conversely, if the firm orders the smallest number of units possible in each order, its carrying cost is minimized, but its ordering cost is maximized. Total inventory cost is minimized when carrying cost and ordering costs are balanced.

**FIGURE 17.2 Economic Order Quantity**

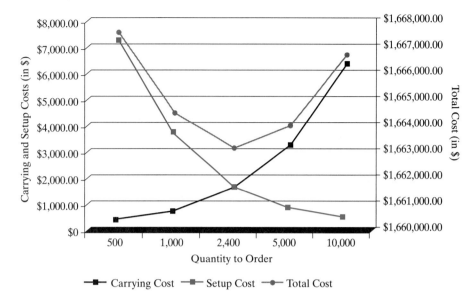

Let us return to our lawnmower manufacturer and compute its economic order quantity, EOQ, using the following formula:

$$D = 400,000 \text{ wheels}$$
$$S = \$9.00 \text{ per order}$$
$$H = \$1.25 \text{ per wheel}$$
$$\text{EOQ} = \sqrt{\frac{2 \times D \times S}{H}}$$
$$= \sqrt{\frac{2 \times 400,000 \times \$9.00}{\$1.25}}$$
$$= 2,400 \text{ wheels}$$

To minimize total inventory cost, the lawnmower manufacturer should order 2,400 wheels at a time. Furthermore,

$$\text{Number of orders per year} = \frac{D}{Q}$$
$$= \frac{400,000}{2,400}$$
$$= 166.67 \text{ orders}$$

This manufacturer will place approximately 167 orders this year at a minimum total cost of $623,000, computed as follows:

$$\text{Total cost} = (D \times C) + \left(\frac{Q}{2} \times H\right) + \left(\frac{D}{Q} \times S\right)$$
$$= (400,000 \times \$4.15) + (2,400/2 \times \$1.25) + (400,0000/2,400 \times \$9.00)$$
$$= \$1,660,000 + \$1,500 + \$1,500$$
$$= \$1,663,000$$

**TABLE 17.6 Economic Order Quantity and Total Cost**

| If Q is . . . | D × C, Cost of Units, Is . . . | Q/2 × H, Carrying Cost, Is . . . | D/Q × S, Ordering Cost, Is . . . | TC, Total Cost, Is . . . |
|---|---|---|---|---|
| 500 | $1,660,000 | $312.50 | $7,200.00 | $1,667,512.50 |
| 1,000 | $1,600,000 | $625.00 | $3,600.00 | $1,664,225.00 |
| **2,400** | **$1,660,000** | **$1,500.00** | **$1,500.00** | **$1,663,000.00** |
| 5,000 | $1,660,000 | $3,125.00 | $720.00 | $1,663,845.00 |
| 10,000 | $1,660,000 | $6,250.00 | $360.00 | $1,666,610.00 |

### Economic Order Quantity with Usage

The preceding EOQ model assumes that orders are filled instantaneously; that is, fresh inventory arrives all at once. Because that assumption does not hold true for many small manufacturers, it is necessary to consider a variation of the basic EOQ model that allows inventory to be added over a period of time rather than instantaneously. In addition, a manufacturer is likely to be taking items from inventory for use in the assembly process over the same time period. For example, the lawn mower manufacturer may be producing blades to replenish his supply, but, at the same time, assembly workers are reducing the supply of blades to make finished mowers. The key feature of this version of the EOQ model is that inventories are used while inventories are being added.

Using the lawn mower manufacturer as an example, we can compute the EOQ for the blades. To make the calculation, we need two additional pieces of information: the usage rate for the blades, $U$, and the plant's capacity to manufacture the blades, $P$. Suppose that the maximum number of lawn mower blades the company can manufacture is 480 per day. We know from the previous illustration that annual demand for mowers is 100,000 units (therefore, 100,000 blades). If the plant operates 5 days per week for 50 weeks (250 days), its usage rate is

$$U = \frac{100{,}000 \text{ units per year}}{250 \text{ days}} = 400 \text{ units per day}$$

It costs \$325 to set up the blade manufacturing line and \$8.71 to store one blade for one year. The cost of producing a blade is \$24.85. To compute EOQ in this situation, we modify the basic formula:

$$\text{EOQ} = \sqrt{\frac{2 \times D \times S}{H \times \left(1 - \dfrac{U}{P}\right)}}$$

For the lawnmower manufacturer,

$$D = 100{,}000 \text{ blades}$$
$$S = \$325 \text{ per production run}$$
$$H = \$8.71 \text{ per blade per year}$$
$$U = 400 \text{ blades per day}$$
$$P = 4.80 \text{ blades per day}$$

$$\text{EOQ} = \sqrt{\frac{2 \times 100{,}000 \times \$325}{8.71 \times \left(1 - \dfrac{400}{480}\right)}}$$

$$= 6{,}692 \text{ blades}$$

Therefore, to minimize total inventory cost, the lawnmower manufacturer should produce 6,692 blades per production run. Also,

$$\text{Number of production runs per year} = \frac{D}{Q}$$

$$= \frac{100{,}000 \text{ blades}}{6{,}692 \text{ blades/run}}$$

$$= 14.9 \approx 15 \text{ runs}$$

The manufacturer will make 15 production runs during the year at a total cost of:

$$\text{Total cost} = (D \times C) + \left(\left(1 - \frac{U}{P}\right) \times \frac{Q}{2} \times H\right) + \left(\frac{D}{Q} \times S\right)$$

$$= (100{,}000 \times \$24.85) + \left(\left(1 - \frac{400}{480}\right) \times \frac{6{,}692}{2} \times \$8.71\right) + \left(\frac{100{,}000}{2} \times \$325\right)$$

$$= \$2{,}485{,}000 + \$4{,}857 + \$4{,}857$$

$$= \$2{,}494{,}714$$

Business owners must remember that the EOQ analysis is based on estimates of cost and demand. The final result is only as accurate as the input used. Consequently, this analytical tool serves only as a guideline for decision making. The final answer may not be the ideal solution because of intervening factors, such as opportunity costs or seasonal fluctuations. Knowledgeable entrepreneurs use EOQ analysis as a starting point in making a decision and then use managerial judgment and experience to produce a final ruling.

### Price

For the typical small business owner, price is always a substantial factor when purchasing inventory and supplies. In many cases, an entrepreneur can negotiate price with potential suppliers on large orders of frequently purchased items. In other instances, perhaps when small quantities of items are purchased infrequently, entrepreneurs must pay list price. The typical entrepreneur shops around before ordering from the supplier that offers the best price. Still, this does not mean that a business owner should always purchase inventory and supplies at the lowest price available. The best purchase price is the lowest price at which the owner can obtain goods and services *of acceptable quality*. As quality guru W. Edwards Deming said, "Price has no meaning without a measure of the quality being purchased." This guideline usually yields the best value more often than simply purchasing the lowest-priced goods.

Recall that one of Deming's 14 points is *"Don't award business on price alone."* Without proof of quality, an item with the *lowest* initial price may produce the *highest* total cost. Deming condemned the practice of constantly switching suppliers in search of the lowest initial price because it increases the variability of a process and lowers its quality. Instead he recommended that businesses establish long-term relationships built on mutual trust and cooperation with a single supplier.

When evaluating a supplier's price, small business owners must consider not only the actual price of goods and services but also the selling terms accompanying them. In some cases, the selling terms can be more important than the price itself. Sometimes a vendor's terms might include some type of purchase discount. Vendors typically offer three types of discounts: trade discounts, quantity discounts, and cash discounts.

### Trade Discounts

*4.* Differentiate among the three types of purchase discounts that vendors offer.

**Trade discounts** are established on a graduated scale and depend on a small firm's position in the channel of distribution. In other words, trade discounts recognize the fact that manufacturers, wholesalers, and retailers perform a variety of vital functions at various stages in the channel of distribution and compensate them for providing these needed activities. Figure 17.3 illustrates a typical trade discount structure.

### Quantity Discounts

**Quantity discounts** are designed to encourage businesses to order large quantities of merchandise and supplies. Vendors are able to offer lower prices on bulk purchases because the

**FIGURE 17.3 Trade Discount Structure**

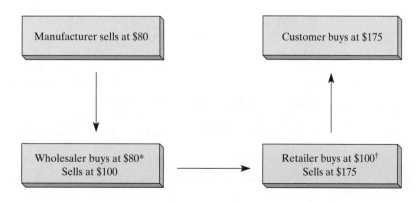

\* Wholesale discount = 54% of suggested retail price.
† Retail discount = 43% of suggested retail price.

**TABLE 17.7 Non-Cumulative Quantity Discount Structure**

| Order Size | Price |
| --- | --- |
| 1–1,000 units | List price |
| 1,001–5,000 units | List price −2% |
| 5,001–10,000 units | List price −4% |
| 10,001 units and above | List price −6% |

cost per unit is lower than for handling small orders. Quantity discounts normally exist in two forms: non-cumulative and cumulative. Non-cumulative quantity discounts are granted only if a certain volume of merchandise is purchased in a single order. For example, a wholesaler may offer small retailers a 3 percent discount only if they purchase 10 gross of Halloween masks in a single order. Table 17.7 shows a typical non-cumulative quantity discount structure.

Cumulative quantity discounts are offered if a firm's purchases from a particular vendor exceed a specified quantity or money value over a predetermined time period. The time frame varies, but a yearly basis is most common. For example, a manufacturer of appliances may offer a small business a 3 percent discount on subsequent orders if its purchases exceed $50,000 per year.

Some small business owners who normally buy in small quantities and are unable to qualify for quantity discounts can earn such discounts by joining buying groups, purchasing pools, or buying cooperatives. For example, the Independent Pharmacy Cooperative is an organization that allows small, independent pharmacies to achieve discounts on more than 1,000 pharmaceutical and other items they purchase. More than 3,000 independent pharmacies receive discounts on their purchases of items ranging from aspirin to gauze.[14]

*Jay DeFoor and DeFoor Drywall & Acoustical Supply Inc.*

Jay DeFoor, CEO of DeFoor Drywall & Acoustical Supply Inc., joined Amarok, a drywall buying cooperative with more than 150 members, so his company could get better prices from large drywall suppliers. In just one year, DeFoor says the lower prices the cooperative negotiated saved his company $250,000. "There's no way I could have negotiated that on my own," says DeFoor, whose company generates annual sales of $20 million. "That's a huge part of our bottom line"[15]

## Cash Discounts

**Cash discounts** are offered to customers as an incentive to pay for merchandise promptly. Many vendors grant cash discounts to avoid being used as an interest-free bank by customers who purchase merchandise and then fail to pay by the invoice due date. To encourage prompt payment of invoices, many vendors allow customers to deduct a percentage of the purchase amount if the customer remits payment within a specified time. Cash discount terms "2/10, net 30" are common in many industries. This notation means that the total amount of the invoice is due 30 days after its date, but if the customer pays the bill within 10 days, he or she may deduct 2 percent from the total. A discount offering "2/10, EOM" (EOM means "end of month") indicates that the buyer may deduct 2 percent if the bill is paid by the tenth of the month after purchase.

In general, it is sound business practice to take advantage of cash discounts. The money saved by paying invoices promptly is freed up for use elsewhere.

*Jeff Schreiber and Hansen Wholesale*

When Jeff Schreiber, owner of Hansen Wholesale, a small distributor of home products, attended a January trade show, he purchased $40,000 of ceiling fans from a manufacturer. The contract gave Schreiber until July to pay for the fans, but the manufacturer also included a cash discount: If Schreiber paid before May 1, he could earn a 3 percent discount on the purchase. By paying in February, Schreiber could save another 1.5 percent of the purchase price. For Schreiber, who manages his company's cash flow meticulously, the decision was an easy one; he paid the invoice in February and saved $1,800. "Your money works better if you take advantage of the discounts," says Schreiber, who recently saved $15,000 in cash discounts for his company in just one year.[16]

There is an implicit (opportunity) cost of forgoing a cash discount. By forgoing a cash discount, a business owner is, in effect, paying an annual interest rate to retain the use of the discounted amount for the remainder of the credit period. For example, suppose the Print Shop receives an invoice for $1,000 from a vendor offering a cash discount of 2/10, net 30. Figure 17.4 illustrates this situation and shows how to compute the cost of forgoing the cash discount. Actually, it costs the Print Shop $20 to retain the use of its $980 for an extra 20 days. Translating this into an annual interest rate:

$$I = P \times R \times T$$

where

$$I = \text{Interest (\$)} = \$20$$
$$P = \text{Principle (\$)} = \$980$$
$$T = \text{Time (number of days/360)} = 20/260$$
$$R = \text{Rate of interest (\%)}$$

To compute R, the annual interest rate,

$$R = \frac{I}{P \times T}$$

In our example,

$$R = \frac{\$20}{980 \times \dfrac{20}{360}}$$
$$= 36.735\%$$

The cost to the Print Shop of forgoing the cash discount is 36.735 percent per year! If there is $980 available on day 10 of the trade credit period, the entrepreneur should pay the invoice unless he is able to earn more than 36.735 percent on that money. If the entrepreneur does not have $980 on day 10 but can borrow it at less than 36.735 percent, he should do so to take advantage of the cash discount. Table 17.8 summarizes the cost of forgoing cash discounts offering various terms.

Although it is a good idea for business owners to take advantage of cash discounts, it is not a wise practice to stretch accounts payable to suppliers beyond the payment terms specified on the invoice. Letting payments become past due can destroy the trusting relationship a small company has built with its vendors.

**FIGURE 17.4 A Cash Discount**

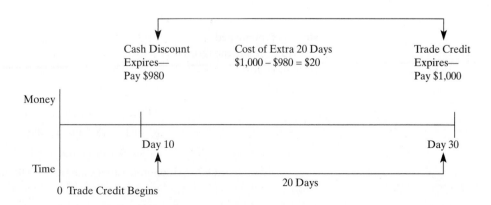

**TABLE 17.8 Cost of Forgoing Cash Discounts**

| Cash Discount Terms | Cost of Forgoing Cash Discounts (Annually) |
|---|---|
| 2/10, net 30 | 36.735% |
| 2/30, net 60 | 34.490% |
| 2/10, net 60 | 13.693% |
| 3/10, net 30 | 55.670% |
| 3/10, net 60 | 22.268% |

## Timing—When to Order

**5.** Calculate a company's reorder point.

Timing the purchase of merchandise and supplies is also a critical element of a purchasing plan. Entrepreneurs must schedule delivery dates so that their companies do not lose customer goodwill from stockouts. In addition, they must concentrate on maintaining proper control over the firm's inventory investment without tying up an excessive amount of working capital. There is a trade-off between the cost of running out of stock and the cost of carrying additional inventory.

When planning delivery schedules for inventory and supplies, owners must consider the lead time for an order, the time gap between placing an order and receiving it. In general, business owners cannot expect instantaneous delivery of merchandise. As a result, managers must plan reorder points for inventory items with lead times in mind. To determine when to order merchandise for inventory, entrepreneurs must calculate the reorder point for key inventory items. Developing a reorder point model involves determining the lead time for an order, the usage rate for the item, the minimum level of stock allowable, and the economic order quantity (EOQ). The **lead time** for an order is the time gap between placing an order with a vendor and actually receiving the goods. It may be as little as a few hours or as long as several weeks to process purchase requisitions and orders, contact the supplier, receive the goods, and add them to the company's inventory. Obviously, owners who purchase from local vendors encounter shorter lead times than those who rely on distant suppliers.

Business owners can determine the usage rate for a particular product from past inventory and accounting records. A business owner must estimate the speed at which the supply of merchandise will be depleted over a given time. The anticipated usage rate for a product determines how long the supply will last. For example, if an entrepreneur projects that she will use 900 units in the next six months, the usage rate is five units per day (900 units/180 days). The simplest reorder point model assumes that the firm experiences a linear usage rate; that is, depletion of the firm's stock continues at a constant rate over time.

Business owners must determine the minimum level of stock allowable. If a firm runs out of a particular item (i.e., incurs stockouts), customers will lose faith in the business and begin to shop elsewhere. To avoid stockouts, many firms establish a minimum level of inventory greater than zero. In other words, they build a cushion, called **safety stock**, into their inventories in case demand runs ahead of the anticipated usage rate. If that occurs, the owners can dip into the safety stock to fill customer orders until their stock is replenished.

To compute the reorder point for an item, the owner must combine this inventory information with the product's EOQ. The following example illustrates the reorder point calculation:

$$L = \text{Lead time for an order} = 5 \text{ days}$$
$$U = \text{Usage rate} = 18 \text{ units per day}$$
$$S = \text{Safety stock (minimum level)} = 75 \text{ units}$$
$$\text{EOQ} = \text{Economic order quantity} = 540 \text{ units}$$

**FIGURE 17.5 Reorder Point Model**

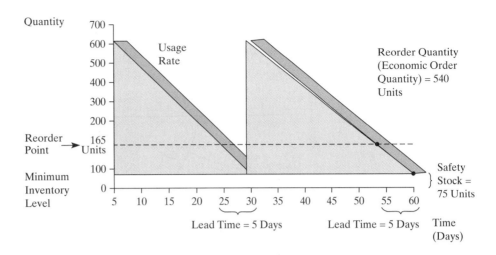

The formula for computing the reorder point is:

$$\text{Reorder point} = (L \times U) + S$$

In this example,

$$\text{Reorder point} = (5 \text{ days} \times 18 \text{ units/day}) + 75 \text{ units}$$
$$= 165 \text{ units}$$

This business owner should order 540 more units when inventory drops to 165 units. Figure 17.5 illustrates the reorder point situation for this small business.

The simple reorder technique makes assumptions that may not be valid in some companies. First, the model assumes that the firm's usage rate is constant, when in fact for most small businesses demand varies daily. Second, the model assumes that lead time for an order is constant when, in fact, few vendors deliver precisely within lead time estimates. Third, in this model, the owner never taps safety stock; however, late deliveries or accelerated demand may force the owner to dip into this inventory reserve. More advanced models relax some of these assumptions, but the simple model can be a useful inventory guideline for making inventory decisions in a small company.

Another popular reorder point model assumes that the demand for a product during its lead time is normally distributed (see Figure 17.6). The area under the normal curve at any given point represents the probability that a particular demand level will occur. Figure 17.7 illustrates the application of this normal distribution to the reorder point model *without* safety stock. The model recognizes that three different demand patterns can occur during a product's lead time. Demand pattern 1 is an example of below-average demand during lead time; demand pattern 2 is an example of average demand during lead time; and demand pattern 3 is an example of an above-average demand during lead time.

If the reorder point for this item is the average demand, $\overline{D}_L$, for the product during lead time, 50 percent of the time, demand will be below average (note that 50 percent of the area under the normal curve lies below average). Similarly, 50 percent of the time, demand during

**FIGURE 17.6 Demand During Leading**

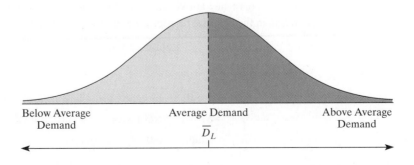

**FIGURE 17.7 Reorder Point without Safety Stock**

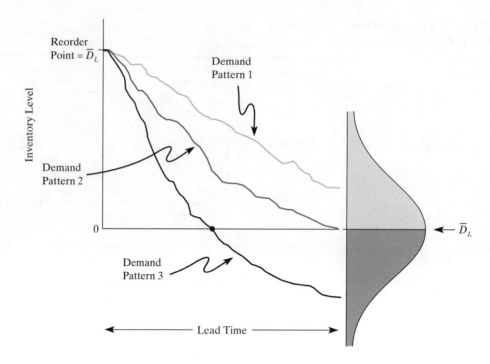

lead time will exceed the average, and the firm will experience stockouts (note that 50 percent of the area under the normal curve lies above average).

To reduce the probability of inventory shortage, a business owner can increase the reorder point above $\overline{D}_L$ (average demand during lead time). But how much should the owner increase the reorder point? Rather than attempt to define the actual costs of carrying extra inventory versus the costs of stockouts (remember the trade-off described earlier), this model allows the small business owner to determine the appropriate reorder point by setting a desired customer level. For example, the owner may want to satisfy 95 percent of customer demand for a product during lead time. This service level determines the amount of increase in the reorder point. In effect, these additional items serve as a safety stock:

$$\text{Safety stock} = SLF \times SD_L$$

where:

$$SLF = \text{Service level factor (the appropriate Z score)}$$
$$SD_L = \text{Standard deviation of demand during lead time}$$

Table 17.9 shows the appropriate service level factor (Z score) for some of the most popular target customer service levels.

Figure 17.8 shows the shift to a normally distributed reorder point model with safety stock. In this case the manager has set a 95 percent customer service level; that is, the manager wants to meet 95 percent of the demand during lead time. The normal curve in the model without safety stock (from Figure 17.7) is shifted up so that 95 percent of the area under the curve lies above the zero inventory level. The result is a reorder point that is higher than the original reorder point by the amount of the safety stock:

$$\text{Reorder point} = \overline{D}_L + (SLF \times SD_L)$$

where

$$\overline{D}_L = \text{Average demand during lead time (original reorder point)}$$
$$SLF = \text{Service level factor (the appropriate Z score)}$$
$$SD_L = \text{Standard deviation of demand during lead time}$$

**TABLE 17.9 Service Level Factors and Z Scores**

| Target Customer Service Level | Z Score* |
|---|---|
| 99% | 2.33 |
| 97.5% | 1.96 |
| 95% | 1.645 |
| 90% | 1.275 |
| 80% | 0.845 |
| 75% | 0.675 |

*Any basic statistics book provides a table of areas under the normal curve, which gives the appropriate Z score for any service level factor.

To illustrate, suppose that the average demand for a product during its lead time (one week) is 325 units with a standard deviation of 110 units. If the desired service level is 95 percent, the service level factor (from Table 17.9) would be 1.645. The reorder point would be:

$$R = 325 + (1.645 \times 110) = 325 + 181 = 506 \text{ units}$$

Figure 17.9 illustrates the shift from a system without safety stock to one with safety stock for this example. With a reorder point of 325 units ($\bar{D}_L$), this small business owner will experience inventory shortages during the lead time 50 percent of the time. With a reorder point of 506 units (i.e., a safety stock of 181 units), the business owner will experience inventory stockouts during the lead time only 5 percent of the time.

**FIGURE 17.8 Reorder Point with Safety Stock**

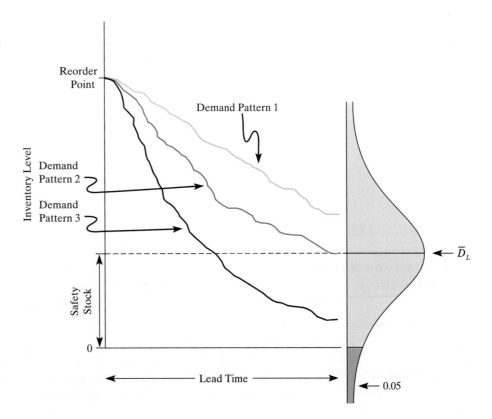

**FIGURE 17.9 Shift from a No-Safety Stock System to a Safety Stock System**

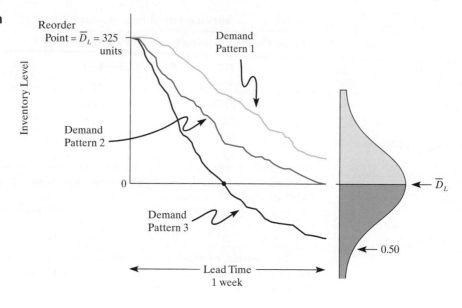

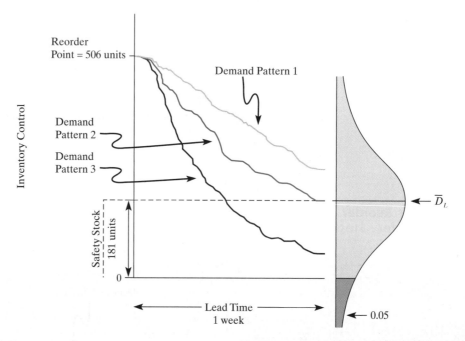

## In the Entrepreneurial Spotlight

### ■ This Cartoon Network Is Not So Funny

The 30-something investment banker works on Wall Street and lives in a spacious, three-bedroom apartment in a chic New York City neighborhood. Like many New Yorkers, he relies on a cadre of couriers to make deliveries to satisfy his wants. He has dinner delivered to his apartment most nights, and the dry cleaner picks up and delivers his suits to his front door. He even orders his groceries online and has them delivered as well.

Tonight, as he does once a month, he is about to request another delivery. When he dials a telephone number listed on a colorful business card, he reaches an answering service, punches in his own telephone number, and hangs up. A few minutes later, his telephone rings and the caller asks him for a special code word. "Cartoon," he replies and hangs up. Two hours later, a clean-cut young man wearing a backpack shows up at his door. Once inside the apartment, the courier opens his backpack to reveal dozens of clear, four-inch-long plastic boxes, each filled with up to two grams of high-grade marijuana, which ranges from $50 to $400. "It's convenient, the weed is good, and it feels safe," says the investment banker.

This delivery, although for an illegal substance, is the result of a highly organized and carefully coordinated supply chain put together by an entrepreneur of sorts named John Nebel. Until he was finally nabbed by police, Nebel was the head of the Cartoon Network (named after the cable television network), a sophisticated supplier of marijuana to upscale clients in New York City. Although police were successful in taking apart the Cartoon Network, they admit that there could be dozens, perhaps hundreds, of similar operations making deliveries of illicit drugs to customers across the city. Only after a former disgruntled employee sent a letter to the police about the organization's operations were authorities able to take it down.

The Cartoon Network was a fluid, technology-savvy organization that changed locations frequently and relied on a well-coordinated supply chain (see accompanying figure). Most of the marijuana was grown in the basements of dozens of private homes in New York and nearby states. A typical grower tended 300 to 400 plants, which were harvested up to four times a year. Each cutting produced 30 to 40 pounds of marijuana, which was worth $150,000 to $200,000 at wholesale

and $540,000 to $720,000 at retail. A wholesale distributor purchased the marijuana and delivered a few pounds at a time to a group of executive managers at the Cartoon Network. "They kept the increments small so they could move it quickly and never have too much on hand," says one of the detectives who finally solved the case. The executives repackaged the marijuana into one-pound containers and delivered them to the network's call center, which rotated weekly and sometimes daily among hotel rooms in New York City or one of Nebel's seven houses in the New York metropolitan area to avoid detection by police.

An executive managed up to six employees in the call center. Two or three employees repackaged the marijuana into 1.5- to 2-gram amounts, placed them into the plastic canisters, and labeled them according to the type, such as Strawberry Cough, NYC Diesel, and AK-47. The higher-priced types always were the best sellers. One employee handled the call center's database, which Nebel had custom-built for $50,000. When a call came in, the employee checked the telephone number against the Cartoon Network database, which produced the caller's vital information, his complete buying history, and the name of the last courier who made a delivery to him. "This was one of their safety valves to weed out police calls," says the police detective. The call center received as many as 600 calls each day. If a caller's number matched the database, the dispatcher returned the call and asked for a code word.

If a customer supplied the correct code word, the dispatcher passed on the order to one of the company's

**Smoke Screen**
The Cartoon Network and other pot delivery services rely on intricate, hard-to-trace webs to get their goods from the producer to the customer. Growers ❶ sell the pot to a wholesale distributor ❷ who, in turn, sells it to a group of executive managers ❸. The marijuana is sent to a call center, where it's broken down and packaged ❹. From there, courier managers get hold of it ❺, and pass it on to backpack-toting street couriers ❻. The customer ❼ contacts the call center. If his number clears the database ❽, the call center phones him back for a code word, and then dispatches a street courier, who delivers the dope.

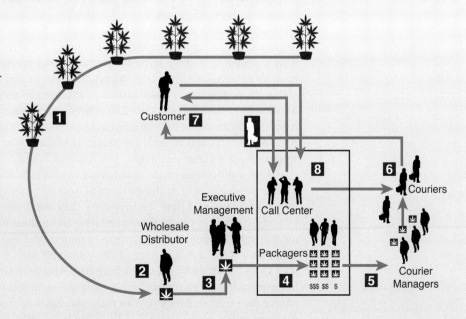

*(continued)*

four street managers, who handed the marijuana to a courier. Couriers limited the amount of marijuana they carried at any time to no more than 8 ounces to avoid felony charges in case they were caught, and they traveled by foot, bike, subway, or bus to make their deliveries. At the end of their 12-hour shifts (11 A.M. to 11 P.M.), couriers, who made $200 a day, met with their street managers and turned in the money that they had collected and any leftover marijuana. Street managers and dispatchers earned $300 a day. Even though the illegal operation incurred daily costs of $9,000, it usually netted $17,000 a day, for an annual net income of $6 million—tax free, of course, until the police were able to crack the network and send Nebel to jail.

1. What lessons can legitimate companies learn from Cartoon Network's supply chain?
2. Identify at least three ways that Cartoon Network could improve its supply chain.

*Source:* Adapted from Monte Burke, "Inside Dope," *Forbes,* March 26, 2007, pp. 78–81.

## Managing the Supply Chain: Vendor Analysis and Selection

**6.** Develop a vendor rating scale.

Businesses have discovered that managing their supply chains for maximum effectiveness and efficiency not only can increase their profitability but it also can provide them with an important competitive advantage in the marketplace. Proper **supply chain management (SCM)** enables companies to reduce their inventories, get products to market much faster, increase quality, and improve customer satisfaction. SCM requires businesses to forge long-term partnerships with reliable suppliers rather than to see vendors merely as "someone trying to sell me something." Doing so can produce an impressive payoff; experts note that implementing a successful SCM system yields an average savings of 15 percent by controlling unnecessary spending, negotiating lower prices, maintaining lower inventory levels, and reducing waste and inefficiency in the purchasing process.[17] One consulting firm that specializes in setting up supply chain management systems says that its clients have seen their inventory levels decline as much as 60 percent, saving those companies vast amounts of money.[18]

Companies are learning that, to make SCM work, they must share information with their suppliers and make their entire supply chains transparent to everyone involved in them. In the early days, that meant linking suppliers and companies as if they were parts of a single business on private data networks using electronic data interchange (EDI), which allowed companies and vendors to exchange orders and invoices electronically. The Internet takes EDI a step further. Web-based supply chain management, or e-procurement, allows companies to share information concerning production plans, shipment schedules, inventory levels, sales forecasts, and actual sales on a real-time basis with their vendors, enabling the companies to make instant adjustments to their orders and delivery schedules. Many studies have found a correlation between the amount of information shared among supply chain members and the efficiency of the entire chain. Costs are significantly lower for retailers, wholesalers, and manufacturers when they are connected in a supply chain network with open communication.[19]

With e-procurement, companies are connected via the Web to their customers and to their suppliers, which allows them to respond rapidly to changing buyer preferences by modifying in real time the inventory they purchase. In turn, suppliers can make the fast adjustments in production scheduling to produce the items that customers actually are buying. Companies "are starting to understand that the 'supply' side of the supply chain isn't worth a hill of beans if the 'demand' side is disconnected," says one industry expert.[20] A study by the consulting firm Aberdeen Group reports that companies that use e-procurement to connect seamlessly the members of their supply chains are able to reduce the prices that they pay for their purchases by 7 percent and cut the delivery time for their orders by 67 percent.[21] With these systems, valuable information flows from the small business that sells suits to customers all the way up the supply chain to the sheep shearer who harvests wool!

A Web-based SCM process works like this: Software at a retail store captures data from sales as they happen and looks for underlying trends for use in calculating quantities of which products to purchase in the future. For instance, SCM software at a retail store may notice that sales of black low-rise jeans are selling more briskly than anticipated and forecasts the quantity of jeans the store should order. That information then goes up the supply chain to the jean maker. Taking into account delivery times and manufacturing speed, the software helps the jean maker create a detailed production plan for cutting, sewing, and shipping the garments on time. Then the software determines how much fabric the jean maker must have to produce the required number of black low-rise jeans and orders it from the textile producer. The software can track everything from the location of the raw materials in the production process to the quality of the finished product for everyone in the supply chain. "Supply chain analytics can boost the bottom line because they produce greater efficiency, less scrap, better quality, and lower production costs and can improve the top line through greater customer satisfaction," says a top manager at International Data Corporation (IDC), a research company that has studied the impact of SCM on companies' performance. "This is basic business made better."[22] A study by IDC found that analytics applied to a company's supply chain produced an impressive 277 percent return over five years, far higher than the returns on those that are applied to financial performance (139 percent) and customer service (55 percent).[23]

To function smoothly, a small company's supply chain should follow the "three A's": agility, adaptability, and alignment.[24] An *agile* supply chain is one that is fast, flexible, and responsive to changes in demand. Agile supply chains are able to deal with the inevitable disruptions and fluctuations by creating strong partnerships with suppliers, adequate but not excessive levels of safety stock, contingency plans for catastrophic events, and an information system that provides everyone in the chain with timely information. An *adaptable* supply chain is one that changes as a company's needs change and is able to accommodate a small company's growth. Adaptable supply chains are predictive, able to anticipate changes in companies' buying and selling process and to help them to adapt to the changes in real time. A supply chain is properly *aligned* when all the companies in it work together as a team for the benefit of the entire group. In the past, some companies were hesitant to share information with the businesses in their supply chains. Success today requires that companies not only share information seamlessly but that they also synchronize their efforts to maximize efficiency throughout the entire chain.

*The North Face*

The North Face, a maker of outdoor apparel whose logo is well known among college students, was generating sales of $238 million but was incurring losses of $100 million because of serious problems with its supply chain. "[The] North Face was producing too much inventory and could not match this inventory to orders or even ship effectively," says one manager. "The company didn't know what its orders were or where its purchases were logistically. Everything had come unglued from an information and service standpoint." On-time delivery to retailers had slipped below 50 percent, which is bad for any business but particularly bad for The North Face because its products were in high demand. The company was in crisis mode because its supply chain was broken. VF, a large apparel company, saw potential in The North Face and purchased the company. VF's first priority was to fix the supply chain. Managers replaced the antiquated manual system that The North Face had been using in a vain attempt at managing its supply chain with a more sophisticated automated system based on business intelligence software. The software compares sales for each of the company's products with inventory records to determine how many of each item The North Face should order from its suppliers. It also specifies the timing of orders to meet or precede customers' requested delivery dates. The resulting reports are sent to key decision makers at The North Face via e-mail. Since implementing the new system, inventory at The North Face has fallen by more than 65 percent, freeing untold millions of dollars in cash flow. Lower costs have improved the company's profit margin to an impressive 14 percent of sales.[25]

Experienced business owners realize that a key link in supply chain management is finding reliable vendors that can supply them with quality merchandise, equipment, supplies, and services at reasonable prices in a timely manner. Selecting the right vendors or suppliers for a business can have an impact well beyond simply obtaining goods and services at the lowest costs. Although searching for the best price will always be an important factor, successful small business owners must consider other factors in vendor selection such as reliability, reputation, quality, support services, speed, and proximity.

## Vendor Certification

To add objectivity to the vendor selection process, many companies are establishing vendor certification programs, agreements to give one supplier the majority of their business if that supplier meets rigorous quality and performance standards. Today, businesses of all sizes and types are establishing long-term "partnering" arrangements with vendors that meet their certification standards. When creating a vendor certification program, entrepreneurs should remember the three Cs: *commitment, communication,* and *control. Commitment* to consistently meeting the company's quality standards must be paramount. No company can afford to do business with vendors that cannot meet its quality targets. Second, a company must establish two-way *communication* with vendors. Communication implies trust, and trust creates working relationships that are long-term and mutually beneficial. Treating suppliers like partners can reveal ways to boost quality and lower costs for both parties. Finally, a company must make sure that its vendors and suppliers have in place the *controls* that enable them to produce quality results and to achieve continuous improvements in their processes. In today's competitive marketplace, entrepreneurs expect all vendors to demonstrate that they operate processes built on continuous improvement.

Creating a vendor certification program requires entrepreneurs to develop a vendor rating scale that allows them to evaluate the advantages and disadvantages of each potential vendor. The scale allows entrepreneurs to score potential vendors on measures of the purchasing criteria that are most important to their companies' success. The first step to developing a scale is to determine the criteria that are most important to selecting a vendor (e.g., price, quality, prompt delivery). The next step is to assign weights to each criterion to reflect its relative importance. The third step involves developing a grading scale for comparing vendors on the criteria. Developing a usable scale requires that the owner maintain proper records of past vendor performances. Finally, the owner must compute a weighted total score for each vendor and select the vendor that scores the highest on the set of criteria. Consider the following example. Bravo Bass Boats Inc. is faced with choosing from among several suppliers of a critical raw material. The company's owner has decided to employ a vendor rating scale to select the best vendor using the following procedure.

**Step 1**    *Determine important criteria.* The owner of Bravo has selected the following criteria:

Quality

Price

Prompt Delivery

Service

Assistance

**Step 2**    *Assign weights to each criterion to reflect its relative importance.*

| Criterion | Weight |
|---|---|
| Quality | 35 |
| Price | 30 |
| Prompt delivery | 20 |
| Service | 10 |
| Assistance | 5 |
| **Total** | 100 |

**Step 3**     *Develop a grading scale for each criterion.*

| Criterion | Grading Scale |
|---|---|
| Quality | $\dfrac{\text{Number of acceptable lots from Vendor X}}{\text{Total number of lots from Vendor X}}$ |
| Price | $\dfrac{\text{Lowest quoted price of all vendors}}{\text{Price offered by Vendor X}}$ |
| Prompt delivery | $\dfrac{\text{Number of on-time deliveries from Vendor X}}{\text{Total number of deliveries from Vendor X}}$ |
| Service | A subjective evaluation of the variety of service offered by each vendor |
| Assistance | A subjective evaluation of the advice and assistance provided by each vendor |

**Step 4**     *Compute a weighted score for each vendor.*

| Criterion | Weight | Grade | Weighted Score (weight × grade) |
|---|---|---|---|
| **Vendor 1** | | | |
| Quality | 35 | 9/10 | 31.5 |
| Price | 30 | 12.5/12.5 | 30.0 |
| Prompt delivery | 20 | 10/10 | 20.0 |
| Service | 10 | 8/10 | 8.0 |
| Assistance | 5 | 5/5 | 5.0 |
| **Total weighted score** | | | 94.5 |
| **Vendor 2** | | | |
| Quality | 35 | 8/10 | 31.5 |
| Price | 30 | 12.5/12.5 | 27.8 |
| Prompt delivery | 20 | 8/10 | 16.0 |
| Service | 10 | 8/10 | 8.0 |
| Assistance | 5 | 4/5 | 4.0 |
| **Total weighted score** | | | 83.8 |
| **Vendor 3** | | | |
| Quality | 35 | 7/10 | 24.5 |
| Price | 30 | 12.5/12.5 | 30.0 |
| Prompt delivery | 20 | 6/10 | 12.0 |
| Service | 10 | 7/10 | 7.0 |
| Assistance | 5 | 1/5 | 1.0 |
| **Total weighted score** | | | 74.5 |

Using this analysis of the three suppliers, Bravo should purchase the majority of this raw material from Vendor 1.

This vendor analysis procedure assumes that business owners have a working knowledge of their supplier network. Start-up companies seldom will, however. Owners of start-up companies must find suppliers and gather data to conduct a vendor analysis. One of the best ways to do that is to ask potential vendors for references. In some cases, industry trade associations have knowledge regarding the integrity of suppliers or vendors. Other sources for information on vendors include trade association shows, the local chamber of commerce, and publications such as *MacRae's Blue Book* (www.macraesbluebook.com), which includes information on more than 500,000 North American industrial companies, and the *Thomas Register of American Manufacturers* (www.thomasnet.com), which includes information on more than

## How to Build a Base of Competent Suppliers

Many small companies pay prices for goods and services that are too high, and they find that their options are limited by the lack of a base of competent suppliers. The broader the base of potential suppliers a business has, the higher is the likelihood it will find the best price. The following steps in the process of scanning potential vendors are never ending:

1. *Establish your company's criteria for selecting a vendor.* What characteristics would the ideal vendor have? You must know up front what you are looking for in a vendor.

2. *Interview prospective vendors with the same level of intensity that you interview prospective employees.* Both relationships influence how successful a company is at achieving quality objectives. "It's not easy to put aside the time," says James Walker, president of Octagon Research Solutions, a 60-person software company, "but for us, it's all about whether we can have a good relationship with [our vendors.]" Use the criteria you established in Step 1 to establish a list of questions to ask potential vendors.

3. *Be assertive.* Ask tough questions and be a knowledgeable buyer. Don't allow suppliers to make their typical "sales pitches" before you have time to ask your questions.

4. *Check potential vendors' credit ratings.* Judging a potential vendor's financial strength and stability is important. Dealing with a vendor that is undergoing financial woes creates unnecessary complications for business owners.

5. *Get referrals.* Ask all potential vendors to supply a list of referrals of businesses that they have served over the past five years or more. Then make the necessary contacts.

6. *Visit potential vendors' businesses.* The best way to judge a vendor's ability to meet your company's needs is to see the operation first hand. Nancy Connolly, president of Lasertone Corporation, a maker of copier and laser toner, insists on "a personal meeting between me and the president of the company," she says, before establishing a relationship with a vendor. The goal is to judge the level of the potential vendor's commitment to meeting Lasertone's needs.

7. *Don't fixate on price.* Look for value in what they sell. If your only concern is the lowest price, vendors will push their lowest priced (and often lowest quality) product lines.

8. *Ask "What if?"* The real test of a strong vendor-customer relationship occurs when problems arise. Smart entrepreneurs ask vendors how they will handle particular types of problems when they arise. James Walker of Octagon Research Solutions says that Dell won his company's loyalty after he purchased five laptops from the computer maker. Two of the computers were defective, but a technician quickly analyzed the problem and offered to replace the motherboards on the defective machines. When Walker asked the technician to replace the motherboards of the three other computers, he agreed to do so even though they showed no signs of the problem.

9. *Attend trade shows.* Work the room. A visit to a trade show is not a vacation; it's business. Find out whether the next booth has a valuable new vendor who has the potential to increase your company's profits!

10. *Don't forget about local vendors.* Because of their proximity, local vendors can sometimes provide the fastest service. Solving problems often is easier because local vendors can make on-site service calls.

11. *Test a vendor before committing completely.* Susan Gilbert, owner of Café in the Park, a restaurant in San Diego, California, says, "Inventory is cash flow. When I'm dealing with a vendor, I need to know how quickly they can deliver, how quickly I can turn over the inventory, and keep it all tight." Rather than place an order for 100 Danish pastries with a new vendor, for instance, Gilbert starts with an order of several dozen pastries to judge the vendor's performance.

12. *Work with the vendors.* Tell your suppliers what you like and don't like about their products and service. In many cases, they can resolve your concerns. Most vendors want to build long-term

relationships with their customers. Give them a chance to do so.

13. *Do unto others . . .* Treat your vendors well. Be selective but pay on time and treat them with respect.

*Sources:* Adapted from Kelly L. Frey, "Selecting a Vendor: RFPs and Responses to RFPs," Baker, Donelson, Bearman, Caldwell, and Berkowitz, www.bakerdonelson.com/Documents/Selecting%20a% 20Vendor.pdf; Allison Stein Wellner, "Finding the Right Vendor," *Inc.*, July 2003, pp. 88–95; Jan Norman, "How to Find Suppliers," *Business Start-ups*, October 1998, pp. 44–47.

500,000 North American industrial companies, and the *Thomas Register of American Manufacturers* (www.thomasnet.com), which lists more than 650,000 industrial companies. Both of these sources provide lists of products and services and the names, addresses, telephone numbers, and ratings of their manufacturers.

The *U.S. Industrial Directory* is similar to the *Thomas Register* although its coverage is not as broad. Business owners also should contact state chambers of commerce about state directories of manufacturers. Entrepreneurs whose product lines have an international flair may look to the *Thomas Global Register* and *Kelly's Manufacturers and Merchants Directory* for information on companies throughout the world dealing in practically every type of product or service.

The Web is another rich source of information on potential suppliers. Purchasing agents in companies of all sizes are stepping up their use of the Internet as a tool for locating and buying merchandise, equipment, and supplies. A quick search produces directories of suppliers in particular industries, countries, or product lines.

### The Final Decision

Once business owners identify potential vendors and suppliers, they must decide which one (or ones) to do business with. Entrepreneurs should consider the following factors before making the final decision about the right supplier.

**NUMBER OF SUPPLIERS.** One important question entrepreneurs face is "Should I buy from a single supplier or from several different sources?" Concentrating purchases at a single supplier (or sole sourcing) results in special attention from the supplier, especially if orders are substantial. Second, a business may be able to negotiate quantity discounts if its orders are large enough. Finally, a small company can cultivate a closer, more cooperative relationship with the supplier. Suppliers are more willing to work with companies that prove to be loyal customers. The result of this type of partnership can be better-quality goods and services. Stratsys, a company that makes plastic prototypes for the aerospace, automotive, and medical industries, purchases some of its most important raw materials from a single source. Company managers admit that doing so involves risk, but they believe that their company produces better quality products by eliminating the variability that multiple sources of supply would introduce into their production process.[26]

However, using a single vendor also has disadvantages. A company can experience shortages of critical materials if its only supplier suffers a catastrophe, such as a fire, strike, or bankruptcy.

*Grubby Clark and
Clark Foam*

Surfboard shapers and owners of retail surfboard shops began scrambling for alternatives when Clark Foam, an icon in the surfing industry and supplier of 90 percent of the foam cores used in the United States to make surfboards, closed suddenly after 30 years of operation. Clark customers were shocked. "Overnight, our number one source is gone," says Brent Hudson, owner of Neptune Surfboards in California. Some surfboard shop owners and shapers turned to suppliers in Australia, Brazil, and other countries for their board cores, and others began purchasing cores made from other materials. "Since the Clark Foam shakeout, a lot of shop owners are taking a hard look at their business practices," says Travis Wilkerson of the Surf Industry Manufacturers Association.[27]

To offset the risks of sole sourcing, many companies rely on the 80/20 rule. They purchase 80 percent of their supplies from their premier supplier and the remaining 20 percent from several "backup" vendors. Although this strategy may require a compromise on getting the lowest prices, it removes the risk of sole sourcing and lets a company's premier suppliers know that they have competition.

**RELIABILITY.** Business owners must evaluate a potential vendor's ability to deliver adequate quantities of quality merchandise when it is needed. One common complaint small businesses have against their suppliers is late delivery. Late deliveries or shortages cause lost sales and create customer ill will. Large customers often take precedence over small ones when it comes to service.

**PROXIMITY.** A supplier's physical proximity is an important factor when choosing a vendor. The cost of transporting merchandise can increase significantly the total cost of merchandise to a buyer. Foreign manufacturers require longer delivery times, and because of the distance that shipments must travel, a hiccup anywhere in the distribution channel often results in late deliveries. In addition, entrepreneurs can solve quality problems more easily with nearby suppliers than with distant vendors.

*Jamey Bennett
and LightWedge*

When Jamey Bennett decided to start a company to sell the LightWedge, an idea he came up with when he was 17, he looked to foreign manufacturers to produce the sheet of clear acrylic that contained light-emitting diodes that softly illuminated a page, allowing one to read in bed without disturbing a sleeping partner. With orders in hand from bookseller Barnes and Noble and catalog retailer Levenger, Bennett purchased equipment and tooling from a factory in China's Guangdong Province. Things ran smoothly for a few months until Bennett introduced a LightWedge designed for paperbacks. The factory ignored Bennett's repeated requests to modify the original design, and he switched production to another Chinese factory where things quickly got worse. Bennett ordered 5,000 Light-Wedges, but only 2,000 arrived—four months late—and many had lenses that were so scratched or were marred by "some kind of mysterious goop" that they were unusable. Because of the problems, LightWedge lost an estimated $1.5 million in sales, and Bennett decided that it was time to bring production back to his home country, the United States. Today a factory in the state of Virginia manufactures the LightWedge, and although costs are 20 percent higher than they were in China, Bennett knows that he will get quality products delivered on time. LightWedge recently was named to the *Inc.* 500, the magazine's list of America's fastest growing private companies.[28]

Despite potential problems such as the ones that Jamey Bennett encountered, outsourcing purchases of materials and components to foreign manufacturers, who can offer lower prices than their domestic competitors, has become increasingly popular in the last decade. According to the Manufacturing Performance Institute's Census of Manufacturers, more than one-third of manufacturers have no supply chain integration with their foreign suppliers, many of whom are located in the Far East (particularly China), South America, and India.[29]

**SERVICES.** Entrepreneurs must evaluate the range of services vendors offer. Do salespeople make regular calls on the firm, and are they knowledgeable about their product line? Will the sales representatives assist in planning store layout and in creating attractive displays? Will the vendor make convenient deliveries on time? Is the supplier reasonable in making repairs on equipment after installation and in handling returned merchandise? Are sales representatives able to offer useful advice on purchasing and other managerial functions? Is the supplier willing to take the time to help you solve problems that inevitably will crop up?

*PayCycle*

CPA Charles Ross uses payroll services company PayCycle to handle the payroll function for his own business and for many of his small business clients. PayCycle won Ross as a loyal customer after he discovered that he had entered a client's payroll information incorrectly, creating a problem that PayCycle remedied quickly. It was Friday afternoon, and the client's tax-employment forms had to go out the following Monday, which meant that PayCycle had to recalculate an entire year's payroll. Even though it required almost a full day's work for someone at PayCycle over a weekend, the payroll service fixed the problem, and the forms went out on schedule on Monday. That level of service explains why Ross is a lifelong customer and why 90 percent of PayCycle's customers refer new customers to the company.[30]

**COLLABORATION.** The goal is to find a supplier that is eager to join forces with the intent of building a long-term partnership with your company. Other small companies make ideal candidates.

*Scott Fischer and Center for Systems Management and Harriet Donnelly and Technovative Marketing*

When the U.S. National Aeronautical Space Administration (NASA) approached Scott Fischer, president of the Center for Systems Management (CSM), a company that provides training and consulting services for corporations and government agencies, about creating a video for an internal marketing campaign, Fischer knew that the job was beyond his company's ability. Wanting the chance to expand his work with the space agency, Fischer began looking for a company with which he could partner to create the video. He had to work quickly because NASA needed the video in just 45 days. Fischer and a team of employees selected Technovative Marketing, a seven-person marketing firm headed by Harriet Donnelly. Donnelly worked on the video herself and attended every meeting that Fischer had with NASA officials. (On every project, Donnelly assigns both a staff person and a senior manager to every Technovative project to make sure that clients always have two points of contact.) Because of the partnership that CSM and Technovative Marketing forged, the project turned out to be a huge success. NASA has enlisted CSM for similar projects, and, in turn, CSM is partnering with Technovative Marketing.[31]

**PRICE NEGOTIATIONS.** Small firms usually must pay market or list price for items that are of lower value and purchased infrequently. This is not the case for goods purchased on a regular basis and that are essential components or supplies. An entrepreneur should not hesitate to attempt to purchase the goods or services it needs at the best price and terms of sale. The terms of sale, as mentioned previously, can be a significant factor in the final price that an entrepreneur pays.

## In the Entrepreneurial Spotlight

### ■ That Ducati "Lean"

When motorcycle enthusiasts hear the words "lean" and "Ducati," they picture one of the company's sleek V-twin bikes leaning into a sweeping turn as the rider takes it at speed. Company managers have a different picture in mind—one that includes the company's lean and efficient supply chain. The improvements for which the company's supply chain is responsible are as impressive as the Italian motorcycle maker's record of racing success. Since Ducati

revamped its supply chain in "Operation Turnaround" using principles such as kaizen (continuous improvement), TQM, Six Sigma, just-in-time inventory control, and others, the impact has been nothing short of amazing. Production costs have declined 25 percent, cycle time has decreased by 50 percent, and measures of manufacturing quality have increased 70 percent. In addition, production volume has increased more than threefold, from 12,000 motorcycles a year to more than 40,000 a year.

*(continued)*

Founded in 1926 in Bologna, Italy, as an industrial components manufacturer, Ducati produced its first motorcycle engine in 1946 and went on to build a great reputation for building off-road bikes. In the 1970s, the company became known for making stellar racing bikes, but by 1999, it was facing serious challenges and had to make key strategic changes. "We wanted to eliminate all non-value-adding activity, eliminate waste, and improve quality—all without any major new investment," says Filippo Pellerey, one of Ducati's top managers. "We conducted a careful analysis of our production processes, which revealed problems." For instance, the company's flow of materials through the factory was inefficient, requiring workers to move parts long distances for no reason. Revamping the work flow and implementing a predictive maintenance system for all of the factory equipment produced huge improvements in productivity, costs, and machine downtime. Pellerey says that those changes alone reduced the hourly cost of operation by 23 percent.

Ducati gained control over its inventory of raw materials by implementing a system that uses assembly kits for each motorcycle that are put together in areas known as "supermarkets" and follow a motorcycle through the production process. As part of their analysis, Ducati workers discovered that just 8 percent of the cost of a typical motorcycle was produced internally; the remaining 92 percent came from the company's supply chain. That meant that the company had to involve its supply chain partners in "Operation Turnaround" if the effort was to succeed. Transferring the culture and the techniques for creating a lean and efficient supply chain to 380 suppliers was no easy task, but Ducati's persistence and hard work paid off. Some suppliers simply refused to participate, which forced Ducati to trim its roster of vendors to 175. "We introduced an integration program that involved Ducati employees and supplier staff working in teams," says Giovanni Contino, another top manager. "We consider our suppliers to be an extension of Ducati so we connected them via the Web to accelerate the flow of information such as production planning, parts price lists, invoices, and quality reports." That means linking suppliers that are as close as a few blocks away as well as many that are scattered across Europe and as far away as Japan.

Ducati's new supply chain management process also allows the company to respond more quickly to shifts in customers' preferences and to operate with more flexibility, both important factors given that the life cycle for a particular motorcycle model is growing shorter. Pellerey is pleased with Ducati's progress but admits that achieving a lean and efficient supply chain is a journey rather than a destination. "We want a customer to be able to walk into a Ducati dealer and get one in the shortest possible time," he says. "That will require further development of the information process between our dealer network and the factory. We are working on that now."

1. What lessons can other companies learn from Ducati's experience of reworking its supply chain?
2. To achieve results such as those at Ducati, how important is the free flow of information among members of a company's supply chain? Explain.
3. What barriers exist to the free flow of information among the members of a company's supply chain, and what can managers do to overcome those barriers?

*Sources:* Adapted from Peter Rae, "Ducati Rides Lean," *Profit,* November 2005, pp. 61–64; "Ducati Aims for New Angle of Lean with Oracle," *Manufacturing and Logistics IT,* 2006, www.logisticsit.com/absolutenm/templates/article-critical.aspx?articleid=710&zoneid=31.

## Legal Issues Affecting Purchasing

**7.** Describe the legal implications of the purchasing function.

When a small business purchases goods for a supplier, ownership passes from seller to buyer. But when do title and risk of loss to the goods pass from one party to the other? The answer is important because any number of things could happen to the merchandise after it has been ordered but before it has been delivered. When small business owners order merchandise and supplies from their vendors, they should know when the ownership of the merchandise—and the risk associated with it—shifts from supplier to buyer.

## Title

Before the U.S. Uniform Commercial Code (UCC) was enacted, the concept of title—the right to ownership of goods—determined where responsibility for merchandise fell. Today, however, the UCC has replaced the concept of title with three other concepts: identification, risk of loss, and insurable interest.

### Identification

Identification is the first requirement that must be met. Before title can pass to the buyer, the goods must already be in existence and must be identifiable from all other similar goods. Specific goods already in existence are identified at the time the sales contract is made. For example, if Graphtech Inc. orders a Model 477-X plotter, the goods are identified at the time the contract (oral or written) is made. Generic goods are identified when they are marked, shipped, or otherwise designated as the goods in the contract. For example, an order of fuel oil may not be identified until it is loaded into a transfer truck for shipment.

### Risk of Loss

**Risk of loss** determines which party incurs the financial risk if the goods are damaged, destroyed, or lost before they are transferred. Risk of loss does *not* always pass with title. Three particular rules govern the passage of title and the transfer of risk or loss.

*Rule 1: Agreement.* A supplier and a business owner can agree to the terms under which title passes. Similarly, the two parties can agree (preferably in writing) to shift the risk of loss at any time during the transaction. In other words, any explicit agreement between buyer and seller determines when title and risk of loss will pass.

*Rule 2: F.O.B. Seller.* Under a sales contract designated F.O.B. (free on board) seller, title passes to the buyer as soon as the seller delivers the goods into the care of a carrier or shipper. Similarly, risk of loss is transferred to the small business owner when the supplier delivers the goods to the carrier. In addition, an **F.O.B. seller contract** (also a **shipment contract**) requires that the buyer pay all shipping and transportation costs. For example, a British manufacturer sells 100,000 capacitors to a buyer in Singapore with terms "F.O.B. U.K." Under this contract, the Singapore firm pays all shipping costs, and title and risk of loss pass from the manufacturer as soon as the carrier takes possession of the shipment. If the goods are lost or damaged in transit, the buyer suffers the loss. Of course, the buyer has legal recourse against the carrier. If a contract is silent on shipping terms, the courts assume that the contract is a shipment contract (F.O.B. seller), and the buyer bears the risk of loss while the goods are in transit.

*Rule 3: F.O.B. Buyer.* A sales contract designated F.O.B. buyer requires that the seller deliver the goods to the buyer's place of business (or to an agent of the buyer). Title and risk of loss are transferred to the small business when the goods are delivered there or to another designated destination. Also, an **F.O.B. buyer contract** (also called a **destination contract**) requires the seller to pay all shipping and transportation costs. In the example above, if the contract were "F.O.B. U.K.," the British manufacturer pays the cost of shipping the order, and title and risk of loss passes to the Singapore company when the shipment is delivered to its place of business. In this case losses due to goods lost or damaged in transit are borne by the seller.

### Insurable Interest

Insurable interest ensures the right of either party to the sales contract to obtain insurance to protect against lost, damaged, or destroyed merchandise as long as that party has "sufficient interest" in the goods. In general, if goods are identified, the buyer has an insurable interest in them. The seller has a sufficient interest as long as the seller retains the title to the goods. However, under certain circumstances both the buyer and the seller have insurable interests even after title has passed to the buyer.

### Receiving Merchandise

Once the merchandise is received, the buyer must verify its identity and condition. When the goods are delivered, the owner should check the number of cartons unloaded against the carrier's delivery receipt so that none are overlooked. It is also a good idea to examine the boxes for damage; if shipping cartons are damaged, the carrier should note the type and extent of the damage on the delivery receipt. The owner should open all cartons immediately after delivery and inspect the merchandise for quality and condition and also check it against the invoices to eliminate discrepancies. If merchandise is damaged or faulty, the buyer should contact the supplier immediately and follow up with a written report. The owner should never destroy or dispose of damaged or flawed merchandise unless the supplier specifically authorizes it. Proper control techniques in receiving merchandise prevent the small business owner from paying for suppliers' and shippers' mistakes.

### Selling on Consignment

Small business owners who lack the necessary capital to invest or are unwilling to assume the risk of investing in inventory may be able to sell goods on consignment. Selling on **consignment** means that the small business owner does not purchase the merchandise carried from the supplier (called the consignor); instead, the owner pays the consignor only for the merchandise actually sold. For providing the supplier with a market for his or her goods, the entrepreneur normally receives a portion of the revenue on each item sold. The business owner (called the consignee) may return any unsold merchandise to the supplier without obligation. Under a consignment agreement, title and risk of loss do not pass to the consignee unless the contract specifies such terms. In other words, the supplier (consignor) bears the financial costs of lost, damaged, or stolen merchandise. The small business owner who sells merchandise on a consignment basis realizes the following advantages.

- The owner does not have to invest money in these inventory items, but the merchandise on hand is available for sale.
- The owner does not make payment to the consignor until the item is sold.
- Because the consignment relationship is founded on the law of agency, the consignee never takes title to the merchandise and does not bear the risk of loss for the goods.
- The supplier normally plans and sets up displays for the merchandise and is responsible for maintaining them.

Before selling items on consignment, the small business owner and the supplier should create a workable written contract, which should include the following items:

- A list of items to be sold and their quantities
- Prices to be charged
- Location of merchandise in store
- Duration of contract
- Commission charged by the consignee
- Policy on defective items and rejects
- Schedule for payments to consignor
- Delivery terms and merchandise storage requirements
- Responsibility for items lost to pilferage and shoplifting
- Provision for terminating consignment contract

If managed properly, selling goods on consignment can be beneficial to both the consignor and the consignee.

# Chapter Review

1. Understand the components of a purchasing plan.
   - The purchasing function is vital to every small business's success because it influences a company's ability to sell quality goods and services at reasonable prices. Purchasing is the acquisition of needed materials, supplies, services, and equipment of the right quality, in the proper quantities, for reasonable prices, at the appropriate time, and from the right suppliers.

2. Explain the principles of total quality management (TQM) and Six Sigma and their impact on quality.
   - Under the total quality management (TQM) philosophy, companies define a quality product as one that conforms to predetermined standards that satisfy customers' demands. The goal is to get delivery and invoicing to installation and follow-up—and get it all right the first time.
   - To implement TQM successfully, a small business owner must rely on 10 fundamental principles: Shift from a management-driven culture to a participative, team-based one; modify the reward system to encourage teamwork and innovation; train workers constantly to give them the tools they need to produce quality products and to upgrade the company's knowledge base; train employees to measure quality with the tools of statistical process control (SPC); use Pareto's Law to focus TQM efforts; share information with everyone in the organization; focus quality improvements on astonishing the customer; don't rely on inspection to produce quality products and services; avoid using TQM to place blame on those who make mistakes; and strive for continuous improvement in processes as well as in products and services.
   - Like TQM, Six Sigma relies on quantitative tools to improve quality. At its core is the DMAIC process: Define the quality problem, Measure current process performance to establish a baseline, Analyze the process and identify potential root causes of the problem, Improve the system by implementing solutions to remove the root causes, and Control the new process by establishing standards of measurement and procedure.

3. Conduct economic order quantity (EOQ) analysis to determine the proper level of inventory.
   - A major goal of the small business is to generate adequate inventory turnover by purchasing proper quantities of merchandise. A useful device for computing the proper quantity is economic order quantity (EOQ) analysis, which yields the ideal order quantity: the amount that minimizes total inventory costs. Total inventory costs consist of the cost of the units, holding (carrying) costs, and ordering (setup) costs. The EOQ balances the costs of ordering and of carrying merchandise to yield minimum total inventory cost.

4. Differentiate among the three types of purchase discounts vendors offer.
   - Trade discounts are established on a graduated scale and depend on a small firm's position in the channel of distribution.
   - Quantity discounts are designed to encourage businesses to order large quantities of merchandise and supplies.
   - Cash discounts are offered to customers as an incentive to pay for merchandise promptly.

5. Calculate a company's reorder point.
   - There is a time gap between the placing of an order and actual receipt of the goods. The reorder point model tells the owner when to place an order to replenish the company's inventory.

6. Develop a vendor rating scale.
   - Creating a vendor analysis model involves four steps: Determine the important criteria (i.e., price, quality, prompt delivery, service, etc.); assign a weight to each criterion to reflect its relative importance; develop a grading scale for each criterion; and compute a weighted score for each vendor.

7. Describe the legal implications of the purchasing function.
   - Important legal issues for purchasing goods involve title, or ownership of the goods; identification of the goods, risk of loss and when it shifts from seller to buyer; and insurable interests in the goods. Buyer and seller can have an insurable interest in the same goods at the same time.

## Discussion Questions

1. What is purchasing? Why is it important for the small business owner to develop a purchasing plan?
2. What is TQM? How can it help small business owners achieve the quality goods and services they require?
3. One top manager claims that to implement total quality management successfully, "You have to change your company culture as much as your processes." Do you agree? Explain.
4. Visit the Web site of the National Institute of Standards and Technology (www.quality.nist.gov/), the organization that grants the Malcolm Baldrige National Quality Award, the highest quality award in the United States. Research one of the companies that received the Baldrige Award and prepare a one-page summary of its quality initiative and the results that it produced.
5. List and briefly describe the three components of total inventory costs.
6. What is the economic order quantity? How does it minimize total inventory costs?

7. Should a small business owner always purchase the products with the lowest prices? Why or why not?
8. Briefly outline the three types of purchase discounts. Under what circumstances is each the best choice?
9. What is lead time? Outline the procedure for determining a product's reorder point.
10. Explain how an entrepreneur launching a company could locate suppliers and vendors.
11. What factors are commonly used to evaluate suppliers?
12. Explain the procedure for developing a vendor rating scale.
13. Explain briefly the three concepts that have replaced the concept of title. When do title and risk of loss shift under an FOB seller contract? An FOB buyer contract?
14. What should a small business owner do when merchandise is received?
15. Explain how a small business would sell goods on consignment. What should be included in a consignment contract?

# Business PlanPro

Entrepreneurs can improve the quality of the products and services they offer, control the cost of purchasing or producing those products and services, and enhance the level of service that they provide their customers through effective management of supply chains. The issues of purchasing, quality management, and vendor analysis cut across all of the functions of an organization and, in many cases, play a significant role in determining a company's ability to compete successfully. If your business is product-based, supply chain management issues will represent a significant part of your business and your business plan. Supply chain management factors are an important part of a product-based business plan.

## On the Web

The Companion Website at www.prenhall.com/scarborough for Chapter 17 offers additional information in the areas of supply chain management including purchasing, quality management, and vendor analysis. Review these sites and determine whether these sources may be useful to you as you build your plan.

## In the Software

Confirm that you have selected the "product" type of plan outline within Business PlanPro. You can do this by clicking on the "Plan Setup" icon and looking at the "Type of business" comments below. It will state, "I sell products" or "I sell services," depending on your choice. If you do sell products, select the proper choice to indicate whether you manufacture those products or purchase and resell them. The outline within Business PlanPro will automatically adjust to your choice. Complete the information in the "Product" section of your business plan. Make sure you also review your financial information regarding product and inventory expenses.

## Building Your Business Plan

Once you have completed the "Product" section, step back and review your plan. By now, you have completed most of the sections in your plan, and it should tell a cohesive story about your business.

# Managing Inventory

If a product isn't selling, I want to get it out of there because it's taking up space that can be devoted to another part of my line that moves. Besides, having a product languish on the shelves doesn't do much for our image.

—Norman Melnick, chairman of Pentech International

Those you trust the most can steal the most.

—Lawrence Lief

## Learning Objectives

**Upon completion of this chapter, you will be able to:**

1 Explain the various inventory control systems and the advantages and disadvantages of each.

2 Describe how just-in-time (JIT) and JIT II inventory control techniques work.

3 Describe methods for reducing losses from slow-moving inventory.

4 Discuss employee theft and shoplifting and how to prevent them.

S upply chain management and inventory control are closely linked. The previous chapter focused on managing a company's supply chain—purchasing the correct materials of the proper quality, in the correct quantity, at the best price, from the best vendors. This chapter will continue that process by discussing various inventory control methods, how to move "slow" inventory items, and how to protect inventory from theft. An entrepreneur's goal is to maximize the value of a company's inventory while reducing both the cost and the risks of owning inventory. The issue is significant; the largest expenditure for many small businesses is in inventory: raw materials, work-in-process, or finished goods.

Business owners now understand the dangers of carrying excess inventory. For years, businesses maintained high levels of inventory so that the manufacturing or sales process ran smoothly. Now managers realize that inventory simply masks other problems that a company may have such as poor quality, sloppy supply chain management, improper pricing, inadequate marketing, inefficient layout, low productivity, and others. Reducing the amount of inventory a company carries exposes these otherwise hidden problems. Only then can managers and employees solve them.

Another reason that business owners are lowering inventory levels is the high cost of carrying excess inventory. Carrying costs add up quickly, the majority of it in the form of taxes, depreciation, insurance, and obsolescence.[1] Holding inventory requires renting or purchasing additional warehouse space, increasing labor costs, boosting borrowing, and tying up a company's valuable cash unnecessarily. Companies with lean inventory levels lower their costs of operation, and those savings go straight to the bottom line. The potential payoff for managing inventory efficiently is huge; companies that switch to lean inventory systems can increase their profitability 20 to 50 percent.

The information age has made techniques such as just-in-time (JIT) inventory systems available to even the smallest of businesses. Electronic networks that connect a company seamlessly with its suppliers have dramatically reduced the time for needed parts or material to arrive and the need to hold inventory. At the other end of the pipeline, a company's customers expect to have what they need when they need it. In today's competitive market, few customers will wait beyond a reasonable time for items they want. Managing inventory properly requires business owners to master an intricate balancing act, keeping enough inventory on hand to meet customers' expectations but maintaining inventory levels low enough to avoid incurring excessive costs.

Managing inventory effectively requires an entrepreneur to implement the following seven interrelated steps:

1. ***Develop an accurate sales forecast.*** The proper inventory level for each item is directly related to the demand for that item. A business cannot sell merchandise that it does not have, and conversely, an entrepreneur does not want to stock inventory that customers will not buy.

**ENTREPRENEURIAL**
**Profile**

*DreamWorks Animation and* Shrek 2

After the success of its hit movie *Shrek 2* in theaters, DreamWorks Animation anticipated brisk sales when it released the DVD, which has become the most profitable segment of the film business. In fact, DVDs now account for 60 percent of a typical movie's revenues. DreamWorks' sales forecast was inaccurate, however, in part because the company had missed a major shift in the DVD market. Studios now unleash a flood of new DVDs every week, which means that the sales cycle for a new title has shrunk dramatically. DreamWorks managers expected sales to peak about one month after they released *Shrek 2*; instead, the title generated more than 50 percent of its total sales in the first week and began tapering off quickly, leaving the studio with millions of unsold copies of the movie.[2]

2. ***Develop a plan to make inventory available when and where customers want it.*** Inventory will not sell if customers have a difficult time finding it. If a company is constantly running out of items customers expect to find, its customer base will dwindle over time as shoppers look elsewhere for those items. An important component of superior customer service is making sure adequate quantities of items are

available when customers want them. Two ways of measuring this aspect of customer service include calculating the percentage of customer orders that a company ships on time and the percentage of the sales volume of orders that it ships on time. Tracking these numbers over time gives business owners sound feedback on how well they are managing their inventory levels from the customer's perspective.

3. ***Build relationships with your most critical suppliers to ensure that you can get the merchandise you need when you need it.*** Business owners must keep suppliers and vendors aware of how their merchandise is selling and communicate their needs to them. Vendors and suppliers can be an entrepreneur's greatest allies in managing inventory. Increasingly, the word that describes the relationship between world-class companies and their suppliers is *partnership*.

4. ***Set realistic inventory turnover objectives.*** Keeping in touch with their customers' likes and dislikes and monitoring their inventory enable owners to estimate the most likely buying patterns for different types of merchandise. As we learned in Chapter 7, "Creating a Solid Financial Plan," one of the factors that has the greatest impact on a company's sales, cash flow, and ultimate success is its inventory turnover ratio.

5. ***Compute the actual cost of carrying inventory.*** Many business owners do not realize how expensive carrying inventory actually is. Without an accurate cost of carrying inventory, it is impossible to determine an optimal inventory level. Carrying costs include items such as interest on borrowed money, insurance expenses associated with the inventory, inventory-related personnel expenses, obsolescence, and others. When new product introductions make existing products obsolete, companies must hold inventory to an absolute minimum. For instance, in the computer industry, the onrush of new technology causes the value of a personal computer held in inventory to decline one percent each week! This gives computer makers big incentives to keep their inventories as lean as possible.

6. ***Use the most timely and accurate information system the business can afford to provide the facts and figures necessary to make critical inventory decisions.*** Computers and modern point-of-sale terminals that are linked to a company's inventory records enable business owners to know exactly which items are selling and which ones are not. The owner of a chain of baby products stores uses a computer network to link all of his stores to the computer at central headquarters. Every night, after the stores close, the point-of-sale terminals in each store download the day's sales to the central computer, which compiles an extensive sales and inventory report. When he walks into his office every morning, the owner reviews the report and can tell exactly which items are moving fastest, which are moving slowest, and which are not selling at all. He credits the system with the company's above-average inventory turnover ratio and much of his chain's success.

7. ***Teach employees how inventory control systems work so that they can contribute to managing the firm's inventory on a daily basis.*** All too often, the employees on the floor have no idea of how the various information systems and inventory control techniques operate or interact with one another. Consequently, the people closest to the inventory contribute little to controlling it. Well-trained employees armed with information can be one of an entrepreneur's greatest weapons in the battle to control inventory.

The goal is to find and maintain the proper balance between the cost of holding inventory and the requirements to have merchandise on hand when customers demand it. Either extreme can be costly. If entrepreneurs focus solely on minimizing cost, they will undoubtedly incur stockouts, lost sales, and customer ill will because they cannot satisfy their customers' needs. For instance, researchers studying inventory control systems at Bulgari, a jewelry manufacturer headquartered in Rome, Italy, discovered that stockouts of just one popular item had lowered the company's profits by five percent of sales.[3] At the other extreme, entrepreneurs who attempt to hold enough inventory to meet every peak customer demand will find that high inventory costs have diminished their chances of remaining profitable. Walking this inventory tightrope is never easy, but the following inventory control systems can help business owners strike a reasonable balance between the two extremes.

# Inventory Control Systems

*1.* Explain the various inventory control systems and the advantages and disadvantages of each.

Regardless of the type of inventory control system business owners choose, they must recognize the importance of **Pareto's Law** (or the **80/20 rule**), which holds that about 80 percent of the value of a company's sales revenue is generated by 20 percent of the items in its inventory. Sometimes a company's best selling items are its highest-priced items, but more often they are low-priced items that sell in high volume. Because most sales are generated by a small percentage of items, entrepreneurs should focus the majority of their inventory control efforts on this 20 percent. Observing this simple principle ensures that entrepreneurs will spend time controlling only the most productive—and, therefore, most valuable—inventory items. With this technique in mind, we now examine three basic types of inventory control systems: perpetual, visual, and partial.

## Perpetual Inventory Systems

**Perpetual inventory systems** are designed to maintain a running count of the items in inventory. Although a number of different perpetual inventory systems exist, they all have a common element: They keep a continuous tally of each item added to or subtracted from the firm's stock of merchandise. A typical system uses a perpetual inventory sheet that includes fundamental product information such as the item's name, stock number, description, economic order quantity (EOQ), and reorder point.

These perpetual inventory sheets are usually placed next to the merchandise in the warehouse or storage facility. Whenever a shipment is received from a vendor, the quantity is entered in the receipt column and added to the total. When the item is sold and taken from inventory, it is simply deducted from the total. As long as this procedure is followed consistently, an entrepreneur can determine quickly the number of each product on hand. Bar-coding the inventory allows the process to be done by handheld scanners that are tied directly to a computerized inventory control system. Automating the perpetual inventory system makes it more accurate and reliable, and when inventory levels drop to the reorder trigger-point, the system generates purchase orders to replenish the supply.

Although consistent use of the system yields accurate inventory counts at any moment, sporadic use creates problems. If managers or employees take items out of stock or place them in inventory without recording them, the perpetual inventory sheet will yield incorrect totals and can foul up the entire inventory control system. Another disadvantage of this system is the cost of maintaining it. If not computerized, keeping perpetual inventory records for a large number of items and ensuring the accuracy of the system can be excessively expensive. Therefore, these systems are used most frequently and most successfully in controlling expensive items that require strict monitoring. Management must watch these items closely and ensure that inventory records are accurate.

Advances in computerized cash registers have overcome many of the disadvantages of using the basic perpetual inventory system. Small businesses now are able to afford computerized **point of sale (POS) systems** that perform all of the functions of a traditional cash register and maintain an up-to-the minute inventory count. Although POS systems are not new (major retailers have been using them for more than 30 years), their affordable prices are. Not so long ago, most systems required mini- or mainframe computers and cost $20,000 or more. Today, small business owners can set up POS systems on personal computers for less than $1,000. Combining a POS system with Universal Product Code (bar code) labels and high-speed scanners gives a small business a state-of-the-art checkout system that feeds vital information into its inventory control system. These systems rely on an inventory database; as items are rung up on the register, product information is recorded and inventory balances are adjusted. Using the system, business owners can tell how quickly each item is selling and how many items are in stock at any time. In addition, their inventory records are more accurate and are always current. They also can generate instantly a variety of reports to aid in making purchasing decisions. The system can be programmed to alert owners when the supply of a particular item drops below a predetermined reorder point or even to print automatically a purchase order for the EOQ indicated. Finally, modern POS systems allow business owners to generate an array of inventory reports instantly. Entrepreneurs can slice and dice data in a multitude of ways, which allows them to determine which items are selling the fastest and which are moving the slowest. Timely reports such as these give entrepreneurs the ability to make sound decisions about scheduling advertising, running special promotions, offering discounts, and arranging store displays. Computerized POS systems also make it possible for the owner to use a basic perpetual inventory system for a large number of items, a task that, if performed manually, would be virtually impossible.

**MANUAL PERPETUAL INVENTORY CONTROL SYSTEMS.** Small companies that lack computerized perpetual inventory systems often use one of the following methods: the sales ticket method, the sales stub method, and the floor sample needed.

- *The sales ticket method.* Most small businesses use sales tickets to summarize individual customers' transactions. These tickets serve two major purposes: They provide the customer with a sales receipt for the merchandise purchased, and they provide the owner with a daily record of the number of specific inventory items sold. The **sales ticket method** operates by gathering all the sales tickets at the end of each day and transcribing the data onto the appropriate perpetual inventory sheet. By posting inventory deductions to the perpetual inventory system from sales tickets, entrepreneurs can monitor sales patterns and keep close control on inventory. The primary disadvantage of using such a system is the time required to make it function properly. Most managers find it difficult to squeeze in the time needed to post sales tickets to the perpetual inventory system.

- *The sales stub method.* The principle behind the **sales stub method** of inventory control is the same as the sales ticket method, but its mechanics are slightly different. Retail stores often attach a ticket with two or more parts containing relevant product information to each inventory item in stock. When employees sell an item, they remove a portion of the stub and place it in a container. At the end of the day, someone posts the inventory deductions recorded by the stubs to the proper perpetual inventory sheets.

- *The floor sample method.* The **floor sample method** of controlling inventory is commonly used by businesses selling big-ticket items with high unit cost such as appliances and furniture. In many cases, these items are somewhat bulky and are difficult to display in large numbers. For example, the owner of a small furniture store might receive a shipment of 15 roll-top desks in a particular style. A simple technique for maintaining control of these items is to attach a small pad to the display desk with sheets numbered in descending order from 15 to 1. Whenever an employee sells a roll-top desk, he removes a sheet from the pad. As long as the system is followed consistently, the owner is able to determine accurate inventory levels with a quick pass around the sales floor. When the supply of a particular item dwindles, the owner simply calls the vendor to replenish the inventory. The procedure is simple and serves its purpose.

## Visual Inventory Control Systems

The most common method of controlling inventory in a small business is the **visual control system**, in which managers simply conduct periodic visual inspections to determine the quantity of various items they should order. As mentioned earlier, manual perpetual inventory systems can be excessively costly and time-consuming. These systems are impractical when the business stocks a large number of low-value items with low sales volumes. Therefore, many owners rely on the simplest, quickest inventory control method: the visual system. Unfortunately, this method is also the least effective for ensuring accuracy and reliability. Oversights of key items often lead to stockouts and resulting lost sales. The biggest disadvantage of the visual control system is its inability to detect and to foresee shortages of inventory items.

In general, a visual inventory control system works best in firms in which daily sales are relatively consistent, the entrepreneur is closely involved with the inventory, the variety of merchandise is small, and items can be obtained quickly from vendors. For example, small firms dealing in perishable goods use visual control systems very successfully, and rarely rely on analytical inventory control tools. For these firms, shortages are not likely to occur under a visual system; when they do occur, they are not likely to create major problems. Entrepreneurs who rely on visual systems must be alert to shifts in customer buying patterns that alter required inventory levels.

## Partial Inventory Control Systems

For small business owners with limited time and money, the most viable option for inventory management is a partial inventory control system. These systems rely on the validity of Pareto's Law (80/20 rule). For example, if a small business carries 5,000 different items in stock, roughly 1,000 of them account for about 80 percent of the firm's sales volume. Experienced business owners focus their inventory control efforts on those 1,000 items. Unfortunately, many owners seek to maintain tight control over the remaining 4,000 items, a frustrating and wasteful practice. Entrepreneur John Payne says that Pareto's Law applied to the consumer electronics business that he ran for years; about 75 percent of his company's sales came from just 20 percent of the items he carried in inventory.[4] Smart entrepreneurs design their inventory control systems with this principle in mind. One of the most popular partial inventory control systems is the ABC system.

**THE ABC METHOD OF INVENTORY CONTROL.** Too many managers attempt to apply perpetual inventory control systems universally when a partial control system would be much more practical. Partial inventory systems minimize the expense involved in analyzing, processing, and maintaining records, a substantial cost of any inventory control system. The ABC method is one such approach, focusing control efforts on that small percentage of items that accounts for the majority of the firm's sales. The typical **ABC system** divides a firm's inventory into three major categories:

A *items* account for a high dollar usage volume.

B *items* account for a moderate dollar usage volume.

C *items* account for low dollar usage volume.

The **dollar usage volume** of an item measures the relative importance of that item in a company's inventory. Note that value is *not* necessarily synonymous with high unit cost. In some instances, a high-cost item that generates only a small sales volume can be classified as an A item. More frequently, however, A items are those that are low to moderate in cost and high volume.

The initial step in establishing an ABC classification system is to compute the annual dollar usage volume for each product (or product category). **Annual dollar usage volume** is simply the cost per unit of an item multiplied by the annual quantity used. For instance, the owner of a stereo shop may find that she sold 190 pairs of a popular brand of speakers during the previous year. If the speakers cost her $75 per unit, their annual dollar usage volume would be as follows:

$$190 \times \$75 = \$14,250$$

The next step is to arrange the products in descending order on the basis of the computed annual dollar usage volume. Once so arranged, they can be divided into appropriate classes by applying the following rule:

A *items*: roughly the top 15 percent of the items listed

B *items*: roughly the next 35 percent

C *items:* roughly the remaining 50 percent

For example, Florentina's small retail shop is interested in establishing an ABC inventory control system to lower losses from stockouts, theft, or other hazards. Florentina has computed the annual dollar usage volume for the store's merchandise inventory as shown in Table 18.1. (For simplicity, we show only 12 inventory items.)

**TABLE 18.1 Calculating Annual Dollar Usage Volume and an ABC Inventory Analysis for Florentina's**

| Item | Annual Dollar Usage Volume | % of Annual Dollar Usage |
|---|---|---|
| Paragon | $374,100 | 42.00% |
| Excelsior | 294,805 | 33.10 |
| Avery | 68,580 | 7.70 |
| Bardeen | 54,330 | 6.10 |
| Berkeley | 27,610 | 3.10 |
| Tara | 24,940 | 2.80 |
| Cattell | 11,578 | 1.30 |
| Faraday | 9,797 | 1.10 |
| Humboldt | 8,016 | 0.90 |
| Mandel | 7,125 | 0.08 |
| Sabot | 5,344 | 0.06 |
| Wister | 4,453 | 0.05 |
| **Total** | **$890,678** | 100.00 |

| Classification | Items | Annual Dollar Usage | % of Total |
|---|---|---|---|
| A | Paragon, Excelsior | $668,905 | 75.1 |
| B | Avery, Bardeen, Berkeley, Tara | 175,460 | 19.7 |
| C | Cattell, Faraday, Humboldt Mandel, Sabot, Wister | 46,313 | 5.2 |
| **Total** | | **$890,678** | 100.00 |

The ABC inventory control method divides the firm's inventory items into three classes depending on the items' value. Figure 18.1 graphically portrays the segmentation of the items listed in Table 18.1.

The purpose of classifying items according to their annual dollar usage volume is to establish the proper degree of control over each item held in inventory. Clearly, it is wasteful and inefficient to exercise the same level of control over C items and A items. Items in the A classification should be controlled under a perpetual inventory system with as much detail as necessary. Analytical tools and frequent counts may be required to ensure accuracy, but the extra cost of tight control for these valuable items is usually justified. Managers should not retain a large supply of reserve or safety stock because doing so ties up excessive amounts of money in inventory, but they must monitor the stock closely to avoid stockouts and the lost sales that result.

Control of B items should rely more on periodic control systems and basic analytical tools such as EOQ and reorder point analysis (discussed in Chapter 17, "Supply Chain Management"). Managers can maintain moderate levels of safety stock for these items to guard against shortages and can afford monthly or even bimonthly merchandise inspections. Because B items are not as valuable to the business as A items, less rigorous control systems are required.

C items typically constitute a minor proportion of the small firm's inventory value and, as a result, require the least effort and expense to control. These items are usually large in number and small in total value. The most practical way to control them is to use uncomplicated records and procedures. Large levels of safety stock for these items are acceptable because the cost of carrying them is usually minimal. Substantial order sizes often enable the business to take advantage of quantity discounts without having to place frequent orders. The cost involved in using detailed record keeping and inventory control procedures greatly outweighs the advantages gleaned from strict control of C items.

One practical technique for maintaining control over C items simply is the **two-bin system**, which keeps two separate bins full of material. The first bin is used to fill customer orders, and the second bin is filled with enough safety stock to meet customer demand during the lead time. When the first bin is empty, the owner places an order with the vendor

**FIGURE 18.1 ABC Inventory Control**

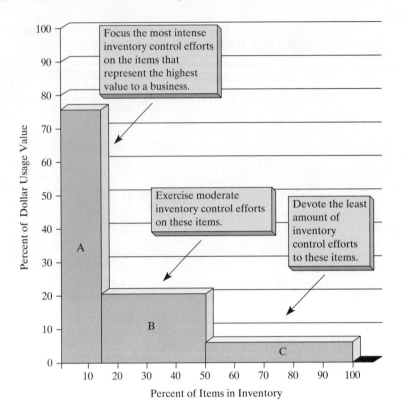

large enough to refill both bins. During the lead-time for the order, the manager uses the safety stock in the second bin to fill customer demand.

When storage space or the type of item makes a two-bin system impractical, an entrepreneur can use a **tag system**. Based on the same principles as the two-bin system, which is suitable for many manufacturers, the tag system applies to most retail, wholesale, and service firms. Instead of placing enough inventory to meet customer demand during lead time into a separate bin, the owner marks this inventory level with a brightly colored tag. When the supply is drawn down to the tagged level, the owner reorders the merchandise. Figure 18.2 illustrates the two-bin and tag systems of controlling C items.

In summary, business owners minimize total inventory costs when they spend time and effort controlling items that represent the greatest inventory value. Some inventory items require strict, detailed control techniques; other items simply do not justify the additional cost of tight controls. Because of its practicality, the ABC inventory system is commonly used in industry. In addition, the technique is easily computerized, speeding up the analysis and lowering its cost. Table 18.2 summarizes the use of the ABC control system.

## Physical Inventory Count

Regardless of the type of inventory control system used, every small business owner must conduct a periodic physical inventory count. Even when a company uses a perpetual inventory system, the owner still must count the actual number of items on hand because errors will occur. A physical inventory count allows owners to reconcile the actual amount of inventory in stock with the amount reported through the inventory control system. These counts give managers a fresh start when determining the actual number of items on hand and enable them to evaluate the effectiveness and the accuracy of their inventory control systems.

The typical method of taking inventory involves two employees; one calls out the relevant information for each inventory item, and the other records the count on a tally sheet. There are two basic methods of conducting a physical inventory count. One alternative is to take inventory at regular intervals. Many businesses take inventory at the end of the year. In an attempt to minimize counting, many managers run special year-end inventory reduction sales. This **periodic count** generates the most accurate measurement of inventory. The other method of taking inventory, called **cycle counting**, involves counting a number of

**FIGURE 18.2 The Two Bin and Tag Systems of Inventory Control**

The Two-Bin System

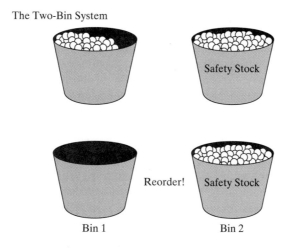

Bin 1     Reorder!     Bin 2

The Tag System

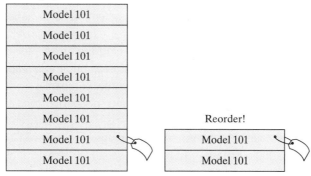

**TABLE 18.2 ABC Inventory Control Features**

| Feature | A Items | B Items | C Items |
|---|---|---|---|
| **Level of control** | Monitor closely and maintain tight control. | Maintain moderate control. | Maintain loose control. |
| **Reorder point** | Based on forecasted requirements. | Based on EOQ calculations and past experience. | When level gets low, reorder. |
| **Record keeping** | Keep detailed records of receipts and disbursements. | Use periodic inspections and control procedures. | No records required. |
| **Safety stock** | Keep low levels of safety stock. | Keep moderate levels of safety stock. | Keep high levels of safety stock. |
| **Inspection frequency** | Monitor schedule changes frequently. | Check on changes in requirements periodically. | Make few checks on requirements. |

items on a continuous cycle. Instead of waiting until year-end to tally the entire inventory of items, an entrepreneur counts a few types of items each day or each week and checks the numbers against the inventory control system. Performing a series of "mini-counts" each day or each week allows for continuous correction of mistakes in inventory control systems and detects inventory problems faster than an annual count does.

Once again, technology can make the job of taking inventory much easier for small business owners. Web-based supply chain management and electronic data interchange (EDI) systems enable business owners to track their inventories and to place orders with vendors quickly and with few errors by linking them to their vendors electronically. These systems often rely on handheld computer terminals equipped with a scanning wand. An employee runs the wand across a bar-code label on the shelf that identifies the inventory item; then the employee counts the items on the shelf and enters that number using the number pad on the terminal. Then, by linking the handheld terminal to a personal computer, the employee can download the physical inventory count into the company's inventory control software in seconds.

In the past, suppliers simply manufactured a product, shipped it, and then sent the customer an invoice. To place an order, employees or managers periodically would estimate how much of a particular item they would need and when they would need it. Today, however, in many EDI or Web-based supply chain management systems, the vendor is tied directly into a company's POS (point-of-sale) system, monitoring it constantly; when the company's supply of a particular item drops to a preset level, the vendor automatically sends a shipment to replenish its stock to an established level. Information that once traveled by mail (or was never shared at all) such as shipping information, invoices, inventory balances, and sales now travel instantly between businesses and their suppliers. The result is a much more efficient system of purchasing, distribution, and inventory control.

*Michael Fidenza and Ideal Supply Company*

When one of Ideal Supply Company's top customers asked the small supplier of industrial pipes and valves to set up an EDI system, general manager Michael Fidenza decided that doing so would give his company an edge over its rivals. "Our industry is old-fashioned," says Fidenza. "We tend to lag behind the times." Ideal Supply not only forged an even closer relationship with its big customer, but it also reaped benefits from its suppliers. Because Ideal Supply was one of the few companies in the industry with EDI capability, Fidenza was able to negotiate higher discounts from its suppliers because of increased efficiencies in the purchasing process. "One of our vendors offered us an extra 5 percent in discounts," he says. "Another plugs in an extra $10,000 worth of product with every $50,000 purchase—just because we're EDI." Ideal Supply has earned an impressive return on its original investment of $5,000 for EDI hardware and software. Today, 80 percent of the company's purchases and 15 percent of its sales are processed through its EDI system.[5]

### Radio Frequency Identification Tags (RFID)

Inventory control systems that use bar codes to track the movement of inventory through the supply chain have been around for years. Increasingly, businesses are replacing their bar code systems with more flexible systems based on **radio frequency identification (RFID)** tags that are attached to individual items or to shipments and transmit data to a company's inventory management system. Each tag, which is about the size of a grain of sand, contains a tiny microchip that stores a unique electronic product code (EPC) and a tiny antenna. Because the tags use short-range radio frequencies, they can transmit information under almost any condition, avoiding the line-of-sight restrictions bar code systems experience. Once activated, the tags perform like talking bar codes and enable business owners to identify, count, and track the inventory items to which they are attached, providing them with highly accurate, real-time information constantly. When a shipment arrives at a warehouse or retail store, the RFID tags signal an inventory system reader, an object about the size of a coin that records the identity, the quantity, and characteristics of each item now in stock. The reader relays the information to a central inventory control system so that business owners can have access to all of this information online. Some stores have installed "smart" shelves equipped with readers that detect the identity and quantity of the items placed on them. When a customer makes a purchase, the smart shelf sends a message to the inventory control system, telling it to reduce the number on hand by the number of items the customer buys. In essence, RFID technology allows business owners to locate and track an item at any point in the supply chain—from the raw material stage to the finished product.

Other retailers use RFID technology to make inventory counts a breeze. Employees simply walk the aisles of the store holding a special reader that scans the RFID tags of the items on store shelves. At some stores, fully integrated RFID systems allow cashiers to ring up customers' purchases by scanning the contents of an entire shopping cart in just seconds, minimizing the time that customers have to stand in checkout lines. The cost of RFID tags continues to fall, from $1 per tag in 2000 to less than five cents today. As costs decline further and the reliability of the tags improve, more businesses will be adopting the technology to improve the degree of control they have over their inventory.

*Reno*

Reno, a shoe retailer based in Germany that operates more than 700 stores in 15 countries, recently began installing wafer-thin RFID tags in its shoes. Reno has been using RFID technology for years to track shipments from its factories to its stores, but the new application is designed to combat employee theft and shoplifting.[6]

One winery attaches RFID tags equipped with sensors to the bottles of wine it ships to restaurants and retail stores. Not only can the winery track each wine bottle on the Internet during shipment, but it also can detect whether the temperature of those bottles reaches a point that could compromise their quality by sitting, for example, on a hot loading dock.[7] The impact of RFID technology, which actually dates back to World War II, on inventory control is enormous. "This is an innovative technology similar to the Internet," says Mark Roberti, editor of *RFID Journal*. "You can now make any object smart."[8] International consulting firm McKinsey & Company estimates that once in use, RFID technology has the ability to increase companies' revenues by as much as 6 percent by reducing the time and energy that staff spend finding merchandise.[9]

## Just-In-Time Inventory Control Techniques

### Just-in-Time Techniques

*2.* Describe how just-in-time (JIT) and JIT II inventory control techniques work.

Many businesses have turned to a popular inventory control technique called **just-in-time (JIT)** to reduce costly inventories and turn around their financial fortunes. Until recently these companies had accepted the following long-standing principles of manufacturing: Long production runs of standard items are ideal; machines should be up and running as much as possible; machines must produce a large number of items to justify long setup times and high costs; similar processes should be consolidated into single departments; tasks should be highly specialized and simplified; and inventories (raw materials, work-in-process, and finished goods) should be large enough to avoid emergencies such as supply interruptions, strikes, and breakdowns.

The just-in-time philosophy, however, views excess inventory as a blanket that masks problems and as a source of unnecessary costs that inhibit a firm's competitive position. Under a JIT system, materials and inventory flow smoothly through the production process without stopping. They arrive at the appropriate location just in time instead of becoming part of a costly inventory stockpile. Just-in-time is a philosophy that seeks to improve a company's efficiency. One key measure of efficiency is the level of inventory on hand; the lower the level of inventory, the more efficient is the production system.

The heart of the JIT philosophy is eliminating waste in whatever form it may take—time wasted moving work in process from one part of a factory to another, money wasted when employees must scrap or rework an item because of poor quality, cash tied up unnecessarily in excess inventory because of a poorly designed process, and many others. Figure 18.3 illustrates Shigeo Shingo's Eight Wastes that just-in-time, TQM, Six Sigma, and other continuous improvement strategies are designed to eliminate.

Companies using JIT successfully embrace a broader philosophy of continuous improvement ("*kaizen*"), which was discussed in the previous chapter. These companies encourage employees to find ways to improve processes by simplifying them, making them more efficient, and redesigning them to make them more flexible. A cornerstone of the JIT philosophy is making waste in a company visible. The idea is that hidden waste is easy to ignore; visible waste gives everyone an incentive to eliminate it. Managers at a small company that manufactures fabrics for use in the paper making industry set off an area in the middle of the production floor and put all of the wasted fabrics there on display. The not-so-subtle message was "help us find ways to reduce this waste." Within a matter of months,

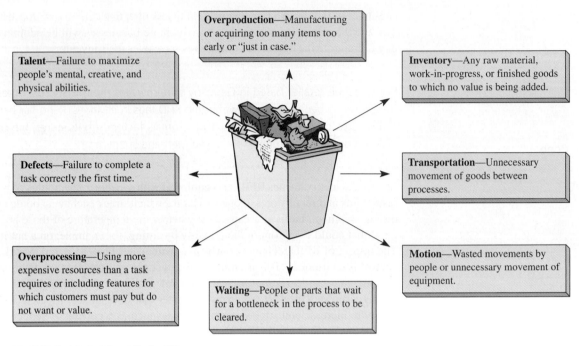

**FIGURE 18.3 The Eight Wastes**

with the help of suggestions from both individuals and teams of employees, the pile of waste shrank dramatically.

In the past, only large companies could reap the benefits of computerized JIT and inventory control software, but now a proliferation of inexpensive programs designed for PCs gives small companies that ability. The most effective business owners know that what is required is not simply the technology but the critical strategic alliances with suppliers who are themselves technologically sophisticated enough to interact on a real-time basis to deliver what is needed when it is needed. The ultimate goal is to drive excess inventory to as close to zero as possible.

**ENTREPRENEURIAL Profile**

*Topshop*

For British clothing retailer Topshop, a lean, just-in-time inventory control system is a key part of the company's strategy. Topshop has found a unique niche tucked between discount stores that sell cheap "fast fashion" and luxury retailers that sell pricey haute couture. Its most expensive items top out around $200, and its cutting-edge fashions have made its stores popular with a broad demographic base ranging from teens to women in their forties looking for the latest fashions. The company was struggling in the 1990s, when managers decided to stop competing on price and to "make a stand that we would become *the* fashion authority." To implement the new strategy of becoming a fashion destination, Topshop began working with its suppliers to speed deliveries of small batches of items to its stores, particularly its 90,000-square-foot flagship London store, which company buyers and designers see as a fashion laboratory. Three shipments of goods arrive each day at the London store, which means that merchandise turns over so quickly that many customers come back every week to see what is new. The London store allows managers to determine which items will sell best, and Topshop's supply chain is set up so that shipments arrive at its other outlets within two weeks, compared to six or eight weeks at most clothing retailers. With Topshop's lean inventory, customers know that if they find an item that they like, they had better purchase it then. The result is that the flagship London store sees an average of 30,000 customers a day, half of whom make a purchase. Topshop says that it sells 30 pairs of knickers per minute, 6,000 pairs of jeans per day, and 35,000 pairs of shoes per week. "It's mad," says a brand director. "The stock goes straight in and out the door."[10]

By managing inventory carefully, Jane Shepherdson turned Topshop into one of the hottest clothing retailers in the world.

Advocates claim that when JIT is successfully implemented, companies experience five positive results:

1. Lower investment in inventory
2. Reduced inventory carrying and handling costs
3. Reduced cost from obsolescence of inventory
4. Lower investment in space for inventories and production
5. Reduced total manufacturing costs from improved coordination among departments to operate at lower inventory levels

Despite the many benefits JIT systems offer, they do carry risks. Any disruption in a company's supply chain, even for inexpensive, commonplace items, can cause the entire operation to come to a halt. Recently, nearly 70 percent of Japan's automobile production was paralyzed for several days after an earthquake damaged the Riken Corporation, which supplies piston rings (which costs only $1.50 each) for all major Japanese automakers. Japanese carmakers rely heavily on the just-in-time philosophy, and they keep their inventories of parts extremely lean. Because piston rings are customized for each car model, automakers could not switch to alternate suppliers, and the interruption in the supply chain forced assembly plants to shut down temporarily.[11]

For JIT systems to be most productive, entrepreneurs must consider the human component of the equation as well. Two elements are essential:

1. *Mutual trust and teamwork.* Managers and employees view each other as equals, have a commitment to the organization and its long-term effectiveness, and are willing to work as a team to find and solve problems.
2. *Empowerment.* Effective organizations provide their employees with the authority to take action to solve problems. The objective is to have the problems dealt with at the lowest level and as quickly as possible.

JIT is most effective in repetitive manufacturing operations where companies traditionally have relied on holding significant levels of inventory, where production requirements can be forecast accurately, and where suppliers and customers work together as partners throughout the supply chain. Experience shows that companies with the following characteristics have the greatest success with JIT:

- Reliable deliveries of all parts and supplies
- Short distance between customers and their vendors
- Consistently high quality of vendors' products
- Stable and predictable product demand that allows for accurate production schedules

### Just-in-Time II Techniques

In the past, some companies that adopted JIT techniques discovered an unwanted side effect: increased hostility resulting from the increased pressure they put on their suppliers to meet tight and often challenging schedules. To resolve that conflict, many businesses have turned to an extension of JIT, **just-in-time II (JIT II)**, which focuses on creating a close, harmonious relationship with a company's suppliers so that both parties benefit from increased efficiency. Lance Dixon, who created the JIT II concept when he was a manager at Bose Corporation, a manufacturer of audio equipment, sought to create a working environment that empowered the supplier *within* the customer's organization. To work successfully, JIT II requires suppliers and their customers to share what was once closely guarded information in an environment of trust and cooperation. Under JIT II, customers and suppliers work hand in hand, acting more like partners than mere buyers and sellers.

In many businesses practicing JIT II, suppliers' employees work on site at the customer's plant, factory, or warehouse almost as if they were employees of the customer. These on-site workers are responsible for monitoring, controlling, and ordering inventory from their own companies. While at Bose, Dixon decided to try JIT II because it offered the potential to reduce sharply the company's inventories of materials and components, to cut purchasing costs, and to generate cost-cutting design and production tips from suppliers who understood Bose's process. This new alliance between suppliers and their customers formed a new supply chain that lowered costs at every one of its links. To protect against leakage of confidential information, Dixon had all of the employees from Bose's suppliers who would work in its plant sign confidentiality agreements. Dixon also put a ceiling on the amount each supplier's employee could order without previous authorization from Bose.

Growing numbers of small companies are forging JIT II relationships with their suppliers and customers.

*Joseph St. Martin and Northern Polymer Corporation*

Northern Polymer Corporation, a seven-person plastics maker, sells plastic resin to G&F Industries, a 170-employee injection molding company under a JIT II arrangement. Northern employees visit G&F's plant several times each month to check its inventory and consumption levels. Northern has set up a resin storage facility near G&F's plant so that it can restock its resin supply within just a few hours, if necessary. The arrangement "secures that piece of business for a long period," says Northern's founder, Joseph St. Martin.[12]

Web-based systems such as those mentioned earlier in this chapter allow many companies to operate JIT II systems without having an employee from the supplier work in-house. G&F Industries has a JIT II relationship with one of its biggest customers, Bose Corporation, and G&F does keep an employee in Bose's plant on a full-time basis.[13]

Manufacturers are not the only companies benefiting from JIT II. In a retail environment, the concept is more commonly known as **efficient consumer response (ECR)**, but the principles are the same. Rather than build inventories of merchandise that might sit for months before selling (or worse, never sell at all), retailers that use ECR replenish their inventories constantly on an as-needed basis. Because vendors are linked electronically to the retailer's point-of-sale system, they can monitor the company's inventory and keep it stocked with the right merchandise mix in the right quantities. Both parties reduce the inventories they must carry and experience significant reductions in paperwork and ordering costs. JIT II and ECR work best when two companies transact a significant amount of business that involves many different parts or products. Still, maintaining trust is the biggest barrier the companies must overcome.

## Turning Slow-Moving Inventory into Cash

*3.* Describe methods for reducing losses from slow-moving inventory.

Managing inventory effectively requires a business owner to monitor the company's inventory turnover ratio and to compare it with that of other firms of similar size in the same industry. As you recall from Chapter 17, the inventory turnover ratio is calculated by dividing a company's cost of goods sold by its average inventory. This ratio expresses the number of times per year the business turns over its inventory. In most cases, the higher the inventory turnover ratio, the better the small firm's financial position will be. A very low inventory turnover ratio indicates that much of the inventory may be stale and obsolete or that inventory investment is too large.

In the Entrepreneurial Spotlight

### ■ Zara: Zipping Fashions to Market

Zara, the flagship brand of private textile company Inditex, is the fastest-growing fashion retailer in the world; yet the company spends almost nothing on advertising. Founded in 1963 by then-24-year-old Amancio Ortega Gaona with just 5,000 pesetas (the equivalent of $25 today), Zara has become a powerhouse in the world of fashion, offering customers stylish, inexpensive clothing in its 650 stores located in 50 countries. From its headquarters in La Coruña situated on the northwest coast of Spain, Zara coordinates a lightning fast supply chain that makes competitors look as if they are moving in slow motion.

The company's innovative use of information, technology, and inventory control give it a significant competitive advantage in a market driven by rapidly changing fashions. Competitors such as Gap and Hennes & Mauritz (H&M) require about five months to move merchandise from the design stage to store shelves, something Zara manages to accomplish in just three weeks even though it produces more than 10,000 different styles in a typical year! None of Zara's styles lasts for more than four weeks, which is ideal for an industry in which customers' fashion tastes change almost as frequently as the direction of the wind. Many of the styles Zara creates resemble the latest couture creations but sell at a fraction of the cost.

Because Zara stocks most items in five or six colors and five to seven sizes, the company must manage about 300,000 stock-keeping units (SKUs). To do that effectively, Zara has developed a supply chain that depends on the constant exchange of information from top to bottom that allows it to create fast fashions. All of Zara's stores are linked electronically to headquarters,

where designers are constantly monitoring sales patterns to discern which styles are selling and which ones are not. Store managers transmit customer requests to designers, and a team of fashion scouts canvass the globe looking for the hottest new fashion trends. All of this real-time information feeds into Zara's headquarters, where designers, managers, and others work together to specify the fabrics, cuts, features, and price points of the flurry of new designs that the company is constantly turning out. Once these teams select items for production, they refine the colors and fabrics using a computer-aided design system, which allows them to transmit production specifications directly to the cutting machines inside the factories that will manufacture them. A sophisticated bar code system tracks the cut pieces through the factory as they are assembled and sewn into finished garments.

Another key feature of Zara's competitive advantage is its manufacturing strategy. Most retailers outsource their manufacturing to textile makers, many of which are located in the Far East. Because Zara is a retail division of textile maker Inditex, the company has 60 percent of its garments made in-house, which also saves a significant amount of time in getting products onto store shelves. Even though the cost to produce garments in Spain is 10 to 15 percent higher than manufacturing them in Asia, Zara does so to maintain its advantage in getting them to market fast. The company's high-tech factory weaves and colors fabrics, which are then cut and sewn into finished garments by Inditex. The combination of real-time information sharing among retail stores, designers, and factories and the in-house production of garments means that Zara keeps very little inventory in stock. The company's

*(continued)*

inventory is just 7 percent of annual revenues compared to 13 percent at rival retailer H&M. At the typical fashion retailer, 17 to 20 percent of inventory items are considered "slow-moving." At Zara, the percentage of slow moving merchandise is less than 10 percent, which means that the company has to rely on discounts to move merchandise much less than the typical fashion retailer.

A single distribution center in La Coruña sorts every garment and ships them out in pre-programmed lots based on what is selling best in that particular location. Zara ships fresh, stylish merchandise to its stores twice a week, far more frequently than the one shipment every six weeks that competitors can deliver. What drives Zara's sizzling growth rate is the company's ability to get new reasonably priced, glamorous fashions in front of style-conscious customers faster than anyone else, and it all starts with a less-than-glamorous supply chain strategy that works.

1. How does Zara's approach to supply chain management and inventory control give the company a competitive advantage?
2. What advantages does Zara reap by managing its inventory so carefully?

*Sources:* Adapted from Kasra Ferdows, Michael A. Lewis, and Jose A.D. Machuca, "Zara's Secret for Fashion," *Harvard Business School's Working Knowledge,* February 21, 2005, http://hbswk.hbs.edu/item.jhtml?id-4652&t=operations; Richard Heller, "Galician Beauty," *Forbes,* May 28, 2001, www.forbes.com/forbes/2001/0528/098; Geoffrey Colvin, "Inside Business: Zara," *Fortune,* September 12, 2000, www.fortune.com/fortune/insidebus ness/0,15704,372095,00.html; "Who We Are," Inditex, www.inditex.com/en/who_we_are/our_ group; Hau Lee, "The Three A's of Supply Chain Excellence," Electronics Supply & Manufacturing, October 1, 2004, www.myesm.com/showArticle.jhtml?articleID=47903369; "Here Today, Discounted Tomorrow: Strategic Shoppers Know When to Buy and at What Price," *Knowledge@Wharton,* May 30, 2007, http://knowledge.wharton.upenn edu/article.cfm?articleid=1750&CFID=32689696&CFTOKEN=98635623&jsessionid=9a309d749a8046f184d7.

Because of the variability in demand and the cyclical nature of the market, auto dealers often struggle to maintain an adequate number of inventory turns and to keep the number of cars on their lots from ballooning, which drives up their operating costs. The longer a car sits on a dealer's lot, the greater is the cost of borrowing to pay for it (recall the discussion of floor planning in Chapter 15, "Sources of Debt Financing"). Auto companies consider 50 to 60 days' worth of cars to be an adequate inventory. As gasoline prices increased, however, dealers began to see large gas-guzzling SUVs languish on their lots with inventories increasing to 100 days' worth. Sales of fuel-efficient and hybrid models fell to record lows. After one spike in gas prices, Toyota reported that its Scion line, which it markets to young people, was down to 7.2 days' supply and its hybrid Prius inventory stood at just 6 days' worth.[14]

As gas prices increased, Toyota's fuel-efficient Scion became so popular that dealers' inventories fell to just 7 days' supply. At the same time, inventories of large, gas-guzzling SUVs increased to more than 100 days' supply.

## Best Practices in Inventory Management

Many entrepreneurs have discovered the dangers of excess inventory. Not only does it tie up a company's valuable cash unnecessarily, but it also hides a host of other operating problems that a company has and needs to address. When it comes to managing inventory, small business owners often face four problems:

1. They have too much of some products.
2. They have too little of other products.
3. They don't know what they have in stock.
4. They know what they have in stock but cannot find it.

Addressing these four problems requires business owners to create a system of inventory management based on best practices. "Effective inventory management allows a distributor to meet or to exceed customers' expectations of product availability by maintaining the amount of each item that will also maximize their company's net profit," says one expert. The following inventory management best practices will help accomplish that goal:

*Recognize the difference between your company's "stock" and its "stuff."* "Stock" is made up of the inventory that customers want and expect a company to have available. "Stuff" is everything else that is in the warehouse or stock room and typically includes slow-moving items. The goal is to manage the stock in such a way that the company can meet customers' demand for items and make a profit and to get rid of everything else—the "stuff."

*Set up an inventory management process that recognizes the value of your company's stock.* Remember that Pareto's Law, the 80/20 rule, applies to many situations, particularly inventory control. About 20 percent of the items in a typical company's inventory account for about 80 percent of its sales. The idea is to set up a system that exercises the greatest degree of control over the most valuable 20 percent of the company's items.

*Work with vendors and suppliers to keep the inventory of essential items as lean as possible.* Even companies that utilize just-in-time techniques find it necessary to carry inventory; however, they keep their levels of stock to a minimum. Look for suppliers that can meet your company's quality requirements and provide rapid deliveries on short notice. Sharing information with the members of your company's supply chain and connecting with them electronically are excellent ways to shorten the lead time on the items you order.

*Use computerized inventory control systems to monitor your company's stock.* Computerized inventory control systems that are linked to point-of-sale (POS) terminals allow entrepreneurs to know which items they have in stock at any time. The reports that these systems generate also help them to know which items are selling best and which items are not selling at all. This information leads to improved inventory decisions in the future and allows entrepreneurs to adjust their buying decisions on the fly.

*Organize your warehouse or stockroom to make it easy to find the items you need.* Organizing a warehouse or stockroom based on the knowledge of which items are in highest demand and which ones are seldom needed allows businesses to minimize the cost of filling orders. Placing the fastest moving items in the most accessible location, preferably nearest the packing and shipping area, minimizes the time that employees spend walking around the warehouse or stock room. Once again, computerized inventory control systems can help by printing the warehouse "address" of the items that employees must "pick" to fill orders.

*Get rid of the "stuff."* Eliminating unwanted or unnecessary inventory frees up valuable cash and simplifies the inventory management process. Possible ideas include:

■ Reducing the price of the items to get rid of them.

■ Offering incentives to salespeople to sell slow-moving "stuff."

■ Offering the items for sale at an online auction house.

*Sources:* Adapted from Jon Schreibfeder, *The First Steps to Achieving Effective Inventory Control*, Microsoft Business Solutions, http://download.microsoft.com/download/b/f/3/bf334d7f-ad07-458e-a716-fdf46a0 cf63c/eimwp1_invcontrol.pdf; "Inventory Best Practices," *The Bottom Line*, Manufacturing Extension Partnership, June 2003, pp. 1–2.

Slow-moving items carry a good chance of loss resulting from spoilage or obsolescence. Firms dealing in trendy fashion merchandise or highly seasonal items often experience losses as a result of being stuck with unsold inventory for long periods of time. Some small business owners are reluctant to sell these slow-moving items by cutting prices, but it is much more profitable to dispose of this merchandise quickly than it is to hold it in stock at the regular prices. A business owner who postpones marking down stale merchandise, fearing it will reduce profit and hoping that the goods will sell eventually at the regular price, is making a huge mistake. The longer the merchandise sits, the dimmer are the prospects of ever selling it, much less selling it at a profit. Pricing these items below regular price or even below cost is difficult, but it is much better than having valuable working capital tied up in unproductive assets.

The most common technique for liquidating slow-moving merchandise is the markdown. Not only is the markdown effective in eliminating slow-moving goods, but it also is a successful promotional tool. Advertising special prices on such merchandise helps the small business garner a larger clientele and contributes to establishing a favorable business image. Using special sales to promote slow-moving items helps create a functional program for turning over inventory more quickly. To get rid of a large supply of out-of-style neckties, one small business offered a "one-cent sale" to customers purchasing neckwear at the regular price. One retailer of stereos and sound equipment chooses an unusual holiday— President's Day—to sponsor an all-out blitz, including special sales, prices, and promotions to reduce its inventory. Other techniques that help eliminate slow-moving merchandise include the following:

- Middle-of-the-aisle display islands that attract customer attention
- One-day-only sales
- Quantity discounts for volume purchases
- Bargain tables with a variety of merchandise for customers to explore
- Eye-catching lights and tickets marking sale merchandise

As inventory control techniques become increasingly sophisticated and accurate, slow-moving inventory will never be "lost" in the supply chain. Aggressive methods of selling slower-moving inventory allow business owners to convert inventory into cash and to produce an acceptable inventory turnover ratio. The inventory management tools described in this chapter also play an important role in avoiding slow-moving merchandise. They highlight those items that are slow-moving, enabling business owners to avoid the mistake of ordering them again. In effect, this information on what *isn't* selling influences entrepreneurs' decisions about the merchandise they order in the future as much as information on those items that *are* selling well. The ability to avoid slow-moving items in the first place means that business owners can invest their working capital more effectively and produce faster inventory turnover ratios, lower costs, and higher profits.

## Protecting Inventory from Theft

*4.* Discuss employee theft and shoplifting and how to prevent them.

Small companies are a big target for crime. The Association of Certified Fraud Examiners estimates that businesses lose $652 billion annually, about five percent of their total sales, to criminals, although the actual loss may be even greater because so many business crimes go unreported.[15] Whatever the actual loss is, its effect is staggering. If a company operates at a five percent net profit margin, it must generate additional sales of $20 for every $1 lost to theft. Small companies are especially vulnerable. Small businesses often lack the sophistication to identify early on the illegal actions of employees or professional thieves and the processes to prevent theft and fraud. A study by the Association of Certified Fraud Examiners reports that the median loss to fraud for all companies is $159,000, but the median loss for small businesses is $190,000.[16] When a company has a small asset base, a loss from theft can be a crippling blow and can threaten its very existence.

Many entrepreneurs believe that the primary sources of theft originate outside the business. In reality, most firms are victimized by their own employees.

### Employee Theft

Ironically, the greatest criminal threat to small businesses comes from inside. Employee theft accounts for the greatest proportion of the criminal losses businesses suffer. On average, dishonest employees steal 5.7 times more than do shoplifters.[17] Unfortunately, employee theft is more prevalent than ever. Tim Dimoff, president of Mogadore, SACS Consulting & Investigative Services Inc., gives one reason for the increased prevalence. "I call the attitude employees take in the workplace 'entitlement,'" he says. "They justify in their minds that they are entitled to take things because they work so hard." Dimoff adds that some businesses all but encourage employee theft. How? By failing to file criminal charges against employees caught stealing. Many business owners do not want the negative publicity that results from prosecuting employee thieves. Others worry about the cost to the company to prosecute, how the time away from management will affect the organization, and the impact that the incident will have on employee morale. Often it is easier just to ask the guilty employee to leave.[18]

The average length of time it takes an employer to catch an employee who is stealing is 18 months, and they usually discover the theft only by accident.[19] How can thefts go undetected for so long? Most thefts occur when employees take advantage of the opportunities to steal that small business owners unwittingly give them. Typically, small business owners are so busy building their companies that they rarely even consider the possibility of employee theft—until disaster strikes.

*Alan Bridges and Allpoints Equipment*

Alan Bridges, owner of Allpoints Equipment, a small Tampa, Florida-based company that sells warehouse equipment, was one of those unsuspecting entrepreneurs who discovered that his company had been a victim of employee theft almost 50 times! One worker in the accounting department used Allpoints' money to pay her own utility bills, and a top executive included his family vehicles on the company insurance plan. Another employee stole $24,000 worth of tools, equipment, and scrap metal from a work site. "I was shell-shocked when it happened to me," says Bridges. "Then I started digging and found out just how extensive the problem is. Most small business owners are blind to this, and most of them say, 'It won't happen to me.'"[20]

In addition, many small companies do not have adequate financial, audit, and security procedures in place. Fewer than 20 percent of small companies have internal audit teams, use unannounced audits, or conduct fraud training for their managers and employees.[21] Add into this mix of sloppy control procedures the high degree of trust that most small business owners place in their employees, and you have a perfect recipe for employee theft.

*Mike Zic and Bevinco*

Mike Zic works with bar owners to minimize their losses from waste, spillage, and theft. Although a typical retailer loses 1.5 percent of its merchandise to shoplifting and employee theft, the average bar owner loses 25 percent of his or her alcoholic beverage stock, costing the company about $3,000 each week. Zic's company conducts secret audits and implements tight control procedures to reduce bar owners' losses to negligible amounts.[22]

**WHAT CAUSES EMPLOYEE THEFT?** Security experts estimate that 30 percent of workers will steal from their employers at some point in their careers.[23] Employees steal from their companies for any number of reasons. Some may have a grudge against the company; others may have a drug, alcohol, or gambling addiction to support. Employees steal from the company for four reasons: need, greed, temptation, and opportunity. A business owner can minimize the last two reasons. To minimize their losses to employee theft, business owners must understand how both the temptation and the opportunity to steal creep into their companies. The following are conditions that lead to major security gaps in small companies.

***The Trusted Employee.*** The fact is that any employee can be a thief although most are not. Studies show that younger, less devoted employees steal from their companies most often, but long-time employees can cause more damage. It is very easy in a small business to view long-time employees almost as partners. Such a feeling, although not undesirable, can develop into a security breach. Many owners refuse to believe that their most trusted employees present the greatest security threat, but these workers have the greatest accessibility to keys, cash registers, records, and even safe combinations. Because of their seniority, these employees hold key positions and are quite familiar with operations, and they know where weaknesses in control and security procedures lie. Alan Bridges, owner of Allpoints Equipment, was shocked when his accounting firm informed him that one of his most trusted employees, his payroll manager, had been stealing from the company for some time.[24]

Small business owners should also be wary of "workaholic" employees. Is this worker really dedicated to the company, or is he working so hard to cover up theft? Employee thieves are unwilling to take extended breaks from their jobs for fear of being detected. As long as a dishonest employee remains on the job, he can cover up theft. As a security precaution, business owners should require every employee to take vacations long enough so that someone else has to take over their responsibilities (at least five consecutive business days). Most schemes are relatively simple and require day-to-day maintenance to keep them going. Business failure records are filled with stories of firms in which the "ideal" employee turned out to be a thief. "In 90 percent of the cases in which people steal from their companies, the employer would probably have described this person, right up to the time the crime was discovered as a trusted employee," says one expert.[25]

***Disgruntled Employees.*** Business owners also must monitor the performance of disgruntled employees. Employees are more likely to steal if they believe that their company treats workers unfairly, and the probability of their stealing goes even higher if they believe that they themselves have been treated unfairly. Employees dissatisfied with their pay or their promotions may retaliate against an employer by stealing. Dishonest employees will make up the difference between what they are paid and what they believe they are worth by stealing. Many believe pilfering is a well-deserved "perk."

***Organizational Atmosphere.*** Many entrepreneurs unintentionally create an atmosphere that encourages employee dishonesty. Failing to establish formal controls and procedures invites theft. Nothing encourages dishonest employees to steal more than knowing they are unlikely to be caught. Four factors encourage employee theft:

1. The need or desire to steal (e.g., to support a habit or to cope with a sudden financial crisis)
2. A rationalization for the act (e.g., "They owe me this.")
3. The opportunity to steal (e.g., access to merchandise, complete control of financial functions)
4. The perception that there is a low probability of being caught (e.g., "Nobody will ever know.")

Owners must recognize that they set the example for security and honesty in the business. Employees place more emphasis on what owners *do* than on what they *say*. Entrepreneurs who install a complete system of inventory control and then ignore it are telling employees that security is unimportant. No one should remove merchandise, materials, or supplies from inventory without recording them properly. There should be no exceptions to the rules, even for bosses and their relatives. Managers should develop clear control procedures and establish penalties for violations. The single biggest deterrent to employee theft is a strong, top-down policy that is well communicated to all employees that theft will not be tolerated and that anyone caught stealing will be prosecuted—*no exceptions*.

Entrepreneurs must constantly emphasize the importance of security and use every available opportunity to reduce employees' temptation to steal. One business owner relies on payroll inserts to emphasize to employees how theft reduces the funds available for growth, expansion, and higher wages. Another useful tool is a written code of ethics that spells out penalties for violations that every worker signs. Workers must understand that security is a team effort. Security rules and procedures must be reasonable, and owners must treat workers equitably. Unreasonable rules are no more effective—and may even be more harmful—than poorly enforced procedures. A work environment that fosters honesty at every turn serves as an effective deterrent to employee theft.

***Physical Breakdowns.*** Another major factor contributing to employee theft is weak physical security. The owner who pays little attention to the distribution of keys, safe combinations, and other entry devices is inviting theft. In addition, owners who fail to lock doors and windows or to install reliable alarm systems literally are leaving their businesses open to thieves both inside and outside the organization.

Open windows and unattended doors give dishonest employees a prime opportunity to slip stolen merchandise out of the plant or store. One security expert worked with a small manufacturing operation that was experiencing high levels of employee theft during the night shift. His investigation revealed that employees could exit the building through 14 different doors with little or no supervision. The company closed most of the exits, installed security cameras at those that remained open, and assigned managers to supervise the night shift. After implementing these simple changes, employee theft plummeted to nearly zero.[26]

Many businesses find that their profits go out with the trash, literally. When collecting trash, a dishonest employee may stash valuable merchandise in with the refuse and dump it in the receptacle. After the store closes, the thief returns to collect the loot. One drugstore owner lost more than $7,000 in merchandise in just six months through trash thefts.

***Improper Cash Control.*** Many small business owners encourage employee theft by failing to implement proper cash control procedures. Without a system of logical, practical audit controls on cash, a firm will likely suffer internal theft. Dishonest employees quickly discover there is a low probability of detection and steal cash with impunity.

Cashiers clearly have the greatest accessibility to the firm's cash and, consequently, experience the greatest temptation to steal. The following scenario is all too common: A customer makes a purchase with the exact amount of cash and leaves quickly. The cashier fails to ring up the purchase and pockets the cash without anyone's knowledge. Some small business owners create a cash security problem by allowing too many employees to operate cash registers and handle customer payments. If a cash shortage develops, the owner is unable to trace responsibility.

A daily inspection of cash register transactions can point out potential employee theft problems. When register reports indicate an excessive number of voided transactions or no-sale transactions, the owner should investigate. A no-sale transaction could mean the register was opened to give a customer change or to steal cash. A large number of incorrect register transactions also are a sign of foul play. Clerks may be camouflaging cash thefts by voiding transactions or by under-ringing sales amounts.

*Famous Footwear*

To cut its losses to shrinkage, Famous Footwear, a chain of retail shoe stores, recently installed a cash register monitoring system in every store. The system records every cash register transaction and looks for suspicious patterns. Within a short time, the monitoring system cut the company's unexplained inventory losses in half. When she learned about the new system, one store manager, convinced that she would soon be caught, admitted to stealing more than $2,000 in cash.[27]

Cash shortages and overages are also clues that alert managers to possible theft. All small business owners are alarmed by cash shortages, but few are disturbed by cash overages. However, cash discrepancies in either direction are an indication of inept cashiering or of poor cash controls. The manager who investigates all cash discrepancies can greatly reduce the opportunity for cashiers to steal.

**PREVENTING EMPLOYEE THEFT.** Many incidents of employee theft go undetected, and of those employees who are caught stealing only a small percentage is prosecuted. The burden of dealing with employee theft falls squarely on the owner's shoulders. Although business owners cannot eliminate the possibility of employee theft, they can reduce its likelihood by using some relatively simple procedures and policies that are cost-effective to implement.

*Screen Employees Carefully.* Statistics show that one out of every 27 employees is caught committing employee theft.[28] Perhaps a business owner's greatest weapon against crime is a thorough pre-employment screening process. The best time to weed out prospective criminals is before hiring them! One security company conducted an analysis of more than 19,000 applicants for retail jobs and rated 19.3 percent of them as "high risk" candidates for employee theft.[29] Although the regulations in many countries prohibit employers from invading job applicants' privacy and from using discriminatory devices in the selection process, employers have a legitimate right to determine job candidates' integrity and qualifications. A comprehensive selection process and reliable screening devices greatly reduce the chances that an entrepreneur will hire a thief. Smart entrepreneurs verify the information applicants provide on their résumés because they know that some of them will either exaggerate or misrepresent their qualifications. A thorough background check with references and previous employers also is essential. (One question that sheds light on a former employer's feelings toward a former employee is "Would you hire this person again?")

Some security experts recommend the use of integrity tests, paper-and-pencil tests that offer valuable insight into job applicants' level of honesty. Business owners can buy integrity tests for $20 or less that are already validated (to avoid charges of discrimination) and that they can score on their own. Because drug addictions drive many employees to steal, employers also should administer drug tests consistently to all job applicants. The most reliable drug tests cost the company from $35 to $50 each, a small price to pay given the potential losses that can result from hiring an employee with a drug habit. In addition, business owners should conduct criminal background checks on every candidate they are considering hiring.

*Create an Environment of Honesty.* Creating an environment of honesty and integrity starts at the top of an organization. This requires business owners to set an impeccable example for everyone else in the company. In addition to creating a standard of ethical behavior, business owners should strive to establish high morale among workers. A positive work environment in which employees see themselves as an important part of the team is an effective deterrent to employee theft. Establishing a written code of ethics and having employees sign "honesty clauses" offer tangible evidence of a company's commitment to honesty and integrity.

*Establish a System of Internal Controls.* The basis for maintaining internal security on the job is establishing a set of reasonable internal controls designed to prevent employee theft. An effective system of checks and balances goes a long way toward deterring internal crime; weak or inconsistently enforced controls are an open invitation for theft. The most basic rule is to separate among several employees related duties that might cause a security breach if assigned to a single worker. For instance, owners should avoid letting the employee who issues checks reconcile the company's bank statement. Similarly, the person who orders merchandise and supplies should not be the one who also approves those invoices for payment. Spreading these tasks among a number of employees makes organizing a theft more difficult. The owner of a small retail art shop learned this lesson the hard way. After conducting an inventory audit, he discovered that more than $25,000 worth of art supplies was missing. The owner finally traced the theft to the company bookkeeper, who was creating fictional invoices and then issuing checks to herself for the same amount.

Business owners should insist that all company records be kept up to date. Sloppy record keeping makes theft difficult to detect. All internal documents—shipping, ordering, invoicing, and collecting—should be numbered. Missing numbers should arouse suspicion. One subtle way to test employees' honesty is to commit deliberate errors occasionally to see if employees detect them. If you send an extra case of merchandise to the loading dock for shipment, does the supervisor catch it, or does it disappear?

Finally, business owners should demonstrate zero tolerance for theft. They must adhere strictly to company policy when dealing with employees who violate the company's trust. When business owners catch an employee thief, the best course of action is to fire the perpetrator and to prosecute. Too often, owners take the attitude: "Resign, return the money, and we'll forget it." Letting thieves off, however, only encourages them to move on

**FIGURE 18.4 Causes of Inventory Shrinkage**

*Source: 2006 National Retail Security Survey,* National Retail Federation.

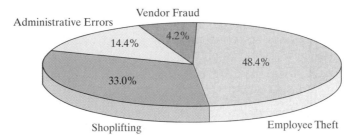

to other businesses where they will steal again. Prosecuting a former employee for theft is never easy, but it does send a clear signal about how the company views employee crime.

For a closer look at where inventory shrinkage occurs, refer to Figure 18.4.

### Shoplifting

The most frequent business crime is shoplifting.[30] Retail businesses lose billions to shoplifters each year, and small businesses suffer a significant share of those losses.[31] Shoplifting takes an especially heavy toll on small businesses because they usually have the weakest lines of defense against shoplifters. Shoplifting losses, which ultimately are passed on to the consumer, account for approximately 3 to 4 percent of the average price tag.

**TYPES OF SHOPLIFTERS.** Anyone who takes merchandise from a store without paying for it, no matter what the justification, is a shoplifter. Shoplifters look exactly like other customers. They can be young children in search of a new toy or elderly people who are short

Retail businesses lose an estimated billions to shoplifters each year.

## ■ Confessions of an Embezzler

Studies show that because small companies often lack proper internal controls and security measures, they are more likely to be victims of business crimes such as employee theft, shoplifting, and embezzlement. In addition to being more susceptible to crime, small companies are less able to tolerate it than their larger counterparts. Although a $100,000 loss can harm a large business, that same loss often drives a small company out of business. Bill and Linda Carey, founders of Hollow Metal Door Company (HMDC), a nine-employee business that sells, installs, and services a variety of doors, were victims of embezzlement by a trusted employee over the course of several years. Although they have managed to keep their business going, they are struggling because of the financial hardship the theft imposed on the company, which generates annual revenues of $2 million to $3 million. "I've worked 10 to 14 hour days for 30 years," says Bill with a touch of bitterness. "She wiped out years of my hard work."

In many ways, Hollow Metal Door's story is typical. Sandra (not her real name) was the company's bookkeeper. She came to work for the Careys in 1987, answering phones and helping with the company's bookkeeping. Sandra, who fit the girl-next-door stereotype, including being a high school cheerleader, was one of the first non-family members hired at HMDC. Before long, the Careys were treating Sandra like a daughter, taking an interest in her life away from the office. "They saw me get married, have kids, and grow up," Sandra says. "They were very good to me."

Unfortunately, Sandra was not good to the Careys. In 1992, Sandra, now married to her high school sweetheart, was a working mother trying to raise two sons. The family budget was always tight, and there never seemed to be enough money left at the end of the month. Sandra handled the family's finances, and she had resorted to charging regular living expenses on high interest rate credit cards. The debt was climbing, and she had not been able to make a payment on the credit card balances in months. "I panicked," she recalls.

For the previous five years, Sandra had written checks for HMDC almost every day, and one day she decided to write a company check to pay off the family's credit card balance. The total amount was just $672. "I thought, 'Just this one time—just to get back on my feet. No one will know,'" she recalls. She knew, however, that what she had done was wrong, so she covered the theft by entering the check as if she had written it as payment to a company vendor. She carried the check in her purse for a week, trying to come up with another solution to her financial woes. The credit card company kept calling, however, and, feeling trapped, she finally mailed the check. "I can't believe I did it," she says, calling it "the stupidest idea" she ever had.

The check cleared, and no one at HMDC suspected that anything was wrong. After all, Sandra was a longtime, trusted employee, and the check was for such a small amount. Had it all stopped there, Sandra's theft might never have been discovered. Instead of "just one time" though, Sandra wrote another check, and then another . . . She learned to cover her tracks by disguising the checks as payments to phony vendors that she had concocted. Sandra never used the money she stole foolishly—gambling or supporting a drug habit. She used it to pay for the family's living expenses. "Maybe we ate a little better," she says.

For seven years, Sandra told no one, not even her husband, what she was doing. Whenever HMDC's bank called, Sandra panicked, worried that the bank had detected her embezzling. "I just knew it was going to be about a check," she says, "but it never was." Sandra made sure that she was in the office the first week of every month because that's when HMDC's bank statement arrived. She had to get to the statement first to hide her cancelled checks. "It was so easy after a while," she says. "It had gotten to the point where it didn't truly feel like I was doing anything wrong."

But she was.

After seven years of embezzling, Sandra's theft was finally uncovered while she was on a family vacation at the beach. One of her old cancelled checks turned up, and Bill Carey could not believe what he was seeing. When she returned, he met her at the door with the cancelled check in his hand. "He asked me if I did this, and all I could say was 'Yeah,'" she recalls. Carey fired Sandra on the spot, and the mild-mannered business owner watched as she cleared out her desk. Sandra realized for the first time that she might go to jail. Still, not even

Sandra realized just how much she had stolen from HMDC over the seven years. The subsequent investigation showed that she had embezzled $248,383 to pay her credit card bills. "We just lived," she recalls tearfully. "We used that money to just live." Although faced with a possible sentence of 16 years in jail, a judge sentenced Sandra to the minimum sentence, 18 months, so she could begin paying restitution to the Careys. Today, she has a menial job running errands for a business and pays $100 a month to HMDC, an amount that obviously cannot repay all that she stole. "I'm not a bad person," she says. "But I did a really bad thing."

1. Why are small companies more likely than large businesses to become victims of business crime?
2. What conditions make a small company ripe for employee theft?
3. What steps could the Careys have taken at Hollow Metal Door Company to avoid Sandra's embezzlement?

*Source:* Adapted from David G. Propson, "Inside Job," *Small Business Computing,* November 2001, pp. 27–30; Cora Daniels, "Confessions of an Embezzler," *FSB,* May 2002, pp. 48–51.

of money. *Anyone* can be a shoplifter, given the opportunity, the ability, and the desire to steal. For instance, actress Winona Ryder was convicted of stealing more than $5,500 worth of designer merchandise from a Beverly Hills Saks Fifth Avenue store.

Fortunately for small business owners, most shoplifters are amateurs who steal because the opportunity presents itself. Many steal on impulse, and the theft is the first criminal act. Many of those caught have the money to pay for their "five-finger discounts." Observant business owners supported by trained store personnel can spot potential shoplifters and deter many shoplifting incidents; however, they must understand the shoplifter's profile. Experts identify five types of shoplifters.

***Juveniles.*** Juveniles account for approximately one-fourth of all shoplifters. Many juveniles steal as a result of peer pressure. Most have little fear of prosecution, assuming they can hide behind their youth. When owners detect juvenile shoplifters, they must not let sympathy stand in the way of good judgment. Many hard-core criminals began their careers as shoplifters, and small business owners who fail to prosecute the youthful offender do nothing to discourage a life of crime. Juvenile offenders should be prosecuted through proper legal procedures just as any adult shoplifter would be.

***Impulse Shoplifters.*** Impulse shoplifters steal on the spur of the moment when they succumb to temptation. These shoplifters do not plan their thefts, but when a prime opportunity to shoplift arises, they take advantage of it. For example, a salesperson may be showing a customer several pieces of jewelry. If the salesperson is called away, the customer might pocket an expensive ring and leave the store before the employee returns.

The most effective method of fighting impulse shoplifting is prevention. To minimize losses, the owner should remove the opportunity to steal by implementing proper security procedures and devices.

***Shoplifters Supporting Other Criminal Behaviors.*** Shoplifters motivated to steal to support a drug or alcohol habit often are easy to detect because their behavior is usually unstable and erratic. One recently apprehended shoplifter was supporting a $100-a-day heroin habit by stealing small items from local retailers and then returning the merchandise for refunds. (The stores almost never asked for sales receipts.) Small business owners should exercise great caution when handling these shoplifters because they can easily become violent. Criminals deranged by drugs or alcohol might be armed and could endanger the lives of customers and employees if they are detained. It is best to let the police apprehend these shoplifters.

***Kleptomaniacs.*** Kleptomaniacs have a compulsive need to steal even though they have little, if any, need for the items they shoplift. In many cases, these shoplifters could afford to purchase the merchandise they steal. Kleptomaniacs account for less than 5 percent of shoplifters, but their disease costs business owners a great deal. They need professional psychological counseling, and the owner only helps them by seeing that they are apprehended.

***Professionals.*** Although professional shoplifters account for 32 percent of shoplifting incidents, the impact of their thefts is disproportionately large. Losses to professional shoplifters are 54 times greater than the average shoplifting loss.[32] Because professional shoplifters' business is theft, they are very difficult to detect and deter. Career shoplifters tend to focus on expensive merchandise they can sell quickly to their "fences," such as stereo equipment, appliances, guns, or jewelry. Usually the fences don't keep the stolen goods long, often selling them at a fraction of their value. Therefore, apprehending and prosecuting professional shoplifters is quite difficult. Police have apprehended professional shoplifters with detailed maps of a city's shopping districts, showing target stores and the best times to make a "hit." Furthermore, many professional shoplifters are affiliated with organized crime, and they are able to rely on their associates to avoid detection and prosecution. Table 18.3 provides some interesting facts about shoplifting.

**TABLE 18.3 Shoplifting Facts**

- More than $13.5 billion worth of goods are stolen from retailers each year. That's nearly $37 million per day.
- There are approximately 23 million shoplifters (or 1 in 11 people) in the U.S. alone. More than 10 million people have been caught shoplifting in the last five years.
- Shoplifting affects more than the offender. It overburdens the police and the courts, adds to a store's security expenses, increases the cost of goods for legitimate shoppers, reduces sales taxes that go to communities, and hurts children and families.
- There is no such thing as a "typical" shoplifter. *Anyone* can be a shoplifter. Men and women shoplift about equally as often.
- Approximately 25 percent of shoplifters are kids, and 75 percent are adults. Fifty-five percent of adult shoplifters say they started shoplifting in their teens.
- Many shoplifters buy and steal merchandise in the same visit. Shoplifters commonly steal from $2 to $200 per incident depending upon the type of store and item(s) chosen.
- Shoplifting is often an impulse crime: 73 percent of adult and 72 percent of juvenile shoplifters don't plan to steal in advance.
- Eighty-six percent of kids say they know other kids who shoplift, and 66 percent say they hang out with those kids.
- Shoplifters say they are caught an average of only once in every 48 times they steal. They are turned over to the police just 50 percent of the time.
- Approximately 3 percent of shoplifters are "professionals" who steal solely for resale or profit as a business. These include drug addicts who steal to feed their habit, hardened professionals who steal as a lifestyle and international shoplifting gangs who steal for profit as a business. "Professional" shoplifters are responsible for 10 percent of the total losses.
- The majority of shoplifters are "non-professionals" who steal, not out of financial need or greed, but as a response to social and personal pressures in their lives.
- The excitement generated from "getting away with it" produces a chemical reaction that results in what shoplifters describe as an incredible "rush" or "high" feeling. Many shoplifters will tell you that this high is their "true reward," rather than the merchandise itself.
- Drug addicts who have become addicted to shoplifting describe shoplifting as equally addicting as drugs.
- Even after getting caught, 57 percent of adults and 33 percent of juveniles say it is hard for them to stop shoplifting.
- Most non-professional shoplifters don't commit other types of crimes. They'll never steal an ashtray from your house and will return to you a $20 bill that you drop. Their criminal activity is restricted to shoplifting and, therefore, any rehabilitation program should be "offense specific" for this crime.
- Shoplifters steal an average of 1.6 times per week.

*Source: 2005 National Retail Security Survey* by Dr. Richard Hollinger. Published online by the University of Florida. Reprinted with permission.

**DETECTING SHOPLIFTERS.** Although shoplifters can be difficult to detect, small business owners who know what to look for can spot them in action. They must always be on the lookout for shoplifters, but merchants should be especially vigilant on Saturdays and around holidays, when shoplifters can hide their thefts more easily in the frenzy of a busy shopping day.

Shoplifters can work alone or in groups. In general, impulse shoplifters prefer solitary thefts, whereas juveniles and professionals operate in groups. A common tactic for group shoplifters is for one member of the gang to create some type of distraction while other members steal the merchandise. Business owners should be wary of loud, disruptive gangs that enter their stores.

Solitary shoplifters are usually quite nervous. They avoid crowds and shy away from store personnel, preferring privacy to ply their trade. To make sure they avoid detection, they constantly scan the store for customers and employees. These shoplifters spend more time nervously looking around the store than examining merchandise. Also, they shop when the store is most likely to be understaffed, during early morning, lunch, or late evening hours. Shoplifters frequently linger in the same area for an extended time without purchasing anything. Customers who refuse the help of sales personnel or bring in large bags and packages (especially empty ones) also arouse suspicion.

Shoplifters have their own arsenal of tools to assist them in plying their trade. They often shop with booster boxes, shopping bags, umbrellas, bulky jackets, baby strollers, or containers disguised as gifts. These props often have hidden compartments that can be tripped easily, allowing the shoplifter to fill them with merchandise quickly.

Some shoplifters use specially designed coats with hidden pockets and compartments that can hold even large items. Small business owners should be suspicious of customers wearing out-of-season clothing (e.g., heavy coats in warm weather or rain gear on clear days) that could conceal stolen goods. Hooked belts also are used to enable the shoplifter to suspend items on hangers without being detected.

Another common tactic is "ticket switching," in which the shoplifter exchanges price tickets on items and pays a very low price for an expensive item. An inexperienced or unobservant cashier may charge $9.95 for a $30.00 item that the shoplifter re-marked while no one was looking. A more elaborate scheme is one in which shoplifters create counterfeit bar codes that they paste over existing bar codes on packages so that when the item is scanned, it rings up at a much lower price. After three years, police finally nabbed a shoplifter who used this technique to steal more than $600,000 worth of toy LEGOS from dozens of stores in five U.S. states. His phony bar codes caused $100 LEGO sets to ring up for just $19 at checkout counters. He then resold the LEGO sets at a markup on a Web site for toy collectors.[33]

One variation of traditional shoplifting techniques is the "grab-and-run" in which a shoplifter grabs an armload of merchandise located near an exit and then dashes out the door into a waiting getaway car. The element of surprise gives these thieves an advantage, and they are often gone before anyone in the store realizes what has happened.

**DETERRING SHOPLIFTERS.** The problem of shoplifting is worsening. Every year, business losses due to customer theft increase, and many companies are declaring war on shoplifting. Funds allocated for fighting shoplifting losses are best spent on *prevention*. By focusing on preventing shoplifting rather than on prosecuting violators after the fact, business owners take a strong stand in protecting their firms' merchandise. Of course, no prevention plan is perfect. When violations occur, owners must prosecute; otherwise the business becomes known as an easy target. Retailers say that when a store gets a reputation for being tough on shoplifters, thefts drop off.

Knowing what to look for dramatically improves a business owner's odds in combating shoplifting:

- ■ *Watch the eyes.* Amateurs spend excessive time looking at the merchandise they're about to steal. Their eyes, however, are usually checking to see who (if anyone) is watching them.
- ■ *Watch the hands.* Experienced shoplifters, like good magicians, rely on sleight of hand.

- *Watch the body.* Amateurs' body movements reflect their nervousness; they appear to be unnatural.
- *Watch the clothing.* Loose, bulky clothing is the uniform of the typical shoplifter.
- *Watch for devices.* Anything a customer carries is a potential concealing device.
- *Watch for loiterers.* Many amateurs must work up the nerve to steal.
- *Watch for switches.* Working in pairs, shoplifters will split duties; one will lift the merchandise, and, after a switch, the other will take it out of the store.

Store owners can take other steps to discourage shoplifting:

***Train Employees to Spot Shoplifters.*** One of the best ways to prevent shoplifting is to train store personnel to be aware of shoplifters' habits and to be alert for possible theft. In fact, most security experts agree that alert employees are the best defense against shoplifters. Employees should look for nervous, unusual customers and monitor them closely. Shoplifters prefer to avoid sales personnel and other customers, and when employees approach them, shoplifters know they are being watched. Even when all salespeople are busy, an alert employee should approach the customer and mention, "I'll be with you in a moment." Honest customers appreciate the clerk's politeness, and shoplifters are put off by the implied surveillance.

All employees should watch for suspicious people, especially those carrying the props of concealment. Employees in clothing stores must keep a tally of the items being taken into and out of dressing rooms. Some clothing retailers prevent unauthorized use of dressing rooms by locking them; customers who want to try on garments must check with a store employee first.

An alert cashier can be a tremendous boon to the store owner attempting to minimize shoplifting losses. A cashier who knows the store's general pricing policy and is familiar with the prices of many specific items is the best insurance against the ticket-switching shoplifter. A good cashier also should inspect all containers being sold; toolboxes, purses, briefcases, and other items can conceal stolen merchandise.

Employees should be trained to watch for group shoplifting tactics. A group of shoppers that enters the store and then disperses in all directions may be attempting to distract employees so that some gang members can steal merchandise. Sales personnel should

© Mike Baldwin / Cornered

"The clerk's back is turned – go for it."

watch closely the customer who lingers in one area for an extended time, especially one who examines a lot of merchandise but never purchases anything.

The sales staff should watch for customers who consistently shop during the hours when most employees are on breaks. Managers can help eliminate this cause of shoplifting by ensuring that their stores are well staffed at all times. Coordinating work schedules to ensure adequate coverage is a simple, but effective, method of discouraging shoplifting.

The cost of training employees to be alert to shoplifting "gimmicks" can be recouped many times over by preventing losses from retail theft. The local police department or chamber of commerce may be able to conduct training seminars for local small business owners and their employees, or security consulting firms might sponsor a training course on shoplifting techniques and protective methods. Refresher courses every few months can help keep employees sharp in spotting shoplifters.

***Pay Attention to Store Layout.*** A well-planned store layout also can be an effective obstacle in preventing shoplifting losses. Proper lighting throughout the store makes it easier for employees to monitor shoppers, whereas dimly lit areas give dishonest customers a prime opportunity to steal without detection. In addition, display cases should be kept low, no more than three or four feet high, so store personnel can have a clear view of the entire store. Display counters should have spaces between them; continuous displays create a barrier between customers and employees.

Business owners should keep small expensive items such as jewelry, silver, and electronics behind display counters or in locked cases with a sales clerk nearby. Valuable or breakable items also should be kept out of customer reach and should not be displayed near exits, where shoplifters can pick them up and quickly step outside. All merchandise displays should be neat and organized so that it will be noticeable if an item is missing.

Cash registers should be located so that cashiers have an unobstructed view of the entire store. Other protective measures include prominently posting anti-shoplifting signs describing the penalties involved and keeping unattended doors locked (within fire regulations). Exits that cannot be locked because of fire regulations should be equipped with noise alarms to detect any attempts at unauthorized exit.

***Install Mechanical Devices.*** Another option a small business owner has in the attempt to reduce shoplifting losses is to install mechanical devices. A complete deterrence system can be expensive, but failure to implement one is usually more expensive. Tools such as two-way mirrors allow employees at one end of the store to monitor a customer at the other end, and one-way viewing windows enable employees to watch the entire store without being seen.

Other mechanical devices, such as closed-circuit TV cameras, convex wall mirrors, and peepholes, also help the owner protect the store from shoplifters. Not every small business can afford to install a closed-circuit camera system, but one clever entrepreneur got the benefit of such a system without the high cost. He installed one "live" camera and several "dummy" cameras that did not work. The cameras worked because potential shoplifters thought they were all live. Another high-tech weapon used against shoplifters is a mannequin named Anne Droid, which is equipped with a tiny camera behind one eye and a microphone in her nose!

An owner can deter ticket-switching shoplifters by using tamper-proof price tickets: perforated gummed labels that tear away if a customer tries to remove them or price tags attached to merchandise by hard-to-break plastic strips. Some owners use multiple price tags concealed on items to deter ticket switchers. One of the most effective weapons for combating shoplifting is the electronic article surveillance (EAS) system, small tags that are equipped with electronic sensors that set off sound and light alarms if customers take them past a store exit. These tags are attached to the merchandise and can be removed only by employees with special shears. Owners using these electronic tags must make sure that all cashiers are consistent in removing them from items purchased legitimately; otherwise, they may be liable for false arrest or, at the very least, may cause customers embarrassment.

**APPREHENDING SHOPLIFTERS.** Despite all of the weapons business owners use to curtail shoplifting, the sad reality is that most of the time shoplifters are successful at plying their trade. Shoplifters say they are caught an average of only once in every 48 times they steal

# ENTREPRENEURSHIP
## *In Action*

### How Would You Handle This Customer?

Patricia Caldwell was shopping in a retail store. A store security employee became suspicious when he saw that she was carrying a large purse and was handling many small items. As she shopped, Caldwell went into several departments and bent down out of sight of the security guard. She says she bent down to look at items displayed on low shelves. She also removed her glasses to read labels and returned them to her purse several times. The guard, believing he had seen Caldwell put some items in her purse, followed her into the parking lot and accused her of shoplifting. He asked Caldwell to open her purse. She did, but the guard found none of the store's merchandise inside.

Rather than releasing her, he told Caldwell to return to the store with him, where he escorted her back to areas where she had been shopping. They walked around the store for approximately 15 minutes, during which time the guard told her six or seven times that he had seen her conceal merchandise in her purse. No one touched Caldwell or searched her. With no evidence of stolen merchandise, another employee told Caldwell she could leave the store.

Caldwell brought a lawsuit against the retailer for slander, making false defamatory statements, and false imprisonment (depriving a person of his or her liberty without justice). The court allowed the retailer's loss prevention manual to be introduced as evidence. The manual spelled out the company's guidelines for employees in making shoplifting arrests. For instance, the manual stated that before apprehending a suspected shoplifter, an employee "must see the shoplifter take our property." It also stated that an employee should watch the suspect continuously and should apprehend him or her after he or she has had the opportunity to pay for the merchandise and is outside the store. The manual said that apprehension should be made in the presence of a witness and that any interrogation should be done in the privacy of the Loss Prevention Office.

The jury in the case awarded Caldwell $75,000 in total damages and the retailer appealed. The appellate court affirmed the lower court's ruling.

1. What did the retailer in this case do wrong?
2. What guidelines should store employees follow when dealing with a suspected shoplifter?

*Source: Caldwell v. K-Mart Corporation,* No. (17) (S.C. Ct. App. filed October 14, 1991).

and that they are turned over to the police just 50 percent of the time. Of those shoplifters who do get caught, less than half are prosecuted. The chance that any shoplifter will actually go before a judge is about 1 in 100.[34] Building a strong case against a shoplifter is essential; therefore, small business owners must determine beforehand the procedures to follow once they detect a shoplifter. The storeowner has to be certain that the shoplifter has taken or concealed the merchandise and has left the store with it. Although laws vary, owners must do the following to make the charges stick:

1. *See* the person take or conceal the merchandise.
2. *Identify* the merchandise as belonging to the store.
3. *Testify* that it was taken with the intent to steal.
4. *Prove* that the merchandise was not paid for.

Most security experts agree that an owner should never apprehend the shoplifter if he or she has lost sight of the suspect even for an instant. In that time, the person may have dumped the merchandise.

Another primary consideration in apprehending shoplifters is the safety of store employees. In general, employees should never directly accuse a customer of shoplifting and should never try to apprehend the suspect. The wisest course of action when a shoplifter is detected is to alert the police or store security personnel and let them apprehend the suspect.

Apprehension *outside* the store is safest. This tactic strengthens the owner's case and eliminates unpleasant in-store scenes that upset other customers or that might be dangerous. Of course, if the stolen merchandise is very valuable, or if the criminal is likely to escape once outside, the owner may have no choice but to apprehend the shoplifter in the store.

Once business owners detect and apprehend a shoplifter, they must decide whether to prosecute. Many small business owners fail to prosecute because they fear legal entanglements or negative publicity. However, failure to prosecute encourages shoplifters to try again and gives the business the image of being an easy target. Of course, each case is an individual matter. For example, the owner may choose not to prosecute elderly or senile shoplifters or those who are mentally incompetent. In most cases, prosecuting the shoplifter is the best option, especially for juveniles and first-time offenders. The business owner who prosecutes shoplifters consistently soon develops a reputation for toughness that most shoplifters hesitate to test. It is in the interest of every business owner to have that reputation.

## Conclusion

Inventory control is one of those less-than-glamorous activities that business owners must perform if their businesses are to succeed. Although it doesn't offer the flash of marketing or the visibility of customer service, inventory control is no less important. In fact, business owners who invest the time and the resources to exercise the proper degree of control over their inventory soon discover that the payoff is huge!

## Chapter Review

1. Explain the various inventory control systems and the advantages and disadvantages of each.
   - Inventory represents the largest investment for the typical small business. Unless properly managed, the cost of inventory will strain the firm's budget and cut into its profitability. The goal of inventory control is to balance the cost of holding and maintaining inventory with meeting customer demand.
   - Regardless of the inventory control system selected, business owners must recognize the relevance of Pareto's Law, the 80/20 rule, which states that roughly 80 percent of the value of the firm's inventory is in about 20 percent of the items in stock. Because only a small percentage of items account for the majority of the value of the firm's inventory, managers should focus control on those items.
   - Three basic types of inventory control systems are available to the small business owner: perpetual, visual, and partial. Perpetual inventory control systems are designed to maintain a running count of the items in inventory. Although they can be expensive and cumbersome to operate by hand, affordable computerized point-of-sale (POS) terminals that deduct items sold from inventory on hand make perpetual systems feasible for small companies. The visual inventory system is the most common method of controlling merchandise in a small business. This system works best when shortages are not likely to cause major problems. Partial inventory control systems are most effective for small businesses with limited time and money. These systems operate on the basis of the 80/20 rule.
   - The ABC system is a partial system that divides a firm's inventory into three categories depending on each item's dollar usage volume (cost per unit multiplied by quantity used per time period). The purpose of classifying items according to their value is to establish the proper degree of control over them. A items are most closely controlled by perpetual inventory control systems; B items use basic analytical tools; and C items are controlled by very simple techniques such as the two-bin system, the level control method, or the tag system.
2. Describe how just-in-time (JIT) and JIT II inventory control techniques work.
   - The just-in-time system of inventory control sees excess inventory as a blanket that masks production problems and adds unnecessary costs to the production

operation. Under a JIT philosophy, the level of inventory maintained is the measure of efficiency. Materials and parts should not build up as costly inventory. They should flow through the production process without stopping, arriving at the appropriate location just in time.

- JIT II techniques focus on creating a close, harmonious relationship with a company's suppliers so that both parties benefit from increased efficiency. To work successfully, JIT II requires suppliers and their customers to share what was once closely guarded information in an environment of trust and cooperation. Under JIT II, customers and suppliers work hand in hand, acting more like partners than mere buyers and sellers.

3. Describe methods for reducing losses from slow-moving inventory.
   - Managing inventory requires monitoring the company's inventory turnover ratio; slow-moving items result in losses from spoilage or obsolescence.
   - Slow-moving items can be liquidated by markdowns, eye-catching displays, or quantity discounts.

4. Discuss employee theft and shoplifting and how to prevent them.
   - Employee theft accounts for the majority of business losses due to theft. Most small business owners are so busy managing their companies' daily affairs that they fail to develop reliable security systems. Thus, they provide their employees with prime opportunities to steal.
   - The organizational atmosphere may encourage employee theft. The owner sets the organizational tone for security. A complete set of security controls, procedures, and penalties should be developed and enforced. Physical breakdowns in security invite employee theft. Open doors and windows, poor key control, and improper cash controls are major contributors to the problem of employee theft. Employers can build security into their businesses by screening and selecting employees carefully. Orientation programs also help the employee to get started in the right direction. Internal controls, such as division of responsibility, spot checks, and audit procedures, are useful in preventing employee theft.
   - Shoplifting is the most common business crime. Fortunately, most shoplifters are amateurs. Juveniles often steal to impress their friends, but prosecution can halt their criminal ways early on. Impulse shoplifters steal because the opportunity suddenly arises. Simple prevention is the best defense against these shoplifters. Alcoholics, vagrants, and drug addicts steal to supply some need and are usually easiest to detect. Kleptomaniacs have a compelling need to steal. Professionals are in the business of theft and can be very difficult to detect and quite dangerous.
   - Three strategies are most useful in deterring shoplifters. First, employees should be trained to look for signs of shoplifting. Second, store layout should be designed with theft deterrence in mind. Finally, anti-theft devices should be installed in the store.

## Discussion Questions

1. Describe some of the incidental costs of carrying and maintaining inventory for the small business owner.
2. What is a perpetual inventory system? How does it operate? What are the advantages and disadvantages of using such a system?
3. List and describe briefly the four versions of a perpetual inventory system.
4. Give examples of small businesses that would find it practical to implement the four systems described in question 3.
5. What advantages and disadvantages does a visual inventory control system have over other methods?
6. For what type of business product line is a visual control system most effective?
7. What is the 80/20 rule, and why is it important in controlling inventory?
8. Outline the ABC inventory control procedure. What is the purpose of classifying inventory items using this procedure?

9. Briefly describe the types of control techniques that should be used for A, B, and C items.
10. What is the basis for the JIT philosophy? Under what condition does a JIT system work best?
11. What is JIT II? What is its underlying philosophy? What risks does it present to businesses?
12. Outline the two methods of taking a physical inventory count. Why is it necessary for every small business manager to take inventory?
13. Why are slow-moving items dangerous to the small business? What can be done to liquidate them from inventory?
14. Why are small companies more susceptible to business crime than large companies?
15. Why is employee theft a problem for many small businesses? Briefly describe the reasons for employee theft.
16. Construct a profile of the employee most likely to steal goods or money from an employer. What four elements must be present for employee theft to occur?
17. Briefly outline a program that could help the typical small business owner minimize losses due to employee theft.
18. List and briefly describe the major types of shoplifters.
19. Outline the characteristics of a typical shoplifter that should arouse a small business manager's suspicions. What tools and tactics is a shoplifter likely to use?
20. Describe the major elements of a program designed to deter shoplifters.
21. How can proper planning of a store layout reduce shoplifting losses?
22. What must an owner do to have a good case against a shoplifter? How should a suspected shoplifter be apprehended?

# Business PlanPro

For many product-oriented businesses, inventory control represents a major investment. Unfortunately, many entrepreneurs fail to manage their inventory investments carefully, and this can lead to serious financial, managerial, and customer service problems. Fortunately, small companies can now afford to purchase inventory control systems that once were available only to large organizations. Technological solutions supported by a sound inventory control system enable even the smallest companies to reap the benefits of maintaining proper inventory control systems.

## On the Web

The Companion Website at www.prenhall.com/scarborough for Chapter 18 offers a series of links that provide additional information regarding inventory control resources. Review these sites, specifically those that relate to your industry, and determine whether these sources may be useful to you as you build your plan.

## In the Software

Review the "Products" section of your plan to make certain that you have included the inventory management issues discussed in this chapter. Does it describe how you plan to manage your inventory? What type of inventory control system will you use in your business? Is it perpetual, visual, or partial? Have you incorporated a description of that system into the plan?

## Building Your Business Plan

Your business plan should describe your company's inventory control strategy. If inventory represents a significant investment for your business, you should invest the time required to develop this section of your plan and make sure that your financial forecasts capture this information as well. If you plan to purchase an inventory control system, be sure to include this as one of your expenses.

# Staffing and Leading a Growing Company

If your actions inspire others to dream more, learn more, do more, and become more, you are a leader.

—John Quincy Adams

Leaders are made, they are not born. They are made by hard effort, which is the price which all of us must pay to achieve any goal that is worthwhile.

—Vince Lombardi

*Learning Objectives*

**Upon completion of this chapter, you will be able to:**

1 Explain the challenges involved in the entrepreneur's role as leader and what it takes to be a successful leader.

2 Describe the importance of hiring the right employees and how to avoid making hiring mistakes.

3 Explain how to build the kind of company culture and structure to support the entrepreneur's mission and goals and to motivate employees to achieve them.

4 Understand the potential barriers to effective communication and describe how to overcome them.

5 Discuss the ways in which entrepreneurs can motivate their employees to achieve higher levels of performance.

## The Entrepreneur's Role as Leader

*1.* Explain the challenges involved in the entrepreneur's role as leader and what it takes to be a successful leader.

As a business grows, the entrepreneur must relinquish control and learn to depend on the productive energy of others to achieve results. Leadership becomes the critical entrepreneurial variable that fuels success. **Leadership** is the process of influencing and inspiring others to work to achieve a common goal and then giving them the power and the freedom to achieve it. Without leadership ability, entrepreneurs—and their companies—never achieve the full potential of the organization or that of the employees.

There is no simple formula for leadership success. In today's rapidly changing business environment, entrepreneurs must adapt their leadership styles to accommodate the changing nature of the workforce. People of various generations and different ethnic and cultural backgrounds have different personal and professional needs and expectations regarding the style and behavior of their leaders. Becoming an effective leader requires a willingness to remain open to the changing needs of people, a deep commitment to the long-term well-being of employees, and a high level of sensitivity. Leaders are always "on stage" because employees constantly judge their actions and give more importance to what their leaders *do* than what they *say*.

**ENTREPRENEURIAL Profile**

*Carley Roney and The Knot*

"You have to let go," says Carley Roney, cofounder and editor-in-chief of The Knot, a company that provides resources for brides and grooms to plan their weddings. "Leading a company is like parenting: It's one long process of pulling back and letting it become its own organism. You have to make sure you have created an organization that is able to operate with or without you."[1] Thanks to the adaptive management styles of Roney and cofounder David Liu, The Knot has become the world's leading wedding media and services company, extending its content and tools through TheKnot.com and a series of books and magazines bearing The Knot brand.

### Management versus Leadership

It is important to differentiate between management and leadership. Stephen Covey, author of *Principle-Centered Leadership,* explains the difference between management and leadership this way:

> Leadership deals with people; management deals with things. You manage things; you lead people. Leadership deals with vision; management deals with logistics toward that vision. Leadership deals with doing the right things; management focuses on doing things right. Leadership deals with examining the paradigms on which you are operating; management operates within those paradigms. Leadership comes first, then management, but both are necessary.[2]

Management and leadership are not the same, yet both are essential to a small company's success. Leadership without management is unbridled; management without leadership is uninspired. Leadership *gets* a small business going, and management *keeps* it going. Effective leaders provide vision, direction, value, and purpose; they inspire, motivate, and build complementary teams that leverage an individual's strengths. Managers provide systems and procedures, define roles, and solve problems. Strong managers organize resources to achieve higher objectives and produce bottom-line results.[3] In short, leadership and management are intertwined; a small business that has one but not the other will go nowhere.

Understanding how the brain operates may explain why some people are great managers but poor leaders, and vice versa. The left side of the brain is logical, sequential, rational, analytical, and objective, and the right side is random, intuitive, holistic, creative, subjective, and emotional. In general, businesses tend to favor the left brain while downplaying the right brain. As a result many organizations have great management systems and controls but lack heart. Others have heart but lack effective processes and structure. The same can be said about individuals. An excellent manager may be organized and have great procedures, but unless he shows heart, he will never evolve into being a great leader. This leads to one of Covey's suggestions: Manage from the left, and lead from the right. The best corporate cultures and leaders span both sides. A successful strategic leader who uses both sides of the brain provides both direction and vision—and has learned how to motivate with the heart.[4]

### ENTREPRENEURIAL Profile

*David Wolfskehl and Action Fast Print*

"I thought I had to have all the right answers," says David Wolfskehl, who launched Action Fast Print at age 24. He believed presiding and deciding were the essence of leadership. Wolfskehl, who built his business to $1.5 million in annual sales before selling it, recalls standing before his 16 employees at weekly meetings and telling them what to do. "We were talking about *my* issues, not the employees' issues," he says. "I would leave those meetings thinking we had accomplished something. But the employees wouldn't buy into what I said we should do." After reading a book about leadership, Wolfskehl mustered the courage to change his leadership style. At the next weekly meeting, he began by saying, "Today we're going to start talking about *your* problems and how I can help you." He recalls, "Once I started asking how I could help, amazing things started happening in my organization. In a two-year period, we had a 30-plus percent improvement in productivity. The solution was so obvious. It's just sad that it took me 15 years to get there."[5]

### Entrepreneurial Leadership

The Corporate Leadership Council estimates that 97 percent of public and non-profit organizations have significant leadership gaps, and more than 40 percent of companies say the gaps are acute.[6] Effective leaders exhibit certain behaviors. They consistently:

■ *Create a set of values and beliefs for employees and passionately pursue them.* Employees look to their leaders for guidance when making decisions. True leaders focus attention on the principles, values, and beliefs on which they founded their companies.

■ *Respect and support their employees.* To gain the respect of their employees, leaders must first respect those who work for them.

■ *Set the example for their employees.* Leaders' words ring hollow if they fail to "practice what they preach." Few signals are transmitted to workers faster than the hypocrisy of leaders who sell employees on one set of values and principles and then act according to a different set.

■ *Focus employees' efforts on challenging goals and keep them driving toward those goals.* Effective leaders have a clear vision of where they want their companies to go, and they are able to communicate their vision to those around them. Leaders must repeatedly reinforce the goals they set for their companies.

■ *Provide the resources employees need to achieve their goals.* Effective leaders know that workers cannot do their jobs well unless they have the tools they need. They provide workers with not only the physical resources they need to excel but also the necessary intangible resources such as training, coaching, and mentoring.

■ *Communicate with their employees.* Leaders recognize that helping workers see the company's overarching goal is just one part of effective communication; encouraging employee feedback and then listening is just as vital. In other words, they know that communication is a two-way street.

■ *Value the diversity of their workers.* Smart business leaders recognize the value of their workers' varied skills, abilities, backgrounds, and interests. When channeled in the right direction, this diversity can be a powerful weapon in achieving innovation and maintaining a competitive edge.

■ *Celebrate their workers' successes.* Effective leaders recognize that workers want to be winners and do everything they can to encourage top performance among their people. The rewards they give are not always financial; in many cases, a reward may be as simple as a handwritten congratulatory note.

■ *Value risk-taking.* Effective leaders recognize that in a rapidly changing competitive environment, they must make decisions with incomplete information and must be willing to take risks to succeed.

■ *Understand that leadership is multidimensional.* Smart leaders know that there is no single "best" style of leadership. The dimensions of leadership change depending on the people involved, the conditions and circumstances of the situation, and the desired outcome.

■ *Value new ideas from employees.* Successful leaders know that because employees work every day on the front lines of the business, they see ways to improve quality, customer service, and business systems. Effective leaders solicit suggestions for improving quality and service from employees.

■ *Understand that success really is a team effort.* Small companies typically depend more on their founding entrepreneurs than on anyone else. After all, someone has to take responsibility for the toughest decisions. However, effective leaders understand that their roles are only a small piece of the entire company puzzle. *Now Who's Boss,* a six-part TLC television series, filmed six CEOs who took jobs on the front lines of their companies, where the "real work" is performed. The cofounders of the California Pizza Kitchen, for example, worked as dish washers, pizza makers, and food servers. In addition to seeing firsthand just how difficult many jobs can be, all of the CEOs had a superb refresher course in how important every worker's role is in the success of a company.[7]

■ *Encourage creativity among their workers.* Rather than punish workers who take risks and fail, effective leaders are willing to accept failure as a natural part of innovation and creativity. They know that innovative behavior is the key to future success and do everything they can to encourage it among workers.

■ *Maintain a sense of humor.* One of the most important tools a leader can have is a sense of humor. Without it, work can become dull and unexciting for everyone.

■ *Behave with integrity at all times.* Real leaders know that they set the ethical tone in the organization. Even small lapses in a leader's ethical standards can have a significant impact on a company's ethical climate. Workers know they can trust leaders whose actions support their words. Similarly, they quickly learn not to trust leaders whose day-to-day dealings belie the principles they preach.

■ *Keep their eyes on the horizon.* Effective leaders are never satisfied with what they and their employees accomplished yesterday. They know that yesterday's successes are not enough to sustain their companies indefinitely. They see the importance of building and maintaining sufficient momentum to carry their companies to the next level.

Entrepreneurs cannot bestow the mantle of leadership on themselves. Managers may inherit their subordinates, but leaders have to *earn* their followers. An entrepreneur's employees—the followers—are the ones who determine whether he or she is worthy of leadership. *Without followers, there are no leaders.* Astute leaders know that their success depends on their employees' success. After all, the employees are the ones who actually do the work, implement the strategies, and produce the results. To be effective, leaders must establish for their workers an environment in which they can achieve success.

One expert identifies six conditions that leaders must create for their followers if a company is to succeed. Followers must:

1. Know what to do.
2. Know how to do it.
3. Understand why they are doing it.
4. Want to do it.
5. Have the right resources to do it.
6. Believe they have the proper leadership to guide them.[8]

# Gaining a Competitive Edge

## Eight Characteristics of Great Leaders

An entrepreneur may possess the entire assortment of personal traits that everyone admires, but without the knowledge of running a business, that person can be a recipe for disaster. Ram Charan's book , *Know-How: The 8 Skills that Separate People Who Perform from Those Who Don't,* outlines eight key leadership attributes.

1. *Positioning the business to make money.* The business must be in sync with its customers' needs at all times and properly aligned with the external environment. Figuring out what to add, what to take out, what new opportunities to pursue for profitable growth, and which technologies to adopt are among the most demanding requirements of the twenty-first century leader. Given the current pace of change, a leader may have to reposition a company four or five times during his or her career.

2. *Pinpointing and taking action on patterns of external change.* Success depends on the ability to detect emerging trends and patterns of change clearly and precisely. A leader must have a broad view of the business—from the outside in—and have the tenacity and the imagination to fill in the gaps until the foggy picture becomes clear. This ability allows effective leaders to stay on the offensive rather than to constantly put out fires.

3. *Getting people to work together by managing the social system of the business.* One of a leader's most important tasks is to shape the way people work together. A company's performance depends on the leader's ability to coordinate the actions of people so that they work toward a common goal.

4. *Judging, selecting, and developing leaders.* A leader's job is to put the right people in the right jobs and then unleash their natural talents. Getting the right match depends on a leader's ability to observe and judge people accurately based on their decisions, actions, and behaviors.

5. *Molding a team of leaders.* Every entrepreneur wants to hire "stars," but sometimes an even greater challenge than recruiting stars is persuading them to submit their own agendas to the best interest of the company. Convincing high-powered people (many of them with high-powered egos) to work together for the greater good of the company is the leader's job.

6. *Determining and setting the right goals.* Leaders must set aggressive goals based on the opportunities that lie ahead and the organization's ability to achieve them. Too often, managers choose goals by looking in the rearview mirror and adding some incremental adjustment. Backward-looking goal setting rarely results in stellar performance.

7. *Setting laser-sharp dominant priorities.* Establishing the right priorities keeps the truly important things from being driven off the company's radar screen. When a leader makes a company's priorities unmistakably clear, people know what should be getting their attention.

8. *Dealing with uncontrollable forces.* Effective leaders anticipate the outside groups and forces that are likely to throw a monkey wrench into the company's plans. They also prepare for the threats that these groups and forces pose to the company's business model.

*Source:* Adapted from Ram Charan, "The 8 Characteristics of Great Leaders," *CIO Insight,* December 21, 2006, www.cioinsight.com/article2/0,1540,2075948,00.asp.

Great leaders do everything in their power to make these conditions thrive in their companies. To be effective, entrepreneurial leaders must perform four vital tasks:

1. Hire the right employees and constantly improve their skills.
2. Build an organizational culture and structure that allows both workers and the company to reach their potential.
3. Communicate the vision and the values of the company effectively and create an environment of trust among workers
4. Motivate workers to higher levels of performance.

# Hiring the Right Employees: The Company's Future Depends on It

**2.** Describe the importance of hiring the right employees and how to avoid making hiring mistakes.

The decision to hire a new employee is an important one for every business. The impact on a small company is much greater—employees' roles in a small company's success are magnified by the company's size and entrepreneurs can *least* afford to make hiring mistakes. "As an entrepreneur, every single hire is critical," says Stephen Fairley, CEO of the Rainmaker Institute, a business coaching firm.[9]

Bad hires are expensive, especially for small companies. The Bureau of Labor Statistics estimates that it costs at least $14,000 to replace one employee.[10] A study for sales positions estimates that the first year cost of a bad hire typically runs 2.5 times the person's salary.[11] There are also intangible costs—the time invested in the job search, training the new employee, lost opportunities, reduced morale among coworkers, and business setbacks. The total cost to a small company of one hiring mistake is *many* times the cost of the worker's salary. Most often, those hiring mistakes come about because entrepreneurs rush into a hiring decision or they neglect to investigate thoroughly a candidate's qualifications and suitability for a job (see Figure 19.1). Some small businesses invest more time and effort deciding which copy machine to lease than selecting an employee to fill a key position.

Although the importance of hiring decisions is magnified in small companies, small businesses are most likely to make hiring mistakes because they lack human resources experience and the disciplined hiring procedures large companies use. In the early days of a company, entrepreneurs rarely take the time to create job descriptions and job specifications. Instead, they hire people they know or trust rather than for their job skills and expertise. As the company grows, business owners hire people to fit in around existing employees, often creating an unusual, inefficient organizational structure comprised of jobs that are poorly planned and designed.

According to a survey by NFI Research, managers in small businesses are more likely to make hiring and promotion decisions based on personality than based on skill.

**The Question:**

When hiring and/or promoting in your business, which of the following do you rely on?

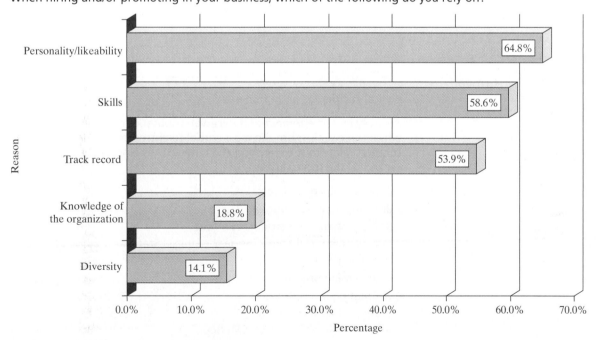

**FIGURE 19.1 Like Me? Hire Me!**

*Source:* "Like Me? Hire Me!" *FSB,* November 2006, p. 20.

Attracting and retaining qualified employees remains a challenge for many companies, and the problem is especially acute among rapidly growing small businesses. The following factors will play a role in the future of hiring, managing, and retaining employees:

- Staffing costs are rising, despite the efficiencies that online recruiting offers.
- Hiring and retaining quality workers is a top priority for entrepreneurial companies (see Figure 19.2).[12]
- Over the next two decades, 78 million baby boomers will turn 65, the traditional retirement age, creating a talent shortage in many industries.[13]
- The current workforce shortage will worsen.[14]
- In the United States, for example, immigrants will account for nearly two-thirds of the population growth between 2007 and 2050. In addition, in 2050 minority groups will account for almost half of the population and the workforce. Leaders must understand how to manage, motivate, and retain employees from many different cultures.[15]

The following guidelines can help small business managers avoid making costly hiring mistakes.

## Create Practical Job Descriptions and Job Specifications

Small business owners must recognize that what they do *before* they ever start interviewing candidates for a position determines how successful they will be at hiring winners. The first step is to perform a **job analysis**, the process by which a company determines the duties and nature of the jobs to be filled and the skills and experience required of the people who are to fill them. An entrepreneur can determine these attributes by addressing the following areas:

- *The mental/physical tasks involved*—ranging from judging, planning, and managing to cleaning, lifting, and welding
- *How the job will be done*—the methods and equipment to be used
- *The reason the job exists*—including an explanation of job goals and how they relate to other positions in the company
- *The qualifications needed*—training, knowledge, skills, and personal traits

A potential resource for acquiring information for a job analysis is to talk to employees and supervisors at other companies with similar positions.[16] A job analysis forms the foundation for developing job descriptions.

**FIGURE 19.2 Critical Factors for Entrepreneurs**
*Source:* Mark Henricks, "A Look Ahead—Mission Critical," *Entrepreneur,* January 2007, p. 73.

---

**Critical Factors for Entrepreneurs**

A survey by *Entrepreneur* and PricewaterhouseCoopers asked business owners which three factors are the most crucial to entrepreneurial success. The top two concerns relate to the retention and hiring of key employees. The top 10 concerns ranked by the survey are:

| | |
|---|---|
| 1. Retaining key workers | 68% |
| 2. Hiring qualified workers | 53% |
| 3. Developing new products/services | 32% |
| 4. Expanding to markets inside the United States | 26% |
| 5. Cutting costs | 22% |
| 6. Increasing productivity | 22% |
| 7. Creating business alliances | 21% |
| 8. Upgrading technology | 17% |
| 9. Better management of cash flow | 13% |
| 10. Merging with or acquiring another company | 12% |

**JOB DESCRIPTION.** A results-oriented job description explains what a job entails and the duties the person filling it is expected to perform. A **job description** is a written statement of the duties, responsibilities, reporting relationships, working conditions, and materials and equipment used in a job. The components should include the job title, job summary, duties to be performed, nature of supervision, job's relationship to others in the company, working conditions, definitions of job-specific terms, and general comments needed to clarify any of these items. A job description also should outline how a job fits within the company. For a one-person business hiring its first employee, these steps may seem unnecessary, but a good job description lays the foundations for a personnel policy, which is essential as the company grows.[17]

Preparing job descriptions may be one of the most important parts of the hiring process because it creates a "blueprint" for the job. Without this blueprint, managers tend to hire the person with experience whom they like the best. Useful sources of information for writing job descriptions include the manager's knowledge of the job, the workers currently holding the job, and the *Dictionary of Occupational Titles (DOT),* available at most libraries. The *Dictionary of Occupational Titles* lists more than 20,000 job titles and descriptions and serves as a useful tool for getting a small business owner started when writing job descriptions.

**JOB SPECIFICATIONS.** A **job specification** is a written statement of the qualifications and characteristics needed for a job stated in terms such as education, skills, and experience. A job specification shows an entrepreneur the kind of person to recruit and helps establish the standards an applicant must meet to be hired. Like a job description, a job specification also includes the job title, the person reports to, and a summary of the position. It lists educational requirements, desired experience, and required specialized skills or knowledge along with the salary range and benefits. Job specifications also should address the physical or other special requirements associated with the job and any occupational hazards the employee faces. Writing job descriptions and job specifications helps an entrepreneur determine whether he or she needs a part- or full-time employee, whether the person should be permanent or temporary, and whether an independent contractor rather than an employee could fill the position.[18]

A job specification defines the traits a candidate needs to do a job well. Does the person have to be a good listener, empathetic, well organized, decisive, or a self-starter? A business owner about to hire a new employee who will be telecommuting from home, for instance, would look for someone with excellent communication skills, problem-solving ability, a strong work ethic, and the ability to use technology comfortably. Table 19.1 provides an example that links the tasks for a sales representative's job (drawn from a job description) to the traits or characteristics a small business owner identified as necessary to succeed in that job.

## Plan an Effective Interview

Once entrepreneurs know what they must look for in a job candidate, they can develop a plan for conducting an informative job interview. Entrepreneurs who go into an interview unprepared often fail to get the information they need to accurately assess the candidate's qualifications, qualities, and suitability for the job. Conducting an effective interview requires entrepreneurs to know what they want to get out of the interview and develop a series of questions to extract that information. The following guidelines will help business owners develop interview questions that will give them meaningful insight into an applicant's qualifications, personality, and character.

- ■ *Develop a series of core questions and ask them of every candidate.* To give the interview process consistency, smart entrepreneurs rely on a set of relevant questions they ask in every interview. Of course, they can still "customize" each interview using impromptu questions based on an individual's responses.
- ■ *Ask open-ended questions.* Open-ended questions demanding more than a "yes or no" response are most effective because they encourage candidates to talk about their work experience in a way that will disclose the presence or the absence of the traits and characteristics business owners are seeking.

**TABLE 19.1 Linking Tasks from the Job Description to the Traits Needed to Perform the Job**

| Job Task | Trait or Characteristic |
|---|---|
| Generate new leads and close new sales. | Outgoing, strong communication skills, persuasive, friendly |
| Make 15 "cold calls" per week. | A self-starter, determined, optimistic, independent, confident |
| Analyze customer needs and recommend proper equipment. | Good listener, intuitive, patient, empathetic |
| Counsel customers about options and features required. | Organized, polished speaker, other–oriented |
| Prepare and explain financing methods; negotiate finance contracts. | Honest, mathematically oriented, comfortable with numbers, understands basics of finance, computer literate |
| Retain existing customers. | Relationship builder, customer focused |

- ◼ *Create hypothetical situations candidates are likely to encounter on the job and ask how they would handle them.* Building the interview around these hypothetical situations gives owners a preview of the candidate's work habits and attitudes. Rather than telling interviewers about what candidates *might* do, these scenarios give them an idea of what candidates *would* do (or have done) in job-related situations.
- ◼ *Probe for necessary traits and characteristics.* Asking the candidate to talk about their work experiences that demonstrate attractive attributes. A common mistake interviewers make is failing to get candidates to provide the details they need to make an informed decision.
- ◼ *Discuss the candidate's recent successes and failures.* Smart entrepreneurs look for candidates who describe both their successes and failures with equal enthusiasm because entrepreneurs know that peak performers put as much into their failures as they do their successes and usually learn something valuable from their failures. Ask the candidates to provide examples of their successes and failures.
- ◼ *Arrange a "non-interview" setting that allows several employees to observe the candidate in an informal setting.* Taking candidates on a plant tour or setting up a coffee break gives everyone a chance to judge a candidate's interpersonal skills and personality outside the formal interview process. These informal settings can be revealing. One business owner was ready to extend a job offer to a candidate for a managerial position until he saw how the man mistreated a waitress who had made a mistake in his lunch order.

Table 19.2 shows an example of some interview questions one manager uses to uncover the traits and characteristics he seeks in a top-performing sales representative.

### Conduct the Interview

An effective interview contains three phases: breaking the ice, asking questions, and selling the candidate on the company.

**BREAKING THE ICE.** In the opening phase of the interview, the entrepreneur's primary job is to create a relaxed environment. Many skilled interviewers use the job description to explain the nature of the job and the company's culture to the applicant. They then use icebreakers—questions about a hobby or special interest—to get the candidate to relax. These "icebreaker" questions may also allow the interviewer an opportunity to gain valuable insight into the person. These are questions that generate little or no pressure, and the interviewee can feel free to expound on something he or she knows a great deal about such as a favorite pastime or hobby.

**ASKING QUESTIONS.** During the second phase of the interview, employers ask the questions from their question bank to determine the applicant's suitability for the job. Employers' primary job at this point is to *listen*. Effective interviewers spend about 25 percent of the

**TABLE 19.2 Interview Questions for Candidates for a Sales Representative Position**

| Trait or Characteristic | Question |
|---|---|
| Outgoing, persuasive, friendly, a self-starter, determined, optimistic, independent, confident | How do you persuade reluctant prospects to buy? |
| | Can you give an example? |
| Good listener, patient, empathetic, organized, polished speaker, other-oriented | What would you say to a fellow salesperson that was getting more than his or her share of rejections and was having difficulty getting appointments? |
| Honest, customer-oriented, relationship builder | How do you feel when someone questions the truth of what you say? |
| | Can you give an example of successfully overcoming this situation? |

### Other Questions

- If you owned a company, why would you hire yourself?
- If you were head of your department, what would you do differently? Why?
- How do you acknowledge the contributions of others in your department?

interview talking and about 75 percent listening. They also take notes during the interview to help them ask follow-up questions based on a candidate's comments and to evaluate a candidate after the interview is over. Experienced interviewers also pay close attention to a candidate's nonverbal clues, or body language, during the interview. They know that candidates may be able to say exactly what they want with their words but that their body language does not lie! Figure 19.3 describes 10 questions that business owners most frequently ask job candidates.

Some of the most valuable interview questions attempt to gain insight into the candidate's ability to reason, be logical, and to be creative. Known as **puzzle interviews**, the goal is to determine how job candidates think by asking them offbeat, unexpected questions such as, "How would you weigh an airplane without scales?" "Why are man-hole covers round?" or "How would you determine the height of a building using only a barometer?" Usually, the logic and creativity a candidate uses to derive an answer is much more revealing than the answer itself.

Another type of interview that is becoming popular is the **situational interview**, in which the interviewer gives candidates a typical job-related situation (sometimes in the form of a role-playing exercise) and presents a series of open-ended questions to assess how they might respond. One entrepreneur had a candidate deal with an "angry customer," who was played by a fellow interviewer. Studies show that situational interviews have a 54 percent accuracy rate in predicting future job performance, much higher than the seven percent accuracy rate of the traditional interview.[19]

ENTREPRENEURIAL
Profile

*IAC/InterActiveCorp*

Johnny C. Taylor, Jr., senior vice president for human resources at IAC/InterActiveCorp, recommends situational interviewing. "By the time you see the finalists," he says, "you can be fairly sure they possess the technical skills. What you want to focus on is fit with the company's culture because when someone fails, it's almost always because they don't fit in well." Questions such as "Give me an example of how you responded when a tight deadline threatened the quality of a project," or "How have you handled situations in which your ideas on how to proceed haven't met with much enthusiasm?" can take candidates off-script and help entrepreneurs learn about their working styles and their personalities.[20]

The **peer-to-peer interview** may provide a closer look at how prospective employees will get along with other staff. In this type of interview, applicants meet one-on-one with potential peers to ask questions about the job and the company. Later, employees share their assessment with the entrepreneur. This interviewing technique is becoming common at

**FIGURE 19.3 Top 10 Interview Questions**

*Sources:* Adapted from Tom Musbach, "Six Common Job Interview Questions," Yahoo! Hot Jobs, http://hotjobs.yahoo.com/ jobseeker/tools/article_print.html?id =Six_common_jobinterview_ questions__20061109-090925.xml; "Answering 6 Common Interview Questions," *CNN.com,* www.cnn. com/2005/US/Careers/12/09/six. questions/index.html; "Common Interview Questions," *USA Today,* www.usatoday.com/careers/ resources/interviewcommon.htm; "Common Interview Questions," Emurse.com, www.emurse.com/ blog/2007/02/07/common-interview-questions.

**Top 10 Interview Questions**

Following are 10 job interview questions that business owners most frequently ask candidates.

1. Tell me about yourself.
2. Why do you want to work for us?
3. Why did you leave your last job?
4. What are your best skills?
5. What is your major weakness?
6. Do you prefer to work by yourself or with others?
7. What do you see yourself doing five years from now? Ten years from now?
8. What are your career goals?
9. What did you learn from your last job/internship/educational experience?
10. What would your last boss say about your work performance?
11. What is your most notable accomplishment?

companies that operate in a team-based environment. "In a small organization, you're going to spend a lot of time together," says Michael Harris, a management professor at the University of Missouri, St. Louis, who has participated in peer-to-peer interviews. "It becomes even more important for the entrepreneur to share some of the [hiring] responsibility with the other employees."[21] Employees involved in the process also feel more empowered and "buy-in" to the hiring process, which can be good for morale and productivity. Applicants also benefit by gaining meaningful insight into an organization's culture. It is important for employees to understand that their feedback is a valuable part of the hiring process, but that the final decision rests with the entrepreneur.[22]

*Bruce Fenton and Atlantic Financial Inc.*

When Bruce Fenton, founder of investment company Atlantic Financial Inc., is excited about a job applicant, he has the applicant meet a few of the company's employees before extending a job offer. "If someone is abrasive to the junior people, we're not interested. They wouldn't be a fit," says Fenton. However, as Fenton learned a few years ago, there are risks. After allowing an unhappy employee to spend time with an applicant the company hoped to hire, the applicant turned down the job offer. Employees bent on turning off talented applicants they see as potential competition for promotions pose another risk. "You've got to make sure the right employees [are doing the interviews]," Fenton says. Ideally employees who participate in peer-to-peer interviews have great people skills, are upbeat about the company, and understand its mission. Fenton says that peer-to-peer interviewing has decreased his company's turnover in a high-turnover industry.[23]

In interviews, entrepreneurs must be careful to avoid asking candidates illegal questions. Interviewing can be problematic and companies are more vulnerable to job discrimination lawsuits now than ever before. Although the U.S. Equal Employment Opportunity Commission (EEOC), the government agency responsible for enforcing employment laws, does not outlaw specific interview questions, it recognizes that some questions can result in employment discrimination. If a candidate files charges of discrimination against a company, the burden of proof shifts to the employer to prove that all pre-employment questions were job related and nondiscriminatory. In addition, many U.S. states have passed laws that forbid the use of certain questions or screening tools in interviews. To avoid discriminatory questions, business owners should keep in mind why they are asking a particular question. The goal is to find someone who is qualified to do the job well. By steering clear of questions about subjects that are peripheral to the job itself, employers are less likely to ask questions that will land them in court. Wise business

## TABLE 19.3 Is It Legal?

Some interview questions can lead an employer into a lawsuit. Review the following questions and then decide whether they are legal or illegal in your country.

| Legal | Illegal | Interview Question |
|:---:|:---:|---|
| ❏ | ❏ | 1. Are you currently using illegal drugs? |
| ❏ | ❏ | 2. Have you ever been arrested? |
| ❏ | ❏ | 3. Do you have any children or do you plan to have children? |
| ❏ | ❏ | 4. When and where were you born? |
| ❏ | ❏ | 5. Is there any limit on your ability to work overtime or travel? |
| ❏ | ❏ | 6. How tall are you? How much do you weigh? |
| ❏ | ❏ | 7. Do you drink alcohol? |
| ❏ | ❏ | 8. How much alcohol do you drink each week? |
| ❏ | ❏ | 9. Would your religious beliefs interfere with your ability to do the job? |
| ❏ | ❏ | 10. What contraceptive practices do you use? |
| ❏ | ❏ | 11. Are you HIV positive? |
| ❏ | ❏ | 12. Have you ever filed a lawsuit or worker's compensation claim against a former employer? |
| ❏ | ❏ | 13. Do you have physical/mental disabilities that would interfere with doing your job? |
| ❏ | ❏ | 14. Are you a citizen of this country? |

Answers (U.S.): 1. Legal. 2. Illegal. Employers cannot ask about an applicant's arrest record, but they can ask if a candidate has ever been *convicted* of a crime. 3. Illegal. Employers cannot ask questions that could lead to discrimination against a particular group (e.g., women, physically challenged, etc.). 4. Illegal. The U.S. Civil Rights Act of 1964 bans discrimination on the basis of race, color, sex, religion, or national origin. 5. Legal. 6. Illegal. Unless a person's physical characteristics are necessary for job performance (e.g., lifting 100-pound sacks of mulch), employers cannot ask candidates such questions. 7. Legal. 8. Illegal. Notice the fine line between question 7 and question 8; this is what makes interviewing challenging. 9. Illegal. This question would violate the Civil Rights Act of 1964. 10. Illegal. What relevance would this have to an employee's job performance? 11. Illegal. Under the U.S. Americans with Disabilities Act, which prohibits discrimination against people with disabilities, people that are HIV positive or have AIDS are considered "disabled." 12. Illegal. Workers who file such suits are protected from retribution by a variety of federal and state laws. 13. Illegal. This question would also violate the Americans with Disabilities Act. 14. Illegal. This question violates the Civil Rights Act of 1964.

owners ask their attorneys to review their bank of questions before using them in an interview. Table 19.3 offers a quiz to help you understand which kinds of questions are most likely to create charges of discrimination. Table 19.4 describes a simple test for determining whether an interview question might be considered discriminatory.

**SELLING THE CANDIDATE ON THE COMPANY.** In the final phase of the interview, when employers have a "high potential" candidate, they should try to sell the benefits of working for the organization. This phase begins by allowing the candidate to ask questions

## TABLE 19.4 A Guide for Interview Questions

Small business owners can use the "OUCH" test as a guide for determining whether an interview question might be considered discriminatory:

- Does the question *Omit* references to race, religion, color, sex, or national origin?
- Does the question *Unfairly* screen out a particular class of people?
- Can you *Consistently* apply the question to every applicant?
- Does the question *Have* job-relatedness and business necessity?

about the company, the job, or other issues. Experienced interviewers note the nature of these questions and the insights they give into the candidate's personality. This part of the interview also offers employers a prime opportunity to explain to the candidate why the company is an attractive place to work. The best candidates will have other offers, and it is up to the entrepreneur to make sure they leave the interview wanting to work for the company. Finally, before closing the interview, employers should thank the candidates and tell them what happens next. For example, "We will be contacting you about our decision within two weeks."

## In the Entrepreneurial  Spotlight

### ■ Sure Footed

Vail Horton, the cofounder and CEO of Keen Mobility (www.keenmobility.com), likes to glide along the hallway of his headquarters in the U.S. state of Oregon on his wooden skateboard. He enjoys checking in with employees who might need an extra jolt of encouragement or a laugh with their morning coffee. Wearing Dragon sunglasses and a dazzling smile, the man who runs this medical-device manufacturer might seem like any other brash, 30-year-old entrepreneur—with one striking difference: Horton leaves his legs behind in his office, propped up against his desk.

Doctors told Horton's parents he would never be able to walk. After consultations with rehabilitation experts and months of intense physical therapy at home, Horton took his first steps at the age of 4 with the aid of crutches and prostheses. He has been exceeding expectations ever since.

While still in college, Horton developed chronic pain in his shoulders from the prolonged wear and tear of walking on crutches. Instead of resorting to a wheelchair, he came up with a new kind of crutch that uses shock absorbers at the base to reduce impact. Realizing that he had discovered a promising business opportunity, Horton and his roommate, Jerry Carleton (now vice president of business development), decided to start a company that could help others overcome disabilities. The two launched Keen Mobility in 2002 with a lofty goal: to better the lives of customers who are elderly or disabled.

Today Keen Mobility designs and manufactures about 35 "assistive devices" that range from collapsible wheelchairs and pressure-relieving foam cushions to adjustable walkers. With a staff of 17, Horton has built a profitable business with revenues of $2 million and an

envious growth curve. That growth, however, has not come easily. Horton faces a challenge common to many small-business owners: attracting and retaining talent in a tight labor market where big competitors can offer higher pay and better perks. Three of Horton's best employees have defected to larger competitors.

Horton stresses that Keen Mobility is an exciting, innovative place to work when he meets with prospective employees. He does not attract employees with high salaries; instead, he targets job candidates who care about helping the disabled and the elderly. He tells them that by selling Keen Mobility's cutting-edge products, they will be making a difference in people's lives. "I hire those," he says, "who have enough passion to sustain them through a job that's extremely difficult." He also emphasizes Keen's ability to create exciting new products.

Innovation also led the company into a successful expansion into nursing homes and veterans hospitals in the Southeast region, which required Horton to expand his sales force and open new offices around the country. Instead of looking for sales professionals, however, he sought nurses, therapists, and other medical workers who had used Keen Mobility's products, understood the difference they made for their users, and could appreciate their value. For instance, in Boston, Massachusetts, Horton hired a physical therapist and an occupational therapist in Milwaukee as sales representatives. The new sales representatives brought experience in both patient care and the intricacies of Medicare and Medicaid regulations. Horton thought

that they would be better at persuading hospitals and nursing homes to pay a premium for his quality products. (Keen's wheelchairs and walkers are priced from $10 to $30 more than the competition's.)

Will Horton be able to take his company to the next level of success without diluting its spirit? The past has demonstrated that you can never count Horton out. When he was young, his mother stored his favorite cereal on a high kitchen shelf, forbidding anyone else in the family to help him reach it. After multiple tries and assorted bruises, he attained his goal—and he's been reaching higher ever since.

1. What are the most significant hiring and retention challenges facing Keen Mobility?
2. What are key attributes of the culture at Keen Mobility and how does that environment benefit the organization?

## Alternative Hiring and Screening Techniques

Traditional interview procedures do have flaws. The process is time consuming and may not correlate with work performance. Employers are often looking for ways that offer greater efficiency and reliability in the search process. One technique for recruiting and screening candidates is through internship programs. Growing numbers of employers are establishing internship programs because they offer the opportunity to "test drive" potential employees before hiring them. Internships, both paid and unpaid, can begin at graduate, college and even high school levels.

*PricewaterhouseCoopers*

The New York office of accounting and consulting firm PricewaterhouseCoopers targets students early with internships, scholarships, employment opportunities, and college grants with the goal of building long-term relationships that give the company an edge when recruiting full-time employees. "We begin looking for potential interns as early as high-school seniors and train them through their college graduation," says Amy Van Kirk, vice president of recruiting for PricewaterhouseCoopers. Van Kirk says interns who are hired full time have the advantage of previous training and a deeper knowledge of the company. "We end up offering 85 percent of our [college-senior] interns" full-time posts, and 90 percent of those accept the offers," says Van Kirk.[24]

Other employers use social networking and referral programs to find new hires.

*Scott Glatstein and Imperatives*

Scott Glatstein, founder and owner of the consulting firm Imperatives, has found that the usual recruiting tools work poorly for his business. "It's hard to advertise for independent consultants," says Glatstein. He has used a variety of recruitment tools, including online advertising, but now relies almost exclusively on recommendations from his 40 existing employees. "In the past six months, we've hired eight people and haven't run a single ad," says Glatstein. "Those hires came [from] referrals." The cost of using referrals is 75 percent lower than using advertising or agencies, and using referrals also reduces turnover among both new and existing employees because applicants are essentially prescreened for culture fit.[25]

More small companies are turning to popular social networking sites such as Facebook and MySpace, where they create pages designed to attract job candidates. Other companies have posted recruiting videos on YouTube. Interested candidates click on links to the company's Web site to learn more about the business and the job and can apply online. These techniques are most effective for companies that are searching for young recruits.[26]

### Check References

Entrepreneurs should take the time to check *every* applicant's references. Although many business owners see checking references as a formality and pay little attention to it, others realize the need to protect themselves (and their customers) from hiring unscrupulous workers. Is a reference check really necessary? Absolutely! A survey by Background Information Services reports that more than half of all job seekers lie on their résumés, often by inflating their job titles.[27] Checking references thoroughly can help an employer uncover false or exaggerated information. Failing to do so can be costly. Rather than rely only on the references candidates list on their résumés, experienced employers call an applicant's previous employers and talk to their immediate supervisors to get a clear picture of the applicant's job performance, character, and work habits.

*Andy Levine
and Development
Counsellors
International*

Andy Levine, president of Development Counsellors International, now requires 12 references for the final stage of the interview process. "It can be pretty amusing when you ask for 12 references. Some candidates have an e-mail to us within an hour; some we never hear from again" says Levine. "When I call references, I start by trying to get them comfortable. I make it clear that what they say will not travel back to the person. Then I often ask, 'If you had to pick three words to describe this person, what are the first ones that come to mind?' It's very interesting, the picture that emerges after you've done eight or nine of these interviews." Levin says, "Before we started this process, our average length of stay was 2.3 years. Since then, it's gone to 4.7 years."[28]

### Background Checks

Background checks may be prudent. In addition to turning up convictions for crimes such as sexual assault, a background check can show if a job candidate has been convicted of stealing from a previous employer, and a check of a candidate's driving records can show convictions for drunk driving or other traffic violations. A criminal records check, which costs $50 or less, can save a business owner thousands of dollars by avoiding a serious hiring mistake. "A lot of times, employers argue that a background check is too expensive," says Zuni Corkerton, president of RefCheck Information Services Inc. "But the litigation that comes as a result of not having done their due diligence and having been negligent in their hiring process can be far greater."[29]

A basic background check takes just three or four days and costs as little as $10. Conducting background checks is wise because courts today are more likely to hold employers liable for "negligent hiring," failing to check the background of a prospective employee. For example, a pizza chain failed to conduct a background check on a delivery driver the company hired. When the driver sexually assaulted a woman after delivering a pizza to her home, evidence showed that the employee had a prior sexual-assault conviction that a simple background check would have revealed. It proved to be a costly mistake; a court ordered the pizza chain to pay the victim $175,000 in damages. Even if a hiring mistake does not result in a lawsuit, bad publicity can destroy a business.[30]

### Conduct Employment Tests

Although various laws have made using employment tests as screening devices more difficult in recent years, many companies find them quite useful. To avoid charges of discrimination, business owners must be able to prove that the employment tests they use are both valid and reliable. A **valid test** is one that measures what it is intended to measure: for example, aptitude for selling, creativity, and integrity. A **reliable test** is one that measures consistently over time. Employers must also be sure that the tests they use measure aptitudes and factors that are job related. Many testing organizations offer ready-made tests that have been proved to be both valid and reliable, and business owners can use these tests safely. In today's environment, if a test has not been validated and proven to be reliable, or is not job-related, it is best not to use it.

Experienced small business owners do not rely on any one element in the employee selection process. They look at the total picture painted by each part of a candidate's portfolio. They know that the hiring process provides them with one of the most valuable raw materials their companies count on for success—capable, hard-working people. They also recognize that hiring an employee is not a single event but the beginning of a long-term relationship.

## Building the Right Culture and Organizational Structure

*3.* Explain how to build the kind of company culture and structure to support the entrepreneur's mission and goals and to motivate employees to achieve them.

**Company culture** is the distinctive, unwritten code of conduct that governs the behavior, attitudes, relationships, and style of an organization. It is the essence of "the way we do things around here." In many entrepreneurial companies, culture plays as important a part in gaining a competitive edge as strategy does. According to the Great Places to Work Institute, companies that have created a positive corporate culture have better financial performances than those that do not.[31]

A company's culture has a powerful impact on the way people work together in a business, how they do their jobs, and how they treat their customers. Company culture manifests itself in many ways—from how workers dress and act to the language they use. At some companies, the unspoken dress code requires workers to wear suits and ties, but at many high technology companies, employees routinely show up in jeans, T-shirts, and flip-flops. At one such company, an employee says, "If someone shows up for work in a suit, everyone immediately assumes that he is interviewing for another job."

In many companies, the culture creates its own language. At Disney theme parks, workers are not "employees;" they are "cast members." They do not merely go to work; their jobs are "parts in a performance." Customers are referred to as "guests." Whenever cast members are in sight of guests, they are "on stage." If a cast member treats someone to lunch, it's "on the mouse." Anything negative—such as a cigarette butt on a walkway—is "a bad Mickey," and anything positive is "a good Mickey."

A company's culture arises from an entrepreneur's consistent and relentless pursuit of a set of core values that everyone in the company can believe in. Nurturing the right culture in a company can enhance a company's competitive position by improving its ability to attract and retain quality workers and by creating an environment in which workers can grow and develop. In fact, as a younger generation of employees enters the workforce, companies are finding that offering a more open and relaxed culture gives them an edge in attracting the best workers. These companies embrace nontraditional, relaxed, fun cultures that incorporate concepts such as casual dress, virtual teams, telecommuting, flexible work schedules, on-site massages, cappuccinos in company cafeterias, and other cutting-edge concepts.

*Neal Rothermel and Virtual Meeting Strategies*

At Virtual Meeting Strategies (VMS), a small company that facilitates online communication, CEO Neal Rothermel is serious about creating a fun culture. Rothermel often ties company objectives to fun events with creative themes. Recently, for example, VMS launched a "Big Picture" event with a meeting for company employees at a local theater that also included popcorn and a preview of upcoming movies. When the company needed to generate a record amount of business in a short time, Rothermel declared that the company was in "survivor mode" and created an environment reminiscent of the reality television show. Managers cleared a conference room and set up tiki torches. Employee teams selected tribal names and wore headbands. Every week, the teams met, not to vote some-one off of the island, but to nominate their top survivors, employees who had excelled in their work on the project. "I wanted to find a way to share war stories across teams and celebrate above-and-beyond efforts," says Rothermel. "The returns on productivity and morale have been exponential."[32]

Today's organizational culture relies on several principles that are fundamental to cre-ating a productive, fun, and supportive workplace. These qualities include:

- *Respect for the quality of work and a balance between work life and home life.* Modern companies must recognize that their employees have lives away from work. These businesses offer flexible work schedules, part-time work, job sharing, telecommuting, sabbaticals, and conveniences such as on-site day care or concierge services that handle employees' errands. Work/life balance issues are becoming more important to employees, and companies that address them have an edge when it comes to recruiting and retaining a quality workforce. "Employers realize that by of-fering work/life programs, they are getting a lot in return in terms of productivity and commitment to the organization," says one consultant.[33]
- *A sense of purpose.* Forward-thinking companies rely on a strong sense of purpose to connect employees to the company's mission. At motorcycle legend Harley-Davidson, employees are so in tune with the company's mission that some of them have tattooed the company's name on their bodies!
- *Diversity.* Companies with appealing cultures not only accept cultural diversity in their workforces, they embrace it, actively seeking out workers with different back-grounds. They recognize that a workforce that has a rich mix of cultural diversity gives their companies more talent, skills, and abilities from which to draw. Because the entire world is now a potential market for many small companies, entrepreneurs realize that having their workforces look, act, and think like their customers, with all of their ethnic, racial, religious, and behavioral variety, is a strength.
- *Integrity.* Employees want to work for a company that stands for honesty and in-tegrity. They do not want to have to check their personal value systems at the door when they report to work. Indeed, many workers take pride in the fact they work for a company that is ethical and socially responsible. We will discuss the issues of ethics, integrity, and social responsibility in more detail in Chapter 21, "Ethics, So-cial Responsibility, and the Entrepreneur."
- *Participative management.* Modern managers recognize that employees expect a participative management style to be part of a company's culture. Today's workforce does not respond well to the autocratic management styles of yesteryear. To maxi-mize productivity and encourage commitment to accomplishing the company's mis-sion, entrepreneurs must trust and empower employees at all levels of the organization to make decisions and to take appropriate actions to do their jobs well.
- *Learning environment.* Progressive companies encourage and support lifelong learning among their employees. They are willing to invest in their employees, im-proving their skills and helping them to reach their full potential. That attitude is a strong magnet for the best and brightest workers, who know that to stay at the top of their fields, they must always be learning.
- *A sense of fun.* Smart entrepreneurs recognize that creating a culture that incorpo-rates fun into work allows them to attract and retain quality employees.

**ENTREPRENEURIAL**
**Profile**

*Paul Spiegelman and
Beryl Companies*

Beryl Companies, a call-center company with $25 million in annual sales that connects callers to hospitals and other health care organizations, operates in an industry known for low morale and high attrition. The work environment is one in which many live in fear of their jobs being outsourced and, to meet productivity standards, each person takes 80 or 90 phone calls a day. The job is tedious, but CEO Paul Spiegelman works to transform the potentially stressful environment into an over-the-top, fun workplace. "Employees don't always love the work. But they sure love coming to work," says Spiegelman. "We once staged a murder mystery on the call-center floor; teams spent eight weeks solving it. It's important to have traditions, events people get revved up for. The point is consistency. Employees should always expect fun just around the corner." Spiegelman proudly states, "We win a lot of best-place-to-work awards. That sets the bar high. People always tell me what a special place this is to work. Hearing that is what's fun for me."[34]

Companies that build their cultures on these principles have an edge when it comes to attracting, retaining, and motivating workers. In other words, creating the right culture helps a small company compete more effectively.

### Jonathan Bush and Athenahealth

Employees at Jonathan Bush's Athenahealth office ride Razor scooters around the office—and it is not just because the office is a thousand feet long. "Scooters make us more productive. At our user conference this year, our people from client operations came dressed like the [the band] Beatles—in flawless Yellow Submarine regalia—and as the Pink Ladies and T-Birds from [the musical] Grease. Why? Because in service companies like ours, when something goes wrong people often get defensive. We want our clients to see we're not like that—that we're human and accessible," says Bush.[35]

**MANAGING GROWTH AND A CHANGING CULTURE.** As companies grow, they often experience dramatic changes in their culture. Procedures become more formal, operations grow more widespread, jobs take on more structure, communication becomes more difficult, and the company's personality begins to change. As more workers come on board, employees find it difficult to know everyone in the company and to understand what their jobs entail. This transition presents a new set of demands for entrepreneurs. Unless entrepreneurs work hard to maintain their company's unique culture, they may wake up one day to find that they have sacrificed that culture—and the competitive edge that went with it—all in the name of growth.

Ironically, growth can sometimes be a small company's biggest enemy, causing a once successful business to spiral out of control. The problem stems from the fact that the organizational structure—or lack of it—and the style of management that makes an entrepreneurial start-up so successful often cannot support the business as it grows into adolescence and maturity. As a company grows, its culture tends to change and so does the need for a management infrastructure capable of supporting that growth. Compounding the problem is the entrepreneur's tendency to see all growth as good. Who would not want to be the founder of a small company whose rapid growth makes it destined to become the next rising star in the industry? Yet achieving rapid growth and managing it are two distinct challenges. Entrepreneurs must be aware of the challenges rapid growth brings with it; otherwise, they may find their companies crumbling around them as they reach warp speed.

In many cases, small companies achieve impressive growth because they bypass the traditional organizational structures, forgo rigid policies and procedures, and maintain maximum flexibility. Small companies often have an edge over their larger rivals because they are naturally quick to respond, they concentrate on creating new product and service lines, and they are willing to take the risks necessary to conquer new markets.

Growth brings with it change: changes in management style, organizational strategy, and methods of operation. Growth introduces organizational complexity. In this period of transition, an entrepreneur's challenge is to walk a fine line between retaining the small company traits that are the seeds of the company's success and incorporating the elements of infrastructure that are essential to supporting and sustaining its growth.

### Organizational Evolution

When the opportunity to grow and the organization's resources and capabilities support expansion, a small company's success may depend on the founder's willingness to transform the firm from a top-down, single leader structure to one that is team based. The founder must accept that size and complexity create situations that require delegating authority and empowering

employees. People who build successful teams understand that each team member has a role to play and that every role plays a part in contributing to the "bigger picture."

Today companies are experimenting with different kinds of teamwork as competition and complexity increase and business problems cross departmental or geographic boundaries. The consulting firm Accenture Ltd. has scores of globally dispersed teams serving clients, teams at IBM collaborate using "wiki" technology, and Google assembles teams of three or four employees to assess new ideas.[36] Entrepreneurial organizations also continue to realize the value of teams.

### Team-Based Management

Team-based management allows the founder to draw on the talents and skills of the entire organization. Workplaces with employee involvement programs, such as self-managed works teams, demonstrate a 2 to 5 percent increase in productivity.[37] Although large companies have been using self-directed work teams to improve quality, increase productivity, raise morale, lower costs, and boost motivation, team-based management also is now growing in popularity in smaller firms. In some situations, a team approach may be best suited for small companies. Even though converting from a traditional management style to a team approach requires a major change in management style, it is often easier to implement with a small number of workers.

A **self-directed work team** is a group of workers from different functional areas of a company who work together as a unit, largely without supervision, making decisions and performing tasks that once belonged only to managers. Some teams may be temporary, attacking and solving a specific problem, but many are permanent components of an organization's structure. As their name implies, these teams manage themselves, performing such functions as setting work schedules, ordering raw materials, evaluating and purchasing equipment, developing budgets, hiring and firing team members, solving problems, and a host of other activities. Teams function best in environments in which the work is interdependent and people must interact to accomplish their goals. The goal is to get people working together to serve customers better.

Managers in companies using teams are just as involved as before, but the nature of their work changes dramatically. Before teams, managers were bosses who made most of the decisions affecting their subordinates alone and hoarded information and power for themselves. In a team environment, managers take on the role of coaches who empower those around them to make decisions affecting their work and share information with workers. As facilitators, their job is to support and to serve the teams functioning in the organization and to make sure they produce results.

Companies have strong, competitive reasons for using team-based management. Companies that use teams effectively report significant gains in quality, reductions in cycle time, lower costs, increased customer satisfaction, and improved employee motivation and morale. A team-based approach is not for every organization, however. Although teams have been a salvation from failure and extinction for some companies, for others the team approach has failed. Teams are *not* easy to start, and switching from a traditional organizational structure to a team-based one is filled with potential pitfalls. Some experts agree with the criticism of teams that dates back to 1972 when Yale psychology researcher Irving Janis wrote *Victims of Groupthink*. Janis theorized that groups breed a false confidence that lead to unsound decisions that individuals would not have made on their own.[38] What makes the difference? What causes teams to fail? The following errors are common in team-oriented environments:

- Assigning a team an inappropriate task, one in which the team members may lack the necessary skills to be successful (lack of training and support).
- Creating work teams but failing to provide the team with meaningful performance targets.
- Failing to deal with known underperformers and assuming that being part of a group will solve the problem. It doesn't.
- Failing to compensate the members of the team equitably.

## In the Entrepreneurial Spotlight

### ■ When Teams Work

Few companies are as committed to teamwork as ICU Medical Inc. This California manufacturer of medical devices empowers workers to form teams to tackle almost any project. Team members set meetings, assign tasks, and create deadlines themselves. CEO George Lopez says he has never vetoed a team decision, even when he disagreed with it. These teams have altered production processes and set up a 401(k) plan, among other changes. ICU is unusual in that it allows workers to initiate the teams. It is "rare that a company says, 'Go form your own team and go address this issue,'" says Ben Rosen, a U.S. management professor.

Dr. Lopez, an internist, founded ICU in 1984 and by the early 1990s, the company had grown to $10 million in annual revenue and was preparing for an initial public offering. Demand for the company's Clave product, which connects a patient's intravenous systems, was skyrocketing, and Lopez needed to ramp up production.

With fewer than 100 employees, managing the company's rapid growth "was an overwhelming task for one entrepreneur" says Lopez, who, at the time, was still making most decisions himself and often sleeping at the office.

Then he had an epiphany watching his son play hockey. The opposing team had a star, but his son's team won. "The team was better than one player," says Dr. Lopez. He decided to delegate power by letting employees form teams, hoping it would help him spread out the decision making and encourage input from people closest to the problems.

ICU's chief financial officer quit and other executives resisted the new team-based management style. Putting the new system in place, Lopez asked employees to form teams to develop ways to boost production, but it didn't work. With no leaders and no rules, "nothing was getting done, except people were spending a lot of time talking," he says.

After about 18 months of struggling with teams, Lopez decided teams should elect leaders, which

*(continued)*

brought a vast improvement. He also hired Jim Reitz, now ICU's human-resources director, who helped him create a structure with minimal bureaucracy. They developed a set of core values and "Rules of Engagement," ground rules for how teams would work:

### Rules of Engagement

- Challenge the issue, not the person
- Consider all options
- Stand up for your position, but never argue against the facts
- Allow yourself the opportunity to seriously consider opposing views
- Lose the words 'I' and 'they' once the team reaches a decision

Employees embraced the team concept, which proved to be the solution to ICU's growth problem.

ICU also started paying teams rewards based on a percentage of the cumulative salaries of their members. These rewards can create tension, however. An employee once balked at sharing a reward with coworkers she thought had joined a team solely for the money. She proposed dividing the money based on the tasks team members performed. The team agreed. The payment system has been changed to link the size of the reward to the importance of the project. "People started thinking, 'We created a whole new product for the company and these guys painted the lunch room, and they're getting the same amount of money that we are?'" Reitz says. He encourages employees to question whether teams really met their goals and whether a project is significant enough to merit high reward levels.

Team members at ICU don't get a break from their regular jobs. Serving on teams is voluntary but some employees with special expertise are "requested" to join. "It's above and beyond your job," says business-applications manager Colleen Wilder, who has served on many teams in the 10 years at ICU. "You still have to get your job done."

Today 12 to 15 teams finish projects each quarter, often meeting weekly. The typical team has five to seven members, and the company allots $75,000 quarterly to reward those that succeed. Teams have instituted changes over the objections of top executives. Dr. Lopez, worried about the cost, didn't want to institute a 401(k) plan, but acquiesced after a team recommended one. He now concedes the plan has helped to retain employees.

ICU has instituted additional rules to help teams function smoothly. A group of employees created a 25-page handbook that concretely spells out team operations—for instance, listing eight items for "What should we do at the first meeting?"—and addresses frequently asked questions. Teams must post notes of each meeting on the company intranet and allow any employee to offer feedback.

Teams aren't perfect, but Lopez says they are better than the alternative. Once, the information-technology department ordered new laptops that many traveling staffers found too heavy. "That's what happens when you don't form a team," he says. "Top-down decisions are frequently wrong."

Lopez can veto team decisions but says he has yet to do so because he recognizes that employees must believe that they have authority for teams to work. A veto would "really have to be worth it," he says. The team would have to be putting the company "on a pathway to destruction." So far, ICU has not imploded. Last year, revenues grew 28 percent to $201.6 million, and the stock has climbed more than sixfold in the last decade.

1. What does the ICU story say about "high control" entrepreneurs and the growth of their companies?
2. What is unique about the creation and rewards associated with teams at ICU?
3. Would you expect this type of teamwork to function for other organizations? What environment would be necessary in a company for teams to succeed?

*Source:* Erin White, "How a Company Made Everyone a Team Player," *Wall Street Journal,* August 13, 007, pp. B1, B7.

To ensure the success of the teams approach, entrepreneurs must:

- ***Make sure that teams are appropriate for the company and the nature of the work.*** A good starting point is to create a "map" of the company's work flow that shows how workers build a product or deliver a service. Is the work interdependent, complex, and interactive? Would teamwork improve the company's performance?
- ***Form teams around the natural work flow and give them specific tasks to accomplish.*** Teams can be effective only if managers challenge them to accomplish specific, measurable objectives. They need targets to shoot for.

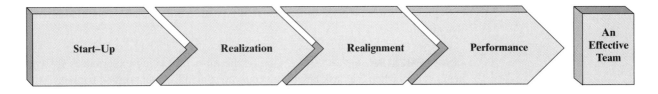

| | Start–Up | Realization | Realignment | Performance | An Effective Team |
|---|---|---|---|---|---|

| | | | | | |
|---|---|---|---|---|---|
| **Description** | • High expectations<br>• Unclear goals and roles<br>• Anxiety and reliance on leader<br>• Avoidance of tasks | • Recognition of time and effort required<br>• Roadblocks<br>• Frustration<br>• Conflict | • Resetting of goals and roles<br>• Development of trust and cooperation<br>• Progress<br>• Structure | • Involvement, openness, and teamwork<br>• Commitment both to process and to task achievement | |
| **Leadership Focus** | • Help team focus on task<br>• Provide goals and structure<br>• Supervise and define accountability | • Emphasize task and process<br>• Clarify expectations and roles<br>• Encourage open discussions and address concerns<br>• Ensure proper skills and resources | • Focus on process<br>• Promote participation and team decision making<br>• Encourage peer support<br>• Provide feedback | • Focus on monitoring and feedback<br>• Let team take responsibility for solving problems and making decisions | |

**FIGURE 19.4 The Stages of Team Development**

- *Provide adequate support and training for team members and leaders.* Team success requires a new set of skills. Workers must learn how to communicate, resolve conflict, support one another, and solve problems as a team. Smart managers see that team members get the training they need.
- *Involve team members in determining how their performances will be measured, what will be measured, and when it will be measured.* Doing so gives team members a sense of ownership and pride about the tasks they are accomplishing.
- *Make at least part of team members' pay dependent on team performance.* Companies that have used teams successfully still pay members individually, but they make successful teamwork a major part of an individual's performance review.

Figure 19.4 illustrates the four stages teams go through on their way to performing effectively and reaching goals.

## Communicating Effectively

*4. Understand the potential barriers to effective communication and describe how to overcome them.*

Entrepreneurs constantly confront dilemmas as they operate their businesses. Entrepreneurs may find they must walk the fine line between the chaos of encouraging creativity and maintaining control over their companies. At other times, they must navigate around questionable actions that might produce large short-term gains toward those actions that are also ethical. As leaders, an important and highly visible part of their jobs is to communicate the values, beliefs, and principles for which their business stands. A leader's foremost job is to communicate the company's vision. It is a never-ending job. "The essence of leadership today is to make sure that the organization knows itself," says one entrepreneur when asked about his role as leader. "There are certain durable principles that underlie the organization. The leader should embody those values. They're fundamental."[39] Nowhere is this skill more important than in small companies, where success is predicated on the founders' ability to communicate a vision and a set of values that everyone in the company can embrace.

### Improving Communication

Managers spend about 80 percent of their time in some form of communication. To some managers communicating means only one thing: sending messages to others. Although talking to people both inside and outside the organization is an important part of an entrepreneur's job, so is the other aspect of an entrepreneur's job as chief communicator: listening.

**COMMUNICATING EFFECTIVELY.** One of the most frustrating experiences for entrepreneurs occurs when they ask an employee to do something and nothing happens. Although entrepreneurs are quick to perceive the failure to respond as the employee's lack of motivation or weak work ethic, often the culprit is improper communication. The primary reasons employees usually don't do what they are expected to do have little to do with their motivation and desire to work. Instead, workers often fail to do what they are suppose to because:

- They don't know what to do.
- They don't know how to do it.
- They don't have the authority to do it.
- They get no feedback on how well or how poorly they are doing it.
- They are either ignored or punished for doing it right.
- They realize that no one ever notices even if they *are* doing it right.

The common thread running through all of these causes is poor communication between the business owner and the employee. What barriers to effective communication must entrepreneurs overcome?

- *Managers and employees don't always feel free to say what they really mean.* CEOs and top managers in companies of any size seldom hear the truth about problems and negative results from employees. This less-than-honest feedback results from the hesitancy of subordinates to tell "the boss" bad news. Over time, this tendency can paralyze the upward communication in a company.
- *Ambiguity blocks real communication.* The same words can have different meanings to different people, especially in modern companies, where the workforce is likely to be highly diverse. For instance, a business owner may tell an employee to "take care of this customer's problem as soon as you can." The owner may have meant "solve this problem by the end of the day" but the employee may think that fixing the problem by the end of the week will meet the owner's request.
- *Information overload causes the message to get lost.* With information from mail, telephone, faxes, e-mail, face-to-face communication, and other sources, employees in modern organizations are literally bombarded with messages. With such a large volume of information washing over workers, it is easy for some messages to get lost.
- *Selective listening interferes with the communication process.* Sometimes people hear only what they want to hear, selectively tuning in and out on a speaker's message. The result is distorted communication.
- *Defense mechanisms block a message.* When people are confronted with information that upsets them or conflicts with their perceptions, they immediately put up defenses. Defense mechanisms range from verbally attacking the source of the message to twisting perceptions of reality to maintain one's self-esteem.
- *Conflicting verbal and nonverbal messages confuse listeners.* Nonverbal communication includes a speaker's mannerisms, gestures, posture, facial expressions, and other forms of body language. When a speaker sends conflicting verbal and nonverbal messages, research shows that listeners will believe the nonverbal message almost every time.

How can entrepreneurs overcome these barriers to become better communicators? The following tips will help:

- *Clarify your message before you attempt to communicate it.* Before attempting to communicate your message, identify exactly what you want the receiver to think and do as a result of the message. Then focus on getting that point across clearly and concisely.
- *Use face-to-face communication whenever possible.* Although not always practical, face-to-face communication reduces the likelihood of misunderstandings because it allows for immediate feedback and nonverbal clues.

- *Be empathetic.* Try to put yourself in the place of those who will receive your message and develop it accordingly. Be sure to tell your audience up front what's in it for them.
- *Match your message to your audience.* Business owners would be very unlikely to use the same words, techniques, and style to communicate their company's financial position to a group of industry analysts as they would to a group of workers on the factory floor.
- *Be organized.* Effective communicators organize their messages so that their audiences can understand them easily.
- *Encourage feedback.* Allow listeners to ask questions and to offer feedback. Sometimes employees are hesitant to ask the boss any questions for fear of "looking stupid." One useful technique, especially when giving instructions, is to ask workers to repeat the message to make sure they understand it correctly.
- *Tell the truth.* The fastest way to destroy your credibility as a leader is to lie.
- *Don't be afraid to tell employees about the business, its performance, and the forces that affect it.* Too often, entrepreneurs assume that employees don't care about such details. Employees *are* interested in the business that employs them and want to understand where it is headed and how it plans to get there.

CH2MHILL

Executives at CH2MHILL, a full-service engineering and construction company, attribute their company's success to a corporate culture that is based on using positive strategies to motivate employees and then rewarding and celebrating their victories. CH2MHILL has spent more than $5 million to put 700 senior managers though a university training program that focuses on a philosophy called "positive organizational scholarship." The program is built on the idea that by using positive communication, companies can demonstrate superior performance. The company, which puts 120 executives through the program each year, estimates its annual overall training budget is more than $20 million.[40]

### Active Listening

When one thinks about communications, listening may not come to mind. Too often, entrepreneurs fail to develop good listening skills. A study by Brussels, Belgium-based training company, Krauthammer International, reports that managers' listening skills fail to measure up to employee expectations at least half the time. Although 95 percent of employees prefer to analyze problems with their managers, only 41 percent of employees say this happens. Eight-two percent want their managers to listen to new ideas and encourage them to think independently, but unfortunately, this happens only 41 percent of the time.[41]

The employees who work on the "front line" and interact with the company's customers every day are the *real* experts in the company's day-to-day activities and are in closer contact with potential problems and opportunities at the operating level. By encouraging employees to develop creative solutions to problems and innovative ideas and then listening to and acting on them, business owners can make their companies more successful. Wal-Mart's legendary founder Sam Walton once said, "The key to success is to get out into the store and listen to what the associates have to say. Our best ideas come from clerks and stockboys."[42]

Encouraging employees to contribute great ideas depends on entrepreneurs' ability to engage in active listening. **Active listening** avoids the rush to judgment by learning the skills of paraphrasing, summarization, and restatement. "Active listening is a state of mind that involves paying full and careful attention to the person who is speaking—it's a willingness and an ability to hear and to understand and most of all, to offer respect to the speaker," says one expert in communication.[43] An entrepreneur who develops this level of listening skill often discovers clues to improved performance and profitability. To hone their active listening skills, entrepreneurs can use the PDCH formula: identify the speaker's *purpose*, recognize the *details* that support that purpose, see the *conclusions* they can draw from what the speaker is saying, and identify the *hidden* meanings communicated by body language and voice inflections.

### The Informal Communication Network: The "Grapevine"

Despite all of the modern communication tools available, the **grapevine**, the informal lines of communication that exist in every company, remains an important link in a company's communication network. The grapevine carries vital information—and sometimes rumors—through every part of the organization with incredible speed. It is not unusual when management makes an important change in the organization for most employees to hear the news first by the grapevine. One study found that 46 percent of employees say they first hear about major changes at work through the grapevine. However, only 17 percent of their employers think that employees hear about changes this way.[44] Instant messaging and text messaging enhance the efficiency of the grapevine, allowing communication to occur within nanoseconds, all under the radar of management.

Knowing that employees are connected through the grapevine allows business owners to send out ideas to obtain reactions without making a formal announcement. The grapevine can be an excellent source of informal feedback when management is also connected. In many companies, training and information still flow downhill and not uphill. Over the next decade, successful companies will bring the knowledge economy full circle by making sure knowledge flows up, down, and sideways, increasing innovation and competitiveness. "The only way they're going to do that," says Mark Loschiavo, executive director of the Laurence A. Baiada Center for Entrepreneurship in Technology at Drexel University in Philadelphia, "is if they break down the barriers that say, 'Because you work for me, I can't learn from you.'"

*Kim Seymour
and Cravings*

One entrepreneur, Kim Seymour, founder and owner of Cravings, a retail company that sells trendy maternity clothing and accessories, has learned the value of listening to the employee grapevine for feedback. Seymour seeks advice from her three employees, who have taught her about merchandising, marketing, and customer relations. One employee had spent nine years as a retail manager, experience Seymour didn't have when she started the company. "There's no way someone is going to be an expert in every aspect of running a business," says Seymour.[45]

## The Challenge of Motivating Workers

**5.** Discuss the ways in which entrepreneurs can motivate their employees to achieve higher levels of performance.

**Motivation** is the degree of additional effort an employee exerts to accomplish a task; it shows up as excitement about work. Motivating workers to higher levels of performance is one of the most difficult and challenging tasks facing a small business manager. Few things are more frustrating to a business owner than an employee with a tremendous amount of talent who lacks the desire to use it. This section discusses four aspects of motivation: empowerment, job design, rewards and compensation, and feedback.

### Empowerment

One motivating principle is empowerment. **Empowerment** involves giving workers at every level of the organization the authority, the freedom, and the responsibility to control their own work, to make decisions, and to take action to meet the company's objectives. Research indicates that employees experience increased initiative and motivation when they are empowered. Empowerment affects their self-confidence and the level of tenacity they display when faced with setbacks. Empowered people take responsibility for making decisions and following them through to completion—they feel energized and excited by what they do, and are more likely to achieve mutually agreed goals.[46] Empowerment complements a team-based management style discussed earlier in this chapter. Competitive forces, growth, and a more demanding workforce challenge business owners to share power with everyone in the organization, even if they do not use a team-based approach.

Empowering employees requires a different style of management and leadership from that of the traditional manager. Business owners who share information, responsibility, authority, and power soon discover that their success (and their company's success) is magnified many times over. Even when the information being shared is not positive, the results can be.

Empowered workers become more successful on the job, which means the entrepreneur's firm has a better chance of survival and ultimate success. Empowerment builds on what real

## The Power of Empowerment

Empowering people involves seven important steps:

1. *Create the vision.* To empower people, you must harness their enthusiasm and their creativity. This means painting a meaningful picture of what the future could look like and how they can contribute to it. Even if it seems beyond credibility or beyond reach, try to create a sense of "we're in this together" and invite people to add their efforts to the collective goal. If they accept your invitation, you can strengthen their commitment by allowing them to use their talents to make that vision of the future become reality.

2. *Motivate.* Work to understand the values, goals, and motivations of the people who are critical to your success. Understanding their passions and motivations helps align their energy with the tasks that must be done. Ask them to share their aspirations within the company and how they want to contribute to achieve their goals.

3. *Identify barriers.* Organizations often ask for one set of behaviors while systematically encouraging another. For example, if a company wants to achieve its goals through teamwork, its compensation system should not reward only individual achievements. An organization that wants to be known for its responsiveness to customers should give employees the authority to resolve customers' problems without having to get management's approval. For instance, at the hotel chain Hampton Inn, any employee, from desk clerk or housekeeper to breakfast hostess or hotel manager, has the power to resolve a guest's problems, including giving a disgruntled guest a free stay. "You don't have to call an 800 [toll-free] number," says one top manager. "Just mention it at the front desk or to any employee—a housekeeper, maintenance person or breakfast hostess—and, on the spot, your stay is free."

4. *Ensure that necessary resources are in place.* Empowering people involves training, access to resources, and support from top managers. Determine the resources people need to get the job done and make sure that they have them.

5. *Provide encouragement and support.* Think about how to support empowered behavior. Identify the existing channels of communication that allow employees to share the information that is necessary to do their jobs. Are these channels clear and free flowing, or are they blocked by restrictive politics or etiquette? Be proactive when asking teams about the changes the company must make to allow empowerment to work. Plan to act as a sounding board for employees' concerns, frustrations, and disappointments rather than allow them to provide negative fodder for the grapevine.

6. *Eliminate fear.* Most people find change threatening. Remember: You are asking them to do something that they have not done before. As a result, they are likely to feel uncertain and vulnerable. They may be asking themselves what will happen if they "get it wrong." When things fail to go according to plan, it is important to respond properly. The *worst* thing a manager can do is punish employees who make mistakes. The goal is to create an atmosphere of positive learning rather than of criticism.

7. *Monitor and celebrate success.* When an empowered employee or team solves a problem or provides outstanding customer service, be sure to celebrate the accomplishment *publicly.* Tangible rewards can be effective but are not always as effective as simple recognition. Circulate stories about empowered employees' successes within the company so that they become part of the company's folklore. Theater and drama, effectively done, can emphasize a point well, making room for imaginative celebrations and rewards.

*Source:* Adapted from "Empowering Your Employees," *bNet.com,* www.bnet.com/2410-13059_23-95573.html; Gary Stoller, "Companies Give Front-Line Employees More Power," *USA Today,* June 26, 2005, www.usatoday.com/money/companies/management/2005-06-26-service-usat_x.htm.

business leaders already know: that the people in their organizations bring with them to work an amazing array of talents, skills, knowledge, and abilities. Workers are willing—even anxious—to put these to use; unfortunately, in too many businesses, suffocating management styles and poorly designed jobs quash workers' enthusiasm and motivation. Enlightened business owners recognize their workers' abilities, develop them, and then give workers the freedom and the power to use them. Empowered employees are more likely to display creativity and initiative in problem solving when they believe that management respects their ideas and talents

When implemented properly, empowerment can produce impressive results, not only for the business but also for newly empowered employees. For the business, benefits typically include significant productivity gains, quality improvements, more satisfied customers, improved morale, and increased employee motivation. For workers, empowerment offers the chance to do a greater variety of work that is more interesting and challenging. Empowerment challenges workers to make the most of their creativity, imagination, knowledge, and skills. This method of management encourages them to take the initiative to identify and solve problems on their own and as part of a team. As empowered workers see how the various parts of a company's manufacturing or service systems fit together, they realize their need to acquire more skills and knowledge to do their jobs well. Entrepreneurs must realize that empowerment and training go hand in hand.

Not every worker *wants* to be empowered, however. Some will resist, wanting only to "put in their eight hours and go home." Companies that move to an empowerment philosophy will lose about five percent of their workforce because they simply are unwilling or are unable to make the change. Another 75 percent of the typical workforce will accept empowerment and thrive under it, and the remaining 20 percent will pounce on it eagerly because they want to contribute their talents and their ideas.

Empowerment works best when entrepreneurs:

- ■ *Are confident enough to give workers all of the authority and responsibility they can handle.* Initially, this may involve giving workers the power to tackle relatively simple assignments. As their confidence and ability grow, most workers are eager to take on additional responsibility.
- ■ *Play the role of coach and facilitator.* Smart entrepreneurs empower their workers and then get out of the way so they can do their jobs.
- ■ *Recognize that empowered employees will make mistakes.* The worst thing an entrepreneur can do when empowered employees make mistakes is to hunt them down and punish them. That teaches everyone in the company to avoid taking risks and to always play it safe—something no innovative small business can afford.
- ■ *Hire people who can blossom in an empowered environment.* Empowerment is not for everyone. Entrepreneurs quickly learn that as costly as hiring mistakes are, these errors are even more costly in an empowered environment. Ideal candidates are high-energy self-starters who enjoy the opportunity to grow and to enhance their skills.
- ■ *Train workers continuously to upgrade their skills.* Empowerment demands more of workers than traditional work methods. Managers are asking workers to solve problems and make decisions they have never made before. To handle these problems well, workers need training, especially in effective problem-solving techniques, communication, teamwork, and technical skills.
- ■ *Trust workers to do their jobs.* Once workers are trained to do their jobs, entrepreneurs must learn to trust them to assume responsibility for their jobs. After all, they are the real experts; they face the problems and challenges every day.
- ■ *Listen to workers when they have ideas, solutions, or suggestions.* Because they are the experts on the job, employees often come up with incredibly insightful, innovative ideas for improving them—if business owners give them the chance. Surveying employees, for example, can be a critical part of companies' efforts to bolster employees' commitment to their jobs, a concept human-resource pros call employee engagement. Engaged workers are more willing to "pitch in" when needed and to promote the company outside of work. More employers are adopting employee-engagement surveys instead of relatively simplistic assessments of job satisfaction. These surveys track employees' commitment and motivation using questions on attitudes toward

coworkers, understanding of responsibilities, and the quality of feedback they receive. However, these efforts can backfire if companies don't act on problems workers identify. "That undermines the credibility of the process," says Robert Kelley, a U.S. business professor.[47] Regardless of the process, failing to acknowledge or to act on employees' ideas sends them a clear message: Your ideas really don't count.

*Yum! Brands Inc.*

At Yum! Brands Inc., parent of fast-food restaurants including KFC and Long John Silver's, new employees take a survey after a few weeks to assess how well their managers covered job basics—such as scheduling, benefits, and uniform requirements. Yum! handles these surveys with an automated process: Employees call a toll-free number and their anonymous answers are sent by e-mail to managers. Yum! reports that turnover among workers who take the surveys is lower than that among workers who do not. Yum! says restaurants that have adopted the program also score high on customer surveys on cleanliness, accuracy, and speed. Houston KFC restaurant manager Jonathan McDaniel says the surveys seem to make workers more enthusiastic. "They really love giving their opinions," he says. "That's the most important part of it—that they have a voice and that they're heard."[48]

■ *Recognize workers' contributions.* One of the most important tasks a business owner has is to recognize positive employee performance. In the book *The Carrot Principle,* authors Adrian Gostick and Chester Elton point out that recognition must be frequent, specific, and timely—not to mention deserved.[49] Some businesses reward workers with monetary awards; others rely on recognition and praise; still others use a combination of money and praise. Whatever system an owner chooses, the key to keeping a steady flow of ideas, improvements, suggestions, and solutions is to recognize the people who supply them. Some employers are implementing programs to allow coworkers to recognize the contributions of employees.

*Kimley-Horn and Associates*

Kimley-Horn and Associates, a civil-engineering company, has found that it pays to have employees reward other employees. At any time and without management's permission, any Kimley-Horn employee can award a $50 bonus to any other employee—no strings attached. "It works because it's real time, and it's not handed down from management," says Barry Barber, Kimley-Horn's human resources director. "Any employee who does something exceptional receives recognition from their peers within minutes." To make an award, an employee downloads a form, explains his thinking, signs it, and—if possible—delivers it to the recipient in person. The recipient sends the form to payroll to cash it, but everyone knows that the *real* reward is the recognition from a fellow employee.[50]

■ *Share information with workers.* For empowerment to succeed, entrepreneurs must make sure workers get adequate information, the raw material for good decision making. Some companies have gone beyond sharing information to embrace **open-book management**, in which employees have access to *all* of a company's records, including its financial statements. The goal of open-book management is to enable employees to understand why they need to raise productivity, improve quality, cut costs, and improve customer service. Under open-book management, employees:
  1. See and learn to understand the company's financial statements and other critical numbers in measuring its performance.
  2. Learn that a significant part of their jobs is making sure those critical numbers move in the right direction.
  3. Have a direct stake in the company's success through profit sharing, ESOPs, or performance-based bonuses.
In short, open-book management establishes a solid link between employees' knowledge and their performance.

## Job Design

Managers have learned that the job itself and the way it is designed can be a source of motivation for workers. During the industrial age, work was organized on the principle of **job simplification**. This involved breaking the work down into its simplest form and standardizing each task, as in assembly line operations. The scope of jobs organized in such a way is extremely narrow, resulting in impersonal, monotonous, and boring work that creates little challenge or motivation for workers. The result can be apathetic, unmotivated workers who care little about quality, customers, or costs.

To break this destructive cycle, some companies have redesigned jobs so that they offer workers intrinsic rewards and motivation. Three job design strategies are common: job enlargement, job rotation, and job enrichment.

- *Job enlargement* (or *horizontal job loading*) adds more tasks to a job to broaden its scope. For instance, rather than having an employee simply mount four screws in computers as they come down an assembly line, the worker might assemble, install, and test the entire motherboard, perhaps as part of a team. The idea is to make the job more varied and to allow employees to perform a more complete unit of work.

- *Job rotation* involves cross-training employees so they can move from one job in the company to others, giving them a greater number and variety of tasks to perform. As employees learn other jobs within an organization, both their skills and their understanding of the company's purpose and processes increase. Cross-trained workers are more valuable because they give a company the flexibility to shift workers from low-demand jobs to those where they are most needed. As an incentive for workers to learn to perform other jobs within an operation, some companies offer **skill-based pay**, a system under which the more skills workers acquire, the more they earn.

- *Job enrichment* (or *vertical job loading*) involves building motivators into a job by increasing the planning, decision-making, organizing, and controlling functions—the traditional managerial tasks—that workers perform. The idea is to make every employee a manager—at least a manager of his or her own job. Notice that empowerment, discussed earlier in the chapter, is based on the principle of job enrichment. To enrich employees' jobs, a business owner must build five core characteristics into them:
    1. *Skill variety* is the degree to which a job requires a variety of different skills, talents, and activities from the worker. Does the job require the worker to perform a variety of tasks that demand a variety of skills and abilities, or does it force the worker to perform the same task repeatedly?
    2. *Task identity* refers to the degree to which a job allows the worker to complete a whole or identifiable piece of work. Does the employee build an entire piece of furniture (perhaps as part of a team), or does the employee merely attach four screws?
    3. *Task significance* describes the degree to which a job substantially influences the lives or work of others—employees or final customers. Does the employee get to deal with customers, either internal or external? One effective way to establish task significance is to put employees in touch with customers so that they can see how customers use the product or service they make.
    4. *Autonomy* is the degree to which a job gives a worker freedom, independence, and discretion in planning and performing tasks. Does the employee make decisions affecting his or her work, or must the employee rely on someone else—the owner, a manager, or a supervisor—to "call the shots"?
    5. *Feedback* is the degree to which a job gives workers direct, timely information about the quality of their performance. Does the job give employees feedback about the quality of their work, or does the product (and all information about it) simply disappear after it leaves the worker's station?

As the workforce and employers continue to change, business is changing the way people work, moving away from a legion of full-time employees in traditional 8-to-5, on-site jobs. Organizational structures, even in small companies, are flatter than ever before, as the lines between traditional "managers" and "workers" become blurred.[51] Rather than resembling a pyramid, more organizations now resemble a spider's web, with a network of interconnected employee specialists working in teams and using a variety of communication links to make decisions without having to meet or go through layers of management.

Changes in workplace design and the integration of technology has resulted in an economy where productivity per employee continues to grow. The nature of how work is done has also changed as workers demand more flexibility in their jobs. One study found that 51 percent of employees say they prefer a job that offers flexible working hours more than one that offers the opportunity for advancement.[52] Many companies are providing that flexibility in the form of flextime, job sharing, and flexplace.

**Flextime** is an arrangement under which employees build their work schedules around a set of "core hours"—such as 11 A.M. to 3 P.M.—but have flexibility about when they start and stop work. For instance, one worker might choose to come in at 7 A.M. and leave at 3 P.M. to attend her son's soccer game, and another may work from 11 A.M. to 7 P.M. Flextime not only raises levels of job satisfaction and worker morale, but it also makes it easier for companies to attract and retain high-quality young workers who want rewarding careers without sacrificing their lifestyles. One recent survey found that employees with high flexibility in their work arrangements reported more than twice the level of job satisfaction as workers with low flexibility in their work arrangements.[53] In addition, companies using flextime schedules often experience lower levels of tardiness and absenteeism.

**Job sharing** is a work arrangement in which two or more people share a single full-time job. For instance, two college students might share the same job, one working mornings and the other working afternoons. Employees who job share often cite "quality of life" issues as the main reason for the arrangement.[54] Although job sharing affects a relatively small portion of the nation's workforce, it is an important job design strategy for some companies that find it difficult to recruit capable, qualified full-time workers. Job sharing has become extremely popular among retired workers who want to supplement their retirement income while remaining active, alert, and having a feeling of remaining valuable contributors to society. Experts do caution that without clear and close coordination between the job sharers, neither the employees nor the company will benefit. The job sharers must invest time to coordinate their activities.[55]

**Flexplace** is a work arrangement in which employees work at a place other than the traditional office, such as a satellite branch closer to their homes or, in some cases, at home. Flexplace is an easy job design strategy for companies to use because of **telecommuting**. Technology enables employees greater flexibility in choosing where they work. Today, it is quite simple for workers to hook up electronically to their workplaces (and to all of the people and the information there) from practically anywhere on the planet!

*ENTREPRENEURIAL*
*Profile*

*Best Buy*

Employees at the corporate headquarters of Best Buy, the electronics retailer, can work whenever and wherever they want, as long as they get their work done. Welcome to ROWE—Results-Only Work Environment. The experiment started within Best Buy's communications and properties divisions and now includes about 80 percent of the company's corporate employees. Since the program began, the productivity of ROWE teams has increased an average of 35 percent over the past two years, and turnover rates in the company's dotcom, sourcing, and logistics divisions are down 90 percent, 75 percent, and 50 percent, respectively. This success means Best Buy will bring ROWE to its retail stores as well. Productivity is up at Best Buy because "people are not just putting in time—when they're working, they're working," says Jody Thompson, who implemented ROWE with coworker Cali Ressler. The duo are now the principals of CultureRX, a Best Buy consulting subsidiary that is spreading the results-only approach, which can work for a growing, teamwork-oriented company with processes that are not highly complicated and not clock-driven.[56]

Jody Thompson (left) and Cali Ressler implemented a flexible work environment at Best Buy, and productivity climbed.

A majority of workers prefer telecommuting because it offers flexibility and reduces commuting costs, time, and hassles.[57] Telecommuting makes it easier for employees to strike a balance between their work and home lives and leads to higher productivity. Studies show that telecommuters are from 4 percent to 12 percent more productive than office-bound workers.[58] Companies also benefit from telecommuting in other ways. Management Recruiters International estimates that employers can save $10,000 annually for each telecommuting worker by reduced absenteeism and job retention costs alone.[59] Managers at Sun Microsystems say they have reduced the company's office space expense by $71 million since employees began telecommuting.[60]

Before shifting to telecommuting, entrepreneurs must address the following questions.

1. *Does the nature of the work fit telecommuting?* Obviously, some jobs are better-suited for telecommuting than others. Positions in which employees work independently, use computers frequently, or spend a great deal of time calling on customers and clients are good candidates for telecommuting.
2. *Can you monitor compliance with wage and hour laws for telecommuters?* In general, employers must keep the same employment records for telecommuters that they do for traditional office workers.
3. *Which workers are best suited for telecommuting?* Those who are self-motivated, are disciplined, and have been around long enough to establish solid relationships with coworkers make the best telecommuters.
4. *Can you provide the equipment and the technical support telecommuters need to be productive?* Telecommuting often requires an investment in laptop computers, fax machines, extra telephone lines, high speed Internet access, and software. Workers usually need technical training as well because they often assume the role of their own technical support staff.
5. *Are you adequately insured?* Employers should make certain the telecommuting equipment employees use in their homes is covered under their insurance policies.
6. *Can you keep in touch?* Telecommuting works well provided long-distance employees stay in touch with headquarters. Frequent telephone conferences, regular e-mail messages, and occasional personal appearances in the office prevent employees from losing contact with what's happening "at work."

**Hoteling** is a variation of telecommuting that has become a significant trend in professional office management.[61] Office hoteling allows employees who spend most of their time away from the office to share the same office space at different times, just as travelers use the same hotel rooms on different days. Today the concept is used by diverse businesses including real estate agencies, consulting firms, law firms, manufacturers' representatives, telecommuters, and flex-time workers.[62] Employees retain their own telephone number extensions and voice mailboxes. Some companies provide special rooms that are designed specifically for hoteling that are equipped with tables, chairs, and even food service.[63] These flexible office designs and furnishings allow workers to configure these "hot offices" (so called because they turn over so quickly that the seats are still hot from the previous user) to suit their individual needs. Workers can connect their laptops, forward their telephone calls to their temporary offices, and even move mobile file cabinets in when they need them. Hoteling reduces the amount of physical office space, lowering overhead costs while (ideally) ensuring that every worker can access office resources when necessary.

## Rewards and Compensation

The rewards an employee gets from the job itself are intrinsic rewards, but managers have at their disposal a wide variety of extrinsic rewards to motivate workers. The key to using rewards to motivate involves tailoring them to the needs and characteristics of the workers. Effective reward systems tap into the values and issues that are important to people. Smart entrepreneurs take the time to learn what makes their employees "tick" and build their reward systems around those. For instance, to a technician making $30,000 a year, a chance to earn a $5,000 bonus would most likely be a powerful motivator. To an executive earning $200,000 a year, it may not be.

One of the most popular rewards is money. Cash is an effective motivator—up to a point. Over the last three decades, many companies have moved to **pay-for-performance compensation systems**, in which employees' pay depends upon how well they perform their jobs. In other words, extra productivity equals extra pay. By linking employees' compensation directly to the company's financial performance, an entrepreneur increases the likelihood that workers will achieve performance targets that are in their best interest and in the company's best interest.

Pay-for-performance systems work only when employees see a clear connection between their performance and their pay. That's where small companies actually have an advantage over large businesses. Because they work for small companies, employees can see more clearly the impact their performance has on the company's profitability and ultimate success than their counterparts at large corporations. To be successful, however, pay-for-performance systems should meet the following criteria:

- *Performance-based.* Employees' incentive pay must be clearly and closely linked to their performances.
- *Relevant.* Entrepreneurs must set up the system so that employees see the connection between what they do every day on the job—selling to customers, producing a product, or anything else—and the rewards they receive under the system.
- *Simple.* The system must be simple enough so that employees understand and trust it. Complex systems that employees have difficulty understanding will not produce the desired results.
- *Equitable.* Employees must believe the system is fair.
- *Inclusive.* The system should be inclusive. Entrepreneurs are finding creative ways to reward all employees, no matter what their jobs might be.
- *Timely.* The company should make frequent payouts to employees. A single annual payout is ineffective—employees have long since forgotten what they did to earn the incentive pay. Many companies pay employees the week after they have achieved an important goal. Regular and frequent feedback is an essential ingredient in any incentive-pay program.

Money is not the only motivator business owners have at their disposal, of course. In fact, non-financial incentives can be more important sources of employee motivation than money. After its initial motivational impact, money loses its impact; it does not have a lasting motivational effect (and for small businesses, with their limited resources, a lasting effect is a plus). Often the most meaningful motivating factors are the simplest ones—praise, recognition, respect, feedback, job security, promotions, and others—things that any small business, no matter how limited its budget, can do. Entrepreneurs can offer praise, recognition, and daily demonstrations of respect for workers on a regular basis at absolutely no cost. When an employee has done an exceptional job, an entrepreneur should be the first to recognize that accomplishment and the first to say "thank you." Praise is a simple, yet powerful, motivational tool. People enjoy getting praise; it's just human nature. As the writer Mark Twain once said, "I can live for two months on a good compliment." Praise is an easy and inexpensive reward for employees producing extraordinary work.

One of the surest ways to kill high performance is simply to fail to recognize the performance and the employees responsible for it. Failing to praise good work eventually conveys the message that an entrepreneur either doesn't care about exceptional performance or cannot distinguish between good work and poor work. In either case, through inaction, the entrepreneur destroys employees' motivation to excel.

Because they lack the financial resources of bigger companies, small business owners must be more creative when it comes to giving rewards that motivate workers. In many cases, however, using rewards other than money gives small businesses an advantage. These rewards often have more impact on employee performance over time. In short, rewards do *not* have to be expensive to be effective, but they should be creative and should have a direct link to employee performance. Consider how the following rewards for exceptional performance both recognize the employee's contribution while also building a positive organizational culture:

- The company CEO washes the top performing employee's car at lunchtime in front of the building.
- A small firm that historically suffered from high levels of tardiness created a poker game with a weekly $25 prize. Employees who are on time every morning receive a card. The best hand on Friday wins the prize.
- The best employee's suggestion, as judged by an employee team, wins an evening for two with limousine service and dinner.
- When one company's workers complete a challenging assignment, the owner treats them to company-paid shopping sprees, movie outings, or tickets to a baseball game, all during office hours.

Whatever system of rewards they use, managers will be most successful if they match rewards to employees' interests and tastes. For instance, the ideal reward for one employee might be tickets to a hockey game; to another, it might be tickets to a musical show. Once again, because they know their employees so well, this is an area in which small business owners have an advantage over large companies. The better entrepreneurs know their employees' interests and tastes, the more effective they will be at matching rewards with performance.

For highly skilled people, work is often about more than just money. Standard financial incentives—bonuses, stock options, or the lure of a raise or corner office—do not always motivate highly skilled or extremely creative people to do their best work. They sometimes respond more strongly to intrinsic rewards. The nature of the job and the structure of the work environment must also meet their inner needs and desires. Suppose that a young working mother is working partly for the money, but she has other strong drives and needs. You might effectively harness her energies by offering a tailored mix of intrinsic factors—perhaps a more flexible schedule and a willingness to look at results rather than worry so much about how she gets them. Leslie Perlow of the University of Michigan documented an electronics company that granted this very mix to such a woman, a project team leader. Her next performance review was her best ever.[64]

In the future, managers will rely more on non-monetary rewards—praise, recognition, car washes, letters of commendation, and others—to create a work environment where employees take pride in their work, enjoy it, are challenged by it, and get excited about it—in short, act like owners of the business themselves. The goal is to let employees know that every person is important and that the company notices, appreciates, and recognizes excellent performance.

## Teams, Tightropes, and Profit-Sharing

Guy Laliberte finds managing his team to be a real circus. French Canadian Laliberte is the founder, majority owner, and CEO of Cirque du Soleil, a collection of globetrotting acrobatic troupes. Formerly a fire-breathing accordionist street performer, Laliberte founded Cirque du Soleil with 20 other ambitious street artists in 1984. Today he has to juggle the demands of creative and financial types while walking a tightrope among the 40 nationalities represented by Cirque du Soleil's 3,000 employees, who speak 25 different languages. More than 700 of those employees are performers in the company's shows, and the rest work behind the scenes to provide the support that makes the performances spectacular, audience-pleasing events.

Cirque du Soleil has grown dramatically since 1984. Today the company has nine tours and five permanent shows around the globe and generates $500 million in revenue annually. Getting everyone to work under the same tent requires a delicate managerial balancing act, but Laliberte is a master ring leader. "Cirque du Soleil depends on its capacity to balance creativity and business," says Laliberte, who works from the company's Montreal headquarters.

A key moment came in 1987 when Cirque first entered the U.S. market. With profits soaring, performers wanted to reinvest the money into the show, but Laliberte wanted to start a second troupe. "We'll use the profit to start the next troupe and then reinvest in the show you're working on," he explained. "Let's build an armada." Since then, the Cirque du Soleil portfolio has grown to 13 troupes that travel to 100 cities on four continents. Every year, Laliberte returns 10 percent of the company's profits to the employees.

To ensure the long-term cooperation of the core management team—the COO, CFO, and vice president of creation—Laliberte offered them a percentage of the company if they agreed to 10-year employment contracts with the company. The core team meets 10 times a year, and each member is expected to travel to find people to establish permanent shows in new countries. "We need to enroll people who come from those cultures," Laliberte says.

For a company with such far-flung operations as Cirque du Soleil's, hiring the right people and sustaining its supportive culture are crucial to long-term success. Sorting through the "beautiful piles" of 50,000 résumés that job seekers submit each year is a challenging task, admits Suzanne Gagnon, vice-president of human resources. To make the process more effective and more efficient, Gagnon began working with a professional staffing company. The result is a Web-based tool that allows candidates to apply for jobs online and

*(continued)*

enables Cirque managers to control the recruitment process electronically from initial contact to the final hiring decision.

Managing people who have run away from home to join the circus presents challenges for Laliberte and the management team. In addition to maintaining a global human resources department with branches in Montreal, Las Vegas, and Amsterdam, Cirque du Soleil sends a human resources manager on every touring show to handle issues such as insurance coverage, immigration, and work/life balance. A constant challenge is helping performers plan for the day when the spotlight dims and they no longer will be able to perform as acrobats, tightrope walkers, and other on-stage roles. "Because our artists are so passionate and so intense, you have to work things a little differently," explains Gagnon. "You can't just put together a traditional career planning program and have them go with the flow." To address the issue, in 2003 Cirque du Soleil launched Crossroads, a career transitions program that helps performers plan for their post-performing years. Crossroads helps performers discover alternative careers within the industry (and often within the company itself) such as stage manager, make-up artist, fitness coach, and others by connecting them with professionals already in those careers to serve as advisors and mentors.

Laliberte credits his ability to picking the right team members to his experience as a street performer. "You develop the ability to read people," he says. At Cirque du Soleil, Laliberte has built a self-policing corporate culture. "If somebody is trying to take advantage, there's a natural rejection," he explains. "In some ways, we're still a bunch of little street kids."

1. Use the Internet to research the challenges that companies that hire performing artists face. What does Laliberte mean when he says, "Cirque du Soleil depends on its capacity to balance creativity and business"?
2. Why do you think Cirque du Soleil receives 50,000 résumés each year? What impact does Cirque du Soleil's profit-sharing plan have on its ability to recruit employees?
3. Explain the benefits that the company's Crossroads program provides employees and Cirque du Soleil.

*Sources:* Adapted from Telis Demos, "Cirque du Balancing Act," *Fortune,* June 12, 2006, p. 114; Cindy Waxer, "Cirque du Soleil's Balancing Act," *Workforce Management,* January 25, 2005, pp. 52–53.

## Performance Feedback

Business owners not only must motivate employees to excel in their jobs, but they must also focus their efforts on the right targets. Providing feedback on progress toward those targets can be a powerful motivating force in a company. To ensure that the link between their vision for the company and its operations is strong, entrepreneurs must build a series of performance measures that serve as periodic monitoring points. For each critical element of the organization's performance (e.g., product or service quality, financial performance, market position, productivity, employee development), entrepreneurs should develop specific measures that connect daily responsibilities with the company's overall strategic direction. These standards become the benchmarks for measuring employees' performance and the company's progress. The adage "what gets measured and monitored gets done" is true for most organizations. By connecting the company's long-term strategy to its daily operations and measuring performance, entrepreneurs make it clear to everyone in the company what is most important.

Getting or giving feedback implies that business owners have established meaningful targets that serve as standards of performance for them, their employees, and the company as a whole. One characteristic successful people have in common is that they set goals and objectives, usually challenging ones, for themselves. Business owners are no different. Successful entrepreneurs usually set targets for performance that make them stretch to achieve, and then they encourage their employees to do the same. The result is that they keep their companies constantly moving forward.

For feedback to have impact as a motivating force in a business requires business owners to follow the procedure illustrated in Figure 19.5, the feedback loop.

**DECIDING WHAT TO MEASURE.** The first step in the feedback loop is deciding what to measure. Every business is characterized by a set of numbers that are critical to its success, and these "critical numbers" are what entrepreneurs should focus on. Obvious critical

**FIGURE 19.5 The Feedback Loop**

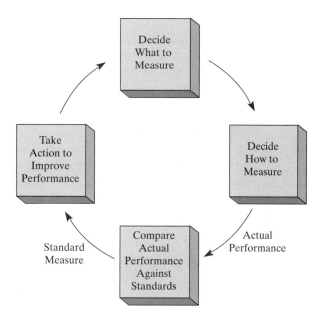

numbers include sales, profits, profit margins, cash flow, and other standard financial measures. However, running beneath these standard and somewhat universal measures of performance is an undercurrent of critical numbers that are unique to a company's operations. In most cases, these are the numbers that actually drive profits, cash flow, and other financial measures and are the company's *real* critical numbers.

In a conversation with another business owner, a hotel franchisee said that his company's critical number was profit and that the way to earn a profit was to control costs. His managerial efforts focused on making sure that his employees knew exactly what to do, how to do it, and how much they could spend doing it. The only problem was that the hotel was losing money.

"Tell me," said his friend, "how do you make money in this business?"

"We fill rooms," said the hotelier.

"How many rooms do you have to fill to break even?"

"Seventy-one percent," came the reply, "but we're only running at 67 percent."

"How many people know that?" asked his friend.

"Two," he said.

"Maybe that's your problem," observed his friend.

The hotel owner quickly realized that one of his company's most important critical numbers was occupancy rate; *that's* what drove profits! His managerial focus had been misguided, and he had failed to get his employees involved in solving the problem. The hotel owner put together an incentive plan for employees based on occupancy rate. Once the rate surpassed 71 percent, all employees qualified for bonuses, and the higher the occupancy rate, the higher the bonuses. Working with his employees, he identified other critical numbers, such as customer satisfaction levels and retention rates, and began tracking results and posting them for everyone to see. Since then, the hotel's occupancy rate, customer satisfaction scores, and customer retention rate have shot up. The hotel owner had learned not only what his company's critical numbers were but also how to use them to motivate employees.[65]

**DECIDING HOW TO MEASURE.** Once business owners identify their companies' critical numbers, the issue of how to best measure them arises. In some cases, identifying the critical numbers defines the measurements owners must make, and measuring them simply becomes a matter of collecting and analyzing data. In other cases, the method of measurement is not as obvious—or as tangible. For instance, in some businesses, social responsibility is a key factor, but how should managers measure their company's performance on such an intangible concept? One of the best ways to develop methods for measuring such factors is to use brainstorming sessions involving employees, customers, and even outsiders. For example, one company used this technique to develop a "fun index," which used the results of an employee survey to measure how much fun employees had at work (and, by extension, how satisfied they were with their work, the company, and their managers).

**COMPARING ACTUAL PERFORMANCE AGAINST STANDARDS.** In this stage of the feedback loop, the idea is to look for deviations *in either direction* from the performance standards the company has set for itself. In other words, opportunities to improve performance arise when there is a gap between "what should be" and "what is." The most serious deviations usually are those in which actual performance falls far below the standard. Managers and employees must focus their efforts on figuring out why actual performance is substandard. The goal is *not* to hunt down the guilty party (or parties) for punishment but to discover the cause of the poor performance and fix it. Managers should not ignore deviations in the other direction, however. When actual performance consistently exceeds the company's standards, it is an indication that the standards are set too low. The company should look closely at "raising the bar another notch" to spur motivation.

**TAKING ACTION TO IMPROVE PERFORMANCE.** When managers or employees detect a performance gap, their next challenge is to decide on a course of action that will eliminate it. Typically, several suitable alternatives to solving a performance problem exist; the key is finding an acceptable solution that solves the problem quickly, efficiently, and effectively.

### Performance Appraisal

One of the most common methods of providing feedback on employee performance is through **performance appraisal**, the process of evaluating an employee's actual performance against desired performance standards. Most performance appraisal programs strive to accomplish three goals:

1. To give employees feedback about how they are doing their jobs, which can be an important source of motivation.
2. To provide business owners and employees the opportunity to create a plan for developing employee skills and abilities and for improving their performance.
3. To establish a basis for determining promotions and salary increases.

Although the primary purpose of performance appraisals is to encourage and to help employees improve their performance, too often they turn into uncomfortable confrontations that do nothing more than upset the employees, aggravate the business owner, and destroy trust and morale. Why? Because most business owners do not understand how to conduct an effective performance appraisal. For example, although U.S. businesses have been conducting performance appraisals for about 75 years, most companies, their managers, and their employees are dissatisfied with the entire process. A survey by Watson Wyatt, a global human resources company, found that 60 percent of workers say that performance appraisals do not produce any useful feedback and fail to help them set meaningful objectives.[66] Common complaints include unclear standards and objectives, managers who lack information about employees' performances, managers who are unprepared or who lack honesty and sincerity, and managers who use general, ambiguous terms to describe employees' performances.

Perhaps the biggest complaint concerning appraisals is that they happen only periodically: in most cases, just once a year. Employees do not have the opportunity to receive any ongoing feedback on a regular basis. All too often, managers save up all of the negative feedback to give employees and then dump it on them in the annual performance review. Not only does it destroy employees' motivation, but it does *nothing* to improve their performance. What good does it do to tell an employee that six months before, he botched an assignment that caused the company to lose a customer? Performance reviews that occur once or twice a year in an attempt to improve employees' performance is similar to working out once or twice a year in an attempt to get into top physical condition!

Lack of ongoing feedback is similar to asking employees to bowl in the dark. They can hear some pins falling, but they have no idea how many or which ones are left standing for the next frame. How motivated would you be to keep bowling? Managers should address problems when they occur rather than wait until the performance appraisal session.

Continuous feedback, both positive and negative, is a much more effective way to improve employees' performance and to increase their motivation.

If done properly, performance appraisals can be effective ways to provide employee feedback and to improve workers' performance. However, it takes some planning and preparation on the business owner's part. The following guidelines can help a business owner create a performance appraisal system that actually works:

- **Link the employee performance criteria to the job description discussed earlier in this chapter.** To evaluate an employee's performance effectively, an entrepreneur must understand the employee's job well.
- **Establish meaningful, job-related, observable, measurable, and fair performance criteria.** The criteria should describe behaviors and actions, not traits and characteristics. What kind of behavior constitutes a solid performance in this job?
- **Prepare for the appraisal session by outlining the key points you want to cover with employees.** Important points to include are employees' strengths and weaknesses and developing a plan for improving their performance.
- **Invite employees to provide an evaluation of their own job performance based on the performance criteria.** In one small company, workers rate themselves on a one-to-five scale in categories of job-related behavior and skills as part of the performance appraisal system. Then they meet with their supervisor to compare their evaluations with those of their supervisor and discuss them.
- **Be specific.** One of the most common complaints employees have about the appraisal process is that managers' comments are too general to be of any value. Offer the employees specific examples of their desirable or undesirable behavior.
- **Keep a record of employees' critical incidents—both positive and negative.** The most productive evaluations are those based on managers' direct observation of their employees' on-the-job performance. These records also can be vital in case legal problems arise.
- **Discuss employees' strengths and weaknesses.** An appraisal session is not the time to "unload" about everything employees have done *wrong* over the past year. Use it as an opportunity to design a plan for improvement and to recognize employees' strengths, efforts, and achievements.
- **Incorporate employees' goals into the appraisal.** Ideally, the standard against which to measure employees' performance is the goals they have helped create. Workers are likely to be motivated to achieve goals that they have helped establish.
- **Keep the evaluation constructive.** Avoid the tendency to belittle employees. Do not dwell on past failures. Instead, point out specific things they should do better and help them develop meaningful goals for the future and a strategy for getting there.
- **Praise good work.** Avoid focusing only on what employees do wrong. Take the time to express your appreciation for hard work and solid accomplishments.
- **Focus on behaviors, actions, and results.** Problems arise when managers move away from tangible results and actions and begin to critique employees' aptitudes and attitudes. This kind of criticism sets a negative tone for the appraisal session and undercuts its primary purpose.
- **Avoid surprises.** If entrepreneurs are doing their jobs well, performance appraisals should contain no surprises for employees or the entrepreneurs. The ideal time to correct improper behavior or slumping performance is when it happens, not months later. Managers should provide employees with continuous feedback on their performance and use the appraisal session to keep employees on the right track.
- **Plan for the future.** Smart business owners use appraisal sessions as gateways to workers' future success. They spend only about 20 percent of the time discussing past performance; they use the remaining 80 percent of the time to develop goals, objectives, and a plan for the future. When one sales manager worked with a sales representative whose performance had been mediocre to set meaningful goals and objectives, her performance improved immediately. As a result of the productive performance appraisal, the sales representative increased her sales by 40 percent in less than a year.[67]

*Chip Prince and City Wholesale*

When Chip Prince took over as sales manager at City Wholesale, a company that sells food service products, employees underwent performance appraisals only once a year, and even then, they were not very effective. After talking with sales representatives, Prince decided to establish quarterly performance appraisals to give workers the more timely feedback they requested. In every appraisal, Prince makes it a habit to ask employees for specific things he and the company can do to improve sales representatives' performance. Then he makes sure to act on what he hears. Since making the changes in the performance appraisal process, City Wholesale's employee annual turnover rate has dropped from 50 percent to just 15 percent, and profit margins have climbed an average of 15 percent a quarter. "People are telling us they know where they're supposed to go and are more in tune with what they are supposed to be doing," says Prince.[68]

Many companies are encouraging employees to evaluate each others' performance in **peer reviews** or to evaluate their boss's performance in **upward feedback**, both part of a technique called **360-degree feedback**. Peer appraisals can be especially useful because an employee's coworkers see his or her on-the-job performance every day. As a result, peer evaluations tend to be more accurate and more valid than those of some managers. In addition, they may capture behavior that managers might miss. Disadvantages of peer appraisals include potential retaliation against coworkers who criticize, the possibility that appraisals will be reduced to "popularity contests," and the refusal of some workers to offer any criticism because they feel uncomfortable evaluating others. Some bosses using upward feedback report similar problems, including personal attacks and extreme evaluations by vengeful subordinates.

## Chapter Review

1. Explain the challenges involved in the entrepreneur's role as leader and what it takes to be a successful leader.
   - Leadership is the process of influencing and inspiring others to work to achieve a common goal and then giving them the power and the freedom to achieve it.
   - Management and leadership are not the same; yet both are essential to a small company's success. Leadership without management is unbridled; management without leadership is uninspired. Leadership gets a small business going; management keeps it going.
2. Describe the importance of hiring the right employees and how to avoid making hiring mistakes.
   - The decision to hire a new employee is an important one for every business, but its impact is magnified many times in a small company. Every "new hire" a business owner makes determines the heights to which the company can climb or the depths to which it will plunge.
   - To avoid making hiring mistakes, entrepreneurs should develop meaningful job descriptions and job specifications; plan and conduct an effective interview; and check references before hiring any employee.
3. Explain how to build the kind of company culture and structure to support the entrepreneur's mission and goals and to motivate employees to achieve them.
   - Company culture is the distinctive, unwritten code of conduct that governs the behavior, attitudes, relationships, and style of an organization. Culture arises from an entrepreneur's consistent and relentless pursuit of a set of core values that everyone in the company can believe in. Small companies' flexible structures can be a major competitive weapon.
4. Understand the potential barriers to effective communication and describe how to overcome them.
   - Research shows that managers spend about 80 percent of their time in some form of communication; yet their attempts at communicating sometimes go wrong.

Several barriers to effective communication include: managers and employees don't always feel free to say what they really mean; ambiguity blocks real communication; information overload causes the message to get lost; selective listening interferes with the communication process; defense mechanisms block a message; and conflicting verbal and nonverbal messages confuse listeners.

- To become more effective communicators, business owners should clarify their messages before attempting to communicate them; use face-to-face communication whenever possible; be empathetic; match their messages to their audiences; be organized; encourage feedback; tell the truth; not be afraid to tell employees about the business, its performance, and the forces that affect it.

5. Discuss the ways in which entrepreneurs can motivate their workers to higher levels of performance.
   - Motivation is the degree of effort an employee exerts to accomplish a task; it shows up as excitement about work. Four important tools of motivation are empowerment, job design, rewards and compensation, and feedback.
   - Empowerment involves giving workers at every level of the organization the power, the freedom, and the responsibility to control their own work, to make decisions, and to take action to meet the company's objectives.
   - Job design techniques for enhancing employee motivation include job enlargement, job rotation, job enrichment, flextime, job sharing, and flexplace (which includes telecommuting and hoteling).
   - Money is an important motivator for many workers, but not the only one. The key to using rewards such as recognition and praise to motivate involves tailoring them to the needs and characteristics of the workers.
   - Giving employees timely, relevant feedback about their job performance through a performance appraisal system can also be a powerful motivator.

# Discussion Questions

1. What is leadership? What is the difference between leadership and management?
2. What behaviors do effective leaders exhibit?
3. Why is it so important for small companies to hire the right employees? What can small business owners do to avoid making hiring mistakes?
4. What is a job description? A job specification? What functions do they serve in the hiring process?
5. Outline the procedure for conducting an effective interview.
6. What are some alternative techniques to traditional interviews?
7. What is company culture? What role does it play in a small company's success? What threats does rapid growth pose for a company's culture?
8. What mistakes do companies make when switching to team-based management? What might companies do to avoid these mistakes? Explain the four phases teams typically experience.
9. What is empowerment? What benefits does it offer workers? The company? What must a small business manager do to make empowerment work in a company?
10. Explain the differences among job simplification, job enlargement, job rotation, and job enrichment. What impact do these different job designs have on workers?
11. Is money the "best" motivator? How do pay-for-performance compensation systems work? What other rewards are available to small business managers to use as motivators? How effective are they?
12. Suppose that a mail-order catalog company selling environmentally friendly products identifies its performance as a socially responsible company as a "critical number" in its success. Suggest some ways for the owner to measure this company's "social responsibility index."
13. What is a performance appraisal? What are the most common mistakes managers make in performance appraisals? What should small business managers do to avoid making those mistakes?

# Business PlanPro

This chapter discusses the importance of leadership, culture, organizational design, staffing, and managing the people who will work in your business. The "Management" section is where these issues are most often addressed within the business plan. This section of the plan captures the key information about your management team, including both its strengths and weaknesses. The management section of the business plan also addresses other personnel issues for your venture.

## On the Web

Visit the Companion Website at www.prenhall.com/ scarborough and review the links associated with Chapter 19. You will find resources that address leadership issues, interviewing techniques, employee motivation programs, culture, organizational structure, and other topics that you may find helpful. These resources may offer additional insight for the human resource and managerial aspects of your business that you may want to incorporate into your business plan.

## In the Software

Review the management section of your business plan and make certain that it addresses the important management and personnel issues for your venture. Check to see that your plan includes the relevant concepts presented in the chapter. Think about the business culture that you plan to build. Assess the leadership abilities of the current management team. Are additional managers or other positions needed? Have you accounted for new hires and the anticipated expenses associated with adding these employees? Does your plan address factors that will allow you to retain existing employees? How do you plan to motivate employees to achieve high levels of performance?

# Management Succession and Risk Management Strategies in the Family Business

When it works right, nothing succeeds like a family firm. The roots run deep, embedded in family values. The flash of the fast buck is replaced with long-term plans. Tradition counts.

—Eric Calonius

Walk sober off before the sprightlier age comes titt'ring on and shoves you from the stage.

—Alexander Pope

## *Learning Objectives*

**Upon completion of this chapter, you will be able to:**

1 Explain the factors necessary for a strong family business.

2 Understand the exit strategy options available to an entrepreneur.

3 Discuss the stages of management succession.

4 Explain how to develop an effective management succession plan.

5 Understand the four risk management strategies.

6 Discuss the basics of insurance for small businesses.

7 Describe various techniques for controlling insurance costs.

## Family Businesses

*1.* Explain the factors necessary for a strong family business.

Worldwide, family-managed businesses employ half the world's workforce and generate well over half the world's GDP. Yet family-owned businesses, those in which family members control ownership and/or decision making, are often overlooked by the media that focus most of their attention on the larger companies in our economy. In the U.S. alone, family businesses generate 64 percent of the country's gross domestic product, account for 62 percent of all employment and 78 percent of job creation, and pay 65 percent of all wages.[1] Despite common perceptions, not all family businesses are small. Worldwide, there are around 200 family businesses with annual revenues of at least $2 billion.[2] Indeed, Sam Walton's heirs own 39 percent of the stock in the world's largest company, Wal-Mart, and those shares are worth an estimated $82 billion, an amount that exceeds the GDP of 126 countries in the world.[3]

When a family business works right, it is a thing of beauty. Family members share deeply rooted values that guide the company and give it a sense of harmony. Family members understand and support one another as they work together to achieve the company's mission. That harmony can produce a significant financial payoff. A study by university professor Jim Lee shows that family-owned businesses are more profitable and experience faster employment and revenue growth over time than non-family businesses.[4] Another study of companies in the Standard & Poor's 500 Index by Ronald Anderson, David Reeb, and Sattar Mansi found that family firms outperformed their non-family counterparts on a variety of financial measures.[5] Other research comparing the financial performances of similar sets of family and nonfamily businesses has concluded that "firms controlled by the founding family have greater value, are operated more efficiently, and carry less debt than other firms."[6]

Family businesses also have a dark side, and it stems from their lack of continuity. Sibling rivalries, fights over control of the business, and personality conflicts often lead to nasty battles that can tear families apart and destroy once thriving businesses. Long-standing feuds can make family relationships difficult, and when mixed with business decisions and the wealth family businesses can create, the result can be explosive. Unfortunately, 70 percent of first-generation businesses fail to survive into the second generation, and of those that do, only 12 percent make it to the third generation. Just 3 percent of family businesses survive to the fourth generation.[7] The leading causes of family business failures are inadequate estate planning, failure to create a management succession plan, and lack of funds to pay estate taxes.[8]

**ENTREPRENEURIAL Profile**

*Kenneth Wilson and Wilson Products Inc.*

When Kenneth Wilson, second generation owner of Wilson Products Inc., a successful aircrafts parts business, died unexpectedly, his three daughters found themselves at the helm of the family business. Even though all three had worked in the business, none of them had ever been groomed to manage it. "You know a little bit about [the business], but running it is a whole other ball game," says Vicky Wilson, one of Kenneth's daughters. Without their father's guidance, the sisters struggled, and so did the company. Within two years of Kenneth's death, Wilson Products filed for bankruptcy, and the company's assets were auctioned off.[9]

As Kenneth Wilson's daughters learned, the stumbling block for most family businesses is management succession. Just when they are ready to make the transition from one generation of leaders to the next, family businesses are most vulnerable. As a result, the average life expectancy of a family business is 24 years, although some last *much* longer (see Table 20.1).[10] Once the oldest family business in the world, Kongo Gumi, a construction company in Japan that specialized in building temples, fell on hard times and in 2006 was acquired by Takamatsu, a large Japanese construction firm. Established in 578, the business had navigated management succession issues successfully for more than 1,400 years across 40 generations of the Kongo family before being sold.[11]

The best way to avoid deadly turf battles and conflicts and to ensure a successful transition from one generation of family owners to the next is to develop a succession plan for the company. Although business founders inevitably want their businesses to survive them

**TABLE 20.1 The World's Oldest Family Businesses**

William O'Hara, director of the Institute for Family Enterprise at Bryant College, and Peter Mandel have compiled a list of some of the world's oldest family businesses.

| Company | Country | Nature of Business | Year Established |
|---|---|---|---|
| Hoshi Ryokan | Japan | Hotel | 718 |
| Château de Goulaine | France | Vineyard, museum, butterfly collection | 1000 |
| Fonderia Pontifica Marinelli | Italy | Bell foundry | 1000 |
| Barone Ricasoli | Italy | Wine and olive oil | 1141 |
| Barovier & Toso | Italy | Artistic glassmaking | 1295 |
| Hotel Pilgram Haus | Germany | Innkeeping | 1304 |
| Richard de Bas | France | High-quality paper maker | 1326 |
| Torrini Firenze | Italy | Goldsmiths | 1369 |
| Antinori | Italy | Wine | 1385 |
| Camuffo | Italy | Shipbuilding | 1438 |
| Baronnie de Coussergues | France | Wine | 1495 |
| Grazia Deruta | Italy | Ceramics | 1500 |
| Fabbrice D'Armi Beretta | Italy | Firearms production | 1526 |
| William Prym GmbH & Company | Germany | Copper, brass, haberdashery | 1530 |
| John Brooke & Sons | Great Britain | Textiles | 1541 |
| Codorniu | Spain | Wine | 1551 |
| Fonjallaz | Switzerland | Wine | 1552 |

*Source:* William T. O'Hara and Peter Mandel, "The World's Oldest Family Companies," *Family Business*, www.familybusinessmagazine.com/oldworld.html.

and almost 80 percent intend to pass them on to their children, they do not always support their intentions by a plan to accomplish that goal. A recent study by the Monitor Group reports that 82 percent of business owners had no written plan that described what they wanted to happen to their companies when they leave (see Figure 20.1).[12] Another survey of family business owners by MassMutual Financial Group and the consulting group Arthur Andersen reports that 19 percent had not engaged in any kind of estate planning other than creating a will.[13] For most family businesses, the greatest threat to survival comes from *within* the company rather than from outside it. Many entrepreneurs dream of their businesses continuing in the family but take no significant steps to make their dreams a reality.

David Bork, founder of the Aspen Family Business Conference, has identified several qualities that are essential to a successful family business: shared values, shared power, tradition, a willingness to learn, family behavior, and strong family ties.[14]

## Shared Values

The first, and probably most overlooked, quality is a set of shared values. What family members value and believe about people, work, and money shapes their behavior toward the business. All members of a family business should talk openly to determine, in a nonjudgmental fashion, each one's values. Without shared values, it is difficult to create a sense of direction for a business.

To avoid the problems associated with conflicting values and goals, family business owners should take the following actions:

- Make it clear to all family members that they are not required to join the business on a full-time basis. Family members' goals, ambitions, and talents should be foremost in their career decisions.

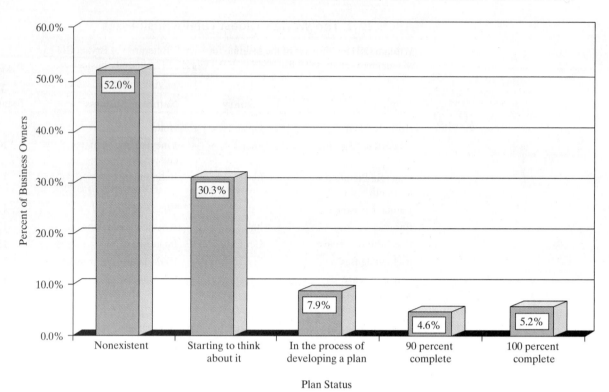

**FIGURE 20.1 Status of Management Succession Plans in Small Businesses**
*Source: Entrepreneur Magazine* and PriceWaterHouse Coopers 2007, "Entrepreneurial Challenge Survey."

■ Do not assume that a successor must come from within the family. Simply being born into a family does not guarantee that a person will make a good business leader.
■ Give family members the opportunity to work outside the business initially to learn firsthand how others conduct business. Working for others allows family members to develop knowledge, confidence, and credibility before stepping back into the family business.

### Shared Power

Shared power is not necessarily equal power. Rather, shared power is based on the simple idea that the skills and talents of each family member may run in different directions. Shared power is based on the idea that family members should allow those with the greatest expertise, ability, and knowledge in particular areas to handle decisions in those areas. Dividing responsibilities along the lines of expertise is an important way of acknowledging respect for each family member's talents and abilities.

*Thad, Harold, and Ralph Garner and T.W. Garner Food Company*

When Thad Garner invented a concoction of red peppers and vinegar called Texas Pete Hot Sauce during the Great Depression, he and his brothers, Harold and Ralph, built a business, T.W. Garner Food Company, around the product. Each assumed responsibilities in a different area of the company based on their individual talents and interests. Thad (known as "Mr. Texas Pete") took over the sales and marketing side of the business, Harold managed its financial and operational aspects, and Ralph handled production. Working together, the brothers built the company into a very successful business, selling millions of dollars' worth of Texas Pete a year.[15]

### Tradition

Tradition is necessary for a family business because it serves to bond family members and to link one generation of business leaders to the next. However, founders must hold tradition in check when it becomes a barrier to change. The key is to maintain those traditions that provide stability for the business while taking care not to restrict the future growth of the company. "The companies that are successful change their strategy after each generation," says Joachim Schwass, a professor of family business at Switzerland's IMD business school. "Bringing in the new generation and saying, 'Son, do as I did,' will not work."[16]

*Maximilian Riedel and Riedel Glas Austria*

Maximilian Riedel, head of North American operations for Austrian glassmaker Riedel, which for generations has been famous for its feather-light, fine crystal wine glasses, is next in line to take control of the family business. Like his father and grandfather did, Maximilian created a new line of wine glasses that has become one of the company's best selling products. The eleventh generation glassmaker created a sensation among oenophiles (wine lovers) with his revolutionary stemless "O" series of wine tumblers that are designed to convey the nuances of the aroma and the flavor of wine. (The wine glass is "the messenger of the wine," he says.) Every business decision that Maximilian makes is steeped in 250 years of family business history, but already he has shown that he is willing to take bold steps to innovate and keep the family business in tune with the demands of the twenty-first century.[17]

### A Willingness to Learn

A willingness to learn and grow is the hallmark of any successful firm, and it is essential to a family business. The family business that remains open to new ideas and techniques is likely to reduce its risk of obsolescence. The current generation of leadership must set the stage for new ideas by involving the next generation in today's decisions. In many cases, a formal family council serves as a mechanism through which family members can propose new ideas. Perhaps more important than a family council is fostering an environment in which family members trust one another enough to express their ideas, thoughts, and suggestions openly and honestly. Open discussion of the merits of new ideas is a tradition that has proved valuable for many family businesses' ability to sustain their competitive advantages.

### Behaving Like Families

Families that play together operate family businesses that are more likely to stay together. Time spent together outside the business creates the foundation for the relationships family members have at work. Too often, life in a family business can degenerate into nothing but day after day of work and discussions of work at home. In some cases, work is the only way some parents interact with their children. When a family adds activities outside the scope of the business, however, new relationships develop in a different arena. A family should not force members to "play together" but instead should create an environment that welcomes every member into fun family activities. Planned activities should be broad enough in scope to involve all family members. In time, trust, respect, openness, and togetherness will lead to behavior that communicates genuine caring and concern for the well-being of each family member, and that spills over into the working relationship as well.

### Strong Family Ties

Strong family ties grow from one-on-one relationships. Shared time conveys the message that the family business is *more* than just a business; it is a group of people who care for one another working together for a common goal. The bond that a family business creates among relatives can be strong and enduring. "There's a love and a trust and a respect that can be very powerful when they are brought into a business environment," says Ross Nager, director of a center for family business.[18]

The same emotions that hold family businesses together can also rip them apart if they run counter to the company's and the family's best interest. Emotions run deep in family businesses, and the press is filled with examples of once successful companies that have been ruined by family feuds over who controls the company and how to run it. Conflict is a natural part of any business but can be especially powerful in family businesses because family relationships magnify the passions binding family members to the company. Without a succession plan, those passions can explode into destructive behavior that can endanger the family business.

*The Noboa Family and
Fruit Shippers Ltd.*

After living in a family that struggled for a meager existence in Ecuador, Luis Noboa co-founded a coffee and banana business and earned his first million by age 39. Noboa later bought out his partner, and when he died at the age of 78, his company, Fruit Shippers Ltd., held $800 million in assets. Unfortunately, Noboa had neglected to develop a management succession plan, and a lengthy and costly battle among his four children ensued. Nine years and $20 million later, Noboa's youngest son Alvaro emerged as the "winner" in the fierce battle over control of the business. However, the Noboa family was divided from the nasty accusations, underhanded tactics, and lengthy lawsuits that characterized one of the most expensive family business conflicts in history.[19]

## Exit Strategies

**2.** Understand the exit strategy options available to an entrepreneur.

Most family business founders want their companies to stay within their families, although in some cases maintaining family control is not practical. Sometimes no one in the next generation of family members has an interest in managing the company or has the necessary skills and experience to handle the job. Under these circumstances, the founder must look outside the family for leadership if the company is to survive. Whatever the case, entrepreneurs must confront their mortality and plan for the future of their companies. Having a solid management succession plan in place well before retirement is near is absolutely critical to success. Entrepreneurs should examine their options once they decide it is time to step down from the businesses they have founded. Three options are available to entrepreneurs planning to retire: sell to outsiders, sell to (non-family) insiders, or pass the business on to family members with the help of a management succession plan. We turn now to these three exit strategies.

### Selling to Outsiders

As you learned in Chapter 5, "Buying an Existing Business," selling a business to an outsider is no simple task. Done properly, it takes time, patience, and preparation to locate a suitable buyer, strike a deal, and make the transition. Advance preparation, maintaining accurate financial records, and timing are the keys to a successful sale. Too often, however, business owners, like some famous athletes, stay with the game too long until they and their businesses are well past their prime. They postpone selling until the last minute when they reach retirement age or when they face a business crisis. Such a "fire sale" approach rarely yields the maximum value for a business.

A straight sale may be best for those entrepreneurs who want to step down and turn the reins of the company over to someone else. However, selling a business outright is not an attractive exit strategy for those who want to stay on with the company or for those who want to surrender control of the company gradually rather than all at once.

*James Beck and
Precision Twist
Drill Company*

James Beck founded the Precision Twist Drill Company in 1952, and by 1997, the small family business had become the leading drill-bit manufacturer in the nation with sales of $124 million. Over time, Beck had distributed shares of stock in the family business to his children, grandchildren, great-grandchildren, and key employees of the company. After receiving offers from several large businesses, Beck decided that it was time to sell the business and accepted a bid from Sandvik, a Swedish corporation, for $135 million. "My grandfather made a lot of people millionaires," says Randy Beck, one of Beck's grandsons.[20]

The financial terms of a sale also influence the selling price of the business and the number of potential bidders. Does the owner want "clean, cash only, 100 percent at closing" offers, or is the owner willing to finance a portion of the sale? The 100 percent, cash-only requirement dramatically reduces the number of potential buyers. On the other hand, the owner can exit the business "free and clear" and does not incur the risk that the buyer may fail to operate the business in a profitable fashion and not be able to complete the financial transition.

## Selling to Insiders

When entrepreneurs have no family members to whom they can transfer ownership or who want to assume the responsibilities of running a company, selling the business to employees is often the preferred option. In most situations, the options available to owners are (1) sale for cash plus a note, (2) a leveraged buyout, and (3) an employee stock ownership plan (ESOP).

**A SALE FOR CASH PLUS A NOTE.** Whether entrepreneurs sell their businesses to insiders, outsiders, or family members, they often finance a portion of the sales price. The buyer pays the seller a lump-sum amount of cash up-front and the seller holds a promissory note for the remaining portion of the selling price, which the buyer pays off in installments. Because this method offers many creative financial options, it is popular with buyers. They can buy promising businesses without having to come up with the total purchase price all at one time. Sellers also appreciate the security and the tax implications of accepting payment over time. They receive a portion of the sale up-front and have the assurance of receiving a steady stream of income in the future. In addition, they can stretch their tax liabilities from the capital gains on the sale over time rather than having to pay them in a single year. In many cases, sellers' risks are lower because they may even retain a seat on the board of directors to ensure that the new owners are keeping the business on track.

*Hudson Family*

When Jim and Lorraine Hudson decided to retire from the successful auto dealership they had operated for 26 years, they decided to sell the business to their daughter, Lynne, and her husband, Chad Millspaugh. The founding couple was confident in turning over the decision making to Lynne and Chad, but they needed help structuring the sale so that it would give them the retirement income they sought and not put the new owners in a difficult financial position. Because the land the dealership occupied had become so valuable, they separated it from the business. They sold the dealership to the Millspaughs for $2 million, accepting a down payment and financing the balance. The Hudsons kept the real estate and will receive lease payments from it, providing them with a healthy retirement income.[21]

**LEVERAGED BUYOUT.** In a **leveraged buyout (LBO)**, managers and/or employees borrow money from a financial institution and pay the owner the total agreed-upon price at closing; then they use the cash generated from the company's operations to pay off the debt. The drawback of this technique is that it creates a highly leveraged business. Because of the high levels of debt they take on, the new managers have very little room for error. Too many management mistakes or a slowing economy has led many highly leveraged businesses into bankruptcy.

If properly structured, LBOs can be attractive to both buyers and sellers. Because they get their money up-front, sellers do not incur the risk of loss if the buyers cannot keep the business operating successfully. The managers and employees who buy the company have a strong incentive to make sure the business succeeds because they own a piece of the action and some of their capital is at risk in the business. The result can be a highly motivated workforce that works hard and makes sure that the company operates efficiently.

*Jack Stack and Springfield Remanufacturing Corporation*

In one of the most successful LBOs in recent years, Jack Stack and a team of managers and employees purchased an ailing subsidiary of International Harvester. The new company, Springfield Remanufacturing Corporation (SRC), which specializes in engine remanufacturing for automotive, trucking, agricultural, and construction industries, began with a debt to equity ratio that was astronomically high, but the team of motivated managers and employees turned the company around. Today SRC has more than 1,000 employees and $200 million in sales.[22]

**EMPLOYEE STOCK OWNERSHIP PLAN (ESOP).** Unlike LBOs, **employee stock ownership plans (ESOPs)** allow employees and/or managers (that is, the future owners) to purchase the business gradually, which frees up enough cash to finance the venture's growth. With an ESOP, employees contribute a portion of their earnings over time toward purchasing shares of the company's stock from the founder until they own the company outright. (Although in leveraged ESOPs, the ESOP borrows the money to buy the owner's stock up front. Then, using employees' contributions, the ESOP repays the loan over time. Another advantage of a leveraged ESOP

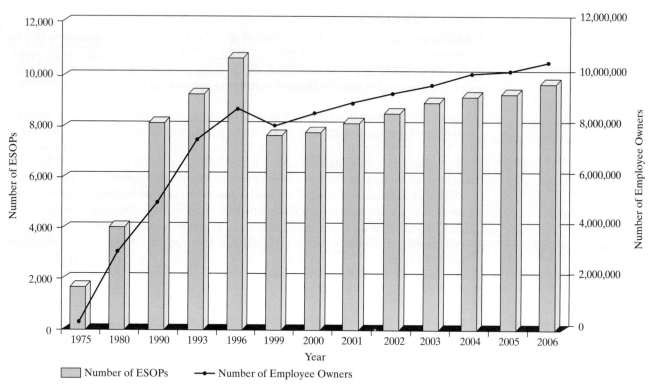

**FIGURE 20.2 Employee Stock Ownership Plans**

*Source:* "A Statistical Profile of Employee Ownership," National Center for Employee Ownership, 2007. Reprinted with permission.

is that the principal and the interest the ESOP borrows to buy the business are tax deductible, which can save thousands or even millions of dollars in taxes.) Transferring ownership to employees through an ESOP is a long-term exit strategy that benefits everyone involved. The owner sells the business to the people he or she can trust the most—his or her managers and employees. The managers and employees buy a business they already know how to run successfully. In addition, because they own the company, the managers and employees have a huge incentive to see that it operates effectively and efficiently. One recent study of employee stock ownership plans in privately held companies found that ESOPs increase sales, employment, and sales per employee by 2.4 percent a year.[23] Figure 20.2 shows the trend in the number of ESOPs and the number of employee owners.

The third exit strategy available to company founders is transferring ownership to the next generation of family members with the help of a comprehensive management succession plan.

## Gaining a Competitive Edge

### How to Set up an ESOP

Eileen Fisher, who in 1984 founded a design company known for its stylish, flowing women's clothing, faced the dilemma that many baby boomer entrepreneurs are facing: How do I cash out some of the value of my company, diversify my investments, and maintain control of the business? For Fisher, 56, the answer was to set up a leveraged employee stock ownership plan (ESOP), which allowed her to transfer nearly one-third of the ownership of the company to her 624 employees. In exchange for the shares in her company, Fisher received $30 million in cash without incurring a huge tax bill, thanks to federal laws that encourage employee ownership of businesses.

Because Fisher retained 69 percent of the company's stock, she also keeps control of the company and its future. "The combination of both selling and giving a piece of the business to the employees felt right." In addition, "it allows me to get some money out," says Fisher, who has two children who will be entering college soon. The move also allows Fisher to plan for her retirement and protect her children's inheritance.

Eileen Fisher Inc., which has 37 stores across the United States and sells clothing through other retail outlets, generates annual sales of $225 million. Fisher was not interested in making an initial public offering because she believes that publicly held companies focus too much on short-term shareholder returns rather than on sound long-term strategies. "I don't want to bring in outsiders," she says. "I want to keep the company intact with the people who've grown it."

After setting up the ESOP, Fisher transferred 31 percent of her company's stock to an ESOP trust that, in turn, used the stock as collateral to borrow $30 million from a consortium of banks to purchase her company stock. The company made a guarantee to the banks on behalf of the trust for payment of the loan principal and interest. Over the next eight years, Fisher's company will make tax deductible contributions from its revenue to the trust to repay the loan from the banks. Over that time, the trust will distribute shares of the company stock to employees' accounts using a predetermined formula that is based on compensation. Favorable tax treatment in the United States allows the company to deduct the interest as well as the principal of the loan. ESOPs allow entrepreneurs to transfer as much or as little of their companies to employees as gradually or as quickly as they want. Fisher says that over the course of the decade, she most likely will transfer more of her company—perhaps all of it—to her employees through the ESOP.

What steps should an entrepreneur who is interested in setting up an ESOP take?

## Step 1. Conduct a feasibility analysis to determine whether an ESOP is right for you and your company.

A company should be profitable and should have at least 20 employees to make an ESOP work. Creating the necessary plan documents and filing them with the proper government agencies costs about $10,000. A business valuation, which can range from $5,000 to $10,000 for a small company, is a necessity. Fixed costs of administering the ESOP run about $2,000 plus $20 to $30 per employee participant. A final consideration is whether the company will generate enough revenue to be able to repay the loan

## Step 2. Hire an attorney who specializes in ESOPs to help you develop a plan for creating and implementing an ESOP.

ESOPs can take many different forms, and an expert can help you determine the advantages and disadvantages of each one so that you can identify the one that is best for you and your company.

## Step 3. Find the money to fund the ESOP.

About 75 percent of ESOPs are leveraged, which means that, like Eileen Fisher's company, they borrow the money to purchase the owner's stock from the ESOP trust. Banks and other financial institutions usually find loans to ESOPs quite attractive.

## Step 4. Establish a process to operate the ESOP.

Companies most often create an ESOP committee of managers and employees to provide guidance to the ESOP trust for managing the ESOP. The team also is responsible for communicating the details of the ESOP and the benefits of investing in it to company employees.

Barbara Gabel, who with her husband, Zach Zachowski, launched Zachary's Chicago Pizza in California in 1984, recently established an ESOP to transfer ownership of their business to their employees. "It's the ultimate exit strategy," says Gabel, referring to the benefits ESOPs provide to both entrepreneurs and employees. Employees at Zachary's receive each year an amount of stock that is equal to 25 percent of their salaries. General Manager J.P. LaRussa, who began working as a part-time dishwasher at Zachary's the day it opened, says, "This breathes new life into the business in a very positive way."

*Sources:* Adapted from Theo Francis, "Inside Eileen Fisher's Employee Stock Plan," *Wall Street Journal*, January 22, 2007, pp. B1, B3; Alec Rosenberg, "Employees to Slice Up Zachary's Pizza," *Oakland Tribune*, June 27, 2003, www.zacharys.com/news_oakland_tribune.html; "ESOP Statistics," ESOP Association, www.esopassociation.org/media/media_statistics.asp; "How Small Is Too Small for an ESOP?" National Center for Employee Ownership, www.nceo.org/library/howsmall.html; "Steps to Setting Up an ESOP," National Center for Employee Ownership, www.nceo.org/library/steps.html.

## Management Succession

*3.* Discuss the stages of management succession.

Experts estimate that between 2001 and 2017, $12 trillion in wealth will be transferred from one generation to the next, representing the greatest transfer of wealth in history and much of it funneled through family businesses.[24] Most of the family businesses in existence today were started after World War II, and many of the founders who have not yet transferred ownership to the next generation now are in their seventies and eighties and are ready to pass the torch of leadership. Eighty-five percent of business owners who have identified a successor say that that person is a family member.[25]

For a smooth transition from one generation to the next, family businesses need a succession plan. Without a succession plan, family businesses face an increased risk of faltering or failing in the next generation. Those businesses with the greatest probability of surviving are the ones whose owners prepare a succession plan well *before* it is time to transfer control to the next generation. Succession planning also allows business owners to minimize the impact of taxes on their businesses, their estates, and their successors' wealth as well and to avoid saddling the next generation of ownership with burdensome debt.

Why, then, do so many entrepreneurs postpone succession planning until it is too late? Many business founders hesitate to let go of their businesses because their personal identities are so wrapped up in their companies. Over time, a founder's identity becomes so intertwined in the business that, in the entrepreneur's mind, there is no distinction between the two. The attitude is "I am the company, and the company is me."

*Michael and Emily Powell and Powell's Books*

At age 66, Michael Powell, who for 27 years has managed Powell's Books, the largest privately held chain of bookstores in the United States, knows that it is time to begin transferring control of the company to his daughter, Emily, 28, by relying on the ten-year transition plan he created seven years ago. When Michael, who took over the family business from his father, talks about retiring from the company he built, however, he covers his face with his hands and his voice grows soft. "There are emotional issues in giving up control and ownership," he admits. "Half my brain says, 'Do it,' and the other half says, 'What are you doing?' This is business and family."[26] Many entrepreneurs share Powell's feelings. According to a survey by The Monitor Group, less than 17 percent of business owners say that they expect to retire after leaving their businesses. (In fact, 45 percent say that they plan to start another company.)[27]

Michael Powell, right, owner of Powell's Books, poses with his daughter, Emily Powell, at their downtown store in Portland, in the U.S. state of Oregon. Powell's Books' flagship store is so large, visitors get a map at the door.

Another barrier to succession planning is that, in planning the future of the business, owners are forced to accept the painful reality of their own mortality. In addition, turning over the reins of a business they have sacrificed for, fretted over, and dedicated themselves to for so many years is extremely difficult to do—even if the successor is a son or daughter! Paul Snodgrass, son of the founder of Pella Products, a maker of apparel for work and outdoor activities, who accepted leadership of the company from his father, explains, "Dad loves you and wants you to take over the business, but he also put heart and soul into that business, and he's not going to let anybody screw it up—not even you."[28] Finally, many family business founders believe that controlling the business also gives them a degree of control over family members and family behavior.

Planning for management succession protects not only the founder's, successor's, and company's financial resources, but it also preserves what matters most in a successful business: its heritage and tradition. "Real succession planning involves developing a strategy for transferring the trust, respect, and goodwill built by one generation to the next," explains Andy Bluestone, who took over as president of the financial services company his father founded.[29] Management succession planning requires, first, an attitude of trusting others. It recognizes that other family members have a stake in the future of the business and want to participate in planning its future. Planning is an attitude that shows that decisions made with open discussion are more constructive than those without family input. Second, management succession is an evolutionary process and must reconcile an entrepreneur's inevitable anguish with the successors' desire for autonomy. Owners' emotional ties to their businesses usually are stronger than their financial ties. On the other side of the equation are the successors, who yearn to have the autonomy to run the business their way. These inherent conflicts can—and often do—result in skirmishes.

Succession planning reduces the tension and stress created by these conflicts by gradually "changing the guard." A well-developed succession plan is like the smooth, graceful exchange of a baton between runners in a relay race. The new runner has maximum energy; the concluding runner has already spent his or her energy by running at maximum speed. The athletes never come to a stop to exchange the baton; instead, the handoff takes place on the move. The race is a skillful blend of the talents of all team members—an exchange of leadership so smooth and powerful that the business never falters, but accelerates, fueled by a new source of energy at each leg of the race.

Management succession involves a lengthy series of interconnected stages that begin very early in the life of the owner's children and extends to the point of final ownership transition (see Figure 20.3). If management succession is to be effective, it is

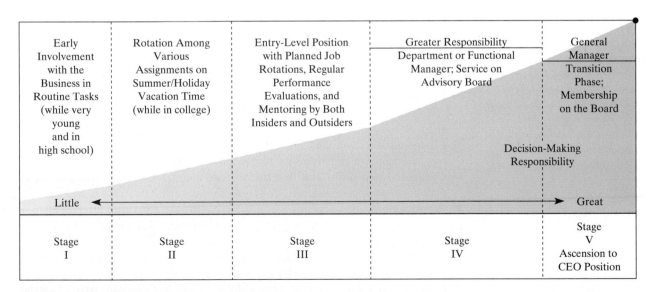

**FIGURE 20.3 Stages in Management Succession**

necessary for the process to begin early in the successor's life (Stage I). For instance, the owner of a catering business recalls putting his son to work in the family-owned company at age 7. On weekends, the boy would arrive at dawn to baste turkeys and was paid in his favorite medium of exchange—doughnuts![30] In most cases, family business owners involve their children in their businesses while they are still in junior high or high school. In this phase, the tasks are routine, but the child is learning the basics of how the business operates. Young adults begin to appreciate the role the business plays in the life of the family. They learn firsthand about the values and responsibilities of running the company.

While in college, the successor moves to Stage II of the continuum. During this stage, the individual rotates among a variety of job functions to both broaden his or her base of understanding of the business and to permit the parents to evaluate his or her skills. Upon graduation from college, the successor enters Stage III. At this point, the successor becomes a full-time worker and ideally has already begun to earn the respect of coworkers through his or her behavior in the first two stages of the process. In some cases, the successor may work for a time outside of the family business to gain experience and to establish a reputation for competency that goes beyond "being the boss's kid." Stage III focuses on the successor's continuous development, often through a program designed to groom the successor using both family and non-family managers as mentors.

*The Joyner Family and C. Dan Joyner Real Estate*

From the time that Danny Joyner was a young boy "helping" his father, Dan, in the real estate business that the elder Joyner was building, he knew that he wanted to join his father's company. "I've always known that this is what I would do," says Danny, who joined the company full-time after graduating from college. Danny heads the successful company's commercial real estate division, and Dan's two daughters and a son-in-law also work in the family business. With a succession plan in place and all of his children in leadership positions in the company, founder Dan Joyner says that the company is positioned to make a smooth transition into the second generation of ownership.[31]

As the successor develops his or her skills and abilities, he or she moves to Stage IV, in which real decision-making authority grows rapidly. Stage IV of the succession continuum is the period when the founder makes a final assessment of the successor's competence and ability to take full and complete control over the firm. The skills the successor needs include the following:

- *Financial abilities.* Understanding the financial aspect of a business, what its financial position is, and the managerial implications of that position are crucial to success.
- *Technical knowledge.* Every business has its own body of knowledge, ranging from how the distribution system works to the trends shaping the industry, that an executive must master.
- *Negotiating ability.* Much of business, whether buying supplies and inventory or selling to customers, boils down to negotiating, and a business owner must be adept at it.
- *Leadership qualities.* Leaders must be bold enough to stake out the company's future and then give employees the resources, the power, and the freedom to pursue it.
- *Communication skills.* Business leaders must communicate the vision they have for their businesses; good listening skills also are essential for success as a top manager.
- *Juggling skills.* Business owners must be able to handle multiple projects effectively. Like a juggler, they must maintain control over several important assignments simultaneously.
- *Integrity.* To be an effective leader of a family business, a successor must demonstrate honesty and integrity in business dealings.
- *Commitment to the business.* It helps if a successor has a genuine passion for the business. Leaders who have enthusiasm for what they do create a spark of excitement throughout the entire organization.[32]

There has been a changing of the guard

The final stage in the management succession process involves the ultimate transition of organizational leadership. It is during this stage that the founder's role as mentor is most crucial.

ENTREPRENEURIAL
**Profile**

*Laura Michaud and
Beltone Electronics
Corporation*

Laura Michaud, who in 1980 became the third generation owner of Beltone Electronics Corporation, a very successful maker of hearing aids that her grandfather founded in 1940, says that the training and mentoring that her father provided was key to her success to managing the family business. Her father insisted on an extensive training program that involved Michaud in all aspects of the company, including having her actually build a hearing aid. "You need to work in all areas of operations," says Michaud, who ran the company for 17 years before selling it to a larger company.[33]

In Stage IV, the successor may become the organization's CEO, while the former CEO retains the title of chairman of the board. In other cases, the best solution is for the founder to step out of the business entirely and give the successor the chance to establish his or her own identity within the company. "Any leader's final legacy is building the next generation," says one business consultant.[34]

## Developing a Management Succession Plan

**4.** Explain how to develop an effective management succession plan.

Families that are most committed to ensuring that their businesses survive from one generation to the next exhibit four characteristics: (1) They believe that owning the business helps achieve their families' missions. (2) They are proud of the values their businesses are built on and exemplify. (3) They believe that the business is contributing to society and makes it a better place to live. (4) They rely on management succession plans to assure the continuity of their companies.[35] Developing a plan takes time and dedication, yet the benefits are well worth the cost. A sound succession plan enables a company to maintain its momentum and sense of purpose and direction.

It is important to start the planning process early, well before the founder's retirement. Succession planning is not the kind of activity an entrepreneur can do in a hurry, and the sooner an entrepreneur starts, the easier and more effective it will be. Unfortunately, too many entrepreneurs put it off until it's too late. "Very few privately owned business make it through several generations, and one reason is the failure of the senior generation to do any planning at all until it is too late in the game," says one expert.[36] Creating a succession plan involves the following steps.

### Step 1: Select the Successor

The average tenure of the founder of a family business has remained constant at 25 years for the past decade.[37] Yet there comes a time for even the most dedicated founder to step down and hand the reins of the company to the next generation. Entrepreneurs should never assume that their children want to take control of the business, however. Above all, they should not be afraid to ask the question: "Do you really want to take over the family business?" Too often, children in this situation tell mom and dad what they want to hear out of loyalty, pressure, or guilt. It is critical to remember at this juncture in the life of a business that children do not necessarily inherit their parents' entrepreneurial skills and desires. By leveling with the children about the business and their options regarding a family succession, the owner will know which heirs, if any, are willing to assume leadership of the business.

**Herman and Jan Berghoff and the Berghoff Restaurant**

The Berghoff Restaurant, a Chicago landmark for 108 years, recently closed after Herman, 70, and Jan, 68, third-generation owners of the German restaurant, decided that they were ready to retire. None of the Berghoff's four children were interested in taking on the challenge of running the restaurant and the 65-plus hours per week that requires. No buyer emerged, and the Berghoffs simply closed the restaurant, much to the dismay of its following of loyal patrons.[38]

One of the worst mistakes entrepreneurs can make is to postpone naming a successor until just before they are ready to step down. One study by the Raymond Institute and Mass-Mutual reports that 55 percent of family business owners age 61 or older have not yet designated a successor![39] The problem is especially acute when more than one family member works for the company and is interested in assuming leadership of it. Sometimes founders avoid naming successors because they don't want to hurt the family members who are not chosen to succeed them. However, both the business and the family will be better off if, after observing family members as they work in the business, the founder picks a successor based on skill and ability. When naming a successor, merit is a better standard to use than gender or birth order. The key is to establish standards of performance, knowledge, education, and ability and then to identify the person who best meets those standards. As part of his company's succession plan, Joe De La Torre selected his daughter Gina to take over Jaunita's Foods rather than his two sons because her financial skills and her ability to solve problems were what the company needed most.[40] Gina La Torre is part of a growing trend among family businesses; 34 percent of family business founders expect the next CEO to be a woman, quite a change from just a generation ago.[41]

**Victoria Ross and Teal Lake Lodge and Golf Club**

When her father was ready to retire from the golf course and resort his father had founded in 1921, Victoria Ross was the natural choice to take over leadership of the business. Ross literally grew up in the family business and knew every aspect of it intimately. "I was in a waitress uniform at age six and have worked every position [in the business]," she says. When she was just 18, Ross assumed management positions at Teal Lake Lodge and Golf Club before going on to earn a degree in business administration with a concentration in small business. She even found time to work at another resort, something she says proved to be quite helpful in managing the family business today.[42]

### Step 2: Create a Survival Kit for the Successor

Once he or she identifies a successor, an entrepreneur should prepare a survival kit and then brief the future leader on its contents, which should include all of the company's critical documents (wills, trusts, insurance policies, financial statements, bank accounts, key contracts, corporate bylaws, and so forth). The founder should be sure that the successor reads and understands all of the relevant documents in the kit. Other important steps the owner should take to prepare the successor to take over leadership of the business include:

- Create a strategic analysis for the future. Working with the successor, entrepreneurs should identify the primary opportunities and the challenges facing the company and the requirements for meeting them.
- On a regular basis, share with the successor their vision of the business's future direction, describing key factors that have led to its success and those that will bring future success.
- Be open and listen to the successor's views and concerns.
- Teach and learn at the same time.
- Identify the industry's key success factors.
- Tie the key success factors to the company's performance and profitability.
- Explain the company's overall strategy and how it creates a competitive advantage.
- Discuss the values and philosophy of the business and how they have inspired and influenced past decisions.
- Discuss the people in the business and their strengths and weaknesses.
- Describe the philosophy underlying the firm's compensation policy and explain why employees are paid what they are.
- Make a list of the firm's most important customers and its key suppliers or vendors and review the history of all dealings with the parties on both lists.
- Discuss how to treat these key players to ensure the company's continued success and its smooth ownership transition.
- Develop a job analysis by taking an inventory of the activities involved in leading the company. This analysis can show successors those activities on which they should be spending most of their time.
- Document as much process knowledge—"how we do things"—as possible. After many years in their jobs, business owners are not even aware of their vast reservoirs of knowledge. For them, making decisions is a natural part of their business lives. They do it effortlessly because they have so much knowledge and experience. It is easy to forget that a successor will not have the benefit of those years of experience unless the founder communicates it.
- Include an ethical will, a document that explains to the next generation of leaders the ethical principles on which the company operates. An ethical will gives company founders the chance to bequeath to their heirs not only a business but also the wisdom and ethical lessons learned over a lifetime.

*Kevin Van Tuinen and West Michigan Uniform*

Every Tuesday morning, Ken Van Tuinen, second generation owner of West Michigan Uniform meets with his son and his two nephews who work in the family business to work on a family covenant that spells out the values and principles by which they will operate their business. They also have regular updates on the company's management succession plan. Once a month, the Van Tuinens meet for frank discussions about the progress the members of the next generation of leadership are making towards their performance goals and to complete their self assessments. "We want to define what it will take to be successful for ourselves and for the next generation," explains Kevin. "My goal is to be able to see my nephews and my son be more successful than I was by continuing the values that my Dad taught me."[43]

### Step 3: Groom the Successor

The process by which business founders transfer their knowledge to the next generation is gradual and often occurs informally as they spend time with their successors. Grooming the successor is the founder's greatest teaching and development responsibility, and it takes time, usually five to ten years.

*Brian Tuberman
and SCTR Systems*

The founder of SCTR Systems, a company created in 1967 that sells computerized retail systems to independent grocers, began looking for a successor (from outside the family because none of his children were interested in taking over the family business) 12 years before he planned to retire. He recruited Brian Tuberman and immediately began grooming him to take over the company. Tuberman purchased the business from the founder in 2005 and credits the smooth transition of ownership to the lessons he learned from his mentor. "Everyone thought I was crazy to quit what I was doing to make plans for 12 years down the road," says Tuberman, "but the previous owner and I believed in each other and in the company and made it happen."[44]

To implement the succession plan, the founder must be:

■ Patient, realizing that the transfer of power is gradual and evolutionary and that the successor should earn responsibility and authority one step at a time until the final transfer of power takes place.
■ Willing to accept that the successor will make mistakes.
■ Skillful at using the successor's mistakes as a teaching tool.
■ An effective communicator and an especially tolerant listener.
■ Capable of establishing reasonable expectations for the successor's performance.
■ Able to articulate the keys to the successor's success.

Teaching is the art of assisting discovery and requires letting go rather than controlling. When problems arise in the business, the founder should consider delegating some of them to the successor-in-training. The founder also must resist the tendency to wade in and fix the problem unless it is beyond the scope of the successor's ability. Most great teachers and leaders are remembered more for the success of their students than for their own success.

### Step 4: Promote an Environment of Trust and Respect

Another priceless gift a founder can leave a successor is an environment of trust and respect. Trust and respect on the part of the founder and others fuel the successor's desire to learn and excel and build the successor's confidence in making decisions. Empowering the successor by gradually delegating responsibilities creates an environment in which all parties can objectively view the growth and development of the successor. Customers, creditors, suppliers, and staff members can gradually develop confidence in the successor. The final transfer of power is not a dramatic, wrenching change but a smooth, coordinated transition.

A problem for some founders at this phase is the meddling retiree syndrome, in which they continue to show up at the office after they have officially stepped down and get involved in business issues that no longer concern them. This tendency merely undermines the authority of the successor and confuses employees as to who really is in charge. Helen Dragas, who succeeded her father at the Dragas Company, a residential construction business, praises her father for handing the reins of the company over to her and then trusting her to handle them. "He gave me the authority and then he stepped back," she says of the successful transfer of leadership.[45]

### Step 5: Cope with the Financial Realities of Estate and Gift Taxes

The final step in developing a workable management succession plan is structuring the transition to minimize the impact of estate, gift, and inheritance taxes on family members and the business. Entrepreneurs who fail to consider the impact of these taxes may force their heirs to sell a successful business just to pay the estate's tax bill. Despite facing potentially large tax bills, 19 percent of senior generation owners have done no estate planning at all![46]

*Gordon Perkins
and Perkins Flowers*

Ella Perkins, co-owner of Perkins Flowers, and her son Gordon saw the need to develop an estate plan to minimize the impact of estate and gift taxes on the company, which Gordon was running. Each year, Ella gave Gordon $10,000 worth of stock in the company, the maximum amount the law allowed at the time without triggering gift taxes. She also transferred majority ownership in the company to Gordon using other estate planning tools so that estate taxes would be smaller on her minority share of the business. Gordon also purchased enough life insurance for his mother to pay the estimated estate tax bill. When Ella died at age 83, Gordon discovered that despite their attempts at estate planning, the amount of tax due was more than he had expected. "At the very least," he says, "it's going to repress the growth of my business for some significant amount of time." He says that he may have to sell a 43-acre tree farm the company owns to pay the full tax bill.[47]

Although tax laws currently allow individuals to pass up to $2 million of assets to their heirs without incurring any estate taxes, the tax rate on transfers above that amount starts at 45 percent! Although the United States is one country that has overhauled the estate and gift tax (see Table 20.2), without proper estate planning, an entrepreneur's family members will incur a painful tax bite when they inherit the business. Entrepreneurs should be actively engaged in estate planning no later than age 45; those who start businesses early in their lives or whose businesses grow rapidly may need to begin as early as age 30. A variety of options exist that may prove to be helpful in reducing the estate tax liability. Each operates in a different fashion, but their objective remains the same: to remove a portion of business owners' assets out of their estates so that when they die, those assets will not be subject to estate taxes. Many of these estate planning tools need time to work their magic, so the key is to put them in place early on in the life of the business.

### TABLE 20.2 Changes in Estate and Gift Taxes in the United States

After years of complaints from family business owners, the United States finally overhauled the often punishing structures of estate and gift taxes. The federal estate tax is actually interwoven with the gift tax, but under the modified law, the impact of the two taxes began to differ in 2004. The estate tax is scheduled to be repealed in 2010, but under current provisions, it will reappear in 2011! The following table shows the exemptions and the minimum tax rates for the estate and gift taxes as they currently stand:

| Year | Estate Tax Exemption | Gift Tax Exemption | Maximum Tax Rate |
| --- | --- | --- | --- |
| 2001 | $675,000 | $675,000 | 55% |
| 2002 | $1 million | $1 million | 50% |
| 2003 | $1 million | $1 million | 49% |
| 2004 | $1.5 million | $1 million | 48% |
| 2005 | $1.5 million | $1 million | 47% |
| 2006 | $2 million | $1 million | 46% |
| 2007 | $2 million | $1 million | 45% |
| 2008 | $2 million | $1 million | 45% |
| 2009 | $3.5 million | $1 million | 45% |
| 2010 | Tax repealed | $1 million | 35% (gifts only) |
| 2011 | $1 million | $1 million | 55% |

However the laws governing estate taxes may change over the next few years, entrepreneurs whose businesses have been successful must not neglect estate planning. Even though the federal estate tax burden has eased somewhat (at least for a while), many U.S. states have increased their estate tax rates.

*Sources:* Tom Herman, "Estate Taxes Will Turn Sharply Lower on Jan. 1," *Wall Street Journal*, November 20, 2003, p. D2; Jeanne Lee, "Death and Estate Taxes," *FSB*, April 2004, p. 96; "Tax Law Changes for Gifts and Estates and Trusts," Internal Revenue Service, www.irs.gov/formspubs/article/0,,id=112782,00.html#estate_tax_rate_2007.

**BUY-SELL AGREEMENT.** One of the most popular estate planning techniques is the buy-sell agreement. A **buy-sell agreement** is a contract that co-owners often rely on to ensure the continuity of a business. In a typical arrangement, the co-owners create a contract that states that each agrees to buy the others out in case of the death or disability of one. That way, the heirs of the deceased or disabled owner can "cash out" of the business while leaving control of the business in the hands of the remaining owners. The buy-sell agreement specifies a formula for determining the value of the business at the time the agreement is to be executed. One problem with buy-sell agreements is that the remaining co-owners may not have the cash available to buy out the disabled or deceased owner. To resolve this issue, many businesses buy life and disability insurance for each of the owners in amounts large enough to cover the purchase price of their respective shares of the business.

*Junab Ali and Jay Uribe and Mobius Partners*

Junab Ali and Jay Uribe, founders of Mobius Partners, a $25 million a year company that specializes in enterprise IT solutions, created a buy-sell agreement to protect themselves and their business in the event of the death or disability of a partner. Their agreement is supported by insurance policies on each partner, giving them the income security they need for their families and providing the remaining partner the financial resources to buy the shares of the missing partner.[48]

Without the support of adequate insurance policies, a buy-sell agreement offers virtually no protection.

**LIFETIME GIFTING.** The owners of a successful business may transfer money to their children (or other recipients) from their estate throughout the parents' lives. Currently in the United States, federal tax regulations allow individuals to make gifts of $12,000 per year, per parent, per recipient, that are exempt from federal gift taxes. Each child would be required to pay income taxes on the $12,000 gift they receive, but the children usually are in lower tax brackets than those of the giver. For instance, husband-and-wife business owners could give $1.44 million worth of stock to their three children and their spouses over a period of ten years without incurring any estate or gift taxes at all.

**SETTING UP A TRUST.** A **trust** is a contract between a grantor (the founder) and a trustee (generally a bank officer or an attorney) in which the grantor gives to the trustee legal title to assets (e.g., stock in the company), which the trustee agrees to hold for the beneficiaries (children). The beneficiaries can receive income from the trust, or they can receive the property in the trust, or both, at some specified time. Trusts can take a wide variety of forms, but two broad categories of trusts are available: revocable trusts and irrevocable trusts. A **revocable trust** is one that the grantor can change or revoke during his or her lifetime. Under present tax laws, however, the only trust that provides a tax benefit is an **irrevocable trust**, in which the grantor cannot require the trustee to return the assets held in trust. The value of the grantor's estate is lowered because the assets in an irrevocable trust are excluded from the value of that estate. However, an irrevocable trust places severe restrictions on the grantor's control of the property placed in the trust. Business owners use several types of irrevocable trusts to lower their estate tax liabilities:

*Bypass Trust.* The most basic type of trust is the **bypass trust**, which allows a business owner to put up to $3 million (beginning in 2009) into a trust naming his or her spouse as the beneficiary upon the owner's death. The spouse receives the income from the trust throughout his or her life, but the principal in the trust bypasses the surviving spouse's estate and goes to the couple's heirs free of estate taxes upon the spouse's death. A bypass trust is particularly useful for couples who plan their estates together. By leaving assets to one another in bypass trusts, they can make sure that their assets are taxed only once between them. However, entrepreneurs should work with experienced attorneys to create bypass trusts because the IRS requires that they contain certain precise language to be valid.

*Irrevocable Life Insurance Trust (ILIT).* An **irrevocable life insurance trust** allows a business owner to keep the proceeds of a life insurance policy out of his or her estate and away from estate taxes, freeing up that money to pay the taxes on the remainder of the estate. To get the tax benefit, business owners must be sure that the business or the trust (rather than themselves) owns the insurance policy. The primary disadvantage of an irrevocable life insurance trust is that if the owner dies within three years of establishing it, the insurance proceeds *do* become part of the estate and *are* subject to estate taxes. Because the trust is irrevocable, it cannot be amended or rescinded once it is established. Like most trusts, ILITs must meet stringent requirements to be valid, and entrepreneurs should use experienced attorneys to create them.

*Irrevocable Asset Trust.* An **irrevocable asset trust** is similar to a life insurance trust except that it is designed to pass the assets in the parents' estate on to their children. The children do not have control of the assets while the parents are still living, but they do receive the income from those assets. Upon the parents' death, the assets in the trust go to the children without being subjected to the estate tax.

*Grantor Retained Annuity Trust (GRAT).* A **grantor retained annuity trust (GRAT)** is a special type of irrevocable trust and has become one of the most popular tools for entrepreneurs to transfer ownership of a business while maintaining control over it and minimizing estate taxes. Under a GRAT, an owner can put property in an irrevocable trust for a maximum of ten years. While the trust is in effect, the grantor (owner) retains the voting power and receives the interest income from the property in the trust. At the end of the trust (not to exceed ten years), the property passes to the beneficiaries (heirs). The beneficiaries are required to pay the gift tax on the value of the assets placed in the GRAT but no estate tax on them. However, the United States, for example, taxes GRAT gifts only according to their discounted present value because the heirs did not receive use of the property while it was in trust. The primary disadvantage of using a GRAT in estate planning is that if the grantor dies during the life of the GRAT, its assets pass back into the grantor's estate. These assets then become subject to the full estate tax.

Establishing a trust requires meeting many specific legal requirements and is not something business owners should do on their own. It is much better to hire experienced attorneys, accountants, and financial advisors to assist in creating them. Although the cost of establishing a trust can be high, the tax savings they generate are well worth the expense.

**ESTATE FREEZE.** An **estate freeze** attempts to minimize estate taxes by having family members create two classes of stock for the business: (1) preferred voting stock for the parents and (2) nonvoting common stock for the children. The value of the preferred stock is frozen whereas the common stock reflects the anticipated increased market value of the business. Any appreciation in the value of the business after the transfer is not subject to estate taxes. However, the parents must pay gift tax on the value of the common stock given to the children. The value of the common stock is the total value of the business less the value of the voting preferred stock retained by the parents. The parents also must accept taxable dividends at the market rate on the preferred stock they own.

**FAMILY LIMITED PARTNERSHIP.** Creating a **family limited partnership (FLP)** allows business-owning parents to transfer their company to their children (thus lowering their estate taxes) while still retaining control over it for themselves. To create a family limited partnership, the parents (or parent) set up a partnership among themselves and their children. The parents retain the general partnership interest, which can be as low as 1 percent, and the children become the limited partners. As general partners, the parents control both the limited partnership and the family business. In other words, nothing in the way the company operates has to change. Over time, the parents can transfer company stock into the limited partnership, ultimately passing ownership of the company to their children.

One of the principal tax benefits of an FLP is that it allows discounts on the value of the shares of company stock the parents transfer into the limited partnership. Because a family business is closely held, shares of ownership in it, especially minority shares, are not as marketable as those of a publicly held company. As a result, company shares transferred into the limited partnership are discounted at 20 to 50 percent of their full market value, producing a large tax savings for everyone involved. The average discount is 40 percent, but that amount varies based on the industry and the individual company involved. A business owner should consider an FLP as part of a succession plan "when there has been a buildup of substantial value in the business and the older generation has a substantial amount of liquidity," says one expert.[49]

Because of their ability to reduce estate and gift taxes, FLPs have become one of the most popular estate planning tools in recent years. However, a tax court ruling in 2005 against a Texas entrepreneur who, two months before he died, established an FLP that contained both business and personal assets, cast a pall over the use of FLPs as estate planning tools. Another case, however, calmed estate planners' fears and reestablished the use of FLPs as legitimate estate planning tools as long as entrepreneurs create them properly. The following tips will help entrepreneurs establish an FLP that will withstand legal challenges:

- Establish a legitimate business reason other than avoiding estate taxes—such as transferring a business over time to the next generation of family members—for creating the FLP and document it on paper.
- Make sure all members of the FLP make contributions and take distributions according to a predetermined schedule. "Don't allow partners to use partnership funds to pay for personal expenses and do not time partnership distributions with personal needs for cash," says one attorney.[50]
- Do not allow members to put all of their personal assets (such as a house, automobiles, or personal property) into the FLP. Commingling personal and business assets in an FLP raises a red flag to the IRS.
- Expect an audit of the FLP. The IRS tends to scrutinize FLPs; be prepared for a thorough audit.[51]

*Ken Van Tuinen and West Michigan Uniform*

Gordon Van Tuinen founded West Michigan Uniform (WMU) in Holland, Michigan, in 1963 and managed it until he retired in 1983, when his son Ken took over as CEO. To transfer the family business to Ken and his four other children, Gordon relied on a variety of estate planning tools, including lifetime gifting and an estate freeze. Ken, who owns the majority of shares in WMU, is now engaged in planning to give control of the company to the third generation of family members with the goal of minimizing the impact of estate taxes. In addition to using lifetime gifting to transfer shares of the company to his three children, one of whom works in the business, Ken created three family limited partnerships that will allow the children to assume ownership of the company over time without incurring oppressive tax bills.[52]

## In the Entrepreneurial Spotlight

### ■ The Third Generation at Powell's Is Booked

Encouraged by friends and professors, Michael Powell, a graduate student at the University of Chicago in 1970, borrowed $3,000, assumed a lease on an existing bookstore, and began selling used books. Powell was so successful that he repaid the loan within two months. Michael's father, Walter, who had recently retired in Portland, Oregon, as a paint contractor, went to Chicago to help his son run the bookstore for a summer. Walter enjoyed the experience so much that when he returned to

Portland, he opened his own used bookstore in the city's downtown district. In 1979, Michael returned to Portland to work with his father in the bookstore, and together the two built Powell's Books on the foundation of a unique strategy, that although viewed as unorthodox at the time, proved to be very successful: used and new books, hardcover and paperback, all on the same shelf, in a store that is open 365 days a year and staffed by knowledgeable and dedicated book lovers. "Used and new on the same shelf? It seemed crazy," admits Michael. However, combining books "had synergy way beyond what we expected; they drive each other." To house their voluminous inventory, the Powell's purchased a cavernous former auto dealership that, after many expansions, became Powell's City of Books, now a landmark in downtown Portland that contains more than one million books and occupies an entire city block. Couples have met—and even married—at the bookstore, and one very loyal customer requested that his ashes be placed inside a Tower of Books statue that stands near an entrance.

Michael took over the business from his father in 1982 and worked hard for two decades, adding stores, launching a Web site in 1994 (before Amazon even existed), and building Powell's Books into the largest privately held bookstore chain in the nation with more than $50 million in annual sales. Now 66, Powell is passing the baton of leadership at Powell's to his only daughter, Emily. Like most children in family businesses, Emily, 28, grew up in the store, shelving books and running cash registers. On Christmas Eve when she was just eight years old, Emily was standing on a box next to a cash register helping make change for customers, a woman asked her, "My dear, when you grow up, are you going to be a cashier?" "When I grow up, I am going to own this place," Emily told the woman. Twenty years later, Emily's statement proved to be prescient when her father officially announced that she would take over as CEO, assuring the company's 500 employees and thousands of devoted customers that Powell's would remain a family business. "I think it hasn't even fully hit me yet. At some point I have to figure out how to make all of this work," she says, making a sweeping gesture around the store.

Emily's rise to the top of the family business has followed an indirect route. After graduating from Haverford College with a degree in urban planning, she wondered what to do with her life. An internship at Powell's did not work out the way she had hoped, and she moved to San Francisco, California, where she worked as a lingerie clerk, a pastry chef, and a real estate analyst. In the meantime, Michael, who was hoping that Emily would one day take charge of the family business, began creating a succession plan. "I never had any

interest in selling," he admits. "I wanted to keep it local, independent, and, if I could, family owned." He knew that passing a family business to the next generation was a perilous event and that forcing Emily into the business would be the worst thing he could do. "I didn't want to blackmail her or bribe her into a decision that she was not going to feel good about, but I always felt like she should at least kick the tires and know what she was walking away from," he says.

Emily agrees with her father's approach. "There was never any pressure," she says. "He let me know that I could follow my own path." In 2004, Emily returned to Powell's and began working in each of the company's different divisions to learn all aspects of the business. "You need to earn your stripes and regain some credibility you might have lost when you were here for that [internship]," advised a family business consultant that Michael had hired. Emily gradually began assuming more responsibility, becoming the director of used books, which represents Powell's most profitable line of business.

Like most independent bookstores, Powell's faces significant opportunities and threats, but Michael is confident that Emily can handle them. "It's an iPod world," he philosophizes. "It's a blogger's world. That's not me. That never will be me. Emily is the one who can delve into this world, and that's what this company needs."

1. Do you think the challenges that Powell's Books faces as a family business are typical of most family-owned companies? What factors cause most family businesses to fail to make the intergenerational transfer of power successfully?

2. What recommendations would you make to the Powells to ensure a smooth transition as Emily assumes the mantle of leadership in the family business?

*Sources:* Adapted from Claire Cain Miller, "Chapter Two," *Forbes,* December 25, 2006, pp. 72–74; Hal Bernton, "The Future Is Booked," *Seattle Times,* May 21, 2006, http://seattletimes.nwsource.com/html/books/2003005918_emilypowell21.html; "Powell's Books' History," Powell's Books, www.powells.com/info/briefhistory.html.

Developing a succession plan and preparing a successor requires a wide variety of knowledge and skills, some of which the business founder will not have. That's why it is important to bring into the process experts when necessary. Entrepreneurs often call on their attorneys, accountants, insurance agents, and financial planners to help them build a succession plan that works best for their particular situations. Because the issues involved can be highly complex and charged with emotion, bringing in trusted advisors to help improves the quality of the process and provides an objective perspective.

## Risk Management Strategies

**5.** Understand the four risk management strategies.

Insurance is an important part of creating a management succession plan because it can help business owners minimize the taxes on the estates they pass on to their heirs and can provide much needed cash to pay the taxes the estate does incur. However, insurance plays an important role in many other aspects of a successful business—from covering employee injuries to protecting against natural disasters that might shut a business down temporarily. When most small business owners think of risks such as these, they automatically think of insurance. However, insurance companies are the first to point out that insurance does not solve all risk problems. A more comprehensive strategy is risk management, which takes a proactive approach to dealing with the risks that businesses face daily. One study shows that only 10 percent of small and midsized companies have developed plans to ensure business survival in the face of a business crisis. "Small companies often spend more time planning the company picnic than planning for an event that could put them out of business," says one insurance expert.[53] Dealing with risk successfully requires a combination of four risk management strategies: avoiding, reducing, anticipating, and transferring risk.

Avoiding risk requires a business to take actions to shun risky situations. For instance, conducting credit checks of customers can help decrease losses from bad debts. Wise managers know that they can avoid some risks simply by taking proactive management actions. Workplace safety improves when business owners implement programs designed to make all employees aware of the hazards of their jobs and how to avoid being hurt. Business owners who have active risk identification and prevention programs can reduce their potential insurance costs as well as create a safer, more attractive work environment for their employees. Because avoiding risk altogether usually is not practical, however, a strategy of reducing risk becomes necessary.

A risk-reducing strategy requires a company to take steps to lower the level of risk associated with a situation. For instance, businesses can reduce risk by following common safety practices, such as installing a sprinkler system to lower the threat of damage from fire. A sprinkler system does not guarantee that a fire will not occur, but it can minimize the damage that results if a fire does break out. Risk reduction strategies do not eliminate risk, but they lessen its impact. Even with avoidance and reduction strategies, the risk is still present; thus, losses can occur.

Risk-anticipation strategies promote self-insurance. Knowing that some element of risk still exists, a business owner puts aside money each month to cover potential losses. Sometimes a self-insurance fund set aside may not be large enough to cover the losses from a particular situation. When this happens, a business stands to lose despite its best efforts to anticipate risk, especially in the first few years when the fund is insufficient to cover large losses. Most businesses, therefore, include in their risk strategies some form of insurance to transfer risk.

*Racine Federated*

Managers at Racine Federated, a small company that sells industrial instruments, machinery, and tools, grew tired of watching the cost of health care coverage for their 110 employees climb every year and decided to establish a self-insurance fund to cover employees' health care benefits. If employees' claims were low in a given year, Racine would save money over what it would have paid in insurance premiums. If several workers suffered catastrophic injuries or illnesses at once, however, the company could face a cash crisis. Recognizing that a self-insurance strategy alone could be risky, Racine purchased a "stop-loss" policy, which takes over payment if any individual employee's health care costs exceed $55,000 a year. Racine also hired a company to handle all of the insurance paperwork. In the seven years since switching to self-insurance, Racine has saved $300,000 over the cost of the company's old insurance plan without reducing its coverage.[54]

Self-insurance is not for every business owner, however. For businesses with fewer than 50 employees, self-insurance is usually not a wise choice because there is so much variation in the number and size of annual claims. Self-insuring also is time-consuming, requiring business owners to take a more active role in managing their companies' insurance needs. Companies using self-insurance should be financially secure with a relatively stable workforce and should see it as a long-term strategy for savings.

Risk transfer strategies depend on using insurance. Insurance is a risk transfer strategy because an individual or a business transfers some of the costs of a particular risk to an insurance company, which is set up to spread out the financial burdens of risk. During a specific time period, the insured business pays money (a premium) to an insurance carrier (either a private company or a government agency). In return, the carrier promises to pay the insured a certain amount of money in the event of a loss. Small companies across the United States are feeling the pinch of rapidly escalating insurance costs and are devising creative ways to control their insurance costs.

**Captive insurance**, which is a hybrid of self-insurance and risk transfer strategies, is a technique that large businesses have used for years and is gaining popularity among small businesses. To implement a captive insurance strategy, small companies band together to create their own insurance company and contribute enough capital to cover a defined level of risk. The group outsources the daily management of the insurance company to a business that specializes in that area and then purchases reinsurance to cover losses above the amount that they have contributed. Over time, if the group experiences no large losses, the excess capital paid into the insurance company goes back to the businesses as dividends. Currently, 27 states and the District of Columbia have passed legislation authorizing insurance captives.

*Dudley Miles and J.D. Miles & Sons*

Dudley Miles, CEO of J.D. Miles & Sons, a roofing contractor founded by his grandfather in 1910, was plagued by escalating insurance premiums that threatened his company's profitability. Working through Roof Connect, an industry association, Miles convinced 25 other roofing contractors to band together to create a captive insurance company. The small businesses agreed to self-insure losses up to $500,000 and purchased reinsurance to cover larger losses. They also adopted several risk reduction strategies such as quarterly safety inspections and random drug tests for employees. The result has been a reduction in the number of claims, improved safety records, and lower premiums than the members of the plan were paying before.[55]

## The Basics of Insurance

*6.* Discuss the basics of insurance for small businesses.

**Insurance** is the transfer of risk from one entity (an individual, a group, or a business) to an insurance company. Without insurance, many of the products and services that businesses provide would be impossible because the risk of overwhelming financial loss would be too great given the litigious society in which we live. Yet many small business owners ignore their companies' insurance needs or fail to buy enough insurance coverage to protect their companies from the most basic risks such as property damage, fire, theft, and liability. Home-based business owners, in particular, put their companies at risk. According to the Independent Insurance Agents & Brokers of America, 58 percent of home-based business owners lack adequate insurance to protect them against liability, property damage or loss.[56]

To be insurable, a situation or hazard must meet the following requirements:

1. It must be possible to calculate the actual loss being insured. For example, it would probably not be possible to insure an entire city against fire because too many variables are involved. It is possible, however, to insure a specific building.
2. It must be possible to select the risk being insured. No business owner can insure against every potential hazard, but insurance companies offer a wide variety of policies. One company even offers an alien abduction policy ($150 a year for $150 million of coverage) and has actually paid one claim! Another offers werewolf insurance, but the policy pays only if the insured turns into a werewolf.[57] Famous insurer Lloyd's of London once wrote a policy to insure against "worry lines" developing on a famous model's face, and *Entertainment Tonight* host Mary Hart has her legs insured for $1 million.[58]

3. There must be enough potential policyholders to assume the risk. A tightrope walker who specializes in walking between tall downtown buildings would have difficulty purchasing insurance because there are not enough people engaging in that activity to spread the risk sufficiently.

Perhaps the biggest barrier facing entrepreneurs is the difficulty of understanding the nature of the risks that they and their businesses face. The risk management pyramid (see Figure 20.4) can help entrepreneurs decide how they should allocate their risk management dollars. Begin by identifying the primary risks your company faces: for example, a fire in a manufacturing plant, a lawsuit from a customer injured by your company's product, an earthquake, and so on. Then rate each event on three factors:

1. *Severity.* How much would the event affect your company's ability to operate?
2. *Probability.* How likely is the event to occur?
3. *Cost.* How much would it cost your company if the event occurred?

Rate the event on each of these three factors using a simple scale: A (high) to D (low). For instance, a small company might rate a fire in its manufacturing plant as ABA. On the other hand, that same company might rank a computer system crash as CBA. Using the risk management pyramid, a business owner sees that the event rated ABA is higher on the risk scale than the event rated CBA. Therefore, this company would focus more of its risk management dollars on preventing a fire in its plant than on dealing with a computer system crash.

### Types of Insurance

No longer is the cost of insurance an inconsequential part of doing business. Now the ability to get adequate coverage and to pay the premiums is a significant factor in starting and running a small business. Sometimes just *finding* coverage for their businesses is a challenge for entrepreneurs.

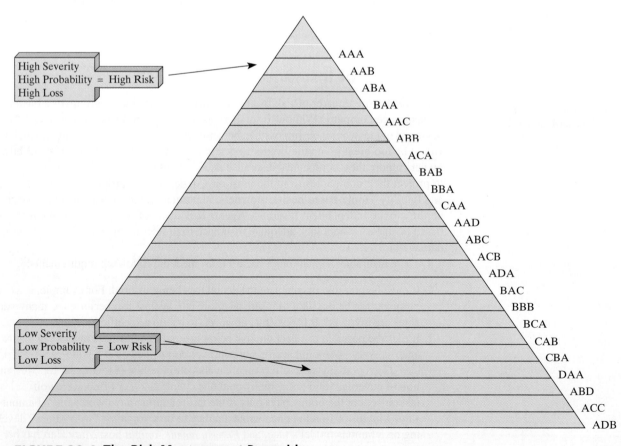

**FIGURE 20.4 The Risk Management Pyramid**

*Jane Reifert and
Incredible Adventures*

For Incredible Adventures, a small company that offers customers the opportunity to fly in a Russian MiG jet fighter, experience weightlessness, go to the edge of space, swim with sharks, or make a high-altitude, low-opening (HALO) sky dive, and experience many other exciting adventures, purchasing insurance is a challenge. President Jane Reifert says that she spends as much time with lawyers and insurance agents as she does with customers. "You can insure people swimming in shark-infested waters, but you can't insure people inside shark cages," she says incredulously.[59]

A customer enjoys a high–flying
adventure coordinated by
Incredible Adventures.

A wide range of business, individual, and group insurance is available to small business owners, and deciding which ones are necessary can be difficult. Some types of insurance are essential to providing a secure future for the company; others may provide additional employee benefits. The four major categories of insurance are property and casualty insurance, life and disability insurance, health insurance and workers' compensation coverage, and liability insurance. Each category is divided into many specific types, each of which has many variations offered by insurance companies. Business owners should begin by purchasing a basic **business owner's policy (BOP)**, which typically includes basic property and casualty insurance and liability insurance coverage. BOPs alone are not sufficient to meet most small business owners' insurance needs, however. Entrepreneurs should start with BOPs and then customize their insurance coverage to suit their companies' special needs by purchasing additional types of coverage.

**PROPERTY AND CASUALTY INSURANCE.** Property and casualty insurance covers a company's tangible assets, such as buildings, equipment, inventory, machinery, signs, and others that might be damaged, destroyed, or stolen. Business owners should be sure that their policies cover the replacement cost of their property, not just its value at the time of the loss, even if this coverage costs extra. One business owner whose policy covered the replacement cost of his company's building was glad he had purchased the extra coverage when he suffered a devastating fire loss. When he began rebuilding, he discovered that the cost to comply with current building code regulations was much higher than merely replacing the previous structure.

Specific types of property and casualty insurance include property, surety, marine and inland marine, crime, liability, business interruption, motor vehicle, and professional liability insurance.

**Property insurance** protects a company's assets against loss from damage, theft, or destruction. It applies to automobiles, boats, homes, office buildings, stores, factories, and other items of property. Some property insurance policies are broadly written to include all of an individual's property up to some maximum amount of loss, whereas other policies are written to cover only one building or one specific piece of property, such as a company car. Many natural disasters such as floods and earthquakes are not covered under standard property insurance; business owners must buy separate insurance policies for those particular events.

Within the past decade, business owners across the United States have suffered billions of dollars in losses from natural disasters such as the string of hurricanes that devastated the Gulf Coast of the United States. Many of the businesses that lacked proper insurance coverage were forced to close for good, and others are still struggling to recover.

*The Brennan Family and Ralph Brennan Restaurant Group*

Even with adequate insurance, reopening the celebrated Commander's Palace restaurant took the Brennans, a famous family of restaurateurs, more than a year after Hurricane Katrina severely damaged the historic Garden District building in New Orleans that housed it. Almost all of the interior of the building, which was constructed in 1880, had to be rebuilt because of water damage, and more than 80 percent of the kitchen equipment had to be replaced. Charlie Williamson, vice-president of the Ralph Brennan Restaurant Group, says that the company's disaster preparation plan has grown from two pages before the hurricane to a 68-page booklet that covers not only operating plans but also technology and communications plans.[60]

A company's BOP may insure the buildings and contents of a factory for loss from fire or natural disaster, but the owner may also buy insurance, called extra expense coverage, to cover expenses that occur while the destroyed factory is being rebuilt. **Extra expense coverage** pays for the costs of temporarily relocating workers and machinery so that a business can continue to operate while it rebuilds or repairs its factory. A similar type of insurance, called **business interruption insurance**, covers business owners' lost income and ongoing expenses in case their companies cannot operate for an extended period of time. As devastating as interruptions can be to a small company, studies show that 55 percent of small business owners do not purchase business interruption coverage and that 63 percent of them do not know how the coverage works.[61] Even more alarming is the fact that 25 percent of the businesses whose operations are interrupted by a disaster never reopen.[62]

*Nick El Deek and Al Sanabel*

Four years after Al Sanabel, a California bakery specializing in pita-based entrées, opened, the building housing Nick El Deek's business was damaged by a fire that started in the restaurant next door. The damage was so severe that El Deek's bakery was closed for more than five months, a devastating event because Al Sanabel finally had established a solid customer base, and sales were growing rapidly. Fortunately, El Deek had fire insurance and business interruption insurance, which provided enough money for him to reopen the Al Sanabel. Extended negotiations with the insurance company required him to borrow $37,000 from friends and family to complete the repairs and renovations. Although sales have not returned to their pre-fire levels, El Deek is optimistic. "I can make it. It just takes time," he says philosophically.[63]

**Machinery and equipment insurance** is a common addition for many businesses and covers a wide range of problems with equipment such as production machinery, electrical systems, HVAC systems, and others. For instance, a restaurant that loses thousands of dollars' worth of food when a freezer breaks down would be covered for its loss under machinery and equipment insurance.

**Auto insurance policies** offer liability coverage that protects against losses resulting from injuries, damage, or theft involving the use of company vehicles. A typical BOP does not include liability coverage for automobiles; business owners must purchase a separate policy for auto insurance. The automobiles a business owns must be covered by a commercial policy, not a personal one.

*Bob Foutz and Purity Pool Service*

Bob Foutz, owner of Purity Pool Service in Huntington Beach, California, counted on his auto insurance policy when a thief stole his service truck from the driveway of his home. Not only did the thief take the vehicle, but he also stole Foutz's inventory of equipment, tools, and parts, some of which were custom-fitted to his customers' pools. Without adequate insurance coverage, Foutz knows that he would have been out of business.[64]

**Electronic data processing (EDP) insurance** covers losses from the theft or loss of computers and data, the impact of computer viruses and computer system failures, intrusion by hackers, and invasion of customer information stored in company databases. EDP insurance has become more important as businesses have moved their operations online and engage in increasing volumes of e-commerce. Thomas Shipley, whose company sells business accessories, generates 30 percent of his sales from the company's Web site. Shipley purchased an EDP policy that protects his business from, among other things, hackers and viruses. The policy costs $14,000 a year, but Shipley says it is well worth the price to protect his company that now brings in more than $10 million in sales a year.[65]

A business may also purchase **surety insurance**, which protects against losses to customers that occur when a company fails to complete a contract on time or completes it incorrectly. Surety protection guarantees customers that they will get either the products or services they purchased or the money to cover losses from contractual failures.

Businesses also buy insurance to protect themselves from losses that occur when either finished goods or raw materials are lost or destroyed while being shipped. **Marine insurance** is designed to cover the risk associated with goods in transit. The name of this insurance goes back to the days when a ship's cargo was insured against high risks associated with ocean navigation.

**Crime insurance** does not deter crime, but it can reimburse the small business owner for losses from the "three Ds": dishonesty, disappearance, and destruction. Business owners should ask their insurance brokers or agents exactly what their crime insurance policies cover; after-the-fact insurance coverage surprises are seldom pleasant. Premiums for crime policies vary depending on the type of business, store location, number of employees, quality of the business's security system, and the business's history of losses. Coverage may include fidelity bonds, which are designed to reimburse business owners for losses from embezzlement and employee theft. Forgery bonds reimburse owners for losses sustained from the forgery of business checks.

**LIFE AND DISABILITY INSURANCE.** Unlike most forms of insurance, life insurance does not pertain to avoiding risk because death is a certainty for everyone. Rather, **life insurance** protects families and businesses against loss of income, security, or personal services that results from an individual's untimely death. Life insurance policies are usually issued with a face amount payable to a beneficiary upon the death of the insured. Life insurance for business protection, although not as common as life insurance for family protection, is becoming more popular. As you learned in the section on management succession, life insurance policies are an important part of many estate planning tools. In addition, many businesses insure the lives of key executives to offset the costs of having to make a hurried and often unplanned replacement of important managers.

When it comes to assets that are expensive to replace, few are more costly than the key people in a business, including the owner. What would it take to replace a company's top sales representative? Its production supervisor? Clearly, money alone cannot solve the problem, but it does allow a business to find and train their replacements and to cover the profits lost because of their untimely deaths or disabilities. That is the idea behind **key-person insurance**, which provides valuable working capital to keep a business on track while it reorganizes and searches for the right person to replace the loss of someone in a key position in the company.

Pensions and annuities are special forms of life insurance policies that combine insurance with a form of saving. With an annuity or pension plan, the insured person's premiums go partly to provide standard insurance coverage and partly to a fund that is invested by the insurance company. The interest from the invested portion of the policy is then used to pay an income to the policyholder when he or she reaches a certain age. If the policyholder dies before reaching that age, either the policy converts to income for the spouse or family of the insured or the insurance proceeds (plus interest) go to the beneficiary as they would in ordinary life insurance.

**Disability insurance**, like life insurance, protects an individual in the event of unexpected and often very expensive disabilities. Because a sudden disability limits a person's ability to earn a living, the insurance proceeds are designed to help make up the difference between what that person could have expected to earn if the accident had not occurred. Sometimes called income insurance, these policies usually guarantee a stated percentage of an individual's income—usually around 60 percent—while he or she is recovering and is unable to run a business. In the United States, short-term disability policies cover the 90-day gap between the time a person is injured and when workers' compensation payments begin. Long-term disability policies pay for lost income after 90 days or longer. In addition to the portion of income a policy will replace, another important factor to consider when purchasing disability insurance is the waiting period, the time gap between when the disability occurs and the disability payments begin. Although many business owners understand the importance of maintaining adequate life insurance coverage, fewer see the relevance of maintaining proper coverage for disabilities. For most people, the likelihood of a disability is three to five times greater than the risk of death; nearly 30 percent of workers between the ages of 35 and 65 will be unable to work for 90 days or longer due to a disability.[66]

Business owners can supplement traditional disability policies with **business overhead expense (BOE) insurance**. Designed primarily for companies with fewer than 15 employees, a BOE policy will replace 100 percent of a small company's monthly overhead expenses such as rent, utilities, insurance, taxes, and others if the owner is incapacitated. Payments typically begin 30 days after the owner is incapacitated and continue for up to two years.

**HEALTH INSURANCE AND WORKERS' COMPENSATION.** According to the National Federation of Independent Businesses (NFIB), small business owners' greatest concern for the last two decades has been the skyrocketing cost of health insurance.[67] The average small company spends $4,248 per year on health care insurance premiums for each employee. Because of the high cost of providing health care coverage for employees, only 60 percent of small businesses offer health insurance to their employees (compared to 98 percent of large companies). However, just 48 percent of the smallest companies, those with fewer than 10 employees, offer their employees health insurance, and both numbers have declined over the last five years.[68] As health care costs continue to climb and the average age of the workforce has increased, fewer small companies can afford to provide coverage for their employees. "The corporate world really spoiled me," says Sandy Dixon, who left a large company to start Interior Arrangements, an interior design company in the U.S. state of Colorado. "[When I started my business,] I was really surprised by the high cost of health insurance and suddenly had a new appreciation for this corporate perk."[69]

Yet health insurance has become an extremely important benefit to most workers. Small companies that offer thorough health care coverage often find that it gives them an edge in attracting and retaining quality workers. A key to providing proper health care coverage while keeping costs in check is to offer the benefits that are most important to your employees and to avoid spending money unnecessarily on coverage that does not apply to them. Four basic health care options are available to employers:

*Traditional Indemnity Plans.* Under these plans, employees choose their own health care providers, and the insurance company either pays the provider directly or reimburses employees for the covered amounts.

*Managed Care Plans.* As part of employers' attempts to put a lid on escalating health care costs, these plans have become increasingly popular. Two variations, the health maintenance organization (HMO) and the preferred provider organization (PPO) are most common. An HMO is a prepaid health care arrangement under which employees must use health care providers who are employed by or are under contract with the HMO their company uses. Although they lower health care costs, employees have less freedom in selecting physicians under an HMO. Under a PPO, an insurance company negotiates discounts for health care with certain physicians and hospitals. If employees choose a health care provider from the approved list, they pay only a small fee for each office visit (often just $10 to $25). The insurance company pays the remainder. Employees may select a provider outside the PPO, but they pay more for the service.

*Health Savings Accounts (HSAs).* Created as part of the United States' major Medicare overhaul in 2003, health savings accounts (HSAs) are similar to IRAs except employees' contributions are used for medical expenses rather than for retirement. An HSA is a special savings account coupled with a high-deductible ($1,000 to $5,000 for an individual) insurance policy that covers major medical expenses. Employees or employers contribute pre-tax dollars (up to a defined ceiling) from their paychecks into the fund and use them as they need to. Withdrawals from an HSA are not taxed as long as the money is used for approved medical expenses. Unused funds can accumulate indefinitely and earn tax-free interest. HSAs offer employees incentives to contain their health care costs, but the employer must choose both an insurance carrier to provide coverage and a custodial firm to manage employees' accounts. Although critics contend that consumer-driven plans push a greater portion of health care expenses onto employees, these plans will grow in popularity among small businesses because of their potential to rein in escalating costs. The average annual premium for an HSA for a small company is $2,836, nearly one-third lower than the cost of traditional health care plans.[70] Although self-employed individuals find HSAs attractive, employers are adding them to their menu of healthcare options for employees. Healthcare research company Information Services says that 24 million HSAs will exist in 2010, up from 3.6 million today.[71]

ENTREPRENEURIAL
Profile

*Andrew Field and
PrintingforLess.com*

Andrew Field, owner of PrintingforLess.com, a Web-based printing company, had seen health care costs for his company's 130 employees increase at double-digit rates year after year and decided to switch from a traditional plan to a health savings account plan. The change allowed him to provide his employees with better, more flexible coverage and the freedom to decide how to spend their health care dollars without any increase in cost. Although PrintingforLess.com did encounter a few problems in making the switch, Field and his employees are pleased with the HSA. "We were worried that it might have some bad side effects," he says, "but it's better than we thought."[72]

*Self-Insurance.* As you learned earlier in this chapter, some business owners choose to insure themselves for health coverage rather than to incur the costs of fully insured plans offered by outsiders. The benefits of self-insurance include greater control over the plan's design and the coverage it offers, fewer paperwork and reporting requirements, and, in some cases, lower costs. The primary disadvantage, of course, is the possibility of having to pay large amounts to cover treatments for several employees' major illnesses at the same time, which can strain a small company's cash flow. Many self-insured businesses limit their exposure to such losses by purchasing stop-loss insurance.

Another type of health-related coverage is **workers' compensation**, which is designed to cover employees who are injured on the job or who become sick as a result of their work environment. Before passage of workers' compensation legislation, any employee injured on the job could bring a lawsuit to prove the employer was liable for the worker's injury. Because of the red tape and expenses involved in these lawsuits, many employees were never compensated for job-related accidents and injuries. Although the details of coverage vary from state to state, workers' compensation laws require employers to provide benefits and medical and rehabilitation costs for employees who are injured on the job. The amount of compensation an injured employee will receive is determined by a fixed schedule of payment benefits based on three factors: the wages or salary that the employee was earning at the time of the accident or injury, the seriousness of the injury, and the extent of the disability to the employee. For instance, the producers of the hit Broadway musical *The Phantom of the Opera* experienced a large workers' compensation claim when a maintenance worker was injured on the set. The worker was polishing the show's huge chandelier as it sat on the floor when another employee unknowingly hit the switch to retract the chandelier into the ceiling. The chandelier knocked the worker into the orchestra pit, seriously injuring him. That one claim ran "well into six figures," says the agent representing the insurance company.[73]

Only three U.S. states, New Jersey, South Carolina, and Texas, do not require companies to purchase workers' compensation coverage once they reach a certain size (usually three or more employees). Usually, the state sets the rates businesses pay for workers' compensation coverage, and business owners purchase their coverage from private insurance companies. Rapidly escalating workers' compensation rates, driven in large part by rising medical expenses, have become a major concern for small businesses across the nation.

## Be Healthy or Be Gone

According to the Centers for Disease Control and Prevention, insurance premiums and absenteeism by sick workers cost businesses $15 billion a year. About 70 percent of healthcare costs arise from *preventable* chronic diseases, a fact that has led many businesses to implement wellness programs that are designed to improve employees' health and to prevent many of the diseases that push the cost of healthcare ever higher. One-third of small companies offer wellness programs that include onsite fitness centers or memberships in offsite fitness centers, smoking cessation programs, online tools for tracking their progress, onsite health checks, and others. Not only do wellness programs improve employees' health, but they also produce an impressive return on investment: more than three dollars on average for every dollar invested.

Jeff Bedard, CEO of Crown Laboratories, a company that makes skin-care products, had watched his company's health insurance costs escalate at 30 percent per year for the three previous years and knew that the time had come to do something about it. One day, as he saw six employees standing outside smoking cigarettes, Bedard thought about Crown Lab's motto: Creating a healthier world through technology. He also knew that Crown Lab employees were absent on average 9 days per year, compared to a national average of 3.8 days per year. The first onsite health review revealed that more than two-thirds of the company's workers were obese and that half of them never exercised.

Crown Lab was paying 100 percent of employees' healthcare insurance premiums, and Bedard wanted to maintain good coverage without imposing costs on his workers. He decided to implement a tough new wellness program designed to improve the health of Crown Lab's 61 employees. Each worker is required to have an onsite health assessment each year, which produces a "wellness number" up to 24. Employees who improve their scores by at least 3 points a year or maintain a score of 20 or more receive a $500 bonus and extra days off. Monthly seminars on topics such as eating a healthy diet or lowering cholesterol levels are mandatory. Perhaps

the most controversial component is the program's smoking policy. Crown Lab has banned smoking—even during off hours—for all of its employees, and nicotine levels are measured in the annual health assessment. Crown offers a smoking cessation program, and employees who continue to smoke must pay their own health insurance premiums.

It's a tough policy, but employers across the United States. are implementing similar plans, some of them even more stringent. Weyco, an employee benefits company in the U.S. state of Michigan, imposed a similar ban on smoking but went one step farther: Employees who fail to stop smoking are fired. "We're not saying that you can't smoke," says CEO Gary Climes. "We're saying that you can't smoke and work here." Three employees were forced to leave Weyco when they could not give up their smoking habit, but 20 others were successful at quitting. Weyco's policy is legal in Michigan and in several other states but not all. Twenty-eight states have passed legislation that protects workers from termination for certain types of behavior away from the workplace. Thirty states forbid companies from firing or demoting smokers. "Even if there is no statute, employers [who implement these policies] are risking a lawsuit on a variety of issues," says an employment lawyer.

Scotts Miracle-Gro, a maker of garden fertilizer and supplies based in the U.S. state of Ohio, also instituted a total ban on smoking for its employees. One worker who was fired because he refused to quit smoking has filed a lawsuit alleging discrimination and asking the court to prohibit Scotts from enforcing its anti-smoking policy. The case is pending, but Scotts hopes that the court will dismiss it.

At Crown Lab, Bedard is pleased with his company's program, saying that helping employees become healthier is an honorable goal. He expects that, over time, the program will produce benefits for the company in the form of reduced absenteeism rates and lower health care costs.

1. What are the advantages and disadvantages of wellness policies such as the one that Crown Lab has implemented?

2. What are the ethical implications of policies such as this? How much control should companies have over employees' lifestyles away from the workplace?
3. Does Crown Lab's policy go too far? Explain your reasoning.

*Sources:* Adapted from Michelle Conlin, "Get Healthy—Or Else," *Business Week,* February 26, 2007, www.businessweek.com/magazine/content/07_09/b4023001.htm?chan=search; Joseph McCafferty, "Light Up and You're Fired," *CFO,* April 2005, p. 19; Lisa Takeuchi, "The Company Doctor," *Time,* June 14, 2007, www.time.com/time/magazine/article/0,9171,1633062,00.html; Brian Nadel, "The Right Prescription," Advertising Insert in *Fortune,* October 3, 2005, pp. S1–S6; Dee Gill, "Get Healthy . . . or Else," *Inc.,* April 2006, pp. 35–37.

Companies in California and Alaska face the highest workers' compensation costs in the nation. McGraw's Custom Construction in Sitka, Alaska, saw its workers' compensation costs go from $146,950 to $315,110 in just two years![74] Rates vary by industry, business size, and the number of claims a company's workers make. For instance, workers' compensation premiums are higher for a timber cutting business than for a retail gift store.

Whatever industry they are in, business owners can reduce their workers' compensation costs by improving their employees' safety records.

*Core Systems*

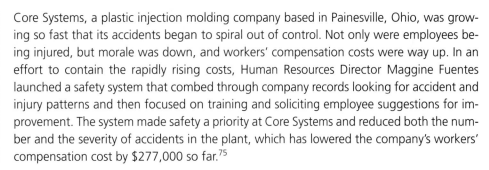

Core Systems, a plastic injection molding company based in Painesville, Ohio, was growing so fast that its accidents began to spiral out of control. Not only were employees being injured, but morale was down, and workers' compensation costs were way up. In an effort to contain the rapidly rising costs, Human Resources Director Maggine Fuentes launched a safety system that combed through company records looking for accident and injury patterns and then focused on training and soliciting employee suggestions for improvement. The system made safety a priority at Core Systems and reduced both the number and the severity of accidents in the plant, which has lowered the company's workers' compensation cost by $277,000 so far.[75]

**LIABILITY INSURANCE.** One of the most common types of insurance coverage is liability insurance, which protects a business against losses resulting from accidents or injuries people suffer on the company's property, from its products or services, and damage the company causes to others' property. Most BOPs include basic liability coverage; however, the limits on the typical policy are not high enough to cover the potential losses many small business owners face. For example, one "slip-and-fall" case involving a customer who is injured by slipping and falling on a wet floor could easily exceed the standard limits on a basic BOP. Claims from customers injured by a company's product or service are also covered by its liability policy.

Even though courts have dismissed them, some small companies have been targets of frivolous lawsuits because they are seen as easy targets. Frivolous lawsuits can cost a small company thousands of dollars to defend, however. Jin and Soo Chung, owners of Custom Cleaners in Washington, D.C., recently were hit with a $54 million lawsuit by a customer after the dry cleaner lost a pair of the customer's pants! The trial court ruled for Custom Cleaners, but plaintiff Roy Pearson filed an appeal, extending the legal nightmare for the small business owners, who incurred $83,000 in legal fees to defend themselves.[76] With jury awards in product liability cases often reaching into the millions of dollars, entrepreneurs who fail to purchase sufficient liability coverage may end up losing their businesses. Most insurance experts recommend purchasing a commercial general liability policy that provides coverage of at least $2 million to $3 million for the typical small business.

Another important type of liability insurance for many small businesses is **professional liability insurance** or **"errors and omissions" coverage**. This insurance protects against damage a business causes to customers or clients as a result of an error an employee makes or an employees' failure to take proper care and precautions. For instance, a land surveyor may miscalculate the location of a customer's property line. If the landowner relies on that property line to build a structure on what he thinks is his land and it turns out to be on his neighbor's land, the surveyor would be liable for damages. Doctors, dentists, attorneys, and other professionals protect themselves through a similar kind of insurance, malpractice insurance, which protects them against the risk of lawsuits arising from errors in professional practice or judgment.

**Employment practices liability insurance (EPLI)** provides protection against claims arising from charges of employment discrimination, wrongful termination, sexual harassment, and violations of the Americans with Disabilities Act, the Family and Medical Leave Act, and other employment legislation. Because the number of lawsuits from these sources has climbed dramatically in the past several years, this is one of the fastest-growing forms of insurance coverage. Although most violations of these employment laws are not intentional but are the result of either carelessness or lack of knowledge, the company that violates them is still liable. Losing an employment practices liability case can be very expensive; the median jury award in EPL cases exceeds $276,000.[77] Because they often lack full-time human resources professionals, small companies are especially vulnerable to charges of improper employment practices, making this type of insurance coverage all the more important to them.

*Burlington Railroad*

Sheila White worked as a forklift operator for Burlington Railroad at the rail yard in Memphis, Tennessee, where she was the only woman. After only a few months on the job, White complained that her supervisor was sexually harassing her. As a result of her complaint, White was suspended during an investigation and then was reassigned to a position as a track laborer, a job that provided the same level of pay but was much more physically demanding and dirtier. Six months later, White filed a complaint with the Equal Employment Opportunity Commission and then initiated a lawsuit, charging Burlington Railroad with both sexual harassment and discriminatory job retaliation because of the reassignment. The court dismissed the sexual harassment charges but ordered the railroad to pay White $43,500 (plus $55,000 in attorney's fees) for retaliatory employment discrimination.[78]

Cases such as this one are the reason that employers need employment practices liability insurance.

Figure 20.5 shows the trend in jury awards in various types of liability cases.

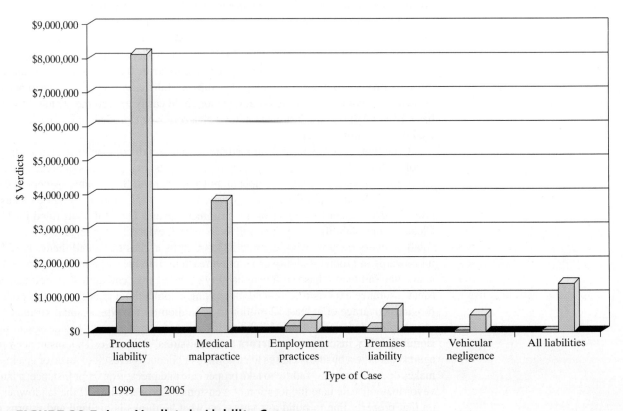

**FIGURE 20.5  Jury Verdicts in Liability Cases**

*Source:* Insurance Information Institute, www.iii.org/media/facts/statsbyissue/litigiousness.

## ■ Not Again!

On August 10, at 5:30 A.M., Sally Eason, second-generation owner of Sunburst Trout Farm, received a phone call that changed the future of her business. The company, founded 56 years before by her father, Richard Jennings, and perched on 17 acres along the Pigeon River in the shadow of Cold Mountain in the U.S. state of North Carolina, was on fire. As Eason approached the business, she could see flames leaping above the 80-foot-tall pine trees that surrounded the company's office, concrete runs that hold the trout, and the processing plant that turned out caviar and trout fillets for upscale grocers such as Whole Foods and the Fresh Market and for posh restaurants such as New York's Gramercy Tavern and 21. By 7 A.M., the fire was extinguished, but the blaze had destroyed everything except a small kitchen that was separated from burned out buildings by fire doors.

An investigation revealed that an arsonist was responsible for the fire. The criminal, who apparently had inside knowledge of the operation, also had stolen $67,000 worth of Sunburst's finest caviar but left behind 330 pounds of a lower quality caviar even though neither was marked. Eason was devastated by the loss. Sunburst was just recovering from a series of setbacks and was on its way to one of the best years in its history. Eason considered closing the business altogether, but because she already had saved the family business from near death experiences on two other occasions, she decided to reopen it. Two days after the fire, Eason and her employees moved into the small kitchen space and had Sunburst running at one-third its normal capacity. They were processing everything by hand because all of the company's equipment had been destroyed in the fire, but what mattered most is that they were still in business.

Getting the capital to rebuild the business proved to be a challenge. Because of the arson investigation, the insurance company's adjusters flagged the claim as suspicious. Eventually, the insurer paid $460,000, but Eason claims that the value of the lost property was $575,000. Eason and her husband took out a $120,000 home equity loan to cover the remaining cost of rebuilding. Eason and the employees at Sunburst also received a small financial donation when restaurant owners and caterers in nearby Asheville, North Carolina held a "Celebrate Sunburst" weekend that raised $5,000. "The [money]

they raised wasn't much," she says, "but the gesture was huge." Eason's father invested $30,000 to give the company some much-needed working capital.

Eason bulldozed through every obstacle that popped up just as she had done twice before when natural disasters had threatened to put Sunburst out of business. In 1985, Eason began working at the company when an employee left unexpectedly and learned firsthand every aspect of the business—from cutting fish to keeping the books. The next year, warm, dry weather throughout the winter and spring pushed the temperature of the water in Sunburst's raceways (concrete runs that pull water from the nearby Pigeon River and hold the trout) above 73 degrees, the survival threshold for trout, a cold water

*(continued)*

species. Sunburst lost 99 percent of its fish, which cost the small company $250,000, and worse, had no insurance against drought. Eason and her father decided to rebuild the business, and Jennings invested $250,000 to get the company back up and running. This time they built bigger raceways, and five months later, Sunburst was back in the market. Eason, who was now running the company, expanded the product line to include smoked fillets, trout sausage, chowder, mousse, and caviar.

In the fall of 2004, Hurricane Frances slammed into the North Carolina coast, and, after diminishing to a tropical storm, hovered over the mountains, dumping 20 inches of rain in just two weeks and flooding all of the area streams and rivers. Thousands of Sunburst's trout were swept downstream by the torrential floods, once again costing the small company $250,000 in lost fish. Floodwaters also destroyed the company's raceways and water intake systems. Eason had insurance coverage but not *flood* insurance. A $48,000 grant from disaster relief agencies and lots of sweat equity got Sun-

burst back in operation once again but just barely. Then a state agency came through with a $202,000 grant, enough for the company to rebuild once again.

The fire provided the third chance to rebuild Sunburst, and Eason saw it as an opportunity to expand. Bigger raceways, more floor space, better machinery, and larger coolers and freezers have allowed Sunburst to more than double its processing volume to 5,000 pounds per day. Eason seems to take the company's peaks and valleys with grace and poise. A group of bankers recently asked her about her specialty. "Disaster management," she replied without missing a beat.

1. What lessons can other business owners learn about risk management and insurance from Sunburst Trout Farm?

2. What types of insurance do you recommend for Sunburst? Explain your reasoning.

*Source:* Adapted from Monte Burke, "She Shall Overcome," *Forbes,* April 9, 2007, pp. 72–73.

Every business's insurance needs are somewhat unique, requiring owners to customize the insurance coverage they purchase. Entrepreneurs also must keep their insurance coverage updated as their companies grow; when companies expand, so do their insurance needs.

## Controlling Insurance Costs

*7.* Describe various techniques for controlling insurance costs.

Small business owners face constantly rising insurance premiums. Entrepreneurs can take steps to lower insurance costs, however. To control the cost of insurance, owners should take the following steps:

1. *Pursue a loss-control program by making risk reduction a natural part of all employees' daily routine.* As discussed earlier in this chapter, risk reduction minimizes claims and eventually lowers premiums. Establishing a loss-control program means taking steps such as installing modern fire alarms, sprinkler systems, safety programs, and sophisticated security systems.

2. *Increase their policies' deductibles.* If a business can afford to handle minor losses, the owner can save money by raising the deductible to a level that protects the business against catastrophic events but, in effect, self-insures against minor losses. Business owners must determine the amount of financial exposure they can reasonably accept.

3. *Work with qualified professional insurance brokers or agents.* Business owners should do their homework before choosing insurance brokers or agents. This includes checking their reputation, credentials, and background by asking them to supply references.

4. *Work actively with brokers to make sure they understand business owners' particular needs.* To provide proper insurance coverage, brokers must understand an entrepreneur's businesses and objectives. They can help only if they know their clients' needs and the degree of risk they are willing to take.

5. *Work with brokers to find competitive companies that want small companies' insurance business and have the resources to cover losses when they arise.* The price of the premium should never be an entrepreneur's sole criterion for selecting insur-

ance. The rating of the insurance company should always be a primary consideration. What good is it to have paid low premiums if, after a loss, a business owner finds that the insurance company is unable to pay? Many small business owners learned costly lessons when their insurance companies, unable to meet their obligations, filed for bankruptcy protection.

6. *Utilize the resources of your insurance company.* Many insurers will provide risk management inspections designed to help business owners assess the level of risk in their companies either for free or for a minimal fee. Smart entrepreneurs view their insurance companies as partners in their risk management efforts.

7. *Conduct a periodic insurance audit.* Reviewing your company's coverage annually can ensure that insurance coverage is adequate and can lead to big cost savings as well.

*Keith Alper and Creative Products Group*

Keith Alper, owner of Creative Products Group (CPG), a business that produces videos for *Fortune* 500 companies, was surprised to discover that CPG was wasting thousands of dollars on policies it did not need. Many employees were classified incorrectly for workers' compensation coverage, several policies duplicated the coverage of others, and the company was paying for auto insurance on four cars when it had only three! In all, Alper was able to shave more than $10,000 off of the company's $75,000 annual insurance bill.[79]

8. *Compile discrimination, harassment, hiring, and other employment policies into an employee handbook and train employees to use them.* Companies that take an active approach to avoiding illegal employment practices have less exposure to lawsuits and therefore, may be able to negotiate lower premiums.

When it comes to health insurance, the sky seems to be the limit for costs. A recent survey by the National Small Business Association reports that the cost of health care ranks second only to economic uncertainty as business owners' greatest concern.[80] Traditionally, businesses have been and continue to be the principal suppliers of health insurance in our society. To control the cost of health insurance, small business owners should consider the following:

1. *Increase the dollar amount of employee contributions and the amount of the employee's deductibles.* Neither option is desirable, but rising medical costs will inevitably result in individuals becoming, to some degree, self-insured to cover the high deductibles.

2. *Switch to HMOs or PPOs.* Higher premium costs have encouraged some small business owners to reevaluate health maintenance organizations (HMOs) and preferred provider organizations (PPOs) as alternatives to traditional health insurance policies. Although some employees resent being told where they must go to receive treatment, the number of businesses offering the HMO and PPO options to employees is rising.

3. *Consider joining an insurance pool.* Small businesses can lower their insurance premiums by banding together to purchase coverage. In many states, chambers of commerce, trade associations, and other groups form insurance pools that small businesses can join, spreading risk over a larger number of employees. In Pennsylvania, for example, two dozen chambers of commerce have formed an insurance pool that covers 30,000 people employed at small businesses at rates well below those that the owners could negotiate separately.[81]

4. *Conduct a yearly utilization review.* A review may reveal that your employees' use of their policies is statistically lower, which may provide you leverage to negotiate lower premiums or to switch to an insurer that wants a business with your track record and offers lower premiums.

5. *Make sure your company's health plan fits the needs of your employees.* One of the best ways to keep health care costs in check is to offer only those benefits that employees actually need. Getting employee input is essential to the process.

6. *Create a wellness program for all employees.* We have all heard the old adage that an ounce of prevention is worth a pound of cure, but when it comes to the high cost of medical expenses, this is especially true! Companies that have created wellness

programs report cost savings of $6 for every $1 they invest. Employees involved in wellness programs not only incur lower health care expenses, but they also tend to be more productive as well. Providing a wellness program does not mean building an expensive gym, however. Instead, it may be as simple as providing routine checkups from a county nurse, incentives for quitting smoking, weight-loss counseling, or after-work athletic games that involve as many employees as possible.

7. *Conduct a safety audit.* Reviewing the workplace with a safety professional to look for ways to improve its safety has the potential for saving some businesses thousands of dollars a year in medical expenses and workers' compensation claims. The National Safety Council offers helpful information on creating a safe work environment.

8. *Create a safety manual and use it.* Incorporating the suggestions for improving safety into a policy manual and then using it will reduce the number of on-the-job accidents. Training employees, even experienced ones, in proper safety procedures is also effective.

9. *Create a safety team.* Assigning the responsibility for workplace safety to workers themselves can produce amazing results. When one small manufacturer turned its safety team over to employees, the plant's lost time due to accidents plummeted to zero for three years straight! The number of accidents is well below what it was when managers ran the safety team, and managers say that's because employees now "own" safety in the plant.

The key to controlling insurance costs is aggressive prevention. Entrepreneurs who actively manage the risks to which their companies are exposed find that they can provide the insurance coverage their businesses need at a reasonable cost. Finding the right insurance coverage to protect their businesses is no easy matter for business owners. The key to dealing with those differences is to identify the risks that represent the greatest threat to a company and then to develop a plan for minimizing their risk of occurrence and insuring against them if they do.

## Chapter Review

1. Explain the factors necessary for a strong family business.
   - Several factors are important to maintaining a strong family business, including shared values, shared power, tradition, a willingness to learn, behaving like families, and strong family ties.
2. Understand the exit strategy options available to an entrepreneur.
   - Family business owners wanting to step down from their companies can sell to outsiders, sell to insiders, or transfer ownership to the next generation of family members. Common tools for selling to insiders (employees or managers) include sale for cash plus a note, leveraged buyouts (LBOs), and employee stock ownership plans (ESOPs).
   - Transferring ownership to the next generation of family members requires a business owner to develop a sound management succession plan.
3. Discuss the stages of management succession.
   - Unfortunately, 70 percent of first-generation businesses fail to survive into the second generation, and, of those that do, only 12 percent make it to the third generation. One of the primary reasons for this lack of continuity is poor succession planning. Planning for management succession protects not only the founder's, successor's, and company's financial resources, but it also preserves what matters most in a successful business: its heritage and tradition. Management succession planning can ensure a smooth transition only if the founder begins the process early on.

**4.** Explain how to develop an effective management succession plan.

- A succession plan is a crucial element in transferring a company to the next generation. Preparing a succession plan involves five steps: (1) Select the successor. (2) Create a survival kit for the successor. (3) Groom the successor. (4) Promote an environment of trust and respect. (5) Cope with the financial realities of estate taxes.
- Entrepreneurs can rely on several tools in their estate planning, including buy-sell agreements, lifetime gifting, trusts, estate freezes, and family limited partnerships.

**5.** Understand the four risk management strategies.

- Four risk strategies are available to the small business: avoiding, reducing, anticipating, and transferring risk.

**6.** Discuss the basics of insurance for small businesses.

- Insurance is a risk transfer strategy. Not every potential loss can be insured. Insurability requires that it be possible to estimate the amount of actual loss being insured against and identify the specific risk and that there be enough policyholders to spread out the risk.
- The four major types of insurance small businesses need are property and casualty insurance, life and disability insurance, health insurance and workers' compensation coverage, and liability insurance.
- Property and casualty insurance covers a company's tangible assets, such as buildings, equipment, inventory, machinery, signs, and others that have been damaged, destroyed, or stolen. Specific types of property and casualty insurance include extra expense coverage, business interruption insurance, surety insurance, marine insurance, crime insurance, fidelity insurance, and forgery insurance.
- Life and disability insurance also comes in various forms. Life insurance protects a family and a business against the loss of income and security in the event of the owner's death. Disability insurance, like life insurance, protects an individual in the event of unexpected and often very expensive disabilities.
- Health insurance is designed to provide adequate health care for business owners and their employees. Workers' compensation is designed to cover employees who are injured on the job or who become sick as a result of a work environment.
- Liability insurance protects a business against losses resulting from accidents or injuries people suffer on the company's property, from its products or services, and damage the company causes to others' property. Typical liability coverage includes professional liability insurance or "errors and omissions" coverage, which protects against damage a business causes to customers or clients as a result of an error an employee makes or an employee's failure to take proper care and precautions. Doctors, dentists, attorneys, and other professionals protect themselves through a similar kind of insurance, malpractice insurance, which protects them against the risk of lawsuits arising from errors in professional practice or judgment. Employment practices liability insurance provides protection against claims arising from charges of employment discrimination, sexual harassment, and other violations of employment legislation.

**7.** Describe various techniques for controlling insurance costs.

- To control the cost of insurance, entrepreneurs can pursue a loss-control program, increase their policies' deductibles, work with qualified insurance brokers or agents, find insurance companies that value small companies' business, use the resources of their insurance companies, conduct periodic insurance audits, and create employee handbooks that cover the company's employment policies.

## Discussion Questions

1. What factors must be present for a strong family business?
2. Discuss the stages of management succession in a family business.
3. What steps are involved in building a successful management succession plan?
4. What exit strategies are available to entrepreneurs wanting to step down from their businesses?
5. What strategies can business owners employ to reduce estate and gift taxes?
6. Can insurance eliminate risk? Why or why not?
7. Outline the four basic risk management strategies and give an example of each.
8. What problems occur most frequently with a risk anticipating strategy?

9. What is insurance? How can insurance companies bear such a large risk burden and still be profitable?
10. Describe the requirements for insurability.
11. Briefly describe the various types of insurance coverage available to small business owners.
12. What kinds of insurance coverage would you recommend for the following businesses?
    - A manufacturer of steel beams.
    - A retail gift shop.
    - A small accounting firm.
    - A limited liability partnership involving three dentists.
13. What can business owners do to keep their insurance costs under control?

# Business PlanPro

Family-owned businesses dominate the business landscape, but they face a dangerous threat from within: management succession. Most family businesses fail to survive into the second generation and beyond. The problem usually is the result of a lack of planning for a smooth transition from one generation of management to the next. The business plan can assist in this process.

## On the Web

Under the "Chapter 20" tab on the Companion Website at www.prenhall.com/scarborough is a list of online resources that deal with succession planning and risk management. You will find resources that address issues related to managing a family business, planning for management succession, and managing business risk.

## In the Software

If the business has issues regarding succession planning, capture those thoughts in your plan. This is also an opportunity to discuss risk management and exit strategies. What types of insurance coverage does your company require? Be sure to incorporate the cost of insurance coverage in your financial forecasts. Remember: You can add or modify outline topics within Business Plan Pro by right-clicking on the outline in the left-hand navigation of the software.

## Building Your Business Plan

One of the best ways to prevent a family-owned business from becoming just another management succession failure statistic is to develop a management succession plan early on in the life of the company. The business plan can be a vehicle to help with this discussion and document the plan to make this transition. The plan can also enable an entrepreneur to document ideas and plans regarding risk management and potential exit strategies.

# Ethics and Social Responsibility: Doing the Right Thing

> Relativity applies to physics not to ethics.
>
> —Albert Einstein

> Integrity is doing the right thing even if nobody is watching.
>
> —Jim Stovall

## *Learning Objectives*

**Upon completion of this chapter, you will be able to:**

1. Define business ethics and describe the three levels of ethical standards.

2. Determine who is responsible for ethical behavior and why ethical lapses occur.

3. Explain how to establish and maintain high ethical standards.

4. Define social responsibility.

5. Understand the nature of businesses' responsibility to the environment.

6. Describe businesses' responsibility to employees.

7. Explain businesses' responsibility to customers.

8. Discuss businesses' responsibility to investors.

9. Describe businesses' responsibility to the community.

**B**usiness ethics involves the moral values and behavioral standards that businesspeople draw on as they make decisions and solve problems. It originates in a commitment to do what is right. Ethical behavior—doing what is "right" as opposed to what is "wrong"—starts at the top of an organization with the entrepreneur. Entrepreneurs' personal values and beliefs influence the way they lead their companies and are apparent in every decision they make, every policy they write, and every action they take. Entrepreneurs who succeed in the long term have a solid base of personal values and beliefs that they articulate to their employees and put into practice in ways that others can observe. Values-based leaders do more than merely follow rules and regulations; their consciences dictate that they do what is right.

In some cases, ethical dilemmas are apparent. Entrepreneurs are keenly aware of the ethical entrapments awaiting them and know that society will hold them accountable for their actions. More often, however, ethical issues are less obvious, cloaked in the garb of mundane decisions and everyday routine. Because they can easily catch entrepreneurs off guard and unprepared, these ethical "sleepers" are most likely to ensnare business owners, soiling their reputations and those of their companies. To make proper ethical choices, entrepreneurs must first be aware that a situation with ethical implications exists.

Complicating the issue even more is that, in some ethical dilemmas, no clear-cut, right or wrong answers exist. There is no direct conflict between good and evil, right and wrong, or truth and falsehood. Instead, there is only the issue of conflicting interests among a company's **stakeholders**, the various groups and individuals who affect and are affected by a business. These conflicts force entrepreneurs to identify their stakeholders and to consider the ways in which entrepreneurs will deal with them (see Figure 21.1). For instance, when the founders of a small producer of frozen foods make business decisions, they must consider the impact of those decisions on many stakeholders, including the team of employees who work

**FIGURE 21.1 Key Stakeholders**

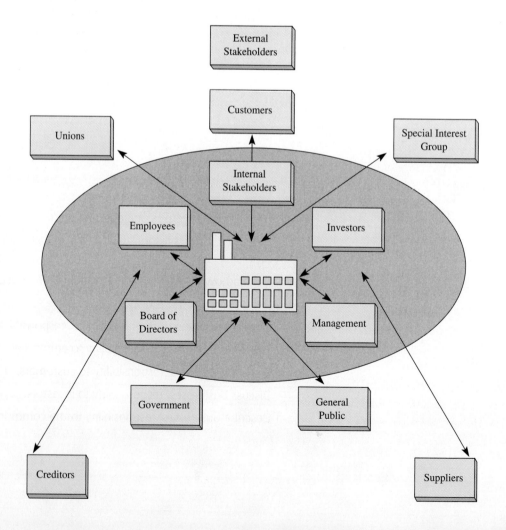

there, the farmers and companies that supply the business with raw materials, the union that represents employees in collective bargaining, the government agencies that regulate a multitude of activities, the banks that provide the business with financing, the stockholders who own shares of the company's stock, the general public the business serves, the community in which the company operates, and the customers who buy the company's products. When making decisions, entrepreneurs often must balance the needs and demands of a company's stakeholders, knowing that whatever the final decision is, not every group will be satisfied.

Ethical leaders approach their organizational responsibilities with added dimensions of thought and action. They link ethical behaviors to organizational outcomes and incorporate social responsibility into daily decisions. They establish ethical behavior and concern for society and the environment as an integral part of organizational training and eventually as part of company culture. What does this mean from a practical standpoint? How does a commitment to "doing the right thing" apply to employees, customers, and other stakeholders, and how does it affect an entrepreneur's daily decision making? Consider the following situation:

**ENTREPRENEURIAL Profile**

*Harry M. Jansen Kraemer, Jr., and Baxter International*

Harry M. Jansen Kraemer, Jr., chairman and CEO of Baxter International, a medical equipment and supplies company, faced an ethical situation when several kidney dialysis patients in Spain died mysteriously. One of the possible causes of the tragedy was a filter made by Baxter, and the company hired an independent testing company to evaluate the filters. They could find nothing wrong; yet, several days later, there were more dialysis-related deaths, this time in Croatia. A team of Baxter experts finally determined that a fluid (which was made by another company) that Baxter used in testing the quality of the filters during manufacturing turned to gas when heated in the bloodstream, causing a pulmonary embolism. When faced with the dilemma of what to do with this information, Kraemer and his management team had three choices: hide these findings, blame others, or step forward and "do the right thing." What did they do? The managers publicly apologized, stopped manufacturing the product, shut down the two plants that made the filters, and settled with all the families affected. The company took a $189 million hit, and Kraemer recommended to the board that because the filter problems had occurred on his watch, his bonus should be reduced by 40 percent and other executives' bonuses should be reduced by 20 percent. "We try to do the right thing" Kraemer says. "I think there's a tendency to make things more complex than they are. If we live the values we profess, we'll add shareholder value. I don't see a conflict."[1]

Business operates as an institution in our often complex and ever evolving society. Therefore, every entrepreneur is expected to behave in ways that are compatible with the value system of our society. It is society that imposes the rules of conduct for all business owners in the form of ethical standards of behavior and the responsibility to act in ways that benefit the long-term interest of all. Society expects business owners to earn a profit on their investment. Ethics and social responsibility simply set behavioral boundaries for decision makers. Ethics is a branch of philosophy that studies and creates theories about the basic nature of right and wrong, duty, obligation, and virtue. Social responsibility involves how an organization responds to the needs of the many elements in society including shareholders, lenders, employees, consumers, governmental agencies, and the environment. Because business is allowed to operate in society, it has an obligation to behave in ways that benefit all of society.

## An Ethical Perspective

*1. Define business ethics and describe the three levels of ethical standards.*

**Business ethics** consist of the fundamental moral values and behavioral standards that form the foundation for the people of an organization as they make decisions and interact with stakeholders. Business ethics is a sensitive and highly complex issue, but it is not a new one. In 560 B.C., the Greek philosopher Chilon claimed that a merchant does better to take a loss than to make a dishonest profit.[2]

Maintaining an ethical perspective is essential to creating and protecting a company's reputation, but it is no easy task. Ethical dilemmas lurk in the decisions—even the most mundane ones—that entrepreneurs make every day. Succumbing to unethical temptations ultimately will destroy a company's reputation, one of the most precious and most fragile possessions of any business.

Building a reputation for ethical behavior typically takes a long time; unfortunately, destroying that reputation requires practically no time at all, and the effects linger for some time. One top manager compares a bad reputation to a hangover. "It takes a while to get rid of, and it makes everything else hurt," he says.[3] Some businesses flounder or even fail after their owners or managers are caught acting in an unethical fashion.

*Martha Stewart*

Martha Stewart, who built an empire out of her flair for entertaining, gardening, and crafts, was convicted of lying to investigators about a personal stock sale and was forced to resign as an officer and board member of the company she founded. After her conviction, Martha Stewart Living Omnimedia Inc. posted large quarterly losses as advertising revenue plunged and the company moved to distance itself from its founder. The company also downplayed Martha Stewart's name on the flagship magazine *Martha Stewart Living* as part of efforts to identify its brand name with overall quality instead of with an expert personality. Regardless of these actions, the stock fell about 40 percent within the few weeks after a New York jury convicted Stewart. Stewart's company continues to recover from the damage caused by the founder's conviction.[4]

### Three Levels of Ethical Standards

There are three levels of ethical standards:

1. *The law,* which defines for society as a whole which actions are permissible and which are not. The law merely establishes the minimum standard of behavior. Actions that are legal, however, may not be ethical. Simply obeying the law is insufficient as a guide for ethical behavior; ethical behavior requires more. Few ethical issues are so simple and one dimensional that the law can serve as the acid test for making a decision.
2. *Organizational policies and procedures,* which serve as specific guidelines for people as they make daily decisions. Many colleges and universities have created honor codes, and companies rely on policies covering everything from sexual harassment and gift giving to hiring and whistle-blowing.
3. *The moral stance* that employees take when they encounter a situation that is not governed by levels one and two. The values people learn early in life at home, in the church or synagogue, and in school are key ingredients at this level. One primary determinant of ethical behavior is *training*. As Aristotle said thousands of years ago, you get a good adult by teaching a child to do the right thing. A company's culture can serve either to support or undermine its employees' concept of what constitutes ethical behavior.

Ethics is something that every businessperson faces daily; most decisions involve some degree of ethical judgment. Over the course of a career, entrepreneurs can be confident that they will face some tough ethical choices. But that is not necessarily bad! Situations such as these give entrepreneurs the opportunity to flex their ethical muscles and do what is right. Entrepreneurs set the ethical tone for their companies. The ethical stance employees take when faced with a difficult decision often reflects the entrepreneur's values and commitment to doing what is right.

### Establishing an Ethical Framework

To cope successfully with the many ethical decisions they face, entrepreneurs must develop a workable ethical framework to guide themselves and their organizations. Although many such frameworks exist, the following four-step process can work quite well:

**Step 1**      ***Recognize the ethical dimensions involved in the dilemma or decision.***
Before entrepreneurs can make informed ethical decisions, they must recog-

nize that an ethical situation exists. Only then is it possible to define the specific ethical issues involved. Too often business owners fail to take into account the ethical impact of a particular course of action until it is too late. To avoid ethical quagmires, entrepreneurs must consider the ethical forces at work in a situation—honesty, fairness, respect for the community, concern for the environment, trust, and others—to have a complete view of the decision.

**Step 2**  *Identify the key stakeholders involved and determine how the decision will affect them.* Every business influences, and is influenced by, a multitude of stakeholders. Frequently, the demands of these stakeholders conflict with one another, putting a business in the position of having to choose which groups to satisfy and which to alienate. Before making a decision, managers must sort out the conflicting interests of the various stakeholders by determining which ones have important stakes in the situation. Although this analysis may not resolve the conflict, it will prevent the company from inadvertently causing harm to people it may have failed to consider. More companies are measuring their performance using a **triple bottom line** (3BL) that, in addition to the traditional measure of profitability, includes the commitment to ethics and social responsibility and the impact on the environment. Nature's Path Foods, a maker of organic cereal and breakfast products founded by Arran Stephens in 1985, uses the 3BL and places equal emphasis on all three components: social, environmental, and financial.[5]

**Step 3**  *Generate alternative choices and distinguish between ethical and unethical responses.* When entrepreneurs are generating alternative courses of action and evaluating the consequences of each one, they can use the questions in Table 21.1 to guide them. Asking and answering questions such as these ensure that everyone involved is aware of the ethical dimensions of the issue.

**Step 4**  *Choose the "best" ethical response and implement it.* At this point, there likely will be several ethical choices from which managers can pick. Comparing these choices with the "ideal" ethical outcome may help managers make the final decision. The final choice must be consistent with the company's goals, culture, and value system as well as those of the individual decision makers.

## Who Is Responsible for Ethical Behavior?

**2.** Determine who is responsible for ethical behavior and why ethical lapses occur.

Although companies may set ethical standards and offer guidelines for employees, the ultimate decision on whether to abide by ethical principles rests with the *individual.* In other words, companies really are not ethical or unethical; individuals are. Managers, however, can greatly influence individual behavior within the company. And that influence must start at the *top.* A founder or chief executive officer who practices ethical behavior establishes the moral tone for the entire organization. Table 21.2 summarizes the characteristics of the three ethical styles of management: immoral, amoral, and moral.

*Immoral Management.*  Immoral managers are motivated by selfish reasons such as their own gains or those of the company. The driving force behind immoral management is *greed:* achieving personal or organizational success at any cost. Immoral management is the polar opposite of ethical management; immoral managers do what they can to circumvent laws and moral standards and are not concerned about the impact that their actions have on others.

**ENTREPRENEURIAL Profile**

*Larry Owen and Carolina Investors*

Larry Owen, CEO of Carolina Investors, a small financial institution in upstate South Carolina, was sentenced to eight years in prison for his role in defrauding more than 12,000 investors of $278 million after the company ran out of cash despite Owen's assurances that the investment company was financially sound. Four other top managers of the company were sentenced to jail terms for their roles in the scandal, which was the largest bankruptcy in the U.S. state's history. A court ruled that the five managers fraudulently promoted the sale of bonds to investors even though they knew that Carolina Investors had no ability to repay them. Manager Ronald Sheppard was indicted for using nearly $1 million of the company's money to finance a personal trainer and a motor home for his family's personal use.[6]

*Amoral Management.* The principal goal of amoral managers is to earn a profit, but their actions differ from those of immoral managers in one key way: They do not purposely violate laws or ethical standards. Instead, amoral managers neglect to consider the impact their decisions have on others; they use free-rein decision making without reference to ethical standards. Amoral management is not an option for socially responsible businesses.

*Moral Management.* Moral managers also strive for success but only within the boundaries of legal and ethical standards. Moral managers are not willing to sacrifice their values and violate ethical standards just to make a profit. Managers who operate with this philosophy see the law as a minimum standard for ethical behavior.

### TABLE 21.1 Questions to Help Identify the Ethical Dimension of a Situation

## Principles and Codes of Conduct

- Does this decision or action meet my standards for how people should interact?
- Does this decision or action agree with my religious teachings or beliefs (or with my personal principles and sense of responsibility)?
- How will I feel about myself if I do this?
- Do we (or I) have a rule or policy for cases like this?
- Would I want everyone to make the same decision and take the same action if faced with these circumstances?
- What are my true motives for considering this action?

## Moral Rights

- Would this action allow others freedom of choice in this matter?
- Would this action involve deceiving others in any way?

## Justice

- Would I feel this action was just (right) if I were on the other side of the decision?
- How would I feel if this action were done to me or someone close to me?
- Would this action or decision distribute benefits justly?
- Would it distribute hardships or burdens justly?

## Consequences and Outcomes

- What will be the short- and long-term consequences of this action?
- Who will benefit from this course of action?
- Who will be hurt?
- How will this action create good and prevent harm?

## Public Justification

- How would I feel (or how will I feel) if (or when) this action becomes public knowledge?
- Will I be able to explain adequately to others why I have taken the action?
- Would others feel that my action or decision is ethical or moral?

## Intuition and Insight

- Have I searched for all alternatives? Are there other ways I could look at this situation? Have I considered all points of view?
- Even if there is sound rationality for this decision or action, and even if I could defend it publicly, does my inner sense tell me it is right?
- What does my intuition tell me is the ethical thing to do in this situation? Have I listened to my inner voice?

*Source:* Sherry Baker, "Ethical Judgment", *Executive Excellence*, March 1992, pp. 7–8.

**TABLE 21.2  Approaches to Business Ethics**

| Organizational Characteristics | Immoral Management | Amoral Management | Moral Management |
|---|---|---|---|
| Ethical norms | Management decisions, actions, and behavior imply a positive and active opposition to what is moral (ethical). | Management is neither moral nor immoral; decisions are not based on moral judgments. | Management activity conforms to a standard of ethical, or right, behavior. |
| | Decisions are discordant with accepted ethical principles. | Management activity is not related to any moral code. | Management activity conforms to accepted professional standards of conduct. |
| | An active negation of what is moral is implicit. | A lack of ethical perception and moral awareness may be implicit. | Ethical leadership is commonplace. |
| Motives | Selfish. Management cares only about its or its company's gains. | Well-intentioned but selfish in the sense that impact on others is not considered. | Good. Management wants to succeed but only within the confines of sound ethical precepts such as fairness, justice, and due process. |
| Goals | Profitability and organizational success at any price. | Profitability. Other goals are not considered. | Profitability within the confines of legal obedience and ethical standards. |
| Orientation toward law | Legal standards are barriers that management must overcome to accomplish what it wants. | Law is the ethical guide, preferably the letter of the law. The central question is, what can we do legally? | Obedience toward letter and spirit of the law. Law is a minimal ethical behavior. Prefer to operate well above what law mandates. |
| Strategy | Exploit opportunities for corporate gain. Cut corners when it appears useful. | Give managers free rein. Personal ethics may apply but only if managers choose. Respond to legal mandates if caught and required to do so. | Live by sound ethical standards. Assume leadership position when ethical dilemmas arise. Enlightened self-interest. |

*Source:* Archie B. Carroll, "In Search of the Moral Manager," reprinted from *Business Horizons*, March/April 1987, pp. 7–15. Copyright 1987 by the Foundation for the School of Business at Indiana University. Used with permission.

## The Benefits of Moral Management

One of the most common misconceptions about business is that there is a contradiction between earning a profit and maintaining high ethical standards. In reality, companies have learned that these two goals are consistent with one another. Jeffrey Swartz, third-generation CEO of Timberland, a company known almost as well for its ethical and socially responsible behavior as it is for its footwear and outdoor clothing, says, "I honestly believe doing good and doing well are inextricably linked."[7] Many entrepreneurs launch businesses with the idea of making a difference in society. They quickly learn that to "do good," their companies must first "do well." Fran Rathke, CFO of Vermont-based Green Mountain Coffee Roasters, a small company known for its commitment to social responsibility, says, "We are motivated to achieve success because the more profitable we are, the more good we can do in the world."[8]

*Robert McGraw and Longjiang River Health Products*

Robert McGraw, who in 2000 launched Longjiang River Health Products (LRHP), a company that markets herbal supplements around the globe, recently built a modern factory in Longjiang Village, China. The company's research and development teams in China, Hong Kong, Singapore, and the United States are dedicated to improving the efficacy of centuries-old herbal formulas in healing a variety of diseases. McGraw, who believes that being a good corporate citizen is important, financed the village's first waste-management facility, donated more than 40 computers to the local school, and started a fund to provide textbooks for schoolchildren. LRHP employees also serve as tutors for children and work on local community projects.[9]

Although behaving ethically has value in itself, there are many other benefits to companies that adhere to high ethical standards. First, companies avoid the extremely damaging fallout from unethical behavior on their reputations. Unethical businesses usually gain only short-term advantages; over the long run, unethical decisions don't pay. It's simply not good business.

Second, a solid ethical framework guides managers as they cope with an increasingly complex network of influence from external stakeholders. Dealing with stakeholders is much easier if a company has a solid ethical foundation on which to build.

Third, businesses with solid reputations as ethical companies find it easier to attract and retain quality workers. Explaining why she came to work for Timberland, Helen Kellogg, a senior manager, says, "I was looking for a company that had a conscience." Timberland gives every employee 40 hours of paid leave every year to work on volunteer projects. Bonnie Monahan, the Timberland vice president who organized a bike-a-thon that raised $50,000 for a local charity, says that she has turned down "several lucrative job offers" from larger companies to stay with Timberland, where "you don't have to leave your values at the door." Every year, Timberland sponsors Serv-a-palooza, a one-day blitz of community service that involves 170 projects in 27 countries.[10]

Timberland employees engaged in a service project that is part of the company's Serv-a-palooza.

Finally, a company's ethical philosophy has an impact on its ability to provide value for its customers. The "ethics factor" is difficult to quantify, yet it is something that customers consider when deciding where to shop and which company's products to buy. "Do I want people buying Timberland boots as a result of the firm's volunteer efforts?" asks CEO Jeffrey Swartz. "You bet."[11] Timberland's commitment to "doing good" in addition to "doing well" is expressed in its slogan, "Boots, Brand, Belief." Like other social entrepreneurs, Swartz's goal is to manage the company successfully so that he can use its resources to combat social problems.

Entrepreneurs must recognize that ethical behavior is an investment in the company's future rather than merely a cost of doing business. Table 21.3 shows the results of a comprehensive study that was conducted by the American Management Association of global human resources directors, who were asked about the reasons for their companies' engaging in ethical behavior and the factors that drive business ethics today.

## Why Ethical Lapses Occur

Even though most small business owners run their companies ethically, business scandals involving Enron, WorldCom, Tyco, and other high-profile companies have sullied the reputations of businesses of all sizes. The best way for business owners to combat

**TABLE 21.3** Reasons to Run a Business Ethically and the Factors That Drive Business Ethics

## Top Five Reasons to Run a Business Ethically

1. Protect brand and company reputation
2. It is the right thing to do
3. Maintain customers' trust and loyalty
4. Maintain investors' confidence
5. Earn public acceptance and recognition

## Top Five Factors That Drive Business Ethics

1. Corporate scandals
2. Marketplace competition
3. Demands by investors
4. Pressure from customers
5. Globalization

*Source: The Ethical Enterprise: A Global Study of Business Ethics 2005–2015*, American Management Association/Human Resource Institute, 2006, p. 2.

these negative public perceptions is to run their business ethically. When faced with an ethical dilemma, however, not every entrepreneur or employee will make the right decision. In fact, a recent study conducted by LRN, an ethics research and consulting firm, reports that 74 percent of workers say that they have observed ethical lapses on the job.[12] Many unethical acts are committed by normally decent people who believe in moral values. What causes ethical lapses to occur? Consider the following causes:

**AN UNETHICAL EMPLOYEE.** Ethical decisions are individual decisions, and some people are corrupt. Try as they might to avoid them, organizations occasionally find that they have hired a "bad apple." Eliminating unethical behavior requires the elimination of these bad apples.

**AN UNETHICAL ORGANIZATIONAL CULTURE.** In some cases, the company culture has been poisoned with an unethical overtone; in other words, the problem is not the "bad apple" but the "bad barrel." Pressure to prosper produces an environment that creates conditions that reward unethical behavior, and employees act accordingly. To create an environment that encourages ethical behavior, entrepreneurs should:

- *Set the tone.* "The character of the leader casts a long shadow over the organization and can determine the character of the organization itself," says one business executive. What you do, how you do it, and what you say sets the tone for your employees. The values you profess must be aligned with the behaviors you demonstrate.
- *Establish and enforce policies.* Set appropriate policies for your organization. Communicate them on a regular basis, and adhere to them personally for others to see. Show zero tolerance for ethical violations and realize that the adage "Don't do as I do; do as I say" does *not* work. Without a demonstration of real consequence and personal accountability, policies are useless.
- *Educate and recruit.* Consider using a formal education program to enhance the understanding of and commitment to ethical behavior. Find colleges and universities that incorporate business ethics into courses and make them prime recruiting sources. Tina Byles Williams, owner of FIS Group, an investment advising and management firm, understands how important it is to hire honest employees with a strong sense of ethics. Although Williams knows that there is no foolproof hiring method, she has redesigned her company's selection process with an emphasis on screening for integrity.[13]
- *Separate related job duties.* This is a basic organizational concept. Not allowing the employee who writes checks to reconcile the company bank statement is one example.

- *Reward ethical conduct.* The reward system is a large window into the values of an organization. If you reward a behavior, people have a tendency to repeat the behavior.
- *Eliminate "undiscussables."* One of the most important things entrepreneurs can do to promote ethical behavior is to instill the belief that it is acceptable for employees to question what happens above them. Doing away with undiscussables makes issues transparent and promotes trust both inside and outside the company.[14]

**MORAL BLINDNESS.** Sometimes, fundamentally ethical people commit unethical blunders because they are blind to the implications of their conduct. Moral blindness may be the result of failing to realize that an ethical dilemma exists, or it may arise from a variety of mental defense mechanisms. One of the most common mechanisms is rationalization:

- "Everybody does it."
- "If they were in my place, they'd do it too."
- "Being ethical is a luxury I cannot afford right now."
- "The impact of my decision/action on (whomever or whatever) is not my concern."
- "I don't get paid to be ethical; I get paid to produce results."

Training in ethical thinking and creating an environment that encourages employees to consider the ethical impact of their decisions can reduce the problem of moral blindness.

**COMPETITIVE PRESSURES.** If competition is so intense that a company's survival is threatened, managers may begin to view what were once unacceptable options as acceptable. Managers and employees are under such pressure to produce that they may sacrifice their ethical standards to reduce the fear of failure or the fear of losing their jobs. Without a positive organizational culture that stresses ethical behavior regardless of the consequences, employees respond to feelings of pressure and compromise their personal ethical standards to ensure that the job gets done.

**OPPORTUNITY PRESSURES.** When the opportunity to "get ahead" by taking some unethical action presents itself, some people cannot resist the temptation. The greater the reward or the smaller the penalty for unethical acts, the greater is the probability that such

"It used to be all about truth and justice.
Now, mostly I fight for market share."

**TABLE 21.4  Ethics Research Reveals Causes of Ethical Breaches and Features of Ethical Cultures**

### Factors That Are Most Likely to Cause People to Compromise Ethical Standards

1. Pressure to meet unrealistic business objectives or deadlines
2. Desire to further one's own career
3. Desire to protect one's job and livelihood
4. Working in an environment characterized by cynicism and low morale
5. Improper training or ignorance that an act is unethical

### Ethics-Related Global Workplace Issues

1. Forced labor, child labor, and excessive working hours
2. Health and safety of working conditions
3. Discrimination and harassment
4. Fraud or theft
5. Gift-giving and bribes

### Characteristics of an Ethical Culture

1. Leaders support and model ethical behavior
2. Consistent communications come from all company leaders
3. Ethics are integrated into the organization's goals, business processes, and strategies
4. Ethics are part of the performance management system
5. Ethics are part of the company's selection criteria and its selection process

*Source: The Ethical Enterprise: A Global Study of Business Ethics 2005–2015*, American Management Association/Human Resource Institute, 2006, pp. 5, 6, and 10.

behavior will occur. If managers, for example, condone or even encourage unethical behavior, they can be sure it will occur. Those who succumb to opportunity pressures often make one of two mistakes: They overestimate the cost of doing the right thing, or they underestimate the cost of doing the wrong thing. Either error can lead to disaster.

**GLOBALIZATION OF BUSINESS.** The globalization of business has intertwined what once were distinct cultures. This cultural cross-pollination has brought about many positive aspects, but it has created problems as well. Companies have discovered that there is no single standard of ethical behavior applying to all business decisions in the international arena. Practices that are illegal in one country may be perfectly acceptable, even expected, in another. Actions that would send a businessperson to jail in Western nations are common ways of working around the system in others.

Table 21.4 provides a summary of important ethics research concerning the factors that business leaders say most often cause people to compromise ethical standards, the top ethics-related global issues, and the characteristics that are most important to establishing an ethical culture.

## Establishing Ethical Standards

*3.* Explain how to establish and maintain high ethical standards.

A study by the Southern Institute for Business and Professional Ethics found that small companies are less likely than large ones to have ethics programs.[15] Although they may not have formal ethics programs, entrepreneurs can encourage employees to become familiar with the following ethical tests for judging behavior.

- *The utilitarian principle.* Choose the option that offers the greatest good for the greatest number of people.
- *Kant's categorical imperative.* Act in such a way that the action taken under the circumstances could be a universal law or rule of behavior.
- *The professional ethic.* Take only those actions that a disinterested panel of professional colleagues would view as proper.

- ■ *The Golden Rule.* Treat other people the way you would like them to treat you.
- ■ *The television test.* Would you and your colleagues feel comfortable explaining your actions to a national television audience?
- ■ *The family test.* Would you be comfortable explaining to your children, your spouse, and your parents why you took this action?[16]

Although these tests do not offer universal solutions to ethical dilemmas, they do help employees identify the moral implications of the decisions they face. People must be able to understand the ethical impact of their actions before they can make responsible decisions. Table 21.5 describes ten ethical principles that differentiate between right and wrong, thereby offering a guideline for ethical behavior.

### TABLE 21.5 Ten Ethical Principles to Guide Behavior

The study of history, philosophy, and religion reveals a strong consensus about certain universal and timeless values that are central to leading an ethical life.

1. *Honesty.* Be truthful, sincere, forthright, straightforward, frank, and candid; do not cheat, lie, steal, deceive, or act deviously.
2. *Integrity.* Be principled, honorable, upright, and courageous, and act on convictions; do not be two-faced or unscrupulous or adopt an ends-justifies-the-means philosophy that ignores principle.
3. *Promise-keeping.* Be worthy of trust, keep promises, fulfill commitments, and abide by the spirit as well as the letter of an agreement; do not interpret agreements in a technical or legalistic manner in order to rationalize noncompliance or to create excuses for breaking commitments.
4. *Fidelity.* Be faithful and loyal to family, friends, employers, and country; do not use or disclose information earned in confidence; in a professional context, safeguard the ability to make independent professional judgments by scrupulously avoiding undue influences and conflicts of interest.
5. *Fairness.* Be fair and open-minded, be willing to admit error, and, when appropriate, change positions and beliefs and demonstrate a commitment to justice, the equal treatment of individuals, and tolerance for diversity; do not overreach or take undue advantage of another's mistakes or adversities.
6. *Caring for others.* Be caring, kind, and compassionate; share, be giving, and serve others; help those in need and avoid harming others.
7. *Respect for others.* Demonstrate respect for human dignity, privacy, and the right to self-determination for all people; be courteous, prompt, and decent; provide others with the information they need to make informed decisions about their own lives; do not patronize, embarrass, or demean.
8. *Responsible citizenship.* Obey just laws [if a law is unjust, openly protest it]; exercise all democratic rights and privileges responsibly by participation [voting and expressing informed views], social consciousness, and public service; when in a position of leadership or authority, openly respect and honor democratic processes of decision making, avoid secrecy or concealment of information, and ensure others have the information needed to make intelligent choices and exercise their rights.
9. *Pursuit of excellence.* Pursue excellence in all matters; in meeting personal and professional responsibilities, be diligent, reliable, industrious, and committed; perform all tasks to the best of your ability, develop and maintain a high degree of competence, and be well informed and well prepared; do not be content with mediocrity, but do not seek to win "at any cost."
10. *Accountability.* Be accountable; accept responsibility for decisions, for the foreseeable consequences of actions and inactions, and for setting an example for others. Parents, teachers, employers, many professionals, and public officials have a special obligation to lead by example and to safeguard and advance the integrity and reputation of their families, companies, professions, and the government; avoid even the appearance of impropriety and take whatever actions are necessary to correct or prevent inappropriate conduct by others.

*Source:* Michael Josephson, "Teaching Ethical Decision Making and Principled Reasoning," *Ethics: Easier Said Than Done,* Winter 1988, pp. 28–29.

## Maintaining Ethical Standards

Establishing ethical standards is only the first step in an ethics-enhancing program; implementing and maintaining those standards is the real challenge facing management. What can entrepreneurs do to integrate ethical principles into their companies?

**CREATE A COMPANY CREDO.** A **company credo** defines the values underlying the entire company and its ethical responsibilities to its stakeholders. It offers general guidance in ethical issues. The most effective credos capture the elusive essence of a company—what it stands for and why it's important—and they can be a key ingredient in a company's competitive edge. A company credo is especially important for a small company, where the entrepreneur's values become the values driving the business. A credo is an excellent way to transform those values into employees' ethical behavior.

**DEVELOP A CODE OF ETHICS.** A **code of ethics** is a written statement of the standards of behavior and ethical principles a company expects from its employees. Codes of ethics do not ensure ethical behavior, but they do establish minimum standards of behavior throughout the organization. A code of ethics spells out what kind of behavior is expected (and what kind will not be tolerated) and offers everyone in the company concrete guidelines for dealing with ethics every day on the job. Although creating a code of ethics does not guarantee 100 percent compliance with ethical standards, it does tend to foster an ethical atmosphere in a company. Workers who will be directly affected by the code should have a hand in developing it.

**ENFORCE THE CODE FAIRLY AND CONSISTENTLY.** Managers must take action whenever they discover ethical violations. If employees learn that ethical breaches go unpunished, the code of ethics becomes meaningless. Enforcing the code of ethics demonstrates to everyone that you believe that ethical behavior is mandatory.

**CONDUCT ETHICS TRAINING.** Instilling ethics in an organization's culture requires more than creating a code of ethics and enforcing it. Managers must show employees that the organization truly is committed to practicing ethical behavior. One of the most effective ways to display that commitment is through ethical training designed to raise employees' consciousness of potential ethical dilemmas. Ethics training programs not only raise employees' awareness of ethical issues, but they also communicate to employees the core of the company's value system.

**HIRE THE RIGHT PEOPLE.** Ultimately, the decision in any ethical situation belongs to the individual. Hiring people with strong moral principles and values is the best insurance against ethical violations. To make ethical decisions, people must have: (1) *ethical commitment*—the personal resolve to act ethically and do the right thing; (2) *ethical consciousness*—the ability to perceive the ethical implications of a situation; and (3) *ethical competency*—the ability to engage in sound moral reasoning and develop practical problem-solving strategies.[17]

**PERFORM PERIODIC ETHICAL AUDITS.** One of the best ways to evaluate the effectiveness of an ethics system is to perform periodic audits. These reviews send a signal to employees that ethics is not just a passing fad.

**ESTABLISH HIGH STANDARDS OF BEHAVIOR, NOT JUST RULES.** No one can legislate ethics and morality, but managers can let people know the level of performance they expect. It is essential to emphasize to *everyone* in the organization the importance of ethics. All employees must understand that ethics is *not* negotiable. The role that an entrepreneur plays in establishing high ethical standards is critical; no one has more influence over the ethical character of a company than its founder. One experienced entrepreneur offers this advice to business owners: "Stick to your principles. Hire people who want to live by them, teach them thoroughly, and insist on total commitment."[18]

## ■ Adding Real Value to a Value Meal

George Propstra founded Burgerville USA, a family-owned fast-food restaurant, in Vancouver, Washington, in 1922 with a "made fresh from local ingredients" mentality that still exists today. When Propstra was still running the business, he was featured in quirky television commercials that showed him using a frozen hamburger patty as a hockey puck, a clever way of communicating to customers that Burgerville, which had never used frozen patties, used only the freshest ingredients. Propstra always took pride in selling onion rings made from onions grown in nearby Walla Walla in the U.S. state of Washington.

Although Burgerville has expanded to 39 locations in the northwest United States, half of which are in Portland, Oregon, and is now run by Propstra's son-in-law, Tom Mears, the "fresh, local" concept remains a key element in the company's strategy. In fact, Mears says that the company is using its emphasis on fresh, local products to move out of the fast-food industry and into the fast-casual dining sector, a niche in the restaurant industry between fast-food and fine dining in which restaurants offer a more upscale yet casual atmosphere and higher quality food that is served quickly. Mears saw the need for a strategic change when Burgerville began to lose market share to national franchised chains about a decade ago. "We decided that we weren't going to play the cheap hamburger game," he says.

As a result, Burgerville's $7 average check is higher than those of its national chain competitors, whose average check is $4.55, but the company's average sales per outlet ($1.5 million) are slightly lower than the national chains' sales per unit ($1.7 million). Burgerville's menu includes items that customers cannot find at most national chains. Dishes such as a wild Coho salmon and Oregon hazelnut salad, Tillamook cheeseburger, Halibut fish and chips, and milkshakes made with real ice cream and fresh fruit keep customers coming back. In 2003, *Gourmet* magazine named Burgerville as the restaurant with the nation's freshest fast food.

In 2004, Mears spotted another way to make Burgerville stand out in the hotly competitive fast-casual segment of the restaurant market: emphasize the company's stand as a socially responsible restaurant. Extending its "fresh and local" strategy, Burgerville began purchasing all of its beef, which is never frozen, from the nearby Country Natural Beef cooperative, which raises grain-fed, humanely treated cattle without using growth hormones. The company once again began purchasing onions from Walla Walla for its onion rings. Cheese comes from Tillamook, Oregon, and the berries for its milkshakes are grown locally. In fact, Burgerville recently stopped offering one of its best-selling milkshakes made from huckleberries when the company realized that it was over-harvesting the berries. Customers were disappointed, but Mears saw the move as an opportunity to prove to customers that the company was committed to operating in a socially and environmentally responsible, sustainable way. "At first people didn't care about what was local and sustainable, but now the public is changing," says Mears. The items on Burgerville's menu are free of transfats, and all of the cooking oil used is converted into biodiesel fuel. Mears purchases all of the company's electricity from nearby wind generators even though doing so costs $200,000 more than getting electricity from traditional sources. Buying from a clean energy source, however, is the equivalent of taking 1,700 cars off of the road. Kid's meals at Burgerville come with gardening tools and seeds rather than action figures from the latest movie.

Operating in a socially environmental manner is not necessarily the least expensive way to run a restaurant, however. Although Burgerville does not release its financial statements, industry analysts estimate that its net profit margin is about 10 percent of sales, compared to an estimated 15 percent for chains such as McDonald's. (However, a significant share of McDonald's income is derived from franchise royalty fees and rent.) Top managers at Burgerville are not concerned, however. They think that incurring somewhat higher costs is an acceptable trade-off for running their company in a socially responsible manner. "Our hope is to challenge the industry [to change its ways]," says Jeff Harvey, Burgerville's chief operating officer.

1. Do you think that incurring higher operating costs is an acceptable trade-off for running a company in a socially responsible manner? Explain.

2. What other steps could restaurants such as Burgerville take to operate their businesses in a more socially responsible, environmentally friendly way?

**SET AN IMPECCABLE ETHICAL EXAMPLE AT ALL TIMES.** Remember that ethics starts at the top. Far more important than credos and codes are the examples the company's leaders set. If managers talk about the importance of ethics and then act in an unethical manner, they send mixed signals to employees. Workers believe managers' *actions* more than their words.

**CREATE A CULTURE THAT EMPHASIZES TWO-WAY COMMUNICATION.** A thriving ethical environment requires two-way communication. Employees must have the opportunity to report any ethical violations they observe. A reliable, confidential reporting system is essential to a whistle-blowing program, in which employees anonymously report breaches of ethical behavior through proper channels.

**INVOLVE EMPLOYEES IN ESTABLISHING ETHICAL STANDARDS.** Encourage employees to offer feedback on how to establish standards. Involving employees improves the quality of a company's ethical standards and increases the likelihood of employee compliance.

## Social Responsibility and Social Entrepreneurship

*4.* Define social responsibility.

The concept of social responsibility has evolved from that of a nebulous "do-gooder" to one of "social steward" with the expectation that businesses will produce benefits not only for themselves but also for society as a whole. Society is constantly redefining its expectations of business and now holds companies of all sizes to high standards of ethics and social responsibility. Companies must go beyond "doing well"—simply earning a profit—to "doing good"—living up to their social responsibility.

Entrepreneurs in particular are using their resources and sphere of influence not only to generate a profit but also to tackle challenging problems confronting the global economy, including pollution, habitat destruction, human rights, AIDS, hunger, poverty, and others. These **social entrepreneurs**, people who start businesses so that they can create innovative solutions to society's most vexing problems, see themselves as change agents for society. Social entrepreneurs use their creativity to develop solutions to social problems that range from cleaning up the environment to improving working conditions for workers around the world; their goal is to use their businesses to make the world a better place to live. Bill Drayton, founder of Ashoka, an organization that promotes social entrepreneurship, says, "Social entrepreneurs are not content just to give a fish or teach [someone] how to fish. They will not rest until they have revolutionized the fishing industry."[19]

*Rodrigo Baggio and CDI*

Rodrigo Baggio grew up in a middle-class neighborhood in Rio de Janeiro where everyday he could see a *favela* (a Brazilian shanty town) known as Santa Marta, where homes are made of scrap materials or even garbage, perched on the hillside that overlooked his home. As a child, Baggio loved computers and eventually grew up to become a computer consultant; he never forgot about the young people in the favela, however. In 1995, he created the first Information Technology and Citizenship School, which was designed to bridge the digital divide between the technology "haves and have nots." Shortly afterward, Baggio launched the Committee for the Democratization of Information Technology (CDI) with the goal of using technology to fight poverty and social exclusion. Baggio convinced the Inter-American Development bank to donate used computers, the Brazilian Air Force to transport them to Rio de Janeiro, and Brazilian customs officials to allow them to enter the country despite an embargo on computers. CDI forms partnerships with schools and community associations to provide computers, software, and training for young people and future teachers, who, in turn, train others to use technology. More than 700,000 students have graduated from CDI schools in locations across South and Central America and Asia. "I believe in the power of communities to transform their social reality by mastering new information and communications technologies," says Baggio.[20]

In a free enterprise system, companies that fail to respond to their customers' needs and demands soon go out of business. Today, customers are increasingly demanding the companies they buy goods and services from to be socially responsible. When customers shop for "value," they no longer consider only the price-performance relationship of the product or service; they also consider the company's stance on social responsibility. A study by consulting firm Hill and Knowlton found that 79 percent of U.S. consumers consider a company's reputation when evaluating products, and 36 percent consider reputation to be an important factor in their purchasing decision.[21] Other studies report that when price, service, and quality are equal among competitors, customers buy from the company that has the best reputation for social responsibility.

Other studies show a connection between social responsibility and profitability. One team of researchers evaluated 52 studies on corporate social responsibility that were conducted over 30 years and concluded that a positive correlation existed between a company's profitability and its reputation for ethical, socially responsible behavior. The relationship also was self-reinforcing. "It's a virtuous cycle," says Sara Rynes, one of the researchers. "As a company becomes more socially responsible, its reputation and financial performance go up, which causes them to become even more socially responsible."[22] The message is clear: Companies that incorporate social responsibility into their competitive strategies outperform those that fail to do so.

## Putting Social Responsibility into Practice

**5.** Understand the nature of businesses' responsibility to the environment.

One problem facing businesses is defining just what socially responsible behavior is. Is it manufacturing environmentally friendly products? Is it donating a portion of profits to charitable organizations? Is it creating jobs in inner cities plagued by high unemployment levels? The nature of a company's social responsibility efforts will depend on how its owners, employees, and other stakeholders define what it means to be socially responsible. Typically, businesses have responsibilities to several key stakeholders, including the environment, employees, customers, investors, and the community.

### Businesses' Responsibility to the Environment

Driven by their customers' interest in protecting the environment, companies have become more sensitive to the impact their products, processes, and packaging have on the planet. Environmentalism has become, and will continue to be, one of the dominant issues for companies worldwide because consumers have added another item to their list of buying criteria: environmental friendliness and safety. Companies have discovered that sound environmental practices make for good business. In addition to lowering their operating costs, environmentally safe products attract environmentally conscious customers and can give a company a competitive edge in the marketplace. Socially responsible business owners focus on the three Rs: reduce, reuse, and recycle:

- *Reduce* the amount of materials used in your company, from the factory floor to the copier room.
- *Reuse* whatever you can.
- *Recycle* the materials that you must dispose of.

*Angela Greene and Ken Kobrick and Passchal*

After Angela Greene purchased a backpack that was made from recycled tire inner tubes, she and Ken Kobrick began creating prototypes of handbags made from truck and tractor tire inner tubes that she got free of charge from local tire stores. After a two-to-three day cleaning process (the inner tubes "are dirty and smell like rotten eggs," says Greene), the recycled material is transformed into stylish, handcrafted purses, iPod cases, DVD holders, baby bags, totes, and messenger bags. The bags light up when opened, thanks to a clever fiber optic light. Passchal customizes bags with hemp, leather, or faux leather trim to add a splash of color and guarantees them for 50,000 miles or life—whichever comes first! Not only does Passchal sell its stylish cases and bags, which range in price from $55 to $250, in stylish boutiques, but the company also counts recycling organizations and automotive and tire stores among its distributors.[23]

Many progressive small companies are taking their environmental policies a step further, creating redesigned, "clean" manufacturing systems that focus on *avoiding* waste and pollution and using resources efficiently. That requires a different manufacturing philosophy. These companies design their products, packaging, and processes from the start with the environment in mind, working to eliminate hazardous materials and by-products and looking for ways to turn what had been scrap into salable products. This approach requires an ecological evaluation of every part of the process, from the raw materials that go into a product to the disposal or reuse of the packaging that contains it.

**ENTREPRENEURIAL**
**Profile**

*Joshua Onysko and Pangea Organics*

Joshua Onysko, founder of Pangea Organics, incorporates these principles into his business, which uses organic, all-natural ingredients such as beeswax, almond oil, and sweet basil to produce its line of soaps and body lotions. Pangea's packaging is made from 100 percent recycled paper using a "zero waste" process. The packages even include the seeds of herbs such as basil and amaranth. Once they remove the product, customers simply soak the package in water for one minute, plant it, and wait for the seeds to sprout! Pangea's 10,000-square-foot factory is powered completely by wind, and a 2,500-square-foot-garden provides lunch for the company's 22 employees seven months out of the year. Onysko says that Pangea is gearing up for an audit of its environmental impact so that the company can be even more environmentally sensitive.[24]

Table 21.6 offers a list of questions that environmentally responsible entrepreneurs should ask themselves.

### Businesses' Responsibility to Employees

*6.* Describe businesses' responsibility to employees.

Few other stakeholders are as important to a business as its employees. It is common for managers to *say* that their employees are their most valuable resource, but the truly excellent ones actually *treat* them that way. Employees are at the heart of increases in productivity, and they

**TABLE 21.6 Environmentally Responsible Questions**

What can companies do to be more environmentally friendly? The following questions can help entrepreneurs evaluate their companies' impact on the environment.

- Are we trying to reduce the volume of our packaging?
- How do we deal with disposal?
- Are we recycling in the office?
- Can we get beyond the concept of volume sales to build products that last?
- Are we reducing waste and substituting toxic substances with nontoxic ones?
- Are we reformulating waste for resale?
- Do we have a formal environmental policy?
- Do we go beyond compliance?
- Are we uniformly stringent environmentally in operations outside, as well as inside, the United States?
- Do we educate employees about the hazards of working with toxic materials?
- Do we encourage employees to submit proposals on how to reduce waste?
- Do we conserve energy?
- Are we avoiding paying taxes, when those tax dollars might go to support environmental programs?
- How do our operations affect the communities they're in, including indigenous people in other countries?

*Source:* Therese R. Welter, "A Farewell to Arms," *Industry Week*, August 20, 1990, p. 42.

## ■ Not the Summit but the Journey

By any measure, Yvon Chouinard is a successful business owner, but he never set out to become one. In fact, many people describe Chouinard, founder of Patagonia, the highly regarded outdoor gear company, as an anti-businessman businessman. Chouinard followed a contrarian path to business success by putting social responsibility and ethics above making a profit, a concept that was particularly foreign when he started Patagonia in 1970. Very much an environmentalist, Chouinard accuses American business of being "unimaginative at best and evil at worst." Chouinard, who says that he intended to spend exactly zero days of his life behind a desk, and his wife Malinda were committed from the outset to running their business their way—with a conscience. Patagonia would not release chemicals into the environment and would produce products of the highest quality in the most efficient and responsible way. If an employee's child was sick, he or she would be right where he or she should be: with the child. When the surf was up or the snow on the slopes was perfect powder, employees could be there. The company always would remain privately held because involving outside investors could cause the company to move away from its core values. Chouinard is famous for saying, "I don't want a Wall Street greaseball running my company." In other words, the Chouinards simply would say "no" to *anything* that might compromise their values or those of the company that reflected their values.

For those who know Chouinard, it is no surprise that Patagonia is a radical business. Patagonia was one of the first companies in America to use recycled material and to provide onsite daycare, flextime, and both maternity and paternity leave for employees. It was the first company in California to use alternative energy sources such as wind and solar power to run its operations and was one of the first businesses to print its catalogs on recycled paper. Chouinard saw his catalog as more than just a way to market Patagonia's products. Every issue carried messages about preserving and protecting the environment from pollution, overfishing, and other dangers. Chouinard's goal was to operate Patagonia so that it leaves no negative footprint on the earth. As much progress as Chouinard has made toward that goal, he realizes that achieving it is virtually impossible. In his book,

*Let My People Go Surfing,* he writes, "Patagonia will never be completely socially responsible. It will never make a totally sustainable, non-damaging product. But it is committed to trying."

Patagonia owes its existence to Chouinard's passion for rock climbing, a sport he fell in love with at age 15. He and a group of friends ("fellow misfits," he calls them) scaled the faces of cliffs but had difficulty finding reliable equipment. Chouinard installed a coal forge in his parents' garage and taught himself the art of blacksmithing, forging pitons—three-inch steel devices that anchored climbing ropes. His simple, elegant design produced pitons that were far superior to anything on the market, and Chouinard scratched out a living selling them out of the back of his car for $1.50 each. He gradually expanded the company, which he called Chouinard Equipment, mainly to finance his wilderness adventures.

Chouinard married Malinda in 1970, and in 1972, the couple expanded the tiny company's product line to include clothing and changed its name to Patagonia. The company's first breakthrough product came in 1977 in the form of a jacket made of polyester pile that repelled moisture and retained heat, important traits to climbers. Patagonia worked with Malden Mills to refine the fabric, creating a finer, softer version called Synchilla, which it used to make the first fleece jacket. Sales exploded, and Patagonia was on its way to becoming an established, if nontraditional, business.

Chouinard began studying the environmental impact of the materials that Patagonia used in its products and realized that cotton was an "environmentalist's nightmare" because of the noxious chemicals used to grow it. In 1994, he commanded the company to make the switch to organic cotton, a rare commodity at the time. The move was a huge risk because cotton products accounted for 20 percent of Patagonia's sales and organic cotton costs between 50 percent and 100 percent more than regular cotton. Patagonia marketed the benefits of organic cotton to its customers, who responded by purchasing even more cotton products. In 2001, Patagonia worked with a Japanese partner to create a process that uses polyester fabric that can be recycled almost endlessly, and the result is a 76 percent savings in the resources used to create the fabric.

Always the entrepreneur, Chouinard also is leading Patagonia into uncharted waters: the surfing market. Why? Climate change. "It's never going to snow again, and the waves are going to get bigger and bigger," he says. "I see an opportunity." Already, Patagonia's designers have developed a new, improved wetsuit fabric that is made from crushed limestone, recycled polyester, and organic wool. Chouinard's son, Fletcher, is developing a line of surfboards that are made from non-toxic materials that are lighter, stronger, and more eco-friendly than those currently in use.

Chouinard is a generous donor to causes that are important to him. Since 1985, Patagonia has donated $26 million to charitable causes. In 2001, he created One Percent for the Planet, an organization that has grown to 500 companies that have pledged to donate one percent of their gross revenues to environmental causes.

Chouinard sees many parallels in his journey as an entrepreneur and the journeys that he makes when he climbs peaks. He knows that reaching the summit in business, just like on a climb, is not nearly as important as the journey you take to get there. Chouinard believes that if he focuses on doing things right, the profits will come. So far, he's been right.

1. Some experts have criticized Chouinard for paying more attention to operating a socially responsible business than on earning a profit. How would you respond?
2. Chouinard often gets calls from would-be buyers who tell him that Patagonia is an undervalued company. If he were to sell the company to them, they argue, they could help Patagonia realize its full potential. Chouinard refuses every offer, and Patagonia remains a privately held company. Do you agree with his decision? Explain.
3. Identify some of the costs and the benefits of Patagonia's commitment to operating in a socially responsible manner.

*Sources:* Adapted from Susan Casey, "Éminence Green," *Fortune,* April 2, 2007, pp. 62–70.

add the personal touch that puts passion in customer service. In short, employees produce the winning competitive advantage for an entrepreneur. Entrepreneurs who understand the value of their employees follow a few simple procedures by:

- Listening to employees and respecting their opinions.
- Asking for their input; involving them in the decision-making process.
- Providing regular feedback—positive and negative—to employees.
- Telling them the truth—always.
- Letting them know exactly what's expected of them.
- Rewarding employees for performing their jobs well.
- Trusting them; creating an environment of respect and teamwork.

Starbucks Coffee Company, the successful Seattle-based coffee retailer with more than 10,000 locations around the world, recognizes the special role its employees (or "partners" in company lingo) play in keeping customers coming back to its retail locations, and it shows employees that it appreciates their contributions. Reflecting on the importance of having satisfied partners, 65 percent of whom are women, interacting with customers in the retail business, CEO Howard Schultz explains, "We built the Starbucks brand first with our people, not with consumers. Because we believed the best way to meet and exceed the expectations of our customers was to hire and train great people, we invested in employees." At Starbucks, employee-partners come first. Great benefits, constant training, respect, and a team approach keep costs low and employee turnover down to just one-eighth of the industry average. Company surveys show that 82 percent of Starbucks partners, who volunteer more than 200,000 hours a year to their local communities, are either satisfied or very satisfied with their jobs.[25]

Several important issues face entrepreneurs who are trying to meet their social responsibility to employees, including cultural diversity, drug testing, AIDS, sexual harassment, and privacy.

**CULTURAL DIVERSITY IN THE WORKPLACE.** The United States has always been a nation of astonishing cultural diversity, a trait that has imbued it with an incredible richness of ideas and creativity. Indeed, this diversity is one of the driving forces behind the greatest

**FIGURE 21.2  U.S. Population by Demographic Group**
*Source:* U.S. Census Bureau, 2007.

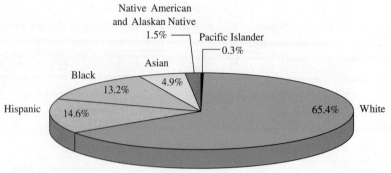

*Does not equal 100% because of rounding.

entrepreneurial effort in the world, and it continues to grow. The United States, in short, is moving toward a "minority majority," and significant demographic shifts will affect virtually every aspect of business. Nowhere will this be more visible than in the makeup of the nation's workforce. Today one in three residents of the United States, a total of more than 100 million people, is a member of a minority group (see Figure 21.2). The Hispanic population is the fastest growing sector in the United States, and Hispanics now comprise the largest minority population in the nation.[26]

This rich mix of cultures within the workforce presents both opportunities and challenges to employers. One of the chief benefits of a diverse workforce is the rich blend of perspectives; skills, talents, and ideas employees have to offer. The changing composition of the nation also is changing the customer base. What better way is there for an entrepreneur to deal with culturally diverse customers than to have a culturally diverse workforce? "No matter who you are, you're going to have to work with people who are different from you," says Ted Childs, vice president of global workforce diversity for IBM. "You're going to have to sell to people who are different from you, buy from people who are different from you, and manage people who are different from you."[27]

Managing a culturally diverse workforce presents a real challenge for employers, however. Molding workers with highly varied beliefs, backgrounds, and biases into a unified team takes time and commitment. Stereotypes, biases, and prejudices present barriers that workers and managers must constantly overcome. Communication may require more effort because of language differences. In many cases, dealing with diversity causes a degree of discomfort for entrepreneurs because of the natural tendency to associate with people who are similar to ourselves. These reasons and others cause some entrepreneurs to resist the move to a more diverse workforce, a move that threatens their ability to create a competitive edge.

How can entrepreneurs achieve unity through diversity? The only way is by *managing* diversity in the workforce. In its *Best Practices of Private Sector Employers,* an Equal Employment Opportunity Commission task force suggests following a "SPLENDID" approach to diversity:

- *Study.* Business owners cannot solve problems they don't know exist. Entrepreneurs must familiarize themselves with issues related to diversity, including relevant laws.
- *Plan.* Recognizing the makeup of the local population, entrepreneurs must set targets for diversity hiring and develop a plan for achieving them.
- *Lead.* A diversity effort starts at the top of the organization with managers communicating their vision and goals to everyone in the company.
- *Encourage.* Company leader must encourage employees at all levels of an organization to embrace the diversity plan.
- *Notice.* Entrepreneurs must monitor their companies' progress toward achieving diversity goals.
- *Discussion.* Managers must keep diversity on the company's radar screen by communicating the message that diversity is vital to business success.
- *Inclusion.* Involving employees in the push to achieve diversity helps break down barriers that may arise.
- *Dedication.* Achieving diversity in a business does not happen overnight, but entrepreneurs must be persistent in implementing their plans.[28]

The goal of diversity efforts is to create an environment in which all types of workers—men, women, Hispanic, African American, white, disabled, homosexual, elderly, and others—can flourish and can give top performances to their companies. In fact, researchers at Harvard University report that companies that embrace diversity are more productive than those that shun diversity. A distinguishing factor the companies supporting diversity share is the willingness of people to learn from their coworkers' different backgrounds and life experiences.[29]

Managing a culturally diverse workforce requires a different way of thinking, however, and that requires training. In essence, diversity training will help make everyone aware of the dangers of bias, prejudice, and discrimination, however subtle or unintentional they may be. Managing a culturally diverse workforce successfully requires a business owner to:

*Assess your company's diversity needs.*  The starting point for an effective diversity management program is assessing a company's needs. Surveys, interviews, and informal conversations with employees can be valuable tools. Several organizations offer more formal assessment tools—cultural audits, questionnaires, and diagnostic forms—that also are useful.

*Learn to recognize and correct your own biases and stereotypes.*  One of the best ways to identify your own cultural biases is to get exposure to people who are not like you. By spending time with those who are different from you, you will learn quickly that stereotypes simply don't hold up. Giving employees the opportunity to spend time with one another is an excellent way to eliminate stereotypes. The owner of one small company with a culturally diverse staff provides lunch for his workers every month with a seating arrangement that encourages employees to mix with one another.

*Avoid making invalid assumptions.*  Decisions that are based on faulty assumptions are bound to be flawed. False assumptions built on inaccurate perceptions or personal bias have kept many qualified minority workers from getting jobs and promotions. Make sure that it does not happen in your company.

*Push for diversity in your management team.*  To get maximum benefit from a culturally diverse workforce, a company must promote nontraditional workers into top management. A culturally diverse top management team that can serve as mentors and role models provides visible evidence that nontraditional workers can succeed.

*Concentrate on communication.*  Any organization, especially a culturally diverse one, will stumble if lines of communication break down. Frequent training sessions and regular opportunities for employees to talk with one another in a nonthreatening environment can be extremely helpful.

*Make diversity a core value in the organization.*  For a cultural diversity program to work, top managers must "champion" the program and take active steps to integrate diversity throughout the entire organization.

*Continue to adjust your company to your workers.*  Rather than pressure workers to conform to the company, those entrepreneurs with the most successful cultural diversity programs are constantly looking for ways to adjust their businesses to their workers. Flexibility is the key.

As business leaders look to the future, an increasingly diverse workforce stares back. People with varying cultural, racial, gender, and lifestyle perspectives seek opportunity and acceptance from coworkers, managers, and business owners. Currently, women make up 46.4 percent of the U.S. workforce, and minority workers comprise about 30.5 percent of the labor force.[30] However, minorities account for more than half of all workers who are entering the workforce.[31] Businesses that value the diversity of their workers and the perspectives they bring to work enjoy the benefits of higher employee satisfaction, commitment, retention, creativity, and productivity than those companies that ignore the cultural diversity of their workers. In addition, they deepen the loyalty of their existing customers and expand their market share by attracting new customers. In short, diversity is a winning proposition from every angle!

**DRUG TESTING.** One of the realities of our society is substance abuse. The second reality, which entrepreneurs now must face head on, is that substance abuse has infiltrated the workplace. In addition to the lives it ruins, substance abuse takes a heavy toll on business and society, costing employers more than $200 billion a year.[32] Drug and alcohol abuse by employees results in reduced productivity (an estimated $81 billion per year), increased medical costs, higher accident rates, and higher levels of absenteeism. Unfortunately, small companies bear a disproportionate share of the burden because 76.8 percent of all substance abusers are employed.[33] Because small companies are less likely to have drug-testing programs than large companies, they are more likely to hire people with substance abuse problems. Abusers who know that they cannot pass a drug test simply apply for work at companies that do not use drug tests. Because the practice of drug testing remains a controversial issue, its random use can lead to a variety of legal woes for employers, including invasion of privacy, discrimination, slander, or defamation of character.

An effective, proactive drug program should include the following four elements:

1. *A written substance abuse policy.* The first step is to create a written policy that spells out the company's position on drugs. The policy should state its purpose, prohibit the use of drugs on the job (or off the job if it affects job performance), specify the consequences of violating the policy, explain the drug testing procedures the company will use, and describe the resources available to help troubled employees.

2. *Training for supervisors to detect substance-abusing workers.* Supervisors are in the best position to identify employees with alcohol or drug problems and to encourage them to get help. The supervisor's job, however, is not to play "cop" or "therapist." The supervisor should identify problem employees early and encourage them to seek help. The focal point of the supervisor's role is to track employees' performances against their objectives to identify the employees with performance problems. Vigilant managers look for the following signs:
   - Frequent tardiness or absences accompanied by questionable excuses
   - Long lunch, coffee, or bathroom breaks
   - Frequently missed deadlines
   - Withdrawal from or frequent arguments with fellow employees
   - Overly sensitive to criticism
   - Declining or inconsistent productivity
   - Inability to concentrate on work
   - Disregard for personal safety or the safety of others
   - Deterioration of personal appearance

3. *An employee education program.* Business owners should take time to explain the company's substance abuse policy, the reasons behind it, and the help that is available to employees who have substance abuse problems. Every employee should participate in training sessions, and managers should remind employees periodically of the policy, the problem, and the help that is available. Some companies have used inserts in pay envelopes, home mailings, lunch speakers, and short seminars as part of their ongoing educational efforts.

4. *A drug testing program, when necessary.* Experts recommend that business owners seek the advice of an experienced attorney before establishing a drug testing program. Preemployment testing of job applicants generally is a safe strategy to follow, as long as it is followed consistently. Testing current employees is a more complex issue, but, again, consistency is the key.

5. *An employee assistance program (EAP).* No drug-battling program is complete without a way to help addicted employees. An **employee assistance program (EAP)** is a company-provided benefit designed to help reduce workplace problems such as alcoholism, drug addiction, a gambling habit, and other conflicts and to deal with them when they arise. Although some troubled employees may balk at enrolling in an EAP, the company controls the most powerful weapon in motivating them to seek and accept help: *their jobs.* The greatest fear that substance-abusing employees have is losing their jobs, and the company can use that fear to help workers recover. EAPs,

which cost between $18 and $30 per employee each year to operate, are an effective weapon in the battle against workplace substance abuse. Research shows that EAPs can pay for themselves quickly by reducing absenteeism and tardiness by 25 percent and increasing productivity by 25 percent.[34]

*Eastern Industries*

Eastern Industries, a company that produces building supplies, concrete, asphalt, and stone, operates in an industry that traditionally has been plagued by substance abuse problems. (A recent study shows that 15.1 percent of workers in the construction industry have substance abuse problems, second only to the food service industry.) Before 1996, Eastern's substance abuse policy was simple: We test for drugs, and if you fail the test, you are fired. The all-or-nothing policy affected the company's ability to keep and retain skilled workers, and company managers decided to change it to a policy that includes prevention, testing, and rehabilitation. Eastern includes educational sessions on substance abuse in its employee orientation program and ongoing programs for all workers. If an employee fails a drug test, he or she can enroll in an employee assistance program that includes rehabilitation that, once successfully completed, allows the worker to return to his or her job. Managers at Eastern say the program has been a tremendous success, allowing them to keep good workers they would have lost under the old policy and giving employees the opportunity to correct bad decisions and keep their jobs.[35]

**AIDS.** One of the most serious health problems to strike the world is AIDS (acquired immune deficiency syndrome). Experts estimate that 1.2 million people in the United States have AIDS.[36] This deadly disease, for which no cure yet exists, poses an array of ethical dilemmas for businesses, ranging from privacy to discrimination. AIDS has had an impact on our economy in the form of billions of dollars in lost productivity and increased health care costs. For most business owners, the issue is not one of *whether* one of their employees will contract AIDS but *when*.

Coping with AIDS in the workplace is not like managing normal health care issues because of the fear and misunderstanding the disease creates among coworkers. When confronted by the disease, many employers and employees operate on the basis of misconceptions and fear, resulting in "knee-jerk" reactions that are illegal, including firing the worker and telling other employees. Unfortunately, many entrepreneurs know very little about their legal obligation to employees with AIDS. In fact, AIDS is considered a disability in the United States and is covered by the Americans with Disabilities Act (ADA). This legislation prohibits discrimination against any person with a disability, including AIDS, in hiring, promoting, discharging, or compensation. In addition, employers are required to make "reasonable accommodations" that will allow an AIDS-stricken employee to continue working. Some examples of these accommodations include job sharing, flexible work schedules, job reassignment, sick leave, and part-time work.

Coping with AIDS in a socially responsible manner requires a written policy and an educational program, ideally implemented *before* the need arises. When dealing with AIDS, entrepreneurs must base their decisions on facts rather than on emotions, which requires them to be well informed. As with drug testing, it is important to ensure that a company's AIDS policies are legal. In general, a company's AIDS policy should include the following:

*Employment.* Companies must allow employees with AIDS to continue working as long as they can perform the job.

*Discrimination.* Because AIDS is a disability, employers cannot discriminate against qualified people with the disease who can meet job requirements.

*Employee benefits.* Employees with AIDS have the right to the same benefits as those with any other life-threatening illness.

*Confidentiality.* Employers must keep employees' medical records strictly confidential.

*Education.* An AIDS education program should be a part of every company's AIDS policy. The time to create and implement one is *before* the problem arises. As part of its AIDS program, one small company conducted informational seminars, distributed brochures and booklets, established a print and video library, and even set up individual counseling for employees.

*Reasonable accommodations.* Under the ADA, employers must make "reasonable accommodations" for employees with AIDS. These may include extended leaves of absence, flexible work schedules, restructuring a job to require less-strenuous duties, purchasing special equipment to assist affected workers, and other modifications.

**SEXUAL HARASSMENT.** As the number of women in the workforce has increased, so has the number of sexual harassment charges filed. One survey reports that 31 percent of women and 7 percent of men had experienced sexual harassment on the job, but 62 percent of employees who had been harassed never reported the incident to the company.[37] Sexual harassment is a violation of Title VII of the U.S. Civil Rights Act of 1964 and is considered to be a form of sex discrimination. Studies show that sexual harassment occurs in businesses of all sizes, but small businesses are especially vulnerable because they typically lack the policies, procedures, and training to prevent it. Even cartoon strip characters are not immune to sexual harassment charges. In Mort Walker's long-running *Beetle Bailey* comic strip, Miss Buxley once filed charges against General Halftrack because of his leering stares and sexual and untoward comments.[38]

**Sexual harassment** is any unwelcome sexual advance, request for sexual favors, and other verbal or physical sexual conduct made explicitly or implicitly as a condition of employment. Women bring about 85 percent of all sexual harassment charges. Jury verdicts reaching into the millions of dollars are not uncommon. Retaliation such as demotions and assignments to less attractive work against employees who file a complaint of sexual harassment occurs too often. The most common form of employer retaliation is termination. Several types of behavior may result in sexual harassment charges:

*Quid Pro Quo Harassment.* The most blatant, and most potentially damaging, form of sexual harassment is *quid pro quo* ("something for something"), in which a superior conditions the granting of a benefit (promotion, raise, etc.) upon the receipt of sexual favors

Studies show that sexual harassment occurs in businesses of all sizes, but small businesses are especially vulnerable because they typically lack the policies, procedures, and training to prevent it.

from a subordinate. Only managers and supervisors, not coworkers, can engage in *quid pro quo* harassment.

***Hostile Environment.*** Behavior that creates an abusive, intimidating, offensive, or hostile work environment also constitutes sexual harassment. A hostile environment usually requires a *pattern* of offensive sexual behavior rather than a single, isolated remark or display. In judging whether a hostile environment exists, U.S. courts, at least, base their decisions on how a "reasonable woman" would perceive the situation. (The previous standard was that of a "reasonable person.") Although not easily defined, a hostile work environment is one in which continuing unwelcome sexual conduct in the workplace interferes with an employee's work performance. Most sexual harassment charges arise from claims of a hostile environment.

***Harassment by Nonemployees.*** An employer can be held liable for third parties (customers, sales representatives, and others) who engage in sexual harassment if the employer has the ability to stop the improper behavior. For example, one company required a female employee to wear an extremely skimpy, revealing uniform. She complained to her boss that the uniform encouraged members of the public to direct offensive comments and physical contact toward her. The manager ignored her complaints, and later she refused to wear the uniform, which resulted in her dismissal. When she filed a sexual harassment claim, the court held the company accountable for the employee's sexual harassment by nonemployees because it required her to wear the uniform after she complained of the harassment.[39]

No business wants to incur the cost of defending itself against charges of sexual harassment, but those costs can be devastating for a small business. Multi-million-dollar jury awards in harassment cases are becoming increasingly common because the Civil Rights Act of 1991 allows victims to collect punitive damages and emotional distress awards. Recently, a jury in the U.S. state of Missouri awarded a woman who worked for a logistics company $6.75 million in damages after she won a lawsuit in which she claimed that her supervisor engaged in inappropriate actions and made sexual comments on five occasions over a two-month period. Even though the company transferred the woman to another shift, she still had to work with the supervisor on occasion. The company also failed to investigate her complaints about the harassment, which was a key factor in the size of the award against the company.[40]

The United States Supreme Court has expanded the nature of an employer's liability for sexual harassment, rejecting the previous standard that the employer had to be negligent to be liable for a supervisor's improper behavior toward employees. In *Burlington Industries vs. Ellerth,* the court ruled that an employer can be held liable *automatically* if a supervisor takes a "tangible employment action" such as failing to promote or firing an employee whom he or she has been sexually harassing. The employer is liable even if he or she was not aware of the supervisor's conduct. If a supervisor takes no tangible employment action against an employee but engages in sexually harassing behavior such as offensive remarks, inappropriate touching, or sexual advances, the employer is not *automatically* liable for the supervisor's conduct. However, an employer would be liable for such conduct if, for example, he or she knew (or should have known) about the supervisor's behavior and failed to stop it.[41]

A company's best weapons against sexual harassment are education, policy, and procedures.

***Education.*** Preventing sexual harassment is the best solution, and the key to prevention is educating employees about what constitutes sexual harassment. Training programs are designed to raise employees' awareness of what might be offensive to other workers and how to avoid sexual harassment altogether.

***Policy.*** Another essential ingredient is a meaningful policy against sexual harassment that management can enforce. The policy should:

- Clearly define the behaviors that constitute sexual harassment.
- State in clear language that harassment will not be tolerated in the workplace.

- Identify the responsibilities of supervisors and employees in preventing harassment.
- Define the sanctions and penalties for engaging in harassment.
- Spell out the steps to take in reporting an incident of sexual harassment.

In another case, the United States Supreme Court ruled that an employer was liable for a supervisor's sexually harassing behavior even though the employee never reported it. The company's liability stemmed from its failure to communicate its sexual harassment policy throughout the organization. This ruling makes employers' policies and procedures on sexual harassment the focal point of their defense.

*Procedure.* Socially responsible companies provide a channel for all employees to express their complaints. Choosing a person inside the company (perhaps someone in the human resources area) and one outside the company (a close adviser or attorney) is a good strategy because it gives employees a choice about how to file a complaint. At least one of these people should be a woman. When a complaint arises, managers should:

- Listen to the complaint carefully without judging. Taking notes is a good idea. Tell the complainant what the process involves. *Never* treat the complaint as a joke.
- Investigate the complaint *promptly,* preferably within 24 hours. Failure to act quickly is irresponsible and illegal. Table 21.7 offers suggestions for conducting a sexual harassment investigation.
- Interview the accused party and any witnesses who may be aware of a pattern of harassing behavior *privately* and *separately.*
- Keep findings confidential.
- Decide what action to take, relying on company policy as a guideline.
- Inform both the complaining person and the alleged harasser of the action taken.
- Document the entire investigation.[42]

The accompanying "Gaining a Competitive Edge" feature includes a quiz on sexual harassment for both employees and managers.

### TABLE 21.7  What to Do When an Employee Files a Sexual Harassment Complaint

When an employee in the United States files a sexual harassment complaint, the U.S. Equal Employment Opportunity Commission (EEOC) recommends that employers (1) question both parties in detail, and (2) probe for corroborative evidence. Here is a checklist to help when following these EEOC recommendations.

- Analyze the victim's story for sufficient detail, internal consistency, and believability.
- Do not attach much significance to a general denial by the accused harasser.
- Search completely and thoroughly for evidence that corroborates either person's story. You can do this by:
  - interviewing coworkers, supervisors, and managers
  - obtaining testimony from individuals who observed the accuser's demeanor immediately after the alleged incident of harassment
  - talking to people with whom the alleged victim discussed the incident (e.g., coworkers, a doctor, or a counselor)
- Ask other employees if they noticed changes in the accusing individual's behavior at work or in the alleged harasser's treatment of him or her.
- Look for evidence of other complaints, either by the victim or other employees.
- Follow up on evidence that other employees were sexually harassed by the same person.

To make a fair and legal decision on a sexual harassment complaint, you need to find out as much information as you can, not only on the incident itself, but also on the victims and accuser's personalities, surroundings, and relationships. To accomplish this task, you need to ask many questions not only of the victim and the accuser but also of any witnesses to the incident.

*Source:* Women's Studies Database at the University of Maryland, www.mith2.umd.edu/ WomensStudies/GenderIssues/SexualHarassment/questions-for-investigations.

## How Much Do You Know About Sexual Harassment?

Do you know sexual harassment when you see it? Consider the following case:

Catherine was exposed to photographs of nude women posted in various areas of the plant in which she worked. She eventually complained about the photos to the plant manager, who (1) made inappropriate personal and sexual remarks to her, (2) addressed her as "honey" and "dear," and (3) insinuated that she was a troublemaker. Thereafter, some, but not all, of the pictures were removed, despite the employer's policy to remove sexually explicit materials upon discovery.

When Catherine's immediate supervisor heard of her complaint, he indicated that he disapproved of "women's liberation" and recited a story to Catherine about employees who had quit their jobs after the jobs were made intolerable. Other employees (including another supervisor) also expressed to Catherine their annoyance over her complaint, and she was subjected to "catcalls" and harassing whistles. These instances of harassment were also reported by Catherine to her immediate supervisor and the plant manager, who indicated to her that she was somehow encouraging the harassment. Management failed to put an end to the whistling and catcalls.

In its defense, the company cited the fact that it had instituted a policy of using gender-neutral terms in its job titles.

Does Catherine have a legitimate sexual harassment complaint? Explain.

Yes, although the company had a mechanism for employees to complain about sexual harassment, managers failed to take any action to stop the harassment. Indeed, the managers to whom she complained participated in the harassment. Catherine prevailed in court.

One of the primary causes of sexual harassment in the workplace is the lack of education concerning what constitutes harassment. The following quiz asks you to assume the roles of an employee and of a manager when answering the questions.

### A Test for Employees

Answer the following true/false questions.

1. If I just ignore unwanted sexual attention, it will usually stop.
2. If I don't mean to sexually harass another employee, there's no way my behavior can be perceived by him or her as sexually harassing.
3. Some employees don't complain about unwanted sexual attention from another worker because they don't want to get that person in trouble.
4. If I make sexual comments to someone and that person doesn't ask me to stop, then I guess my behavior is welcome.
5. To avoid sexually harassing a woman who comes to work in a traditionally male workplace, the men simply should not haze her.
6. A sexual harasser may be told by a court to pay part of a judgment to the employee he or she harassed.
7. A sexually harassed man does not have the same legal rights as a woman who is sexually harassed.
8. About 90 percent of all sexual harassment in today's workplace is done by males to females.
9. Sexually suggestive pictures or objects in a workplace don't create a liability unless someone complains.
10. Displaying "girlie" pictures can constitute a hostile work environment even though most workers in the workplace think they are harmless.
11. Telling someone to stop his or her unwanted sexual behavior usually doesn't do any good.

Answers: (1) False, (2) False, (3) True, (4) False, (5) False, (6) True, (7) False, (8) True, (9) False, (10) True, (11) False.

### A Test for Managers

Answer the following true/false questions.

1. Men in male-dominated workplaces usually have to change their behavior when a woman begins working there.
2. Employers are not liable for the sexual harassment of one of their employees unless that employee loses specific job benefits or is fired.
3. Supervisors can be liable for sexual harassment committed by one of their employees against another.

*(continued)*

4. Employers can be liable for the sexually harassing behavior of management personnel even if they are unaware of that behavior and have a policy forbidding it.

5. It is appropriate for a supervisor, when initially receiving a sexual harassment complaint, to determine if the alleged recipient overreacted or misunderstood the alleged harasser.

6. When a supervisor is telling an employee that an allegation of sexual harassment has been made against the employee, it is best to ease into the allegation instead of being direct.

7. Sexually suggestive visuals or objects in a workplace don't create a liability unless an employee complains about them and management allows them to remain.

8. The lack of sexual harassment complaints is a good indication that sexual harassment is not occurring.

9. It is appropriate for supervisors to tell an employee to handle unwelcome sexual behavior if they think that the employee is misunderstanding the behavior.

10. The *intent* behind employee A's sexual behavior is more important than the *impact* of that behavior on employee B when determininng whether sexual harassment has occurred.

11. If a sexual harassment problem is common knowledge in a workplace, the courts assume that the employer has knowledge of it.

Answers: (1) False, (2) False, (3) True, (4) True, (5) False, (6) False, (7) False, (8) False, (9) False, (10) False, (11) True

*Sources: Industry Week,* November 18, 1991, p. 40; *Sexual Harassment Manual for Managers and Supervisors* (Chicago: Commerce Clearing House, 1992), p. 22: Andrea P. Brandon and David R. Eyler, *Working Together* (New York: McGraw-Hill, 1994).

**PRIVACY.** Modern technology has given business owners the ability to monitor workers' performances as they never could before, but where is the line between monitoring productivity and invasion of privacy? With a few mouse clicks, it is possible for managers to view e-mail messages employees send to one another, listen to voice mail or telephone conversations, and actually see what is on their monitors while they are sitting at their computer terminals. Managers use electronic monitoring to track customer service representatives, word-processing clerks, data entry technicians, and other workers for speed, accuracy, and productivity. Even truck drivers, the lone rangers of the road, are not immune to electronic tracking. Almost two-thirds of the major trucking companies now have communications devices in their trucks that allow them to monitor drivers' exact locations at all times, to regulate their speed, to make sure they stop only at approved fueling points, and to ensure that they take the legally required hours of rest. Although many drivers support the use of these devices, others worry about their tendency to create an overbearing work atmosphere.

E-mail also poses an ethical problem for employers. Experts estimate that Internet users send more than 183 billion e-mails each day.[43] Although many of the e-mails sent are unwanted spam, e-mail has become a common method of communication among employees. Forrester Research reports that workers in the average company send 23 million e-mail messages per year.[44] Most of those workers do not realize that, in many states, employers legally can monitor their e-mail and voice mail messages without notification. Only in a few states are companies required to have the consent of all parties involved in a communication before they can monitor it. According to the Electronic Monitoring & Surveillance Survey, 55 percent of businesses monitor employees' e-mail.[45] To avoid ethical (and legal) problems, business owners should follow these guidelines:

■ *Establish a clear policy for monitoring employees' communications.* Employees should know that the company is monitoring their e-mails and other forms of communication, and the best way to make sure they do is to create an unambiguous policy. Once you create a policy, be sure to follow it. Some managers ask employees to sign a consent form acknowledging that they have read and understand the company's monitoring policy.

■ *Create guidelines for the proper use of the company's communication technology, and communicate them to everyone.* A company's policies and guidelines should be reasonable and should reflect employees' reasonable expectations of privacy.

■ *Monitor in moderation.* Employees resent monitoring that is unnecessarily invasive. In addition, excessively draconian monitoring may land a company in a legal battle.

## Think Before You Send That E-mail

Bonita Bourke and Rhonda Hall worked as customer service representatives for Nissan Motor Corporation, where they helped managers and employees at dealerships resolve problems with a new computer system that the company had implemented to help run dealerships more efficiently. During a training session on the system, one of Bonita Bourke's coworkers, Lori Eaton, was demonstrating how dealerships could use the systems' e-mail feature as a management tool. As part of the demonstration, she randomly selected an e-mail that Bourke had sent to an employee at a Nissan dealership. Unfortunately, the e-mail was a personal one rather than one with a business purpose and contained sexual comments.

Eaton reported the incident to her supervisor, who reviewed the e-mails of all of the employees in Bourke's work group. He found a substantial number of e-mails from Bourke and Hall with similar content, much of it sexual and inappropriate in a business setting. The supervisor issued written warnings to both Bourke and Hall for violating the company's policy that prohibits the use of Nissan's e-mail system for personal purposes.

According to previous job evaluations, Bourke's job performance was sub-standard, and after the e-mail incident, her performance declined. Eleven months after the e-mail incident, Bourke's job evaluation was rated "needs improvement," the second lowest category. Hall also received negative performance reviews during this time. Her supervisor wrote that she spent too much time on personal business and that she needed to demonstrate more initiative to learn the new computer system. She received the lowest performance rating, which was "unsatisfactory." Two months later, Bourke and Hall filed complaints with the human resources department, claiming that the company had invaded their privacy by reading their e-mail messages.

Two weeks later, Bourke's supervisor told her that if her performance did not improve over the next three months, that she would be fired. She resigned the next day, the same day that Nissan fired Hall. Bourke and Hall filed a lawsuit against Nissan, alleging invasion of privacy, wrongful termination, and violation of the right to privacy under the U.S. Constitution. They argued that because the company gave them passwords to access the computer system and told them to safeguard their passwords, they believed that their e-mail messages would remain private. In its answer to the lawsuit, Nissan argued that employees had no reasonable expectation of privacy in their e-mail communications. The company pointed to a statement of company policy that the plaintiffs had signed: It is "company policy that employees restrict their use of company-owned computer hardware and software to company business." Furthermore, both employees knew that managers sometimes reviewed the e-mail messages that employees sent. Nissan argued that given these facts, employees could not reasonably expect that their e-mail communications were private.

Many e-mail privacy cases such as *Bourke vs. Nissan Motor Corporation* have landed in courts in recent years. E-mail monitoring is a common practice among companies; a survey by the American Management Association reports that 55 percent of businesses retain and review employees' e-mail messages. Furthermore, 25 percent of companies say that they have fired workers for e-mail abuse. The best way for companies to avoid legal problems over e-mail privacy is to create a policy that states that employees have no expectation that their e-mails are private and that the company reserves the right to monitor e-mail activity. The policy also should address the appropriate use of the company's e-mail system. Employees should sign the policy as well.

Many workers are blissfully unaware that their e-mail activity is anything but private. "If your e-mails are being monitored and you send a message that violates your company's policy and you are terminated for that message, you will have a hard time making a claim of invasion of privacy stick," says one expert. However, some courts have upheld employees' right to e-mail privacy because they require "all party consent" for an employer to monitor e-mail communications. In other words, both the sender and the receiver of the e-mail message must be aware that the company is monitoring their communications.

*(continued)*

1. If you were the judge in the *Bourke vs. Nissan Motor Corporation* case, how would you rule? Explain your reasoning.
2. What steps can companies that monitor employees' e-mail take to protect themselves against invasion of privacy lawsuits?

*Sources:* Adapted from "2005 Electronic Monitoring & Surveillance Survey: Many Companies Monitoring, Recording, Videotaping—and Firing—Employees," American Management Association, www. amanet.org/press/amanews/ems05.htm; Andrea Coombes, "Privacy at Work" Don't Count on It: Employers Are Tracking E-mail, *Career Journal.com,* July 1, 2005, www.careerjournal.com/myc/killers/ 20050701-coombes.html; *Bourke vs. Nissan Motor Corporation,* B068705 (Cal. Ct. App. July 26, 1993).

## Businesses' Responsibility to Customers

**7.** Explain businesses' responsibility to customers.

One of the most important groups of stakeholders that a business must satisfy is its *customers.* Building and maintaining a base of loyal customers is no easy task, it requires more than just selling a product or a service. The key is to build relationships with customers. Socially responsible companies recognize their duty to abide by the Consumer Bill of Rights, first put forth by U.S. President John Kennedy. This document gives consumers the following rights.

**RIGHT TO SAFETY.** The right to safety is the most basic consumer right. Companies have the responsibility to provide their customers with safe, quality products and services. The greatest breach of trust occurs when businesses produce products that, when properly used, injure customers. Product liability cases can be controversial, such as the McDonald's coffee lawsuit, in which a jury found that the fast-food giant's coffee was "too hot" and caused a serious injury when a customer spilled coffee in her lap. In many other situations, the evidence was clear that a product suffers from fundamental flaws in either design or construction and resulted in injury to its user when used properly.

Many companies have responded by placing detailed warning labels on their products that sometimes insult customers' intelligence. Consider the following actual examples from product warning labels:

- "Do not eat toner" on a toner cartridge for a laser printer.
- "Do not use orally" on a toilet bowl cleaning brush.
- "Do not try to dry your phone in a microwave oven" in the instructions for a cellular phone.
- "Caution: Remove infant before folding for storage" on a baby stroller.[46]

**RIGHT TO KNOW.** Consumers have the right to honest communication about the products and services they buy and the companies that sell them. In a free market economy, information is one of the most valuable commodities available. Customers often depend on companies for the information they need to make decisions about price, quality, features, and other factors. As a result, companies have a responsibility to customers to be truthful in their advertising.

Unfortunately, not every business recognizes its social responsibility to be truthful in advertising. The U.S. Federal Trade Commission (FTC), for example, filed a false advertising lawsuit against a small company that was selling an exercise device that the company claimed would allow users "to lose from 4 to 14 inches guaranteed in just 7 days" by "supercharging their blood with fat-burning oxygen." The infomercial that promoted the $54.85 device (including shipping and handling) ran more than 2,000 times on cable channels across the United States. As a result of the FTC's action, the company agreed to refund to customers $2.6 million and to stop their false advertising campaign.[47] Businesses that rely on unscrupulous tactics may profit in the short-term, but they will not last in the long-run.

**RIGHT TO BE HEARD.** The right to be heard suggests that the channels of communication between companies and their customers run in both directions. Socially responsible businesses provide customers with a mechanism for resolving complaints about products and services. Some companies have established a consumer ombudsman to address customer questions and complaints. Others have created customer hotlines, toll-free numbers designed to serve customers more effectively.

Another effective technique for encouraging two-way communication between customers and companies is the customer report card. The Granite Rock Company relies on an annual report card from its customers to learn how to serve them better. Although the knowledge a small business owner gets from customer feedback is immeasurable for making improvements, only one in 12 small companies regularly schedules customer satisfaction surveys such as Granite Rock's. It is a tool that can boost a company's profitability significantly.

**RIGHT TO EDUCATION.** Socially responsible companies give customers access to educational programs about their products and services and how to use them properly. The goal is to give customers enough information to make informed purchase decisions. A product that is the wrong solution to the customer's needs will only result in a disappointed customer who is likely to blame the manufacturer or retailer for the mistake. Consumer education is an inexpensive investment in customer satisfaction and the increased probability that a satisfied customer is a repeat buyer.

**RIGHT TO CHOICE.** Inherent in the free enterprise system is the consumer's right to choose among competing products and services. Socially responsible companies do not restrict competition, and they abide by the United States' antitrust policy, which promotes free trade and competition in the market. The foundation of this policy is the U.S. Sherman Antitrust Act of 1890, which forbids agreements among sellers that restrain trade or commerce and outlaws any attempts to monopolize a market.

## Businesses' Responsibility to Investors

**8.** Discuss businesses' responsibility to investors.

Companies have the responsibility to provide investors with an attractive return on their investment. Although earning a profit may be a company's *first* responsibility, it is not its *only* responsibility; meeting its ethical and social responsibility goals is also a key to success. Investors today want to know that entrepreneurs are making ethical decisions and acting in a socially responsible manner. In a recent survey by Opinion Research Corporation, 76 percent of investors say that they would move their investments from companies that engage in unethical but legal behavior, even if the company's action produced a high return on their investment.[48] Maintaining high standards of ethics and social responsibility translates into a business culture that sets the stage for a profitable business operation.

Companies also have the responsibility to report their financial performances in an accurate and timely fashion to their investors. Businesses that misrepresent or falsify their financial and operating records are guilty of violating the fiduciary relationship with their investors.

*John and Timothy Rigas and Adelphia*

A jury found John Rigas, founder of cable television company Adelphia, and his son Timothy, who served as Adelphia's CFO, guilty of siphoning $60 million from the company to purchase shares of Adelphia stock and personal luxuries such as condominiums, shoes, limousines, and gifts. Prosecutors charged that the Rigases "used Adelphia as a private ATM" and that they "systematically looted" investors in the company. John and Timothy are now serving 15- and 20-year jail terms, respectively, and the company that John founded and built for 50 years is gone, sold in pieces to competitors Time Warner and Comcast.[49]

## Businesses' Responsibility to the Community

**9.** Discuss businesses' responsibility to the community.

As corporate citizens, businesses have a responsibility to the communities in which they operate. In addition to providing jobs and creating wealth, companies contribute to the local community in many different ways. Socially responsible businesses are aware of their duty to put back into the community some of what they take out as they generate profits; their goal is to become a neighbor of choice.

The following are just a few examples of ways small businesses have found to give back to their communities:

- Act as volunteers for community groups such as the Red Cross, literacy programs, and a community food bank.
- Participate in projects that aid the elderly or economically disadvantaged.
- Adopt a highway near the business to promote a clean community.

According to a survey by the Society for Human Resource Management, 80 percent of companies worldwide engage in some type of socially responsible activity.[50] These companies commit talent and know-how, not just dollars, to pressing but carefully chosen social needs and then tell the world about their cause and their dedication to serving it. Through the association, both the businesses and the causes benefited in unique ways. Over the years, associations have helped social causes enjoy financial rewards and unprecedented support both inside and outside companies. They also have helped companies enhance their reputations, deepen employee loyalty, strengthen ties with business partners, and sell more products or services.

**ENTREPRENEURIAL Profile**

*Stewart Spinks and Spinx Company*

Stewart Spinks, founder of the Spinx Company, a business that operates 78 convenience stores and gas stations (some of which include Arby's, Subway, and Burger King franchises), understands the importance of making sure that his company gives back to the communities in which it operates. During the two weeks after Hurricane Katrina, Spinx donated 100 percent of its profits to the Red Cross's hurricane relief effort. The company also gives thousand of dollars each year to the Muscular Dystrophy Association, Red Ribbon, St. Jude's Children's Hospital, and other organizations. Spinks, who started with just a single gas station in 1972, now has more than 1,000 employees, and his company generates annual sales of $285 million. Just as important to Spinks is knowing that the communities that his company serves see Spinx as a good corporate citizen and a generous donor to worthwhile community causes.[51]

One of the stores owned by Stewart Spinks, who makes sure that his business is a good corporate citizen by giving back to the communities in which the company operates.

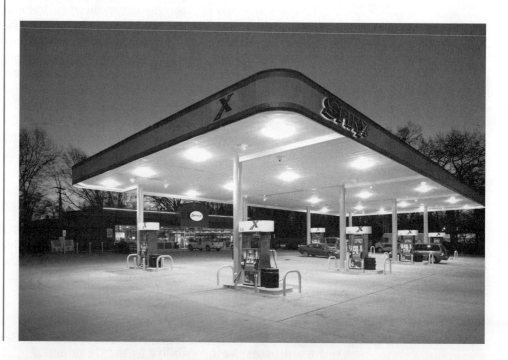

Entrepreneurs such as Spinks who demonstrate their sense of social responsibility not only make their communities better places to live and work but also stand out from their competitors. Their efforts to operate ethical, socially responsible businesses create a strong sense of loyalty among their customers and their employees.

# Conclusion

Businesses must do more than merely earn profits; they must act ethically and in a socially responsible manner. Establishing and maintaining high ethical and socially responsible standards must be a top concern of every business owner. Managing in an ethical and socially responsible manner presents a tremendous challenge, however. There is no universal definition of ethical behavior, and what is considered ethical may change over time and may be different in other cultures.

Finally, business owners and managers must recognize the key role they play in influencing their employees' ethical and socially responsible behavior. What owners and managers *say* is important, but what they *do* is even more important! Employees in a small company look to the owner and managers as models; therefore, these owners and managers must commit themselves to following the highest ethical standards if they expect their employees to do so.

# Chapter Review

1. Define business ethics and describe the three levels of ethical standards.
   * Business ethics involves the fundamental moral values and behavioral standards that form the foundation for the people of an organization as they make decisions and interact with organizational stakeholders. Small business managers must consider the ethical and social as well as the economic implications of their decisions.
   * The three levels of ethical standards are (1) the law, (2) the policies and procedures of the company, and (3) the moral stance of the individual.

2. Determine who is responsible for ethical behavior and why ethical lapses occur.
   * Managers set the moral tone of the organization. There are three ethical styles of management: immoral, amoral, and moral. Although moral management has value in itself, companies that operate with this philosophy discover other benefits, including a positive reputation among customers and employees.
   * Ethical lapses occur for a variety of reasons:
     Some people are corrupt ("the bad apple").
     The company culture has been poisoned ("the bad barrel").
     Competitive pressures push managers to compromise.
     Managers are tempted by an opportunity to "get ahead."
     Managers in different cultures have different views of what is ethical.

3. Explain how to establish and maintain high ethical standards.
   * Philosophers throughout history have developed various tests of ethical behavior: the utilitarian principle, Kant's categorical imperative, the professional ethic, the Golden Rule, the television test, and the family test.
   * A small business manager can maintain high ethical standards in the following ways:
     Create a company credo.
     Develop a code of ethics.
     Enforce the code fairly and consistently.
     Hire the right people.
     Conduct ethical training.
     Perform periodic ethical audits.
     Establish high standards of behavior, not just rules.
     Set an impeccable ethical example at all times.
     Create a culture emphasizing two-way communication.
     Involve employees in establishing ethical standards.

4. Define social responsibility.
   * Social responsibility is the awareness of a company's managers of the social, environmental, political, human, and financial consequences of their actions.

5. Understand the nature of businesses' responsibility to the environment.
   - Environmentally responsible business owners focus on the three Rs: reduce, reuse, recycle: *reduce* the amount of materials used in the company from the factory floor to the copier room; *reuse* whatever you can; and *recycle* the materials that you must dispose of.
6. Describe businesses' responsibility to employees.
   - Companies have a duty to act responsibly toward one of their most important stakeholders: their employees. Businesses must recognize and manage the cultural diversity that exists in the workplace; establish a responsible strategy for combating substance abuse in the workplace (including drug testing) and dealing with AIDS; prevent sexual harassment; and respect employees' right to privacy.
7. Explain businesses' responsibility to customers.
   - Every company's customers have a right to safe products and services; to honest, accurate information; to be heard; to education about products and services; and to choices in the marketplace.
8. Discuss businesses' responsibility to investors.
   - Companies have the responsibility to provide investors with an attractive return on their investments and to report their financial performances in an accurate and timely fashion to their investors.
9. Describe a business's responsibility to the community.
   - Increasingly, companies are seeing a need to go beyond "doing well" to "doing good"—being socially responsible community citizens. In addition to providing jobs and creating wealth, companies contribute to the local community in many different ways.

## Discussion Questions

1. What is ethics? Discuss the three levels of ethical standards.
2. In any organization, who determines ethical behavior? Briefly describe the three ethical styles of management. What are the benefits of moral management?
3. Why do ethical lapses occur in businesses?
4. Describe the various methods for establishing ethical standards. Which is most meaningful to you? Why?
5. What can business owners do to maintain high ethical standards in their companies?
6. What is social responsibility?
7. Describe businesses' social responsibility to each of the following areas:
   - The environment
   - Employees
   - Customers
   - Investors
   - The community
8. What can businesses do to improve the quality of our environment?

9. Should companies be allowed to test employees for drugs? Explain. How should a socially responsible drug testing program operate?
10. Many owners of trucking companies use electronic communications equipment to monitor their drivers on the road. They say that the devices allow them to remain competitive and to serve their customers better by delivering shipments of vital materials exactly when their customers need them. They also point out that the equipment can improve road safety by ensuring that drivers get the hours of rest the law requires. Opponents argue that the surveillance devices work against safety. "The drivers know they're being watched," says one trucker. "There's an obvious temptation to push?" What do you think? What ethical issues does the use of such equipment create? How should a small trucking company considering the use of such equipment handle these issues?
11. What rights do customers have under the Consumer Bill of Rights? How can businesses ensure those rights?

# Business PlanPro

Businesses have a responsibility to both "do well"—earn a profit, remain financially sound, and stay in business—and "do good"—operate ethically and meet their responsibility to society. It is critical for business owners to recognize their obligation to operate their businesses in an ethical and socially responsible manner. They must consider these issues as essential elements of a successful and sustainable business. They must create a culture that encourages employees to recognize ethical dilemmas and to do what is right when faced with ethical dilemmas. Values-based leaders integrate the ethical dimensions of their actions and decisions as well as those of their employees into the fabric of their companies' culture. They establish ethical guidelines, conduct training sessions in ethics, and, most important, set an example for ethical behavior in the organization. These leaders understand that ethical behavior does not simply happen in an organization; it is the result of a conscious effort that involves everyone. They also recognize that their companies have a responsibility to society that extends far beyond merely earning a profit. The business plan must capture this broader sense of ethical and social responsibility to all stakeholders.

## On the Web

The Internet offers a wealth of information regarding business ethics and a company's responsibility to investors, employees, customers, the community, and the environment. You will find some of these resources on the Companion Website at www.prenhall.com/scarborough for Chapter 21.

These links may help you to integrate ethical standards into the fabric of your business plan.

## In the Software

Review all divisions of your plan. Attempt to take an objective look to determine whether your plan communicates a values-based leadership approach. Consider these questions:

- How does your plan describe the company's responsibility to its employees?
- How does the plan describe its responsibility to investors?
- How does your plan describe its responsibility to customers?
- What does the business plan communicate about the company's responsibility to the community?
- Does the plan explain how the business operates in an environmentally responsible manner?
- Does the plan describe a business that offers long-term sustainability?

## Building Your Business Plan

The business plan will help you to identify the key stakeholders in your company, verbalize your philosophy of business ethics, identify the best way to establish high ethical standards, and explain the level of your company's commitment to socially responsible actions. Consider including the description of your philosophy of ethics and social responsibility in the plan's "Strategy and Implementation" section. Your analysis of these important issues also may lead you to modify your company's mission statement.

# The Legal Environment: Business Law and Government Regulation

A law is something that must have a moral basis so that there is an inner compelling force for every citizen to obey.
—Chaim Weizmann

A wise and frugal government, which shall leave men free to regulate their own pursuits of industry and improvement, and shall not take from the mouth of labor the bread it has earned—this is the sum of good government.
—Thomas Jefferson

## Learning Objectives

**Upon completion of this chapter, you will be able to:**

1 Explain the basic elements required to create a valid, enforceable contract.

2 Outline the major components of the U.S. Uniform Commercial Code governing sales contracts.

3 Discuss the protection of intellectual property rights using patents, trademarks, and copyrights.

4 Explain the basics of the law of agency.

5 Explain the basics of bankruptcy law.

6 Explain some of the government regulations affecting small businesses, including those governing trade practices, consumer protection, consumer credit, and the environment.

T he legal environment in which small businesses operate is becoming more complex, and entrepreneurs must understand the basics of business law if they are to avoid legal entanglements. Situations that present potential legal problems arise every day in most small businesses although the majority of small business owners never recognize them. Routine transactions with customers, suppliers, employees, government agencies, and others have the potential to develop into costly legal problems. For example, a manufacturer of lawn-mowers might face a lawsuit if a customer injures himself while using the product, or a customer who slips on a wet floor while shopping could sue the retailer for negligence. A small manufacturer who reneges on a contract for a needed raw material when he or she finds a better price elsewhere may be open to a breach of contract suit. Even when they win a lawsuit, small businesses often lose because the costs of defending themselves can run quickly into thousands of dollars, depleting their already scarce resources.

**Pamela Reeder and Victoria Dauernheim and Haute Diggity Dog**

Luxury goods giant Louis Vuitton Malletier SA of Paris recently filed a lawsuit against Haute Diggity Dog, a Las Vegas-based business with just five employees (counting its two co-owners), claiming that the small company was guilty of trademark infringement because it was selling stuffed toys and pillows for dogs with the name "Chewy Vuitton" on them. Even though a U.S. court in Virginia dismissed the claim and ruled in favor of the Haute Diggity Dog, the small company incurred significant costs as a result of the lawsuit. Legal fees, which co-owners Pamela Reeder and Victoria Dauernheim expected to be $50,000, escalated to $200,000 and will go higher because Louis Vuitton decided to appeal the ruling. "We decided that we had to fight back because [otherwise] we would have had to go out of business," says Pamela Reeder. Before the distractions of the lawsuit, Reeder and Dauernheim expected sales of Haute Diggity Dog to hit $2 million per year; now they are hoping to at least match the $1 million they had generated in sales before the lawsuit even though they are introducing new parody dog toys such as a "Pawda" bag and a "Growlex" watch.[1]

As Reeder and Dauernheim learned, lawsuits also are bothersome distractions that prevent entrepreneurs from focusing their energy on running their businesses. In addition, one big judgment against a small company in a legal case could force it out of business. Judgments, the financial penalties that a company must pay if it loses a lawsuit, take three forms: compensatory, consequential, and punitive damages. As their name implies, **compensatory damages** are the monetary damages that are designed to place the plaintiff in the same position he or she would have been in had a contract been performed. In other words, compensatory damages require the defendant to pay the actual amount of loss the plaintiff incurred because of the defendant's actions. Suppose that a small manufacturer creates a contract to deliver 1,000 plastic barrels for $80 per unit by a particular date. If it fails to do so and the customer must purchase the barrels from another supplier for $88 per unit and pay an additional $500 for rush delivery, the customer's compensatory damages are $8,500 (1,000 barrels × $8 price difference plus $500 rush delivery charges). **Consequential damages** are awarded to offset the losses suffered by the plaintiff that go beyond simple compensatory damages because of lasting effects of the damage. If the customer in the previous example lost $15,000 in sales because it did not receive the barrels on time, it could request consequential damages in that amount. For a party to recover consequential damages, the breaching party must have known the consequences of the breach. Courts typically award **punitive damages** in cases in which the defendant engages in intentionally wrongful behavior or behavior that is so negligent or reckless that it is considered intentional. As the name suggests, punitive damages are intended to punish the wrongdoer. Many states have imposed limits on punitive damages in court cases.

**Cindy Brillman and CGB Inc.**

After seven years of litigation, two trials, and two appeals, a U.S. Court of Appeals reduced a federal trial judge's award of $2 million (A jury originally had imposed $30 million in punitive damages, which the judge reduced to $2 million.) in a case to $750,000, saying that the judge's punitive award, which was 18 times greater than the compensatory damages in the case, was unconstitutionally excessive. In the lawsuit, plaintiff CGB, an occupational therapy firm owned by Cindy Brillman, claimed that Sunrise Assisted Living, a nursing home management company, had committed the tort of wrongful interference with a contractual relationship by inducing two nursing homes to terminate their contracts with CGB and then hire away five of its twenty occupational therapists. In addition to the punitive damages, CGB received $109,000 in compensatory damages.[2]

Small business owners should know the basics of the laws that govern business practices to minimize the chances that their decisions and actions lead to costly lawsuits. This chapter is not designed to make you an expert in business law or the regulations that govern businesses but to make you aware of the fundamental legal issues of which every business owner should be aware. Entrepreneurs should consult their attorneys for advice on legal questions involving specific situations.

## The Law of Contracts

*1.* Explain the basic elements required to create a valid, enforceable contract.

Contract law governs the rights and obligations among the parties to an agreement. It is a body of laws that affects virtually every business relationship. A **contract** is simply a legally binding agreement. It is a promise or a set of promises for the breach of which the law gives a remedy, or the performance of which the law in some way recognizes as a duty. A contract arises from an agreement, and it creates an obligation among the parties involved. Although almost everyone has the capacity to enter into a contractual agreement (freedom of contract), not every contract is valid and enforceable. A **valid contract** has four separate elements:

1. *Agreement.* A valid offer by one party that is accepted by the other.
2. *Consideration.* Something of legal value that the parties exchange as part of a bargain.
3. *Contractual capacity.* The parties must be adults capable of understanding the consequences of their agreement.
4. *Legality.* The parties' contract must be for a legal purpose.

In addition, to be enforceable, a contract must meet two supplemental requirements: *genuineness of assent and form. Genuineness of assent* is a test to make sure that the parties' agreement is genuine and not subject to problems such as fraud, misrepresentation, or mistakes. *Form* involves the writing requirement for certain types of contracts. Although not every contract must be in writing to be enforceable, the law does require some contracts to be evidenced by writing.

### Agreement

Agreement requires a "meeting of the minds" and is established by an offer and an acceptance. One party must make an offer to another, who must accept that offer. Agreement is governed by the **objective theory of contracts**, which states that a party's intention to create a contract is measured by outward facts—words, conduct, and circumstances—rather than by subjective, personal intentions. When settling contract disputes, courts interpret the objective facts surrounding the contract from the perspective of an imaginary reasonable person.

ENTREPRENEURIAL
**Profile**

Carbaugh vs. Klick-Lewis Buick-Chevrolet-Pontiac

Klick-Lewis, a car dealership, offered a new Chevrolet Beretta as a prize to any person who hit a hole-in-one on the ninth hole of a golf tournament. It displayed the car at the tee box of the ninth hole with a sign saying, "HOLE-IN-ONE Wins this 1988 Chevrolet Beretta GI Courtesy of Klick-Lewis Buick-Chevrolet-Pontiac $49.00 OVER FACTORY INVOICE in Palmyra." Amos Carbaugh was playing in the East End Open Golf Tournament and scored a hole-in-one on the ninth hole, but when he attempted to claim the prize, Klick-Lewis refused to sell him the car at $49.00 over invoice. The dealer said that it had offered the car as a prize in another golf tournament that had taken place two days earlier and that it had simply neglected to remove the car and the sign before the tournament in which Carbaugh was playing. Carbaugh filed a lawsuit against Klick-Lewis and won the right to buy the car at $49.00 over invoice. The court said that, based on the objective theory of contracts, an imaginary reasonable person in Carbaugh's position would have believed that the dealership was making an offer, citing the presence of the sign, the car, and no mention of a specific golf tournament. Klick-Lewis's *subjective* intent was irrelevant.[3]

Agreement requires that one of the parties to a contract make an offer and the other an acceptance.

**OFFER.** An **offer** is a promise or commitment to do or refrain from doing some specified thing in the future. For an offer to stand there must be an intention to be bound by it. The terms of the offer must be defined and reasonably certain, and the offeror (the party making the offer) must communicate the offer to the offeree (the party to whom the offer is made). The offeror must genuinely intend to make an offer, and the offer's terms must be definite, not vague. The following terms must either be expressed or be capable of being implied in an offer: the parties involved; the identity of the subject matter (which goods or services); and the quantity. Other terms of the offer should specify price, delivery terms, payment terms, timing, and shipping terms. Although these elements are not required, the more terms a party specifies, the more likely it is that an offer exists.

Courts often supply missing terms in a contract when there is a reliable basis for doing so. For instance, the court usually supplies a time term that is reasonable for the circumstances. It supplies a price term (a reasonable price at the time of delivery) if a readily ascertainable market price exists; otherwise, a missing price term defeats the contract. On rare occasions, courts supply a quantity term, but a missing quantity term usually defeats a contract. For example, the small retailer who mails an advertising circular to a large number of customers is not making an offer because one major term—quantity—is missing. Similarly, price lists and catalogs sent to potential customers are not offers.

In general, an offeror can revoke an offer at any time prior to acceptance, but two exceptions to this rule exist: an option contract and a merchant's firm offer. In an **option contract**, the parties create a separate contract to keep an offer open for a particular time period. Option contracts are common in real estate transactions. For instance, the owner of a fast-food franchise created an option contract with the owner of a piece of land that the franchisee was considering purchasing. The landowner made an offer to sell the property to the franchisee, who wanted time to study the demographics, traffic count, and other data at the potential location but did not want to lose a promising piece of real estate by having the owner sell it to someone else. The franchisee and the landowner created an option contract; the franchisee paid the landowner $5,000 for a six-month option on the land, which meant that the landowner could not revoke his offer to sell the property during the six-month option.

The other exception to the revocation-before-acceptance rule is a **merchant's firm offer**. If a merchant seller (a merchant is defined later in this chapter in the section on the U.S. Uniform Commercial Code) makes a promise or assurance to hold an offer open in writing, the offer is irrevocable for the stated time period or, if no time is stated, for a reasonable time period. Neither time period can exceed 90 days, however.

An offer must always be communicated to the other party because one cannot agree to a contract unless he or she knows it exists. The offeror may communicate an offer verbally, in writing, or by action.

Offers do not last forever. Several actions by either party, the offeror or the offeree, can cause an offer to terminate. In addition, the law itself can cause an offer to cease to exist. As you have learned, an offeror can revoke an offer as long as he or she does so before the offeree accepts it. The offeree can cause an offer to terminate by rejecting the offer (e.g., saying "no" to it) or by making a counteroffer. For instance, suppose that an entrepreneur offers to purchase a piece of land for $175,000. The landowner responds, "Your price is too low, but I'll sell it to you for $190,000." When the landowner made the counteroffer, the entrepreneur's original offer terminated. An offer terminates by operation of the law if the time specified in the offer has elapsed ("This offer is good until noon on October 7."), if the subject matter of the offer is destroyed before the offeree accepts, or if either the offeror or the offeree dies or becomes incapacitated before the offeree accepts the offer.

**ACCEPTANCE.** Only the person to whom the offer is made (the offeree) can accept an offer and create a contract. The offeree must accept voluntarily, agreeing to the terms exactly as the offeror presents them. When an offeree suggests alternative terms or conditions to those in the original offer, he or she is implicitly rejecting the original offer and making a counteroffer. Common law requires that the offeree's acceptance exactly match the original offer. This is called the **mirror image rule**, which says that an offeree's acceptance must be the mirror image of the offeror's offer.

Generally, silence by the offeree cannot constitute acceptance, even if the offer contains statements to the contrary. For instance, when an offeror claims, "If you do not respond to this offer by Friday at noon, I conclude your silence to be your acceptance," no acceptance exists even if the offeree does remain silent. The law requires an offeree to act affirmatively to accept an offer in most cases.

An offeree must accept an offer by the means of communication authorized and within the time limits specified by the offeror. Generally, offers accepted by alternative media or after specified deadlines are ineffective. If the offeror specifies no means of communication, the offeree must use the same medium used to extend the offer (or a faster method). According to the **mailbox rule** (which is more formally known as the **deposited acceptance rule**), if an offeree accepts by mail, the acceptance is effective when the letter is dropped in the mailbox, even if it never reaches the offeror. Also, all offers must be properly dispatched; that is, they must be properly addressed, noted, and stamped.

### Consideration

Contracts are based on promises, and because it is often difficult to distinguish between promises that are serious and those that are not, courts require that consideration be present in virtually every contract. **Consideration** is something of *legal* value (*not* necessarily economic value) that the parties to a contract bargain for and exchange as the "price" for the promise given. Consideration can be money, but parties most often swap promises for promises. For example, when a buyer promises to buy an item and a seller promises to sell it, valuable consideration exists. The buyer's promise to buy and the seller's promise to sell constitute the consideration for their contract. To comprise valuable consideration, a promise must impose a liability or create a duty.

For a contract to be binding, the two parties involved must exchange valuable consideration. The absence of consideration makes a promise unenforceable. A promise to perform something one is already legally obligated to do is not valuable consideration. Because consideration is something that a promisor requires in exchange for his promise ("bargained for"), past consideration is not valid. In addition, under the common law, new promises require new consideration. For instance, if two businesspeople have an existing contract for performance of a service, any modifications to that contract must be supported by new consideration. In some states, promises made in exchange for "love and affection" are not enforceable because the contract lacks valuable consideration.

One important exception to the requirement for valuable consideration is **promissory estoppel**. Under this rule, a promise that induces another party to act can be enforceable without consideration if the promisee substantially and justifiably relies on the promise. Thus, promissory estoppel is a substitute for consideration.

## ENTREPRENEURIAL Profile

**Joseph Hoffman vs. Red Owl Stores**

Joseph Hoffman owned a bakery but wanted to open a Red Owl grocery store. He approached Edward Lukowitz, a division manager for Red Owl, and told him that he had $18,000 to invest in a Red Owl franchise. Lukowitz assured Hoffman that $18,000 was sufficient to set him up in business as a Red Owl franchisee. However, Lukowitz suggested that Hoffman needed experience running a grocery store before he became a Red Owl franchisee, and Hoffman purchased a small grocery store in Wautoma. After several months, Red Owl confirmed that Hoffman was operating the store at a profit. Lukowitz then told Hoffman that he would have to sell the grocery store to purchase a Red Owl franchise, and Hoffman sold the store to one of his employees. In a meeting, Lukowitz assured Hoffman that "everything is ready to go. Get your money together and we are set." Shortly after this meeting Lukowitz told Hoffman that he would have to sell his bakery business and building, and that this was the only "hitch" that remained. Hoffman sold the bakery and the building and moved to Chilton, Wisconsin, where Red Owl had found a potential site for a store. During this time, however, Red Owl Stores raised the price of the franchise from $18,000 to $24,100, and later to $26,100. Hoffman ended negotiations with Red Owl and filed a lawsuit, claiming that although Hoffman had not given any consideration, he had justifiably relied on Red Owl's promises to his detriment. The court applied the doctrine of promissory estoppel and ruled in favor of Hoffman.[4]

In most cases, courts do not evaluate the adequacy of consideration given for a promise. In other words, there is no legal requirement that the consideration the parties exchange be of approximately equal value. Even if the value of the consideration one party gives is small compared to the value of the consideration the other party provides, the bargain stands. Why? The law recognizes that people have the freedom to contract and that they are just as free to enter into "bad" bargains as they to enter into "good" ones. Only in extreme cases (e.g., cases affected by mistakes, misrepresentation, fraud, duress, and undue influence) will the court examine the value of the consideration provided in a trade.

## Contractual Capacity

The third element of a valid contract requires that the parties involved in it must have contractual capacity for it to be enforceable. Not every person who attempts to enter into a contract has the capacity to do so. Under the common law, minors, intoxicated people, and insane people lack or have limited contractual capacity. As a result, contracts these people attempt to enter are considered to be *voidable*—that is, the party can annul or disaffirm the contract at his or her option.

**MINORS.** Minors constitute the largest group of individuals with limited contractual capacity. In most states, anyone under the age 18 is a minor in the United States, for example. With a few exceptions, any contract made by a minor is voidable at the minor's option. In addition, a minor can avoid a contract during minority and for "a reasonable time" afterwards. The adult involved in the contract cannot avoid it simply because he is dealing with a minor.

In most states, if a minor receives the benefit of a completed contract and then disaffirms that contract, he or she must fulfill the *duty of restoration* by returning the benefit. In other words, the minor must return any consideration he or she has received under the contract to the adult and is entitled to receive any consideration he or she gave the adult under the contract. The minor must return the benefit of the contract no matter what form or condition it is in. For instance, suppose that Brighton, a 16-year-old minor, purchases a mountain bike for $415 from Cycle Time, a small bicycle shop. After riding the bike for a little more than a year, Brighton decides to disaffirm the contract. Under the law, all he must do is return the mountain bike to Cycle Time, whatever condition it is in (pristine, used, wrecked, or rubble), and he is entitled to get all of his money back. In most U.S. states, he does not have to pay Cycle Time for the use of the bike or the damage done to it. A few states impose an additional duty on minors. In these states, the *duty of restitution* requires that minors who disaffirm contracts return any consideration they received to the adult and must pay a "reasonable value" for the depreciation of or damage to the item (which is usually less than the actual value of the depreciation of or damage to the item). Adults enter into contracts with minors at their own risk.

Parents are usually not liable for any contracts made by their children, although a cosigner is bound equally with a minor. Entrepreneurs can protect themselves when dealing with minors by requiring an adult to cosign. If the minor disaffirms the contract, the adult cosigner remains bound by it.

**INTOXICATED PEOPLE.** A contract entered into by an intoxicated person can be either voidable or valid, depending on the person's condition when entering into the contract. If a person's reason and judgment are impaired so that he or she does not realize that he or she is making a contract, the contract is voidable (even if the intoxication was voluntary) and the benefit must be returned. However, if the intoxicated person understands that he or she is forming a contract, although it may be foolish, the contract is valid and enforceable.

**PEOPLE WITH MENTAL INCAPACITIES.** A contract entered into by a person with a mental incapacity can be void, voidable, or valid, depending on the mental state of the person. Those people who have been judged to be so mentally incompetent that a guardian is appointed for them cannot enter into a valid contract. If such a person does make a contract, it is *void* (i.e., it does not exist). An insane person who has not been legally declared insane nor appointed a guardian (e.g., someone suffering from Alzheimer's disease) is bound by a contract if he or she was lucid enough at the time of the contract to comprehend its consequences. On the other hand, if at the time of entering the contract, that same person was so mentally incompetent that he or she could not realize what was happening or could not understand the terms, the contract is voidable. Just as with minors, he or she must return any benefit received under the contract.

## Legality

The final element required for a valid contract is legality. The purpose of the parties' contract must be legal. Because society imposes certain standards of conduct on its members, contracts that are illegal (criminal or tortuous) or against public policy are void. Examples of these situations include contracts in which the stated interest rate exceeds the rate allowed by a state's usury laws; interstate gambling that is conducted in states where the type of gambling is illegal (casino games via the Internet); business transactions that violate a state's blue laws (creating certain types of contracts on Sunday); activities that require a practitioner to have a license to perform (e.g., attorneys, real estate brokers, contractors, and others); and free-standing contracts that restrain competition and trade.

If a contract contains both legal and illegal elements, courts will enforce the legal parts as long as they can separate the legal portion from the illegal portion. However, in some contracts, certain clauses are so unconscionable that the courts will not enforce them. Usually, the courts do not concern themselves with the fairness of a contract between parties because individuals are supposed to be intelligent. However, in the case of unconscionable contracts, the terms are so harsh and oppressive to one party that the courts often rule the clause to be void. These clauses, called **exculpatory clauses**, frequently attempt to free one party of all responsibility and liability for an injury or damage that might occur. For instance, suppose that Miguel Ferras signs an exculpatory clause when he leaves his new BMW with an attendant at a parking garage. The clause states that the garage is "not responsible for theft, loss, or damage to cars or articles left in cars due to fire, theft, or other causes." The attendant leaves Miguel's car unattended with the keys in the ignition, and a thief steals the car. A court would declare the exculpatory clause void because the garage owes a duty to its customers to exercise reasonable care to protect their property, a duty it breached because of gross negligence.

**GENUINENESS OF ASSENT AND THE FORM OF CONTRACTS.** A contract that contains the four elements just discussed—agreement, consideration, capacity, and legality—is *valid,* but a valid contract may be unenforceable because of two possible defenses against it: genuineness of assent and form. **Genuineness of assent** serves as a check on the parties' agreement, verifying that it is genuine and not subject to mistakes, misrepresentation, fraud, duress, or undue influence. The existence of a contract can be affected by mistakes that one or both parties to the contract make. Different types of mistakes exist, but only mistakes of *fact* permit a party to avoid a contract. Suppose that a small contractor submits a bid on the construction of a bridge, but the bidder mistakenly omits the cost of some materials. The client accepts the contractor's bid because it is $82,000 below all others. If the client knew or should have known of the mistake, the contractor can avoid the contract; otherwise, the contractor must build the bridge at the bid price.

Fraud also voids a contract because no genuineness of assent exists. **Fraud** is the intentional misrepresentation of a material fact, justifiably relied on, that results in injury to the innocent party. The misrepresentation with the intent to deceive can result from words (making false statements), conduct (taking actions to deceive another), or silence (failing to disclose a serious hidden defect that a seller knows the buyer will be unable to detect in a reasonable inspection). Suppose a small retailer purchases a new security system from a dealer who promises it will provide 20 years of reliable service and lower the cost of operation by 40 percent. The dealer then knowingly installs a used, unreliable system. In this case, the dealer has committed fraud, and the retailer can either rescind the contract with his or her original position restored or enforce it and seek damages for injuries.

**Duress**, forcing an individual into a contract by fear or threat, eliminates genuineness of assent. The innocent party can choose to carry out the contract or to avoid it. For example, if a supplier forces the owner of a small video arcade to enter a contract to lease the supplier's machines by threat of personal injury, the supplier is guilty of duress. Blackmail and extortion used to induce another party to enter a contract also constitute duress.

Generally, the law does not require contracts to follow a prescribed form; a contract is valid whether it is written or oral. Most contracts do *not* have to be in writing to be enforceable, but for convenience and protection, a small business owner should insist that every contract be in writing. If a contract is oral, the party attempting to enforce it must first prove its existence and then establish its actual terms. Although each state has its own rules, the Statute of Frauds, generally requires the following contracts to be in writing:

- Contracts for the sale of land.
- Contracts involving lesser interests in land (e.g., rights-of-way or leases lasting more than one year).
- Contracts that cannot by their terms be performed within one year.
- Collateral contracts such as promises to answer for the debt or duty of another.
- Promises by the administrator or executor of an estate to pay a debt of the estate personally.
- Contracts for the sale of goods (as opposed to services) priced above $500. (A proposal to raise this amount to $5,000 currently is under consideration.)

## Breach of Contract

The majority of contracts are discharged by both parties fully performing the terms of their agreement. Occasionally, however, one party fails to perform as agreed. This failure is called **breach of contract**, and the injured party has certain remedies available. A breach of contract can be either a minor breach in which substantial, but not complete, performance occurs, or a material breach of contract associated with non-performance or inferior performance. In cases where there exists a minor breach of contract, the party "in breach" may agree to complete the specific terms of the contract or compensate the other party for the unperformed component of the contract. If these two remedies are not accepted, the next step is legal action to recover the cost to repair the defect.

In contrast, a *material breach* occurs when a party renders inferior performance that impairs or destroys the essence of the contract. The non-breaching party may either rescind the contract and recover restitution or affirm the contract and recover damages. Of course, the injured party has the duty to mitigate the damages incurred. In other words, the nonbreaching party must make a reasonable effort to minimize the damages incurred by the breach.

**ENTREPRENEURIAL Profile**

Leroy Greer vs. 1-800-FLOWERS

Leroy Greer, a married man who was going through a divorce, filed a $1 million lawsuit for breach of contract against 1-800-FLOWERS for revealing to his wife that he was having an affair with another woman. When Greer ordered a cuddly stuffed animal and a dozen long-stem red roses for his girlfriend, he asked that the company keep his purchase private and was referred to 1-800-FLOWERS' privacy policy, which states that customers can ask the company not to share personal information with "third parties." Greer says that 1-800-FLOWERS violated its privacy policy by sending a thank you note for his order to his home, where his wife saw it. When she called the company, a customer service representative faxed a copy of the receipt from her husband's clandestine purchase. After Greer's wife learned about her husband's affair, she asked for a much larger divorce settlement, $300,000, in addition to child support, and Greer sued 1-800-FLOWERS.[5]

In some cases, monetary damages are inadequate to compensate an injured party for a defendant's breach of contract. The only remedy that would compensate the nonbreaching party might be specific performance of the act promised in the contract. **Specific performance** is usually the remedy for breached contracts dealing with unique item (antiques, land, and animals). For example, if an antique auto dealer enters a contract to purchase a rare Corvette and the other party breaches the contract, the dealer may sue for specific performance. That is, the dealer may ask the court to order the breaching party to sell the classic car. Courts rarely invoke the remedy of specific performance. Generally, contracts for performance of personal services are not subject to specific performance.

# The Uniform Commercial Code (UCC)

*2.* Outline the major components of the Uniform Commercial Code governing sales contracts.

For many years, sales contracts relating to the exchange of goods were governed by a loosely defined system of rules and customs called the *Lex Mercatoria* (Merchant Law). Many of these principles were assimilated into the U.S. common law through court opinions, but they varied widely from state to state and made interstate commerce difficult and confusing for businesses. In 1952, the commission on Uniform State Laws created the **Uniform Commercial Code** (or the **UCC** or the **Code**) to replace the hodge-podge collection of confusing, often conflicting state laws that governed basic commercial transactions with a document designed to provide uniformity and consistency. The UCC replaced numerous statutes governing trade when each of the states, the District of Columbia, and the Virgin Islands adopted it. (Louisiana has adopted only articles 1, 3, 4, and 5.) The Code, which has been updated numerous times over the years, does not alter the basic tenets of business law established by the common law; instead, it unites and modernizes them into a single body of law. In some cases, however, the Code changes some of the specific rules under the common law. The Code consists of ten articles:

1. General Provisions
2. Sales
   a. Leases
3. Negotiable Instruments
4. Bank Deposits and Collections
   a. Wire transfers
5. Letters of Credit
6. Bulk Transfers
7. Documents of Title, Warehouse Receipts, Bills of Lading, and Others
8. Investment Securities
9. Secured Transactions
10. Effective Date and Repealer

This section covers some of the general principles relating to sales (UCC Article 2), but small business owners should also become familiar with the basics of the other part of the Code. The UCC creates a "caste system" of merchants and nonmerchants and requires merchants to have a higher degree of knowledge and understanding of the Code.

## Sales and Sales Contracts

Every sales contract is subject to the basic principles of law that govern all contracts—agreement, consideration, capacity, and legality. However, when a contract involves the sale of goods, the UCC imposes rules that may vary slightly or substantially from basic contract law. Article 2 governs *only* contracts for the *sale of goods,* but it pertains to *every* sale of goods, whether the good involved is a 79-cent pen or a billion-dollar battleship. To be considered a good, an item must be personal property that is tangible and moveable (e.g., not real estate or services), and a "sale" is "the "passing of title from the seller to the buyer for a price" (UCC Sec. 2-106[1]). The UCC does *not* cover the sale of services, although certain "mixed transactions," such as the sale by a garage of car parts (goods) and repairs (a service) will fall under the Code's jurisdiction if the goods are the dominant element of the contract.

In addition to the rules it applies to the sale of goods in general, the Code imposes special standards of conduct in certain instances when merchants sell goods to one another. Usually, a person is considered a **merchant** if he or she "deals in goods of the kind" involved in the contract and has special knowledge of the business or of the goods, employs a merchant agent to conduct a transaction for him or her, or holds himself or herself out to be a merchant.

Although the UCC requires that the same elements outlined in common law be present in forming a sales contract, it relaxes many of the specific restrictions. For example, the UCC states that a contract exists even if the parties omit one or more terms (price, delivery date, place of delivery, quantity), as long as they intended to make a contract and there is a reasonably certain method for the court to supply the missing terms. Suppose a manufacturer orders a shipment of needed raw materials from her usual supplier without asking the price. When the order arrives, the price is substantially higher than the manufacturer expected, and the manufacturer attempts to disaffirm the contract. The Code verifies the existence of a contract and assigns to the shipment a price that is reasonable at the time of delivery.

Common law requires that acceptance of an offer to be exactly the same as the offer; an acceptance that adds some slight modification is no acceptance at all, and no contract exists. Any modification constitutes a counteroffer. However, the UCC states that as long as an offeree's response (words, writing, or actions) indicates a sincere willingness to accept the offer, it is a legitimate acceptance even though varying terms are added. This section of the UCC is known as "the battle of the forms." If at least one of the parties involved in the contract is a nonmerchant, these added terms are merely "proposals for addition." In other words, a contract is formed on the *offeror's* original terms. Between two merchants, however, these additional terms *automatically* become part of the contract unless they materially alter the original contract, the offer expressly states that no terms other than those in the offer will be accepted, or the offeror objects to the particular terms within a reasonable time. In other words, the contract is formed on the *offeree's* modified terms. For example, suppose that an appliance wholesaler (a merchant) offers to sell a retailer (a merchant) a shipment of appliances for $5,000 plus freight. The retailer responds, "I accept" but includes an additional term by stating, "Delivery within 5 days." A contract exists, and the addition will become part of the contract unless the wholesaler objects within a reasonable time.

When the offeree includes a term in the acceptance that contradicts a term in the offeror's original offer, the UCC says that the two terms cancel out each other. What, then, are the terms of the resulting contract? The UCC turns to its gap-filling rules, which establish reasonable terms for prices, delivery dates, warranties, payment times, and other topics, to supply the disputed term.

**ENTREPRENEURIAL Profile**

**Superior Boiler Works vs. R.J. Sanders Company**

The R.J. Sanders Company won a contract to install the heating system at a federal prison and negotiated a contract with Superior Boiler Works to purchase three large commercial boilers for the project. On March 27, Superior sent a letter to Sanders in which it offered to sell three boilers for $156,000 with an estimated delivery time of four weeks. After several discussions, Sanders sent a purchase order (an offer) to Superior on July 20 for three boilers, agreeing to pay $145,827 and stating a delivery date of four weeks (August 20). Superior responded by sending Sanders a sales order (an acceptance) in which it agreed to the price but stated a shipping date of October 1. Superior shipped the boilers on October 1, just as it had promised, and they arrived at Sanders on October 5. This delivery date forced Sanders to rent temporary boilers at a cost of $45,315, and Sanders sent Superior a check for $100,000 with a note explaining that the deduction was to offset the cost of the rented boilers. Superior sued Sanders for the $45,000 difference, claiming that the October 1 shipping date was reasonable. The Supreme Court of the U.S. state of Rhode Island ruled that the parties' conflicting delivery terms canceled out each other. The court then applied the UCC's gap-filling rules (boilers are goods), which state that the time for delivery of the goods must be made "a reasonable time." The court ruled in favor of Superior, stating that the October 1 shipping date was within a reasonable time.[6]

The UCC significantly changes the common law requirement that a contract modification requires new consideration. ("New promises require new consideration.") Under the Code, modifications to contract terms are binding *without* new consideration if they are made in good faith. ("New promises do *not* require new consideration.") For example, suppose that a small building contractor forms a contract to purchase a supply of lumber for $1,200. After the agreement but before the lumber is delivered, a hurricane forces the price of the lumber to double, and the supplier notifies the contractor that the price of the lumber shipment has increased to $2,400. The contractor reluctantly agrees to the additional cost but later refuses to pay. According to UCC, the contractor must pay the higher price because the contract modification requires no new consideration.

The Code also has its own Statute of Frauds provision relating to the form of contracts for the sale of goods. If the price of the goods is $500 or more, the contract must be written to be enforceable. Of course, the parties can agree orally and then follow up with a written memorandum. The Code does not require both parties to sign the written agreement, but it must be signed by the party against whom enforcement is sought (which is impossible to tell before a dispute arises, so it is a good idea for *both* parties to sign the agreement at the outset).

The UCC includes a special provision involving the writing requirement in contracts between merchants. If merchants form a verbal contract for the sale of goods priced at more than $500 and one of them sends a written confirmation of the deal to the other, the merchant receiving the confirmation must object to it *in writing* within 10 days. Otherwise, the contract is enforceable against *both* merchants, even though the merchant receiving the confirmation has not actually signed anything.

Once the parties create a sales contract, they are bound to perform according to its terms. Both the buyer and the seller have certain duties and obligations under the contract. Generally, the Code assigns the obligations of "good faith" (defined as "honesty in fact in the conduct or transaction concerned") and "commercial reasonableness" (commercial standards of fair dealing) to both parties.

The seller must make delivery of the items involved in the contract, but "delivery" is not necessarily physical delivery. The seller simply must make the goods available to the buyer. The contract normally outlines the specific details of the delivery, but occasionally the parties omit this provision. In this instance, the place of delivery will be the seller's place of business, if one exists; otherwise, it is the seller's residence. If both parties know the usual location of the identified goods, that location is the place of delivery (e.g., a warehouse). In addition, the seller must make the goods available to the buyer at a reasonable time and in a reasonable manner. All goods covered by the contract must be tendered in one delivery unless the parties' agreement states otherwise.

A buyer must accept the delivery of conforming goods from the seller. Of course, the buyer has the right to inspect the goods in a reasonable manner and at any reasonable time or place to ensure that they are conforming goods before making payment. However, C.O.D. terms prohibit the right to advance inspection unless the contract specifies otherwise. Under the perfect tender rule in Section 2-601 of the Code, "if goods or tender of delivery fail, in any respect, to conform to the contract," the buyer is not required to accept them.

A buyer can indicate his or her acceptance of the goods in several ways. Usually the buyer indicates acceptance by an express statement that the goods are suitable. This expression can be by words or by conduct. Suppose that a small electrical contractor orders a truck to use in her business. When she receives it, she equips it to suit her needs, including a company decal on each door. Later the contractor attempts to reject the truck and return it. By customizing the truck, the buyer has indicated her acceptance of the truck. In addition, the Code assumes acceptance if the buyer has a reasonable opportunity to inspect the goods and has failed to reject them within a reasonable time.

A buyer has the duty to pay for the goods on the terms stated in the contract when they are received. A seller cannot require payment before the buyer receives the goods. Unless otherwise stated in the contract, payment must be in cash.

## Breach of Sales Contracts

As we have seen, when a party to the sales contract fails to perform according to its terms, that party is said to have breached the contract. The law provides the innocent (nonbreaching) party numerous remedies, including damage awards and the right to retain possession of the goods. The object of these remedies is to place the innocent party in the same position as if the contract had been carried out. The parties to the contract may specify their own damages in case of breach. These provisions, called **liquidated damages**, must be reasonable and cannot be in the nature of a penalty. For example, suppose that Alana Mitchell contracts with a local carpenter to build a booth from which she plans to sell crafts. The parties agree that if the booth is not completed by September 1, Mitchell will receive $500. If the liquidated damages had been $50,000, they would be unenforceable because such a large amount of money is clearly a penalty.

An unpaid seller has certain remedies available under the terms of the Code. Under a seller's lien, every seller has the right to maintain possession of the goods until the buyer pays for them. In addition, if the buyer uses a fraudulent payment to obtain the goods, the seller has the right to recover them. If the seller discovers that the buyer is insolvent, the seller can withhold delivery of the goods until the buyer pays in cash. If goods are shipped to an insolvent buyer, the seller can require their return within ten days after receipt. In some cases, the buyer breaches a contract while the goods are still unfinished in the production process. When this occurs, the seller must use "reasonable commercial judgment" to decide whether to sell them for scrap or complete them and resell them elsewhere. In either case, the buyer is liable for any loss the seller incurs. Of course, the seller has the right to withhold performance when the buyer breaches the sales contract.

When the seller breaches a contract, the buyer also has specific remedies available. For instance, if the goods do not conform to the contract's terms, the buyer has the right to reject them. If the seller fails to deliver the goods, the buyer can sue for the difference between the contract price and the market price at the time that the breach became known. When the buyer accepts goods and then discovers that they are defective or nonconforming, he or she must notify the seller of the breach. In this instance, damages amount to the difference between the value of the goods delivered and their value if they had been delivered as promised. If a buyer pays for goods that the seller retains, the buyer can take possession of the goods if the seller becomes insolvent within ten days after receiving the first payment. If the seller unlawfully withholds the goods from the buyer, the buyer can recover them. Under certain circumstances, a buyer can obtain specific performance of a sales contract; that is, the court orders the seller to perform according to the contract's terms. As mentioned earlier, specific performance is a remedy only when the goods involved are unique or unavailable on the market. Finally, if the seller breaches the contract, the buyer has the right to rescind the contract; if the buyer has paid any part of the purchase price, it must be refunded.

Whenever a party breaches a sales contract, the innocent party must bring suit within a specified period of time. The Code sets the statute of limitations at four years. In other words, any action for a breach of a sales contract must begin within four years after the breach occurred.

## Sales Warranties and Product Liability

Many economies once emphasized the philosophy of *caveat emptor,* "let the buyer beware," but today the marketplace enforces a policy of *caveat venditor,* "let the seller beware." **Tort law** deals with cases in which one party commits a wrong against another party and causes injury or damage to the person and/or his or her property. Tort law covers a wide range of topics, including defamation of character, false imprisonment (e.g., wrongly detaining a suspected shoplifter), fraud, wrongful interference with a contractual relationship, and others. Tort liability represents a significant risk for small companies. A study by the U.S. Chamber Institute for Legal Reform reports that tort liability costs small businesses $98 billion per year. Tort liability costs the typical small business $20.11 for every $1,000 of revenue; in other words, a small company with $5 million in revenue pays, on average, $100,550 in tort related costs each year.[7] Entrepreneurs must be aware of two general categories related to torts that involve the quality and reliability of the products they sell: sales warranties and product liability.

**SALES WARRANTIES.** Simply stated, a **sales warranty** is a promise or a statement of fact by the seller that a product will meet certain standards. Because a breach of warranty is a breach of promise, the buyer has the right to recover damages from the seller. Several different types of warranties can arise in a sale. A seller creates an **express warranty** by making statements about the condition, quality, and performance of the good on which the buyer substantially relies. Express warranties can be created by words or actions. For example, a manufacturer selling a shipment of cloth to a customer with the promise that "it will not shrink" is creating an express warranty. Similarly, the jeweler who displays a watch in a glass of water for promotional purposes creates an express warranty that "this watch is waterproof" even though no such promise is ever spoken. Generally, an express warranty arises if the seller indicates that the goods conform to any promises of fact the seller makes, to any description of them (e.g., printed on the package or statements of fact made by salespersons), or to any display model or sample (e.g., a floor model used as a demonstrator).

Whenever someone sells goods, the UCC automatically implies certain types of warranties unless the seller specifically excludes them. These **implied warranties** take several forms. Sellers, simply by offering goods for sale, imply a **warranty of title**, which promises that their title to the goods is valid (i.e., no liens or claims exist) and that transfer of title is legitimate. A seller can disclaim a warranty of title only by using very specific language in a sales contract.

An implied **warranty of merchantability** applies to every merchant seller, and the only way to disclaim it is by mentioning the term "warranty of merchantability" in a conspicuous manner. An implied warranty of merchantability assures the buyer that the product will be of average quality—not the best and not the worst. In other words, merchantable goods are "fit for the ordinary purposes for which such goods are used" (UCC Sec. 2-314[1-C]). For example, a commercial refrigeration unit that a food store purchases should keep food cold.

What types of warranties do companies that sell goods offer to buyers?

*Source:* Jessica McGowan/The New York Times.

**Profile**

Webster vs. Blue
Ship Tea Room

Priscilla Webster, a long-time New England resident, ordered a bowl of fish chowder at the Blue Ship Tea Room, a Boston restaurant that overlooked the ocean. After eating three or four spoonfuls, Webster felt something caught in her throat. It turned out to be a fish bone that was in the bowl of chowder she had ordered. Webster had to undergo two surgical procedures to remove the bone from her throat and she filed a lawsuit against the restaurant, claiming that it had breached the implied warranty of merchantability. The Supreme Court of the U.S. state of Massachusetts ruled in favor of the Blue Ship Tea Room, stating that "the occasional presence of [fish bones] in chowders is . . . to be anticipated and . . . [does] not impair their fitness or merchantability." Because the fish bone in the fish chowder was not a foreign object, but one that a person could reasonably expect to find in chowders on occasion, the court decided that the restaurant had not breached a warranty of merchantability.[8]

An implied **warranty of fitness for a particular purpose** arises when a seller knows the particular reason for which a buyer is purchasing a product and knows that the buyer is depending on the seller's judgment to select the proper item. For example, suppose a customer

**"Great little product, but liability could eat you up."**

enters a small hardware store requesting a chemical to kill poison ivy. The owner hands over a gallon of chemical, but it fails to kill the weed; the owner has violated the warranty of fitness for a particular purpose.

The Code also states that the only way a merchant can disclaim an implied warranty is to include the words "sold as is" or "with all faults," stating that the buyer purchases the product as it is, without any guarantees. The following statement is usually sufficient to disclaim most warranties, both express and implied: "Seller hereby disclaims all warranties, express and implied, including all warranties of merchantability and all warranties of fitness for a particular purpose." To protect a business, the statement must be printed in bold letters and placed in a conspicuous place on the product or its package.

**PRODUCT LIABILITY.** At one time only the parties directly involved in the execution of a contract were bound by the law of sales warranties. Today, the UCC and U.S. states have expanded the scope of warranties to include any person (including bystanders) incurring personal or property damages caused by a faulty product. In addition, most states allow an injured party to sue *any* seller in the chain of distribution for breach of warranty (a concept known as joint and several liability). Product liability is built on the principle that a person who introduces a product into the stream of commerce owes a duty of care, not only to the person who first purchases the product but also to anyone else who might foreseeably come into contact with it. A company that may be responsible only for a small percentage of the responsibility for a person's injury may end up bearing the majority of the damage award in the case. If a small company is hit with a product liability lawsuit, the results can be devastating. Figure 22.1 shows the number of product liability lawsuits filed in recent years in the United States alone.

Many customers who ultimately file suit under product liability laws base their claims on **negligence**, when a manufacturer or distributor fails to do something that a "reasonable" person would do. Typically, negligence claims arise from one or more of the following charges:

*Negligent design.* In claims based on negligent design, a buyer claims that an injury occurred because the manufacturer designed the product improperly. To avoid liability charges, a company does not have to design products that are 100 percent safe, but it must design products that are free of "unreasonable" risks.

*Negligent manufacturing.* In cases claiming negligent manufacturing, a buyer claims that a company's failure to follow proper manufacturing, assembly, or inspection procedures allowed a defective product to get into the customer's hands and cause injury.

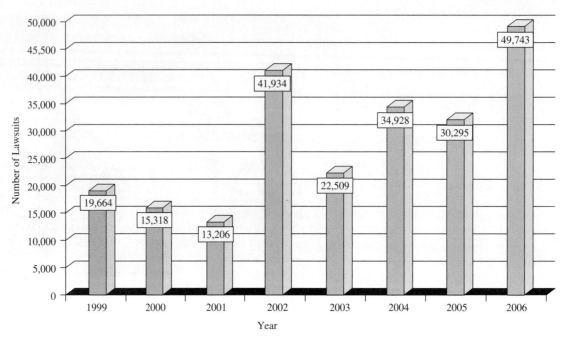

**FIGURE 22.1 Number of Product Liability Lawsuits**

*Source:* "Product Liability Cases Commenced," *Judicial Business of the United States Courts,* 2006.

A company must exercise "due care" (including design, assembly, and inspection) to make its products safe when they are used for their intended purpose.

***Failure to warn.*** Although manufacturers do not have to warn customers about obvious dangers of using their products, they must warn them about the dangers of normal use and of foreseeable misuse of the product. (Have you ever read the warning label on a stepladder?) Many businesses hire attorneys to write the warning labels they attach to their products and include in their instructions.[9]

Another common basis for product liability claims against businesses is **strict liability**, which states that a manufacturer is liable for its actions no matter what its intentions or the extent of its negligence. Unlike negligence, a claim of strict liability does not require the injured party to prove that the company's actions were unreasonable. The injured person must prove only that the company manufactured or sold a product that was defective and that it caused the injury when used in a way that was foreseeable. Whereas negligence charges focus on a party's *conduct,* strict liability focuses on the *product.* For instance, suppose that the head of an axe flies off its handle, injuring the user. To sue the manufacturer under strict liability, the customer must prove that the defendant sold the axe, the axe was unreasonably dangerous to the customer because it was defective, the customer incurred physical harm to person or to property, and the defective axe was the proximate cause of the injury or damage. If these allegations are true, the axe manufacturer's liability is virtually unlimited.

## Protection of Intellectual Property Rights

*3.* Discuss the protection of intellectual property rights using patents, trademarks, and copyrights.

Entrepreneurs excel at coming up with innovative ideas for creative products and services. Many entrepreneurs build businesses around intellectual property, products and services that are the result of the creative process and have commercial value. New methods that are capable of teaching foreign languages at an accelerated pace, hit songs with which we can sing along, books that bring a smile, and new drugs that fight diseases are just some of the ways intellectual property makes our lives better or more enjoyable.

Unfortunately, thieves are escalating their efforts to steal intellectual property.[10] The problem extends far beyond pirated software, DVDs and CDs, and knockoffs of expensive watches or the latest styles of designer clothing. Authorities have discovered pirates selling counterfeit helicopter, airplane, and auto parts, prescription medications (includ-

# ENTREPRENEURSHIP

## *In Action*

### How Hot Is "Too Hot"?

Stella Liebeck, 79, was sitting in the passenger seat of her grandson's car when they pulled up to the drive-in window at McDonald's. Her grandson stopped the car so she could add cream and sugar to the cup of coffee she had just ordered. Liebeck put the Styrofoam cup between her knees to remove the lid, but when she did, the coffee spilled into her lap, soaked into her sweatpants, and burned her severely. She received third-degree burns over 6 percent of her body, was hospitalized for eight days, and had to undergo skin grafts and other treatments.

Liebeck sued McDonald's under product liability law. During the trial, McDonald's documents showed more than 700 claims filed between 1982 and 1992 by people burned by its coffee. McDonald's testified that, at a consultant's advice, it held its coffee at temperatures between 180 and 190 degrees to maintain optimum taste but that it had not studied the safety implications of serving coffee at that temperature. A quality assurance manager for the chain testified that the company actively enforces a requirement that coffee be kept and served at that temperature. Evidence also revealed that other restaurants typically serve their coffee at much lower temperatures and that coffee made at home typically is between 135 and 140 degrees. In addition, attorneys pointed to a warning to the franchise industry from the Shriner's Burn Institute in Cincinnati that some chains were causing unnecessarily serious burns by serving beverages at temperatures above 130 degrees.

An expert witness for Mrs. Liebeck testified that at 180 degrees liquids that come into contact with human skin will cause third-degree burns within two to seven seconds. Liquids at 155 degrees also can produce third-degree burns but the time required to do so is about 60 seconds.

McDonald's claimed that its customers buy coffee on their way to work or home with the intent of drinking it when they arrive at their destinations. The company admitted that it did not warn customers of the risk of incurring severe burns from their coffee if it were spilled. McDonald's argues that its customers know that its coffee is hot and that they prefer it that way. (The company sells about $1.3 million of coffee a day.)

The jury awarded Mrs. Liebeck $200,000 in compensatory damages for her injuries, but that amount was reduced to $160,000 because the jury ruled that Liebeck was 20 percent responsible for the accident. The jury also awarded her $2.7 million in punitive damages, roughly the equivalent of two days' worth of McDonald's coffee sales, but that amount was reduced to $480,000. Ultimately, McDonald's and Mrs. Liebeck entered into a secret post-verdict settlement.

1. On what grounds could Mrs. Liebeck have brought her product liability suit against McDonald's?

2. Do you agree or disagree with the jury's verdict in this case? Explain.

3. What advice would you give to a restaurant owner about serving coffee to customers and avoiding legal liabilities?

4. A customer has filed a similar lawsuit against Starbucks, claiming that he suffered third-degree burns to his hand when the top came off of a cup of hot tea and spilled. He accused Starbucks of "negligently and carelessly" selling unsafe tea. Use the Web to research this case and write a short summary of the facts and an analysis of how you think the court should rule and why.

*Sources:* Adapted from "The McDonald's Scalding Coffee Case," The American Association for Justice, http://justice.org/pressroom/FACTS/frivolous/McdonaldsCoffeecase.aspx; "The Actual Facts About the McDonald's Coffee Case," 'Lectric Law Library, www.lectlaw.com/files/cur78.htm; "Mythbuster! The 'McDonald's Coffee Case' and Other Fictions," Center for Justice and Democracy, www.centerjd.org/free/mythbusters-free/MB_mcdonalds.htm.

ing blood pressure medication and birth control pills), and many other products. A tidal wave of counterfeit products, mostly originating in China, India, Turkey, Malaysia, Brazil, and Russia, are flooding the world. Entrepreneurs can protect their intellectual property from unauthorized use with the help of three important tools: patents, trademarks, and copyrights.

## Patents

A **patent** is a grant from a government's patent and trademark office (PTO) to the inventor of a product. In the United States, it gives the inventor the exclusive right to make, use, or sell the invention in this country for 20 years from the date of filing the patent application. The purpose of giving an inventor a 20-year monopoly over a product is to stimulate creativity and innovation. After 20 years, the patent expires and cannot be renewed. Most patents are granted for new product inventions, but **design patents**, issued in the United States for 3½, 7, or 14 years beyond the date the patent is issued, are given to inventors who make new, original, and ornamental changes in the design of existing products that enhance their sales. Likewise, U.S. inventors who develop a new plant can obtain a **plant patent** (issued for 7 years), provided they can reproduce the plant asexually (e.g., by grafting or cross-breeding rather than planting seeds). To be patented, a device must be new (but not necessarily better; see Figure 22.2), not obvious to a person of ordinary skill or knowledge in the related field, and useful. A device cannot be patented if it has been publicized in print anywhere in the world or if it has been used or offered for sale in this country prior to the date of the patent application. A U.S. patent is granted only to the true inventor, not a person who discovers another's invention. No one can copy or sell a patented invention without getting a license from its creator. A patent does not give one the right to make, use, or sell an invention but the right to exclude others from making, using, or selling it.

In recent years, the PTO in the United States, for example, has awarded companies, primarily Web-based businesses, patents on their business methods. Rather than giving them the exclusive rights to a product or an invention, a business method patent protects the way a company conducts business. For instance, Amazon.com earned a patent on its "1-Click"

---

**FIGURE 22.2 Design Patent #376,811, False Sideburns for Sunglasses**

*Source:* U.S. Patent and Trademark Office.

---

**United States Patent** [19]

Lowe

[11] Patent Number: **Des. 376,811**

[45] Date of Patent: **\*\*Dec. 24, 1996**

[54] **PAIR OF FALSE SIDEBURNS FOR SUNGLASSES**

[76] Inventor: **Allen Lowe, 1148 12th St. S., Birmingham, Ala. 35205**

[\*\*] Term: **14 Years**

[21] Appl. No.: **28,333**

[22] Filed: **Sep. 12, 1994**

**Related U.S. Application Data**

[63] Continuation of Ser. No. 930,048, Aug. 17, 1992, abandoned.

[52] **U.S. Cl.** .................................................. **D16/341**

[58] **Field of Search** ....................... D16/100, 300, D16/306–308, 309, 330, 335, 336, 341, 342, D21/189, 190; D2/741; 2/206; 351/41, 44, 51–52, 122, 123, 158

[56] **References Cited**

U.S. PATENT DOCUMENTS

| | | | |
|---|---|---|---|
| 135,600 | 4/1943 | Stolper | |
| D. 146,601 | 4/1947 | Jaffe | D16/127 |
| 149,007 | 4/1947 | Lewis | D57/1 |
| D. 241,428 | 9/1976 | Bloch | D16/118 |
| D. 274,821 | 7/1984 | Dair | D16/118 |
| D. 282,668 | 2/1986 | Haas | D16/102 |
| 2,233,698 | 3/1941 | Girouard | 2/206 |
| 2,262,993 | 11/1941 | Dessart | 2/206 |
| 2,666,206 | 1/1954 | Mafko | 2/206 |
| 2,914,772 | 12/1959 | Lemelson | D21/190 |
| 3,009,163 | 11/1961 | Beauvais | 2/206 |
| 3,858,589 | 1/1975 | Geiger | D21/190 |
| 4,909,620 | 3/1990 | Saccone | 351/51 |

OTHER PUBLICATIONS

Luminous Catalog. p. 8 insert in Optician Mar. 2, 1973.
Optician Apr. 24, 1987 p. 28.
Optician Aug. 22, 1975 p. 33.
Fendall Catalog Mar. 13, 1980 p. 6.
Spiegel, p. 61, F unny Face Kit" bottom right side of page
Optometric Monthly Apr. 1984 p.161.
Optician Mar. 10, 1972 p.19.
Optician Mar. 10, 1972 p. 24.
Dessart Catalog 1967 p. 2#1.
*Graceland Summer 1992 Gift Catalog* item #070–1150 "Elvis Sunglasses" p.10.

Primary Examiner—Raphael Barkai

[57] **CLAIM**

The ornamental design for a pair of false sideburns for sunglasses, as shown and described.

**DESCRIPTION**

FIG. 1 is a top perspective view of a pair of false sideburns for sunglasses showing my new design;
FIG. 2 is an exterior side view of the left false sideburn show in FIG. 1;
FIG. 3 is an interior side view thereof;
FIG. 4 is a front elevational view thereof;
FIG. 5 is a rear elevational view thereof;
FIG. 6 is a top plan view thereof; and,
FIG. 7 is a bottom plan view thereof.
The broken line showing of the sunglasses in FIG. 1 is for illustrative purposes only and forms no part of the claimed design. The showing of the left false sideburns in FIGS. 2–7 is for ease of illustration only and FIGS. 2–7 the right false sideburn is a mirror image of the left false sideburn.

**1 Claim, 3 Drawing Sheets**

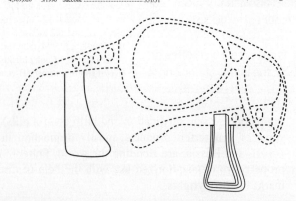

Web-based checkout process, precluding other e-tailers from using it. Priceline.com has a patent on its business model of "buyer-driven commerce," in which customers name the prices they are willing to pay for airline tickets, hotel rooms, and other items.

Although inventors have no guarantee of getting a patent, they can enhance their chances considerably by following the basic steps suggested by the PTO. Before beginning the lengthy and involved procedure, inventors should obtain professional assistance from a patent practitioner—a patent attorney or a patent agent—who is registered with the PTO. Only attorneys and agents who are officially registered may represent an inventor seeking a patent. Approximately 98 percent of all inventors rely on these patent experts to steer them through the convoluted process.[11] One experienced patent attorney says that the cost to obtain a patent ranges from $4,000 for a simple invention to $25,000 or more for a highly complex invention.[12]

**THE PATENT PROCESS.** Since U.S. President George Washington signed the first patent law in 1790, the U.S. Patent and Trademark Office has issued patents on everything imaginable (and some unimaginable items, too), including mouse traps, animals (genetically engineered mice), games, and various fishing devices. To date the PTO has issued more than seven million patents, and it receives more than 400,000 new applications each year. The first patent was issued to Samuel Hopkins on July 31, 1790, for an improved method for making potash, an ingredient in fertilizer and other products.[13] Patent number seven million went to DuPont senior researcher John P. O'Brien for polysaccharide fibers (which have cotton-like properties, are biodegradable, and are useful in textile applications) and a process for producing them. Figure 22.3 shows the trend in the number of U.S. patent applications and number of patents actually granted in recent years.

To receive a patent, an inventor must follow these steps:

***Establish the invention's novelty.*** An invention is not patentable in the United States if it is known or has been used in the United States or has been described in a printed publication in this or a foreign country.

***Document the device.*** To protect their patent claims, inventors should be able to verify the date on which they first conceived the idea for their inventions. Inventors can

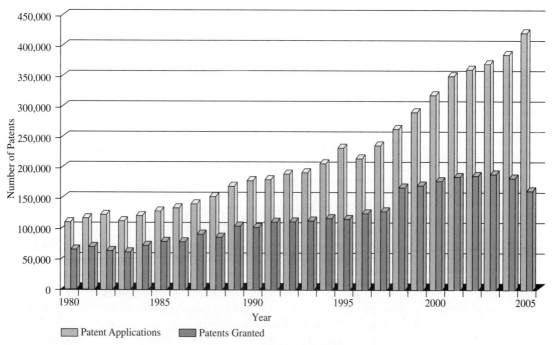

**FIGURE 22.3  Patent Applications and Patents Granted**
*Source:* U.S. Patent and Trademark Office.

document a device by keeping dated records (including drawings) of their progress on the invention and by having knowledgeable friends witness the records. Inventors also can file a disclosure document with the U.S. PTO—a process that includes writing a letter describing the invention and sending a check for $10 to the PTO. A disclosure document is *not* a patent application, but it does provide evidence of the date an inventor conceived an invention.

*Search existing patents.*  To verify that the invention truly is new, non-obvious, and useful, inventors must conduct a search of existing patents on similar products. The purpose of the search is to determine whether the inventor has a chance of getting a patent. Most inventors hire professionals trained in conducting patent searches to perform the research. In some countries, inventors themselves can conduct an online search of all patents.

*Study search results.*  Once the patent search is finished, inventors must study the results of the search to determine their chances of getting a patent. To be patentable, a device must be sufficiently different from what has been used or described before and must not be obvious to a person having ordinary skill in the area of technology related to the invention.

*Submit the patent application.*  An inventor must file an application describing the invention with the PTO. This description, called the patent's claims, should be broad enough so that others cannot easily engineer around the patent, rendering it useless. However, they cannot be so narrow as to infringe on patents that other inventors already hold. The typical patent application runs 20 to 40 pages although some, especially those for biotech or high-tech products, are tens of thousands of pages long.

*Prosecute the patent application.*  Before the U.S. PTO will issue a patent, one of its examiners studies the application to determine whether or not the invention warrants a patent. If the PTO rejects the application, the inventor can amend the application and resubmit it to the PTO. The average time for a patent to be issued is 28 months, and the head of the PTO says that, as the backlog of patent applications grows ever larger, the average time will double within five years.[14]

Defending a patent against "copycat producers" can be expensive and time-consuming but often is necessary to protect an entrepreneur's idea. Patent lawsuits are on the rise, the number filed annually more than tripling since the early 1980s.[15] Unfortunately, the cost of defending a patent has increased as well; the average cost of a patent infringement case is about $2 million for each side.[16] However, the odds of winning are in the patent holder's favor; more than 60 percent of those holding patents win their infringement suits.[17]

## Trademarks

A **trademark** is any distinctive word, phrase, symbol, design, name, logo, slogan, or trade dress that a company uses to identify the origin of a product or to distinguish it from other goods on the market. (A **service mark** is the same as a trademark except that it identifies and distinguishes the source of a service rather than a product.) A trademark serves as a company's "signature" in the marketplace. A trademark can be more than just a company's logo, slogan, or brand name; it can also include symbols, shapes, colors, smells, or sounds. For instance, Coca-Cola holds a trademark on the shape of its bottle, and NBC owns a trademark on its three-toned chime. Components of a product's identity such as these are part of its **trade dress**, the unique combination of elements that a company uses to create a product's image and to promote it. For instance, a Mexican restaurant chain's particular décor, color schemes, design, and overall "look and feel" would be its trade dress. To be eligible for trademark protection, trade dress must be inherently unique and distinctive to a company, and another company's use of that trade dress must be likely to confuse customers.

## ■ Ripped Off!

Zippo, the company that has been making the classic flip-top cigarette lighter for more than 75 years, turns out 50,000 lighters per day at its factory in the U.S. state of Pennsylvania. Factories in China produce almost as many lighters. The only problem is that Zippo has no factories in China! All of the Chinese-made Zippos are counterfeit and cost the company an estimated $42 million in lost sales and one-third of its profits each year. The International Chamber of Commerce estimates that worldwide companies such as Zippo lose $600 billion annually to counterfeit products. Whereas counterfeiters once copied only high-end, luxury items such as Prada shoes, Coach bags, or Rolex watches, today they are copying common products such as lighters and air conditioning components. Part of the problem is that China, the source of about two-thirds of the world's counterfeit merchandise, does little to protect intellectual property and doles out minor penalties for the few counterfeiters who are caught and prosecuted. Another problem is that because companies are outsourcing more production to overseas factories, many of the counterfeit goods are produced in the same factories that turn out authentic goods—usually on an unauthorized "third shift."

Small companies often are victims of pirates. David Pearl, who, with his father and brother, operates Uniweld, a small company that manufactures welding tools and equipment for testing air refrigeration and conditioning compressors, was astonished to learn that knockoffs of his company's products were turning up on shelves in Saudi Arabia. Pirates had duplicated almost everything about the products, from their overall appearance to the packaging. The bogus products, however, were cheaply made, causing users who believed that they had purchased real Uniweld products to complain. Some even switched to competitors' products because of the poor quality of the fakes, which leaked and lacked the ability to provide accurate readings.

Even though Uniweld, which was founded in 1949, is a small company, it knows its way around international markets; the company has offices in Canada, Ecuador, and Lebanon and sells its products all over the world. The low-quality counterfeit products, which the Pearls discovered were selling at 30 percent to 50 percent below

the company's usual wholesale price, were ravaging Uniweld's sales as well as its reputation in the market. "It was a horrible blow," says Pearl, who never suspected that products as unglamorous as the ones his company manufactured would be the target of copycat pirates. Because the fake items came with authentic company documentation, including operation manuals and warranty and contact information, Uniweld was forced to field complaints from disgruntled customers.

The Pearls suspected that the phony products were coming from China but weren't sure how to take the necessary steps to stop the counterfeiting. How were the counterfeiters exporting them to the Middle East? The Pearls began interviewing everyone in their industry who had connections to the Middle East, including a former Uniweld distributor in Saudi Arabia, but no one was able to offer any clues.

The Pearls hired a Saudi law firm to register the Uniweld trademark throughout the countries of the Middle East, but that move failed to stem the tide of the counterfeit products flowing into the area. By now, the bogus items were costing Uniweld $1 million per year in lost revenue, not to mention the cost that they were imposing on the company's reputation for quality. Finally, an industry insider told the Pearls that he had been tipped off: It was the company's former distributor in Saudi Arabia that was importing the fake items from China. The Pearls filed a lawsuit against the distributor in the Saudi court system, demanding reimbursement for lost sales, but the case has crawled along without resolution.

*(continued)*

At a recent trade show, one of Uniweld's new regional sales representatives received an unusual offer from four people. Each one approached the man, who none of them recognized as a Uniweld employee, and offered to sell him Uniweld products. The problem: None of the men were authorized Uniweld dealers. Alarmed, the Pearls realized that the counterfeit products with their company's name on them had spread beyond Saudi Arabia. Their attorneys told them to send company technicians to pose as buyers and to purchase phony products from various distributors as evidence. The technicians returned with plenty of evidence, and the Saudi attorneys immediately sent out "cease and desist letters" to the unauthorized distributors. They introduced the evidence the technicians gathered into the trial of the former distributor. Although fake Uniweld products still crop up in Saudi Arabia, the Pearls' actions appear to have halted their distribution in other parts of the world—at least for now. Legal fees and lost sales have cost the small family business millions of dollars. "We've been working hard to regain the market, but it's not easy," says Pearl. "The only way to survive is by being constantly vigilant."

1. Use the Web to research the problem of counterfeit products. What are the consequences and the costs to companies whose products are being "knocked off by counterfeiters"?

2. What steps can companies take to combat this problem?

*Sources:* Adapted from Deborah Orr, "Pirate's Ball," *Forbes*, April 9, 2007, pp. 102–104; Erik Sherman, "Fighting Fakes," *Inc.*, February 2006, pp. 45–46; Nicholas Zamiska, "A Question of Value," *Wall Street Journal*, June 2, 2006, pp. A13, A16; Geoffrey A Fowler, "Estimates of Copyright Piracy Losses Vary Widely," *Wall Street Journal*, June 2, 2006, pp. A13, A16; "Technologies to Spot Fakes Are Short-Lived," *Wall Street Journal*, May 26–27, 2007, p. A6.

**Pearl Oyster Bar vs. Ed's Lobster Bar**

Rebecca Charles, who founded the Pearl Oyster Bar, a popular restaurant in New York City, filed a lawsuit against Ed McFarland, her former sous chef, claiming that his restaurant, Ed's Lobster Bar, infringes on her company's trade dress. The complaint states that McFarland copied "each and every element" of Pearl Oyster Bar, including its white marble bar, the gray paint on the wainscoting, the wheat-straw backs on the chairs and bar stools, the packets of oyster crackers placed on each table, and the dressing on the Caesar salad, the recipe for which, says Charles, she learned from her mother. "My restaurant is a personal reflection of me, my experience, and my family," says Charles. "That restaurant is me." Pointing out differences in his restaurant and the Pearl Oyster Bar, McFarland, who believes the lawsuit lacks merit, says that he researched many oyster bars in Boston as part of his "homework in designing the dining room." The lawsuit has not yet gone to trial.[18]

There are 1.5 million trademarks registered in the United States, 900,000 of which are in actual use. The law permits a manufacturer to register a trademark, which prevents other companies from employing a similar mark to identify their goods. Before 1989, a business could not reserve a trademark in advance of use. Today, the first party that either uses a trademark in commerce or files an application with the PTO has the ultimate right to register that trademark. Unlike patents and copyrights, which are issued for limited amounts of time, trademarks last indefinitely as long as the holder continues to use them. However, a trademark cannot keep competitors from producing the same product and selling it under a different name. It merely prevents others from using the same or confusingly similar trademark for the same or similar products.

Many business owners are confused by the use of the symbols ™ and ®. Anyone who claims the right to a particular trademark (or service mark) can use the ™ (or ᔆᴹ) symbols without having to register the mark with the PTO. The claim to that trademark or service mark may or may not be valid, however. Only those businesses that have registered their marks with the PTO can use the ® symbol. Entrepreneurs do not have to register trademarks or service marks to establish their rights to those marks; however, registering a mark with the PTO does give entrepreneurs greater power in protecting their marks. Filing an application to register a trademark or service mark is relatively easy, but it does require a search of existing names.

*Barbara Allen and
Mrs. Allen's SHED-STOP*

When Barbara Allen launched a business selling an old family recipe of oils and vitamins that prevented pets from shedding, she named her product Mrs. Allen's SHED-STOP. Rather than applying for a patent for her product, however, Allen chose to register its name as a trademark. "If we went the patent route," she explains, "we'd have to divulge the formula. So we decided on the 'Coca-Cola' approach—trademark the name and keep the formula secret."[19]

An entrepreneur may lose the exclusive right to a trademark if it loses its unique character and becomes a generic name or if the company abandons its trademark by failing to market the brand adequately. Aspirin, escalator, thermos, brassiere, super glue, yoyo, and cellophane all were once enforceable trademarks that have become common words in the English language. These generic terms can no longer be licensed as a company's trademark.

## Copyrights

A **copyright** is an exclusive right that protects the creators of original works of authorship such as literary, dramatic, musical, and artistic works (e.g., art, sculptures, literature, software, music, videos, video games, choreography, motion pictures, recordings, and others). The internationally recognized symbol © denotes a copyrighted work. A copyright protects only the form in which an idea is expressed, not the idea itself. A copyright on a creative work comes into existence the moment its creator puts that work into a tangible form. Just as with a trademark, obtaining basic copyright protection does not require registering the creative work with the U.S. Copyright Office; doing so, however, gives creators greater protection over their work. When author J. K. Rowling wrote the manuscripts for the immensely popular *Harry Potter* series, she automatically had a copyright on her creation. To secure her works against infringement, however, Rowling registered the copyright with the U.S. Copyright Office (and with the copyright offices in other countries). Copyright applications must be filed with the Copyright Office in the U.S. Library of Congress for a fee of $30 per application. A valid copyright on a work lasts for the life of the creator plus 70 years after his or her death. (A copyright lasts 75 to 100 years if the copyright holder is a business.) When a copyright expires, the work becomes public property and can be used by anyone free of charge.

Because they are so easy to duplicate, computer software programs, CDs, and DVDs are among the most-often-pirated items by copyright infringers. The motion picture industry loses an estimated $18 billion a year to piracy.[20] The average cost of a DVD in the United States, for example, is $16.75, but the typical street price for a pirated DVD is just $1.[21] In fact, before the latest *Spiderman* epic was released in theaters, street vendors in Beijing were selling pirated copies of it for $1!

## Protecting Intellectual Property

Acquiring the protection of patents, trademarks, and copyrights is useless unless an entrepreneur takes action to protect those rights in the marketplace. Unfortunately, some businesspeople do not respect others' rights of ownership to products, processes, names, and works and infringe on those rights with impunity. In other cases, the infringing behavior simply is the result of a lack of knowledge about other's rights of ownership. After acquiring the proper legal protection through patents, copyrights, or trademarks, entrepreneurs must monitor the market (and the World Wide Web in particular) for unauthorized copycat users. If an entrepreneur has a valid patent, trademark, or copyright, stopping an infringer usually requires nothing more than a stern "cease and desist" letter from an attorney. Often, offenders don't want to get into expensive legal battles and agree to stop their illegal behavior. If that tactic fails, the entrepreneur may have no choice but to bring an infringement lawsuit, many of which end up being settled out of court.

The primary weapon an entrepreneur has to protect patents, trademarks, and copyrights is the legal system. The major problem with relying on the legal system to enforce ownership rights is the cost of infringement lawsuits, which can quickly exceed the budget of

## Will We Be Sued Out of Existence?

TerraCycle, a small company started in 2003 by Tom Szaky and John Beyer while they were students at Princeton, makes vermiculture compost, a fancy term for an all-natural liquid fertilizer that is made from earthworm excrement. TerraCycle, which packages its liquid fertilizer in recycled soft drink bottles, generates annual sales of $1.5 million, less than one-tenth of one percent of the sales of its largest competitor, Scotts Miracle-Gro. Yet Scotts recently filed a lawsuit against TerraCycle, claiming that the small company's packaging, with its yellow and green color scheme, brand name in the center, and photos of flowers and vegetables at the bottom, infringes on the trade dress of Scotts Miracle-Gro brand of fertilizer. Scotts' complaint, which includes 86 points, also accuses TerraCycle of engaging in false advertising, which is a violation of the Lanham Act, and is asking the court to award all of the gains generated by the alleged violations to Scotts. A court ruling in favor of Scotts would wipe out TerraCycle. Szaky sees irony in the false advertising claims because TerraCycle has done very little advertising in its brief history. "I don't think we have advertised this year at all," he says. "We have only had one printed advertisement in our history."

The battle over trademarks comes just as TerraCycle's rapid growth has landed its organic fertilizer, TerraCycle Plant Food, in more than 7,000 locations, including big-box retail stores. The company is riding the wave of a customer movement toward products that are natural and environmentally friendly. In addition to its environmental benefits, TerraCycle Plant Food also works! An independent study by the Rutgers Eco-Complex concluded that TerraCycle Plant Food performs as well or better than the leading chemical fertilizer (which happens to be Scotts Miracle-Gro). Retailers find the product attractive as well because the company's low cost structure (Earthworms are some of its most important "employees.") means that it can offer its distributors higher profit margins than they can earn on chemical fertilizers.

Small companies such as TerraCycle are at a distinct disadvantage when a larger rival files a lawsuit against them because they lack the resources to fight lengthy and expensive legal battles and because the legal wrangling

Tom Szaky, cofounder of TerraCycle.

distracts managers from running their companies. In addition to hiring an attorney to answer Scotts' claim, Szaky is relying on a guerrilla strategy, turning to the Internet in an effort to enlist a wave of public support and to raise money for the company's legal defense. A company blog, www.suedbyscotts.com, posts Scotts' complaint against TerraCycle, TerraCycle's legal response to the lawsuit (called an answer), facts about the case, and photos that show the drastic differences between the two companies. Szaky says that the lawsuit is unfounded. "The idea of trade dress laws is to protect against knockoffs like fake Prada bags that could confuse consumers," he says.

TerraCycle's answer to the lawsuit denies Scotts' claims and accuses Scotts of falsely advertising the quality of its own products and seeks cancellation of Miracle-Gro's green and yellow trademark. After the Sued by Scotts Web site went live, traffic on TerraCycle's main Web site went from about 1,000 visitors per day to as many as 13,000 per day. One attorney says that TerraCycle's strategy to use public opinion against its larger, deep-pocketed rival carries risks, however. "What if you are wrong about the court of public opinion and you open yourself up to claims of defamation?" he asks.

TerraCycle's attorney says that forcing TerraCycle to change its packaging would cause the company to lose its sales momentum, citing the problem of "the loss of cus-tomer recognition." Still, the small company also must deal with the expense and distraction of the lawsuit. As part of the discovery process, Scotts has asked for thou-sands of documents, ranging from information about new products that the company might have in develop-ment and contracts with retailers to its strategic plan and details about "the composition of the materials con-sumed by worms." Szaky says that legal costs so far have totaled less than $50,000, which is a significant amount for a small company. The two companies recently agreed to a settlement, saving themselves hundreds of thousands of dollars they would have likely spent had they engaged in an extended legal battle in the court system.

1. Use the resources of the Web to research the facts of this case. Pay close attention to the two companies' packaging. Do you think that Scotts has a legitimate complaint?
2. What strategy do you recommend to owners of small companies to minimize the impact of lawsuits such as one that TerraCycle faced?

*Sources:* Adapted from Gwendolyn Bounds, "A Growing Dispute," *Wall Street Journal,* May 22, 2007, pp. B1, B10; Bo Burlingham, "The Coolest Little Start-up in America," *Inc.,* July 2006, pp. 78–85; "Our Story," TerraCycle, www.terracycle.net/story.htm; Doug Eshleman, "TerraCycle Faces Scotts Miracle-Gro Lawsuit," *Daily Princetonian,* April 26, 2007, www.dailyprincetonian.com/archives/2007/04/26/news/18275.shtml.

most small business. Legal battles usually are expensive. Before bringing a lawsuit, an en-trepreneur must consider the following issues:

- Can the opponent afford to pay if you win?
- Do you expect to get enough from the suit to cover the costs of hiring an attorney and preparing a case?
- Can you afford the loss of time, money, and privacy from the ensuing lawsuit?

## The Law of Agency

**4.** Explain the basics of the law of agency.

An **agent** is one who stands in the place of and represents another in business dealings. Al-though he or she has the power to act for the principal, an agent remains subject to the prin-cipal's control. Many small business managers do not realize that their employees are agents while performing job-related tasks. Employers are liable only for those acts that em-ployees perform within the scope of employment. For example, if an employee loses con-trol of a flower shop's delivery van while making a delivery and crashes into several parked cars, the owner of the flower shop (the principal) and the employee (the agent) are liable for any damages caused by the crash. Even if the accident occurred while the employee was on a small detour of his own (e.g., to stop by his house), the owner is still liable for dam-ages as long as the employee is working "within the scope of his employment." Normally, an employee is considered to be within the scope of his or her employment if the employee is motivated in part by the principal's action and if the place and time for performing the act is not significantly different from what is authorized.

Any person, even those lacking contractual capacity, can serve as an agent, but a princi-pal must have the legal capacity to create contracts. Both the principal and the agent are bound by the requirements of a fiduciary relationship, one characterized by trust and good faith. In addition, each party has specific duties to the other. An agent's duties include the following:

- *Loyalty.* Every agent must be faithful to the principal in all business dealings.
- *Performance.* An agent must perform his or her duties according to the principal's instructions.
- *Notification.* The agent must notify the principal of all facts and information con-cerning the subject matter of the agency.
- *Duty of care.* An agent must act with reasonable care when performing duties for the principal.
- *Accounting.* An agent is responsible for accounting for all profits and property received or distributed on the principal's behalf.

A principal's duties include the following:

- **■ *Compensation.*** Unless a free agency is created, the principal must pay the agent for his or her services.
- **■ *Reimbursement.*** The principal must reimburse the agent for all payments made for the principal or any expenses incurred in the administration of the agency.
- **■ *Cooperation.*** Every principal has the duty to indemnify the agent for any authorized payments or any loss or damages incurred by the agency, unless the liability is the result of the agent's mistake.
- **■ *Safe working conditions.*** The law requires a principal to provide a safe working environment for all agents. Workers' compensation laws cover an employer's liability for injuries agents receive on the job.

As agents, employees can bind a company to agreements, even if the owner did not intend for them to do so. An employee can create a binding obligation, for instance, if the business owner represents him or her as authorized to perform such transactions. For example, the owner of a flower shop who routinely permits a clerk to place orders with a supplier has given that employee *apparent authority* for purchasing. Similarly, employees have *implied authority* to create agreements when performing the normal duties of their jobs. For example, the chief financial officer of a company has the authority to create binding agreements when dealing with the company's bank.

One issue related to agency that many businesses confront is whether their workers are employees who are directly under their control or independent contractors who are hired temporarily by contract to perform a job. Because employers do not have to incur payroll taxes or provide health care or other benefits to independent contractors, paying an independent contractor is less expensive than hiring an employee to do the same job. In addition, an employer is liable for negligent acts by an employee but is not liable for the negligent acts of an independent contractor. Some businesses have experienced disputes with the U.S. Internal Revenue Service (IRS) over the status of workers that they claim are independent contractors and the IRS considers employees. The difference boils down to the right of control. The more control that an entrepreneur exercises over a worker, the more likely it is that he or she is an employee. If, on the other hand, the employer controls only the final result of the work, the worker is most likely an independent contractor. The IRS provides guidelines for determining the difference between employees and independent contractors on its Web site, www.irs.gov.

## Bankruptcy

**5.** Explain the basics of bankruptcy law.

**Bankruptcy** occurs when a business is unable to pay its debts as they come due. Although filing for bankruptcy traditionally has had a social stigma attached to it, today it has become an accepted business strategy for troubled companies (see Figure 22.4).

### Forms of Bankruptcy

Many of those filing for bankruptcy are small business owners seeking protection from creditors under one of the eight chapters created by the U.S. Bankruptcy Reform Act of 1978, which was amended in 2005. The Bankruptcy Reform Act of 2005 requires debtors to pay as many of their debts as possible rather than having them discharged by bankruptcy. Under the act, three (Chapters 7, 11, and 13) govern the majority of bankruptcies related to small businesses. Usually, small business owners in danger of failing can choose from two types of bankruptcies: **liquidation** (Chapter 7, in which an owner files for bankruptcy, and the business ceases to exist) and **reorganization** (Chapter 11 in which after filing for bankruptcy, the owner formulates a reorganization plan under which the business continues to operate).

**CHAPTER 7: LIQUIDATION.** The most common type of bankruptcy is filed under Chapter 7 (called straight bankruptcy), which accounts for 70 percent of all filings. Under Chapter 7,

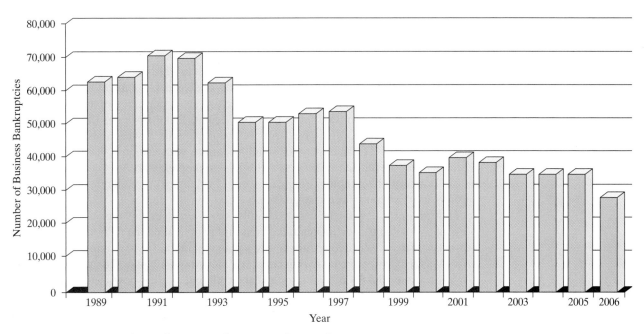

**FIGURE 22.4 Number of U.S. Business Bankruptcies**

*Source:* American Bankruptcy Institute, 2004, www.abiworld.org/ContentManagement/ContentDisplay.cfm?ContentID=8149.

the debtor simply declares all of his or her company's debts; he or she must then turn over all assets to a trustee, who is elected by the creditors or appointed by the court. The trustee sells the assets and distributes all proceeds first to secured creditors and then to unsecured creditors (which include stockholders). Depending on the outcome of the asset sale, creditors can receive anywhere between 0 and 100 percent of their claims against the bankrupt company. Once the bankruptcy proceeding is complete, any remaining debts are discharged, and the company disappears.

Straight bankruptcy proceedings can be started by filing either a voluntary or an involuntary petition. A voluntary case starts when the debtor files a petition with a bankruptcy court, stating the names and addresses of all creditors, the debtor's financial position, and all property the debtor owns. On the other hand, creditors start an involuntary petition by filing with the bankruptcy court. If there are 12 or more creditors, at least 3 of them whose unsecured claims total $12,300 or more must file the involuntary petition. If a debtor has fewer than 12 creditors, only one of them having a claim of $12,300 or more is required to file. As soon as a petition (voluntary or involuntary) is filed in a bankruptcy court, all creditors' claims against the debtor are suspended. Called an automatic stay, this provision prevents creditors from collecting any of the debts the debtor owed them before the petition was filed. In other words, no creditor can begin or continue to pursue debt collection once the petition is filed.

Not every piece of property the individual bankrupt debtor owns is subject to court attachment. According to the code certain assets are exempt, although each state establishes its own exemptions. Most U.S. states make an allowance for equity in a home, interest in an automobile, interest in a large number of personal items, and other personal assets. Federal law allows an $18,450 exemption for a home, $9,850 exemption for household items and clothing, a $2,950 exemption for equity in a car, and several other exemptions.

The law does not allow a debtor to transfer the ownership of property to others to avoid its seizure in a bankruptcy. If a debtor transfers property within two years of the filing of a bankruptcy petition, the trustee can ignore the transfer and claim the assets. In addition, any transfer of property made for the express purpose of avoiding repayment of debts (called fraudulent conveyance) will be overturned. The new law also enables a judge to dismiss a Chapter 7 bankruptcy petition if it is a "substantial abuse" of the bankruptcy code.

**CHAPTER 11: REORGANIZATION.** For a small business weakened by a faltering economy or management mistakes, Chapter 11 provides a second chance for success. The philosophy behind this form of bankruptcy is that ailing companies can prosper again if given a fresh start with less debt. Under Chapter 11, a company is protected from creditors' legal actions while it formulates a plan for reorganization and debt repayment or settlement. In most cases, a small business and its creditors negotiate a settlement in which the company repays a percentage of its debts and is freed of the remainder. The business continues to operate under the court's direction, but creditors cannot foreclose on it, nor can they collect any pre-bankruptcy debts the company owes. One study reports that the average Chapter 11 bankruptcy requires 2.25 years to resolve.[22] An exemption passed in 1994 established a fast-track version of Chapter 11 bankruptcy for small businesses with liabilities that do not exceed $2 million that streamlines the process and is less expensive.

A Chapter 11 bankruptcy filing can be either voluntary or involuntary. Once the petition is filed, an automatic stay goes into effect and the debtor has 120 days to file a reorganization plan with the court. Usually, the court does not replace management with an appointed trustee; instead, the bankrupt party, called the debtor in possession, serves as trustee. If the debtor fails to file a plan within the 120-day limit, any party involved in the bankruptcy, including creditors, may propose a plan. The plan must identify the various classes of creditors and their claims, outline how each class will be treated, and establish a method to implement the plan. It also must spell out the debts that the company cannot pay, those that it can pay, and the methods the debtor will use to repay them.

Once the plan is filed, the court must decide whether to approve it. A court will approve a plan if a majority of each of the three classes of creditors—secured, priority, and unsecured—votes in favor of it. The court will confirm a plan if it has a reasonable chance of success, is submitted in good faith, and is "in the best interest of the creditors." If the court rejects the plan, the creditors must submit a new one for court approval.

Filing under Chapter 11 offers a weakened small business a number of advantages, the greatest of which is a chance to survive (although most of the companies that file under Chapter 11 ultimately are liquidated). In addition, employees keep their jobs, and customers get an uninterrupted supply of goods and services. But there are costs involved in bankruptcy proceedings. Customers, suppliers, creditors, and often employees lose confidence in a company's ability to succeed. Creditors frequently incur substantial losses in Chapter 11 bankruptcies, receiving payments of just pennies for every dollar they are owed.

**CHAPTER 13: DEBT REPAYMENT PLAN FOR INDIVIDUALS.** Chapter 13 bankruptcy is the consumer version of Chapter 11 proceedings. Individual debtors (not businesses) with a regular income who owe unsecured debts of less than $307,675 or secured debts of less than $922,975 may file for bankruptcy under Chapter 13. Many debtors who have the choice of filing under Chapter 11 or 13 find that Chapter 13 is less complicated and less expensive. Chapter 13 proceedings must begin voluntarily. Once the debtor files a petition, creditors cannot start or continue legal action to collect payment. Under Chapter 13, only the debtor can file a repayment plan, whose terms cannot exceed five years. If the court approves the plan, the debtor may pay off the obligations—either in full or partially—on an installment basis. The plan is designed with the debtor's future income in mind, and when the debtor completes the payments under the plan, all debts are discharged.

## Government Regulation

*6.* Explain some of the government regulations affecting small businesses, including those governing trade practices, consumer protection, consumer credit, and the environment.

Although most entrepreneurs recognize the need for some government regulation of business, most believe the process is overwhelming and out of control. Small business owners often feel overwhelmed by the paperwork required to respond to all the governmental agencies trying to regulate and protect them. For instance, a U.S. entrepreneur who wants to start an auto repair shop must contend with 38 sets of regulations from 18 federal, state, and local agencies.[23]

The major complaint that small business owners have concerning government regulation concerns the cost of compliance. The National Federation of Independent Businesses estimates that complying with government regulations cost businesses $1.1 trillion per year.[24] Because of their size, the regulatory burden falls most heavily on small businesses. Large companies can spread the cost of compliance over a larger number of employees, and consequently, have a lower regulatory cost per employee. A study conducted by Mark Crain of Lafayette College for the Small Business Administration shows that the cost of compliance per employee for small companies with 1 to 20 workers is $7,647, which is significantly higher than the $5,411 cost per employee at companies with more than 20 workers.[25] Small manufacturers bear a particularly heavy regulatory burden. The same study reports that complying with federal regulations cost manufacturers with 20 or fewer workers $15,747 per employee, more than three times the $4,970 cost per worker for manufacturers with 21 to 499 employees.[26]

In a competitive market, small companies cannot simply pass these additional costs forward to their customers and, consequently, they experience a squeeze on their profit margins. The U.S. Small Business Regulatory Enforcement and Fairness Act offers business owners some hope. Its purpose is to require government agencies to consider the impact of their regulations on small companies and gives business owners more input into the regulatory process.

Most business owners agree that some government regulation is necessary. There must be laws governing working safety, environmental protection, package labeling, consumer credit, and other relevant issues because some dishonest, unscrupulous managers will abuse the opportunity to serve the public's interest. It is not the regulations that protect workers and consumers and achieve social objectives to which business owners object but those that produce only marginal benefits relative to their costs. Owners of small companies, especially, seek relief from wasteful and meaningless government regulations, charging that the cost of compliance exceeds the benefits gained.

## Trade Practices

**SHERMAN ANTITRUST ACT.** Contemporary society places great value on free competition in the marketplace, and antitrust laws reflect this. The notion of *laissez-faire*—that the government should not interfere with the operation of the economy—that once dominated U.S. markets no longer prevails. One of the earliest trade laws was the Sherman Antitrust Act, which was passed in 1890 to promote competition in the U.S. economy. This act is the foundation on which antitrust policy in the United States is built and was aimed at breaking up the most powerful monopolies of the late nineteenth century. The U.S. Sherman Antitrust Act contains two primary provisions affecting growth and trade among businesses.

Section I forbids "every contract, combination in the form of trust or otherwise, or conspiracy, in restraint of trade or commerce among the several states, or with foreign nations." This section outlaws any agreement among sellers that might create an unreasonable restraint on free trade in the marketplace. For example, a group of small- and medium-size regional supermarkets formed a cooperative association to purchase products to resell under private labels only in restricted geographic regions. The U.S. Supreme Court ruled that their action was an attempt to restrict competition by allocating territories and had "no purpose except stifling of competition."[27]

Section II of the Sherman Antitrust Act makes it illegal for any person to "monopolize or attempt to monopolize any part of the trade or commerce among the several states, or with foreign nations." The primary focus of Section II is on preventing the undesirable effects of monopoly power in the marketplace.

**CLAYTON ACT.** The United States passed the Clayton Act in 1914 to strengthen federal antitrust laws by spelling out specific monopolistic activities. The major provisions of the Clayton Act forbid the following activities:

1. *Price discrimination.* A firm cannot charge different customers different prices for the same product, unless the price discrimination is based on an actual cost savings, is made to meet a lower price from competitors, or is justified by a difference in grade, quality, or quantity sold.

2. *Exclusive dealing and tying contracts.* A seller cannot require a buyer to purchase only his or her product to the exclusion of other competitive sellers' products (an exclusive dealing agreement). Also, the act forbids sellers to sell a product on the condition that the buyer agrees to purchase another product the seller offers (a tying agreement). For example, a computer manufacturer cannot sell a computer to a business and, as a condition of the sale, require the firm to purchase software as well.

3. *Purchasing stock in competing corporations.* A business cannot purchase the stock or assets of another business when the effect may be to substantially lessen competition. This does not mean that a corporation cannot hold stock in a competing company; the rule is designed to prevent horizontal mergers that would reduce competition. The U.S. Federal Trade Commission and U.S. Antitrust Division of the Justice Department enforce this section, evaluating the market shares of the companies involved and the potential effects of a horizontal merger before ruling on its legality.

4. *Interlocking directorates.* The act forbids interlocking directorates—a person serving on the board of directors of two or more competing companies.

**FEDERAL TRADE COMMISSION ACT.** To supplement the Clayton Act, the United States passed the Federal Trade Commission Act in 1914, which created its namesake agency and gave it a broad range of powers. Section 5 gives the FTC the power to prevent "unfair methods of competition in commerce and unfair or deceptive acts or practices in commerce." To be considered deceptive, a company's activity must involve a material misrepresentation that is likely to mislead a consumer who is acting in a reasonable manner.

Recent amendments have expanded the FTC's powers. The FTC's primary targets are those businesses that engage in unfair trade practices, often brought to the surface by consumer complaints. In addition, the agency has issued a number of trade regulation rules defining acceptable and unacceptable trade practices in various industries. Its major weapon is a "cease and desist order," commanding the violator to stop its unfair trade practices.

The FTC Act and the Lanham Trademark Act of 1988 (plus state laws) govern the illegal practice of deceptive advertising. In general, the FTC can review any advertisement that might mislead people into buying a product or service they would not buy if they knew the truth. For instance, if a small business advertised a "huge year-end inventory reduction sale" but kept its prices the same as its regular prices, it is violating the law.

**ROBINSON-PATMAN ACT.** Although the Clayton Act addressed price discrimination and the Federal Trade Commission forbade the practice, the United States found the need to strengthen the law because many businesses circumvented the original rules. In 1936, it passed the Robinson-Patman Act, which further restricted price discrimination in the marketplace. The act forbids any seller "to discriminate in price between different purchases of commodities of like grade and quality" unless there are differences in the cost of manufacturing, selling, or delivering the goods. Even if a price-discriminating firm escaped guilt under the Clayton Act, it violated the Robinson-Patman Act. Traditionally, the FTC has had the primary responsibility of enforcing the Robinson-Patman Act.

**OTHER LEGISLATION.** The Celler-Kefauver Act of 1950 gave the FTC the power to review certain proposals for mergers so it could prevent too much concentration of power in any particular industry.

Congress created the Miller-Tydings Act in 1937 to introduce an exception to the Sherman Antitrust Act. This act made it legal for manufacturers to use fair trade agreements that prohibit sellers of the manufacturer's product from selling it below a predetermined fair trade price. This form of price fixing was outlawed when the country repealed the Miller-Tydings Act in 1976. Manufacturers can no longer mandate minimum or maximum prices on their products to sellers.

## Consumer Protection

Since the early 1960s, legislators have created many laws aimed at protecting consumers from unscrupulous sellers, unreasonable credit terms, and mislabeled or unsafe products.

## Are Your Ads Setting You Up for Trouble?

When an auto dealer in the state of Florida offered a "free four-day, three-night vacation to Acapulco" for any customer purchasing a new car or van, he had no idea of the legal problems his advertisement would create. A customer who bought a van from the dealer felt cheated when he discovered that the "free vacation" was actually a sales promotion for a time-share condominium and was overrun with restrictions, conditions, and qualifications. Believing the ad was deceptive, the customer filed a lawsuit against the dealer. The jury ruled against the car dealer and awarded the customer $1,768 in compensatory damages and $667,000 in punitive damages.

Entrepreneurs sometimes run afoul of the laws concerning advertising because they do not know how to comply with legal requirements. The Federal Trade Commission (FTC) is the federal agency that regulates advertising and deals with problems created by deceptive ads. Under federal and state laws, an advertisement is unlawful if it misleads or deceives a reasonable customer, even if the business owner responsible for it had no intention to deceive. Any ad containing a false statement is in violation of the law although the entrepreneur may not know that the statement is false. The FTC judges an ad by the overall impression it creates and not by the technical truthfulness of its individual parts.

What can entrepreneurs do to avoid charges of deceptive advertising? The following guidelines will help:

- *Make sure that your ads are accurate.* Avoid creating ads that promise more than a product or service can deliver. Take the time to verify the accuracy of every claim or statement in your ads. If a motor oil protects an engine from damage, don't claim that it will repair damage that already exists in an engine—unless you can prove that it actually does.
- *Understand the difference between sales "puffery" and false advertising.* The distinction is not always clear. Sales puffery involves claims that are so general or so exaggerated that they would not confuse customers. (How many times have you seen a small restaurant advertising that it has "the best hot dog in town"?) The more specific and fact-

based the claims in an ad are, the more likely they are to pose problems for a company if they are false or if the company has no factual basis for making them. When Pizza Hut ("Best Pizza Under One Roof") filed a false advertising claim against Papa John's Pizza over a Papa John's ad that claimed "Better Ingredients, Better Pizza," a U.S. court of appeals ruled that Papa John's claim was puffery and that the company could continue to use it *if* it stopped making specific fact-based claims in the same ad that its tomato paste and dough were superior. For instance, the ad for Papa John's claimed that its sauce, which was made from "vine-ripened tomatoes," was superior to Pizza Hut's "remanufactured tomato sauce." Because Papa John's had no facts to prove this claim, the court ruled that this was false advertising.

- *Get permission to use quotations, pictures, and endorsements.* Never use material in an ad from an outside source unless you get written permission to do so. One business owner got into trouble when he inserted a photograph of a famous athlete without his permission into an ad for his company's service.
- *Be careful when you compare competitor's products or services to your own.* False statements that harm the reputation of a competitor's business, products, or services not only may result in charges of false advertising but also in claims of trade libel. Make sure that any claims in your ads comparing your products to competitors' are fair and accurate. You can use a competitor's trademark in your advertising (for purposes of comparison, for example) as long as it does not cause confusion among customers concerning the origin of the product or its affiliation with the competitor.
- *Stock sufficient quantities of advertised items.* Businesses that advertise items for sale must be sure to have enough units on hand to meet anticipated demand. If you suspect that demand may outstrip your supply, state in the ad that quantities are limited.
- *Avoid "bait and switch" advertising.* This illegal technique involves advertising an item for sale at an attractive price when a business has no real

*(continued)*

intention of selling that product at that price. Companies using this technique often claim to have sold out of the advertised special. Their goal is to lure customers in with the low price and then switch them over to a similar product at a higher price.

■ *Use the word "free" carefully and accurately.* Every advertiser knows that one of the most power words in advertising is "free." However, anything you advertise as being free must actually be free. For instance, suppose a business advertises a free paintbrush to anyone who buys a gallon of a particular type of paint for $11.95. If the company's regular price for the paint is less than $11.95, the ad is deceptive because the paintbrush is not really free.

■ *Be careful of what your ad does not say.* Omitting information in an ad that leaves customers with a false impression about a product or service and its performance is also a violation of the law.

■ *Describe sale prices and "savings" carefully.* Business owners sometimes get into trouble with false advertising when they advertise items at prices that offer huge "savings" over their "regular" prices. One jeweler violated the law by advertising a bracelet for $299, a savings of $200 from the item's regular $499 price. In reality, the jeweler had never sold the item at its $499 "regular" price; the item's normal price was $299, which he advertised as the "sale" price.

*Sources:* Adapted from *Guides Against Bait Advertising,* Federal Trade Commission, www.gov/bcp/guides/baitads-gd.htm; *Frequently Asked Questions: A Guide for Small Business,* Federal Trade Commission, www.ftc.gov/bcp/cdnline/pubs/buspubs/ad-faqs.htm; Carlotta Roberts, "The Customer's Always Right," *Entrepreneur,* November 20, 2002, www.entrepreneur.com/article/0,4621.284044.00.html; James Astrachan, "False Advertising Primer," (Baltimore, Maryland: Astrachan, Gunst, Thomas, PLC, 2006), www.aboutfalseadvertising.com/index1files/False%20Advertising%20Primer.pdf, p. 14; "Seven Rules for Legal Advertising," *Inc.,* www.inc.com/search/20153.html; "Consumer protection Laws," *Inc.,* www.inc.com/search/l9691.html.

Early laws focused on ensuring that food and drugs sold in the marketplace were safe and of proper quality. The first law passed in the United States, the Pure Food and Drug Act, passed in 1906, regulated the labeling of various food and drug products. Later amendments empowered government agencies to establish safe levels of food additives and to outlaw carcinogenic (cancer-causing) additives. In 1938, the United States passed the Food, Drug, and Cosmetics Act, which created the Food and Drug Administration (FDA). The FDA is responsible for establishing standards of safe over-the-counter drugs; inspecting food and drug manufacturing operations; performing research on food, additives, and drugs; regulating drug labeling; and other related tasks.

The United States also has created a number of laws to establish standards pertaining to product labeling for consumer protection. Since 1976, manufacturers have been required to print accurate information about the quantity and content of their products in a conspicuous place on the package. Generally, labels must identify the raw materials used in the product, the manufacturer, the distributor (and its place of business), the net quantity of the contents, and the quantity of each serving if the package states the number of servings. The law also requires labels to be truthful. For example, a candy bar labeled "new, bigger size" must actually be bigger. These requirements, created by the Fair Packaging and Labeling Act of 1976, were designed to improve the customers' ability to comparison shop. A 1970 amendment to the Fair Packaging and Labeling Act, the Poison Prevention Packaging Act, required manufacturers to install child-proof caps on all products that are toxic.

With the passage of the Consumer Products Safety Act in 1972, the United States created the CPSC to control potentially dangerous products sold to consumers, and it has broad powers over manufacturers and sellers of consumer products. For instance, the CPSC can set safety requirements for consumer products, and it has the power to ban the production of any product it considers hazardous to consumers. It can also order vendors to remove unsafe products from their shelves. In addition to enforcing the Consumer Product Safety Act, the CPSC is also charged with enforcing the Refrigerator Safety Act, the Federal Hazardous Substance Act, the Child Protection and Toy Safety Act, the Poison Prevention Package Act, and the Flammable Fabrics Act.

The Magnuson-Moss Warranty Act, passed in 1975 by the United States, regulates written warranties that companies offer on the consumer goods they sell. The act does not require companies to offer warranties; it only regulates the warranties companies choose to offer. It also requires businesses to state warranties in easy-to-understand language and defines the conditions warranties must meet before they can be designated as "full warranties."

The Telemarketing and Consumer Fraud and Abuse Protection Act of 1994 put in place the following restrictions on telemarketers:

- Calling a person's residence at any time other than 8:00 A.M. to 8:00 P.M.
- Claiming an affiliation with a government agency where such an affiliation does not exist.
- Claiming an ability to improve a customer's credit record or obtain a loan for a person regardless of that person's credit history.
- Not telling the receiver of the call that it is a sales call.
- Claiming an ability to recover goods or money lost by a consumer.

## Consumer Credit

Another area subject to intense government regulation is consumer credit. This section of the law has grown in importance since credit has become a major part of many consumer purchases. The primary U.S. law regulating consumer credit is the Truth-in-Lending Act of 1969. This law requires sellers who extend credit and lenders to fully disclose the terms and conditions of credit arrangements. The Federal Trade Commission is responsible for enforcing the Truth-in-Lending Act. The law outlines specific requirements that any firm that offers, arranges, or extends credit to customers must meet. The two most important terms of the credit arrangement that lenders must disclose are the finance charge and the annual percentage rate. The finance charge represents the total cost—direct and indirect—of the credit, and the annual percentage rate (APR) is the relative cost of credit stated in annual percentage terms.

The Truth-in-Lending Act applies to any consumer loan for less than $25,000 (or loans of any amount secured by mortgages on real estate) that includes more than four installments. Merchants extending credit to customers must state clearly the following information, using specific terminology:

- The price of the product.
- The down payment and any trade-in allowance made.
- The unpaid balance owed after the down payment.
- The total dollar amount of the finance charge.
- Any prepaid finance charges or required deposit balances, such as points, service charges, or lenders' fees.
- Any other charges not included in the finance charge.
- The total amount to be financed.
- The unpaid balance.
- The deferred payment price, including the total cash price and finance and incidental charges.
- The date on which the finance charge begins to accrue.
- The annual percentage rate of the finance charge.
- The number, amount, and due dates of payments.
- The penalties imposed in case of delinquent payments.
- A description of any security interest the creditor holds.
- A description of any penalties imposed for early repayment of principal.

Another provision of the Truth-in-Lending Act limits the credit cardholder's liability in case the holder's card is lost or stolen. As long as the holder notifies the company of the missing card, he or she is liable for only $50 of any amount that an unauthorized user might charge on the card (or zero if the holder notifies the company before any unauthorized use of the card).

In 1974 the Fair Credit Billing Act, an amendment to the Truth in Lending Act, was passed. Under this law, a credit cardholder may withhold payment on a faulty product, providing he or she has made a good faith effort to settle the dispute first. A credit cardholder also can withhold payment to the issuing company if he or she believes his or her bill is in error. The cardholder must notify the issuer within 60 days but is not required to pay the bill

In the Entrepreneurial **Spotlight**

### ■ "We're Shuttin' You Down"

Five years after launching their business, Boston Billows, a small company that makes nursing pillows for infants, Erik Skoug, 73, and Ken Igoe, 57, received a letter from their largest competitor, Boppy Company, that claimed that the poly-bead filling in its pillows could be "unsafe for use with infants and small children." The entrepreneurs began to realize that Boppy, which uses a different filler in its nursing pillow, saw Boston Billows, whose annual sales had grown to $750,000, as a threat. A few months later, however, they discovered the real threat when they received another letter, this one from the Consumer Product Safety Commission (CPSC), the U.S. government agency charged with ensuring the safety of consumer products, that demanded that Boston Billows recall all of the pillows that the company had sold because they were deemed unsafe. The CPSC said that a tip from a competitor had prompted the recall letter. Skoug and Igoe were shocked because Boston Billows' nursing pillows had never been linked to any injuries or deaths. In fact, hospitals, pediatricians, and lactation consultants (nurses who specialize in helping new mothers breast-feed their babies) enthusiastically endorsed Boston Billows' products because they help newborn babies, especially premature babies, nurse more easily. Diane DiSandro, who has been a lactation consultant for 25 years, says, "Boston Billows' [pillows] provides more support under a baby's head" than competing pillows.

The unwarranted safety challenge stemmed from problems with a completely different product, mattresses, that used the same poly-bead filling and that were related to 35 infant deaths in the late 1980s and early 1990s. Even though scientists and investigators were never able to determine the causes of the infants' deaths, the CPSC banned the mattresses in 1992. After investigators received the tip letter, they spent three weeks examining Boston Billows' nursing pillows in their lab and concluded that their design and filling were too similar to the mattresses that may or may not have been related to the infants' death. The researchers' decision led to the recall letter that threatened to put Boston Billows out of business for good.

Skoug and Igoe believed that the comparison between the two products was unfair. The filling was the same, but nothing else in the two products was even remotely similar. Their pillow was crescent-shaped and designed to support a nursing baby's head; the mattresses were flat, soft slabs on which babies went to sleep. Skoug and Igoe had researched nursing pillows for two years before they launched Boston Billows. They decided to use the poly-bead filling because it offered many advantages over other fillings and had been used in Europe for decades without any problems at all. Hoping to convince CPSC officials to change their minds, the two entrepreneurs flew to the agency's headquarters for a meeting. The meeting was unproductive. The CPSC told Skoug and Igoe to modify their pillow design (The agency offered no advice on what to modify or how to modify it.) and demanded that Boston Billows recall all of the pillows that currently were on the market. "I asked what would happen if we didn't follow through with the recall," says Skoug. "The CPSC said that it would bring all of the resources of the U.S. government down on us."

Lacking the money to engage in an extended legal battle with a powerful government agency, Boston Billows issued a recall, spending $10,000 to contact retailers, write letters to customers, and issue refunds. For the next 18 months, Skoug and Igoe tried to convince the CPSC to change its decision. They made the pillow smaller and more compact, but the agency ignored the redesigned version of the pillow. The entrepreneurs convinced Senator John Sununu and Congressman Judd Gregg, both from the state of New Hampshire, to write letters and to make telephone calls to the CPSC on behalf of Boston Billows. That resulted in a meeting with the head of the CPSC and seven CPSC lawyers at which Skoug and Igoe explained the months of intense research that they had conducted recently and showed how the banned mattresses were completely different from their nursing pillow. They also offered testimony from experts who had conducted recent research into the 35 deaths that had occurred more than a decade earlier that strongly disputed the charges that the filling in the mattresses was the culprit. After the meeting, the CPSC did nothing to change its decision.

Skoug and Igoe recently resorted to their final option, filing official documents with the CPSC requesting that the agency reverse its decision. The CPSC is one of the smallest government agencies and its budget and headcount have been cut by nearly half since 1975. Its

814

workload has increased in that time, however, which means that it will take at least two years before Boston Billows gets a response to its request.

In the meantime, Skoug and Igoe are trying to keep their company together. They have been forced to lay off all seven of their employees, and the cofounders themselves are filling by hand the few orders that trickle in from the ten hospitals that still use their pillows. (Hospitals are exempt from the CPSC recall.) "We just canceled our UPS account," says Igoe because the company could no longer afford the $40 per month fee for daily pickup service. Sales have plummeted to just $15,000 per year, and Skoug and Igoe say that their only remaining expense, $2,000 per month for their factory and warehouse, may force them to shut the company down

completely. "'Frustrating' is an understatement," says Igoe of their ordeal with the CPSC. "The process is structured this way to force small companies like ours to just go away."

1. Evaluate the steps that Skoug and Igoe took to battle the CPSC's recall ruling. Should they have done anything differently?

2. What do you forecast for Boston Billows' future? Work with a group of your classmates to identify other options that Skoug and Igoe could pursue with their company.

*Sources:* Adapted from Maggie Overfelt, "Uncushioned Blow," *FSB,* December 2006/January 2007, p. 18; Maggie Overfelt, "Total Recall," *FSB,* February 2006, pp. 88–93.

until the dispute is settled. The creditor cannot collect any finance charge during this period unless there was no error.

Another credit law designed to protect consumers is the U.S. Equal Credit Opportunity Act of 1974, which prohibits discrimination in granting credit on the basis of race, religion, national origin, color, sex, marital status, or whether the individual receives public welfare payment.

In 1970, the United States created the Fair Credit Reporting Act to protect consumers against the circulation of inaccurate or obsolete information pertaining to credit applications. Under this act, the consumer can request the nature of any credit investigation, the type of information assembled, and the identity of those persons receiving the report. The law requires that any obsolete or misleading information contained in the file be updated, deleted, or corrected.

U.S. Congress enacted the Fair Debt Collection Practices Act in 1977 to protect consumers from abusive debt collection practices. The law does not apply to business owners collecting their own debts, but only to debt collectors working for other businesses. The act prevents debt collectors from doing the following:

- Contacting the debtor at his or her workplace if the employer objects.
- Using intimidation, harassment, or abusive language to pester the debtor.
- Calling on the debtor at inconvenient times (before 8 A.M. or after 9 P.M.).
- Contacting third parties (except parents, spouses, and financial advisers) about the debt.
- Contacting the consumer after receiving notice of refusal to pay the debt (except to inform the debtor of the involvement of a collection agency).
- Making false threats against the debtor.

The Consumer Leasing Act of 1976 amended the Truth in Lending Act for the purpose of providing meaningful disclosure to consumers who lease goods. The lease period must be more than four months, and the dollar value of the lease obligation cannot exceed $25,000.

In 2003, the United States passed the Fair and Accurate Transactions Act (the FACT Act) to address the fastest growing crime in the United States: identity theft. The FTC estimates that 10 million U.S. citizens have been victim of identity theft, most often in the form of credit card fraud.[28] The FACT Act allows victims of identity theft to file theft reports with credit reporting agencies and requires those agencies to include "fraud alerts" in their credit reports.

### Environmental Law

In 1970, the United States created the Environmental Protection Agency (EPA) and gave it the authority to create laws that would protect the environment from pollution and contamination. Although the EPA administers a number of federal environmental statutes, three in particular stand out: the Clean Air Act, the Clean Water Act, and the Resource Conservation and Recovery Act.

**THE CLEAN AIR ACT.** To reduce the problems associated with global warming, acid rain, and airborne pollution, U.S. Congress passed the Clean Air Act in 1970 (and several amendments since then). The act targets everything from coal-burning power plants to automobiles. The Clean Air Act assigned the EPA the task of developing national air quality standards for carbon monoxide, hydrocarbons, sulfur oxide, ozone, lead, and other harmful substances. The agency works with state and local governments to enforce compliance with these standards.

**THE CLEAN WATER ACT.** The Clean Water Act, passed in 1972, set out to make all navigable waters in the United States suitable for fishing and swimming by 1983 and to eliminate the discharge of pollutants into those waters by 1985. Although the EPA has made progress in cleaning up many bodies of water, it has yet to achieve these goals. The Clean Water Act requires each state to establish water quality standards and to develop plans to reach them. The act also prohibits the draining, dredging, or filling wetlands without a permit. The Clean Water Act also addresses the issues of providing safe drinking water and cleaning up oil spills in navigable waters.

**THE RESOURCE CONSERVATION AND RECOVERY ACT.** Congress passed the Resource Conservation and Recovery Act (RCRA) in 1976 to deal with solid waste disposal. The RCRA, which was amended in 1984, sets guidelines by which solid waste landfills must operate, and it establishes rules governing the disposal of hazardous wastes. The RCRA's goal is to prevent solid waste from contaminating the environment. What about those waste disposal sites that are already contaminating the environment? In 1980, Congress passed the Comprehensive Environmental Response, Compensation, and Liability Act (CERCLA) to deal with those sites. The act created the Superfund, a special federal fund set up to finance and to regulate the cleanup of solid-waste disposal sites that are polluting the environment.

The Pollution Prevention Act of 1990 set forth a public policy statement that offered rewards to firms that reduced the creation of pollution. The federal government provides matching funds to states for programs that promote the use of "source reduction techniques" to deal with pollution problems. This is a milestone piece of legislation because it replaces the regulatory "stick" approach resented by business with a "carrot" approach that rewards businesses for positive actions that reduce pollution.

## Chapter Summary

1. Explain the basic elements required to create a valid, enforceable contract.
   - A valid contract must contain these elements: agreement (offer and acceptance), consideration, capacity, and legality. A contract can be valid and yet unenforceable because it fails to meet two other conditions: genuineness of assent and proper form.
   - Most contracts are fulfilled by both parties performing their promised actions; occasionally, however, one party fails to perform as agreed, thereby breaching the contract. Usually, the nonbreaching party is allowed to sue for monetary damages that would place him or her in the same position he or she would have been in had the contract been performed. In cases where money is an insufficient remedy, the injured party may sue for specific performance of the contract's terms.
2. Outline the major components of the Uniform Commercial Code governing sales contracts.
   - The Uniform Commercial Code (UCC) was an attempt to create a unified body of law governing routine business transactions. Of the ten articles in the UCC, Article 2 on the sale of goods affects many business transactions.

- Contracts for the sale of goods must contain the same four elements of a valid contract, but the UCC relaxes many of the specific restrictions the common law imposes on contracts. Under the UCC, once the parties create a contract, they must perform their duties in good faith.
- The UCC also covers sales warranties. A seller creates an express warranty when he or she makes a statement about the performance of a product or indicates by example certain characteristics of the product. Sellers automatically create other warranties—warranties of title, implied warranties of merchantability, and, in certain cases, implied warranties of fitness for a particular purpose—when they sell a product.

3. Discuss the protection of intellectual property rights using patents, trademarks, and copyrights.
   - A patent is a grant from the government that gives an inventor exclusive rights to an invention for a certain number of years. To submit a patent, an inventor must: establish novelty, document the device, search existing patents, study the search results, submit a patent application to the government, and prosecute the application.
   - A trademark is any distinctive word, symbol, or trade dress that a company uses to identify its product or to distinguish it from other goods. It serves as the company's "signature" in the marketplace.
   - A copyright protects original works of authorship. It covers only the form in which an idea is expressed and not the idea itself. In the United States, it lasts for 70 years beyond the creator's death.

4. Explain the basic workings of the law of agency.
   - In an agency relationship, one party (the agent) agrees to represent another (the principal). The agent has the power to act for the principal but remains subject to the principal's control. While performing job-related tasks, employees play an agent's role.
   - An agent has the following duties to a principal: loyalty, performance, notification, duty of care, and accounting. The principal has certain duties to the agent: compensation, reimbursement, cooperation, indemnification, and safe working conditions.

5. Explain the basics of bankruptcy law.
   - Entrepreneurs whose U.S. businesses fail often have no other choice but to declare bankruptcy under one of three provisions: Chapter 7 liquidation, where the business sells its assets, pays what debts it can, and disappears; Chapter 11, reorganization, where the business asks that its debts be forgiven or restructured and then re-emerges; and Chapter 13, which is for individuals only.

6. Explain some of the government regulations affecting small businesses, including those governing trade practices, consumer protection, consumer credit, and the environment.
   - Businesses operate under a multitude of government regulations governing many areas, including trade practices, where laws forbid restraint of trade, price discrimination, exclusive dealing and tying contracts, purchasing controlling interests in competitors, and interlocking directorates.
   - Other areas subject to U.S. government regulations include consumer protection (the Food, Drug, and Cosmetics Act and the Consumer Product Safety Act) and consumer credit (the Consumer Credit Protection Act [CCPA], the Fair Debt Collection Practices Act and the Fair Credit Reporting Act), and the environment (the Clean Air Act, the Clean Water Act, and the Resource Conservation and Recovery Act [RCRA]).

## Discussion Questions

1. What is a contract? List and describe the four elements required for a valid contract. Must a contract be in writing to be valid?
2. What constitutes an agreement?
3. What groups of people lack contractual capacity? How do the courts view contracts that are created with minors? Intoxicated people? Insane people?
4. What circumstances eliminate genuineness of assent in the parties' agreement?
5. What is breach of contract? What remedies are available to a party injured by a breach?
6. What is the Uniform Commercial Code? To which kinds of contracts does the UCC apply? How does it alter the requirements for a sales contract?
7. Under the UCC, what remedies does a seller have when a buyer breaches a sales contract? What remedies does a buyer have when a seller breaches a contract?
8. What is a sales warranty? Explain the different kinds of warranties sellers offer.
9. Explain the different kinds of implied warranties the UCC imposes on sellers of goods. Can sellers disclaim these implied warranties? If so, how?
10. What is product liability? Explain the charges that most often form the basis for product liability claims. What must a customer prove under these charges?
11. What is intellectual property? What tools do entrepreneurs have to protect their intellectual property?
12. Explain the differences among patents, trademarks, and copyrights. What does each protect? How long does each last?
13. What must an inventor prove to receive a patent?
14. Briefly explain the patent application process.
15. What is an agent? What duties does an agent have to a principal? What duties does a principal have to an agent?
16. Explain the differences among the three major forms of bankruptcy: Chapter 7, Chapter 11, and Chapter 13.
17. Explain the statement "For each benefit gained by regulation, there is a cost."

# Business PlanPro

Navigating the increasingly complex waters of the legal and regulatory environment is no easy task for entrepreneurs. Today's entrepreneurs must understand the basics of business law and government regulations if they are to operate successful businesses. Having access to a qualified attorney to serve as a business advisor is wise, but having a fundamental understanding of how to avoid potential legal entanglements is also important. Some entrepreneurs learn the importance of understanding business law and government regulation only after they face an expensive legal battle or are required to pay a costly fine. Solid planning can avoid this and the business plan can be a tool for the entrepreneur to accomplish this important task.

## On the Web

If you have existing or future concerns regarding potential legal issues facing your company, begin by conducting additional research on the Web. The Companion Website at www.prenhall.com/scarborough for Chapter 22 offers some general information that you may find useful. Industry associations also may provide resources that address more common issues. Does your company face special legal issues? Is your business subject to regulation by one or more government agencies? If so, be sure that your plan addresses these matters. The more you know—and plan for now—the better. Incorporate any insights you gain from these resources into your business plan.

## In the Software

At this point, the only section remaining in your business plan is the executive summary. Even though it is the first section in the plan, it is the last section completed. Because many potential lenders and investors read the executive summary first, your plan may be judged on its value and impact alone. An executive summary is a brief overview of your entire plan. Its purpose is to concisely highlight the key points of the business plan, saving readers time and preparing them for the upcoming content. The executive summary must be clear and concise. It should allow readers to grasp the essence of the business plan very quickly. An executive summary should also entice the reader to read the entire plan. It should be compelling, enabling the reader to see your vision for the venture, and motivating them to read on. For these reasons, the executive summary is the most important section of the business plan. If it fails to accomplish its tasks, the business plan may not be read.

Review the executive summary from a sample plan that you have found beneficial. To get an idea of how an executive summary should flow, you may also want to review these plans: Pegasus Sports, Hand's On Children's Museum, Salvador's Inc., and The Daily Perc. Identify attributes within other executive summaries that you find engaging and incorporate those elements into your plan's executive summary.

Write your executive summary in Business Plan Pro. Remember, this section incorporates key highlights of information in the plan ahead. Keep it brief—ideally two pages or less—and to the point.

## Building Your Business Plan

The chapters in this book have guided you through all of the key aspects of creating a business plan. The final task you will complete, and one that many consider to be the single most important section, is the executive summary. Once this section is completed, your business plan is ready. Share your business plan with others whom you trust and respect. Test its effectiveness in describing your business venture. Ask for feedback. Modify sections that are unclear or fail to effectively communicate your business's message to others.

And then . . . when you are ready and the plan feels solid, the ultimate test is the answer to this question: "Would *you* invest in the venture?"

# Appendix

## My Friends' Bookstore Plan

Dana Waters

## Confidentiality Agreement

The undersigned reader acknowledges that the information provided by _____ in this business plan is confidential; therefore, reader agrees not to disclose it without the express written permission of _____.

It is acknowledged by the reader that information to be furnished in this business plan is in all respects confidential in nature, other than information which is in the public domain through other means and that any disclosure or use of same by the reader, may cause serious harm or damage to _____.

Upon request, this document is to be immediately returned to _____.

_____
Signature

_____
Name (typed or printed)

_____
Date

This is a business plan. It does not imply an offering of securities.

# Contents

# 1. Executive Summary

My Friends' Bookstore is a college store that operates out of Presbyterian College (PC). It buys books from students and sells them to other students on campus as well as to millions of students online. It is run by college students in a dorm room, thereby avoiding many of the costs incurred by traditional college stores. By focusing on used textbooks, we are able to capitalize on the 35.1 percent gross margin and under-price our competitors.

By providing dorm room delivery and pick-up of textbooks, lower prices, and a fully functional Web site, My Friends' Bookstore will vault past its competition.

After conducting a very successful trial run during the Fall 2006/Spring 2007 semesters, partners Dana Waters, Scott Mumbauer, and Jonathan Choi were able to learn valuable lessons about running a used textbook store, all while making a profit from an investment of $15,000. Many businesses take up to three years to make profit, but my Friends' Bookstore was able to earn a profit after only two months!

This business plan ultimately serves to show the incredible opportunity of investing in a revolutionary new college store that allows the personal touch of a small business to reach a global market.

## 1.1. Objectives

1. To create an online bookstore that serves the needs of Presbyterian College students.
2. To earn 30 percent market share and achieve name recognition as the "on campus" bookstore by 2008.
3. To achieve a net income of $5,000 by year two and $10,000 by year three (see Figure A1).
4. To provide better prices, convenience, and customer satisfaction than competitors.

## 1.2. Mission

My Friends' Bookstore is dedicated to buying and selling books to students at fair, competitive prices while providing the highest possible level of customer service and satisfaction. We strive to provide convenience and timeliness to all our customers while maintaining a positive relationship with the faculty and administrative staff at Presbyterian College.

## 1.3. Keys to Success

The keys to success for My Friends' Bookstore are:

1. COST LEADERSHIP. Selling textbooks and other course materials at competitive prices across a majority of academic departments. My Friends' Bookstore must provide all relevant materials for all classes that are covered.

**FIGURE A1  Financial Highlights**

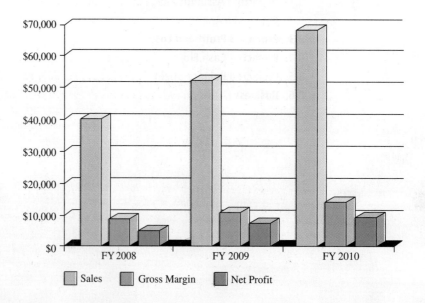

2. LOCATION. Offering convenience through reliable and timely deliveries and pick-ups. There is no physical location, which makes fast response time to customers essential to providing more convenience than a traditional bookstore.

3. CUSTOMER LOYALTY. Buying textbooks from students at competitive and fair prices so that they will recognize the benefits of using My Friends' Bookstore. That loyalty will generate a solid customer base and increase total sales.

4. CUSTOMER SATISFACTION. Provide satisfaction for 100 percent of our customers. My Friends' Bookstore strives to keep a close and positive relationship with every customer through the use of personal greeting strategies, newsletters, customer feedback, and quick response times to customers' questions or complaints.

## 2. Company Summary

***Store Location*** Although My Friends' Bookstore is run entirely online, its storage facility currently is located in a dorm room at Presbyterian College (PC). This allows for storage, deliveries, and pick-ups to be made from a convenient and central location.

***Store Operation*** My Friends' Bookstore uses a Web site that allows for all sales and purchases to be conducted online; therefore, it is technically open 24/7. It also has a phone line in the dorm room for students to call with questions or to make sales and purchases. Book deliveries and purchases are usually conducted between the hours of 12 P.M. and 11 P.M. My Friends' Bookstore is staffed by three full-time partners as well as up to five part-time employees who serve as telephone support representatives, e-mail and Web site technicians, and book delivery persons.

***Store Policies*** My Friends' Bookstore accepts cash on delivery (CODs), all major credit cards, and PayPal. Books sold to My Friends' Bookstore cannot be refunded at any time. Books bought from My Friends' Bookstore can be returned for any reason within 14 days with receipt up until the final day of book sales.

### 2.1. Company Ownership

My Friends' Bookstore is organized as a partnership among the three general partners of G. Dana Waters, Scott B. Mumbauer, and Jonathan H. Choi. Each owns 33.33 percent of the company. Dana Waters handles the accounting and legal duties; Scott Mumbauer works with financing and loan duties; and Jonathan Choi works with pricing, marketing strategies, and the company's Web site design. All partners share daily business duties evenly.

### 2.2. Company History

My Friends' Bookstore was created by two Presbyterian College students on September 5, 2006, to provide students with an alternative to the "typical" campus bookstore that generally overcharged students for textbooks and underpaid them for their used textbooks at the end of the semester. After getting permission from college administrators to set up on campus, My Friends' Bookstore surprised everyone in its almost "overnight" success.

My Friends' Bookstore is privately financed by family members and private investors (or angels). More than $15,000 was invested into the company for its first trial run in December 2006. This money covered start–up costs, including launching a grassroots advertising campaign with t-shirts and hoodies and buying more than 700 books from students and online sources. At the beginning of the next semester, they sold these books to students at competitive prices, most of which were lower than those the campus bookstore offered. They have sold the remaining inventory online through Amazon.com. The company's first major struggles soon began. Several books were reported stolen and campus police confiscated nearly $200 worth of books from My Friends' Bookstore. Tensions rose as My Friends' Bookstore tried to follow the rules established by residence life and campus police, while running a full-time bookstore and going to class full time. Sales were also less than expected, and a large portion of inventory had to be listed on Amazon.com, which charges a 15 percent commission on every book sold. This greatly reduced the store's profit margin, which was already very low to compete with competitors' prices. The founder's of My Friends' Bookstore have learned a great deal from this trial run and implemented changes to increase sales and profits. The owners have changed their strategy to increase their profit margin based on Amazon.com's commission and to increase sales with better and larger advertising campaigns to encourage more PC students to buy. The founders believe that the convenience they offer will increase their customer base when their largest competitor, the campus bookstore, moves to its downtown, off-campus location.

My Friends Bookstore has gained a competitive advantage in the market by providing students with fair and competitive prices, emphasizing the convenience of buying and selling their books on the company's Web site as well as delivering books to students' dorm rooms free of charge, and above all, providing a level of customer satisfaction and knowledge that only students can provide to other students.

## Past Performance

|  | FY 2006 | FY 2007 |
|---|---|---|
| Sales | $ 0 | $16,743 |
| Gross margin | $ 0 | $ 1,257 |
| Gross margin % | 0.00% | 7.51% |
| Operating expenses | $ 0 | $ 1,646 |
| Inventory turnover | 0.00 | 6.23 |

|  | FY 2006 | FY 2007 |
|---|---|---|
| **Balance sheet** | | |
| **Current assets** | | |
| **Cash** | $ 0 | $ 8,290 |
| Inventory | $ 0 | $ 4,974 |
| Other current assets | $ 0 | $ 100 |
| Total current assets | $ 0 | $13,364 |
| **Long-term assets** | | |
| Long-term assets | $ 0 | $ 0 |
| Accumulated depreciation | $ 0 | $ 0 |
| Total long-term assets | $ 0 | $ 0 |
| Total assets | $ 0 | $13,364 |
| **Current liabilities** | | |
| Accounts payable | $ 0 | $ 0 |
| Current borrowing | $ 0 | $ 0 |
| Other current liabilities (interest free) | $ 0 | $ 5,500 |
| Total current liabilities | $ 0 | $ 5,500 |
| Long-term liabilities | $ 0 | $ 0 |
| Total liabilities | $ 0 | $ 5,500 |
| Paid-in capital | $ 0 | $15,500 |
| Retained earnings | $ 0 | ($24,109) |
| Earnings | $ 0 | $16,473 |
| Total capital | $ 0 | $ 7,864 |
| Total capital and liabilities | $ 0 | $13,364 |
| **Other inputs** | | |
| Payment days | 0 | 1 |

## 3. Products

My Friends' Bookstore sells predominantly used textbooks bought from Presbyterian College students and online. Therefore, there is no set supplier. The suppliers are students and online sellers whose prices and products vary greatly from semester to semester, even day-to-day. The textbook market is very competitive and unstable. As new editions come out, the value of previous editions of textbooks greatly depreciates almost immediately. Therefore, knowledge of when new editions are coming out is essential for maintaining a competitive advantage in buying and selling textbooks.

Books from virtually every academic department offered at Presbyterian College are bought and sold. All books are purchased based on the Amazon.com retail price, and on the expected demand of the book and the current quantity in stock. To maintain a strong customer base, the owners must begin to provide all books and materials for PC classes on its Web site instead of offering only some of the materials required for them. This, of course, is not essential when selling books to non-PC customers.

Books are sold first to PC students, and the rest of the inventory is listed online. A new Web site is in the works that will allow customers to buy books directly from the Web site with credit cards and PayPal, whereas the original system involved sending PayPal invoices to individual customers, which was a very tedious and time-consuming process. This Web site will also allow all inventory to be cross-listed on eBay, thus allowing My Friends' Bookstore to reach a broader market.

## 4. Market Analysis Summary

***College Store Industry Information*** The college textbook market totaled $6.5 billion in 2004–2005. The total sales for college stores totaled nearly $11.2 billion in 2004–2005.[1]

### Breakdown of College Store Sales*

| | | |
|---|---|---|
| Course materials | 58.40% | $6.524 billion |
| Computer products | 14.10% | $1.577 billion |
| Insignia merchandise | 11.40% | $1.278 billion |
| Other merchandise | 6.40% | $0.718 billion |
| Student supplies | 5.50% | $0.614 billion |
| General/trade books | 4.20% | $0.465 billion |
| **Total** | 100.00% | $11.172 billion |

*Based on 2004–2005 estimates.

**CAMPUS STORE OWNERSHIP.** According to the National Association of College Stores' approximately 4,450 college stores serve 4,236 institutions in the United States."[2] This is equivalent to 1.05 stores per institution. More than 3,000 of these stores are NACS members. Their members are an accurate representation of the average college store. They are divided by ownership as follows:

**FIGURE A2 Campus Store Ownership/ Operations**

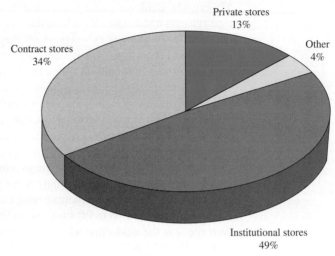

**Campus Store Ownership/Operations**

Private stores
13%

Other
4%

Contract stores
34%

Institutional stores
49%

Source: National Association of College Stores, 2007.

For example, Presbyterian College's bookstore is a contract store, and My Friends' Bookstore is a private store. Many college stores are owned by student associations, and also fall under the Private Stores category.[3]

**COLLEGE STORE ANNUAL SALES.** According to the NACS, college stores' sales vary greatly based on the size of the institution. Average annual sales are approximately $6 million, but most college stores generate sales of less than $3 million (see Figure A3).[4]

**USED TEXTBOOK MARKET.** Textbooks and other course materials make up nearly 59 percent of all college stores' sales.

| | | |
|---|---|---|
| New texts | 40.80% | $4.284 billion |
| Used texts | 17.10% | $1.796 billion |
| Course packs | 1.10% | $0.116 billion |
| **Total course material** | **59.0%** | **$6.195 billion** |
| **Total store sales** | **100.00%** | **$10.5 billion** |

Source: NACS *2007 College Store Industry Financial Report,* National Association of Bookstores, 2007.

New textbooks generate the greatest percentage of the typical college store's sales. My Friends' Bookstore caters mainly to the used book niche of the textbook market. This market may be somewhat overlooked because it represents a small portion of the total market. Only 29.8 percent of college stores' course materials sales come from used textbooks.

**FIGURE A3 NACS Membership by Estimated Sales**

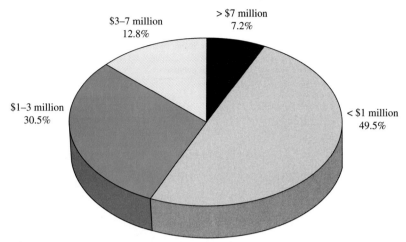

NACS Membership by Estimated Sales

$3–7 million
12.8%

> $7 million
7.2%

$1–3 million
30.5%

< $1 million
49.5%

Source: National Association of College Stores, 2007.

Used textbooks typically sell for about 75 percent of the original price of new textbooks.[5] However, this lower price does not mean a lower profit margin. The margin on used textbooks is 35.1 percent, compared to only 22.3 percent on new textbooks.[6] For Fall 2006 (the latest data available), the average new textbook price is $53, compared to $44 for used textbooks.

Unfortunately, there are additional costs attached with the used textbook market. According to the NACS' analysis of used textbooks:

> The process of acquiring, cleaning, pricing, and re-shelving used books involves significantly more time that that of new textbooks and increases college stores operating expenses.[7] In addition, because used books are non-returnable to publishers (as new books are), college stores assume a higher risk on their used book inventory. There is also the possibility that the publication of a new edition will make inventoried used textbooks obsolete, even though the store has already purchased them.[8]

The higher risks involved in purchasing used textbooks may explain why new textbooks make up a larger portion of most college stores sales. They may be less willing to invest a large portion of their resources into inventory that carries a higher risk of obsolescence. By studying used textbook trends, My Friends' Bookstore can reduce the high risks associated with used textbooks and turn this normally higher-risk market into a higher-profit market.

**WHERE THE NEW TEXTBOOK DOLLAR GOES.** As Figure A4 shows, college stores retain only 22.2 cents per dollar on new textbooks. Therefore, by focusing on the used textbook market, My Friends' Bookstore can avoid the 77.8 cents per dollar publisher/freight fees *and* earn a higher level of profit, all while paying less per book.

## Where the New Textbook Dollar Goes*...

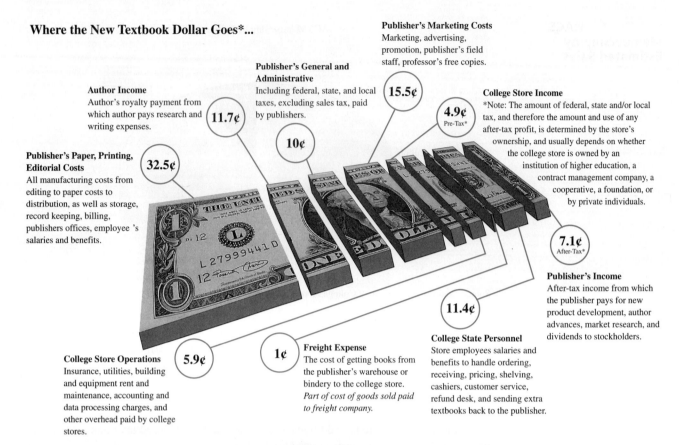

**Publisher's Marketing Costs**
Marketing, advertising, promotion, publisher's field staff, professor's free copies.

**Publisher's General and Administrative**
Including federal, state, and local taxes, excluding sales tax, paid by publishers.

**Author Income**
Author's royalty payment from which author pays research and writing expenses.

**College Store Income**
*Note: The amount of federal, state and/or local tax, and therefore the amount and use of any after-tax profit, is determined by the store's ownership, and usually depends on whether the college store is owned by an institution of higher education, a contract management company, a cooperative, a foundation, or by private individuals.

**Publisher's Paper, Printing, Editorial Costs**
All manufacturing costs from editing to paper costs to distribution, as well as storage, record keeping, billing, publishers offices, employee 's salaries and benefits.

**Publisher's Income**
After-tax income from which the publisher pays for new product development, author advances, market research, and dividends to stockholders.

15.5¢   4.9¢ Pre-Tax*   11.7¢   10¢   32.5¢   7.1¢ After-Tax*   11.4¢   1¢   5.9¢

**College Store Operations**
Insurance, utilities, building and equipment rent and maintenance, accounting and data processing charges, and other overhead paid by college stores.

**Freight Expense**
The cost of getting books from the publisher's warehouse or bindery to the college store. *Part of cost of goods sold paid to freight company.*

**College State Personnel**
Store employees salaries and benefits to handle ordering, receiving, pricing, shelving, cashiers, customer service, refund desk, and sending extra textbooks back to the publisher.

**FIGURE A4  Where the New Textbook Dollar Goes***

*College store numbers are averages and reflect the most current 2004–2005 data gathered by the National Association of College Stores. Publisher numbers are estimates based on data provided by the Association of American Publishers.
(© 2006 by the National Association of College Stores.)

**THE ONLINE COLLEGE STORE ADVANTAGE.** According to the National Association of College Stores (NACS), only 2.8 percent of college sales are from online purchases.[10] This means that only 1.6 percent of college stores' total textbook sales are conducted online. There are many advantages to adding online capabilities to a college store, such as My Friends' Bookstore, including the following:

- Ease of returns
- Ability to pick up items immediately
- One-stop shopping
- Accurate information on which textbooks students need for courses
- The trust and security of buying from a well-known source with an on-campus location
- The primary target audience, college students, is accustomed to making purchases online.

**MY FRIENDS' BOOKSTORE'S ONLINE ADVANTAGE.** This "click and mortar" strategy can be highly successful if implemented properly. My Friends' Bookstore can capitalize on all of these advantages. All books are sold through a Web site with a secure checkout system. These books are then delivered to the students' dorms free-of-charge at the time they request. Refunds are as easy as a phone call or an e-mail. The owners know which textbooks to stock by talking to individual professors to determine which books they require for their classes. Because My Friends' Bookstore has been on campus since Fall 2006, it has made a name for itself as being fast, convenient, and fair to all students. My Friends' Bookstore's online advantage is accomplished by combining the benefits of a traditional college store with the ease and convenience of online purchasing.

**HIGHER EDUCATION STATISTICS.** There are 4,236 institutions of higher education in the United States. Most colleges have fewer than 10,000 students (see Figure A5), which is ideal for My Friends' Bookstore's current capacity. This size allows a relatively small number of students (2 to 3) to have the ability to keep in contact with professors, apply affective marketing strategies for a small campus, and handle the volume of books that students will purchase and sold with relative ease. This smaller size also requires less financing than trying to compete with a college store at a large campus.

**FIGURE A5 College Enrollment Statistics**

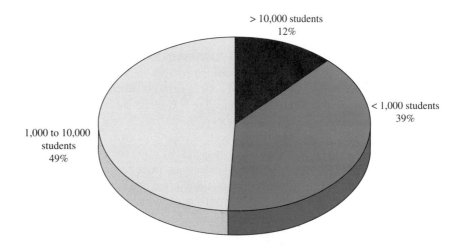

There were 17.3 million college students in 2004, which represents an increase of 21 percent in enrollment since 1994. The number of female students increased faster (25 percent) than male students (16 percent). The number of young students is also increasing; the number of enrolled students under 25 increased nearly 31 percent since 1990.[11]

An *Almanac 2007–2008* survey of college students published by the *Chronicle of Higher Education* reports found the following:

- 86 percent were undergraduates
- 61 percent of students attended four-year institutions
- 43 percent were between the ages of 15 and 21
- 32.9 percent were between the ages of 22 and 30
- 56.6 percent were women
- 59.9 percent of the total attended college or university full time[12]

**FIGURE A6 Ethnic Background of Enrolled Students**

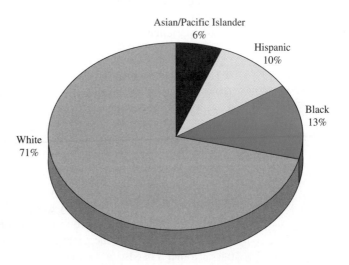

Although the majority of students at higher education institutions are white, nearly 30 percent of students are minorities (see Figure A6). The number of Asian/Pacific Islanders and Hispanics has increased the most (6 percent and 10 percent since 1974, respectively).[13]

**COLLEGE STUDENTS' SPENDING IN COLLEGE STORES.** Students spent an average of $763 at a college store in 2005–2006, up from $720 in the previous academic year. Spending does not differ greatly between public and private or between two-year and four-year higher education institutions. The College Board reports that students, on average, spent between $850 and $942 on textbooks and supplies in 2005–2006, up from $801 to $904 in 2004–2005.[14] Based on these statistics, Presbyterian College's student population of 1,200 yields $864,000 in potential college store sales per academic year.

**COLLEGE STUDENTS' SPENDING AND THE INTERNET.** More than 93 percent of college students, an estimated 16.4 million users, access the Internet in a given month.[15] Nearly 90 percent of college students own a computer, and more than 67 percent have a high-speed Internet connection.[16] College students spend more than $210 billion a year.[17] Approximately 75 percent of students have a job, in which they earn $645 per month on average. Meanwhile, parents contribute an extra $154 a month to their income. This means a typical college student spends $13,000 each year.[18]

College students are price sensitive when they shop. More than 93 percent of college students say that low-price is a determining factor when they make purchases.[19] College students frequently use the Internet to make purchases. One recent survey found that:

- 98 percent of college students have bought something online.
- 54 percent of students have purchased a product because of online advertising.
- 34 percent find online advertising to be the most influential means to get them to learn more about a product.[20]

Another survey found that Facebook, a social-networking site, is the most popular Web site among people ages 17 to 24. Half of females and more than one-third of males list it as their favorite Web site.[21] My Friends' Bookstore began using the marketing power of Facebook during its first semester of operation by creating a My Friends' Bookstore group that Facebook members can join. Within one week, the page had nearly 200 members at a college of 1,200 students. By using Facebook, My Friends' Bookstore sent messages to members about buying and selling textbooks. It also allowed customers to comment on their experiences and list how much money they received for their books. Only a few days after the creation of the Facebook group, the number of views of My Friends' Bookstore's Web site (www.myfriendsbookstore.com) increased more than 285 percent.

College students spend a significant amount of time researching products and companies before making a purchase, and usually that purchase is online.[22] College students also have "considerable swaying power" over their peers.[23] It is essential to market to students effectively so that they visit the Web site and tell their friends about their experience.

### 4.1. Market Segmentation

**MY FRIENDS' BOOKSTORE'S MARKET ANALYSIS.** My Friends' Bookstore has found that it is more profitable to provide for general education classes as opposed to upper-level courses. This is due to the high number of students, on average, that are enrolled in a general education course. The books are also more readily available to buy and sell at Presbyterian College and online because of the high volume of students taking these classes across colleges and universities in the United States. Most Presbyterian College customers, when asked about why they purchased a general education book from My Friends' Bookstore, said that they thought that My Friends' Bookstore would be carrying a high number of general education textbooks, but very few upper-level textbooks. Therefore, focusing on the general education textbook market is essential to provide for the customer's needs.

Market Analysis

| Potential Customers | Growth | 2007 | 2008 | 2009 | 2010 | 2011 | Compound Annual Growth Rate |
|---|---|---|---|---|---|---|---|
| Presbyterian College Students | 5% | 1,200 | 1,260 | 1,323 | 1,389 | 1,458 | 4.99% |
| College Students in United States | 2% | 16,400,000 | 16,744,400 | 17,096,032 | 17,455,049 | 17,821,605 | 2.10% |
| **Total** | 2.10% | 16,401,200 | 16,745,660 | 17,097,355 | 17,456,438 | 17,823,063 | 2.10% |

## 4.2. Target Market Segment Strategy

**TARGET CUSTOMERS.** The primary customer target is Presbyterian College students. Due to PC's small size, marketing campaigns can reach almost everyone on campus with relative ease.

- These customers are predominantly ages 18 to 24.[24]
- There are approximately 1,200 students—48 percent male and 52 percent female.[25]
- 95 percent of students live on campus.[26]
- The average cost for textbooks for each student per semester: $555.00.[27]

As previously mentioned, the typical college student spends $13,000 each year. Therefore, Presbyterian College students spend more than $15,600,000 every year!

The secondary customer target is college students at other universities who purchase textbooks online through Amazon.com or eBay. My Friends' Bookstore's new, proposed Web site will include a cross-listing of all inventory on eBay, thereby reaching a large portion of the online textbook market beyond Presbyterian College.

**PRESBYTERIAN COLLEGE MARKETING STRATEGIES.** Because of the relatively small size of the campus, My Friends' Bookstore has found that word-of-mouth can be the most effective marketing tool. In addition, the following marketing tools were used during the Fall 2006/Spring 2007 period.

- Flyers
- T-shirts and hoodies
- Direct mail advertisements
- Facebook messaging
- E-mailing customers about updates and special offers

Despite the variety of advertising techniques that the founders used, many students still were unaware of My Friends' Bookstore after the first semester of operation. This was because the founders had made only a small investment in marketing because the first semester of operation was meant to be a trial run for the business. In essence, the founders were engaging in business prototyping to determine whether their idea was viable. The owners will implement new marketing strategies on a larger scale for the next buying and selling period, including more personal advertising and efforts to reach people who have not yet purchased from My Friends' Bookstore. The owners are working to retain the company's existing customer base with special offers for returning customers. To date, 228* students have sold books to My Friends' Bookstore, and 131 students have purchased books from the company.

---

*228 includes some repeat customers; it should also be noted that the $14,000 used to buy back books was used over 3 days rather than to the planned 7-day buyback period due to the enormous success of offering better prices for books and the wildfire-like spread of word of our prices across campus.

### 4.3. Industry Analysis

**THE COLLEGE TEXTBOOK INDUSTRY.** The college bookstore industry is unique because sellers for the most part do not get to choose the products they sell. They sell the books that professors choose for their classes. Therefore, the demand of textbooks is governed by professors and students, and the supply of textbooks is provided by publishers and wholesalers. It is the college store's responsibility as a retailer to resell textbooks to college students.[28]

College stores are service-driven, and they try to provide the lowest-priced textbooks instead of trying to make a large amount of profit per book. The *NACS 2006 College Store Industry Financial Report* shows that the average gross margin on new textbooks is 22.3 percent, a figure that has not greatly changed since 1989. The average gross margin for used textbooks is considerably higher, reaching 35.1 percent. This is normal compared to other retail industries where annual gross margins ranging from 19.2 to 50.4 percent. However, there are also higher risks associated with used textbooks, including the fact that stores cannot return them to publishers and that new editions are constantly coming out.[29]

After publisher and store costs, the average college store retains only about 4 cents per dollar on every textbook it sells.[30] My Friends' Bookstore is run out of a college dorm room, and it is able to set lower prices than a typical college bookstore because it has few of these costs (no rent, no utilities, etc).

Many students try to find the lowest-cost textbooks. Textbook prices have steadily been increasing an average of 6 percent annually, almost twice the rate of inflation.[31] Textbooks sold on the Internet often are much cheaper than at a college store because publishers who sell to international markets must compete locally by setting competitive prices in the areas in which they are selling books. In addition, foreign-based textbook suppliers often set their online prices much lower than their U.S.-based competitors.[32]

College students spend a great deal of their income on online purchases. However, according to a 2005 Student Watch™ survey, only 23 percent of students buy their textbooks online. Moreover, one-third of these online sales are made on college stores' Websites.[33] Online retailers such as Amazon.com and eBay account for slightly more than 15 percent of college textbook sales. This is a great advantage for a click-and-mortar strategy such as that of My Friends' Bookstore. By providing the on-campus availability and reliability of a traditional college store and the convenience and lower prices of an online store, My Friends' Bookstore has a strong advantage over both of its major competitors.

#### Major Competitors

1. Traditional college stores (85 percent of the market)
2. Online retailers, such as Amazon.com and eBay (15 percent of the market)

### Traditional College Stores

Traditional college stores typically have higher prices than online stores, operate from established physical locations (off-campus in the case of Presbyterian College), and sell a variety of college-related items in addition to textbooks. They make the most profit from used textbooks, student supplies, and "insignia items" such as apparel displaying the name of the institution. The gross margins of each category of items are shown below:

|  | Average | 25th Percentile | Median (Mid-Point) | 75th Percentile |
|---|---|---|---|---|
| New texts | 22.3% | 19.7 | 22.4 | 24.5 |
| Custom published materials | 23.8% | 15.8 | 23.0 | 31.7 |
| Used texts | 35.1% | 33.1 | 35.8 | 38.3 |
| **Total course books** | 25.9% | 23.3 | 25.8 | 28.6 |
| Trade books | 26.0% | 22.1 | 28.2 | 33.7 |
| Medical reference books | 22.2% | — | 20.5 | — |
| **Total trade books** | 25.5% | 20.4 | 26.7 | 33.7 |

| | | | | |
|---|---|---|---|---|
| **Total book sales** | 25.8% | 23.4 | 26.0 | 28.5 |
| Computer hardware | 7.5% | 3.3 | 7.8 | 12.7 |
| Computer software | 16.6% | 12.2 | 17.0 | 22.2 |
| Computer supplies | 26.2% | 16.8 | 26.1 | 34.5 |
| **Total computer products** | 16.1% | 10.7 | 14.5 | 22.1 |
| Student supplies | 37.9% | 33.1 | 39.0 | 43.6 |
| Medical instruments | 28.1% | — | — | — |
| **Total supplies** | 36.2% | 31.7 | 38.7 | 43.5 |
| Insignia items | 37.7% | 32.4 | 40.3 | 44.7 |
| Other merchandise | 31.5% | 24.9 | 32.5 | 40.1 |
| **Total non-book sales** | 31.5% | 25.1 | 31.3 | 38.6 |
| **Total sales** | **27.2%** | **23.9** | **27.2** | **30.2** |

Source: "2007 College Store Margins," National Association of College Stores, 2007, www.nacs.org/public/research/margins.asp. © NACS 2006 College Store Industry Financial Report.

### Online Retailers

Amazon.com has seen an increase of 18 percent from 2004 to 2005 in its book, music, and DVD sectors. Nearly one-third of the books sold on Amazon.com are through third-party sellers, such as individuals and businesses. Third-party sellers accounted for more than 28 percent of Amazon.com's total sales in 2005.[34] Although these third-party sellers are direct competitors, My Friends' Bookstore has used Amazon.com to its advantage by selling its remaining inventory through the Web site with great success (and often underpricing its competitors).

eBay has seen an increase in textbook sales of 180 percent per year.[35] An eBay textbook marketing forum has the following to say about the booming textbook industry:

> Each year during the months of August–September and January–February, textbook sales soar on eBay. Textbook sellers have found that they can sell very profitably on eBay because of the high average selling price of a textbook (often $70 to $120 per book!) and the significant turnover of textbooks each college semester. Imagine, every few months there is a new source of supply (the end of a semester when students sell their textbooks) and a new source of demand (the beginning of each semester when students need to buy their textbooks). Because of the large volume of quickly turning inventory, profits can be substantial for sellers in this category.[36]

My Friends' Bookstore also takes advantage of eBay by cross-listing all of its inventory with eBay and competing with that market. Therefore, My Friends' Bookstore's uses its two largest online competitors as marketing channels to reach new customers in new markets.

**ANNUAL TEXTBOOK SALES.** Students spend more than $6.5 billion on textbooks annually,[37] an amount that makes up nearly 40 percent of total annual book sales of $16.6 billion.[38] Textbook sales are very seasonal, revolving around the beginning and end of academic semester. As Figure A7 shows, January, August, September, and December produce the highest monthly textbook sales at college bookstores.

**4.3.1 COMPETITION AND BUYING PATTERNS.** Competition in the online textbook industry is based mainly on three factors:

1. Delivery time
2. Price
3. Ability to verify that the book is the right one for a class[39]

Most textbook buyers want to have their books delivered as fast as possible.[40] During its first selling period, My Friends' Bookstore noticed that more than half of all buyers on

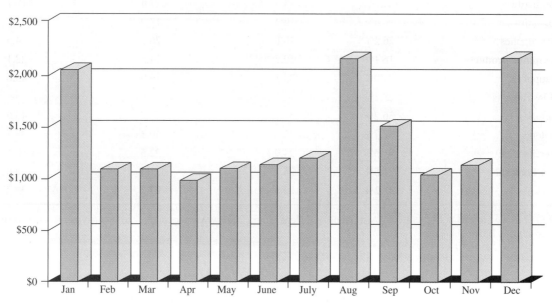

**FIGURE A7 2005 Bookstore Sales in Billions of $**

Source: National Association of College Stores, 2007.

Amazon.com opted to pay for expedited shipping ($5.99 versus $3.49). This need for speedy delivery occurs because most students do not shop for their textbooks until after they have attended a class and learned about the materials that are required for the course. My Friends' Bookstore can capitalize on all of these factors. Textbooks for classes are determined by talking to professors, the price is set to be competitive with both college stores and online markets, and books are delivered in person, thus cutting out shipping time and costs.

Reputation is also an important factor. My Friends' Bookstore is located on campus; it is currently building a strong reputation with Presbyterian College students. Likewise, on Amazon.com, My Friends' Bookstore has 96 percent positive ratings, which lets buyers know that the seller is reliable.

The actual product, textbooks, is bought based on condition. Demand for a textbook is based solely on whether a professor requires it for a class. Therefore, students do not shop around for different textbooks but instead search for the best price and condition. Therefore, My Friends' Bookstore emphasizes buying textbooks in good condition because poor condition books sell for much less than a "like new" book.

Because of the high turnover of inventory, it is essential to keep customers coming back so that they will buy and sell books. The textbook industry is unique because it also buys from the same customers to whom it sells; therefore, college stores must focus on keeping customers satisfied or they will lose twice the amount of business a normal store would lose.

Market Analysis (C.A.G.R.)

**FIGURE A8** Market Analysis (C.A.G.R.)

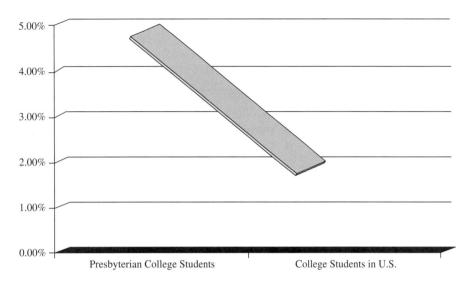

## 5. Web Plan Summary

My Friends' Bookstore's Web site is the source for all of the business's sales. Its e-commerce strategy is based on instilling trust in potential customers and providing easy access, simple payment options, and detailed information about the books that are required for each class. The Web site is PayPal verified, provides the ability to pay with credit card, and lists all the books required for every class in every department on campus. In addition, prices for every book are clearly listed and, when available, the price of the campus bookstore is also listed. We also show the percentage difference in our prices and those of our competitors to illustrate our low prices.

My Friends' Bookstore contacts customers mainly through e-mail, but a phone line is available for customers who prefer to place orders over the phone. A professional company runs the Web site and provides a shopping cart, credit card payment, and inventory uploading. The inventory listed on our Web site is also cross-listed with eBay so that the company reaches the online textbook market without any extra effort.

### 5.1. Web Site Marketing Strategy

Our online marketing strategy involves listing all of the benefits and conveniences of our business to encourage students to buy from us. We clearly list all of our prices and will soon include pictures next to the books that we list for sale to help students verify they are buying the right book. Talking to each professor to determine required textbooks for each course is essential, and this information is listed online so that students can see the books they need to buy before they ever attend class. Prices and price differences are listed to show customers the benefit of buying from a cheaper, online bookstore.

Our online business allows us to process a virtually unlimited number of orders with relative ease. We simply deliver the books, implement the proper marketing strategy, and address customer concerns.

## 5.2. Development Requirements

Ongoing Costs:

- Web site fee, monthly: $24.95
- Yearly domain registration fee: $15.00
- Credit card and PayPal commissions: variable (example: $1.39 + 3 percent of price)
- Site design: Free (done by ourselves)
- Site updates: Free (done by ourselves)
- Traffic reports: Included in Web site fee
- Shopping cart, inventory, and eBay access: Included in Web site fee

# 6. Strategy and Implementation Summary

## 6.1. SWOT Analysis

The SWOT analysis provides us with an opportunity to examine the internal strengths and weaknesses that My Friends' Bookstore must address. It also allows us to examine the opportunities presented to My Friends' Bookstore as well as potential threats.

### 6.1.1. STRENGTHS

1. CLOSE AND PERSONAL RELATIONSHIP WITH CUSTOMERS. The owners of My Friends' Bookstore have personally greeted every one of their more than 300 customers during the first buying and selling period. Because we are students, we know our fellow students better than anyone else. Many of our friends have been very loyal to us, and their positive word-of-mouth has brought in many customers we did not know.

2. DETAILED KNOWLEDGE OF PRODUCTS AND PRICING. We have learned how prices fluctuate online and the general markups of the campus bookstore. We also buy and sell our own textbooks. We maintain a strong relationship with the professors at Presbyterian College so that we know what books will be used each semester for each course.

3. PREVIOUS EXPERIENCE. We have conducted a thorough trial run of the bookstore business and have learned a great deal about the industry. We know how to manage cash flow and inventory, maximize efficiency with deliveries, set competitive prices for books, and market to students. All partners have gained a great deal of knowledge about running a bookstore efficiently.

4. STRONG REPUTATION AT PRESBYTERIAN COLLEGE AND ONLINE. We are known on campus as having fair prices and looking out for students' best interests. Many students strongly and actively support our endeavor and favor us over the campus bookstore based on principle alone. On Amazon.com, we have a positive feedback rating of nearly100 percent, a rating that ensures potential customers who may not be familiar with us that we are reliable and honest sellers.

5. COMPLEMENTARY SKILLS OF FOUNDING PARTNERS. Dana Waters is a business management major, and is currently enrolled in a small business management course to help improve My Friends' Bookstore. He has a vast knowledge of computers, accounting, pricing, and customer service. Scott Mumbauer is a music major and is planning to minor in business. He helped to secure the financial backing, which al-

lowed the business to conduct a successful trial run. Jonathan Choi handles the company's pricing and specializing in managing and updating the My Friends Bookstore Web site.

6. SOUND FINANCIAL BACKING. The founders launched My Friends Bookstore with capital from family members. When the company's rapid growth quickly outstripped the capacity of family financing, the owners presented their business plan to the Palmetto Bank, which granted the business a $15,000 unsecured line of credit. The company used the entire line of credit, repaid it, and now has increased its line of credit to $25,000.

7. COST LEADERSHIP STRATEGY. Because prices are so important to students, pursuing a cost leadership strategy is key to the company's success. This strategy allows us to maintain a price advantage over competitors. Our low costs allow us to underprice competitors and still generate a reasonable profit.

8. A REPUTATION FOR PROVIDING CONVENIENCE FOR CUSTOMERS. My Friends' Bookstore combines the best of both worlds. It provides the convenience of shopping online 24/7 and paying instantly with a credit card, while providing fast dorm room delivery. This gives the company a competitive advantage over traditional college stores with limited hours and online stores that require shipping times and fees.

9. RECOGNITION THAT MY FRIENDS BOOKSTORE IS NOT AN OFFICIAL COLLEGE STORE. Because we are not affiliated with Presbyterian College, we do not have to pay commissions to the college like the campus bookstore does. We also have the freedom to operate however we see fit, and we are not under the influence of the college.

10. POTENTIAL TO EXPAND MARKET SHARE. Many potential customers have not discovered us yet. As we increase our marketing efforts, we will be able to increase our share of the market.

### 6.1.2 WEAKNESSES

1. LIMITED TIME OF PARTNERS. In addition to being entrepreneurs, we are also full-time students. The buyback period is in the middle of exam week, and we must hire friends to help us run the bookstore and limit the strain it puts on our schedules.

2. NOT AN OFFICIAL COLLEGE STORE. This is both a strength and a weakness. As a weakness, Presbyterian College cannot provide us with funding, aid, or guidance. We must talk to professors about textbooks and gather information ourselves.

3. LIMITED STORAGE CAPACITY. We are limited by the size of our dorm room. We have converted one entire dorm room into temporary storage for textbooks until they are sold. We are exploring the possibility of renting a larger storage space not far from campus.

4. OPERATING UNDER THE AUTHORITY OF THE COLLEGE'S RESIDENCE LIFE OFFICE, ADMINISTRATION, AND CAMPUS POLICE. We are allowed to operate on college grounds only as long as we abide by the rules set by the college. Because of the college's contractual relationship with the company that operates the "official" bookstore, we may have to move our operations off campus.

**6.1.3. OPPORTUNITIES.** The most important opportunity in the Presbyterian College market is that the campus bookstore is moving off campus. Its new location requires students to drive downtown to buy and sell textbooks. Therefore, My Friends' Bookstore's convenience will be much more beneficial to Presbyterian College students who do not want to drive downtown.

Another opportunity is the potential to expand our sales to both Presbyterian College and online purchases. As college enrollment increases along with textbook prices, the opportunity for profit increases as well.

**6.1.4. THREATS.** Threats to My Friends' Bookstore include:

1. USED TEXTBOOKS BECOMING OUTDATED WHEN A NEW EDITION COMES OUT. This is especially dangerous over the summer because we must wait four months until our inventory will begin selling again (with the exception of summer school).
2. COMPETITION FROM THE CAMPUS BOOKSTORE. The campus bookstore attempts to compete with our convenience and/or low prices.
3. LOWER PRICES FROM ONLINE SELLERS THAN WE CANNOT MATCH. Occasionally we must list some books at prices that are lower than the purchase price of the book. This usually happens when new editions come out, and the market is "flooded" with older editions at very low prices.
4. THEFT. My Friends' Bookstore stores its books in a dorm room, making security essential. Also, large amounts of cash are necessary to buy back books, and this may attract thieves.

## 6.2. Competitive Edge

My Friends' Bookstore has a competitive edge because it combines the best benefits of traditional college stores and online retailers: convenience, ease of use, 24/7 operation with a Web Site, fast and free delivery, and personal knowledge of the books required for each class are a few of the many examples.

My Friends' Bookstore prides itself on customer service and satisfaction. Our goal to provide not only a monetary benefit of saving students money, but also the intangible benefit of dealing with students who know and understand them. We strive to provide for their best interests while still making profits.

Our reputation as a high quality company will continue to spread across Presbyterian College and the online market. Our superior customer service is unmatched by any of our competitors. Therefore, our market share should steadily increase for many years to come.

## 6.3. Marketing Strategy

Our marketing strategy focuses on the following:

- Offering low prices
- Providing all of the right books for each class
- Building a solid reputation as a good company with total customer satisfaction
- Continuing to increase marketing to reach new customers in both the Presbyterian College and online textbook markets

## 6.4. Sales Strategy

**Our sales strategy focuses on the following:**

- We will offer specials to encourage people to buy and sell books from us.
- There is very little "convincing" customers to buy books. Because our business is conducted entirely online, the best way to close sales is to be up-front about the benefits of our Web site and bookstore offer customers.
- Order processing involves sending confirmation e-mails to customers, fixing any problems that occur along the way, delivering books in a timely fashion, and above all making sure the customer is satisfied.

- Inventory rosters must be as accurate as possible to ensure that we do not accept orders for books that we do not have in inventory.
- We will offer a 14-day return/exchange policy to build trust with our customers and maintain retention and loyalty.

**6.4.1 SALES FORECAST.** The sales forecast is based on an actual net profit margin of 20 to 25 percent, although our goal is to reach 30 percent profit. By investing all of the profits back into the business, we hope to attain a steady 30 percent growth in sales. Sales are based on the typical sales period for textbooks, mainly August and September, and January and February. For each season, we forecast 75 percent of sales occurring in the first month, and the remaining 25 percent occurring in the second month. Virtually all of our expenses are variable costs; therefore, the company's cost of goods sold increases at about 30 percent, the same percentage as the increase in sales.

Sales Forecast

|  | FY 2008 | FY 2009 | FY 2010 |
|---|---|---|---|
| **Sales** | | | |
| Textbooks | $77,460 | $147,140 | $204,210 |
| Total sales | $77,460 | $147,140 | $204,210 |

|  | FY 2008 | FY 2009 | FY 2010 |
|---|---|---|---|
| **Direct cost of sales** | | | |
| Textbook purchases | $52,000 | $94,000 | $134,000 |
| Subtotal direct cost of sales | $52,000 | $94,000 | $134,000 |

**FIGURE A9  Sales Monthly**

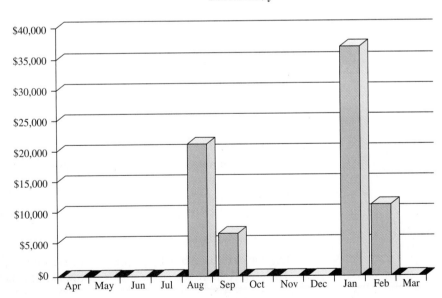

**FIGURE A10 Sales by Year**

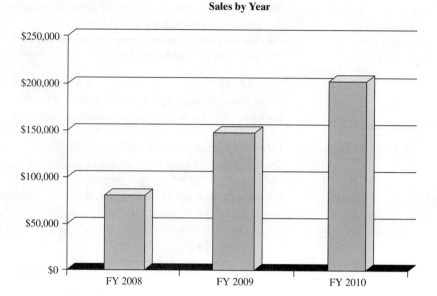

## 7. Management Summary

My Friends' Bookstore is comprised of:

- 3 full-time partners
- Up to 5 part-time employees who work during peak volume periods

Additional partners may be added as the business grows in size.

### 7.1. Personnel Plan

Personnel are needed only during peak volume sales and buyback periods and when the owners are otherwise unable to operate the business themselves. These costs are based on hourly wages, which are $6.00 per hour.

## 8. Financial Plan

We expect our business to grow at a very rapid rate of 30 percent, which is limited by the amount of financing that we can attain for the business through investments and loans. We also plan to reinvest all profit back into the business to further expand our company's growth.

### 8.1. Important Assumptions

Sales occur entirely through our online storefront; therefore, we incur no sales tax. All loans are for a term of one-year. The interest-free loan provided by a private lender can be paid back over the course of several months, but the financial forecasts assume that the amount will be paid back in full one month prior to the next loan.

### 8.2. Breakeven Analysis

Our business has virtually no fixed expenses other than Web site fees and advertising. Therefore, our breakeven point is very low, at just $100 per month.

| Breakeven Analysis | |
| --- | --- |
| Monthly revenue breakeven | $100 |
| **Assumptions** | |
| **Average percent variable cost** | 67% |
| Estimated monthly fixed cost | $ 33 |

**Breakeven Analysis**

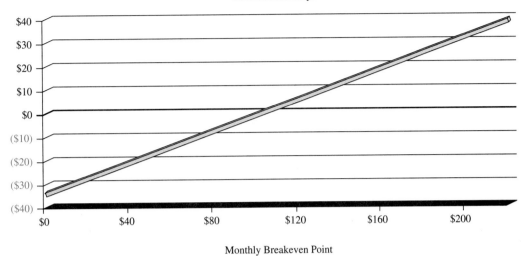

Monthly Breakeven Point

Breakeven point = where line intersects with 0

**FIGURE A11** **Breakeven Analysis**

### 8.3. Projected Profit and Loss

We expect to see rapid growth in our sales as we continue to finance our company through loans and retained earnings, which will allow us to sell more textbooks. A 20 to 25 percent net profit margin also allows a significant amount of profit to be reinvested into the company, which further increases the cash available to buy textbooks. Because of the highly seasonal nature of our business, the company experiences huge swings in profit on a monthly basis (see Figure 10), but its annual profit increases at a steady rate (see Figure 11).

**Pro Forma Profit and Loss**

|  | FY 2008 | FY 2009 | FY 2010 |
|---|---|---|---|
| Sales | $77,460 | $147,140 | $204,210 |
| Direct costs of goods | $52,000 | $ 94,000 | $134,000 |
| Other costs of goods | $    0 | $    0 | $    0 |
| Cost of goods sold | $52,000 | $ 94,000 | $134,000 |
| Gross margin | $25,460 | $ 53,140 | $ 70,210 |
| Gross margin % | 32.87% | 36.12% | 34.38% |
| Expenses |  |  |  |
| Payroll | $    0 | $    0 | $    0 |
| Marketing/promotion | $   80 | $   90 | $  100 |
| Depreciation | $    0 | $    0 | $    0 |
| Web site fee | $  300 | $  300 | $  300 |
| Domain registration fee | $   15 | $   15 | $   15 |
| Total operating expenses | $  395 | $  405 | $  415 |
| Profit before interest and taxes | $25,065 | $ 52,735 | $ 69,795 |
| Earnings before interest, taxes and depreciation | $25,065 | $ 52,735 | $ 69,795 |
| Interest expense | $ 1,039 | $  2,133 | $  3,467 |
| Taxes incurred | $ 7,208 | $ 15,181 | $ 19,899 |
| Net profit | $16,818 | $ 35,421 | $ 46,430 |
| Net profit/sales | 21.71% | 24.07% | 22.74% |

**FIGURE A12 Profit Monthly**

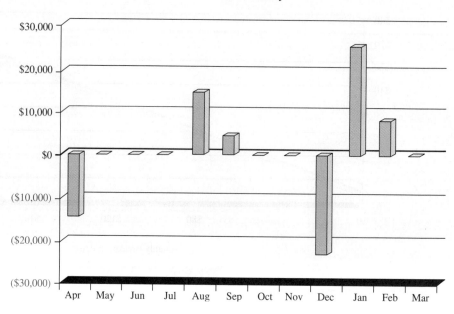

Profit Monthly

**FIGURE A13 Profit Yearly**

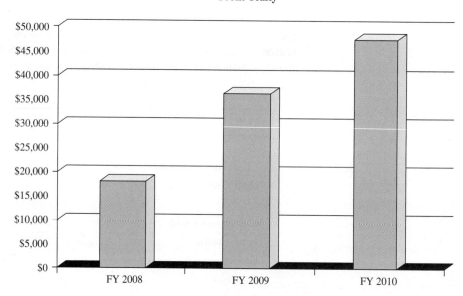

Profit Yearly

**FIGURE A14 Gross Margin Monthly**

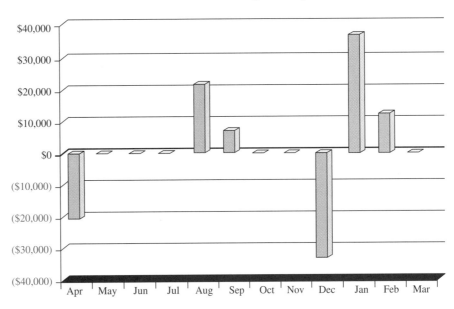

Gross Margin Monthly

**FIGURE A15 Gross Margin Yearly**

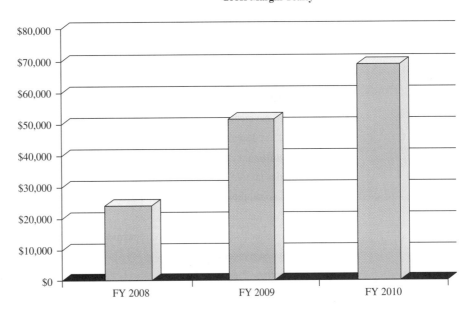

Gross Margin Yearly

## 8.4. Projected Cash Flow

Cash flow is also very important due to the high seasonality of the business. As the business grows, its yearly cash balance greatly increases. Some months show a negative cash flow during periods of low sales, but the monthly cash balance stays relatively high (see Figure A16).

Pro Forma Cash Flow

|  | FY 2008 | FY 2009 | FY 2010 |
| --- | --- | --- | --- |
| **Cash received** | | | |
| **Cash from operations** | | | |
| Cash sales | $ 77,460 | $147,140 | $204,210 |
| Subtotal cash from operations | $ 77,460 | $147,140 | $204,210 |
| **Additional cash received** | | | |
| Sales tax, VAT, HST/GST received | $ 0 | $ 0 | $ 0 |
| New current borrowing | $ 0 | $ 0 | $ 0 |
| New other liabilities (interest-free) | $ 20,000 | $ 20,000 | $ 20,000 |
| New long-term liabilities | $ 32,000 | $ 74,000 | $114,000 |
| Sales of other current assets | $ 0 | $ 0 | $ 0 |
| Sales of long-term assets | $ 0 | $ 0 | $ 0 |
| New investment received | $ 0 | $ 0 | $ 0 |
| Subtotal cash received | $129,460 | $241,140 | $338,210 |
| Expenditures | FY 2008 | FY 2009 | FY 2010 |
| Expenditures from operations | | | |
| Cash spending | $ 0 | $ 0 | $ 0 |
| Bill payments | $ 87,568 | $126,358 | $178,711 |
| Subtotal spent on operations | $ 87,568 | $126,358 | $178,711 |
| **Additional cash spent** | | | |
| Sales tax, VAT, HST/GST paid out | $ 0 | $ 0 | $ 0 |
| Principal repayment of current borrowing | $ 0 | $ 0 | $ 0 |
| Other liabilities principal repayment | $ 20,000 | $ 20,000 | $ 20,000 |
| Long-term liabilities principal repayment | $ 17,335 | $ 60,667 | $100,667 |
| Purchase other current assets | $ 0 | $ 0 | $ 0 |
| Purchase long-term assets | $ 0 | $ 0 | $ 0 |
| Dividends | $ 0 | $ 0 | $ 0 |
| Subtotal cash spent | $124,903 | $207,024 | $299,377 |
| Net cash flow | $ 4,557 | $ 34,116 | $ 38,833 |
| Cash balance | $ 12,847 | $ 46,963 | $ 85,795 |

**Cash Flow**

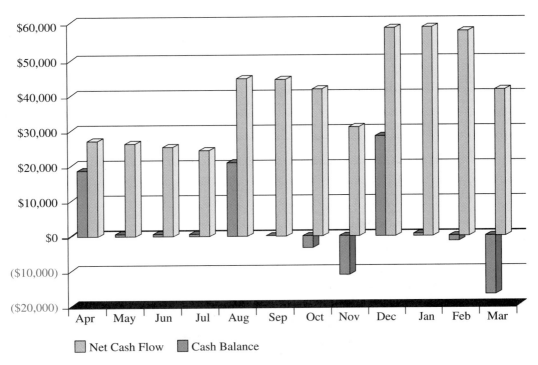

FIGURE A16  Cash Flow

## 8.5. Projected Balance Sheet

Our balance sheet shows that our business will experience rapid growth, leading to a significant increase in inventory, sales, and long-term liabilities in the form of loans. Although liabilities are projected to increase throughout the next several years, capital and retained earnings are also projected to increase. Our net worth is expected to increase substantially as our business becomes more profitable, thus allowing more retained earnings to be reinvested into the business and further expanding the financial capacity of the business.

Pro Forma Balance Sheet

|  | FY 2008 | FY 2009 | FY 2010 |
|---|---|---|---|
| **Assets** | | | |
| **Current assets** | | | |
| Cash | $12,847 | $ 46,963 | $ 85,795 |
| Inventory | $32,000 | $ 57,846 | $ 82,462 |
| Other current assets | $ 100 | $ 100 | $ 100 |
| Total current assets | $44,947 | $104,909 | $168,357 |
| **Long-term assets** | | | |
| Long-term assets | $ 0 | $ 0 | $ 0 |
| Accumulated depreciation | $ 0 | $ 0 | $ 0 |
| Total long-term assets | $ 0 | $ 0 | $ 0 |
| Total assets | $44,947 | $104,909 | $168,357 |

|  | FY 2008 | FY 2009 | FY 2010 |
|---|---|---|---|
| **Liabilities and capital** | | | |
| **Current liabilities** | | | |
| Accounts payable | $ 100 | $ 11,307 | $ 14,991 |
| Current borrowing | $ 0 | $ 0 | $ 0 |
| Other current liabilities | $ 5,500 | $ 5,500 | $ 5,500 |
| Subtotal current liabilities | $ 5,600 | $ 16,807 | $ 20,491 |
| Long-term liabilities | $14,665 | $ 27,999 | $ 41,332 |
| Total liabilities | $20,265 | $ 44,805 | $ 61,823 |
| Paid-in capital | $15,500 | $ 15,500 | $ 15,500 |
| Retained earnings | ($7,636) | $ 9,182 | $ 44,604 |
| Earnings | $16,818 | $ 35,421 | $ 46,430 |
| Total capital | $24,682 | $ 60,104 | $106,533 |
| Total liabilities and capital | $44,947 | $104,909 | $168,357 |
| Net Worth | $24,682 | $ 60,104 | $106,533 |

## 8.6. Business Ratios

Our business ratios are included and compared to a retail bookstore.

Ratio Analysis

| | FY 2008 | FY 2009 | FY 2010 | Industry Profile |
|---|---|---|---|---|
| Sales growth | 362.64% | 89.96% | 38.79% | 6.22% |
| **Percent of total assets** | | | | |
| Inventory | 71.19% | 55.14% | 48.98% | 28.92% |
| Other current assets | 0.22% | 0.10% | 0.06% | 28.31% |
| Total current assets | 100.00% | 100.00% | 100.00% | 84.87% |
| Long-term assets | 0.00% | 0.00% | 0.00% | 15.13% |
| Total assets | 100.00% | 100.00% | 100.00% | 100.00% |
| Current liabilities | 12.46% | 16.02% | 12.17% | 45.48% |
| Long-term liabilities | 32.63% | 26.69% | 24.55% | 15.42% |
| Total liabilities | 45.09% | 42.71% | 36.72% | 60.90% |
| Net worth | 54.91% | 57.29% | 63.28% | 39.10% |
| **Percent of sales** | | | | |
| Sales | 100.00% | 100.00% | 100.00% | 100.00% |
| Gross margin | 32.87% | 36.12% | 34.38% | 12.95% |
| Selling, general, & administrative expenses | 11.16% | 12.04% | 11.64% | 6.26% |
| Advertising expenses | 0.10% | 0.06% | 0.05% | 0.54% |
| Profit before interest and taxes | 32.36% | 35.84% | 34.18% | 0.94% |
| **Main ratios** | | | | |
| Current | 8.03 | 6.24 | 8.22 | 1.62 |
| Quick | 2.31 | 2.80 | 4.19 | 0.85 |
| Total debt to total assets | 45.09% | 42.71% | 36.72% | 65.08% |
| Pre-tax return on net worth | 97.34% | 84.19% | 62.26% | 2.82% |
| Pre-tax return on assets | 53.45% | 48.23% | 39.40% | 8.08% |

| | FY 2008 | FY 2009 | FY 2010 | |
|---|---|---|---|---|
| **Additional ratios** | | | | |
| Net profit margin | 21.71% | 24.07% | 22.74% | n/a |
| Return on equity | 68.14% | 58.93% | 43.58% | n/a |
| **Activity ratios** | | | | |
| Inventory turnover | 2.17 | 2.09 | 1.91 | n/a |
| Accounts payable turnover | 880.08 | 12.17 | 12.17 | n/a |
| Payment days | 27 | 15 | 26 | n/a |
| Total asset turnover | 1.72 | 1.40 | 1.21 | n/a |
| Debt ratios | | | | |
| Debt to net worth | 0.82 | 0.75 | 0.58 | n/a |
| Current liab. to liab. | 0.28 | 0.38 | 0.33 | n/a |
| **Liquidity ratios** | | | | |
| Net working capital | $39,348 | $88,102 | $147,865 | n/a |
| Interest coverage | 24.13 | 24.72 | 20.13 | n/a |
| **Additional ratios** | | | | |
| Assets to sales | 0.58 | 0.71 | 0.82 | n/a |
| Current debt/total assets | 12% | 16% | 12% | n/a |
| Acid test | 2.31 | 2.80 | 4.19 | n/a |
| Sales/net worth | 3.14 | 2.45 | 1.92 | n/a |
| Dividend payout | 0.00 | 0.00 | 0.00 | n/a |

Sales Forecast

| | | Apr-07 | May-07 | Jun-07 | Jul-07 | Aug-07 | Sep-07 | Oct-07 | Nov-07 | Dec-07 | Jan-08 | Feb-08 | Mar-08 |
|---|---|---|---|---|---|---|---|---|---|---|---|---|---|
| **Sales** | | | | | | | | | | | | | |
| Textbooks | 0% | $ 0 | $ 0 | $ 0 | $ 0 | $21,450 | $7,150 | $ 0 | $ 0 | $ 0 | $36,660 | $12,200 | $ 0 |
| Other | 0% | $ 0 | $ 0 | $ 0 | $ 0 | $ 0 | $ 0 | $ 0 | $ 0 | $ 0 | $ 0 | $ 0 | $ 0 |
| **Total sales** | | $ 0 | $ 0 | $ 0 | $ 0 | $21,450 | $7,150 | $ 0 | $ 0 | $ 0 | $36,660 | $12,200 | $ 0 |
| **Direct cost of sales** | | | | | | | | | | | | | |
| Textbook purchases | | $20,000 | $ 0 | $ 0 | $ 0 | $ 0 | $ 0 | $ 0 | $ 0 | $32,000 | $ 0 | $ 0 | $ 0 |
| Other | | $ 0 | $ 0 | $ 0 | $ 0 | $ 0 | $ 0 | $ 0 | $ 0 | $ 0 | $ 0 | $ 0 | $ 0 |
| Subtotal direct cost of sales | | $20,000 | $ 0 | $ 0 | $ 0 | $ 0 | $ 0 | $ 0 | $ 0 | $32,000 | $ 0 | $ 0 | $ 0 |

Pro Forma Cash Flow

| | | Apr-07 | May-07 | Jun-07 | Jul-07 | Aug-07 | Sep-07 | Oct-07 | Nov-07 | Dec-07 | Jan-08 | Feb-08 | Mar-08 |
|---|---|---|---|---|---|---|---|---|---|---|---|---|---|
| **Cash received** | | | | | | | | | | | | | |
| **Cash from operations** | | | | | | | | | | | | | |
| Cash sales | | $ 0 | $ 0 | $ 0 | $ 0 | $21,450 | $7,150 | $ 0 | $ 0 | $ 0 | $36,660 | $12,200 | $ 0 |
| Subtotal cash from operations | | $ 0 | $ 0 | $ 0 | $ 0 | $21,450 | $7,150 | $ 0 | $ 0 | $ 0 | $36,660 | $12,200 | $ 0 |
| **Additional cash received** | | | | | | | | | | | | | |
| Sales Tax, VAT, HST/GST received | 0.00% | $ 0 | $ 0 | $ 0 | $ 0 | $ 0 | $ 0 | $ 0 | $ 0 | $ 0 | $ 0 | $ 0 | $ 0 |
| New current borrowing | | $ 0 | $ 0 | $ 0 | $ 0 | $ 0 | $ 0 | $ 0 | $ 0 | $ 0 | $ 0 | $ 0 | $ 0 |
| New other liabilities (interest-free) | | $10,000 | $ 0 | $ 0 | $ 0 | $ 0 | $ 0 | $ 0 | $ 0 | $10,000 | $ 0 | $ 0 | $ 0 |
| **New long-term liabilities** | | $10,000 | $ 0 | $ 0 | $ 0 | $ 0 | $ 0 | $ 0 | $ 0 | $22,000 | $ 0 | $ 0 | $ 0 |
| **Sales of other current assets** | | $ 0 | $ 0 | $ 0 | $ 0 | $ 0 | $ 0 | $ 0 | $ 0 | $ 0 | $ 0 | $ 0 | $ 0 |
| **Sales of long-term assets** | | $ 0 | $ 0 | $ 0 | $ 0 | $ 0 | $ 0 | $ 0 | $ 0 | $ 0 | $ 0 | $ 0 | $ 0 |
| **New investment received** | | $ 0 | $ 0 | $ 0 | $ 0 | $ 0 | $ 0 | $ 0 | $ 0 | $ 0 | $ 0 | $ 0 | $ 0 |
| **Subtotal cash received** | | $20,000 | $ 0 | $ 0 | $ 0 | $21,450 | $7,150 | $ 0 | $ 0 | $32,000 | $36,660 | $12,200 | $ 0 |

|  | Apr-07 | May-07 | Jun-07 | Jul-07 | Aug-07 | Sep-07 | Oct-07 | Nov-07 | Dec-07 | Jan-08 | Feb-08 | Mar-08 |
|---|---|---|---|---|---|---|---|---|---|---|---|---|
| **Expenditures** | | | | | | | | | | | | |
| Expenditures from operations | | | | | | | | | | | | |
| Cash spending | $ 0 | $ 0 | $ 0 | $ 0 | $ 0 | $ 0 | $ 0 | $ 0 | $ 0 | $ 0 | $ 0 | $ 0 |
| Bill payments | $ 970 | $ 71 | $ 66 | $ 61 | $ 271 | $ 6,357 | $ 2,120 | $ 42 | $ 1,198 | $33,783 | $10,901 | $ 3,656 |
| Subtotal spent on operations | $ 970 | $ 71 | $ 66 | $ 61 | $ 271 | $ 6,357 | $ 2,120 | $ 42 | $ 1,198 | $33,783 | $10,901 | $ 3,656 |
| Additional cash spent | | | | | | | | | | | | |
| Sales Tax, VAT, HST/GST paid out | $ 0 | $ 0 | $ 0 | $ 0 | $ 0 | $ 0 | $ 0 | $ 0 | $ 0 | $ 0 | $ 0 | $ 0 |
| Principal repayment of current borrowing | $ 0 | $ 0 | $ 0 | $ 0 | $ 0 | $ 0 | $ 0 | $ 0 | $ 0 | $ 0 | $ 0 | $ 0 |
| Other liabilities principal repayment | $ 0 | $ 0 | $ 0 | $ 0 | $ 0 | $ 0 | $ 0 | $10,000 | $ 0 | $ 0 | $ 0 | $ 10,000 |
| Long-term liabilities principal repayment | $ 833 | $ 833 | $ 833 | $ 833 | $ 833 | $ 833 | $ 833 | $ 833 | $ 2,667 | $ 2,667 | $ 2,667 | $ 2,667 |
| Purchase other current assets | $ 0 | $ 0 | $ 0 | $ 0 | $ 0 | $ 0 | $ 0 | $ 0 | $ 0 | $ 0 | $ 0 | $ 0 |
| Purchase long-term assets | $ 0 | $ 0 | $ 0 | $ 0 | $ 0 | $ 0 | $ 0 | $ 0 | $ 0 | $ 0 | $ 0 | $ 0 |
| Dividends | $ 0 | $ 0 | $ 0 | $ 0 | $ 0 | $ 0 | $ 0 | $ 0 | $ 0 | $ 0 | $ 0 | $ 0 |
| Subtotal cash spent | $ 1,804 | $28.976 | $ 899 | $ 894 | $ 1,105 | $ 7,190 | $ 2,953 | $10,875 | $ 3,865 | $36,450 | $13,568 | $ 16,323 |
| Net cash flow | $18,196 | ($ 904) | ($ 899) | ($ 894) | $20,345 | ($ 40) | ($2,953) | ($10,875) | $28,135 | $ 210 | ($ 1,368) | ($16,323) |
| Cash balance | $26,486 | $25,582 | $24,683 | $23,789 | $44,134 | $44,094 | $41,141 | $30,266 | $58,401 | $58,611 | $57,243 | $ 40,920 |

# Endnotes

[1] "Higher Education Retail Market Facts and Figures 2007," National Association of College Stores, http://www.nacs.org/public/research/higher_ed_retail.asp.

[2] Ibid.

[3] Ibid.

[4] Ibid.

[5] FAQ on Used Textbooks." National Association of College Stores, June 2007, http://www.nacs.org/common/research/faq_usedbooks.pdf.

[6] "Higher Education Retail Market Facts and Figures 2007," National Association of College Stores, http://www.nacs.org/public/research/higher_ed_retail.asp.

[7] Ibid.

[8] Ibid.

[9] "Fast Facts," National Center for Education Statistics, http://www.nces.ed.gov/fastfacts/display.asp?id=98.

[10] "Higher Education Retail Market Facts and Figures 2007," National Association of College Stores, http://www.nacs.org/public/research/higher_ed_retail.asp.

[11] "Fast Facts," National Center for Education Statistics, http://www.nces.ed.gov/fastfacts/display.asp?id=98.

[12] Higher Education Retail Market Facts and Figures 2007," National Association of College Stores, http://www.nacs.org/public/research/higher_ed_retail.asp.

[13] Robyn Greenspan, "College Students Surf, Spend," ClickZ, February 13, 2003, http://www.clickz.com/showPage.html?page=1583871.

[14] "College Students Tote $122 Billion in Spending Power Back to Campus This Year," Harris Interactive, August 14, 2004, http://www.harrisinteractive.com/news/allnewsbydate.asp?NewsID=835.

[15] Robyn Greenspan, "College Students Surf, Spend," ClickZ, February 13, 2003, http://www.clickz.com/showPage.html?page=1583871.

[16] "College Students Tote $122 Billion in Spending Power Back to Campus This Year," Harris Interactive, August 14, 2004, http://www.harrisinteractive.com/news/allnewsbydate.asp?NewsID=835.

[17] "Higher Education Retail Market Facts and Figures 2007," National Association of College Stores, http://www.nacs.org/public/research/higher_ed_retail.asp.

[18] "Online Advertising Motivates College Students to Buy," *MarketingVox,* February 8, 2006, http://www.marketingvox.com/archives/2006/02/08/online_advertising_motivates_college_students_to_buy/.

[19] "College Students Pick Facebook as Favorite Site," *MarketingVox,* December 4, 2006, http://www.marketingvox.com/archives/2006/12/04/college-students-pick-facebook-as-favorite-site/.

[20] Online Advertising Motivates College Students to Buy," *MarketingVox,* February 8, 2006, http://www.marketingvox.com/archives/2006/02/08/online_advertising_motivates_college_students_to_buy/.

[21] "College Students Tote $122 Billion in Spending Power Back to Campus This Year," Harris Interactive, August 14, 2004, http://www.harrisinteractive.com/news/allnewsbydate.asp?NewsID=835.

[22] "FAQ on College Textbooks," National Association of College Stores," June 2007, http://www.nacs.org/common/research/faq_textbooks.pdf.

[23] Ibid.

[24] Ibid.

[25] Ibid.

[26] Ibid.

[27] Morris Rosenthal, "North American Book Market," Foner Books, http://www.fonerbooks.com/booksale.htm.

[28] "EBay Workshop: Selling Textbooks on eBay," eBay.com. http://forums.ebay.com/db2/thread.jspa?threadID=410167803.

[29] Ibid.

[30] "Higher Education Retail Market Facts and Figures 2007," National Association of College Stores, http://www.nacs.org/public/research/higher_ed_retail.asp.

[31] "EBay Workshop: Selling Textbooks on eBay," eBay.com. http://forums.ebay.com/db2/thread.jspa?threadID=410167803.

[32] Ibid.

## Case 1
## Ted Leonsis and Filmanthropy

It was January of 2007. Ted Leonsis wandered among crowds of people at the Sundance Film Festival. Eyes of passersby lit up as they glanced down at his nametag and said, "*Nanking*! You've got great buzz." *Nanking* was the documentary Leonsis had produced over the last two years with a top tier team, including an academy award winning director and actors Woody Harrelson and Mariel Hemingway. For this brief moment in time, Leonsis was a movie producer. The currency was "buzz" instead of the "eyeballs" and "page views" from AOL, where he served as vice chair.

The new film industry executive commented on how he mixed his intuitive vision with a drive to action:

> You need that balance between the vision and the execution. No matter how excited you might be about a vision, you can never lose sight that customers may not buy an idea. With *Nanking, I* could pitch people on what the story was going to be about. But someone has to pay $10 and sit for 90 minutes in the dark. If the movie stinks, there goes that vision. . . . You can't be a visionary all the time. It is better to be a person who can connect strategy and tactics. The big idea only comes around once every few years.

Leonsis was often quoted as saying that he "could sell one million of anything." Would that mantra carry over to this new industry with his film, *Nanking?* Leonsis was successful by anyone's definition. He had made millions starting and selling two businesses as well as serving on the front line of AOL's leadership team for 14 years. In addition, he owned stakes in three major sports franchises. Now Leonsis was toying with the term "Filmanthropy" to brand the merging of social causes with filmmaking and funding. He could see it, but could the audience? Was he a worthy champion to help lead this cause? The theater darkened and Leonsis sensed that very soon he would have an answer to his questions.

### Case-in-Case

The National Foundation for Teaching Entrepreneurship (NFTE) also champions an important social cause. Julie Kantor, is now a NFTE Executive Director and author of *I Said Yes,* explained: "Our students are in low income communities and, for them, learning entrepreneurship is a way of controlling their own destiny. For instance, one of our top students helped his mom buy a house. As an organization, we live by the double bottom line. We fundraise to support our programs. But we also have to prove our social impact and worth. It's a fun and rewarding challenge."

Sundance was a far cry from Leonsis's early years. He had grown up in tough neighborhoods and witnessed friends getting shot and killed. His best friend and neighbor died of a heroin overdose. He felt thankful to be in this place today: Happy and successful with a wonderful family. It all started with his "ah ha moment" in college after winning a prestigious award for his thesis, which applied the worlds of literature, linguistics, and computers to the works of Ernest Hemingway. He went on to work in the computer industry, ultimately starting his own company—L.I.S.T.—a publication for the industry with a *TV Guide*-like format. Through a connection at E. F. Hutton, Leonsis raised $1 million to build the company. Leonsis was elated when he sold L.I.S.T. for $60 million, but a plane crash changed his perspective on everything. Leonsis elaborated on the 101 list of goals he developed after the crash: "Some of it is goofy. . . . But having it written down compelled me to go and do it. Throughout my career, writing things down had helped me accomplish a great deal." He coined and evangelized the term "new media" and founded his next company, Redgate. In 1993 Redgate was AOL's first acquisition and, from there, Leonsis became AOL's longest-tenured executive. AOL's Chairman and CEO Jonathan Miller said, "Ted Leonsis helped build AOL not once, but twice."[1]

Flash-forward more than 10 years, and Leonsis is reading the *New York Times*. A beautiful Asian face stared back at him from the stark black-and-white newsprint. "Noted Author and Historian Dies at 36," said the obituary from December 2004. Iris Chang was married and had two children. She had committed suicide. Leonsis was on a boat vacationing with his family and reading an obituary about this young and talented woman. The contrast between the two worlds was marked and struck a chord for Leonsis. A single word echoed in his mind: Gratitude.

Leonsis almost threw the paper away, but for a reason he could not explain, he placed it in his padfolio. A week later, Leonsis came home and Googled the author's name. He bought and read her book: *The Rape of Nanking,* a term used to describe the murder, rape, and looting in the Chinese city Nanking (now called Nanjing) after it was seized by Japanese troops in 1937. Leonsis wanted to tell the story. How was it possible that he did not know about this major event in history? The best way to tell the story would be through a movie, but what did he know about making movies? Didn't mainstream movies cost at least $50 million to make? That would be a big risk to take for a first-time producer. Leonsis explained the fast and furious turn of events:

> I called the head of CAA, Hollywood's leading talent agency, and described the movie premise: "It's about China. It's about heroes who stayed back and helped during dire times. It is *Schindler's List* with a Chinese twist." His reaction was sort of like, "Yeah, you and everyone else." He told me I needed a director to which I responded, "Can you introduce me to a director?" The director thought it sounded boring. I sent my son to the Library of Congress to find film footage from 1937 in Nanjing and, after many, many hours he found it. I took the footage back to the director and hired him. I wrote a letter to the Chinese ambassador essentially asking, "How do you make a movie in China?" I approached Woody Harrelson, who bore a striking resemblance to one of the characters. He signed on.

In the span of a few months, Leonsis had dissected an industry with which he had been completely unfamiliar. He and the production team spent a month in China before moving on to Japan. After three months, the team had 900 hours of footage to edit. Leonsis described the new process of filmmaking:

> We were so into it that we didn't know if it was any good. Friday was the deadline to get into Sundance. We heard Robert Redford wanted to see the film. A week later he called me with Sundance Film Festival Co-Director Geoff Gilmore and told me we were in. I didn't know you're not supposed to have that level of success the first time. I didn't know you're not supposed to get into Sundance.

*Nanking* won an award for Best Edited Documentary at Sundance and went on to the Berlin, Hong Kong, Tribeca, and Silver Docs film festivals. The film was picked up for distribution around the world and was bought by HBO. On July 7, 2007, *Nanking* had its first theatrical release in China to rave reviews. Leonsis and his team made worldwide distribution deals including CCTV, China's main TV network, which would broadcast the film to approximately 650,000 viewers. By the fall of 2007, one million tickets had sold in China. The impact continued to reverberate as described by Leonsis:

> There is something here about making films that can activate a discussion, focus on people as heroes, and then have a big charity component around it. . . . Always in the back of my mind I wanted to make a movie, but I didn't want to be dumb money where someone comes to me with an idea and I finance it. . . .

Now I'm probably looking at putting together a studio. I want to make 25 or 50 of these films at around one to three million dollars each.

Despite Leonsis's many interests, everyone knew that family was number one on his list. Over the last few years, Leonsis managed his time closely and committed to fewer engagements that would take him away from his family. Relinquishing the stress of day-to day management at AOL in early 2007 and retiring in the fall of 2007 was also a great help. He continued to manage his sports teams and to pursue new entrepreneurial endeavors, his philanthropic interests, and film projects. He never failed to involve his family in the adventure, whether it was a Friday night hockey game or filming in China. Leonsis was incredibly busy for someone on the self-proclaimed "back 9" of his career and, therefore, retirement remained a humorous subject around the Leonsis household. Leonsis smiled, "I think there is a serial entrepreneur inside me. There is an adrenaline rush. There is something meaningful in creating and launching an endeavor." Would Leonsis's corporate successes carry over to the realm of social entrepreneurship? Determined to make Filmanthropy a worthwhile enterprise, he searched for the right model and approach.

## Exercises

1. Examine the following "Leonsis Equation" table. Where is he in the equation with Filmanthropy?
2. Research social entrepreneurship and, specifically, the film industry using the Internet. Also review points from the text. Develop a "top five" list with information that could be helpful in building Filmanthropy.
3. Develop a mini feasibility plan for Filmanthropy using the following categories: Service/product provided, benefit, target population and market, strategy (e.g., cost leadership, differentiation, or focus), financial viability, and social responsibility (triple bottom line).
4. Discuss Leonsis's pattern of idea generation and execution. What do you think is the necessary balance of idea generation versus execution for a successful entrepreneur?
5. What is your "big idea?" Provide statistics to validate the market size and growth opportunity for your potential business. Does a viable market opportunity exist?
6. How would you leverage your resources and network of contacts at this point in your life to begin to accomplish your goal? List target resources, network members, and strategies for making inroads with them.

*Source:* Katherine Korman Frey, "Ted," The Cool Daddies Project Case Database, www.visionforward.com, 2007.

Go to www.VisionForward.com for printable cases, more on Ted Leonsis and Filmanthrophy, plus additional exercises and resources.

## TABLE 1 The Leonsis Equation*

| Step | Leonsis's Notes & Quotes: |
|---|---|
| 1. *Envision.* Idea inspired by interdisciplinary thinking. | • "You could say I've never had an original idea. All I've ever done is take one from column a, one from column b, and one from column c, shake it up, and bring it out differently."<br>• Examples: College thesis, L.I.S.T. |
| 2. *Assess.* Analyze "big" potential. Talk to experts, talk to consumers. If possible, contribute to making a market. | • "I go out and talk to lots and lots of people. I'm very high on the intuitive."<br>• "I won't do anything around a vision or idea that doesn't get big fast."<br>• "You can never lose sight that customers may not buy an idea."<br>• "Once I go out and talk to people, my gut instinct kicks in."<br>• Examples: "I usually like to see a market of 10 million clients before I'll get involved."<br>"I then develop a product to serve this burgeoning market." |
| 3. *Develop.* Create a product, build a business around it. | • "I make sure it is something customers will buy."<br>• "I raise funding and build the right team."<br>• Examples: "Enamored with personal computers, I came up with the idea of L.I.S.T., pitched it, raised money, and made some key hires." |
| 4. *Commit.* Never turn back. | • "Once I say I'm gonna do it, I don't stop. I am fearless. The path can remain malleable and open. But I am 100 percent convinced it's going to work. I would never go into something half way."<br>• "Even if your idea isn't the best idea, you will work it, analyze it, push it until you win."<br>• "There's more than one way to skin that cat. Effort, tenacity, passion, and 'stickwithitness' are traits that everyone can have."<br>• Example: *Nanking*—finding footage, convincing director. |
| 5. *Evangelize.* Sell 1 million, 10 million, 100 million, or 1 billion of something. | • "I've been quoted as saying I think I could sell 1 million of anything. The next is 1 million to 10 million. Then 10 million to 100 million. Then 100 million to 1 billion. . . . That's what I've been good at."<br>• Example: "My goal with *Nanking* was to have one billion people see it. With the CCTV deal, I got 650,000 right there." |
| 6. *Connect.* Link vision and strategies with tactics and execution to get where you need to be. | • "You can't be a visionary all the time. It is better to be a person that can connect strategy and tactics. The big idea only comes around once every few years."<br>• "I make lots of lists. And then there is a lot of execution."<br>• Example: "I said 'I want 1 billion people to see *Nanking*.' Everything else trickled down from that. Our strategy was to seek distribution partners, and our tactics were to call one major player a day until we reached that goal." |
| 7. *No bad days.* Follow up and manage. | • "I have this motto of 'You can't have a bad day.' Bad day, bad week. Bad week, bad month. Bad month, bad quarter. Bad quarter, bad year. I try to keep people up, focused, understanding that you can't have a bad day. It's not a happy thing. You do better than the day before to meet growth goals."<br>• Example: "At AOL, I had morning meetings, lunchtime water-cooler talk, and end of day e-mails to make sure my team was on-track." |
| 8. *Higher calling.* | • "There is an adrenaline rush. There is something meaningful in creating and launching an endeavor."<br>• "As Steve Case said during our first meeting: 'Life is too short to drink bad wine'."<br>• Example: "I am incredibly proud of the movie I made. I'd like to do it again." |

*Time Warner press release, September 15, 2006.

# Case 2
# Brian Scudamore and 1-800-Got-Junk

**B**rian Scudamore, founder and CEO of 1-800-Got-Junk, rushed down the hall for his 10:55 A.M. meeting. Every day, the entire staff at 1-800-Got-Junk participates in what Scudamore calls a "daily huddle." The meeting lasts about 5 minutes, and all staff remains standing. The agenda that day consisted of a discussion of the company's key metrics (critical numbers) and some words of encouragement from Scudamore about hitting these numbers. As Scudamore viewed the jam-packed "huddle room," he could hardly believe that just a few years ago it was he who was manning the phones and driving the trucks. Now his primary role was quite different at the company that had become the world's largest junk removal company. He acted as visionary to anchor the company's long-term goals and supported his teams to help them plan and execute. "I'm a visionary and cheerleader," Scudamore summarized.

The company regularly tracks 5 or 6 pages of metrics in a homegrown Microsoft Excel spreadsheet. Certain numbers might play an important role at various times depending on the company's focus, but a handful of metrics are always in the center of the radar screen: revenue, cash flow, and franchise partner success. The company's 2012 revenue goal is a whopping $1 billion. Scudamore hoped that the company would be able to generate enough cash to finance its growth internally and to maintain or improve on its 94 percent franchisee satisfaction rating. There were complexities with growth, as Scudamore explained:

> I'd heard this from a lot of CEOs, and it's true: Beyond $100 million (in revenue), it's a different ballgame. The complexity is greater. It forces you to have a different style of leadership . . . to be less reactive and more proactive. It's all about the right systems.

The company was changing some of its systems and processes, and the changes would impact the company's lifeblood: 1-800-Got-Junk's 320 franchise partners. The company's franchise partners each operated within specified territories. In exchange for an initial investment and an 8 percent royalty on every dollar earned, the partners are able to participate in a proven, successful business system and a comprehensive support system including training, coaching, field visits, and benefits resulting from national commercial alliances that 1-800-Got-Junk had developed. Franchise partners sign a five-year agreement. During that time, if the company made changes, franchise partners would be unaffected until the end of their agreements. At that time, they would have the choice to accept the new changes or relinquish their franchises. Scudamore described how the franchise model came about:

> Between 1989 and 1999 I did *a lot* of research. I learned that the right franchise has a great chance of success. I also liked the idea of a network of franchise partners. You're putting all these brilliant minds and saying "let's innovate together." We really believe that our franchise partners are partners. We allow the partners to work more on the business than in the business because we have a call center that does all of the dispatching. This allows them to work on building fleets of trucks, not answering phones.

Scudamore and his team receive continuous feedback from the franchise partners with the assistance of the 1-800-Got-Junk Franchise Advisory Council (FAC): A group of 6 franchise partners elected by their peers. The group collects feedback from franchise partners in their region, summarizes it, and then go to headquarters twice per year to meet with top management who use the information to make improvements.

"Last time it was all about marketing," Scudamore explained. "There were too many materials, and franchise partners wanted an updated Web site. That was the focus for our changes this past year." Before implementing new operating procedures, 1-800-Got-Junk managers presented them to the FAC first. After managers work with these groups, they communicated the changes to the entire network of franchise partners.

## Case-in-Case

Ingenia Group, an interactive marketing agency based in Mexico City, uses a non-traditional method for communication. Company founder Pablo O'Hagan Hernandez explained, "When there is a problem, solving it fast is not enough. I create a system to prevent it from happening again. One effective system we have is a simple email address that every single person at Ingenia receives. Any client can use the email to complain or praise! It has worked well for us, because nobody wants to receive a complaint. The results have been very positive for customer service and team motivation."

The latest change that was communicated through the FAC and the network of partners had to do with territory sizes. The change had resulted in some concerns among franchisees. Scudamore knew that part of the challenge had to do with the company's size. In the past, a small change would produce a small ripple effect. Now, with 320 partners, even a small change could produce a large ripple effect. Changing territory structure? That was a *large* change. Scudamore explained:

> Recently, we cut the territory sizes down for our franchise partners. The territory size population base went from 125,000 to 62,500. So, this means our partners need to have a truck for every 62,500 people in their territory. We've got a top franchise partner who joined at the 125,000 per truck model. They must have 16 trucks running at any given point in time. Now, under the new agreement, someone [in that situation] must have 32 trucks running. These are tougher requirements. We did not get buy-in on this from some of our top partners.

The company offers one of the best franchise models available, but hearing about unhappy franchise partners was hard for Scudamore. He secretly wondered whether there was anyway the announcement could have gone a bit smoother.

Would a different approach have helped? Was the company so large that it would be impossible to make every partner happy?

## Exercises

1. What advantages and disadvantages do 1-800-Got-Junk franchisees experience?
2. Why did 1-800-Got-Junk change the sizes of its franchisees' territories?
3. Is there a better way for 1-800-Got-Junk to have rolled out the communication about the territory size change to its franchisees? Do you think the result would have been different? Explain.
4. Comment on 1-800-Got-Junk's system for setting goals and tracking performance. Is it effective?
5. How do you think 1-800-Got-Junk is capitalized?

*Source:* Katherine Korman Frey, "Brian," The Vision Forward Case Database, http://www.visionforward.com, 2007.

Go to http://www.VisionForward.com for printable cases, more on Brian Scudamore and 1-800-Got-Junk, plus additional exercises and resources.

### TABLE 1  Summary of the 1-800-Got-Junk Value Proposition

*Low investment and high potential for growth*

| | |
|---|---|
| • Franchise fee per exclusive territory (62.5k population): | $ 16,000 |
| • Each additional exclusive territory (62.5k population): | $ 8,000 |
| • Marketing package: | $ 12,000 |
| • Start-up investment (down payments, office expenses, etc.): | $ 9,000 |
| • Working capital: | $ 45,000 |
| Minimum capital requirement: | $ 90,000 |

***Our guarantee:*** If you do not hit the minimum revenue goal of $100,000 within your first 12 months of business, we will refund 100 percent of your franchise fee on your first territory, and allow you to give back your franchise.

***Support summary:*** Training, coaching, field visits, peer support, help desk, national accounts and strategic alliances, national public relations and marketing, call center for appointment booking, awards.

# Case 3
# Jason Beans and RISING Medical Solutions, Inc

Jason Beans, the founder of RISING Medical Solutions Inc., couldn't believe what was happening in his own company. Beans, his operations manager, and other staff gathered in celebration to give an employee a performance reward: Baseball tickets. The staffer was happy and surprised; then her demeanor quickly changed. She meekly asked, "May I please make a personal call to see if my mom can come to the game tonight?" The manager turned to Beans and grinned, content that her authoritarian management style had taken effect. Beans felt nauseous . . . *May she make a call to her mom? For tickets we just gave her?* "We had created mice. That's the only way I can think to describe it. My manager was proud of what had happened. I was horrified," he said.

RISING Medical Solutions helps employers and insurance companies contain healthcare costs. Lots of employees and insured individuals mean lots of healthcare and insurance bills. A key service of RISING helps customers organize and analyze the many complicated items on their bills. The average savings? For every $1 paid to RISING medical, a client saves between $8 and $78 dollars. The savings come from a variety of areas, but errors and fraud are the biggest problems when controlling healthcare costs. RISING is on top of it. Clients are quite surprised by some of the discoveries RISING makes on their bills: Provider offices that did not exist, phantom medical supply companies, unlicensed providers, and double-billing under multiple facilities.

It is a complicated industry, but the bottom line is this: Beans is an astute businessman, and he is the type of person who wanted to make things better. Even his approach to RISING is about improvement. Beans explained:

Our products are in commodity markets, but I refuse to let us be seen as a commodity product. I strive daily to give medical cost containment a good name. If you are an employer and save $40,000 in medical fees, that could mean another job at that company. It could mean better coverage for the employees already there. We teach that to our staff. These are not just a bunch of numbers. These are lives.

Looking back, Beans realized his philosophies differed from those of his operations manager. However, when Beans hired her, he was strapped and needed help. He had not paid himself in months, and he was performing every executive position in the company, from Chief Executive Officer to Chief Marketing Officer. When he implemented flextime, some staff claimed to be coming in at 5.00 A.M. In-

stead, they would punch in and then go out to breakfast. Beans commented on his next move:

I needed to hire someone a little tougher than I was to do the day-to-day management. I brought in someone I knew from before, gave her the goals, and then I didn't micromanage. She essentially managed everyone by the time clock. If they punched in 5 minutes late, she would e-mail them. She was videoing staff computer screens. It was about catching them doing something wrong. After about 6 months, I talked with her about lightening up, but she just couldn't evolve from the negative management style. I knew it had to change.

Beans hired a new Human Resources/Talent Manager. The job description? Make RISING one of the best places to work in the country. He wanted people to be accountable, but in a supportive way. "You don't have to be mean to be accountable," Beans said.

It was a new dawn at RISING, and Beans liked what he was seeing. When thinking about "ideal" environments, Beans remembered his martial arts classes. He was a Jujitsu black belt and was very familiar with Bushido, a Samurai code. The code resulted in a tremendous sense of trust among the members of his class. "All of these years later, I could still call any of those guys from my class for anything," he said. He wanted to replicate that feeling at his company. In doing so, however, he would have to overcome some obstacles.

The baseball ticket episode flashed through Beans's mind. Why had this event produced such a visceral reaction for him? The incident ran counter to his values. How could he translate those values to his company? Beans stopped pacing around his office and created what would become the company's guiding document: The RISING Medical Solutions Core Values.

---

## Case-in-Case

Values-based messages can influence internal and external audiences. The Alzheimer's Association, the world's first and largest organization supporting Alzheimer's research and families (www.alz.org), has many chapters across the United States. "We've all been part of the campaign for the first National Memory Walk," noted Anthony Sudler, president and CEO of the National Capital Area chapter. "The three pillars are: OPEN, VOICE, and MOVE. It's about opening your mind, using your voice, and moving to action. It's not a just a campaign anymore. It permeates all that we do."

---

Beans worked for months on the values statement before sharing it with advisors and experts in the field. "One advisor told me I had too many things I was trying to teach people," Beans recounted. "He explained that people learn best in multiples of up to 7, so, I knew that was going to be the number."

After researching successful high-growth companies, Beans realized that his message and vision were not effectively trickling down to all levels of his company. When the company was small, catching up with the CEO was easy. As RISING grew, however, Beans was no longer directly involved with the hiring and mentoring of all new employees. Without guidance and coaching, employees simply relied on the habits that had worked for them at their former employers. RISING had become a parking lot for mismatched company cultures. Now, Beans was changing all of that. He explains the process:

> We promoted [core values] in our internal communications, meetings, and company social events. Employees received a framed set of our values to hang at their workstations. We printed t-shirts with our values on them. We created "Rock Star Awards" whereby employees rewarded each other for applying core values in "rock-star-worthy" ways. We even named our conference rooms after them. From time to time, I would randomly approach employees and ask them to recite the core values. If they could, they received a $100 bill on the spot. Our core values quickly became the guiding force our company was lacking.

RISING's accountability structures also began falling into place. Beans hired more senior managers. Together, they revamped the company's annual goals and quarterly milestones. Beans described how he tracks progress daily: "I have a morning call with all of my managers for 12 minutes. Be-fore they meet with me, they are supposed to meet with their staff. I want to hear what they are doing to drive those top 5 goals as well as any barriers." Based on the outcome of the meeting, managers post the goals on their office doors with red, yellow, and green visual indicators: red, the company is going to miss their goal; yellow, the company is close to the danger zone; green, the company is on track. "It's been working for managers so now we're rolling it down to the whole company," Beans said. "When we discuss 'red' or off-track goals, it's never about punishment. It's about problem solving." It was a far cry from the baseball ticket episode, but with measurable improvements in turnover and client satisfaction, Beans has confidence in his new management system.

## Exercises

1. Summarize RISING's management systems. Use the information in the chapters in your textbook on strategic management, organizational management, and leadership.
2. Describe three values you have that translate into your professional and personal activities.
3. How do entrepreneurs' values affect the companies they create? Find examples on the Internet of entrepreneurs who operate their businesses using a set of core personal values.
4. As a leader, what could Jason Beans have done to prevent the "baseball ticket episode?"

*Source:* Katherine Korman Frey, "Jason," The Vision Forward Case Database, http://www.visionforward.com, 2007.

Go to http://www.VisionForward.com for printable cases, more on Jason Beans and RISING Medical Solutions Inc., plus additional exercises and resources.

Josh Frey enjoyed a cigar while walking his dog, Foxy. These were the times, Frey found, that he could really think and reflect. He looked around at his neighborhood and appreciated how beautiful it was. Appreciation of the good things in his life was never a problem for Frey, until it came to business. Even though Frey had taken his company from his parents' basement to seven figures in revenue, he still found himself wanting more. He was never satisfied. Yet he felt completely the opposite as he looked at his wife, their son, their daughter on the way, and their great home and lifestyle. How was it that he could be so satisfied with one area of his life and feel continual unrest with another?

Frey's company, On Sale Promos (OSP), sold promotional products, which meant that the company coordinated the application of a company's logo onto one or more of millions of products ranging from pens, mugs, and bags to high-end gift sets, apparel, and awards. Whenever Frey felt a sense of unease about his business, it was usually due to one of two things: sales or cash flow. Cash was his biggest source of anxiety for many years. "We just need to sell more," Frey would say in an effort to solve the company's cash flow problems. However, as Frey later realized, that was not the answer:

> We had to give a 50 percent deposit to manufacturers on merchandise that went in the packages. We still had not received one dollar from the client at that point. Then we had to make the remainder of the payment when the product was delivered. We really needed to get on top of our accounts payable and accounts receivables policies—not just our sales. To be honest, some of the problem was just the way the industry worked. We couldn't come in and say, "You know how everyone gives you 50 percent? We're not going to."

## Case-in-Case

Dave Burnett is founder and owner of Canadian-based An Opportunity Knocks, a promotional products company like On Sale Promos. Burnett noted, "Cash flow is one of the biggest challenges we've had to face. . . . When I was in business school, I wasn't taught the importance of cash flow. . . . If the $3,000,000 manufacturer account payable is due tomorrow and the $5,000,000 accounts receivable from your customers isn't coming in 30 days you have a MAJOR problem."

To help, Frey took on an operational partner: Kaeser and Blair (K&B). In exchange for a percentage of each sale, K&B paid OSP's manufacturers and billed its clients. Frey completely reversed his cash flow cycle as K&B paid OSP at the time an order was placed. Frey breathed a sigh of relief as K&B took over the company's back office and financing functions. OSP quickly became one of K&B's top partners in the nation.

When OSP did accrue more cash, it was plowed into growth, primarily in the form of new salespeople. Frey's sales process is very methodical, but it must be to have a replicable system that Frey could teach to staffers, most of whom were top students or recent graduates from a nearby university. Frey trained the salespeople how to network and find leads. "There is an equation . . . phone calls, meetings, and e-mails leads to prospects leads to proposals leads to sales," Frey would tell his sales team. "At each step, the number is getting smaller, so you have to cast a wide net." Frey also mapped out the OSP client base: First, there are strategic partners such as a large events promotion company using OSP exclusively for promotional products. Second, there are large customers planning specific events. The last group of clients is comprised of smaller—but more consistent—orders, some of which are submitted through the company's online store. OSP focused on a handful of key industries in which staff attended tradeshows. The rest of the company's clients were referrals in a variety of industries and geographies.

## Case-in-Case

Dave Burnett's philosophy? Return on investment (ROI) on every sales and marketing dollar spent. He explained, "I have a reasonably strong dislike for big budget items like commercials and billboard advertising. Stats like 0.1 percent response rate on a direct mail piece means you failed with the other 99.9 percent! The way we generate new business is by becoming active members in our customers' organizations. Otherwise you are just another phone call they won't return."

OSP was in the middle of a competitive bid for a client with a large order. This was a six-figure opportunity and, as he always did in large bidding situations, Frey pondered his strategy repeatedly. He decided to use a fresh approach and prepared a memo for the team to use as talking points for OSP's Monday afternoon sales meeting. Frey knew this would keep him up at night until the proposal was submitted at the end of the week.

**To:**      **On Sale Promos sales team**
**From:**   **Josh**
**Re:**      **Artemis\* Bid**

### Background

- Artemis needs 100,000 units of 4 different products. The contract is up for bid.
- The RFP (Request for Proposal) is extended to 3 vendors, including On Sale Promos.
- OSP worked with the client in the past. Due to spending cuts shortly after 9/11, OSP has not worked with Artemis in several years. Now the company is buying again.
- Cost consciousness: They have a lot of need (units) but not a lot of money on a per-unit basis.
- The products are a pen, a notepad, a key chain, and a magnet. All will be imprinted with the Artemis logo. Artemis needs 100,000 units of each.

### Next Step

- After the first round of bids, one of the vendors has been eliminated based on price.
- The marketing director is making the ultimate decision. There are two managers under the marketing manager: One has a relationship with OSP, the other has a relationship with the second vendor. They are responsible for soliciting the bid from the vendor with which they have the relationship.
- Current OSP pricing is as follows:

| Pen | $0.40 per unit | Key chain | $0.10 per unit |
|---------|----------------|-----------|----------------|
| Notepad | $0.40 per unit | Magnet | $0.10 per unit |

- In this round, OSP has also offered (after conversations leveraging a relationship with a manufacturer):
  - Free stocking of merchandise for 6 months.
  - Free inventory management and shipping service (not actual cost of shipping) so the client does not have to store items at its office and can have them shipped, as needed, to the various corporate locations/events/etc.

### Last Step

- The other vendor has matched OSP's offer. In response, we offered an additional $1,000 off the order in addition to the discounts that we already had offered to get to a low per-unit cost. (Part of the way OSP arranged for this was by delivering 20 percent of the product right away, then working with the manufacturer to have the remainder made in Asia and delivered 90 days later.)
- OSP also sent a Coach umbrella to the contact as a thank-you gift for the opportunity to bid.

\*This was a real sales situation. The prospect's actual name has been substituted with Artemis.

### Exercises

1. Draw a diagram of OSP's cash flow cycle. Explain the cash flow difficulties described by Josh Frey and Dave Burnett (refer to the Case-in-Case). Why did Frey's strategy of more sales fail to improve OSP's cash flow?
2. Discuss OSP's "replicable sales process." Why is this issue so important to OSP's success?
3. Draw a diagram of the "sales equation" that Frey describes in his memo. Estimate the numbers at each step.
4. Prepare for an in class sales role-play meeting between the OSP team and Artemis. Develop a list of key questions and concerns that the Artemis team might have as well as an approach for the OSP team. Goal for both teams: Close the deal during the meeting.
5. Why do you think that Frey "never feels satisfied" with his business. Do you think this is common among entrepreneurs?

*Source:* Katherine Korman Frey, "Josh," The Vision Forward Cool Daddies Project Case Database, http://www.visionforward.com, 2006.

Go to http://www.VisionForward.com for printable cases, more on Josh Frey and On Sale Promos, plus additional exercises and resources.

## Case 5
## Kathryn From and Bravado! Designs

**K**athryn From felt like a deer in headlights. The banker's voice seemed to play in slow motion, "Are you Bravado! Designs' new owner? We're pulling your line of credit." From had left her high-powered job for this? Bravado! Designs is a niche lingerie company located in Ontario, Canada, that From had worked with as a consultant. She described her actions after the company's owner asked From to invest:

> I sold all of my possessions and borrowed money. I'm not sure the company had ever hit breakeven, but I saw potential. Everyone thought I was crazy for buying into it, but it had such a great name and reputation. With a manufacturing business, you need to hit a certain point before you break even, and they were on the cusp.

With the phone receiver in one hand and a bottle of aspirin in the other, From wondered about her decision to become CEO of the company. She began reviewing the company's supply chain to see whether she could make improvements:

### From's Notes on the Bravado! Supply Chain

- **Design.** Create own product with in-house designers.
- **Materials requisition and payment.** Find sources of materials and pay for them; suppliers will require a cash outlay six months before delivery.
- **Materials.** Receive materials and store them in our offices. (Fabric on big bolts is stored offsite.) Some raw materials have to be checked for quality before sending them to the factories.
- **Distribution.** Ship material to three to five local factories.
- **Garment assembly.** Factory handles this part of the process.
- **Quality control.** Verify quality of final garments before shipping them.

Bravado! was in control of most parts of its supply chain. In addition, if Bravado! called its local manufacturers about a new order, the factory could sew up garments in a day or two. Furthermore, bankers liked From because of her MBA, consulting background, and general knowledge of business. She thought like they thought, which made

bankers comfortable. When she got the call about the line of credit, From believed that in all likelihood she would be able to develop a relationship with a new bank. However, what really hit Bravado! was the decline in value of the U.S. dollar. From explained:

> The U.S. dollar lost about 45 percent against the Canadian dollar very quickly. Boy, it really affects a Canadian company that is shipping the bulk of its sales into the United States. Before, for one U.S. dollar, we'd get $1.63 Canadian; we now get $1.04. Our product, which sells for $32 U.S. dollars, would translate into $52 Canadian dollars. Now, with the currency decline, that translates into $33 Canadian dollars. The apparel industry is not a high-margin industry like the liquor or perfume industries. A 10 percent profit margin is a solid return. You take 45 percent off your top line, and you can imagine what a hole you're in.

---

### Case-in-Case

Judy Leissner, CEO of China-based Grace Vineyards, recounts her experience in building relationships abroad, "I grew up in China and got my college degree in the States. My background is very different from those I work with in China, especially in working with government officials. Bridging this gap and building a close working relationship with them has been a good challenge."

Grace Vineyards encountered unique growth challenges as a result of operating in China. Leissner described, "The government wants us to expand as fast as possible so that they can earn more tax income. On a regular basis, we deal with roughly 30 government departments. Then, multiply that number by village, county, city, province, and national levels."

---

Kathyrn's list of "might do" changes in the Bravado! supply chain quickly moved to the "must do" list. Without them, the company would be out of business in six months. First, the company had to move its manufacturing base from Canada. This was extremely difficult because the company was founded on the idea of keeping jobs in Canada. The company had developed partnerships with two factories in Mexico. One factory worked with well-known lingerie company Victoria's Secret, and the other worked with La Perla. Under the new arrangement, the factory in Mexico negotiated and purchased fabric. Bravado! then bought garments for $6 each instead of buying all the raw materials.

**864**

Bravado! paid the factories on 30-day terms when the garments were completed. To ensure quality, Bravado! staff checked a percentage of the garments by lots. The changes made a big difference, as From described:

> Two to three months after we had sent our production to Mexico, we started making profits again. We lowered our cost of goods sold by 25 to 30 percent overnight. We are now a design, marketing, and branding firm that happens to source lingerie. We don't have much clout, but we are a solid number-two or number-three partner with the companies that manufacture our garments. In the future, I'd like to be able to get better economies of scale.

Some of the changes necessitated new operating procedures at the company. Previously, Bravado! wrote checks over a period of time: first for materials, then for the factory work, and so on. After the supply chain changes From made, Bravado! received very few invoices for several months; then it received a $250,000 invoice from a manufacturer. From explained the new skill set this required:

> You have to be better at managing the highs and lows, and you have to be pretty good at forecasting. We do purchase orders three or four months in advance. These are skills we're all learning as we go. We're better now than we were even six months ago.

The need to forecast sales and cash flow forced From to focus on the Bravado! customer base. Bravado typically sold to specialty boutiques and through online stores. In an attempt to make sales more stable, From decided to establish minimum order sizes for stores. Looking toward future growth, the company was beginning to make its way into department stores. Specialty businesses focused on pregnant and nursing mothers, and getting shelf space in them was much easier than getting the Bravado! Line into department stores. From explained:

> Take Nordstrom, for instance. They agree that [lingerie for pregnant women] is a hot category. . . . Young

celebrity moms get a lot of press, and about one percent of the population is pregnant at any given time. . . . But it's still too small a category to dedicate a lot of space to it in a store. If you go to Nordstrom and ask for one of our products, they might go in the back and get it for you. But online is a really huge thing for them. The inventory is centralized, and they don't need to dedicate the shelf space in every single store.

From was looking to take the next big step. She laughed as she recounted the words of her CEO coaching group: "Stop making bras and start making deals!" Now that the business is finally getting somewhere, she might just take their advice.

## Exercises

1. Make 3 columns: "Before," "After," and "Impact." Track the changes in the Bravado! supply chain in the first two columns. Use the third column to analyze the overall impact of the changes.
2. Is a financial or banking relationship still necessary for Bravado!? Explain. If so, do you recommend debt or equity financing?
3. What does From mean when she refers to manufacturing "clout' and "economies of scale?"
4. What does From mean when she says Nordstom's inventory is "centralized?" What challenges and opportunities does this pose for her company?
5. Are you surprised at the impact that fluctuations in the value of the U.S. dollar have on Bravado!? What steps can global entrepreneurs take to minimize the negative impact of currency fluctuations on their businesses?
6. What steps do you advise From to take next? What kinds of "deals" should she make?

*Source:* Katherine Korman Frey, and Susan G. Duffy, "Kathyrn," The Vision Forward Hot Mommas Project Case Database, http://www.visionforward.com, 2007.

Go to http://www.VisionForward.com for printable cases, more on Kathryn From and Bravado! Designs, plus additional exercises and resources.

**K**imberly Wilson sat in her office at Tranquil Space yoga studio, remembering somewhat fondly the time when she performed every function in the business: Serving as teacher, Web master, and front desk staffer. Now there were new challenges to ponder. Wilson was wrestling with the type of employee the studio tended to attract versus the type of employee the studio actually needed:

> I think a lot of people just come here to work . . . they aren't dedicated to the business as much as I would like. The studio is not as "chill" as you would think. We create a tranquil space for the students, but for the staff it's pretty intense. There is a lot that goes into running this business. It is important for staff to think about the company and its needs, not just their own perspective. That is number one. Finding people with a strong work ethic is a challenge.

Recently, Tranquil Space had opened a second studio. However, Wilson was not just the owner of a couple of yoga studios. To some outside observers, she was building a yoga empire. *Hip Tranquil Chick,* Wilson's book promoting a yoga lifestyle "on and off the mat," was published in 2006. Her weekly podcasts reach thousands globally. In addition, Wilson has developed a clothing line, TranquiliT, which is sold at the yoga studios and online. Finally, Wilson started a foundation to help channel dollars from her business success toward a worthy cause. She shared a typical workday and to-do list:

Thursday

| | |
|---|---|
| **9:00** A.M. | Wake up, check e-mail and handle urgent matters, make green tea, walk Louis (dog) |
| **10:00** A.M. | Handle other emails, check in w/ studio, breakfast |
| **11:00** A.M. | Contacts with consultants and mentors, head to studio |
| **12:00** P.M. | Additional e-mail responses, quick lunch while working |
| **1:00** P.M. | Team updates |
| **2:00** P.M. | PR work |
| **3:00** P.M. | Work on clothing line/consultant meeting |
| **4:00** P.M. | Meet with managing director on studio operations and projects |
| **5:00** P.M. | Take and teach yoga classes, work at studio |
| **8–12** P.M. | Blog, read, e-mail responses, meetings with consultants, dinner, date with beau or friend |

## Case-in-Case

Deborah Driskill, owner of human resource IT and consulting company CDG & Associates, shared lessons from her challenging leadership transition, "What I learned is that feeling appreciated and acknowledged is more important to our employees than anything else. I learned to find a way to effectively communicate with a different style than they had been used to. And I learned that as long as I am open and honest, employees can deal with just about anything that comes our way, because we have trust."

## Key Questions to Begin Tackling Today

| | |
|---|---|
| **11:00** A.M. | *Layout of clothing line.* Online sales seem to be okay, but I want our strategy to be selling in-studio. I want to test it at the original Tranquil Space studio. Wondering what would be the best way to display and how to set up: Upstairs by classrooms, or downstairs by the cash register? |
| **1:00** P.M. | *Team update time.* Discuss employees' roles in my multiple business ventures. |
| **3:00** P.M. | *Confer with consultants.* Discuss legal structure of businesses (multiple LLCs and a non-profit 501c3 corporation) |
| **4:00** P.M. | *Recruiting the right people.* How to do this? I feel as though I'm starting at ground level. |

While reviewing her to-do list for the day, Wilson had some additional thoughts. Her 11:00 A.M. appointment was set aside to consider her clothing line. TranquiliT is a line of yoga wear made from organic, breathable bamboo fabric. She had developed the line, gone to the trade shows, and was now beginning to feature the line in the studio and on her company's Web site. The original studio was a two-level commercially zoned townhouse with the entryway and cash register on the first floor and the yoga classrooms upstairs. Wilson's primary goal was to wholesale the TranquiliT line. However, always the prepared businessperson, she wanted to understand how to sell the line in her own studio so that she could advise other yoga studios that would carry the line in the future.

Next on her list of questions was the 1:00 P.M. team update. Given what was on her mind, Wilson thought the staff should clear some additional time on their calendars. She reviewed her organization chart and tried to re-think how her employees' roles and responsibilities supported the multiple business lines. She could organize around product lines such as the studio, the clothing line, and the book. But, how much revenue would these divisions need to generate to justify hiring line managers? Was that even the right approach? She had to keep one thing at the forefront: Getting the staff to buy into her vision of the company. Wilson explained:

> We used to be a tighter clan . . . I know that is part of growth. My challenge is (A) to show how this growth affects them individually and (B) to involve them in thinking about the business's goals.

The team meeting was the perfect segue to her 3:00 P.M. consultation with a business advisor. As the product lines grew, Wilson wanted to be sure she had the right structure. A former paralegal, Wilson considers herself well educated on the topic of ownership structures and intellectual property. She trademarked the words "Hip Tranquil Chick" and the associated logo and had set up several business entities for each of her ventures. There was a separate LLC for the studio, her *Hip Tranquil Chick* book, the TranquiliT clothing line, and a 501c3 corporation for her new nonprofit foundation. Was this the ideal structure to support her company's growth, Wilson wondered?

## Case-in-Case

Pinnacle Pursuits is an experiential training company run by husband and wife team Jonathan and Cheryl Wilcocks. Growth has driven major company changes, as Jonathan Wilcocks explained: "Pinnacle Pursuits is its own entity. What began as a company that I started as a personal expression of myself and my passion, now has developed its own personality and has a group of people who contribute to its personality and presence as it unfolds into the world."

Last on her agenda of questions was the meeting with her managing director. Since founding Tranquil Space more than six years ago, Wilson had hired a managing director to take over the day-to-day operations in addition to the three part-time managers and 13 teachers already on board. The studio also had a volunteer staff of 30 people who worked at the desk and performed other tasks for the studio in exchange for free yoga lessons. Did she have a good thing going with an arsenal of part-timers? Wilson was unsure. She wanted to focus on building the overall brand of "Hip Tranquil Chick" and the TranquiliT clothing line. Together with the yoga studios, the brand and product lines melded into what Wilson considered a picture of future success. Whatever organizational structure facilitated this goal was the one in which Wilson would be most interested.

### Exercises

1. What advice would you give to Wilson regarding the layout of her studio's retail space?
2. Develop an agenda for Wilson's team meeting. What problems might her employees have in understanding Wilson's vision for her business? What can she do to involve them in creating and accomplishing the company's vision?
3. Which form of ownership do you recommend for the Tranquil Space studios, *Hip Tranquil Chick* book, TranquiliT clothing line, and Wilson's foundation? Why? Refer to Chapter 3, "Choosing a Form of Ownership."
4. Review the Tranquil Space organization chart in Figure 1. What changes, if any, do you recommend?
5. What types of employees should Wilson seek, and how should she go about recruiting them? What kind of company culture should Wilson establish? What tips can you offer her for building this culture?

*Source:* Katherine Korman Frey, "Kimberly," The Hot Mommas Project Case Database, http://www.visionforward.com, 2006.

Go to http://www.VisionForward.com for printable cases, more on Kimberly Wilson and Tranquil Space, plus additional exercises and resources.

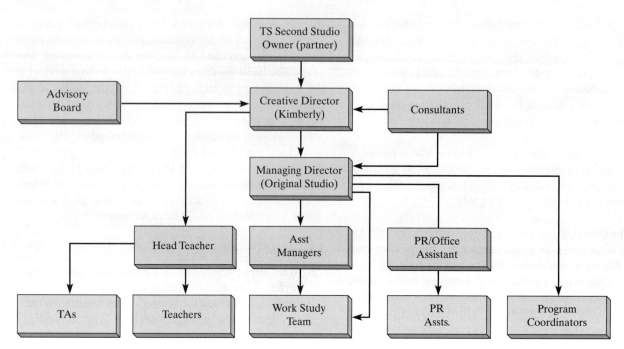

**FIGURE 1  Tranquil Space Organization Chart**

# Laura Lee Williams-Murphy and Laura Lee Designs

As Laura Lee Williams-Murphy sat in Starbucks sipping her latte, another customer approached her. "What a beautiful purse!" the woman exclaimed. "It's like a work of art!" So went a day in the life of Williams-Murphy, high-energy purse designer, triathelete, friend, daughter, and wife. A former *Fortune* 500 corporate executive hailing from the ranks of Apple, Nike, and American Express, Williams-Murphy set out on her own to design a purse inspired by her extensive time working in Asia. Her elegant, brightly colored purses held a special significance for Williams-Murphy. In her eyes, her purses represented an expression of herself:

> Did I envision at a young age that I was going to be a designer? No. Did I know I was going to do something different that really melded and molded into what I'm all about? Yes. And I think the purses speak for themselves. It's a piece of art. It's an individual style. It's something that's a unique and individual way of expression.

Starting her company was not an easy task; it required Williams-Murphy to make countless trips overseas to personally visit bead, textile, and manufacturing companies. Within the business itself, perhaps the biggest challenge she faced was creating a marketing strategy for her company. Concerned with balancing growth and brand integrity, Williams-Murphy weighed several options including public relations, sales reps, trade shows, showrooms, and e-commerce. Each one presented risks and benefits, and she had to consider each one carefully now that her line of purses was starting to take off. No matter how many celebrities carried her purses, Williams-Murphy could not lose sight of the fact that her business was still small.

Williams-Murphy recalled the birth of her business idea. While working in Asia, she visited an outdoor market in Thailand. She loved the market. It was alive with people . . . bustling . . . exotic foods . . . bright colors. Out of the corner of her eye, Williams-Murphy saw a beautiful piece of fabric and felt drawn to it. She asked the woman if it could be made into a bag. "Give me one day," instructed the woman, and she would sew the bag Williams-Murphy had sketched out on a crumpled piece of paper. On her way to the airport the next day, Williams-Murphy stopped at the market, picked up her bag, and placed the colorful creation over her shoulder. She had almost forgotten about it until people began staring and stopping her in the airport. "Where did you get that?" one woman asked. These positive comments began to plant the seeds of entrepreneurship.

Six months later, Williams-Murphy sat in her hotel room fanning through her journal of notes, design ideas, and material that she had collected. Was she really going to leave her cushy job to start her own line of purses? The idea seemed crazy. She was accomplished in her career and had a great deal to lose. However, what started as a zany idea was now her life's dream. Williams-Murphy turned to a fresh page in her journal and began to outline the Williams-Murphy Designs business plan. She was going to see this dream through.

The realization of Williams-Murphy's entrepreneurial dream was a challenge on many levels. She recalled a trip to the small Chinese factory town of Sham Shui Po:

> I had to take two trains to reach the village where I was scheduled to meet with these factory representatives. It was a hot 120-degree day. Rice fields lined one side of the dirt road I was walking along; on the other side of the road were dead chickens. An old man came by in a rickshaw, went through a puddle, and doused me. I was head to toe in mud. I was so upset, but knew I had to get to the meetings. I had no idea what I looked like until later when I went back to my hotel. I looked in the mirror and all I saw were streaks—tear marks down the mud on my face.

## Case-in-Case

Richard Barney, co-founder of Corus Home Realty, explained how his firm took a nontraditional approach to the real estate market, and what marketing approaches worked: "Corus has salaried sales agents and a team-based approach to service. Our advanced technology and 9-to-9, 7-day-a-week office hours are not typical in this industry. To showcase our unique model, we tried glossy direct mail, radio advertisements, and keyword searches on Google. But the only thing that has really worked for us over the years is referrals. So, we set up several formal referral partnerships and that is how we now get most of our business."

Despite these early hardships, Williams-Murphy was able to persevere and start manufacturing her distinctive bags. She drew on her experience in product development at Apple and on her marketing background at Nike, Ralph Lauren, and American Express to fabricate a top-of-the line product and portray it as such. The sales floodgates opened when the exclusive New York department store Henri Bendel hosted a trunk show featuring her product line. Celebrities were seen toting the bags soon thereafter. Magazines featured Laura Lee Designs. Exclusive boutiques all over the United States, and soon—the world—were carrying Laura Lee Designs.

However, each of these achievements was the result of Williams-Murphy's individual effort. She needed a marketing plan that went beyond one person. Stretching herself too thin and making the wrong choices about marketing channels could damage her exclusive brand. There were many nuances of the retail world that she did not understand, but she had to believe that her common sense would allow her to prevail. Williams-Murphy's journal reflected her marketing options dilemma:

## Laura Lee Designs Journal Notes on Marketing Options

- *Target customer:* High-end accessory purchasers. Price points range from $350–$550.
- *Target intermediary:* High-end boutiques and trunk shows at department stores. Up for discussion: Establishing a line at a department store.
- *Marketing options:*
  - *Public relations.* This has worked well for Laura Lee Designs to date. Received good press by sending my own press releases. Considerations: Should I hire a public relations firm? I have been approached by many, but I have small budget.
  - *Sales representatives.* Important. I have existing relationships in the industry with buyers in stores. Are sales reps the best way to enter the market, or should I rely on them for logistics and buying management after the relationship is started?
  - *Trade shows.* Everyone from the boutiques to department store buyers attend trade shows. Booths are expensive, and there is no guarantee of orders. However, if we do get a big order, can I handle it from a manufacturing and financial standpoint? The company cannot risk a decline in product quality.
  - *Showrooms.* This is a way for buyers to see my products, but it would require setting up showrooms near buyers' locations. I would have to change

product lines each season and have my lines designs for buyers to see three seasons in advance! Am I ready for that?
  - *E-commerce.* People on the street are always asking about availability online, but I worry about cheapening the brand with an "eBay feel."

Which marketing tools were appropriate at this stage in the company's life? What parts of Williams-Murphy's marketing strategy and the company operations could she delegate to outsiders? It is hard to know the right answer. The new designer explained, "I have a cornucopia of marketing avenues. The biggest hurdle is trusting someone to help and then delegating because this business is so closely tied to me."

### Exercises

1. Find another designer online from whom Williams-Murphy could gain knowledge about industry marketing techniques. Explain the main lessons the designer has to offer.
2. Consider the four Ps of marketing and how they apply to Laura Lee Designs. List each of the four Ps and include your analysis and recommendations for each one.
3. Assume the role of marketing consultant and brainstorm five guerilla marketing tactics for Laura Lee Designs.
4. What does Williams-Murphy mean by "the manufacturing and financial repercussions of a large order?"
5. Find an example of effective marketing techniques that large companies use. Provide three suggestions for how to adapt this technique to a small business such as Laura Lee Designs.
6. What adjustments do you think Williams-Murphy's has made in transitioning from company executive to entrepreneur?

*Source:* Katherine Korman Frey and Elizabeth Levine, "Laura Lee," The Vision Forward Hot Mommas Project Case Database, http://www.visionforward.com, 2005.

Go to http://www.VisionForward.com for printable cases, more on Laura Lee, plus additional exercises and resources.

# Case 8
# Susan Apgood and News Generation

California Closets arrived at Susan Apgood's house to install her home office. Apgood was the same outgoing, level-headed, organized person she had been since childhood. She chose to approach the melding of her business and home life in the same way. A new baby at home necessitated a home office.

Apgood's company, News Generation, provides public relations services in a very specific niche: Radio. "About 70 percent of the interviews you hear on the radio are set up by people like me," Apgood explained. "For instance, we recently pitched a series of interviews with the host of TLC's show *Trading Spaces*." After building News Generation from the ground up, Apgood was eager to find areas of the business that she could streamline to allow for more time at home. After all, if she *could* figure out a way to spend more time with her son, and still run a thriving business, why *wouldn't* she? That was the beauty of having her own business.

Outsourcing was how Apgood planned to gain hours in her schedule. It was easier said than done, however. Apgood felt a sense of pride in the company that she had created from the ground up and did not want to let that go. She explained:

"We're one of the largest and most successful radio PR companies in the nation. I really don't want to give that up. It is a part of me. We have a great reputation. Two reasons I think we have this reputation are, first, our highly skilled staff members who deliver results. And, second, in a business where many companies will take any and all business, we actually turn down stories we think won't work . . ."

Apgood acquired her first big clients by writing down her "wish list" on a piece of paper, then checking the items off one at a time: (1) Microsoft, (2) Discovery Communications, and (3) PBS. Apgood employed the same approach when deciding which aspects of her business to outsource. She sat at her new desk, grabbed a fresh legal pad, and wrote at the top of the first page: "Goal: CREATE MORE HOURS IN THE DAY." Then she began to scan her company's organization chart and financial statements to look for time-saving opportunities.

One area in which Apgood wanted to make some changes but had not yet was managing the finances of her business. To date Apgood personally had handled all aspects of financial management for the company. Managing the finances helped Apgood feel connected to the business and gave her a sense of control. Apgood had earned her MBA with a concentration in finance. Her degree and her past

work experience contributed to her understanding of the importance of sound financial management. She explained an experience with her former employer in the same industry:

We were doing a project for Miramax Films. We were trying to send out advance copies of a movie for interviews we had booked with radio talk shows. We took the packages downstairs, and the UPS guy looked up our account and said, "Nope, I refuse to take these." I felt guilty. It was a bad reflection on me. I spent so long trying to make good with these people whom we treated so poorly by not paying them for the service they provided. I realized how much time I wasted to try to make up for the company's financial shortfalls.

According to some of her advisors, Apgood had implemented some useful processes for day-to-day financial management of a small business. Apgood regularly entered all financial information into QuickBooks and monitored what she called "key indicators" each week. Apgood had developed News Generation's three key indicators over time. She knew that if these three indicators were on track, her company was on track. Conversely, if the key indicators were not on track, Apgood knew that she had to take in certain action steps:

- **Key Indicator 1: $100,000 in the bank.** This was a basic level of cash that Apgood liked to keep in the company checking account. In addition, Apgood saved money each month in a separate account from which she distributed bonuses and profit sharing payments.
- **Key Indicator 2: $200,000 in receivables.** If Key Indicator 1 or 2 were off, Apgood made collection calls.
- **Key Indicator 3: $250,000 in prospects.** Apgood preferred to have more prospects than receivables as an indicator that the company was growing. Prospects were typically $50,000 (average) more than receivables. Prospects were defined as companies that had a timeline, a budget, and a specific service that they needed. These definitions help weed out interested but unqualified prospects. If the prospect number was off, Apgood got on the phone to generate proposals.

In addition to checking key indicators each week, Apgood went to the bank to deposit checks daily, printed out and reviewed financial statements monthly, and met with her accountant two or three times per year to prepare for tax filing. Occasionally Apgood met with merger and acquisition experts to make sure her cash flow and other financial statements would be attractive to potential acquirers.

## Case-in-Case

Lisa Quadrini, Wealth Management Advisor at Merrill Lynch, commented on personal "key indicators": "Entrepreneurs and high net-worth clients want to build on the money they've made. The best thing they can do is apply their goal-setting skills at home. I advise them to develop a personal mission statement with income goals, and use a financial expert to turn those goals into investment strategies."

Apgood also used a very simple pricing model. News Generation and its staff were paid based on results. No story on the radio meant no payment. Apgood thought that it was important not to diminish her role as the influencer and coach for her staff. She knew that the spreadsheets and QuickBooks would not miss her, but her staff would. As long as she could still have control over her company's financial performance, Apgood would be comfortable outsourcing the financial management of her company to a professional. She estimated that she could save 12 hours per week by freeing herself from some of the task-oriented financial details such as inputting data and generating reports. Twelve hours was worth a lot right now, as she reviewed her tight schedule, and Apgood began to peruse Monster.com and send e-mails to her network of contacts.

### Apgood's Schedule

| | |
|---|---|
| **5:00** A.M. | Up for baby's first feeding (goal = sleep until 6 when baby is older) |
| **5:30** A.M. | Check e-mail, then gym |
| **8:00** A.M. | To Starbucks and office, tackle tough item #1 |
| **8:30** P.M. | Project and client work |
| **11:30** P.M. | Client conference calls |
| **12:30** P.M. | Lunch and go to bank. See baby if time permits. |
| **1:15** P.M. | Internal work, financials, marketing, proposals. Tackle tough item #2 |
| **5:00** P.M. | Plan for next day |
| **5:15** P.M. | Head home to relieve nanny, spend time w/baby, cook dinner. |
| **7:30** P.M. | Put baby to bed, dinner with hubby |
| **9:00** P.M. | Run errands |

## Exercises

**1a.** What option would you suggest for Apgood when outsourcing her company's financial functions?

**b.** Follow through on your suggestions. Using the Internet or your personal network, list and provide qualification summaries for your "top 3" staff candidates for financial outsourcing services.

**2.** Estimate Apgood's sales per hour using the accompanying financial statements in Tables 1–5. Assuming 12 additional hours per week with the addition of an outsourced financial function, what level of additional sales do you think the company could generate? What additional benefits could the company realize with Apgood's free time?

**3.** Review the appendices and determine whether Apgood is on track or off track for her "big 3" financial metrics.

**4.** Review the income statement, balance sheet, statement of cash flows, and accounts receivable reports (refer to the following tables). What numbers stand out? Why? Make a list of each line item or category and the amounts associated with it.

**5.** Perform a ratio analysis using News Generation's financials. Use Chapter 7, "Creating a Solid Financial Plan," as a guide. Select three key ratios and tell your version of the "story behind the numbers."

*Source:* Katherine Korman Frey, "Susan," The Vision Forward Hot Mommas Project Case Database, http://www.visionforward.com, 2005.

Go to http://www.VisionForward.com for printable cases, more on Susan Apgood and News Generation, plus additional exercises and resources.

**TABLE 1** **News Generation Profit and Loss Statement, January 1–December 31, 2005**

| | |
|---|---:|
| Ordinary Income/Expense | |
|   Income | |
|     Fee Income | 1,390,115.00 |
|   Total Income | 1,390,115.00 |
|   Cost of Goods Sold | |
|     Direct Cost of Services | |
|       Audio Broadcasting | 1,135.04 |
|       Fax | 1,508.97 |
|       Long Distance Telephone | 1,777.73 |
|       Teleconferencing | 15,322.49 |
|     Total Direct Cost of Services | 19,744.23 |
|   Total COGS | 19,744.23 |
| Gross Profit | 1,370,370.77 |
|   Expenses | |
|     Automobile Expenses | |
|       Automobile Lease | 6,050.00 |
|       Gas | 1,138.57 |
|       Insurance | 1,514.70 |
|       Parking | 3,278.66 |
|       Service | 337.98 |
|     Total Automobile Expenses | 12,319.91 |
|     Bank Service Charges | 1,916.56 |
|     Contributions | |
|       Charities | 1,400.00 |
|     Total Contributions | 1,400.00 |
|     Dues, Networking, and Development | |
|       Professional Development and Network | 2,944.50 |
|       Subscriptions and Directories | 493.30 |
|       Trade Association Dues | 380.00 |
|     Total Dues, Networking, and Development | 3,817.80 |
|     Employee Tax Witholdings | |
|       Federal | 185,597.86 |
|       GA State | 29,250.88 |
|       MD State | 21,065.94 |
|       Medicare | 12,542.32 |
|       NJ DBL | 244.50 |
|       NJ State | 2,329.10 |
|       NJ SUI | 207.82 |
|       PA State | 193.90 |
|       PA SUI | 5.69 |
|       Social Security | 35,900.23 |
|     Total Employee Tax Witholdings | 287,338.24 |

*(continued)*

**TABLE 1** News Generation Profit and Loss Statement, January 1–December 31, 2005–continued

| | |
|---|---:|
| Employer Tax Expense | |
| FUTA | 610.54 |
| GA SU1 | 553.63 |
| MD SUI | 187.01 |
| Medicare | 12,542.32 |
| NJ DBL | 299.24 |
| NJ SUI | 726.99 |
| PA SU1 | 173.30 |
| Social Security | 35,900.15 |
| Total Employer Tax Expense | 50,993.18 |
| Insurance | |
| Dental Insurance | 1,594.00 |
| Disability Insurance | 1,896.00 |
| Health Insurance | 23,321.00 |
| Liability Insurance | 690.50 |
| Worker's Compensation | 3,171.00 |
| Total Insurance | 30,672.50 |
| Marketing | |
| Advertising | 3,917.44 |
| Award Applications | 2,152.00 |
| Directory Listings | 750.00 |
| Event sponsorship | 7,426.74 |
| Promotion and Holiday Gifts | 6,030.69 |
| Total Marketing | 20,276.87 |
| Office Supplies | |
| Computer Software | 221.07 |
| Radio Production Supplies | 1,420.00 |
| Office Supplies–Other | 2,392.75 |
| Total Office Supplies | 4,033.82 |
| On-line services | 1,450.39 |
| Postage and Delivery | |
| Overnight service | 2,093.32 |
| US Mail | 974.25 |
| Total Postage and Delivery | 3,067.57 |
| Printing | |
| Checks and Invoices | 81.45 |
| Letterhead, Business Cards, etc. | 1,771.24 |
| Marketing Material | 5,711.65 |
| Photocopying | 0.00 |
| Total Printing | 7,564.34 |
| Professional Fees | |
| Accounting | 2,017.52 |
| Consulting | 1,750.00 |
| Design Work | 2,800.00 |

(*continued*)

**TABLE 1** **News Generation Profit and Loss Statement, January 1–December 31, 2005 –continued**

| | |
|---|---:|
| Payroll Service | 1,753.91 |
| Radio Database | 2,355.00 |
| Total Professional Fees | 10,676.43 |
| | |
| Rent | |
| Clerical Services | 150.00 |
| Office Space | 44,864.46 |
| Total Rent | 45,014.46 |
| Repairs | |
| Computer Repairs | 73.49 |
| Total Repairs | 73.49 |
| Salaries | |
| Bonus | 22,984.96 |
| Commission | 73,252.71 |
| Operations | 463,362.49 |
| Sales and Marketing | 46,434.52 |
| Total Salaries | 606,034.68 |
| Taxes | |
| Federal Income Tax | 1,332.00 |
| Personal Property | 555.97 |
| State Income Tax | 653.25 |
| Total Taxes | 2,541.22 |
| Telephone | |
| Cellular Phone | 1,723.09 |
| Phone/fax/modem | 11,550.06 |
| Total Telephone | 13,273.15 |
| Travel and Entertainment | |
| Hotel | 1,666.13 |
| Meals | 1,519.10 |
| Meals—100% | 832.53 |
| Travel | 4,906.56 |
| Total Travel and Entertainment | 8,924.32 |
| Total Expenses | 1,111,388.93 |
| Net Ordinary Income | 258,981.84 |

**TABLE 2** News Generation Balance Sheet, January 1–December 31, 2005

| ASSETS | | |
|---|---|---|
| Current Assets | | |
| Checking/Savings | | |
| Checking Account- First Union | 114,439.27 | |
| Money Market Account- First Union | 131,327.46 | |
| Total Checking/Savings | 245,766.73 | |
| Accounts Receivable | | |
| Accounts Receivable | 168,950.00 | |
| Total Accounts Receivable | 168,950.00 | |
| Other Current Assets | | |
| Prepaid Income Taxes | | |
| Federal | 3,694.00 | |
| Maryland | 1,970.00 | |
| Total Prepaid Income Taxes | 5,664.00 | |
| Total Other Current Assets | 5,664.00 | |
| Total Other Current Assets | 5,664.00 | |
| Total Current Assets | 420,380.73 | |
| Fixed Assets | | |
| Accumulated Depreciation | −50,418.00 | |
| Office Equipment | | |
| Computers | 43,352.04 | |
| Office Furniture | 9,209.73 | |
| Office Equipment-Other | 435.57 | |
| Total Office Equipment | 52,997.34 | |
| Recording/Production Equipment | 7,039.27 | |
| Total Fixed Assets | 9,618.61 | |
| Other Assets | | |
| Deposits | 4,985.00 | |
| Total Other Assets | 4,985.00 | |
| TOTAL ASSETS | 434,984.34 | |
| LIABILITIES & EQUITY | | |
| Equity | | |
| Capital Stock | 1,000.00 | |
| Retained Earnings | 203,665.62 | |
| S-Distributions | −29,182.20 | |
| Net Income | 259,500.92 | |
| Total Equity | 434,984.34 | |
| TOTAL LIABILITIES & EQUITY | 434,984.34 | |

**TABLE 3** News Generation Statement of Cash Flows, January 1–December 31, 2005

| OPERATING ACTIVITIES | |
|---|---|
| Net Income | 259,500.92 |
| Adjustments to reconcile Net Income to net cash provided by operations: | |
| Accounts Receivable | 18,590.00 |
| Accounts Payable | −124,509.14 |
| Net cash provided by Operating Activities | 153,581.78 |
| INVESTING ACTIVITIES | |
| Office Equipment: Computers | −1,319.98 |
| Office: Equipment: Office Furniture | −2,600.00 |
| Recording/Production Equipment | −261.45 |
| Net cash provided by Investing Activities | −4,181.43 |
| FINANCING ACTIVITIES | |
| Opening Bal Equity | 3,850.80 |
| Retained Earnings | −3,850.80 |
| S-Distributions | −29,182.20 |
| Net cash provided by Financing Activities | −29,182.20 |
| Net cash increase for period | 120,218.15 |
| Cash at beginning of period | 125,548.58 |
| Cash at end of period | 245,766.73 |

## TABLE 4 News Generation Accounts Receivable and Prospect List, December 31, 2005

| | Current | 1–30 | 31–60 | 61–90 | >90 | Total |
|---|---|---|---|---|---|---|
| AARP | 5,750.00 | 13,840.00 | 10,500.00 | 0.00 | 0.00 | 30,090.00 |
| Airfoil PR | 0.00 | 8,200.00 | 0.00 | 0.00 | 0.00 | 8,200.00 |
| Blue Cross Blue Shield Association | 4,550.00 | 0.00 | 0.00 | 0.00 | 0.00 | 4,550.00 |
| Bragman Nyman Cafarelli LLC | 0.00 | 0.00 | 0.00 | 0.00 | 0.00 | 0.00 |
| Business Communications | 0.00 | 0.00 | 0.00 | 0.00 | 0.00 | 0.00 |
| Capgemini | 0.00 | 3,350.00 | 0.00 | 0.00 | 0.00 | 3,350.00 |
| Citigate Cunningham | 0.00 | 0.00 | 0.00 | 0.00 | 0.00 | 0.00 |
| Discovery Communications, Inc. | 4,800.00 | 0.00 | 1,050.00 | 0.00 | 0.00 | 5,850.00 |
| E*Trade Financial | 0.00 | 4,430.00 | 0.00 | 0.00 | 0.00 | 4,430.00 |
| ESRB | 0.00 | 11,950.00 | 0.00 | 0.00 | 0.00 | 11,950.00 |
| Fight Crime, Invest in Kids | 3,350.00 | 0.00 | 0.00 | 0.00 | 0.00 | 3,350.00 |
| Fleishman-Hillard, Inc. | 3,350.00 | 8,645.00 | 4,035.00 | 0.00 | 0.00 | 16,030.00 |
| GMMB | 0.00 | 3,350.00 | 7,170.00 | 0.00 | 0.00 | 10,520.00 |
| Goodman Media | 0.00 | 0.00 | 0.00 | 0.00 | 0.00 | 0.00 |
| GYMR | 4,400.00 | 8,800.00 | 0.00 | 0.00 | 0.00 | 13,200.00 |
| Herrie Communications | 0.00 | 3,350.00 | 0.00 | 0.00 | 0.00 | 3,350.00 |
| High Museum of Art | 0.00 | 3,350.00 | 0.00 | 0.00 | 0.00 | 3,350.00 |
| Marriott Itnternational | 0.00 | 0.00 | 5,725.00 | 0.00 | 0.00 | 5,725.00 |
| NIEER | 4,910.00 | 0.00 | 0.00 | 0.00 | 0.00 | 4,910.00 |
| PBS | 3,350.00 | 0.00 | 0.00 | 0.00 | 0.00 | 3,350.00 |
| PR Studio | 0.00 | 0.00 | 1,375.00 | 0.00 | 0.00 | 1,375 00 |
| Preschool California | 0.00 | −1,975.00 | 0.00 | 0.00 | 0.00 | −1,975.00 |
| Ron Sachs Communications | 0.00 | 835.00 | 0.00 | 0.00 | 0.00 | 835.00 |
| Rosa Communications | 0.00 | 1,670.00 | 0.00 | 0.00 | 0.00 | 1,670.00 |
| UPS | 7,315.00 | 0.00 | 0.00 | 0.00 | 0.00 | 7,315.00 |
| WCTV | 3,200.00 | 9,500.00 | 0.00 | 0.00 | 0.00 | 12,700.00 |
| WETA Television | 0.00 | 2,575.00 | 0.00 | 0.00 | 0.00 | 2,575.00 |
| WGBH-TV | 0.00 | 5,750.00 | 0.00 | 0.00 | 0.00 | 5,750.00 |
| WNET-TV | 0.00 | 3,250.00 | 0.00 | 3,250.00 | 0.00 | 6,500.00 |
| TOTAL | 44,975.00 | 90,870.00 | 29,855.00 | 3,250.00 | 0.00 | 168,950.00 |

## TABLE 5 News Generation Prospect List

| | Projected Business |
|---|---|
| AARP | 24,000.00 |
| *Blue Cross Blue Shield Association | 13,000.00 |
| Discovery Communications, Inc. | 45,000.00 |
| E*Trade Financial | 7,000.00 |
| Fight Crime Invest in Kids | 4,500.00 |
| Fleishman-Hillard, Inc. | 48,000.00 |
| Marriott International | 18,000.00 |
| PBS | 57,000.00 |
| UPS | 17,000.00 |
| WCTV | 10,000.00 |
| WETA Television | 15,000.00 |
| WGBH-TV | 18,000.00 |
| WNET-TV | 4,000.00 |
| TOTAL | 280,500.00 |

*Note: Not sure of timeline for project.

# Case 9
# Warren Myer and Myers Internet

**W**arren Myer opened the refrigerator in his office, plugged in his portable burner, and began heating up lunch. Seventeen-hour days didn't leave much time for breaks. Very soon, however, Myer would discover long days were not enough. He picked up the phone and heard his panicked salesperson on the other end: "Warren. We are in trouble. This competitor has all of San Diego in their lap."

At first Myer did not believe what he was hearing. His company, Myers Internet, was the industry leader. Granted, in 1999 the industry of online loan transactions was relatively new. However, Myers was one of the pioneers. Myer evangelized the concept of customers checking rates and actually applying for loans online. He spoke at conferences, wrote whitepapers, and sent daily fax blasts to the mortgage industry. Thousands of mortgage brokerage and real estate firms nationwide had bought into this novel idea and used the Myers Internet platform for their Web sites.

Myer reviewed the customer lists and realized that his salesperson was right: Myers Internet was losing customers, city by city. The competitor had been studying Myers Internet. The CEO, it turned out, had a pattern of approaching the Myers Internet booth at trade shows to gather competitive intelligence. Although Myer considered the competitor's actual product capabilities to be comparable, there were some major differences. Myer explained:

- **Pricing.** "The Myers Internet pricing strategy was to price the product at one or two thousand dollars up front, and another couple hundred dollars a month thereafter. The competitor was essentially giving their product away for free and charging fees later after an introductory period."

- **Scale.** "The competitor was more scalable. They had automated some parts of delivery. In San Diego, for instance, they were able to deliver about four times as many units [mortgage and real estate Web sites] than we could."

- **Capital.** "This competitor was venture backed. Myers Internet had no sources of outside capital. They could afford to go city by city and blitz our customers with their marketing."

## Case-in-Case

Serial entrepreneur Michael Goldstein, founder of www.ContentNow.com, had a college business selling cement blocks that students used to raise their dorm beds.

He described his creative tactics: "When I saw competitors surfacing, I went down to the city and got a 'Hockers and Peddlers Permit.' I then showed it to a police officer who looked at it, scratched his head, and ordered the unpermitted vendors off campus.

---

"We were stumbling around trying to figure out what to do," Myer recalls. As a temporary solution, Myers Internet dropped their prices to retain customers. They were deciding what to do next when Myer received a call that would change everything. The call was from Provident Financial, a large lending institution with a client base of 10,000 mortgage brokers. After a few negotiations, the two companies arrived at a win-win agreement. In exchange for a minority stake in Myers Internet, Provident would market Myers' product.

The partnership went beyond marketing as the two companies figured out a way to produce a free Web site. Next, Provident marketed the free Web site to its contact base of 10,000 mortgage brokers. Finally, Provident provided Myers Internet with an "executive-on-lend": Provident's Chief Technology Officer. Within two months, Myers Internet was capable of producing 150 units per month instead of its former 20 units per month. Myer commented on the transformation:

> We didn't have a diverse senior management team, metrics or KPIs (key performance indicators), or a board of advisors. We were just working long hours trying to survive. Provident brought a more operational mentality. They helped us figure out how to push more volume through the company. That was the key.

Myer made additional changes to help strengthen the company's position against competitive threats. After all, it was the dot-com boom, and Internet businesses were being started by everyone ranging from *Fortune* 500 companies to basement-office software developers. One change was Myer's decision to bring in a new engineering manager. The company was behind in product releases, and products were sometimes released in a less-than-ideal state. "Engineering would say, 'It's done,' but the product would be released with bugs," Myer recounted. Web sites with bugs were not going to succeed in the new, intensely competitive environment. Ultimately, the swift changes Myer and his team made resulted in a market victory:

> The competitive threat really vaulted our company to a new level. It forced us to improve. As a result, our

competition went in another direction. My guess is they initially thought, 'We are going to kill this company and get market share.' But we came back 10 times stronger than they expected. I think our partnership with Provident made it harder for them to get customers. Then they probably had to go back and explain to investors why the initial plan wasn't working and justify another strategy to get a second round of financing.

Myers Internet experienced unprecedented success for the next few years. However, after a 360-degree evaluation Myer administered in the company, he was despondent. Employees considered him a micromanager and were not taking risks as a result. They believed that Myer would come along and change what they produced, anyway, so why try? Myer also reflected on his personal life and took what the employees said to heart. As he looked over his calendar for the past year, he realized that he had only taken off one day—*total:* half of one day for Thanksgiving, and half of one day for Christmas. While growing up in India, his work ethic had been strongly influenced by his entrepreneurial parents . . . but this was ridiculous! Myer set out to make some changes in his business and personal life.

After much deliberation, Myer decided to take the next step with his business. Throughout the years Myer had received calls from prospective acquirers, which he had ignored. Recently, however, he started taking the calls more seriously. MGIC, a *Fortune* 2000 company in the mortgage financing business, purchased Myers Internet in 2005. Even though Myer sat down with MGIC's CEO to do the term sheet at the beginning of the negotiation, months of due diligence ensued. MGIC hired a business broker to conduct a valuation of Myers Internet, and Myer's firm produced so many company documents that when the lawyers printed them all out, the stack of paper stood 8 feet tall. Part of the deal's terms included an employment agreement in which Myer would stay on for one year. Ironically,

selling the company helped him become a better person and leader:

> When I got back the 360-degree evaluation results, I knew I had to make some changes. I joined a couple of CEO groups. They helped me see the light. I also realized that working long hours had a negative effect on the business. We needed to be smart and thinking ahead. Instead, I was just in the trenches.

Myer walked out of the office at 6:00 P.M. and thought about his next mountain-climbing trip on the ride home. His hobby had, in many ways, helped prepare him for the obstacles he faced in his career and life. With a smirk on his face, Myer wondered how, and when, he would encounter his next challenge.

## Exercises

1. Conduct a SWOT (strengths, weaknesses, opportunities, and threats) analysis of Myers Internet at the time of the competitive threat. Next, list the key actions the company took in response. Comment on the balance of responsive versus proactive on the part of Myers Internet.

2. Why did Myer conclude that working long hours was not enough to ensure his company's success? How can entrepreneurs avoid falling victim to this myth?

3. Discuss a hobby that has taught you something about personal/leadership values. What lessons have you learned?

4. Conduct a Google search of terms in this case that you would like to understand better (e.g., 360-degree evaluation, KPI, etc.) and make your own glossary. Be sure to cover exit strategy terms and comment on the following: Does selling a company sound fun or tedious?

*Source:* Katherine Korman Frey, "Warren," The Vision Forward Case Database, http://www.visionforward.com, 2007.

Go to http://www.VisionForward.com for printable cases, more on Warren Myer and Myers Internet, plus additional exercises and resources.

# Case 10
# Woodie Neiss and FLAVORx

Woodie Neiss had always been a details guy: Financial records, papers on his desk, and to-do lists in Microsoft Outlook; even his apartment was neat and organized. When Woodie and the senior executives at FLAVORx were preparing the company for sale, Woodie's detail-orientation became a major asset.

FLAVORx produced flavorings for children's medicine. FLAVORx was the number-one behind-the-counter system available at pharmacies nationwide. It provided medically designed and scientifically tested flavorings to pharmacies and pharmaceutical companies to combat the bad taste of over-the-counter and prescription liquid medicines. Neiss was CFO and co-owner of FLAVORx. When the time came to sell the company, Neiss knew it would be a tremendous amount of work. He even described selling his company as a second full-time job.

The steps involved in preparing for the sale were many and detailed. First, Neiss organized an internal team to collaborate on the acquisition process. But there was a catch: Only a few individuals in the company were aware of the plans to sell FLAXORx. Because an eminent company sale can cause a great deal of tension in a company, Neiss strongly believed it was best to involve a limited number of employees. Initially, the team consisted of the CEO, the finance team, and Neiss.

Second, Neiss needed to find the right investment bank to run the acquisition process. "I spent 3 months researching banks, interviewing them, listening to their presentations and negotiating the project scope and fees," he explained.

## Case-in-Case

Brothers Jim and Steve Reznikoff, founders and owners of IT company Microsystems Automation Group (MSAG), are backing into their company's sale price. Jim explained, "First, we said, 'When we retire, how much do we want in income each year?' Next, we figured out what amount of principal would throw off that amount of annual interest. That principal number is our target sale price. Our company strategies and goals now all lead us to that number."

Third was the paper. Neiss and his finance team assembled every pertinent document related to the operations of the business and loaded them into a virtual "data room." Neiss elaborated, "The data room allowed interested parties access to documents so they could perform their due diligence without interrupting the daily operations of the company."

Next Neiss worked with his team and the bank to write what was called "the book." "The book is like a business plan on steroids," laughed Neiss. "It provides an entire breakdown of the company, historic analysis, and future potential all with detailed financials and proformas." The numbers in the book are set in stone between the time the book is printed and the time when the company is sold. "You miss a number on those published figures and your value is reduced," Neiss noted.

Neiss breathed a sigh of relief when the bank took over. In this case, the bank's job was to contact as many buyers that fit within FLAVORx's "sweet spot" (target buyer profile), as Neiss described:

> For FLAVORx, there were two types of buyers: (1) Strategic buyers—pharmaceutical companies and retail pharmacies. These were our customers. They were familiar with our product and our business. Additional strategic buyers included wholesale distribution companies, flavoring companies, and a variety of international conglomerates. (2) The second type of company in our "sweet spot" was a financial buyer. These were venture capital and private equity firms, hedge funds, and the like.

After contacting more than 270 buyers and sending out the book to 70 interested parties, FLAVORx received 15 initial bids.

The FLAVORx team spoke with each of the potential acquirers. After reducing the list, the team made formal five-hour presentations to each potential buyer. Neiss explained:

> This is where a person really needs to perform. I often joked that a little acting class would have helped. We were put under a microscope and asked very detailed questions about the company, its financials, and how we could substantiate the projections. We also spent a lot of time talking about our successes and what we learned from our failures. This conversation was repeated over and over as we whittled the list down to find the right buyer. *Then* the hard work began.

After the selection of the buyer, a term sheet was negotiated and signed, and the buyers' due diligence began. At that point it was necessary to include many of the FLAVORx senior managers in the acquisition discussion as the potential buyer wanted to meet with them. Neiss elaborated on the interaction with the senior managers: "It was important to really explain what was happening, get buy-in to the idea of selling the company, and make sure there was incentive in it for them." In this case, all employees had options in the privately held FLAVORx. Thus, the sale of the company would provide staff with liquidity.

Fast-forward nine weeks: The buyer revisited the data room, interviewed employees, called customers and vendors, and performed other due diligence. "A lot of energy was spent making the potential acquirer comfortable with the organization at that point so that the transition would be easy," Neiss explained. Also during this stage, attorneys became involved to negotiate the acquisition and draw up an agreement. Neiss elaborated:

> The document the attorneys produced turned out to be longer than *The Odyssey* and about one-tenth as interesting. However, it was critical that I read it and familiarized myself and agreed with everything in there because the team and I would be held accountable for any misrepresentations. My advice would be to pour yourself 100 cups of coffee, sit down for a long read, and try not to faint when you get the legal bill.

While performing the tasks associated with selling the company, Neiss and the entire team had to be performing at 110 percent in their "other jobs," which in Neiss's case was CFO. Throughout the process, he continued to manage the finances of the company, ensured FLAVORx was on budget, strategized about goals, and kept the operations running smoothly.

After almost one year, FLAVORx sold. Neiss described it as the most mentally and emotionally intense experience he'd ever been through. However, he learned a great deal and shared his top tip for entrepreneurs:

My number one tip is to *be organized!* Believe it or not, we were able to streamline much of this process because we had prepared for a year or so prior to the decision to sell. Companies that don't often take longer to sell at much lower valuations.

Neiss's final step turned out to be the most enjoyable. He put his money in the bank, interviewed financial planners, and took off for a year of travel around the world. "I'll do it again for sure," Neiss said. "It's just a question of when."

## Exercises

1. Are you surprised by the level of effort required to sell FLAVORx? Do you think every company approaches acquisition with this level of effort and detail?
2. Look up three entrepreneurial acquisition stories on the Internet and summarize the ways in which the acquisition experiences were similar to or different from Neiss's.
3. What do you think of Neiss's decision not to disclose the plans to sell FLAVORx to the entire company? What are the potential tensions to which he alludes? What would you have done?
4. What does Neiss mean when he refers to the FLAVORx employees as having "options."
5. Neiss did not have to sign an employment agreement requiring that he stay on with FLAVORx under the management of the parent company. Why do you think this is the case?

*Source:* Katherine Korman Frey and Woodie Neiss, "Woodie," The Vision Forward Case Database, http://www.visionforward.com, 2007.

Go to www.VisionForward.com for printable cases, more on Woodie Neiss and FLAVORx, plus additional exercises and resources.

# Endnotes

## Chapter 1

1. Robert E. Litan, "What We Know," *Understanding Entrepreneurship: A Research and Policy Report* (Kansas City, MO: Ewing Marion Kauffman Foundation, 2005), p. 8.
2. "Small Business Is Cool Now," *Inc. Special Report: The State of Small Business 1996,* p. 17.
3. Donald F. Kuratko, *Entrepreneurship Education: Emerging Trends and Challenges for the 21st Century,* 2003 Coleman Foundation White Paper Series for the United States Association of Small Business and Entrepreneurship, p. 3.
4. "Global Entrepreneurship Monitor (GEM): The Definitive Study of Entrepreneurship in 2005," Babson College Newsroom, www.babson.edu/Newsroom/Releases/globalgem11206release.cfm.
5. Amanda C. Kooser, "Making Their Mark: Chris Giffiths," *Entrepreneur,* November 2005, p. 91; "Our History," Garrison Guitars, www.garrisonguitars.com/history.asp.
6. Jeffry A. Timmons, "An Obsession with Opportunity," *Nation's Business,* March 1985, p. 68.
7. "Panel Study on Entrepreneurial Dynamics," Kauffman Foundation Entrepreneurship Research Portal, http://research.kauffman.org/ cwp/appmanager/research/researchDesktop?_nfpb=true&_pageLabel=research_dataDetail&awebcurl=Research/DataSet_01.htm.
8. Jerry Useem, "The Risk-Taker Returns," *FSB,* May 2001, p. 70.
9. Joshua Hyatt, "Stuck on You," *Inc.,* December 2005/January 2006, p. 132; "How It Works," StarChase Inc., www.starchase.org/howitworks.html.
10. Devin Comiskey, "Studies Reveal Online Entrepreneurship Thriving," *Small Business Computing,* April 28, 2005, www.smallbusinesscomputing.com/news/article.pho/3501141.
11. David McClellan, *The Achieving Society* (Princeton, NJ: Van Nostrand, 1961), p. 16; Nancy Michaels, "Entrepreneurship: An Alternative Career Choice," *U.S. News & World Report,* March 24, 2003, p. 45; Susan Ward, "So You Want to Start a Small Business? Part 2: The Personality of the Entrepreneur," *Small Business Canada,* http://sbinfocanada.about.com/library/weekly/aa082900b.htm.
12. Charles Gerena, "Nature vs. Nurture," *Region Focus,* Fall 2005, p. 19.
13. Ralph Waldo Emerson, "Essays: First Series," Emerson.com, www.emersoncentral.com/selfreliance.htm.
14. Jeffrey Shuman and David Rottenberg, "Famous Failures," *Small Business Start-Ups,* February 1999, pp. 32–33; Francis Huffman, "A Dairy Tale," *Entrepreneur,* February 1999, p. 182; Gail Borden, "Famous Texans," www.famoustexans.com/GailBorden.htm.
15. Sabin Russell, "Being Your Own Boss in America," *Venture,* May 1984, p. 40.
16. Anne Field, "Bouncing From Start-Up to Start-Up and Loving It," Gathering of Angels, http://gatheringofangels.com/News/bouncing.html; Howard Yellen, "The Making of a Serial Entrepreneur," Larta Institute, January 10, 2005, http://www.larta.org/LAVox/articlelinks/2005/050110_ making.asp.
17. Stephanie N. Mehta, "Young Entrepreneurs Are Starting Business After Business," *Wall Street Journal,* March 19, 1997, p. B2.
18. Roger Rickleffs and Udayan Gupta, "Traumas of a New Entrepreneur," *Wall Street Journal,* May 10, 1989, p. B1.
19. Chris Pentilla, "Model Behavior," *Entrepreneur,* April 2006, pp. 78–81.
20. James Park, "Tea for Two," *Entrepreneur,* April 2006, p. 128; Ayeko Vinton, "Shakers: Cleaning Up," Profiles of African-American Achievers, July 8, 2005, http://blackvoices.aol.com/workmonmain/workmonmain_canv/shakers_a5/_a/shakers-cleaning-up/20050620103809990001.
21. John Case, "The Origins of Entrepreneurship," *Inc.,* June 1989, p. 52.
22. Sara Wilson, "Learning from the Best," *Entrepreneur,* March 2006, pp. 62–65; "Starwich Story," www.starwich.com/.
23. Lindsey Gerdes, "Sunken Treasure," *FSB,* December 2005/January 2006, pp. 104–109; "About Us," Goodwin Heart Pine, www.goodwinheartpine.com/aboutus/.
24. Mitch Stacy, "PODS Removing Big Chunk of Moving, Storage Market," *Greenville News,* August 5, 2006, pp. 13A–17A.
25. "Alaska Entrepreneur Hopes to Turn Glacial Mud into Gold," *Greenville News,* September 2, 2006, p. 12A.
26. April Y. Pennington, "Baby Steps," *Entrepreneur,* December 2005, p. 172.
27. John Boyanoski, "Hot Idea Comes to Downtown," *GSA Business,* June 30, 2006, p. 22.
28. "Higher Purpose," *Entrepreneur,* May 2003, p. 32.
29. Cheryl Dahle, "Filling the Void," *Fast Company,* January 2006, www.fastcompany.com/magazine/102/open_social-capitalists-intro.html; Beth Potier, "From Law School Roots, BELL Puts Kids on 'Success Spiral,'" *Harvard Gazette,* November 21, 2002, www.hno.harvard.edu/gazette/2002/11.21/03-comm.html.
30. Roger P. Levin, "You've Got to Love It or Leave It," *Success,* December 2000/January 2001, p. 22.
31. "What Builds a Fortune?" *Money,* August 2003, p. 78.
32. Matthew Miller and Tatiana Serafin, "The Forbes 400," *Forbes,* October 9, 2006, pp. 80–90.
33. Mary Diebel, "4.6 Million Americans Are Millionaires," *The Sacramento Bee,* July 16, 2001, http://24hour.sacbee.com/24hour/business/story/632161p-678117c.html; Sheryl Nance, "You Can Be a Millionaire," *Your Company,* June/July 1997, pp. 26–33.
34. Carlye Adler, "The Fresh Prince of Software," *FSB,* March 2003, pp. 42–48; "Marc Benioff," Salesforce.com, www.salesforce.com/us/company/board.jsp?name= benioff; Salesforce.com Annual Report 2006, www.salesforce.com/us/pdf/investor/CRM_2006_Annual_ Report.pdf, p. 41.
35. *NFIB National Small Business Poll: Retirement,* National Federation of Independent Business Owners, Volume 5, Issue No. 3, November 2, 2005, (Washington, DC), p. 3.
36. Alice Feiring, "French Bliss," *FSB,* April 2006, pp. 67–69.
37. Gayle Sato-Stodder, "Never Say Die," *Entrepreneur,* December 1990, p. 95.
38. *NFIB Small Business Policy Guide* (Washington, DC: NFIB Education Foundation, 2000), p. 22.
39. Anne Fisher, "Is Your Business Ruining Your Marriage?" *FSB,* March 2003, pp. 63–71.
40. *NFIB Small Business Policy Guide* (Washington, DC: NFIB Education Foundation, 2000), p. 16.
41. Mark Henricks, "Not All Business Owners Keep Slavish Hours," *Startup Journal: Wall Street Journal Center for Entrepreneurs,* June 27, 2002, www.startupjournal.com/columnists/startuplifestyle/20020627-lifestyle.html.
42. Emily Lambert, "No Free Lunch," *Forbes,* June 9, 2003, pp. 154–156.
43. Geoff Williams, "Guiding Light," *Entrepreneur B.Y.O.B.,* August 2003, p. 84.
44. Mark Henricks, "Parent Trap?" *Entrepreneur,* September 2005, pp. 17–18.
45. Pattie Simone, "You Can Do It!" *Entrepreneur,* July 2006, pp. 94–101.
46. Patricia B. Gray, "Can Entrepreneurship Be Taught?" *FSB,* March 2005, pp. 34–51; Raymund Flandez, "An Education in Itself," *Wall Street Journal,* September 25, 2006, p. R10.
47. Jim Hopkins, "Venture Capital 101: Entrepreneur Courses Increase," *USA Today,* January 5, 2004, p. 1B.
48. "USTR Focus on Services," Office of the United States Trade Representative, www.ustr.gov/Trade_Sectors/Services/Section_Index.html.
49. Maggie Overfelt, "Start-ups on Fire: PrepMe," *FSB,* November 2005, pp. 34–36.
50. Samantha Sordyl, "Scott Adams, Drawing the Line," *Washington Post,* May 10, 2005, www.washingtonpost.com/wp-dyn/content/article/2005/05/09/AR2005050901066.html; Larry Keller, "Scott Adams: Cubicle Refugee," *CNN.com,* October 6, 2000, http:// archives.cnn.com/2000/CAREER/trends/10/05/scott.adams/index.html; Anne Stuart, "A World of His Own," *Inc. Technology 2001,* No. 2, pp. 33–36.

51. John Symons, "Forrester Research U.S. E-Commerce Forecast: Online Retail Sales to Reach $329 Billion by 2010," Forrester Research, September 19, 2005, www.forrester.com/ER/Press/Release/0,1769,1033,00.html.

52. "Interland's Small- and Medium-sized Business Barometer Reveals Majority of Businesses Are Generating Sales Online," Interland, September 29, 2005, http://phx.corporate-ir.net/ phoenix.zhtml?c= 120781&p=irol-newsArticle&ID= 762405&highlight.

53. Ryan McCarthy, "The Young and the Restless: Jacquelyn Tran, Perfume Bay," *Inc.*, July 2006, p. 89; Les Christie, "The Sweet Smell of Success," *CNN/Money,* June 6, 2005, http://money.cnn.com/2005/06/01/smbusiness/perfume_ bay/index.htm.

54. Lara Chamberlain, *NFIB National Small Business Poll: International Trade,* Volume 4, Issue 1, 2004, National Federation of Independent Businesses, pp. 1, 4.

55. "Small California Manufacturer Grows by Exporting to the World," National Association of Manufacturers, 2006, www.nam.org/s_nam/doc1.asp?CID=201840&DID =233946.

56. Meredith Bagby, "Generation X," *Success,* September 1998, pp. 22–23; Debra Phillips, "Great X-Pectations," *Business Start-Ups,* January 1999, pp. 31–33.

57. Maria Minniti, William Bygrave, and Erkko Autio, *Global Entrepreneurship Monitor: Executive Summary,* Babson College and the London Business School, January 2006, p. 33.

58. Elaine Pofeldt and Brandi Stewart, "Start-ups on Fire," *FSB,* November 2005, pp. 32–46.

59. Angus Loten, "The Young and the Restless: Mark Zuckerberg," *Inc.,* July 2006, pp. 86–91; April Y. Pennington, "Friendly Faces," *Entrepreneur,* June 2006, p. 40.

60. Nichole L. Torres, "Girls Club," *Entrepreneur,* July 2006, pp. 130–131; Dawn Klingensmith, "Entrepreneurs Become Desirable Slice of Market," *Chicago Tribune,* August 6, 2006, www.chicagotribune.com/entertainment/chi-0608090155aug09,1,2998437.story?page=1&ctrack= 1&cset=true.

61. Anne Fisher, "The Sky's the Limit," *Fortune,* May 1, 2006, pp. 124[B]–124[H].

62. Jasmine D. Adkins, "The Young and the Restless: Theranos," *Inc.,* July 2006, pp. 86–91.

63. "Women-Owned Businesses Continue to Outpace Growth Rates for All Other Firms," Center for Women's Business Research, September 12, 2006, www.womensbusinessresearch.org/press/details.php?id=135.

64. April Y. Pennington, "In on the Action," *Entrepreneur,* July 2006, p. 30.

65. Cora Daniels, "Minority Rule," *FSB,* December 2003/January 2004, pp. 65–66; *The Entrepreneur Next Door: Characteristics of Individuals Starting Companies in America* (Kansas City, MO: Ewing Marion Kauffman Foundation, 2002), pp. 15–16.

66. *The State of Minority Business* (Washington, DC: Minority Business Development Agency, August 2006), www.mbda.gov/documents/mbda2.pdf, p. 2.

67. Amanda Kooser, April Y. Pennington, Nichole L. Torres, and Sara Wilson, "Making Their Mark," *Entrepreneur,* November 2005, pp. 83–97.

68. April Y. Pennington, "Beyond Their Years: Chai Ling," *Entrepreneur,* November 2003, pp. 78–81.

69. Mike Bergman, "Half of U.S. Businesses Are Home-based, Majority of Firms Self-financed, Reports Census Bureau," *U.S. Census Bureau News,* September 27, 2006, www.census.gov/Press-Release/www/releases/archives/business_ownership/007537.html.

70. John McDowell, "Home-based Sole Proprietors Generate $102 Billion in Annual Revenue," Small Business Administration Office of Advocacy, May 31, 2006, www.sba.gov/advo/press/06-14.html.

71. "The Ticker," *Information Week,* March 8, 2006, p. 18.

72. McDowell, "Home-based Sole Proprietors Generate $102 Billion in Annual Revenue," Small Business Administration Office of Advocacy, May 31, 2006, www.sba.gov/advo/press/06-14.html.

73. Madeleine Marr, "Home Business No Half-Baked Idea," *Greenville News,* January 1, 2006, p. 1F; Joan Fleischman, "Cookin' Good," *Miami Herald,* September 20, 2006, www.miami.com/mld/miamiherald/news/columnists/joan_fleischman/15560111.htm?template=contentModules/printstory.jsp.

74. "Facts and Figures on Family Business in the U.S.," The Family Firm Institute, www.ffi.org/looking/fbfacts_ us.cgi.

75. Erick Calonius, "Blood and Money," *Newsweek,* Special Issue, p. 82.

76. Liz Welch, "Things I Can't Live Without: Donna Grucci Butler," *Inc.,* July 2006, p. 70; "About Us," Fireworks by Grucci, www.grucci.com/aboutus.html.

77. "Facts and Perspectives on Family Business in the U.S.," The Family Firm Institute, www.ffi.org/looking/fbfacts_us.pdf

78. Nichole Seymour, "Copreneurs," Kauffman Center for Entrepreneurial Leadership Clearinghouse on EntrepreneurialEducation, June 2002, www.celcee.edu/publications/digest/Dig02-03.html.

79. "Love and the Bottom Line: Couples in Business Find High Rewards and Risks," *Nando Times News,* http://archive.nandotimes.com/newsroom/nt/0212bizcpl.html

80. Allison Fass, "Safari Guide," *Forbes,* December 12, 2005, pp. 220–223.

81. Donna Kato, "Changing Course, Burning Suits," *Greenville News,* June 6, 1993, p. 1D.

82. Jessica Seid, "Ditching the Daily Grind," *CNNMoney.com,* May 11, 2006, http://money.cnn.com/2006/05/11/smbusiness/corporate_refugees/index.htm.

83. Kelly Spors, "Building a Start-up after Retirement," *Wall Street Journal's Startup Journal,* October 2, 2006, www.startupjournal.com/howto/soundadvice/20061002-spors.html.

84. Eileen Blass, "The New Entrepreneurs: Americans Over 50," *USA Today,* January 17, 2005, www.usatoday.com/money/smallbusiness/2005-01-17-older-entrepreneurs_ x.htm; "Our Story," Cookies on Call, www.cookiesoncall.com/story.htm.

85. "Small Business FAQ," U.S. Small Business Administration, Office of Advocacy, December 2000, p. 1; *NFIB Small Business Policy Guide* (Washington, DC: NFIB Education Foundation, 2000), p. 25.

86. John McDowell, "Small Business Continues to Drive Economy," U.S. Small Business Administration Office of Advocacy, October 3, 2005, www.sba.gov/advo/press/05-46.html.

87. *NFIB Small Business Policy Guide* (Washington, DC: NFIB Education Foundation, 2000), p. 30; "Help Wanted," *Inc Special Report: The State of Small Business 1997,* pp. 35–41; "The Job Factory," *Inc Special Report: The State of Small Business 2001,* pp. 40–43; "The Gazelle Theory," *Inc. Special Report: The State of Small Business 2001,* pp. 28–29.

88. Preston McLaurin, "Small Businesses Are Winners," *S.C. Business Journal,* May 2000, p. 10.

89. John McDowell, "Small Business Continues to Drive Economy," U.S. Small Business Administration Office of Advocacy, October 3, 2005, www.sba.gov/advo/press/05-46.html.

90. *Small Business by the Numbers* (Washington, DC: U.S. Small Business Administration, 2004), www.sba.gov/advo/stats/sbfaq.pdf, p. 1.

91. Lev Grossman, "Best Inventions 2006," *Time,* November 13, 2006, www.time.com/time/2006/techguide/bestinventions/inventions/youtube.html; "The Hug Shirt," CuteCircuit, www.cutecircuit.com/now/projects/wearables/fr-hugs/.

92. Lev Grossman, "Best Inventions 2006," *Time,* November 13, 2006, www.time.com/time/2006/techguide/bestinventions/inventions/youtube.html; "Introducing Pleo," UGOBE, http://ugobe.com/pleo/index.html.

93. "Middle-Aged Spread," *Inc. Special Report: The State of Small Business 2001,* p 54.

94. Michael Warshaw, "Great Comebacks," *Success,* July/August 1995, p. 43.

95. Michael Barrier, "Entrepreneurs Who Excel," *Nation's Business,* August 1996, p. 28.

96. Clint Willis, "Try, Try Again," *Forbes ASAP,* June 2, 1997, p. 63.

97. Geoff Williams, "I Quit," *Start-Ups,* December 2000, pp. 47–49.

98. Stephanie Barlow, "Hang On!" *Entrepreneur,* September 1992, p. 156.

99. Jared Sandberg, "Counting Pizza Slices, Cutting Water Cups—You Call This a Budget?" *Wall Street Journal,* January 21, 2004, p. B1.

100. Rhonda Abrams, "Building Blocks of Business: Great Faith, Great Doubt, Great Effort," *Business 2.0,* March 4, 2001, p. 2.

# Chapter 2

1. Fred Vogelstein, "Mastering the Art of Disruption," *Fortune,* February 6, 2006, pp. 23–24; Chris Pentilla, "All Shook Up," *Entrepreneur,* December 2005, pp. 112–113.

2. Alvin Toffler, "Shocking Truths About the Future," *Journal of Business Strategy,* July/August 1996, p. 6; Russ Juskalian, "Knowledge Drives Future, Creates Wealth, Authors Say," *USA Today,* May 15, 2006, p. 5B.

3. Norm Brodsky, "Be Prepared," *Inc.,* January 2006, pp. 53–54.

4. Samuel Greenguard, "Knowledge Management Can Turbocharge Your Company," *Beyond Computing,* November/December 2000, p. 28.

5. Thomas A. Stewart, "You Think Your Company's So Smart? Prove It," *Fortune,* April 30, 2001, p. 188.

6. Thomas A. Stewart, "Intellectual Capital: Ten Years Later, How Far We've Come," *Fortune,* May 28, 2001, p. 188.

7. Gary Hamel, "Innovation's New Math," *Fortune,* July 9, 2001, p. 130.

8. Geoffrey Colvin, "Managing in Chaos," *Fortune,* October 2, 2006, pp. 76–82.

9. Samual Fromartz, "Greener Tea," *FSB,* April 2006, pp. 85–89.

10. Richard Breeden, "By the Numbers: Small vs. Big," *Wall Street Journal,* January 3, 2006, p. A23.

11. Ron Stodghill, "Who's on Deck? Play Well with Others," *FSB,* May 2006, p. 49.

12. Ray Smilor, *Daring Visionaries: How Entrepreneurs Build Companies, Inspire Allegiance, and Create Wealth* (Avon, MA: Adams Media Corporation, 2001), pp.12–13.

13. Thomas A. Stewart, "Why Values Statements Don't Work," *Fortune,* June 10, 1996, p. 137.

14. Nancy Brown Johnson, "Low-Cost Competition in the U.S.," Labor and Employment Relations Association, *Proceedings of the 58th Annual Meeting,* January 6–8, 2006, www.press.uillinois.edu/journals/irra/proceedings 2006/johnson.html;

15. Danny Meyer, "The Saltshaker Theory," *Inc.,* October 2006, p. 70.

16. Bill Thomas, "Rhapsody in Beige: How I Did It," *Inc.,* June 2006, pp. 104–106; Staci Kusterbeck, "All Star Salute: Bills Khakis," *Apparel,* December 1, 2005, www.apparelmag.com/articles.dec.dec05_4.shtml; Bill Thomas, "Developing a Passion for a Product," *Nation's Business,* December 1993, p. 84; Jay Koenig, "Interview with Bill Thomas, CEO of Bills Khakis," Hoovers Business Center, www.hoovers.com/business-information/—pageid_ 14529--/global-hoov-index.xhtml.

17. Tom Chappell, "Heart, Soul, and Toothpaste," *Your Company,* September 1999, pp. 64–68; "The Tom's of Maine Story," Tom's of Maine, www.tomsofmaine.com/about/mission.asp.

18. "About Our Winery: Mission Statement," Fetzer Vineyards, www.fetzer.com/fetzer/wineries/philosophy.aspx.

19. Karen E. Spaeder, "Ticket to Ride," *Entrepreneur,* May 2006, p. 28.

20. Andy Serwer, "Extreme Makeover," *Fortune,* May 29, 2006, pp. 108–116.

21. Kate Kelly, "The Multiplex Under Siege," *Wall Street Journal,* December 24–25, 2005, pp. P1, P5; Andy Serwer, "Extreme Makeover," *Fortune,* May 29, 2006, pp. 108–116.

22. Nicole L. Torres, "Roast of the Town," *Entrepreneur B.Y.O.B.,* March 2003, p. 118; "Retail Shops," Mayorga Coffee Roasters, www.mayorgaimports.com/html/.

23. "Executive Outlook," *Sales and Marketing Management's Performance Newletter,* May 29, 2006, p. 1.

24. Alison Stein Wellner, "Spy vs. Spy," *Inc.,* June 2003, pp. 39–41.

25. Carolyn Z. Lawrence, "Know Your Competition," *Business Startups,* April 1997, p. 51.

26. "Know Thy Enemy," *Entrepreneur,* July 2003, p. 103.

27. David Whitford, "Sandwich Superheroes," *FSB,* June 2003, p. 20; "Our History," Geno's Steaks, www.genosteaks.com/; "History," Pat's King of Steaks, www.patskingofsteaks.com/history.htm.

28. Julia Boorstin, "Cruising for a Bruising?" *Fortune,* June 9, 2003, pp. 143–150; Martha Brannigan, "Cruise Lines Look to the Land to Get Boomers on Board," *Wall Street Journal,* December 6, 1999, p. B.4.

29. Shari Caudron, "I Spy, You Spy," *Industry Week,* October 3, 1994, p. 36.

30. Stephen D. Solomon, "Spies Like You," *FSB,* June 2001, pp. 76–82.

31. Dan Brekke, "What You Don't Know Can Hurt You," *Smart Business,* March 2001, pp. 64–76.

32. David H. Freedman, "Somebody's Watching You," *Inc.,* September 2005, pp. 75–76.

33. Mark Henricks, "In the BHAG," *Entrepreneur,* August 1999, pp. 65–67.

34. Jim Collins and Jerry Poras, *Built to Last: Successful Habits of Visionary Companies* (New York: HarperBusiness, 1994), p. 232.

35. "Supply Meets Demand at Dell Computer," *Accenture Access,* www.accenture.com/Global/Services/By_Industry/Communications/Access_Newsletter/Article_Index/SupplyComputer.htm.

36. Joseph C. Picken and Gregory Dess, "The Seven Traps of Strategic Planning," *Inc.,* November 1996, p. 99.

37. Kambiz Foroohar, "Step Ahead—and Avoid Fads," *Forbes,* November 4, 1996, pp. 172–176.

38. Saul Hansell and John Markoff, "A Search Engine That's Becoming an Inventor," *New York Times,* July 3, 2006, www.nytimes.com/2006/07/03/technology/03google.html?ei=5088&en=11ad7f241098c6e2&ex=1309579200&adxnnl=1&partner=rssnyt&emc=rss&adxnnlx=1151888719-NxrsEO+IzRvSa28feeFzfw& pagewanted=all&pagewanted=all; Rich Karlgaard, "The Cheap Decade," *Forbes,* March 31, 2003, p. 37; Jonathan Thaw, "Google Passes Yahoo as Second Most-Visited Site," *Bloomberg.com,* December 22, 2006, www.bloomberg.com/apps/news?pid=20601103&sid=akmPwI7HOrjQ&refer=news.

39. "The Steady, Strategic Assent of JetBlue Airways," *Knowledge@Wharton,* January 6, 2006, http://knowledge.wharton.upenn.edu/article.cfm?articleid=1342&CFID=3461527&CFTOKEN=87628687; Nancy Brown Johnson, "Low-Cost Competition in the U.S.," Labor and Employment Relations Association, *Proceedings of the 58th Annual Meeting,* January 6–8, 2006, www.press.uillinois.edu/journals/irra/proceedings2006/johnson.html; Shawn Tully, "Airlines: Why the Big Boys Won't Come Back," *Fortune,* June 14, 2004, pp. 101–104; Melanie Wells, "Lord of the Skies," *Forbes,* October 14, 2002, pp. 130–138; Barney Gimbel, "Southwest's New Flight Plan," *Fortune,* May 16, 2005, pp. 93–98; Donna Rosato, "The Plane Truth About Flying Cheap," *Money,* May 2004, pp. 83–86; David Whelan, "The Slipper Solution," *Forbes,* May 24, 2004, p. 64; Susan Carey, "Amid Jet Blue's Rapid Ascent, CEO Adopts Big Rivals' Traits," *Wall Street Journal,* August 25, 2005, pp. A1, A6; "JetBlue 101," JetBlue Airlines, http:// www.jetblue.com/learnmore/air101.html.

40. Matthew Boyle, "The King of Cheap Stuff," *Fortune,* November 14, 2005, p. 220; Ann Zimmerman, "Behind the Dollar-Store Boom: A Nation of Bargain Hunters," *Wall Street Journal,* December 13, 2004, pp. A1, A10; Brendan Coffey, "Every Penny Counts," *Forbes,* September 30, 2002, pp. 68–70; Amber McDowell, "Discount Retailers Prosper Amid Economic Instability," *Greenville News Business,* December 23, 2002, pp. 6, 13; Tony Taylor, "S.C. a Growth Center for Discount Retailer," *GSA Business,* November 25, 2005, pp. 3, 9; Debbie Howell, "Dollar General Market to Grow to 70 in 2006," *DSN Retailing Today,* December 19, 2005, www.findarticles.com/p/articles/mi_m0FNP/is_23_44/ai_n15969632.

41. Debra Phillips, "Leaders of the Pack," *Entrepreneur,* September 1996, p. 127.

42. Bridget Finn, "For Petco, Success Is a Bitch," *Business 2.0,* November 2003, p. 54.

43. Siri Schubert, "The New (Age) Drugstore," *Business 2.0,* May 2006, pp. 48–51.

44. Siri Schubert, "The New (Age) Drugstore," *Business 2.0,* May 2006, pp. 48–51; "Elephant Pharm Announces Los Altos Store Opening," Elephant Pharmacy, www. strauscom.com/ elephant/press.php?id=pr112906.
45. Phillips, "Leaders of the Pack," p. 127.
46. Sibylla Brodzinsky, "Protects Like Armor, Fits Like Armani," *Business 2.0,* August 2006, p. 60.
47. Robert Johnson, "This Pair of Shoes Are Soles of Indiscretion; That's the Point," *Wall Street Journal,* February 25, 2000, pp. A1, A4. "The Scott Family," www.folkvine.org/scotts/scotts.html.
48. Brandi Stewart, "A Butterfly Business Takes Flight," *FSB,* November 2006, p. 23.

49. Jenny Mero, "You Do What? IMAX Screen Cleaner," *Fortune,* May 29, 2006, p. 34.
50. Ron Stodghill, "Who's on Deck? Seek Value," *FSB,* May 2006, p. 50.
51. Jacob Hale Russell, "Unhappy Feet: Ballerinas' New Lament," *Wall Street Journal,* December 23–24, 2006, pp. P1, P11.
52. Joel Kurtzman, "Is Your Company Off Course? Now You Can Find Out Why," *Fortune,* February 17, 1997, p. 128.
53. Robert S. Kaplan and David P. Norton, "The Balanced Scorecard—Measures That Drive Performance," *Harvard Business Review,* January–February 1992, pp. 71–79.
54. Kevin Ferguson, "Mission Control," *Inc.,* November 2003, pp. 27–28.

# Chapter 3

1. Janelle Elms, "Law and Orders," *Entrepreneur,* March 2006, p. 110.
2. "Total Number of U.S. Businesses," BizStats.com, www.bizstats. com/businesses.htm.
3. Steve Nubie, "Naming Names—Why a Good Business Plan Can Help You Name Your Company," *Entrepreneur,* May 2000, www. entrepreneur.com/magazine/businessstartupsmagazine/2000/may/ 26080.html.
4. Ian Mount, "Business Licenses to Go," *FSB,* March 2007, p. 14.
5. Norm Brodsky, "Sam and Me," *Inc.,* June 2006, p. 65.
6. Emily Lambert, "The Odd Couple," *Forbes,* September 4, 2006, p. 73.
7. Marc Diener, "Real Deal," *Entrepreneur,* March 2006, p. 74.
8. Stephanie Clifford, "Until Death, or Some Other Sticky Problem, Do Us Part," *Inc.,* November 2006, pp. 104–110.
9. Personal communication with Jason Landau, June 30, 2007.
10. Nichole L. Torres, "Left in the Lurch?" *Entrepreneur,* May 2006, p. 108.

11. Ibid.
12. "Dispute Resolution," Australian Government, Department of Industry, Tourism and Resources, January 2, 2007, www. nml.csiro.au/content/itrinternet/cmscontent.cfm?objectid= B3057698-8E48-4532-A6DA75C31CFC1762 &indexPages=/ content/azindex.cfm,/content/azindex.cfm?keyword=guidelines.
13. Henry R. Cheeseman, *Business Law,* 5th ed. (Upper Saddle River, NJ: Pearson Prentice Hall, 2004), p. 675.
14. Grace Wong, "Kozlowski Gets up to 25 Years," CNN/Money.com, September 19, 2005, http://money.cnn.com/2005/09/19/news/ newsmakers/kozlowski_sentence.
15. Jane Easter Bahls, "Behind the Mask," *Entrepreneur,* March 2006, p. 80.
16. Crystal Detamore-Rodman, "S Corps Are Coming Under Closer Scrutiny. How Will It Affect You?" *Entrepreneur,* January 2006, p. 24.
17. *Statistics of Income Bulletin,* Internal Revenue Service, October 2006.
18. C. J. Prince, "Take Cover," *Entrepreneur,* November 2006, p. 86.

# Chapter 4

1. David J. Kaufmann, "What a Ride!" *Entrepreneur,* May 2007, pp. 108–109.
2. Maria Anton and Janean Chun, "Best of the Best," *Entrepreneur,* January 2007, p. 94.
3. Hachemi Aliouche, "Rosenberg Center Study Confirms Global Franchise Growth," *Franchising World,* August 1, 2006, www. allbusiness.com/retail-trade/1189645-1.html.
4. "What Is Franchising?" U.S. Small Business Administration, May 20, 2007, www.sba.gov/smallbusinessplanner/start/buyafranchise/ serv_sbp_s_franov.html.
5. Gregory Matusky, "The Franchise Hall of Fame," *Inc.,* April 1994, pp. 86–89.
6. Personal contact with Nicholas A. Bibby, The Bibby Group, www. bibbbygroup.com, May 2, 2007.
7. Catherine Siskos, "Franchises That Work Out," *Kiplinger's Personal Finance Magazine,* October 2003, pp. 73–75.
8. Ibid.
9. Sara Wilson, "Pushing Forward," *Entrepreneur,* December 2005, p. 124.
10. Sara Wilson, "Look Who's Buying," *Entrepreneur,* January 2007, pp. 118–125.
11. David J. Kaufmann, "The Big Bang," *Entrepreneur,* January 2004, pp. 86–101.
12. Siskos, "Franchises That Work Out," pp. 73–75.
13. Wilson, "Look Who's Buying," pp. 118, 120.
14. Nichole, L. Torres, "Full Speed Ahead," *Entrepreneur,* January 2007, pp. 162–163.
15. Janean Huber, "Franchise Forecast," *Entrepreneur,* January 1993, p. 73.
16. Richard Landesberg, "A New Career for You Might Start at Franchise U," *Success,* July/August 2000, pp. 82–83.

17. Louise Witt, "Franchising: The Great Entrepreneurial Gambit," *FSB* Special Advertising Section, December 2002/January 2003, pp. 51–52; Mark Jones, "Getting Hip with Plato's Closet," *GSA Business,* September 22, 2003, pp. 3, 7.
18. Janean Huber, "Franchise Forecast," *Entrepreneur,* January 1993, p. 73.
19. "The Profile of Franchising," *Franchising World,* March 2007, p. 69.
20. The Franchise Registry, www.franchiseregistry.com/Registry.
21. April Y. Pennington "Show Me The Money—Smoothie Sailing," *Entrepreneur,* September 2005, www.entrepreneur.com/magazine/ entrepreneur/2005/september/79462.html.
22. Stephanie Barlow, "Sub-Stantial Success," *Entrepreneur,* January 1993, p. 126.
23. Charles C. Miler, "Hot Litigation Tops in Franchising," BartkoZankel Attorneys, www.bztm.com/pub_hot_lit.html.
24. Vylene Enterprises vs. Naugles, FindLaw, http://caselaw.lp. findlaw.com/cgi-bin/getcase.pl?court=9th&navby=case&no= 9456470; Nicole Harris and Mike France, "Franchisees Get Feisty," *Business Week,* www.businessweek.com/1997/08/ b351592.htm; Richard Gibson, "Court Decides Franchisees Get Elbow Room," *Franchise Law Update,* Luce, Forward, Hamilton, & Scripps LLP. vol. 1, No. 6, (October 1996), www.lice.com/ publicat/flu_16-3.html
25. Siskos, "Franchises That Work Out," pp. 73–75.
26. Devlin Smith, "Want a Franchise with That?" *Entrepreneur B.Y.O.B.,* May 2002, pp. 102–106.
27. "Red Flags, Green Flags," *Entrepreneur,* January 2007, p. 106.
28. Siskos, "Franchises That Work Out," pp. 73–75.
29. Carol Tice, "Meet Your Match," *Entrepreneur,* January 2007, 96–107.

30. "Illinois Franchisees File Class Action Suit Against Quiznos Sub," *PR Newswire,* April 19, 2007.
31. Steve Cooper, "Creative Endeavors," *Entrepreneur,* January 2003, pp. 126–128.
32. "Notable Franchise Facts," McDonald's, www.mcdonalds.com/ corporate/franchise/facts/index.html; Matusky, "The Franchise Hall of Fame," pp. 86–89.
33. Janet Adamy, "For McDonald's, It's a Wrap," *Wall Street Journal,* January 30, 2007, pp. B1–B2.
34. Dan Morse, "Individual Owners Set Up Own E-Commerce Sites," *Wall Street Journal,* March 28, 2000, p. B2.
35. Siskos, "Franchises That Work Out," pp. 73–75.
36. Amy Covington, "Fantastic Sam's: The John McCurry Story," April 2007, www.franchiseprospector.com/success/fantastic-sams-john-mccurry.php.
37. Jeff Elgin, "Ten Signs of a Great Franchise," *Entrepreneur,* December 11, 2006, www.entrepreneur.com/article/printthis/ 171432.html.
38. Amy Covington, "Microtel Inns & Suites; The Rocco Valluzo Story," *Franchise Prospector,* April 2007, www.franchiseprospector.com/success/microtel-rocco-valluzo.php.
39. Jeannie Ralston, "Before You Bet Your Buns," *Venture,* March 1988, p. 57.
40. Hachemi Aliouche, "Rosenberg Center Study Confirms Global Franchise Growth," *Franchising World,* August 2006, pp. 21–23.
41. Kaufmann, "What a Ride!"
42. Asia Pacific Economic Cooperation, "Consultative Survey on Franchising in APEC Member Economies," www.strategis.ic.gc.ca/SSG/ae00275e.html.
43. John Sotos and Sam Hall, "African Franchising: Cross-Continent Momentum," *International Franchise Association,* July 2007, www.franchise.org/Franchise-Industry-News-Detail.aspx?id= 34922.
44. Zaheera Wahid, "Twist and Shout," *Business Start-Ups,* February 2000, p. 85; Elizabeth Bernstein, "Holy Frappuccino," *Wall Street Journal,* August 31, 2001, pp. W1, W8; "Holy Fries," ABC13.com, http://abclocal.go.com/ktrk/news/020601_sn_holyfries.html.
45. Richard C. Hoffman and John F. Preble, "Convert to Compete: Competitive Advantage Through Conversion Franchising," *Journal of Small Business Management,* Vol. 41, No. 2, July 2003, pp. 187–204.
46. "McBusiness," *Inc. Special Report: State of Small Business 2001,* pp. 34–35; Kaufmann, "The Big Bang," p. 95.
47. Brian O'Keefe, "From NBA to MBA: Shaq Suits Up for Business," *Fortune,* September 18, 2006, p. 40; "Hoopster Shaq Buys Area Pretzel Franchise," *Buffalo Business First,* October 12, 2007, buffalo.bizjournals.com/buffalo/stories/2007/10/08/daily41.html.
48. Dunkin' Donuts/Baskin-Robbins/Togo's Franchise Opportunities, www.dunkin-baskin-togos.com; Bruce Horovitz, "The Latest Fast-Food Combo: Restaurants," *Greenville News,* March 16, 2002, p. 1D.
49. Devlin Smith, "Good as Gold," *Entrepreneur,* January 2004, pp. 106–110.
50. Mark Seibert, "Should You Franchise Your Business?" *Entrepreneur,* July 19, 2004, www.entrepreneur.com/franchises/franchisingyourbusinesscolumnistmarksiebert/article71886.html.
51. Amy Joyce, "The Art of the Successful Franchise," *Washington Post,* April 30, 2007, p. D1.
52. Amy Joyce, "The Art of the Successful Franchise."
53. Seibert, "Should You Franchise Your Business?"
54. Ibid.
55. Personal contact with Jim Thomas, May 16, 2007.
56. Amy Joyce, "The Art of the Successful Franchise."
57. Personal contact with Jim Thomas, May 16, 2007.

# Chapter 5

1. David E. Gumpert, "Buying a Biz Instead of Starting One," *Business Week,* August 21, 2006, www.businessweek.com/smallbiz/content/aug2006/sb20060821_514069.htm?chan=search.
2. Julie Bawden Davis, "Buying an Existing Business? You'd Better Shop Around," *Entrepreneur,* August 1999, http:// www.entrepreneur.com/magazine/entrepreneur/1999/august/18132.html.
3. Lin Grensing-Pophal, "Decide Whether You'll Buy an Existing Business, a Business Opportunity, a Franchise, or Go It Alone," *Business Start-Ups,* December 2000.
4. Lil Sawyer, "Buying a Business: The Safer Alternative," About.com, http://entrepreneurs.about.com/od/buyingabusiness/a/buyingabusiness.htm.
5. Bill Broocke, "Buy—Don't Start—Your Own Business: Why Not Take a Common Sense Approach to Entrepreneurship, and Consider the Option of Buying an Already Established Business?" *Entrepreneur,* March 22, 2004, www.Entrepreneur.com/article/0,4621,314869,00.html.
6. "Buying a Business," Small Business Administration, www.sba.gov/smallbusinessplanner/start/buyabusiness/SERV_SBP_S_BUYB.html.
7. Ira Nottonson, *Entrepreneur Magazine's Ultimate Guide to Buying or Selling a Business* (New York: Entrepreneur Press, 2004), p. 153.
8. Personal contact with Joe Rubenstein, November 5, 2007.
9. B. G. Yovovich, "Why Start a Business When You Can Buy One?" *Satisfaction,* www.satisfactionmag.com/index.php/2006/10/why-start-a-business-when-you-can-buy-one/.
10. Mark Blayney, *Buying a Business and Making It Work* (Oxford: How To Books Ltd., 2005), p. 420.
11. Robert F. Klueger, *Buying and Selling a Business: A Step by Step Guide* (John Wiley & Sons, 2004), p. 12.
12. Ibid.
13. Edward Karstetter, "How Intangible Assets Affect Business Value," *Entrepreneur,* May 6, 2002, http://Entrepreneur.com/article/0,4621,299514,00.html.
14. B. G. Yovovich, "Why Start a Business When You Can Buy One?"
15. Elaine Appleton Grant, "Sails and Services," *Inc.,* August 2007, p. 28.

# Chapter 6

1. Timothy Faley, "Start-Up," *Inc.,* www.inc.com/resources/startup/tfaleybio.html.
2. Michael E. Porter, *Competitive Advantage* (New York: Free Press, 1985), pp. 7–29.
3. Charles Fishman, "The Wal-Mart You Don't Know," *Fast Company,* December 2003, www.fastcompany.com/magazine/77/walmart.html.
4. "The Home-Based Business Blog: Using eBay for Product Market Testing," *Small Business Blog Center,* www.allbusiness.com/blog/TheHomeBasedBusinessBlog/8180/003338.html?RSS=XXXX.
5. Karen J. Bannan, "Companies Save Time, Money with Online Surveys," *BtoB,* June 6, 2003, www.btobonline.com/article.cms?articleId=11115.
6. Don Debelak, "Join Hands," *Entrepreneur's Be Your Own Boss,* October 2000, pp. 138–140.
7. Jeffrey Gangemi, "The Afterlife of Business Plan Contest Winners," *Business Week,* December 12, 2006, http:// businessweek.com/smallbiz/content/dec2006/sb20061212_410722.htm.
8. Timothy Faley, "Start-up."

9. William A. Sahlman, "How to Write a Great Business Plan," *Harvard Business Review,* July/August 1997, p. 105.

10. David H. Bangs, Jr., *The Business Planning Guide,* 9th ed. (Chicago: Dearborn Trade Publishing, 2002), p. 2.

11. Garrett Sutton, Esq., *The ABC's of Writing Winning Business Plans* (New York: Warner Business Books, 2005), pp. 169–170.

12. Nicole Gull, "Plan B (and C and D and . . .)," *Inc.,* March 2004, p. 40.

13. Greg Sands, "The Return of the Business Plan," *FSB,* April 2001, p. 31.

14. Steve Marshall Cohen, "Money Rules," *Business Start-Ups,* July 1995, p. 79.

15. Kelly K. Spors, "Do Start-Ups Really Need Formal Business Plans?" *Wall Street Journal,* January 10, 2007, p. B9.

16. Donna Fenn, "The Making of an Entrepreneurial Generation," *Inc.,* www.inc.com/30under30/2007/6-myers.html.

17. Dusty Donaldson, "Entrepreneurial MBA Students Pitch Winning Business Plans During Two-Minute Elevator Ride with Venture Capitalists," *Babcock News and Events,* March 26, 2003.

18. "Advice from the Great Ones," *Communication Briefings,* January 1992, p. 5.

19. Adam McCulloch, "Prefab with a View," *Business 2.0,* May 2005, p. 70.

20. Edward Clendaniel, "The Professor and the Practitioner," *Forbes ASAP,* May 28, 2001, p. 57.

21. "Business Plan Competition 2007: The 'Eight Great' Make Their Pitch," *Knowledge@Wharton,* http://knowledge.wharton.upenn.edu/article.cfm?articleid=1738&CFID=34214186&CFTOKEN=67394551&jsessionid=9a308e717020131243d5.

22. Ibid.

23. Jeff Wuorio, "Get an 'A' in Researching a Business Idea," *Microsoft bCentral,* www.bcentral.com/articles/wuorio/140.asp.

24. Eileen Figure Sandlin, "The Ingredients of Restaurant Success," *Entrepreneur,* www.entrepreneur.com/restaurantsuccess/index.html.

25. Sahlman, "How to Write a Great Business Plan," p. 100.

26. "Raising Money," *Entrepreneur,* July 2005, p. 58.

27. Michael V. Copeland, "How to Make Your Business Plan the Perfect Pitch," *Business 2.0,* September 2005, p. 88.

28. Karen Axelton, "Good Plan, Stan," *Business Start-Ups,* March 200, p. 17.

29. Sahlman, "How to Write a Great Business Plan," p. 105.

30. "Prepping Yourself for Credit," *Your Company,* April/May 1997, p. 9.

31. Evanson, "Capital Pitches That Succeed," p. 41.

32. Jill Andresky Fraser, "Who Can Help Out with a Business Plan?" *Inc.,* June 1999, p. 115.

## Chapter 7

1. Benjamin B. Gaunsel, "Toward a Framework of Financial Planning in New Venture Creation," presented at United States Association for Small Business and Entrepreneurship Annual Meeting, January 2005, Palm Springs, CA, www.sbaer.uca.edu/research/usasbe/2005/pdffiles/papers/25.pdf.

2. Eileen Davis, "Dodging the Bullet," *Venture,* December 1988, p. 78.

3. C. J. Prince, "Number Rustling," *Entrepreneur,* March 2003, pp. 43–44.

4. Mike Hogan, "Pocket Books," *Entrepreneur,* March 2006, pp. 42–43.

5. Norm Brodsky, "The Magic Number," *Inc.,* September 2003, pp. 43–46.

6. Jeff Nachtigal, "The Greenest Office in America," *Business 2.0,* September 2006, pp. 52–54.

7. Jared Sandberg, "Counting Pizza Slices, Cutting Water Cups—You Call This a Budget?" *Wall Street Journal,* January 21, 2004, p. B1.

8. Diedrich Von Soosten, "The Roots of Financial Destruction," *Industry Week,* April 5, 1993, pp. 33–34.

9. G. Dean Palmer, "Marketing and Management Strategies of Small Rural Retailers in South-Side Virginia," Small Business Advancement National Center, University of Central Arkansas, 1995, Conway, AR, www.sbaer.uca.edu/Research/1995/SSBIA/95swi052.txt.

10. Lori Ioannou, "He's Preaching the Power of Thrift," *Fortune,* October 30, 2000, p. 208[P].

11. Michael Brush, "Trump, You're Fired," *MSN Money,* September 27, 2006, http://articles.moneycentral.msn.com/Investing/Company Focus/TrumpYoureFired.aspx; Christina Binkley, "Trump's Casinos Risk Bankruptcy, Auditors Warn," *Wall Street Journal,* March 31, 2004, pp. A3, A8; Jeffrey Gold, "Trump Casinos Seek Bankruptcy Protection," *Los Angeles Times,* November 22, 2004, www.latimes.com/business/investing/wire/sns-ap-trump-casino-bankruptcy,1,2258616.story?coll=sns-ap-investing-headlines.

12. Herb Greenberg, ""The Hidden Dangers of Debt," *Fortune,* July 21, 2003, p. 153.

13. "Analyzing Creditworthiness," *Inc.,* November 1991, p. 196.

14. "Ratings Movers: Denny's Debt Smokin', Lifecare Outlook Bleak," *Bank Loan Report,* November 27, 2006, p. 11; "Denny's Applies $62 M to Debt from Sale of 60 Units," *Nation's Restaurant News,* October 16, 2006, p. 160.

15. Jill Andresky Fraser, "Giving Credit to Debt," *Inc.,* November 2000, p. 125.

16. "Michael's Stores Inc.: SWOT Analysis," *DataMonitor,* September 1, 2006, p. 6.

17. Alan Johnson, "Dell Upgrades Local Supply Chain," *Manufacturers' Monthly,* September 2006, p. 30; Russ Banham, "Does Dell Stack Up?" *CFO-IT,* Fall 2003, pp. 39–43.

18. Jeff Bailey, "Small Car Lots: a Basic, Gritty Loan Business," *Wall Street Journal,* July 8, 2003, p. B9.

19. Ilan Mochari, "Give Credit to the Small Business Owner," *Inc.,* March 2001, p. 88.

20. Jim Mueller, "Understanding the Cash Conversion Cycle," *Investopedia,* July 12, 2006, www.investopedia.com/articles/06/cashconversioncycle.asp.

21. Paul Frumkin, "NYC Restaurateurs Face Fierce Competition, Price Pressures," *Nation's Restaurant News,* November 13, 2006, pp. 1, 43–46.

22. Jon E. Hilsenrath, "Adventures in Cost Cutting," *Wall Street Journal,* May 10, 2004, pp. R1, R3.

23. Kathy Gulli, "The New, Frugal Face of Air Travel," *Maclean's,* July 6, 2006, p. 35.

24. Pat Croce, "Taking Your Own Pulse," *FSB,* December 2003/January 2004, p. 36.

25. Joshua Hyatt, "Planes, Trains, and . . . Buses," *FSB,* February 2004, p. 20.

26. Croce, "Taking Your Own Pulse," p. 36.

27. Brodsky, "The Magic Number," pp. 43–46.

28. William F. Doescher, "Taking Stock," *Entrepreneur,* November 1994, p. 64.

29. Ibid.

30. Hyatt, "Planes, Trains, and . . . Buses?" p. 20.

## Chapter 8

1. Philip Campbell, "Cash Flow Projections Made Easy," *Inc.,* October 1, 2004, www.inc.com/resources/finance/articles/20041001/cashprojection.html.

2. Mike Hofman, "Archive," *Inc.,* January 2002, p. 104.

3. "Paul Moore's Cruise Control," *Travel Trade Gazette UK & Ireland,* October 14, 2005, p. 7; Samantha Mayling, "Moore Blames Cash Flow and Critics for Collapse," *Travel Trade Gazette,* November 4, 2004, p. 10.

4. "Are You Ready for the Major Leagues?" *Inc.,* February 2001, p. 106.

5. Daniel Kehrer, "Big Ideas for Your Small Business," *Changing Times,* November 1989, p. 58.

6. Daniel Lyons, "Wool Gatherer," *Forbes,* April 16, 2001, p. 310.

7. Jason Leopold, "Enron But Not Forgotten," *Entrepreneur,* January 2003, p. 63.

8. Douglas Bartholomew, "4 Common Financial Mistakes . . . And How to Avoid Them," *Your Company,* Fall 1991, p. 9.

9. Karen M. Kroll, "Ca$h Wears the Crown," *Industry Week,* May 6, 1996, pp. 16–18.

10. David Armstrong, "The Segway: Bright Idea, Wobbly Business," *Wall Street Journal,* February 12, 2004, pp. B1, B6; "Segway Slump," *FSB,* March 2004, p. 12.

11. Kortney Stringer, "Neither Anthrax Nor the Economy Stops the Fruitcake," *Wall Street Journal,* December 19, 2001, pp. B1, B4; Dirk Smillie, "Signs of Life," *Forbes,* November 11, 2002, p. 160.

12. Sam Walker, "Wardrobe Malfunctions, Inc.," *Wall Street Journal,* February 2, 2007, pp. W1, W12.

13. Ed Engel, "Number One with a Bullet," *Inc.,* April 2002, p. 34.

14. Bartholomew, "4 Common Financial Mistakes . . . And How to Avoid Them," p. 9.

15. Jill Andresky Fraser, "Monitoring Daily Cash Trends," *Inc.,* October 1992, p. 49.

16. George Anders, "Truckers Trials: How One Firm Fights to Save Every Penny As Its Profits Plummet," *Wall Street Journal,* April 13, 1982, pp. 1, 22.

17. Mark Henricks, "Losing Stream," *Entrepreneur,* September 2003, pp. 77–78.

18. C. J. Prince, "Give 'Em Credit," *Entrepreneur,* April 2004, pp. 59–60.

19. Michael Selz, "Big Customers' Late Bills Choke Small Suppliers," *Wall Street Journal,* June 22, 1994, p. B1.

20. Tony Taylor, "Developer's Money Woes Impact Other Businesses," *GSA Business,* November 13, 2006, pp. 1, 6.

21. Richard G.P. McMahon and Scott Holmes, "Small Business Financial Practices in North America: A Literature Review," *Journal of Small Business Management,* April 1991, p. 21.

22. Howard Muson, "Collecting Overdue Accounts," *Your Company,* Spring 1993, p. 4.

23. Elaine Pofeldt, "Collect Calls," *Success,* March 1998, pp. 22–24.

24. Kimberly Stansell, "Tend to the Business of Collecting Your Money," *Inc.,* March 2, 2000, http://www2.inc.com/search/17568. html; Frances Huffman, "Calling to Collect," *Entrepreneur,* September 1993, p. 50.

25. "Collections Information," ACA International, www. acainternational.org/?cid=5431.

26. "Time Shrinks Value of Debts," *Collection,* Winter 1992, p. 1.

27. "Make Them Pay!" *Inc.,* August 2003, p. 50.

28. John Gorham, "Revenge of the Lightweight," *Forbes,* March 6, 2000, p. 54.

29. C. J. Prince, "Vulture Capital," *Entrepreneur,* February 2003, pp. 47–48.

30. Bill Breen, "Living In Dell Time," *Fast Company,* November 2005, p. 86.

31. Jill Andresky Fraser, "How to Get Paid," *Inc.,* March 1992, p. 105.

32. "Copier Toner Scam," Mid-South Better Business Bureau, February 13, 2006, www.midsouth.bbb.org/newsrelease. html?newsid=83&newstype=1; Elizabeth Olson, "When the Check in the Mail Is a Bill," *New York Times,* April 22, 2004, p. C5; "Protect Your Business from Phony Invoices," *GSA Business,* December 4, 2000, p. 28.

33. Crystal Detamore-Rodman, "Cash In, Cash Out," *Entrepreneur,* June 2003, pp. 53–54.

34. William G. Shepherd, Jr., "Internal Financial Strategies," *Venture,* September 1985, p. 68.

35. Roberta Maynard, "Can You Benefit from Barter?" *Nation's Business,* July 1994, p. 6.

36. "33 Ways to Increase Your Cash Flow and Manage Cash Balances," *The Business Owner,* February 1988, p. 8.

37. Carol Pickering, "The Price of Excess," *Business 2.0,* February 6, 2001, pp. 38–42.

38. Kroll, "Ca$h Wears the Crown," pp. 16–18; Lynn Cook, "Requiem for a Business Model," *Forbes,* July 24, 2000, pp. 60–63.

39. Jeffrey Lant, "Cash Is King," *Small Business Reports,* May 1991, p. 49.

40. Kelly K. Spors, "Trade You a Laptop? Online Sites Promote the Art of the Barter," *Wall Street Journal,* November 14, 2006, pp. B1, B5; "Statistics," International Reciprocal Trade Association, www.irta.com/

41. Richard J. Maturi, "Collection Dues and Don'ts," *Entrepreneur,* January 1992, p. 328.

42. "Testimonials," Art of Barter, www.artofbarter.com/testimonials. html.

43. "Overview of the Equipment Leasing and Finance Industry," Equipment Leasing Association, www.elaonline.com/research/ overview.cfm.

44. "Overview of the Equipment Leasing and Finance Industry," Equipment Leasing Association, www.elaonline.com/research/ overview.cfm.

45. Bob Violino, "What's the Deal?" *CFO-IT,* Spring 2004, pp. 15–8.

46. Roger Thompson, "Business Copes with the Recession," *Nation's Business,* January 1991, p. 20.

47. Ibid.

48. Bruce G. Posner, "Skipped Loan Payments," *Inc.,* September 1992, p. 40.

49. Mike Hogan, "Go Retro," *Entrepreneur,* April 2003, pp. 41–42.

50. Michael Russell, "Fraud—Check Fraud Statistics," *Ezine@articles,* January 20, 2006, http://ezinearticles.com/ ?Fraud—Check-Fraud-Statistics&id=131847.

51. Jill Andresky Fraser, "Better Cash Management," *Inc.,* May 1993, p. 42.

52. C.J. Prince, "Money to Burn?" *Entrepreneur,* July 2004, pp. 51–52.

53. Mary Paulsell, "The Problem of Employee Theft," Missouri Small Business Development Centers, October 10, 2002, www. missouribusiness.net/docs/problem_employee_theft.asp.

54. Julia Boorstin, "Alcohol Auditor," *Fortune,* June 27, 2005, p. 40.

55. Robert A. Mamis, "Money In, Money Out," *Inc.,* March 1993, p. 103.

# Chapter 9

1. Ellen Neuborne, "Gag Marketing," *Inc.,* February 2006, pp. 35–36; Judith Blake, "Jones Soda Founder Is Tuned into Youths' Taste," *Seattle Times,* March 10, 2004, http:// www.jonessoda.com/ media_archives/040410%20-%20pop %20psychology.pdf; Melanie Wells, "Cult Brands," *Forbes,* April 16, 2001, pp. 198–205; Victoria Neal, "Gourmet Bubbly," *Entrepreneur,* September 1999, www. entrepreneur.com/Magazines/MA_SegArticle/0,1539, 230624—1-, 00.html; "The Jones Soda Story," Jones Soda Company, www. jonessoda.com/stockstuff/story.html.

2. Joe Crews, "New Products Provide NASCAR Fans Options," *Daytona Beach News-Journal,* February 17, 2007, http:// www. news-journalonline.com/NewsJournalOnline/Speed/Headlines/ racBIZ02NEXT021307.htm; Michael A. Prospero, "On with the Show: NASCAR," *Fast Company,* September 2006, pp. 52–53.

3. Howard Fana Shaw, "Customer Care Checklist," *In Business,* September/October 1987, p. 28.

4. Lynn Rosellini, "The High Life of Crime," *U.S. News & World Report,* November 20, 2000, pp. 76–77.

5. Sara Wilson, "The Lush Life," *Entrepreneur,* December 2006, p. 34; "Fast 50: Go-Getter: Beverage or Bust," *Fast Company,* www.fastcompany.com/fast50_02/ profile/index.html?adler601; Amy Spector, "San Diego-Based Dlush Blends Smoothie, Coffee Concepts," *Nation's Restaurant News,* May 24, 2004, pp.108–110.

6. Jim Jvicala, "Buying Power of U.S. Minorities Continues Upward Climb, Says University of Georgia's Selig Center for Economic

Growth," September 30, 2005, www.terry.uga.edu/news/releases/2005/minority_buying_2005.html.

7. Ryan Chittum, "Buenos Días, Shopper," *Wall Street Journal,* July 19, 2006, pp. B1, B10; Edward Iwata, "Immigrants Courted as Good Customers," *USA Today,* May 11, 2006, p. 3B; Kim T. Gordon, "Se Habla Español?" *Entrepreneur,* June 2003, pp. 83–84; Miriam Jordan, "Hispanic Magazines Gain Ad Dollars," *Wall Street Journal,* March 3, 2004, p. B2.

8. Ryan Chittum, "Buenos Días, Shopper," *Wall Street Journal,* July 19, 2006, pp. B1, B10; Edward Iwata, "Immigrants Courted as Good Customers," *USA Today,* May 11, 2006, p. 3B; "Company Overview," La Curacao, www.lacuracao.net/english/overview.htm.

9. Kimberly L. McCall, "Fielding Questions," *Entrepreneur,* September 2001, pp. 14–15.

10. Kim Komando, "Three Reasons to Use Online Customer Surveys," Microsoft Small Business Center, www.microsoft.com/smallbusiness/resources/marketing/market_research/3_reasons_to_use_online_customer_surveys.mspx.

11. Damon Brown, "Online Customer Surveys for Small Business," *Inc. Technology,* December 2006, http:// technology.inc.com/internet/articles/200612/onlinesurveys.html.

12. Avery Johnson, "Hotels Take 'Know Your Customer' to New Level," *Wall Street Journal,* February 7, 2006, pp. D1, D3.

13. Shari Caudron, "Right on Target," *Industry Week,* September 2, 1996, p. 45.

14. Michael Meltzer, "Using Data Mining on the Road to Successful BI," *Data Mining Review,* October 2004, www.dmreview.com/editorial/newsletter_article.cfm?nl=bireport&articleId=1011392&issue=20082; "About Us," Henry Singer Fashion Group, www.henrysinger.com/company/index.asp.

15. Thomas Mucha, "The Builder of Boomtown," *Business 2.0,* September 2005, http://money.cnn.com/magazines/business2/business2_archive/2005/09/01/8356515/index.htm; Josephine Lee, "If You Build It, They Will Make You Rich," *Forbes,* November 10, 2003, pp. 130–132.

16. Nick Wreden, "From Customer Satisfaction to Customer Loyalty," *Beyond Computing,* January/February 1999, pp. 12–14.

17. Liz Welch, "Jalem Getz," *Inc.,* October 2006, p. 82; Eric Decker, "Costume Jewelry," *Small Business Times,* April 14, 2006, www.biztimes.com/news/2006/4/14/costume-jewelry.

18. Roberta Maynard, "Rich Niches," *Nation's Business,* November 1993, p. 41.

19. Dale D. Buss, "Entertailing," *Nation's Business,* December 1997, p. 18.

20. Ibid., pp. 12–18.

21. "Hot Growth Special Report: Build-A-Bear Workshop," *Business Week,* June 5, 2006, www.businessweek.com/hot_growth/2006/company/40.htm; Allison Fass, "Bear Market," *Forbes,* March 1, 2004, p. 88; Elizabeth Goodgold, "Talking Shop," *Entrepreneur,* September 2003, pp. 62–65; Sharon Nelton, "Building an Empire One Smile at a Time," *Success,* September 2000, pp. 34–37; Teresa F. Lindeman, "Former Payless Chief Hits Pay Dirt with Build-A-Bear," *Post-Gazette.com,* www.post-gazette.com/businessnews/20010803bears0803bnp1.asp.

22. Sara Wilson, "Getting Personal," *Entrepreneur,* March 2006, p. 71; "Who Are We?" Title Nine, www. titlenine.com/jump.jsp?itemID=220&itemType= CATEGORY&path=1%2C3.

23. April Y. Pennington, "Firm Foundation," *Entrepreneur,* July 2006, p. 38.

24. Dave Sifry, "Blog Usage Statistics and Trends," *MasterNewMedia,* November 8, 2006, www.masternewmedia.org/news/2006/11/08/blog_usage_ statistics_and_trends.htm.

25. John Nardini, "Create a Blog to Boost Your Business," *Entrepreneur,* September 27, 2005, www.entrepreneur.com/article/0,4621,323598,00.html.

26. Cullen Poythress, "MySpace Marketing," *Transworld Business Magazine,* May 11, 2005, www.twsbiz.com/twbiz/features/article/0,21214,1060360,00.html.

27. "Network-based Marketing: Using Existing Customers to Help Sell to New Ones," *Knowledge@Wharton,* January 10, 2007, http://knowledge.wharton.upenn.edu/ article.cfm?articleid=1637&CFID=3117765.

28. Liz Welch, "Jalem Getz," *Inc.,* October 2006, p. 82; Eric Decker, "Costume Jewelry," *Small Business Times,* April 14, 2006, www.biztimes.com/news/2006/4/14/costume-jewelry.

29. Joseph R. Garber, "Know Your Customer," *Forbes,* February 10, 1997, p. 128.

30. Jenny C. McCune, "Becoming a Customer-Driven Company," *Beyond Computing,* May 2000, pp. 18–24.

31. David J. Wallace, "e=crm$^2$," *Small Business Computing,* November 2000, pp. 55–57.

32. "Beware Dissatisfied Cosumers: They Like to Blab," *Knowledge@Wharton,* March 9, 2006, http://knowledge.wharton.upenn.edu/index.cfm?fa= printArticle&ID=1422.

33. "Ways and Means," *Reader's Digest,* January 1993, p. 56.

34. "Encourage Customers to Complain," *Small Business Reports,* June 1990, p. 7.

35. Dave Zielinski, "Improving Service Doesn't Require a Big Investment," *Small Business Reports,* February 1991, p. 20.

36. Brian Caufield, "How to Win Customer Loyalty," *Business 2.0,* March 2004, pp. 77–78.

37. Susan Greco, "Fanatics," *Inc.,* April 2001, pp. 36–48.

38. Ibid.

39. Rahul Jacob, "Why Some Customers Are More Equal Than Others," *Fortune,* September 19, 1994, pp. 215–224.

40. Robert B. Tucker, "Earn Your Customers' Loyalty," Economics Press Techniques, Strategies, and Inspiration for the Sales Professional, www.epic.co/SALES/selltips.htm#earn_loyalty.

41. Patricia Sellers, "Companies That Serve You Best," *Fortune,* May 31, 1993, p. 75.

42. Willian A. Sherden, "The Tools of Retention," *Small Business Reports,* November 1994, pp. 43–47.

43. Richard Stone, "Retaining Customers Requires Constant Contact," *Small Business Computing,* January 11, 2005, www.smallbusinesscomputing.com/biztools/print.pho/3457221.

44. Patricia Neale, "John Ratzenberger's 'Made in America' Season Premiere Features Allen Edmonds Shoe Corporation," Company Press Release, November 21, 2005, www.allenedmonds.com/wcsstore/AllenEdmonds/about/Made%20in%20America%20PR%2011.21.05.pdf.

45. Ibid.

46. Faye Rice, "How to Deal with Tougher Customers," *Fortune,* December 3, 1990, pp. 39–40.

47. Rahul Jacobs, "TQM: More Than a Dying Fad," *Fortune,* October 18, 1993, p. 67.

48. Ibid.

49. Kim Clark, "Customer Disservice," *U.S. News & World Report,* August 18/August 25, 2003, pp. 28–38.

50. Mina Kimes, "Kind Cuts for a Dot-Com Stylist," *FSB,* November 2006, p. 21.

51. Karen Edwards, "Shop and Go," *Entrepreneur,* June 2006, p. 97.

52. Paul Lukas, "Whither the Checkout Girl?" *Fast Company,* November 2006, pp. 50–52.

53. Emily Nelson, "Marketers Push Individual Portions and Families Bite," *Wall Street Journal,* July 23, 2002, pp. A1, A6.

54. Lucy McCauley, "Measure What Matters," *Fast Company,* May 1999, p. 100.

55. Mike Doherty, "The Best vs. the Rest," *Innovation.net,* November 1, 2004, http://venture2.typepad.com/innovationnet/2004/11/the_best_vs_the.html.

56. "William Rees Instruments: A Snapshot of Small Business Innovation and Entrepreneurship," *Where America Stands: Entrepreneurship Competitiveness Index,* Council on Competitiveness, February 2007, www.compete.org/pdf/ew_deeper_dive.pdf, p. 6; "The Scoop," Harpsicle Harp Company, http://harpsicleharps.com/.

57. *Where America Stands: Entrepreneurship Competitiveness Index,* Council on Competitiveness, February 2007, www.compete.org/pdf/ew_deeper_dive.pdf, p. 4.

58. Michael Schrage, "Getting Beyond the Innovation Fetish," *Fortune,* November 13, 2000, p. 230.

59. Joseph R. Mancuso, "How Callaway Runs His Idea Factory," *Your Company,* April/May 1997, p. 72.

60. Alan Deutschman, "America's Fastest Risers," *Fortune,* October 7, 1991, p. 58.

61. Jonathan Karp, "Hey, You! How About Lunch?" *Wall Street Journal,* April 1, 2004, pp. B1, B5.

62. Gwen Moran, "Power to the People," *Entrepreneur,* June 2006, pp. 21–24.

63. Matthew Maier, "Home Sweet Home Networking," *Business 2.0,* February 2003, pp. 23–24.
64. Roberta Maynard, "The Heat Is On," *Nation's Business,* October 1997, p. 14–23.
65. Greco, "Fanatics," p. 38.
66. "Poor Customer Service Causes Churn," *Sales & Marketing Management Magazine's Performance Newsletter,* August 21, 2006, p. 1.
67. Angela R. Garber, "Hook, Line, and Sinker," *Small Business Computing,* February 2000, pp. 41–42.
68. Richard Gibson, "Can I Get a Smile with My Burger and Fries?" *Wall Street Journal,* September 23, 2003, p. D6.
69. Chris Penttila, "Brand Awareness," *Entrepreneur,* September 2001, pp. 49–51.
70. Thomas A. Stewart, "After All You've Done for Your Customers, Why Are They Still NOT HAPPY?" *Fortune,* December 11, 1995, pp. 178–182; Gile Gerretsen, "Special Tools Are Used by Super Markets," *Upstate Business,* June 14, 1998, p. 4.
71. Anne Fisher, "For Happier Customers, Call HR," *Fortune,* November 28, 2005, p. 272.
72. Debbie Salinsky, "Insanely Great Customer Service," *Success,* September 2000, p. 61.
73. Peter Sanders, "Takin' Off the Ritz—A Tad," *Wall Street Journal,* June 23, 2006, pp. B1, B3; Brian Caufield, "How to Win Customer Loyalty," *Business 2.0,* March 2004, pp. 77–78.
74. Elena Malykhina, "Pocket PCs on a Mission," *Information Week,* February 20, 2006, p. 60.
75. Jennifer Saranow, "Selling the Special Touch," *Wall Street Journal,* July 18, 2006, pp. B1, B8.
76. Brian Dumaine, "How Managers Can Succeed Through Speed," *Fortune,* February 13, 1989, pp. 54–59.
77. Mark Henricks, "Time Is Money," *Entrepreneur,* February 1993, p. 44.
78. Kerry A. Dolan, "Speed: the New X Factor," *Forbes,* December 26, 2005, pp. 74–7; Fred Vogelstein, "Mastering the Art of Disruption," *Fortune,* February 6, 2006, pp. 23–24.
79. Julie Sloane, "Play Big," *FSB,* November 2006, pp. 26–36.
80. "Forrester Research U.S. E-Commerce Forecast: Online Retail Sales to Reach $329 Billion by 2010," *CRM Today,* September 20, 2005, www.crm2day.com/news/crm/115557.php.
81. Radhika Praveen, "Study: Poor Web Sites Lose Business," *Small Business IT World,* June 16, 2006, http:// smallbusiness.itworld.com/4408/060616poorwebsites/pfindex.html.
82. Stanley J. Winkelman, "Why Big Name Stores Are Losing Out," *Fortune,* May 8, 1989, pp. 14–15.
83. "Soft-Wired," *Fast Company,* July/August 2006, p. 107; Evan Blass, "Thomas Pink's iPod-Concealing Commuter Shirt," *Engadget,* May 12, 2006, www.engadget.com/2006/05/12/thomas-pinks-ipod-concealing-commuter-shirt/.
84. Tim Carvell, "Shorts Circuit," *Fortune,* February 6, 2006, p. 116.
85. "Silly Putty History 101," www.sillyputty.com/history_101/history101.htm.
86. Brett Nelson, "Fore!-Boding," *Forbes,* April 14, 2003, p. 60.
87. Alyssa Danigelis, "Party On," *Fast Company,* May 2006, p. 30.
88. Speech by Doris Christopher given at the United States Association for Small Business and Entrepreneurship Annual Conference, Orlando, Florida, January 12, 2007; "Company Facts," The Pampered Chef, www.pamperedchef.com/our_company/statistics.html; Danigelis, "Party On," p. 30.
89. Lynn Cook, "How Sweet It Is," *Forbes,* March 1, 2004, pp. 90–92; "About Blue Bell," Blue Bell Creameries, http:// www.bluebell.com/about.htm.

# Chapter 10

1. Lin Grensing-Pophal, "Who Are You?" *Business Start-Ups,* September 1997, pp. 38–44.
2. Meg Whittemore, "PR on a Shoestring," *Nation's Business,* January 1991, p. 31.
3. Sara Wilson, "Learning from the Best: Coffee 101," *Entrepreneur,* March 2006, p. 64.
4. Eilene Zimmerman, "Big Marlin, Big Money," *FSB,* October 2006, pp. 104–110.
5. Debra Phillips, "Fast Track," *Entrepreneur,* April 1999, p. 42.
6. Elaine Appleton Grant, "A Token Strategy," *Inc.,* May 2006, www.inc.com/magazine/20060501/priority-promos.html.
7. Joanna L. Krotz, "'Cause Marketing' Tips: Boost Business by Giving Back," Microsoft Small Business Center, www.microsoft.com/smallbusiness/resources/marketing/advertising_branding/cause_marketing_tips_boost_business_by_giving_back.mspx.
8. Peggy Linial, "Small Business and Cause Related Marketing: Getting Started," Cause Marketing Forum, www. causemarketingforum.com/framemain. asp?ID=189.
9. Catharine Livingston and Gordy Megrose, "Adventure Altruism: Giving Large," *Outside Online,* January 2006, http://outside.away.com/outside/altruism.html.
10. Barry Farber, "Sales Shape-Up," *Entrepreneur,* August 2006, p. 72.
11. Barbara K. Mednick, "Behavior Counts in Sales," *Minneapolis St. Paul Star Tribune,* May 28, 2004, http:// www.startribune.com/working.
12. "Most Salespeople Can't Sell," *Small Business Reports,* September 1990, p. 10.
13. Eric Anderson and Bob Trinkle, *Outsourcing the Sales Function: The Real Cost of Field Sales* (Mason, OH: Thomson Publishing, 2005) p. 8.
14. "Salespeople Don't Prep Enough for Calls," *Sales & Marketing Management's Performance Newsletter,* December 12, 2005, p. 2.
15. Norm Brodsky, "Keep Your Customers," *Inc.,* September 2006, pp. 57–58.
16. Sara Wilson, "All Systems Yo," *Entrepreneur,* February 2007, p. 38; "About Us," Pinkberry, www.pinkberry.com.
17. Jennifer Alsever, "Flying Off the Shelves," *Business 2.0,* December 2006, pp. 47–49.
18. "In a Flash: Data Storage Makers Step Up Sponsorship Activity," *IEG Sponsorship Report,* March 13, 2006, p. 7.
19. Solano Avenue Events and News, www.solanoavenueassn.org/scut_past/scut04_7.html.
20. Kim T, Gordon, "Tips for Event Sponsorship," *Entrepreneur,* March 2006, www.entrepreneur.com/magazine/entrepreneur/2006/march/83672.html.
21. Sara K. Goo, "Apple Gets Big Slice of Product Placement Pie," *Washington Post,* April 15, 2006, www.washingtonpost.com/wp-dyn/content/article/2006/04/14/AR2006041401670.html.
22. "And Now a Word from Our Sponsor . . ." Media Awareness Network, www.media-awareness.ca/english/resources/educational/teachable_moments/word_from_our_sponsor.cfm.
23. "Advertisers Chase News Consumers," *Sales and Marketing Management's Manage Smarter Newsletter,* March 5, 2007, p. 1.
24. Steven Ratner, "Red All Over," *Wall Street Journal,* February 15, 2007, p. A19.
25. *Radio Marketing Guide and Fact Book,* Radio (New York: Radio Advertising Bureau, 2006), pp. 4–6.
26. Paul R. La Monica, "Superbowl Ads Through the Ages," *CNN/Money,* February 1, 2007, http://money.cnn.com/2007/02/01/news/funny/superbowlads_history/index.htm; "Industry Statistics," National Cable and Telecommunications Association, June 2007, www.ncta.com/Statistic/Statistic/Statistics.aspx.
27. Darren Dahl, "TV Advertising for the Rest of Us," *Inc.,* June 2006, pp. 48–50.
28. "Media Trends Track," Television Bureau of Advertising, www.tvb.org/nav/build_frameset.asp.
29. Ibid.
30. "Television and Health," The Sourcebook for Teaching Science, www.csun.edu/science/health/docs/tv&health.html.
31. "AAF: MySpace and YouTube, Yes; Blogs, Not Really Very Much," June 13, 2006, www.resonancepartnership.com/resonance_partnership/buzz_marketing.html.

32. "Average U.S. Home Now Receives a Record 104.2 Channels, According to Nielsen," *PR Newswire,* March 19, 2007, http://sev. prnewswire.com/television/20070319/NYM16319032007-1.html.

33. "Viewers Warm to Infomercials," *B&T,* March 8, 2007, www. bandt.com.au/news/2A/0C04A42A.asp.

34. Don Debelak, "Put a Lid on It!" *Entrepreneur,* December 2005, www.entrepreneur.com/startingabusiness/inventing/ distributionandlicensing/article81080.html.

35. Karen E. Spaeder, "Beyond the Big Idea," *Entrepreneur,* October 2004, www.entrepreneur.com/magazine/entrepreneur/ 2004/october/72624.html.

36. *The Magazine Handbook: A Comprehensive Guide 2006/07* (New York: Magazine Publishers of America, 2007), pp. 6, 57.

37. Ibid., p. 23.

38. "Historical Advertising/Editorial Ratios," American Society of Magazine Editors, www.magazine.org/editorial/editorial_ trends_and_magazine_handbook/15539.cfm.

39. POPAI Library, Point-of-Purchase Advertising International, www. popai.com/Content/NavigationMenu/Resources/Research/ Research.htm.

40. "Facts & Figures," Outdoor Advertising Association of America, www.oaaa.org/outdoor/facts/.

41. "Case Studies: Bennett Infiniti Inc.," Outdoor Advertising Association of America, www.oaaa.org/images/upload/research/ 200312916163668014966.pdf.

42. American Fact Finder, U.S. Census Bureau, http://factfinder. census.gov/servlet/ADPTable?_bm=y&-geo_id=01000US&- qr_name=ACS_2005_EST_G00_DP3&-gc_url=null&- ds_name=&-_lang=en&-redoLog=false.

43. "Why Mobile Ads," MobileMetroMedia, 2007, http:// mobilemetromedia.com/benefits_mobile_ads.html.

44. *Arbitron National In-Car Study* (New York: Arbitron Inc/Edison Media Research, December 2003), p. 2, www.oaaa.org/pdf/ Incarstudy_summary.pdf.

45. "Special Report: Catalog Marketing," *Direct,* July 26, 2005, http:// directmag.com/exclusive/specialreports/2005_05_20_especial_ report/.

46. "Mail Moves America," *NPES News,* April 2007, p. 5, www.npes. org/news/newsapril07.pdf.

47. "Direct Mail Tips for Manufacturers' Letters," Koch Group, www. kochgroup.com/directmail.html.

48. "Mail Moves America," *NPES News,* p. 5.

49. *DMA 2006 Response Rate Trends* (New York: Direct Marketing Association, 2006), p. 8.

50. "Success Stories: Dartmouth Pharmaceuticals," U.S. Postal Service, www.usps.com/directmail/dartmouthpharmaceuticals.htm; "Company Info," Dartmouth Pharmaceuticals, www.ilovemynails. com/elonhome.html.

51. Amanda Kooser, "The Basics of Local Online Advertising," *Entrepreneur,* March 2007, www.entrepreneur.com/marketing/ onlinemarketing/article174700.html; "Customer Showcase: Blonde Bear Bed & Breakfast," *MerchantCircle,* www.merchantcircle. com/corporate/showcase/blonde-bear-bed-and-breakfast.html.

52. Joanna L. Krotz, "Rise to the Top of Search Results," *bCentral,* www.bcentral.com/articles/krotz/110.asp?.

53. Shuman Ghosemajumber, "Why Third-Party Click Fraud Estimates Don't Add Up," January 31, 2007, Shumans.com, http:// shumans.com/articles/000048.php.

54. "Worldwide Daily E-mail Traffic Climbs to 171 Billion, Spam Rises to 71 Percent, Says Radicati Group," Tekrati Weblog, May 9, 2006, http://weblog.tekrati.com/?p=1546.

55. Ibid.

56. "Spa Relies on E-mail Marketing to Fill Appointments," *Constant Contact,* www.constantcontact.com/email-marketing-success/ case-studies/balance-spa.jsp.

57. Skip Cox, "The Unique Value of Exhibitions in Accelerating the Sales Process," Exhibition Surveys, presented at the Exhibition and Convention Executives Forum, June 15, 2006, www.exhibit surveys.com/files/File/whitepapers/AcceleratingSalesProcess.pdf.

58. Max Chafkin, "Ads and Atmospherics: Outdoor Campaigns Are Suddenly Hip," *Inc.,* February 2007, pp. 39–41; Jennifer Pollock, "Can Your Banner Ad Do This?" *Fast Company,* July/August 2006, p. 51; Sara Wilson, "Hawking on Eggshells," *Entrepreneur,* February 2007, p. 75.

59. Suzanne Vranica, "Hangar Ads Ensure Message Gets Home," *Wall Street Journal,* March 12, 2007, p. B4.

60. Steven Heller, "Going Overground," *Metropolis,* March 14, 2007, www.metropolismag.com/cda/ story.php?artid=2557.

# Chapter 11

1. Christopher T. Heun, "Dynamic Pricing Boosts Bottom Line," *Information Week,* October 29, 2001, www.informationweek.com/ story/showArticle.jhtml?articleID=6507202.

2. "Study: New Motor Vehicle Sales, Year in Review," *The Daily,* April 23, 2007, www.statcan.ca/Daily/English/070423/d070423a. htm; Sue Zesiger Callaway, "Bachelor Meets Bugatti," *Fortune,* March 19, 2007, pp. 214–216.

3. Rick Bruns, "Tips for Coping with Rising Costs of Key Commodities," *Fast Company,* December 1997, pp. 27–30.

4. Rick Brooks, "More Businesses Slap on Fuel Fees," *Wall Street Journal,* May 4, 2006, pp. D1, D2; GiddyUp Fishing Charters, www.captgiddyup.net/.

5. Jeffrey A. Trachtenberg, "Borders Slashes Buyer Rewards, Cuts Discounts," *Wall Street Journal,* March 28, 2007, pp. D1, D4.

6. "Gas Prices Could Affect the Price of Pizzas, Flowers," *Greenville News,* April 29, 2006, p. 3A.

7. Jeannie Mandelker, "Pricing Right from the Start," *Profit,* September/October 1996, p. 20.

8. Kate Dubose Tomassi, "Southwest Best Prepared for Rising Fuel Prices," *Forbes,* July 19, 2006, www.forbes.com/markets/2006/07/ 19/southwest-airlines-markets06.html.

9. Stacy Meichtry, "What Your Time Is Really Worth," *Wall Street Journal,* April 7–8, 2007, pp, P1, P4, P5; Adam McCollum, "The Big Time," *Forbes Life,* September 18, 2006, http://members. forbes.com/fyi/2006/0918/114.html.

10. Michael V. Marn, Eric V. Roegner, and Craig C. Zawada, "Pricing New Products," *The McKinsey Quarterly,* Number 3, 2003, www. mckinseyquarterly.com/ article_ abstract.aspx?ar=1329&l2= 16&l3=19&srid=190&gp=0.

11. Jeff Shulman and Richard Miniter, "Discounting Is No Bargain," *Wall Street Journal,* September 18, 2002, p. A30.

12. Elizabeth Bernstein, "Shopping Around," *Wall Street Journal,* March 23, 2006, p. D3; Lauren Young, "Bugaboo Leaps Past Frog," *Business Week,* August 31, 2005, www.bugaboo.com; Kate Bonamici, "The Latest Fashion: Kid Stuff Goes Mod," *Fortune,* November 28, 2005, p. 45; "Cameleon," Bugaboo, www.bugaboo.com/; Susanna Hamner, "Baby Got Bucks," *Business 2.0,* March 2006, p. 62.

13. Nadine Heintz, "Flexing Your Pricing Muscles," *Inc.,* February 2004, p. 25.

14. Andy Patrizio, "Price Competition Hurt Intel Sales in 2006," *Internet News,* March 16, 2007, www.internetnews.com/bus-news/ article.php/3666291; "Price War Burdens Global Chip Sales," *CNNMoney,* April 17, 2007, http://money.cnn.com/2007/04/30/ technology/chip_ prices.reut/index.htm.

15. Richard Gibson, "Big Price Cut at McDonald's Seems a McFlop," *Wall Street Journal,* May 9, 1997, pp. B1, B2; Richard Gibson, "Prices Tumble on Big Macs, But Fries Rise," *Wall Street Journal,* April 25, 1997, pp. B1, B2; Cliff Edwards, "Some McDonald's Franchisees Quietly Boosting Prices to Offset Cost of Promotion," *Greenville News,* April 26, 1997, p. 8D.

16. Alison Stein Wellner, "Boost Your Bottom Line by Taking the Guesswork Out of Pricing," *Inc.,* June 2005, p. 78.

17. Joshua Hyatt, "For You? Our Special Price," *Inc.,* March 2006, p. 110.

18. Ibid, p. 80.

19. Norm Brodsky, "Dealing with Cost Hikes," *Inc.,* August 2005, p. 49.

20. Carolyn Z. Lawrence, "The Price Is Right," *Entrepreneur,* October 1994, p. 54.

21. Gladys Edmunds, "Price Is Right? Not If It's Too Low," *USA Today,* June 8, 2005, www.usatoday.com/money/smallbusiness/columnist/edmunds/2005-06-08-price_x.htm.

22. Rachel Dodes and Cheryl Lu-Lien Tan, "What Price Beauty? Costly Face Creams Lift Prices, Spirits," *Wall Street Journal,* December 19, 2006, pp. A1, A12.

23. "Dynamic Pricing: DVD vs. CD Strategies," *The Big Picture,* http://bigpicture.typepad.com/comments/2005/03/dynamic_pricing.html.

24. Raymund Flandez, "Small Makers of Children's DVDs Unite to Take on Big Rival," *Wall Street Journal,* February 6, 2007, p. B4.

25. "City Swingers," *Forbes Life,* September 2006, p. 30; "Swing Set," *Men's Vogue,* April 2007, www.mensvogue.com/health/regimen/articles/2007/04/drive_495.

26. Hiroshi Suzuki, "Nintendo's Japan Wii Sales Double Those of Sony's PlayStation 3," *Bloomberg News,* April 2, 2007, www.bloomberg.com/apps/news?pid=conewsstory&refer=conews&tkr=NTDOY:US&sid=a_A5anLn.xE8; Brian Bremmer, "Will Nintendo's Wii Strategy Score?" *Business Week,* September 20, 2006, www.businessweek.com/globalbiz/content/sep2006/gb20060920_163780.htm; Kathleen Sanders and Casamassina, "U.S. Wii Price, Launch Date Revealed," *IGN Entertainment,* September 13, 2006, http://wii.ign.com/articles/732/732669p1.html;

"Playing a Different Game," *Economist,* October 26, 2006, www.economist.com/business/displaystory.cfm?story_id=8080787.

27. David Worrell, "Time Well Spent," *Entrepreneur,* June 2006, p. 63.

28. *"Frontline: Secret History of the Credit Card,"* PBS, www.pbs.org/cgi-registry/generic/trivia.cgi; Mark Brinker, "Credit Card Debt Statistics," June 2007, Hoffman, Brinker, and Roberts, www.hoffmanbrinker.com/credit-card-debt-statistics.html.

29. *Credit Card Practices: Fees, Interest, and Grace Periods,* United States Senate Committee on Homeland Security and Government Affairs, March 7, 2007, http://hsgac.senate.gov/_files/OPENINGLEVINwithExhibits.pdf; Carly Zander, "Federal Reserve Releases New Statistics about Credit Cards, Reports Lowcards.com," *Send2Press,* March 2, 2006, www.send2press.com/newswire/2006-03-0302-002.shtml.

30. "Credit Counseling Statistics," Consumer Credit Counseling Service, http://creditcounselingbiz.com/credit_counseling_statistics.htm.

31. "Statistics for General and Online Card Fraud," *ePayNews,* www.epaynews.com/statistics/fraud.html.

32. Michael Bloch, "Preventing Credit Card Chargebacks—Anti-Fraud Strategies," *Taming the Beast,* www.tamingthebeast.net/articles2/card-fraud-strategies.htm.

# Chapter 12

1. International Business Owners Survey 2006: Key Findings, Grant Thornton, June 2006, www.international businessreport.com/main/index1.php?page=14&lang=en&id=120811&country_id=0; "U.S. Business Embraces Global Growth," *Sales & Marketing Management's Performance Newsletter,* October 15, 2006, p. 1.

2. Michael V. Copeland, "The Mighty Micro-Multinational," *Business 2.0,* July 2006, pp. 106–114.

3. "Company Background," Elk River, Inc., www.elkriver.com/html/about_us.html; "University-Government Partnership Helps Local Small Businesses Export," Alabama International Trade Center, www.aitc.ua.edu/images/AITC&%;20Success&%;20Stories&%%;20ElkRiver.pdf.

4. *International Trade Statistics 2006: World Merchandise Exports by Region and Selected Economy,* World Trade Organization, www.wto.org/english/res_e/statis_e/its2006_e/its06_overview_e.pdf, p. 28.

5. Robyn Meredith with Suzanne Hoppough, "Why Globalization Is Good," *Forbes,* April 16, 2007, pp. 64–68.

6. Lowell L. Bryan and Jane N. Fraser, "Getting to Global," *The McKinsey Quarterly,* Number 4, 1999, pp. 1–9; Bradford W. Ketchum, "Going Global: East Asia-Pacific Rim," *Inc.,* May 20, 1997, Special Advertising Section.

7. Jack Stack with Bo Burlingham, "My Awakening," *Inc.,* April 2007, pp. 93–97.

8. Leigh Buchanan, "Going Global," *Inc.,* April 2007, p. 91.

9. Ted Miller, "Can America Compete in the Global Economy?" *Kiplinger's Personal Finance Magazine,* November 1991, p. 8.

10. Bernard Wysocki, Jr., "Going Global In The New World," *Wall Street Journal,* September 21, 1990, p. R3.

11. Michael V. Copeland, "The Mighty Micro-Multinational," *Business 2.0,* July 2006, pp. 106–114.

12. Riva Richmond, "Entrepreneurs with Big Dreams Tap Global Market," *Wall Street Journal,* April 17, 2007, p. B6.

13. Andy Raskin, "How to Bulletproof Your Product (Hint: Take It to Japan)," *Business 2.0,* September 2003, p. 54.

14. *Economic Report of the President* (Washington, DC: U.S. Government Printing Office, 2007), p. 169.

15. "Globesmanship," *Across The Board,* January/February 1990, p. 26.

16. Michael Barrier, "Why Small Looms Large in The Global Economy," *Nation's Business,* February 1994, p. 9; Vivian Pospisil, "Global Paradox: Small is Powerful," *Industry Week,* July 18, 1994, p. 29.

17. Michael Barrier, "A Global Reach For Small Firms," *Nation's Business,* April 1994, p. 66.

18. Jeremy Main, "How To Go Global—And Why," *Fortune,* August 8, 1989, p. 70.

19. Janelle Elms, "Go Global," *Entrepreneur,* September 2006, pp. 130–131.

20. "Think Global," Kentucky World Trade Center, July 14, 2006, www.kwtc.org/enews/071406/eleven.htm; "About Us," IMPEX, www.rgrana.com/about.htm; "About Arch Environmental," Arch Environmental, www.aeec.com/Help/About.aspx.

21. Nichole L. Torres, "Biz 101," *Entrepreneur,* October 2006, p. 124.

22. Joseph E. Pattison, "Global Joint Ventures," *Overseas Business,* Winter 1990, p. 25.

23. Polly Larson, "Opening Doors to Emerging Markets," International Franchise Association, www.ifa.org/intl/News/Prjf6.asp.

24. "Impart Media Group Announces Plans for a Joint Venture in China," *Yahoo! Finance,* May 17, 2007, http://biz.yahoo.com/iw/070517/0254299.html.

25. Patrick J. Sauer, "Update: Firing Up Sales," *Inc.,* September 2006, www.inc.com/magazine/20060901/handson-casestudy-update.html.

26. "California Pizza Kitchen Inks Franchise Deal for Mexico," *Pizza Marketplace,* February 16, 2007, www.pizzamarketplace.com/article.php?id=6855&prc=133&page=114; "Company Overview," California Pizza Kitchen, www.cpk.com/company_information/company_overview.aspx.

27. Howard Dahl, "How I Did It," *Inc.,* April 2007, pp. 102–105.

28. Elizabeth Clark, *Small and Medium-Sized Exporting Companies: A Statistical Handbook,* International Trade Administration, Office of Trade and Industry Information (Washington, DC: U.S. Government Printing Office, 2005), p. 2.

29. Elizabeth Clark, *Small and Medium-Sized Exporting Companies: A Statistical Handbook,* International Trade Administration, Office of Trade and Industry Information (Washington, DC: U.S. Government Printing Office, 2005), p. 1; Elizabeth Wasserman, "Happy Birthday, WTO?" *Inc.,* January 2005, pp. 21–23; C. J. Prince, "Foreign Affairs," *Entrepreneur,* March 2005, pp. 56–58.

30. Geoff Williams, "It's a Small World After All," *Entrepreneur,* May 2004, pp. 39–43; Kurlantzick, "Stay Home?" pp. 58–59; Clark, *Small and Medium-Sized Exporting Companies: A Statistical Handbook,* p. 1.

31. Paul C. Hsu, "Profiting From a Global Mind-Set," *Nation's Business,* June 1994, p. 6.

32. David Newton, "Shipping News," *Entrepreneur,* February 2004, p. 22.

33. "Success Stories: J&N Enterprises," Indiana Small Business Development Center, www.isbdc.org/ default.aspx?action=SuccessStories&id=29.

34. Jan Alexander, "To Sell Well Overseas, Customize," *Your Company,* Fall 1995, p. 15.

35. Kurlantzick, "Stay Home?," pp. 58–59.

36. Frances Huffman, "Hello, World!" *Entrepreneur,* August 1990, p. 108.

37. *Foresight 2020: Economic, Industry, and Corporate Trends,* Economist Intelligence Unit, *The Economist,* 2006, p. 7.

38. Alexander, "To Sell Well Overseas, Customize," p. 15.

39. Eric Decker, "The Art of the Trade Mission," *Small Business Times,* June 8, 2007, www.biztimes.com/news/2007/6/8/the-art-of-the-trade-mission.

40. "Trade Missions Testimonials," Automation Alley, www.automationalley.com/autoalley/International+Business+Center/Trade+Missions/Testimonials.htm; "Past Missions," Automation Alley, www.automationalley.com/autoalley/International+Business+Center/Trade+Missions/Past+Missions/China2002.htm.

41. "Featured Companies: Annual Report 2006," Export-Import Bank, www.exim.gov/about/reports/ar/ar2006/PTSI.pdf, p. 7.

42. Charlotte Mulhern, "Fast Forward," *Entrepreneur,* October 1997, p. 34.

43. Daniel Kaufmann and Shang-Jin Wei, "Does 'Grease Money' Speed Up the Wheels of Commerce?" World Bank, www.worldbank.org/wbi/governance/pdf/grease.pdf.

44. *International Business Attitudes to Corruption,* Simmons & Simmons, 2006, p. 7.

45. Leigh Buchanan, "Six Ways to Open an Office Overseas," *Inc.,* April 2007, www.inc.com/magazine/20070401/features-six-ways-open-office-overseas.html.

46. "More Reliability, Less Potholes," Fieldglass, November 8, 2004, www.fieldglass.com/news/11_8_04_MoreLess_Purchasing.htm.

47. Jim Hopkins, "To Start Up Here, Companies Hire Over There," *USA Today,* February 11, 2005, www. usatoday.com/money/economy/employment/2005-02-10-offshore-usat_x.htm.

48. Sheree R. Curry, "A Shore Thing?" *Entrepreneur,* June 2005, www.entrepreneur.com/magazine/entrepreneur/2005/june/77748.html.

49. Mark Henricks, "The New China?" *Entrepreneur,* February 2006, pp. 17–18.

50. "Total Merchandise and Service Trade," World Trade Organization, http://stat.wto.org/StatisticalProgram/ WSDBViewData.aspx?Language=E.

51. *The Economic Effects of Significant U.S. Import Restraints, Fifth Update,* United States International Trade Commission

(Washington, DC: U.S. Government Printing Office, February 2007), http://hotdocs.usitc.gov/docs/pubs/332/pub3906.pdf, p. xvii.

52. John Fischer, "Will Chinese Quotas Pinch?" *Multichannel Merchant,* June 26, 2005, http://multichannelmerchant.com/mag/chinese_quotas_pinch/.

53. Paula L. Miller, "Reeling in China's Movie Fans," *China Business Review,* March 1, 2007, www.chinabusinessreview.com/public/0703/miller.html.

54. "China TV Exporter in Dispute with Its U.S. Distributor," *All Business,* January 3, 2005, www.allbusiness.com/retail-trade/4299402-1.html; "Antidumping Disputes," Institute for International Economics, pp. 73–74.

55. Michelle Tsai, "Shanghai Surprises: The Perils of Opening an Office in China," *Inc.,* March 2007, pp. 47–49.

56. John L. Graham and N. Mark Lam, "The Chinese Negotiation," *Harvard Business Review,* October 2003, p. 87.

57. Stephen J. Simurda, "Trade Secrets," *Entrepreneur,* May 1994, p. 120.

58. Edward T. Hall, "The Silent Language of Overseas Business," *Harvard Business Review,* May–June 1960, pp. 5–14.

59. Ibid.

60. Lawrence Van Gelder, "It Pays to Watch Words, Gestures While Abroad," *Greenville News,* April 7, 1996, p. 8E.

61. Anton Piéch, "Speaking in Tongues," *Inc.,* June 2003, p. 50.

62. Anton Piéch, "Lost in the Translation," *Inc.,* June 2003, p. 50.

63. "U.S. Exports Fact Sheet," U.S. Department of Commerce, February 13, 2007, p. 1.

64. "Benefits to Small and Medium-Sized Exporters," Export.gov, www.export.gov/fta/complete/CAFTA/ SME_Ben.asp?dName=CAFTA; "Think Global," Kentucky World Trade Center, July 14, 2006, www.kwtc.org/enews/071406/eleven.htm.

65. John S. McClenahen, "Sound Thinking," *Industry Week,* May 3, 1993, p. 28.

66. Jeremy Main, "How To Go Global—And Why," *Fortune,* August 28, 1989, p. 70.

67. "Businesses Capitalising on Opportunities in the World's Fastest Growing Economies," Grant Thornton, February 2007, www.internationalbusinessreport.com/ main/index1.php?page=131&lang=en&id=114557&country_id=0.

68. Orit Gadiesh and Jean-Marie Pean, "Think Globally, Market Locally," *Wall Street Journal,* September 9, 2003, p. B2.

# Chapter 13

1. Nick Wingfield, "Amazon, Mail-Order Retailers Reheat Online Food Sales," *Wall Street Journal,* June 23, 2003, pp. B1, B3; Anne D'Innocenzio, "Online Grocery Hopes Fresh Take on Concept Helps Business Ripen," *Greenville News,* April 19, 2003, p. 12A; Tim Laseter, Barrie Berg, and Martha Turner, "What FreshDirect Learned from Dell," *Strategy + Business,* Spring 2003, pp. 20–25.

2. "Internet Usage Statistics: The Big Picture," Internet World Stats, 2007, www.internetworldstats.com/stats.htm.

3. Dan Muse, "Shoppers Are More Savvy. Are You?" *E-Commerce Guide,* November 16, 2006, www.ecommerce-guide. com/solutions/advertising/article.php/3644396.

4. Jerry Useem, "Our 10 Principles of the New Economy, Slightly Revised," *Business 2.0,* August/September 2001, p. 85.

5. "JupiterResearch Forecasts Online Retail Spending Will Reach $144 Billion in 2010, A CAGR of 12% from 2005," February 6, 2006, JupiterResearch, www.jupitermedia. com/corporate/releases/06.02.06-newjupresearch.html.

6. "Interland Survey Finds Web Sites are Key to Driving Credibility, Marketing, and Sales for Small Businesses," October 1, 2003, *Yahoo! Finance,* www.biz.yahoo.com/bw/031001/15400_1.html.

7. Wingfield, "Amazon, Mail-Order Retailers Reheat Online Food Sales," pp. B1, B3; "About Us," The Cheesecake Factory, www.cheesecakefactory.com.

8. "Online Sales to Surpass $200 Billion This Year," *CRM Today,* May 29, 2006, www.crm2day.com/news/crm/118774.php.

9. Nick Timiraos, "Web Can Pay Off for Traditional Retailers," *Wall Street Journal,* December 23–24, 2006, p. A7.

10. "Marketing on the World Wide Web," Alaska Internet Marketing, www.alaskaoutdoors.com/Misc/info.html

11. "Business Purchasing Survey Shows 93 Percent of Small Businesses Value Internet for Research Over Online Purchasing," BuyerZone, www.buyerzone.com/corporate/about_buyerzone/pr051705.html.

12. Laseter, Berg, and Turner, "What FreshDirect Learned from Dell," pp. 20–25.

13. Nick Timiraos, "Facts," *Wall Street Journal,* December 23–24, 2006, p. A7.

14. "A Perfect Market," *The Economist,* May 15, 2004, p. 4.

15. Jeffrey Gangemi, "Secrets of Online Business Success," *Business Week,* September 5, 2006, www.businessweek.com/smallbiz/content/sep2006/sb20060901_464008.htm; "American Pearl.com Helps Clients String Together Pearl Knowledge," National Jeweler, September 16, 2006, p. 16; "Charlie—A Pearl Legend," American Pearl, www.americanpearl.com/ourfounder.html.

16. *National Survey of Small and Mid-Sized Businesses: Executive Summary,* National Small Business Association, Washington, DC, 2007, p. 4; Elizabeth Holmes, "Going Online Isn't a 'Must' Move for All Entrepreneurs," *Wall Street Journal,* April 24, 2007, p. B4.

17. Lauren Simonds, "Web Sites: They're Not Just for E-Commerce," *Small Business Computing,* February 15, 2007, www.smallbusinesscomputing.com/news/article.php/3660186.

18. Elizabeth Holmes, "Going Online Isn't a 'Must' Move for All Entrepreneurs," p. B4.

19. Gwen Moran, "Time for Change," *Entrepreneur,* November 2006, pp. 67–71.

20. Frank Fortunato, "Search Engine Strategy Expo Exposes Valuable Tips," *E-Commerce Guide,* May 1, 2007, www.ecommerce-guide.com/solutions/article.php/3675066.

21. Robert McGarvey, "Connect the Dots," *Entrepreneur,* March 2000, pp. 78–85.

22. Candace Lombardi, "Blog Researcher Talks Blog Success," *CNETNews.com,* June 28, 2007, http://news.com.com/8301-10784_3-9737081-7.html; Peter Alexander, "Should You Start a Business Blog?" *Entrepreneur,* February 28, 2007, www.entrepreneur.com/technology/techtrendscolumnistpeteralexander/article175236.html.

23. "A Solid Corporate Blog Case Study," Fleishman-Hiller Blogs, March 16, 2007, http://fhcsr.typepad.com/wandered/2007/03/finally_a_solid.html; Candace Lombardi, "Blog Researcher Talks Blog Success," *CNETNews.com,* June 28, 2007, http://news.com.com/8301-10784_3-9737081-7.html; "Nuts About Southwest," www.blogsouthwest.com/.

24. Claire Tristram, "Many Happy Returns," *Small Business Computing,* May 1999, p. 73.

25. "Gartner Says Nearly $2 Billion Lost in E-commerce Sales in 2006 Due to Security Concerns of U.S. Adults," Gartner Inc., November 27, 2006, www.gartner.com/it/page.jsp?id=498974.

26. "Survival of the Fastest," *Inc. Technology,* No. 4, 1999, p. 57.

27. "The Smart Business 50: Dell Computer," *Smart Business,* September 2001, p. 74.

28. Steve Bennett and Stacey Miller, "The E-Commerce Plunge," *Small Business Computing,* February 2000, p. 50.

29. "The Zappos Story," Zappos.com, www.zappos.com/about.zhtml; Sidra Durst, "Shoe In," *Business 2.0,* December 2006, p. 54; "Beyond Their Years," *Entrepreneur,* November 2003, www.entrepreneur.com/article/0,4621,311420,00.html; "Zappos.com on Pace to More Than Double Sales This Year," *Internet Retailer,* November 3, 2003, www.internetretailer.com/ dailynews.asp?id=10577; Jane Bennett Clark, Robert Frick, Sean O'Neill, Ronaleen Roha, and Alison Stevenson, "Point Click Buy," *Kiplinger's,* June 2003, pp. 90–93.

30. Muse, "Shoppers Are More Savvy. Are You?" *E-Commerce Guide,* November 16, 2006, www.ecommerce-guide.com/solutions/advertising/article.php/3644396.

31. Errol Denger, "Transforming the Shopping Experience with Web 2.0," IBM Whitepaper, September 2006, http://software.ibm.com/software/genservers/commerce/library/Web20_wp_091806a.pdf, p. 3.

32. Ibid

33. *The State of Retailing Online,* Forrester Research and Shop.org, 2007, p. 12.

34. "Why Do We Abandon Shopping Carts?" Vovici, January 2006, www.vovici.com/efm-innovation/reference/website-visitors/shopping-cart-abandonment-survey.asp.

35. Eisenberg, "20 Tips to Minimize Shopping Cart Abandonment," (Part 1), pp. 1–2.

36. David Bell, "How the Offer of 'Free Shipping' Affects Online Shopping," *Knowledge@Wharton,* April 19, 2006, http://knowledge.wharton.upenn.edu/ article.cfm?articleid=1449.

37. "Customer Case Study: Blue Jeans Cable," PayPal, 2006, www.paypal.com/en_US/pdf/bluejeanscableCaseStudy.pdf.

38. Bronwyn Fryer, "When Something Clicks," *Inc. Technology,* No. 1, 2000, pp. 62–72; Tristram, "Many Happy Returns," pp. 70–75; Mardesich, "The Web Is No Shopper's Paradise," *Fortune,* November 8, 1999, pp. 188–198.

39. *Retail Web Site Performance: Consumer Reaction to a Poor Online Shopping Experience,* New York: JupiterResearch, June 1, 2006, p. 1.

40. Melanie Trottman, "Travelocity Streamlines Its Web Site," *Wall Street Journal,* March 25, 2004, p. D5.

41. Fred Vogelstein, "A Cold Bath for Dot-Com Fever," *U.S. News & World Report,* September 13, 1999, p. 37.

42. Karen Kroll, "Virtual Inventories Get Real," *MultiChannel Merchant,* June 1, 2006, http://multichannelmerchant.com/opsandfulfillment/virtual_inventories_05302006/index.html.

43. Timiraos, "Web Can Pay Off for Traditional Retailers," *Wall Street Journal,* December 23–24, 2006, p. A7.

44. Muse, "Shoppers Are More Savvy. Are You?" *E-Commerce Guide,* November 16, 2006, www.ecommerce-guide.com/solutions/advertising/ article.php/3644396; Timiraos, "Web Can Pay Off for Traditional Retailers," *Wall Street Journal,* December 23–24, 2006, p. A7.

45. "The Smart Business 50: REI," *Smart Business,* September 2001, p. 73.

46. "U.S. Census Bureau E-Stats," U.S. Department of Commerce, May 25, 2007, www.census.gov/eos/www/2005/2005reportfinal.pdf.

47. Robert McGarvey, "From: Business To: Business," *Entrepreneur,* June 2000, pp. 96–103.

48. Ibid.

49. Greg Howlett, "Trade PPV for VLV: Visitor Lifetime Value Metric Makes Money," *E-Commerce Guide,* May 23, 2007, www.ecommerce-guide.com/solutions/building/article.php/3679441.

50. Bronwyn Fryer and Lee Smith, ".com or Bust," *Forbes Small Business,* December 1999/January 2000, p. 41.

51. "Equal Time Spent on TV and Web," *eMarketer,* July 3, 2007, www.emarketer.com/Article.aspx?id=1005105.

52. Heidi Dawley, "Time-Wise, Internet Is Now TV's Equal," *Media Life,* February 1, 2006, http://medialifemagazine.com/artman/publish/article_2581.asp.

53. Stephenson, Lockwood, and Raven, "The Entrepreneur's Guide to the Strategic Use of the Internet," p. 3.

54. Kim T. Gordon, "Become a Business Evangelist," *Entrepreneur,* September 2006, www.entrepreneur.com/marketing/findingcustomers/article165864.html; "Community," Bike Friday, www.bikefriday.com/webclub.

55. Ralph F. Wilson, "The Five Mutable Laws of Web Marketing," *Web Marketing Today,* www.wilsonweb.com/wmta/basic-principles.htm, April 1, 1999, pp. 1–7.

56. "Success Stories: Communiqué Public Relations," Constant Contact, www.constantcontact.com/email-marketing-success/case-studies/communique.jsp.

57. Morgan Stewart, "E-Mail Marketing: 2005 Response Rate Study," ExactTarget, 2006, http://email.exacttarget.com/pdf/2005_Response_Study.pdf; "Industry Research: E-mail Delivers!" Datran Media, http://success.datranmedia.com/research/index.php.

58. "Ninety Percent of E-Mail Will be Spam by Year-end," *ITNews,* February 23, 2007, www.itnews.com.au/newsstory.aspx?CIaNID=46299.

59. Jan Gardner, "10 Ideas for Growing Business Now," *Inc.,* October 29, 2001, http://www2.inc.com/search/23629.html

60. Ellen Neuborne, "Taming the Beast," *Inc.,* February 2004, p. 32.

61. Ron Stodghill, "Sharing a Lobster," *FSB,* October 2006, pp. 45–48.

62. "The Top Ten Languages Used on the Web," Internet World Stats, July 14, 2007, www.internetworldstats.com/stats7.htm.

63. Dylan Tweney, "Think Globally, Act Locally," *Business 2.0,* November 2001, pp. 120–121.

64. Chris Pentilla, "D'Oh!" *Entrepreneur,* July 2007, www.entrepreneur.com/magazine/entrepreneur/2007/july/180518.html.

65. Scott Woodward, "Online Marketing with Offline Conversions," *Marketing Pilgrim,* January 5, 2007, www.marketingpilgrim.com/2007/01/online-marketing-with-offline-conversions.html.

66. Mary Meeker and David Joseph, "The State of the Internet, Part 3," Morgan Stanley, www.morganstanley.com/institutional/techresearch/pdfs/Webtwopto2006.pdf, p. 16.

67. "Search Engine Ad Spending Forecast Up 39 Percent in '07," *Outsell,* January 29, 2007, www.outsellinc.com/press/press_releases/ad_spending_online_search_engine print.

68. Justin Martin, "Get Right with Google," *FSB,* September 2006, pp. 70–78.

69. Kevin J. Delaney, "How Search Engine Rules Cause Sites to Go Missing," *Wall Street Journal,* March 13, 2007, pp. B1, B4.

70. Martin, "Get Right with Google," pp. 70–78.

71. Enid Burns, "U.S. Search Engine Rankings, April 2007," *ClickZStats,* www.clickz.com/showPage.html?page=3626020.

72. Martin, "Get Right with Google," pp. 70–78.

73. Martin, "Get Right with Google," pp. 70–78.

74. Frank Fortunato, "PPC Fraud: Every Click Counts . . . or Does It?" *E-commerce Guide,* May 22, 2007, p. 2.

75. Mylene Mangalindan, "Playing the Search-Engine Game," *Wall Street Journal,* June 16, 2003, pp. R1, R7.

76. Herman Miller, www.hermanmiller.com; "Design Matters," *Fortune Tech Guide,* 2001, pp. 183–188.

77. "Santa's Helpers," *The Economist,* May 15, 2004, pp. 5–8.

78. Alfred Gingold, "Click Here," *My Generation,* July–August 2001, p. 51.

79. Christopher Saunders, "How Do I: Attract and Keep Customers?" *E-Commerce Guide,* June 8, 2004, http:// www.ecommerce-guide.com/news/article.php/3365551.

80. Melissa Campanelli, "Good Incentive," *Entrepreneur,* August 2001, pp. 82–84.
81. Ibid.
82. Melissa Campanelli, "The Right Stuff," *Entrepreneur,* April 2007, p. 54.
83. Carol Stavraka, "There's No Stopping E-Business. Are You Ready?" *Forbes,* December 13, 1999, Special Advertising Section.
84. James Maguire, "The 'Mystery Shopping' Report," *E-Commerce Guide,* February 21, 2006, www.e-commerce-guide.com/solutions/customer_relations/article.php/3586441.
85. "Online Shoppers Will Pay Extra to Protect Privacy, Study Shows," PhysOrg.com, June 6, 2007, www.physorg.com/news100357431.html.
86. Lena West, "Frauds and Hacks," *E-commerce Guide,* January 23, 2007, www.ecommerce-guide.com/news/news/article.php/3655526.

87. Sharon Gaudin, "Study: Seventy Percent of Web Sites Are Hackable," *Information Week,* February 13, 2007, www.informationweek.com/showArticle.jhtml;jsessionid=PKT0LYYDTF1XYQSNDLPSKHSCJUNN2JVN?articleID=197005784&queryText=%22Web+Sites+Are+Hackable%22.
88. Larry Greenemeier, "Largest Data Breach Ever," *Information Week,* April 2, 2007, p. 21.
89. Michael Bertin, "The New Security Threats," *Smart Business,* February 2001, pp. 78–86.
90. "Seventh Annual Online Fraud Report," Cybersource Corporation, 2006, www.cybersource.com/resources/collateral/Resource_Center/whitepapers_and_reports/CYBS_2006_Fraud_Report.pdf, p. 3.
91. Adam Stone, "Small E-Stores Avoid Credit Card Fraud," *Small Business Computing,* December 23, 2003, www.smallbusinesscomputing.com/emarketing/print.php/3291231.

# Chapter 14

1. Paul DeCeglie, "What About Me?" *Business Start-Ups,* June 2000, pp. 45–51.
2. Alison Stein Wellner, "Blood Money," *Inc.,* December 2003, pp. 48–50.
3. Elizabeth Holmes, "Show Me the Money—Maybe," *Wall Street Journal,* June 25, 2007, p. R6.
4. Mark Henricks, "The Money Market," *Entrepreneur,* July 2006, pp. 69–74.
5. Ibid.
6. Silva Sansoni, "Burned Angels," *Forbes,* April 19, 1999, pp. 182–185.
7. *Global Entrepreneurship Monitor: National Entrepreneurship Assessment—United States of America, 2004–2005 Executive Report,* Global Entrepreneurship Research Association, 2006, p. 23.
8. Stephanie Clifford, "How to Start a Business for (Almost) Nothing," *Inc.,* July 2006, pp. 101–107.
9. "Fast-Growing MyYearbook.com Gets $4.1 Million," *Yahoo! Tech,* January 29, 2007, http://tech.yahoo.com/blogs/devlin/7486; Henricks, "The Money Market," pp. 69–74; Sara Wilson, "Most Likely to Succeed," *Entrepreneur,* May 2007, p. 41.
10. *Global Entrepreneurship Monitor 2006 Financing Report,* Global Entrepreneurship Research Association, 2006, p. 8.
11. *Global Entrepreneurship Monitor: National Entrepreneurship Assessment—United States of America, 2004–2005 Executive Report,* Global Entrepreneurship Research Association, 2006, p. 22.
12. Paul Kvinta, "Frogskins, Shekels, Bucks, Moolah, Cash, Simoleans, Dough, Dinero: Everybody Wants It. Your Business Needs It. Here's How to Get It," *Smart Business,* August 2000, pp. 74–89.
13. Pamela Sherrid, "Angels of Capitalism," *U.S. News & World Report,* October 13, 1997, pp. 43–45.
14. "The Angel Investor Market in 2006," Center for Venture Research, University of New Hampshire, www.unh.edu/cvr.
15. "Is He an Angel or a Beatle?" *FSB,* October 2000, p. 39.
16. Wendy Taylor and Marty Jerome, "Pray," *Smart Business,* July 2000, p. 45; John Heylar, "The Venture Capitalist Next Door," *Fortune,* November 13, 2000, pp. 293–312.
17. Jeanne Lee, "Building Wealth," *FSB,* June 2006, p. 43.
18. Geoff Williams, "Shoot for the Stars," *Entrepreneur,* March 2004, p. 27.
19. Rhonda Abrams, "More Entrepreneurs Finding Angelic Help," *Greenville News,* October 1, 2006, p. 1F; Jim Melloan, "Angels With Angels," *Inc.,* July 2005, pp. 93–104.; Roger Barnes, "Touched by an Angel," *Black Enterprise,* June 2001, pp. 242–247; Susan Greco, "Get$$$Now.com," *Inc.,* September 1999, pp. 35–38; "Digging for Dollars," *Wall Street Journal,* February 24, 1989, p. R25; Quentin Hardy, "Where Angels Dare to Tread," *Forbes,* October 28, 2002, pp. 303–304.
20. David Worrell, "Customer Appreciation," *Entrepreneur,* March 2007, p. 65.
21. Henricks, "The Money Market," p. 72.
22. Jennifer Lawton, "Making Friends: The Name of the Angel Game," *EntreWorld,* February 1, 2000, www.entreworld.org

23. Crystal Detamore-Rodman, "Angels in Flight," *Entrepreneur,* January 2007, pp. 38–40.
24. Rosalind Resnick, "Guardian Angels," *Entrepreneur,* July 2007, p. 92; Lee, "Building Wealth," p. 38.
25. "Vital Statistics," Band of Angels, www.bandangels.com; Bonnie Azab Powell, "Angel Investors Fill Void Left by Risk Capital," *New York Times,* July 6, 2001, p. 28; Loren Fox, "Heaven Can't Wait," *Business 2.0,* March 20, 2001, pp. 123–124; Anne Ashby Gilbert, "Small Stakes in Small Business," *Fortune,* April 12, 1999, p. 162[H]; Sherrid, "Angels of Capitalism," pp. 43–45; Heylar, "The Venture Capitalist Next Door," pp. 293–312.
26. Bruce J. Blechmna, "Step Right Up," *Entrepreneur,* June 1993, pp. 20–25.
27. Heylar, "The Venture Capitalist Next Door," pp. 293–312.
28. Anne Fisher, "Changing Course," *Fortune,* November 27, 2006, p. 278.
29. *Corporate Venture Capital: Annual Analysis 2006,* National Venture Capital Association, www.nvca.org/pdf/corporateVCthrough2006.pdf.
30. Jennifer Pellett, "In Good Company," *Entrepreneur,* March 2007, p. 22; "Virtual Iron Raises $8.5 Million. Intel Capital Leads Series C Round," Virtual Iron, www.virtualiron.com/news_events/releaseDate-9-26-05.cfm.
31. Max Chafkin and Bobbie Gossage, "Need Money?" *Inc.,* October 2006, pp. 25–26.
32. David Worrell, "School Ties," *Entrepreneur,* November 2006, pp. 88–90.
33. Brian Caulfield, "The Pentagon's Venture Capitalists," *Business 2.0,* April 2003, p. 28.
34. David Worrell, "Safe Bet," *Entrepreneur,* February 2004, p. 24; "About Us," Sourcefire Network Security Inc., www.sourcefire.com/about.html.
35. Roy Harris, "Capital Without the Venture," *CFO,* February 2004, pp. 31–32.
36. Mabel Brecrick-Okereke, "Report to U.N. Cautions that Focus on Venture Capital Can Hinder Entrepreneurial Economy," United Nations Association of the United States of America, http://unusa.school.aol.com/newsroom/NewsReleases/ean_venture.asp; Cara Cannella, "Where Seed Money Really Comes From," *Inc.,* August 2003, p. 26.
37. PricewaterhouseCoopers MoneyTree Survey, www.pwcmoneytree.com/stage.asp?year=2001&qtr=3; National Venture Capital Association, www.nvca.org
38. P.B. Gray, "Helping Hands," *CFO,* May 2006, pp. 89–92.
39. Jeff Bailey, "Rethinking a Return to Venture Capital Funding," *Wall Street Journal,* September 30, 2003, p. B4.
40. Tracy T. Leteroff, "In Full Bloom," *Entrepreneur,* July 2006, p. 78.
41. Harris, "Capital Without the Venture," pp. 31–32.
42. Karl Rhodes, "The Venture Adventure," *Region Focus,* Fall 2003, pp. 22–26.
43. Amy Feldman, "Putting Founders First," *Inc.,* March 2007, pp. 29–31.
44. Henricks, "The Money Market," p. 74.
45. Harris, "Capital Without the Venture," pp. 31–32.

46. Tracy T. Lefteroff and Nichole L. Torres, "The Thrill of the Chase," *Entrepreneur*, July 2003, pp. 56–63.

47. Dave Pell, "What's Old Is New Again," *FSB*, July/August 2000, p. 122.

48. Kvinta, "Frogskins, Shekels, Bucks, Moolah, Cash, Simoleans, Dough, Dinero: Everybody Wants It. Your Business Needs It. Here's How to Get It," p. 87.

49. Jay Ritter, "Some Factoids About the 2006 IPO Market," University of Florida, http://bear.cba.ufl.edu/ritter/ IPOs2006Factoids%204-26-07.pdf, p. 11.

50. Ibid., p. 6.

51. "Heely's Prices 6.425 Million Shares Well Above the Range," *IPO Home*, www.ipohome.com/marketwatch/iponews2.asp?article= 2368.

52. Kevin Delaney, "Google Looks to Boost Ads with YouTube," *Wall Street Journal*, October 10, 2006, p. B1.

53. Susan Carey and Paulo Prada, "Course Change: Why JetBlue Shuffled Top Rank," *Wall Street Journal*, May 11, 2007, pp. B1–B2; Chris Isidore, "Jet Blue Founder Ousted as CEO," *CNNMoney*, May 10, 2007, http://money.cnn.com/2007/05/10/ news/companies/jetblue/index.htm.

54. Tony Taylor, "A Going (Public) Concern," *GSA Business*, February 20, 2006, p. 15.

55. "CompuPay and PayMaxx Finalize Agreement," CompuPay, June 24, 2005, www. compupay.com/about_compupay.cfm?subpage=426; Lynn Stephens and Robert C. Schwartz, "The Chilling Effects of Sarbanes-Oxley: Myth or Reality?" *CPA Journal*, June 2006, www.nysscpa.org/cpajournal/2006/606/infocus/p14.htm.

56. Thomas Johansmeyer, "Alternatives to the American IPO: Listing on the AIM," Swiss Management Center, www.swissmc.ch/article/ 17/alternatives_to_the_american_ipo_listing_on_aim.

57. Darren Dahl, "Assessing Vonage's Grim IPO," *Inc.*, August 2006, p. 26; Shawn Young, "Vonage Customers Withhold Payment for IPO Shares," *Wall Street Journal*, August 2, 2006, p. B1; Shawn Young and Randy Smith, "How Vonage's High Profile IPO Stumbled on the Stock Market," *Wall Street Journal*, June 3–4, 2006, pp. A1, A6.

58. Joseph McCafferty, "The Long View," *CFO*, May 2007, p. 48.

59. Reason, "Off the Street," *CFO*, May 2003, p. 58.

60. Joanna L. Ossinger, "Stock Answers," *Wall Street Journal*, June 25, 2007, p. R6.

61. Pui-Wing Tam, "The Venture Capital Tangle," *Wall Street Journal*, May 8, 2007, pp. C1, C3; Pui-Wing Tam, "Venture Capital's New Adventure," *Wall Street Journal*, December 21, 2006, pp. C1, C4.

62. David Worrell, "Waiting in the Wings," *Entrepreneur*, January 2004, pp. 21–22.

63. "The Bare Escentuals Makeup Story," Bare Escentuals, www. bareescentuals.com/about/story.html; "Bare Escentuals," IPO Home, www.ipohome.com/ common/ipoprofile.asp?ticker=BARE.

64. "Heely's Prices 6.425 Million Shares Well Above the Range," *IPO Home*, www.ipohome.com/ marketwatch/iponews2.asp?article= 2368.

65. David M. Katz, "A Tough Act to Follow," *CFO*, March 2006, pp. 65–72; Unica Corporation, IPO Home, http:// www.ipohome.com/common/ipoprofile.asp?ticker=UNCA.

66. Mirenco, Inc., www.mirenco.com/Company/SECFilings.asp; Tom Stewart-Gordon, SCOR-Report, www.scor-report.com.

67. "Force Protection, Inc. Announces $41 Million Equity Financing," *Swamp Fox*, July 24, 2006, www.swampfox.ws/force-protection- inc-announces-41-million-equity-financing/.

68. Phaedra Hise, "Off the Grid IPOs," *Inc.*, December 2006, pp. 40–42.

69. Chinaberry Inc. 2002 Annual Report, p. 11; "Case Studies: Chinaberry Inc.," Drew Fields Direct Public Offerings, www. dfdpo.com/clientsum13.htm.

70. David Worrell, "London Calling," *Entrepreneur*, July 2006, pp. 62–64.

---

# Chapter 15

1. Mara Der Hovanesian, "Tapped Out?" *Business Week*, Winter 2007, www.businessweek.com/magazine/content/07_09/b4023443.htm.

2. Cynthia E. Griffin, "Something Borrowed," *Entrepreneur*, February 1997, p. 26; Business Lenders Inc., www. businesslenders.com/q&a.htm

3. Charles Ou, *Banking and SME Financing in the United States*, SBA Office of Advocacy, June 2006, www.sba.gov/advo/research/ rs277tot.pdf, p. 7.

4. Jim Hopkins, "Where Do Start-ups Get Their Money?" *USA Today*, October 24, 2006, www.usatoday.com/money/smallbusiness/ 2006-10-18-small-finance-usat_x.htm.

5. *Small Business and Micro Business Lending in the United States 2005*, SBA Office of Advocacy, December 2006, www.sba.gov/ advo/research/sbl_05study.pdf, p.6.

6. Mark Henricks, "The State of Small Business Funding," *Entrepreneur*, July 2006, www.entrepreneur.com/money/financing/ article159798.html.

7. Daniel M. Clark, "Banks and Bankability," *Venture*, September 1989, p. 29.

8. Rosalind Resnick, "Loan Woes," *Entrepreneur*, April 2007, p. 96.

9. William J. Dennis, "NFIB National Small Business Poll: The Cash Flow Problem," *National Federation of Independent Businesses* 1, no. 3, 2001, p. 1.

10. Crystal Detamore-Rodman, "Bounce Back," *Entrepreneur*, June 2007, p. 56.

11. "Thrifty Names President of Thrifty Car Sales; Announces Strategic Alliances with Bank of America, APCO, Manheim, and Others," Dollar Thrifty Automotive Group, February 8, 2005, www.dtag.com/ phoenix.zhtml? c=71946&p=irol- newsArticle&ID=27723&highlight=.

12. Tim Reason, "Borrowing Big Time," *CFO*, November 2003, pp. 87–94.

13. Juan Hovey, "Want Easy Money? Look for Lenders Who Say Yes," *FSB*, November 2000, pp. 41–44.

14. "Let's Make a Deal," Insert in *Fortune*, August 21, 2006, p. S3.

15. "What Is Business Credit?" National Association of Credit Management, www.nacm.org/aboutnacm/what.html; "Financing Small Business," *Small Business Reporter*, C3, p. 9.

16. Jack Stack with Bo Burlingham, "My Awakening," *Inc.*, April 2007, www.inc.com/magazine/20070401/features-my- awakening_pagen_2.html.

17. *Small Business and Micro Business Lending in the United States 2005*, p. 6.

18. David Worrell, "The Other Colors of Money," *Entrepreneur*, July 2004, p. 67.

19. Worrell, "The Other Colors of Money," p. 67.

20. "Hardee's Franchisee Acquires $8.5 Million to Buy Atlanta Stores," *Nation's Restaurant News*, July 12, 2007, www. nrn.com/breakingNews.aspx?id=342950& menu_id=1368.

21. Crystal Detamore-Rodman, "Work with Me," *Entrepreneur*, April 2006, pp. 65–68.

22. Scott McMurray, "Personal Loans from Brokers Offer Low Rates," *Wall Street Journal*, January 7, 1986, p. 31.

23. John R. Walter, "Not Your Father's Credit Union," *Economic Quarterly*, Federal Reserve Bank of Richmond, Fall 2006, pp. 353–377.

24. Der Hovanesian, "Tapped Out?" www.businessweek.com/ magazine/content/07_09/b4023443.htm.

25. *U.S. Credit Union Profile*, Credit Union National Association Economics & Statistics (Alexandria, Virginia: Credit Union National Association, 2004), http://advice.cuna.org/download/ uscu_profile_1q07.pdf, pp. 5–6.

26. Crystal Detamore-Rodman, "A Perfect Union," *Entrepreneur*, October 2006, pp. 77–80.

27. Rodman, "A Perfect Union," pp. 77–80.

28. Sean P. Melvin, "Itsy-Bitsy Bonds," *Entrepreneur,* January 2002, pp. 78–81.

29. "Sweet Success Raises $3.3 Million in Private Placement," *San Antonio Business Journal,* August 23, 2006, http:// sanantonio. bizjournals.com/sanantonio/stories/2006/08/21/daily18.html? surround=lfn.

30. *2007 SBIC Program Guide,* National Association of Small Business Investment Companies, www.magnetmail.net/images/ clients/NASBIC/attach/2007_SBIC_ Program_ Guide.pdf, p. 4.

31. Ibid.

32. *SBIC Program Overview,* National Association of Small Business Investment Companies, June 13, 2007, http:// www.magnetmail. net/images/clients/NASBIC/attach/6_13_07_SBIC_Program_ Overview.pdf, p. 3.

33. Ibid.

34. Dan Kehrer, "A Hidden Trove of Small Business Capital," *Business.com,* 2006, www.business.com/directory/advice/money- and-finance/loans-and-financing/a-hidden-trove-of-small-biz- capital/; "Buying Power: Austin's Sosa Brothers Create a Debit Card for the Masses," *HispanicTrends.com,* May/June 2005, www. hispaniconline.com/trends/2005/May-June/briefcase/trendsetters. html; "Our Company," NetSpend, https://www.netspend.com/info/ corp/corp_company.shtml.

35. "Section 108 Case Studies," U.S. Department of Housing and Urban Development, www.hud.gov/offices/cpd/ communitydevelopment/programs/108/casestudies.cfm.

36. Sarah Zajaczek, "Local Manufacturer Gets Minority Ownership Funding," *Clinton Chronicle,* July 25, 2001, p. 4A.

37. "SBA Technology: Small Business Innovation Research Program (SBIR)," U.S. Small Business Administration, www.sba.gov/SBIR/ sbir.html.

38. "SBIR/STTR Hallmarks of Success Videos: Digiray Corporation," NASA Small Business Innovation Research Program, http://sbir. gsfc.nasa.gov/SBIR/video/digiray.html; "Small Business Innovations," Johnson Space Center, National Aeronautic and Space Administration, http:// www1.jsc.nasa.gov/er/seh/pg112s95. html; "Company Overview," Digiray, Inc., www.digiray.com/ digiray_corporation.htm.

39. Thomas G. Tolan, "Small Business Administration's Loan Programs Receive Boost," *Cascade,* Spring 2005, www.phil.frb. org/cca/spring05_5.html.

40. "Overview and History of the SBA," U.S. Small Business Administration, www.sba.gov/aboutsba/history.html.

41. Art Beroff and Dwayne Moyers, "SBA Guaranteed Loans," *Entrepreneur,* www.entrepreneur.com/article/0,4621,261896,00.html

42. Julie Monahan, "Quick Fix," *Entrepreneur,* April 2004, p. 27.

43. Tolan, "Small Business Administration's Loan Programs Receive Boost," www.phil.frb.org/cca/spring05_5.html.

44. "Spotlight on Success: Navy Pilots Aim for Business Success on Land," *BLX Lending Report* 1, no. 1, www.blxonline.com/Files/ Public/BLX-Success-Story-Jet-Stream-Car-Wash.pdf.

45. "Aquatech International Wins Significant Export Contracts, Backed by PNC Working Capital Loan Under Ex-Im Bank's New Fast Track Program," Export-Import Bank of the United States, May 22, 2006, www.exim.gov/pressrelease.cfm/62EC206C-08B3-CDE0- CC9A88613EFDCFF4/.

46. "Success Stories: Lindar Corporation," Minnesota Business Finance Corporation, www.mbfc.org/SStories/SStories_Index. asp?sid=8.

47. *SBA Microloan Program: FY 2007,* Women Impacting Public Policy, www.wipp.org/news_details.asp?story_id=204& memberonly=False.

48. Gwendolyn Bounds, "Risky Businesses May Find Loans Even Scarcer," *Wall Street Journal,* April 13, 2004, p. B8.

49. Rick Haney, "Success Story: West Virginia District Office," U.S. Small Business Administration, www.sba.gov/idc/groups/public/ documents/wv_clarksburg/wv_budgetblinds.pdf.

50. Anne Marie Frawley, "Record SBA Disaster Loan Approvals Surpass $6 Billion Following 2005 Gulf Coast Hurricanes," U.S. Small Business Administration, March 13, 2006, www.sba.gov/idc/groups/ public/documents/sba_homepage/news_cbr_2006_0617.pdf.

51. Crystal Detamore-Rodman, "Public Works," *Entrepreneur,* June 2004, pp. 60–62.

52. Ziona Austrian and Zhongcai Zhang, "An Inventory and Assessment of Pollution Control and Prevention Financing Programs," Great Lakes Environmental Finance Center, Levin College of Urban Affairs, Cleveland State University, www. csuohio.edu/glefc/inventor.htm#.

53. Mike Ramsey, "Main Street Paving Way for Growth," Capitol Places, www.capitolplaces.com/MISC/article2.htm; "Commercial Revolving Loan Fund Success Stories," ColumbiaBusinessLoans.com, www.columbiabusinessloans.com/ success_stories.asp.

54. *CDFI Data Project, FY 2005 Data Fifth Edition,* http:// www.cdfi. org/Uploader/Files/cdp_fy_2005_full.pdf, p. 2.

55. Sean P. Melvin, "Hidden Treasure," *Entrepreneur,* February 2002, pp. 56–58.

56. Mark Henricks, "Something Old, Something New," *Entrepreneur,* July 2006, p. 74.

57. "SurePayroll Insights Survey," SurePayroll, April 16, 2007, www. surepayroll.com/spsite/press/releases/2007/release041607.asp.

58. James Park, "Game Face," *Entrepreneur,* April 2007, p. 119.

59. Jill Andresky Fraser, "Business Owners, Beware!" *Inc.,* January 1997, pp. 86–87.

# Chapter 16

1. Mark Henricks, "Hot Spots," *Entrepreneur,* October 2005, pp. 68–74.

2. "The Final Word on 2005: Commerce Dept. Reports Online Sales Grow 24.6%," *Internet Retailer,* www.internetretailer.com/internet/ marketing-conference/04300-final-word-2005-commerce-dept- reports-online-sales-grow-246.html.

3. "How to Start a Retail Store," Entrepreneur Magazine's SmallBizBooks.com, www.smallbizbooks.com/cgi-bin/ SmallBizBooks/00101.html.

4. Mark Henricks, "Is That a Stretch?" *Entrepreneur,* May 2007, p. 26.

5. Vivian Wagner, "Site Management Software Deployed by Bank," *Bank Systems & Technology Online,* May 27, 2003, www. banktech.com/story/techFocus/BNK20030527S0014.

6. Conor Dougherty, "Take the Money and Don't Run," *Wall Street Journal,* June 11, 2007, pp. R1, R3.

7. Ibid.

8. Timothy Aeppel, "Sticks and Stones May Break Bones, But Warsaw, Ind., Makes Replacements," *Wall Street Journal,* October 26, 2006, pp. B1, B4.

9. Amanda C. Kooser, "Tech Towns," *Entrepreneur,* June 2003, pp. 24–26; Kurt Badenhausen, "Wide Open for Business," *Forbes,* May 26, 2003, pp. 116–120; Paul Kaihla, "Boom Towns," *Business 2.0,* March 2004, pp. 94–102.

10. State Individual Income Taxes 2007, Taxadmin.org, www. taxadmin.org/FTA/rate/ind_inc.html.

11. Personal contact with Judy Wilson, owner, Dept. of the Interior Decorator Fabrics LLC, September 7, 2007.

12. Emily Richmond, "1 Million More Residents Projected by 2024," *Las Vegas Sun,* May 19, 2004, www.lasvegassun. com/sunbin/stories/text/ 2004/may/19/516881766.html.

13. Ken Ritter, "Developer, Las Vegas Officials Tout Plan for Jewelry Marketplace," *Las Vegas Sun,* October 23, 2006, www.lasvegassun. com/sunbin/stories/nevada/2006/oct/23/102310894.html.

14. Jesse M. Cubbinson, "Fitness Centers Get Quite a Workout Finding Locations," *Real Estate & Construction Quarterly,* July 25, 2005, p. 17.

15. "Businesses Use Data to Gain Competitive Advantage," U.S. Census Bureau, www.census.gov/econ/census07/uses.htm.

16. Mark Henricks, "Moving On Up: Neighborhood Renewals Open New Doors for Entrepreneurs," *Entrepreneur,* October 2006, pp. 19–20.

17. Kerry A. Dolan, "San DNAgo," *Forbes,* May 26, 2003, pp. 122–126.

18. Matt Rosenberg, About Reilly's Law of Retail Gravitation, About.com, http://geography.about.com/cs/citiesurbangeo/a/aa041403a.htm; G.I. Thrall and J.C. del Valle, "The Calculation of Retail Market Areas: The Reilly Model," *GeoInfoSystems* 7, No. 4, 1997, pp. 46–49.

19. Mike Ramsey, "Borders Going Places Other Stores Dare Not Go," *Business,* June 13, 2004, p. 6.

20. Scope U.S. 2006, International Council of Shopping Centers, http://icsc.org/srch/rsrch/scope/current/UnitedStates06.pdf.

21. Caryssa Wyant, "MOA Signs Great Wolf Water Park for Phase 2," *Minneapolis/St. Paul Business Journal,* July, 26, 2007, www.bizjournals.com/twincities/stories/2007/07/23/daily30.html.

22. Ibid.

23. "ISCS Shopping Center Definitions—U.S.," International Council of Shopping Centers, http://icsc.org/srch/about/impactofshoppingcenters/03_Definitions.pdf#xml=http://icscsearch.icsc.org/texis/search/pdfhi.txt?query=ICSC+Shopping+Center+Definitions&pr=IcscLiveNew&prox=page&rorder=500&rprox=500&rdfreq=500&rwfreq=500&rlead=500&sufs=0&order=r&cq=&id=46ddeab6a9.

24. Ibid.

25. Stan Sesser, "The New Spot for Giant Malls: Asia," *Wall Street Journal,* September 16, 2006, p. P6.

26. Ibid.

27. Mike Bergman, "Half of U.S. Businesses Are Home-Based, Majority of Firms Self-Financed, Census Bureau Reports," U.S. Census Bureau, www.census.gov/Press-Release/www/releases/archives/business_ownership/007537.html, September 27, 2006.

28. Timothy Aeppel, "Still Made in the USA," *Wall Street Journal,* July 8, 2004, pp. B1, B4.

29. Ian Pulsipher, "Evaluating Enterprise Zones," *National Conference of State Legislatures,* May 6, 2005, www.ncsl.org/programs/econ/evalentzones.htm; Kristin Ohlson, "EZ Answers," *Entrepreneur,* July 2007, www.entrepreneur.com/magazine/entrepreneur/2007/july/180334.html.

30. "Imperial Valley EZ Update," California Association of Enterprise Zones, August 21, 2007, www.caez.org/documents/IVEZ_Helps_Small_Biz_Success.pdf.

31. "Business Incubators," *Entreprenuer,* www.entrepreneur.com/article/printthis/52802.html.

32. "Business Incubation Success Stories," National Business Incubation Association, www.nbia.org/resource_center/success/martek.php.

33. "What Is Business Incubation?" National Business Incubation Association, March 31, 2006, www.nbia.org/resource_center/what_is/index.php.

34. Ibid.

35. Marci McDonald, "The Latte Connections," *U.S. News & World Report,* March 20, 1999, pp. 63–66.

36. Jeffrey Pfeffer, "Thinking Outside the Cube," *Business 2.0,* April 2007, p. 60.

37. Michal Lev-Ram, "How to Make Your Workspace Work Better," *Business 2.0,* November 2006, pp. 58–60.

38. Laura Tiffany, "The Rules of . . . Retailing," *Business Start-Ups,* December 1999, p. 106; Paul Keegan, "The Architect of Happy Customers," *Business 2.0,* August 2002, pp. 85–87.

39. Elizabeth Razzi, "Retailers' Siren Song," *Kiplinger's Personal Financial Magazine,* November 2000, pp. 130–134.

40. Tiffany, "The Rules of . . . Retail," p. 106.

41. "Educational Kit," President's Committee on Employment of People with Disabilities, http://www50.pcepd.gov/pcepd/archives/pubs/ek99/wholedoc.htm#decisions.

42. Susanna Hamner, "Filling the Gap," *Business 2.0,* July 2005, p. 30; Matthew Maier, "The Department Store Rises Again," *Business 2.0,* August 2004, pp. 56–57; Ellen Byron, "Rethinking the Men's Department," *Wall Street Journal,* October 8–9, 2005, p. P9.

43. "Proposal for an Ergonomics Program Standard," The Occupational Health and Safety Administration, www.osha-slc.gov/ergonomics-standard/ergo-faq.html.

44. Leigh Gallagher, "Get Out of My Face," *Forbes,* October 18, 1999, pp. 105–106.

45. Linda Tischler, "Death to the Cubicle!" *Fast Company,* June 2005, pp, 29–30.

46. Jennifer Alsever, "Showing Products in a Better Light," *Business 2.0,* September 2005, p. 62.

47. Linda Tischler, "Smells Like a Brand Spirit," *Fast Company,* August 2005, pp. 52–59.

48. Suzanne Hoppough, "What's That Smell?" *Forbes,* October 2, 2006, p. 76.

49. Kara Newman, "How to Sell with Smell," *Business 2.0,* April 2007, p. 36.

50. Hoppough, "What's That Smell?" p. 76.

51. Colleen Bazdarich, "In the Buying Mood? It's the Muzak," *Business 2.0,* March 2002, p. 100.

52. Nadine Heintz, "Play Bach, Boost Sales," *Inc.,* January 2004, p. 23.

53. Theunis Bates, "Volume Control," *Time,* August 2, 2007, www.time.com/time/printout/0,8816,1649304,00.html.

54. Ibid.

55. Paul Keegan, "The Architect of Happy Customers," *Business 2.0,* August 2002, pp. 85–87.

56. Russell Boniface, "I Spy a Shopper," *AIArchitect,* June 23, 2006, www.aia.org/aiarchitect/thisweek06/0623/0623paco.cfm.

57. "Business Bulletin," *Wall Street Journal,* April 15, 1999, p. A1.

58. Thomas Mucha, "Target Thinks Outside the Box Wine," *Business 2.0,* February 2003, pp. 46–47.

59. Jane J. Kim, "A Latte With Your Loan?" *Wall Street Journal,* May 17, 2006, p. D1.

60. Ray Davis, ThinksExist.com, http://en.thinkexist.com/search/searchquotation.asp?search=store%20design&page=2.

61. Tom Stevens, "Practice People," *Industry Week,* March 17, 1997, pp. 33–36.

62. Paul Keegan, "The Architect of Happy Customers," *Business 2.0,* August 2002, pp. 85–87; Kenneth Labich, "This Man Is Watching You," *Fortune,* July 19, 1999, pp. 131–134.

63. Keegan, "The Architect of Happy Customers," pp. 85–87.

64. Boniface, "I Spy a Shopper," *AIArchitect,* www.aia.org/aiarchitect/thisweek06/0623/0623paco.cfm.

65. "Release Me," *Entrepreneur,* January 1998, pp. 48–49.

# Chapter 17

1. Ian Mount and Brian Caulfield, "The Missing Link," *eCompany,* May 2001, p. 84.

2. Randy Myers, "Food Fights," *CFO,* June 2007, pp. 70–74; Adrienne W. Fawcett, "Survey: Most Americans Remain Unaffected by Pet Food Recall," *Marketing Daily,* April 13, 2007, http://publications.mediapost.com/ index.cfm?fuseaction=Articles. showArticleHomePage&art_aid=58672.

3. Beth Bacheldor, "Keeping Risks to a Minimum," *Information Week,* October 10, 2005, pp. 43–45.

4. Stephanie Clifford, "Outlook 2006: Real Estate," *Inc.,* January 2006, www.inc.com/magazine/20060101/outlook-real-estate.html.

5. Rachel Dodes, "A Run on Alligators Sends Designers Scrambling," *Wall Street Journal,* March 18–19, 2006, pp. P1, P9.

6. Randy Myers, "The Spice Trade," *CFO,* June 2007, p. 74.

7. David Blanchard, "Census of Manufacturers: What's Working for U.S. Manufacturers," *Industry Week,* October 1, 2006, www.industryweek.com/ ReadArticle.aspx?ArticleID=12720.

8. Jill Jusko, "Scotsman Ice Systems:IW Best Plants Profile 2006," *Industry Week,* October 1, 2006, www. industryweek.com/ ReadArticle.aspx?ArticleID=12682.

9. Ibid.

10. Joelle Dick, Caroline Kvitka, Aaron Lazenby, and Rich Schwerin, "Four Keys to Lean Six Sigma," *Profit,* November 2004, p. 9.

11. Alex Taylor III, "A Tale of Two Factories," *Fortune,* September 18, 2006, pp. 118–126.

12. Ian Mount and Brian Caulfield, "The Missing Link," *eCompany,* May 2001, p. 84.

13. Doug Bartholomew, "Supply Chains at Risk," *Industry Week,* October 1, 2006, www.industryweek.com/ReadArticle.aspx? ArticleID=12713.

14. Beth Baker, "Our Way of Doing Business," *Rural Electric Magazine,* October 2006, www.nreca.org/main/NRECA/ AboutUs/CooperativeDifference/CoopMonth.htm.

15. Jeff Bailey, "Co-Op Entrepreneur Makes Discounts a Business," *Wall Street Journal,* October 22, 2002, p. B4.

16. Crystal Detamore-Rodman, "Cash In, Cash Out," *Entrepreneur,* June 2003, www.entrepreneur.com/magazine/entrepreneur/2003/ june/61916.html.

17. Connie Winkler, "Where Does the Money Go?" *CFO-IT,* Spring 2005, pp. 45–49.

18. Ian Mount and Brian Caulfield, "The Missing Link," *eCompany,* May 2001, pp. 82–88.

19. "The Value of Sharing Information Up and Down the Supply Chain," *CIO,* January 28, 2005, www.cio.com/article/1887/ The_Value_of_Sharing_Information_ Up_and_ Down_the_ Supply_Chain/1; Imam Baihaqi and Nicholas Beaumont, "Information Sharing in Supply Chains: A Literature Review and Research Agenda," Monash University Department of Management Working Paper Series, June 2005, www.buseco. monash.edu.au/mgt/research/working-papers/2005/wp45-05.pdf.

20. Bob Evans, "Supply Chains Hit Home (Sweet Home)," *Information Week,* February 7, 2007, p. 68.

21. Brian Nadel, "Show Me the Money," Special Advertising Feature in *Fortune,* April 3, 2006, pp. S1–S5.

22. Ian Mount and Brian Caulfield, "The Internet-Based Supply Chain," *eCompany,* May 2001, p. 85.

23. Russ Banham, "Everything Must Go," *CFO-IT,* Summer 2003, pp. 31–37.

24. Hau Lee, "The Three A's of Supply Chain Excellence," *Electronics Supply and Manufacturing,* October 1, 2004, www.my-esm.com/showArticle.jhtml?articleID= 47903369; Tracy Mayor, "The Supple Supply Chain," *CIO,* June 13, 2007, www.cio.com/ article/119301/. Tracy Mayor, "The Supple Supply Chain," *CIO,* June 13, 2007, www.cio.com/article/119301/.

25. Russ Banham, "Everything Must Go," *CFO-IT,* Summer 2003, pp. 31–37.

26. Ian MacMillan, "A Few Good Suppliers," *CFO,* October 2004, p. 26.

27. Maggie Overfelt, "Rough Stuff," *FSB,* February 2006, p. 23; Nathan Myers, "Clark Foam Closes Its Doors," *Surfing Magazine,* December 5, 2005, www.surfingthemag.com/news/surfing-pulse/ clark-foam-120505/; Gwen Mickelson, "Shapers Still Drawing Blanks One Month After Clark's Closure," *Santa Cruz Sentinel,* January 6, 2006, www.santacruzsentinel.com/archive/2006/ January/06/local/stories/03local.htm; Larry Peterson, "It's Time for Surf Shops to Mean Business," *Savannah Now,* January 2, 2007, http://savannahnow.com/node/205653.

28. John Turrettini, "Remade in America," *Forbes,* January 12, 2004, p. 190; "LightWedge," *Inc.,* September 2006, pp. 124–125.

29. David Blanchard, "Census of Manufacturers: Too Many Supply Chains Are Failing to Integrate," *Industry Week,* November 1, 2006, www.industryweek.com/ReadArticle.aspx?ArticleID= 12845&SectionID=10.

30. Michael Fitzgerald, "Turning Vendors into Partners," *Inc.,* August 2005, pp. 94–100.

31. Ibid.

# Chapter 18

1. James A. Cooke, "A Snapshot of the U.S. Logistics Market," *Logistics Management,* July 1, 2006, www. logisticsmgmt.com/ article/CA6352889.html?text=logistics+costs+under+pressure.

2. Merissa Marr, "How DreamWorks Misjudged DVD Sales of Its Monster Hit," *Wall Street Journal,* May 31, 2005, pp. A1, A9.

3. "With Billions of Bytes of Customer Data, How Can Retailers Be 'Starved for Information?'" *Knowledge@ Wharton,* August 2000, http://pf.inc.com/articles/2000/08/20043.html.

4. John Payne, "Pareto's Law—Your Formula for Success," *Ezine,* January 25, 2005, http://ezinearticles.com/?Paretos-Law—Your-Formula-For-Success&id=11091.

5. Phaedra Hise, "Early Adoption Pays Off," *Inc.,* August 1996, p. 101.

6. John Blau, "European Retailer to Put RFID Chips in Shoes," *CIO,* March 2, 2007, www.cio.com/article/29135/European_Retailer_ to_Put_RFID_Chips_in_Shoes.

7. Caroline Kvitka, "RFID: True Supply Chain Transparency," *Oracle Magazine,* July/August 2004, p. 25.

8. Mark Henricks, "Tell and Show," *Entrepreneur,* April 2004, pp. 77–78.

9. Alex Niemeyer, Minsok H. Pak, and Sanjay Ramaswamy, "Smart Tags for Your Supply Chain," *McKinsey Quarterly,* Number 4, 2003, www.mckinseyquarterly.com/article_page.aspx?ar= 1347&L2=1&L3=26.

10. Elizabeth Esfahani, "High Class, Low Price," *Business 2.0,* November 2006, pp. 74–76; Adam Smith," How Topshop Changed Fashion," *Time,* May 24, 2007, www.time.com/time/ globalbusiness/article/0,9171,1625185,00.html; "About Topshop," Topshop.com, www.topshop.com/webapp/wcs/stores/servlet/ StaticPageDisplay?storeId=12556&catalogId=19551&identifier= ts1%20about%20topshop.

11. Amy Chozick, "A Key Strategy of Japan's Car Makers Backfires," *Wall Street Journal,* July 20, 2007, pp. B1, B5.

12. Mark Henricks, "On the Spot," *Entrepreneur,* May 1997, p. 80.

13. Ibid.

14. Neal E. Boudette, "Big Dealer to Detroit: Fix How You Make Cars," *Wall Street Journal,* February 9, 2007, pp. A1, A8; Sholnn Freeman, "Smaller Cars Enjoy New Chic," *Washington Post,* September 28, 2005, www.washingtonpost.com/wp-dyn/content/ article/2005/09/27/AR2005092701812.html.

15. *2006 ACFE Report to the Nation on Occupational Fraud and Abuse,* Association of Certified Fraud Examiners, 2006, p. 4.

16. Ibid., pp. 4–5.

17. "Shoplifters and Dishonest Employees Continue to Steal in Record Numbers from United States Retailers," Jack Hayes International, 2006, www.hayesinternational.com/thft_srvys.html.

18. Serri Pfeil, "Is There a Thief Among Us?" *Employment Review,* December 2000, pp. 37–38.

19. *2006 ACFE Report to the Nation on Occupational Fraud and Abuse,* Association of Certified Fraud Examiners, p. 5; "The Luck of the Fraud," *Sales and Marketing Management's Performance eNewsletter,* December 12, 2005, p. 2.

20. Scott Wescott, "Are Your Staffers Stealing?" *Inc.,* October 2006, pp. 33–35.

21. *2006 ACFE Report to the Nation on Occupational Fraud and Abuse,* Association of Certified Fraud Examiners, p. 5.

22. Julia Boorstin, "Alcohol Auditor," *Fortune,* June 27, 2005, p. 40.

23. Mary Paulsell, "The Problem of Employee Theft," Missouri Small Business Development Centers, October 10, 2002, www. missouribusiness.net/docs/problem_ employee_theft.asp.

24. Scott Wescott, "Are Your Staffers Stealing?" *Inc.,* October 2006, pp. 33–35.

25. Robert T. Gray, "Clamping Down on Worker Crime," *Nation's Business,* April 1997, p. 44.
26. Scott Wescott, "Are Your Staffers Stealing?" *Inc.,* October 2006, pp. 33–35.
27. Calmetta Coleman, "Sticky Fingers," *Wall Street Journal,* September 8, 2000, pp. A1, A6.
28. "Highlights from Jack L. Hayes International Inc.'s 18 Annual Retail Theft Survey," 2006, www.hayesinternational.com/thft_srvys.html.
29. Ibid.
30. Amanda C. Kooser, "Make the Cut?" *Entrepreneur,* February 2006, p. 26.

31. Kathy Grannis, "Retail Losses Hit $41.6 Billion Last Year, According to National Retail Security Survey," National Retail Federation, June 11, 2007, www.nrf.com/modules.php?name=News&op=viewlive&sp_id=318.
32. Richard Hollinger and Lynn Langton, *2005 National Retail Security Survey Final Report,* University of Florida and the National Retail Federation, www.crim.ufl.edu/research/srp/finalreport_2005.pdf, pp. 27, 29.
33. Ann Zimmerman, "As Shoplifters Use High-Tech Scams, Retail Losses Rise," *Wall Street Journal*, October 25, 2006, pp. A1, A12.
34. William Ecenbarger, "They're Stealing You Blind," *Reader's Digest,* June 1996, p. 101.

# Chapter 19

1. Matthew Boyle, "Carley Roney–The Knot," *Fortune,* December 12, 2005, p. 48.
2. Francis Huffman, "Taking the Lead," *Entrepreneur,* November 1993, p. 101.
3. Mary Donato, "Smart Management: Both Sides of the Brain," *Smart Management,* June 29, 2007, www.managesmarter.com/msg/content_display/publications/e3i07b4dbb2a064255c6a88329c403726f6?imw=Y.
4. Donato, "Smart Management: Both Sides of the Brain," www.managesmarter.com/msg/content_display/publications/e3i07b4dbb2a064255c6a88329c403726f6?imw=Y.
5. Leigh Buchanan, "In Praise of Selflessness," *Inc.,* May 2007, www.inc.com/magazine/20070501/managing-leadership.html.
6. Susan Meyers, "Growing Leaders in Your Own Backyard," *Trustee,* June 2007, p. 8.
7. April Y. Pennington, "Big Switch," *Entrepreneur,* August 2004, p. 32.
8. William H. Miller, "The Stuff of Leadership," *Industry Week,* August 18, 1997, p. 100.
9. Chris Penttila, "Hire Away," *Entrepreneur,* June 2007, p. 20.
10. Ibid.
11. Charles R. Emery and Kevin S. Handell, "Selection of Sales Personnel: Love at First Sight," *Proceedings of the Academy of Marketing Studies* 12, No. 1, 2007, p. 17.
12. Mark Henricks, "A Look Ahead—Mission Critical," *Entrepreneur,* January 2007, p. 73.
13. Nitasha Tiku, "Boomer Benefits," *Inc.,* August 2007, p. 44.
14. Mark Hendricks, "A Look Ahead–Risky Business," *Entrepreneur,* January 2007, p. 71.
15. Joshua Hyatt, "Found in Translation," *Inc.,* October, 2006, p. 41.
16. "How to Write a Job Analysis and Description," Start Your Own Business, *Entrepreneur,* www.entrepreneur.com/humanresources/hiring/article56490.html.
17. Ibid.
18. Ibid.
19. Chris Pentilla, "Testing the Waters," *Entrepreneur,* January 2004, pp. 72–73.
20. Scott Leibs, "Gut Check," *CFO,* December 2006, pp. 89–90.
21. Chris Penttila, "Peering In," *Entrepreneur,* January 2005, pp. 70–71.
22. Ibid, p. 70.
23. Ibid, pp. 70–71.
24. Aman Singh, "Firms Court New Hires—In High School," *Wall Street Journal,* August 15, 2006, p. B5.
25. Mark Henricks, "You Know Who?" *Entrepreneur,* May 2007, p. 89–90.
26. Anjali Athavaley, "A Job Interview You Don't Have to Show Up For," *Wall Street Journal,* June 20, 2007, pp. D1, D8.
27. "Smart Questions for Your Hiring Manager," *Inc.,* February 2007, p. 47.
28. Andy Levine, "Dig We Must," *Inc.,* August 2006, p. 97.
29. Richard Slawsky, "Reducing Risk: The Search for Reputable Employees," *QSR Web,* August 9, 2007, www.qsrweb.com/article.php?id=8390&na=1.
30. Ibid.
31. Ibid.

32. Leigh Buchanan, "That's Chief Entertainment Officer," *Inc.,* August 2007, www.inc.com/magazine/20070801/thats-chief-entertainment-officer_pagen_2.html.
33. Julia Chang, "Balancing Act," *Sales & Marketing Management,* February 2004, p. 16.
34. "Whatever It Takes," *Inc.,* August 2007, p. 92.
35. Leigh Buchanan, "That's Chief Entertainment Officer," *Inc.,* August 2007, pp. 88–89.
36. Erin White, "How a Company Made Everyone a Team Player," *Wall Street Journal,* August 13, 2007, p. B1.
37. Beth Baker, "Pass the Pasta, Please, and Hold the Stress," *Washington Post,* July 10, 2007, p. HE01.
38. David Freedman, "The Idiocy of Crowds," *Inc.,* September 2006, pp. 61–62.
39. Mort Meyerson, "Everything I Know About Leadership Is Wrong," *Fast Company's Handbook of the Business Revolution 1997,* p. 9.
40. Marquez, "Kindness Pays . . . Or Does It?," pp. 40–41.
41. Garry Kranz, "Employees to Managers: Shut Up and Listen," *Workforce.com,* May 1, 2007, www.workforce.com/section/quick_takes/48859_2.html.
42. Simran Khurana, "Sam Walton Quotes," About.com, http://quotations.about.com/od/stillmorefamouspeople/a/SamWalton1.htm.
43. Bob Rogers, "The Lost Art of Listening," *GSA Business,* June 25, 2007, p. 22.
44. "Smarts," *Entrepreneur,* January 2004, p. 23.
45. Chris Pentilla, "Live and Learn: You May Be the Boss, But That Doesn't Mean You Can't Let Your Employees Teach You a Thing or Two," *Entrepreneur,* June 2004, pp. 36–39.
46. "Empowering Your Employees," *bNet.com,* www.bnet.com/2410-13059_23-95573.html.
47. Erin White, "How Surveying Workers Can Pay Off," *Wall Street Journal,* June 18, 2007, p. B3.
48. Ibid.
49. Daniel Akst, "The Rewards of Recognizing a Job Well Done," *Wall Street Journal,* January 31, 2007, p. D9.
50. Alex C. Pasquariello, "Grant Makers," *Fast Company,* April 2007, p. 32.
51. Paul Glader, "It's Not Easy Being Lean," *Wall Street Journal,* June 19, 2006, p. B1.
52. Magali Rahault, "On the Job," *Kiplinger's Personal Finance Magazine,* May 2001, p. 24.
53. "Flexible Work Arrangements," Ceridian Corporation, www.ceridian.com/www/content/3/10027/11028/319,32,Flexible_work_arrangements_related_to_job_satisfaction_in_2002.
54. David Javitch, "The Pros and Cons of Job Sharing," *Entrepreneur,* November 10, 2006, www.entrepreneur.com/humanresources/employeemanagementcolumnistdavidjavitch/article170244.html.
55. Ibid.
56. Chris Pentilla, "Off the Clock," *Entrepreneur,* May 2007, p. 36.
57. Sue Shellenbarger, "When Working at Home Doesn't Work: How Companies Comfort Telecommuters," *Wall Street Journal,* August 24, 2006, p. D1.
58. Doug Bartholomew, "Your Place or Mine?" *CFO-IT,* Spring 2004, pp. 32–38.

59. Christine L. Romero, "Telecommuting Popular on Both Ends of the Connection," *Greenville News*, July 20, 2003, p. E1.
60. Bartholomew, "Your Place or Mine?" pp. 32–38.
61. "10 Keys to Office Hoteling Success," *Facility Innovations. com*, http://facilityinnovations.com/10keys.htm.
62. "What Is Hoteling," *SearchCIO.com*, http://searchcio.techtarget.com/sDefinition/0,,sid19_gci1067496,00.html.
63. Ibid.
64. Richard Florida, "The Rise of the Creative Class: Motivating Creative IT Workers to Give Their All Means Going Beyond

Trappings of Foosball Tables and Casual Dress," *Optimize*, May 2002, www.optimizemag.com/issue/007/culture.htm.
65. Jack Stack, "The Logic of Profit," *Inc.*, March 1996, p. 17.
66. John Eckeberg, "Workers Debunk Value of Their Annual Reviews," *Greenville News*, June 11, 2004, p. A18.
67. Jordana Mishory, "Frequency Matters," *Sales & Marketing Management*, July 2004, pp. 36–38.
68. Ibid.

# Chapter 20

1. "Facts About Family Business," S. Dale High Center for Family Business at Elizabethtown College, www.centerforfamilybusiness.org/facts.asp; MassMutual Family Business Network, www.massmutual.com/fbn/index.htm; "Family Business Facts," Family Business Institute, www.ffi.org/looking/fbfacts_us.pdf.
2. James Lea, "Five Ways Family Firms Can Thrive," *Bizjournals.com*, February 2, 2004, www.bizjournals.com/extraedge/consultants/family_business/2004/02/02/column180.html.
3. Carol J. Loomis, "The Fate of the $16 Billion Walton Estate," *Fortune*, May 1, 2007, http://money.cnn.com/magazines/fortune/fortune_archive/2007/05/14/100008717/index.htm.
4. Tony Taylor, "Small Businesses Show Relative Strength," *GSA Business*, September 4, 2006, p. 22; Jim Lee, "Family Firm Performance: Further Evidence," *Family Business Review* 19, No. 2, June 2006, pp. 103–114.
5. "Research Reveals: Family Firms Perform Better," *Family Business Advisor* 7, No. 3, March 2003, p. 1.
6. Nicholas Stein, "The Age of the Scion," *Fortune*, April 2, 2001, pp. 121–128.
7. "Facts and Perspectives on Family Business Around the World: United States," Family Business Institute, http:// www.ffi.org/looking/fbfacts_us.pdf.
8. Ibid.
9. Carol Tice, "Lost in Transition," *Entrepreneur*, November 2006, pp. 101–103; Steve Wilhelm, "A Family's Struggle: Wilson Products Faces Sale or Auction," *Puget Sound Business Journal*, October 21, 1005, http://seattle.bizjournals.com/seattle/stories/2005/10/24/story4.html.
10. "Facts and Perspectives on Family Business Around the World: United States," Family Business Institute, http:// www.ffi.org/looking/fbfacts_us.pdf.
11. James Olan Hutcheson, "The End of a 1,400 Year Old Business," *Business Week*, April 16, 2007, www.businessweek.com/smallbiz/content/apr2007/sb20070416_589621.htm?campaign_id=rss_topEmailedStories.
12. Carol Tice, "Lost in Transition," *Entrepreneur*, November 2006, pp. 101–103.
13. "Facts and Perspectives on Family Business Around the World: United States," Family Business Institute, www.ffi.org/looking/fbfacts_us.pdf.
14. Sharon Nelton, "Ten Keys to Success in Family Business," *Nation's Business*, April 1991, pp. 44–45.
15. "Family Members Fight Over Control of Texas Pete Hot Sauce Empire," *Greenville News*, May 17, 1997, p. 11D.
16. Stein, "The Age of the Scion," p. 124.
17. Eugenia Levenson, "Road Warrior," *Fortune*, November 27, 2006, p. 276; Hsiao-Ching Chao, "Maximilian Riedel Has the Stemware Industry in the Palm of His Hand," *Seattle Post-Intelligencer*, April 13, 2005, http://seattlepi.nwsource.com/food/219827_riedel13.html; Anthony Giglio, "Glass Menagerie," *Boston Magazine*, April 2006, www.bostonmagazine.com/dining_food_wine/articles/boston_magazine_liquids_specialty_wineglasses/.
18. Stein, "The Age of the Scion," p. 124.
19. Daniel Howden and Rick Vecchio, "Presidential Runoff Familiar Ground for Ecuador's Richest Man," *The Agonist*, October 15, 2006, http://agonist.org/20061015/ecuador_set_to_join_pink_tide_washing_across_latin_america; Michael

Freedman, "Slippery Situation," *Forbes*, March 17, 2003, pp. 108–112.
20. Daniel I. Dorfman, "Tips for Tough Transitions," *Business Week*, February 16, 2006, www.businessweek.com/ smallbiz/content/feb2006/sb20060215_080293.htm?chan=smallbiz_smallbiz+index+page_family+owned+business.
21. Lori Ioannou, "Keeping the Business All in the Family," *FSB*, November 2001, p. 75.
22. Springfield Remanufacturing Corporation, www.screman.com/index.htm.
23. "Employee Ownership and Corporate Performance," National Center for Employee Ownership, www.nceo.org/library/esop_perf.html.
24. Paul J. Lim, "Putting Your House in Order," *U.S. News & World Report*, December 10, 2001, p. 38.
25. "Facts and Perspectives on Family Business Around the World: United States," Family Business Institute, http:// www.ffi.org/looking/fbfacts_us.pdf.
26. Claire Cain Miller, "Chapter Two," *Forbes*, December 25, 2006, p. 72.
27. Carol Tice, "Lost in Transition," *Entrepreneur*, November 2006, p. 102.
28. TCPN Quotations Center, www.cyber-nation.com/victory/quotations/subject/quotes_subjects_f_to_h.html#f.
29. Andy Bluestone, "Succession Planning Isn't Just About Money," *Nation's Business*, November 1996, p. 6.
30. Shelly Branch, "Mom Always Liked You Best," *Your Company*, April/May 1998, pp. 26–38.
31. Tony Taylor, "Small Businesses Show Relative Strength," *GSA Business*, September 4, 2006, pp. 22, 24.
32. Patricia Schiff Estess, "Heir Raising," *Entrepreneur*, May 1996, pp. 80–82.
33. Carol Tice, "Lost in Transition," *Entrepreneur*, November 2006, pp. 101–103.
34. Jacquelyn Lynn, "What Price Successor?" *Entrepreneur*, November 1999, p. 146.
35. Craig E. Aronoff and John L. Ward, "Why Continue Your Family Business," *Nation's Business*, March 1998, pp. 72–74.
36. Jeremy Quittner, "Creating a Legacy," *Business Week*, June 25, 2007, www.businessweek.com/magazine/content/ 07_26/b4040443.htm?chan=search.
37. Lee Smith, "The Next Generation," *Your Company*, October 1999, pp. 36–46.
38. Daniel I. Dorfman, "Tips for Tough Transitions," *Business Week*, February 16, 2006, www.businessweek.com/smallbiz/content/feb2006/sb20060215_080293.htm?chan=smallbiz_smallbiz+index+page_family+owned+business.
39. "New Nationwide Survey Points to Bright Spot in American Economy-Family-Owned Businesses," MassMutual Financial Group, www.massmutual.com/mmfg/about/pr_2003/01_22_03.html.
40. Annetta Miller, "You Can't Take It With You," *Your Company*, April 1999, pp. 28–34.
41. "Family Business Facts," Family Business Institute, http:// www.ffi.org/looking/fbfacts_us.pdf.
42. Aliza Pilar Sheridan, "Connect the Daughters," *Entrepreneur*, December 2002, pp. 36–37.
43. Jeremy Quittner, "Creating a Legacy," *Business Week*, June 25, 2007, www.businessweek.com/magazine/content/07_26/b4040443.htm?chan=search.

44. Karen E. Klein, "Succession Planning Without an Heir," *Business Week,* June 20, 2007, www.businessweek.com/smallbiz/content/ jun2007/sb20070620_135303.htm?chan=search.

45. Sharon Nelton, "Why Women Are Chosen to Lead," *Nation's Business,* April 1999, p. 51.

46. "New Nationwide Survey Points to Bright Spot in American Economy-Family-Owned Businesses," MassMutual Financial Group, www.massmutual.com/mmfg/about/pr_2003/01_22_03.html.

47. Miller, "You Can't Take It With You," pp. 28–34; Joan Pryde, "The Estate Tax Toll on Small Firms," *Nation's Business,* August 1997, pp. 20–24.

48. Jeremy Quittner, "Creating a Legacy," *Business Week,* June 25, 2007, www.businessweek.com/magazine/content/ 07_ 26/b4040443.htm?chan=search.

49. Joan Szabo, "Spreading the Wealth," *Entrepreneur,* July 1997, pp. 62–64.

50. Gay Jervey, "Family Ties," *FSB,* March 2006, p. 60.

51. Gay Jervey, "Family Ties," p. 60; Tom Herman, "Court Ruling Bolsters Estate Planning Tool," *Wall Street Journal,* May 27, 2004, p. D1.

52. Jeremy Quittner, "Creating a Legacy," *Business Week,* June 25, 2007, www.businessweek.com/magazine/ content/07_26/b4040443.htm?chan=search.

53. Daniel Tynan, "In Case of Emergency," *Entrepreneur,* April 2003, p. 60.

54. Elizabeth Hockerman, "When to Self-Insure?" *Small Business Times,* May 12, 2006, www.biztimes.com/news/2006/5/12/ when-to-self-insure.

55. Jeanne Lee and Brandi Stewart, "Build Your Own Insurance Company," *FSB,* September 2007, pp. 28–31.

56. Tiana Velez, "A Home Business Needs Insurance," *Arizona Daily Star,* June 5, 2006, www.azstarnet.com/allheadlines/132077.

57. Kimberly Lankford, "Weird Insurance," *Kiplinger's Personal Finance Magazine,* October 1998, pp. 113–116.

58. "Weird Insurance Policy: Lloyd's of London Bank," TriviaLibrary.com, www.trivia-library.com/a/weird-insurance-policy-lloyds-of-london-bank.htm; Larry Getlen, "Celebrity Body Parts: Million Dollar Thighs and Smiles," *Bankrate.com,* June 27, 2003, www.bankrate.com/brm/news/insur/20020410a.asp.

59. John Fried, "Having Fun Yet?" *Inc.,* March 2006, pp. 75–77; "Incredible Adventures: Our Story," Incredible Adventures, www. incredible-adventures.com/about_us.html; Esther Dyson, "I Live and Die by Waivers," Esther Dyson's Flight School, May 11, 2007, www.edventure.com/ flightschool/blog/?p=4.

60. Joyce M. Rosenberg, "Preparing a Disaster Plan Gets Serious," *Los Angeles Times,* August 16, 2007, www.latimes.com/business/la-fi-smalldisaster16aug16, 1,4272739.story?coll=la-headlines-business&ctrack= 1&cset=true; "Famed Restaurant Reopens Today," *Greenville News,* October 1, 2006, p. 4B.

61. Larry Kanter, "Smart Questions for Your Insurance Agent," *Inc.,* August 2006, p. 40; Michele Marchetti, "Thrown Off Track," *FSB,* February 2004, pp. 66–69.

62. Heidi Ernst, "The Best Line of Defense," Advertising Insert, *FSB,* July/August 2007, p. 80.

63. Jan Norman, "Business Disaster Can Strike at Any Time," *Greenville News,* April 4, 2004, p. E1.

64. Jan Norman, " Contacts Key When Disaster Hits," *Greenville News,* February 8, 2004, p. 1E.

65. Ilan Mochari, "A Security Blanket for Your Web Site," *Inc.,* December 2000, pp. 133–134.

66. Andrew Smyth, "Council for Disability Awareness Launches Consumer Website," *The Insurance Policy,* November 3, 2006, www.theinsurancepolicy.com/new_insurance_agents/ disability_insurance/.

67. "Small Business Health Care Reform," National Federation of Independent Businesses, July 31, 2007, www.nfib.com/page/ healthcare.html.

68. *Employer Health Benefits 2006,* The Kaiser Family Foundation and Health Research and Educational Trust (Menlo Park, California and Chicago, Illinois: The Kaiser Family Foundation, 2006), pp. 4, 25.

69. Eileen Figure Sandlin, "Finding Health Insurance as a Start-up," *Entrepreneur,* October 2006, www.entrepreneur.com/management/ insurance/typesofinsurance/article168504.html.

70. *Employer Health Benefits 2006,* Kaiser Family Foundation and Health Research and Educational Trust, p. 2.

71. "HSA Penetration Reaches 5% But Varies by State, ISI Study Shows," *HSA Finder,* June 2006, www.hsafinder.com/06-07_02. shtml.

72. Colleen DeBaise, "Small Business Owners Try HSAs to Trim Health Costs," *Smart Money,* July 6, 2007, www.smartmoney. com/smallbiz/index.cfm?story=20060511.

73. Leslie Scism, "If Disorder Strikes This 'Titanic,' Chubb Could Lose Millions," *Wall Street Journal,* April 9, 1997, pp. A1, A4.

74. Greg O'Claray, "Alaska Needs Workers' Compensation Reform Now," *National Federation of Independent Businesses,* March 14, 2005, www.nfib.com/object/IO_20952.html.

75. Aaron Dalton, "Best Practices: Rapid Recovery," *Industry Week,* March 1, 2005, www.industryweek.com/ ReadArticle.aspx?ArticleId=10001.

76. Marc Fisher, "Judge Who Seeks Millions for Lost Pants Has His (Emotional) Day in Court," *Washington Post,* June 13, 2007, www. washingtonpost.com/wp-dyn/content/article/2007/06/12/ AR2007061201667.html; "Dry Cleaner Raises Enough Cash to Pay Legal Fees, *WUSA9.com,* August 13, 2007, www. wusa9.com/news/ news_article.aspx?storyid=61690.

77. "Trends in Employment Practices Liability," Insurance Information Institute, www.iii.org/commerciallines/ whatitdoes/lines/ specialty/?table_sort_685200=3.

78. Steve Strauss, "Retaliate and You May Regret It," *USA Today,* July 3, 2006, www.usatoday.com/money/smallbusiness/columnist/ strauss/2006-07-03-retaliate_ x.htm; "On the Docket: Burlington Northern and Santa Fe Railway," Medill School of Journalism, Northwestern University, http://docket.medill.northwestern.edu/archives/003256.php.

79. Ilan Mochari, "Bug Your Broker," *Inc.,* August 2000, pp. 127–128.

80. *2007 NSBA Survey of Small and Medium-Size Businesses,* National Small Business Association (Washington, DC: U.S. Government Printing Office, 2007), www.nsba.biz/docs/surveynewfinal.pdf, p. 3.

81. Buss, "Cost-Saving Tips for Health Plans," pp. 30–33.

## Chapter 21

1. Michael Sisk, "Do the Right Thing," Harvard Business School: *Working Knowledge,* September 29, 2003, http://hbsworkingknowledge.hbs.edu/item.jhtml?id=3689&t= moral_leadership.

2. Vernon R. Loucks, Jr., "A CEO Looks at Ethics," *Business Horizons,* March–April 1987, p. 2.

3. Susan Caminiti, "The Payoff from a Good Reputation," *Fortune,* February 10, 1992, p. 74.

4. "Martha Stewart's Company Posts Loss, Shares Fall," *Forbes,* May 7, 2004, www.forbes.com/newswire/2004/05/07/rtr1364228.html; Mark Robichaux, "Martha Stewart: TV's Homebody," *Broadcasting & Cable,* December 17, 2007, www. broadcastingcable.com/article/CA6513155.html.

5. Karen Edwards, "The Principle's Office," *Entrepreneur,* December 2006, p. 95; "CSR and Sustainability," Nature's Path Foods, www.naturespath.com/sustainability/csr_and_sustainability.

6. Elliot Blair Smith, "Subprime Lender Indicted," *USA Today,* November 17, 2005, www.usatoday.com/money/industries/ banking/2005-11-17-carolina-usat_x.htm; Noelle Phillips, "Home Gold/Carolina Investors Victims Still Bitter Despite Sentences," *The State,* February 17, 2007, http://findarticles.com/p/articles/ mi_km4472/is_200702/ai_n18686501.

7. Joseph Pereira, "Doing Good and Doing Well at Timberland," *Wall Street Journal,* September 9, 2003, pp. B1–B10.

8. Kate O'Sullivan, "Virtue Rewarded," *CFO,* October 2006, p. 51.

9. Chris Pentilla, "Give a Little," *Entrepreneur,* May 2006, p. 89.

10. Kate O'Sullivan, "Virtue Rewarded," *CFO,* October 2006, p. 51; Jennifer Reingold, "Walking the Walk," *Fast Company,* November 2005, pp. 81–85; Joseph Pereira, "Doing Good and Doing Well at Timberland," pp. B1–B10.

11. Joseph Pereira, "Doing Good and Doing Well at Timberland," *Wall Street Journal,* September 9, 2003, pp. B1–B10.

12. Nicole Solis, "Are Businesses Serious About Ethics?" BNET, June 22, 2007, http://blogs.bnet.com/intercom/?p=386&tag=nl.e713.

13. Mark Henricks, "Well, Honestly!" *Entrepreneur,* December 2006, p. 103.

14. Patricia Wallington, "Total Leadership–Ethical Behaviour Is Essential," CIO, March 15, 2003, www.cio.com/article/31779/Total_Leadership_Ethical_Behaviour_Is_ Essential.

15. Joshua Kurlantzick, "Liar, Liar," *Entrepreneur,* October 2003, pp. 68–71.

16. Gene Laczniak, "Business Ethics: A Manager's Primer," *Business,* January–March 1983, pp. 23–29.

17. Michael Josephson, "Teaching Ethical Decision Making and Its Principled Reasoning," *Ethics: Easier Said Than Done,* Winter 1988, p. 28.

18. John Rutledge, "The Portrait on My Wall," *Forbes,* December 30, 1996, p. 78.

19. "What Is a Social Entrepreneur?" Ashoka, www.ashoka.org/social_entrepreneur.

20. "Social Entrepreneurs: Rodrigo Baggio," Global Generations Policy Institute, www.genpolicy.com/initiatives/brazilian_social_entrepreneur.html; Bill Drayton, "Everyone a Changemaker: Social Entrepreneurship's Ultimate Goal," *Innovations,* Winter 2006, pp.1–3.

21. Lori Ioannou, "Corporate America's Social Conscience," *Fortune* Advertising Insert, May 26, 2003, pp. S1–S10; "Americans Are Looking for Good Corporate Citizens But Aren't Finding Them," *CSR Wire,* July 3, 2001; Lori Ioannou, "Corporate America's Social Conscience," pp. S1–S10.

22. Edward Iwata, "Businesses Grow More Socially Conscious," *USA Today,* February 14, 2007, www.usatoday.com/money/companies/2007-02-14-high-purpose-usat_x.htm.

23. Alethea, "Environment Shines on New Fashion Bags," *BrooWaha Los Angeles Edition,* December 5, 2006, http://losangeles.broowaha.com/article.php?id=456; April Y. Pennington, "Trash to Treasure," *Entrepreneur,* March 2006, p. 29; "Our Story," Passchal, www.passchal.com/About%20Us.html.

24. Chris Pentilla, "Shades of Green," *Entrepreneur,* August 2007, pp. 19–20; "Nature Meet Nurture," Pangea Organics, www.pangeaorganics.com/home.html.

25. John Moore, "The Starbucks 'Employee First' Philosophy," *Brand Autopsy,* January 15, 2007, http://brandautopsy.typepad.com/brandautopsy/2007/01/the_starbucks_e.html; "Starbucks Validates Commitment to Corporate Transparency in New Corporate Social Responsibility Report," GreenMoneyJournal.com, www.greenmoneyjournal.com/article.mpl?newsletterid=29&articleid=316; Mary Scott, "Howard Schulz," *Business Ethics,* November/December 1995, pp. 26–29; "100 Best Companies to Work For 2007: Starbucks," Fortune, http://money.cnn.com/magazines/fortune/bestcompanies/2007/snapshots/16.html.

26. Robert Bernstein, "Minority Population Tops 100 Million," *U.S. Census Bureau News,* May 17, 2007, www.census.gov/Press-Release/www/releases/archives/population/010048.html.

27. Keith H. Hammonds, "Difference Is Power," *Fast Company,* July 2000, p. 58.

28. "Best Practices of Private Sector Employers," Equal Employment Opportunity Commission, www.eeoc.gov/abouteeoc/task_reports/prac2.html.

29. Martha Lagace, "Racial Diversity Pays Off," Harvard Business School: *Working Knowledge,* June 21, 2004, http://hbsworkingknowledge.hbs.edu/item.jhtml?id=4207&t=organizations.

30. "Charting the U.S. Labor Market," Bureau of Labor Statistics, www.bls.gov/news.release/empsit.t01.htm.

31. "Entrants to the Workforce," Diversity Central, www.diversitycentral.com/business/diversity_statistics.html#entrants.

32. "The Economic Cost of Drug Abuse in the United States 1992–2002," Office of National Drug Control Policy, www.whitehousedrugpolicy.gov/publications/economic_ costs/e_summary.pdf, p. vi.

33. "You Are Not Alone," Partnership for a Drug-Free America, March 21, 2006, www.drugfree.org/Intervention/WhereStart/You_Are_Not_Alone.

34. Gina Ruiz, "Expanded EAPs Lend a Hand to Employer's Bottom Line," *Workforce Management,* January 16, 2006, pp. 46–47.

35. *The President's National Drug Control Strategy,* February 2007, www.whitehousedrugpolicy.gov/publications/policy/ndcs07/, pp. 14–15; "Nationwide Survey Shows Most Illicit Drug Users and Heavy Alcohol Users Are in the Workplace and May Pose Special Problems," Substance Abuse and Mental Health Services Administration, U.S. Department of Health and Human Services, July 17, 2007, http://oas.samhsa.gov/work2k7/press.htm.

36. "U.S. HIV/AIDS Statistics," Global Health Reporting, 2007, www.globalhealthreporting.org/diseaseinfo. asp?id=23#us.

37. "Sexual Harassment Training and Prevention," The Training Network, www.hr-training-network.com/products/harassment.shtml.

38. Amy Wilson, "Inappropriate Behavior Lands Beetle Bailey's General in Hot Water," *Greenville News,* November 22, 1992, p. 20D.

39. *Sexual Harassment Manual for Managers and Supervisors* (Chicago: Commerce Clearing House, 1992), pp. 25–26.

40. Mark Kind, "Jury Awards $6.8M in Sexual Harassment Case," *Kansas City Business Journal,* January 17, 2006, www.bizjournals.com/kansascity/stories/2006/01/16/daily18.html.

41. *Burlington Industries vs. Ellerth* (97-569) 123 F.3d 490 (1998); "Employer Liability for Harassment," Equal Employment Opportunity Commission, www.eeoc.gov/types/harassment.html.

42. Nicole P. Cantey, "High Court Rules Same Sex Harassment Is Against the Law," *South Carolina Business Journal,* August 1998, p. 3; Jack Corcoran, "Of Nice and Men," Success, June 1998, pp. 64–67.

43. Heinz Tschabitscher, "How Many E-Mails Are Sent Every Day?," About.com, http://email.about.com/od/emailtrivia/f/emails_per_day.htm

44. "E-mail Usage/Penetration," EmailStatCenter, www.emailstatcenter.com/Usage.html.

45. "2005 Electronic Monitoring and Surveillance Survey: Many Companies Monitoring, Recording, Videotaping—and Firing—Employees," American Management Association, May 18, 2005, www.amanet.org/press/amanews/ems05.htm.

46. "M-Law's Tenth Annual Wacky Warning Label Contest," Wacky Warning Labels, January 4, 2007, www.wackywarnings.com/; "Things People Said: Warning Labels," Rinkworks.com, www.rinkworks.com/said/warnings.shtml.

47. "FTC Charges BodyFlex with False Advertising," ConsumerAffairs, November 10, 2003, http://consumeraffairs.com/news03/bodyflex.html; "BodyFlex to Offer $2.6 Million in Refunds," ConsumerAffairs.com, September 1, 2004, www.consumeraffairs.com/news04/bodyflex.html.

48. Thomas Kostigen, "Ethics Trumps Returns," *Market Watch,* July 13, 2007, www.marketwatch.com/news/story/story.aspx?guid=%7BC3CA306A-4BD5-4250-85C2-98D60F699CAB%7D&siteid=rss.

49. Brooke A. Masters and Ben White, "Adelphia Founder, Son Convicted of Fraud," *Washington Post,* July 9, 2004, http:// www.washingtonpost.com/wp-dyn/articles/A39143-2004Jul9.html; Leslie Cauley, "John Rigas Tells His Side of the Adelphia Story," *USA Today,* August 5, 2007, www.usatoday.com/money/companies/management/2007-08-05-Rigas_N.htm.

50. "Corporate Social Responsibility Growing," *Inc.,* April 11, 2007, www.inc.com/news/briefs/200704/0411study.html.

51. "Company Profile," Spinx Company, www.spinxco.com/profile.htm.

# Chapter 22

1. Raymund Flandez, "A Tiny Firm Wins 'Chewy Vuitton' Suit, But Still Feels the Bite," *Wall Street Journal,* November 28, 2006, p. B1, B5.
2. Shannon P. Duffy, "Third Circuit Slashes Punitive Damages Award," Law.com, August 27, 2007, www.law.com/jsp/article.jsp?id=1187946144676.
3. *Carbaugh vs. Klick-Lewis,* 561 A.sd 1248 (Pa 1989).
4. *Hoffman v. Red Owl Stores, Inc.,* 133 N.W. 2ed 267 (1965) 26 Wis. 2ed 683.
5. Scott Michels, "Man Sues for Revealing Affair," *ABC News,* August 10, 2007, http://news.aol.com/story/ar/_a/man-sues-florist-for-revealing-affair/20070810160709990001; Noah Oppenheim, "Man Sues Florist for Revealing Affair," *MSNBC,* August 13, 2007, http://allday.msnbc.msn.com/ archive/2007/08/13/314223.aspx?p=1.
6. *Superior Boiler Works vs. R.J. Sanders, Inc.,* 1998 R.I. Lexis 153, Supreme Court of Rhode Island, 1998.
7. Judyth W. Pendell and Paul J. Hinton, "Tort Liability Costs for Small Business," U.S. Chamber Institute for Legal Reform, Washington, DC, May 2007, pp. 4–10.
8. *Webster v. Blue Ship Tea Room,* 198 N.E. 2d 309 (Mass. 1964); 347 Mass. 421.
9. "Product Liability Basics," *Inc.,* February 2000, http:// www.inc.com/articles/2000/02/17249.html.
10. Thomas Claburn, "Cracking Down," *Information Week,* September 26, 2005, p. 19.
11. Anne Field, "How to Knock Out Knock Offs," *Business Week,* March 14, 2005, www.businessweek.com/ magazine/content/05_11/b3924446.htm.
12. Eugene R. Quinn, "Cost of Obtaining a Patent," *IP Watchdog,* August 15, 2007, www.ipwatchdog.com/patent_cost.html.
13. "U.S. Patent History," The Great Idea Finder, www.ideafinder.com/history/inventions/uspatent.htm; "U.S. Patent and Trademark Office Issues Seven Millionth Patent," U.S. Patent and Trademark Office, February 14, 2006, www.uspto.gov/web/offices/com/speeches/06-09.htm.
14. Molly M. Peterson, "Reducing Patent Backlog Could Take Years, Patent Official Says," *Government Executive,* April 26, 2005, www.govexec.com/dailyfed/0405/042605cdam1.htm; "Patent Performance," U.S. Patent and Trademark Office, http://www1.uspto.gov/web/offices/com/annual/2005/040201_patentperform.html.
15. James Bessen and Michael Meurer, "The Patent Litigation Explosion," *Technological Innovation and Intellectual Property,* October 24, 2005, www. researchoninnovation.org/ WordPress/?p=59.
16. David Whitford, "Vision Quest," *FSB,* April 2006, pp. 45–46.
17. Kris Frieswick, "License to Steal?" *CFO,* September 2001, pp. 89–91; Megan Barnett, "Patents Pending," *U.S. News & World Report,* June 10, 2002, pp. 33–34; Tomima Edmark, "On Guard," *Entrepreneur,* August 1997, pp. 92–94; Tomima Edmark, "On Guard," *Entrepreneur,* February 1997, pp. 109–111.
18. Pete Wells, "Chef Sues Over Intellectual Property (the Menu)," *New York Times,* June 27, 2007, www.nytimes.com/2007/06/27/nyregion/27pearl.html?ex=1189137600&en=7192883eabea4c1d&ei=5070.
19. Lance Frazer, "A Small Biz Guide to Trademarks, Patents, and Copyrights," *E-Merging Business,* Fall/Winter 2000, pp. 112–115.
20. Harry Harris and William Brand, "Oakland Sewer Employee Arrested for Selling Hundreds of Counterfeit DVDs," *Content Agenda,* August 24, 2007, www.contentagenda.com/articleXml/LN660265083.html?industryid=45187.
21. "A Darkening Picture," *Fast Company,* December 2005, pp. 54–55.
22. Arturo Bris, Ivo Welch, and Ning Zhu, "The Costs of Bankruptcy: Chapter 7 Liquidation vs. Chapter 11 Reorganization," *Journal of Finance,* June 2006, p. 1270.
23. Andrea James, "Small Business Owners Vent Their Regulation Frustrations," *Seattle Post-Intelligencer,* August 20, 2007, www.sba.gov/advo/research/rs264.pdf.
24. Jack Faris, "Small Business Focus: Climbing Mount Regulation," National Federation of Independent Businesses, October 19, 2005, www.nfib.com/object/IO_25133.html.
25. W. Mark Crain, "The Impact of Regulatory Costs on Small Firms," *Small Business Research Summary,* No. 264, September 2005, www.sba.gov/advo/research/rs264.pdf.
26. James Mehring, "A Heavy Regulatory Load," *Business Week,* Winter 2005, www.nfib.com/object/IO_25133.html.
27. *United States vs. Topco Associates Inc.,* 405 U.S. 596, (1972).
28. *Consumer Fraud and Identity Theft Complaint Data,* Federal Trade Commission, January 2006, www.consumer.gov/sentinel/pubs/Top10Fraud2005.pdf, p. 3; Brian Koerner, "General Identity Theft Statistics," About.com, http://idtheft.about.com/od/dataandstat1/p/GeneralStats.htm.

# Photo Credits

**Chapter 1,** page 26, Goodwin Heart Pine Company; page 26, R.A. Simerl/Corbis –NY; page 11, Frank Rogozienski; page 30, Boston Globe/Mathhew J. Lee/ Landow LLC; page 32, Nicola Jones/Cartoon Stock

**Chapter 2,** page 57, Honest Tea; page 61, Tom's of Maine, Inc.; page 62, Nicola Jones/Cartoon Stock; page 64, Michael Dunning/Getting Images, Inc.-Photographer's Choice-Rights Ready

**Chapter 3,** page 98, Charles Rex Arbogast/AP Wide World Photos; page 101, Capsule; page 109, Nicola Jones/Cartoon Stock

**Chapter 4,** page 123, Dresdene Flynn-White; page 124, Jeffery Allan Salter/Corbis/Saba Press Photos, Inc.; page 142, Nicola Jones/Cartoon Stock; page 144, Scott McDermott/Corbis-NY

**Chapter 5,** page 157, Chris Pietsch; page 159, Nicola Jones/ Cartoon Stock; page 178, Kerry L. Werry/Shutterstock; page 181, Colin & Linda McKie/Shutterstock

**Chapter 6,** page 198, Littlearth Productions, Inc.; page 202, Inogen; page 218, Nicola Jones/Cartoon Stock

**Chapter 7,** page 229, Jeff Greenberg/Omni-Photo Communications, Inc.; page 231, Lorentz Gullachsen/Getty Images Inc.-Stone Allstock; page 250, LBS Publications, Inc.; page 253, Nicola Jones/Cartoon Stock

**Chapter 8,** page 267, H.J. Heinz Company; page 267, Nicola Jones/Cartoon Stock; page 268, Ibex Outdoor Clothing, Inc.; page 271, The Goltz Group

**Chapter 9,** page 301, AP Wide World Photos/Ted S. Warren page 305, Nicola Jones/Cartoon Stock; page 311, Roark Johnson; page 321, Kimberly White/Landov LLC

**Chapter 10,** page 340, Nicola Jones/Cartoon Stock; page 349, Pinkberry, Inc.; page 353, Fox-TV/ Picture Desk Inc./Kobal Collection; page 361, Wilkins' Oklahoma Truck Supply

**Chapter 11,** page 379, AP Wide World Photos; page 386, Bizuayehu Tesfaye/ AP Wide World Photos; page 390, Mike Bladwin/Cornered Cartoons; page 392, Drive 495

**Chapter 12,** page 408, Sundia Corp.; page 410, Nicola Jones/Cartoon Stock; page 421, Steven Harris/Getty Images Inc.-Hulton Archive Photos; page 427, Pharmaceutical Trade Services, Inc. (PTSI)

**Chapter 13,** page 447, ©Carol Cable from cartoonbank.com. All Rights Reserved; page 456, Brad Swonetz/ Redux Pictures; page 464, Green Gear Cycling, Inc.; page 466, Lobster Gram Intl, Inc.

**Chapter 14,** page 488, ©The New Yorker Collection 2002/ Robert Mankiff from cartoonbank.com. All Rights Reserved; page 491, Mark Schafer; page 508, Getty Images/Dave Hogan page 510, Bare Essentials

**Chapter 15,** page 527, AllPoints Research; page 528, Cartoon Stock; page 535, Mobilight Inc.; page 550, eDimensional, Inc.

**Chapter 16,** page 561, The Indianapolis Star/Nikki Kahn/AP Wide World Photos; page 572, Cartoon Stock; page 589, Rick Bowmer/AP Wide World Photos

**Chapter 17,** page 598, Creative Eye/MIRA.com; page 600, Vahan Shirvanian/Cartoon Stock; page 605, Vineyard 29; page 608, Getty Images; page 630, Filippo Monteforte/A/Getty Images

**Chapter 18,** page 647, Dan Burn-Forti; page 650, Scott Olson/Getty Images; page 657, Getty Images Inc-Photodisc; page 622, Cartoon Stock

**Chapter 19,** page 680, John W. Clark; page 686, Cartoon Stock; page 698, Bright House Inc.; page 701, Frederick M. Brown/Getty Images

**Chapter 20,** page 718, Don Ryan/AP Wide World Photos; page 721, Cartoon Features Syndicate; page 733, Incredible Adventures, Inc.; page 741, Davis Turner

**Chapter 21,** page 754, Timberland; page 756, Cartoon Stock; page 763, Pangea Organics; page 770, Dorling Kindersley Media Library; page 778, The Spinx Company, Inc.

**Chapter 22,** page 794, Jessica McGowan/New York Times Agency; page 795, Cartoon Bank; page 801, Uniweld Products, Inc.; page 804, TerraCycle, Inc.

# Index